W9-BKP-879

ENCYCLOPEDIA OF THE RENAISSANCE

Peter Paul Rubens. ***The Reception of Marie de Médicis at Marseille.*** *The Reception at Marseille* is one of twenty-four paintings in the Medici Cycle, which depicts events in the life of the queen of Henry IV of France and mother of Louis XIII, painted by Rubens between 1622 and 1625. [See the entry on Rubens in this volume.] MUSÉE DU LOUVRE, PARIS/GIRAUDON/ART RESOURCE, NY

ENCYCLOPEDIA OF THE

ENAISSANCE

Paul F. Grendler

Editor in Chief

Published in Association with
The Renaissance Society of America

VOLUME 5

Peucer – Sforza

CHARLES SCRIBNER'S SONS

An Imprint of The Gale Group

NEW YORK

Charles Scribner's Sons
1633 Broadway
New York, New York 10019

1 3 5 7 9 11 13 15 17 19 20 18 16 14 12 10 8 6 4 2

PRINTED IN THE UNITED STATES OF AMERICA

Library of Congress Cataloging-in-Publication Data
Encyclopedia of the Renaissance / Paul F. Grendler, editor in chief.
p. cm.
Includes bibliographical references and index.
ISBN 0-684-80514-6 (set) — ISBN 0-684-80508-1 (v. 1) — ISBN 0-684-80509-X (v. 2) — ISBN 0-684-80510-3 (v. 3) — ISBN 0-684-80511-1 (v. 4) — ISBN 0-684-80512-X (v. 5) — ISBN 0-684-80513-8 (v. 6)
1. Renaissance—Encyclopedias. I. Grendler, Paul F. II. Renaissance Society of America.
CB361.E52 1999
940.2′3′03—dc21 99-048290

The paper used in this publication meets the requirements of ANSI/NISO Z39.48-1992 (Permanence of Paper).

The typeface used in this book is ITC Garamond, a version of a typeface attributed to the French publisher and type founder Claude Garamond (c. 1480–1561).

CONTENTS OF OTHER VOLUMES

COMMON ABBREVIATIONS USED IN THIS WORK

A.D.	*Anno Domini,* in the year of the Lord
A.H.	*Anno Hegirae,* in the year of the Hegira
b.	born
B.C.	before Christ
B.C.E.	before the common era (= B.C.)
c.	*circa,* about, approximately
C.E.	common era (= A.D.)
cf.	*confer,* compare
chap.	chapter
d.	died
D.	Dom, Portuguese honorific
diss.	dissertation
ed.	editor (pl., eds.), edition
e.g.	*exempli gratia,* for example
et al.	*et alii,* and others
etc.	*et cetera,* and so forth
f.	and following (pl., ff.)
fl.	*floruit,* flourished
HRE	Holy Roman Empire, Holy Roman Emperor
ibid.	*ibidem,* in the same place (as the one immediately preceding)
i.e.	*id est,* that is
MS.	manuscript (pl. MSS.)
n.	note
n.d.	no date
no.	number (pl., nos.)
n.p.	no place
n.s.	new series
N.S.	new style, according to the Gregorian calendar
O.F.M.	*Ordo Fratrum Minorum,* Order of Friars Minor; Franciscan
O.P.	*Ordo Predicatorum,* Order of Preachers; Dominican
O.S.	old style, according to the Julian calendar
p.	page (pl., pp.)
pt.	part
rev.	revised
S.	*san, sanctus, santo,* male saint
ser.	series

S.J.	*Societas Jesu,* Society of Jesus; Jesuit
SS.	*sancti, sanctae,* saints; *sanctissima, santissima,* most holy
Sta.	*sancta, santa,* female saint
supp.	supplement
vol.	volume
?	uncertain, possibly, perhaps

ENCYCLOPEDIA OF THE RENAISSANCE

(CONTINUED)

PEUCER, KASPAR (1525–1602), German humanist historian, physician, and professor. Born in Upper Lusatia, Peucer began his education at a Latin school in Goldberg (Lower Silesia) under its rector Valentin Trotzendorf, a student of Philipp Melanchthon. In 1540 he enrolled at the University of Wittenberg, where he lived in Melanchthon's house and, in 1550, married his host's youngest daughter, Magdalena. Peucer received his master of arts degree in 1545 and in 1554 became professor of mathematics. At the death of the physician and teacher Jakob Milich, he joined the medical faculty, receiving his doctorate in medicine in 1560. In the same year he was elected rector of the university.

In the following years Peucer ingratiated himself to the electoral Saxon court. He became not only the elector August's chief advisor for higher education in Saxony but also his personal physician and counselor to both the elector and his Danish-born wife, Anna. In the midst of renewed theological disputes over the Lord's Supper, Peucer favored and had appointed to the University of Wittenberg theologians who insisted, in contrast to other Lutheran theologians, that Christ's humanity was in heaven at God's right hand and not directly in the supper. When their true position became public in 1574, the more Lutheran elector arrested Peucer and his collaborators, in part because of disparaging comments about the electoress in private letters that described the court as a gynecocracy. Shortly after her death in 1585, Peucer was released and became counselor and physician to the Count Joachim Ernst of Anhalt.

In Melanchthon's later years, Peucer was his father-in-law's chief confidant and physician, accompanying him on several important journeys. Upon Melanchthon's death, Peucer published his father-in-law's speeches, letters, and collected works and took over university lectures on world history, which had ceased with Charlemagne. In part using orations and prefaces composed by the older man before his death, Peucer completed the work so that it traced world history from Adam and Eve to the election of Charles V. Called the *Chronicon Carionis* after the work by the humanist Johann Carion on which it was loosely based, the work went through scores of printings in its Latin version and was translated into German, French, Dutch, and Swedish. It combined Melanchthon's concern for the biblical history of salvation with the generally held Protestant conviction that the Middle Ages had experienced an overwhelming growth of papal power.

As a professor in the medical faculty, Peucer wrote several orations dealing with such things as pleurisy and contagious diseases. Living in an age that connected the movement of the planets with disease, he also produced several lengthy works on astronomy, combining Ptolemy's theories with those of Copernicus. He wrote works on mathematics and geography and in 1553 published an exhaustive study of the interpretation of omens, *Commentarius de praecipuis generibus divinationum* (Commentary on the chief types of divinations). While in prison he wrote a lengthy poem in praise of his homeland, Lusatia, as well as several defenses of his position on the Lord's Supper, all of which he published after his release. Entanglements in the theological disputes of his day cut short his promising career as a humanist scholar, so that after his incarceration he never regained the leading role among Melanchthon's students he had earlier enjoyed.

BIBLIOGRAPHY

Kolb, Robert. *Caspar Peucer's Library: Portrait of a Wittenberg Professor of the Mid-Sixteenth Century*. St. Louis, Mo., 1976. Provides a fascinating glimpse at the resources in Peucer's personal library.

Neddermeyer, Uwe. "Kaspar Peucer (1525–1602): Melanchthons Universalgeschichtsschreibung." In *Melanchthon in seinen Schülern*. Edited by Heinz Scheible. Wiesbaden, Germany, 1997. Pages 69–101. Shows the connection between Melanchthon's and Peucer's work on world history.

TIMOTHY J. WENGERT

PEURBACH, GEORG (1423–1461), astronomer, mathematician. Little is known of Peurbach's early life. He matriculated at the University of Vienna in 1446. He received a bachelor's degree in 1448 and his master's degree in 1453, the same year he was appointed a member of the arts faculty. It is not clear whether Peurbach studied astronomy at the university, but he had access to the books of John of Gmunden, the last notable astronomer in Vienna, who had died in 1442. Peurbach traveled in Germany, France, and Italy from 1448 to 1453 and may have lectured on astronomy. After his return to Vienna he was appointed court astrologer to King Ladislaus V of Hungary and later to Emperor Frederick III. His duties at the university, however, appeared to be mostly concerned with humanistic studies.

In the mid-1450s Peurbach began to collaborate with his student Regiomontanus on observations and calculations. Peurbach's *Theoricae novae planetarum* (New theory of the planets) was completed in 1454. This work, which popularized solid sphere Ptolemaic planetary models, went through nearly sixty editions until it became obsolete in the seventeenth century.

Cardinal Johannes Bessarion arrived in Vienna in 1460 as legate of Pius II. He hoped to increase knowledge of ancient Greek texts among intellectuals in the Latin West and sought a Latin translation of Ptolemy's *Mathematical Syntaxis,* commonly known as the *Almagest,* that would supersede both Gerard of Cremona's twelfth-century translation from the Arabic and one completed in 1451 from the Greek by George of Trebizond, which Bessarion considered inferior. He also hoped for a Latin summary that would make the work more accessible in the West. Peurbach did not know Greek but he knew Gerard's translation almost by heart, according to Regiomontanus, so he agreed to prepare a summary, the *Epitome of the Almagest*. Peurbach had completed only the first six books of the *Almagest* when he died in 1461. Regiomontanus was at his side and promised to complete the work, which he did.

See also **Astronomy**; *biography of Regiomontanus.*

BIBLIOGRAPHY

Primary Work

Peurbach, Georg. *Theoricae novae planetarum*. In *Joannis Regiomontani Opera collectanea*. Edited by Felix Schmeidler. Osnabrück, Germany, 1972. Pages 755–793.

Secondary Work

Zinner, Ernst. *Leben und Wirken des Joh. Müller von Königsberg genannt Regiomontanus*. 2d ed. Osnabrück, Germany, 1968.

SHEILA J. RABIN

PEUTINGER, KONRAD (1465–1547), German humanist and antiquarian. Peutinger was the descendant of an old merchant family in Augsburg. After studies in Basel, he traveled in Italy, attending lectures in law and literature at Padua and Bologna, where he studied with Giason del Maino, Ermolao Barbaro, and Filippo Beroaldo, the Elder. Proceeding to Florence and Rome, he made the acquaintance of Giovanni Pico della Mirandola, Angelo Poliziano, and Pomponio Leto. Contact with these scholars deepened his interest in and appreciation for the culture and history of classical antiquity. Inspired by Leto's Roman Academy, he organized a literary sodality in Augsburg.

On his return to Germany in 1488, he entered the service of his native city and, in 1497, became town clerk. In 1498 he married Margarethe Welser (1481–1552), an exceptionally well-educated woman who actively shared his interest in biblical and classical studies. Emperor Maximilian I made Peutinger a councillor, a position he retained under his successor, Charles V. He went on a number of diplomatic missions abroad, participated in diets, and acted as the representative of the Swabian League. Because of his standing at the imperial court, he was able to obtain important fiscal and judicial privileges for his city. In recognition of his services he was elevated to the patriciate (1538) and the nobility (1547).

Peutinger at first sympathized with Luther's ideas, but withdrew his support when he recognized the schismatic nature of Luther's movement. When Augsburg turned Protestant, he resigned his office (1534) and devoted himself to scholarly pursuits. He was interested in epigraphy and published a collection of Roman inscriptions: *Romanae vetustatis fragmenta in Augusta Vindelicorum et eius diocesi*

(Fragments of Roman antiquity in Augsburg and its diocese; Augsburg, 1505). He discussed historical questions in *Sermones conviviales de mirandis Germaniae antiquitatibus* (Convivial talks about the marvelous antiquities of Germany; Strasbourg, 1506). He was also interested in architectural design, supervising the construction of Maximilian's famous tomb in Innsbruck and the renovation of the Augsburg city hall by Jörg Breu. Peutinger collected ancient coins and owned a number of valuable manuscripts, among them the so-called *Tabula Peutingeriana,* a map of military roads in the Roman Empire from late antiquity. He was also instrumental in publishing manuscripts, for example, the *Chronicle of Ursberg,* which he himself had discovered, Jordanes's *History of the Goths,* and Paulus Diaconus's *History of the Langobards.*

Peutinger maintained contacts with a wide circle of humanists in Germany. His correspondents included Johannes Reuchlin, Desiderius Erasmus, Ulrich von Hutten, Willibald Pirckheimer, and Beatus Rhenanus. A portrait of Peutinger by Christoph Amberger is in the Städtische Kunstsammlung, Augsburg.

See also **Humanism,** *subentry on* **Germany and the Low Countries.**

BIBLIOGRAPHY

Primary Works

Die Peutingersche Tafel. Edited by Konrad Miller. Stuttgart, 1962. A facsimile edition of the *Tabula Peutingeriana.*

Peutinger, Konrad. *Briefwechsel.* Edited by Erich König. Munich, 1923.

Secondary Works

Borchardt, Frank L. *German Antiquity in Renaissance Myth.* Baltimore, 1971.

Lutz, Heinrich. *Conrad Peutinger: Beiträge zu einer politischen Biographie.* Augsburg, Germany, 1958.

ERIKA RUMMEL

Philip II. Portrait by Titian. 1551. MUSEO DEL PRADO, MADRID/ANDERSON/ALINARI/ART RESOURCE

PHILIP II (1527–1598), regent of Spain (1545–1556), king of Spain (1556–1598). The only surviving son of the emperor Charles V and Isabella of Portugal, Philip began governing Spain as regent, in his father's absence, from 1543. In 1548–1551 he made a historic tour of Italy, southern Germany, and the Netherlands, which gave him practical experience of European politics and a permanent taste for Flemish and Italian Renaissance culture. Philip was married four times: in 1543 to Maria of Portugal (d. 1545), mother of Don Carlos; in 1554 to Mary I of England (d. 1558); in 1560 to Elizabeth of Valois (d. 1568), mother of the infants Isabella and Catalina; in 1570 to Anna of Austria (d. 1580), mother of the next king, Philip III.

Imperial Commitments. As husband of Mary I and joint ruler (during her lifetime only) of the kingdom of England, Philip spent little more than a year there before going to the Netherlands to assist at Charles V's abdication and participate in his father's wars against France. He took part in the campaign leading to the notable victory of Saint-Quentin (1557) and negotiated the peace of Cateau-Cambrésis (1559), but the spread of the Reformation threatened to bring instability to the realms he inherited at his father's abdication in 1556: Spain, America, the Netherlands, Franche-Comté, and the Italian possessions (mainly Naples and Milan). Undecided about the application of force against heresy in England (where he was unenthusiastic about the Marian persecution) and the Netherlands (where he spent more than four years, 1554–1559), Philip supported the full use of the Inquisition against Protestant groups in Spain (1558–1562), to which he returned finally in 1559.

Philip attempted to reform the structure and finances of the government in Castile, but the serious debts left by Charles V, which had forced Philip to suspend treasury payments in 1557, continued to provoke further suspensions (1560, 1576, 1596). Most expenditure went to war and to building ships in the Mediterranean. The major threat was the Turks, who inflicted a severe defeat on Spanish forces at Djerba (1560) but were checked by a Spanish force that relieved Malta (1565); subsequently, the Spanish-Italian forces of the Holy League won a striking naval victory over the Turks at Lepanto (1571). The long-term problem with gravest implications was the revolt of the Netherlands, which Philip hoped to crush by tough measures (through the duke of Alba in 1567–1573), but which resisted all possible solutions, caused spiraling costs, and invited military intervention by both the French and the English. The revolt (known to the Dutch as the Eighty Years' War) was led from the late 1570s by William of Orange.

When Portugal faced a succession crisis as the result of the death of King Sebastian in battle in Africa (1578), France and Spain showed their interest by supporting Antonio of Crato as the next ruler. This made Philip decide to invade the country (1580) in support of his own claim to the throne. Fixing his capital at Lisbon, he soon decided that England was the principal threat to Spanish interests in both America and Europe. Plots against Elizabeth of England, fostered by the Spanish ambassador in favor of Mary Stuart, were revealed and led to Mary's execution (1587). By then Philip had already decided to attempt an invasion of England, but the result was the costly failure of the Armada (1588). His military commitments—essential to maintaining Spain's global empire, which by the 1580s included the Philippines and most of South America—affected the country's already limited economic capacity. In the 1580s Philip also intervened militarily in France in order to prevent a Protestant succession there. Despite some gains in western Europe (such as the recovery of Antwerp by the troops of Alessandro Farnese in 1585) most of the ventures toward the end of Philip's reign tended to be unproductive.

Domestic Problems. Residing continuously in the Iberian Peninsula from 1559, Philip dedicated himself assiduously to the tasks of government. He reformed the structure of the treasury, negotiated tax agreements with the Cortes (assembly), restructured the central administration to allow more effective control of war, built up a Mediterranean fleet, and supervised the holding of church provincial councils (1565) to improve the state of religion. Before him the crown had no significant court and no capital city; in 1561 he chose Madrid as the site for both. A firm enemy of rebellion, he was ruthless to those who participated in the Morisco uprising in the kingdom of Granada (1569–1570), but he also firmly respected the autonomy of his different peninsular realms, attended their Cortes, and visited all his provincial capitals. Though the non-Castilian provinces were tranquil under his reign, tensions increased in Castile during the latter part of it. From the 1570s taxation rose in Castile and the king began to be criticized by his own people; the Armada failure made further taxes necessary and provoked riots. In 1591 he was also faced by disturbances in Aragon stirred up by his former secretary Antonio Pérez, who had been under arrest for murder since 1579 but escaped and attempted to incite rebellion against the king.

Reputation and Achievement. Despite his diligence as a ruler, his reputation did not survive untarnished—the repression of rebels in the Netherlands and the subsequent Armada campaign provoked a tide of hostile propaganda from the English and the Dutch. Enemies abroad spread sinister stories of his killing his son Don Carlos and his own wife, Elizabeth of Valois; Protestants created bizarre legends of his tyranny, his lugubrious court, his hostility to free thought. Even in Castle his ministers criticized his bureaucratic devotion to paperwork. A more favorable view was taken of his achievements as patron of the arts. He restored and constructed palaces, of which the greatest was the palace-monastery of the Escorial (1563–1584); developed landscape gardens for the first time in Spain (the supreme example was in Aranjuez); supported the leading painters of the Netherlands (notably Antonis Mor, known as Antonio Moro), Spain (excepting only El Greco), and Italy; and invited foreign musicians to court. He financed a new polyglot version of the Bible (directed by the Hebraist Arias Montanus), built up a unique collection of rare books and manuscripts, financed historical and scientific studies of his various realms, and ordered (with limited success) geographical surveys to be made of Castile and America. His artistic preferences when young are reflected in the sensual series known as the Poésies by Titian; later paintings he commissioned were meant for solemn palaces and are religious in tone.

An unswerving Catholic, Philip permitted himself sexual lapses when younger; when older, he was unbending in religious matters but no fanatic, even supporting modification of the "purity of blood" regulations that discriminated against people of Jewish origin and accepting (reluctantly) the necessity for some toleration in the Netherlands. An ardent promoter of church reform, he was in great measure responsible for the success of the last sessions of the Council of Trent (ended 1564), but he also consistently opposed those papal policies with which he disagreed. A firm believer in the efficacy of the Inquisition, he supported all its actions (including even the arrest of the archbishop of Toledo, Bartolomé Carranza, in 1559) and used it in Aragon in 1592 to punish supporters of Antonio Pérez, but it played no significant part in his system of government.

Reputed in his lifetime and later to be an "absolute" ruler, Philip neither claimed to be one nor ever made decisions alone, always relying on his advisers for support; in 1586 he downgraded his own status by ordering that he be addressed as "Sir" and not as "Majesty." A negative personal image extended into mythical depictions of him as a recluse (in fact, after his father he was the most widely traveled of all the Habsburg rulers of Spain). He was inevitably blamed for the failures of his reign: the Armada, the wars, the taxes, and inflation. However, his reign was subsequently dubbed a "golden age," not so much for its imperialist ventures as for its striking achievements in art, literature, and architecture, most of them derived from contact with Renaissance civilization. The roots of Spain's contact with the Renaissance lay in preceding reigns, but under Philip they were substantially extended, always with foreign help: the printing press (pioneered in Seville, Barcelona, and Valencia by northern Europeans) offered new editions to readers; poets (Juan Boscán) imitated Italianate forms; painters went to Italy to be trained. To develop his palaces Philip invited a stream of Italian architects, artists, and decorators to Spain, and virtually all the technological improvements of his reign were carried out under the aegis of northern European or Italian engineers. The most striking of the many portraits of Philip are by Titian, done in Augsburg (1551; held by the Prado), and by Antonis Mor, done in England (1554; held by the Bilbao Art Museum). El Greco included Philip in his *Adoration of the Name of Jesus* (1580; held by the Escorial; see the color plates in this volume).

See also **Armada, Spanish**.

BIBLIOGRAPHY

Braudel, Fernand. *The Mediterranean and the Mediterranean World in the Age of Philip II*. Translated by Sian Reynolds. 2 vols. New York, 1972.

Fernández Álvarez, Manuel. *Felipe II y su tiempo*. Madrid, 1998.

Kamen, Henry. *Philip of Spain*. New Haven, Conn., 1997.

Parker, Geoffrey. *Philip II*. Boston, 1978.

Pierson, Peter. *Philip II of Spain*. London, 1975.

Thompson, I. A. A. *War and Society in Habsburg Spain*. Aldershot, U.K., and Brookfield, Vt., 1992.

HENRY KAMEN

PHILIP III (1578–1621), king of Spain (1598–1621). An unimpressive successor to his father, Philip II, in 1599 Philip III was married to Margaret of Austria, daughter of the archduke Charles of Styria, who died in 1611 having borne him eight children during their marriage. Uninterested in politics, he devoted himself to court life and left government policy in the hands of his ministers. Internal affairs were directed by the court favorite, Francisco Gómez de Sandoval y Rojas, duke of Lerma, and external affairs by Juan de Idiáquez, veteran of Philip II's regime. Lack of royal direction allowed Philip's ministers to pursue policies they had long demanded. Costly wars abroad were terminated by peace with England (Treaty of London, 1604) and a twelve-year truce with the Dutch (1609); the peace with France (Treaty of Vervins, 1598) was sealed by a marriage alliance between Philip's son Philip, the future king, and the French king's sister Isabel (1615). The ministers expressed support for religious peace between Catholics and Protestants and backed proposals to end discrimination in Spain against persons of Jewish origin.

During Philip III's reign political attitudes became more liberal: theorists expressed opposition to the concept of absolutism; religious thinkers (Juan de Mariana and Francisco Suárez) asserted the rights of subjects against rulers and the justice of killing tyrants; in the Castilian Cortes (assemblies) deputies claimed that grievances should be redressed before grants were voted to the government. In 1618 the Junta for Reform, a committee of the Council of Castile that aimed to reform political life, was formed. Perhaps the only retrogressive measure of the period was the forcible expulsion of the Morisco minority, some 300,000 of whom were made to leave the country in stages (1609–1614). Though widely criticized by Spaniards, the act that expelled the Moriscos had few negative consequences for the Castilian economy, which did decline but for other reasons. Valencia, however, lost one-third of its population; twenty years later many villages remained deserted.

The years of peace, a veritable *pax hispanica,* were maintained in part by the energy of an incomparable team of Spanish ambassadors who worked in foreign courts, the most notable of whom was Diego Sarmiento de Acuña, count of Gondomar, who wielded great influence at the court of James I of England. Despite the wish for peace, it proved impossible to avoid the impact of two key events: the rebellion of 1618–1620 in Bohemia, which sparked off the Thirty Years' War; and the expiry in 1621 of the truce with the Dutch, which obliged the government to have its armies active already in 1620, when the Spanish occupied the Rhine Palatinate. The duke of Lerma enriched himself as the king's favorite, placed his relatives in positions of importance, and inspired the removal of the capital from Madrid to Valladolid for five years (1601–1606). Plots against him by fellow nobles led to his dismissal by the king in 1618; he was replaced as chief minister by his son, Cristobál de Sandoval y Rojas, duke of Uceda. The king this time retained a good part of his executive authority and for the first time began to govern. He helped to pilot through a famous report of the council of state in 1619, calling for sweeping reforms in economy and administration. Following a visit to Portugal that year, he fell ill and died shortly after.

Despite the subdued role of the late-Renaissance court under Philip III, during the years of peace Spain developed its relations with Netherlandish culture (through artists such as Rubens, who visited Spain, and thinkers such as Justus Lipsius) and with numerous Italian artists. Aspects of Castilian culture, notably the vogue for the picaresque novel and Spanish styles of dress, were disseminated throughout Europe; the works of Cervantes and Teresa of Ávila became known to an international readership, as did those of Mariana and Suárez.

See also **Moriscos; Thirty Years' War.**

BIBLIOGRAPHY

Pérez Bustamante, Ciriaco. *La España de Felipe III: La política interior y los problemas internacionales.* Vol. 15 of *Historia de España,* edited by Ramón Menéndez Pidal. Madrid, 1979.

Lynch, John. *The Hispanic World in Crisis and Change, 1598–1700.* Cambridge, Mass., 1992.

Tomás y Valiente, Francisco. *Los validos en la monarquía española del siglo dies y siete: Estudio institucional.* Madrid, 1963.

Williams, Patrick. "Philip III and the Restoration of Spanish Government, 1598–1603." *English Historical Review* 88 (1973): 751–769.

Williams, Patrick. "La política interior." In *Historia general de España y América.* Vol. 8, *La crisis de la hegemonía española.* Madrid, 1986. Pages 419–443.

Henry Kamen

PHILOSOPHY. Historians of philosophy speak of "Renaissance philosophy" as encompassing developments in philosophy throughout western Europe roughly from the mid-fourteenth to the early seventeenth century. Obviously no single definition of philosophy would be applicable over these 250-odd years. Philosophy then was rich and varied, constantly changing in conceptions of its scope and purpose, its objects, and its methods.

The mid-fourteenth-century development resulted from a complex interaction between Scholasticism and studies in the humanities. The humanities benefited greatly from linguistic advances and the recovery of ancient sources, whereas Scholasticism languished for being overly speculative and from intramural disputes. The two fundamental authorities in the medieval world, the papacy and the Holy Roman Empire, were in disarray, and new social institutions were rapidly being formed. God, man, and nature continued to occupy philosophers' thought, but their ways of thinking, while not opposed to theology, no longer could be said to be in service of theology. Under the influence of humanism, man came on center stage, in philosophy as in other disciplines.

This article attempts to chronicle this changing scene, first by tracing philosophy's evolution during the period, then by detailing its relationship to other disciplines, the various traditions it encompassed, and its legacy to the modern period.

Historical Overview. The growth of philosophy in the Renaissance was of necessity episodic, with various individuals and themes assuming importance at different places and times. It is generally agreed that the factors most influencing philosophy's development first took form in Italy and then worked their way across the Alps into northern Europe. The resulting temporal and geographical differentiation may conveniently be discussed as pertaining first to the Italian Renaissance, then to the northern Renaissance.

Italian Renaissance. The seminal figure here was Petrarch (1304–1374), who returned to a conception of philosophy rooted in the Greco-Roman tradition. He opposed the classical notion of *sapientia* (wisdom) to the haughty pretensions of the "moderns" (*recentiores*), whose search for the secrets of nature he saw as futile and misleading. Instead one should focus on man's destiny and his struggle to achieve nobility as a creature of God. An enthusiastic manuscript hunter himself, Petrarch led others in the revival of "humane letters" (*litterae hu-*

manae) as the first step in an intellectual renewal. Among those he influenced were Coluccio Salutati (1331–1406), Leonardo Bruni (c. 1370–1444), and Poggio Bracciolini (1380–1459), all of whom promoted humanistic learning (*studia humanitatis*) in distinctive ways.

Among fifteenth-century thinkers Lorenzo Valla (1407–1457) was a towering figure because of his contributions to history, philology, and rhetoric. His dialogues on pleasure treated Epicureanism sympathetically but still showed the superiority of the Christian view. In other works he combated the Aristotelianism of his day and was much concerned with the problem of free will and how human freedom could be reconciled with God's foreknowledge and predestination.

Valla's concern with humanist philosophy was complemented, in the second half of the century, by the more speculative interests of Marsilio Ficino (1433–1499). Trained in the humanities, philosophy, and medicine, and strongly opposed to Averroës's secularism, Ficino proposed a "holy philosophy" (*pia philosophia*) that would link ancient wisdom with Christian dogma. Also interested in astrology and magic, he saw man as the center of the universe, a microcosm who recapitulates the order of the macrocosm. He was preoccupied with man's immortality and the ultimate happiness he would attain with God when freed from his mortal body.

Influenced by Ficino, Giovanni Pico della Mirandola (1463–1494) became more interested in finding the truth that underlay Platonism, Aristotelianism, and the Jewish Kabbalah. He is known for a celebrated *Oration* he was to give in 1487 that began with a special affirmation of the dignity of man and went on to stress harmonies among his philosophical predecessors.

More explicitly Aristotelian in his philosophy was Pietro Pomponazzi (1462–1525), who aimed to discover the real Aristotle under the layers of Scholasticism that obscured his thought. He too focused on man's personal immortality, in which he firmly believed, but he was equally convinced that it could not be demonstrated on Aristotelian principles. His writings provoked further controversies over immortality throughout the sixteenth century.

Other philosophers of that period were less sympathetic to Aristotle. Bernardino Telesio (1509–1588) rejected Aristotle's teaching on matter and form and tried to explain nature with his own principles. He taught that man has a material spirit that vivifies his body and, in addition, a soul created by God and infused into his body.

Even more reactionary against Aristotle was Giordano Bruno (1548–1600), an influential Dominican who was executed for heresy by the Roman Inquisition. Bruno combined Neoplatonism and the Hermetic tradition with Copernican astronomy in a philosophy that was strongly suggestive of pantheism. For him an infinite number of solar systems combine to form an infinite universe in which God vivifies matter in much the same way as the human soul vivifies the body.

In the realm of political philosophy the most famous figure was the Florentine Niccolò Machiavelli (1469–1527). A commentator on political history, Macchiavelli sought for Italy the national unity then emerging in other European countries. In 1513 he wrote *Il principe* (The Prince), essentially a handbook for grasping and retaining power in a predatory society. As opposed to medieval treatises on the governance of rulers, his work was completely amoral in outlook. Macchiavelli regarded human nature as brutal, avaricious, power hungry, and collectively cowardly. His concept of *virtù* favored aggressive daring and opportunism over concern for the virtue of justice.

Northern Renaissance. A transitional figure in Germany was Nicholas of Cusa (1401–1464), a philosopher and theologian who was also a cardinal of the Roman church. Cusa was interested in solving the paradoxes of infinity by a combination of opposites, a theme he develops in his *De docta ignorantia* (On learned ignorance; 1440). Breaking with Aristotle's categories, he proposed that the universe is an infinite sphere whose circumference is nowhere and whose center is everywhere. For Cusa, God is paradoxically the maximum and minimum of all things. Basically Neoplatonic in his thought, he was much influenced by the Dominican mystic theologian Meister Eckhart (c. 1260–1327?). In abandoning the Aristotelian world view, Cusa prepared the way for Nicholas Copernicus (1473–1543).

What Petrarch was to Italian humanism Rudolph Agricola (1443/44–1485) was to German humanism. More a rhetorician than a philosopher, he preferred Cicero over Aristotle. Agricola's principal work, *De inventione dialectica* (On dialectical invention; 1479), stressed discovery over judgment and privileged a logic of topics over a logic of syllogisms. He was also interested in history and scripture and made important contributions to educational reform.

Agricola exerted a marked influence over the French humanist Petrus Ramus (1515–1572), whose *Dialecticae partitiones* (Divisions of dialectic; 1543) simplified and greatly popularized Agricola's teachings. Likewise an educational reformer, Ramus wrote textbooks that were widely circulated in northern Europe. He was vigorously anti-Aristotelian and anti-Scholastic and, when murdered in rioting on St. Bartholomew's Day (24 August 1572), came to be regarded as a martyr of the new humanistic learning.

A different line of German humanism was developed by Johann Reuchlin (1455–1522). When studying in Italy he became intrigued with the magic symbolism of the Jewish Kabbalah. Like Pico della Mirandola he sought to use this tradition in support of his Catholic faith, combining number mysticism with the Neoplatonic tendencies he inherited from Nicholas of Cusa. When overzealous Christians proposed destroying Hebrew books so as to promote the conversion of the Jews, at great cost to himself Reuchlin defended the value of Hebrew knowledge in his *Augenspiegel* (Opthalmoscope, or eye mirror) of 1511.

The most important figure of the northern Renaissance, Desiderius Erasmus (c. 1466–1536), contributed only indirectly to philosophy. An outstanding scholar, he placed his learning at the service of religion with a Greek edition of the New Testament, translations of the Church Fathers, and numerous publications, including his *Moriae encomiom* (*Praise of Folly;* 1509). Very interested in the problem of human freedom and God's foreknowledge, Erasmus attacked the denial of free choice by Martin Luther (1483–1546) in a diatribe published in 1524. This provoked a polemical reply from the German reformer in 1525.

In the field of medicine as related to philosophy, the most important figure was the Swiss Theophrastus Bombastus von Hohenheim, better known as Paracelsus (1493–1541). Educated in mineralogy, botany, and natural philosophy by his physician father, Paracelsus wrote mainly in German, scorning classical scholarship and organized religion. In medicine he rejected the authority of Galen and Aristotle, stressing empirical observation but also importing magic and the occult into his medical practice. Regarded as the father of medical chemistry, Paracelsus exerted an important influence on Johannes Baptista van Helmont (1579–1644) and Robert Boyle (1627–1691).

In France, Ramus's humanism was complemented by that of the political philosopher Jean Bodin (1530–1596). Whereas Machiavelli is associated with the absence of morality in political thinking, Bodin is known for bringing natural law to bear on political questions. Bodin acknowledged that sovereign power is the ultimate source of authority in society, but for him the sovereign still remains subject to the moral law. In an age of religious persecution he issued a plea for natural religion and tolerance. Bodin also wrote with discernment on the nature of history and historical writing.

Dame Philosophy Enthroned. Woodcut from Conrad Celtis, *Quatuor Libri Amorum* (1502). PRIVATE COLLECTION/THE BRIDGEMAN ART LIBRARY

The Valencian Juan Luis Vives (1492–1540) was the Spanish contemporary of Erasmus and, like him, was concerned with education and man. Vives studied at Paris in the early sixteenth century but was repelled by the logical hairsplitting there and became a vigorous anti-Scholastic. He spent most of his life in the Low Countries but also lectured in England. In thought he was indebted to the writings of Lorenzo Valla. Vives's contributions were mainly in psychology, where he sought to study man's actions rather than focus simply on man's nature.

Disciplinary Aspects. From this brief sketch one may gather that Renaissance philosophers, in the main, were not immersed in the arduous problems of metaphysics, logic, and theology that attracted the attention of the Scholastics. Nor were they captivated by nominalism and the application of calculatory techniques to studies of time and motion. Rather they were concerned with attaining a sapiential knowledge of all things human and divine that would be persuasively expressed and meet the everyday needs of people in a changing society. Areas hitherto neglected, such as ethics, politics, and rhetoric, got increasing attention, as did practical arts such as philology, history, sculpture, architecture, and poetry.

University teaching. Innovations in Renaissance philosophy came mainly from outside the universities, from authors engaged in public or ecclesiastical life. Within the universities learning continued to be more or less in continuity with that of the later Middle Ages. Academic philosophers continued to expose the Aristotelian corpus, with lectures and disputations on the master's various works. Platonism was introduced in a few universities, but Plato's thought did not lend itself readily to systematic exposition. The same difficulty presented itself with Epicureanism, Stoicism, and skepticism, treated below.

Aristotle was taught mainly in Latin translation, but with increasing care for accuracy in interpreting the Greek text and with attention to hitherto unavailable Greek commentaries. Humanists made important contributions in establishing the text and supplying new translations, although some of them privileged words over ideas and obscured the sense of the original.

The philosophical curriculum in most universities was fairly uniform during the Renaissance. Prerequisites were basic instruction in grammar, mainly for Latin but also for some Greek and in a few cases for Hebrew, an introduction to rhetoric, and the reading of classics in Latin literature. Formal studies then covered three years, the first year devoted to logic, the second to natural philosophy, and the third to metaphysics and study of the soul.

The detail in which these matters were treated can be seen from the philosophy course taught at the Collegio Romano by the Jesuit Ludovicus Rugerius (Luigi Ruggiero) from 1589 to 1592. Fortunately Rugerius left a manuscript in which he numbered and dated all of his lectures over this three-year period. These came to a total of 1,088 lectures, of which 310 were devoted to logic, 481 to natural philosophy (some of this extending into the third year), and 297 to metaphysics and the soul.

The main works read in the first year were the *Summulae logicale* (Little summaries of logic) of Peter of Spain, Porphyry's *Isagoge,* and Aristotle's *Categories, On Interpretation, Prior Analytics,* and *Posterior Analytics.* In addition some students took on complementary studies in Euclid's *Elements.* In the second year 207 lectures were devoted to Aristotle's *Physics,* 74 to his *On the Heavens,* and 75 to his *Meteorology.* These were accompanied by varying numbers of lectures on *Sphaera* (Spheres), a work of astronomy by Johannes Sacrobosco. The third year saw natural philosophy completed, with 125 lectures on Aristotle's *On Generation,* then metaphysics begun, with 99 lectures on selected books of his *Metaphysics.* Following this came 198 lectures on Aristotle's *On the Soul,* plus readings in moral philosophy taken mainly from his *Nicomachean Ethics.*

Rugerius's teaching was undoubtedly elitist, representing the peak of the Collegio Romano's curricular development from its foundation in 1551 to the end of the century. Nonetheless it mirrored in its detail the curriculum prescribed at other Italian universities, including those at Bologna, Pisa, and Padua. The main difference was that professors in these institutions drew a sharper distinction between philosophy and theology and resisted any attempt to subordinate Aristotle's teachings to the truths of religion. Many were prone to defend Aristotle's views, for example, on the human soul, which denied personal immortality, and the eternity of the world, which denied creation in time, when these were being rejected by the church. Otherwise they covered the entire Aristotelian syllabus, affirming, in contrast to the humanists, the superiority of speculative over practical and poetical philosophy.

Philosophy as method. Throughout the Renaissance there was no clear demarcation between natural science and the special branches of natural philosophy, and mathematics had not yet been excluded from the philosophical domain. The humanist interest in Greek sources helped immeasurably in bridging the gap to antiquity, particularly in recovering the classics of mathematics, astronomy, optics, and mechanics. And the sense of adventure springing from voyages of discovery stimulated novel but imaginative theories of the cosmos.

A point of agreement between humanists and Aristotelians was the need for a general methodology, a believable account of how knowledge should be acquired and organized. Renaissance thinkers debated important issues such as the role of philosophy in the sciences, the rhetorical or logical character of knowledge, and the relationship between teaching and research. Humanists favored rhetorical and dialectical procedures, and, as in the work of Agricola and Ramus, sought a unified method for creating systematic and encyclopedic knowledge.

The English word "method" came from the Greek *methodos,* which was transliterated as *methodus* by postclassical Latin scholars, against the objection of humanists such as Mario Nizzoli (1498–1566). Originally it meant the way or order to be followed in rational inquiry. The Greek teaching on method derived from Hippocrates (460–c. 370 B.C.), as described in a section of Plato's *Phaedrus.* In this context it was closely associated with art or *technē,* but it was soon extended to the sciences. The term was taken up by Plato's students, especially Aristotle and the Stoics, each with distinctive emphases.

An equally important influence came from Galen (c. 129–c. 200), who drew on these sources and applied their ideas in his medical researches. Similar applications were made by Ptolemy (c. 100–c. 170) in his scientific works and by Pappus (fl. 300–350) in his mathematical treatises. The culmination of this line of thought in the Renaissance may be seen in the methodological writings of Jacopo Zabarella (1533–1589) and Francis Bacon (1561–1626) and in the experimental achievements of William Gilbert (1544–1603) and Galileo Galilei (1564–1642).

Humanists, in general, took a different view of method. They favored an interpretation advanced by Latin scholars such as Quintilian (A.D. c. 38–c. 100) and John of Salisbury (c. 1110–1180), who regarded method as a brief summary (*breve compendium*) and way (*via*) of communicating knowledge. The interest of many humanists in education then led them to elevate method into a "philosophy" that guided their reforms. As opposed to the Aristotelians in the universities, they privileged art over science, adopting a Stoic conception of art as a system of precepts that could be exercised together toward some useful end in life. This view was seminal in Petrarch and Bruni and influenced Agricola in his critique of scholastic dialectics and Philipp Melanchthon (1497–1560) in his theology and general educational reforms. Others extended the movement into fields such as grammar, rhetoric, history, law, and medicine.

The greatest simplification of humanist method came in the works of Ramus, who advocated a single method for communicating all the intellectual disciplines. His proposals were received enthusiastically by educators, and his textbooks enjoyed great popularity, particularly in northern Europe. But they were at root simplistic and were attacked strenuously by philosophers, especially those who taught Aristotelian logic in the universities. By the end of the sixteenth century they ceased to have any significant influence on philosophy.

Philosophical Traditions. Apart from Aristotelianism, several systematic philosophies were resurrected during the Renaissance and contributed to the rich diversity of its thought. For purposes here it may suffice to document briefly the status of Platonism, Epicureanism, Stoicism, and skepticism respectively.

Platonism. Second only to Aristotle, Plato exerted a dominant influence throughout the Renaissance. Platonism was brought to Italy by George Gemistus Pletho (c. 1360–c. 1452), who trained Ficino in Greek and set him to work translating Plato's works into Latin. Ficino also translated, in addition to the writings attributed to the mythical Hermes Trismegistus, the *Enneads* of Plotinus (c. 205–270) and the *Elements of Theology* of Proclus (c. 410–485), among other works. Not surprisingly, a strong admixture of ancient theology (*prisca theologia*), magic, and Neoplatonism can be found in Ficino's thought. Another of Pletho's students was Cardinal Bessarion (c. 1403–1472), who defended his teacher against the charge leveled against his philosophy by George of Trebizond (1396–1484) that it was unchristian and actually a new religion.

Others with Platonic sympathies included Giovanni Pico della Mirandola, Jacopo Mazzoni (1548–1598), and Francesco Patrizi da Cherzo (1529–1597). Pico prepared to defend nine hundred theses in a public disputation in Rome, fifty-five of which were based on Proclus's *Platonic Theology;* undoubtedly he saw a basic harmony between Plato and Aristotle. Mazzoni, the second professor of Platonic philosophy at Pisa, also worked on a detailed concordance of Platonic-Aristotelian teachings. But Patrizi, the first professor of Platonic philosophy at Ferrara, was harshly critical of the Aristotelian tradition.

Epicureanism. Renaissance thinkers were also interested in the teachings of the Greek philosopher Epicurus (341–270 B.C.), particularly as taken up by the Roman authors Cicero (106–43 B.C.), Lucretius (c. 95–c. 55 B.C.), and Seneca (c. 4 B.C.–A.D. 65). Epicurus was one of the atomists of antiquity, and this aspect of his thought was systematically developed by Lucretius in his *On the Nature of Things,* whose Latin text was recovered by Poggio Bracciolini sometime in 1417. Epicurus's ethical teachings, and particularly his view of pleasure as the supreme good, became known through the *Lives of the Philosophers* by Diogenes Laertius (c. 412–323 B.C.), which was available in Latin translation by the late 1420s. The pros and cons of Epicureanism, its various interpretations, and how these might be reconciled with Christianity, exercised a large number of thinkers from Petrarch and Bruni to Melanchthon.

Stoicism. Somewhat opposed to Epicureanism was a Greek philosophy founded by Zeno of Citium (c. 366–c. 264 B.C.) and named after the place (the *Stoa*) where he taught in Athens. Stoicism stressed the seriousness of life and emphasized the individual and the concrete as opposed to Plato's abstract ideas and Aristotle's universals. Characteristic teachings were the primacy of the practical, the ideal of mental tranquility, and a pervasive materialism, the last of which Stoicism shared with Epicureanism.

Stoic concepts of the supreme good and of virtue were discussed by Valla, Poggio, and Salutati, and their concept of the emotions by Michel de Montaigne (1533–1592), among others. Critiques of Stoic ethics were advanced by Erasmus and religious thinkers generally. Yet some Renaissance philosophers were intent on developing a neo-Stoicism that showed a fundamental compatibility of Stoic thought with Christian moral teachings. The Flemish scholar Justus Lipsius (1547–1606) was the leader of this movement, further advanced by the French statesman and philosopher Guillaume du Vair (1556–1621). Other strains of Stoic thought were its view of fate and free will, which attracted the attention of Pomponazzi, and its teachings on spirit (Greek *pneuma,* Latin *spiritus*) and magical influences, which figured importantly in the works of Ficino and Telesio.

Skepticism. This option inevitably arose during the Renaissance from the chorus of philosophers presenting their dissenting views, leaving doubt as the only safe position. The resulting skepticism assumed many forms in the Renaissance, including the academic, Pyrrhonian (from Pyrrho, the fourth-century B.C. Greek philosopher), Socratic, and Ciceronian varieties. The early forms were known mainly through the Greek writings of Sextus Empiricus (fl. c. A.D. 200), whose manuscripts circulated in Italy from the early fifteenth century onward but were not edited until 1621. Gianfrancesco Pico della Mirandola summarized Sextus's thought in Latin in a work published in 1520. Full Latin texts became available in the 1560s and were quickly put to use by Montaigne in his essays.

The way was prepared for Montaigne by Nicholas of Cusa's teaching on "learned ignorance" and by Erasmus's fideistic skepticism as manifested in his writings on free will and in *Praise of Folly.* Another possible influence came from the German occultist philosopher Heinrich Cornelius Agrippa of Nettesheim (1486–1535), who held that nothing was more pernicious to human salvation than the arts and the sciences. Other notable Renaissance skeptics included Montaigne's disciple Pierre Charron (1541–1603), who favored suspension of judgment on all matters save divine truths, and Francisco Sanches (1550/1–1623), the title of whose work *Quod nihil scitur* (That nothing is known; 1581), revealed his conviction that all human knowledge is open to suspicion.

The Legacy of Renaissance Philosophy. As can be seen from the above account, the Renaissance provided a rich seedbed from which modern science and modern philosophy would gradually emerge. It was a period of transition, and by the death of Galileo in 1642, no definite resolution of the many issues raised had been achieved. But by the end of the period materials were at hand for their resolution, and these perhaps constitute its most enduring legacy.

A most important contribution was its making available accurate texts and translations of the classics of antiquity, not only in philosophy and Bible studies but in science and mathematics as well. Related to this were advances in philology and the arts, and in national literatures as the vernacular languages developed. A transition from humanism to the humanities was very much in progress. This involved a greater appreciation for history and for poetics and rhetoric, fields much neglected in the Middle Ages. Another humanist strength lay in recognizing the importance of education at all levels, not merely in the universities, and in promoting new and more practical educational methods. In higher education, by the end of the sixteenth century the Jesuits were well on their way to becoming "the schoolmasters of Europe," emulated in the north as well as the south.

In science a great achievement of the Renaissance was the development of new cosmological views, some imaginative and creative, the more important both theoretical and observational in the modern sense. The astronomy of Copernicus, Galileo, and Johannes Kepler (1571–1630) contributed substantially to the scientific revolution of the later seventeenth century. Related advances were made with experiments in mechanics and optics, and electricity and magnetism emerged as new fields for scientific study. Anatomical research grew apace, with detailed portrayals of the human body by Andreas Vesalius (1514–1564) and experimental studies of the blood's circulation by William Harvey (1578–1647).

In philosophy itself methodological studies predominated, with significant advances made in scientific method. Ethics and politics began to assume systematic form, after long periods of neglect. A crisis of knowledge was also in evidence, arising partly from the religious debates of the Reformation and Counter-Reformation, partly from challenges presented by the new sciences. Skepticism had a transitory appeal, foreshadowing the "methodic doubt" that René Descartes (1596–1650) employed to become "the father of modern philosophy." A new branch of philosophy, epistemology, was thus on the horizon, and it would dominate the discipline for the next three hundred years. Its scholastic ties with theology had been severed, but not before the complex relationships between God's causality, divine grace, human freedom, and predestination had been argued to an impasse by philosopher-theologians of the "second Scholasticism."

See also **Aristotle and Aristotelianism; Epicurus and Epicureanism; Hermeticism; Humanity, Concept of; Logic; Metaphysics; Moral Philosophy; Natural Philosophy; Plato, Platonism; Political Thought; Skepticism; Stoicism;** *and biographies of figures mentioned in this entry.*

BIBLIOGRAPHY

Cassirer, Ernst, et al., eds. *The Renaissance Philosophy of Man.* Chicago, 1948, 1956.

Copenhaver, Brian P., and Charles B. Schmitt. *Renaissance Philosophy.* Oxford and New York, 1992.

De Santillana, Giorgio. *The Age of Adventure.* New York, 1956.

Gilbert, Neal Ward. *Renaissance Concepts of Method.* New York, 1960.

Henry, John, and Sarah Hutton, eds. *New Perspectives on Renaissance Thought: Essays in the History of Science, Education and Philosophy in Memory of Charles B. Schmitt.* London, 1990.

Kretzmann, Norman, et al., eds. *The Cambridge History of Later Medieval Philosophy.* Cambridge, U.K., 1982.

Kristeller, Paul Oskar. *Renaissance Thought and Its Sources.* New York, 1979.

Kristeller, Paul Oskar. *Renaissance Thought and the Arts.* Princeton, 1980.

Kristeller, Paul Oskar. *Studies in Renaissance Thought and Letters.* Rome, 1956.

Kristeller, Paul Oskar. *Studies in Renaissance Thought and Letters, II.* Rome, 1985.

Mahoney, Edward P., ed. *Philosophy and Humanism: Renaissance Essays in Honor of Paul Oskar Kristeller.* New York, 1976.

Randall, John Herman. *The Career of Philosophy.* Vol. 1, *From the Middle Ages to the Enlightenment.* New York, 1962. Pages 1–360.

Schmitt, Charles B., et al., eds. *The Cambridge History of Renaissance Philosophy.* Cambridge, U.K., 1988.

Spitz, Lewis William. *The Religious Renaissance of the German Humanists.* Cambridge, Mass., 1963.

Trinkaus, Charles. *In Our Image and Likeness: Humanity and Divinity in Italian Renaissance Thought.* 2 vols. Chicago, 1970.

Trinkaus, Charles. *The Scope of Renaissance Humanism.* Ann Arbor, Mich., 1983.

WILLIAM A. WALLACE

PHYSICS. The term "physics" had a different meaning in the Renaissance than it has in modern times, referring then primarily to a work of Aristotle—known in Greek as *Phusika,* and in latin as *Physica*—that lays the foundations for his philosophy of nature. Knowledge of this branch of philosophy was required of medical students, and in some universities, mainly in Italy, it was sometimes taught by professors of medicine and took on the medical connotation of the English term "physic." This meaning aside, however, some components of the modern science of physics began to assume recognizable form in the Renaissance. The main advances were made in mechanics, optics, and the study of magnetism.

Aristotle's *Physics* continued to provide the intellectual background for scientific progress in the Renaissance, but it was another work attributed to Aristotle, the *Mechanics,* that provided positive stimulus to study in this field. The treatise is otherwise titled *Questions of Mechanics* or *Mechanical Problems.* Actually it was not written by Aristotle but by a member of his Lyceum in the generation after his death; thus, authorship is now ascribed to Pseudo-Aristotle. Lost for centuries, the Greek text was published at Venice in 1497, translated into Latin in 1517 and 1525, and then, to make it available to engineers, into Italian in 1582. Other works from Greek antiquity relating to statics and hydrostatics were made widely available in text and translation after the invention of printing. Of special importance are Niccolò Tartaglia's translations into Italian of the works of Euclid and Archimedes, published at Venice in 1543. To these should be added treatises from the late Middle Ages on the science of weights as well as those of the English "calculators" and their followers, who laid foundations for the disciplines now known as kinematics and dynamics. Typical is Gaetano da Thiene's commentary on William Heytesbury's *Regule solvendi sophismata* (Rules for solving sophisms), published at Venice in 1491. The influence of such writings extended all the way to Galileo and Newton.

Optics, the study of light rays in reflection and refraction, was another science that was well developed among the Greeks and then further advanced in the Middle Ages. The basic treatises were recovered and made available in print during the Renaissance. Noteworthy is the collection of works by Alhazen and Witelo that was edited by Friedrich Risner, a protégé of Peter Ramus, and published at Basel in 1572 with the title *Opticae thesaurus* (Treasury of optics). These studies were known to Johannes Kepler and guided his researches in the theory of vision.

Renaissance thinkers were fascinated with magic and the occult but made little progress in their study. The major exception was William Gilbert (1554–1603). In his treatment of the lodestone in *De magnete* (On the magnet), published in London in 1600, he advanced considerably beyond Girolamo Cardano's *De subtilitate rerum* (On the subtlety of things; Nürnberg, 1550). The first full experimental study of electrical and magnetic phenomena, Gilbert's work opened a new century and heralded the dawn of an experimental era.

See also **Mechanics**; **Optics**; *and biography of William Gilbert.*

BIBLIOGRAPHY

Drake, Stillman, and I. E. Drabkin, eds. *Mechanics in Sixteenth-Century Italy.* Madison, Wis., and London, 1969. Selections from Tartaglia, Benedetti, Guido Ubaldo, and Galileo, translated and annotated by the editors.

Lindberg, David C. *Theories of Vision from al-Kindi to Kepler.* Chicago, 1976.

Rose, Paul Lawrence, and Stillman Drake. "The Pseudo-Aristotelian *Questions of Mechanics* in Renaissance Culture." *Studies in the Renaissance* 18 (1971):65–104.

Wallace, William A. "The 'Calculatores' in Early Sixteenth-Century Physics." *The British Journal for the History of Science* 4 (1969): 221–232.

WILLIAM A. WALLACE

PIBRAC, GUY DU FAUR, SIEUR DE (1529–1584), French magistrate and writer. Born in Toulouse into a well-established family of magistrates, Guy du Faur, sieur de Pibrac played an important political role at the court of Henry III. He studied rhetoric and law at Toulouse and at Pavia, was elected a representative to the Estates General of Orléans in 1560, and became in 1562 royal ambassador to the Council of Trent where he spoke forcefully on behalf of the Gallican church. As chancellor for Henry, duc de Anjou, he defended in Poland the latter's claim to the throne. In 1578 he was appointed chancellor for Margaret of Valois, and in 1580 he became a member of Henry III's Privy Council. Eventually Pibrac convinced the high court at the Parlement of Paris to create an academy of poetry and music, which became the Palace Academy under Henry III.

In addition to being a talented orator and Latin rhetorician, Pibrac is remembered as a defender of the Saint Bartholomew's Day massacre. In 1573 he wrote an anonymous epistle in which he used official court arguments to justify the demise of the Protestants. Critics believe that Catherine de Médicis commanded Pibrac to write this work. Pibrac is also remembered for his *Quatrains moraux* (Moral quatrains: 50 quatrains published in 1574; 104 quatrains in *La continuation* [The continuation] in 1575) and for his *Plaisirs de la vie rustique* (The pleasures of country life; 1574). Both the quatrains and *Plaisirs* contain moral precepts and popular wisdom. Although they were written in a serious and pessimistic tone, the quatrains became highly popular and were translated into Latin and Greek as school texts.

BIBLIOGRAPHY

Primary Works

Pibrac, Guy du Faur. *Un essai de propagande française au seizième siècle: L'apologie de la Saint-Barthelemy.* Paris and Auch, France, 1922.

Pibrac, Guy du Faur. *Les quatrains: Suivis de ses autres poésis.* Edited by Jules Claretie. Paris, 1874. Reprint, Geneva, 1969.

Secondary Work

Cabos, Alban. *Guy du Faur de Pibrac, un magistrat poète au seizième siècle.* Auch, France, 1922. Standard work on Pibrac.

ANNE R. LARSEN

PICARESQUE NOVEL. The picaresque novel recounts the autobiographical, humorous misadventures of marginalized, lower-class youths who survive by their wits chiefly in an urbanized environment. Initially such narratives were written to counter the idealized pastoral and chivalric narratives of sixteenth-century Spain; their fictional protagonists relate their ordeals through episodes, in a realistic or a grotesque manner, and embody their authors' critique of an increasingly materialist and dehumanizing society. The genre's first notable example, the anonymous *Lazarillo de Tormes* (1554), is written as an epistolary response to an unknown superior. The seemingly simple tale narrates Lazarillo's experiences with a series of miserly masters representing various social and religious hierarchies.

The ironic first-person narrative compels the reader to judge whether the adult narrator makes a degrading marriage to the servant of his last master, the archpriest of Toledo, out of corruption or out of need.

Lazarillo was popular and generated two second parts and an expurgated edition (1599). Not until Mateo Alemán's *Guzmán de Alfarache* (part 1, 1599; part 2, 1604; trans. *The Rogue, or The Life of Guzman de Alfarache*), however, was the term *pícaro* (rogue) identified with the protagonist. This lengthy and rhetorically complex novel is considered Spain's first "best-seller." The author divides its chapters into picaresque escapades and moral sermons addressing his reformist concerns. Guzmán's preference for the picaresque life over that of a merchant reflects Alemán's preoccupation with Spain's economic stagnation and seriously engages the theme of free will. The *pícaro*'s supposed conversion from his picaresque life, after he is sentenced to the galleys for theft, has been questioned.

Circulated in manuscript at the Valladolid court, Francisco de Quevedo's *Buscón* (1624; trans. *The Swindler*) has been considered a parody of the picaresque. The novel's satirical brilliance often detracts from its somber message, in which the author's conservative values condemn the character's behavior. Miguel de Cervantes's exemplary novel *Rinconete y Cortadillo* (1614) is narrated in the third person. Although it recounts only one episode in the lives of the two young *pícaros* in the title, it is thematically linked to the picaresque by their experiences in the rigidly organized criminal underworld bound symbiotically to Sevillian society. In *El coloquio de los perros* (The colloquy of the dogs; 1614), Cervantes exploits the beast fable along with the picaresque mode to question in a similar way the concepts of individual liberty, social responsibility, and moral choice.

Novels with female protagonists form a subgenre of the picaresque. All stem from Fernando de Rojas's novel in dialogue, *La tragicomedia de Calisto y Melibea* (1499, 1507; trans. *The Celestina*), known for its protagonist, the old bawd Celestina. While they often do not deal explicitly with philosophical issues, the narratives nevertheless reveal the social constraints imposed on women. As in *The Celestina,* the *pícaras* depend on their sexual attraction to subsist through prostitution. Francisco Delicado's *La lozana andaluza* (Portrait of Lozana, the lusty Andalusian woman, 1528) interweaves a seemingly realistic depiction of Roman prostitution with premonitions of the city's impending sack as it traces the riotous life and loves of a young Spanish woman of Jewish descent who succeeds both as prostitute and procuress.

Later female picaresque tales highlight their authors' misogynist views. Despite its undecipherable burlesque code, Francisco López de Ubeda's *La pícara Justina* (The rogue Justina; 1604) exposes prevailing attitudes on acceptable female behavior. Other novels with female protagonists, such as Alonso Jerónimo de Salas Barbadillo's *La hija de la Celestina* (Celestina's daughter; 1614) and Alonso de Castillo Solórzano's *La niña de los embustes, Teresa de Manzanares* (The trickster girl, Teresa of Manzanares; 1632), present the *pícaras'* aspirations to improve their positions in society, but also the author's rejection of their mobility.

Soldiers' tales comprise another picaresque subgenre, although most lack the ironic separation between author and fictional character that conveys the genre's critical perspective on social values. *La vida del capitán Alonso de Contreras* (1630) and *Estebanillo González* (1646), deemed the last Spanish picaresque, assimilate the genre's conventions in their autobiographical stance and episodic adventures. Thus, although *Estebanillo González*'s soldier/buffoon survives the Thirty Years' War through role-playing, his narrative gives testimony to the degradation of the Habsburg military.

The many editions and translations of Spanish picaresque novels confirm the genre's enduring popularity throughout Europe. The *Lazarillo* was translated into French in 1560; the *Guzmán de Alfarache* into English in 1622. The genre's influence in European literature was first felt in Germany, with Hans Jakob Grimmelshausen's *Simplicius Simplicissimus* (1668) and *Runagate Courage* (1670); imitations followed in France, with Alain Le Sage's *Gil Blas* (1715); and in England, with Daniel Defoe's *Moll Flanders* (1722) and Tobias Smollett's *Roderick Random* (1748).

See also biographies of Alemán, Mateo; Cervantes Saavedra, Miguel de; Quevedo, Francisco de; Rojas, Fernando de.

BIBLIOGRAPHY

Primary Works

Alemán, Mateo. *The Rogue, or The Life of Guzman de Alfarache.* Translated by James Mabbe. Reprint, London, 1924; New York, 1967.

The Celestina: A Novel in Dialogue. Translated by Lesley Byrd Simpson. Berkeley, Calif., 1955.

Cervantes, Miguel de. *Exemplary Stories.* Translated by C. A. Jones. Harmondsworth, U.K., 1972.

Delicado, Francisco. *Portrait of Lozana, the Lusty Andalusian Woman*. Translated by Bruno M. Damiani. Potomac, Md., 1987.

The Spanish Libertines; Or, the Lives of Justina, the Country Jilt; Celestina, the Bawd of Madrid; and Estevanillo Gonzales, the Most Arch and Witty of Scoundrels. . . . London, 1707. Reprint, London, 1889.

Two Spanish Picaresque Novels: Lazarillo de Tormes; The Swindler. Translated by Michael Alpert. Harmondsworth, U.K., 1969.

Secondary Works

Cruz, Anne J. *Discourses of Poverty: Social Reform and the Picaresque Novel in Early Modern Spain*. Toronto, 1999.

Dunn, Peter N. *Spanish Picaresque Fiction: A New Literary History*. Ithaca, N.Y., 1993.

Parker, Alexander A. *Literature and the Delinquent: The Picaresque Novel in Spain and Europe, 1599–1753*. Edinburgh, 1967.

Wicks, Ulrich. *Picaresque Narrative, Picaresque Fictions: A Theory and Research Guide*. New York and London, 1989.

ANNE J. CRUZ

PICCOLOMINI, AENEAS SILVIUS. *See* **Pius II.**

PICCOLOMINI, ALESSANDRO (1508–1579), Sienese philosopher and man of letters. Scion of the same noble family as Pius II, Piccolomini began an ecclesiastic career late in life, becoming archbishop of Patrasso in 1574 and coadjutor to the archbishop of Siena. He studied the entire humanistic curriculum in his hometown, and there he entered the world of letters. As a member of the Academy of the Intronati, he wrote *canzoni* (lyric poems); vernacular renderings from Virgil's *Aeneid* (Venice, 1540), Ovid's *Metamorphoses* (Venice, 1541), and Xenophon's *Oeconomicus* (Venice, 1540); and two witty comedies, *Amor costante* (Constant love; Venice, 1540) and *Alessandro* (Rome, 1545). His major literary work, *Dialogo della bella creanza delle donne,* also known as *La Raffaella* (Dialogue concerning good manners in women; Venice, 1539), describes the corruption of a young woman by a procuress, with original psychological introspection and a worldly and wise handling of moral issues.

When Piccolomini moved to Padua in 1538 to continue his philosophical and mathematical studies, his writings took a more serious turn. Although he retained his Aristotelian background, his work from this time shows a larger commitment to the vernacular as a vehicle for education in philosophy and science and the advancement of knowledge. Advancement was his aim in producing Italian translations of Aristotle's *Rhetoric* (Venice, 1565–1572) and *Poetics* (Siena, 1572), both rich sources for discussion, and his Italian commentaries and accounts of Aristotelian philosophy, which are remarkable for their clarity.

These works include his *De la institutione di tutta la vita del'huomo nato nobile, e in città libera . . .* (On the education of a man of noble birth living in a free city . . . ; Venice, 1542), based on a series of lessons on Nichomachean ethics he gave at the Paduan Academy of the Infiammati, and his astronomical tracts *De la sfera del mondo . . .* and *De le stelle fisse . . .* (On the cosmos . . . [and] On the fixed stars . . . ; Venice, 1540). The latter is outstanding for its constellation charts using, for the first time, a lettering system for the stars. His *Filosofia naturale* in two parts (Rome, 1551, and Venice, 1565) is the first systematic account of Aristotelian physics in the vernacular. His *Instrumento della filosofia* (Organon of philosophy; Rome, 1551) explains the Aristotelian canons of scientific logic to be used in the search for both physical and metaphysical truths, and analyzes the dialectical techniques developed by Rudolf Agricola, most suitable for the everyday dealings among men.

He affixed *Commentarium de certitudine mathematicarum disciplinarum* (Commentary on certainty in the mathematical disciplines) to his paraphrase of the pseudo-Aristotelian *Questions of Mechanics* (Rome, 1547), and it caused much lively debate on the status of mathematics. Piccolomini refutes the traditional point of view, held by Ibn Rushd (Averroes) and the Latin commentators, which saw the certainty of mathematics as depending on the method of demonstration. That certainty, instead, has to be reduced to the fact that mathematics operates without connection to physical entities and is thus of itself elementary. His *Annotationi* on Aristotle's *Poetics* (Venice, 1575) contains more original works. It is probably the first commentary on the *Poetics* to anticipate the concept of artistic necessity as the prime mover determining the organization of plot in an epic poem.

BIBLIOGRAPHY

Cerreta, Florindo. *Alessandro Piccolomini letterato e filosofo senese del Cinquecento*. Siena, Italy, 1960.

De Pace, Anna. *Le matematiche e il mondo: Ricerche su un dibattito in Italia nella seconda metà del Cinquecento*. Milan, 1993. Pages 21–75 and 254–256.

Giacobbe, Giulio Cesare. "Il 'Commentarium de certitudine mathematicarum disciplinarum' di Alessandro Piccolomini." *Physis* 14 (1972): 162–193.

Suter, Rufus. "The Scientific Work of Alessandro Piccolomini." *Isis* 60 (1969): 210–222.

ANNA DE PACE

PICCOLOMINI, ENEA SILVIO. *See* **Pius II.**

PICO DELLA MIRANDOLA, GIOVANNI (1463–1494), Italian philosopher. Pico was born to a noble Italian family, the counts of Mirandola and Concordia near Modena in the province of Emilia-Romagna. At the age of fourteen he left for Bologna, intending to study canon law, but after two years moved to Ferrara and then a year later to Padua, where he met one of his most important teachers, Elia del Medigo, a Jew and an Averroist Aristotelian. By the time he left Padua in 1482, he had also felt the attraction of the Platonism revived by Marsilio Ficino, and by 1484 he was corresponding with Angelo Poliziano and Lorenzo de' Medici about the topic of poetry.

In 1485 Pico traveled from Florence to Paris, the great stronghold of Scholasticism. Before he left, at the age of twenty-two, he made his first important contribution to philosophy: a defense of the technical terminology of philosophy, which since Petrarch's time had incited humanist critics of philosophy to attack scholastic Latin as a barbaric violation of classical usage. Having refined his literary talent while developing his philosophical skills, Pico issued his manifesto in the form of a letter to the renowned Ermolao Barbaro, using the occasion and the genre to show, like Plato in the *Phaedrus,* how a virtuoso's rhetoric could equip a philosopher to defend his calling against rhetorical assault.

After less than a year in Paris, Pico came back to Florence, Rome, and then Arezzo, where he caused a scandal by abducting a young woman named Margherita, previously promised to Giuliano Mariotto de' Medici. Despite the support that came from Lorenzo, the commotion that followed and then a plague kept Pico on the move, just at the time he was writing a commentary on a love poem by Girolamo Benivieni and planning his much grander scheme for philosophical concord. At its core this project aimed to discover harmony between Platonists and Aristotelians, but in keeping with Pico's immense ambition, the total scope of the effort was global, striving to join all schools of thought in a single symphony of philosophies. Pico intended to underwrite a magnificent conference on this theme in Rome early in 1487, and in preparation he assembled nine hundred theses on numerous points of philosophy, ancient and medieval, pagan, Christian, Muslim, and Jewish. He had these *Conclusions* printed in Rome at the end of 1486, and to introduce them he composed his most famous work, which after his death acquired the title *De hominis dignitate oratio* (Oration on the dignity of man).

Intervention by the Holy See derailed Pico's plans and blocked the conference. Pope Innocent VIII appointed a commission that first declared six of the theses suspect and condemned seven others, then rejected Pico's clarifications and repudiated all thirteen. When the *Apology* that Pico then published provoked Innocent to denounce all nine hundred *Conclusions,* the venturous young count left for Paris near the end of 1487. At the pope's request, however, he was detained by French authorities and briefly jailed. By the summer of 1488 he was back in Fiesole as the guest of Lorenzo, to whom in 1489 he dedicated a short work called *Heptaplus de septiformi sex dierum geneseos enarratione* (Heptaplus, a sevenfold account of the six days of Genesis).

From 1483 one-third of Pico's income came from his family's estates, which with his Mirandola property he transferred in 1491 to his nephew Gianfrancesco Pico (1469–1533), who was to become an important philosopher in his own right and an early voice for the revival of scepticism as an instrument of Christian faith. At this time, however, even after the dust had settled on the controversial *Conclusions,* contemporaries were unsure of the elder Pico's orthodoxy, and the Kabbalist exegesis of Genesis in the *Heptaplus* did nothing to reassure them. Meanwhile, Pico pursued safer philological inquiries with Poliziano, to whom Pico's little treatise, *De ente et uno* (On being and the one), was dedicated in 1492. Even though this work was meant as the first installment of the great work that would prove Plato's thought in concord with Aristotle's, not all gave their approval to Pico's offering.

In 1493 Pico made peace with the church when Pope Alexander VI pardoned him for his earlier misadventures. In this period he grew closer to Girolamo Savonarola, whom he had known for some years and who was on his way to establishing his power in Florence. Pico also disposed of more of his property, some to the church and some to his family, as his habits became more unworldly. He was working hard on another enormous project, the unfinished *Disputationes adversus astrologiam divinatricem* (Disputations against divinatory astrology), when death (hastened by poison, some said) came to him on 17 November 1494. On the same day Florence fell to the armies of the French king Charles VIII, ending the dazzling age of Florentine culture that Pico's meteoric genius made all the brighter, however briefly.

Thought. Since the nineteenth century, when Jakob Burckhardt and Walter Pater made Pico an icon of humanism, people have read the speech that he did *not* call *De hominis dignitate oratio* as the supreme Renaissance expression of that elusive ideal. Only a scrupulous regard for historical context will distinguish the reverent classicism that shaped Pico from a human-centered secularism completely alien to the pious mentality of his Christian age. Moreover, because he was writing a speech meant to ornament and advertise his nine hundred dense and homely *Conclusions,* it was rhetorical artifice more than philosophical clarity that guided Pico when he composed the *Oration,* which begins with an audacious new myth of Genesis and makes Adam a miracle of limitless choice. Hence, even in the context of earlier fifteenth-century treatments of human dignity, the *Oration*'s famous prelude might distract a modern reader from the goal of freedom as Pico explained it: the goal was to die in the body in order to live in the supreme Mind with all other souls.

While Ficino had glorified humanity by putting it at the center of a cosmic hierarchy, Pico liberated Adam from any such structure and set him free to rise or fall as he chose. The source of Adam's liberty is not himself, however; it is "the great liberality of God the Father." Later in the *Heptaplus,* Pico again makes a special case of humanity by calling it either a fourth world beyond the supercelestial, celestial, and sublunary, or at least the junction of the other three. Made in God's image, humans are most like God in having a soul that reflects the Trinity. God set this image like a statue at the center of the universe for all to admire the divine likeness, the human microcosm that exalts what is lower than itself but degrades what is higher. Like the *Oration,* the *Heptaplus* urges humans to aspire to the angelic life rather than crawl with the beasts. Pico repeats the Hermetic salute to the human miracle that opens the *Oration* and then follows it with a warning: those who break God's law and defile his image will be the prey of avenging demons. Humanity was made in God's image, Christ was made human, and Christ was crucified. In this ultimate sacrifice of embodied divinity, humankind finds safety from the demons.

Christ saved human sinners by denying the body and thereby establishing an ascetic ideal for Christians. Since Pico was a person of great learning, it was natural that the *Oration*'s ascetic regimen should be curricular, prescribing progress through moral philosophy, dialectic, and natural philosophy toward a theology revealed only to the initiate, and thus appealing to a culture preoccupied with educational reform as an aid to salvation. In the manner of his humanist contemporaries, Pico traced the roots of his enterprise to remotest antiquity, making plain its Platonic and Stoic pedigree but also claiming an older ancestry in Pythagorean, Orphic, Chaldean, and Egyptian wisdom. Having learned from Ficino, who had translated fourteen Hermetic treatises in the year of Pico's birth, he accepted and advanced a special framework of cultural history, an "ancient theology" transmitted by gentile sages in the days of Moses to reinforce the revelation of sacred Scripture. To these two channels of ancient wisdom, Pico added a third that he discovered in the writings of the Kabbalists.

In its historical aspect, Pico's version of the ancient theology offered a pattern for the development of human thought. Had he lived to complete his project of harmonizing Plato and Aristotle, he might have achieved something similar as a philosopher by discovering some structure of concordance between Platonic and Peripatetic ideas and hence among the later systems derived from them. He made a start on the difficult metaphysics of being and unity, but what survives in his work *De ente et uno* is fairer to Aristotle than to Plato and lacks the scope of a large philosophical design. In the *Oration* he remarked that just the task of reconciling Plato and Aristotle could have occupied many hundreds of his theses, whereas his plan for the nine hundred was comprehensive, meant to include "all teachers of philosophy, . . . all writings, . . . every school." Pico's grandiose scheme was eclectic in the root sense of that term: because each school offers something of value not found in others, he determined to choose the best from each. Whether he could have achieved a coherent syncretism, a convincing synthesis of the various truths that he discovered, we cannot know. Of his originality and daring, however, we have ample evidence, above all in his declaration that wisdom comes by three routes: classical, biblical, and Kabbalist.

All three traditions encouraged or at least permitted the escape from the world and the flesh that Pico wished to achieve. This austere stance toward the future, grounded in an irenic view of the past, guided his program for salvation and drew strength from a larger hope that he shared with other learned people of his time: that the scholar could improve Christianity with classical learning, despite its paganism. But an effective Christian humanism would have to overcome not only the heathen instincts of the classics, but their elitist dispositions as well. Pico failed brilliantly on both counts, preferring an esoteric wisdom that excluded the uninitiated and founding his piety

Giovanni Pico della Mirandola. Portrait medallion attributed to Niccolò Fiorentino (1430–1514). BIBLIOTHÈQUE NATIONALE, PARIS/GIRAUDON/ART RESOURCE, NY

on sources so arcane that its strongest allure was to polymaths like himself.

Pico and the Kabbalah. One of Pico's major accomplishments was the invention of a Christian Kabbalah. Introduced in the *Oration,* defended in the *Apology,* and applied in the *Heptaplus,* this most cryptic of Pico's undertakings dominates the *Conclusions,* whose 119 Kabbalist theses would have baffled even the most learned Christian until Johann Reuchlin (1455–1522) began to puzzle them out in the year of Pico's death. Even then, a larger grasp of Pico's project had to wait almost five more centuries for the erudite analysis of Chaim Wirszubski.

Meanwhile, as the first Christian who took Kabbalah seriously enough to justify the difficulty of understanding it, Pico had two great advantages: his own remarkable gifts of intellect, especially in languages, and the help of a number of learned Jews, especially Flavius Mithridates. Flavius, called Samuel bin Nissim Abulfaraj before his conversion, was a rabbi in Sicily and then went to work for Pope Sixtus IV before turning many volumes of Kabbalah into Latin for Pico's instruction. Although he learned to read Hebrew and Aramaic at a time when these languages were all but inaccessible to Christians, Pico also depended on the versions prepared by Flavius, who had salted them with the trinitarian and christological clues that Pico was anxious to uncover. Nonetheless, he also learned a great deal of genuine Kabbalah and applied it creatively for his own hermeneutic and theological purposes.

It was these purposes that shaped the architecture of the nine hundred *Conclusions,* which culminate in seventy-two Kabbalist propositions. The seventy-two are part of the five hundred or so that Pico called his own, as distinct from the four hundred not so identified that contain forty-seven theses on Kabbalah. Pico grouped the *Conclusions* by source, arranging them in lists attributed to the ancient and medieval sages whose agreement he aimed to demonstrate. Apart from these obvious divisions, it has been hard to find any other plan in the *Conclusions,* whose terse assertions are often obscure in themselves and connect with one another even more obscurely. In the *Conclusions,* Pico left a riddle that only Hebrew learning equal to his own could unlock, and Kabbalah is the key.

The very last proposition claims that "just as the true astrology teaches us to read in the book of God, in the same way Cabala teaches us to read in the book of the Law." This way of reading the books of scripture and nature treats the signs of the Hebrew alphabet as letters, as numbers, and also as tokens of creative divinity. Thus, the number (900) of the last thesis (and of all the theses) is a form of the Hebrew letter *tsade,* whose cruciform shape embodies the christological messages that Kabbalist exegesis helped Pico find in pre-Christian scripture. Likewise, two forms of the letter *mem,* valued as 40 and 600, turn up in the first of Pico's theses about Plato, which is number 600 in the series and deals with 40 as a Platonic numerical mystery ($3^0 + 3^1 + 3^2 + 3^3 = 40$) linked to a messianic cipher based on Isaiah 9:6–7. The clearest sign that Pico meant his *Conclusions* to be read numerologically is that he saved the final place of honor among exactly nine hundred theses for precisely seventy-two of them about Kabbalah and labeled them as his own. The number 72 is one of great power, especially when displayed as an equilateral triangle of four points on each side and one in the center, ten points in all. If the four points at the base of the triangle are treated as a row of 10s (the Hebrew letter *yod*), the next row of three as 5s (the letter *he*), the next row of two as 6s (*waw*), and the apex as 5 (*he* again), the triangle spells out God's ineffable name, the Tetragrammaton, and sums to 72.

The same potent number appears in Exodus 14: 19–21, whose three verses, each containing seventy-two letters, led the Kabbalists to align the letters, read them vertically as the three-lettered names of seventy-two good angels, and then use them to make stellate hexagrammatic amulets (shaped like the six-pointed Magen David, the Shield or Star of David) to ward off evil angels. Likewise, Pico meant his Kabbalah to invoke the mightiest angel of all, Metatron, as protection against Azazel, the great demon who invented magic and stood ready to devour any who made mistakes in using that art. One of the *Conclusions* condemned by the Church claims that "no knowledge gives us more certainty of Christ's divinity than magic and Cabala," and Pico took great pains here, in the *Oration* and in the *Apology,* to distinguish this good natural magic from evil demonic magic. Like Ficino, he wished to base a learned and beneficent magic on the remains of ancient wisdom, so the threat of dying in the jaws of Azazel was a matter of grave professional risk for him. The aid that he sought from Metatron, however, was not material power but another kind of death, the good ecstatic death, called the death of the kiss, that liberates the soul from the body for a higher destiny.

Thus, the amuletic letter magic of the *Conclusions,* based on Pico's understanding of the secret Hebrew names of God and angels, has the same goal as the *Oration,* where the best exercise of human choice is to choose the cherubic life of an angel in order to die the best kind of death. Even though Pico did not say that his famous speech was about human dignity, he might have done so while remaining true to his project and to his time, when a good death was the desired end of spiritual discipline for all Christian believers.

If Pico meant the severe angelic discipline of the *Oration* and the world-escaping angel magic of the *Conclusions* to show what path he would follow in his own life, his eventual movement toward a close relationship with Savonarola was consistent with that intention. His development will seem erratic only if one takes the *Oration* to be about a conception of human dignity more adaptable than Pico's to later secular and materialist ideologies. Likewise, by ending the *Conclusions* with the ideal of a "true astrology," he made no commitment incompatible with the huge but incomplete polemic against judicial astrology that occupied him in these later years.

Pico and Astrology. For centuries before Pico's time, opponents of astrology had condemned it as determinist or unreliable or irreligious but could not discredit it altogether because the notion of celestial influence was so fundamental to the prevailing post-Aristotelian worldview; after Pico died, another two centuries had to pass before astrology could simply be ignored as part of a failed natural philosophy. Impressed by the strong language of the *Disputations,* Jakob Burckhardt credited Pico with routing the astrologers, but the Royal Society of Newton's time still thought the subject worthy of inquiry. If Pico failed to destroy astrology, he was also no threat to science. Both pictures of his work are anachronistic, as was Ernst Cassirer in claiming that Pico paved the way for Johannes Kepler and Isaac Newton. Frances Yates aggravated Cassirer's misunderstanding by making Pico the Hermetic herald of the new science, even though Hermes Trismegistus is a minor figure in Pico's ancient theology. In this context, Eugenio Garin best captured Pico's meaning by connecting his natural philosophy with his philology, seeing both as challenges to the traditional order. If, as Pico tells us, both nature and scripture are to be read as books, a new reading of one (humanists preparing themselves to demystify sacred scripture by unriddling the secular scriptures of Greece and Rome) may invite a new reading of the other.

With the realization that nature's language is mathematical, Galileo Galilei finally proposed a way to read the book of the world that would displace and indeed subvert the libraries of verbal wisdom to which mankind had long looked for counsel. Although there is no reason to think that Galileo read Pico, and less to suppose that he could have understood him, it is remarkable that both these heroes of originality reached their deepest insights by pushing language past its accustomed limits. The special properties of the Hebrew alphabet—that its signs are both letters and numerals, that God used them for the words of creation and revelation—caused Pico to press his thinking about alphabetic numbers, shapes, and meanings beyond any sense that a contemporary Christian could be expected to grasp. Galileo's innovation was public where Pico's was esoteric, clear where Pico's was enigmatic, and in these crucial ways it stimulated the growth of what we now call "science," as Pico's speculations never could.

Influence and Interpretation. Through the later Renaissance Pico was well remembered, often positively as by Johannes Reuchlin, who developed his Christian Kabbalah, or by his nephew Gianfrancesco Pico, who wrote his biography and admired his austere spirituality. Leone Ebreo (c. 1460–c. 1521), Francesco Giorgi (1460–1540), Agostino Steuco (1497?–1548), and many others found his eclectic concordism inspiring, though some were troubled by its debt to erudition: Tommaso Campanella (1586–1639) criticized Pico for sticking closer to his books than to nature. Jacob Brucker's verdict in his *Historica critica philosophiae* (Critical history of philosophy; 5 vols., 1742–1744) was even harsher. Brucker remembered Pico as the fountainhead of an irresponsible occultist syncretism, not as a proponent of the dignity of man. Since the historiography of Renaissance philosophy first acquired its now-familiar form in this pre-Kantian, eighteenth-century work, the eventual reversal of Brucker's judgment leads one to ask why and how later opinion reshaped Pico's reputation.

Wilhelm Tennemann's post-Kantian *Geschichte der Philosophie* (History of philosophy; 11 vols., 1798–1819), for example, referred to the *Oration* by its usual name and appreciated its value, while G. W. F. Hegel (1770–1831) barely noticed Pico in his *Vorlesungen über die Geschichte der Philosophie* (Lectures on the history of philosophy; 1833). When the neo-Kantian Ernst Cassirer introduced Pico in a blaze of glory to the twentieth century, he placed him in a chapter of the *Erkenntnisproblem* (The problem of knowledge; 1906) on the "renewal of the conception of nature and of history," where Cassirer read the *Oration* in the light of the *Disputations*. Mankind's freedom to choose is freedom from the stars, their demonic force tamed by a regularized conception of nature. Thus hailed as precursor of the new science, Pico could also be praised as prophet of liberal humanism—both in some vague, post-Enlightenment sense.

Yet this extraordinary but unfinished thinker was neither of these. Giovanni Pico della Mirandola was a daringly creative and eclectic philosopher, equipped with the new learning of his humanist contemporaries, whose primary commitments were to an ascetic Christian spirituality and to the peace among philosophical schools that he believed necessary to instruct the world in that discipline.

See also **Hermetism; Humanism; Kabbalah; Magic and Astrology; Skepticism.**

BIBLIOGRAPHY

Primary Works

Pico della Mirandola, Giovanni. *De hominis dignitate; Heptaplus; De ente et uno.* Edited by Eugenio Garin. Florence, 1942.

Pico della Mirandola, Giovanni. *Disputationes adversus astrologiam divinatricem.* 2 vols. Edited by Eugenio Garin. Florence, 1946–1952.

Pico della Mirandola, Giovanni. *On the Dignity of Man; On Being and the One; Heptaplus.* Translated by Charles Glenn Wallis, Paul J. W. Miller, and Douglas Carmichael. Indianapolis, Ind., 1965.

Secondary Works

Breen, Quirinus. "Giovanni Pico della Mirandola on the Conflict of Philosophy and Rhetoric." *Journal of the History of Ideas* 13 (1952): 384–426.

Copenhaver, Brian P., and Charles B. Schmitt. *Renaissance Philosophy.* Vol. 3 of *A History of Western Philosophy.* Oxford, U.K., and New York, 1992.

Garfagnini, Gian Carlo, ed. *Giovanni Pico della Mirandola: Convegno internazionale di studi nel cinquecentisimo anniversario della morte (1494–1994), Mirandola, 4–8 ottobre 1994.* Florence, 1997.

Garin, Eugenio. *Giovanni Pico della Mirandola: Vita e dottrina.* Florence, 1937.

Garin, Eugenio. *Ritratti di umanisti.* Florence, 1967.

Kibre, Pearl. *The Library of Pico della Mirandola.* New York, 1936.

Kristeller, Paul Oskar. *Eight Philosophers of the Italian Renaissance.* Stanford, Calif., 1964.

Kristeller, Paul Oskar. "Giovanni Pico della Mirandola and His Sources." In *L'Opera e il pensiero di Giovanni Pico della Mirandola nella storia dell'umanesimo: Convegno internazionale (Mirandola: 15–18 settembre 1963).* Florence, 1965. Pages 35–142.

Wirszubski, Chaim. *Pico della Mirandola's Encounter with Jewish Mysticism.* Cambridge, Mass., 1989.

Yates, Frances A. *Giordano Bruno and the Hermetic Tradition.* London and Chicago, 1964.

BRIAN P. COPENHAVER

PIEDMONT-SAVOY. The states of the dynasty of Savoy were located in and on either side of the western Alps between the plain of the Po and the Saône-Rhône valley. After 1388 the house of Savoy also ruled the county of Nice and until 1536 the bailiwick of Vaud, north of Lake Geneva. Although these lands constituted a composite state in which the authority of the ruler varied territorially, the Savoyard rulers might have hoped that their title of imperial vicar in Italy would homogenize their status as sovereigns.

Dynastic Territorial Expansion. During the reign of Amadeus VI (1343–1383), the Savoyard domains included several alpine valleys, lands around Lake Geneva and the southern Jura, Savoie proper surrounding the town of Chambéry (administrative capital since the late 1200s), and parts of Piedmont including the town of Turin. Under Amadeus VI and Amadeus VII (1383–1391) the dynasty began playing an international role and acquired new lands. Amadeus VIII (count, 1391–1416; duke, 1416–1434) extended the dynasty's prestige in Europe through, among other things, his election as Pope Felix V by the Council of Basel (1439).

During the fifteenth century tensions emerged between "Savoyard" and "Piedmontese" elites for the political favor of the ruler. Factionalism, periods of regency rule, and short-lived dukes blocked further expansion until 1536 when invading Swiss, French, and Imperial armies occupied most of the states of Duke Charles III (1504–1553). The stunning victory of Duke Emmanuel Philibert (1553–1580) at Saint-Quentin in 1557 and the peace of Cateau-Cambrésis (1559) restored many of the Savoyard domains, whose new capital was established at Turin in 1563. By the early seventeenth century, the territorial center of gravity of the Savoyard domains had shifted unequivocally to the Italian side of the Alps.

Institutions. Key institutions that had been created in Chambéry by the fourteenth century included the counts' chancery, a fiscal court, and a peripatetic council that administered justice. During the 1420s a sedentary appellate law court was set up in Turin to match the Savoyard appellate court established a century earlier. These courts heard appeals from regional, feudal, and town magistrates. They were replaced with *parlements* by French occupiers during the sixteenth century and were renamed senates by Emmanuel Philibert. In lands under the immediate feudal jurisdiction of the ruler, the castellan was the local magistrate-administrator-tax collector. The *Statuta Sabaudiae* (Statutes of Savoy) of Amadeus VIII (1430) were perhaps the first European example of a coherent legislative packaging of public, private, ecclesiastic, economic, and sumptuary norms. Revisions of the statutes were undertaken during the sixteenth century, when the use of the vernacular in public documents was authorized.

Regional assemblies of the three estates first met during the late 1200s and were most prominent under Amadeus VIII, negotiating autonomy and privileges for nobles, clergy, and towns, in exchange for subsidy grants. During the late fifteenth and early sixteenth centuries the estates began to resist ducal requests for assistance. After the early 1560s Emmanuel Philibert stopped convoking the estates and instead negotiated new taxes and subsidies with individual constituent groups. The most important sources of revenues for the dynasty were the salt tax, transit tolls, indirect taxes on meat and wine, and cash drawn by the rulers from their immediate feudal holdings. While Emmanuel Philibert's efforts to supplement his mercenary forces with a peasant militia were unsuccessful, the late sixteenth century was a golden period of military architecture in the Savoyard domains; Francesco Paciotto of Urbino completed construction of the Turin citadel in the 1560s.

Economic and Social Structures. There was no real urban center in the Savoyard lands until the seventeenth century. Between the mid-fourteenth and mid-fifteenth centuries population throughout the domains dropped by about half. By the late 1500s, there were about 520,000 inhabitants in Piedmont and slightly fewer in Savoy. In Piedmont, partible inheritance and land sales during the 1400s led to the dispersion of rural communities; one wonders whether the privatization of communal property and improvement of wastelands during the demographic recovery created a constituency for the protection of property rights by the Savoyard dynasty. Historians have posited that in Savoy domains economic and political power was monopolized by the feudal aristocracy, whereas Piedmontese communes were able to restrain noble influence.

In Savoy, raising livestock was the most important economic activity. Some communities engaged in viticulture, hemp weaving, and small-scale mining, but Savoyard towns were chiefly centers of commercial transit, an activity facilitated by the presence of bankers from Asti and elsewhere. The Piedmontese plain produced far greater supplies of cereals (which served export markets in Genoa and the Swiss cantons) and towns such as Pinerolo, Vercelli, Chieri, Turin, and Racconigi produced textiles, including silks. Occasionally, and particularly after 1559, Savoyard rulers sought to stimulate production and commerce through merchant-friendly legislation, canal building, banking reforms, and the like. Until Emmanuel Philibert openly welcomed Jews into his domains, Savoyard policy toward this group was equivocal.

Culture and Religion. Amadeus VIII had a rich library and three hundred courtiers who were entertained by musicians such as Guillaume Dufay. During the 1400s the cosmopolitan suites of duchesses from France, Burgundy, Cyprus, and Austria included manuscript illuminators and dynastic chroniclers. The court of Emmanuel Philibert and his successors welcomed intellectual dynamism in the areas of engineering, science, architecture, collecting, and mathematics. During the sixteenth century, the court and the University of Turin (founded 1405) attracted scholars such as Claude de Seyssel, Jacques Cujas, and Giovanni Botero. Jesuit colleges were founded during the 1560s in Mondovì, Turin, and Chambéry. Among the monuments of late Gothic architecture in the Savoyard domains are the Sainte-Chapelle in Chambéry (which housed the Holy Shroud until it was transferred to Turin in 1578) and the church of Brou (in Bresse, constructed under the patronage of Margaret of Austria).

Emmanuel Philibert's consort, Margaret of France (1523–1574), was a friend of the Pléaide poets and a protector of Huguenots, even among her own courtiers. She helped persuade her husband to replace his abortive 1561 war against the Waldensian minority in Piedmont with a policy of limited tolerance toward Protestants. Geopolitics and legal-historical claims for authority over Geneva led Duke Charles Emmanuel I (1580–1630) to promote the missionary activity of François de Sales in Savoyard regions bordering Geneva, and to attempt to capture the town by surprise attack (the "Escalade") in 1602.

BIBLIOGRAPHY

Primary Works

Duboin, Felice Amato, ed. *Raccolta per ordine di materie delle leggi, cioè editti, patenti, manifesti, ecc. emanate negli stati di terraferma sino all'8 dicembre 1798 dai sovrani della real casa di Savoia dai loro ministri, magistrati, ecc.* 31 vols. Turin, Italy, 1826–1869. A collection of laws and edicts issued by the counts and dukes of Savoy from the fourteenth through the eighteenth centuries.

Tallone, Armando, ed. *Parlamento sabaudo. Patria cismontana,* part 1, 7 vols. Bologna, Italy, 1933. Reprint, Bologna, Italy, 1971. *Patria oltramontana,* Part 2, 6 vols. Bologna, Italy, 1935. Transcriptions of records of regional representative assemblies and selected town assemblies for the fourteenth through sixteenth centuries, accompanied by useful narrative summaries.

Secondary Works

Brondy, Réjane, Bernard Demotz, and Jean-Pierre Leguay. *La Savoie de l'an mil à la Réforme*. Rennes, France, 1984.

Devos, Roger, and Bernard Grosperrin. *La Savoie de la Réforme à la Révolution française*. Rennes, France, 1985.

Koenigsberger, Helmut. *Estates and Revolutions: Essays in Early Modern European History*. Ithaca, N.Y., 1971 (1952). See "The Parliament of Piedmont during the Renaissance, 1460–1560," pp. 19–79.

Merlin, Pierpaolo, et al. *Il Piemonte sabaudo: Stato e territori in età moderna*. Turin, Italy, 1994.

Nada Patrone, Anna Maria. *Il medioevo in Piemonte*. Turin, Italy, 1986.

Vester, Matthew. "Territorial Politics in the Savoyard Domains, 1536–1580." Ph.D. diss., University of California, Los Angeles, 1997.

MATTHEW VESTER

PIERO DELLA FRANCESCA (c. 1412–1492), Umbrian painter and mathematician. Piero was the second born but eldest surviving son of Benedetto di Piero dei Franceschi of Borgo San Sepolcro, a small town in Tuscany (now called Sansepolcro), and his wife, Romana. The date of Piero's birth is estimated from the fact that his parents' marriage contract is dated 1410. His date of death is known from the record of his burial in the Badia at Borgo (12 October 1492). The family surname was properly dei Franceschi, but the form della Francesca, by which (following Giorgio Vasari) Piero is generally known, was used by Piero's grandfather, also called Piero di Benedetto. The explanation of the feminine form given by Vasari—that the boy was brought up by his widowed mother—may apply to this Piero. The painter's mother died in 1459, about fourteen years before his father. Throughout his life, Piero spent a considerable amount of time in Borgo San Sepolcro; he owned property both in the town and nearby. His fresco *The Resurrection of Christ* was painted for the town hall (now the Museo Civico of Sansepolcro).

Education. We have no direct information about Piero's early education. Studies of educational practices during the appropriate period indicate that he might have attended an "abacus school," one of the schools set up to teach mathematics to boys who intended to pursue a career in, for example, commerce or banking. Piero's father was a moderately prosperous merchant, and Piero seems to have maintained connections with the family firm throughout his life, so it is not surprising that the kind of mathematics in Piero's treatises closely resembles what was taught in abacus schools. However, it is possible that Piero was taught by a private tutor. His autograph marginal comments in Latin manuscripts of his perspective treatise, and his apparently active collaboration in making the Latin version from the vernacular original, suggest strongly that he was able to read some Latin. No specimen of Piero's handwriting is known from his early years, but his later style, a highly legible humanistic cursive with more than enough character for easy identification, suggests contact with the learned tradition of the day. Piero was apprenticed to Antonio da Anghiari, a local painter about whose style nothing is known. In 1438 Piero is recorded as working in Florence with Domenico Veneziano (fl. 1439, d. 1461). By then Piero was no longer an apprentice.

The Mathematical Treatises. Vasari tells us Piero wrote "many" mathematical treatises. Three are now known: *Trattato d'abaco* (Abacus treatise), *Libellus de quinque corporibus regularibus* (Short book on the five regular solids), and *De prospectiva pingendi* (On perspective for painting). Their dates of composition are uncertain. The *Trattato,* in Tuscan and probably composed before 1460, is dedicated to a member of the Picchi family of Arezzo, at whose wish the dedicatory letter says the work was

Piero della Francesca. *Defeat of Chosroes.* From the fresco series *Legend of the Holy Cross* in the church of San Francesco, Arezzo, Italy. The Roman emperor Heraclius (ruled 610–641) defeated the Persian emperor Chosroes (Khosrow II) at Nineveh in 628, recovering the Cross on which Jesus died, which the Persians had taken from Jerusalem in 614. The exposition of the recovered Cross at Jerusalem in 629 was celebrated in the Western Church in the liturgical feast of the Exaltation of the Holy Cross on 14 September. Fresco; series painted between 1455 and 1466; 328 × 747 cm (10.75 × 24.5 ft.). CHURCH OF SAN FRANCESCO, AREZZO/ALINARI/ART RESOURCE

written. It is an ideal version of the textbooks used in abacus schools, dealing with elementary arithmetic, algebra, and geometry. Instruction proceeds by a series of worked examples, with almost no discursive text. The algebra includes very advanced examples, and there is far more geometry than was usual in textbooks, including three-dimensional examples. Both the algebra and the geometry of the *Trattato* are "state of the art." Some of the problems found in the *Trattato* appear in a neater or more developed form in the *Libellus,* which survives in a single Latin copy (probably translated from Piero's vernacular original), dedicated to Guidobaldo da Montefeltro (1472–1508). It thus seems that the *Libellus,* which is almost entirely concerned with geometry, was written after the *Trattato.* Between them, the *Trattato* and the *Libellus* describe six of the "Archimedean solids" (polyhedra with regular faces of more than one kind which meet in the same way at each corner of the solid). Piero seems to have rediscovered these six solids.

De prospectiva pingendi, the earliest known work on the mathematics of perspective, was written in the vernacular, but the Latin title is found in all manuscripts. The treatise is divided into three books. The first deals with basic theorems and then with plane problems, such as how to construct the perspective image of a regular hexagon. The second considers prisms, erected on the bases formed by the figures in the first book, so that we have, for example, a hexagonal wellhead. The method of construction employed in Piero's first two books is close to, but not identical with, that described by Leon Battista Alberti (1404–1472) in *De pictura* (On painting; 1435). The third book employs a different method to draw perspective images of more complicated shapes, such as the human head. This method effectively constructs the lines of individual "visual rays," using front and side views and sections of the solids. All Piero's examples are presented in full detail, as a series of drawing instructions. The text is tremendously repetitive. Comparing the examples proposed with known works by Piero, it seems that *De prospectiva pingendi* was probably completed in the late 1460s.

Piero's Painting. We know only a rather small number of commissions for paintings. Piero never ran a workshop. He probably did not rely exclusively upon his painting for his livelihood but drew income from the family business.

Piero's earliest known commission, apart from a painting on a ceremonial candle, was for the polyptych *Madonna della Misericordia* (1445), but the panels (Sansepolcro, Pinacoteca) seem in fact to have been painted in the period 1460–1462, after

Piero della Francesca. ***The Nativity.*** Oil on poplar; 1480s; 124 × 123 cm (49 × 48.5 in.). NATIONAL GALLERY, LONDON/ANDERSON/ALINARI/ART RESOURCE

Piero had started work on his major fresco cycle, *The Legend of the True Cross* (1455–1466; Arezzo, San Francesco). Part of the difficulty that scholars find in dating Piero's works may be due to his habit of working slowly. He is said to have used cloths to keep the plaster wet so that he could work on frescoes over a longer time. The Arezzo frescoes employed egg tempera and oils as well as standard fresco colors. Infrared reflectograms of both panel paintings and frescoes show extensive use of detailed underdrawings. These are strong evidence that the painstaking methods described in his perspective treatise were part of Piero's practice as a painter.

All Piero's works show a complete absorption of the new classicizing manner of his Florentine predecessors, in particular the powerful figure style of Donatello (1386–1466) and Masaccio (1401–c. 1428), and the concern with lighting of Domenico Veneziano and others. Piero's work is also characterized by his skill in balancing composition in depth with composition in the picture plane, and by the extreme delicacy of his handling of detail. Lighting is often used to impose unity. The construction in depth is usually an art that hides art: there is very little explicit visible use of constructed perspective. The single exception is the small panel painting *The Flagellation of Christ* (Urbino, Galleria Nazionale delle Marche), where it has proved possible to reconstruct a complete ground plan. In contrast, there are no construction clues in the portraits of Federigo da Montefeltro (1422–1482) and his wife, Battista Sforza (1446–1472), the parents of the dedicatee of Piero's *Libellus* (Florence, Uffizi), or in his *Madonna di Sinigallia* (1469–1480; Urbino, Galleria Nazionale delle Marche). Piero's last painting is believed to be the unfinished *Nativity of Christ* (1480s; London, National Gallery).

Vasari says that in his old age Piero lost his sight, but if this is true it must refer only to Piero's very last years, since we have an autograph draft of his will dated 1487.

Pupils and Reputation. There is evidence that the painter Luca Signorelli (1450?–1523) was

Piero's pupil. On stylistic grounds, the same has been asserted of Melozzo da Forlì (1438–1495) and others. Piero never taught mathematics. Luca Pacioli (c. 1445–1517), who used Piero's *Trattato* extensively for his *Summa de arithmetica* (Treatise on arithmetic; Venice, 1494)—a work of great historical importance as the first printed algebra—probably came into possession of Piero's manuscripts after the painter's death. A vernacular text of Piero's *Libellus* appeared, without Piero's name, in Pacioli's *De divina proportione* (On divine proportion; Venice, 1509).

Piero's reputation as a painter declined quickly, overtaken by changes of taste in the sixteenth century. Art historians rediscovered him in the early twentieth century. The perceived formality of Piero's work harmonized with current concern with abstract qualities in art. Unfortunately, this linkage has encouraged persistence in the anachronistic 1920s practice of drawing complicated mathematical figures over reproductions of Piero's pictures, implying that these figures "explain" the composition. Piero's posthumous reputation as a mathematician mainly rested on his perspective treatise. Up to 1600, all perspective treatises show substantial traces of Piero's work. Daniele Barbaro (1513–1570) incorporated large parts of it, sometimes verbatim, into his *La pratica della perspettiva* (The practice of perspective, Venice, 1568, 1569). Like Pacioli's *Summa,* this work was widely read and very influential. However, Piero's mathematical afterlife contained a large dash of anonymity. Only in the last twenty years or so has it become clear that Piero is in fact an important figure in the history of mathematics.

BIBLIOGRAPHY

Primary Works

Piero della Francesca. *De prospectiva pingendi.* Edited by G. Nicco Fasola. 1942. Reprint, Florence, 1984. This edition is essentially based on the autograph manuscript in Parma, but notes indicate variant readings in the two manuscripts in Milan. For the perils of relying on the vernacular text, see Field (1997) below.

Piero della Francesca. *Libellus de quinque corporibus regularibus.* Florence, 1995. This publication is the first volume in a projected, and very welcome, new edition of all Piero's writings.

Secondary Works

Banker, James R. *The Culture of Borgo San Sepolcro in the Time of Piero della Francesca.* Forthcoming (title provisional). The author has carried out extensive archival research.

Battisti, Eugenio. *Piero della Francesca.* Edited by Marisa Dalai Emiliani. 2d ed. 2 vols. Milan, 1992. Deals with Piero almost exclusively as a painter. The second volume includes transcripts of all the documents that were known (in 1992) to refer to Piero.

Field, J. V. *The Invention of Infinity: Mathematics and Art in the Renaissance.* Oxford, 1997. Chapters 4 and 5 deal with Piero della Francesca.

Field, J. V. *Piero della Francesca: A Mathematician's Art.* Forthcoming.

Lavin, M. A., ed. *Piero della Francesca and His Legacy.* Washington, D.C., 1995. Includes a summary of the dates given to Piero's pictures by various scholars.

Lightbown, R. *Piero della Francesca.* London, 1992. Deals with Piero almost exclusively as a painter.

J. V. Field

PIERO DI COSIMO. *See* **Florence,** *subentry on* **Art of the Sixteenth Century.**

PIETY. *See* **Religious Piety.**

PILGRIMAGE. Pilgrimage is a physical journey from a person's normal residence to a site or sites that the person considers sacred. The journey is undertaken primarily for religious reasons, although numerous motives, both interior and exterior, play a role in the decision to make the trip. Some aspect of hardship or sacrifice is included in the concept of making a pilgrimage, such as walking the entire distance.

Although sometimes thought of as a medieval religious practice that withered away quickly under the attacks by Reformation leaders such as Martin Luther during the sixteenth century, Christian pilgrimages continued throughout the Renaissance, although fewer people took part. New shrines continued to be built. After the Council of Trent (1545–1563), considered the onset of the Counter-Reformation, the number of new pilgrimage shrines multiplied markedly in Catholic areas.

Numbers are hard to ascertain, but records for the century preceding the Reformation give an indication of the powerful appeal of pilgrimage. Fairly accurate records exist for some shrines: Wilsnack in Saxony could expect nearly 100,000 pilgrims a year in the fifteenth century; 142,000 pilgrims prayed in Aachen on a single day in 1496; in 1466, at the shrine in Einseideln, Switzerland, 130,000 pilgrim medals were sold in fourteen days.

The Reformation. Attacks on pilgrimage in the fifteenth century began with the Lollards, who decried the veneration of images and considered pilgrimage an expensive moral corruption. The Hussites called pilgrimage immoral. Among Martin Luther's theses of 1517 were attacks on the cult of saints and the sale or granting of indulgences, both integral parts of the much maligned pilgrimage. Desiderius

Erasmus added to the outcry when he ridiculed the excesses possible in pilgrimage in his colloquy *Peregrinatio religionis ergo* (A pilgrimage for religion's sake) in 1526. John Calvin in Switzerland disparaged pilgrimage and the abuse of relics in the Catholic religion, grouping the practices under the term "superstitions."

In those areas that became Protestant, the number of people who trekked to shrines sometimes dropped drastically, but not always. When Henry VIII of England established a national church, he allowed for the despoliation of the nation's shrines. The very popular Holywell, on the northern coast of Wales, where St. Winefred was beheaded in the seventh century and which was the site of numerous miracles in the Middle Ages, was desecrated. Yet there is evidence of continued pilgrimage activity there throughout the epoch of persecution of Catholics, even though this activity resulted in the violent deaths of several priests. On 3 November 1629, Winefred's feast day, fifteen hundred pilgrims came. Of the shrines that were newly established during the era of the Reformation, most have remained minor, with some exceptions, perhaps the most notable being Turin, Italy, where the Holy Shroud was placed in 1578.

As important as the establishment of new pilgrimage sites in Europe is the spread of this facet of Christianity to the New World Hispanic colonies. In 1531 in Mexico, the Indian Juan Diego was said to have witnessed repeated apparitions of the Virgin Mary. Her reported gift to him of a cloak filled with flowers resulted in the establishment of the shrine of the Virgin of Guadalupe over an ancient Mesoamerican holy spot. This marked the beginning of the syncretization of the Old and New World pilgrimage traditions.

Motives for Making a Pilgrimage. If the original motive for visiting a pilgrimage shrine was to enter into a sacred precinct where the human and divine are contiguous, the number of motives soon expanded to include a variety of human-divine interventions. Pilgrimages were commonly imposed by local priests as a form of official penance for sins committed. Communal benefits were sought through pilgrimage as well. During times of catastrophe, towns might hire pilgrims to walk to a specific shrine to plead the case for the entire town. Residents with leprosy, an incurable illness in those days, were sent on pilgrimage to the shrines of St. Roch, St. Lazarus, and St. Anthony. Even if they were not healed, they would probably die elsewhere, not infecting anyone else in the town. Courts sometimes sentenced offenders to make a pilgrimage. In Scandinavian countries, Santiago de Compostela in Spain was the most popular international penitential pilgrimage sentence in the mid-fifteenth century.

Prayers to the saints included requests for aid, for release from sins, or for improvement in physical health. As a sign of thanks, pilgrims often left a memento, an ex-voto at the shrine, sometimes money but often a physical token of the aid received. The desire to witness a miracle or, better yet, receive a miracle from the venerated saint, emerged as a particularly strong motive for making a pilgrimage. In Bavaria, during the years 1346 to 1522, extant collections indicate that eleven shrines recorded twelve thousand miracles, most connected with physical healing.

People needed to know that their prayers were being answered, even if they did not witness miraculous apparitions. A paper trail of indulgences commenced in the Middle Ages and continued throughout the Renaissance. Church officials initially offered indulgences in multiples of forty days or seven years, but the number of years and the number of indulgences spiraled skyward after the 1350s (and the terrifying Black Death). Excesses such as a remission of thirty-three thousand years of penitential reparation for reciting a certain prayer at a pietà in Rome, for example, became common.

Pilgrimage often focused on arrival at special times. A saint's feast day occurred but once a year, and extraordinary celebrations and activities occurred on those days. When the saint's feast day fell on a Sunday, even more celebrations were called for. In addition, the church often responded by offering plenary indulgences, full remission of the temporal penalty attached to pardoned sins, on those holy Sundays. Pope Boniface VIII announced a new tradition of jubilee years in Rome, complete with plenary indulgence, beginning in 1300 and to occur every fifty years. Estimates of the numbers of pilgrims to Rome may be exaggerated, but they point to the continuing importance of pilgrimage: two million pilgrims for the first of the Roman jubilees and forty thousand pilgrims arriving daily for the 1450 jubilee.

Travel to holy sites was not just an act of religious devotion. It was a grueling physical journey; at least 10 percent of all pilgrims died en route. Pilgrims did not often travel alone because wild animals and thieves could attack on the lonely stretches. Fourteenth-century accounts of the voyages from Venice to Acre in the Holy Land speak of week-long storms that blew the boats off course, days lost trying to find their way without wind, pirate attacks, bad food, rats, overcrowding, and seasickness. Once in the Holy Land, pilgrims might be forbidden to journey to Jerusalem or held for ransom by the Muslims. European pilgrimage offered similar risks.

A crucial factor in the continuance of pilgrimage was the Renaissance interest in travel, the desire to see more of the world and test new ideas. Before the invention of the concept of "vacation," for the average citizen pilgrimage offered one of the few legitimate excuses for travel. While a pilgrimage trek was difficult, it could also be fun. Geoffrey Chaucer recognized this when he opened his *Canterbury Tales* (c. 1387–1400) with the bold statement that when it is April and the weather is improving, people "long . . . to go on pilgrimages." Another indication of this interest in travel lies in the journals written by Renaissance travelers, who were not content to list just the journey's itinerary, but commented on wide-ranging facets of their experiences. Some pilgrims never made it back home, not because of illness and death, but because they chose to stay away.

As during the Middle Ages, pilgrims came from everywhere and from every social station, from kings to the poorest beggar. Their identities, sometimes with scant biographical information, can be gleaned from hospice or hospital records, wills that the pilgrims made before leaving on a pilgrimage, legal papers needed for pilgrimage, and transportation records, especially the passenger lists in records of boat crossings. From the records we can conclude that in general the numbers of pilgrims did decline. In addition, the social level of those who made the journey changed to include more of the poor and vagabond, who went to take advantage of the charity available to pilgrims along the way. During the centuries of the Reformation and Counter-Reformation, legislation about pilgrims' rights leads us to believe that the system of charity for pilgrims was atrophying. While records exist of the foundation of new confraternities dedicated to St. James in European countries and of new pilgrims' hospitals, in general new construction of pilgrimage infrastructure was lacking.

However, a strong interest in pilgrimage travel remained, evidenced in the variety of artistic and literary output. Continuing an ancient tradition, some pilgrims wrote itineraries to help other pilgrims find their way to a specific site or to warn future pilgrims of dangers. Other pilgrims wrote accounts of their experiences, ranging from succinct journal entries to detailed narratives. The number of guidebooks and itineraries about the various pilgrimage routes to the three main pilgrimage centers of Jerusalem, Rome, and Compostela more than doubled each century after the thirteenth. Charles Estienne's French guide, *Les voyages de plusieurs endroits de France et encore de la Terre Sancte, d'Espaigne, d'Italie et autre pays,* went through twenty-eight editions between 1552 and 1668. Pilgrimage narratives evolved into travelogues. These writer-pilgrims visited more than just one sacred site. Some pilgrims, such as the Englishwoman Margery Kempe, went to the three major sites as well as several lesser-known sites along the way. Pilgrims to Compostela in the seventeenth century also toured Portugal and Andalucia before heading back home. The information included in their memoirs is not limited to the religious aspect of the site. Some authors note customs of the regions that they pass through. Some accounts of pilgrimages were intended as vicarious pilgrimages for those who could not make the actual journey: Felix Fabri rewrote part of his *Evagatorium in Terre Sancte, Arabiae et Egypti peregrinationem* in the last decade of the fifteenth century in German for Swabian nuns.

Interest in pilgrimage had not been eclipsed. Sixteenth-century Italian and French short dramatic pieces focused on St. James's miracles, especially those that took place on the pilgrimage route. There are signs of this interest in the artistic output during the Renaissance as well. Books of hours, rich people's prayerbooks, were typically decorative, and in the Renaissance pilgrimage motifs became more pronounced. In Spain especially, due in part to the increased income from New World colonies, churches along pilgrimage routes found themselves in a position to afford new altarpieces, reredos, paintings, and to incorporate the new Flemish and Italian styles.

See also **Religious Piety**.

BIBLIOGRAPHY

Primary Works

There are many modern editions of pilgrimage journals, narratives, and itineraries, and of the denunciations of pilgrimage. This list presents only those specifically used in the article. See Hoade and Kollek (below).

Erasmus, Desiderius. "A Pilgrimage for Religion's Sake." In *The Colloquies of Erasmus*. Translated by Craig R. Thompson. Chicago, 1965. Pages 285–312.

Fabri, Felix. *The Wanderings of Felix Fabri*. Translated by Aubrey Stewart. 1893. Reprint, New York, 1971.

Kempe, Margery. *The Book of Margery Kempe*. Edited by W. Butler-Bowdon. New York, 1944.

Secondary Works

Hoade, Eugene, ed. *Western Pilgrims*. 1952. Reprint, Jerusalem, 1970. Edition of three fourteenth-century Jerusalem pilgrims' journals with an appendix listing narratives in English through the nineteenth century.

Hyde, J. K. "Navigation of the Eastern Mediterranean in the Fourteenth and Fifteenth Centuries According to Italian Pilgrims' Books." In *Papers in Italian Archaeology. I: The Lancaster Seminar.* Edited by H. Blake, T. W. Potter, and D. B. Whitehouse. Oxford, 1978. Pages 521–540. Uses fourteenth- and fifteenth-century pilgrims' records.

Kollek, Teddy, and Moshe Pearlman. *Pilgrims to the Holy Land.* London, 1970. Concise information about the development of pilgrimage in the Holy Land, for Jews, Christians, and Muslims, with quotes from pilgrims' narratives and itineraries.

Nolan, Mary Lee, and Sidney Nolan. *Christian Pilgrimage in Modern Western Europe.* Chapel Hill, N.C., 1989. Important presentation of data showing when and why pilgrimage shrines developed.

Soergel, Philip M. *Wondrous in His Saints: Counter-Reformation Propaganda in Bavaria.* Berkeley, Calif. 1993. Shows the revival of pilgrimage practices in Bavaria, especially the publication of pilgrimage books and pamphlets recounting miracles and legends about the shrines.

Sumption, Jonathan. *Pilgrimage: An Image of Mediaeval Religion.* Totowa, N.J., and London, 1975. Uses contemporary original sources to trace the development of pilgrimage in Europe with regard to cults, motives, and travel; one chapter dedicated to Rome.

Swanson, R. N. *Religion and Devotion in Europe, c. 1215–c. 1515.* Cambridge, U.K., 1995. Although lacks documentation of source material, a readable study of the evolution of religion of the period. Sections on indulgences, pilgrimage, and image veneration as part of popular religion.

Vázquez de Parga, Luis. "Le pèlerinage après le moyen âge." *Bulletin de l'Institut Français en Espagne* 46 (1950): 222–224. Focuses on the change in the kind of pilgrim who trekked to Compostela after the Reformation.

Zacher, Christian K. *Curiosity and Pilgrimage. The Literature of Discovery in Fourteenth-Century England.* Baltimore, 1976. Looks at religious and secular motives for pilgrimage in a study of several literary works.

LINDA KAY DAVIDSON

PINTURICCHIO (Bernadino di Betto di Biago; c. 1454–1513), Italian painter. Like his mentor Perugino, Pinturicchio of Perugia was a highly successful painter in the gentle, colorful Umbrian style of the late fifteenth century who lived long enough to see that style and his career eclipsed by the meteoric genius of Raphael. Yet in his heyday, he was one of the most innovative central Italian painters, bringing a sophisticated understanding of ancient Roman pictorial composition and a strong architectonic sense to the large-scale fresco commissions that were a sign of his cachet among some of the era's most important patrons.

Trained in his native Perugia, Pinturicchio moved to Rome in 1481 to work with Perugino on the walls of the new Sistine Chapel (painting completed in 1483) built at the behest of Pope Sixtus IV (reigned 1471–1484). From 1485 to 1489 he provided fresco decorations for a series of chapels for relatives of the same pope in the newly remodeled Santa Maria del Popolo, as well as a splendid chapel for the Bufalini family in the Franciscan church of Santa Maria in Aracoeli (1486). In these commissions Pinturicchio imitated the relief sculpture of Roman sarcophagi in grisaille (black-and-white) fresco and showed his awareness of ancient Roman painting by quoting design motifs from the buried halls of Nero's Domus Aurea (Golden House); his graffito is still legible on one of its vaults, in the corridor known as Cryptoporticus. He also worked with Andrea Mantegna in the Belvedere of Pope Innocent VIII (reigned 1484–1492) on frescoes that survive only in fragments.

Pinturicchio. ***Self-portrait.*** Fresco in the church of Sta. Maria Maggiore, Spello, Italy. SCALA/ART RESOURCE, NY

Pinturicchio's consciously antique variant of Umbrian style must have been instrumental in securing his commission to decorate the apartments of Pope Alexander VI Borgia (reigned 1492–1503) in the Vatican Palace. [See the color plates in this volume.] Between 1492 and 1495, amid copious applications of gold leaf and gilded stucco, Pinturicchio adorned six halls with personifications of the liberal arts and images of the Hebrew prophets, pagan sibyls, saints, and Egyptian deities, as well as a life-size portrait of the pope kneeling in prayer before the resurrected Christ. Unfortunately, a bolt of lightning struck the papal palace in 1500, destroying the centerpiece of Pinturicchio's suite, the Hall of the Popes, and nearly killing the pontiff himself. Another extensive fresco cycle undertaken for the same pope in Castel Sant' Angelo has also disappeared. In 1502 Pinturicchio began a lavish fresco campaign in the Cathedral of Siena, where the wealthy Piccolomini family had endowed a library; here the painter recounted the life of the famous Piccolomini pope, Pius II (reigned 1458–1464), amid lively grotesques, stately architectural forms, and richly clad figures. In 1503 a second Piccolomini pope succeeded Alexander VI; despite the fact that Pius III reigned for only twenty-six days, Pinturicchio continued to work on the library and finished in 1509.

Pinturicchio's work was not confined to Siena during this period. Taking advantage of favorable transportation routes between Siena and Rome, in 1507 Pinturicchio returned to Santa Maria del Popolo to decorate the choir vault of the church for Pope Julius II (reigned 1503–1513), the nephew of his early patron Pope Sixtus IV. Within a year, however, Michelangelo was painting the Sistine Chapel ceiling, Raphael had begun to fresco the papal apartments, and the style of Roman art changed forever. Gold, grotesques, and the delicate tracery of fantasy architecture were replaced by an imposing solidity and epic scale that seemed to capture the grandeur of ancient Roman art and the scope of Pope Julius's ambitions more convincingly than Pinturicchio's delicate touch. He returned to Siena, working for illustrious clients like the local lord Pandolfo Petrucci and the banker Sigismondo Chigi until his death in 1513.

BIBLIOGRAPHY

Carli, Enzo. *Il Pintoricchio*. Milan, 1960.

Dacos, Nicole. *La découverte de la Domus Aurea et la formation des grotesques à la Renaissance*. London, 1969.

Poeschel, Sabine. "Age itaque Alexander: Das Appartamento Borgia und die Erwartungen an Alexander VI." *Römisches Jahrbuch der Bibliotheca Hertziana* 25 (1989): 127–165.

Sandström, Sven. *Levels of Unreality: Studies in Structure and Construction in Italian Mural Painting during the Renaissance*. Uppsala, Sweden, 1963.

Schulz, Jürgen. "Pinturicchio and the Revival of Antiquity." *Journal of the Warburg and Courtauld Institutes* 25 (1962): 35–55.

INGRID D. ROWLAND

PIRACY. The Renaissance did not invent piracy, defined here as "larceny on or by descent from the sea," but as a historical phenomenon piracy grew in both volume and scope after 1350. As Mediterranean and eastern Atlantic seaborne trade—particularly in compact valuables—began to expand in the wake of the Black Death, seafarers inclined to criminal predation began robbing merchant vessels with alarming frequency. They often rowed or sailed small, swift vessels, attacked with lightning speed, and returned with their booty to uncontrolled harbors or ports managed by friendly states.

Piracy in the Mediterranean. In the Mediterranean numerous groups engaged in piracy after 1350, among them the Uskoks of Segna (on the eastern shore of the Adriatic), who were a recurring menace for nearby Venice, and several North African bands based near Tunis, who preyed on Genoese shipping until a 1390 truce. With the growth of Ottoman power along the eastern and southern shores of the Mediterranean, piracy came to exhibit a more pronounced Christian versus Muslim character. This tendency was exacerbated by the Spanish defeat of the Moors in the territory of Granada by 1492 and subsequent expulsions of non-Christians and suspect converts. Swollen with these disgruntled refugees, the Maghrib, or Barbary Coast, of North Africa became nearly dependent on sea raiding, primarily against Christian shipping. Although the Knights of St. John and St. Stephen also raided Muslim ships and settlements in peacetime, the Maghrib became indelibly associated with piracy in the European popular imagination. Especially memorable were Kheir-ed-din and Aruj "Barbarossa," two early sixteenth-century corsair brothers based at Algiers. As a business, Mediterranean piracy went beyond mere looting to include organized extortion, or capturing and holding individuals for ransom, among them Spain's greatest golden age writer, Miguel de Cervantes Saavedra, who was held from 1575 to 1580. Ransoming Christian captives became the business of the Trinitarian and Mercedarian religious orders by the mid-sixteenth century (the orders were founded at the turn of the thirteenth century with the express purpose of redeeming Christian captives taken during the crusades), but piracy was never entirely reduced to religious crusading. The decline of Venice by 1615, for example, has been more closely linked to the cumulative effect of rogue Florentine, Maltese, Spanish, English, and Dutch (that is, fellow Christian) attacks on its merchant shipping than to Muslim piracy.

Pirates. Uskoks attacking merchantmen, from G. Rosaccio, *Viaggio da Venetia a Constantinopoli* (1606). Based in the Adriatic seaport of Senj, *Uskoki* (the name is derived from the Croatian word meaning to board or to jump in) were corsairs in the service of the Habsburgs, who defended the frontier between Habsburg lands to the north and Ottoman lands to the south. The Venetians and Ottomans considered them to be pirates.

Piracy in the Atlantic. In the Atlantic, meanwhile, pirates plied the Basque coast and the British Isles, particularly Ireland. Among the best-remembered of Irish pirate leaders was Grace O'Malley, a contemporary of Elizabeth I of England. As in the case of the so-called Barbary corsairs, the pirates of the eastern Atlantic concentrated their efforts on slow-moving trade vessels sailing through narrow passages such as the Strait of Gibraltar or English Channel. Atlantic piracy grew rapidly after 1500, as Portuguese and Spanish overseas activities began to generate huge profits, often by trading or raiding for gold, slaves, spices, and other exotic goods. The Spanish conquest and settlement of the Americas, in particular, led to regular shipments of gold and silver bullion across the Atlantic (and later Pacific). This traffic in precious metals through unprotected sea lanes quickly caught the attention of Spain's enemies, some of them pirates. These pirates, mostly non-Spaniards but including renegades and runaway slaves, soon joined hurricanes on the growing list of Atlantic maritime insurance hazards. As in the Mediterranean, corsairing could be synonymous with privateering, or state-sanctioned plunder, particularly during episodes of declared war. But whether sanctioned by monarchs or not, wartime pillage differed little from traditional, pecuniary piracy; as on land, one robbed wealthy people to get rich first, to settle national or regionalist scores afterward.

Protestant Pirates. Other pretexts for plunder abounded, and the religious factionalism of the sixteenth and seventeenth centuries found nominally Christian pirates and their prey exchanging insults as to the others' supposed "heresy" or "idolatry." Such was the atmosphere of mutual religious antagonism between the French Huguenot raiders and their Spanish and Portuguese prey in the eastern Atlantic, the Caribbean, and Brazil to around 1570. Notable French Protestant pirates in the Caribbean and eastern Atlantic during this period included Jacques Sores, who captured Havana from the Spanish in 1555, and François le Clerc, also known as "Jambe de Bois," or "Peg-leg," the first wooden-legged pirate on record. Similar Protestant fervor peppers the writings of numerous English raiders during the reign of Elizabeth I (1558–1603), most notably the Hawkinses of Plymouth and their relative, Francis Drake. Another Elizabethan pirate was John Oxenham, who was tried by the Spanish Inquisition for heresy and executed in Lima in 1580. Drake was considerably more lucky, but even he experienced about as many failures as successes in his attempts on Spanish ships and settlements worldwide. He died of dysentery off the Veragua coast of Central

America in 1596 but is perhaps best remembered for capturing several richly laden vessels off the Pacific coast of Spanish America in the course of his global circumnavigation (1577–1580), the second after Ferdinand Magellan. Lavishly illustrated accounts of these and other English, French, and Dutch exploits in Spanish and Portuguese seas fired the imaginations of European readers of Theodor de Bry's widely copied *Historia Americae* after 1598. De Bry, a Flemish refugee who lived in Frankfurt, cast the Spanish in a particularly negative light, which may have helped fuel the so-called "Black Legend."

Nationalist and religious tensions continued to influence sea raiders in the early seventeenth century, by this time largely dominated by Dutchmen in the Americas, Portuguese Indies, and even Mediterranean. The Dutch *zee-rovers,* many of them veterans of the anti-Spanish rebellion of the northern Netherlands (1566–1648), were mostly sponsored by the East or West India Companies and thus could more properly be described as privateers than as pirates. Still, many of their raids occurred during truces with Spain and its then subject kingdom, Portugal, and in general tended more toward unprovoked acts of pillage than open, staged warfare. In any case, notable Dutch plunderers included Joris van Speilbergen, who captured the Peruvian "armada," or navy, in 1615, and Piet Heyn, who captured the New Spain silver fleet in Matanzas Bay, Cuba, in 1628. Heyn was also a veteran of Dutch battles in Portuguese Brazil. The capture of Pernambuco, Brazil, in 1630 capped Dutch overseas ventures in the seventeenth century.

Only at the close of the Renaissance can one begin to speak of a worldwide "age of piracy," a time in which quasi-anarchistic, plunder-seeking individuals coalesced into bands to raid whatever ships or towns they thought worthwhile, regardless of national or religious affiliation. These predatory sea peoples, variously called buccaneers, filibusters, freebooters, *forbans,* and so on, flourished and declined during the second half of the seventeenth century, particularly among the Caribbean islands of Jamaica, Hispaniola, and Tortuga, and in the Indian Ocean on Madagascar. In response, the increasingly powerful English led a nearly successful campaign to eliminate piracy in the Atlantic and Indian Oceans after the 1680s. Although enlightened despotism ended the "sweet trade" in these seas by the 1720s, the corsairs of the Mediterranean kept the tradition alive for another century.

See also **Drake, Francis**; **Mediterranean Sea**.

BIBLIOGRAPHY

Andrews, Kenneth R. *The Spanish Caribbean: Trade and Plunder, 1530–1630.* New Haven, Conn., 1978.

Bradley, Peter T. *The Lure of Peru: Maritime Intrusion into the South Sea, 1598–1701.* New York, 1989.

Braudel, Fernand. *The Mediterranean and the Mediterranean World in the Age of Philip II.* Translated by Sian Reynolds. 2 vols. Berkeley, Calif., 1995.

Gracewell, Catherine W. *The Uskoks of Senj: Piracy, Banditry, and Holy War in the Sixteenth-Century Adriatic.* Ithaca, N.Y., 1992.

Tenenti, Alberto. *Piracy and the Decline of Venice, 1580–1615.* Translated by Brian Pullan and Janet Pullan. Berkeley, Calif., 1967.

Thrower, Norman J., ed. *Sir Francis Drake and the Famous Voyage, 1577–1580: Essays Commemorating the Quadricentennial of Drake's Circumnavigation of the World.* Berkeley, Calif., 1984.

Wolf, John B. *The Barbary Coast: Algiers under the Turks, 1500–1830.* New York, 1979.

KRIS LANE

PIRCKHEIMER, CARITAS (1467–1532), Bavarian humanist abbess. The eldest daughter of Dr. Johannes Pirckheimer and Barbara Löffelholz, a noted patrician family in Nürnberg, Caritas Pirckheimer entered the exemplary and scholarly convent of St. Clare at the age of twelve. A fine Latinist, she helped produce a well-sourced chronicle of her order and convent and was the hub of a lively group of humanist correspondents that included Willibald Pirckheimer, her brother, Sixtus Tucher, and Christoph Scheurl. (Some of her letters to these humanist friends were published in 1515.) Admired by Erasmus and Johann Reuchlin, she had a high reputation in Nürnberg but also became a symbol for humanists, such as Conrad Celtis, of the burgeoning of classical studies in Germany, being likened to the tenth-century poet Hrosvitha von Gandersheim as well as to Jerome's female disciples and earlier classical models. Although her primary concern was that scholarship be a handmaid to piety and her orthodoxy was uncontested, her Franciscan superiors forbade her to produce writings in Latin.

Having become an abbess in 1503, she led a reasoned, scholarly, and politically astute opposition to the crude and hectoring pressures on the convent in 1524 and 1525 that threatened to close it down altogether. Her efforts so impressed the Wittenberg reformer Philipp Melanchthon that in 1525 he urged the city council to grant a reprieve for her convent. She documented these struggles in the "Denkwürdigkeiten" of 1524–1528, which was first published in 1852.

A genuine humility, both personal and spiritual, characterized Pirckheimer's energetic defense of monastic humanism and spiritual freedom.

BIBLIOGRAPHY

Primary Works

Pfanner, Josef, ed. *Briefe von, an und über Caritas Pirckheimer.* Landshut, Germany, 1966.

Pfanner, Josef, ed. *Die "Denkwürdigkeiten" der Caritas Pirckheimer.* Landshut, Germany, 1962.

Secondary Works

Barker, Paula S. and Datsko Barker. "Caritas Pirckheimer: A Female Humanist Confronts the Reformation." *Sixteenth Century Journal* 26 (summer 1995): 259–272.

Bryant, Gwendolyn. "Caritas Pirckheimer: The Nuremberg Abbess." In *Women Writers of the Renaissance and Reformation.* Edited by Katharina M. Wilson. Athens, Ga., 1987. Pages 287–303.

PETER MATHESON

PIRCKHEIMER FAMILY. The most important and well-known members of the patrician Pirckheimer family from Nürnberg were also its last: Willibald, the humanist and friend of Albrecht Dürer, and Caritas, who was an accomplished and resolute abbess.

Early Family Members. Their great-grandfather Franz (1388–1449) received a humanist education before studying law in Pavia. His children received a well-grounded humanist education. The eldest daughter, Katharina, was a phenomenon in her time. Although neither married nor a nun, she apparently had a household of her own and was held in high esteem because of her education. Hans, the oldest son, was a graduate of the University of Cologne and worked for the family business. In later years he studied law in Bologna and Padua and served on the Nürnberg Council (1453–1477). At the same time he was interested in humanism. He copied letters, speeches, and treatises of Italian humanists and made notes on texts of the classics. Hans also completed a summa of moral philosophy in 1462, utilizing excerpts from nearly all the Roman authors up to the late Christian antiquity.

Hans's son Johannes (c. 1440–1501) was probably introduced to humanistic studies by him. From 1458 he studied law at the University of Padua. In the year 1465 he returned to Nürnberg with a doctorate in canon and civil law. Soon afterwards he entered the service of the bishop of Eichstätt, William of Reichenau, around whom a circle of early humanists had gathered. The majority of his twelve children were born in Eichstätt; eight daughters, one of whom was Caritas, survived, along with the son Willibald. After the death of his wife in 1488, he helped to found the School of Poets in Nürnberg in 1496. He became a priest in 1497 and entered the Franciscan monastery shortly before his death.

Johannes owned one of the most important private libraries in Germany, which his son Willibald inherited and of which the largest part still survives at the end of the twentieth century. Apart from a complete collection of legal codices and incunabula, it contains literature from all fields of humanism, in Latin editions of Greek authors, up to medieval chronicles. Among his own literary bequests, the most interesting is a dispute recorded in ten letters between himself and the prior of Tegernsee, Ulrich of Landau, over the question of whether Saint Jerome translated the Bible from Greek to Latin. Johannes was of the opinion that he had only adapted a previous anonymous translation, whereas Ulrich obstinately disputed this, arguing according to the conventional theological method and in each letter producing new authorities. Johannes, on the other hand, based his argument on Latin quotations of the early church fathers from the Bible and on remarks of Jerome himself.

Caritas. Of his eight daughters, only Juliana Geuder was married; she had four sons. The others all entered a convent, four of them became abbesses. The eldest, Barbara, later known as Caritas (1467–1532), became famous beyond Nürnberg. She entered the convent of Saint Klara there in 1479 and soon possessed an astonishing knowledge of Latin, including an ability to write it that her Franciscan superiors forbade her to apply for a time. She contributed to the Latin Chronicle of her convent and was also involved in its German translation. She noted down sermons of her spiritual advisers that were then copied out. A Christmas sermon, delivered in front of her convent, has been preserved as well as numerous letters. From 1500 on she was reputed to be a paragon of a learned woman by the humanists. In 1503 the convent elected her abbess.

But what made Caritas famous into the modern era was her brave opposition, from 1524 on, to the efforts of the Nürnberg Council to move to Protestantism, which she described in her writing, later titled "Denkwürdigkeiten" (Memoirs). From the spring of 1524 the nuns had to live without sacraments and were in continual fear of expulsion. Thanks to Caritas's brother Willibald, who intervened on their behalf by composing their petitions and supplications to the council, and to Philipp Melanchthon, who interceded in November 1525, they were more or less left in peace instead of being

Willibald Pirckheimer. Silver portrait medallion. VICTORIA & ALBERT MUSEUM, LONDON/ART RESOURCE, NY

driven out. However, they were still denied sacraments and the convent was condemned to die out.

Willibald. By far the most important member of the Pirckheimer family was Willibald (1470–1530), born in Eichstätt. He was trained as a nobleman at the court of the bishop of Eichstätt. He received his schooling from his father, who—partly on his travels—taught him Latin and the rudiments of Greek. Willibald then studied law from 1490 to 1495 in Padua and Pavia without graduating, because a law degree would have disqualified him from becoming a councilor. In 1495 he married Crescentia Rieter, who died at childbirth in 1504 together with their son and left him a widower with five small daughters. From 1496 he was a member of the Nürnberg Council with one interruption, until he left at his own request in 1523 because of his gout. Subsequently, he never filled a public office but did undertake several diplomatic journeys, the last of which took place in 1519. In 1499 he took part in the Schweizerkrieg (Swiss war) as an army captain and wrote down his experiences and perceptions.

From 1501 Willibald intensified his humanistic studies. Above all, with great perseverance he learned Greek by himself. In 1513 he had his first translation from Greek into Latin printed. Sixteen further translations followed, especially from Plutarch and Lucian and later from Gregory of Nazianz; in 1525 his translation of Ptolemy's *Geography* was published.

His published works are only of historical interest. His correspondence, however, which he preserved and of which a large part still exists, paints a lively picture of a humanist and his circle. He cultivated many friendships, including those with Albrecht Dürer and Desiderius Erasmus. But the Reformation took its toll: he broke temporarily with Johannes Cochlaeus, an antagonist of Luther's, and permanently with Lazarus Spengler, the protagonist of the Nürnberg Reformation. Willibald, like many humanists, favored the Reformation initially but eventually distanced himself because he rejected the consequences in Nürnberg. He intensified his relation to Erasmus, who like himself, despite all criticism, adhered to the old beliefs. Of his five daughters, two were married; only the eldest, Felicitas, had children. The others entered a convent when they were very young. Their father thought this was a great mistake in 1525, when Nürnberg turned Protestant, but that did not stop him from supporting Katharina, who subsequently became the last abbess of Saint Klara, in her determination to take her vows and remain in the convent.

In 1606 Willibald's great-grandson, Hans Imhoff, wrote a short life of his ancestor. It was based on an autobiographical sketch of the humanist.

See also **Humanism,** *subentry on* **Germany and the Low Countries.**

BIBLIOGRAPHY

Primary Works

Pfanner, Josef, ed. *Caritas Pirckheimer: Quellensammlung.* 3 vols. Landshut, Germany, 1961–1966.

Willibald Pirckheimers Briefwechsel. Vols. 1 (1491–1507) and 2 (1507–1515) edited by Emil Reicke, Munich, 1940 and 1956; vol. 3 (1516–1518) edited by Dieter Wuttke and Helga Scheible, 1989; and vol. 4 (1519–1521) edited by Helga Scheible, 1997.

Secondary Works

Bietenholz, Peter G. *Contemporaries of Erasmus: A Biographical Register of the Renaissance and Reformation.* Vol. 3. Toronto, 1987.

Eckert, Willehad Paul, and Christoph von Imhoff. *Willibald Pirckheimer.* Cologne, Germany, 1982.

Holzberg, Niklas. *Willibald Pirckheimer: Griechischer Humanismus in Deutschland.* Munich, 1981.

Kurras, Lotte, and Franz Machilek, eds. *Caritas Pirckheimer, 1467–1532: Ausstellungskatalog.* Munich, 1982.

Reimann, Arnold. *Die älteren Pirckheimer.* Edited by Hans Rupprich. Leipzig, Germany, 1944.

HELGA SCHEIBLE

PISA. The seaport of Tuscany, Pisa was an independent state and a seagoing power in the Middle Ages. Although it lost its independence to Florence, Renaissance Pisa remained an important commercial center and hosted a prominent university.

According to Emanuele Repetti's *Dizionario* (1841), Pisans numbered 8,571 in the 1551 census, but the people living in four suburban church parishes were not registered. The census ordered by Cosimo I de' Medici in 1558–1562 gave a total of 10,069 inhabitants. David Herlihy reckoned early Renaissance Pisa population as between 10,000 and 15,000.

The commune was ruled in medieval Pisa by twelve (or fourteen) *consoli* (consuls) elected by urban guilds, such as the *ordo mercatorum* (order of merchants), the *ars lane* (guild of wool workers), or the *ordo maris* (order of the sea). The *Senato* was a parliamentary assembly of the commune, set up by forty members appointed by the *consoli*. Both *consoli* and *senatori* (senators) belonged to noble and merchant families of the city. The *Senato* was a depositary of the sovereign power, while the *consoli* decreed on justice and legal affairs through a magistrate of their own, the *Console di Giustizia*. The *popolo* (people), counterbalancing the commune, were represented by the *Anziani* (council of elders), since their thirteenth-century consolidation. Arts and crafts were divided, by their professional and financial importance, in major, middle, and lower guilds; they worked with the government of the commune as did the Order of Merchants and the Guild of Wool Workers.

Since the thirteenth century, growing political functions had been assumed by the merchant orders and the four officially recognized guilds, leading Pisa to be divided in two political factions. An upsurge rooted in the excluded crafts resulted in the recognition of the *ars lane* as an order, or major guild, and in the independence of several artisan guilds by 1267. Pisan noble families lived outside the city in villas with their own armies, councils, and captains, and rented their urban properties to the common people, who suffered under the high cost of living. The guilds also suffered as a result of high rents.

The governing merchant guilds strongly opposed tax-free use of the Port of Pisa by the Florentine textile industry, while the manufacturing guilds were more inclined to allow such use. At the end of war with Florence (1356–1364)—which had tried to use the Sienese trading port of Talamone—old tax ex-

Pisa. *Capture of Pisa* by Giorgio Vasari (1511–1574). The painting, one of several frescoes in the Palazzo Vecchio depicting the wars that Florence waged against Pisa and Siena, celebrates a Florentine victory over Pisa. The baptistery, cathedral, and Leaning Tower are at the far left. SCALA/ART RESOURCE

emptions were renewed and the Gambacorta, manufacturers' chief representatives, had to quit their power. Giovanni dell'Agnello (d. 1387) then became holder of a *dogato* (magistracy) from 1364 to 1368. Subsequent governments of Pietro Gambacorta (1369–1392) and Jacopo d'Appiano (1392–1399) notably marked the ascent of merchant and bureaucratic families coming out of the *popolo*. When Gherardo d'Appiano retired in 1399, he left Pisa in the hands of Gian Galeazzo Visconti, duke of Milan, who was trying to create a large north Italian State. After Visconti's sudden death in 1402, his natural son sold Pisa to Florence in 1406 for 206,000 gold *florins*. Pisa lost its independence, despite a struggle against Florence.

In 1409 the city saw two popes deposed: Gregory XII and the antipope, Benedict XIII, faced each other at the Council of Pisa, which elected Alexander V in an attempt to resolve religious questions posed by the Great Schism (1378–1417).

Until Lorenzo de' Medici's time (1449–1492), the Florentine government feared new turbulence and harshly controlled the city. The Medici helped Pisa recover its prosperity by replacing trade income with large investments in the building of fortifications and in the draining of marshes surrounding the district and the countryside. In 1547 the new *Ufficio dei Fiumi e Fossi* (Office of rivers and canals) was created in Pisa, with the function of looking after lands and rivers. Lorenzo de' Medici revived the University of Pisa, which had ceased to exist in the early fifteenth century. In 1473 Lorenzo moved the University of Florence to Pisa, where it remained, and ordered his subjects to study there. The Medici particularly favored the University of Pisa. As a result it became a major Italian university, especially after 1543.

When the king of France, Charles VIII, invaded Italy (1494), a political crisis began: the Medici were expelled from Florence and the Republic was restored under the leadership of Girolamo Savonarola (ruled 1494–1498). Pisa rose up. This portion of the Wars of Italy lasted fourteen years. The city surrendered in 1509 after three sieges (1499; 1503, when Leonardo da Vinci was charged with planning the diversion of the Arno's flow; and 1505) The peace was signed on 4 June 1509 in the presence of Niccolò Machiavelli, secretary of the Florentine republic. He returned to Pisa two years later (1511), to allow French prelates entrance to the French-sponsored Council of Pisa—the "conciliabolo," as Leo X mocked it. The assembly had been summoned by Louis XII, ostensibly as a general council for the reformation of the Catholic Church.

Late Renaissance Pisa was a favorite dwelling place of Alessandro de' Medici, first duke of Florence (1510–1537). The *Ordine dei Cavalieri di Santo Stefano* (Order of knights of Saint Stephen), whose palace and church are among the most remarkable works of Giorgio Vasari (1511–1574), was created in 1562 by Cosimo de' Medici to reinforce the political consensus as well as to increase sea-trade income with privileges granted to the new aristocracy. The new paths opened by Galileo Galilei, who taught at the University of Pisa from 1589 to 1592, to the modern scientific investigation soon rescued Pisa's lost maritime glory.

See also **Florence; Medici, Lorenzo de'**.

BIBLIOGRAPHY

Primary Work

Repetti, Emanuele. *Dizionario geografico fisico storico della Toscana contenente la descrizione di tutti i luoghi del granducato, ducato di Lucca, Garfagnana, e Lunigiana* (A geographical, physical, historical dictionary of Tuscany). Florence, 1833, 1846.

Secondary Works

Benvenuti, Gino. *Storia della Repubblica di Pisa*. Pisa, Italy, 1982.

Diaz, Furio. *Il Granducato di Toscana: I Medici*. Turin, Italy, 1976, 1987.

Herlihy, David. *Pisa in the Early Renaissance: A Study of Urban Growth*. New Haven, Conn., 1958.

Luzzati, Michele. *Firenze e la Toscana nel Medioevo seicento anni per la costruzione di uno stato*. Turin, Italy, 1986.

PAOLO RENZI

PISANELLO, ANTONIO PISANO, IL (c. 1395–1455), Italian painter, medalist, draftsman. Pisanello was born in Pisa of a Pisan father and a Veronese mother. His early career and training, which took place in northern Italy, are uncertain. Sources attribute to him a (lost) fresco in the Sala del Maggior Consiglio in the Doge's Palace in Venice. Painted in the mid to late teens of the fifteenth century, it depicted an episode in the struggle between Pope Alexander III and the emperor Frederick Barbarossa in the late twelfth century. Of Pisanello's certain works that survive, the earliest was painted when he was over thirty: a fresco of the Annunciation, c. 1426, forming part of the tomb for Niccolò Brenzoni in San Fermo Maggiore, Verona. The work shows the formative influences of Gentile da Fabriano, the most accomplished painter working in northern Italy, and of Stefano da Zevio, the leading painter in early fifteenth-century Verona.

Court Painter and Portrait Medalist. By the early 1420s Pisanello's reputation was estab-

Medallion by Pisanello. Portrait medallion of the Byzantine emperor John VIII Palaeologus (ruled 1425–1448). The emperor attended the Council of Florence in 1438–1439. The artist's name, in Latin and Greek, is on the reverse. Museo Nazionale del Bargello, Florence/Anderson/Alinari/Art Resource

lished, and he had settled into his lifelong pattern of moving among various northern Italian courts, in particular Ferrara and Mantua. In around 1430 he was also working for the duke of Milan, for whom he may have created (lost) fresco cycle(s) in the castle in Pavia, and Pope Eugenius IV, for whom he finished a (lost) cycle on the life of St. John the Baptist with prophets and evangelists in St. John Lateran, Rome, that had been left unfinished at Gentile da Fabriano's death.

Having studied the visual remains of antiquity while in Rome, Pisanello may have been more fully integrated into the humanist interests of the northern Italian princes who employed him than was usual for an artist at this time. His contacts with his compatriot, the humanist Guarino Guarini, who arrived in Ferrara in 1429, and other court humanists, stimulated him virtually to reinvent the antique art form of the bronze portrait medal. His medal of 1438–1439 for John VIII Palaeologus, emperor of Byzantium, is conventionally seen as his earliest such work, followed, during the 1440s, by medals for most of the dominant personalities in northern Italian politics: the rulers Leonello d'Este of Ferrara, Sigismondo Malatesta of Rimini (1445), Domenico Malatesta Novello of Cesena, and Filippo Maria Visconti of Milan (but possibly dating c. 1432–1433), as well as the condottieri (mercenary captains) Niccolò Piccinino (before 1444) and Francesco Sforza (1441?). In 1447 he produced portrait medals for Ludovico Gonzaga of Mantua and his sister Cecilia; the medals for the marchese's father, Gian Francesco Gonzaga, and his tutor Vittorino da Feltre may date from this same period. In 1448 he created a medal for Pier Candido Decembrio that Leonello d'Este had commissioned as a gift for the Milanese humanist.

In Ferrara in 1441, both Pisanello and Jacopo Bellini painted portraits of the future ruler of Ferrara, Leonello d'Este; according to a humanist's sonnet, Bellini's work was preferred to Pisanello's. In the early 1440s these humanists started to celebrate Pisanello's artistic skill in verse, and he became the contemporary artist most praised by the humanists. Ulisse degli Aleotti and Angelo Galli wrote in Italian; Guarino, Tito Vespasiano Strozzi, and Basinio da Parma in Latin. It was the job of the court humanist to articulate his prince's taste and values, and these verses reveal that Pisanello's art corresponded to an ideal fostered in court circles.

In 1448 Pisanello left northern Italy for Naples and the Aragonese court, where King Alfonso V decreed him a member of the royal household with an annual stipend of four hundred ducats. He created three portrait medals for the king and worked on other projects for which only drawings survive. At the end of his life and after his death in 1455, humanists in

Naples and Rome (Pietro Porcellio, Bartolomeo Fazio, Flavio Biondo, Leonardo Dati) were still writing to honor his pictorial and sculptural skill, and in 1504 Pomponio Gaurico cited the artist among the innovative sculptors of his age.

Surviving Works. Little art is left to show for Pisanello's continual travels, his high-powered patronage, and the humanists' unstinting praise. Of the works mentioned, only twenty-three portrait medals, the San Fermo Annunciation, and the *Portrait of Leonello d'Este* (Accademia Carrara, Bergamo) have survived. Giorgio Vasari in 1550 attributed to him the otherwise undocumented fresco of *St. George and the Princess of Trebizond* over the arch of the Pellegrini Chapel in Sant' Anastasia, Verona, and two other (lost) scenes, probably dating from the late 1430s. The only other universally accepted paintings are three small panels: *Portrait of an Este Princess* (Paris, Louvre), and two private devotional panels (London, National Gallery). Pisanello's most important legacy, however, may be one of the largest bodies of drawings to survive from the early Renaissance (primarily Paris, Louvre). The four hundred sheets, of which about a sixth are attributable to Pisanello's own hand, give an excellent idea of the range of varied tasks undertaken by a court artist's workshop. He drew the appurtenances of war, such as helmets, cannon, and armor; objects in precious materials, like rings, crowns, and tableware; animals such as deer, hounds, horses, hares, falcons, peacocks, monkeys, and camels; and his patrons' portraits, as well as the elaborate costumes and headdresses that they loved.

Pisanello. ***Study of the Head of a Horse.*** Ink drawing. MUSÉE DE LOUVRE, PARIS/GIRAUDON/ART RESOURCE.

Such was the catalog of his works until the 1960s, when a major discovery was made of unfinished secular murals—Pisanello's only known large-scale cycle—painted in the Ducal Palace in Mantua, in a hall named, uniquely, after the artist. Their date, ranging from the 1420s through the 1440s, is a point of contention among scholars. The cycle illustrates an episode from the prose *Lancelot,* a thirteenth-century Arthurian romance in French. The episode in question comprises a tournament given at King Brangoire's castle in which the hero Bohort takes part, a banquet following the tournament in which twelve knights make distinctive vows, and the seduction of Bohort by King Brangoire's daughter. The episodes of the knights' vows are labeled by inscriptions in French, indicating that the manuscript on which the decoration was based was written in that language. The discovery included many meters of beautiful underdrawings in green earth and *sinopie* in red earth by a master draftsman, unexpectedly visible because the work is unfinished.

Artistic Achievement. Although Pisanello always signed his medals OPVS PISANI PICTORIS (the work of Pisano the painter), his modern reputation inevitably rests on his surviving medals and drawings rather than on his paintings. Pisanello's subtle medals are among the masterpieces of the genre, and he was the finest Italian draftsman of the early Renaissance. In the case of both medals and drawings, the subject matter is overwhelmingly secular, in a period from which few large-scale secular decorations have survived, and in which small-scale painted portraits were in the process of being invented.

Pisanello's low-relief medal was a new art form: a miniature, portable, sculpted, double-sided portrait, cast in a precious metal, designed to be shared with other art lovers—an audience limited to the aristocrats and patricians whose portraits were being circulated—in the most intimate of circumstances, by being passed from hand to hand. As the only prestigious art form that could be quickly replicated and widely distributed, it was a unique form of communication in an age before printing. The reverse of the medal normally allowed the commissioner, whose portrait was depicted in profile on the obverse, consciously to project an image of his circumstances, achievements, and enthusiasms, while unconsciously revealing his fantasies and illusions. Sigismondo Malatesta, for instance, chose to foreground his reputation as a bellicose condottiere, while Leonello d'Este instead emphasized abstruse visual emblems that have proven difficult to decode.

Many of Pisanello's drawings belong to the exemplum (pattern) or "model-book" tradition; that is, they were carefully finished studies, in which fixed poses and definition of structure and surface texture were emphasized, of motifs that would later be incorporated into his compositions. Other sheets, focusing on the vitality and mobility of the motif, usually an animal, were drawn with rapid and spontaneous pen strokes. The great freedom of treatment of these drawings suggests that Pisanello studied the animals directly from nature, rather than copying the images from earlier drawings, which had hitherto been the usual artistic practice. An interesting outcome of the artist's studies from life are the sketches he made of the authorities attending the church Council of Ferrara and Florence in 1438—the earliest known example of a visual artist functioning as a journalist as the historic event unfolded.

The theme of the humanists' literary exercises was the eternal life that Pisanello's portraits gave to his patrons. Thus the artist's contemporary fame rested primarily on what was perceived, or at least vaunted, as his portraits' verisimilitude or "naturalism"—*al naturale,* as the formula deriving from classical antiquity went. In actual practice, however, naturalism as an artistic ideal was at odds with the princes' desire to be presented to posterity in the best possible light, and they eschewed mimesis when applied too pointedly to their own likenesses. A tacit understanding between artist and sitter on the degree of naturalism to be allowed into the image helps to explain why Pisanello's portraits, to which the term *grazia* (grace) was often applied, were highly idealized.

BIBLIOGRAPHY

Degenhart, Bernhard, and Annegrit Schmitt. *Pisanello und Bono da Ferrara*. Munich, 1995.

Fossi Todorow, Maria. *I disegni del Pisanello e della sua cerchia*. Florence, 1966.

Paccagnini, Giovanni. *Pisanello*. Translated by Jane Carroll. London, 1973.

Pisanello: Le peintre aux sept vertus. Exhibition catalog, Musée du Louvre. Paris, 1996. Together with the forthcoming acts of the conference held in conjunction with the exhibition, this includes the most recent, and most exhaustive, bibliography relating to Pisanello studies.

Pisanello. Actes du colloque, musée du Louvre, 1966. 2 vols. Paris, 1998.

Scheller, Robert W. *Exemplum: Model-book Drawings and the Practice of Artistic Transmission in the Middle Ages (c. 900–c. 1450)*. Amsterdam, 1995.

Woods-Marsden, Joanna. *The Gonzaga of Mantua and Pisanello's Arthurian Frescoes*. Princeton, N.J., 1988.

JOANNA WOODS-MARSDEN

PISANO, ANDREA (c. 1295–1348/1349?), sculptor, goldsmith. Sometimes known as Andrea da Pontedera, Andrea Pisano was *capomaestro* (head) of the cathedral works in Florence and Orvieto; he was not related to the sculptors Nicola and Giovanni Pisano. Nothing is known about his background except that he was the son of the Pisan notary Ugolino di Nino. Andrea is thought to have trained as a goldsmith because his work for the doors of the Florentine Baptistery, a well-documented artistic enterprise, displays a high quality of finish and a sensitivity to ornamental, miniature detail. Perhaps the most important Tuscan sculptor of his day, Andrea contributed to the development of relief sculpture through an attentive study of Giotto di Bondone's art.

The Bronze-Door Reliefs (1330–1336). In 1329 the Arte di Calimala (Guild of Cloth Importers) of Florence selected Andrea to design a pair of bronze doors for the city's baptistery. After the guild had sent a goldsmith to study examples of bronze doors in Pisa and Venice, Andrea set to work on the commission, signing and dating (1330) his reliefs for the doors of the Baptistery's east portal (these doors, which are now on the south portal, were replaced by Lorenzo Ghiberti's work). He executed twenty reliefs on the life of St. John the Baptist (the patron saint of Florence and the baptistery's titular) and eight reliefs of virtues in quatrefoil frames. He unified the appearance of the doors by using a variety of decorative motifs: lions' heads are placed at the corners of each panel, bands of studs and rosettes unite the lions' heads, and dentiled moldings (moldings with a series of small rectangular blocks projecting like teeth) frame each of the quatrefoils. In 1330–1331 he worked on the wax models, which were subsequently cast in bronze in the lost-wax

Andrea Pisano. Florence Baptistery Doors. Pisano made the doors facing the Duomo in 1336; they were moved to the south side of the Baptistery in 1424 when Ghiberti's doors (see the color plates in volume 3) were installed. The panels depict scenes from the life of St. John the Baptist and the virtues theological (faith, hope, and charity) and cardinal (prudence, temperance, fortitude, and justice). The decorations on the frame were added by Lorenzo Ghiberti's son Vittorio between 1452 and 1464. ART RESOURCE

method by Venetian craftsmen. In 1333 the left door was put in place; the second door was not finished until late 1335 due to problems in the casting. The doors were dedicated on the Feast of the Baptist in 1336.

Much of the iconographic program of Andrea's doors is related to that of the mosaic scenes on the life of the Baptist in the interior of the Baptistery and to frescoes by Giotto in the Peruzzi Chapel in Santa Croce. Giotto's art is also reflected in the harmonious balance of Andrea's compositions, in the careful structuring of the reliefs in planes, and in the concentrated grouping and purposeful movements of the figures. But Andrea's scenes, which are held together by decorative framing devices, do not entirely reflect Giotto's interest in creating a convincing pictorial space; instead, Andrea placed his figures in front of a plain background with the occasional motif of a curtain, doorway, or canopy. However, landscape is included in five reliefs on the left-hand door, and in these scenes Andrea used aspects of the natural world in an expressive and subtle way. His reliefs were also influenced by Sienese and French Gothic artistic traditions: they are enriched with rhythmic drapery forms, which introduce a sense of energy, refinement, and elegance to his compositions.

Andrea's work on the doors is of the highest quality, and, as the crisp and delicate details of the gilded bronze surfaces reveal, he took much time over the final chiseling. He was evidently a mature and proficient artist when the Calimala awarded him the commission, and his work was still widely esteemed in the early fifteenth century, when his doors were the model for a second set designed by Ghiberti.

The Florence Cathedral Campanile (1337–c. 1341). Following Giotto's death in 1337, Andrea became capomaestro and worked on the project to build and decorate the campanile (bell tower) according to his great predecessor's designs. Giotto had directed the building of the lower socle and the first floor from 1334, and Andrea supervised work on the remaining sections of the lower third of the bell tower until 1341 (Francesco Talenti completed the central and upper sections by 1359). Andrea's precise role in the project has been widely debated, but it is thought that he worked on the marble reliefs depicting certain scenes from Genesis and practitioners of the arts and sciences and on some freestanding sculptures. Among the works generally attributed to him is the marble relief *Sculpture,* which, like the Baptistery panels, is characterized by an attention to detail, subtle modeling, well-proportioned and solidly defined forms, and an interest in how the figure fits into the design of the frame. Many of the campanile works display a quiet monumentality that is linked to Andrea's enduring contact with the art of Giotto and to his awareness of classical sculpture.

The Final Phase: Pisa and Orvieto (c. 1341–c. 1348). In 1341 or shortly thereafter Andrea returned to Pisa. In his home city he is thought to have worked on a number of statues in marble, including *Virgin Suckling the Infant Christ* (c. 1343; Pisa, Museo Nazionale di San Matteo). But this Pisan group of sculptures has at various times been attributed to Andrea's son Nino (1315?–1368?), who was almost certainly based at his father's workshop. In 1347 Andrea was appointed overseer of works at Orvieto Cathedral, and in the following year a marble statue, *Virgin and Child* (Orvieto, Museo dell'Opera del Duomo), was sent from his Pisan workshop to Orvieto. Andrea is assumed to have died as a victim of the plague in 1348–1349.

Nino and Tommaso Pisano. Nino (active 1334–1360s) and Tommaso (active 1363–1372), Andrea's sons, carried on their father's tradition. Both developed a mainly Gothic formal vocabulary and appear to have been less interested in the classicizing aspects of Andrea's work. Nino's signed *Virgin and Child* (c. 1348; Florence, Santa Maria Novella) is characterized by a delicacy of mood that has much in common with French Gothic sculpture. The grace and poise of this statue are partly achieved through the gently swaying S-curve of the body. The influence of Nino's lyrical style lingered on in northwest Tuscany and beyond until the close of the fourteenth century.

See also **Ghiberti, Lorenzo; Giotto di Bondone; Sculpture.**

BIBLIOGRAPHY

Burresi, Mariagiulia, ed. *Andrea, Nino, e Tommaso scultori pisani.* Milan, 1983.

Clark, Kenneth, David Finn, and George Robinson. *The Florence Baptistery Doors.* New York, 1980.

Kreytenberg, Gert. "Andrea Pisano's Earliest Works in Marble." *Burlington Magazine* 122 (January 1980): 3–7.

Kreytenberg, Gert. *Andrea Pisano und die toskanische Skulptur des 14. Jahrhunderts.* Munich, 1984.

Moskowitz, Anita. *The Sculpture of Andrea and Nino Pisano.* Cambridge, U.K., 1986.

FLAVIO BOGGI

PIUS II (Aeneas Silvius; Enea Silvio Piccolomini; 1405–1464), pope (1458–1464) and author. Piccolomini's parents, impoverished magnates of Siena, raised their son in the small Tuscan town of Corsignano. Only when he went to Siena in 1423 was he immersed in humanistic culture. For the next eight years Piccolomini lived a life of hard study and youthful irresponsibility, contracting habits of amorous indulgence that persisted into middle age. From 1431 he was employed as secretary and envoy by several churchmen and then by the Council of Basel, whose conciliarist, antipapal ideology he adopted.

Piccolomini traveled widely, especially in central Europe and Italy, gaining a deep familiarity with the nations of Europe and their leaders, but never losing a sense of Italian cultural superiority. In 1442 he joined the chancery of the Habsburg ruler of Austria and nominal ruler of Germany, Frederick III (Holy Roman Emperor, 1452–1493). At around this time Piccolomini abandoned conciliarism, and, fearing that Europe was becoming fragmented through nationalism and interstate rivalry, embraced a universalist ideal of Christendom united under the aegis of pope and emperor.

He was a versatile, reliable, and persuasive courtier; from 1445 to 1447 he negotiated the alliance between Frederick III and Pope Eugenius IV that left the Council of Basel moribund. Piccolomini restored his lost credit with the Roman Curia, took holy orders, and was appointed as apostolic secretary and bishop of Trieste in 1447. Nicholas V transferred him to the see of Siena in 1450 and Calixtus III made him cardinal in 1456. The failure of the European powers to organize a military expedition against the Turks in the Balkans became his main concern, and when he was elected pope as Pius II in the conclave of August 1458, a hard-fought contest between himself and the French candidate, he made this expedition his paramount goal.

No other pope rivals his importance in the history of literature. The humanist Latin of the fifteenth century, the language of his daily working life as well as his formal compositions, was a distinctive amalgam of influences from the classical, late antique, and medieval periods. Piccolomini was a prolific writer of both anecdotal private letters, and correspondence and treatises on public affairs. In his conciliar phase he wrote a work he later retracted, *De gestis Concilii Basiliensis* (On the proceedings of the Council of Basel), that recounts the deposition of Eugenius IV in 1439, and expounds the reasons of those who opposed papal absolutism. But in later works on central Europe he defended the Roman Curia against the *gravamina* (complaints) of the German nation, and as pope he anathematized by

Pope Pius II. Bust in the Borgia Apartments in the Vatican Palace. ANDERSON/ALINARI/ART RESOURCE

the bull *Execrabilis* (1460) any appeal from a pope to a church council.

From his youth Piccolomini also practiced the lighter genres, and in 1444 produced his amatory masterpiece, *Historia de duobus amantibus* (The tale of two lovers, Eurialus and Lucretia). This novella, which narrates the seduction in 1432 of a young Sienese matron by a handsome German courtier, their adultery, his abandonment of her, and her death, was one of the most popular works of the fifteenth century. The principal accomplishment of Pius II as patron of the arts was the urbanistic and architectural redesign of Corsignano, which he renamed Pienza. [For a view of the main square in Pienza, see the illustration to Art, subentry on Renaissance Art.]

His *Commentarii* are a memoir of his career and pontificate combined with a survey of Italian and European affairs. The ardent personal involvement of the writer in great and small events, his shrewd assessment of the character and motivation of many prominent contemporaries, and his enjoyment of the beauty and variety of cities, monuments, and landscapes, make this a classic of Renaissance literature. During his reign the Italian states and mercenary captains were drawn into the contest between the house of Anjou, representing France, and Ferrante of Aragon, for the succession to the kingdom of Naples. Pius supported Ferrante, and the war of the Neapolitan succession occupies a large part of the *Commentarii*. The pope's strategic aim was to reconcile the princes of Italy and Europe and make them commit to a united expedition against the Turks. To this end he summoned them to a congress at Mantua in 1459, but they all evaded commitment then or later [see Pinturicchio's painting of the council in Papacy]. This failure (a dramatic high point of the *Commentarii*) foreshadowed that of his last initiative, the assembly of an army and a fleet at Ancona in 1464 to sail against the Turks, with the pope and the cardinals on board. The pope, gravely ill, reached Ancona in time to see what a shambles the expedition had turned into [see Pinturicchio's painting of Pius's arrival in Crusade], and died there on 14 August 1464.

BIBLIOGRAPHY

Primary Works

Pius II. *De gestis Concilii Basiliensis commentariorum libri II.* Edited and translated by Denys Hay and W. K. Smith. Oxford, 1992.

Pius II. *Memoirs of a Renaissance Pope: The Commentaries of Pius II.* Translated by F. A. Gragg. Edited by L. C. Gabel. New York, 1959. Abridged edition of the only complete English translation, published in installments as *The Commentaries of Pius II* in Smith College Studies in History, 1937–1957.

Pius II. *Pii Secundi pontificis maximi commentarii.* Edited by I. Bellus and I. Boronkai. 2 vols. Budapest, Hungary, 1993–1994. Important critical edition, preceded by those of A. van Heck and L. Totaro (with Italian translation), both 1984.

Secondary Works

Mitchell, R. J. *The Laurels and the Tiara: Pope Pius II, 1458–1464.* London, 1962. Popular biography.

Feinberg, Richard. "Aeneas Silvius Piccolomini (1405–1464), Pope Pius II, Model of the Early Renaissance: A Selected, Annotated Bibliography of English-Language Materials." *Bulletin of Bibliography* 49, no. 2 (1992): 135–155.

WILLIAM MCCUAIG

PIUS IV (Giovanni Angelo [also Giovannangelo or Gian Angelo] Medici [also de' Medici]; 1499–1565), pope (1559–1565). Giovanni Angelo Medici was born in Milan, Italy, on 31 March 1499, to Bernardino Medici, a ducal official, and Cecilia Serbelloni. His family was part of the Milanese nobility but was in no way related to the Florentine ducal family of the same name. Giovanni Angelo studied at the universities of Pavia and Bologna, where he obtained a doctorate in civil and canon law in 1525. His legal career, begun during the papacy of Clement VIII, advanced significantly under Paul III, to whom Medici was linked before Farnese became pope.

Medici became known for his administrative ability and negotiating skills. He also maintained the mentality and customs of a Renaissance prelate. Contemporaries said that he had three illegitimate children, although historians have not been able to confirm this. When in 1545 he was nominated archbishop of Ragusa in Dalmatia (now Dubrovnik), he had not received even minor orders. He never set foot in the diocese of Ragusa nor in that of Cassano Ionio in Calabria, where he was transferred in 1553. He was elevated to the cardinalate on 8 April 1549 and was elected pope in December 1559, after a conclave of almost four months following the death of Paul IV.

Pius IV's pontificate began with a denunciation of some relatives of his predecessor. Two of the accused, Cardinal Carlo Carafa and Giovanni Carafa, duke of Paliano, were sentenced to death for their crimes. Pius IV then summoned to Rome his own relatives, whom he trusted with appointments and loaded with honors. The twenty-one-year-old Carlo Borromeo, son of his sister, Margaret, stood out among the appointees; Borromeo was quickly promoted to the cardinalate and became Pius IV's closest collaborator.

Pius IV's greatest accomplishment was to reconvoke and conclude the Council of Trent. The reopening of the council was promised in the capitulations of the conclave, that is, in the obligations the future pope had agreed to respect. After having overcome the reluctance of secular princes, the pope reconvoked the assembly at Trent on 15 January 1562. From Rome the pope closely followed the work of the council: the cardinal legates, nominated by him to preside over the assembly, sent him regular reports while he sent them instructions. The debates, which generally revolved around a program of rigorous disciplinary reform, concluded on 4 December 1563.

Pius IV immediately indicated his intention to implement the council's decisions. He confirmed the decrees orally on 26 January 1564 and then in writing on 30 June with the *Benedictus Deus* bull, backdated to the day of prior oral approval. In the meantime, on 24 March, the pope had the full Index of Prohibited Books published, which the council had not completed. On 2 August he instituted a permanent congregation of cardinals to ensure the observance of the conciliar decrees. On 13 November he promulgated the text of the Tridentine profession of

Pope Pius IV. Engraving; 1559. © The British Museum, London

faith, which was both a public profession of faith in Catholic doctrine and a vow of obedience to the Roman church. It was required of all bishops, clergymen caring for souls, superiors of religious orders, and other groups, including university professors and students receiving doctorates. The pope himself set the example by reforming some offices of the Curia and by establishing the seminary of Rome.

Endowed with a solid humanist culture, Pius IV was an excellent Latin scholar. Even as pope he delighted in reciting entire passages of classical authors by heart. He supported learned men such as Guglielmo Sirleto (whom he elevated to cardinal in 1565), Latino Latini, and Mariano Vittorio. In 1561 he had the printer Paolo Manuzio (son of the famous Aldo) called to the Eternal City to run a publishing house destined to print the works of church fathers and other ecclesiastical authors. Pius IV also promoted various artistic projects in the Vatican, especially those by Pirro Ligorio (the completion of the Belvedere courtyard and the so-called Casino of Pius IV or the Villa Pia (where Federico Zuccari, Santi di Tito, and Federico Barocci decorated the walls with paintings). Construction and urban-renewal projects were even more common in the city; examples are the construction of Porta Pia, the reconstruction of Porta del Popolo, and the completion of the Palazzo dei Conservatori. Pius IV not only supported Michelangelo in his position as architect of the basilica of Saint Peter but also gave him the commission to build the church of Saint Mary of the Angels over the ruins of the Baths of Diocletian. Pius IV's remains were transferred to this church in 1583, in conformity with his last will and testament.

See also **Trent, Council of.**

BIBLIOGRAPHY

Besozzi, Leonida. "Giovannangelo Medici (Pio IV) nei documenti dell'Archivio di Frascarolo." *Libri e documenti* 11, no. 2 (1985): 1–23; no. 3 (1985): 14–30.

Ganzer, Klaus. *Kirche auf dem Weg durch die Zeit: Institutionelles Werden und theologisches Ringen. Ausgewälte Aufsätze und Vorträge.* Edited by Heribert Smolinsky and Johannes Meier. Münster, Germany, 1997. Some of the articles in this collection cast new light on Pius IV's attitude toward the last phase of the Council of Trent and on the problem of church reform.

Jedin, Hubert. *Geschichte des Konzils von Trient.* 2 vols. Vol. 4, *Dritte Tagungsperiode un Abschluss.* Freiburg, Germany, 1975. The text outlines the action undertaken by the pope while the council was in session.

Pastor, Ludwig von. *The History of the Popes.* Vols. 15–16. Edited by Ralph Francis Kerr. London, 1928. This text remains the fundamental work on the history of the papacy.

Agostino Borromeo

Translated from Italian by Elizabeth Bernhardt

PIUS V (Antonio Ghislieri; 1504–1572), pope (1566–1572) and Catholic saint. From a poor family, Ghislieri was a shepherd as a boy. He entered the Dominican order at the age of fourteen, taking the name Michele. Studious, austere, and zealous, he was ordained a priest in 1528. Cardinal Gian Pietro Carafa, one of the founders of the Roman Inquisition, was instrumental in Ghislieri's appointment as inquisitor in Bergamo and Como. Later, as Pope Paul IV, Carafa made Ghislieri a cardinal (1557) and head of the Inquisition (1558). Elected pope in January 1566 with the support of Saint Charles Borromeo, the reform-minded archbishop of Milan and cardinal, Ghislieri took the name Pius V.

As pontiff, Pius V had a clear program. His first concern was the implementation of the decrees of the Council of Trent, which had concluded its sessions in 1563. Thus he embarked on a sweeping moral and disciplinary reform of the clergy, enforcing the residency of priests in their parishes and bishops in their dioceses, and setting a personal example of austerity and piety at the papal court. In accordance with the work begun by the council, Pius V continued the move toward uniformity of and central control over church ritual. Under him the Roman Catechism for the doctrinal instruction of the laity was published in 1566, followed by the Roman Breviary (the book of obligatory daily prayers and scriptural readings for priests). The revised Roman Missal of 1570 established a standard text of the mass for most of the Catholic Church, whether in Europe or the missions in the non-European world.

Pius V's second aim was the extirpation of heresy. To that end he strengthened the Roman Inquisition, often attending its meetings. A number of prominent suspects were executed, among them the Florentine Pietro Carnesecchi. Another measure in the war against heresy was the establishment of the Congregation of the Index, charged with enforcing control over what was printed through the Index of Forbidden Books. The pope also banished most Jews from the Papal States.

The relations of Pius V and European rulers were thorny. He excommunicated Queen Elizabeth I of England, thereby making the lot of English Catholics very difficult. In France he supported the queen-regent Catherine de Médicis against Huguenots without any sympathy for the predicament of the French monarchy or understanding for her attempts to placate the Protestants. Unwilling to accept the Spanish tradition of state control over many aspects of the church, he clashed with King Philip II of Spain over jurisdictional issues. The one great success of papal foreign policy was the formation of the Holy League, an alliance with Spain and Venice that led to the great naval victory against the Turks at Lepanto in October 1571. In commemoration, Pius V instituted the feast of Our Lady of Victory (the Madonna of the Rosary).

His intransigence makes Pius V a less than sympathetic figure to the modern mind. His canonization in 1712, however, testifies to his reputation for personal holiness, reform activity in the church, efforts to establish a disciplined and well-trained clergy, and support of worldwide missions.

BIBLIOGRAPHY

Lemaitre, Nicole. *Saint Pie V.* Paris, 1994. A biography that remains too general.

Pastor, Ludwig von. *The History of the Popes from the Close of the Middle Ages.* 3d ed. Vols. 17–18. Edited by Ralph Francis Kerr, St. Louis, Mo., 1951–1952. Still indispensable.

ELISABETH G. GLEASON

PIZAN, CHRISTINE DE (1364–c. 1430), French writer. Although known primarily as a French courtly writer, Christine de Pizan was born in Venice, where her father, Thomas de Pizan, was an adviser to the city government. The family had originated in Pizzano, near Bologna.

Education, Marriage, and Widowhood. In 1369, Christine moved with her family to Paris, where her father had been appointed astrological and medical adviser to the French king, Charles V (ruled 1364–1380). An Italian intellectual tradition, along with a youth spent in the shadow of an unusually cultivated French court, undoubtedly influenced Christine's intellectual development. She probably shared some years of schooling with her two brothers, a common practice in Italian families of her day, but this was brought to an early end by her marriage in 1380, at the age of fifteen, to a young notary from a Picard family, Étienne du Castel, who in that year was given a promising appointment as a royal secretary at the French court.

This marriage produced three children before Étienne, away from Paris on a mission for the king, died in an epidemic in 1390. Christine, thus widowed at the age of twenty-five, was left with her children and an elderly mother to care for. Inexperienced in the ways of the world, she was the victim of unscrupulous financial advisers with whom her husband had had dealings. When she later wrote in *Le livre de la mutacion de fortune* of having been obliged to change into a man, she was not merely inventing a symbol but describing her situation.

After a period of struggle and profound sorrow, Christine began to create a new life for herself through reading and eventually through writing. Among the works she read early on were Boethius's *Consolation of Philosophy* and the medieval *Ovide moralisé* (Ovid moralized). In her early writing, she relied on the poetic forms popular in her day: ballades, rondeaux, and virelays. At first her poems expressed grief at her husband's death, but later she broadened their subjects through participation in poetic contests, especially those held at the court of the duc d'Orléans, where she had found a place.

Literary Works. Her continuing self-education making her more ambitious, Christine composed a long allegorical and mythological work titled *L'epistre d'Othéa la déesse à Hector* (The letter of the goddess Othea to Hector; c. 1400). In her advice to the young hero of Troy, the goddess of wisdom sets forth precepts, in prose and verse, for the proper moral and spiritual education of a young man

Christine de Pizan. Miniature; c. 1410–1415. BRITISH LIBRARY, LONDON/THE BRIDGEMAN ART LIBRARY

approaching knighthood. Education of the young would be an enduring interest throughout Christine's career, directed first toward her son Jean and later toward the French dauphin, Louis de Guyenne.

Christine's writing attracted attention when she became involved in a literary debate concerning Jean de Meun's part in writing the continuation of Guillaume de Lorris's popular poem *Le roman de la rose* (The romance of the rose). She had already raised the issue of Jean de Meun's misogyny in one of her longer poems, *L'epistre au dieu d'amour* (The letter to the god of love; 1399), in which she took exception to his attitude toward women. But in 1402 she became more publicly involved in a discussion of this question with members of the royal chancellery, young men who were especially attuned to early humanistic ideas coming from Italy.

Her receptiveness to these ideas is evident in a long poem she composed in 1403 titled *Le livre du chemin de long estude* (The book of the long road of study). This work suggests that she had been reading Boccaccio's *De genealogia deorum gentilium* (On the genealogy of the gods), in which poetry is represented as inspired truth veiled in fiction or fable. She had evidently come to consider allegory a more effective poetic form than society verse. In this poem she uses a dream vision in which she embarks on a long journey, guided by the Cumaean sibyl. Her voyage begins on earth and eventually leads to the heavens, where she and the sibyl encounter, seated on four thrones, four queens who govern the universe. In their midst sits Queen Reason. The queens are engaged in a discussion of the qualities needed by the ideal prince to rule the world. Although they do not reach a conclusion, they commission Christine to carry a message to the French princes, so she returns to earth with a mission. She shows evidence here of the early Renaissance idea that a writer has a duty to influence the thinking of political figures.

Christine's participation in the debate surrounding *Le roman de la rose* inspired her to write *Le livre de la cité des dames* (The book of the city of ladies; 1405), which was influenced in large measure by Boccaccio's *De claris mulieribus* (On famous women), which recently had been translated into French. In this poem she offers a new interpretation of the historical role of women through her description of a city built especially for them under the supervision of three allegorical assistants: Reason, Rectitude, and Justice. This work was followed by *Le livre des trois vertus* (The book of the three virtues; 1406), in which these same three women guide young ladies to a suitable life in contemporary society. Christine dedicated this book to the dauphin's young wife, Marguerite de Bourgogne, but the number of surviving manuscripts, along with three early printed editions, suggests that Christine's ideas influenced young women for more than a hundred years.

Political Works. Another aspect of Christine's thinking found expression in a long allegorical poem titled *Le livre de la mutacion de fortune* (The book of the changes of fortune; 1403), a treatise on the role of fortune in human affairs that includes a long discourse on universal history. The success of this work led to a commission from the duc de Bourgogne, Philip the Bold, to write a biography of his late brother Charles V. To fulfill this commission, Christine wrote *Le livre des fais et bonnes meurs du sage roy Charles V* (The book of the deeds and good customs of the wise king Charles V; 1404), which was conceived to honor and preserve the fame of a distinguished ruler and to serve as an example for those who followed, especially his grandson, Louis de Guyenne. This concept of biography as a means of instruction was influenced by ideas spreading from Italy.

Unfortunately, the death of the duc de Bourgogne in 1404 brought on a devastating rivalry between his son, John the Fearless, and Louis, duc d'Orléans. In response to this tense political situation, Christine composed several works admonishing the rulers of France. In 1405 she wrote a letter to Queen Isabeau of Bavaria, reminding her of her duties to France. In 1407 she wrote *Le livre du corps de policie* (The book of the body politic), which she addressed to Louis de Guyenne. In this treatise she outlines her suggestions for a well-organized society, specifically the roles to be played by the individual classes, and reminds the dauphin, the military, and the middle classes of their duty to maintain a stable government. In 1410 she wrote *Lamentacions sur les maux de la guerre civile* (Lamentations on the evils of civil war) to the duc de Berri, Charles V's remaining brother. The situation in France did not improve, however, and in 1410, probably directed by John the Fearless, duc de Bourgogne, she addressed to Louis de Guyenne *Le livre des faits d'armes et de chevalerie* (The book of deeds of arms and of chivalry), instructing him in his duties as a military leader in a turbulent country. In 1413 Christine dedicated to Louis de Guyenne her *Livre de la paix* (The book of peace), in which she expressed the need for leadership to calm contentious factions and restore the welfare of the country, but to no avail. France was headed toward its disastrous defeat at Agincourt (1415). There is some evidence that Louis de Guyenne was progressing in his skills as a leader, but all was lost with his early and unexpected death at the end of 1415.

In other works written in the second decade of the fifteenth century, Christine more directly addressed the effects on women of the country's travails. In 1410 she wrote *La lamentacion sur les maux de la France* (Lamentation on the woes of France), in which she expresses her fear of civil war and accuses the French princes of acting more like the country's enemies than its sons. She also makes a special appeal to the women of France, who are in danger of losing their male relatives. The deaths of a number of friends at Agincourt inspired Christine to share her dismay with other women equally bereft in *L'epistre sur la prison de vie humaine* (Letter on the prison of human life; 1418).

As France's situation deteriorated, Christine withdrew to the Abbey of Poissy, where her daughter had been a member of the Dominican community for some years. She did not, however, completely disappear from view. To express her joy at the appearance of Joan of Arc, she composed *Le ditié de Jeanne d'Arc* (The tale of Joan of Arc; 1429), the first literary tribute to France's heroine. Although her death date is not known, Christine must have died before 1434 because Martin Le Franc referred to her in the past tense in *Le champion des dames* (The champion of ladies) published in that year.

Evaluation and Influence. Christine de Pizan's early poetry was encouraged not only by her widowhood but also by contact with members of the so-called Court of Love, founded in 1402, presumably to honor women, although she noted that this ideal was not always observed, a principal cause of her involvement in the debate over *Le roman de la rose*.

Christine de Pizan was the first fully independent professional woman writer in Europe, and perhaps the world. Like many women writers since, she dealt with issues involving women's proper role and status in society, and she has attracted attention among modern readers for her feminism. It is true that she insisted on proper respect for women at a time when this was generally missing in society; however, this was not her only concern. The range of her interests is a significant aspect of her career as a writer. Although her political writings have attracted less interest among modern readers than her concern for women, they provide a valuable insight into the France of her day.

BIBLIOGRAPHY

Primary Works

Blumenfeld-Kosinski, Renate, ed. *The Selected Writings of Christine de Pizan: New Translations, Criticism*. New York, 1997.

Cerquiglini-Toulet, Jacqueline, ed. *Cent ballades d'amant et de dame*. Paris, 1982.

Kennedy, Angus, ed. *Christine de Pizan's* Epistre de la prison de vie humaine. London, 1984.

Kennedy, Angus, ed. *Le livre du corps de policie*. Paris, 1998.

Moreau, Thérèse, and Eric Hicks, trans. *Le livre de la cité des dames*. Paris, 1986. In modern French.

Willard, Charity Cannon, ed. *The Writings of Christine de Pizan*. New York, 1994.

Secondary Works

Hicks, Eric, ed. *Le débat sur le roman de la rose*. Paris, 1977.

Kennedy, Angus. *Christine de Pizan: A Bibliographical Guide*. London, 1984. Supplement, 1994.

Solente, Suzanne. "Christine de Pizan." In *Histoire littéraire de la France*. Vol. 40. Paris, 1969.

Willard, Charity Cannon. *Christine de Pizan: Her Life and Works*. New York, 1984.

CHARITY C. WILLARD

PIZARRO, FRANCISCO (c. 1478–1541), Spanish conqueror of Peru. Pizarro spent most of his adult life in the Indies, as the Americas were then known. Following the conquest of Peru he became the new territory's first governor and received the noble title of marquis. The title was a far cry from his humble origins as the illegitimate son of a middling hidalgo (low-ranking noble) in the Spanish city of Trujillo, in the Extremadura region. Raised by his mother's family of humble farmers, Francisco was illiterate and uneducated. He used the surname of his father, Gonzalo Pizarro, who subsequently had a number of other children, illegitimate and legitimate, all of whom, unlike Francisco, grew up in the large Pizarro household.

Francisco left for the Indies in 1502 with the expedition that accompanied Fray Nicolás de Ovando, who had been named governor of Hispaniola, possibly intending to join his father's brother, Juan Pizarro. By the time he went to the isthmian region in 1509 he was already a prominent figure. When Panama was founded ten years later he became a member of the town council and one of the largest *encomenderos,* well-positioned to claim leadership of the expedition to Peru in the 1520s. (*Encomenderos* were granted the right to control the labor of and collect tributes from an Indian community.) When he went to the royal court in 1529 to secure authorization to conquer the Andean empire of the Incas, Pizarro recruited his half-brothers Hernando, Juan, and Gonzalo Pizarro, and Francisco Martín de Alcántara (his maternal half-brother), as well as other relatives and compatriots in Trujillo and its region to participate in the expedition. Hernando Pizarro, educated and the only legitimate sibling, worked closely with Francisco.

In 1539 Hernando returned to Spain, where he spent years in prison for his role in the execution of Francisco's rival and former partner, Diego de Almagro, and eventually settled in Trujillo. None of the other brothers left Peru. Juan Pizarro perished in the siege of Cuzco during the indigenous uprising of the mid-1530s; Francisco and Francisco Martín were assassinated in 1541; and Gonzalo Pizarro was executed in 1548 after the defeat of the rebellion he led against the crown's officials. Francisco Pizarro never married, although he had children with two Indian noblewomen. One of his daughters, Doña Francisca, married her uncle Hernando, and the extensive holdings in lands, mines, and *encomiendas* that the family had accumulated in Peru and Extremadura came to be concentrated in their hands.

BIBLIOGRAPHY

Lockhart, James. *The Men of Cajamarca: A Social and Biographical Study of the First Conquerors of Peru.* Austin, Tex., 1972. Includes excellent short biographies of the Pizarros and other participants in the events at Cajamarca.

Varón Gabai, Rafael. *Francisco Pizarro and His Brothers: The Illusion of Power in Sixteenth-Century Peru.* Translated by Javier Flores Espinosa. Norman, Okla., 1997. A study emphasizing the economic enterprises of the Pizarros.

IDA ALTMAN

PLAGUE. Recurrent bubonic plague in Europe coincides with the Renaissance. Petrarch both witnessed and survived the first pandemic wave, wondering

> How can posterity believe there was once a time without . . . visible disaster, in which not only this part or that part of the world, but almost all of it remained without a dweller? When was anything similar either seen or heard? In what chronicles did anyone ever read that dwellings were emptied, cities abandoned, countrysides filthy, fields laden with bodies, and a dreadful and vast solitude covered the earth? (*Rerum familiarum libri,* book 8, p. 417)

Petrarch's assessment proved true: there has been no recorded epidemic mortality so devastating in Europe. Estimates of the losses have been steadily revised upward in recent decades as archaeologists and historical demographers now believe that from 30 to 50 percent in each affected locale perished in the epidemic of 1347–1350. No war, pestilence, or famine since has been so unforgiving, nor so uniformly unstinting as the Black Death.

Until the mid-seventeenth century, plague struck every region of Europe at least once in every generation. Then, after a final apocalyptic appearance in Marseille in 1720, plague receded from western Europe almost as mysteriously as it came. Thus, the temporal extension of the plague in Europe overlaps directly with the broadest temporal construction of the Renaissance. Yet little connects these two historical phenomena. Neither caused the other, and neither was appreciably changed by the other, so their histories have for the most part been written independently. Two broadly different approaches define historians' interest in plague in Europe. Some begin with the view that plague is a biomedical phenomenon understandable and appreciable in modern terms; others approach the subject with a primary interest in the social and historical contexts of human experience in epidemics.

Recurrent Plague and the History of Disease. Most chronicle, diary, and literary accounts

The Plague's Harvest. *The Triumph of Death,* attributed to Francesco Traini (fl. 1321–1363) or to an artist known as the Maestro del Trionfo della Morta, in the Camposanto, Pisa. At the upper left St. Macarius, a fourth-century Egyptian ascetic, holds an unrolled scroll and points to three corpses, warning passing noblemen of the inevitability of death. Fresco; mid-fourteenth century. ALINARI/ART RESOURCE

of the 1340s epidemic describe the sudden appearance of large swellings on its victims, a human pathological response characteristic of bacterial infection with *Yersinia pestis*. Histories written before the 1970s use the former name for this microorganism, *Pasturella pestis,* but the point remains that the bodies of plague victims in 1348 bore unequivocal evidence that a particular microbe was responsible for much of the mortality. From Giovanni Boccaccio's time onward, the bubo (a swelling of a lymph node) trained Renaissance observers to focus on the human body and its morbid appearances. In his introduction to the *Decameron* (c. 1350), he writes: "It began in both men and women with certain swellings either in the groin or under the armpits, some of which grew to the size of a normal apple and others to the size of an egg" (p. 4).

Y. pestis is highly virulent in humans because they are not its customary host. Instead, rodents and their fleas maintain *Y. pestis* within a complex ecological system, and only when the organism infects highly susceptible rodents, such as the common house rat (*Rattus rattus*), do humans become part of a widening dying off. Medieval and Renaissance accounts not only focus attention on the anatomical location of the swellings; many eyewitnesses and survivors also describe dramatic instances of lung infection—pneumonic plague—with frightening, bloody sputum and high fatality. Subsequent epidemics that were attributed to *peste* or *pestilentia* or a general mortality may well have included other pathogens. Indeed, contemporaneous accounts of plague and *peste* throughout this period retain the nonspecific sense of a generalized, nonspecific, acute mortality, which makes Renaissance descriptive sources an uncertain reflection the behavior of *Y. pestis* across time and space.

Acknowledging such difficulties, we nonetheless can be sure that *Y. pestis* infection in European populations, whether rural or urban, came suddenly and recurrently; provoked crisis-level mortality rates of from two to ten times above the normal rates; and, for the most part, occurred during warm summer months. Some speculation about the incidence of epidemics of plague pneumonia during winter exists wherever crisis mortality can be documented during that season, but the symptoms of pneumonic plague are not as specific to *Y. pestis* as the bubo is to bubonic plague. Bio-historical interest in plague from 1348 to 1720 has thus fueled demographic studies of population loss and recovery subsequent to pestilence, as well as progressive public health history.

Demographic studies of recurrent plague. Population losses from the pandemic of 1347 to 1350 were in some respects uniform. A few individual locales seem to have been spared (most notably the city of Milan), but wherever careful demographic analysis has been undertaken, overall adult population losses range from 20 to 60 percent, a staggering proportion. When reconstruction of the age distribution of survivors is possible, the evidence suggests that younger adults better weathered the initial catastrophe than did those over forty years in age. Petrarch, in his late forties, was an atypical survivor, Boccaccio, then in his mid-thirties, was more representative of those who inherited the post-plague world. The more favorable survival rates of younger adults may explain the perception of the second wave of bubonic plague in the 1360s as a "plague of children." Although *Y. pestis* does not produce long-lasting immunity among those who survive infection, a baby boom in the initial recovery phase may have placed more children at risk when plague returned. Subsequent fourteenth-century pestilences may also have included infectious diseases more deadly to the young, compromising long-term population recovery. The available demographic data for the century following the Black Death reveal a steadily contracting European population, in both rural and urban areas. For example, Florence shrank from a pre-1348 population of over 100,000 to a city with approximately 40,000 inhabitants in 1430. These survivors of the plagues enjoyed a higher standard of living than those who lived before 1348.

By the late fifteenth century, first in northern Italy, Aragon, and the Low Countries, and later spreading to areas along all of the great river basins of Europe, gradual population recovery was accompanied by new patterns of settlement and land usage. Europeans now preferred to live in cities. Most of the great urban areas of modern Europe emerged as such during the sixteenth and seventeenth centuries. Plagues of the 1500–1700 period were no less brutal than those of the earlier centuries, but they did not impede accelerating urbanization. Plague's disappearance after 1720 may have contributed to the early phases of the most important demographic feature of recent centuries: the modern rise of population.

Plague and public health. In cities, plague had always been more dramatic and visible than elsewhere, more likely to inspire eyewitness testimony. City life naturally demanded much higher rates of literacy and depended on trade and commerce; both of these facts are related to the disproportionate number of urban records of plague in the Renaissance period.

But while the perception that plague was largely an urban problem may thus be artifact, Renaissance cities did develop new governmental responses to epidemic threats. Evidence of organized efforts to minimize plague losses occurred even during the Black Death. Florence, Venice, and a few smaller city states created committees of prominent citizens to manage the enforcement of street cleaning and other existing sanitary laws in a desperate attempt to minimize local sources of putrefaction that were believed to fuel plague. In his introduction to the *Decameron,* Boccaccio noted that "quantities of filth were removed from the city by officials charged with this task; the entry of any sick person into the city was prohibited; and many directives were issued concerning the maintenance of good health" (pp. 3–4)—all to no avail.

New public health approaches to recurrent plague were invented in Renaissance Italy between 1350 and 1500, and were gradually adopted and modified elsewhere over the next 150 years. The most formalized early approach to banning trade and travel from areas affected by plague was the quarantine, originally established in Ragusa in 1377 as a passive thirty-day (or *trentino*) waiting and watching period to see if passengers on an incoming vessel developed plague. The quarantine technically meant forty days, but the observed length of isolation varied considerably. Unlike our modern use of the term to denote the isolation of the sick, the original concept of quarantine was the isolation of well individuals or goods that might harbor plague; thus, it was a true preventive measure.

The isolation and medical care of individuals believed to be ill with plague led to the designation of specific plague hospitals, called *lazzaretti*. Early pesthouses were an urban management solution to the problem of provisioning the poor during a plague. Corralled into temporary camps or preexisting hospitals and monasteries, those without resources thus presented less of a danger to the elite and its properties. By the late fifteenth century, pesthouses began to be planned that would serve the exclusive function of isolating plague victims from the well. During nonplague years, use of the new pesthouses was often limited to the temporary housing of vagrants, the incarceration of groups deemed dangerous, and the isolation of suspect merchandise. In great maritime cities, formal quarantine stations multiplied in the sixteenth century and included both isolation facilities for plague victims and holding and disinfection spaces for uninfected people and suspect goods.

Finally, the passive quarantine practices and the active isolationist pesthouse initiatives required levels of external and internal surveillance that could only be managed by the re-creation of governmental bureaucracies such as the emergency council that Boccaccio described. Health magistracies with vastly expanded powers and objectives developed anew in fifteenth-century urban Italy, first as temporary plague-oriented directories, later as permanent public health and public order units. The information gathering and record keeping such magistracies required depended upon the same clerical skills so important to the artistic and literary Renaissance. Both served a nascent state, however routine, prosaic, and nonideological the health bureaucracies now appear.

Monitoring plague in the seventeenth century became a transregional, quasi-diplomatic, merchant-sensitive government activity. Local controls of plague expanded secular authorities' policing powers. Long after plague had disappeared from Europe, it remained the quintessential feared disease. Thus, sporadic cases of plague in the Middle East helped to inspire the nineteenth-century creation of international sanitary congresses, the beginning of global epidemic disease surveillance.

Social and Cultural History of Plague in the Renaissance. Giovanni Boccaccio's introduction to the *Decameron* best illustrates how an early humanist created a powerful construction of plague realities. Plague degrades individuals and civil society, elevating lowly grave diggers to mock and lord over their betters, leading gentlewomen to flaunt conventions of modesty and their obligations in mourning dead kinsmen. Plague thus exposes all the frailties to which the flesh is heir. Boccaccio's tales gradually move from the self-centeredness of a little company of privileged young men and women telling each other bawdy, distracting stories to the reaffirmation of the Christian doctrine and the traditional social order.

Not all contemporary formulations of the meaning and importance of the initial catastrophe so deliberately focused on the here and now as did those of Boccaccio and Petrarch. Most who wrote in the aftermath of the Black Death were churchmen focused on the message of human sin and redemption that God was providing in this severe chastisement. Religious responses to plague were dominated by public penance (typically processional) and the appeal to saints, and they continued to be so throughout the Catholic world. Similarly, medical scholars who wrote plague treatises before, during, and after 1348 confirmed traditional knowledge of God's created natural order, and viewed the origins of plague within the cosmos and within the human body as explicable. Surprisingly little changed within these two great synthetic ideologies. Plague remained both God's punishment for sin and a manifestation of change in the natural order best understood through a study of Galen, Aristotle, and their medieval commentators.

However, larger cultural and religious changes altered discussions and descriptions of plague in ways that did not so much undermine Catholic and scholastic synthesis as add new metaphors and meanings to the experience of plague. Influenced by Renaissance ideas, particularly the Renaissance emphasis on historical change, later plague treatises tended to provide a review of previous plagues. The most notable instance was the sixteenth-century interest in Thucydides's description of the Plague of Athens (420 B.C.). While plague was never seen as an entirely new disease, unheard-of in antiquity, Renaissance attention to how diseases might change over time or come into existence dominated discussion of the "Great Pox" and influenced renewed inquiry into contagionist ideas that challenged traditional medicine. Girolamo Fracastoro wrote his 1546 work, *De contagione et contagiosis morbis* (On contagion and contagious diseases), in this Renaissance climate while attending the Council of Trent.

The anatomical revolution in medical teaching, gathering momentum by the end of the fifteenth century, increasingly emphasized the bodily meaning and anatomically based diagnosis of plague, a change reflected even in the growing preference for St. Roch over St. Sebastian as the best plague saint. Sebastian, depicted pierced through with arrows of pestilence, less specifically represented plague in the new climate of representation than did Roch, who lifts his pilgrim's skirt to show a bubo in the groin.

Finally, the Protestant Reformation created deep religious divisions in the public ways that sin, still the primary cause of plague for Christians, would be expiated. Protestants abandoned the saints as effective intermediaries; Catholics identified new saints who could relay human contrition to God. Protestants abandoned processions in favor of private prayers. Plague art and literature reflected broad religious divides.

Most importantly, by the later centuries of plague all Christian Europeans settled on a view of plague as a disease of the poor, who were perceived to be its primary victims and who were now placed most directly in plague's way with developing quarantine and isolation practices. In ways only partly envisioned by Boccaccio, plague became a disease of the disordered body and state for both Protestants and Catholics, rather than a reflection of the fallen state of man and civil society.

See also **Demography**; **Medicine**; **Sickness and Disease**; *and biography of Giovanni Boccaccio.*

BIBLIOGRAPHY

Primary Works

Boccaccio, Giovanni. "The Author's Introduction." In *The Decameron.* Translated and edited by Mark Musa and Peter Bondanella. New York, 1977. Pages 3–17.

Fracastoro, Girolamo. *De contagione et contagiosis morbis et eorum curatione, libri III.* Translated and edited by W. C. Wright. New York, 1930.

Horrox, Rosemary, ed. and trans. *The Black Death.* New York, 1994.

Petrarca, Francesco (Petrarch). *Rerum familiarum libri.* Translated and edited by Aldo S. Bernardo. Albany, N.Y., 1975. See Book 8, no. 7, pp. 415–420.

Secondary Works

Bernardo, Aldo S. "The Plague As Key to Meaning in Boccaccio's *Decameron.*" In *The Black Death: The Impact of the Fourteenth-Century Plague.* Edited by Daniel Williman. Binghamton, N.Y., 1982. Pages 39–64.

Calvi, Giulia. *Histories of a Plague Year: The Social and the Imaginary in Baroque Florence.* Berkeley, Calif., 1989.

Cipolla, Carlo. *Public Health and the Medical Profession in the Renaissance.* Cambridge, U.K., and New York, 1976.

Herlihy, David. *The Black Death and the Transformation of the West.* Edited and with an introduction by Samuel K. Cohn Jr. Cambridge, Mass., 1997.

Jones, Colin. "Plague and Its Metaphors in Early Modern France," *Representations* 53 (1996): 97–127.

Nutton, Vivian. "The Reception of Fracastoro's Theory of Contagion: The Seed that Fell among Thorns?" *Osiris,* second series, 6 (1990): 196–234.

Pullan, Brian. "Plague and Perceptions of the Poor in Early Modern Italy." In *Epidemics and Ideas.* Edited by Terence Ranger and Paul Slack. Cambridge, U.K., and New York, 1992. Pages 101–123.

Slack, Paul. *The Impact of Plague in Tudor and Stuart England.* London and Boston, 1985.

ANN G. CARMICHAEL

PLANTIN, CHRISTOPHE (c. 1520–1589), bookbinder, printer, and publisher in Antwerp. Plantin, French by birth, was born in Saint-Avertin near Tours, the son of a servant in a modest family torn apart by the plague. Plantin spent his formative years in Caen, where he arrived in the late 1530s and later married Jeanne Riviere in 1545 or 1546. In 1548 or 1549 he moved from Paris to the rapidly growing port of Antwerp. Initially Plantin was involved in the leather trade and worked as a bookbinder, then was officially admitted to the booming local printing business before the Council of Brabant in 1555. What scarce evidence is available suggests that Hendrik Niclaes, the heterodox sect leader of the Family of Love, played an important role in the setting up of the Plantin printing press.

In spite of his personal inclination to mysticism, he complied outwardly with Catholicism and remained aloof from the revolt against Spanish authority. In 1562 some of his journeymen secretly published Calvinist writings. This obliged him to close his press temporarily and for a while live in exile in Paris. In 1563 he reopened his business, collaborating with the Calvinist van Bomberghens for the next four years. Gradually, however, he distanced himself from the anti-Catholic and anti-Spanish presses, and sought contact with influential Catholics such as Cardinal Granvelle.

With the financial support of King Philip II, the superb *Biblia polyglotta* (1568–1573), a new critical five-language edition of the Bible, was produced in the Plantinian office under the leadership of the Spanish humanist and king's chaplain Benito Arias Montano. As a royal printer Plantin received government orders for the printing of ordinances and the Index of Prohibited Books (1569–1570). He also secured the highly lucrative monopoly on the production of liturgical and religious works for Spain and overseas colonies in 1571. While remaining true to his motto "Work and Persistence," Plantin reached

Plantin's Printer's Mark.

the pinnacle of his career. His workshop, the Golden Compass, flourished as a humanist center and a printing house that regularly operated sixteen presses and employed more than seventy men. The Spanish Fury (1576) interrupted Plantin's royal connection. Financial difficulties forced him to find favor with the leaders of the revolt and the Calvinists who had gained virtual power in Antwerp. In 1581 Plantin readily printed the works of an erstwhile follower of Niclaes, called Barrevelt, but he remained outwardly loyal to Catholicism.

In 1582, with the impending Spanish siege of Antwerp, he established a reserve office in Leiden on the insistence of Justus Lipsius. There, in 1583, he laid the foundations for academic publishing as official printer to the local Dutch university. In Antwerp his sons-in-law Jan I Moretus and Franciscus Raphelengius produced less neutral publications for various parties during this period of reasonably tolerant Calvinist rule. Plantin returned to Antwerp immediately after the capitulation in 1585. The Calvinist Raphelengius moved to the Leiden branch. Together with Jan I Moretus, Plantin made the Antwerp firm the most important printing and publishing business of the Netherlands.

Plantin and the eminent scholars around him contributed significantly to the expansion of Antwerp as a European cultural center. He was the largest printer and publisher of humanist, academic, and Counter-Reformation literature of his time. As an industrial entrepreneur Plantin produced around 2,450 titles, or an average of seventy-two editions a year. He successfully combined French, Italian, and domestic methods, techniques, and artistic elements to form a unique high-quality Renaissance book style. Plantin's works received international recognition and their distribution reached as far as North Africa, India, China, and Japan.

See also **Printing and Publishing**.

BIBLIOGRAPHY

Primary Work

Rooses, Max, and Jean Denucé, eds. *Correspondence de Christophe Plantin*. 8 vols. Antwerp, Belgium, 1883–1918.

Secondary Works

Materné, Jan. "Ex Officina Plantiniana. Les impressions anversoises à caractère religieux destinees au marché du livre Ibéro-Américain." In *Flandre et Amérique Latine: 500 ans de confrontation et métissage*. Edited by E. Stols and R. Bleys. Antwerp, Belgium, 1993. Pages 139–153.

Schepper, Marcus de, and Francine de Nave, eds. *Ex Officina Plantiniana: Studia in memoriam Christophori Plantini (ca. 1520–1589)*. Antwerp, Belgium, 1989.

Voet, Leon B. *The Golden Compasses: A History and Evaluation of the Printing and Publishing Activities of the Officina Platiniana at Antwerp*. 2 vols. Amsterdam and London, 1969–1972.

Voet, Leon B., and Jenny Voet-Grisolle. *The Plantin Press (1555–1589). A Bibliography of the Works Printed and Published by Christopher Plantin at Antwerp and Leiden*. 6 vols. Amsterdam, 1980–1983.

JAN MATERNÉ

PLATINA, BARTOLOMEO (Bartolomeo Sacchi; 1421–1481), Roman humanist, Vatican librarian, and biographer of the popes. Born in obscurity in the village of Piadena, Platina may have been educated in nearby Cremona before spending four years as a mercenary soldier, in which capacity he was initially employed by Francesco Sforza (1401–1466). In 1449 or soon thereafter he went to Mantua to study under Ognibene da Lonigo in the school that Ognibene's teacher, the famous humanist educator Vittorino da Feltre (1378–1446), had founded. There Platina gained the favor of Ludovico Gonzaga and his wife, Barbara. After Ognibene's departure in 1453, they hired Platina to tutor their children, including Francesco (1444–1483), who later proved his foremost advocate. With support and encouragement from Ludovico, Platina left Mantua for Florence in 1457 to study Greek under John Argyropoulos (c. 1415–1487), in whose classes he formed lasting friendships with prominent Florentine scions such as Donato Acciaiuoli (1429–1478) and Lorenzo de' Medici (1449–1492).

Soon after Francesco Gonzaga was created cardinal (18 December 1461), Platina went to Rome to enjoy the patronage of his erstwhile pupil. There he attended scholarly discussions that Cardinal Bessarion (c. 1403–1472) hosted, and he became active in the Roman Academy founded by Pomponio Leto (1428–1498). In part through the agency of Cardinals Bessarion and Gonzaga, Platina purchased a post within the papal bureaucracy in the College of Abbreviators, which prepared shortened versions of bulls and supervised their revision.

Shortly after succeeding Pope Pius II (reigned 1458–1464), Paul II (reigned 1464–1471) dissolved the College of Abbreviators. Outraged, Platina obtained a papal audience, where he demanded the decision be reversed and even dared to question the validity of Paul's election, sentiments he then elaborated upon in an inflammatory letter to the pontiff. In response Paul had him imprisoned in the Castel Sant'Angelo (September 1464). Platina's contemptuous outbursts may have resulted in part from overfamiliarity, for as a resident in Cardinal Gonzaga's household he would surely have become acquainted with his patron's friend Cardinal Pietro Barbo (the future Paul II). In any case Gonzaga's influence proved crucial: in January of 1465 he persuaded the pontiff to have Platina released. Three years later Paul II once again ordered Platina imprisoned (February 1468), this time along with several other members of Leto's Academy, on charges including sodomy, paganism, conspiracy, and heresy. Paul II appears at least initially to have given the accusations some credence, but within a few months all charges were dropped and the prisoners released.

Platina's fortunes improved dramatically with the elevation of Paul's successor, Sixtus IV (reigned 1471–1484). Owing in part to Platina's friendship with Sixtus's favorite nephew, Pietro Riario, the pontiff showered favors upon Platina, including appointing him the first official librarian of the Vatican Library (1475), an event commemorated in a fresco of the scene by Melozzo da Forlì (1438–1494; see the color plates in volume 4). Platina oversaw the expansion of the collection, the renovation and decoration of rooms in the Vatican Palace to house it properly and elegantly, and the establishment of generous access and borrowing privileges. Thus he helped Pope Sixtus to realize the goal of making the Vatican Library a splendid and lasting monument to the pontiff's largesse and to the cultural preeminence of papal Rome. By the time of his death from plague in 1481, Platina had at last attained a position of respect commensurate with his lofty ambitions. A memorial service in April 1482 drew numerous mourners, including his friend Pomponio Leto, who delivered the eulogy.

A scholar more passionate and prolific than insightful or original, Platina often borrowed verbatim and at length from the writings of others. He addressed a variety of subjects in tracts such as *De honesta voluptate et valetudine* (On right pleasure and good health; composed 1465), a handbook on foods and cooking; a history of Mantua and of its ruling family, the Gonzaga (*Historia urbis Mantuae Gonzagaeque familiae;* 1469); and a panegyric of Cardinal Bessarion (1470). After composing a treatise on princely rule for Federico Gonzaga (*De principe;* 1471), Platina dedicated to Lorenzo de' Medici the strikingly similar *De optimo cive* (On the best citizen; 1474), which modified the text of *De principe* so as to accommodate the civic values of republican Florence. His biographical history of the popes (*Liber de vita Christi et omnium pontificum;* 1474), dedicated to Sixtus IV, ostensibly celebrated the papacy, but its juxtaposition of Christ's life with those of recent pontiffs resulted in implied criticisms that Martin Luther would take as supporting his critique of the papacy.

If Platina's contributions as Vatican librarian ultimately overshadowed his literary accomplishments, in both pursuits he exhibited eclectic tastes and an ardent commitment to the revival and dissemination of the learning of antiquity.

BIBLIOGRAPHY

Primary Works

Platina, Bartolomeo. *Liber de vita Christi et omnium pontificum*. Edited by Giacinto Gaida. Città di Castello, Italy, 1932.

Platina, Bartolomeo. *De optimo cive* (On the best citizen). Edited by Felice Battaglia. Bologna, Italy, 1944.

Platina, Bartolomeo. *On Right Pleasure and Good Health*. Edited and translated by Mary Ella Milham. Tempe, Ariz., 1998. Translation and critical edition of *De honesta voluptate et valetudine* (printed c. 1470). Editor's introduction includes biography and extensive bibliography.

Secondary Works

Campana, Augusto, and Paola Medioli Masotti, eds. *Bartolomeo Sacchi, detto Il Platina*. Padua, Italy, 1986. Acts of a conference held at Cremona in 1981 to mark the five hundredth anniversary of Platina's death.

Grafton, Anthony. "The Vatican and Its Library." In *Rome Reborn: The Vatican Library and Renaissance Culture*. Edited by Anthony Grafton. Washington, D.C., and New Haven, Conn., 1993. Pages 3–45.

Lee, Egmont. *Sixtus IV and Men of Letters*. Vatican City, Italy, 1978.

KENNETH GOUWENS

PLATO, PLATONISM, AND NEOPLATONISM. To read Plato had been the unfulfilled dream of Petrarch, who owned a Greek manuscript of the great philosopher but knew no Greek. The revival of Platonism in the Renaissance depended in the first instance on the discovery and acquisition of new Greek manuscripts that were brought to Italy in the fifteenth century by the collectors hired to enrich signorial libraries; and it was pioneered by humanists eager to learn and promote Greek (though Plato's Greek text was not published until 1513). Their attempts at translation had literary, educational, and political aims, and although their scholarly contributions were not of lasting importance, they bear eloquent witness to their enthusiasms and classicizing ideals. However, beginning obliquely with Nicholas of Cusa (1401–1464), the most speculative, independent and yet medieval of the thinkers indebted to Platonism, and then more centrally with Bessarion (1403–1472), Marsilio Ficino (1433–1499), and Giovanni Pico della Mirandola (1463–1494), the revival was transformed into a theological-philosophical apology for Plato and an exploration of his philosophy and myths. It swiftly impacted the intellectual and cultural life of the European Renaissance and continued to play a major role in the development of its thought and culture in the sixteenth and early seventeenth centuries, partly because it reformulated one of the perennially attractive ways of looking at Plato and Platonism through Christian eyes. In the works of Ficino, the revival made a lasting contribution to scholarship. Nevertheless, Plato never supplanted Aristotle in the universities, though various scholars in the sixteenth century lectured on the dialogues, most notably Francesco Patrizi, who occupied a professorship of Platonic philosophy at Ferrara, and Jacopo Mazzoni similarly at Pisa.

Plato's dialogues, with a few signal exceptions—especially the first half of the *Timaeus* and parts of the *Parmenides*—had been unknown to the Latin Scholastics. As the humanists' contacts with Byzantium intensified in the years preceding its fall in 1453, they became aware that the canon, along with the succession of Platonic commentators, ancient and Byzantine, had played a central role in Byzantine education, culture, and scholarship. Some of Plato's views nevertheless had long been anathema and others the object of constant Aristotelian refutation: abortion and the community of wives and goods in the *Republic,* the homosexual play in the *Symposium* and *Charmides,* the theories of reincarnation and transmigration in the *Timaeus,* the many references to Socrates's "daemon" and the gods, and so on.

Latin Translations. Several humanists tried their hand at rendering selected dialogues into Latin (vernacular editions appeared later). Manuel Chrysoloras, a distinguished Byzantine émigré who served the Visconti after 1400, helped Uberto Decembrio translate the *Republic,* though the result was much criticized. Uberto's son, Pier Candido Decembrio, who likewise served the Visconti, retranslated the *Republic* while making continual reference to his father's version (foes branded it a "remake"). A third and better translation was made during the 1440s by Antonio Cassarino, a schoolmaster in Genoa, who also translated the pseudonymous *Axiochus* and *Eryxias.* Meanwhile Leonardo Bruni, the illustrious Florentine chancellor, by 1427 had translated the *Apology, Crito,* and *Phaedo*—the dialogues dramatizing the death of Socrates—along with the first part of the *Phaedrus,* the *Gorgias,* and some of the *Letters.* The *Axiochus* and *De virtute* were rendered by Cencio de' Rustici; the *Ion* by Lorenzo Lippi; the *Crito, Axiochus,* and *Euthyphro* by Rinuccio Aretino (the *Euthyphro* brilliantly); three of the *Letters* by Francesco Filelfo; and a fragment of the *Charmides* by the accomplished Poliziano. George of Trebizond (1396–c. 1472), a Cretan convert to Catholicism, eventually a papal secretary, and a brilliant but rabid Aristotelian, was a hostile translator: he rushed through the *Laws* and *Epinomis* in 1450–1451 at the request of Pope Nicholas V (reigned 1447–1455), making many errors, some malevolently, and then similarly botched the *Parmenides* in 1458–1459 for Cardinal Nicholas of Cusa (at least according to Bessarion).

The humanists' choices depended partially on manuscript availability. Nonetheless—leaving aside George of Trebizond—the list has two foci: first, some of the Socratic dialogues, including pseudepigrapha, variously remarkable for their playfulness, verve and drama; and second, the *Republic,* with its abiding fascination for those interested in politics and the claims of various polities, most notably the republican versus the princely. The patronage of the Decembrii by the Visconti was not coincidental: the Milanese tyrants wanted to have Plato on their side. Even the best of these attempts, however, were flawed. They lacked a comprehensive understanding of both Plato's philosophy and the complex interpretative tradition; and they avoided, bowdlerized, or explained away many of the difficulties a Christian reader necessarily encounters in Plato—

predictably so, since they wished the dialogues to serve as edifying educational texts.

Interpreting Plato. By 1462, when Cosimo de' Medici first asked Ficino to translate Plato for him, the majority of the thirty-six canonical dialogues were still unavailable in Latin and Plato's philosophy was still a mystery to the West. One desideratum was therefore the translation and elucidation of the canon, and this Ficino accomplished triumphantly with his *Platonis opera omnia* (Complete works of Plato; 1484) and his *Commentarium in Platonem* (Commentary on Plato; 1496). But the architects of the second phase of Renaissance Platonism were also committed to a profound reengagement with the thought and spirit of Plato as part of an irenic and concordist goal: to heal the terrible and long-standing divisions separating religion from true philosophy. Bessarion, Ficino, and Pico were all three wide-ranging scholars drawn to the knotty speculations of Plato's middle and late dialogues (which the earlier humanists had neglected or misunderstood) in the conviction that these contained the kernel of his wisdom. For this they were indebted to the interpretative tradition in its twofold pagan and Christian elaborations (which again the humanists had largely ignored).

Of central importance here were the fifty-four visionary, if highly technical, treatises of the *Enneads* by the mystical founder of Neoplatonism, the third-century philosopher Plotinus. Indeed, Plotinus played such a magisterial role in the interpretation of Plato's dialogues that we should more properly refer to these Renaissance Platonists, and above all to Ficino, as Neoplatonists. Significantly, Ficino's greatest scholarly achievement, excelling even his 1484 Plato, was his translation of, and commentary on, the *Enneads,* which he published in a magnificent volume in 1492. But they were also drawn, as Nicholas of Cusa had been before them, to the comparably difficult works of two of Plotinus's most illustrious fifth-century followers, the voluminous Proclus and the mysterious Pseudo-Dionysius the Areopagite. The latter we now suppose a follower of Proclus but medieval and Renaissance thinkers, with a few dissenting voices, identified him with the Dionysius mentioned in Acts 17:34 as one of St. Paul's first Athenian converts on the hill of Mars (the Areopagus). His writings became central to medieval theology after they were translated by John Scotus Erigena in the ninth century and were the object of numerous medieval and Renaissance commentaries. They are imbued with a speculative Christian, and

Platonism Detail from a bust by Donatello (c. 1386–1466) of a medallion depicting the soul drawn to God by the twin horses of intellect and will. MUSEO NAZIONALE DE BARGELLO, FLORENCE/ALINARI/ART RESOURCE

(we now realize) a Proclan, Neoplatonism; and they explore the hierarchy of spiritual being, the nine angelic orders, and the corresponding ecclesiastical orders. More important, they set forth the "negative way" of contemplating God by denying every predication of a Deity beyond being and non-being, ineffable, incomprehensible, a deep but dazzling darkness.

This Dionysian presentation of the negative or apophatic way is rooted in the second part of Plato's sublime exercise in dialectic, the *Parmenides,* where the aged Eleatic monist sets up what the ancient Neoplatonists later decided were nine hypotheses, the first five exploring the consequences of supposing the One's existence, the last four of supposing the One's non-existence. To attribute Dionysius's works to the first century is thus to endow them with apostolic authority and to postulate a fully developed Neoplatonism at the fountainhead of Christian theology, one learned at the feet of St. Paul, but centered on the *Parmenides* as interpreted by Proclus's weighty commentary. It is to postulate a metaphysical, dialectical, theological, ecstatic Parmenidean Plato as the guardian angel of Christianity's apostolic, transformational years.

The Augustinian Tradition. The Renaissance Neoplatonists turned for guidance and authority to the works of other Church Fathers besides Dionysius, particularly to Augustine. His *Contra Academicos* (Against the Platonists) describes the emergence of skepticism in the Academy in the generations after Plato's immediate disciples, and then with Plotinus the reemergence of Plato's pure doctrines. His *Confessions* likewise tells of his rejecting Manichean dualism and returning to Christianity after encountering "certain books of the Platonists"—Latin versions by Marius Victorinus of selections from Plotinus or Porphyry, Plotinus's pupil and biographer. Augustine's witness that the "Platonists" (Neoplatonists) had been the handmaids to his own conversion thus testified to their being the ancient philosophical school that had best anticipated Christian Truth. His own Neoplatonizing theology, moreover, had come to dominate the early Middle Ages, nourished in part by Latin works with Platonic themes—Boethius's *Consolation of Philosophy* with its echoes of the creation myth of *Timaeus;* various treatises, essays, and letters of Cicero, Seneca, Apuleius, Macrobius, Martianus Capella, and so on. After the revival of Aristotle in the twelfth century, the treatise had continued to thrive and to transmit many Neoplatonic features, especially in its epistemology, to a succession of Schoolmen, aided in part by the continuing authority of the Areopagite and by the study of Calcidius's late ancient Latin commentary on the *Timaeus*. Even in the heyday of Scholasticism in the thirteenth century, the accessible Neoplatonic texts had retained their authority: witness Aquinas's request to a fellow Dominican, William of Moerbeke, that he translate Proclus's *Elements of Theology* and part of his commentary on the *Parmenides* (which included lemmata). Significantly, it was Proclus's chief work, the *Theologia Platonica* (a title Ficino adopted for his own masterpiece), that Pietro Balbi translated for Nicholas of Cusa in 1462.

It is not the scattered translation attempts of the earlier humanists, but this long medieval Augustinian tradition, derived from the *Parmenides,* Plotinus, Proclus, and the Areopagite, that sets the scene for the climactic contributions of the later fifteenth century. Yet a Byzantine intellectual, George Gemistus (c. 1360–1452), who adopted the Platonic surname Pletho, also played a role. He accompanied the Palaeologus emperor John VIII to the Council of Ferrara–Florence in 1438–1439 to debate the union of the Greek Orthodox and the Roman Catholic churches. Since he was opposed to yielding to the West's theological demands, he antagonized Orthodox proponents of union and their Aristotelian allies in the Roman party. But on his visit he also made influential friends, and Ficino later claimed he had inspired Cosimo de' Medici to patronize the study of Plato—to found a Platonic Academy in Florence (though this claim may be figurative).

Renaissance Neoplatonism. However, as the founding father of Renaissance Neoplatonism, Pletho was and is a controversial figure. His major treatise, *De legibus* (On the laws), was destroyed by the unionist George Scholarius (later the first post-Byzantine Orthodox patriarch) on the grounds it had advocated the supersession of Christianity by a revived polytheistic Platonism. Scholarius was seconded by George of Trebizond who also accused Pletho of being a crypto-Muslim. These charges are unconvincing in light of Pletho's prominence as one of the emperor's most distinguished advisers at a council where Orthodoxy was being defined and defended; and in light, too, of his illustrious defenders, among them his pupil, Bessarion, who had been appointed a cardinal in December 1439. Yet Pletho's views were syncretistic and perhaps inconsistent. A Greek patriot, he dreamed of reviving Neoplatonic Platonism, "the Hellenic theology" he called it, as Greece's priceless legacy, even composing hymns to Platonic abstractions such as Light and Goodness and devising a Platonic calendar. The key to understanding him is probably again Proclus, whom Scholarius had declared was Pletho's true master, not Christ!

Whatever our final verdict on his "paganism," Pletho seemed the embodiment of a Platonic sage, a Plotinus reborn, for a circle of Italian admirers who looked to Cosimo de' Medici among others for patronage. One of his arguments, derived from Proclus, was particularly influential: namely, that the tree of ancient wisdom—which such early Church Fathers as Eusebius, Clement, and Lactantius had eagerly acknowledged was the Gentile parallel to, if not the equivalent of, the Mosaic wisdom of the Hebrews—had the Persian sage, Zoroaster, as its root. Ficino made this Proclan-Plethonian Zoroaster into the originary and original Neoplatonist, whose disciples centuries later had been the three Magi worshiping the Christ Child, the new Zoroaster, the new Plato, the Platonic Idea of Man in Bethlehem. He adopted the notion of a line of ancient theologians, a succession that arced back across Plato's Pythagorean teachers to Pythagoras, to Orpheus, to Hermes Trismegistus, to Zoroaster. But he saw the line itself as consummated in Christ, like its Hebrew prophetic counterpart, and its theology as perfected in the opening of St. John's Gospel, in the epistles of St. Paul, in the treatises of the Areopagite, and in the *Enneads*. The Hebrew and the Gentile traditions had thus been fulfilled in the revelation of a Christian-Neoplatonic metaphysics of the One, and of the soul's ascent to God as the One. Agostino Steuco (1497/8–1548) later developed this Ficinian archaeology of wisdom into a theory of the "perennial" philosophy.

Defense of Plato. Bessarion took up Pletho's defense against the attack of George of Trebizond in what had become by the 1460s a running battle between Aristotelians and Platonists. Written initially in Greek and running through several drafts before a final Latin version, his *In Calumniatorem Platonis* (Against Plato's slanderer; 1469) is a four-book defense of Platonic positions and of Plato's compatibility with Christian dogma by an authoritative Hellenist and theologian. Effectively, it introduced the Italians to the intricacies of the ongoing (and age-old) controversy among the Byzantines on the relative merits of Plato and Aristotle, while drawing on the Greek Fathers and on the metaphysics of the Neoplatonists. The cardinal's work must have done much to reestablish Plato (if not Pletho) as a theological visionary, even as it carefully distinguished between Plato's positions and those of Christian orthodoxy. Not to insist on a complete accommodation in fact was the Renaissance apologists' most effective strategy. It was refined by Ficino, who, without actually attributing the dogma of the Trinity to Plato and the ancient theologians, subtly unfolded it from their metaphysical and oracular dicta and enigmas.

Ficino and Pico, followed by Agrippa, Paracelsus, Patrizi, Giordano Bruno, and others, also revived the Plotinian account of Nature as animate in the now abandoned sense of ensouled. This entailed reconsidering ancient notions of a natural, a demonic, and an astral magic functioning by way of the World-Spirit linking the World-Soul to the World-Body. Their revival of Neoplatonic magic theory was colored by their familiarity with medieval and Arab magic and with talismanic medicine and pharmacology; and like them it was based on the notion of natural sympathies, loves, and harmonies. Yet its goal was not to manipulate nature and natural effects, but rather to establish human—individual and societal—consonances with the World-Soul. Hence it called upon incantation, song, and instrumental music; upon harmony, ratio and number symbolism; and upon a fine-spun astrology concerned not so much with horoscopic prediction as with unravelling the threads of planetary and stellar affiliations. Its enemies attacked it for revalorizing demons or at least for linking human souls with airy and fiery demonic natures or spirits. Did they also fear a revival of the Docetist heresy that Christ's bodily nature was demonic or phantasmal (that is, mere appearance), never truly incarnated, or of the Gnostic heresy that postulates a special knowledge for His chosen ones? Regardless, they were probably correct in seeing Ficino's and Pico's Neoplatonism as a revival both of an Arian subordinationist metaphysics and of a Pelagian ethics with its notion that we can rise by virtue of our own intellect and will to a lost godhead that is ours. If only indirectly, the positions articulated by these two major ancient heresies were explored and rearticulated by the Renaissance Neoplatonists, in part because of their conviction that the philosopher's soul, like Socrates's, could be caught up, albeit momentarily, to St. Paul's third heaven (2 Corinthians 12:2).

Metaphysics of Neoplatonism. The Neoplatonists' new soul-centered metaphysics, unlike its intellect-centered ancient Plotinian counterpart, focused on the interdependent roles of the individual soul, of the World-Soul (which Peter Abelard in the twelfth century had daringly identified with the Holy Spirit), and of Soul as a unique substance or hypostasis. This animatological orientation is a prominent and special feature of their thought; and it has many implications, notably for the theory of the soul's immortality, as in Ficino's *Platonic Theology;* for christology, as in Pico's *Heptaplus;* and for cosmology, astrology, and holistic therapy, as in Ficino's speculative *De Vita.* But if the soul aspires to knowledge, it is also moved by love, anciently defined as the longing or desire for beauty, and in Platonic metaphysics, for Beauty as an Idea, as the splendor of all the Ideas in their collectivity as Truth. The Renaissance, as Jakob Burckhardt famously argued, can be characterized as an age dedicated to seeing Beauty as an ideal and an Idea. Certainly, Ficino's commentaries on Plato's *Symposium* and *Phaedrus* elaborated a psychology both of desire, its sublimation or ideation, and of the will, traditionally the faculty counterpoised to the intellect. The former particularly, though mediated by other works—Cristoforo Landino's *Disputationes Camaldulenses* (Camaldulensian Disputations; c. 1472), Lorenzo de' Medici's poetry, Baldassare Castiglione's *Il cortegiano* (1528; trans. *The Book of the Courtier*), the love treatises of Leone Ebreo—resonated through three centuries, creating an erotic or amatory aesthetic that rapidly seduced European court culture. It influenced and inspired a host of painters, composers, poets, and writers, among them Sandro Botticelli, Michelangelo, the French Pléiade, and Edmund Spenser, as well as philosophers and scientists like Bruno, Galileo, Johannes Kepler, and the Cambridge Platonists.

Yet Renaissance Platonism remains in essence metaphysical, and not magical, psychological, or even spiritual. Committed to a metaphysical notion of God, it is committed to a metaphysical notion of Man made in the image and likeness of God as the One and the Good. Despite its multifarious impact on the society, art, science, religion, and culture of its age, at heart it is an elite, transcendentalist philosophy that envisions the individual as an empowered intellectual soul yearning to contemplate, to be united to, an intelligible Nature, the intelligible Ideas, the trans-intelligible One. Though Christian, it hardly needs Christ except as the Idea of deiform Man, and it rarely evokes such central Christian themes as the Incarnation, Passion, and Redemption, the gift of the sacraments, the power of unmerited grace, the community of belief. It treats rather of the soul as an ingathered unity returning to Unity, "the flight of the alone to the alone," in the haunting valedictory phrase of the *Enneads*. For the Neoplatonic ecstasy is rare, noetic, and solitary.

See also biographies of figures mentioned in this essay.

BIBLIOGRAPHY

Allen, Michael J. B. *Synoptic Art: Marsilio Ficino on the History of Platonic Interpretation*. Florence, 1998. Includes chapters on Ficino's views on the ancient theology and the later history of Platonism.

Cassirer, Ernst. *The Individual and the Cosmos in Renaissance Philosophy*. Translated by Mario Domandi. New York, 1964. Four remarkable essays, two of them on Nicholas of Cusa.

Copenhaver, Brian, and Charles B. Schmitt. *Renaissance Philosophy*. Oxford and New York, 1992. Excellent introduction to the context.

Field, Arthur. *The Origins of the Platonic Academy of Florence*. Princeton, N.J., 1988. Fine, detailed study.

Hankins, James. *Plato in the Italian Renaissance*. 2 vols. Leiden, Netherlands, and New York, 1990. The synoptic account.

Hankins, James. "Plato in the Middle Ages." In *Dictionary of the Middle Ages*. Edited by Joseph Strayer, et al. 13 vols. New York, 1982–1989. Vol. 9, pp. 694–704. Comprehensive survey.

Kristeller, Paul Oskar. *The Philosophy of Marsilio Ficino*. Translated by Virginia Conant. New York, 1943. Reprint, Gloucester, Mass., 1964. Authoritative study of Ficino as a formal philosopher.

Kristeller, Paul Oskar. *Renaissance Thought and Its Sources*. Edited by Michael Mooney. New York, 1979. Pays special attention to Platonism.

Kristeller, Paul Oskar. *Studies in Renaissance Thought and Letters*. Rome, 1956. Important essays on Ficino's context and influence.

Kristeller, Paul Oskar. *Studies in Renaissance Thought and Letters. III*. Rome, 1993. More essays on Renaissance Platonism and on individual Platonists.

Trinkaus, Charles. *In Our Image and Likeness: Humanity and Divinity in Italian Humanist Thought*. 2 vols. London, 1970. Wide-ranging analysis of a Christian-Platonic theme.

Walker, D. P. *Spiritual and Demonic Magic: from Ficino to Campanella*. London, 1958. Reprint Notre Dame, Ind., 1975. A seminal study on magic theory and its influence.

Wind, Edgar. *Pagan Mysteries in the Renaissance*. Rev. ed., New York, 1968. A rich book on Platonism's influence on Renaissance mythography, art, and culture.

Yates, Frances. *Giordano Bruno and the Hermetic Tradition*. London, 1964. A speculative reframing of Renaissance Neoplatonism.

Michael J. B. Allen

PLATTER FAMILY. For three generations in the sixteenth century, the Platters, a family of Swiss scholars and physicians, produced autobiographical writings of high quality. They offer a case study of the ascent of the urban bourgeoisie in the Renaissance period.

Thomas Platter Sr. (1499–1582) was born in Grächen, Switzerland. Much information about his life is drawn from his own account, a memoir of a peasant youth that is perhaps unique for the Renaissance. His father died of plague soon after Thomas was born, and he was cared for by various relatives. From Thomas's earliest childhood, his relatives wanted him to become a priest. However, at an early age, he was sent out as a goatherd and lived in very harsh conditions.

He was then sent out to beg on the road in Germany, perhaps in the hope that he would learn to read, perhaps in the hope that he would no longer be a burden on his family. The boy joined a band of child beggars supervised by adolescents and young delinquents, who made their living pilfering from passersby. They subsisted on a diet that was sometimes tolerable, at other times no more than roasted acorns and wild plums. Platter traveled east and perhaps visited Hungary; he certainly visited Silesia and German-speaking parts of Poland.

Although largely self-taught, Thomas did have some formal if haphazard schooling, in particular from the age of eighteen. In Basel, he worked as a rope-maker, but by studying on his own and seizing what chances he could to study with others, he became an intellectual in the humanist style, an illiterate who transformed himself into a renowned professor of Latin, Greek, and Hebrew. Later he established himself as a printer in the city, which had adopted a relatively moderate form of Protestantism early in the Reformation. Platter published the first Latin edition of John Calvin's *Institutes of the Christian Religion* in 1536. Although his fortunes fluctuated, Thomas was able to acquire a country estate and to pay for his son Felix to study medicine at the University of Montpellier, a highly regarded institution, as well as to journey through France on a sort of grand tour.

Felix Platter (1536–1614) enjoyed a brilliant career. After completing his studies, he married the daughter of one of Basel's important surgeons. He became the city physician of Basel as well as a professor of medicine, a dean, a director of education, and an author of books on medicine and physics. He maintained ties with the Reformer David Joris and the French essayist Michel de Montaigne. Thus a practitioner became a patrician.

In 1574, at the age of seventy, Thomas Platter Sr. and his second wife had a son, Thomas Jr. (1574–1628), who represents in a sense a third generation—he was raised in part by his older brother. Thomas Jr. traveled in France, Catalonia, England, and the Low Countries; he also became a physician and he also recorded certain episodes of his life.

These three men's writings span in time and space the Europe of the Renaissance, the Reformation, and the baroque. Their memoirs and the information they collected illuminate their personalities and the world in which they lived. Their lives represent a remarkable social ascent: the beggar who himself becomes a scholar and makes of his son a great professor and physician. Products of the Europe of the Rhine, these Protestants embodied the character of men of the early modern period in Europe.

BIBLIOGRAPHY

Primary Works

Platter, Felix. *Tagebuch*. Edited by V. Lötscher. Basel, Switzerland, 1976. Includes text and notes.

Platter, Thomas, Sr. *Lebensbeschreibung*. Edited by A. Hartmann. Basel, Switzerland, 1944. A fundamental source.

Platter, Thomas, Jr. *Beschreibung der Reisen durch Frankreich, Spanien, England, und den Niederlanden*. Edited by Rut Keiser. 2 vols. Basel, Switzerland, 1968. A fundamental source.

Secondary Work

Le Roy Ladurie, Emmanuel. *The Beggar and the Professor: A Sixteenth-Century Family Saga*. Chicago, 1997. Translation by Arthur Goldhammer of *Le siècle des Platter, 1499–1628*. Vol. 1: *Le mendiant et le professeur*. Paris, 1995.

EMMANUEL LE ROY LADURIE

Translated from French by Sylvia J. Cannizzaro

PLAUTUS, TITUS MACCIUS (c. 254–184 B.C.), Roman playwright. After the rediscovery of twelve plays by Plautus in 1427, his contribution to Renaissance comedy became even greater than that of Terence. Despite some humanists' objections to his panache, his plays, based on the tradition of Greek New Comedy, which superseded the Old Comedy of Aristophanes in Athens from the late fourth century B.C., provided Renaissance playwrights with a wealth of suggestions as to comic scenes, plots, stock figures, and the play with language, of which Plautus is a great master.

Whereas his influence was only moderate in Spain and Portugal and less obvious in Germany, it was clearly recognizable in France—for example, in Jean de Rotrou's work and later in Molière's *Amphitryon* (1668) and *L'avare* (1668)—and even more so in Italy and England. Along with the plays of Terence and what was known of Menander, the Plautine comedies were considered comic prototypes and provided examples for Ludovico Ariosto's early comedy *La cassaria* (1508) and other plays, especially *La calandria* by Bernardo Dovizi (called il Bibbiena), first performed around 1514. However, the aesthetic goal of the Italian comedic plays was a skillful fusion of Plautine suggestions with other disparate sources.

In England the reception of Plautus was intense. Not only were new plays written in imitation of Plautine models, but humanist playwrights such as John Lyly and Ben Jonson learned a great deal from him. Throughout Shakespeare's development as a comic playwright, a Plautine influence can be felt, most strongly in *The Comedy of Errors* (1589–1593), which he based on *Menaechmi* with further suggestions from *Amphitruo,* which Plautus called a *tragicocomoedia*.

See also **Terence**.

BIBLIOGRAPHY

Clubb, Louise George. *Italian Drama in Shakespeare's Time*. New Haven, Conn., 1989.

Grismer, Raymond Leonard. *The Influence of Plautus in Spain before Lope de Vega*. New York, 1944.

Riehle, Wolfgang. *Shakespeare, Plautus, and the Humanist Tradition*. Cambridge, U.K., 1990.

Salzmann, Wolfgang. *Molière und die lateinische Komödie*. Heidelberg, Germany, 1969.

WOLFGANG RIEHLE

PLÉIADE. A constellation of seven French poets active in the third quarter of the sixteenth century under the preeminent leadership of Pierre de Ronsard. Initially calling itself the "brigade," this group was renamed Pléiade in 1553 after the seven third-century B.C. Greek poets belonging to the court of Ptolemy Philadelphus. These Greek poets were thought to have been transformed into stars of the Pleiades constellation, thus becoming immortal.

Origin and Identification. The French group was not close enough to be remembered as a school, but members were linked by similar principles of imitation and by poet Joachim Du Bellay's manifesto, *Défense et illustration de la langue française* (Defense and illustration of the French language; Paris, 1549). This text urged the renewal of a national poetic French language and embodied the poetic and linguistic principles of Ronsard's reform. Du Bellay called for the imitation of Greco-Roman and Italian writers in order to enrich the French language. A heightened importance was placed on technique and especially on inspiration described as "divine madness." Poets, now considered as intermediaries between the gods and man, acquired an elevated status. This movement of poetic renewal and innovation rejected as outdated medieval poetic genres in favor of the models and forms of classical antiquity (elegy, eclogue, epigram, ode, satire, epic, tragic and comic theater) and of Italy (sonnet). In addition to experimenting with a variety of metrical forms, the Pléiade poets explored a wide range of subjects (love poetry, religious and scientific verse, political discourse, satirical and official writings, tragedies and comedies, the pastoral, and epic poetry) since they were educated in all fields of learning, from Greek and Latin to mathematics and astronomy.

The Pléiade was exclusive but not a closely knit group. Its members were hardly recognized as any different in stature from other poets of the period; they tended not to know one another personally, nor did they live in proximity to each other. In fact, it has been difficult for historians to identify all seven members of the Pléiade at a specific moment in time. These poets were grouped together because they were followers of Ronsard. Ronsard first drew up a list of these poets in 1553 in his "Elegie à J. de La Péruse" (Elegy to J. de La Péruse; fifth book of *Odes*), where the poets mentioned are Du Bellay, Pontus de Tyard, Antoine de Baïf, Guillaume Des Autels, Étienne Jodelle, and Jean de La Péruse. When a poet died, Ronsard replaced him in order to keep the group membership at seven. Thus, La Péruse, upon his death in 1554, was the first to be replaced, by Rémy Belleau, and Guillaume Des Autels was replaced by Peletier du Mans. Later, Claude Binet, in his biography of Ronsard (1586), replaced Peletier with Jean Dorat, who had been principal in 1547 of the Collège de Coqueret, where Ronsard, Du Bellay, and Baïf were educated. The other Parisian college associated with the formation of the Pléiade poets was the Collège de Boncourt, the training ground of the poets Jodelle, Belleau, and La Péruse. Other figures like Amadis Jamyn, Olivier de Magny, Nicolas Denisot, Marc-Antoine Muret, Jean Tagaut, Jacques Grévin, and Robert Garnier gravitated as well around the new poetic movement.

Principal Members of the Pléiade. Rémy Belleau's (1528–1577) celebrated translation of the odes of Anacreon (1556) earned him Ronsard's immediate praise and inclusion among the Pléiade poets. His *Petites inventions* (Brief imitations; 1556) showed him adept at the genre of the descriptive *blason,* and *Les amours et nouveaux échanges des pierres précieuses* (Love poems and a new commentary on precious stones; Paris, 1576) reaffirmed his predilection for descriptive realism. His annotations on Ronsard's *Second livre des amours* (Second book of love; 1560) was followed by his major work, *Bergerie* (Pastoral; Paris, 1565, 1572), written at the family estate of the marquis of Elbeuf at Joinville, where Belleau was preceptor to the marquis's son, Charles of Lorraine. A posthumous collection of his works (1578) contains his interesting verse comedy *La reconnue* (The recognized one; composed c. 1563).

Guillaume Des Autels (1529–1581) is mainly remembered for his role in the mid-century controversy over Louis Meigret's proposed reform of French orthography. In his 1548 treatise condemning Meigret's proposal and in his 1553 reply to Meigret, Des Autels takes the opportunity as well to critique Du Bellay's rejection of translation in favor of imitation. Des Autels argues that there is little difference between the two and that the enrichment of the language requires complete independence from Greco-Roman and Italian predecessors. Eventually Des Autels came to agree with Du Bellay that imitation was the best way to reform French poetry. Ronsard originally included him in his listing because Des Autels endorsed Ronsard's new treatment of the ode.

Jean Dorat (1508–1588) was a translator and the teacher of Ronsard, Du Bellay, and Baïf at the Collège de Coqueret from 1547 on. He taught Greek and Latin literature, interpreting the works of Greek dramatists and of poets such as Homer, Pindar, and Callimachus. He published an annotated Greek edition of Aeschylus's *Prometheus Bound* (1548) and *Poemata* (1548), a collection of French and Latin verse. He greatly influenced Ronsard's career; Ronsard credited Dorat with his own learning of poetry and adopted his elevation of the poet as a seer.

Amadis Jamyn (c. 1540–1593) was Ronsard's secretary and friend. Educated by Dorat and Adrien Turnèbe, he was associated with a group of court poets that included Philippe Desportes. Jamyn is remembered for his love poetry, his religious verse, and partial translations of the *Iliad* and the *Odyssey*.

Jacques Peletier du Mans (1517–1582), a poet, philosopher, and mathematician, translated Homer, Virgil, Horace, and Petrarch. In 1555 he published his *L'amours des amours* (Loves of loves), a collection that combines abstract love lyrics with cosmological and scientific verse. His *Art poétique* (Poetic theory; Lyon, 1555) is at once a philosophical manifesto for poetry as a superior form of knowledge and a manual detailing the principles of poetic writing.

Scévole de Sainte-Marthe (1536–1623), a distinguished magistrate and mayor of Poitiers, was a poet and a humanist who published several collections of writings in Latin and French. His admired *Elogia* (Praises; 1598) of contemporary French and neo-Latin poets and writers was translated into French by Guillaume Colletet in 1644. His equally celebrated *Paedotrophiae* (1584), a manual on the upbringing of infants and children dedicated to the childless Henry III, was translated into French and English in the following century.

Pontus de Tyard (1521–1605), a poet, translator, scientist, and bishop, published three Petrarchan sonnet sequences entitled *Erreurs amoureuses* (Amorous errors; 1549, 1551, 1555); *Vers lyriques* (Lyrical verse; 1552, 1553), revealing the influence of Ronsard; *Oeuvres poétiques* (Poetic works; 1573), Petrarchist poems celebrating Catherine of Clermont, the erudite maréchale of Retz whose Parisian salon Tyard attended from 1568 on; and a translation of Leone Ebreo's *Dialoghi d'amore* (Dialogues on love; 1551). Between 1552 and 1558 he wrote a collection of Neoplatonic philosophical treatises on astrology and divination (*Mantice,* 1550), on poetry (*Solitaire premier,* 1552), on music (*Solitaire second,* 1552), on time (*Discours du temps, de l'an, et de ses parties* [Discourse on time, on the year, and its parts]; 1556), and on the spiritual and physical universe; *L'univers* [The universe; Lyon, 1557]).

BIBLIOGRAPHY

Bellenger, Yvonne. *La Pléiade: La poésie en France autour de Ronsard*. Paris, 1988. Complete survey of the Pléiade poets.

Castor, Graham. *Pléiade Poetics: A Study in Sixteenth-Century Thought and Terminology*. Cambridge, U.K., 1964. Classic analysis of the poetic principles of the Pléiade poets.

Chamard, Henri. *Histoire de la Pléiade*. 4 vols. Paris, 1939–1940.

Clements, Robert J. *Critical Theory and the Practice of the Pléiade*. Cambridge, Mass., 1942.

Laumonier, Paul. *Ronsard, poète lyrique*. Paris, 1909.

Stage international d'études humanistes. *Lumières de la Pléiade*. Paris, 1966. A classic anthology of articles on the poetic practices of the Pléiade poets.

ANNE R. LARSEN

PLINY THE ELDER (Gaius Plinius Secundus; 23–79 A.D.), Roman author who was a major influence on Renaissance thinking in many fields. Pliny's *Historia naturalis* (trans. *Natural History*) was the most important Roman work on natural science and a major source for knowledge about the ancient world. Born at Como in northern Italy, he pursued a military and administrative career. According to the letters of his nephew, Pliny the Younger, he spent every leisure moment engaged in study and observation of the world. He wrote books on military science, grammar, oratory, and history as well as natural philosophy; but only *Natural History* survives. A letter of the nephew describes his uncle's death when, as commander of the Roman fleet in the bay of Naples, he went ashore during the eruption of Mount Vesuvius that destroyed Pompeii, partly out of scientific curiosity and partly out of concern for the inhabitants. His industriousness is faithfully reflected in *Natural History*. It is jammed with a wealth of information, some of it fantastic and unbelievable but most of it as accurate as a well-informed man of the Roman ruling class of his day could make it; and all of it indispensable to those in the Middle Ages and the Renaissance, and even those in modern times, who wanted to discover what the Romans knew about their world.

Pliny was proudly Roman, suspicious of other peoples, especially the Greeks, whom he recognized as intelligent and erudite but disdained as arrogant and deceitful. He preferred Italic folk medicine to the learned medicine of Greek physicians. Yet more than half of his listed sources are Greek. Among the principal attractions of *Natural History* for medieval, Renaissance, and modern readers are the citations from earlier scientific writers whose works have perished.

Natural History covers a multitude of topics: the structure of the universe, human nature, astronomy, physics, geology, geography (treated in great detail, region by region), anthropology, zoology, botany, agriculture, medicine, medicinal substances, magic, minerals and gems, and even a survey of famous works of art. Pliny tries to distinguish between what he has personally observed and what comes from others, but he never manages to impose a true intellectual order on the data he reports.

Natural History is a prime example of a classical text that was never lost. Hardly a single medieval century lacks at least some witness to its influence as a source of knowledge, even though medieval authors regularly amalgamated the two Plinys into one. The elder Pliny served as a source for Roman writers like Quintus Gargilius Martialis (third century A.D.) and the third-century geographer Solinus, and also for medieval encyclopedists from Isidore of Seville (c. 560–636) and Bede (672/73–735) to late-medieval authors like Thomas de Cantimpré (c. 1201–c. 1270/72) and Vincent de Beauvais (c. 1190–c. 1264). He was second only to Aristotle as an authoritative source for encyclopedists. Humanist scholars of the Renaissance could not fail to be attracted to such a rich storehouse of information about antiquity. As specialists in classical Latin, they were especially attracted by the lexicographical treasures of *Natural History:* a hoard of first-century Latin terms, particularly scientific and technical terms.

The invention of printing increased the book's influence. It was printed early and, despite the high cost of such a long book, often: there were fifteen editions before 1501. Since it was not used as a schoolbook in the Middle Ages, there were no medieval commentaries; but almost immediately after the first printed edition appeared (1469) the obvious defects of the text attracted attention, and humanists began producing commentaries to clarify corrupt passages. The most important commentary of the fifteenth century was a work published in 1492–1493 by Ermolao Barbaro (1454–1493); this work and the essays of Angelo Poliziano (1454–1494) (*Miscellanea,* 1489) strongly influenced subsequent editors. The Ferrarese physician Niccolò Leoniceno (1428–1524), a determined Hellenist who criticized Pliny for preferring Roman medical knowledge to that of Greek authors like his contemporary Dioscorides, stirred up debate in 1492 by blaming Pliny, not subsequent scribes, for medical errors in the text. This was a significant controversy: it shifted attention from the humanistic goal of restoring the text to the medical goal of determining which of the ancient texts provided the best treatment for patients.

In the sixteenth century the major commentators were non-Italians: Nicolas Berault (1473–1550) of Paris, who compiled a composite commentary (1516) drawn from several humanists including Erasmus (c. 1466–1536) and Guillaume Budé (1467–1540), Beatus Rhenanus (1485–1547), and Sigismund Gelen (1497–1554), Erasmus's associates at the Froben press; the Spanish humanist Fernando Nuñez de Guzmán (1475–1553); and the French physician and botanist Jacques Daléchamps (1513–1588). The sixteenth-century commentaries emphasize Pliny's value for medicine and other scientific fields; many of those who wrote on Pliny were trained as physicians.

See also **Botany.**

BIBLIOGRAPHY

Primary Work

Pliny. *Natural History.* Edited by Horace Rackham et al. Rev. ed. 10 vols. Cambridge, Mass., 1938–1963. The convenient Loeb Classical Library edition, with Latin and English texts on facing pages.

Secondary Works

Beagon, Mary. *Roman Nature: The Thought of Pliny the Elder.* Oxford, 1992. An overview of Pliny's place in the intellectual history of ancient Rome.

Copenhaver, Brian P. "A Tale of Two Fishes: Magical Objects in Natural History from Antiquity through the Scientific Revolution." *Journal of the History of Ideas* 52 (1991): 373–398. Examines Renaissance efforts to understand references to occult forces in classical authors, including Pliny.

French, Roger, and Frank Greenaway, eds. *Science in the Early Roman Empire: Pliny the Elder, His Sources and Influence.* London, 1986. A collection of essays; especially pertinent are B. S. Eastwood, "Plinian Astronomy in the Middle Ages and Renaissance," pp. 197–251; and R. K. French, "Pliny and Renaissance Medicine," pp. 252–281.

Nauert, Charles G. "Gaius Plinius Secundus." In *Catalogus translationum et commentariorum.* Edited by Paul Oskar Kristeller, et al. Washington, D.C., 1980. Vol. 4, pp. 297–422. A survey of all known commentaries on *Natural History,* with an extended introduction on the textual history of the work.

Nauert, Charles G. "Humanists, Scientists, and Pliny: Changing Approaches to a Classical Author." *American Historical Review* 84 (1979): 72–85.

CHARLES G. NAUERT

PLOTINUS (204/5–270 C.E.), perhaps of Lycopolis in Egypt, generally regarded as the founder of Neoplatonism. Almost all of what we know about the life of Plotinus comes from a biography, *The Life of Plotinus,* written by his pupil the philosopher Porphyry. According to Porphyry, in his twenty-eighth year Plotinus discovered in himself a thirst for philosophy. This led him to Alexandria and the school of Ammonius Saccas. After some ten or eleven years with Ammonius, Plotinus conceived a plan to study Persian and Indian philosophy. To this end, he attached himself to a military expedition led by the emperor Gordian III in 243. After the assassination of Gordian by his troops and the aborting of the expedition, Plotinus traveled to Rome, where he remained until his death.

All of Plotinus's known writings are extant. They are contained in an edition compiled by Porphyry and titled *Enneads,* after the Greek word meaning nine. It was apparently Porphyry who decided to divide the essays of Plotinus into six groups of nine. Although the division was probably made by Porphyry, the six *Enneads* do have a perspicuous order. The first *Ennead* contains what Porphyry calls "ethical matters." *Enneads* 2 and 3 contain treatises on natural philosophy or cosmology. *Ennead* 4 concerns the soul or psychology; *Ennead* 5 investigates intellect and other epistemological matters; and *Ennead* 6 treats being, number, and the One, the first principle of all. Thus, the treatises move from the external to the internal, from the earthly to the heavenly.

Although Plotinus is regarded as the founder of Neoplatonism, he certainly regarded himself not as an innovator, but merely as a disciple of Plato. Plotinus's discipleship, however, is filtered through the nearly six hundred years of philosophy separating him from his master. Owing to the critical and partisan nature of this philosophy, Plotinus found himself obliged to defend, and not simply expound, Plato's teachings. In doing so, he came to offer accounts of philosophical matters that were, *malgré lui,* new and perhaps even incompatible with those of his master. Porphyry tells us that the *Enneads* are full of concealed Stoic and Peripatetic doctrines. What this apparently means is that, primarily in natural philosophy and ethics, Plotinus was led to take serious account of what the two most serious competitors to Platonism had to offer. Plotinus accepts what he can from these two schools and rejects that which is impossible to assimilate to his understanding of Plato.

The principal way in which Plotinus's Neoplatonism differs from Platonism has to do with his account of the One, or the first principle of all. According to Plotinus, the One is that upon which absolutely everything else depends for its being. Although his account of our knowledge and experience of the One is a controversial matter, there is little dispute about this. For Plato, however, the Form of the Good, evidently his first principle, is explicitly the source of the being only of the Forms, whereas, at least in his dialogue *Timaeus,* a principle of matter or passivity is posited as independent. The differences between making everything dependent on the first principle and not doing so are far-reaching. For example, Plotinus, who, like Plato, assumes the perfect goodness of the first principle, must give an account of evil that does not make the One responsible for it.

Plotinus's writings were transmitted to the West in Marsilio Ficino's translation with commentary (1484–1492). In his personal writings, Ficino tried to demonstrate the harmony of Platonic and Christian principles. Giovanni Pico della Mirandola and Francesco Patrizi both contributed to the transmission of broadly Platonic and Neoplatonic ideas to the mixture that is Renaissance philosophy.

See also **Plato, Platonism, and Neoplationism**; *and the biographies of Ficino, Patrizi, and Pico della Mirandola.*

BIBLIOGRAPHY

Gerson, Lloyd P. *Plotinus: The Arguments of the Philosophers.* London and New York, 1994.

Lloyd, A. C. *The Anatomy of Neoplatonism.* Oxford, 1990.

O'Meara, Dominic J. *Plotinus: An Introduction to the Enneads.* Oxford, 1993.

LLOYD P. GERSON

PLUTARCH. *See* **Historiography,** *subentry on* **Classical Historians.**

PODESTÀ. The podestà was the chief executive and judicial official (in later years, exclusively a judicial official) in most of the city-states of Italy, excluding Venice, Naples, and Sicily, from the twelfth through the fifteenth centuries. The name podestà was also given to the heads of judicial systems in minor cities within Renaissance territorial states, although they had less authority. The podestà originally developed in the twelfth and thirteenth centuries as an official of the city governments called communes; the podestà was sometimes appointed by the Holy Roman Emperor. The Holy Roman Emperor Frederick Barbarossa played an important role in the development of the office.

The podestà was head of the Council of the Commune, which maintained the authority over all the important acts of government. The podestà convened the council and put material in order for presentation to it, but the council deliberated and made decisions. At first the podestà was chosen from among the citizens, but very soon foreign citizenship, usually from another Italian city-state, was required. Still, the podestà had to come from a friendly city-state. The developing city-states had to overcome factionalism caused by competition among local aristocrats. The requirement that the podestà be a foreigner was meant to insulate him from kinship ties, patronage, and local influence. For similar reasons, the podestà had a very short term of office, usually six months to a year. He was forbidden to receive local people as guests or to accept gifts from them.

As city-state government grew in complexity and volume, administering both government and the judicial system became too great a task for the podestà. His executive power passed to other officials and he became exclusively a judicial and police official. The judicial sphere required considerable attention: Roman law was relatively technical and sophisticated. Each newly appointed podestà was required to bring with him civil and criminal judges, a police chief, police officials, and pages. Upon arrival, the podestà and his entourage had only a couple of weeks in which to read the local statutes before beginning to act. This system was functional because, despite differences between local statutes, the *ius commune* (literally, "common law," but in practice a fusion of feudal law, Roman law, and canon law) was in effect all across Italy from 1000 to 1700. The podestà did not need to be a doctor of law, though it helped, but he had to be a noble. As government and the judicial system expanded in the fourteenth century, the job of the podestà grew. Regular policing, handling of arrests at the scene, and collecting evidence became more prominent among the duties of the podestà and his staff.

The system of the traveling foreign podestà and his cadre of judicial officials declined during the late fifteenth century as rule by a single powerful prince became the norm in the city-states of northern and central Italy. The podestà system had always been very expensive; it became more so as the podestà's duties increased. Judicial systems began to rely on committees of citizen judges. These panels, which did not rely on the principles of Roman law, could be manipulated more easily by a prince.

See also **City-State**; **Law**.

BIBLIOGRAPHY

Chambers, David, and Trevor Dean. *Clean Hands and Rough Justice: An Investigating Magistrate in Renaissance Italy.* Ann Arbor, Mich., 1997.

Stern, Laura Ikins. *The Criminal Law System of Medieval and Renaissance Florence.* Baltimore, 1994.

LAURA IKINS STERN

POETICS. [This entry includes two subentries, a general survey and a discussion of French poetics. For discussion of English poetics, see Literary Theory, Renaissance.]

Survey

Throughout the Middle Ages, there was no shortage of poets and scholars who wrote about the nature of poetry and about how to distinguish good poetry from bad. Many of their ideas originated in Greece and Rome, and many of the poets they most admired, their *auctores,* came from antiquity as well. Yet by the end of the Middle Ages, poetics had evolved in a number of decidedly unclassical directions. Treatises like the thirteenth-century *artes poetriae* (arts of poetry) taught schoolboys how to compose poems that sounded quite different from those produced in ancient Rome, and the major documents of classical theory and criticism were either little read or seriously distorted.

The claims of the Renaissance humanists in this area, therefore, have considerable validity. Beginning even before Petrarch and reaching its definitive form in the fifteenth century, Renaissance humanism sought a cultural renewal that would rest on a more accurate historical and intellectual understanding of the ancient world and the texts produced in it. Part of this renewal involved a curricular reform in the schools that placed greater emphasis on certain disciplines, one of which was poetry. As a result, Renaissance writers produced an extraordinary series of documents that used the key works of ancient literary criticism and theory to defend the status of poetry and explore its nature and power.

For purposes of analysis, Renaissance poetics can be divided into three phases. The first coincides with the late-fourteenth and fifteenth centuries, and unfolds in opposition to a number of articulate, well-reasoned attacks on poetry as a pagan and morally corrupting influence. This phase presents a wide variety of writings that defend poetry on ontological and moral grounds. The second phase, coinciding roughly with the sixteenth century, includes commentaries on ancient texts, arts of poetry, and evaluative disputes about major poems, and moves from general assertions to increasingly detailed analyses of how literature can and should function. During the third phase, extending from the sixteenth century into the seventeenth, the insights gained in Italy spread throughout Europe and played an important role in the discussions about literature in Renaissance England, France, and the Netherlands.

From Pre-humanism to the Fifteenth Century. In the thirteenth and fourteenth centuries a number of conservative scholars, especially clerics, opposed the study of poetry. Their objections fell into two basic areas. First, the opponents of poetry turned to two works of Thomas Aquinas, his commentary on the *Metaphysics* of Aristotle and his *Summa theologiae* (Summary of theology; 1266–

1273), to claim that poetry is the lowest of all the sciences and that poets lie. The other basic objection followed from those of Aquinas: poets knew so little that they often incited their readers to immoral action.

The first major clash between the conservative opposition and the defenders of a new poetics took place in Padua in 1315–1316. In a series of documents the Dominican Giovannino of Mantua argued that poetry is totally devoid of truth and far removed from the divine science of theology. The pre-humanist Albertino Mussato (1261–1329) responded by claiming that the poet was in fact a kind of theologian who either consciously or unconsciously concealed some parts of religious truth in his poetry. In defending the concept of the *poeta theologus,* which became a commonplace of humanist theory, Mussato offered nine reasons to consider poetry divine, including such claims that poetry was given to the human race by God and that poetry can be interpreted so that it is in accordance with the Bible.

Petrarch (1304–1374), who gave humanism its decisive literary cast, defended the power of poetry in a number of places, especially in his *Invective contra medicum* (Invective against a doctor; 1355) and in the *Collatio laureationis* (Discussion at the laurel crowning), the speech he prepared to mark his coronation as poet laureate of Rome (1341). Allegory, he argued, was necessary to uncover the Christian truth hidden in all great poetry, including that of the pagans. Petrarch was also unusually sensitive to the nuances of poetic language, as revealed by the careful marginal notes he left in his copies of the classical authors.

Many of the points made by Petrarch are also made by Boccaccio (1313–1375) in his *Trattatello in laude di Dante* (Treatise in praise of Dante; 1351, 1360, 1373), which discusses the civilizing effects of poetry, the parallelisms between pagan poetry and the Bible, and the importance of allegory. The last two books of his *Genealogie deorum gentilium* (Genealogy of the pagan gods; 1350–1375) add a general defense of pagan poetry to the preceding discussion of classical myth. Here Boccaccio draws again on the *poeta theologus* motif, arguing that poetry proceeds from God and can lead the reader back to its divine source. Both poetry and scripture, Boccaccio admits, can be difficult to understand, but the effort to interpret the allegory in them actually aids the comprehension and retention of the truth.

Humanistic studies in Florence were maintained in the next generation by the city's chancellor, Coluccio Salutati (1331–1406), whose writings on poetry include a famous exchange with the Dominican Giovanni Dominici. In his *Lucula noctis* (The firefly), Dominici admits that pagan poetry contains some lines that are consonant with the Christian faith, but intermingled with what is true are many things that are false; why, moreover, should the Christian risk being led astray when the pure truth of the Bible is available? Salutati's defense rests primarily in the arguments made by his humanist predecessors, though he also adds an unusually clear statement of the moral and rhetorical power of poetry. Paraphrasing Quintilian's definition of the orator, Salutati defines the poet as the best of men, skilled in the praise of virtue and the condemnation of vice.

Education. There is also a vigorous defense of pagan poetry in the educational theory of the early humanists. The principal documents are five treatises: Pier Paolo Vergerio's *De ingenuis moribus et liberalibus studiis* (On noble character and liberal studies; 1402–1403), Leonardo Bruni's *De studiis et litteris* (On literary studies; c. 1424), Enea Silvio Piccolomini's *De liberorum educatione* (On the education of children; c. 1445), Battista Guarini's *De ordine docendi et discendi* (On the order of teaching and learning; 1459), and Maffeo Vegio's *De educatione liberorum clarisque eorum moribus* (On education and distinction of character in children; completed by 1443, published c. 1460). The authors of these works acknowledge that lyric, satire, and comedy sometimes introduce themes that should not be taught to schoolboys, but they argue that in general pagan poetry reinforces the moral development that was the proper goal of a humanist education.

These arguments remained controversial, however, as we see in two disputes from the middle of the century. When the cleric Giovanni of Prato attacked pagan poetry for being immoral (1450), the famous schoolmaster Guarino Guarini argued that the church fathers knew the classics, that the *De legendis libris gentilium* (On reading pagan books) of Basil the Great (c. 329–379) shows how this material should be read, and that poetry is necessary to support the teachings of theology. The other dispute from this period is particularly interesting because in this case the author of the *Orationes contra poetas* (Speeches against the poets; 1455–1459), an attack on poetry, is the humanist bishop of Verona, Ermolao Barbaro il Vecchio (c. 1410–1471). Barbaro argues that it is pointless to rest a defense of poetry in allegory, for removing the allegorical shell from pagan poetry only exposes a Jove who commits adultery and rape. Immoral in content and associated with false gods, poetry is far removed from theology for Barbaro, whose attack shows that more than a century after Mussato, poetry's place was not secure even among the humanists, who were its most consistent defenders.

Poetics. In the last decades of the fifteenth century, three Florentines produced discussions of literature that foreshadow the directions that sixteenth-century poetics would follow. The first of these men was Cristoforo Landino (1424–1498), whose poetics were deeply influenced by the Platonism of Marsilio Ficino (1433–1499). The poet, Landino argues, is inspired by God, so that by using allegory, poetry arrives at the same truth as philosophy. However, Landino also emphasized the stylistic and rhetorical analysis of poetry, a tradition drawn from Horace's *Ars poetica* (Art of poetry), on which he published a commentary in 1482.

Angelo Poliziano (1454–1494) was close to Landino and the other Florentine Neoplatonists, but toward the end of his life he moved away from Plato toward the literary criticism of Aristotle. He was the first scholar in fifteenth-century Florence to own a copy of the *Poetics,* and in his commentary to Terence's *Andria,* for example, Poliziano notes that poetry originates in imitation and cites Aristotle to support his position. This interest in Aristotle led Poliziano away from his earlier tendencies to "mix poetry with philosophy" and toward a new interest in poetic language.

The first Renaissance treatise devoted exclusively to poetics is the *De poetice* (On the art of poetry; 1490–1492) of Bartolomeo della Fonte, Landino's student and Poliziano's colleague at the Florentine university. Della Fonte first discusses inspiration, the position of poetry among the arts and science, its utility, and its moral value. Then he turns to Horace, but recasts the classical principles as guides to poetic composition in his own day, picking up rhetorical points in particular and advocating imitation of classical authors. Finally, he provides a brief history of poetry.

Sixteenth-century Criticism. Landino, Poliziano, and della Fonte set the tone for the remarkable flurry of critical activity in the sixteenth century. This activity involved, first, the systematic recovery of the ideas of Horace, Plato, and Aristotle on poetry; then the development of the art of poetry as a genre in its own right; and, finally, the refinement of critical ideas in disputes over the masterworks of Italian literature.

Horace's poetics. From Horace, Renaissance critics took a number of well-turned phrases that helped ground their discussions—poetry is like a picture (*ut pictura poesis*), into the middle of things (*in medias res*), and above all, poets aim either at profit or delight (*aut prodesse volunt aut delectare poetae*)—along with a number of key concepts like decorum, or the importance of what is appropriate in different circumstances. Decorum in origin is a rhetorical term, and Horace's *Ars poetica* (Art of poetry) was regularly analyzed for its affinities with parts of the rhetorical tradition, like the three styles of rhetoric and the movement from invention through disposition to style by the major commentators of the Renaissance: Cristoforo Landino (1482), Iodocus Badius Ascensius (Josse Bade, 1500), Aulo Giano Parrasio (1531), Giovanni Battista Pigna (1561), and Giovanni Fabrini, the author of the only commentary published in Italian during the sixteenth century (1566).

In 1546 Francesco Filippo Pedemonte's *Ecphrasis in Horatii Flacci Artem poeticam* (Explanation of Horace's *Art of Poetry;* 1546) added Aristotle's *Poetics* to the texts that were regularly brought to bear on Horace, and Francesco Robortello and Vincenzo Maggi both added appendices to their commentaries on the *Poetics* that argued a fundamental parallelism between Horace and Aristotle. In the 1560s and 1570s Horatian criticism took a more practical turn, while the last twenty years of the sixteenth century were marked by a series of shorter treatises such as Tommaso Correa's *De elegia* (On the elegy; 1590) and Federico Ceruti's *Dialogus de comoedia* (Dialogue on comedy; 1593), describing particular genres according to Horatian principles.

***Aristotle's* Poetics.** Unlike Horace's more casual approach, Aristotle's literary theory demands to be approached systematically. *Poetics* focuses on tragedy, but Aristotle's basic ideas on the other genres are easily worked out as well, and a number of key ideas in Renaissance poetics can be traced directly to this treatise: the primacy of plot, the catharsis of pity and fear as the end of tragedy, the importance of unity and verisimilitude, and the relationship of genre and moral character.

Aristotle's text entered Italian criticism in the garbled Latin translation that Hermannus Alemannus had made of Averroes (written 1256, first printed in 1481), and the first phase of scholarly activity involved restoring an accurate text and providing a basic exegesis of it. The earliest significant efforts to do this, Francesco Robortello's *In librum Aristotelis de arte poetica explicationes* (Commentary on Aristotle's book concerning the art of poetry; 1548) and Bartolomeo Lombardi and Vincenzo Maggi's *In Aristotelis librum de poetica communes explicationes* (Public commentary on Aristotle's book concerning the art of poetry; 1550), show that *Poetics* was read at first through a Horatian filter by critics who had real difficulty distinguishing what is unique about it.

The next group of scholars succeeded in using *Poetics* as the source of ideas for their own arts of poetry and for some innovative speculations on genre, but the major treatise of this period, Pietro Vettori's *Commentarii in primum librum Aristotelis de arte poetarum* (Commentary on the first book of Aristotle concerning the art of poetry; 1560), still sounds more like Horace than Aristotle in places. The next few years saw the publication of two great vernacular commentaries. Lodovico Castelvetro's *Poetica d'Aristotele vulgarizzata et sposta* (Aristotle's *Poetics* translated and explained; 1570) declares boldly that pleasure is the primary end of poetry and tightens the constraints on the unities of time, place, and plot, while Alessandro Piccolomini's *Annotazioni nel libro della Poetica d'Aristotele* (Annotations on Aristotle's book on the art of poetry; 1575) clarifies two essential Aristotelian points: the primacy of plot and the distinction between nature and art.

Over the next decade Aristotle was made to serve in the literary quarrels of the day, as theorists used Dante, Sperone Speroni, Ludovico Ariosto, Torquato Tasso, and Battista Guarini to argue about whether generic rules were fixed in antiquity or evolved over time. Aristotle was made to serve both sides; the traditionalists argued that ancient descriptions of ancient genres were eternally valid, the "modernists" that Aristotelian principles could be extended to allow modern adaptations of ancient genres. These same points were developed further in the final years of the sixteenth century; the major figure of the day was Antonio Riccoboni, whose *Compendium artis poeticae Aristotelis ad usum conficiendorum poematum* (Summary of Aristotle's art of poetry to be used for making poems) appeared in 1591.

Plato's poetics. Unlike his student Aristotle, Plato never wrote a poetics, but he did write dialogues on other topics—the *Phaedrus,* the *Ion,* and especially the *Republic*—that take up literature in relation to other, largely social and moral, concerns. Renaissance critics were especially interested in inspiration, Plato's idea that poets speak in a sort of divine madness; in imitation, the idea that literature is ontologically deficient because it is so far removed from the forms in which reality inheres; and in the banishment of the poet from Plato's ideal republic because his erroneous ideas and the passions he stirs up threaten the moral development of the young.

Bernardino Tomitano's *Ragionamenti della lingua toscana* (Discussions on the Tuscan language; 1545) relates poetry to the forms of reality and discusses the need for censorship, while Francesco Patrizi's *Discorso della diversità dei furori poetici* (Discourse on the diversity of poetic madnesses; 1553) takes up inspiration and Sperone Speroni's *Dialogo sopra Virgilio* (Dialogue on Virgil; 1564) deals with imitation. During the last thirty years of the sixteenth century, Platonic criticism merged with an increasingly conservative Catholicism to generate documents like Lorenzo Gambara's *Tractatio de perfectae poëseos ratione* (Treatise on the method of perfect poetry; 1576), in which Plato's republic becomes Christian and the key elements of Platonic philosophy, including Plato's ideas on poetry, are adapted to the post-Tridentine age. In part because Renaissance Platonists did not have an authoritative text focused directly on poetry, however, many treatises in this group have pronounced Aristotelian and Horatian overtones.

Art of poetry. Renaissance literary criticism is also marked by a series of treatises written not as commentaries on the ancient authors, but as independent arts of poetry in their own right. Some of them, like Marco Girolamo Vida's *De arte poetica* (On the art of poetry; 1527) or Bernardino Daniello's *La poetica* (Art of poetry; 1536), remain close to one classical text (here Horace), but others blend various strands of ancient criticism into eclectic treatises that are sometimes quite original. Girolamo Fracastoro's *Naugerius sive de poetica dialogus* (Naugerius or dialogue on the art of poetry; composed c. 1540), for example, begins with Horatian utility and pleasure as ends for poetry but then rejects them for a Platonic assertion that poetry aims at the most perfect expression a subject allows. Antonio Sebastiano Minturno's *De poeta* (On the poet; 1559) is a fascinating eclectic study that creates a series of nine different genres that are described in essentially Ciceronian terms.

Perhaps the most famous treatise in this group is Julius Caesar Scaliger's *Poetices libri septem* (Seven books on the art of poetry; 1561), an unusually systematic document that starts out by focusing on language as the essence of poetry but ends up by denying an independent art of poetry in arguing that literature must be discussed in relation either to the natural world it describes or the human audience it is written for. Two treatises from the end of the century, finally, are interesting for the different directions in which they go. Francesco Patrizi's *Della poetica* (On the art of poetry; 1586) is highly original, arguing (against Aristotle) that the fundamental characteristic of poetry is not imitation but the marvelous; his approach draws from Plato in its emphasis on inspiration, but it also shows the influence of first-century Greek critic Longinus's *On the Sublime,* a treatise that occupied a comparatively minor position in most literary discussions of the Renaissance. Tommaso Campanella's *Poetica* (Art of poetry; c. 1596), in turn, represents the critical strain of conservative Catholicism that also flourished at the end of the sixteenth century, one that rested in a Christianized Plato and a throwback to a moralized Horace.

Literary debates. The ideas developed in sixteenth-century criticism received practical application in a series of quarrels over the great masterworks of Italian literature. While the arguments were developed with great subtlety and sophistication, several issues appeared over and over again in the debates: Do the genres represent eternal, immutable literary forms, or do they evolve as the times change? Do intellectual precepts guide the creation of art, or does authority rest in nature and the senses? Do genres require unity, or is variety of plot and subject allowable? Are literary rules limited to those that can be found in the ancient theorists, or can new rules be developed that follow the spirit of the earlier writers? Does authority rest in an erudite audience that knows the rules of the ancients or in the ignorant masses that follow shifting changes in taste?

The dispute over Dante, which was explored at greatest length in Jacopo Mazzoni's *Della difesa della Comedia di Dante* (On the defense of Dante's *Divine Comedy;* part 1 was published in 1587), ranged from language and genre to the moral efficacy of poetry among various types of audiences. Discussions about tragedy at this time, focused in part around Sperone Speroni's *Canace e Macareo* (1546), revealed that it was one thing to decide to write a modern drama according to Aristotelian principles and another to agree on exactly what those principles were and how they should be implemented.

Another dispute arose over Ariosto's *Orlando furioso* (1516), a wildly popular work that was not easy to reconcile with the generic demands of ancient epic. This dispute took an interesting turn at the publication of Tasso's *Gerusalemme liberata* (Jerusalem delivered; 1581), which Ariosto's opponents seized upon as proof that good literature could still be written according to epic norms, although Tasso himself described his own work with more subtlety than some of his defenders. The dispute over Battista Guarini's *Il pastor fido* (1590; trans. *The Faithful Shepherd*) also centers around genre, with the critics complaining that "tragicomedy" is neither authorized by the ancients nor reducible to the one end which every proper genre should have.

The Spread of Italian Critical Ideas. French criticism entered the Renaissance with Joachim Du Bellay's *Défense et illustration de la langue française* (Defense and elucidation of the French language; 1549). Drawing from ancient criticism through its Italian mediators, Du Bellay argued that French could be perfected as a literary language through imitation of the classics. Pierre de Ronsard's *Abrégé de l'art poëtique françois* (Summary of the French art of poetry; 1565) in turn imports the need for the poet to be a good man and the relationship between poetry and theology that could be developed through allegory. Julius Caesar Scaliger's *Poetics* introduced Aristotelian canons to French criticism, and Jean Vauquelin's *Art poétique* (Art of poetry; 1605) can serve as a useful summation of how Aristotle, Horace, and the sixteenth-century Italian critics Vida and Minturno all contributed to the French critical climate at the turn of the century. By this point everything was in place for a reaction against the sixteenth-century poetics of the *Pléiade,* so that under the guidance of Honoré de Balzac and Jean Chapelain, the critical standard shifted to a pure French diction and logical argumentation that culminated in the inviolability of literary rules, especially as reflected in the dramatic unities that Nicolas Boileau described in his *Art poétique* (Art of poetry; 1674).

Much of the earliest literary criticism in England was mostly rhetorical; Thomas Wilson's *Arte of Rhetorike* (1553) or Roger Ascham's *Scholemaster* (1563–1568) serve as examples. The next group of treatises, which include George Puttenham's *Arte of English Poesie* (1589), blend metrical studies with efforts to classify poetic forms, subjects, and rhetorical figures. English Renaissance poetics, however, climaxes definitively with Sir Philip Sidney's *Defense of Poesie* (1583), a skillful blending of Aristotelian imitation and Horatian utility and delight with the ideas of Renaissance critics ranging from Boccaccio and Scaliger to Castelvetro and Minturno. Though many of the ideas are borrowed, Sidney represents the best of Renaissance criticism, offering a defense of poetry in the best tradition of the early Renaissance, a sensitivity to literary history and genre that equals the best of Italian criticism, and a belief in the literary potential of his own native language that points him firmly toward the literary theory of the future.

Renaissance poetics concludes in the Netherlands. The Low Countries had attracted famous scholars from abroad, like the Spaniard Juan Luis Vives (1492–1540), to join native sons like Justus Lipsius (1547–1606) in the sixteenth century, but it was not until the seventeenth century that Dutch scholarship on poetics dominated Europe. Daniel Heinsius (1580–1655), for example, began within the tradition of sixteenth-century Italian scholarship, but his edition of Aristotle's *Poetics* (1610) and the essay he wrote on it, *De tragoediae constitutione* (On the structure of tragedy; 1611), broke with that tradition to reestablish the primacy of plot and the importance of emotion as the organizing principle on which tragic unity must be based. Heinsius also edited Horace's *Ars poetica* (1610), which he read through an Aristotelian filter. The *Poetical Institutions* (1647) of Gerardus Johannes Vossius (1577–1649), in turn, began from Julius Caesar Scaliger's *Poetics* but reorganized and modified Scaliger's principles from an Aristotelian perspective that was more congenial to his age. Heinsius's work came close to a modern understanding of Aristotle, and Vossius's treatise was the last of the great humanist surveys, so that the effort to survey the field of poetics comprehensively and systematically might be said to end here.

See also **Allegory; Aristotle and Aristotelianism; Aristotle and Cinquecento Poetics; Horace; Plato, Platonism, and Neoplatonism; Rhetoric.**

BIBLIOGRAPHY

Primary Works

Gilbert, Allan H., ed. *Literary Criticism: Plato to Dryden*. Detroit, 1962. Contains the basic texts from antiquity in English translation along with a selection of important Renaissance treatises.

Weinberg, Bernard, ed. *Trattati di poetica e retorica del Cinquecento*. 4 vols. Bari, Italy, 1968–1974. The major treatises of sixteenth-century criticism in the original Latin and Italian.

Secondary Works

Aguzzi-Barbagli, Danilo. "Humanism and Poetics." In *Renaissance Humanism: Foundations, Forms, and Legacy*. Edited by Albert Rabil Jr. Vol. 3, *Humanism and the Disciplines*. Philadelphia, 1988. Pp. 85–169.

Buck, August. *Italienische Dichtungslehren vom Mittelalter bis zum Ausgang der Renaissance*. Tübingen, Germany, 1952.

Greenfield, Concetta C. *Humanist and Scholastic Poetics, 1250–1500*. Lewisburg, Pa., 1981.

Hathaway, Baxter. *The Age of Criticism: The Late Renaissance in Italy*. Ithaca, N.Y., 1962.

Hathaway, Baxter. *Marvels and Commonplaces: Renaissance Literary Criticism*. New York, 1968.

Herrick, Marvin T. *The Fusion of Horatian and Aristotelian Literary Criticism, 1531–1555*. Urbana, Ill., 1946.

Herrick, Marvin T. *Italian Comedy in the Renaissance*. Urbana, Ill., 1960.

Herrick, Marvin T. *Italian Tragedy in the Renaissance*. Urbana, Ill., 1965.

Sellin, Paul R. "The Contribution of Humanist Poetics in the Netherlands to Critical Theory in the Early Seventeenth Century." In *Acta Conventus Neo-Latini Hafniensis: Proceedings of the Eighth International Congress of Neo-Latin Studies*. Copenhagen, 12 August to 17 August 1991. Edited by Rhoda Schnur. Binghamton, N.Y., 1994. Pp. 899–906.

Spingarn, Joel E. *A History of Literary Criticism in the Renaissance*. New York, 1899.

Tateo, F. *Retorica e poetica fra Medioevo e Rinascimento*. Bari, Italy, 1960.

Trabalza, Ciro. *La critica letteraria nel Rinascimento*. Milan, 1915.

Vasoli, C. "L'estetica dell'umanesimo e del Rinascimento." In *Momenti e problemi di storia dell'estetica*. Milan, 1959. Pp. 348–433.

Vossler, Karl. *Poetische Theorien in der italienischen Frührenaissance*. Berlin, 1900.

Weinberg, Bernard. *A History of Literary Criticism in the Italian Renaissance*. 2 vols. Chicago, 1961. The standard survey of this material.

CRAIG KALLENDORF

French Poetics

French Renaissance poetry emerged as a result of three factors. First, it was intentionally created by poets and scholars who sought to develop a "national" linguistic and literary body of work. Their efforts marked a midpoint, a kind of "literary adolescence," as French poetry matured in style. This process involved venerating and imitating great predecessors from antiquity, then rejecting or revising their characteristics and replacing them with the poet's own voice. On a smaller scale, female poets of the time went through much the same process to distinguish themselves from their male contemporaries. Second, French Renaissance poets wrote in accordance with significant and well-thought-out theories. Thinkers and poets such as Joachim du Bellay (1522–1580), Thomas Sébillet (1512–1589), and Jacques Peletier Du Mans (1517–1582) drafted tracts instructing fellow poets how to write verse, how to enrich the French language, what to include or reject from dialect, and how to "discover" and imitate an existing poet. Similarly, the French Renaissance is the period during which scholars reflected on, established, and exemplified nearly all the literary genres that constitute and illustrate the body of writing conceived of as belles lettres. Third, French Renaissance poetry draws from many disciplines. It was influenced and shaped by varied inspirations: art, religion, architecture, and politics all played roles in fostering poetical creation. French Renaissance poetry refers to these sources; it is a highly philosophical but also engagé body of work.

Models and Forms. Poets and orators like Tertullian, Lucian, Juvenal, Horace, Seneca, Cicero, Ovid, and Virgil spoke in a language that appealed to French writers of the sixteenth century, who were at first uncertain whether their own idiom, not yet even officially stabilized as a national tongue, might be used to produce poetry of equal value. Poetry was the preeminent literary form. Prose, required primarily to record history or transmit popular tales from oral to written form, did not possess the cachet of poetry as the most important courtly genre.

Renaissance poets throughout Europe practiced *imitatio* (the imitation and subtle revision of precursor models). The poet selected a poem to imitate, slightly reworked its verses—sometimes so minimally that the result would today be called plagiarism—and then claimed authorship of the resulting version. The poets chose the themes to be elucidated using *inventio,* the process of identifying the primary foci of the earlier poem. Much like *translatio,* the physical transfer from one culture to another of something that might enhance the latter, this practice marks the first phase in the development of the craft of French Renaissance poetry.

That poets could find these sources and read them in their original languages was directly attributable to the great new Renaissance learning method that sought a return to the sources (*ad fontes*). This philosophy, called humanism, revived the study of Greek and Roman literature and made many of the great texts of antiquity available in reliable and accurate translations. Humanism also offered new sources of inspiration beyond the purely Christian by rehabilitating pagan mythology and philosophies such as Epicureanism. French humanism was a vast, interdisciplinary attempt to retrieve the great classical models of inspiration, infuse them with a French poetic flavor, and thereby create a national literature. Francis I was an important supporter of humanism in France; he patronized the arts and imported great Italian writers, artists, and architects to work in France, thereby bringing the Italian Renaissance of a century earlier.

Several poetic forms predominated in the French Renaissance. One is the epic, a long poem of heroic dimensions, themes, and aspirations. The sonnet is composed of fourteen verses divided into two quatrains, or groups of four, and two tercets, or groups of three. Du Bellay introduced the sonnet into France and modeled it on the work of Petrarch. The ode, or long poem was often encyclopedic, philosophical, didactic, or some combination of these. It was introduced to France by the Pléiade, a circle of poets, who were inspired by the great odes of ancient Greece and Rome. The satirical poem lampoons aspects of daily life and is modeled on the work of the ancient satirical writer Juvenal. The lyric poem, often following the example of the great Greek poet Pindar, eulogizes the poet's love object or experience, his country, or nature. Initially a form of song, meant to be sung to the accompaniment of a lyre, the ode is recognized for its attractive meter. The religious poetry of the French Renaissance is either Catholic or Protestant, and may take the form of a meditation on the Psalms in verse or some other biblical passage (for example, Théodore de Bèze's *Chréstienne méditations*); a polemical exchange during the Wars of Religion (such as Théodore-Agrippa d'Aubigné's *Les tragiques*); a metaphysical meditation on the transitory nature of this world (Jean-Baptiste Chassignet; Jean de Sponde); a passionate hymn of praise to the godhead (Jean de La Ceppède); an allegorical description of the Christian life (Margaret of Navarre); or an emblematic poem, in which caption, brief verse, and prose commentary join to represent one aspect of religious experience or understanding (as in Georgette de Montenay or contemporary Jesuit emblems as those by Dominic Bouhours and Pierre Le Moyne).

Neo-Latin poetry marks the transition between the discovery and translation of ancient models and the emergence of an individual and original poetic voice during the French Renaissance. The Neo-Latin poets predominantly translated, but also imitated, Greek and Latin poets. A highly erudite circle primarily active in Lyon, these poets often composed collaboratively, wrote in Latin, French, and Italian, and practiced especially the genres of the pastoral, epistle, eclogue, and epigram.

Poets such as Jean Lemaire de Belges (c. 1475–c. 1525), Jean Marot (c. 1463–c. 1526; father of Clément Marot), and Jean Molinet (c. 1435–c. 1507) are called the Rhétoriqueurs. Their poetry is elegant, witty, elaborately adorned, and sometimes didactic, transposing into French the principles of Latin versification and rhetoric. The poets were more concerned that their work be melodious, pleasingly arranged, and brilliantly written than deep thematic explorations or meditations. Although the Rhétoriqueurs were playful innovators who sparked enthusiasm for French poetry, they did not rely on any underlying theory in writing their verse in any consistent, thorough, or systematic way. Thus, as it moved beyond the Rhétoriquer poetry of the fifteenth century, sixteenth-century poetry made a major contribution with the publication of several very influential *arts poétiques* (brief manifestos wherein poets explain what they have intended to convey with their literary creations).

Theoretical Tracts. These scholars were conscious of the need to develop a poetic language and vocabulary that could create a national poetic literature. The *arts poétiques* address the issues of the nature of poetry and its inspiration; the enrichment of the French language; the development of a noble poetic style (*style élevé*); and the proper use of different poetic genres.

Jacques Peletier du Mans composed *L'art poétique* in 1555. He is considered one of the promoters of the poetic revolution of 1549. Peletier devised his own phonetic spelling in an attempt to standardize French orthography of the day. In 1561, Julius Caesar Scaliger (1484–1558), part of an important literary circle in Lyon of which Peletier had also been a member, published another extremely influential text entitled *Poetices*. This work was well known to members of the Pléiade and exercised, at least, an indirect influence on them. *Poetices,* the first French poetical treatise to appeal to the authority of Aristotle, attempted to systematize poetry by dealing with the origin and cultivation of language; the matter and technique of poetry; genres; and basic rhetorical principles of style. Scaliger, unlike du Bellay, was a philosophical philologist rather than a practicing poet and so was able to craft an explicitly theoretical language that codified poetry's aspects, forms, and functions.

Other theorists include Michel de Boteau and his *L'art de métriffier françois* (1497); Jean de La Taille's *La manière de faire des vers en français* (1573) and *Art de la tragédie* (1572); and Jean-Antoine de Baïf. In broad terms, the literary scholars of the century were concerned with creating standards for the description and further crafting of poetic forms.

Clément Marot (c. 1497–1544), member of the evangelical circle of Margaret of Navarre, inherited and retained much from his Rhétoriqueur father. However, in his work he intensified the philosophical qualities and added an element of psychological penetration; he also wrote poetry that reflected the events of his time, such as the *Epitre à son amy Lyon, pour avoir mangé le lard* (1526). He was stylistically innovative; with his friend Peletier du Mans he introduced into France two different arrangements for the rhyming scheme of the Petrarchan sonnet, which were widely practiced in France by the end of the sixteenth century. Much influenced by the writings of Martin Luther, Marot was protected by Renée, the duchess of Ferrara, and stayed for a time in Calvin's Geneva, where he extended his translation of the Psalms.

Ronsard, the Pléiade, and After. The next poet to influence French Renaissance poetry decisively was Pierre de Ronsard (1524–1585), who developed his theory of literary creation from his own career. He believed in divine inspiration; the poet *vates* (prophet) would enter a frenzied state, during which he would receive inspiration for his verses from the gods. Ronsard did not deny the need for hard work, as poetry is the craft not only of a seer, but also of an artisan. His *La lyre* (1539) provides an early self-portrait of the poet as prophet, asserting the moral value of Neoplatonic aesthetics and espousing the Horatian dictum of *ut pictura poesis* (poetry should be like a picture), in which art is enjoined to represent nature.

So admired was Ronsard that a circle of poets and friends, most of whom were fellow students under the noted Hellenist Jean Dorat (1508–1588), joined him, imitating and enhancing his poetic theories and efforts. Stars clustering around the brightest star in the constellation, they termed themselves the Pléiade. Among them were du Bellay, Pontus du Tyard, Jean-Antoine de Baïf, Peletier, Rémy Belleau, and Étienne Jodelle. The Pléiade poets followed Ronsard's example in preaching the indissoluble union of form and content, rather than continuing the artificial conceits and clever wordplay that made Rhétoriqueur poetry so self-conscious.

Ronsard practiced almost every poetic genre then known, among them the Horatian or Anacreonic *odelette* (minor ode); Pindar's great ode; the hymn or philosophical poem of Neo-Latin origin; the *élégie* or *épître;* Petrarchan sonnet; and Juvenalian satire. He attempted to write the first French epic, but was not able to sustain the desired heroic verve of *La Franciade* (The hymn of France; 1572); renewed contact with the *gaulois* vein of bawdy inspiration dear to some of the Rhétoriqueurs in his *Livret de folastries* (1553); and armed himself with pen to defend Catholicism against the Calvinist heresy in the *Discours des misères de ce temps* (1562). His love poetry, particularly the *Sonnets pour Cassandre*

(1552), *Marie* (1555), and *Hélène* (1578; in two books), is rich and varied, evoking, respectively, the haughtiness of Cassandre Salviati, a banker's daughter, the naive, bucolic landscape of a pretty Angevin peasant, Marie, and the courtly sophistication of Hélène de Surgères. Together they comprise a lyrical autobiography and love story.

The last quarter of the sixteenth century might be dubbed the post-Pléiade period. Poets such as Amadis Jamyn (1540–1593); Guy du Faur de Pibrac (1529–1584); the tragedian Robert Garnier (1545–1590); and Jean Passerat (1534–1602) penned verses. Vauquelin de la Fresnaye (c. 1536–1606)—author of *Epîtres,* two volumes of *Idillies, Diverses poésies,* five books of *Satires,* and an *Art poétique*—was a leader in the field. He witnessed the beginning of the transition from the ideal of Ronsard to the stern, sober classicism of Boileau in the late seventeenth century. At court, Philippe Desportes (1546–1606), a mannerist poet, enjoyed official favor from 1571 on due to his *Stances, Meslanges, Premières oeuvres, Dernières amours,* and *Elégies*. He was known chiefly for his renewal of Petrarchan forms and his reworking of some of Ronsard's poetic conventions, especially in his Epicurean love poetry. However, his chief rival, François de Malherbe (1555–1628), was quickly recognized for his lyrical skill, elegance, and ease of composition, if not his brilliance or overwhelming creativity. His *Premières oeuvres* appeared in 1573. Malherbe was extremely critical of Desportes, and his work reflects these criticisms. His own systematized poetics inaugurated a very technical definition and execution of French poetry. In his work he rejected Ronsard's style—reliance on divine inspiration—in favor of a disciplined, highly rationalized approach to the writing of verse, one that mirrored the political tenor of Bourbon kingship. Malherbe consistently moved the poetry of the century away from baroque stylistics toward classicism—simple, carefully crafted verses stressing a common stock of fairly predictable themes.

Several generations of poets and theorists of poetry—ranging from the late medieval Rhétoriqueurs through the Pléaide school and culminating with Malherbe's proto-classical poetic style—helped accomplish the goals that Joachim du Bellay had early elucidated in the *Deffense et illustration de la langue françoyse:* the consolidation of the French language; versification in French that rivaled the work of classical poets; and the development of a new, young, French literature. Pan-European influences permeated and helped form French poetry, yet artists such as Ronsard and Desportes infused their models and inherited forms with a peculiarly French accent and flavor.

See also **French Literature and Language; Pléiade; Rhétoriqueurs;** *and biographies of figures mentioned in this entry.*

BIBLIOGRAPHY

Primary Works

Ceppède, Jean de la. *Les théorèmes sur le sacré mystère de notre rédemption.* Toulouse, France, 1613. Reprint, Geneva, 1966.

Chassignet, Jean. *Le mespris de la vie et consolation contre la mort.* Edited by Hans Lope. Geneva, 1967.

Desportes, Philippe. *Oeuvres.* Edited by Alfred Michiels. Paris, 1858.

Peletier, Jacques du Mans. *L'art poétique.* Lyon, 1555. Reprint, edited by A. Boulanger. Paris, 1930.

Secondary Works

Cave, Terence. *Devotional Poetry in France, c. 1570–1613.* London, 1968.

Cave, Terence, ed. *Ronsard the Poet.* London, 1973.

Chamard, Henri. *Histoire de la Pléiade.* Paris, 1961.

Chatelain, Henri. *Recherches sur le vers français au XVe siècle.* 1908. Reprint, Geneva, 1974.

Jeanneret, Michel. *Poésie et tradition biblique au XVIe siècle.* Paris, 1969.

McClelland, John. *L'humanisme français au début de la Renaissance.* Paris, 1973.

Martin, John R. *Baroque.* New York, 1977.

Rubin, David. *The Knot of Artifice: A Poetic of the French Lyric in the Early Seventeenth Century.* Columbus, Ohio, 1981.

Russell, Daniel. *The Emblem and the Device in Renaissance France.* Lexington, Ky., 1986.

Zumthor, Paul. *Le masque et la lumière: La poétique des grands rhétoriqueurs.* Paris, 1978.

CATHERINE RANDALL

POETRY. [This entry includes four subentries:

Classical Poetry
Religious Poetry
The Sonnet outside England
The English Sonnet

For discussion of English poetry, see the following entry, Poetry, English. For discussion of poetic miscellanies, see Poetry, English, subentry on Early Tudor Poetry.]

Classical Poetry

Beginning with the earliest moments of cultural renewal and continuing through to the seventeenth century, Greek and Latin poetry played a central role in the Renaissance. The intellectual foundation of Renaissance life, humanism, honored poetry as one of the five key disciplines in its educational program, and during this time poetry meant first and foremost the poetry of classical antiquity, the period whose rebirth the cultural avant-garde was advocating.

The Reception of the Classical Poets. Access to and appreciation of the Greek and Latin poets increased enormously in the Renaissance. Latin had remained the language of learning throughout the Middle Ages, but the vocabulary and syntax of medieval Latin differed from Roman practice, and the reliance of medieval verse on stress accents rather than the quantitative system used in antiquity also impeded the appreciation of Roman poetry for hundreds of years. Humanist scholarship sought to recover the ability to encounter Roman poetry on its own terms, and this ability quickly trickled down from the great scholars like Petrarch (1304–1374) and Erasmus (c. 1466–1536) to the isolated schoolmasters toiling in lonely obscurity throughout Europe.

Few people in the West could read Greek during the Middle Ages, but Petrarch understood that the cultural renewal he wanted demanded access to Greek literature as well as Latin. He never learned more than the basics of Greek, but those who came after him did, so that early in the fifteenth century one could learn enough Greek in Florence to read the poets of antiquity in the original. Instruction in Greek spread throughout Europe, and while real facility in the language never became widespread, the effective recovery of Greek literature remains one of the great achievements of Renaissance humanism.

Knowledge of the Classical Poets. It is surprisingly difficult, however, to assess the precise impact of Greek and Roman poetry on Renaissance culture. On the one hand, there is no question that many people had an intimate knowledge of a great deal of classical literature during the Renaissance. The humanist curriculum that rested decisively on classical poetry slowly came to dominate the schools, and then many of the university faculties as well. And while the effect of the printing press on book prices has been overstated by a number of modern scholars, there also is no question that printing lowered the cost of books and allowed new groups of people to own their own texts of the Greek and Roman poets.

However, while printed copies of most of the Greek and Roman poets were available by the middle of the sixteenth century, this does not mean that all these texts had equal impact on Renaissance culture. For one thing, work in the schools rested primarily on Latin writers. *De liberorum educatione* (On the education of children; c. 1445) by Enea Silvio Piccolomini and Battista Guarini's *De ordine docendi et discendi* (On the order of teaching and learning; 1459) recommend Virgil, Lucan, Statius, Ovid, Claudian, Horace, Juvenal (with reservations), Plautus, Terence, and Seneca. This is a good-size list, but records indicate that most teachers actually covered much less. Paul Grendler's survey of what Venetian teachers taught in 1587–1588, for example, found that Virgil, Terence, and Horace were being taught with some regularity, Ovid on occasion, and Plautus once. It is therefore likely that a graduate of a typical humanist school had more than a passing acquaintance with only a few Latin authors.

What is more, the humanist schools primarily served the elite. Vernacular schools were not focused on ancient literature, and the vast majority of people in the Renaissance would have received little direct exposure to the classics. It is worth remembering, however, that there were many avenues linking high and low culture during this period—Sebastian Brant's famous edition of Virgil, for example, had woodcut illustrations so that the illiterate could also follow the story. Thus a popular dramatist like Shakespeare could parody Ovid's Pyramus and Thisbe story in *A Midsummer Night's Dream* (1595–1596) and be reasonably confident that his audience would get at least the main point.

Interpretation and Imitation of the Classical Poets. Another problem revolves around how Greek and Latin literature was interpreted in the Renaissance. The best evidence for how readers of this period approached classical poetry lies in the margins of the books they bought, studied, and annotated. This evidence suggests that sometimes they read a book straight through, much as we do, but two other possibilities were at least as common: skipping around from one isolated episode to another, and mining the text as a source for easily memorized proverbs and ready-made expressions. This last option in particular is the result of how classical literature was taught in the humanist schools of the day. The schoolmaster generally directed his students to keep two commonplace books, one to record lines that illustrated moral virtues, common sentiments, and social practices, the other to record models of felicitous expression organized according to the figures of speech and so forth. That is, Renaissance readers learned in school that the classical poets could teach them to write Latin well and to edify themselves morally, and their books show that they carried what they learned into adult life as well.

These commonplace books in turn served their owners as sources for their own literary composition. Much Renaissance poetry was still written in Latin, so that works ranging from Petrarch's epic, the *Africa,* to Cristoforo Landino's collection of love poems, *Xandra,* can only be appreciated by those readers who are able to hear the echoes of classical verse they contain and to recognize the scenes their authors rewrote from Greek and Latin poetry. The same is true of Renaissance vernacular literature. In pastoral, for example, Theocritus and Virgil serve as the models for Clément Marot and Edmund Spenser. Ancient lyric poetry effectively enters French literature with the Pléiade poets, and Horace runs from Thomas Wyatt and Ben Jonson through Andrew Marvell and Abraham Cowley. Shakespeare drew from Plautus, Terence, and Seneca, and French theater would be unimaginable without Greek drama. Ludovico Ariosto and Torquato Tasso in turn produced very different kinds of poems from the same source, Virgil's *Aeneid,* a phenomenon repeated in English with Spenser and John Milton.

Early Renaissance art continued to be dominated by religious themes, but paintings such as Botticelli's *Pallas and the Centaur* and *Primavera* demand to be interpreted in relation to the classical poetry which both painter and patron knew. The same is true of sculpture ranging from Michelangelo's *Bacchus* to Gian Lorenzo Bernini's *Aeneas, Anchises, and Ascanius.* Sometimes the connections to classical poetry are obvious, as in Raphael's *Parnassus;* at other times they are not, as in the pictorial reference to book 2 of the *Aeneid* at the corner of the same artist's *Fire in the Borgo.* But these connections were an inextricable part of Renaissance culture, so that even Claudio Monteverdi's early opera *Orfeo* (1607) sends us back to Ovid's *Metamorphoses.*

See also **Classical Scholarship; Education; Horace; Humanism; Ovid; Printing and Publishing; Terence; Virgil.**

BIBLIOGRAPHY

Bolgar, R. R. *The Classical Heritage and Its Beneficiaries.* Cambridge, U.K., 1954. The classic study of how classical authors were studied and transmitted through the ages.

Gaisser, Julia Haig. *Catullus and His Renaissance Readers.* Oxford, 1993. An excellent case study of how one classical poet influenced the literary culture of the Renaissance.

Greene, Thomas M. *The Light in Troy: Imitation and Discovery in Renaissance Poetry.* New Haven, Conn., 1982. The definitive treatment of how Renaissance poets imitated their classical models.

Grendler, Paul F. *Schooling in Renaissance Italy: Literacy and Learning, 1300–1600.* Baltimore and London, 1989.

Highet, Gilbert. *The Classical Tradition: Greek and Roman Influences on Western Literature.* Oxford, 1949. Not restricted to the Renaissance, but still the best beginning place for specific information on which early modern authors drew from which classical ones.

CRAIG KALLENDORF

Religious Poetry

Miles Coverdale's *Ghoostly Psalms and Spirituall Songes* (c. 1538), based on Martin Luther's 1524 hymnbook, marks the beginning of Protestant sacred poetry in England. Like much Tudor religious verse, this was popular poetry, intended, as its preface claims, for women "spynnynge at the wheles" and for "carters & plow men . . . to whistle upon." The early Reformers generally shared Coverdale's desire to make scripture accessible to low and high alike. The antagonism between popular and Protestant culture did not emerge until the 1570s, as attested by the mid-century outpouring of metrical psalms and godly ballads, often set to the latest dance tunes. The title page of John Daye's 1562 *The Whole Booke of Psalmes* (a revision of the psalter originally made by Thomas Sternhold before 1549 and expanded by John Hopkins in 1557) describes it as "mete to be used of all sortes of people"—and so it was, running to over two hundred editions by 1640 and sung in parish churches throughout England for over a century. Yet for all its "rude & homely maner of vulgar Poesie," this was, in inception, a courtly project; Sternhold wrote his metrical psalms for his fellow courtiers and at royal command.

The sacred poetry of the English Renaissance (as opposed to the English Reformation) begins with Thomas Wyatt's *Certayne Psalmes,* posthumously published in 1549. Wyatt replaced Sternhold's ballad meters with the new verse forms of the continental Renaissance, notably the sonnet. Through the next century, biblical translation remained a major type of sacred poetry. Henry Surrey, Philip Sidney, the countess of Pembroke (Mary Herbert), George Herbert, Francis Bacon, Thomas Carew, John Denham, and John Milton all tried their hands at verse translations of the Psalms, as did King James I and Archbishop Matthew Parker (the latter's 1567 *Whole Psalter* printed with music by Thomas Tallis). These often free, personalized, and metrically experimental adaptations of passionate interior and personal piety of the Hebrew provide a crucial context for the flowering of the devotional lyric in the seventeenth century.

Other parts of scripture were also translated into verse not to mention two attempts at versifying the entire Bible. The French poet Guillaume Du Bartas's 1574 *La Judit* (translated into English, at James VI's request, by Thomas Hudson as *The Historie of Judith;* 1584) inspired a series of biblical epics from Michael Drayton's 1604 *Moses* to Abraham Cowley's unfinished history of David, *Davideis* (1656). Du Bartas's hexameral epic, *La sepmaine* (1578)—*Bartas His Devine Weekes & Workes* in Sylvester's translation (1608)—had even greater impact. Both Milton and the seventeenth-century poets termed the "metaphysicals," C. S. Lewis notes, "sound as if they had been brought up on him." A similar fusion of scriptural narrative and secular form produced the sacred complaint, in which biblical sinners poured forth their tales of guilt and pain in language reminiscent of the ghosts who rehearse their sad histories in *Mirror for Magistrates* (1559) and the abandoned women of Ovid's *Heroides.* In this category fall Anthony Munday's *The Mirrour of Mutability* (1579), Nicholas Breton's *The Blessed Weeper* (1601), and the Jesuit Robert Southwell's *Saint Peter's Complaint* (1595; fifteen editions before 1620), whose striking conceits and focus on inner conflict anticipate the devotional lyrics of the next century.

Christian allegory and the Italian romantic epic come together in the sacred poetry of the first and (unfinished) final books (1590, 1609) of Edmund Spenser's *The Faerie Queene.* Those who followed Spenser in the seventeenth century, drawing on these, are primarily religious poets: Giles Fletcher, author of *Christ's Victorie and Triumph in Heaven and Earth* (1610); his brother, Phineas, whose *The Locusts* (1627), an attack on the Jesuits, treats the Gunpowder Plot; and the Civil War poets—Henry More (*Psychozoia;* 1642, 1647), Joseph Beaumont (*Psyche, or Love's Mystery;* 1648), and Edward Belowes (*Theophilia;* 1652)—who transform the romantic epic into vast allegories of interior and personal spiritual warfare and mystic ascent that hark back both to Spenser's epic and his *Fowre Hymnes* (1596). This latter work belongs among the handful of Renaissance sacred verse-treatises, along with Sir John Davies's *Nosce Teipsum* (1599), Fulke Greville's *Of Religion* (written sometime between 1610 and Greville's death in 1628; excised from the 1633 edition of Greville's *Works;* published 1670), and John Davies of Hereford's *Mirum in Modum* (1602), *Microcosmos* (1603), and *Summa Totalis* (1607).

The publication of Sidney's *Astrophil and Stella* in 1591 inspired not only numerous Petrarchan sonnet sequences but several attempts to fashion a devotional counterpart, including Henry Lok's *Sundry Christian Passions* (1593), Barnabe Barnes's *A Divine Centurie of Spirituall Sonnets* (1595), Henry Constable's *Spirituall Sonnettes to the Honour of God and His Sayntes* (written c. 1593), William Alabaster's moving prison sonnets (written 1597), and the religious lyrics of Fulke Greville's *Caelica,* which begins as an unusually edgy Petrarchan sequence but whose final sonnets turn from ladies' love to dark grapplings with penitence and politics.

Caelica, although probably begun a half-century earlier, appeared posthumously in 1633—as did the two greatest collections of Renaissance devotional poetry: Donne's *Poems* and Herbert's *The Temple.* Both include various "kinds" of sacred poetry (and Donne's *Poems* includes his secular verse), but the majority are deeply personal lyrics of spiritual inwardness, registering the movements and motives of the soul in language simultaneously capable of introspective precision and passionate expressiveness.

The other major type of Renaissance sacred poetry—often referred to as "baroque"—treats salvation history and the mysteries of faith rather than the spirit's inner weather. Richard Crashaw (c. 1612–1649) is the most consistently "baroque" of English poets, but Amelia Lanyer's *Salve Deus Rex Judaeorum* (1611), Herbert's "The Sacrifice," Milton's "On the Morning of Christ's Nativity" (1629), and Francis Quarles's once immensely popular *Divine Fancies* (1632) and *Emblems* (1635) belong here as well. These works treat much the same themes as late medieval religious verse (that is, the Nativity and Passion). However, they complicate its simple emotional piety either by theological elaboration—the vast historical sweep of Milton's ode; Lanyer's intertwining of the Passion narrative with feminist apologetics; Quarles's lyrics on ritual nonconformity, iconoclasm, and future contingents—or by emotional heightening of the sort that infuses Crashaw's and (at moments) Lanyer's poems with their extravagant sanguinary pathos and flights of voluptuous rapture, as in Crashaw's description of martyrs' wounds as "Fair, purple Doores, of love's devising" ("To the Name above Every Name") or Lanyer's of Saint Lawrence "Yielding his naked body to the fire, / To taste this sweetness, such was his desire" (*Salve Deus Rex Judaeorum*).

Robert Herrick's *Noble Numbers* (1648) and Henry Vaughan's *Silex Scintillans* (1650, 1655)—the former a sacred transposing of the Jonsonian plain style, the latter deeply influenced by Herbert's *Temple*—mark the end of the period. The disestablishment of the English Church divides the sacred poets of the earlier seventeenth century from Herrick and Vaughan. Both royalists, they forged a poetry of defeat (as Milton was to do in the aftermath of a subsequent defeat)—of paradise within, divinized nature, and the lost innocence of Eden, infancy, and England.

BIBLIOGRAPHY

Bush, Douglas. *English Literature in the Earlier Seventeenth Century, 1600–1660.* New York, 1945.

Campbell, Lily B. *Divine Poetry and Drama in Sixteenth-Century England.* Cambridge, U.K., 1959.

Guiney, Louise Imogen, ed. *Recusant Poets.* New York, 1939.

Lewalski, Barbara Kiefer. *Protestant Poetics and the Seventeenth-Century Religious Lyric.* Princeton, N.J., 1979.

Smith, Nigel. *Literature and Revolution in England, 1640–1660.* New Haven, Conn., 1994.

Summers, Claude J. "Herrick, Vaughan, and the Poetry of Anglican Survivalism." In *New Perspectives on the Seventeenth-Century English Religious Lyric.* Edited by John R. Roberts. Columbia, Mo., 1994. Pages 46–74.

Watt, Tessa. *Cheap Print and Popular Piety, 1550–1640.* Cambridge, U.K., 1991.

DEBORA K. SHUGER

The Sonnet outside England

The sonnet was invented by Giacomo da Lentino, a notary at the court of the Holy Roman Emperor Frederick II, in the first half of the thirteenth century. It was probably derived from the Sicilian peasant song, the *canzuna*, eight lines of hendecasyllables, rhyming *abababab,* or the more literary *strambotto,* which consisted of six or eight hendecasyllable lines, rhyming variously *ababab[ab], ababcc[dd], aabbcc[dd],* or *abababcc*. To this eight-line form Giacomo added a six-line sestet to create what we now call a sonnet. His fifteen sonnets follow the form *abababab,* with a sestet rhyming *cdcdcd* or *cdecde.* The form was imitated by way of poetic debate in one sonnet by Jacopo Mostacci (d. after 1277), one sonnet by Pier della Vigna (c. 1190–1249), and two by the abbot of Tivoli. These nineteen sonnets constitute the beginning of the tradition of writing sonnets.

The Sonnet Sequence. Whatever the sonnet's peasant or courtly origins may have been, its future as a literary form was assured when Dante (1265–1321) chose the sonnet as the poetic form to depict his new life, *La vita nuova,* composed between 1292 and 1300. Dante's story of his love for Beatrice permanently set the role of this new form as an instrument for a poet to declare his unrequited devotion to that unyielding blonde and blue-eyed pillar of virtue. His combination of prose narrative and sonnet in *La vita nuova,* almost certainly derived from the *De consolatione philosophiae* of Boethius, also initiated the genre of the sonnet sequence.

At least it must have seemed so to Dante's younger Florentine exile, Petrarch (1304–1374), who realized that Dante had won the epic palm in writing *La divina commedia* in the vernacular. Petrarch withdrew from that poetic fray to write his own never-to-be-completed epic, *Africa*, in Latin, but he saw that he might surpass Dante in writing sonnets in the vernacular. He set out to compose his *Canzoniere,* or *Rime sparse,* as a collection of 366 sonnets and other poetic forms to celebrate his unrequited love for Laura, who soon was to become as famous as Beatrice. She too was to succumb to that early death of the unyielding lady so common to sonnet literature in Italian. With Beatrice and Laura in place, the floodgates opened in Italy, and the whole peninsula was deluged with grieving sonneteers who had lost their unyielding ladies. That we can identify so few of these ladies historically strongly suggests a literary topos rather than a real-life encounter between poet and lady. The search for Beatrice or Laura or Shakespeare's Dark Lady has not proven successful. Any shred of biographical fact turns almost at once to mythical use of a topos powerful in Western literature since Dante and Petrarch: sexual infatuation, no matter how cleverly the sonneteer writes poetry, does not end successfully, especially when the lady is most often already married to someone else. The poet is really demonstrating that human desire obscures the object of his protagonist's search. In all the sonnet sequences we learn more about the fatuity of that search than we do about the lady, who is seldom given a chance to speak. Sonnet sequences become the means for a poet to show how cleverly he can write about sexual infatuation in order to make the moral point: What fools these mortals be! The persona of the sonnet sequences revels in his agony, reviles the tyranny of the lady, contradicts himself with abandon, and whips his wit to hyperbolic frenzy, but he also uses the sonnet to chastise the vanities of the world beyond his obsessive love—the court and church for their avarice and hypocrisy (*Canzoniere* 53 and 137–139)—and thus extends the sonnet form as a mode of invective and satire.

The Petrarchan Tradition. To trace the development of the sonnet in the Renaissance is to follow the Petrarchan tradition of the fourteenth and fifteenth centuries. Petrarch's *Canzoniere* was first printed in 1470, and by 1600 there were more than 170 editions. In the same period there were fifty-two editions of *La divina commedia.* The imitation began even during Petrarch's life, when his friend Giovanni Boccaccio made use of two of his sonnets in *Filostrato* (c. 1340). Also in the fourteenth century Geoffrey Chaucer closely imitated *Canzoniere* 130: "S'amor non è" in his *Troilus and Criseyde,* 1.400–420, the so-called Cantus Troili. Chaucer may have met Petrarch since they were both in attendance at the marriage of Edward III's son Prince Lionel to Violante Visconti, daughter of the duke of Milan, in 1368, but Chaucer certainly knew at least that one sonnet, even though he imitated the sonnet in the rhyme royal stanza of his poem, and therefore must be credited with being the first Petrarchist in English.

Ernest Hatch Wilkins defines the development of Petrarchism in Italy under several headings, the most important of which for us are "Il Cariteo" (1450–1514) and Pietro Bembo (1470–1547). Il Cariteo was born in Barcelona and came to the Aragonese court in Naples in 1467/68, establishing himself as the leading poet of a group developing Petrarchan sonnet literature. This group included Serafino Aquilano (1466–1500), a gifted musician who set many of Petrarch's sonnets to music and disseminated this art to most of the city courts of Italy at the time, and Antonio Tebaldeo (1463–1537), whose *Rime* (eleven pirated editions from 1499; authorized version 1534) was written to a young Sienese, Flavia, to rival Petrarch's Laura and Catullus's Lesbia. Il Cariteo's *Endimione* (1506), a sonnet sequence to a supposed woman named Luna, takes up the myth of Apollo's pursuit of Daphne, celebrated by Petrarch, and translates it into the even more unlikely myth of Diana and Endymion, including political and ecclesiastical invectives along the way. This school, if such it may be called, is the first major thrust putting the Petrarchan impulse into motion.

This southern impulse was severely criticized by Pietro Bembo, the Venetian patrician whose *Prose della volgar lingua* (Writings on the vernacular language; 1525) was to settle the problem of the Italian language in favor of the Tuscan dialect written by Petrarch and Boccaccio and to criticize the Cariteans for their excessive development of Petrarchan rhetorical devices. His *Rime* (1530, 1535, 1548) set the standard for Petrarchan imitation in the sonnet. In 1545 the Venetian publisher Gabriele Giolito de' Ferrari brought out *Rime diverse,* a collection of almost one hundred imitators of Petrarch in the Bembist mode, and this volume sold wildly to foreign travelers and made the Petrarchan sonnet the true Italian sonnet. From this point on the Petrarchan model of the sonnet was to sweep literary Europe for the rest of the sixteenth century.

Naples was not to be put off by Tuscan purism, and in 1552 Giolito published another anthology, *Rime di diversi illustri napoletani,* which included the work of Luigi Tansillo (1510–1568), in many ways the most brilliant of the sixteenth-century *petrarchisti.* A spate of sonnet literature spread across Europe in the second half of the sixteenth century, part of which was the innumerable editions of Petrarch's poems, part of which was the Petrarchan imitations of the Cariteans, the Bembists, and the later Neapolitans. At this time it is very hard to distinguish what is attributable to any of these possible sources, but the impulse to carry over into another language what has come to be known as Petrarchism, or Petrarchanism, was a tidal wave that covered the lyric poetry of most European countries.

The name of Petrarch became an adjective to denote sonnet literature that talked about a love for a reluctant lady who either died or refused to yield and the resulting despair of the poet-lover. The adjective "Petrarchan" has become so debased as a critical term that it means hardly more than a poetry that we no longer read. But this was not the case for all those countries that wanted to bring sonnet literature into their own languages, to incorporate the Italian achievement into their own emerging vernacular literature.

The sonnet arrived in France, Spain, and Portugal in the first half of the sixteenth century. In Spain it was the work of Juan Boscán (c. 1490–1542) and Garcilaso de la Vega (1503–1536). In France it was the work of Clément Marot (c. 1496–1544), Mellin de Saint-Gelais (1491–1558), and Maurice Scève (c. 1500–1560) and later the Pléiade group, most notably Pontus de Tyard (1521–1605), Joachim du Bellay (c. 1522–1560), Jean-Antoine du Baïf (1532–1589), and finally Pierre de Ronsard (1524–1585). In Portugal it was Sá de Miranda (1481?–1558). In England it was the work of Sir Thomas Wyatt (1503–1542) and Henry Howard, earl of Surrey (1517?–1547), as published in *Tottel's Miscellany* (1557). After these beginnings it was open season for the sonnet.

One interesting example of the productivity of the sonnet must suffice. Petrarch's *Canzoniere* 323, "Standomi un giorno solo à la fenestra," is a series of six visions that come to the lover: a beast with a human face, a ship, a laurel tree, a fountain, a phoenix, and a beautiful lady. The poem is an allegorical reassessment of his love for Laura and a parallel to his six *Trionfi:* the triumph of love, the triumph of chastity, the triumph of death, the triumph of fame, the triumph of time, and finally the triumph of eternity. It is also a reassessment of *Canzoniere* 23, the first of the sequence of canzoni, which leads the poet through a number of metamorphic changes derived from Ovid. This poem was translated into French by Clément Marot as *Le chant des visions de Petrarque* (1533), and later by Joachim du Bellay as *Songe ou vision* (1558). Marot's work is an effort to translate Petrarch's poem within the context of Petrarch's myth of his lost Laura. Du Bellay's translation, however, since it was appended to his *Les antiquitez de Rome,* a complaint about the vanities of this world, seems to globalize the significance of the lamented loss beyond the specifics of Petrarch's loss of Laura. Or so it seemed to an otherwise little-known Dutchman, Jan van der Noot, who used most of du Bellay's translation of *Canzoniere* 323 to illustrate his Calvinist polemic against the tyranny of the Roman Catholic Church in his *Het theatre oft toon-neel* (A theatre for voluptuous worldings; 1566). This Dutch edition, since van der Noot was living in London as an exile, was printed by Henry Bynneman and dedicated to Roger Martens, lord mayor of London. In the same year another English printer, John Day, brought out a French edition, dedicated to Queen Elizabeth, with the Petrarch poem in the French translation of Marot as well as the translation of du Bellay. In 1569 Bynneman brought out an English edition, using the same copperplate engravings as the Dutch and French editions, which makes the *Theatre* the first emblem book in English. The *Theatre* also marks the first appearance in print of the teenage Edmund Spenser, who contributed the English translations of the Marot and du Bellay poems (reprinted as regular sonnets in his *Complaints* volume of 1591). A German edition was published in 1572. Petrarch had become international and, even more important, his poetic myth of his love for Laura had become a vehicle for religious and political polemics—an aspect of his influence that has not been adequately studied.

See also **Bembo, Pietro; Petrarch; Petrarchism.**

BIBLIOGRAPHY

Bellenger, Yvonne, ed. *Le sonnet à la Renaissance*. Paris, 1988.
Davis, C. Roger. "Petrarch's *Rime* 323 and Its Tradition through Spenser." Ph.D. diss., Princeton University, 1973.
Greene, Roland. *Post-Petrarchism: Origins and Innovations of the Western Lyric Sequence*. Princeton, N.J., 1991.
John, Lisle Cecil. *The Elizabethan Sonnet Sequence*. New York, 1938.
Lever, J. W. *The Elizabethan Love Sonnet*. London, 1956.
Parker, Tom W. N. *Proportional Form in the Sonnets of the Sidney Circle*. Oxford, 1998.
Prescott, Anne Lake. *French Poets and the English Renaissance*. New Haven, Conn., 1978.
Roche, Thomas P., Jr. *Petrarch and the English Sonnet Sequences*. New York, 1989.
Scott, Janet. *Les sonnets elizabethains*. Paris, 1929.
Smith, Hallett. *Elizabethan Poetry*. Cambridge, Mass., 1952.
Vaganay, Hugues. *Le sonnet en Italie and en France au XVIe siècle*. Lyon, France, 1902–1903.
Wilkins, Ernest Hatch. *The Invention of the Sonnet and Other Studies in Italian Literature*. Rome, 1959.

THOMAS P. ROCHE JR.

The English Sonnet

The sonnet came into the English language and the French language about the same time, the second decade of the sixteenth century, and remained in favor with poets until the death of John Milton (1674), the last major poet to use the sonnet form until William Wordsworth. Although it is not quite true that the Augustan age produced no sonnets, the English sonnet and the sonnet sequence belong distinctively to the periods of the Renaissance and romanticism.

It is convenient to think of the British sonnet, singly or in sequences, as having passed through three phases during the Renaissance: a developmental phase from about 1527 to 1580, in which writers experimented with the form but were not always clear about what it was or what others were doing; a vogue phase from 1580 to about 1610, when there was a craze for sonnet writing, particularly of sequences, by writers associated with the royal capitals of London and Edinburgh; and an aftermath from 1610 to about 1674, in which some major writers (Drummond of Hawthornden, Milton) and some old-fashioned ones (Fulke Greville, Lady Mary Wroth) went their own way in what was by then an unfashionable genre.

The Developmental Phase. The sonnet gained enormous popularity in Italy between its invention about 1235 and the beginning of the sixteenth century. When the young Thomas (later Sir Thomas) Wyatt (1503–1542) went to France and Italy in 1526–1527, he probably met French and Italian sonnet writers, and he began writing sonnets on his return, although we have no precise dates for any of what he produced. Wyatt was the best English poet of his time, but his particular contribution to the sonnet was less to quality than to form: in introducing the sonnet to England, he retained in English the octave of the Italian sonnet (*abba abba*) but added a distinctive "English" sestet, *cddc ee* (or *cdcd ee*), thus giving the English sonnet its typical final couplet.

Wyatt's younger contemporary and friend at the court of Henry VIII of England, Henry Howard, earl of Surrey (1517?–1547), also wrote a number of sonnets. Like Wyatt he left no record of his aims or sources, but he made a further change to the Italian sonnet as Wyatt and he must have encountered it, altering the octave so that the rhymes change in the second quatrain: *abba cddc* (or *abab cdcd*). Though many later writers in English used the Italian or Petrarchan form, Wyatt's and Surrey's alterations gave British poets what has become known as the English or (because Shakespeare used it exclusively) Shakespearean sonnet. The invention of this form produced a fondness for concluding a sonnet with a "punch line" (or lines), which the final couplet invites.

Thanks to an enterprising publisher, the sonnets of Wyatt and Surrey, which were not published in the authors' lifetimes, became widely known and imitated in the following decades. Richard Tottel's *Songes and Sonettes* (1557), a poetic anthology now generally known as *Tottel's Miscellany,* went through ten editions in thirty years. It undoubtedly popularized the sonnet as a literary form and established Wyatt and Surrey as leading English poets. A young London merchant's wife, Anne Locke (1533?–1595?) got the idea of using Surrey's sonnet form to write the first sonnet sequence in English. Her *Meditation of a Penitent Sinner* (1560), which gives a religious sequence of twenty-six English sonnets, is a fluently written meditation upon Psalm 51. It precedes by more than twenty years Sir Philip Sidney's *Astrophel and Stella.* By 1569 the young Edmund Spenser was experimenting with sonnet translations from Italian and French, which speaks to the growing awareness in England that the courts of Italy, France, and Spain could already boast a fashionable national literature and that if English speakers wished to compete, they had to domesticate the sonnet themselves.

Renaissance princes used poetry for prestige just as they used art and architecture, and James VI of Scotland (later also James I of England; 1566–1625) patronized the sonnet by writing a sonnet sequence himself (in *Essayes of a Prentise in the Divine Art of Poesie,* 1584) and encouraged a number of poets to write sonnets, notably Alexander Montgomerie (c. 1550–1598).

The sonnet in England, with its much larger and more diffused patronage system, was not dependent on the direct encouragement of the sovereign. The great nobles of Elizabeth I (ruled 1558–1603) responded to current notions of fashion and prestige by favoring poets in or connected with their households. Thomas Watson, for instance, published England's first Petrarchan love sequence in 1582 and dedicated it to the earl of Oxford, Edward de Vere. No subsequent poet departed from or subverted the Petrarchan template, except for those who wrote religious sonnet sequences. Philosophical, moral, and satirical sonnets normally appear as individual poems or in very small groups.

The Sonnet Vogue. The most famous Petrarchan sonnet sequence, and by common critical consent one of the two or three greatest in English literature, is Sir Philip Sidney's *Astrophel and Stella,* written about 1582 but published only in 1591, five years after Sidney's death in 1586. When Sidney decided to write the story of his love for "Stella" (Penelope Devereux, later Lady Rich) in traditional unrequited Petrarchan fashion, he became posthumously responsible for a craze for sonnet sequences in England that lasted for nearly twenty years. The sequence craze also enhanced the popularity of the individual, unsequenced sonnet, which continued to be used for occasional poetry, and in particular for complimentary verses (as by Hugh Holland, for example, in Shakespeare's *First Folio* of 1623)

The most popular sonnet writers after Sidney were Samuel Daniel (*Delia,* 1592) and Michael Drayton (*Ideas Mirrour,* 1594). John Donne, whose religious sonnets (*La Corona,* written about 1607, and *Holy Sonnets,* written at various times up to 1620, both published in 1633) are now very famous, wrote no secular love sonnets. Daniel's gentle plangency was much indebted to the French sonneteers, particularly Philippe Desportes (*Les amours de Diane,* 1573), and he passed this elegiac mode and its techniques on to other writers. Drayton started off in the same way, like Shakespeare, but became tougher, more ironic, and self-mocking as the age of Elizabeth gave way to that of James I, who acceded to the English throne in 1603.

The poet who towered above his contemporaries in the sonnet's vogue years was Edmund Spenser (1552/53–1599), author of *The Faerie Queene* (1590–1596). Connoisseurs of the sonnet appreciate Spenser's very Italianate and mannered, but subtle and sophisticated sequence *Amoretti* (1595), written to his fiancée, Elizabeth Boyle. With Milton, Spenser is a "poet's poet," and his intricate version of the English sonnet, rhyming *abab bcbc cdcd ee* and known as the "Spenserian sonnet," attracted admiration but may have been too difficult for sustained imitation;

it was used, independently, by some of the Scots poets around King James VI.

William Shakespeare, whose verse shows that he thoroughly absorbed what his contemporaries in the 1590s were doing, also went his own way. He circulated love sonnets before 1598 but does not seem to have borrowed specifically from anyone (Daniel is closest) and apparently had no interest in developing its form. In his 154 sonnets, published in 1609, he used Surrey's well-established form, *abab cdcd efef gg,* almost always arranged in three quatrains and a couplet. The content was and has remained baffling, if compelling, in a way that has allowed each age to see its own desires reflected in his work. As in more conventional Petrarchan sequences, the sonnets set up a relationship without giving clues as to the actual context. Strangely, nothing in the sonnets suggests that the writer thought of them as a sequence, and subsequent scholarly attention has failed to turn up any fact that dates a single sonnet, or confirms or denies Shakespeare's involvement in their publication. The interest in the themes of transience, aging, and immortality that dominated romantic reading of the *Sonnets* has since about 1980 been supplemented by postmodernist ideas that have allowed critics to talk intelligibly about the way in which, seemingly intentionally, Shakespeare's peculiarly intense wordplay fragments call into question the components of traditional sonnet sequences: the Self, the Other whom the self desires, and the identities that the "love" between them constructs. Existential questions have been the material of sonnets and sonnet sequences since Dante's *Vita nuova* (c. 1292), but Shakespeare's intensity and obliquity is distinctive and fascinating, and is compounded by the fact that his sonnets fall into two parts. The first part (to sonnet 127) deals with either a dependent friendship or a homoerotic relationship with a younger man, and the second with a heterosexual and bitter attachment to an adulterous older woman. Shakespeare's sonnet form, however, remains traditional, and even his wordplay, as extraordinary in his sonnets as it is in his dramas, can be seen as extending late sixteenth-century rhetorical practice.

The Aftermath. The sonnet in Scotland and England was handled conservatively: no tailed sonnets, no hieroglyphic or acrostic sonnets, no curtailed or doubled sonnets, no sonnets on the sonnet, and very few corona sequences—all quite common in France and Italy. Its strict and predictable form gave it a secure place from which to attack the stability of meaning itself, with puns, antitheses, antanaclasis (repetition of a word in different senses), and ploce (iteration of a word). The writers of the vogue period, culminating chronologically at least in Shakespeare, took such attacks about as far as they could go. A loss of interest and a reaction was probably inevitable; few sonnet sequences were printed from 1600 to 1610, and these were mostly from the 1590s. The second and last woman sonnet-sequence writer of the British Renaissance, Lady Mary Wroth, published *Pamphilia to Amphilanthus* in 1621, very much in imitation of the sonnets of her uncle, Sir Philip Sidney.

The expressive capacity of the sonnet was in those years developed by poets who for various reasons were not concerned to publish for patronage or favor. William Drummond of Hawthornden, near Edinburgh in Scotland, published a Petrarchan sequence in *Poems* (1616) and twenty-six devotional sonnets in *Flowers of Zion* (1623); George Herbert wrote a small number of devotional sonnets, *The Temple,* not published until 1633; and John Donne wrote occasional sonnets to friends and two short devotional sequences (*Poems,* 1633).

Drummond, who favored the mixed Italian and English sonnet (*abba abba cdcd ee*), had both the means to acquire a fine private library of continental and British authors and the leisure to use it in his own poetry. Though formally and thematically conservative, he produced a Petrarchan sequence with an astonishingly international textuality, drawing on Italian, French, and Spanish sources in translation, paraphrase, and allusion. This kind of borrowing had been a feature of European Petrarchism for most of the sixteenth century: Drummond almost alone inserted the English sonnet into this literary community. Herbert and Donne, who were probably acquainted as young men, developed the eloquence of the sonnet by introducing enjambment (running the syntax across the line ends), hyperbaton (distortion of normal word order), and suspension of syntax, techniques much admired among the Italian Petrarchists.

Probably, but unprovably, the sonnet was saved for posterity (that is, for the romantic poets of the late eighteenth and early nineteenth centuries and their successors) by John Milton. His brilliant personal, political, and civic sonnets—ten printed in 1645, collected with another ten in his *Poems &c.* of 1673, with four posthumously from manuscript—opened up a new life for the sonnet and enabled later writers and critics to find apparently similar moral and philosophical sonnets in the works of Shakespeare and Spenser.

Milton wrote only what are called "occasional" sonnets, mostly to friends or to public figures, such as Oliver Cromwell, and nearly all of them adopt the persona of a Renaissance civic humanist, not a Petrarchan lover. He used the Italian form of the sonnet almost exclusively (only four of twenty-four have a couplet ending) and is one of the very few British Renaissance figures to have written sonnets in the Italian language. He experimented very little with the rhyme scheme, but he did develop the technique of enjambment as it was famously practiced in Italy by Giovanni della Casa (1503–1556), whose poems he owned.

Partly because of its shortness, and partly because it was usually about love, the sonnet was considered by sixteenth-century rhetoricians to be a light and "passionate" form of poetry, rather than a grave and wise form, like epic or the ode. The use of enjambment, however, with all that it implied for the use of complex sentences with embedded clauses and grammatical suspensions, was thought to confer weight, or *gravità*. Milton's *gravità* inspired the romantic poets, particularly Wordsworth. Moreover, with the return to favor of Petrarch and Dante at the end of the nineteenth century, the Miltonic sonnet became a favorite with both British and American poets; it was seen as uniting personal intensity with moral or civic humanism in a succinct and epigrammatic form.

See also biographies of figures mentioned in this entry.

BIBLIOGRAPHY

Primary Works

Du Bellay, Joachim. *La déffence et illustration de la langue françoyse* (A defense and celebration of the French tongue; Paris, 1549). The standard edition is edited by Henri Chamard (Paris, 1948), uniform with his edition of du Bellay's *Oeuvres Poetiques.* 7 vols. Paris, 1908–1931.

James VI, king of Scotland. *The Essayes of a Prentise, in the Divine Art of Poesie.* Edinburgh, 1585. Reprinted in *The Poems of James VI of Scotland.* Edited by James Craigie. 2 vols. Edinburgh, 1955–1958.

Klein, Holger M., ed. *English and Scottish Sonnet Sequences of the Renaissance.* 2 vols. Hildesheim, Germany, 1984. Facsimile texts of most of the sonnet sequences left out of Sidney Lee (see below).

Lee, Sidney. *Elizabethan Sonnets.* 2 vols. Westminster (London), 1904. Along with Holger Klein, this old but widely available edition gives readable texts of most of the minor sonnet sequences of the Elizabethan and Jacobean periods

Puttenham, George. *The Arte of English Poesie.* London, 1589. Menston, U.K., 1968. A rhetorical handbook that gives insights into the relationship between poetry and courtly behavior.

Tottel, Richard, ed. *Songes and Sonettes.* London, 1557. Edited as *Tottel's Miscellany* by Hyder Rollins. 2 vols. Cambridge, Mass., 1965. The first printing of the first English sonnets by Thomas Wyatt, Henry Howard, earl of Surrey, and others.

Wroth, Lady Mary. *The Poems of Lady Mary Wroth.* Edited by Josephine A. Roberts. Baton Rouge, La., 1983.

Secondary Works

Donow, Herbert S. *The Sonnet in England and America: A Bibliography of Criticism.* Westport, Conn., and London, 1982. Sections 2 and 3 of this invaluable work cover the Renaissance (including Scotland), listing published criticism, though not editions, of all known sonnet writers.

Espiner, Janet G. (Scott). *Les sonnets élisabéthains.* Paris, 1929. Despite its age, this diligent study is a useful overview of French borrowings by British sonneteers.

Lever, J. W. *The Elizabethan Love Sonnet.* London, 1956.

Prince, F. T. *The Italian Element in Milton's Verse.* Oxford, 1954.

Spiller, Michael R. G. *The Development of the Sonnet.* London and New York, 1992. Covers the sonnet from its beginnings in Italy up to Milton, for the student of English literature.

Vendler, Helen. *The Art of Shakespeare's Sonnets.* Cambridge, Mass., 1997. The most detailed twentieth-century study of Shakespeare's wordplay, it also provides a facsimile of the 1609 printing and a modernized text. It has an excellent bibliography of criticism and editions of Shakespeare's *Sonnets.*

Waller, Gary. *English Poetry of the Sixteenth Century.* London and New York, 1986.

Wilson, Katharina, ed. *Women Writers of the Renaissance and Reformation.* Athens, Ga., 1987.

MICHAEL R. G. SPILLER

POETRY, ENGLISH. [This entry consists of four subentries:

Neo-Latin Poetry in England
Tudor Poetry before Spenser
Elizabethan Poetry
Early Stuart and Metaphysical Poetry]

Neo-Latin Poetry in England

Neo-Latin poetry was written and printed in England in a significant quantity from the time of the introduction of printing until well into the eighteenth century, though it flourished in the century from 1540 to 1640 in particular. Such poetry was written almost without exception by graduates of the universities, where Latin verse composition was taught and practiced as an aid to competence in the Latin language. A small number of privately educated and exceptional women (the Catholic exile Elizabeth Weston, Bathsua Reynolds, and the daughters of the duke of Somerset) also published volumes of Latin poetry. Some English writers, notably Sir Thomas More, achieved international renown for their Latin verse, as did other poets from the British Isles, such as the Welshman John Owen and the Scots George Buchanan, who was acquainted with the members of the Pléiade and who wrote mostly in France. Most, however, were content with a merely national reputation. Some wrote for private pleasure, others at the behest of the wealthy and influential or in the hope of attracting their patronage. The new university presses of Cambridge (1584) and Oxford (1585) widely disseminated the verses of their alumni. The more learned London printers, such as John Day, Henry Bynneman, and Thomas Vautrollier, also printed English neo-Latin poets, and many were published by continental presses.

The poetry thus produced is very various. There are mythological poems, poems based on English history, versifications of parts of the Bible and of biblical incidents, saints' lives, epigrams, many obituary verses, and didactic and political poems. Great national events such as the defeat of the Spanish Armada, the birth or marriage of a prince, the death of a sovereign or prominent aristocrat, and the Gunpowder Plot of 1605 called forth much specially commissioned commemorative poetry. A great mass of occasional verse also survives, some of it never printed. Books of all types, whether English or Latin, are frequently prefaced by often lengthy Latin verses by leading poets praising and validating the work concerned. Throughout the period, English writers showed a marked fondness for self-consciously "artificial" forms such as pattern poems, acrostics, anagrams, palindromes, riddles, and "echo" verses where the end of a line repeats with a different meaning a syllable from the line's middle.

Many famous English vernacular poets also wrote a considerable amount of Latin poetry. Notable among them are John Milton, whose English poem *Lycidas* first appeared in the *Iusta Edouardo King,* a predominantly Latin university anthology of 1638; Thomas Campion, whose Latin poetry, including an unusual sequence of love elegies and many mordant epigrams, comprises roughly a third of his total poetical output; and George Herbert, Abraham Cowley, and Richard Crashaw. John Donne and Ben Jonson also wrote a few Latin verses. Edmund Spenser's *Shepherd's Calendar* was translated into Latin poetry by Theodore Bathurst.

The English neo-Latin poets mark and exemplify the reception and assimilation of humanism in England. Though always fluent and competent, they are not, however, to be numbered among the world's great poets, and only rarely attained a fame that lasted for more than one or two generations or reached beyond the confines of their native land.

BIBLIOGRAPHY

Binns, J. W. *Intellectual Culture in Elizabethan and Jacobean England: The Latin Writings of the Age.* Leeds, U.K., 1990.

Binns, J. W., ed. *The Latin Poetry of English Poets.* London, 1974.

Bradner, Leicester. *Musae Anglicanae. A History of Anglo-Latin Poetry, 1500–1925.* New York, 1940.

Schleiner, Louise. *Tudor and Stuart Women Writers.* Bloomington, Ind., 1994.

J. W. BINNS

Tudor Poetry before Spenser

From Henry VIII's monarchy through the early years of his daughter Elizabeth's reign, English writers creatively mixed and moved between late medieval and Renaissance forms, styles, and themes. It was a time of vital poetic experimentation and transition.

Although Henry VII's reign (1485–1509) had begun the Tudor consolidation of state power and ushered in a period of peace, his court had little contact with the continental Renaissance; its few notable poets (Stephen Hawes, Alexander Barclay, John Skelton) worked primarily within the native medieval tradition. With the ascension of Henry VIII, humanists such as Sir Thomas More and scholars such as Skelton (who had served as Henry's tutor) saw an opportunity for the advancement of poetry; the king himself composed lyrics to be set to his own music. During the years of Henry's marriage to Catherine of Aragon, poets began to import, translate, and adapt new forms from the Continent—most notably the sonnets of Petrarch. Later in his reign, however, Henry contributed to the premature silencing of his court's greatest poets and scholars: More, Sir Thomas Wyatt, and Henry Howard, earl of Surrey.

The potential risk of speech and writing in the wake of the king's break with the Roman church extended through the short, tumultuous reigns of his Protestant son Edward VI (1547–1553) and Catholic daughter Mary (1553–1558). Nevertheless, from midcentury onward, printed anthologies of poems appeared; the most influential was Richard Tottel's *Songs and Sonnets* (1557), commonly called *Tottel's Miscellany,* which made the work of both Henry's "courtly makers" and younger poets available to a wider audience. Within an emerging print culture, self-conscious composition mingled with the older habit of using verse to aid memory in "unliterary" forms such as almanacs and instruction books: Thomas Tusser's gardening manual in verse was among the most popular. From Elizabeth's accession (1558) through the publication of Edmund Spenser's *Shepheardes Calender* (1579), poets such as Barnabe Googe, Thomas Sackville, Isabella Whitney, George Turberville, and most notably George Gascoigne imitated and experimented with form and voice—establishing the iambic line and accentual/syllabic meter as the norms for modern English poetry and introducing a range of poetic genres and ambitions. In concert with the growing body of popular verse circulated in print and manuscript, often anonymously (as broadside ballads, songs from plays and entertainments, and in commonplace books and anthologies), they set the stage for the later Elizabethan poetic Renaissance.

The Court of Henry VIII (1509–1547). John Skelton (c. 1460–1529) was the most innovative of the earliest Tudor poets, although his work derived from the grammar and rhetoric of fourteenth- and fifteenth-century poetry rather than adapting new European models. After writing *The Bowge of Courte* (1498), an allegorical satire presenting a ship of state plagued by the corruption of court life, he took holy orders and retired to Norfolk. He returned to public life early in Henry VIII's reign and tried to make a space for play mixed with seriousness, defending vernacular poetry against those who trivialized it (*The Garland of Laurel;* 1523). Skelton's verse possessed distinctive energy and wit, concrete diction, and individuated voices. In his lively short-lined poems such as "Philip Sparrow" (c. 1504), written in what are now called "Skeltonics," he created a new rhyming form in English indebted to medieval Latin poetry. His love of sound and realism also appears in "The Tunning of Elinour Rumming," a celebration of pub low life, and "Colin Clout," the report of a plain-speaking commoner who sees "wrong with each degree." Skelton also penned two dangerously pointed attacks on Cardinal Thomas Wolsey, "Speak, Parrot" and "Why Come Ye Not to Court?," and the "Ballad of the Scottish King" commemorating the English victory at Flodden Field (1513), which some regard as the first printed broadside ballad.

Although Sir Thomas More (1478–1535) wrote poems in the vernacular, he composed his biting political poetry, including a series of epigrams, in Latin. Like other humanists, he regarded purified neoclassical Latin as the proper language for serious literature. It was thus left to Sir Thomas Wyatt (1503–1542) to become the fountainhead of English Renaissance vernacular poetry. Wyatt, as his fellow poet Surrey eulogized, "taught what might be said in rhyme." Returning in 1527 from diplomatic missions in Italy and France, Wyatt freely translated many of Petrarch's *Rime* from eleven-syllable Italian lines into iambic pentameter sonnets of internal struggle, among them "My galley charged with forgetfulness," "I find no peace," "Whose list to hunt," and "The long love that in my thought doth harbor." Imprisoned on treason charges, his 1541 acquittal was testimony to his rhetorical ability and a reminder of the close links between poetry and rhetoric stressed by Renaissance humanists. It also gives a sense of their precarious involvement with politics. This difficulty and the desire to assert an authentic personal voice appear in Wyatt's shorter-lined lyrics, which draw on medieval forms ("Blame not my lute," "My lute awake"). Conflict between his blunt persona and courtly ways animates two masterpieces, "They flee from me" (three stanzas of rhyme royal) and "Mine own John Poins" (a terza rima neoclassical satire). Wyatt asserts his bemusement with "newfangledness" even as he innovates poetically.

Later poets regarded Wyatt as the initiator; they saw Henry Howard, earl of Surrey (1517–1547), as the perfector. His smoothness and attention to the natural world in sonnets such as "The soote season" and "Alas, so all things now" contrast with Wyatt's rough struggles (see, for example, Surrey's "Love, that doth reign" versus Wyatt's "The long love," adaptations of the same Petrarch sonnet). Surrey established what became the standard English sonnet form, three quatrains followed by a couplet; seven different rhyming sounds made it more amenable to English. His translations of books 2 and 4 of the *Aeneid* are credited as the first blank verse in English (published 1557). As he paid tribute to his forerunner in "Wyatt resteth here," so would the Elizabethan Turberville laud Surrey: "Our mother tongue by him hath got such light / As ruder speech thereby is banished quite."

Much poetry from Henry's era has been lost, including most of the writings of Thomas, Lord Vaux (1510–1556), and undoubtedly some by minor lyricists such as William Cornish. A miscellany from the 1530s, *The Court of Venus,* exists only in fragments. Powerful lyrics remain unattributed, such as "Western wind" (and later, "Greensleeves"); genre took precedence over individuated authorship. Throughout the first three-quarters of the century, poets were eager to praise one another, and authorship of particular poems may have been collaborative (as plays and poetic collections certainly were). The primacy of place given to Wyatt and Surrey as "reformers" of English verse—a project sometimes linked with England's religious independence—is thus in part a retrospective creation attributable to their ample representation in *Tottel's Miscellany.*

Poetry at Midcentury (1547–1558). Tottel's *Songs and Sonnets* included Henrican poetry previously circulated only in manuscript. Tottel's aim was clarity and smoothness, as in the "regularizing" of Wyatt's meter—often to ill effect. Nevertheless, such editing played an important part in establishing the iambic norm of modern English poetry, moving away from the four- and five-stress lines of fourteenth-century verse to a metrical system that considered both accent and the number of syllables. Later poets would reconcile spoken word stress with metrical accent more artfully.

Testifying to the increasing dominance of the iambic line, Tottel dismissed metrical subtlety but allowed variety in stanza and line length. Poulter's measure, alternating lines of six and seven iambic feet, was among the most popular forms and deemed appropriate for serious writing; even in the 1570s Gascoigne regarded poulter's as the "commonest sort of verse which we use now adayes." To modern ears it sounds like a quatrain of trimeter and tetrameter lines, more suited to light topics. "The Agèd Lover Renounceth Love" by Lord Vaux is among the more successful examples of broken poulter's, connecting poetry and prodigal youth—a reiterated trope throughout the period.

The iambic septameter line or "fourteener" was also esteemed. Judged an English equivalent to the long lines of classical poetry, it was chosen by Thomas Phaer for his translation of the *Aeneid* (seven books, 1558) and by Arthur Golding for his version of Ovid's *Metamorphoses* (books 1–4, 1565; complete, 1567). Nevertheless, fourteener couplets tended to sound like shorter-lined quatrains of "eight and six" (syllables), as attested by the use of this "common meter" form in the immensely popular translation of the *Psalms* initiated by Thomas Sternhold and John Hopkins (book 1, 1547; complete, 1562).

The publication of Sternhold and Hopkins obviously did more than popularize fourteeners: it made scripture immediately available for the English to sing in their own vernacular, contributing powerfully to the Protestant Reformation. But between Sternhold's first translations and the complete volume's appearance, the state religion changed twice and the monarch thrice. Tottel might well seek regularity in verse, for these were irregular times. The moralizing and elegiac tenor of midcentury poetry appears in Nicholas Grimald's "What path list you to tread?" and "A funeral song, upon the decease of Anne, his mother." Political upheavals silenced some and drove others away: John Heywood (c. 1497–c. 1580), self-described as the poet "with the mad merry wit" and another notable contributor in Tottel, survived as court entertainer for Henry, Edward, and Mary, but left the country upon Elizabeth's accession. He had produced a collection of epigrams, a verse dialogue on marriage, and a religious satire, *The Spider and the Fly* (1556). Other publications were merely delayed by the increasing precariousness of Mary's reign: *A Mirror for Magistrates,* suppressed in 1555, became an Elizabethan best-seller.

Early Elizabethan Trends (1558–1579). The popularity of verse anthologies continued: Richard Edwards's *The Paradise of Dainty Devices* (1576) ran to ten editions by 1606. It mixed Henrican poems by Lord Vaux with those of Elizabethan courtiers such as Edward de Vere, earl of Oxford, testifying to continuities in style and theme. But a new mode of presenting verse also emerged, and with it the nascence of a modern conception of a poet: the publication of single-authored volumes at their authors' behest. One motivation appears in the frank profession of Barnabe Googe (1540–1594), who writes in his *Eclogues, Epitaphs, and Sonnets* (1563), "Give money me, take friendship whoso list." George Turberville (1540?–1595?), influenced by Googe, published his *Epitaphs, Epigrams, Songs, and Sonnets* in 1567. Turberville's work illustrates how English poets now routinely placed themselves in relation to the European Continent and the Renaissance recovery of classical forms: he wrote a carpe diem poem, translated Ovid and Mantuan (Giovanni Battista Spagnoli), and later drew on his experience as secretary to the ambassador to Russia to personalize his lyrics.

Similar patterns appear, more remarkably, in the work of Isabella Whitney (flourished 1567–1573), apparently the first publishing female poet in England. With a straightforwardness of topic and diction akin to Googe and Turberville, Whitney mixed classical allusions with autobiographical references to her middle-class background and experience as a London servant. *The Copy of a Letter* (1567?) addresses an inconstant love, but rather than simply mourning she argues energetically for his returning to her. *A Sweet Nosegay* (1573) appends her "Will and Testament" to London, a vivid, affectionate urban portrait, to a collection of short verses and epistles. Whitney's self-assertion is the most public indication of increasing access to literacy and interest in writing among women.

If one poet captures the new ambitiousness of Elizabethan authors and the risks they ran, it is George Gascoigne (1535?–1577). His surreptitious publication of *A Hundreth Sundrie Flowers* in 1573 attests to the continuing stigma of print for gentlemen and the dangers of autobiographical verse. Attacked for immorality and slander, he nevertheless published an elaborately prefaced, reedited version two years later as *The Posies of George Gascoigne, Esquire*. Nor did he shy away from self-advertisement in his verse. Numerous poems announce him by name ("The arraignment of a Lover," "Gascoigne's De profundis"), including one of his most esteemed poems, "Gascoigne's Woodmanship," in which he transforms a prodigal's past failures into an apologia for the poet, combining the moral forthrightness found in Wyatt with tongue-in-cheek playfulness that foreshadows Philip Sidney's more extensive irony as "Astrophil." Gascoigne organized his poems into categories in *The Posies,* in part to avoid further charges of immorality. He pioneered what David Norbrook calls the "new possibilities offered by the printing-press in controlling the reader's response . . . in the structuring of whole volumes of poems" (*Penguin Book of Renaissance Verse,* p. xxxvi). Displaying great range as a lyricist, Gascoigne also mastered longer forms. Among the most memorable are his exposé of war based on his experience in the Netherlands, "Dulce bellum inexpertis," and what may be the first complete original blank verse poem in English, the moral satire *The Steel Glass* (1576).

Original blank verse had already appeared in the Inns of Court drama *Gorboduc* (1561), coauthored by Thomas Sackville, earl of Dorset (1536–1608). That Sackville's other published verse appeared in the collection of English historical tragedies, *A Mirror for Magistrates* (edited by William Baldwin; 1563), reflects the generic hierarchies that continued to place the vernacular lyric low on moral and aesthetic scales: Sackville went on to a distinguished career as courtier and peer, whereas Gascoigne remained on the margins of respectability. *The Mirror* also serves as a reminder that Tudor poetry mixed medieval and modern: its *de casibus* stories of the falls of princes mingled with even more popular tales of less elevated sorts, such as Thomas Churchyard's tragedy of Edward IV's mistress, "Shore's Wife." Sackville's "Induction" and "Complaint of Henry, Duke of Buckingham" for the *Mirror* deployed the medieval frame of a dream vision in rhyme royal but conjured up historical English alongside allegorical figures. With fine attention to nature, pounding iambic stress, and new emphasis on national history, Sackville's tragedy brings the dead past, and past dead, to life. That endeavor reappears, in a more elegant and densely textured way, in the *Shepheardes Calender,* when Spenser brings Tudor poetry full circle by resurrecting Skelton's character, Colin Clout, to serve as a figure for the younger poet. Looking back, Spenser proclaimed and came to be interpreted as a new beginning: the confidently self-conscious start of an Elizabethan Renaissance.

See also biographies of figures mentioned in this entry.

BIBLIOGRAPHY

Primary Works

Gascoigne, George. *The Complete Works of George Gascoigne.* Edited by John W. Cunliffe. 2 vols. Cambridge, U.K., 1907–1910.

Googe, Barnabe. *Selected Poems.* Edited by Alan Stephens. Denver, Colo., 1961.

Muir, Kenneth, ed. *Collected Poems of Sir Thomas Wyatt.* London, 1949.

Surrey (Henry Howard, Earl of). *Poems.* Edited by Enrys Jones. Oxford, 1964.

Sylvester, Richard S., ed. *English Sixteenth-Century Verse: An Anthology.* New York, 1984.

Tottel, Richard. *Tottel's Miscellany.* Edited by Hyder Edward Rollins. Cambridge, Mass., 1965.

Travitsky, Betty, ed. *The Paradise of Women: Writings by Englishwomen of the Renaissance.* New York, 1989.

Williams, John, ed. *English Renaissance Poetry: A Collection of Shorter Poems from Skelton to Jonson.* 2d ed. Fayetteville, Ark., 1990.

Secondary Works

Helgerson, Richard. *The Elizabethan Prodigals.* Berkeley, Calif., 1976.

Norbrook, David. Introduction to *The Penguin Book of Renaissance Verse 1509–1659.* Edited by H. R. Woudhuysen. London, 1993.

Peterson, Douglas L. *The English Lyric from Wyatt to Donne: A History of the Plain and Eloquent Styles.* Princeton, N.J., 1967.

Prouty, Charles Tyler. *George Gascoigne: Elizabethan Courtier, Soldier, and Poet.* New York, 1942.

Stevens, John. *Music and Poetry in the Early Tudor Court.* 1961. Reprint, Cambridge, U.K., and New York, 1979.

Thompson, John. *The Founding of English Metre.* New York, 1961.

Waller, Gary. *English Poetry of the Sixteenth Century.* New York, 1986.

Winters, Yvor. "The Sixteenth Century Lyric in England: A Critical and Historical Reinterpretation." In *Elizabethan Poetry: Modern Essays in Criticism.* Edited by Paul J. Alpers. London, 1967. Pages 93–125.

DIANA E. HENDERSON

Elizabethan Poetry

Elizabeth Tudor (1533–1603) acceded to the throne of England on 17 November 1558, when she was twenty-five. She reigned for forty-five years until she was succeeded in 1603 by James Stuart (1566–1625), who was James I of England, but James VI of Scotland from the time of his father's murder in 1567. Both wrote poetry, Elizabeth preferring a plain style, James the aureate or golden, which was more elaborate in its diction and sound patterns. Underlying both styles is an acknowledgment of the divine origins of poetry, as in the Psalms, and a determination to write in a manner suitable to the dignity of the genre. James published several volumes, the earliest of which was *The Essayes of a Prentise, in the Divine Art of Poesie* (1584). In addition to poems, *Essayes* contained *Ane Schort Treatise, conteining some reulis and cautelis to be obseruit and eschewit in Scottis Poesie*.

Styles of Elizabethan Poetry. Edmund Spenser's *Shepheardes Calender* (1579) marks a watershed in English poetry. It contains one of the earliest sophisticated expressions of the new politicized literary nationalism brought about in response to fear that the queen would marry a French Roman Catholic prince. It was ingeniously complex, self-evidently witty, cuttingly ironic, a linguistic and poetic tour de force, and a scathing commentary on contemporary events and figures. It was dedicated to Philip Sidney, who with Spenser set new levels of sophistication in English creative writing, inspiring generations of future poets.

The writing of Spenser and Sidney is outstanding in an era during which Tudor poetry continued to exert its influence through new publications and reprints. Throughout Elizabeth's reign, Tudor poetry provided models for imitation. Arthur Goldin's translation of Ovid's *Metamorphoses,* of which there were seven editions between 1567 and 1612, was quarried for classical tales and imagery. The outstanding exemplars of Tudor verse are the publisher Richard Tottel's *Songes and Sonettes Written by Henry Haward Late Earl of Surrey and Other* (1557), frequently referred to as *Tottel's Miscellany,* and the *Mirror for Magistrates* (1574). *Songes and Sonettes* contained 271 poems, including ninety-seven attributed to Sir Thomas Wyatt, forty to Henry Howard, earl of Surrey, forty to Nicholas Grimald, and ninety-four to uncertain authors. The popularity of this work demanded that it was reprinted with additions and deletions nine times between 1557 and 1587. These successive editions ensured that virtually every poet with London connections had access to the principal court poetry of the earlier half of the century. In consequence, much of the shorter Elizabethan poetry, including sonnets, bears a striking resemblance to that of an earlier generation. Verse by weaker poets, many of whom did not publish, tends to be imitative. Poetry by more self-confident writers such as Sidney in both versions of his *Arcadia,* Spenser in *The Shepheardes Calender* and *The Faerie Queene,* Marlowe in *Hero and Leander,* and Shakespeare in *Venus and Adonis* and *The Rape of Lucrece,* as well as in the plays, ranges from originality to self-assured parody.

Later Elizabethan poets, preeminently represented by Sidney and Spenser, can be regarded as expressing a genial synthesis of Protestant Christianity and classical humanism. The growing volume of mid- to late-sixteenth-century publication of ancient Greek and Roman history, philosophy, science, and literature stimulated interest in nationalistic self-expression. Motivated to a large extent by French criticism, Spenser skillfully adapts the ancient pastoral eclogue into a vehicle for a veiled commentary on politics and the church. His *Shepheardes Calender* (1579) welds the Roman poet Virgil's *Eclogues* onto the much reprinted book of versified monthly agricultural instructions, *The kalender of shepherdes* (1506), itself published from 1570 onward as *The shepardes kalendar.* In the manner of the Greco-Roman revival of ancient or Attic Greek, Spenser also experiments with the revival of his own native language. When E. K., the annotator of the *Shepheardes Calender,* writes to Spenser's Cambridge friend and critic Gabriel Harvey, he defends the author's 'choyse of old and vnwonted words.' E. K., who may be Harvey himself, complains that many less thoughtful poets have corrupted English by introducing French, Italian, and Latin words, 'So now they haue made our English tongue, a gallimaufray or hodgepodge of al other speches.'

Demonstrating the poetic power of unsullied English, Spenser opens the April eclogue, 'Tell me good Hobbinoll, what garres thee greete?' In a parody of translations of Italian and French love poetry, E. K. glosses this for his fashionable London readers as 'causeth thee weepe and complain.' In his letter to Ralegh, Spenser describes the ancient (Homer and Virgil) as well as the Renaissance (Ludovico Ariosto and Torquato Tasso) models for his allegorical nationalistic epic *The Faerie Queene.* Though incomplete, it remains one of the longest poems in English. Even in its opening lines, 'A Gentle Knight was pricking on the plaine, / Y Cladd in mightie armes and siluer shielde,' archaic spelling and diction simultaneously invoke the medieval spirit of Geoffrey Chaucer and the ideals of a prelapsarian Arthurian court.

Sidney's nationalism manifests itself in his anglicizing of Greek and Latin forms in his verse, drama, and prose, all of which he regarded as created literature or poetry. The result is a stunning combination of stark clarity combined with metaphor, and plainness blended into ornamentally rhythmic passages constructed out of words in Greco-Roman patterns, as in this description of the dying Parthenia from the revised or *New Arcadia* (1582–1584; pub. 1590): 'her roundy, sweetly swelling lips a little trembling, as though they kissed their neighbour, death; in her cheeks, the whiteness striving by little and little to get upon the rosiness of them; her neck (a neck indeed of alablaster) displaying the wound which with most dainty blood laboured to drown his own beauties, so as here was a river of purest red, there, an island of perfittest white, each giving lustre to the other.'

This baroque richness is more apparent in Sidney's poetic prose than in his verse. In the *Old Arcadia* (1579–1581), virtually all the seventy-seven poems are dramatic songs that experiment with "words derived out of other languages . . . as they are denizened in English," and are in complex Greek or Italian forms. Thus the Petrarchan theme of the forlorn lover may be expressed in the innovative, argumentative sonnets of *Astrophil and Stella* (1581; pub. 1591), or in lengthy Greek "elegiacs": "Unto the caitiff wretch whom long affliction holdeth, / and now fully believes help to be quite perished, / Grant yet, grant yet a look, to the last monument of his anguish." Sidney's poems in quantitative verse are far more successful than those of his friends Gabriel Harvey, Spenser, and Abraham Fraunce. Liberating contemplative erotic verse from the fourteeners (verses consisting of fourteen syllables) and poulters' measure (a meter in which lines of twelve syllables and fourteen syllables alternate) fashionable among the Tudor poets, Sidney's poems are valued for the intellectual prowess of their metric and rhetorical ingenuity, their linguistic dexterity, and for their outstandingly sincere expression of Protestant Greco-Roman philosophical values through secular verse.

Another mode of Protestant expression in verse was psalm translation. Sidney only finished forty-three; Psalms 44 to 150 were translated by his sister Mary Sidney Herbert, countess of Pembroke. A manuscript of the complete Psalms, presented with a lengthy verse dedication to Elizabeth I, opens with Mary Sidney Herbert's best known poem, "To the Angel Spirit of the most excellent Sir Philip Sidney," acknowledging her debt of inspiration to her deceased brother. Drawing upon a great number of continental translations, principally French, she worked with a variety of inventive metrical forms and stanzas, striving to represent the musicality of King David's prayers in song, in the manner of Philip Sidney's twenty-third Psalm: "The lord the lord my shepherd is, / And so can never I / Tast misery. // He rests me in green pastures his. / By waters still and sweet / He guides my feet."

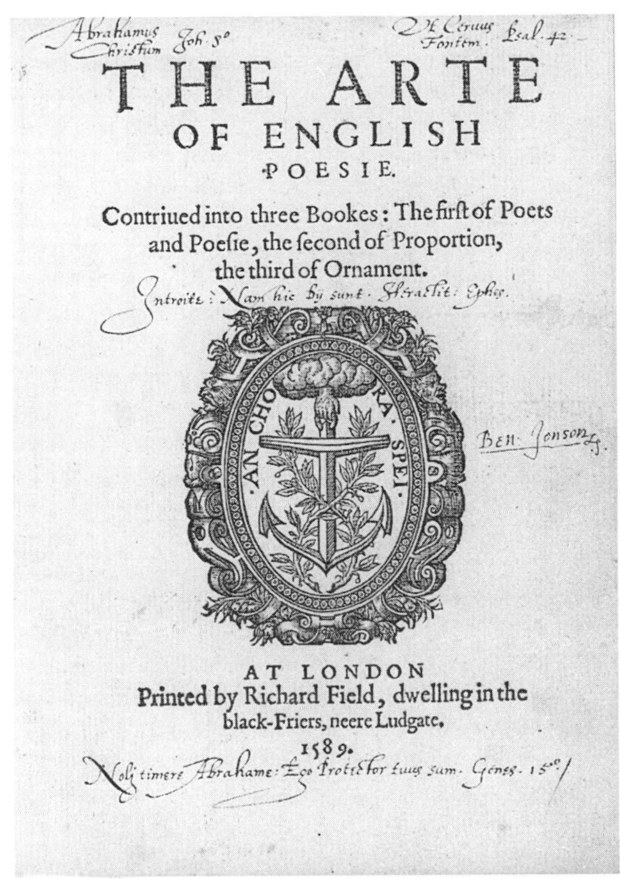
THE ARTE
OF ENGLISH
POESIE.
Contriued into three Bookes: The first of Poets and Poesie, the second of Proportion, the third of Ornament.
AT LONDON
Printed by Richard Field, dwelling in the black-Friers, neere Ludgate.
1589.

Elizabethan Poetry. Title page of George Puttenham's *The Arte of English Poesy* (London, 1589) with annotations by Ben Jonson. BY PERMISSION OF THE BRITISH LIBRARY. G11548

The verbal patterns that characterize the figured ornamentation seen in Sidney's prose are found in much of Shakespeare's drama, as well as in his erotic narratives. Shakespeare imitates Sidney's description of Parthenia in *The Rape of Lucrece.* There he draws on Sidney's distinctive image of blood flowing from a wound as rivers around islands: "bubbling from her breast it doth divide / In two slow rivers, that the crimson blood / Circles her body in on every side, / Who like a late-sack'd island vastly stood, / Bare and unpeopled in this fearful flood" (ll. 1737–1741). Both writers give the illusion of revelling in the macabre, but they are actually filling out their stories through the use of copious detail, an esteemed Renaissance device effected here through the accretion of metaphors.

The Faerie Queene is built of multilayered metaphors in praise of Elizabeth I. Elizabethan poets were fond of using sustained metaphors throughout a story in order to create an allegory. After being raped, Shakespeare's Lucrece compares herself at length to the betrayed city of Troy. The poem could be interpreted as a warning against an invasion by Spain. The clarity of Robert Southwell, the Jesuit, masks brief allegories of self-sacrifice expressed through paradox, as in the poem "Decease Release": "Alive a Queen, now dead I am a Saint; / Once Mary called, my name now Martyr is." Although paradox becomes a seventeenth-century obsession, it forms the basis of the remarkable poem by Chidiock Tichborne, "written by his own hand in the Tower before his execution" in 1586: "My prime of youth is but a frost of cares, / My feast of joy is but a dish of pain / . . . / The day is past, and yet I saw no sun, / And now I live, and now my life is done."

In Sir John Davies's *Orchestra,* Antinous, one of Penelope's disorderly suitors while her husband Odysseus was absent during the Trojan War, invites her to dance. This invitation celebrates universal order in every part of the macrocosm and microcosm. The 1596 version qualifies the celebration of order because the question of who might succeed to the English throne remained unsettled. Order had not been insured throughout the body politic. In the 1622 version, which may reflect Davies's nostalgia for the Elizabethan court, the poet adds concluding stanzas in which Penelope appears to accept Antinous's invitation to dance.

Metaphors form the basis of many Elizabethan sonnets. Shakespeare interrogated conventional use of metaphor in love poetry through his question, "Shall I compare thee to a summer's day?" and "My mistress' eyes are nothing like the sun." The compounding and compressing of metaphor, sometimes to the point of obscurity, is particularly typical of John Donne, who heaped images upon images in both his prose and his verse. His metaphors form logical puzzles such as in the first lines of "The Flea": "Mark but this flea, and mark in this, / How little that which thou deny'st me is." Donne is outstanding both for the density of his arguments and for the stunning clarity of his abrupt openings: "For God's sake hold your tongue, and let me love" ('The Canonization'). He is boldly anti-Petrarchan in celebrating the integration of body and spirit in fulfilling sexual relations, and reminiscent of Sir Thomas Wyatt in chiding women for infidelity.

Religious, meditative, and satirical verse also could employ a plainer classical style as a complement to truth. Many exponents of the plain style grew up in Calvinist families with mothers who wrote poetry, as did Philip, Mary, and Robert Sidney, whose mother was Mary Dudley. Similarly, Henry Lok (c. 1553–1608) was the son of the poet Ann Lok or Locke. The lyrics of George Gascoigne (c. 1525–1577) and Sir Walter Ralegh (1554–1618) make use of the plain style to express with simple diction a haunting, gnomic wisdom, as in Ralegh's sonnet to his son: "The wood is that, which makes the gallows tree; / The weed is that, which strings the hangman's bag; / The wag, my pretty knave, betokeneth thee." Even Ralegh's allegorical *Ocean to Cynthia* is couched in clear terms: "Sufficeth it to you, my joys interred, / In simple words that I my woes complain."

The agricultural lyrics of Thomas Tusser (1524–1580), Thomas Churchyard's tales in verse (c. 1520–1604), the personal narrative of Isabella Whitney (fl. 1567–1573, sister of Geoffrey Whitney, famous for his book of emblems), and Nicholas Breton's (c. 1553–c. 1625) lyrics of court and country demonstrate the continued interest in easily understood poetry throughout the Elizabethan era. Both Samuel Daniel (c. 1562–1619) and Ben Jonson (1572–1637) make a particular effort to write with uncluttered clarity. Daniel becomes so successful at plainness that if it were not for his insistence on rhyme, much of his history in verse *The Civil Wars* would read like straightforward prose. As a protegé of the Countess of Pembroke, he used plainness to signal his intention to use poetry to tell the truth, as if strengthening Sir Philip Sidney's denial in his *Defence of Poetry* that all poets are liars.

There is still a great deal to be learned about Elizabethan poets and their writing. A much more representative picture is emerging through the research of Steven W. May, whose *Bibliography and First Line Index of English Verse, 1559–1603,* increases the number of known Elizabethan poems from around 18,000 to 30,000.

Imitation and Convention. Literary fads were a natural outgrowth of an epistemology that valued imitation. It was assumed that authors would imitate existing forms—preferably those with classical authority, although French and Italian models were also common. Originality was largely suspect; even social reformers were likely to argue that a particular reform was a return to traditional practice rather than an "innovation." Poems were especially valued if they offered English equivalents of classical or continental models. Michael Drayton's *Englands Heroical Epistles* imitates Ovid's *Heroides:* Drayton's verse letters are the imagined correspondence of famous lovers, but he uses English history rather than classical mythology as his source for the lover's laments. These epistolary poems were extremely popular and went through more editions in the same time period than *The Faerie Queene*. Imitation could also involve general literary ideas, images, and motifs, such as the pastoral convention. Conventional verse mediates between literary tradition and personal experience or emotion. An author who decides to write a pastoral elegy on the occasion of the death of a friend or patron—such as Spenser did with the "November" elegy in his *Shepheardes Calender*—asks: what form does the tradition of poetry suggest I give to my feelings? The poet may even reread Theocritus's *Idylls* and Virgil's *Eclogues* or examine continental models. These pastoral conventions represented to the Elizabethans information shared by the poet and the reader: the reader is supposed to respond to the poet's use of the tradition as well as to the feelings and ideas expressed in the poem. Conversely, when the conventions are unknown or have been rejected, pastorals in which nymphs and shepherds engage in singing contests, lament a lost patron, or complain about unrequited love may seem artificial and alienating. The positive connotations they had for the Elizabethans become negative.

Pastoral. The specific history of later Elizabethan poetry begins with the pastoral convention and Edmund Spenser's publication of the *Shepheardes Calender* (1579). He appropriately began his literary career in emulation of Virgil by writing pastoral eclogues in the *Shepheardes Calender* and then moved to epic in *The Faerie Queene*. Spenser invites us to recognize his imitation of models by using the format of the almanac and by adopting the persona of Colin Clout, a name borrowed from John Skelton's "Colyn Cloute" (1530), a satirical monologue on clerical abuses. He also identifies Chaucer as his master and, possibly in imitation of Chaucerian Middle English, deliberately characterizes his shepherds as speaking in archaic or dialect forms. This elaborate and illustrated set of twelve eclogues, one for each month in the year, was reprinted at least four times in separate quarto editions after its initial appearance.

The pastoral emphasizes the achievement of the good life, an ideal of rural contentment. Pastoral is related to the classical ideal of "otium," or leisure, and celebrates the rejection of the aspiring mind. It was also highly political. There are biblical as well as classical sources for the pastoral, blending together concrete details and moral treatment. Francis Bacon allegorized the story of Cain and Abel as images of the active and contemplative life. God favored the shepherd (the contemplative) over the husbandman who tilled the ground (active). Michael Drayton's *Idea: The Shepheards Garland* is unusual in that it specifically imitates Spenser's *Shepheardes Calender,* but unlike that work it is also a poetic manifesto. Drayton's nine eclogues form a garland that will crown his mistress, the Idea of Poetry, while paying tribute to the nine muses who preside over the arts. This kind of specific generic imitation was unusual. The pastoral furnished writers in many genres with numerous themes and images, ranging from court entertainments such as Sidney's *Lady of May,* to narratives interspersed with songs and eclogues, like Sidney's *Arcadia* or Thomas Lodge's *Rosalynde,* which Shakespeare was to adapt into *As You Like It*.

Verse miscellanies, important to early Tudor poetry, continued to be compiled in manuscript and print throughout the century. *Englands Helicon* (1600; 1614) contains twenty-four anonymous as well as 126 signed poems, and it serves as a storehouse of pastoral forms: complaints, lyrics, love dialogues, blazons, palinodes, songs and ayres from books of musical arrangements. The close connection between the English pastoral lyric, and musical forms such as the madrigal or the ayre for a single voice, cannot be overestimated.

Complaint. The celebration of the simple life in the pastoral is echoed in more overtly political works related to the "mirror for magistrates" tradition. These complaints, related to the medieval didactic tradition of the "fall of princes," relate the misadventures of former governors to illustrate the principles of good government. Many of the poems follow a formula in which the ghost of a famous person asks the poet to describe his or her downfall. Critical of the dangers of the aspiring mind, these poems, like pastoral celebrations of humble pleasures, illustrate the folly of vaulting ambition.

Edmund Spenser's *Complaints* (1591) contained a number of meditations on mutability, such as *The Ruines of Rome* and *The Ruines of Time,* but Samuel Daniel seems to have established the vogue of the love complaint. He published *The Complaint of Rosamond* (1592) at the conclusion of his sonnet sequence *Delia,* and his account of the fair Rosamond, mistress of Henry II, brought a new Ovidian richness to the *ubi sunt* ("where have they gone?") theme and the complaint tradition. Thomas Churchyard's earlier account of Jane Shore, mistress of Edward IV, in the *Mirror for Magistrates* (1563) depicted Jane as a repentant wife who warned her audience that chastity was the better course. In contrast, Rosamond's ghost is troubled by her obscurity; her tomb at Godstowe nunnery has been destroyed and she herself is forgotten.

Ovidian minor epic. Thomas Lodge, an innovator in a number of genres, wrote *Scillaes Metamorphosis* in 1589 and so may have written the first of the extremely popular Ovidian wooing poems. Lodge uses the framework of the love complaint; the poet is on the banks of the Isis when the sea god tells of his lady's disdain. When Scylla later complains of Glaucus's indifference, she is attended by personifications of Fury, Rage, and Despair. The more strictly Ovidian poems—represented most notably by Marlowe's *Hero and Leander* and Shakespeare's *Venus and Adonis*—have been variously labeled minor epics, mythological narratives, erotic narratives, and perhaps most aptly—even though the term was not coined until the nineteenth century—epyllia, little epics. These highly wrought mythological and amatory poems are loosely based on episodes occurring in or related to an epic. Ovid almost always serves as the model for these poems, but Spenser's *Muiopotmos* (1591) and *The Faerie Queene* (1590) also contributed models for mythological embroidery.

Hero and Leander was first entered in the Stationers' Register as a book to be published in 1593, the year of Marlowe's death. In addition to the main plot in which Leander seduces Hero, Venus's nun, Marlowe relates a story at the end of the first sestiad that purports to explain why the Fates are not favorable to love and incidentally explains why scholars are always poor. This formal digression, containing a macrocosm-microcosm parallel, is frequently a convention of this genre. In Shakespeare's *Venus and Adonis* the amorous advances of the goddess of love and beauty are thwarted by the reluctant, even petulant, Adonis. In the digression, Adonis's horse suffers no such inhibitions with a passing filly. The digression on animals comments upon the narrative concerning the gods. Numerous imitations followed, including Thomas Edwards's *Cephalus and Procris* (1593) and *Narcissus* (1595), Thomas Heywood's *Oenone and Paris* (1594), Richard Barnfield's *Cassandra* (1595), Michael Drayton's *Endymion and Phoebe* (1595), George Chapman's *Ovid's Banquet of Sence* (1595) and his completion of Marlowe's *Hero and Leander* (1598). Michael Drayton was undecided about whether to use Daniel's complaint or Marlowe and Shakespeare's Ovidian wooing poems as his models. His publications and revisions illustrate the vicissitudes of taste in the 1590s. His *Piers Gaveston* (1593) is called a "tragicall discourse" and *Matilda* (1594) is a "tragicall Historie." When they were republished in 1596, Drayton added twenty-five new stanzas to *Piers Gaveston* and twenty-six to *Matilda:* these already heavily embellished poems were given even more rhetorical flourishes. By 1618 he had renamed these poems "legends" and severely cut them to become historical narratives.

Satire. Like the pastoral, satire can be a generalized convention or a specific genre such as the beast epic, formal verse satire, or epigram. Spenser's "Mother Hubberds Tale" appeared in his *Complaints* (1591), and it is the topical satire in this poem that was most frequently copied into the commonplace books of his contemporaries. Thomas Lodge, always the experimenter, could claim to be the first satirist; he published *A Fig for Momus* (1595), a satirical miscellany containing eclogues, satires, and epistles. John Donne's five satires circulated in manuscript from 1593 to 1597, but were not published until after his death in 1631. Joseph Hall's *Virgidemiarum Sixe Bookes* appeared in two parts, the first three books in 1597 and the last three in 1598. Hall took Juvenal and Persius as models and claimed to be the first English satirist.

John Marston took up Hall's challenge to be the second English satirist with *The Metamorphosis of Pigmalions Image and Certaine Satyres* (1598). Pigmalion is modeled on the Ovidian wooing poems, but satirizes many of their conventions. Marston followed his attack on Hall with *The Scourge of Villainie* (1598), a dark poem that depicts the world itself as enveloped in lust. Everard Guilpin, Marston's friend, entered the satirical battle with *Skialetheia or A Shadowe of Truth, in certaine Epigrams and Satyres* (1598). Guilpin imitated Donne's first satire in his fifth, demonstrating that Donne's poetry circulated widely enough in manuscript to have an impact on some of his contemporaries. On 1 June 1599 an order suppressing epigrams, satires, unauthorized plays, and English histories was entered in the Stationers' Register. Books already in print were to be collected and burned by the Bishop of London. This order seems to have had little effect on the publication of satires. John Weever united the Ovidian poem and satire when he published *Faunus and Melliflora, or the Original of our English Satyres* (1600). Numerous writers—Cyril Tourner, John Lane, Thomas Bastard, Samuel Rowlands, Thomas

Middleton, and William Rankins, to mention only a few—published satires before the end of the century.

Sonnet, Sonnet Sequence, and Epic. The story of the Petrarchan love sonnet and its influence on English poetry begins with Chaucer, Petrarch's younger contemporary. He translates a Petrarchan sonnet as a song for his hero in *Troilus and Criseyde*. Translations of Petrarch by Wyatt and Surrey appeared in Tottel's *Songes and Sonnets* (1557–1587). Thomas Watson translated Petrarch into Latin and in 1582 published *Hekatompathia or Passionate Centurie of Loue*. These one-hundred sonnets derived from Petrarch, Serafino, Pierre de Ronsard, and many other French and Italian poets.

Whatever the specific influence of Petrarch, or of French adaptations, on the English sonnet, the most important influence on the English sonnet sequence was Sir Philip Sidney's delightfully ironic and self-mocking *Astrophil and Stella*. After his sonnets appeared in 1591, along with selections from Samuel Daniel's *Delia*, every would-be writer in the 1590s tried his hand at writing sonnets. The most successful collections are the dark and complex; *Caelica* by Sidney's lifelong friend Fulke Greville, Spenser's emblematic *Amoretti*, Drayton's *Idea*, and Shakespeare's *Sonnets*. John Donne's *Songs and Sonets* (1633), which circulated widely in manuscript, largely consists of satirical erotic poetry in complex forms. In spite of the popularity of the sonnet sequence, the epic remained the acme of poetic achievement. Sidney, in his *Defence of Poetry* (1595), identifies the essential ingredient of poetry as "fiction," the product of the poet's invention. In contrast, Julius Caesar Scaliger's *Poetices* (1561) holds that meter (systematically arranged rhythm in verse) characterizes poetry and differentiates it from ordinary language. He argues that all language is representative and imitates reality, but that all language is not poetry. These issues had an impact on sixteenth-century views of what constituted the epic and differentiated it from the historical, or heroic, poem and the romance. At one extreme, an epic was to be based on historical events while a romance might be entirely invented; at the other, poetry had to be distinguished from history. Was Lucan's *Pharsalia* versified history because he wrote about what had happened even though he used meter? Alternatively, was Livy, who wrote in prose, a poet because he invented orations to insert in his history? Sixteenth-century conceptions of epic tended to be eclectic and would probably have included works such as Samuel Daniel's *Civil Wars*, Michael Drayton's *Barons Wars*, and William Warner's *Albion's England* as well as Spenser's *Faerie Queene*. Contemporary estimates of poetic achievement would have concurred in celebrating Sidney and Spenser as the major poets of the Elizabethan age.

BIBLIOGRAPHY

Primary works

Breton, Nicholas. *Poems*. Edited by Jean Robertson. Liverpool, 1952.

Brittons Bowre of Delights, 1591. Edited by Hyder E. Rollins. Cambridge, Mass., 1933. Repr. New York, 1968.

Daniel, Samuel. *Poems and a Defence of Ryme*. Edited by Arthur Colby Sprague. Cambridge, Mass., 1930.

Davies, John. *The Poems of Sir John Davies*. Edited by Robert Krueger. Oxford, 1975.

Drayton, Michael. *The Works of Michael Drayton*. Edited by J. William Hebel. 5 vols. Oxford, 1932.

Elizabethan Minor Epics. Edited by Elizabeth Story Donno. New York, 1963. Introduction to the Ovidian mythological poem.

England's Helicon, 1600, 1614. Edited by Hyder E. Rollins. 2 vols. Cambridge, Mass., 1935.

Hall, Joseph. *Collected Poems of Joseph Hall, Bishop of Exeter and Norwich*. Edited by Arnold Davenport. Liverpool, 1949.

Lodge, Thomas. *The Complete Works of Thomas Lodge*. Edited by Edmund W. Gosse. 4 vols. 1883. Repr. New York, 1963.

Marston, John. *The Poems of John Marston*. Edited by Arnold Davenport. Liverpool, 1962.

May, Steven W. *The Elizabethan Courtier Poets: The Poems and Their Contexts*. Columbia, Mo., and London, 1991.

Phoenix Nest, 1593. Edited by Hyder E. Rollins. Cambridge, Mass., 1931.

A Poetical Rhapsody, 1602–1621. Edited by Hyder E. Rollins. Cambridge, Mass., 1932.

Secondary Works

Brink, Jean R. *Michael Drayton Revisited*. Boston, 1990.

Crane, Mary Thomas. "Review Essay. Women and the Early Modern Canon: Recent Editions of Works by English Women, 1500–1660." *Renaissance Quarterly* 51 (1998): 942–956.

Fowler, Alastair. *Kinds of Literature: An Introduction to the Theory of Genres and Modes*. Cambridge, Mass., and Oxford, 1982.

Greenblatt, Stephen. *Renaissance Self-Fashioning from More to Shakespeare*. Chicago, 1980.

Hamilton, A. C. *The Structure of Allegory in the* Faerie Queene. Oxford, 1961.

Hardison, O. B. *Prosody and Purpose in the English Renaissance*. Baltimore and London, 1989.

Heninger, S. K., Jr. *Sidney and Spenser: The Poet as Maker*. University Park, Pa., and London, 1989.

Lewis, C. S. *English Literature in the Sixteenth Century Excluding Drama*. Oxford, 1954.

May, Steven W. *Bibliography and First-Line Index of English Verse, 1559–1603*. London, 2001.

Nelson, William. *The Poetry of Edmund Spenser*. New York, 1963.

Norbrook, David. *Poetry and Politics in the English Renaissance*. London and Boston, 1984.

Patterson, Annabel. *Censorship and Interpretation: The Conditions of Writing and Reading in Early Modern England*. Madison, Wis., 1984.

Perry, Curtis. *The Making of Jacobean Culture*. Cambridge, U.K., 1997.
Rees, Joan. *Samuel Daniel: A Critical and Biographical Study*. Liverpool, 1964.
Roche, Thomas. *The Kindly Flame: A Study of the Third and Fourth Books of Spenser's* Faerie Queene. Princeton, N.J., 1964.
Smith, Hallett. *Elizabethan Poetry: A Study in Conventions, Meaning, and Expression*. Cambridge, Mass., 1952.
The Spenser Encyclopedia. Edited by A. C. Hamilton et al. Toronto, 1990. Useful articles and bibliography.
Tillyard, E. M. W. *The Elizabethan World Picture*. Rev. ed. New York and London, 1956.

JEAN R. BRINK and VICTOR SKRETKOWICZ

Early Stuart and Metaphysical Poetry

When Sir Herbert Grierson published his *Metaphysical Lyrics and Poems of the Seventeenth Century* in 1921, he could not have fully anticipated the effect it would have, but in conjunction with T. S. Eliot's review in the same year, it served to lay the groundwork for a modern understanding of the poetry of this period. Grierson had already edited John Donne's poetry, with great learning, and Donne consequently plays a large part in this anthology—in both the number of poems included and the weight given to them as the truest representative of "metaphysical" poetry in English.

Critical Overview. By "metaphysical," Grierson meant something different from either John Dryden or Samuel Johnson, who preceded him in applying this term to Donne's verse. For Grierson, the term defined not only the significant presence of scholastic wit in Donne's poetry, the purpose of which Dryden had subtly derogated when he assumed that Donne had written in order to perplex "the minds of the fair sex." It also identified, more importantly, a habit of mind reflected in the verse, in which feeling and thought were viewed as inseparable. "Passionate thinking is always apt to become metaphysical," Grierson wrote, "probing and investigating the experience from which it takes its rise." Eliot shortly raised Grierson's ante by proposing that Donne's poetry belonged to a prelapsarian moment in literary history when thinking and feeling were yet to be dissociated.

Grierson's and Eliot's remarks are still worth recalling for their literary perceptions and the canonical force they gave Donne in subsequent discussions of seventeenth-century verse, and because the term "metaphysical" is sometimes thought to be synonymous with seventeenth-century poetry more generally. It is not, and Grierson, in fact, tried to suggest as much in the title of his anthology. But the lack of a single suitable umbrella term to comprehend the first sixty or so years of the seventeenth century—a period that saw the reign of two Stuart kings, civil war, regicide, a decade of Puritan rule, and, along the way, great experimentation with lyric verse especially—has occasionally meant that a distinguishing feature of some of the poetry has, as a matter of convenience, been asked to stand for the whole.

When modern critics speak of a "metaphysical" strain in seventeeth-century verse, they usually have the following in mind: the Italian origins of its "conceited" language ("conceit" deriving from the Italian "*concetto*" for "concept"); the conspicuous role allotted to shocking metaphors that violently yoke together the most heterogeneous ideas, as Johnson observed; the speaker's frequently hyperbolic or dramatic mode of address; the attention given to terse argumentation throughout a poem; and the frequent choice of love as the usual subject matter, whether secular or devotional. Besides Donne, the most important poets often regarded as exhibiting at least some of these features include George Herbert (1593–1633), Richard Crashaw (1613–1649), Henry Vaughan (1621–1695), and Andrew Marvell (1621–1678). Among the many (now) lesser-read poets are Herbert's older brother Edward, Lord Herbert of Cherbury (1582–1648); the executor of Donne's estate, Henry King (1592–1669); Crashaw's Cambridge classmate and friend Abraham Cowley (1618–1667); Francis Quarles, the popular emblematist (1592–1644); John Cleveland (1613–1658); and Katherine Philips (1632–1664)—to name those whose verse can still readily be found in modern anthologies.

Donne's great contemporary and occasional critic, Ben Jonson (1572–1637), although grouped with this "race of writers" by Samuel Johnson on the basis of "the ruggedness of his lines," is more often regarded by modern scholars as forming another circle (with an overlapping membership), one whose subjects, themes, literary models, and modes of address are more decisively classical than "metaphysical." Robert Herrick (1591–1674) is the most thoroughly obliging of Jonson's many "sons" in this regard. But other poets, like Thomas Randolph (1605–1635), Edmund Waller (1606–1687), Sir John Denham (1615–1669), Richard Lovelace (1618–1657), and early Vaughan, learned much of their craft from Jonson; and still others, like the Caroline poet Thomas Carew (1595–1640) and (again) Andrew Marvell, fully assimilated the influence of both metaphysical and classical "strains" in nearly equal amounts. The greatest poet of the century, John Milton (1608–1674), does not fit comfortably into either group. Almost singlehandedly, he continues to give meaning to the notion of a Spenserian school of poetry in the early seventeenth century. Nor does either help identify traditions available to women poets of the period.

Metaphysical Impulses, Profane and Sacred. If "metaphysical" poetry often took love as its subject—a topic that Jonson deliberately rejected—it did so, however, in a manner decidedly different from that typically found in the great wave of Petrarchan sonneteering that swept through courtly circles in the last decade of the sixteenth century under Queen Elizabeth. With Donne often serving as both catalyst and model, less attention was lavished on revering the ultimately unattainable, usually female, object of address—describing the woman's many virtues, often in the octave, and then complaining, often in the sestet, of her "cruelty" for refusing to bestow her favors on her suitor—and more attention was paid to describing, sometimes impudently and graphically, the mutual experience of love, in lyrics that prized stanzaic variety and a language that combined the earthy with the esoteric. Donne's "The Good-Morrow," from his *Songs and Sonnets* (1633), is a characteristic example of this new "realism"—its abrupt beginning and indecent demeanor still allowing for a recondite joke about the cave or den in which seven Christian youths, fleeing the persecution of Decius (A.D. 249), slept for nearly two centuries:

> I wonder by my troth, what thou, and I
> Did, till we lov'd? were we not wean'd till then?
> But suck'd on countrey pleasures, childishly?
> Or snorted we in the seaven sleepers den?

This kind of familiar thinking about love—immediate, playful, and dramatic—can be found among many of Donne's followers (for example, in Cowley's *The Mistress;* 1647), as can Donne's animated concern with the connection of body and soul in this and other poems.

At the most abstract level, Donne's inquiries into the properties or elements of love helped revive a discourse of mannered Neoplatonism as found in the poems of Edward Herbert ("An Ode upon a Question Moved, Whether Love Should Continue for Ever") and, as the century progressed, among Carolines like Thomas Stanley in his 1647 *Poems* (Stanley also translated Giovanni Pico della Mirandola's *Platonick Discourse upon Love*). Likewise, many changes were rung on Donne's "A Valediction: Forbidding Mourning." Marvell's "The Definition of Love," for instance, is a late response to this Donnean habit of inquiry, while Katherine Philips's *Poems* (1664), with its many imagined partings, borrows frequently and pointedly from Donne in describing the bonds of female friendship. At a more graphic level, Donne's erotic verse, represented most commandingly in Ovidian elegies like "To His Mistress Going to Bed," helped charge sexually explicit poems like Thomas Carew's "A Rapture" as well as the casual misogyny that runs throughout John Suckling's lyrics, first published in his *Fragmenta Aurea* (1646). On a related but distinctly graver note, the witty, melancholic, and morbid Donne, the death-obsessed poet of "A Nocturnal upon St. Lucy's Day," tuned many a later poet's sense of personal grief. The following from Bishop Henry King's passionately intense "Exequy," usually thought to commemorate the death of his wife, is a celebrated example:

> Dear Losse! since thy untimely fate
> My task hath been to meditate
> On thee, on thee, thou art the book,
> The Library whereon I look,
> Though almost blind. For thee, loved clay,
> I languish out, not live, the day,
> Using no other exercise
> But what I practice with my eyes.

The most important lessons of Donne's love poetry, however, were perhaps learned not by fellow amorists but by George Herbert, England's greatest devotional lyricist. In *The Temple* (1633), Herbert mastered in a more artful and personable key the full array of Donnean effects, especially the variety of lyric forms and dramatic situations on display in *The Songs and Sonnets,* which Herbert probably read in manuscript. (Herbert's learned mother, Magdalen, was a longtime patron of Donne's.) In poems like "The British Church," Herbert gave voice to the very idea of a via media in religion, although without passing over what he elsewhere called "a picture of the many spiritual conflicts that have passed betwixt God and my soul." "The Collar," "The Forerunners," "The Flower," and "Love (III)" are among the most moving examples of this latter impulse.

Although Herbert died only two years after Donne and, as rector of Bemerton, never rose to a level of comparable importance as the dean of Saint Paul, his poetry, more than Donne's, inspired the very different devotional verse of both the Counter-Reformation sympathizer Richard Crashaw—beginning with his *Steps to the Temple* (1646) and continuing in *Carmen Deo Nostro* (1652)—and the politically rebuffed Royalist and Welsh physician,

Henry Vaughan, in his two versions of *Silex Scintillans* (1650, 1655). Primarily a poet of sacred epigrams, songs, and hymns, Crashaw is most notable for his "baroque" conceits and extravagant emotionalism, and for his celebration of the feminine, especially in the persons of the Spanish mystic St. Teresa of Avila and Mary Magdalen. "The Weeper," with its thirty-one stanzas on the penitent Mary's tears, is perhaps the most (in)famous example of Crashaw's ingenuity. But "secular" poems, like "Wishes to His Supposed Mistress" and "Music's Duel," published in his *Delights of the Muses* (1646), reveal a stylistic exuberance that looks forward to the long impassioned poems on the seraphic St. Teresa ("The Flaming Heart" and "A Hymn to the Name and Honor of the Admirable Sainte Teresa"). A frequent visitor to Little Gidding while living in nearby Cambridge, Crashaw's eventual conversion to Catholicism seems utterly unsurprising, as does perhaps his pilgrimage to Loreto, Italy, where he died shortly after arriving.

Vaughan's turn toward religion is a different matter. Sudden and decisive, it is not at all predictable from the preceding secular verse in *Poems* (1646) and the belatedly published *Olor Iscanus* (1651). Herbert served Crashaw as a point of departure; he offered Vaughan a source of continual renewal, so indebted are his "private ejaculations" to Herbert's. In *Silex Scintillans,* it is impossible to fully separate devotional from poetic "regeneration," the title of the first poem in the collection, even if the best results are some distance from Herbert's. Vaughan's poetry swirls and flashes with a dark sublimity and mystical longing, as exemplified in the last stanza of "The Night":

> There is in God (some say)
> A deep but dazzling darkness, as men here
> Say it is late and dusky, because they
> See not all clear.
> Oh for that night, where I in him
> Might live invisible and dim!

The metaphysical in Vaughan arises from a keen sense of his still inhabiting a universe of occult sympathies, of which Herbert remains one of the points of attraction, and nature, as a manifestation of God's presence, another.

Although initially confused with Vaughan's poetry when discovered early in the twentieth century, the verse of Thomas Traherne (1637–1674) is almost exclusively preoccupied with the wonder of childhood felicity and is better read as a visionary anticipation of Blake than an artful extension of Herbert.

Jonsonian Attitudes and Followers. Meditative, often private in its point of view, metaphysical poetry has been readily received by modern readers for its attention to the personal "I." Poetry indebted to Jonson showed a more social, although not fully public, face. Self-presentation in the form of verse epistles to friends predominates, as does an interest in formal symmetries and the couplet, and in the notion that the poet should perform a variety of ethical, social, and moral purposes: eulogizing the dead, instructing the living, commemorating places and events, praising pleasure in moderation. With the pages of Horace and Martial open, Jonson did all of these things with great authority, as spelled out especially in his 1616 *Works* and the two influential, classically inspired collections of verse it contained, *The Epigrams* and *The Forest*—the latter including the celebrated "country-house" poem "To Penshurst" and his elegant adaptations into English tetrameter verse of Catullus's "Vivamus mea Lesbia" (Let us live, my Lesbia). Those who came after him refined and, in some cases, improved on their predecessor.

The versatile, courtly Thomas Carew, without forsaking Donne, managed both the "song" and the verse epistle with a sophisticated polish befitting someone who had spent time in Italy in the company of Sir Dudley Carleton, the English ambassador to Venice, and Thomas Howard, the second earl of Arundel and England's first great art collector. Carew's own epistle to Jonson, correcting "deare *Ben*" for his bad behavior, shows an acute critical intelligence at work, as does his great elegy to Donne; and his two "country-house" poems reveal a characteristically decorous adjustment to the different circumstances of his patrons, a practice found elsewhere in this most representatively Caroline collection of verse. In his epistle to Aurelian Townsend, with its stated courtly preference for "lyric feet" over heroic verse, Carew gives an insider's view of the "halcyon days" under Charles I that is belied only by a subsequent turbulent history that Carew did not live to see. His *Poems* appeared posthumously in 1640.

Among "Cavalier" poets, Robert Herrick in *Hesperides* (1648) best caught the spirit of festivity in Jonson: not the grave tones as revealed in Jonson's "Inviting a Friend to Supper," but a whimsy suitable to the mock heroics of a thirsty Falstaff reluctantly swearing off, then fully embracing, drink in "His Farewell to Sack" and "The Welcome to Sack." Although a writer of odes, epithalamia (poems celebrating a marriage), and verse epistles, too—on that most popular of Horatian themes, country retirement—Herrick was a lyricist at heart. He took a sweet delight in small forms (songs, ballads, epitaphs) and in thinking titillating thoughts about women, as in his famous *carpe diem* poem "To the Virgins, to Make Much of Time," or in the incitingly loose tercets that make up his celebrated lyric "Upon Julia's Clothes":

> Whenas in silks my Julia goes,
> Then, then methinks, how sweetly flows
> That liquefaction of her clothes.
>
> Next, when I cast mine eyes and see
> That brave vibration each way free,
> Oh, how that glittering taketh me!

A bachelor clergyman from London, Herrick landed in Devon, where in "Discontents in Devon" he speaks of his "discontents" there as also having led to the making of much verse. With the publication of the smaller *Noble Numbers* (1648), dedicated to religious subjects, Herrick's lyric output grew to a hefty 1,400 poems.

As England entered into civil war in the early 1640s, the note of Royalist resolve among Jonson's "sons" came increasingly to the fore. Herrick's "Delight in Disorder" winsomely pursues an anti-precisian (or anti-Puritan) bias, and other poems announce in journalistic fashion their support for the king. But it is with Richard Lovelace that loyalism and lyricism intertwine and resonate most fully. Songs like "To Althea from Prison," written while Lovelace was imprisoned in the Gatehouse for his part in the Kentish petition in support of the king just prior to the outbreak of civil war, formed a Royalist cri de coeur expressed more fully in the "Epodes" and "Odes" of *Lucasta* (1649). (More poems were included in the second, posthumously published volume in 1659.) For the elegant swashbuckling Lovelace—the portrait of him in the Dulwich Picture Gallery shows him in armor and sash—addressing the unidentified Althea in the high mode of transcendent love (and in now familiar lines like "Stone walls do not a prison make / Nor iron bars a cage") also allowed him to celebrate a version of "liberty" that was anathema to Puritans, as in the opening stanza:

> When Love with unconfined wings
>   Hovers within my gates,
> And my divine Althea brings
>   To whisper at the grates;
> When I lie tangled in her hair
>   And fettered to her eye,
> The gods that wanton in the air
>   Know no such liberty.

Milton would call this not "liberty" but libertinism. The note of unswerving political loyalty sounded in the third stanza of this song also looks forward to Lovelace's most memorable poem, the mythologically and tonally rich "Grasshopper" ode, which Lovelace addressed to his friend Charles Cotton, father of the poet Charles Cotton and translator of Michel de Montaigne. Where other Lovelace poems can falter, sometimes grammatically, this one is struck with full confidence from the outset:

> Oh thou that swing'st upon the waving haire
> Of some well-filled Oaten Beard,
> Drunke ev'ry night with a Delicious teare,
> Dropt thee from Heaven, where now th'art reared.

Based on the Aesopian fable of the improvident insect, Lovelace's ode reflects many of the Horatian themes associated with Cavalier ideas of retreat amid the "winter" of civil war, including resisting, in its pointed festivity, Puritan hostility toward the notion of Christmas itself. The warm comfort found in loyal friendships is inseparable from loyalty to the crown itself and the warm celebrations they inspire when "Dropping December shall come weeping in."

Lovelace is the more interesting for being slightly ahead of his time in his knowledge of the visual arts. No doubt furthered while in exile in Holland in the 1640s, it is best glimpsed in his poem to Peter Lely, subtitled "On that Excellent Picture of His Majesty, and the Duke of York, Drawn by Him at Hampton Court." (After Sir Anthony Van Dyck, Lely was the most important painter associated with the English court.) The Royalist perspective underscored in this poem is taken in an altogether different direction by Sir John Denham in "Cooper's Hill," first published while Lovelace was languishing in the Gatehouse. Along with Marvell's "Upon Appleton House," "Cooper's Hill" is the most important topographical poem of the midcentury, in part for its significant redeployment of the Jonsonian couplet, now in the service of a more consciously political aesthetic, and in part for its infusion of English history into the imagined landscape and the subtle and not-so-subtle coding that emerges. Its most celebrated lines, addressed to the river Thames, have often been read as anticipating the sharp parallels and antitheses associated with the Augustan poetics of Dryden and Alexander Pope:

> O could I flow like thee, and make thy stream
> My great example, as it is my theme!
> Though deep, yet clear, though gentle, yet not dull,
> Strong without rage, without ore-flowing full.

And though these lines include an argument for moderation, the view from "Cooper's Hill" is resolutely Royalist throughout.

One last distant Jonsonian needs mentioning, mainly because he was reputed to have provided the proverbial sweetness to the Jonsonian couplet that Denham had supposedly strengthened. Few poets have been treated with greater indifference in this century than Edmund Waller; but in his day his *Poems* (1645) easily outsold Milton's collection of lyrics brought out in the same year by the same publisher, Humphrey Mosely, and for a short while the well-heeled Waller was regarded as a model of genteel writing. Panegyric came easily to him, regardless of the subject, but his two "Penshurst" poems compare poorly with Jonson's. For the most part, his poetry remains interesting for the opportunity it provided others with improvement, an activity in which Marvell took special delight in his "Last Instructions to a Painter." Waller's song "Go Lovely Rose" is deservedly his most anthologized poem.

Spenserian and Women Poets. In its brevity, seventeenth-century lyric poetry remains readily accessible, whether in printed form or, as in the case of Herbert especially, through ongoing musical adaptations and church hymnals. Even Jonson's "Drink to me only with thine eyes" still makes the rounds. But with the exception of Milton, writers of the long poem in the seventeenth century have remained largely the preserve of specialists. Often loosely referred to as "Spenserians," in deference to Edmund Spenser's vast legacy as a *vates* (seer), the long-lived Michael Drayton (1563–1631) is probably the best known of this group. But even Drayton's hard-won fame derives in part from his work with the sonnet ("Since there's no help, come let us kiss and part" is perhaps the best known) as well as from his massive (and rarely read) *Poly-Olbion* (1612, 1622), a shire-by-shire "chorographical" description of England and Wales, written in durable hexameter verse. An early experimenter with the ode, among many other kinds of verse, Drayton gave his poetry a strong nostalgic and patriotic flavor (perhaps best sampled in his ode "To the Virginian Voyage" and "Ballad of Agincourt"). As he identified more with the country than the court, he helped keep alive a version of pastoral in the early seventeenth century that Milton returned to in his description of Sabrina in *A Mask*.

After Drayton, William Browne (1590/01?–1643/45?), George Wither (1588–1667), Phineas (1582–1650) and Giles (1585/86–1623) Fletcher, and Henry More (1614–1687) all drew on Spenser's examples in different ways. Browne and Wither, close acquaintances of Drayton's, furthered the strain of Spenserian pastoral in the early seventeenth century. In *Britannia's Pastorals* (1613–1616), the patriotic Browne, writing from the Inner Temple in London but hailing from Devon, celebrated the local English countryside in an often pleasing mixture of pastoral genres that ranged from contemporary satire (and allegory) to heroic romance, passing through a georgic appreciation for nature, and composed in fluent pentameter couplets frequently interspersed with pastoral lyrics and quick octosyllabics that anticipate Milton's "L'Allegro." Browne's fellow collaborator in *The Shepheard's Pipe* (1616), the popular George Wither, with his "free-born" muse drew on pastoral early in his exceptionally long, frequently harried career. In *The Shepheards Hunting* (1615), Wither exploited the eclogue's association with veiled political criticism (used by both Spenser and Drayton) to protest the first of his several imprisonments in Marshalsea Prison.

Although Wither went on to write many other kinds of poems—hymns, emblem poems, jeremiads—he would occasionally return to a distantly vatic impersonation of the inspired poet. But it belonged to Phineas and Giles Fletcher to amplify, in light of the xenophobia ignited by the Gunpowder Plot (1605), the apocalyptic and Protestant elements in Spenser. Phineas emphasized the apocalyptic in the five-cantos' worth of modified Spenserian stanzas that form *The Locusts, or Apollyonists* (1627; the title alludes to Revelation 9 when the angel of the abyss is loosed upon the wicked), and Giles celebrated the Protestant cause in his lengthy, heroic song, *Christ's Victory and Triumph* (1610), with its prefatory nod toward Spenser as a model for divine hymns. In spite of their bombastic sentiments, the Fletchers form an important thematic and ideological link to Milton, most evident in "On the Morning of Christ's Nativity" and *Paradise Regained*. The Spenserian (and Lucretian) tradition of using poetry for purposes of philosophical speculation, intermittently present in the Fletchers, continues not only in *Paradise Lost* but in the writings of Milton's Cambridge contemporary, the Neoplatonist Henry More. More's 1647 antimaterialist championing of the preexistence of the soul, in the work with that title, is set forth in 104 Spenserian stanzas.

The most adept pastoral lyricist of the century, Andrew Marvell is probably best described as a Spenserian by generic association, not by temperament. In his many pastoral poems, including the four "mower poems," as well as "A Nymph Complaining for the Death of Her Faun," "The Garden," and "Upon Appleton House," Marvell's concentrated emphasis falls on the psychological, the playful, or the portentous rather than the spaciously prophetic or allegorical associations of the genre. Marvell was also too much of a classicist in verse for his speakers to sound rustical, however naive they might be. Given his subtle mind, it is probably right that his most audible Spenserian reminiscence is the syntactically complicated alexandrine that uncoils at the end of each stanza of "The Mower's Song," to remind us of the speaker's ensnared heart.

A century that witnessed so much versifying—in print, at court, among the elite, for God and the godly—also saw the cautious beginnings of individually female-authored collections of poetry. Sidney's niece, Mary Wroth (1587?–1651?), praised by Jonson among others for her courtly accomplishments, continued her uncle's Petrarchan legacy especially, but from the point of view of a female speaker in the extended sonnet sequence *Pamphilia to Amphilanthus*. Appended to her massive prose romance, *The Countess of Montgomery's Urania* (1621), the sonnets are the first of this kind to be published by a woman in England. Wroth's Jacobean contemporary, Aemelia Lanyer (1569–1645), took the tradition of the "complaint," popular under Elizabeth among male poets (including Drayton), in a protofeminist direction in *Salve Deus Rex Judaeorum* (1611), especially in the section glossed as "Eve's Apology," near the middle of this 1,840-line poem, written in ottava rima. Prompted by a desire for patronage, Lanyer's sole publication is directed to a number of powerful women in Jacobean England, identified by name in the many accompanying commendatory poems. Her "Description of Cooke-ham" laments an idyllic time Lanyer spent in the company of Anne Clifford; as an early example of the "estate" poem in English it has been often compared with Jonson's "Penshurst." And finally, recently discovered poems in manuscript, like Martha Moulsworth's undated "Memorandum," and rarely read volumes like An Collins's *Divine Songs and Meditacions* (1653) are beginning to participate in the more general revival of interest in women authors of the period, especially as affecting those slightly later in the century: the already mentioned Katherine Philips, Margaret Cavendish (1623–1673; her *Poems and Fancies* were published in 1653), and Aphra Behn (1640–1689) England's first professional woman author.

BIBLIOGRAPHY

Primary Works

Baker, Herschel, ed. *The Later Renaissance in England: Nondramatic Verse and Prose, 1600–1660*. Boston, 1975.

Greer, Germaine, et al., eds. *Kissing the Rod: An Anthology of Seventeenth-Century Women's Verse*. London, 1988.

Grierson, John Clifford, ed. *Metaphysical Lyrics and Poems of the Seventeenth Century*. New York, 1959.

Hunter, William B., Jr., ed. *The English Spenserians: The Poetry of Giles Fletcher, George Wither, Michael Drayton, Phineas Fletcher, and Henry More*. Salt Lake City, Utah, 1977.

Kenner, Hugh, ed. *Seventeenth Century Poetry: The Schools of Donne and Jonson*. New York, 1964.

Norbrook, David, and H. R. Woudhuysen, eds. *The Penguin Book of Renaissance Verse: 1509–1659*. London, 1992.

Roberts, Josephine A., ed. *The Poems of Lady Mary Wroth*. Baton Rouge, La., 1983.

Woods, Susanne, ed. *The Poems of Aemilia Lanyer: Salve Deus Rex Judaeorum*. New York, 1993.

Secondary Works

Bush, Douglas. *English Literature in the Earlier Seventeenth Century*. 2d ed. Oxford, 1962.

Corns, Thomas N., ed. *The Cambridge Companion to English Poetry: Donne to Marvell*. Cambridge, U.K., 1993.

Eliot, T. S. "The Metaphysical Poets." In *Selected Essays of T. S. Eliot*. New York, 1964. Pages 241–250.

Grundy, Joan. *The Spenserian Poets*. London, 1969.

Johnson, Samuel. "Life of Cowley." In *Lives of the English Poets*. Edited by George Birkbeck Hill. 3 vols. Oxford, 1905. Pages 1–69.

Lewalski, Barbara Kiefer. *Protestant Poetics and the Seventeenth-Century Religious Lyric*. Princeton, N.J., 1979.

Martz, Louis L. *The Poetry of Meditation*. Rev. ed. New Haven, Conn., 1962.

Miner, Earl. *The Cavalier Mode from Jonson to Cotton*. Princeton, N.J., 1971.

Post, Jonathan F. S. *English Lyric Poetry: The Early Seventeenth Century*. London, 1999.

Smith, Nigel. *Literature and Revolution in England, 1640–1660*. New Haven, Conn., 1994.

Summers, Joseph H. *The Heirs of Donne and Jonson*. New York, 1970.

JONATHAN F. S. POST

POETRY AND MUSIC.

> Blest pair of sirens, pledges of heaven's joy,
> Sphere-borne harmonious sisters, Voice, and Verse,
> Wed your divine sounds, and mixed power employ.

In "At a Solemn Music" (1633), Milton entwines within twenty-eight lines almost all the strands that composed the ideal view of the relationship between poetry and music in the Renaissance. His picture of the sister arts as an image and enactment of cosmic harmony draws on the classical notion that the mathematical proportions of the universe were reflected in the proportions of music and of poetry; more specifically, he alludes to the neo-Pythagorean belief that the spheres of the heavens themselves made a celestial music that human music dimly echoed, but which, in our fallen condition, we can no longer hear (a notion given memorable expression by Shakespeare in the dialogue of Lorenzo and Jessica in *The*

Merchant of Venice, 5.1). At the same time the poem invokes the Judeo-Christian tradition of God's creation of the universe by "number, weight and measure" and also recalls the mythic figure of Orpheus, whose power as a singer not only charmed Pluto in Hades but was capable of giving life to "dead things" by making rocks, stones, and trees move to his music. (Orpheus was but the most frequently invoked of such figures—Milton might equally have alluded to Amphion, whose music caused stones to build the walls of Thebes, or to the biblical king David, held to be the composer of the Psalms.)

Theories and Debates. The ideas and allusions compressed in Milton's masterly poem are an expression of beliefs and attitudes that had, in various forms, been continuously deployed from classical times until the Renaissance, providing a repertoire of images and allusions that could be invoked readily in drama and in poetry both religious and secular. These notions also had a significant effect upon the ways in which writers and composers discussed their art and approached the practical task of producing musical works. In particular, the Renaissance focused on the possibility of recovering the potent effects of music upon the minds and emotions of the listener that were seen as deriving specifically from the close union of poetry and music in classical Greece. Precisely what the nature of that union had been, and what modern equivalent might be devised, however, was a matter of debate.

The French academies of the late sixteenth century explored the possibilities of uniting a verse scanned quantitatively, after the classical manner, with a musical notation that exactly reproduced the pattern of long and short syllables—experiments known as *musique mesurée.* The austere practice of such neoclassical theories by the members of Jean-Antoine de Bäif's Academie de Poésie et Musique (founded 1570) was short-lived and limited in its effect on other writers and composers (though Thomas Campion in England was clearly influenced by them and produced, in his song "Come Let Us Sound," a thoroughgoing attempt to match a poem in classical quantitative meter which celebrated God as "Author of Number" to a musical setting which reproduced exactly its metrical shape). Perhaps the most important product of such thinking in France was the *Ballet comique de la reine* (1581), a work whose fusion of spectacle, music, words, and dance in a device that claimed not merely to entertain but to educate resonated throughout the history of the court masque in England. Campion in *The Lord's Masque* of 1613 presented Entheus, or poetic fury, united with Orpheus as able to charm and tame disordered passions; Ben Jonson, in *Pleasure Reconciled to Virtue* (1618), claimed that dance "maketh the beholder wise" by its measured and "numerous" patterns.

In Italy, too, humanist musical theorists looked back to the Platonic and Pythagorean formulations and sought to recover the moral effectiveness that music and words seemed once to have achieved. Of particular relevance to the consideration of the relationship of poetry and music was the contest between the polyphonic settings of verse in the madrigal, where composers attempted to represent the words through a wide range of expressive devices, including ingenious "word painting," and the move toward monody and recitative, which, in Claudio Monteverdi's formulation, "considers harmony not commanding but commanded, and makes the words the mistress of the harmony." The address to the reader that prefaced Thomas Campion's *Booke of Ayres* (1601) echoes something of this debate in its ridicule of music "where the nature of everie word is precisely exprest in the Note" and preference for that which graces "no word, but that which is eminent, and emphaticall." Across Europe, then, Renaissance theorists and practitioners debated the nature of the relationship between poetry and music, justifying their experiments by appeals to a rich repertory of belief and symbol derived from classical and biblical sources, even though by the end of the period the focus on the rhetorical expressiveness of music had itself largely emptied the old images of the music of the spheres of anything but figurative significance.

Music and Poetic Practice. When Philip Sidney, in his *Defence of Poesy,* characterized the poet as one who "cometh to you with words set in delightful proportion," either accompanied with, or prepared for, the well enchanting skill of music," he was not describing the universal practice of the poets of his time. When Thomas Wyatt tells his hard-hearted mistress to "blame not my lute," or John Donne wryly sees himself as a "triple fool" when his poem is set to music, they are using the notion of a musical destination for their lyric verse as a conceit, not as a statement of fact. Nonetheless it was true that poets of different kinds did write words for musical settings, and it remains a significant possibility that in the evolution of poetic form, metrical flexibility, and expressive ambition in lyric poetry of the

Renaissance, an awareness of or sensitivity to music may have played a part.

Discussion of the nature of the mutual relationship between music and poetry is fraught with theoretical problems and difficulties. But, to simplify considerably, it is possible to move along a line that begins with poetry written to fit already existing music, through poetry explicitly written with the intention of finding a musical setting, to poetry that may in some more or less metaphorical sense be seen as "like" music or be influenced by it.

The provision of words to existing tunes has a continuous history throughout the sixteenth century and beyond—whether it is the popular balladeer writing to fit a well-known tune, or King Henry VIII taking over the song "De mon triste desplaisir" and giving it the words "Pastime with good company," or an anonymous poet (perhaps the composer himself) supplying the words "Flow My Tears" to fit John Dowland's "Lacrimae" pavane. It can be argued that the translation of madrigal texts, of which the publication of *Musica Transalpina* (1588) and *Italian Madrigals Englished* (1590; with words by the minor poet Thomas Watson) was a manifestation, provided one channel through which varied and irregular poetic structures derived from Italian verse forms made their way into England. Frank Fabry, for example, suggested that Sidney's five poems written to existing Italian tunes generated lyrics which saw "the introduction of trochaics into English poetics, and the reappearance of feminine rhymes."

Writers fitting words to tunes face a task that is the inverse of those who compose lyrics with the explicit purpose of having them set to music. In the latter case poets must provide something that is settable within the particular musical form or idiom for which they write. So the lyrics for a madrigal, where any kind of syntactic complexity is obliterated by the polyphonic setting and frequent repetition of words, will tend to provide opportunities for vivid illustration and mimetic effects, generally in a single stanza. Madrigal verse rarely attempts much complexity of thought or feeling. A great madrigal, like John Wilbye's "Draw on Sweet Night" (1609), can be made out of a neatly turned but commonplace lyric; in reading through Edmund Fellowes's *English Madrigal Verse* one finds a comprehensive repertory of stock themes and images, a good deal of stanzaic variation and metrical dexterity, allied on occasion to an epigrammatic neatness, but few poems that aspire much higher.

Much the same could, indeed, be said of many of the longer stanzaic lyrics set for solo voice and lute. But Thomas Campion (1567–1620), who set his own poems to music, provides a convenient test case for an exploration of some of the ways in which writing for music might pose particular challenges and consequently prompt solutions productive on a wider scale. Perhaps the most obvious constraint upon the poet is the need to provide a lyric in which each stanza may be fitted to the same tune. In order for this to be possible there must be an exact replication not only of rhythm but also of phrasing and patterning of feeling. Campion's preference for largely syllabic setting of his words and his avoidance of detailed word-painting made the task easier. His musical style itself was perhaps dictated by his awareness of the poetic problems in composing stanzaic lyrics. The technical challenge is one which Campion effortlessly surmounted and, in his very best lyrics, turned to powerful effect. "My sweetest Lesbia," for example, transforms Catullus's famous "Vivamus mea Lesbia" into a three-stanza lyric in which successive meditations upon love and mortality, bound together by the return to the words "ever-during night" (the only words repeated in the musical setting), build to a triumph of love over time.

The sureness of Campion's metrical ear, the variation of stanza forms that he employed, and the delicate play of phrase length within and across the line might all be attributed, at least in part, to the productive potential of his practical mastery of both arts, as well as to his theoretical belief in their correspondence, which informed his treatise on quantitative meter, *Observations in the Art of English Poesie* (1602). It is interesting however, that Campion's most elaborate experiments in stanzaic form are to be found in his lyrics for the *Songs of Mourning* (1613), which were set to music by his friend John Coprario. The song addressed to James I's daughter Elizabeth, "So Parted You," is an exquisite poem, whose variation of phrase and line length and delicate patterns of alliteration might justly be thought of as an epitome of "musical" verse writing. Yet Coprario's setting, using a declamatory style owing something to Italian experiment, though it fits the first stanza closely, copes much less successfully with the second. Paradoxically, musical settings that most assiduously devote themselves to an expressive ideal of verbal representation can least cope with the formal repetitions of stanza form, just as the words supplied exactly to match Dowland's "Lacrimae" make a very oddly patterned lyric when read apart from the music. Though Dowland's music reaches an emotional intensity to which Campion can rarely aspire, it frequently poses for the singer problems in accommodating second and subsequent stanzas that Campion rigorously avoids.

As Renaissance turns into baroque, the recitative initiated by the Florentine Camerata, and by Monteverdi and his successors, devoted to subordinating music to words, is actually capable of setting anything—prose or verse—and so is much less capable of suggesting forms and rhythmic shapes that a poet can use. Hence, when considering the poetry, for example, of George Herbert or of Donne, it is impossible to say with confidence that it derived this or that inspiration from music. But it is difficult not to believe that Herbert's fondness for music, attested in "Church-music" and in the complex musical imagery he deploys in poems such as "Easter," did not contribute to the metrical variety and rhythmic sensitivity pervasive throughout his work. Similarly, Northrop Frye argued in *Anatomy of Criticism* that Donne's broken rhythms, complex phrases, and irregular stanza forms are properly to be called "musical," even if his poems had to wait for the development of the declamatory style to find successful settings. But in both cases we are in the realm of analogy. Without imagining their task as preparing words for musical setting, these poets were able to draw on a repertoire of poetic forms whose variety had been much increased through the humanist exploration of the relationship between the two arts.

In this brief entry many issues have necessarily been ignored: the domestic production of much of the surviving repertoire of English secular music of the period; the songs written for dramatic performance in plays and in masques; and perhaps most important of all, the ambiguous and divided attitudes to music and words in Christian worship that underlay both the Puritan expulsion of everything but metrical psalms from church services and the Catholic reformation of ecclesiastical music after the Council of Trent (1545–1563). This was but one symptom of a pervasive anxiety throughout the period about the dangers of music's power to appeal to the emotions, unless that power is contained and directed by words. But suffice it to say that the Renaissance exploration of the relationship between word and music, driven by the imagined ideal that Milton articulated, produced, in the motets of William Byrd and Giovanni Pierluigi da Palestrina, the madrigals of Luca Marenzio and Wilbye, the songs of Campion and Dowland, and the operas of Monteverdi, a rarely balanced fusion of voice and verse that may have contributed significantly to the education of the ear of poets as they developed an increasingly varied and subtle music in their poetry.

See also biographies of figures mentioned in this entry.

BIBLIOGRAPHY

Primary Works

Fellowes, Edmund, ed. *English Madrigal Verse*. 3d ed. Revised by Frederick W. Sternfeld and David Greer. Oxford, 1967. For the lute airs a more thoroughly annotated text is Edward Doughtie, ed, *Lyrics from English Airs, 1597–1622* (Cambridge, Mass., 1970).

Strunk, Oliver, ed. *Source Readings in Music History*. Rev. ed. 7 vols. New York, 1998. An invaluable collection of writings about music. See vol. 3, *The Renaissance,* and vol. 4, *The Baroque*.

Secondary Works

Caldwell, John, Edward Olleson, and Susan Wollenberg, eds. *The Well-Enchanting Skill: Music, Poetry, and Drama in the Culture of the Renaissance*. Oxford, 1990. Wide-ranging collection of essays.

Carter, Tim. *Music in Late Renaissance and Early Baroque Italy*. London, 1992. Discusses both sacred and secular music.

Cazeaux, Isabelle. *French Music in the Fifteenth and Sixteenth Centuries*. Oxford, 1975. Useful account of the French musical scene.

Doughtie, Edward, *English Renaissance Song*. Boston, 1986. Lucid and clear account of both madrigal and lute song.

Finney, Gretchen Ludke. *Musical Backgrounds for English Literature, 1580–1650*. New Brunswick, N.J., 1962. A good survey, strongest on Milton.

Heninger, S. K., Jr. *Touches of Sweet Harmony: Pythagorean Cosmology and Renaissance Poetics*. San Marino, Calif., 1974. Detailed exploration of philosophical backgrounds.

Hollander, John. *The Untuning of the Sky: Ideas of Music in English Poetry, 1500–1700*. Princeton, N.J., 1961. Still the best account of the theories of poetry and music in England.

Lindley, David. *Thomas Campion*. Leiden, Netherlands, 1986. The most comprehensive study of the poet-musician.

McColley, Diane Kelsey. *Poetry and Music in Seventeenth-Century England*. Cambridge, U.K., 1997. Detailed studies of Donne, Herbert, and Milton.

Sternfeld, F. W. *The Birth of Opera*. Oxford, 1993.

Stevens, John E. *Music and Poetry in the Early Tudor Court*. London, 1961. Excellent pioneering study of the social nature of the arts.

Tomlinson, Gary. *Monteverdi and the End of the Renaissance*. Oxford, 1987. Discusses the poets set by Monteverdi in his madrigals.

Walker, D. P. *Studies in Musical Science in the Late Renaissance*. London, 1978. Authoritative account of the philosophical and speculative theories of the period.

Winn, James Anderson. *Unsuspected Eloquence: A History of the Relations between Poetry and Music*. New Haven, Conn., 1981. Perhaps the most wide-ranging and ambitious study of musico-poetic relationships.

Yates, Frances. *The French Academies of the Sixteenth Century*. London, 1947. Thorough exploration of musical humanism in France.

DAVID LINDLEY

POGGIO BRACCIOLINI. *See* **Bracciolini, Poggio.**

POLAND. At the end of the fifteenth century, the kingdom of Poland, ruled by the Jagiellon dynasty and linked with the Grand Duchy of Lithuania by means of a personal union (1385, 1413), occupied an area of about 1,140,000 square kilometers, stretching from the Baltic to the Black Sea. In the course of the sixteenth century, it lost control over Moldavia and the Principality of Siewierz, while gaining wider access to the Baltic in Livonia (about 990,000 square kilometers in 1634). During the same time, the population grew from about 7 million to approximately 11 million. The battle of Mohács (1526), which resulted in a victory for the invading Turks, destroyed Jagiellonian plans for a consolidation of their rule in Bohemia and Hungary, which in that year passed into the hands of the future Holy Roman Emperor Ferdinand I. The advance of the Turks made access to the Black Sea difficult, but commercial relations nevertheless flourished. It was therefore essential to maintain a peaceful relationship with Turkey between 1533 and 1620.

Political Developments. The secularization of the Teutonic Order led to the transformation of its lands into a feudal duchy in 1525. In 1569 Poland and Lithuania became a commonwealth (Union of Lublin), sharing a common ruler, *sejm* (parliament), and foreign policy. Equal rights granted to the nobility of the two countries did not wipe out the identity of Lithuania and Rus', which retained languages, religions, and customs. Apart from Lithuanians and Ruthenians, Poland was also home to other large ethnic groups: Germans, Jews, Armenians, and Tatars.

Up to the death of Sigismund II August (ruled 1548–1572) and the extinction of the Jagiellon line, monarchs were elected from among the descendants of the Jagiellon dynasty. After 1573 the practice of free elections by the assembly of *szlachta* (nobles) became customary. However, prolonged interregnums did not undermine the stability of the state. The nobles elected Henry of Anjou in 1573, binding him to respect their rights. After his escape from Poland (to assume the French throne as Henry III), Stephen Báthory (ruled 1575–1586), prince of Transylvania, was an effective ruler who led a successful military campaign against Ivan IV of Muscovy from 1579 to 1582 and tried to establish royal authority. His successor, Sigismund III (ruled 1587–1632), who was elected king against a Habsburg candidate, was the first of three kings of the Vasa dynasty.

Under the Vasa, Poland embarked upon initiatives aimed at subjugating Muscovy, restoring Catholicism in Sweden, and guaranteeing security to southeastern lands. Despite various outcomes of battles, Poland managed to preserve the status quo thanks to spectacular victories against Sweden (Kircholm, 1605) and Muscovy (Kłuszyn, 1610). Nonetheless, it was incapable of dictating solutions and was forced to defend all its borders. This fact was connected with a concurrence of views regarding political priorities. The nobles increasingly rejected involvement in European conflicts that, in their opinion, posed the threat of reinforcing royal power.

Polish Kings during the Renaissance

Kazimierz Jagiellon (1447–1492)
Jan I Olbracht Jagiellon (1492–1501)
Aleksander Jagiellon (1501–1506)
Sigismund I Jagiellon (1506–1548)
Sigismund II August Jagiellon (1548–1572)
Henryk Valois (1573–1574)
Stefan Batory (1575–1586)
Sigismund III Vasa (1587–1632)

Constitutional and Economic Developments. The state system can be described as a mixed monarchy with a strong republican accent. Royal rule was distinctly limited by the number of privileges granted to the nobility as a whole, and from 1493 to the Chamber of Deputies, representing that estate in Parliament. The nobility, which in Poland totaled 8 percent of the whole population, ensured for itself not only a privileged economic position, but also a public legal status, expressed by such laws as "neminem captivabimus nisi iure victum" (We shall not keep anyone captive unless justly defeated; 1423) and "nihil novi constitui debeat per nos sine communi consensu conciliariorum et nuntiorum terrestrium" (No innovations may be introduced without the consent of the deputies; 1505). During the first half of the sixteenth century, a dominating role was played by the owners of great landed estates and high-ranking church and secular dignitaries, represented in the Senate. The second half of that century witnessed the growing significance of the Chamber of Deputies, which made decisions about taxation. Under the principle of "executio iurium" (execution of the laws)—a program promulgated since 1520—the nobility endeavored to guarantee its domination in the state. The restoration of the prevalence of the magnates at the end of the sixteenth century endowed the Polish system with the features of an oligarchy.

A specific trait of the commonwealth was opposition to centralism, expressed in the restriction of the executive power by the representation of the estates and the absence of a foundation for the emergence of absolutism. At the same time, the nobility experienced a more and more strongly embedded feeling of freedom and an awareness of the supremacy of law over authority; it also increasingly practiced civic obligations and chivalric virtues. These tendencies, dating back to the Middle Ages, became more marked under the influence of Renaissance trends and gave rise to the Polish school of human rights and tolerance.

The economy was based on grain agriculture, which provided constantly growing supplies of commodities for export to western Europe. An essential role was also played by forestry, which provided timber for shipbuilding, and animal husbandry, particularly oxen. Poland was located at the crossroads of east-west routes linking Atlantic Europe with central Asia via the Baltic and the Black Seas and north-south routes linking Muscovy to southern Europe. The greatest profits were enjoyed by owners of large and medium landed estates, lesser ones by smaller urban centers and merchants, and almost none by the state. An insufficient population stimulated the expansion of the *corvée* (compulsory labor) performed by the peasants in the demesnes, and consequently reinforced serfdom. Despite the low productivity of land cultivation and weakly developed domestic exchange, the country was prosperous and did not suffer from famine. Low prices of foodstuffs contrasted with the rising costs of imported industrial and luxury articles. This state of affairs benefited small urban centers, which satisfied the overall consumption needs of the gentry.

Intellectual and Cultural Developments. The University of Cracow, founded in 1364, was the intellectual center of Poland. It produced numerous outstanding scholars: jurists who defended the principle of converting pagans to Christianity without the application of force (Paweł Włodkowic, 1415); a mathematical school led by Wojciech of Brudzewo; and an astronomical school led by Nicolaus Copernicus (1473–1543). At the end of the fifteenth and the beginning of the sixteenth century, Cracow became an important center of philological (Stanisław Warszewicki), historical (Jan Długosz, Marcin Kromer, Marcin Bielski) and geographical (Jan of Głogów, Bernard Wapowski, Maciej of Miechów) studies. *Tractatus de duabus Sarmatiis, Asiana et Europiana* (A tractate concerning two Sarmatias, Asian and European), published by Maciej of Miechów in 1517, provided the basis for modern knowledge about eastern Europe.

At the end of the fifteenth century, the Cracow Academy enjoyed well-deserved acclaim connected with the development of schools that trained ever better educated graduates for state service and involvement in civic affairs. The Reformation brought a further flourishing of the school network. The most outstanding schools included the Polish Brethren academy in Raków; Lutheran gymnasiums in Elblag, Gdańsk, and Toruń; the Calvinist gymnasium in Pińczów; and the Bohemian Brethren gymnasium in Leszno. The mid-sixteenth century witnessed the growth of Jesuit schools patterned on Italian and Spanish models. The newly founded academies included Lubrański College in Poznań (1519), the Jesuit school in Vilnius (1578), and the magnate school in Zamość (1594). The schools flourished against the background of religious disputes and competed as regards the level of instruction; they did not become mere instruments of propaganda.

The gentry did not permit religious differences to limit the privileges of the estates. The idea of *zgoda* (agreement) required the recognition of the right to free activity and thought. This atmosphere of political and intellectual liberty gave rise to Polish tolerance. Despite the successes of the Reformation during the first half of the sixteenth century, followed by strong Catholic reform, Poland retained the principle of freedom of religious belief, which in 1573 was added to the principles of the state system. Consequently, the commonwealth was populated by Catholics, Protestants, followers of the Orthodox Church, Armenians, Jews, and Muslims, living in harmony. In 1596 a union between the Orthodox Church in the commonwealth and Rome gave rise to great social and political conflicts in the mid-seventeenth century, but in eastern Europe it created a permanent Greek Catholic Church, inseparably associated with Ukrainian national consciousness. Even at a time when the opinions voiced by the nobles expressed a decidedly critical attitude toward all adherents of other creeds, Poland remained a refuge for all persons persecuted because of their religious convictions.

Contacts with Italy, extremely vigorous in the fifteenth century, became even closer due to the large-scale presence of Polish students there, especially in Bologna and Padua. Numerous Italians left their im-

print upon the development of Polish thought, art, and architecture.

The writings of Desiderius Erasmus (1466?–1536) were given a wide reception in Poland. The outstanding Polish humanists Jan Dantyszek (Dantiscus), Jodocus Ludovicus Decius, Jan Łaski, Andrzej Krzycki, and Piotr Tomicki belonged to the European intellectual elite of the first half of the sixteenth century and their works were published in Rome, Basel, Antwerp, and other centers. Polish legal thought is represented in the sixteenth century by the renowned writers Stanisław Orzechowski and Andrzej Frycz Modrzewski. The former addressed to Sigismund II Augustus an *Instruction for the Making of a Good Ruler* (1549), in which he assserted that the king was "chosen for the benefit of the kingdom" and that the law was "the soul and mind of the kingdom." Modrzewski was the author of *Commentarium de republica emendanda libri quinque* (Five books on the reform of the commonwealth; 1551), in which he described Poland's mixed constitution as a monarchy in which kings were elected by the estates. The book had its origins in the finest classical tradition and gained a Europe-wide acclaim. Book printing, which developed in Cracow from the late fifteenth century, exerted a distinct impact not only in central-eastern Europe, but also beyond this region (for example, Stanislaus Polonus in Spain).

The legacy of the Polish Renaissance is most distinct in the domain of political thought, literature, and architecture. The many participants in political life created a market capable of absorbing a copious and many-sided literature dealing with public affairs. Moreover, members of the political establishment not only prepared themselves for a future public role, but also exchanged views in letters, pamphlets, and diaries.

Initially, the language dominating public discourse was Latin, which in the course of the sixteenth century not only held its own but even gained enhanced influence in the Lithuanian-Ruthenian regions. Polish-language creativity developed in tandem with Latin. The Polish Renaissance was bilingual, most distinctly so in the domain of political and historical writings.

In the fifteenth century Jan Długosz produced a historical work, *Historiae Polonicae* (1455–1480), that promoted the sense of the Polish realm. During the sixteenth century, historical works that contributed to the self-awareness of the Poles became part of political arguments. Such authors as Stanisław Orzechowski, Swiętosław Orzelski, Reinhold Heidenstein, and Maciej Stryjkowski created a historical synthesis based on civic education. Their vision of the world, concurrent with the Renaissance model, satisfied the needs of the nobility in the throes of a transformation into a political nation. The outstanding role in this process was played by a work by Łukasz Górnicki, a Polish counterpart to Baldassare Castiglione's *Cortegiano,* that was a major work of Polish Renaissance prose. Lively interest in history contrasted with meager involvement in the legal sciences. In the second half of the sixteenth century, Stanisław Górski created a unique collection of documents for the history of Sigismund I (ruled 1506–1548) and Sigismund II August, the era of rivalry between the Jagiellon and Habsburg dynasties for domination in central Europe. Stanisław Iłowski was the author of the first study on historical research (*De perfecto historico;* 1557). Andrzej Patrycy Nidecki collected fragments of Cicero (Venice, 1561). Libraries emerged and printing houses multiplied. The first book in Ruthenian was issued in Cracow at the end of the fifteenth century.

Polish historical vision strove to justify, via the classical tradition, claims for the creation of an eastern Europe envisaged as part of Roman civilization. This search was expressed in the rapid reception of ideas and models originating not only from Italy but also from the Netherlands. At the same time, the historical vision generated an entirely original conception, which took into consideration the specific experiences of the region, expressed in multisided pluralism that favored cultural polonization, with the retention of religious distinctness. A specific feature of the reception of classical antiquity was the considerable and continually growing supremacy of the Latin tradition over the Greek. However, across the territory of Poland the border between Catholic Slavs and Orthodox Slavs continued to exist.

Although the Latin poems by Klemens Janicki, Sebastian Klonowic, Dantyszek, Szymon Szymonowic, and Maciej Kazimierz Sarbiewski (Heratius Polonus) gained acclaim throughout Europe, poetry was a domain in which the Polish language largely ousted Latin. Poles accepted the classical tradition to such a great extent that they were capable of expressing classical contents and models in their own tongue. Following the examples of Mikołaj Rej (1505–1569), Jan Kochanowski (1530–1584), and Mikołaj Sęp Szarzyński (1550–1581), poets became representatives of original qualities precisely due to an increasingly perfect adaptation of their language to universal contents.

In public life, the Polish language was employed to an ever wider degree in the acts of the lesser assemblies and the courts. Polish translations of the Bible appeared in 1553 (Calvinist), 1572 (Arian, or nontrinitarian), and 1561 and 1599 (Catholic). Achievements in the arts were primarily architectural, as the influence of fifteenth-century Italy was transferred north of the Alps (for example, in the Sigismund Chapel at the Wawel). A city conceived as a *città ideale,* Zamość, was built, and tomb art flourished with the contributions of many foreign artists, mainly Italian.

Religious Developments. The Protestant Reformation in Poland was from its beginning a widespread phenomenon affecting all social strata, but, in contrast to the situation in the rest of Europe, it did not lead to social and political radicalism. The Polish nobility treated the Protestant Reformation as a tool but returned to the Catholic Church in large numbers during the Counter-Reformation of the second half of the sixteenth century. The Counter-Reformation was supported by the activity of such persons as Stanisław Hosius, who introduced in Poland the decrees of the Council of Trent, and Piotr Skarga, who established the Polish ethos as defenders of Catholicism.

The period of the acceptance and development of Renaissance culture in Poland was a time of great and varied activity in politics, education, intellectual pursuits, and the arts. It was a counterpart of a European expansive tendency and consolidated European civilization in the vast eastern regions. True, permanent Polish hegemony in eastern Europe did not last, but well-defined boundaries of civilization were delineated both in the east and the south. This period, later called the Golden Age, in its idealized form became an important part of the historical memory of the nation and served as a reference point in discussions about the formation of a modern state in the nineteenth and beginning of the twentieth centuries.

See also **Cracow; East Central Europe, Art in.**

BIBLIOGRAPHY

Axer, Jerzy, ed. *Tradycje antyczne w kulturze europejskiej: Perspektywa polska* (The classical tradition in European culture: Polish perspective). Warsaw, 1995.

Davies, Norman. *God's Playground: A History of Poland.* 2 vols. New York, 1982.

Fiszman, Samuel, ed. *The Polish Renaissance in Its European Context.* Bloomington and Indianapolis, Ind., 1988.

Jobert, Ambroise. *De Luther à Mohila: La Pologne dans la crise de la chrétienté, 1517–1648.* Paris, 1974.

Konopczyński, Władysław. *Dzieje Polski nowozytnej.* 2 vols. Warsaw, 1986.

Maczak, Antoni, Henryk Samsonowicz, and Peter Burke, eds. *East-Central Europe in Transition from the Fourteenth to the Seventeenth Century.* Cambridge, U.K., 1985.

Segal, Harold B. *Renaissance Culture in Poland: The Rise of Humanism, 1470–1543.* Ithaca, N.Y., 1989.

Tazbir, Janusz. *A State without Stakes: Polish Religious Toleration in the Sixteenth and Seventeenth Centuries.* New York, 1972.

Williams, George Huntston. *The Radical Reformation.* 3d ed. Kirksville, Mo., 1992.

Ziornek, Jerzy. *Renesans.* Warsaw, 1995.

JERZY AXER and JAN KIENIEWICZ

POLE, REGINALD (1500–1558), cardinal, archbishop of Canterbury. Grandson of the duke of Clarence, brother of Edward IV, Pole benefited from the rehabilitation of his family by Henry VIII, at whose expense he was humanistically educated, first at Oxford and then on the Continent at Padua and Paris. Henry expected recompense for his support and gave Pole his first assignment in 1529 in the form of a mission to secure favorable opinions on Henry's divorce from the doctors of the University of Paris. Pole succeeded. Nevertheless, he failed to capitalize on the opportunity; instead, six months later he sent Henry his own opinion opposing the divorce. In early 1532, with Henry's blessing, Pole left England for Avignon and then Padua, where he remained until the summer of 1536. During this time he underwent a religious conversion, becoming a firm proponent of justification by faith, at nearly the same moment as he made contact with Charles V, the Holy Roman Emperor and Henry's enemy.

Pole's opposition to Henry came to its first climax in the form of his *Pro ecclesiasticae unitatis defensione* (Defense of the unity of the church), known as *De unitate,* a polemical defense of Catholic unity written in 1535–1536. In July 1536, just as *De unitate* reached England, Pope Paul III summoned Pole to Rome and five months later made him a cardinal. From then until his departure from Rome in 1553, Pole was always close to the pope and a figure of importance. He immediately joined the commission that produced the *Consilium de emendanda ecclesia*

Reginald Pole. Anonymous portrait; 1556. BY COURTESY OF THE NATIONAL PORTRAIT GALLERY, LONDON

(Legal opinion on the reform of the church; 1537), which would have disassembled the papal monarchy. Shortly thereafter Pole undertook his first diplomatic assignment for Paul, an effort to enlist the emperor's support for Henry's overthrow. Like most of Pole's missions, this one and another in 1539 failed.

In 1541 Pole became legate of Viterbo and quickly gathered around him many of the surviving evangelicals in Italy, especially Marcantonio Flaminio. In 1542 and 1545 Pole served as one of the papal legates to the Council of Trent. Despite his high status, he failed to defend justification by faith at the council in 1546, just as he had failed to uphold the compromise formula on that doctrine worked out by his close friend and patron Gasparo Contarini at the Colloquy of Regensburg in 1541. During the 1540s Pole and his circle began to come under suspicion of heresy, but in the conclave of 1549–1550 Pole nonetheless missed election as pope by only one vote, largely because of his own inaction. The successful candidate, Julius III, leaned heavily on Pole and protected him to the maximum degree. In 1553, when

Mary I acceded to the throne in England, Julius and Pole flung themselves into an effort to restore England to the church. Pole was also made legate for peace between the emperor and the king of France.

Largely because of obstacles thrown up by his own stubbornness, Pole did not reach England until late 1554. In early 1556 he became archbishop of Canterbury as well as papal legate. He thus held more power over the English church than anyone since Cardinal Wolsey. Partly for reasons of time, partly for reasons of money, and partly because of his and his advisers' slowness to grasp the situation in an England that had been officially Protestant for almost twenty years, Pole's efforts at reform met with only limited success. The legatine synod he held in late 1555 and early 1556 marked the high point of his efforts, perhaps especially in its legislation establishing seminaries for the education of the clergy, a plan later taken up by the Council of Trent. Pole also took part in two high-profile cases of heresy, those of John Cheke and Thomas Cranmer. Pole persuaded Cheke to recant but had less success with Cranmer, whom he blamed for England's departure from the true faith. One of Pole's long letters to Cranmer was later published as *Epistola de sacramento eucharistiae* (Letter on the sacrament of the eucharist; 1584). However bitterly Pole may have attacked Cranmer, he was apparently not in favor of the more general policy of repression that proved to be one of Mary's biggest failures.

Pole had not much more success as papal legate for peace, despite strong support from the Crown, wrecking the Conference of Marcq (1555) by his refusal to concede anything to political realities. Shortly thereafter, both Pole's legations were revoked. His former ally and now serious enemy, Gianpietro Carafa, had become Pope Paul IV in 1555, and he pursued a political vendetta against Pole as part of his campaign to bring down Philip II, the king of Spain and husband of Queen Mary. Pole, at Mary's insistence, refused the summons to Rome, but his position in England was seriously weakened. He died in an epidemic that wiped out much of the governing class of England.

Despite his long and active career, Pole was probably happiest when writing and produced an enormous number of words, if very few formal writings. Uncomfortable taking responsibility for publication, Pole mainly wrote for very limited audiences or for himself. His most famous work, *De unitate,* Pole insisted was intended for Henry alone. His other important writings were not published during his lifetime; in addition to printed versions of no obvious authority, they also exist in multiple manuscript versions, making their interpretation exceedingly difficult. They include two dialogues on the papal office, one of them written during the conclave of Julius III; *De concilio,* his reflections on the legates' role at Trent, written in 1545 but not published until 1562; a large and almost impossibly complicated dialogue, "De reformatione ecclesiae" (On the reformation of the church), left in manuscript; a large number of letters, some of them apparently collected for an aborted publication; and his *Discorso di pace* (Discourse on peace) written to Charles V and Henry II of France in 1554. In most of these texts, Pole leans heavily on scripture to develop a new humanistic, rhetorical theology that included what must be called a charismatic view of papal primacy and the office of a good minister. Pole preferred study and one-on-one contacts to more traditional forms of action, and through his writing he hoped to persuade a number of audiences of the necessity of spirited convention.

See also biography of Richard Morison.

BIBLIOGRAPHY

Primary Works

Pole, Reginald. *De concilio. De baptismo Constantini. Reformatio Angliae ex decretis eiusdem.* Rome, 1562. Reprint, Farnborough, U.K., 1962.

Pole, Reginald. *Défense de l'unité de l'église.* Edited by Nöelle Marie Egretier. Paris, 1967. A translation of *Reginaldi Poli cardinalis Britanni ad Henricum octavum Britanniae regem, pro ecclesiasticae unitatis defensione* (Reginald Pole the British cardinal to Henry VIII, king of Britain, for the defense of the unity of the church), originally published at Rome by Antonio Blado in 1539.

Pole, Reginald. *Friedenslegation des Reginald Pole zu Kaiser Karl V. und König Heinrich II. (1553–1556).* Edited by Heinrich Lutz. Tübingen, Germany, 1981. Includes (pp. 381–403) *Discorso di pace di Mons. Reginaldo Polo Cardinale Legato a Carlo V. Imperatore et Henrico II. Re di Francia* (Discourse on peace by the legate Cardinal Reginald Pole to the emperor Charles V and Henry II, king of France; 1554).

Pole, Reginald. *Pole's Defense of the Unity of the Church.* Translated with an introduction by Joseph G. Dwyer. Westminster, Md., 1965. A translation of *Reginaldi Poli cardinalis Britanni ad Henricum octavum Britanniae regem, pro ecclesiasticae unitatis defensione,* originally published at Rome by Antonio Blado in 1539; this edition is available in a reprint (Farnborough, U.K., 1965).

Pole, Reginald. *Reformatio Angliae. The Reformation of England, by the Decrees of Cardinal Pole.* In *The Anglican Canons 1529–1947.* Translated and edited by Gerald Bray. Woodbridge, U.K., 1998. Pages 68–162. See also J. P. Marmion, "The London Synod of Reginald, Cardinal Pole, 1555–6" (M.A. thesis, Keele University, 1974, vol. 2, pp. 1–65).

Secondary Works

Fenlon, Dermot. *Heresy and Obedience in Tridentine Italy: Cardinal Pole and the Counter Reformation.* Cambridge, U.K., 1972.

Hallé, Marie (writing as Martin Haile). *Life of Reginald Pole*. London, 1911.
Schenk, Wilhelm. *Reginald Pole, Cardinal of England*. London, 1950.
Zeeveld, W. Gordon. *Foundations of Tudor Policy*. Cambridge, Mass., 1948.

THOMAS F. MAYER

POLITICAL THOUGHT. The *Decameron* has, obviously enough, no claim to a place in the history of political thinking. Yet, in its imaginative structure, Boccaccio's masterpiece provides a parable of some central issues in Renaissance political discourse. The characters have fled from the threat of plague in the city to the peace and security of the countryside; yet the tales they tell one another belong, for the most part, to the real (and plaguey) world of human relationships. It does no harm to remember that the society that produced the early Renaissance also experienced the trauma of the Black Death; but the point here is rather different.

Like the company in the *Decameron,* Renaissance humanists withdrew from society and yet were involved in it and concerned with its problems. They faced a recurrent dilemma. Did wisdom lead to detachment and retirement from the world? Or did the possession of wisdom impose the duty of placing it at the service of others—indeed, of society at large? The second alternative carried the risk of contamination and corruption; but the first might entail a breach of moral obligations—the obligation, above all, of justice. Now justice was central in the teaching of both Plato and Cicero, luminaries to whom humanists looked with particular keenness in their thinking about society. Platonic and Ciceronian guidance might, however, point in varying directions. And there were, of course, other persuasive voices resounding from the ancient world. Renaissance political thought could not and would not be monolithic.

Italian Humanism, 1350–1550.

The dilemma between *otium* (private leisure) and *negotium* (public activity) was firmly resolved in favor of *otium* by Boccaccio's friend Petrarch (1304–1374), disconcerted though he evidently was to find that Cicero, whom he so revered, had taken the opposing view. Faced with the undeniable fact of Cicero's intense political involvement Petrarch exclaimed, "How much better it would have been for a philosopher to grow old in the quiet countryside!" The tranquillity that this ideal presupposed depended, to be sure, on the maintenance of social and political order; but that, in Petrarch's view, was the responsibility of the prince. Rulers like the Carrara lords of Padua, where Petrarch spent his last years, must guarantee peace and security for their subjects by governing justly. Under firm princely authority, everyone would be able to "live his life in freedom and security." Such social order must, in this view, be at risk under any political system that failed to repress factional strife; and only princely rule could pass that test. Two or three decades later, again in Padua, Pier Paolo Vergerio (1370–1444), writing *De monarchia* (On monarchy) for the Carrara lords, argued that the rule of "a good king" was "the best form of government" and the only secure guarantee of "true liberty."

Civic humanism. Yet Vergerio reveals another aspect of humanist political thinking. Even if political power was best exercised by a prince, it might not follow that the wise course for his subjects was simply, and in all cases, to withdraw from public life. At much the same time as his work on monarchy, Vergerio assumed the character of Cicero in a letter intended to refute Petrarch's advocacy of withdrawal and solitary contemplation. As "Cicero" sees it, "the man who surpasses all others . . . is one who bestows his efforts on the government of the body politic and in working for the benefit of all." And if this kind of excellence is exemplified supremely in the prince, it may yet be shared by the scholar who, as teacher or counselor, contributes to its triumph. The copious "mirror of princes" literature, in which humanists added to what their scholastic predecessors and contemporaries had long been amassing, was to testify throughout the Renaissance to the importance of the education of rulers and the corresponding worth of those who taught them. Hence the value ascribed to such works as Vergerio's *De ingenuis moribus et liberalibus studiis* (Concerning character and liberal studies; c. 1401/02). Counsel too was a theme to which substantial scholastic attention had been devoted; and humanists, when considering princely rule, likewise had much to say of the courtiers and counselors whose influence, for better or for worse, might so largely determine the character of that rule. Humanist writing of these kinds developed extensively during the fifteenth century, and reached its apogee at the end of that century and the beginning of the next.

Long before that, however, the theme of princely government had been joined, contrapuntally, by the republican element in Renaissance political thought. Vergerio once again provides a hint; for his work on monarchy is matched by his treatise *De republica veneta* (On the Venetian republic). Writing in or about 1400, Vergerio praised Venice, with its constitutional blend of monarchy, aristocracy, and democracy, as the exceptional case of a republic achieving both greatness and stability. That view of Venice was to have a long history in Renaissance thinking and later; but it was only one factor in humanist republicanism. At least as influential was the example of Florence. It is above all in the Florentine context that we encounter the concept, much discussed and not uncontentious, of civic humanism.

Here, we may say, disciples of Cicero came fully to terms with their mentor's political commitment; and here the issue of liberty was fully joined in humanist political discourse. When, in the 1390s, Vergerio wrote of the realization of "true liberty" under monarchical rule, it is clear that he had in mind what would later be called "negative liberty"—the freedom to pursue private ends in the peace and security afforded by firm government from above. In the Florentine republic of the early fifteenth century liberty had a different connotation. On the one hand it meant the independence of the state, its freedom both from the juridical claims of the Holy Roman Empire and from the external threat posed above all by the Visconti regime in Milan. On the other hand—and this indeed was seen as the ultimate guarantee of the state's independence—liberty meant the active participation of the citizens in the government and defense of the city. This was the core of the "civic humanism" proclaimed especially by Vergerio's exact contemporary Leonardo Bruni (c. 1370–1444), following the lead given by Coluccio Salutati (1331–1406), chancellor of Florence from 1375 until his death; and the theme was taken up by Bruni's own followers, notably Poggio Bracciolini (1380–1459) and Leon Battista Alberti (1404–1472).

Civic humanism involved above all the theory and practice of active citizenship, conceived, sometimes at least, in broad (*largo*), inclusive terms rather than the restricted (*stretto*), oligarchic view characteristic of the Venetian republic. Thus, for Bruni, liberty and justice prevailed in Florence because of the principle that "what concerns the many is to be determined by the opinion of the many." The case for republican against princely government is built both on Ciceronian doctrine and on a reading of Roman history in Livy and Sallust in which the expulsion of Rome's kings inaugurates an era of "true liberty." It is striking to find that term used in a sense diametrically opposed to its interpretation by Vergerio: the freedom he saw as dependent on princely rule consists here in government by all the citizens. Nor is the antithesis at all blunted by the diverse ways in which "citizenship" might be defined. "Citizens" in any sense of the term were not "subjects."

The strictly political element, again, was only part of the "civic-humanist" compound: the republic was to be the vehicle for a morality in which individual action for the common good would shape nobility of character. Nobility, a recurrent theme in both humanist and scholastic discourse, was interpreted as reflecting not birth or wealth, but virtue. It may indeed be best to preserve the Latin *virtus* at this stage, just as, later, the Italian *virtù* may be used to distinguish another shade in the spectrum of meaning. *Virtus* is the quality of a man (*vir*) whose human potential has been fully actualized, and its prominence in civic-humanist discourse supports the claim of such thinking to centrality in Renaissance political thought.

Princely rule. Yet the civic humanism of Bruni and his followers was in a sense a lost cause. Even in Florence the rise of the Medici reflected the wider preponderance of princely rule, a preponderance surely manifest in the prolific literature on the training and formation of rulers, courtiers, and counselors, rather than of citizens. It is also important to bear in mind that southern Italy was governed by the more traditional hereditary monarchy of the kingdom of Naples: this too attracted humanist advice, some of which drew on the Platonic image of the philosopher-king. In the northern city-states the dominant themes were the honor and glory to be achieved by rulers whose *virtù* was equal to the opportunities afforded by power and to the challenges thrown down by an unpredictable Fortune. These themes were characteristic of such writers as the Sienese Francesco Patrizi (1413–1494), Giovanni Pontano (1426–1503) at Naples, and, in his influential work *Il cortegiano* (*The Book of the Courtier*), Baldassar Castiglione (1478–1529); but they took more problematic forms in the enigmatic writings of Niccolò Machiavelli (1469–1527).

There may be as many views of Machiavelli as there have been scholars and others to interpret him, but it can scarcely be denied that his avowed purpose in *Il principe* (*The Prince;* 1513) was to advise rulers on how best to establish and preserve their power under the sway of necessities that must be accepted and of the vagaries of Fortune, which might be dominated by *virtù*. This, notoriously, involved willingness to defy the rules of ordinary morality when to keep them would endanger political survival. It meant a capacity to rule by fear rather than love, and sufficient self-discipline to curb appetites that might otherwise threaten the economic and sexual interests of subjects. It also required concentration upon the art and demands of war, demands to be met—in Machiavelli's somewhat anachronistic view—by relying on citizen-soldiery rather than mercenary forces. That last point, however, indicates another aspect of Machiavelli's political thought and serves as a reminder that the republican tradition still survived.

Machiavelli had served the republican government of his native Florence during its restoration between 1494 and 1512, and his *Discorsi sopra la prima deca di Tito Livio* (Discourses on the first ten books of Livy; 1513–1519) evinces his belief that the best hope of political permanence in an unstable world lies in a well-constituted republic. Its constitution, however, depends less on institutions than on a certain balance and tension between social forces that will ensure the liberty of all by preventing the dominance of any. And, again, such conditions will prevail only in certain historical epochs; for, following Polybius, Machiavelli saw human history as moving cyclically in a process that may be halted by the efforts of civic *virtù* but that cannot be indefinitely suspended. And here too outstanding personal *virtù* has an indispensable part to play. Whether as lawgiver and founder, or as the restorer of a corrupt state, the commanding individual remains at the center of Machiavelli's political landscape.

Meanwhile, it was not in Florence but in Venice that republican government survived in practice. The century-old humanist admiration of Venetian "serenity" was encapsulated in the political thought of Francesco Guicciardini (1483–1540) and Donato Giannotti (1492–1573). Both hoped for the revival, through reform, of the Florentine republic, and each took Venice as the model. As we have seen, that model embodied a mixed constitution; and one of its merits, for Florentine reformers, was the countervailing authority by which the *ottimati* (the aristocracy) checked the power of the *popolo* (the people). There was implicit criticism here of Machiavelli's more "democratic" vision, and explicit rejection of his favorable view of "class conflict." In any case, neither version of the republican ideal prevailed in Florence against the increasingly absolute power of the grand dukes of Tuscany.

Northern and Western Europe, 1450–1550. By the mid-fifteenth century, the influence of the Italian Renaissance was becoming apparent north of the Alps, beyond the Rhine, across the English Channel, south of the Pyrenees. This was evident not only in educational and cultural activity but also in the business of government, especially in the part played as diplomats and officials by men trained in humanist rhetoric. In political thought, however, it would be hard to find a distinctive contribution from the north before the early sixteenth century. Even then the numerous mirrors of princes and books of counsel in various vernacular languages were largely derivative and repetitive. That should perhaps be qualified by taking account of a characteristically strong emphasis on the strictly pedagogic aspect of the subject. This is noteworthy, for instance, in *De l'institution du prince* (The education of the prince) by Guillaume Budé (1467–1540) and *Relox de príncipes* (Mirror of princes; 1529) by Antonio de Guevara (c. 1481–1545). It is, however, in the title of the most celebrated work in this group that we may see what is more strikingly distinctive in these transalpine humanists.

Erasmus. *Institutio principis Christiani* (The education of a Christian prince; 1516) by Desiderius Erasmus (c. 1466–1536) poses the question of whether it is indeed a Christian humanism that is reflected in the political thought of the northern Renaissance. There are pitfalls to avoid here. A simple antithesis between Italian secularism (or even neopaganism) and transalpine Christian piety is not sustained by the evidence. Yet to cross the Alps in this context is certainly to become aware of a cultural environment where the issues of Christian faith and practice assume far greater prominence. A relevant factor here is the application of humanist scholarship to biblical texts, of which Erasmus's edition of the Greek New Testament was an outstanding example. Relevant too is the influence of the so-called *devotio moderna* (modern devotion), with its emphasis on a Christ-centered personal religion directly available to ordinary lay people. Much of this was, to be sure, continuous with essentially nonhumanist developments in the fourteenth and fifteenth centuries; but there can be no doubt that "Erasmian humanism" made a distinctive contribution. What did this mean for political discourse?

To Erasmus it meant, above all, taking seriously the teaching of Matthew 20:25–28: the ruler must not be the lord and master of his subjects, but their servant—indeed their slave. And to serve them well called for wisdom: scriptural and Platonic elements come together here in the figure of a "Christian prince" who is "fit to rule," not for personal or dynastic gain, but for the common good. This implies, among other things, rejection of the chivalric model of the warrior-king: condemnation of warfare was to be a major element in Christian humanism. Authority is to look within rather than beyond the borders of the realm and to seek justice and well-being for its people. This contrasts sharply with the oppression and exploitation seen as typical of those who ruled societies professedly Christian but in practice disastrously at odds with the teachings of the gospel. Social criticism of this kind was to be prominent in Christian-humanist writing; and the most celebrated—and difficult—example of it was the *Utopia* (1516) of Erasmus's friend Thomas More (1478–1535).

Thomas More. More is arguably as enigmatic a figure in his context as Machiavelli is in his. Even if we set aside such problems as the apparent contradiction between the tolerance of More the humanist and the repression of heresy by More as chancellor, we shall still find ambiguities in *Utopia* itself. It is a work shot through with irony and satire; and it is also affected by the persistent Renaissance dilemma, noted above, between involvement in and detachment from the world of practical politics. Should the wise man embrace or eschew the life of the court? Does Utopian society embody an ideal or simply a contrasting alternative intended to point up the deficiencies of a supposedly Christian society that, for all its faults, has access, by God's merciful revelation, to a higher ideal than unaided human reason could conceive? Are we to take seriously such radical notions as the abolition of private property? Does More, as author, retreat in the end from positions that "Morus" in the dialogue had seemed to accept? Such questions are likely to remain disputed and unresolved; and this indeed may have been part of More's intention. Yet some points at least seem clear enough to be regarded as substantive elements in Christian-humanist political thought.

First among these is the harsh critique of society as it was in More's day—its pursuit of delusive and destructive chivalric goals, its travesty of justice, its greed, its deafness to the cry of the poor. Whatever ambiguities there are, readers of *Utopia* cannot suppose that More means them to accept or approve the cruelty and inequity of such a society. The theme was vigorously taken up by other English writers, notably in the *Dialogue between Pole and Lupset,* completed about 1535 by More's younger contemporary Thomas Starkey (c. 1499–1538). Endorsing much of the criticism of society in *Utopia* but envisioning a more feasible reform program, Starkey looked to an aristocracy taught to recognize their responsibilities as overseers of a "politic order and good civility" grounded "not in the weal and prosperous state of any particular part . . . but in every part coupled together . . . as members of one body by love." The *Dialogue* remained unpublished at the time; and in this sense the radical socioeconomic doctrine of commonwealth writers and preachers in the mid-century England of Edward VI may be still more important. A significant example is the anonymous *Discourse of the Common Weal* (written 1549, published 1581), possibly the work of Sir Thomas Smith (1513–1577).

Other English theorists. Smith is better known as the author of *De republica Anglorum* (On the Commonwealth of England; written c. 1565, published 1583), a work that serves as a reminder that *respublica* (commonwealth) had a specifically political as well as a wider social connotation. The principal title of More's *Utopia* was *De optimo reipublicae statu* (Concerning the best state of a commonwealth), and that state depended, in some degree, on the form of government. The Utopians lived, in each of their fifty-four cities, under a mixed constitution. The structure was pyramidal, with the household as the base and, at the apex, a prince elected for life by a body comprising the leaders of groups of families to govern with the advice of a senate. Matters affecting the whole island were dealt with by an annual assembly of three members from each city, but there was no executive government at that level.

Such a contrived republican system was not, of course, available to the actual states of sixteenth-century Europe. When humanists and others moved closer to the practicalities of government, they were faced with the fact of monarchy, usually hereditary and part of a largely "feudal" institutional system. This, however, need not mean the abandonment of republican values and goals. Indeed, to reconcile *respublica* and *regnum* (kingdom) may be regarded both as a major concern of Renaissance political thought and as an important element of continuity between scholastic and humanist conceptions of government. Starkey, for instance, shared a widespread humanist distrust of monarchy, and his years in Padua had made him an admirer of Venetian institutions. Yet his *Dialogue* was written for an England where hereditary kingship was clearly a permanent feature of the political landscape; and Starkey's scheme for its reform included a role in restraining royal power for the impeccably feudal figure of the Constable, a point reiterated a generation later by John Ponet (1516–1556) in his *Shorte Treatise of Politike Power* in 1556.

Ponet's "mixed state" is in fact a "mixed monarchy," and this is a common theme in the political thought of the early sixteenth century. A notable humanist exposition of it is the *Le monarchie de France* of Claude de Seyssel (c. 1450–1520). Seyssel accepts the need for strong monarchical rule; but he insists that it be subject to restraints imposed by the "bridles" of religion, justice, and *la police.* By the third of these he means the framework of customary institutions within which royal power must operate—in effect, what would later be called the constitution. Half a century later Smith, in *De republica Anglorum,* argued that government in England was certainly monarchical, for it was "the Prince" who gave "the last and highest commandment." Yet "the most high and absolute power of the realm . . . consisteth in the Parliament," where all orders and estates in "the multitude of free men" united in a *respublica* met with the king "to advertise, consult and show what is good and necessary for the commonwealth."

The Late Renaissance, 1550–1625. Seyssel and Smith were both jurists, trained in (Roman) civil law, and it was juristic thinking that gave birth to the concept of sovereignty. The circumstances in which European states faced the problem of locating Smith's "most high and absolute power," whence issued "the last and highest commandment," were in large part the product of politico-religious conflicts generated by the Reformation and Counter-Reformation. Such conflicts also fostered a growing preoccupation with the need to uphold at all costs a social order threatened by confessional and social divisions: hence the prominence in late-Renaissance political discourse of the notion of "reason of state."

Jean Bodin. It was another jurist, Jean Bodin (1530–1596), who crystallized the concept of sovereignty in his *Six livres de la république* (Six books of the commonwealth; 1576; in Latin, 1586). This was a work both of erudition and of urgent propaganda in a country torn by strife between Catholics and Huguenots. Bodin's "commonwealth" (*république; respublica*) is "the state" (*l'état*)—political society as such. That society, he argues, requires for its coherence, its stability, its very survival, a sovereign power to make law by command, a power precisely located and firmly maintained. Such power rightly belonged, in France, to the monarchy; and in the divisive confusion of the religious wars, it was essential to uphold it, even at the sacrifice of the religious unity of the Most Christian King's realm. The absolutism Bodin proposes, however, does not imply arbitrary power. The ultimately Aristotelian concept of participatory citizenship is, to be sure, rejected. Bodin's "citizen" is a "subject" of sovereign power, but a "free subject." His freedom (masculinity is inescapable here) derives from his independent status as head of a patriarchal household whose *res privatae* (private property and interests) are accessible to the *respublica* only with their owner's consent. The sovereign, moreover, is checked not only by the inviolable threshold of the family, not only by divine and natural law, but also by the *lois politiques* (constitutional laws) that establish and define his authority. Nor has the notion of "mixed monarchy" simply disappeared. Distinguishing "sovereignty" from "government," Bodin envisages a "royal monarchy" where there is a place in administration (though not in legislation) for aristocratic and democratic elements.

Bodin's massive work contained much more than the theory of sovereignty just outlined, but it was that theory that entered rapidly and powerfully into the mainstream of European political thought. In England, for instance, Bodin's ideas played their part in the ideological debates over royal and parliamentary sovereignty before and during the civil wars of the mid-seventeenth century. The reception of Bodin was not by any means uniformly positive. Both criticism and adjustment of his theory were especially significant among German scholars. In the Holy Roman Empire it was not merely difficult, but impossible to locate the absolute and undivided sovereign Bodin prescribed. Unwilling to accept either that the empire was not a state at all, or that its constitution was not monarchical, such writers as Henning Arnisaeus (1576/79–1636) and Christoph Besold (1577–1638) wrestled with the problem and, while reaching different conclusions, achieved new insights into the possibilities of divided sovereignty. Transmitted especially by the study of public law in the German universities, notably at Jena during the long career of Dominicus Arumaeus (1579–1673), these ideas were to have continuing importance in the political science of the eighteenth-century Enlightenment.

Reason of state. Arnisaeus and Besold also figure in the other aspect of late-Renaissance political thought mentioned above. Each has a place in his theory for the *arcana imperii* or *arcana rerum publicarum,* the secrets of state. Besold, in his *Politicorum libri duo* (Politics, in two books; 1618), identified these with the Aristotelian concept of equity (*epieikeia*), on the basis of which ordinary law could be overridden. It is clear, however, that he had also been influenced by the extensive literature of reason of state built up since the 1580s. The term in its original Italian form seems to have been coined in the mid-sixteenth century; but its vogue may be dated from the publication, in 1589, of *Della ragione di stato* (Reason of state) by Giovanni Botero (1544–1617). Botero and his many followers—in Italy alone the phrase "reason of state" was used in the titles of at least eight other books by 1635—were arguing in defense of extraordinary measures necessary for the public good, especially when it was a matter of saving the state itself from subversion or destruction. In doing so they clearly took their cue from Machiavelli; but that was not a debt to be acknowledged without some embarrassment.

By the late sixteenth century the figure of "murderous Machiavel" was well established in political demonology. Accordingly, reason of state theory was complicated by the need to distinguish the legitimate uses of the concept from its illegitimate Machiavellian abuse. When, for example, the theme—though not in this case the actual phrase—was taken up by the Flemish scholar Justus Lipsius (1547–1606), in his *Politicorum sive civilis doctrinae libri sex* (Politics, or civil doctrine in six books; 1589), he distinguished degrees of dissimulation for the purpose of maintaining the state along a scale ranging from what was positively recommended, through what might be tolerated, to what must be condemned. Others drew a line between what was justifiable because it was done for the common good and what counted as "false reason of state" because it was done in the selfish interest of the ruler or statesman concerned. The slippery nature of such distinctions is obvious, and there were always those who denied the moral legitimacy of reason of state, notably the Spaniards Pedro de Ribadeneyra (1527–1611) and Francisco de Quevedo (1580–1645).

Yet reason of state doctrine continued to spread across Europe, encouraged in part by a significant shift in the late-humanist reading of history, in particular the history of Rome. Sallust and Livy yielded their primacy as influential authorities to Tacitus, who had lived through and written of events and personalities likely to breed skepticism, if not cynicism, as to political motivation and behavior: his was the Rome, not of Cicero, Caesar, and Augustus, but of Tiberius, Nero, and Domitian. What has come to be called "Tacitism" in the political thought of the later Renaissance reflected this; or it might be more accurate to say that the glass through which the Tacitists read the *Annals* and the *Histories* was shaped and colored by the factors that made theirs the great age of reason of state. Certainly the two genres of political writing—commentaries on Tacitus and reason of state treatises—developed in parallel: one of the earliest attempts to define *regione di stato* was by Scipione Ammirato (1531–1601) in his 1594 *Discorsi sopra Cornelio Tacito* (Discourses on Tacitus). And it is noteworthy that Lipsius, while critical early in his career of some forms of Tacitism, made his reputation as a classical scholar by editing Tacitus, on whom he drew extensively in his *Politics*. There may be uncertainty as to the Roman historian's own political stance, but there can be no doubt that his irony and skepticism made his writings a rich source for the political pragmatism of reason of state.

Neo-Stoicism and after. There was a high degree of mutual respect between Lipsius and the author who most perfectly expresses ironic distaste for the frenzied doctrinal controversies of the late sixteenth century. Michel de Montaigne (1533–1592) lived in virtual (and deliberate) seclusion from public office and thus from the conflicts that made Lipsius's life one of peripatetic uncertainty. Indeed, their diverse experiences offer another parable of the humanist dilemma between *otium* and *negotium*. Yet they shared basic (though potentially contradictory) attitudes, a further reminder that Renaissance political thought lacked monolithic unity. On the one hand, they regarded existing institutions with skeptical realism: what gives laws their efficacy, Montaigne argued, is not their justice but the mere fact that "they are the laws" and must be obeyed as such. On the other hand, this late-Renaissance skepticism was combined with a persistent (or renewed) Stoicism, now perhaps the Stoicism of Seneca rather than of Cicero. Lipsius is again a key figure: his *De constantia* (On constancy; 1584) has a quintessentially Senecan theme, taken up a decade later by Guillaume du Vair (1556–1621) in *De la constance et consolation ès calamités publiques* (On constancy and consolation in public calamities; 1593). Arguably, such neo-Stoic doctrine was intended to persuade subjects to accept with resignation the authority of rulers who should themselves be guided by "true" reason of state, directed to the common good. Yet when the Scottish humanist George Buchanan (1506–1582) published his radical dialogue *De jure regni apud Scotos* (On the right of the kingdom in Scotland; 1579), he appended a passage from Seneca's *Thyestes* celebrating the virtues of the ideal Stoic ruler (*rex stoicus*). And it may not be safe to assume that this is no more than the survival, from an earlier generation, of an older Stoicism now yielding to its renovated form.

By the early decades of the seventeenth century, however, Renaissance humanism as a whole was itself giving way to, or mingling with, other currents of thought. A revitalized Scholasticism—exemplified, especially for political discourse, by Francisco Suárez (1548–1617)—emerged in Spain and Italy. The "modern theory of natural law" would soon be magisterially expounded by Hugo Grotius (1583–1645). The new science represented by Galileo and the new philosophy of Descartes introduced basic intellectual changes. New, or at least modified, political theologies were generated by a now-divided western Christendom. Each of these developments owed something to Renaissance humanism; yet, taken together, they marked the end of Renaissance political thought in its distinctive forms.

See also **Civic Humanism; Constitutionalism; Law; Monarchy; Prince; Republicanism; Utopias;** *and biographies of figures mentioned in this entry.*

BIBLIOGRAPHY

Primary Works

Alberti, Leon Battista. *The Family in Renaissance Florence.* Translated by Renée Neu Watkins. Columbia, S.C., 1969. Translation of *Della famiglia* (c. 1433–1441).

Bodin, Jean. *The Six Bookes of a Commonweale.* Translated by Richard Knolles. London, 1606. Reprint, Cambridge, Mass., 1962. This is based on a conflation of *Les six livres de la république* (1576) and *De republica libri sex* (1586).

Bodin, Jean. *On Sovereignty.* Edited by Julian H. Franklin. Cambridge, U.K., 1992. A modern translation of a very limited, though crucial, part of this very long text.

Botero, Giovanni. *The Reason of State.* Translated by Pamela J. Waley and Daniel P. Waley. London, 1956. Translation of *Ragione di stato* (1589).

Bruni, Leonardo. *Laudatio Florentinae urbis.* In Hans Baron. *From Petrarch to Leonardo Bruni.* Chicago, 1968. Pages 217–263. Latin text of Bruni's praise of the city of Florence.

Bruni, Leonardo. *The Humanism of Leonardo Bruni: Selected Texts.* Translated and introduced by Gordon Griffiths, James Hankins, and David Thompson. Binghamton, N.Y., 1987. See pages 116–121 for an English translation of the concluding section four of *Laudatio Florentinae urbis* (c. 1403–1404).

Castiglione, Baldassar. *The Book of the Courtier.* Translated by George Bull. Harmondsworth, U.K., 1967. Translation of *Il cortegiano* (1528).

Erasmus, Desiderius. *The Education of a Christian Prince.* Translated by Lester K. Born. New York, 1965. Translation of *Institutio principis Christiani* (1516).

Guicciardini, Francesco. *Dialogue on the Government of Florence.* Edited and translated by Alison Brown. Cambridge, U.K., 1994. Translation of *Dialogo del reggimento di Firenze* (c. 1521/25).

Lipsius, Justus. *Two Bookes of Constancie.* Translated by Sir John Stradling. Edited by Rudolf Kirk. New Brunswick, N.J., 1939. Translation (1595) of *De constantia libri duo* (1584).

Lipsius, Justus. *Sixe Bookes of Politickes or civil doctrine.* Translated by William Jones. London, 1594. Reprint, Amsterdam, 1970. Translation of *Politicorum sive civilis doctrinae libri sex* (1589).

Machiavelli, Niccolò. *Discourses on Livy.* Translated by Harvey C. Mansfield and Nathan Tarcov. Chicago, 1996. The most recent of several translations of *Discorsi sopra la prima deca di Tito Livio* (c. 1513–1519).

Machiavelli, Niccolò. *The Prince.* Edited by Quentin Skinner and Russell Price. Cambridge, U.K., 1988. Translation of *Il principe* (1513). The earlier translation by Allan H. Gilbert is used in *Machiavelli: The Prince, Selections from "The Discourses" and Other Writings.* Edited by John Plamenatz. London, 1972.

More, Thomas. *Utopia.* Edited by George M. Logan and Robert M. Adams. Cambridge, U.K., 1989. Translation of *De optimo reipublicae statu deque nova insula Utopia libellus vere aureus* (1516).

Petrarch, Francesco. *The Life of Solitude.* Translated by Jacob Zeitlin. Urbana, Ill., 1924. Translation of *De vita solitaria* (c. 1337).

Petrarch, Francesco. *Letters of Old Age: Rerum senilium libri I–XVIII.* Translated by Aldo S. Bernardo, Saul Levin, and Reta A. Bernardo. Volume 2. Baltimore and London, 1992. Pages 521–552. A translation of Petrarch's letter on government.

Seyssel, Claude de. *The Monarchy of France.* Edited by Donald R. Kelley. Translated by J. H. Hexter. New Haven, Conn., 1981. Translation of *La monarchie de France* (1519).

Smith, Thomas. *De republica Anglorum.* Edited by Mary Dewar. Cambridge, U.K., 1982. Written about 1565, first published 1583.

Starkey, Thomas. *A Dialogue between Pole and Lupset.* Edited by Thomas F. Mayer. London, 1989. This is a rigorous "diplomatic transcription" from the manuscripts, completed about 1535. Nonspecialist readers may prefer *A Dialogue between Reginald Pole and Thomas Lupset.* Edited by Kathleen M. Burton. London, 1948.

Vergerio, Pier Paolo. *De ingenuis moribus.* Translated by William H. Woodward. In *Vittorino da Feltre and Other Humanist Educators.* New York, 1963. Pages 96–118. Translation of *De ingenuis moribus et liberalibus studiis* (c. 1401–1402).

Vergerio, Pier Paolo, *Epistolario.* Edited by Leonardo Smith. Rome, 1934. See "P. P. Vergerio in nome di Cicerone a Francesco Petrarca" (Letter in the name of Cicero to Petrarch), pp. 436–445, and "De monarchia sive de optimo principatu" (On monarchy or the best form of government), pp. 447–450.

Vergerio, Pier Paolo. *De republica veneta* (On the Venetian republic; c. 1400). In David Robey and John Law. "The Venetian Myth and the *De republica veneta* of Pier Paolo Vergerio." *Rinascimento,* ser. 2, 15 (1975): 36–50.

Secondary Works

Baron, Hans. *The Crisis of the Early Italian Renaissance.* 2d ed. Princeton, N.J., 1966.

Burns, J. H., and Mark Goldie, eds. *The Cambridge History of Political Thought, 1450–1700.* Cambridge, U.K., 1991. See especially chapters 1–3 and 10–11.

Keohane, Nannerl O. *Philosophy and the State in France: The Renaissance to the Enlightenment.* Princeton, N.J., 1980.

Pagden, Anthony, ed. *The Languages of Political Theory in*

Early-Modern Europe. Cambridge, U.K., 1987. See especially chapters 2, 3, and 6.

Pocock, J. G. A. *The Machiavellian Moment: Florentine Political Thought and the Atlantic Republican Tradition*. Princeton, N.J., 1975. See especially chapters 1–9.

Skinner, Quentin. *The Foundations of Modern Political Thought*. Vol. 1: *The Renaissance*. Cambridge, U.K., 1978.

Skinner, Quentin. "Political Philosophy." In *The Cambridge History of Renaissance Philosophy*. Edited by Charles B. Schmitt, Quentin Skinner, Eckhard Kessler, and Jill Kraye. Cambridge, U.K., 1988. Pages 389–452.

Tuck, Richard. *Philosophy and Government, 1572–1651*. Cambridge, U.K., 1993. See especially chapters 1–4.

J. H. BURNS

POLITIQUES. *See* **Wars of Religion.**

POLIZIANO, ANGELO (Politian; 1454–1494), Italian philologist and poet. Angelo Poliziano was born in Montepulciano (Mons Politianus in Latin) in the Siena province of Tuscany. His birth name was Angelo di Benedetto Ambrogini, but he later assumed the surname derived from the Latin name of his birthplace. His mother, Antonia Salimbeni, belonged to a prominent family, and his father, Benedetto, was a doctor of law and held a number of public offices in the town of Montepulciano and elsewhere.

Early Career. By 1469 Poliziano was living in Florence, most likely with his cousin Cino di Matteo Ambrogini. In Florence Poliziano came under the protection of Lorenzo de' Medici and attended the University of Florence courses of Giovanni Argiropulo, Andronico Callisto, Cristoforo Landino, and Marsilio Ficino. This academic experience helped Poliziano strengthen his knowledge of ancient philosophy and ancient Greek. The year 1473 represents a turning point in Poliziano's career. He translated the *Iliad* into Latin hexameters and dedicated books 2 and 3 of this groundbreaking translation to Lorenzo de' Medici, who, moved by the precocious talent of Poliziano, invited him to take up quarters in his palace on Via Larga in Florence. Here Poliziano was able to continue his studies in humanist culture thanks to the vast collection of important and rare codices held in the Medici library and to the presence of significant intellectual figures who were friends of the Medici court.

In 1475 Poliziano became Lorenzo de' Medici's private secretary and tutor of his son Piero. To celebrate the victory of Lorenzo's younger brother Giuliano in a jousting match in 1475, Poliziano began writing the unfinished poem *Stanze cominciate per la giostra del magnifico Giuliano di Piero de Medici* (Stanzas begun for the jousting match of the magnificent Giuliano di Piero de' Medici). Poliziano had stopped working on the *Stanze* by 26 April 1478, the day that Giuliano de' Medici died. Critics have described the poem as the most extraordinary phenomenon of fifteenth-century Italian poetry. Some critics argue that the *Stanze* is the first poem since Dante and Petrarch to have offered an acceptable solution to the question of a new poetic voice. The *Stanze* is divided into two books that offer a poetic account of the love relation between Julio (Giuliano de' Medici) and Simonetta (Simonetta Cattaneo). The poem begins in a pseudo-classical landscape around Florence. The world of the *Stanze* is one that intersects history with classical mythology. The dominating philosophical mind-set of the poem is Ficinian Neoplatonism. According to many, the *Stanze* is a Janus-faced entity that rethinks the origins of Italian literature but also traces future literary paths for the vernacular. The *Stanze*'s subtextual universe is densely populated by biblical, classical, and medieval writers. But Poliziano's use of these authors is not rooted in artistic subservience, but rather in the attempt to transform himself into the original literary source. The *Stanze* is a powerful experiment, as far as linguistic and poetic invention are concerned, based on Poliziano's notion of *docta varietas* (learned variety). This critical notion, which runs counter to Pietro Bembo's theory of "single model" imitation, is a highly refined form of eclecticism. Some critics have observed that the *Stanze* is characterized by the idea of "reawakening," both as a theme found throughout the poem and as an ideological element that points to the rebirth of a literary and cultural tradition.

In 1476 Poliziano wrote "Dum pulchra effertur nigro Symonetta feretro" in honor of Simonetta Cattaneo, wife of Marco Vespucci, love interest of Giuliano de' Medici, and an important personage in the *Stanze,* who had died on 19 April of that year. In 1477 Poliziano received from Lorenzo de' Medici an ecclesiastical gift in the form of the priorship of San Paolo. He was ordained as a priest sometime before 1486, the year in which he was named canon of the Florentine cathedral of Santa Maria del Fiore. All of this facilitated Poliziano's vocation for humanistic research.

Poliziano's tranquil existence was sent into upheaval with the infamous "congiura dei Pazzi" (conspiracy of the Pazzi). On 26 April 1478 Lorenzo de' Medici and his brother Giuliano were attacked in the Duomo by a rival family. Giuliano died but Lorenzo

Angelo Poliziano. Portrait of Giovanni Pico della Mirandola, Marsilio Ficino, and Poliziano. Detail from *The Miracle of the Blessed Sacrament* by Cosimo Rosselli (1439–1507) in the church of Sant'Ambrogio, Florence. ALINARI/ART RESOURCE

was spared thanks to the intervention of Poliziano, among others. In fact, the first work Poliziano published was a pro-Medici account of the attack, *Pactianae coniurationis commentarium* (Commentary on the Pazzi conspiracy; 1478), which was modeled on Sallust's *Conspiracy of Catiline* and printed by Niccolò di Lorenzo della Magna. As a result of the political uncertainty that arose in the wake of the attack, including Pope Sixtus IV's excommunication of Lorenzo and his supporters on 1 June 1478, and the outbreak of the plague, it was no longer safe for Poliziano to remain in Florence.

By early 1479 Poliziano was in Careggi with his students, including Lorenzo's son Giovanni (the future Pope Leo X). After an argument with Lorenzo's wife Clarice Orsini (who disliked Poliziano's insistence on a humanistic curriculum for her children's education), Poliziano was sent to the Medici villa in Fiesole. Here he translated into Latin Epitectus's *Enchiridion* (Manual). After some pleading with his lord, Poliziano was readmitted to the Medici palace in Via Larga, Florence. But by 1480 we find Poliziano traveling throughout northern Italy, to Venice, Padua, Verona, and Mantua, where on April 21 he was made chaplain and commensal (table companion) by Cardinal Francesco Gonzaga. It was probably in Mantua during the carnival of 1480 that Poliziano wrote the *Fabula di Orfeo,* a dramatic work in Italian that recounts the mythical story of Orpheus. *Orfeo* is usually cited as the first nonreligious work in the history of Italian literature that was meant to be represented on stage. While in northern Italy Poliziano also began a lasting friendship with Ermolao Barbaro, who encouraged him to study Aristotelian philosophy.

Professorship and Later Career. Poliziano returned to Florence, where in November 1480 he was hired as professor of rhetoric and poetics at the University of Florence with a salary about four times greater than many of the other professors. After staying at the priory of San Paolo, he moved into a small villa in Fiesole given to him by Lorenzo.

In November 1480 Poliziano began the academic year with a course on Quintilian's *Oratory Institutions* and Statius's *Sylvae* (which was to inspire Poliziano's poetic *Sylvae*), while in the following academic year he gave a course on Ovid's *Fasti* and on the Latin treatise on oratory *Rhetorica ad Herennium.* In 1482 Poliziano's *sylva* entitled *Manto* was published by Antonio Miscomini.

In November 1484 Poliziano was part of the Florentine diplomatic entourage that went to Rome to congratulate Pope Innocent VIII (Giovanni Battista Cibo) on his election, which had taken place on 29 August. Innocent VIII commissioned Poliziano to do a Latin translation of Herodian, which was completed in 1487 and dedicated to the pope.

On 19 September 1489 Miscomini published Poliziano's *Miscellaneorum centuria prima,* an encyclopedic work that put forward revolutionary ideas in the field of philological research. For example, diametrically opposed to his contemporaries, Poliziano re-creates the variant reading of ancient codices; for the first time, the codex is referred to with the name of the owner or the library where it is held, along with the classification of the paleography and other external features and reference to the tradition to which it belongs. Poliziano's philological scholarship anticipated the future methods of textual criticism.

In the early part of June 1491, Poliziano was instructed by Lorenzo to travel to Bologna, Ferrara, Padua, and Venice with the objective of acquiring books and manuscripts as well as to recruit renowned professors for the University of Florence. The most important detail of Poliziano's trip (he was accompanied by Giovanni Pico della Mirandola) was that as a guest at Bernardo Bembo's home in Venice, he collated an ancient Terence codex with the assistance of Bembo's son Pietro.

While Poliziano had every right to claim a sense of satisfaction for the fame he acquired for his scholarship, the death of his benefactor and protector Lorenzo on 8 April 1492 provoked a strong sense of uncertainty in his life. With the support of Cardinal Ascanio Sforza, the brother of Ludovico Sforza, ruler of Milan, he sought an appointment as librarian of the Vatican Library. However, the reigning Borgia pope, Alexander VI, hired a relatively unknown Spanish bishop instead. Poliziano's next move was to seek an ecclesiastical appointment. In fact, in 1493 Piero de' Medici sought to convince Alexander VI to make Poliziano a cardinal. This too failed.

Poliziano passed his final years in hard work and conflict. The *Miscellanea,* while admired by many, attracted the anger and envy of various individuals, including Giorgio Merula, who accused him of plagiarism, as well as Michele Marullo and Bartolomeo Scala (Poliziano was apparently in love with Scala's daughter Alessandra, who was also Marullo's wife). We even find figures such as Jacopo Sannazaro reacting against Poliziano's work. Critics speculate that the attacks against Poliziano were also directed against the power of the Medici family.

Poliziano died sometime between 28 and 29 September 1494 in Florence. Girolamo Savonarola fulfilled Poliziano's last wish and instructed that he be given his funeral rites dressed in the habit of a Dominican friar and buried at the church of San Marco. As many have observed, Poliziano's death was part of the end of an era, if we consider that Matteo Franco (a key figure in the Medici court) died on 6 September of that year, Baccio Ugolini (the first to interpret the role of Orfeo) died on 27 September, Piero was expelled from Florence on 9 November, and Giovanni Pico della Mirandola died on 17 November, the same day on which Charles VIII of France entered Florence.

See also **Humanism**, *subentry on* **Italy**; **Manuscripts**.

BIBLIOGRAPHY

Primary Works

Poliziano, Angelo. *Opera Omnia*. Edited by Ida Maïer. 3 vols. Turin, Italy, 1970–1971.

Poliziano, Angelo. *Prose volgari inedite e poesie latine e greche edite e inedite*. Edited by Isidoro Del Lungo. Florence, 1867.

Poliziano, Angelo. *The Stanze of Angelo Poliziano*. Translated by David Quint. Amherst, Mass., 1979. Translation of the *Stanze de messer Angelo Poliziano cominciate per la giostra del magnifico Giuliano di Piero de' Medici* (1494).

Poliziano, Angelo. *A Translation of the Orpheus of Angelo Politian and the Aminta of Torquato Tasso*. Introduction by Louis E. Lord. 1931. Reprint, Westport, Conn., 1986.

Secondary Works

Branca, Vittore. *Poliziano e l'umanesimo della parola*. Turin, Italy, 1983.

Colilli, Paul. *Poliziano's Science of Tropes*. New York, 1989.

Godman, Peter. *From Poliziano to Machiavelli: Florentine Humanism in the High Renaissance*. Princeton, N.J., 1998.

Grafton, Anthony. *Joseph Scaliger: A Study in the History of Classical Scholarship*. Oxford, 1983. Contains an important chapter on Poliziano's philological research.

Mencken, F. O. *Historia vitae et in literis meritorum*. Leipzig, Germany, 1736. Contains one of the earliest biographical accounts of Poliziano.

PAUL COLILLI

POMPONAZZI, PIETRO (1462–1525), Italian Aristotelian philosopher. Pomponazzi was born in Mantua. He entered the University at Padua in 1484 and was awarded his arts doctorate in 1487. He began teaching there the next year. He was awarded a doctorate in medicine in 1494. He left Padua in 1496, studied with Alberto Pio, and married in 1497. He returned to Padua in 1499 and stayed there almost continually until 1511. He then went to Bologna, where he taught until his death.

A popular teacher, many of his lectures at Padua on natural philosophy, psychology, and logic were recorded by students and have been published only recently. His interest in natural philosophy continued throughout his career, and he published works in Bologna on such topics as the intention and remission of forms, in which he criticized the thought of Richard Swineshead. In 1516 he published his famous work the *Tractatus de immortalitate animi* (Treatise on the immortality of the soul). In 1518 and 1519 he wrote and published defenses of this work. He also wrote *De incantationibus* (On incantations; 1556) and *De fato* (On fate; 1567) while at Bologna, but both these works were published posthumously.

The Immortality Controversy. Pomponazzi is famous for his denial that philosophy can demonstrate the immortality of the human soul. While this was not a new position in the Latin West, Pomponazzi explored the issue with an unparalleled vigor. In his *De immortalitate* Pomponazzi canvassed a wide variety of arguments to show the mortal nature of the human soul. He took care at the beginning of the treatise to stress that he was dealing with the question of what Aristotle held concerning the soul and would set aside revelation and deal with the constraints of natural reason. Since it was generally agreed that the intellect was the most obvious candidate for immortality because of its immaterial nature, Pomponazzi's primary project was to show that the human intellect itself is mortal. He affirmed that the intellect in itself is immaterial and found evidence in our ability to comprehend universal notions. Despite this immaterial function of the intellect, Pomponazzi was quick to point out that the intellect depends essentially on the body insofar as it is unable to operate without making use of the sensory faculties, especially "imagination." By imagination, Pomponazzi is referring to the internal sense power that fashions images, or "phantasms," based on the input of the external senses. This internal sense power, Pomponazzi held, is entirely organic. Because the intellect cannot function without phantasms, even when thinking of universals, it is dependent on the body and perishes when the body perishes. While recognizing that the intellect knows universals, Pomponazzi was also emphatic that that knowledge of universals is never "pure." Instead, it is always rooted in some particular phantasm. More formally, Pomponazzi stated that the intellect is absolutely mortal and relatively immortal, by which he meant that the intellect is bound to the body by its need for phantasms (absolutely mortal), but can function universally within the limits provided by phantasms (relatively immortal).

Pomponazzi recognized that the argument for mortality faced grave problems. One he particularly concerned himself with was the argument that if the soul is mortal, there is no reason to be moral. In other words, without the prospect of punishment beyond the grave, no one would have any reason to lead a blameless life. Pomponazzi responded by arguing that virtue is a reward in itself since the virtuous person never suffers from guilt. Moreover, if the only reason to be moral is the fear of punishment, this would mean that humans are incapable of being virtuous in any but a servile manner. In response to the assertion that without immortality humans would be most unhappy, Pomponazzi stressed that humans can be happy in this life in a way proportionate to human nature by living a virtuous life based on human abilities.

The publication of the *De immortalitate* set off a large controversy. Pomponazzi was denounced throughout Italy by churchmen and even had his book publicly burned in Venice. A series of books were written against him by philosophers and theologians, including works by his old Paduan rival Agostino Nifo (c. 1470–1538) and one of Pomponazzi's students, Gasparo Contarini (1484–1542). Pomponazzi wrote replies to both Nifo and Contarini in which he reiterated that he was merely arguing that Aristotle and reason show that the human soul is mortal and was saying nothing against a faith that teaches that the soul is immortal.

Causation and Human Freedom. Pomponazzi's *De fato,* written by 1520, juxtaposes two radically different views. In the first two books Pomponazzi advocated a strong form of determinism in respect both to the natural world and the human will. Defining "fate" as the divine ordering of causes, that is, providence, he argued that all events can be traced back to a first cause. The consequence is that everything that happens does so of necessity. All talk of contingency is a matter of human ignorance. Because we cannot know all the elements in a causal chain, we cannot know the necessary effect. Ignorance of the necessity of the cause of the effect, however, in no way alters the fact that the effect must occur. Pomponazzi extended this necessary causation into the realm of human decision-making. While the human will is able to deliberate between competing choices, this deliberation must be understood properly. We can always ask why the will chooses one alternative over another. The reason such a question can be asked is that the answer ultimately resides in some cause external to us. Again, the appearance of deliberative freedom is due to human ignorance—our inability to recognize hidden causes of the results of our deliberation.

In the remaining three books of *De fato,* Pomponazzi distanced himself from the determinism espoused in the earlier books. Instead, he argued from a position of faith. Relying on Thomas Aquinas (1225–1274) and John Duns Scotus (c. 1266–1308), he presented a view of the human will as free and a position on divine foreknowledge that is compatible with human freedom. Divine omniscience contains a truly contingent element, one that leaves the future open for human determination. The human will is free because it is able to prescind from the options available to it. The view of human freedom, then, is essentially negative and consists of the ability to resist the options presented to it by the intellect.

On Miracles. In *De incantationibus,* written by 1520, Pomponazzi subjected the very notion of miracles to searching criticism. He repeatedly tried to find natural explanations for apparently unnatural actions. Pointing to the hidden, but nonetheless natural, powers of herbs and animals, Pomponazzi extended the reach of such "occult" powers even to humans. Some humans are gifted with natural, although not obviously perceptible, abilities to affect the course of natural events. This is at least one possible explanation for so-called miraculous cures. In fact, the cure is traceable back to the hidden powers of the doctor and the doctor's knowledge of the hidden power of various herbs and other such natural objects. Pomponazzi stated that prayer has no effect on others, but rather functions as a way to purify the human soul by demonstrating a love for God. Finally, even biblical miracles can be reduced to natural causes.

Pomponazzi also offered a naturalistic account of religion. Religion comes about from the workings of the planetary intelligences. Indeed, religions are nothing more than aspects of the endless and recurring cycles of the planets. Founders of religion are given natural, but occult, powers to perform wonders that will cement the public's perception of the apparently miraculous foundation of the religion in question.

Philosophy and Religion. Many of Pomponazzi's claims were in conflict with the claims of Christianity. Pomponazzi was careful to point out, however, that philosophy and religion are two different activities. Some remarks at the end of the *De immortalitate* are particularly relevant. Pomponazzi argued that faith has its own proper procedures, revelation, and scripture. These separate faith from his philosophical project and make it immune from his criticisms of miracles, immortality, and freedom. However, following Averroes (Ibn Rushd), Pomponazzi claimed that there is a philosophically useful function that the thesis of immortality performs. The philosophically false thesis of immortality helps keep the majority of people under control by holding out the threat of eternal punishment. Without such a threat, Pomponazzi believed that the ordinary human would quickly descend into venality and hedonism. Such an apparently cynical use of the thesis of immortality has led some scholars to doubt the sincerity of Pomponazzi's view of the superiority of theology. It must be noted, however, that there are other passages in his writings where his sincerity does not seem feigned.

BIBLIOGRAPHY

Primary Works

Pomponazzi, Pietro. *Corsi inediti dell' insegnamento padovano.* 2 vols. Edited by Antonino Poppi. Padua, Italy, 1966–1970.

Pomponazzi, Pietro. "On the Immortality of the Soul." Translated by William H. Hay. Revised by John H. Randall, Jr. Annotated by Paul O. Kristeller. In *The Renaissance Philosophy of Man.* Edited by Ernst Cassirer. Chicago, 1948. Pages 280–381.

Pomponazzi, Pietro. *Petri Pomponatii Mantuani Libri quinque de fato, de libero arbitrio, de praedestinatione.* Edited by Richard Lemay. Lugano, Italy, 1957.

Secondary Works

Kristeller, Paul O. *Eight Philosophers of the Italian Renaissance.* Stanford, Calif., 1964.

Kristeller, Paul O. "The Myth of Renaissance Atheism and the French Tradition of Free Thought." *Journal of the History of Philosophy* 6 (1968): 233–243.

Mahoney, Edward P. "Saint Thomas and the School of Padua at the End of the Fifteenth Century." *Proceedings of the American Catholic Philosophical Association* 48 (1974): 277–285.

Nardi, Bruno. *Studi su Pietro Pomponazzi.* Florence, 1965.

Pine, Martin L. *Pietro Pomponazzi: Radical Philosopher of the Renaissance.* Padua, Italy, 1986.

JAMES B. SOUTH

PONTANO, GIOVANNI (Jovianus Pontanus; 1426–1503), Neapolitan diplomat and humanist. Pontano, a distinguished cultural and political figure at the royal court of Naples, won recognition as one of the most prominent Italian humanists of the fifteenth century. He was thoroughly familiar with classical Latin literature, and throughout his adult life he composed poetry, literary works, and treatises on moral themes. He was an important member of the Neapolitan Academy, known from 1471 as the Accademia Pontaniana, a forum for discussions on po-

Giovanni Pontano. Portrait medallion by Adriano Fiorentino.

litical, moral, literary, and religious issues. Like many of his humanist counterparts in Florence, Venice, Milan, and other Italian cities, Pontano also participated actively in political and diplomatic affairs. His writings clearly reflect his efforts to balance the conflicting demands of classical values, Christian ethics, and contemporary experience.

Political and Diplomatic Career. Born in Umbria, near Spoleto, Pontano received his early education at Perugia. In 1447 he came to the attention of Alfonso I of Aragon, known as Alfonso the Magnanimous (king of Naples, ruled 1442–1458), who was then campaigning in Umbria; in 1448 Pontano moved to Naples to assume a post at the royal court. He continued his studies at Naples and spent most of his life in the southern kingdom. He served as a tutor at the court of the Aragonese kings of Naples and later as an ambassador and a secretary in the Neapolitan chancellery. From the 1460s to the 1490s he was a councillor and close adviser to King Ferdinand I of Naples (ruled 1458–1494) and his successors Alfonso II (ruled 1494–1495) and Ferdinand II (ruled 1495–1496).

Pontano's political and diplomatic services at the royal court introduced him to the turbulent world of Italian politics in the fifteenth century. He lived through two serious rebellions by the Neapolitan barons—one after the death of Alfonso the Magnanimous, as Ferdinand I consolidated his claim to the throne (1459–1463), the other later in Ferdinand I's reign (1485–1487)—as well as the invasions of Italy and the kingdom of Naples by French and Spanish armies after 1494. Pontano was especially active in Neapolitan diplomacy during the second barons' revolt. As secretary to Ferdinand I, he coordinated efforts to win support for the king's policies and to forestall the formation of an Italian alliance against Ferdinand I, and he negotiated an end to the conflict with Pope Innocent VIII, who was the barons' main supporter outside Naples. Pontano's task was particularly difficult because Ferdinand I did not hesitate to violate agreements with the pope and other Italian powers who supported the barons. In representing Ferdinand I's policies and justifying his actions, Pontano received a practical education in power politics.

During the late 1480s and early 1490s Pontano worked energetically to improve Neapolitan relations with the papacy and to stabilize political affairs throughout Italy so as to reduce the threat of a French invasion. While Duke Ludovico il Moro of Milan organized an Italian coalition against Naples and allied with King Charles VIII of France, Pontano instructed Neapolitan ambassadors to argue that a French invasion would lead to disaster for all of Italy. When it became clear that his diplomatic campaign was not succeeding, he attempted to organize Neapolitan military defenses as the French army made its way south through the Italian peninsula. King Ferdinand II fled Naples just before the arrival of the invading force, leaving Pontano, as royal secretary, to deliver the keys of the city to Charles VIII. There is no evidence to support the story told by the Florentine historian Francesco Guicciardini that Pontano welcomed Charles with a warm speech that vilified the kings of Naples. His consistent loyalty to the Neapolitan monarchy and his strenuous efforts to deflect the invasion both testify against the probability of Guicciardini's report being accurate.

Writings. Pontano was a prolific author, and many of his works reflect his political experience. His poetry and literary dialogues are mostly undistinguished, but his political and moral treatises are lively documents that consider ethical issues from the perspective of Pontano's public experience. He composed several treatises while working on behalf of the Neapolitan kings: they include *De principe* (1468), *De obedientia* (1470), *De fortitudine* (1481), *De liberalitate* (1493), and *De beneficentia* (1493). After retiring as royal secretary following the French occupation of Naples in 1495, Pontano devoted much more of his time to literary affairs and composed eight new treatises on moral and philosophical themes before his death in 1503: *De magnificentia, De splendore, De conviventia, De magnanimitate, De prudentia, De immanitate, De fortuna,* and *De sermone*. (His early treatises were published in 1490, and first publication of others continued until 1520.)

Pontano believed strongly that monarchy was the best form of government. In *De obedientia* he associated monarchy with stability and social harmony while condemning republican governments that encouraged the unbridled pursuit of individual self-interest. In *De principe* he outlined the qualities of an ideal monarch, including liberality, moderation, self-control, courtesy, humanity, and majesty. He often took an Aristotelian approach to the analysis of moral qualities, seeking a virtuous mean between vicious extremes. Thus in *De fortitudine* he advocated the cultivation of courage as a mean between the extremes of timidity and temerity. The treatise *De fortuna* represented Pontano's efforts to understand the influence of the heavens and the role of unexpected events in human affairs. He regarded fortune as a providential force operating through stellar influence and shaping all earthly developments except those controlled by the human will. Thus conscious and purposeful human action could forestall the ill effects of fortune. The treatise *De prudentia* discussed the qualities that would enable rulers and administrators to avoid fortune's snares. Prudence was the most important of these qualities, since it was the foundation of civil society and made it possible for individuals to lead their lives in accordance with reason and virtue. Prudence required rulers and administrators to tend diligently to public affairs, keep their eyes open for danger, and adapt flexibly to changing situations.

Although Pontano despised lies, deceit, and hypocrisy, he contended that rulers and administrators must stand prepared to employ cunning and misrepresent the truth in the interests of public welfare. Thus, like his younger Florentine contemporary Niccolò Machiavelli, Pontano drew on his experience in the tumultuous world of practical politics in reconsidering traditional moral thought.

BIBLIOGRAPHY

Bentley, Jerry H. *Politics and Culture in Renaissance Naples*. Princeton, N.J., 1987.

Percopo, Erasmo. *Vita di Giovanni Pontano*. Naples, Italy, 1938.

Tateo, Francesco. *L'umanesimo etico di Giovanni Pontano*. Lecce, Italy, 1972.

Trinkaus, Charles. "The Astrological Cosmos and Rhetorical Culture of Giovanni Gioviano Pontano." *Renaissance Quarterly* 38 (1985): 446–472.

JERRY H. BENTLEY

PONTORMO, JACOPO DA. *See* **Florence,** *subentry on* **Art of the Sixteenth Century.**

POPULAR CULTURE. The term "popular culture" was not in use in the fifteenth and sixteenth centuries, although the French essayist Michel de Montaigne referred on occasion to *poésie populaire* (*Essays,* Book 1, chapter 55, 1580). What have been known since the end of the eighteenth century as "folksongs," "folktales," and so on were described in this period simply as "songs" or "stories" and were known to and appreciated by the upper classes—male and female, clerical and lay.

High and Low Cultures. In contemporary terms, the upper classes may be described as bicultural because they participated in both high and low cultures. The humanist Giovanni Pontano and the poet Ludovico Ariosto are two well-known examples of members of the elite who enjoyed the popular performances of *cantastorie,* Italian singers of tales. Ordinary people, on the other hand, were excluded from high culture, including Renaissance art and literature, by a number of barriers, the first being language. Much of high culture centered on Latin culture, but the vast majority of the population did not study Latin. The second barrier was literacy. Only a minority—composed mostly of urban males—of the population could read and write. Ordinary people were also excluded from high culture by the economic barrier that prevented them from buying books or paintings, although some of them could afford prints.

Consequently, the culture of ordinary people was in many ways an oral culture. Within the household children learned songs, stories, and proverbs; beyond the household rumor and gossip were the main channels of information. This "homemade" culture was supplemented, especially in the towns, by the work of professional communicators such as preachers or actors. Popular material culture, however poor it may seem by the standards of later centuries, was also important in shaping the lives of individuals. Although most of what we call "folk art" dates from the eighteenth century or later, some visual representations of the Renaissance have survived.

Finally, oral communication and images were supplemented by rituals, some unofficial (like the

Popular Pastimes. *Battle between Carnival and Lent* by Pieter Brueghel the Elder (c. 1525 or 1530–1569). KUNSTHISTORISCHES MUSEUM, VIENNA/BILDARCHIV FOTO MARBURG/ART RESOURCE, NY

charivari or "rough music" played outside the house of a couple whose marriage was contrary to the local norms) and some official (notably the liturgy of the church).

Popular Religion. The popular religion of this period is usually presented by historians as a system of beliefs and rituals, the main function of which was security or relief from anxiety. Saints were regarded as powerful protectors and healers with virtually autonomous miraculous powers, and many of them were viewed as specialists. Saint Sebastian and Saint Roche offered protection against the plague, Saint Margaret against the dangers of childbirth, Saint Blaise against sore throats, and so on, while the Virgin Mary was regarded as a "general practitioner." Patron saints of cities, guilds, or individuals looked after the general safety and interests of their clients. The proverb "You can't get to heaven without saints" implied the importance of patrons and mediators in the next world as in this one.

In cases of emergency, such as epidemics, famines, wars, or individual accidents, collective processions would take place and individual vows would be made—to go on pilgrimage to a particular shrine, to light candles, to commission a painted "ex-voto" (a plaque acknowledging a blessing received or a prayer answered), or to offer gifts such as a silver hand or foot in return for a cure for the corresponding part of the body. A particularly rich collection of ex-votos from the fifteenth and sixteenth centuries has survived in the church of Santa Maria del Monte in Cesena. In Florence, a local miracle-working image of the Virgin, Santa Maria Impruneta, was frequently taken in procession through the city in order to ask for rain or avert political crises. Unofficial prayers were recited to cure sickness, assist childbirth, or find stolen objects.

This security system generated anxieties of its own. The saints required propitiation with offerings, were sensitive to neglect, and might punish their lukewarm devotees. On the other hand, the faithful might punish the saints if they failed to provide the help requested, by dunking their images in water in order to coerce them into future cooperation.

Festivals. Unlike later regimes of everyday leisure and consumption, the popular culture of this period focused on ephemeral events (it is generally the case that the poorer the society, the richer the festivals). One of the major festivals of sixteenth-century Europe was Carnival, especially in the Mediterranean world (in colder areas, such as Britain, Scandinavia, and Russia, spring and summer festivals were more important and took similar forms). The carnival season, which began in late December but generally reached its climax in the week culminating on Shrove Tuesday (the Tuesday before Ash Wednesday), was an officially tolerated time of license. The most popular activities included gluttony, sex, and violence. Participants ate meat and drank alcohol on the grandest possible scale, wore masks (or complete fancy dress), harassed members of the opposite sex, and engaged in more or less ritualized aggression: throwing eggs, oranges, fireworks, or water; tormenting animals; exchanging insulting words and gestures; and enacting various kinds of combat from football to mock tournaments and mock jousts (like the one unforgettably portrayed in the Netherlander Pieter Brueghel the Elder's painting *The Combat of Carnival and Lent;* 1559).

In some cities, notably Florence and Nürnberg, a procession or parade of decorated floats was a central part of the festival. In Rome there were races in which Jews, prostitutes, and old men were forced to take part. In Venice the public executioner beheaded a bull and twelve pigs on Piazza San Marco. In Nürnberg, the butchers danced in the marketplace, and in Königsberg in 1583, ninety butchers carried a gigantic sausage through the streets, doubtless a reference to the phallus as well as to the pleasures of eating meat. Young adult males, organized in guilds or festive societies like the French Abbeys of Misrule, usually played the leading roles in the proceedings, which were frequently sponsored by town councils, but women were also able to participate to some extent, notably by dressing as men or by launching missiles from their balconies. In short, Carnival allowed participants to enact the popular ideal of "the world turned upside down."

Imitation of High Culture. One feature of the secular culture of the period that has made a considerable impression on later scholars is the way in which popular culture imitated the content and the forms of high culture, sometimes centuries later. Romances of chivalry, written about (and originally for) knights and ladies, appealed by the sixteenth century to ordinary people as well. Many traditional oral narrative poems—in English, ballads—are concerned with the courts of Charlemagne, King Arthur, and other rulers. According to some historians the popular interest in knights and ladies was a form of escapism that indicates the cultural hegemony of the upper classes and helps explain the relative rarity of revolts. Some scholars have wondered if the individual heroes of these stories—Roland, Lancelot, Ogier the Dane, and so on—might not have had meanings for listeners in cottages that differed from the ones they were given in the great hall of the castle.

In any case it can be misleading to identify particular classes of texts and other objects as popular, and more illuminating to think in terms of items from a more or less common stock as being appropriated for different reasons and put to different uses by various social groups. One argument against the so-called two-tier model of learned and popular culture is its inadequacy with respect to the culture of artisans, shopkeepers, and other townspeople. The inhabitants of large towns in particular enjoyed relatively easy access to schools, plays, and works of art displayed in public places such as churches or town halls. Another argument against the two-tier model is that it does not account for the many mediators between the two cultures, such as parish priests, servants in the houses of the elites, and noblewomen, whose access to formal education was as limited as that of the popular classes.

These mediators played a crucial role in the interaction between popular culture and the elite movement known as the Renaissance. From one side came the dissemination of forms and ideas of the Renaissance from the elite to the people; using a simple spatial metaphor, we may call this a downward movement. From the other side, there was upward movement, in which Italian artists and writers drew on the heritage of popular culture. Diffusion was, as usual, accompanied by creative adaptation. Hence it might be useful to employ the terms "folklorization," for the process of appropriation by ordinary people, and "defolklorization," for appropriations by the elite of aspects of popular culture.

The Popularization of the Renaissance. Some ordinary people were familiar with at least a small part of the classical tradition. For example, works by the ancient Roman writers Cicero, Ovid, and Virgil had been translated into the vernacular by this time. The story about the Roman matron Lucretia

Popular Songs. Lorenzo de' Medici *(left)* watches as masked singers serenade women with his songs. Frontispiece to *Canzone per andare in maschera per Carnesciale* by Lorenzo and others. Woodcut; after 1497. BIBLIOTECA NAZIONALE CENTRALE, FLORENCE, E.6.5.47 FRONTISPIECE

and her suicide following her rape by King Tarquin appears to have been especially well known and was the subject of woodcuts, songs, and plays in Italy, Germany, and elsewhere.

A relatively clear-cut example of movement downward is that of Ariosto's *Orlando furioso* (1516). The poem was written by a noble for nobles, and in its published form was relatively expensive. However, the "laments" of the poem's characters such as Bradamante, Isabella, Rodomonte, and Ruggiero (as well as other verse paraphrases, supplements, and summaries) were available in the sixteenth century in the form of small booklets, the language and the price of which suggests that they were available to ordinary people. The popular appeal of *Orlando furioso,* cantos of which were frequently to be heard in the streets, was noted by some contemporary observers, among them Montaigne on his visit to Italy in 1580. Ariosto's poem was taught in some schools along with the Latin classics, a practice unusual in the sixteenth century. There is also evidence from archives, mainly from heresy trials, of interest in Ariosto on the part of ordinary Italians. In Venice, for example, a swordsmith's apprentice, a silk merchant, and a prostitute all testified to reading *Orlando furioso*.

The high art of the Italian Renaissance was generally produced by men with the training and status of craftsmen. The Florentine painter Sandro Botticelli, for example, left school in early adolescence, and the classical references in his paintings, notably the *Primavera* (1477–1478), were probably suggested to him by humanists he knew, such as Marsilio Ficino or Angelo Poliziano. Secular paintings of this kind were not widely visible during the Renaissance. It was, however, possible for a wider public to view graphic versions of some of them, notably the engravings after Raphael of Urbino made by Marcantonio Raimondi.

By the Renaissance period, the work of art had already entered the age of mechanical reproduction. Like printing, engraving was a great popularizer, at least in the sense that it allowed a larger number and variety of people access to the images. Ceramics offered another means of diffusing images more widely, since the raw material was inexpensive. The majolica plates and jugs produced in Faenza, Urbino, Deruta, and elsewhere were frequently decorated with scenes from classical mythology and ancient history. Some were based on the Raimondi engravings after Raphael. Although some of these ceramics were made for wealthy patrons, others were simple and practical (drugpots for apothecary shops, for example). Painted terracotta images produced by the Della Robbia family workshop in Florence might be regarded as poor man's sculptures. This workshop produced many small images for wayside shrines and private individuals as well as large expensive altarpieces for churches. Although it would be an exaggeration to use the term "mass production," signs of hasty work have been found, and it is not uncommon to find a particular image (an Adoration, say, or a Madonna and Child) surviving in ten or even twenty almost identical copies.

Drama also helped introduce ordinary people to Renaissance culture. Troupes practicing the new genre of *commedia dell'arte*—a semi-improvised comedy built around certain stock characters or masks such as Capitano, the boastful soldier, Gratiano, the pedant, or Pulcinella, the cunning servant—performed in cities as well as courts, and this style of acting was appropriated by charlatans who performed in town squares in Italy and sometimes in France to attract crowds to buy their medicines. The permanent public theaters founded in the later sixteenth century in major cities such as Paris, London, and Madrid were attended by ordinary people (such as apprentices) as well as by elites. Playwrights such as William Shakespeare, Christopher Marlowe, and Felix Lope de Vega had to provide something for everyone, and many of their plays vary in tone from scene to scene, ranging from clowning to tragedy.

Popular Inspiration in the Renaissance. Conversely, the high culture of the Renaissance was often inspired by low or popular traditions. For example, plays were frequently performed during the time of Carnival; like Carnival itself, comedies often represented a world turned upside down. A classic example of popular inspiration is writing by François Rabelais, a friar turned physician involved in the humanist movement. In a famous study, known in English as *Rabelais and His World,* the Russian critic Mikhail Bakhtin (1895–1975) argued that the author of *Gargantua and Pantagruel* (1532) drew heavily on the "culture of folk humor," in particular, the grotesque and the carnivalesque, popular styles that used festive laughter to subvert authority in church and state. Unfortunately, Bakhtin's account of the relation between high and low cultures was neither precise nor explicit. At times the contrast or opposition with which he is concerned seems to be that between the cultures of two social groups, the elite and the "people." At other times the two opposed cultures are defined in functional terms as the "official" and the "unofficial." These distinctions may overlap but they do not coincide. The students of Montpellier in France, for example, whose festivities Bakhtin includes in his category of "folk humor," had developed a lively unofficial culture while still belonging to a social elite. All the same, Bakhtin's work, which is full of insights into the language of the marketplace, the meanings of festive violence, and the function in various arts of images of "the lower bodily stratum," has been taken as a model for later studies of William Shakespeare and other artists and writers of the sixteenth century. That it continues to be useful for the incomplete task of assessing the importance of popular elements in the art and literature of the Renaissance will be argued here by means of four case studies: Boccaccio, Brueghel, Shakespeare, and Cervantes.

Boccaccio. Giovanni Boccaccio (1313–1375) was a learned man who wrote treatises in Latin and lectured on Dante. His Tuscan dialect was canonized in the sixteenth century (along with Dante's and Petrarch's) as a model of pure Italian. Nevertheless, it is clear that many of the stories in his famous *Decameron* (completed c. 1351–1353) were taken from popular oral tradition, and that they illustrate some of Bakhtin's favorite themes. Carnival and the carnivalesque occupy an important place in Boccaccio's stories, and a number of these stories include episodes of what Bakhtin calls "grotesque realism" or "degradation." The plots of a number of stories turn on practical jokes or *beffe,* a central genre in Tuscan popular culture. Whether the author or his intended readers were supposed to participate in this world or regard it from a distance is not always easy to deduce.

Brueghel. In this respect the case of sixteenth-century Netherlands painter Pieter Brueghel the Elder (c. 1525–1569) is somewhat clearer. His work frequently represents peasants working, dancing, eating, or drinking, and the paintings also illustrate a number of themes from popular culture such as games, proverbs, and Carnival. The earliest biography of Brueghel describes him as attending peasant weddings in order to gather information. All the same, the painter's work cannot be described as a simple instance of popular culture. A citizen of Antwerp, Brueghel frequented a circle of learned men around the geographer Abraham Ortelius. If he did not have the advantage of a classical education himself, he could, like Botticelli, at least learn about antiquity from conversations with humanists, and one of his most famous paintings, *Landscape with the Fall of Icarus* (c. 1558), has been shown to illustrate a passage from the *Metamorphoses* of the ancient Roman poet Ovid. His patrons were townspeople and it is likely that—whether they took the paintings lightly or seriously—these patrons understood the paintings as satires on the peasants, the "other" against which they defined themselves.

Shakespeare. Like Brueghel, William Shakespeare (1564–1616) represented ordinary people as comic figures, notably in *A Midsummer Night's Dream* (1595–1596) in such characters as Bottom the weaver and Snout the tinker. Shakespeare's comedies also draw on popular festive traditions. Holofernes and Armado in *Love's Labour's Lost* (1594–1595), for example, have been described as typical examples of the masks of the Pedant and the Captain from the *commedia dell'arte*. Similarly, Falstaff, "that stuffed cloak bag of guts," is a carnivalesque character if not a representation of Carnival, always eating, drinking, and making merry. Even the celebrated abandonment of Falstaff by an increasingly sober Prince Hal in *Henry IV, Part II* (c. 1598) follows the traditional framework of the trial of Carnival, which in many areas of Europe dramatized the end of the festive season. *Twelfth Night* (c. 1601) has a festive setting in which Sir Toby Belch plays a carnivalesque role, and *A Midsummer Night's Dream* follows the plot of what Elizabethans called a "May Game," the traditional English spring festival.

Cervantes. Miguel Cervantes (1547–1616) in his *Don Quixote* (1605–1615) draws on traditional folktales or retells them within the framework of the novel. Like Falstaff, Don Quixote's companion Sancho Panza (whose surname means "Belly") is something of a carnivalesque figure, a mighty eater and sleeper, though his combination of credulity and cunning, together with his malapropisms, refer to other popular comic traditions.

Changes in Popular Culture. The Renaissance period witnessed the beginning of a withdrawal of elites from participation in popular culture for both religious and secular reasons. The movements of religious reform we now describe as the Reformation and Counter-Reformation included a series of attempts to purify traditional popular culture of paganism, immorality, and rusticity. The variety of elite attitudes toward witchcraft at this time may be taken to illustrate the process of reform and withdrawal. That Gianfrancesco Pico della Mirandola (1469–1533), nephew of the humanist Giovanni Pico (1463–1494), for example, believed in witchcraft but attributed it to ordinary people and did his best to root it out, is revealed by his activity in witch trials (in his principality of Mirandola in northern Italy) between 1522 and 1523 as well as by his dialogue on the subject, "The Witch" (*Strix*). The Neapolitan physician Giambattista Della Porta (c. 1535–1615), on the other hand, had a more relaxed or empiricist attitude toward witchcraft. He tested the power of witches' ointments experimentally to see whether they would allow the users to fly.

In different ways, however, both Pico and Della Porta reveal their detachment from popular beliefs. The Renaissance movement itself encouraged a withdrawal of elites from popular culture. The more carefully the readers of Baldassare Castiglione's *Il cortegiano* (*The Book of the Courtier;* 1528), for example, followed the author's model of elegant behavior, the further they were bound to move from popular traditions. In retrospect it appears that Rabelais, Bruegel, Shakespeare, and Cervantes all created their masterpieces at a point of unstable equilibrium between the practice of participation and the trend toward withdrawal. While more distant from popular culture than their medieval predecessors, they were much closer to ordinary people than their modern successors. The wealth of evidence of interaction between the two cultures may prompt the reader, as it has already prompted a number of scholars, to call for the rejection of the binary opposition between learned and popular and high and low. But what other means have we for speaking about this very interaction?

See also **Carnival; Catholic Reformation and Counter-Reformation; Ceramics; Charivari; Chivalry,** *subentry on* **Romance of Chivalry; Commedia dell'arte; Festivals; Graphic Arts; Parades, Processions, and Pageants; Protestant Reformation; Religious Piety; Translation; Witchcraft;** *and biographies of figures mentioned in this entry.*

BIBLIOGRAPHY

Bakhtin, Mikhail. *Rabelais and His World.* Translated by Helene Iswolsky. Cambridge, Mass., 1968. Translation of *Tvorchestvo Fransua Rable i narodnaia kultura Srednevekovia i Renessansa* (1965). A controversial but fundamental study of popular culture as subversion.

Barber, C. L. *Shakespeare's Festive Comedy: A Study of Dramatic Form and Its Relation to Social Custom.* Princeton, N.J., 1959.

Bristol, Michael D. *Carnival and Theater: Plebeian Culture and the Structure of Authority in Renaissance England.* London and New York, 1985. Uncritically Bakhtinian.

Burke, Peter. *Popular Culture in Early Modern Europe.* 2d ed. New York, 1994. A Europewide survey.

Chartier, Roger. "Culture as Appropriation: Popular Cultural Uses in Early Modern France." In *Understanding Popular Culture: Europe from the Middle Ages to the Nineteenth Century.* Edited by Steven L. Kaplan. Berlin and New York, 1984. Pages 229–254. An important theoretical formulation.

Davis, Natalie. *Society and Culture in Early Modern France.* Stanford, Calif., 1975. Pioneering and influential essays.

Ginzburg, Carlo. *Cheese and Worms: The Cosmos of a Sixteenth-Century Miller.* Translated by Anne and John Tedeschi. Baltimore, 1980. Translation of *Il Formaggio e i Vermi* (1976). A classic of history "from below."

Molho, Maurice. *Cervantes: Raíces folklóricas.* Madrid, 1976.

Scribner, Robert W. *Popular Culture and Popular Movements in Reformation Germany.* London, 1987. Stimulating essays.

Sullivan, Margaret A. *Bruegel's Peasants: Art and Audience in the Northern Renaissance.* Cambridge, U.K., and New York, 1994.

Thomas, Keith V. *Religion and the Decline of Magic.* London and New York, 1971. A classic of historical anthropology.

PETER BURKE

POPULAR RELIGION. *See* **Religious Piety.**

POPULAR REVOLTS. Popular revolts were a consequence of stresses and dysfunctions in a usually stable society. Though "peasant" revolts were the best-known form of protest, generically there were few purely "peasant" or rural revolts, since town and country were closely connected. At a local level discontent was a symptom of stresses in the fabric of traditional social relationships; at a national level it reflected the conflicting aspirations of status groups. At both of these levels the motives and ideology for revolt did not necessarily originate among the popular classes, who were often the led rather than the leaders.

The Incidence of Revolt. Protest was normal and therefore frequent; it was an accepted feature of relations between seigneurs (lords) and tenants, or princes and their subjects. The most common causes of instability were changes in political organization or fiscal obligation, and a changing perception of social relationships. By the late Renaissance the local communities—the fundamental unit of early modern Europe—were changing their external status and their internal structure. Problems that did not threaten the basic structure of the community were solved through internal confrontations (murder of the lord, riots of taxpayers against the tax-exempt, persecution of witches) and seldom led to an outward explosion.

For revolt to occur, two things were essential: an outrage or threat to the moral conscience of the community and the projection of protest from a local to a universal plane. A threat might come in the form of a violation of the norms of survival (crippling taxes and maldistribution of food would both threaten the basic right to exist) and would instantly lower the threshold of violence, precipitating collective action that might not occur at other times. Any violence would naturally be conservative, not revolutionary; that is, it would aim to conserve and restore disregarded norms. Revolt was not normally a blind act of violence, but a carefully coordinated movement, usually agreed on by the leadership of several villages at some regional function such as a fair (in Swabia in 1524) or a carnival (in Romans-sur-Isère in 1580), and carried out with maximum coercion against those individuals or villages that refused to take part.

Our knowledge of the frequency of revolt is necessarily determined by availability of documentation. Though the 1430s and 1440s have been identified as a period of popular upheaval in Denmark and Sweden, for example, no comparable documentation for revolts in central or southern Europe can be found. Resistance to seigneurs was commonplace everywhere, as instanced by the famous incident at Fuenteovejuna (southern Spain) in 1476, when an entire village claimed joint responsibility for the murder of its lord, an action that emphasized the tradition of communal revolt. In Germany there were millennial movements such as that of the piper of Niklashausen (1476) and the Bundschuh (peasant boot) rebellions (from 1493, mainly in the Black Forest in southwest Germany). From the sixteenth century onward, documentation of uprisings becomes more available. The first major revolt of the sixteenth century was that of the Hungarian peasants in 1514; there was also a large uprising of Slovene peasants in 1515 in Carniola and Carinthia. In spring 1520, as Charles V was leaving Spain for Germany, the major revolt of the *comunidades* (Castilian cities) broke out, followed shortly after by that of the Germanías (brotherhoods) in Valencia.

The classic popular revolt of the early century was that of the German peasants (1525). Confined neither to Germany nor to the peasants, it was a vast unintegrated wave of protest that swept over the whole of central Europe and in some areas was primarily urban. The events have been described as a war or even as a revolution. Their long-term cause must be sought in the slow encroachment of seigneurs on the peasant economy: lords enforced and extended their fiscal and jurisdictional privileges, and in so doing came into conflict with strong village communities whose leaders helped to coordinate resistance. The first resort to arms was in June 1524 in Stühlingen (Swabia). By the autumn there were uprisings all around Lake Constance and toward the Black Forest. The core of uprisings in south and central Germany (February to May 1525) extended into Upper Swabia and then spread along the Danube down to Bavaria and the Alps. In April there were risings by peasants, miners, and townspeople in Württemberg, northern Switzerland, Alsace, Thuringia, and the Rhineland down to Mainz, the Palatinate, and Franche-Comté. By summer the revolts had spread to Saxony, Salzburg, Styria, and Austria, then into French-speaking Lorraine and Burgundy. In the Rhineland the movement was largely urban, with a notable city revolt in Frankfurt. The heart of the revolution was in Upper Swabia, where the original Twelve Articles of the peasants were drawn up at Memmingen in March 1525. This astonishing series of uprisings was led for the most part not by peasants but by artisans, preachers, lesser nobles, and bourgeois. All groups found a common ideology less in their social grievances than in the appeal to "God's law." Although Luther had pioneered this concept, and many rebels looked to him for support, he fiercely denounced the uprising.

Among the notable urban revolts of this time were the Grande Rebeyne at Lyon (April 1529) and the urban revolt at Ghent (1540), both in defense of traditional privileges. A more broadly based revolt was the Pilgrimage of Grace (1536) in England. Though social protest remained strong within the movement, the Pilgrimage quickly became a traditionalist pro-Catholic uprising. In 1548 the first of a series of major uprisings broke out in Aquitaine, protesting the introduction of a salt tax (*gabelle*). Rural areas such as Santonge and Angoumois established communes, and the revolt of the Pitauds (the poor) spread into the city of Bordeaux, which was taken over by the rebels. The mid-1580s, particularly the period between 1585 and 1587, was a time of bad harvests and political crisis throughout western Europe, accompanied by wars in France and the Netherlands. In the town of Romans-sur-Isère in the winter of 1580, a rebellious alliance was formed between the peasants of the countryside and the artisans of the town; encouraged by support from the townsmen, the peasants refused to pay their tithes (to the church) and *taille* (taxes). The revolt was repressed by February 1580. In 1585 in Naples a similar event occurred when, after a bad harvest, the authorities raised the price of bread and authorized the export of flour. In May an angry mob lynched one of the magistrates responsible, a man named Starace, whose body was mutilated and dragged through the streets; a large urban revolt followed. In the subsequent repression more than eight hundred people were brought to trial. In the same period, the city of Paris experienced an uprising provoked by the politics of the religious wars. On 12 May 1588, the Day of Barricades, a general uprising of the population in favor of the duke of Guise took place. When the duke and the cardinal of Guise were assassinated on the king's orders in 1588, authority in the anarchic city devolved into a commune led by the so-called Council of Sixteen.

The conditions of the 1590s were catastrophic: from 1590 to 1597 harvests were bad, prices crippling. There was famine in 1595 in parts of England, Languedoc, and Naples. Prices in Rome from 1590 to 1599 were double those for 1570 to 1579. The crisis touched England, France, Austria, Finland, Hungary, Lithuania, and the Ukraine. In Finland a peasant revolt occurred from 1596 to 1597. A few English laborers in the Midlands attempted an uprising in 1596, but the authorities responded swiftly, arrested the leaders, and snuffed out the insurrection. The great revolt of the Croquants (the poor) in France was concentrated in the years 1593 to 1595. It began in Bas-Limousin and eventually covered Périgord, Quercy, Limousin, and Languedoc. Originally a peasant rebellion, it became more complex in its social composition and grew to include a large proportion of urban laborers in its ranks. The main grievance of the Croquants was the fiscal system: they firmly opposed both tithe and *taille* as well as seigneurial taxes. Upper Austria, "beyond the river Enns" (*ob der Enns*), with Linz as its capital, was the theater of almost continuous peasant uprisings in 1525 and subsequent years. Since the territory was Lutheran, the uprisings had a strong religious inspiration, although secular grievances were deeply intermixed. The revolt of 1594 there was significant and lasted more than three years.

The Dynamics of Popular Revolt. In Renaissance Europe the precipitants of revolt can be reduced very generally to three: bad harvests, extraordinary taxation, and marauding of the soldiery. However, the causes of revolt did not necessarily coincide with these precipitants. Bad harvests were a normal occurrence, and as long as the common people believed that everyone else was starving they would endure the hardship. Only when it was clear that others were profiting from distress did they revolt; for example, food-hoarders were the target of an uprising in Naples in 1585. Extraordinary taxation features in nearly every revolt as a direct or proximate cause but was invariably no more than a trigger to release other long-standing grievances.

The tradition of revolt was also an important aspect of many insurrections. Certain localities seem to have been at the forefront of rebellions; the small town of Gourdon in Quercy (France) was at the center of peasant agitation three times in three centuries. On a larger scale, endemic regionalism was a self-evident reason for the persistence of a tradition of rebellion. At times the tradition took the form of a myth: names like Croquants, Levellers, and Germanías were adopted repeatedly by subsequent rebels as if to draw legitimacy from their predecessors. The urge to legitimate a rebellion by establishing continuity from a respected past was constant. Swiss rebels tended to appeal directly to the tradition of their mythical national hero, William Tell, who resisted foreign oppression.

The leaders and instigators of uprisings emerged from the rural elite, urban artisans, and, at the topmost level, nobility. This was not surprising since many major revolts, once they had transcended the local level of grievances, mushroomed out to become large movements embracing all classes and interests. Nobles also wished to rescue their people from the taxation and political authority of the state. Clergy were prominent participants and leaders. A *Croquant* priest in the Angoumois justified his role "because priests are not forbidden to go to war . . . and he was defending the public good." In Spain, clergy had a long tradition of rebellion; the preaching of friars in Salamanca in 1520 put the city firmly on the side of the *comunidades*.

Popular agitation has often been viewed as fragmentary and short-lived, and consequently of no political importance. Where community structures were weak or even nomadic (as on the Russian frontier), peasant risings degenerated into skirmishes, all too easily suppressed. However, where peasant communities were firmer, protracted struggle was possible: the Croquant rebellion of 1594 lasted nearly two years, and the Austrian peasant uprising of 1594 continued for three. In numbers, too, the uprisings could not be ignored, rebel armies reaching the size of forty thousand persons in Austria in 1595.

A common misapprehension about popular uprisings is that they were purely sanguinary in their goals. Luther denounced the peasants as "murderous," but the reality was different. Most rebels respected both life and property, and the violence of revolts was usually quite distinctive. The primary purpose of rebellion was always to achieve justice, which was therefore visited, in a primeval and almost symbolic way, on doers of evil and enemies of the community. Tax collectors, particularly those who originated from outside the community, were regular victims. The ritual of cannibalism practiced at Romans-sur-Isère in 1580 and the ritualistic mutilation of the sort committed on Starace in Naples in 1585 were further examples of popular justice.

All rebels took great pains to establish their legitimacy. Lacking any basis for their authority, they appealed to history, to myth, and to God. Side by side with this pseudo-ideology went a formal belief and trust in the king. It is exceptional to meet cases such as that recorded by the soldier Blaise de Lasseran Massencôme, marshal of France, in his *Commentaires* (written 1521–1574, published 1592), of peasant rebels in the late sixteenth century who reacted to a mention of the king by saying, "What king? It is we who are the kings; the one you speak of is just a little turd."

Role reversals of various types were commonplace in most uprisings: rebels might dress themselves up as lords and clergy; men might dress up as women. The symbolism was subversive but modeled on the otherwise nonsubversive role reversal practiced in carnivals. Turning the world upside down, a common enough feature of the carnival tradition, became a logical recourse of rebels.

See also **Comuneros, Revolt of the; Peasants' War; Violence.**

BIBLIOGRAPHY

Bercé, Yves-Marie. *Révoltes et révolutions dans l'Europe moderne, XVIe–XVIIIe siècles*. Paris, 1980. English edition: *Revolt and Revolution in Early Modern Europe*. Translated by Joseph Bergin. Manchester, U.K., 1987.

Blickle, Peter, ed. *Resistance, Representation, and Community*. Oxford and New York, 1997. Has an excellent and comprehensive bibliography of recent works.

Hill, Christopher. *The World Turned Upside Down*. London and New York, 1972.

Le Roy Ladurie, Emmanuel. *Carnival in Romans*. New York, 1979. Translated by Mary Feeney. Translation of *Carnaval de Romans*.

Pillorget, Rene. *Les mouvements insurrectionnels de Provence entre 1596 et 1715*. Paris, 1975.

Schulze, Winfried, ed. *Aufstände, Revolten, Prozesse*. Stuttgart, Germany, 1983.

Schulze, Winfried, ed. *Europäische Bauernrevolten der frühen Neuzeit*. Frankfurt am Main, Germany, 1982.

HENRY KAMEN

POPULATION. *See* **Census; Demography.**

PORNOGRAPHY. Did the Renaissance have a kind of pornography? If "pornography" is taken to mean sexually explicit and obscene material, then the answer is certainly yes. An important and relatively neglected aspect of Renaissance humanism concerns its engagement with the sexual mores and practices of Greek and Roman culture, whose erotic statuary and poetry celebrated not only nudity but a wide array of sexual behavior that was explicitly condemned by Christianity. In recuperating the objects and texts of antiquity, Renaissance scholars confronted a sexual world that was, in certain fundamental respects, different from their own. Ancient gods enjoyed their sexuality without shame; indeed, one of the household gods of ancient Greece and Rome, Priapus, was popularly identifiable by his large, erect penis. Similarly, the ancient world did not condemn sodomy but routinely depicted liaisons between men and boys as a natural part of human sexuality.

Latin Writings. Both the sexualized gods and sexual practices of antiquity challenged Christian humanists' belief that antiquity could be wholly compatible with Christianity. The responses to this moral dilemma were varied. Some scholars chose to ignore these parts of antiquity, circulating only the salutary writings of reputable ancients such as Cicero and Tacitus rather than the bawdy poems of Catullus; in other instances they exercised their moral authority as educators of the young, expurgating the most salacious passages from works such as Ovid's *Metamorphoses.* Some scholars felt that the inaccessibility of ancient eroticism, confined to the private studies of humanists and to languages known by only a few, precluded it from falling into the wrong hands. Learning itself, they argued, was its own guarantor of moral probity. Such attitudes were effectively satirized by a Sienese writer, Antonio Vignali (1500 or 1501–1559). In *La cazzaria* (Bunch of pricks; 1525–1526), Vignali, writing under the pseudonym Intronato Arsiccio, imagined the humanist study as a pornographer's den filled with nothing but erotic and obscene works for visitors to peruse. In short, education was never an absolute barrier to the obscene.

In some instances education seemed to encourage the obscene, suggesting that Renaissance values and ancient mores were not so far apart as moralists claimed. In the fifteenth and sixteenth centuries, as knowledge of the ubiquity of Priapus in antiquity grew, writing priapic poems became enormously popular. Many authors justified writing erotic and obscene poetry by reference to ancient precedent; the twenty-two editions of the ancient *Carmina priapea* (Priapic poems) in circulation by 1517 suggest how popular these writings already were in the early days of printing. Humanists circulated erotic manuscripts by the ancients and by their own hand among friends, often attributing them to well-known authors such as Ovid and Virgil. They treated such texts with the same philological rigor as they did the less objectionable histories, letters, and poetry of the ancients, indicating that these works had a place in the widening literary canon.

Not everyone agreed with this perspective. Yet another aspect of pornography has to do with distinctions between tasteful eroticism and unacceptable obscenity or sexual vulgarity. As early as the fifteenth century controversies arose over the humanist celebration of ancient sexuality. In 1425 Antonio Beccadelli (1394–1471) published *Hermaphroditus* (The hermaphrodite), a priapic poem that he dedicated to Cosimo de' Medici (he described one half of the poem as a vagina and the other half as a penis). Within a year praise had become vituperation. The poem was condemned by preachers and the pope, and copies were publicly burned in several cities. Fellow humanists seem to have been more ambivalent, since Beccadelli's poem belonged to a genre they recognized as witty imitation of ancient writing. Yet this episode potentially concerned the controversial act of public dissemination: as a private joke *Hermaphroditus* may not have qualified as pornography since it offended few of its more learned readers, but as a text dedicated to one of the leading political and cultural figures in Renaissance Italy it outraged guardians of public morality. By this definition and in this context it was pornographic.

Undoubtedly the concerns raised by preachers such as Bernardino of Siena about Beccadelli coincided with their general sense that the new literary culture of the late fourteenth and the fifteenth century openly critiqued and subverted the values they sought to uphold. Its popularity explicitly challenged Christian morality. Latin works such as *Hermaphroditus* and Poggio Bracciolini's bawdy *Facetiae* (Witty tales; 1473) had their vernacular counterpart in the earthy materialism and anticlericalism of Giovanni Boccaccio's *Decameron* (1353). While not pornographic in that they did not focus exclusively and explicitly on sexuality, Boccaccio's tales frequently made sexual transgressions by husbands, wives, and clerics an object of hilarity. The widespread popularity of these tales, and Boccaccio's ability to mediate between high and low culture, led moralists to fear that acceptance of more openly obscene works in the learned form, such as *Hermaphroditus,* would lead to the circulation of more popular equivalents among a less discerning readership.

Vernacular Writings. Developments in erotic and obscene literature in the sixteenth century suggest that this was a well-placed concern. After a century of humanists' exchanging Latinate pornography in the form of priapic poems and bawdy epigrams, vernacular writers began to capitalize on the new medium of the printing press to popularize these genres. Vernacular languages became the preferred medium of pornography in the sixteenth and seventeenth centuries in order to reach the widest possible readership. Words no longer were enough. Engraved images helped to visualize the sexual acts that words described.

The writings of Pietro Aretino (1492–1556) and his associates in Venice played a central role in defining popular genres of pornography. The author of *Sonetti lussuriosi* (Lewd sonnets; 1527) and *Ragionamenti* (Dialogues; 1534–1536), Aretino gave shape to a new kind of pornography. In *Sonetti* he described in verse sixteen sexual positions that had originally been depicted by the Roman artist Giulio Romano (c. 1499–1546); they were subsequently engraved by the prolific Marcantonio Raimondi (c. 1480–c. 1534), who helped to distribute them widely throughout Rome. Aretino capitalized on the scandal by recognizing, with Raimondi, its commercial possibilities. He supplied the words that made the intent of the images unmistakable. Ever since, *Sonetti* has marked the origins of pornography for both historians and aficionados of pornography. So coveted and scandalous were the Aretine postures, as they came to be called, that only one copy of the original edition has survived intact. Imitations proliferated. By the middle of the seventeenth century readers could find pseudo-Aretine works that had increased the number of positions threefold.

Scandal is surely another feature of pornography. By actively cultivating a scandalous reputation, through his outrageous satires of society and audacious requests of powerful patrons, artists, and writers, Aretino helped to create the image of the venal author who wrote to outrage and to profit. Spending the majority of his life in Venice, the center of the Renaissance publishing industry, Aretino understood well that there was a market for obscenity in his society and provided readers with what they desired. By the end of the sixteenth century his works were so well known in countries such as England and France that the term "Aretine" was as synonymous with vice and corruption as the more well known phrase "Machiavellian."

Aretino's *Ragionamenti* expanded the definition of pornography to include writing by and about prostitutes (following the etymology of the word *pornographos*). In these dialogues between an older prostitute, Nanna, and her young protégée, Pippa, Aretino enhanced Boccaccio's and Poggio's tales of wayward clergy and vice-ridden spouses by creating an encyclopedia of sexual vices and insincerity that would not be rivaled until the work of the Marquis de Sade two and a half centuries later. The premise of the dialogues alone was bound to outrage many readers. On the first day young Pippa attempts to decide which path would be the best for her to pursue: that of a nun, wife, or prostitute. Nanna responds that she has tried them all and recounts her adventures, making it amply clear that prostitution is the most honest profession for a woman to follow. She persuades Pippa of the truth of her experience and assists her in becoming the best prostitute in Rome, teaching her all the tricks used by high-class courtesans to attract learned courtiers and humanists who wish to spend time with women as much for their conversation as for their sex.

Ragionamenti strikes modern readers as belonging more to the genre of social satire than to pornography; for all its sexual explicitness, the book targets society more than sex. Yet Renaissance readers did not necessarily make such a distinction (nor admittedly do some modern readers). Part of the pornography in *Ragionamenti* lay in its exposure, in the vulgar language of the marketplace, of the lives and pretensions of the upper classes as seen in their bedroom behavior. Aretino, in essence, had turned the tables on his patrons, making them appear weak, debauched, and silly to a broad reading public. Such material was very popular among English readers who wished to believe the worst about the corruption of the Italians and the papacy. Aretino not only exposed the social and intellectual pretensions of the papal court but also enhanced its weaknesses through long, voyeuristic accounts of the imagined sexual life of the clergy.

Attempts at Control. In 1559 Aretino's works appeared on the Catholic Church's Index of Prohibited Books. This official announcement of their scandalous nature only increased their popularity in the clandestine book market; London publishers printed Italian copies, along with the banned works of Machiavelli, and smuggled them to Venice for booksellers to distribute. That it took more than twenty years formally to censure Aretino's writings is in itself telling. The Catholic Church only developed formal mechanisms of censorship in the wake of the Reformation and initially concentrated on heretical rather than obscene or lascivious works. Only belatedly did it realize that the popularity of morally questionable books, poems, and prints might prove an additional threat to the purification and restoration of Catholicism.

By the late sixteenth century the morality of culture had become a battleground for many prominent religious reformers, who used formal mechanisms such as the Index of Prohibited Books to help sharpen the public's appreciation for the boundaries between good and bad culture. All works of art and literature deemed excessively concerned with the sins and pleasures of the flesh were labeled pagan—a term that increasingly signaled the pornographic. Repudiating the earlier and more tolerant humanism that had embraced all aspects of antiquity, reforming clerics sought to clean up the imagery of their society. They began in the churches, clothing the nudes of Michelangelo's *Last Judgment,* removing the most carnal images of Christ, Mary, and the saints, and placing the naked statues in the Belvedere gardens in Rome behind curtains so that casual visitors would not be overcome by the sight of lustful, pagan art. Undoubtedly, it was in response to this new climate that some patrons of the works of Titian, such as Philip II of Spain, placed his more erotic paintings behind curtains in their palaces. Such actions fit the new moral guidelines of the Catholic Reformation but also created a titillating aura around Renaissance and ancient depictions of nudity that may not have been there previously.

Neither the placement of books on the Index of Prohibited Books nor the reformed guidelines for art checked the appreciation of erotic and obscene words and images in late Renaissance society. Followers of Aretino, such as the Venetian writer Nicolò Franco (1515–1570), imitated his successes, publishing vernacular priapic poems and parodies of the catalogs of whores for which Venice was famous. By the early seventeenth century libertine academies such as the Venetian Accademia degli Incogniti boasted of several scandalous authors among their members. Works such as Ferrante Pallavicino's *La rettorica delle puttane* (Whore's rhetoric; 1642) and Antonio Rocco's *L'Alcibiade fanciullo a scola* (Alcibiades the schoolboy; 1652) continued two of the primary themes of Renaissance pornography: the revelations of the lascivious, knowing whore and the pederastic scandals of the humanist schoolroom, where boys were initiated by schoolmasters into Latin and vice.

The subjects chosen by Renaissance writers and artists determined the nature of a great deal of early modern pornography. Courtly and clerical scandals, schoolroom trysts, and the antics of whores entertained readers for the next two centuries. By the late seventeenth century the English, Dutch, and French increasingly played a greater role than the Italians in the publication of pornography. This transition reflected not only the shifting centers of the publishing industry but also a sense that, after 1650, Italy was no longer a region of powerful states whose scandals delighted foreigners. There were new political and sexual scandals to consume to the north. Because research on northern European pornography has focused on the period after the Renaissance, we do not yet know to what degree an equivalent literature flourished in Shakespeare's England or Montaigne's France.

See also **Aretino, Pietro; Prostitution.**

BIBLIOGRAPHY

Barkan, Leonard. *Transuming Passion: Ganymede and the Erotics of Humanism.* Stanford, Calif., 1991.

Findlen, Paula. "Humanism, Politics, and Pornography in Renaissance Italy." In *The Invention of Pornography: Obscenity and the Origins of Modernity, 1500–1800.* Edited by Lynn Hunt. New York, 1993. Pages 49–108.

Frantz, David O. *Festum Voluptatis: A Study of Renaissance Erotica.* Columbus, Ohio, 1989.

Ginzburg, Carlo. *Myths, Emblems, Clues.* Translated by John Tedeschi and Anne C. Tedeschi. London, 1990. See "Titian, Ovid, and Sixteenth-Century Codes for Erotic Illustration," pp. 77–95.

Hunt, Lynn, ed. *The Invention of Pornography: Obscenity and the Origins of Modernity, 1500–1800.* New York, 1993.

Kendrick, Walter. *The Secret Museum: Pornography in Modern Culture.* New York, 1987.

Talvacchia, Bette. *Taking Positions: On the Erotic in Renaissance Culture.* Princeton, N.J., 1999.

Thompson, Roger. *Unfit for Modest Ears: A Study of Pornographic, Obscene, and Bawdy Works Written or Published in England in the Second Half of the Seventeenth Century.* Totowa, N.J., 1979.

PAULA FINDLEN

PORTA, GIAMBATTISTA DELLA. *See* **Della Porta, Giambattista.**

PORTUGAL. The common image of Renaissance Portugal has long reflected the leading role this small kingdom on the western rim of the Iberian Peninsula played in the early European overseas expansion. Contemporaries were dazzled by the reports of Portuguese oceanic explorations; the influx of African gold, slaves, and Eastern spices; accounts of victories against Muslims in Morocco and the Indian Ocean; and the exotic wonders of Asia. Renaissance writers celebrated the Portuguese for not only matching but exceeding the military and exploration exploits of classical antiquity. For the nineteenth century, the overseas expansion became deeply fused with the idea of progress and the victory of science and technology over a premodern "darkness." Twentieth-century historians, despite stark differences in their ideological and methodological outlooks, mostly continued to acknowledge the Portuguese navigations and conquests as one of the fundamental factors involved, for better or for worse, in the making of the modern world.

Nation and Dynasty. As a result of these factors, the Portuguese overseas ventures have generally received much more attention than the social, political, and cultural context from which they sprang and that gave them momentum. This context was shaped by the demographic, economic, and religious upsets that had, in the fourteenth century, so profoundly shaken western Europe and the Mediterranean world: the plague of 1348–1349 and the

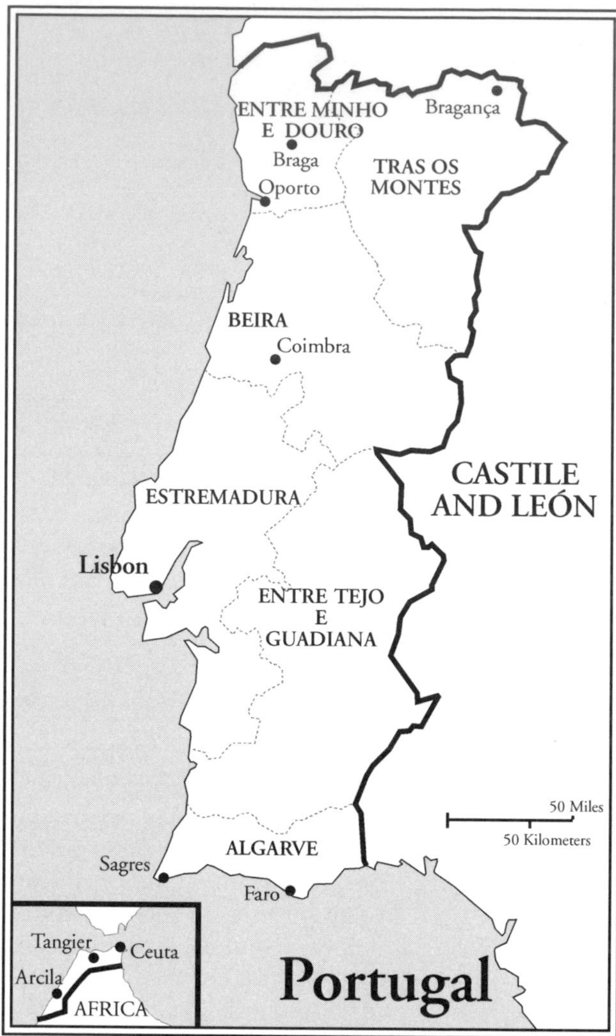

subsequent epidemics, chronic local and general warfare, recurring famines, scarcity of bullion, declining revenues and rising expenditures of the elites, and the papal schism. Although Portugal was no less affected by these problems than were other European countries, its small size, sense of identity, and dynastic strength afforded it more stability than its neighbors enjoyed in the fifteenth century, and endowed it with many of the attributes of an early nation-state.

The vibrant sense of national identity in late medieval Portugal is associated with the rise of the Avis dynasty, which ruled the country throughout its age of prominence, the fifteenth and sixteenth centuries. The dynasty's founder, Dom João, the master of the military order of Avis, emerged victorious from a power struggle that followed the death in 1383 of Dom Fernando, the last Burgundian king of Portugal, who did not leave a male heir. Dom Fernando's daughter, Dona Beatriz, was married to Dom Juan of Trastamara, the reigning king of Castile. Dom João, Fernando's illegitimate half-brother, profited from his supporters' deep hostility against a personal union with Castile, as well as from the social tensions pitting the Portuguese grandees against lesser nobility, the towns, and the poverty-stricken urban poor. In 1385 the Cortes, the assembly of the three Portuguese estates, declared the throne vacant and elected Dom João king (ruled 1385–1433).

Throughout the first twenty-five years of Avis rule, Portugal lived in an intermittent state of war with its much larger and more powerful neighbor, the Kingdom of Castile and Leon. Castile, however, unlike Portugal, suffered not only from demographic problems, epidemics, and warfare, but also from its rulers' inability to tame powerful noble factions and pursue effective fiscal policy. Portuguese victory became assured in the early stages of the war, following decisive engagements fought in 1385. By 1389 Dom Juan I of Castile had to acknowledge defeat and sign a truce. Over the next fifteen years, hostilities took the form of border raids and counterraids, in which the Portuguese as a rule had the upper hand. The foundations of a long-term peace were laid only in 1411.

Ironically, it was the state of war during the early decades of Avis rule that helped to forge the cohesive character of the Portuguese state, strengthened the central government, and established a sound fiscal base. The need for defense justified levying an internal sales tax, the *sisa,* year after year, until it became a permanent pillar of royal revenue. Similarly, the prolonged state of emergency gave the crown greater scope of power than peacetime conditions would have allowed. Also, the war made the opponents of Avis rule not only dynastic but also national traitors. Finally, the wars and confiscations of enemy property gave Dom João I the means to reward his noble followers with suitable opportunities and gifts.

The official end of hostilities in 1411 was thus a very mixed blessing. On the positive side, it promised a peace dividend: security, end of wartime expenditures, and economic prosperity. At the same time, it exposed some inherent constraints. Chief among these was that without war, the crown could not command the means to keep a volatile nobility occupied and satisfied. This was a very serious problem at a time when severe monetary devaluations and a shrinking population base whittled down the nobility's revenues. The crown soon found itself short of land to bestow on those who merited rewards or who needed to be placated. Moreover, appanages, grants of land or revenue, had to be created

Kings of Portugal

Dom Pedro I (1357–1367)
Dom Fernando (1367–1383)

Avis Dynasty
Dom João I (1385–1433)
Dom Duarte (1433–1438)
Dom Afonso V (1438–1481)
Dom João II (1481–1495)
Dom Manuel (1495–1521)
Dom João III (1521–1557)
Dom Sebastião (1557–1578)
Dom Henrique (1578–1580)

Habsburg Dynasty
Philip I (1580–1598) (Philip II, king of Spain)
Philip II (1598–1621) (Philip III, king of Spain)
Philip III (1621–1640) (Philip IV, king of Spain)

Bragança Dynasty
João IV (1640–1656)

both for Dom João's sons and for the numerous descendants of Dom João's father, King Pedro I, whose claims to the throne had to be bought out.

The 1415 military campaign against the North African city of Ceuta, whose conquest is often taken to mark the beginning of the European overseas expansion, was thus not only an expected source of booty, but also an expedient way to divert the energies of the Portuguese nobility and a commonly recognized prestige-generating enterprise, designed to bolster the image of the Avis dynasty as not only a factual but legitimate royal house. The success of the venture indeed much enhanced the international recognition of both Portugal and of the house of Avis, which already had sound foundations by a dynastic alliance with the ruling house of England. In the first half of the fifteenth century, the prestige of the house of Avis was further promoted through travels and state visits by members of the royal family, and through marriages of Portuguese princesses to prestigious rulers and nobles, including the Holy Roman Emperor (1451), two kings of Castile (1447 and 1455), and the duke of Burgundy (1430).

Domestic Difficulties. External diplomatic and military success, however, could not resolve mounting domestic difficulties. Monetary problems, declining incomes, social tensions, and a slipshod justice system created a dangerous atmosphere of discontent that plagued Portugal throughout much of the fifteenth century. Various levels of the nobility felt particularly strongly affected, and the crown oscillated between a policy of confrontation and appeasement. Appeasement involved large giveaways of royal lands and, increasingly, generous monetary pensions and other annuities, further depleting crown resources. Dom João II (ruled 1481–1495) joked bitterly that his father, Dom Afonso V (ruled 1438–1481), had left him king of only the highways of Portugal.

Internal constraints forced both the crown and its subjects to look outside the borders for new opportunities. Many nobles, including princes, left or considered leaving Portugal in search of better living elsewhere, or, like Prince Henry the Navigator, sought fame and fortune in the Atlantic islands and in Morocco. The Madeiras, Azores, and Cape Verde Islands, explored and colonized between the 1420s and 1460s, offered new lands and agricultural possibilities; western Africa yielded profitable commodities, in particular gold and slaves; and Morocco, the most conventional outlet, provided socially suitable "work" for the nobility and seemingly prestigious territorial acquisitions. Undeterred by the cost of maintaining Ceuta and by a humiliating defeat at Tangier in 1437, the Portuguese embarked on a series of campaigns in Morocco in the 1450s and 1460s, which by 1471 resulted in the capture of Alcacer Seguer (Qsar al seghir), Arzila (Asilah), and Tangier (Tanja), and left Portugal in control of the northern coast of Morocco.

The early overseas expansion helped to alleviate some of the internal pressures, but at the same time it reinforced others. Meritorious service overseas now called for generous rewards and gave rise to numerous ennoblements and knightings that could not be supported by suitable endowment. As a result, lawless bands of "knights" and men-at-arms began to roam the countryside, protected by landowning magnates who hid them behind the shield of private feudal jurisdiction. Furthermore, Dom João I's policy of creating strategically located land grants for his progeny, based on the assumption of enduring family loyalty, and his grandson Dom Afonso V's commitment to liberality and princely largesse, backfired seriously in the second half of the century. The House of Bragança, founded by Dom João's illegitimate son Dom Afonso, and the House of Viseu/Beja, based on the patrimony of Prince Henry and his nephew and adoptive son Dom Fernando, both wielded sufficient power to cripple the crown.

Matters came to a head in the early 1480s, when Dom João II sought to reassert his power and rebuild the crown's territorial and financial power base. The

The King and Queen of Portugal. Marriage of Dom Manuel I (ruled 1495–1521) and Eleonor of Austria in 1518 by Garcia Fernandes (fl. 1518–1565). MUSEU DA MISERICORDIA DE LISBOA, PORTUGAL

noble conspiracies of 1483 and 1485 gave him sufficient ground to suppress the most important of his noble relatives and dispossess the Bragança. Dom João's heavy-handed policy of centralization and confrontation may have cost him his life: he died prematurely in 1495, a delayed consequence, according to some, of having been poisoned several years earlier.

Dom João's cousin and successor, Dom Manuel (ruled 1495–1521), employed more subtle tactics in his search to further strengthen the crown, softened by appeasing the nobility through generous gifts, pensions, and profitable offices. He restored the Bragança and reversed many of Dom João's more severe decisions, in exchange for the high nobility's cooperation. Additional income from the African and especially the Asian trade more than doubled the revenues of the Portuguese state and made Dom Manuel's generosity practicable. Even so, however, the cost of appeasement was high: some 80 percent of the state budget was earmarked for the support of the nobility.

Portuguese Successes and Failures. Although neither Dom João II nor Dom Manuel was able to resolve the domestic problems, their reigns nevertheless marked the peak of the Avis dynasty. Both kings placed key emphasis on overseas expansion. Dom João II personally promoted the development of trade with Africa and relations with African states and was the first to support a concerted effort to reach India. The refusal to back Christopher Columbus deprived the Portuguese of any claim to the Western Hemisphere, but in the 1494 Treaty of Tordesillas they secured what truly seemed to matter: a guaranteed access to Africa and Asia. Dom Manuel was able to reap the benefits of Dom João II's vision. The two decades following Vasco de Gama's 1498 landing in India were filled with dazzling achievements in exploration, trade, and naval warfare. The Portuguese made their way to Brazil, southeast Asia, Indonesia, and China. A mixture of ruthlessness, ingenuity, naive self-confidence, and naval superiority allowed them to dominate the shipping lanes of the Indian Ocean and for a short time to assume control of the spice trade. Dom Manual was able to make a grandiose addition to his royal title: the "Lord of Conquest, Navigation, and Commerce of Ethiopia, Arabia, Persia, and India," complementing the appellation of "Lord of Guinea" adopted by Dom João II.

Notwithstanding his subjects' exploits in distant parts of the globe, Dom Manuel's dearest ambitions were focused closer to home and were deeply rooted in medieval values. As had the earlier members of the Avis dynasty, Dom Manuel saw war against Muslims as his most cherished goal and conquest in Morocco as his most prestigious undertaking. He hoped to free the Holy Land and to assume an imperial title based on his overseas possessions. Regardless of the nature of his ideological motivation, Dom Manuel epitomized Machiavelli's Renaissance prince: all his energies focused on "great enterprises" and on promoting his international image. His court glittered and overwhelmed with sartorial splendor and exotic display, blending late gothic and Renaissance forms in architecture, painting, theater, and literature.

Dom Manuel came very close to uniting the Iberian Peninsula under his rule, thanks to the dynastic misfortune that deprived both Dom João II and the Catholic kings of their male heirs. Although his expectations were frustrated, his dynastic policy and the policy of his son, Dom João III, remained focused on the Habsburg heirs to the Spanish throne. The double marriage between Dom João III and Dona Catarina, sister of the Holy Roman Emperor Charles V, in 1525, and between João's sister Isabela and the Holy Roman Emperor in 1526, constituted a stunningly prestigious diplomatic victory for Portugal and a testimony to its wealth. In the 1540s, a similar double marriage, between the crown princes of Portugal and Spain and their respective sisters, prepared the ground for the eventual union of Portugal and Habsburg Spain in 1580.

However, the dynastic union of 1580 could not have been foreseen at that time: it became possible only through the extraordinary misfortunes that befell the descendants of Dom Manuel. Both Dom Manuel and Dom João III produced sons, some of whom lived to be adults, and there seemed no danger that the Avis line might come to an end. Yet when Dom João III died in 1557, he was survived only by his brother Cardinal Dom Henrique, and a grandson, Dom Sebastião, a young child who now embodied all the hopes of the dynasty. Dom Sebastião was chronically ill, both physically and mentally. Although he lived into adulthood, his weakness and unwillingness to procreate left considerable doubts about the dynasty's future. These doubts became reality in 1578 when the king was killed in the battle of Alcacer Kebir (Qsar al-kabir), in an ill-conceived attempt to rekindle the Portuguese conquest in Morocco. His elderly great-uncle, Cardinal Dom Henrique, a caretaker king, proved unable to manage a smooth dynastic transition. A brief war of succession followed his death in 1580, but Philip II of Spain, the most powerful European monarch of his day, found little difficulty in making good his claim to the throne of Portugal, temporarily uniting the Iberian Peninsula under one ruler.

The dynastic weakness that marked the last decades of the Avis rule was only one aspect of the growing problems Portugal faced in the sixteenth century. Despite the prosperity and demographic growth that had characterized the reigns of Dom Manuel and Dom João III, contemporaries were keenly aware of the overwhelming burden of military and administrative commitments overseas and of insatiable expectations of royal largesse at home. This crippling combination was aggravated by the prestige imperative: these rulers had not only to maintain the impressive achievements of the past, but to surpass them. Dom João III found this impossible to accomplish. Despite opposition, he chose to concentrate all Portuguese overseas efforts on Asia. The Portuguese enhanced their positions in the Indian Ocean and established outposts as far as China and Japan. Subsequently, however, Dom João was

Rulers of Portugal: The Avis Dynasty

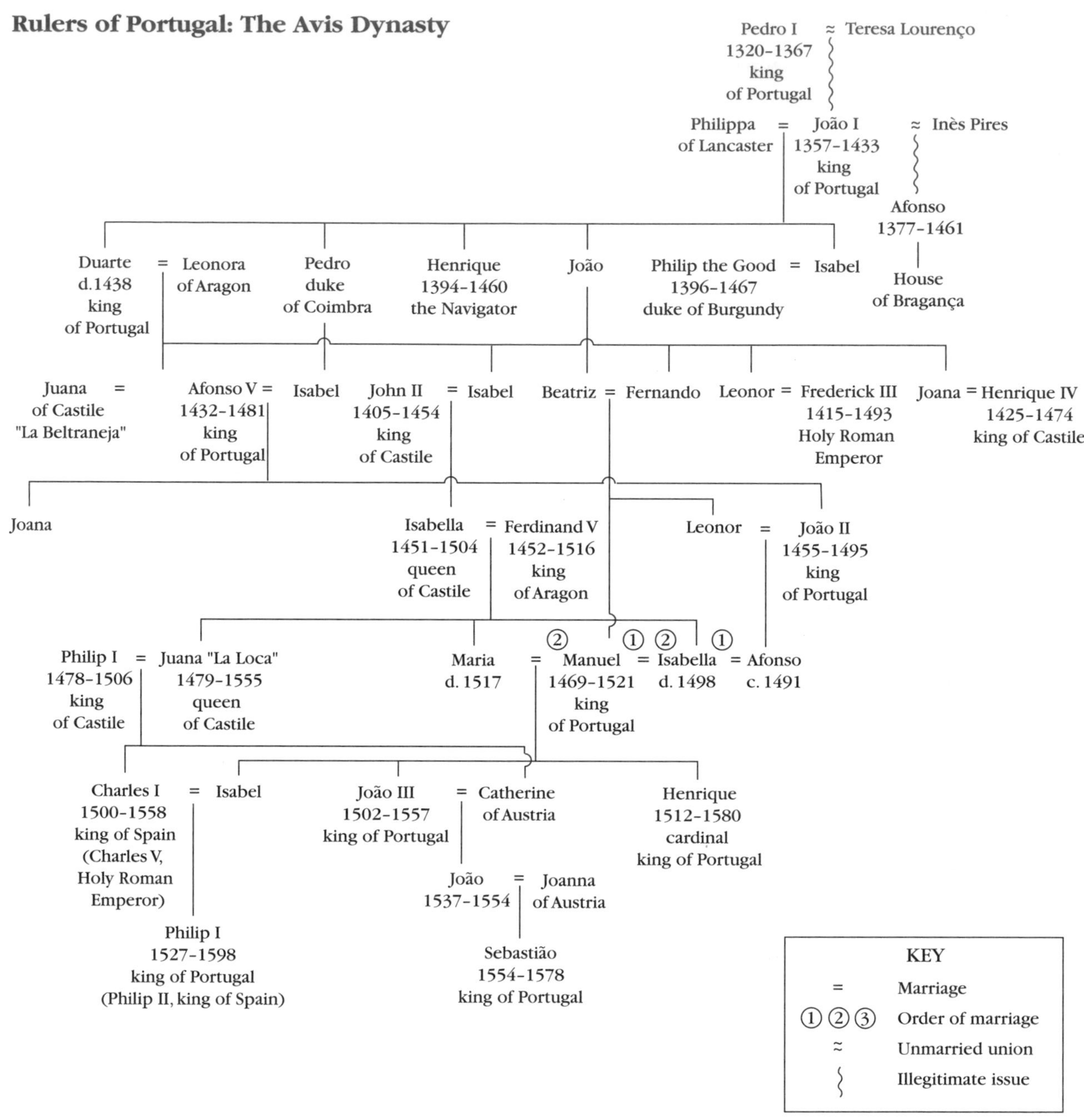

forced to abandon key holdings in Morocco, and, harassed by the French, he experienced great difficulty maintaining Portuguese control over navigation in the South Atlantic. In the long run, the decision to retreat in Morocco proved very costly: not only did it stain Dom João III's reputation, but the need to redress the perceived dishonor became an obsession for his successor, Dom Sebastião, one that led to the catastrophe of 1578.

The waning of Portugal's golden age, however, began long before Dom Sebastião's death on a Moroccan battlefield. The overseas expansion, a key source of the country's flash of prosperity, brought some material rewards to most Portuguese, but only postponed the social and political crisis that had faced late medieval Portugal. The response to renewed difficulties was a growing entrenchment of social privilege, and heavy-handed enforcement of conformity. The ruthless persecution of New Christians by the Inquisition, founded in 1536, deprived Portugal of some of its most talented entrepreneurs and administrators. The suppression of the Erasmian

Renaissance, which had flourished in Portugal earlier in the sixteenth century, and the surveillance and rigidity brought about by the Jesuits, the Inquisition, and the post-Tridentine reformation of the Catholic Church, stultified Portuguese culture and crippled higher education.

The inability to sustain the intoxicating pace of expansion that had given the Manueline period its self-confidence created now an atmosphere of pessimism about the future and nostalgia for the heroic past, which combined with overtones of cynicism and self-mockery. This attitude resounds loudly in the works of post-Manueline artists and historians, such as Luís Vaz de Camões, author of the national epic *Os Lusíadas* (The Lusiads; 1572) and Diogo do Couto, who wrote *O soldado prático* (The practical soldier; c. 1588) and completed João de Barros's monumental history of the Portuguese expansion, *Décadas da Ásia* (1552–1615). Well before the Spanish takeover, Portugal was thus slipping into a condition that, perhaps unfairly, would later make it a symbol of backwardness and repression for Voltaire and other Enlightenment thinkers.

See also **Asia, East; Coimbra, University of; Exploration; Humanism,** *subentry on* **Portugal; Lisbon; Portuguese Literature and Language;** *and biography of Camoēs, Luiz Vaz de.*

BIBLIOGRAPHY

Dias, João José Alves, ed. *Portugal do Renasci mento à crise dinástica.* Vol. 5 of *Nova História de Portugal.* Directed by Joel Serrão and A. H. de Oliveira Marques. Lisbon, Portugal, 1998.

Diffie, Bailey W., and George D. Winius. *Foundations of the Portuguese Empire, 1415–1580.* Minneapolis, Minn. 1977.

Godinho, Vitorino Magalhães. *Os descubrimentos e a economia mundial.* 4 vols. 2d ed. Lisbon, Portugal, 1984.

Homem, Amadeu Carvalho, ed. *Descobrimentos, expansão e identidade nacional.* Coimbra, Portugal, 1992.

Hower, Alfred, and Richard A. Preto-Rodas, eds. *Empire in Transition: The Portuguese World in the Time of Camões.* Gainesville, Fla., 1985.

Marques, A. H. de Oliveira. *History of Portugal.* 2d ed. New York, 1976.

Marques, A. H. de Oliveira. *Portugal na Crise dos séculos XIV e XV.* Vol. 4 of *Nova História de Portugal.* Directed by Joel Serrão and A. H. de Oliveira Marques. Lisbon, Portugal, 1987.

Marques, A. H. de Oliveira, ed. *A expansão quatrocentista.* Vol. 2 of *Nova História da expansão Portuguesa.* Directed by Joel Serrão and A. H. de Oliveira Marques. Lisbon, Portugal, 1998.

Mattoso, José, ed. *História de Portugal.* Vols. 2 and 3. Lisbon, Portugal, 1993.

Russell-Wood, A. J. R. *A World on the Move: The Portuguese in Africa, Asia, and America, 1415–1808.* Manchester, U.K., and New York, 1992.

Sousa, Armindo de. "Portugal." In *The New Cambridge Medieval History.* Vol. 7, *c. 1415–c. 1500.* Edited by Christopher Allmand. Cambridge, U.K., and New York, 1998. Pages 627–644.

Subrahmanyam, Sanjay. *The Career and Legend of Vasco da Gama.* Cambridge, U.K., and New York, 1997.

Subrahmanyam, Sanjay. *The Portuguese Empire in Asia, 1500–1700: A Political and Economic History.* London and New York, 1993.

Thomaz, Luís Filipe F. R. *De Ceuta a Timor.* Lisbon, Portugal, 1994.

Winius, George D. *Portugal, the Pathfinder: Journeys from the Medieval World toward the Modern World, 1300–ca. 1600.* Madison, Wis., 1995.

IVANA ELBL

PORTUGAL, ART IN. *See* **Spain,** *subentry on* **Art in Spain and Portugal.**

PORTUGUESE LITERATURE AND LANGUAGE. The Portuguese Renaissance coincided with the height of the maritime voyages and overseas discoveries that built what historian C. R. Boxer has termed Portugal's "seaborne empire." It extended from Brazil to Japan and was mythologized in the Western imagination by Vasco da Gama's voyage to India (1497–1499) and the first voyage to circumnavagate the globe (1519–1522), led by Ferdinand Magellan (d. 1521). In Portugal the five hundredth anniversary of the discoveries was marked by the publication of a substantial library of primary and secondary texts. These have brought the historical, literary, and intercultural perspectives of the Portuguese Renaissance to the forefront of Portuguese society, posing a constructive dialogue between the global interests of the seaborne empire and the contemporary dynamics of the European community. Contacts with previously unknown places, peoples, and cultures brought about by the maritime discoveries had a profound impact on literature, linguistics, and learning. Humanistic and commercial perspectives made possible by the voyages conflicted with an ecclesiastical and inquisitional social and religious background.

Development of General Literary Genres. "The Old Man of the Restelo" (1572), created by Luís Vaz de Camões (c. 1524–1580), and *Soldado prático,* by Diogo do Couto (c. 1542–1616), defended a humanistic outlook, questioning the ethics and the philosophy of the colonial system. Tensions and conflicting perceptions in the Portuguese world, heightened by the establishment of the Inquisition in 1536, promoted early development of mannerist and baroque qualities of the Manueline style in the reign of Dom Manuel (1495–1521).

João de Barros (c. 1496–1570) produced a vast work reflecting the range of a Renaissance man of letters. Perhaps influenced by his post in the Casa da India, which was in charge of all commerce arriving from the overseas possessions, Barros planned a monumental project: a geographical, economic, and historical account of the overseas expansion. He first wrote a chivalry novel, *Crónica do Imperador Clarimundo* (Chronicle of the reign of Clarimundo; 1522), celebrating the genealogy and aristocratic virtues of the heroes of the Portuguese monarchy, then a grammar, *Gramática da língua portuguesa* (1539) and moral dialogues, represented by the colloquy *Ropicapnefma* (Spiritual merchandise; 1531). The latter, comparable to works of the Spanish humanist Juan Luis Vives, is written as a dialogue in which Reason defends orthodox doctrine, amid the questioning of heretical voices and the calming reflections of Time, Understanding, and Will. Barros is most widely known as the chronicler of Portuguese expansion in Asia in the early sixteenth century. In his four *Décadas da Ásia* (1552–1563; 1615), Barros refined the historiographical style founded by Fernão Lopes (c. 1380–c. 1460) in the first half of the fifteenth century, and continued by Gomes Eanes de Zurara (c. 1410–1474) and Rui de Pina (1440–1521), by placing this tradition in a broader perspective of regions and continents, linking history to geography, and using the heroic and epic frames of classical rhetoric.

Humanist, scholar, and chronicler Damião de Góis (1502–1574) spent twenty-two years outside of Portugal, first in commerce in Antwerp, and later as a student in Italy and France. A friend of Desiderius Erasmus, Góis was the author of Latin essays on topics including rituals of the faith. After his return to Portugal in 1545, Góis became chief archivist of the Torre do Tombo (national archives) in Lisbon in 1548 and was denounced by the Inquisition, before which he defended humanist orthodoxy. Francisco de Holanda (1517–1584), the son of a Dutch painter in Portugal, studied in Italy as did Góis, where he became a disciple of Michelangelo. His essays in *Da pintura antiga* (On ancient painting; 1548) regarded painting as human and divine creation.

Historiography drew on early chronicles of the nation's historical past and its literary traditions to compose epic relations of the voyages in writing characterized by a renewed assimilation and influence of Greco-Latin culture. The voyages to India and the Far East marked the life and works of many of the most prominent intellectuals, clerics, writers, and soldiers of the sixteenth century, including Afonso de Albuquerque, Diogo do Couto, Garcia da Orta, Fernão Mendes Pinto, and St. Francis Xavier. They culminated in the epic poem *Os Lusíadas* (1572), lyrical poetry (such as "Babel e Sião"), and letters, all by Camões, who spent seventeen years in Portuguese Asia. All incorporated a vision of Asia and a dimension of personal experience in their works, preserving the impact of the voyages on European writing and anticipating modern currents of orientalism and exoticism in Western literature.

India was the center of attention in the four editions of *Décadas da Ásia* by Barros; nine by Diogo do Couto; the *História da conquista e descobrimento da Índia pelos Portugueses* (8 vols.; 1551–1561), by Fernão Lopes de Castanheda (d. 1559); the *Chronica do felicissimo rei Dom Emanuel* (2 vols. in 4 parts; 1566–1567), by Góis; the *Comentários* (1557) of Afonso de Albuquerque, and numerous works on the conquests of Diu and Goa. The description of lands, peoples, and cultures encountered by the Portuguese produced a literature of its own, including the *Livro* (1510) of Duarte Barbosa (d. 1521) and the *Lendas da Índia* (Legends of India; 1518), with ink engravings, by Gaspar Correa (fl. sixteenth century). The Portuguese wrote early descriptions of China, such as *Tratado das cousas da China* (Treatise on Chinese affairs; 1569), by Gaspar da Cruz (d. 1570). As the first Westerners to enter Japan, they produced a significant body of historical and descriptive literature on that country, including *História de Japam,* by Luís Fróis, and writings of João Rodrígues Tsuzzu.

The variety of genres represented increased rapidly with circumstances; they include maps, letters, verse, essays, travel diaries, shipwreck accounts, religious theater, ballads, legends, vocabularies, grammars, routes, itineraries, documents, designs, blueprints of forts, and portraits of viceroys and governors. Navigational and natural science were represented in travel routes and charts, including *Primeiro roteiro da costa da Índia desde Goa até Diu* (First logbook of the coast of India from Goa to Diu) by Don João de Castro (1500–1548) (published 1843), and the log of Vasco da Gama's voyage (published in 1838). Garcia da Orta's horticultural treatise, the *Colóquios dos simples, e drogas he cousas mediçinais de Índia* (Colloquies on the simples and drugs of India) was published in Goa in 1563. The great mass of religious literature included letters from the religious orders and biographies such as the *História da vida de Padre Francisco de Xavier* (The life of Father Francis Xavier; 1600) by João de Lucena (c. 1549–1600).

Prose. Chivalric and bucolic prose works evolved into moral and doctrinal allegories or the long sentimental monologue. An example is *Diana*

(1559), by Jorge de Montemayor (1520?–1561), a pastoral fiction incorporating intrigue, devices of classical comedy, and bucolic poetry; another is a sentimental novel of love and feminine psychology, *Menina e Moça* (1554), by Bernardim Ribeiro (1482–1552), which relates the tragic love of Binmarder for Aónia and of Avalor for Arima. The cycles of *Amadis de Gaula* (1508) and *Palmeirim de Inglaterra* (3d ed. 1564–1567), by Francisco de Morais (c. 1500–1572), continued the vogue of chivalric novels and ideals of gallantry, service to the monarchy, and the crusades.

Voyage literature included dramatic narratives of shipwrecks that documented the tragic fate of one-third of the India fleets, later collected in the *História trágico-marítima* (The tragic history of the sea; 1735). The major prose work of the discoveries is *Peregrinação* (Travels; 1614), by Fernão Mendes Pinto (d. 1583), a fantastic first-person account of his travels and adventures throughout Portuguese Asia and one of the most widely read books of the seventeenth century. The constant encounters between the Portuguese narrator and Asians, amounting to an early form of anthropology, enabled the narrator to objectify himself and the Portuguese from the other's critical point of view. Long considered to contain fabrications and mystifications, the *Peregrinação* has proved to be substantially accurate in the light of recent investigations. The novel contributed to the development of the picaresque or self-conscious hero and to narrative style.

Theater. Sixteenth-century Portuguese theater featured religious allegories staged onboard ships, while court theater drew on popular characters and moral conceits. In the *Comedia Eufrosina* (1566), by Jorge Ferreira de Vasconcelos (1515–1585), a letter from Goa was read on stage, representative of many true letters commenting on the vicissitudes of life in India. The major playwright, Gil Vicente (c. 1465–c. 1536), wrote and produced some forty-five plays for the Lisbon court from 1502 until 1536, publishing only a few in chapbooks before the incomplete and defective edition prepared in 1562 by his son, who divided them arbitrarily into the categories of devotion, farce, comedy, tragi-comedy, and lesser works. Characterized by poetic versatility, complexity, and variety of dramatic structure, Vicente's plays satirize the clergy and nobility, as well as local administrators and artisans. The *Auto da Índia* (India play) portrays a soldier's wife who enjoys a free existence in his absence, while in the farce *Quem tem farelos?* a village girl tries to change her condition through marriage to a squire, who proves worthless. In *Juiz da Beira,* an ignorant half-mad peasant judges normal people, arriving at decisions that are the reverse of the law and customs of the day.

António Ferreira (1528–1569) represents the apogee of literary classicism and humanism through his use of Italian poetic forms and defense of the Portuguese language. Ferreira's tragedy, *Castro* (1587), dramatizes the historical theme of the assassination of Inês de Castro (1355), recast with the classical dialogues and choruses of Greek tragedy.

Poetry. The oral tradition, consisting of ballads, folktales, popular and religious verses, aphorisms, riddles, and so on, spread throughout the empire, at times becoming creolized with the contact languages. The *Cancioneiro geral* (1516) of Garcia de Resende (c. 1470–1536) is a collection of poetry in peninsular forms, including *redondilha, vilancete,* and *cantiga.* Francisco de Sá de Miranda (1481–1558), who contributed to the *Cancioneiro,* later brought the Italian forms of the *dolce stil nuovo* (sweet new style) to Portugal after a prolonged visit to Italy from to 1521 to 1526. His poetry treats Petrarchian love themes, applying a classical erudition critical of the court and praising values of rural life. The lyrical works of Camões include traditional peninsular forms while perfecting the Italianate forms, particularly with his sonnets, which remain among the best-known poems in the Portuguese language.

Camões's epic poem in ten cantos, *Os Lusíadas,* draws together major conflicting forces in Portugal's Renaissance in one of the classic works of Western literature. The theme is drawn from the history of Portugal, recited in the poem by Vasco da Gama during his voyage to India. Gama's voyage becomes the advancing line of present time. Progress depends on intrigues among classical gods who observe the expedition, with Venus as protector of the Portuguese and Bacchus opposed to them. Action is advanced by magical devices, dreams, and intercessions of the gods. The interior episodes of "Inês de Castro," "Adamastor," and the "Island of Love" carry historical action to a pan-erotic plane, suggesting a journey to paradise through sensual desire. The voyage assumes universality as Tetis and Gama survey the known and future world of the Portuguese from a mountain peak. Full of keen observation, *Os Lusíadas* is also a naturalist encyclopedia of unusual phenomena. The poetry is dense in musical rhythm and imagery, approaching the naturalist painters such as the German Renaissance painter Albrecht Dürer. Achieving unity through diversity, Camões synthesizes the conflicts of a civilization, which he lived as a soldier-poet in Asia and then incorporated into the ideals of his poetic art.

Linguistic changes. The early development of historiographical prose after the time of Fernão Lopes was decisive in the evolution of the modern Portuguese language. Renaissance grammarians emphasized the close relationship between Portuguese and classical Latin. Barros, for example, composed poetry that could be read as either language. Latin dictionaries and grammars by Estêvão Cavaleiro (b. 1540) and Jerónimo Cardoso (d. 1569) appeared in 1516 and 1570, respectively; lexical and syntactical latinization of literary language emerged alongside them. The first Portuguese grammars, by Fernão de Oliveira (d. 1576) in 1536 and Barros in 1539, as well as the orthographies by Magalhães Gândavo (d. 1576) in 1562 and Duarte Nunes do Leão (1530?–1608) in 1576, demonstrate that the Portuguese language was fully developed by the mid-1500s.

The presence of Portuguese in Asia and their contact with languages there constituted one of the principal topics of research that stimulated linguistic activity. The Portuguese language contributed extensive vocabulary to contact languages in Africa and Asia, also making possible the development of creoles based on Portuguese. Works printed in Asia included grammars, vocabularies, dictionaries, etymologies, glossaries, phrases, and dialogues. The production of grammars and vocabularies, from Brazil to Goa and Japan, resulted in the creation of comparative linguistics, placing Portuguese alongside indigenous or local languages, such as Konkani, Tamil, and Japanese.

See also biographies of Afonso de Albuquerque, Luíz Vaz de Camões, António Ferreira, Jorge de Montemayor, Gil Vicente, and Juan Luis Vives.

BIBLIOGRAPHY

Primary Works

Albuquerque, Afonso de. *Albuquerque, Caesar of the East: Selected Texts.* Edited and translated by T. F. Earle and John Villiers. Warminster, England, 1990.

Camões, Luís de. *The Lusiads.* Oxford and New York, 1997. Translation of *Os Lusíadas* (1572).

Correa, Gaspar. *The Three Voyages of Vasco da Gama and His Viceroyalty, from the Lendas da India of Gaspar Correa.* New York, 1963. Translated from *Lendas da Indioa* (1518).

Cruz, Gaspar da et al. *South China in the Sixteenth Century: Being the Narratives of Galeote Pereira, Fr. Gaspar da Cruz, O.P., [and] Fr. Martin de Rada, O.E.S.A. (1550–1575).* Edited and translated by C. R. Boxer. London, 1953.

Ferreira, António. *The Comedy of Bristo, or, The Pimp.* Ottawa, Canada, 1990. Translation of *Comédia do Fanchono ou de Bristo* (1562).

Ferreira, António. *The Tragedy of Ines de Castro.* Coimbra, Portugal, 1987. Translation of *Tragédia de Inês de Castro* (1587).

Galvão, Antonio. *The Discoveries of the World from their First Original unto the Year Our Lord 1555, by Antonio Galvano. Corrected, quoted, and Published in England, by Richard Hakluyt, 1601. Now reprinted, with the Original Portuguese Text: and Edited by Vice-Admiral Bethune.* New York, 1971. Translation of *Tratado dos descobrimentos* (1563).

Góis, Damião de. *Lisbon in the Renaissance: A New Translation of the* Urbis Olisiponis descriptio. Translated by Jeffrey S. Ruth. New York, 1996.

Orta, Garcia de. *Colloquies on the Simples and Drugs of India.* Edited by the Conde de Ficalho. London, 1913. Translation of *Colóquios dos simples, e drogas he cousas mediçinais de India* (1563).

Pinto, Fernão Mendes. *The Travels of Mendes Pinto.* Edited by Rebecca D. Catz. Chicago, 1989. Translation of *Peregrinação* (1614).

Pires, Tomé et al. *Travel Accounts of the Islands (1513–1787).* Manila, Philippines, 1971.

Velho, Alvaro. *A Journal of the First Voyage of Vasco da Gama, 1497–1499.* Edited by Ernest George Ravenstein. 1898. Reprint, New York, 1963. Translation of *Roteiro da viagem de Vasco da Gama.*

Vicente, Gil. *The Boat Plays.* London, 1997. Translation of *Autos das barcas.*

Vincente, Gil. *A Critical Edition with Introduction and Notes of Gil Vicente's* Floresta de enganos. Edited by Constantine C. Stathatos. Chapel Hill, N.C., 1972. Translation of *Floresta de enganos.*

Secondary Works

Boxer, C. R. *João de Barros, Portuguese Humanist and Historian of Asia.* New Delhi, India, 1981.

Colloque international d'études humanistes. *L'Humanisme Portugais et l'Europe.* Actes due XXIe Colloque international d'études humanistes. Paris, 1984.

Cooper, Michael, S. J. *Rodrigues the Interpreter: An Early Jesuit in Japan and China.* New York and Tokyo, 1974.

Hart, Henry H. *Luis de Camoëns and the Epic of the Lusiads.* Norman, Okla., 1962.

Hirsch, Elisabeth Feist. *Damião de Góis: The Life and Thought of a Portuguese Humanist, 1502–1574.* The Hague, Netherlands, 1967.

Russell-Wood, A. J. R. *A World on the Move: The Portuguese in Africa, Asia, and America, 1415–1808.* Manchester, U.K., 1992.

Saraiva, António José, and Óscar Lopes. *História da Literatura Portuguesa.* 1945. 17th ed. Porto, Portugal, 1996.

K. David Jackson

POSTEL, GUILLAUME (1510–1581), French humanist. Born at Barenton, France, Postel was acclaimed as a mathematician, cartographer, cosmographer, printer, world traveler, linguist, translator, grammarian, and philosopher. His published works, numbering more than sixty, and his unpublished texts of several thousands of pages demonstrate his vast erudition in many fields. Postel was a polymath whom King Charles IX of France called his own philosopher and whom Francis Bacon described as a marvel of the world.

Obsessed with a desire for knowledge, he taught in the village of Sagy while still in his teens until he earned enough money to go to Paris to continue his studies. Arriving in the French capital around 1530, he plunged immediately into the study of languages, quickly mastering Greek, Latin, Spanish, and Portuguese. His self-taught knowledge of Hebrew and his brilliance in many disciplines earned him a position in the circle of "royal readers" in the court of King Francis I who chose him to accompany Jean de la Forêt to the court of Süleyman the Great. Postel collected books for the king in Hebrew, Arabic, Samaritan, and Syriac; these became the basis of the Oriental collection of the Library of Paris.

Postel's first contributions to Renaissance scholarship were translations from original texts in Greek and Latin; he published a French translation of Xenocrates's *Axiochus,* and translated Greek poetry into Latin. He considered Hebrew the parent of all other languages, since God spoke to Adam in this language to teach him the names of things. From this concept of a common origin of languages, Postel developed a theory of the unity of all things.

Believing that a "divine voice" led him to devote himself to reform and, consequently, to relinquish his benefices, Postel lost favor with Francis I when he incessantly demanded that the king reform himself, his court, and his realm. In 1544 Postel joined Ignatius Loyola in Rome and became a member of the nascent Society of Jesus. His visions of reform and of universal concord returned; he became a liability to the Jesuits and was given license to depart. Arriving in Venice in 1546, he began work as a priest at the Ospedaletto of Saints John and Paul, where he met a mystical woman who had founded the hospice in 1528. Postel called her the Venetian Virgin, and her influence on him was enduring. She taught Postel that God wanted "all the sheep [to] be gathered into one sheepfold," and that one must demonstrate one's love of God through ministry to the poor and the infirm. Throughout his life Postel worked to accomplish this mystic's vision of a *respublica mundana* (world commonwealth) under God, in which praise of God and universal brotherhood would be the guiding principles.

Postel returned to the East on several occasions to increase his knowledge of ancient languages and to collect rare books. In 1553 the Emperor Ferdinand appointed him to a chair at the University of Vienna. Postel's visions of universal reform and a world state, coupled with his belief that the Venetian Virgin was the "Mother of the World," caused him problems. He was condemned by the Venetian Inquisition in 1555 and imprisoned in Rome until 1559.

Postel's dreams of a united world in which religion would be catholic enough to include all who worshipped God; his theory that all languages had a common parent, namely Hebrew; and his emphasis on the feminine principle that directs the lower world demonstrated the modernity of this Renaissance polymath. He died in the Monastery of Saint Martin des Champs on 6 September 1581.

BIBLIOGRAPHY

Primary Works

These works represent only a small portion of Postel's more than sixty printed texts. His important unpublished texts can be found in the British Library; the Bibliothèque Nationale, Paris; the Biblioteca Apostolica Vaticana, Rome; the Biblioteca Nazionale, Florence; and elsewhere.

Cosmographicae disciplinae compendium. Basel, Switzerland, 1561.

Divinationis sive divinae summaeque veritatis discussio. Paris, 1571.

Des Histoires orientales et principalement des Turkes. Paris, 1575.

De Orbis terrae concordia libri 4. Basel, Switzerland, 1545.

De Originibus seu de Hebraicae linguae et gentis antiquitate. Paris, 1538.

Quaternariae rei compendium ad disciplinas omnes scientiasve maxime autem metaphipicas et divinas mathematicasve. Paris, 1570.

Signorum coelestium vera configuratio. Paris, 1553.

De Universitate liber. Paris, 1552; 1563.

Secondary Works

Bouwsma, William J. *Concordia mundi: The Career and Thought of Guillaume Postel.* Cambridge, Mass., 1957.

Kuntz, Marion Leathers. *Guillaume Postel: Prophet of the Restitution of All Things.* The Hague, Netherlands; Boston; and London, 1981.

Kuntz, Marion Leathers, ed. *Postello, Venezia e il suo mondo.* Florence, 1988.

MARION LEATHERS KUNTZ

POTTERY. *See* **Ceramics and Pottery.**

POVERTY AND CHARITY. In the great cities of Renaissance Europe, between fifty and seventy people in every hundred were in some sense "poor," suffering in varying degrees from financial hardship, lack of power, lack of esteem, and insecurity.

In a town well endowed with organized charities, some 4 to 8 percent of the people, including the very young, the aged, chronic invalids, and those who were mentally afflicted or physically impaired, would be continually dependent on relief. Some were beggars; some were hospital poor; some were infants farmed out to wet nurses; some received relief in their own homes. In famine years their numbers were swelled by refugees from the devastated countryside, who struggled toward the city's gates in a desperate quest for food from its granaries and alms from its citizens.

Beyond the helpless and destitute lay a much larger circle of ill-paid laboring poor, comprising journeymen and their families, porters and other casual workers, women who took on spinning and other tasks in the textile trades, widows burdened with young children, agricultural workers living within town walls, out-of-work servants, and the like. Perilously reliant on irregular, seasonal work, without reserves or savings, they could scrape out a living for much of the time, but sudden rises in the price of bread, a highly unstable commodity, would immediately plunge them into dependence on charity. These people, called by modern historians the "crisis poor" but known to Renaissance tax collectors as *miserabili* or have-nothings, accounted for at least another 20 percent of the urban population.

There was also an outer circle of craftsmen, shopkeepers, and minor officials, with claims to respectability but no real security in the face of illness or personal disaster, or indeed of some protracted public catastrophe such as a plague epidemic. They corresponded, no doubt, to the group described by Carlo Cardinal Borromeo, archbishop of Milan, when he visited Varese in 1567 and mentioned "those who, although they have some possessions, require assistance on account of a large number of children, especially girls whom they have to marry off, or for some other reason." Those in the outer circle of poverty would never have begged openly, but few would have spurned charitable grants toward their daughters' marriage portions.

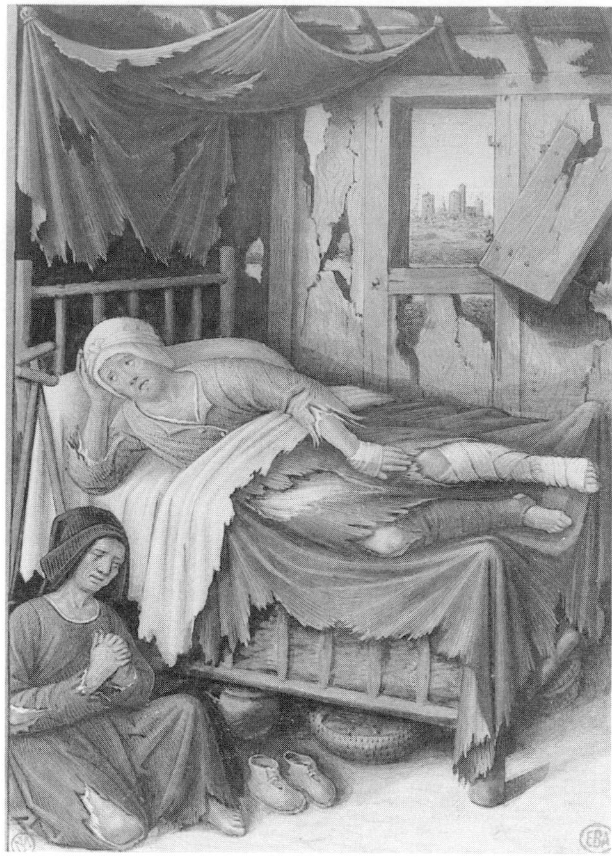

Poverty. Miniature painting by Jehan Bourdichon (c. 1457–1521). BIBLIOTHÈQUE DE L'ÉCOLE DES BEAUX-ARTS, PARIS/GIRAUDON/ART RESOURCE, NY

Classifying Poverty. Most societies recognized a hierarchy of poverty, a series of categories created by superiors. A privileged group of "shamefaced poor" generally claimed the largest allowances and enjoyed the most discreet and considerate treatment at the hands of charitable associations. In the narrowest sense they were nobles or burghers deprived by declining fortunes of the ability to maintain the style of life enjoined by their rank and threatened, not with starvation, but with loss of honor. However, the "shamefaced" poor, as in fifteenth-century Florence, could also include respectable artisans and shopkeepers, who resembled the "house poor" of sixteenth-century Germany or the "decayed householders" of Edward VI's London and were likewise ashamed to beg.

Less socially refined, and equally variegated, were the people loosely described as "the poor of Christ," those best qualified to represent the suffering savior and, by acting as the receivers of God, to transform the donations of their benefactors from earthly goods into heavenly treasure. They included widows and orphans and all poor folk who submitted patiently to misfortune and disability, among them those classified in the more secular language of mid-Tudor England as "poor by impotency" and "poor by casualty."

In Catholic countries clerics and religious, who were poor by virtue of their own decision to renounce worldly goods, were among "the poor of Christ," especially if, like the stricter Franciscans, they owned no property, even as communities, and lived by begging. Pilgrims, vowed to grueling journeys to Rome or Loretto or Compostela, or some less distant destination, had special claims to hospitality.

There was little room, however, for the claims of the religious poor in Protestant societies, where their practices were perceived as mistaken attempts to pursue salvation through socially useless "works." Voluntary poverty, wrote Huldrych Zwingli, the reformer of Zurich in the 1520s, follows the human will, whereas involuntary poverty follows the will of God.

No doubt the largest body of poor people at any one time consisted of the ordinary laboring folk—those who lived precariously and had no assets other than their own physical strength, like the family of Giulia of Gazuolo, near Mantua, the tragic heroine of one of Matteo Bandello's short stories. She was

> the daughter of a poor man of the town, of humble origins, for whom there was nothing but to work with his arms all day, striving to earn a living, nothing more, for himself, his wife, and two daughters. His wife, who was a good woman, struggled to make a bit by spinning and performing other services, as women do.

Below the laboring poor, at the bottom of the moral if not of the economic hierarchy, lay the outcast poor—vagrants, beggars of doubtful credentials, and brothel prostitutes (as distinct from the more prosperous courtesans). Widely accepted, at least from the thirteenth century, was the notion that not all the poor were the poor of Christ, and that they included idlers, false cripples, bogus pilgrims, and fraudulent, canting rogues. From the fifteenth century there was a burgeoning, imaginative literature that depicted them as part of an organized antisociety, devoted to conning the pious and stealing the alms of the truly poor. Prostitution, though to some extent licensed in Spanish and Italian towns, and in France and Germany before the coming of Protestantism, was at the same time stigmatized; in Dijon in 1554 it was perceived, however unjustly, as a feminine form of vagrancy. During the sixteenth century the outcast poor were increasingly portrayed in official rhetoric as brute beasts, who could only be made human by the Christian teachings of which they were woefully ignorant, and as habitual sinners, mired in sloth and vice, lost souls in need of redemption—which could be achieved by confinement in an institution and subjection to a quasi-monastic regime.

Formal and Informal Assistance. Poverty was to a large extent palliated by innumerable unrecorded, small casual transactions between beggars and almsgivers; by the mutual support afforded to each other by neighbors and kinsfolk; by landlords and farmers who parted with grain to the local poor at less than the current market prices; by alehouse keepers and bakers who gave generous credit; and by the tactics for survival that the poor devised for themselves, including the practice of backstreet magic (a resort of former prostitutes in Naples).

Apart from these forms of relief, there was a sophisticated institutional structure in most towns and in some townships and villages, which also had their confraternities, hospitals, and credit institutions on a more modest scale. Towns tended to imitate each other, and they also listened to the exhortations of the same eloquent preachers, so that standard forms of organization were widely disseminated. Management of these institutions afforded social opportunities to well-to-do, leisured citizens: chances to improve their social standing, to exercise patronage by providing beds or pensions for their own favored dependents, and even, as well-commemorated benefactors, to earn a kind of immortality. Hospitals employed a large staff in relation to the number of inmates, and there was often no great difference between the poor admitted to hospitals and the ward attendants who looked after them.

Confraternities. Catholic cities generally contained large numbers of religious brotherhoods, with a much smaller number of sororities. Most of these confraternities were societies of laypersons subscribing to a not-too-onerous religious rule, a body of statutes that taught them how to acquire a store of religious merit by the practice of good works and the correction of faults. Among these good works, sometimes (though not invariably) assuming crucial importance for their regime, were the acts of mercy prescribed in the twenty-fifth chapter of St. Matthew's Gospel: almsgiving, caring for the sick, visiting prisoners, and taking in strangers. Ecclesiastical tradition had added another act of mercy, the burial of the dead, and this pious duty usually extended to financing masses for the souls of the departed, since those suffering the pains of Purgatory were fitting objects for the charity of living people, and mass-foundations provided welcome employment for impecunious priests. After the Black Death, at least in Italy, it became increasingly common to provide relatively large sums in dowries for the marriage of poor girls of good reputation.

Sometimes specializing in particular works of mercy and sometimes covering the whole range of charitable acts, confraternities functioned partly for the benefit of their own members and partly for the benefit of outsiders. From the late fifteenth century, there were increasing numbers of devout confraternities, like the Compagnia del Divino Amore in Genoa and elsewhere, that directed much of their energy outward, toward people too poor or disreputable to belong to a religious brotherhood. Confraternities could be socially exclusive clubs, or they might embrace everyone in a community or parish, making only modest demands on their time and purses. In the Spanish town of Zamora in the late sixteenth century (an extreme case), there were 150 confraternities serving at most 8,600 residents, one organization for every fourteen households; there were five for clerics, ten for nobles, and more than a hundred for plebeians.

Though confraternities were mostly confined to artisans and people above them socially, it was possible, as in Rome, Florence, Milan, and Venice, to organize confraternities of approved beggars, especially blind and lame ones, their elected officers being charged to distribute fairly among the members the alms collected on the street by the more skillful and appealing beggars. In sixteenth-century Bologna, street porters and others formed a Company of the Poor for the purpose of attracting rather than dispensing charity. The more opulent confraternities did not confine themselves to outdoor relief; they were quite capable, for example, of running hospitals or almshouses, and could be dedicated to almost any charitable or pious purpose.

Hospitals. Hospitals provided shelter but not necessarily medical care. To provide hospitality was not their only task, for they might also serve as general almoners to their communities, and infants in their care were put out to foster homes, often in the nearby countryside. Three major functions of hospitals were the reception of pilgrims, the care of orphans and abandoned children, and the care of old people and widows. Attention to the sick could well become a preoccupation, since people were poor because they were sick, and sick because they were poor. Certain hospitals, among them Santa Maria Nuova in Florence, enjoyed a high reputation for the quality of their medical care. Some kept wards for the "shamefaced" poor, but hospitals were unlikely to attract well-to-do people who needed a sophisticated medical treatment not available in their homes.

In the late Middle Ages, innumerable small hospitals were founded by private individuals, lay and clerical, and by associations such as confraternities. In the fifteenth and sixteenth centuries, many large cities in Spain, France, and northern Italy attempted, in the interests of efficiency and incorruptibility, to draw most of their local hospitals together in a single organization run on the community's behalf. In Italy at least, responsibility for these organizations lay, not with unsupervised priors or wardens, but with boards of governors recruited from the principal social orders in the city.

However, these metropolitan superhospitals of the Renaissance seldom succeeded in drawing all hospitals under their wings, and before long new institutions were added. Plague hospitals, in part quarantine centers for suspected people and goods, owed much to the belief that the disease was spread, not only by corruption of the air but also by contagion. Hospitals for "incurables" originated about 1500 in the course of a virulent outbreak of sexually transmitted disease but soon began to deal with other conditions that required protracted treatment. From about 1560, hospitals designed to admit all beggars in the city began to be erected, amid much controversy over the desirability of keeping destitute people away from the public gaze. Certain cities staged "Triumphs of Charity" processions, which involved assembling local beggars and marching or carting them off to their new quarters, accompanied by a selection of their benefactors. Some triumphs were short-lived, as in papal Rome, for few such hospitals possessed the resources to carry out an effective internment of the poorest of the poor.

Credit Institutions. Italian towns, especially, attempted to provide small loans at controlled rates of interest for the "poor of money," who had goods to pawn, as distinct from the "poorer poor," who had none. They might license a Jewish pawnbroker, or (from the 1460s) establish a cut-rate Christian pawnshop known as a *monte di pietà,* or resort to both methods. Similar pawnshops arose in Spain and the southern Low Countries, and also, in the form of the so-called *prêts charitables,* in seventeenth-century France. They served not only as pawnshops but also as disaster banks, from which the commune was entitled to borrow in emergencies. In country districts the equivalents of the urban *monti di pietà* were grain banks, or *monti frumentari,* which lent seed corn to peasant farmers—not, generally, on pledges, but on the strength of guarantees provided by their more prosperous neighbors.

Reforms in Catholic and Protestant Europe. From the early sixteenth century many town councils and some state governments endeavored to establish a more rational and coordinated system of poor relief. Their schemes had several common characteristics: They aimed at the suppression or at least the restriction of public begging; at establishing the principle that each locality should look after its own poor people and turn others away; at organizing censuses of the resident poor; at setting up work schemes for the unemployed; and at providing trade training for beggar children and orphans. Several German towns that broke with Rome decreed that the resources of dissolved religious institutions should be absorbed into Common Chests controlled by boards of laymen and directed toward education and the relief of the deserving poor.

Some Catholic cities, however, also attempted to pool resources and establish central organs for outdoor relief, such as the Aumône Générale in Lyon or the Bureau des Pauvres in Rouen, even as the Italians and others had already endeavored to establish control over their hospitals. They could hardly appropriate monastic property or change the use of bequests from paying for masses for the dead to supporting the living poor. But, amid intense religious conflict, with each confession striving to impose on the people its own norms of conduct, belief, and worship, control of discriminating relief was an instrument too valuable to be neglected. Such control offered a pretext for acquiring intimate knowledge of the circumstances and habits of local residents. The so-called prefects of the poor in Catholic Ypres were instructed to visit the poor and "by certain tokens and conjectures to get the knowledge of their condition, their health, their homely and secret griefs, their manners and (as near as can be) their merits, and to write these in a book or tables ordained for the same purpose."

In the sixteenth and early seventeenth centuries there was a shift, though not a decisive one, away from the tradition of regarding poor relief as a voluntary activity or "charitable imperative," a duty prompted by powerful religious sanctions and social pressures but not by legal coercion. In the 1520s an ordinance for Leisnig in Saxony contemplated imposing a poor rate should voluntary charity prove inadequate. Hitherto most organized assistance had been administered by institutions dependent on gifts, legacies, or collections taken in the town or district; *monti di pietà* were able to draw on deposits of money as well as on outright donations. If the commune supported hospitals, it did so in a piecemeal fashion, which might well include the assignment of certain indirect taxes or certain judicial fines to the institution. Save in the direst emergencies, the public authorities' role was to supervise charities, sometimes in parallel with churchmen, rather than to intervene directly in poor relief.

In the sixteenth century the introduction of rating, the assessing of each citizen's relative wealth and responsibility, often went with the use of the parish and its officers as agents for collecting and distributing relief to the deserving poor. Voluntary principles were reluctantly abandoned even in Tudor and Stuart England, which gradually adopted parish relief as the foundation of a countrywide system authorized by parliamentary statute. By the 1550s the Rouen scheme seemed to depend heavily on "voluntary taxation," called "quotization," on the part of gentry, burghers, artisans, and prelates; in Lyon those failing to subscribe adequately to the Aumône Générale could be pressed to give more generously; in Orléans persons who did not honor their promises might well face legal coercion, for in the reign of Charles IX tax collectors were empowered by royal edict to distrain on their goods. In France, however,

Works of Mercy: Feeding the Hungry. Detail of fresco by Giovanni della Robbia in the Ospedale del Ceppo, Pistoia, Italy. 1514. ALINARI/ART RESOURCE

the practice of levying poor rates diminished in the seventeenth century, if only because the royal government looked askance at rival systems of municipal taxation.

In Europe generally, in the sixteenth and seventeenth centuries, agencies directly administered by public authorities came to play a larger part in poor relief. Public granaries became desirable, though not always effective, defenses against famine. Strong connections were drawn between control of the outcast poor and control of disease; the Board of Health in Venice took charge of measures against begging, vagrancy, and prostitution. There was to some extent a common culture of poor relief in early modern Europe that crossed religious boundaries. In their official pronouncements, Catholics and Protestants condemned idleness and undisciplined begging with equal vigor.

But the institutional structures could be very different—as witness, for example, the prompt disappearance of the theologically unacceptable confraternities from Protestant countries. Louder and more articulate protests against the poor law were heard from a particular segment of the Catholic Church—from the orders of begging friars, especially Charles V's chaplain, Domiñgo Soto. Catholic institutions, such as the great beggars' hospitals which imposed a near-monastic rule on their inmates, had a flavor of their own, even though, by the mid-seventeenth century, they were starting to borrow from the Amsterdam House of Correction or from some similar institution in northern Europe.

See also **Confraternities; Hospitals and Asylums; Orphans and Foundlings; Prostitution; Social Status.**

BIBLIOGRAPHY

Cavallo, Sandra. *Charity and Power in Early Modern Italy: Benefactors and Their Motives in Turin, 1541–1789.* Cambridge, U.K., 1995.

Daunton, Martin, ed. *Charity, Self-interest, and Welfare in the English Past.* London, 1996. Includes essays on Europe.

Davis, Natalie Zemon. *Society and Culture in Early Modern France.* Stanford, Calif., 1975. See chapter 2. "Poor Relief, Humanism, and Heresy: The Case of Lyon," pp. 17–64.

Flynn, Maureen. *Sacred Charity: Confraternities and Social Welfare in Spain, 1400–1700.* Basingstoke, U.K., 1989.

Gutton, Jean-Pierre. *La société et les pauvres: L'exemple de la généralité de Lyon, 1534–1789.* Paris, 1971.

Jütte, Robert. *Poverty and Deviance in Early Modern Europe.* Cambridge, U.K., 1994.

Lindberg, Carter. "'There Should Be No Beggars among Christians': Karlstadt, Luther, and the Origins of Protestant Poor Relief." *Church History* 46 (1977): 313–334.

Martz, Linda. *Poverty and Welfare in Habsburg Spain: The Example of Toledo.* Cambridge, U.K., 1983.

Mollat, Michel. *The Poor in the Middle Ages: An Essay in Social History.* New Haven, Conn., 1986.

Pullan, Brian. *Poverty and Charity: Europe, Italy, Venice, 1400–1700.* Aldershot, U.K., 1994. Reprints of essays published over the previous thirty years.

Pullan, Brian. *Rich and Poor in Renaissance Venice: The Social Institutions of a Catholic State, to 1620.* Oxford and Cambridge, Mass., 1971.

Slack, Paul. *Poverty and Policy in Tudor and Stuart England.* London, 1988.

Wandel, Lee Palmer. *Always among Us: Images of the Poor in Zwingli's Zurich.* Cambridge, U.K., 1990.

BRIAN PULLAN

PRAGUE. The capital of the kingdom of Bohemia, Prague was elevated to the status of a leading European metropolis by Emperor Charles IV (ruled 1355–1378). The city was assured its preeminent place by an extensive building program, the establishment of the office of archbishop (1344), the founding of the first university in Central Europe (1348), and the doubling of the urban area by the creation of the New Town (1348). By the turn of the fifteenth century, artisans were the most numerous section of the population and were the driving force of the religious reform movement inspired by the work and martyrdom of Jan Hus. In 1419 an uprising broke out in Prague, in the course of which the artisans joined forces with the urban poor and seized power. Prague rid itself of the rule of the Czech sovereign as well as of the influence of the nobility and the church. By 1421 the Praguers were at the height of their power, holding sway over most of the territory of Bohemia. However, they then started to turn away from the radicals, who continued to call uncompromisingly for reform and the total equality of all people. After the defeat of the Hussites (1434), Prague was economically devastated. It remained the strongest and most populous Czech city, with at least twenty-five thousand inhabitants. The number of artisans fell while, on the other hand, the unpromising guild system was supported. The only outcome of the Prague uprising in 1419 was the formation of the reformed Utraquist Church by the spiritual descendants of Hus, whose organization was subordinated to the city authorities.

Revival. The renewal of Prague began with the election of George of Poděbrady (ruled 1458–1471) as king of Bohemia at the Prague Old Town Hall, which was still the country's political center. George's election marked the reestablishment of central power that was the precondition for the development of the economy and foreign trade. In view of Prague's geographical location, foreign trade

Prague. Woodcut by Michael Wolgemut (c. 1434 or 1437–1519) from Hartmann Schedel and Anton Koberger, *Liber chronicarum* (The Nürnberg Chronicle; 1493). GIRAUDON/ART RESOURCE

was its traditional source of wealth. With the passage of time its importance increased still further, until by the turn of the seventeenth century it was more significant than the city's artisanal production. George's successor, King Vladislav II (ruled 1471–1516) continued the policy of enhancing the city's appearance, carrying out renovations chiefly at the Prague Castle, where, under his auspices, architect Benedict Ried in 1493 converted the Royal Palace into the first Renaissance building north of the Alps.

During the reign of the Habsburg king Ferdinand I, who became king of Bohemia in 1526 (and ruled until his death in 1564), Prague became a glittering royal residence and the main financial and administrative center of the country. On the other hand, the Habsburgs' arrival in Prague meant that the city lost the independence it had won in the Hussite revolution in the wake of an unsuccessful uprising against Ferdinand in 1547. Ferdinand's building activity was concentrated on the splendid garden, with its Singing Fountain, designed by Francesco Terzio in 1493 at the Prague Castle, where Ferdinand began erecting the Summer Palace of Queen Anna. Following the disastrous fire of 1541, the appearance of the Lesser Town (Malá Strana) was radically altered. Lying directly below the castle, this was the third of Prague's component towns and it was gradually transformed into the local nobility's residential quarter, constructed in the style of the Italian Renaissance. The city's architecture was also enriched by the son of Ferdinand I, the Archduke Ferdinand II of Tyrol (ruled 1547–1567), who erected the Star Pavilion (1555–1560) in the mannerist style.

The great period of Prague's embellishment dates from the early 1580s when it became the city of residence of the Emperor Rudolf II (ruled 1575–1612). Thanks to the emperor's wide interests, the city became a major center of science and the arts and the size of its population roughly doubled to at least sixty thousand. It was in this period that the right-bank settlement (Malá Strana, Hradčany, and Prague Castle), which had close links with the cosmopolitan court and where German, Czech, and Italian were spoken, became distinct in character from the left-bank settlement (the Old and New Towns), where the population consisted of artisans and traders and the Czech language prevailed. A large colony of Italian masons and artisans settled in Prague, where they worked for Rudolf, converting the Prague Castle into a Renaissance residence, and also built magnificent Renaissance palaces for the foremost Czech nobility in the vicinity of the imperial seat. The emperor's art collection, one of the biggest in Europe of the day, was located in Prague. The cultural activities of the court were supplemented by those of the University of Prague and the patronage of educated nobles and patricians.

In 1521 Luther's pupil Thomas Müntzer came to Prague with hopes of propagating the ideas of the German Reformation, but he failed because of opposition from the Utraquists. In 1556, Ferdinand I invited the Jesuits to Prague. Prague now became a center for the restoration of the Roman Catholic faith. The restoration of the Prague archbishopric (1561) was also intended to serve that end. The conflict between the Protestant Czech Estates and the Catholic

Habsburgs came to a head in the early seventeenth century, when the opposition Estates in a famous confrontation threw the imperial governors out of a window in the Prague Castle in 1618. The incident, the Defenestration of Prague, precipitated the Thirty Years' War. In 1620 the troops of the Estates were defeated at the White Mountain near Prague. In the wake of the defeat came crippling fines and confiscations that affected all the non-Catholic inhabitants of the city. Roman Catholicism was proclaimed the country's sole religion and all other denominations were harshly persecuted. A living testimony to the extent of the confiscations is the complex of palaces built by the commander of the imperial troops, Albrecht von Wallenstein, in Prague's Lesser Town in the years from 1623 to 1630. During the Thirty Years' War, Prague was plundered repeatedly. The most destructive looting, however, was committed by the Swedish army in 1648, the last year of the war, when the enormous collection of Rudolf II was taken back to Sweden almost in its entirety. Desolate and depopulated, Prague did not recover until the end of the seventeenth century.

Renaissance Art in Prague. The chief relics of Prague's Renaissance art are held in the Collection of Old Masters in Saint George's Convent at Prague Castle; the remnants of Rudolf II's picture gallery discovered in the 1960s are displayed in the Castle Gallery at Prague Castle. Apart from the architecture already mentioned, extant monuments include the Large Ball Court in the Royal Gardens, (Boniface Wolmut, 1567–1569); the organ loft in Saint Vitus Cathedral (Boniface Wolmut, 1556–1561); the sepulchre of Ferdinand I, Anne Jagiello, and Maxmilian II in Saint Vitus Cathedral (Alexander Colin, 1566–1589); the Palace of John of Lobkowitz in Prague, Hradčany (Agostino Galli, before 1563); the Mathias Gateway, Prague Castle (Giovanni Maria Filippi, 1613–1614); and Town Hall in Prague, Lesser Town (1617–1619).

See also East Central Europe, Art in; *biography of Rudolf II.*

BIBLIOGRAPHY

Janáček, Josef, ed. *Dějiny Prahy*. Prague, 1964. Pages 141–355.
Macek, Josef. *Jagelonský věk v českých zemích, 1476–1526*. 3 vols. Prague, 1992–1998.
Neubert, Karel, and Jan Royt. *Art Treasures of Prague: A Guide to the Galleries, Museums, and Exhibition Rooms of Prague, with Basic Tourist Information*. Prague, 1992.
Neumann, Jaromír. *The Picture Gallery of Prague Castle*. Prague, 1967.

JAN BAŽANT

PRAYER BOOK, ENGLISH. The first Book of Common Prayer was born out of the English Reformation, under the young king Edward VI, in 1549. New and simpler orders of public worship in English were urgently needed to replace the rival Latin "uses" (liturgies), which complicated church life and included legends and other nonbiblical material, as well as too many services in the judgment of English Protestants. That first Prayer Book was based on the best of the Latin "uses," that of "Sarum" (services at Salisbury), and on research into European models and older English devotional material. Thomas Cranmer, then archbishop of Canterbury, stamped the book with his own scholarship, and indeed genius.

As in the oldest church traditions, daily public reading of the Bible, by then translated into English, came first: all the Psalms were to be read or sung every month, the whole New Testament was to be read aloud three times a year, and most of the Old Testament every year. The Psalms were from the version by Miles Coverdale in 1535. His was the first complete Bible printed in English, though not from the original languages. A revision of this, initiated by Cranmer in 1549, prefaced by him, was the only English Bible ever to be authorized. The Prayer Book Psalter withstood later new translations from the Hebrew, including the King James Version of 1611. The many Latin daily services were reduced to Matins and Evensong (which from 1552 became Morning and Evening Prayer), Holy Communion and Baptism (the only sacraments in the English Church), and five other services. Cranmer was the author of much of the detail, particularly the daily short prayers known as "collects," of lapidary beauty in form and cadence. To him we owe, for example, "Lighten our darkness, we beseech thee, O Lord; and by thy great mercy defend us from all perils and dangers of this night." There are many such prayers.

Those services in English, spoken and heard daily from the mid-sixteenth century across much of the English-speaking world, had a literary impact that is incalculable. Cranmer's phrases, with the Bible's, acted as rhetorical authorization and models for a continuing English plain style of timeless simplicity and strength. Plain directness became an aim at all social and cultural levels: it is in Cranmer's own *Homilies* of 1547 and William Latimer's sermons of the mid 1550s. It is the preferred mode of the learned scientists who founded the Royal Society in 1660. High feeling in simple form in the early 1600s is in Shakespeare's "The rest is silence" at the end of *Hamlet* (1600–1601), and in John Bunyan's "and all

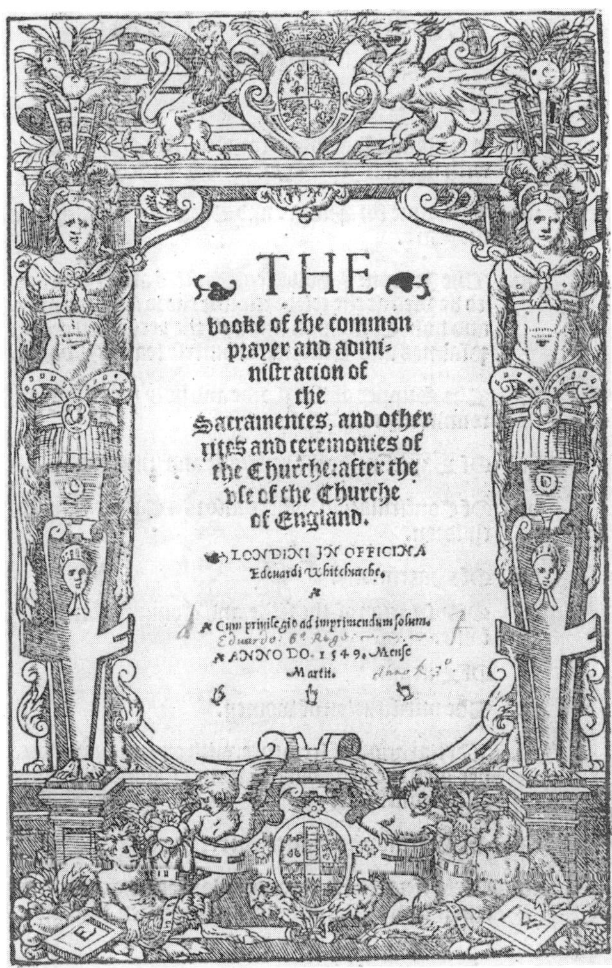

THE
booke of the common
prayer and admi-
nistracion of
the
Sacramentes, and other
rites and ceremonies of
the Churche: after the
vse of the Churche
of England.

LONDINI IN OFFICINA
Edouardi Whitchurche.

Cum privilegio ad imprimendum solum.
ANNO DO. 1549. Mense
Martii.

The Book of Common Prayer. Title page of the 1549 Prayer Book. BY PERMISSION OF THE BRITISH LIBRARY. C25L14

the trumpets sounded for him on the other side" at the end of *Pilgrim's Progress, the Second Part* (1684). Many simple phrases from the Prayer Book are still in use, like "peace in our time," "through fire and water," and "like a giant refreshed." The English Prayer Book has given voice, in its own phrase, to "all sorts and conditions of men."

See also **Bible**, *subentry on* **The English Bible**; **Cranmer, Thomas**.

BIBLIOGRAPHY

Brook, Stella. *The Language of the Book of Common Prayer.* London, 1965.

MacCulloch, Diarmaid. *Thomas Cranmer.* New Haven, Conn., and London, 1996.

DAVID DANIELL

PREACHING AND SERMONS. [This entry includes two subentries, one on Christian preaching, the other on Jewish preaching.]

Christian Preaching and Sermons

"Faith comes from hearing" (Rom. 10:17). Preaching is communicating the Word of God in human speech; its purpose is to awaken faith and make Christians ever mindful of their calling. Evangelists are "to proclaim the message; be persistent whether the time is favorable or unfavorable; convince, rebuke, and encourage, with the utmost patience in teaching" (2 Tim. 4:2). Preaching's importance is grounded in the life of Christ, who "preached the Good News" of "the Kingdom" (Mark 1:14–15) and commanded his apostles "to go and make disciples of all nations" (Matt. 28:19).

As throughout Christian tradition, in the Middle Ages and Renaissance occasions for preaching were various and generally unrestricted. Preaching occurred as a regular part of the eucharistic liturgy after the reading of the gospel. It could also take place at any time outside the liturgy in Advent and Lenten sermons, in panegyrics for the Blessed Virgin or the angels and saints, in confraternities, at funerals or special devotions such as Forty Hours (a devotion originated in sixteenth-century Italy in which the Blessed Sacrament is exposed in a church or chapel for a period of forty hours), in times of plague or famine, in proclaiming indulgences, venerating relics, imparting moral instruction, encouraging penitence in the streets among city dwellers, and so on. Outside the liturgy, preachers might encourage Christians to "take up the Cross" against the Turks. Crusade preaching continued throughout the Renaissance and well after the Christian naval victory at Lepanto (1571).

The office of preaching properly belongs to bishops, who delegate priests as coadjutors in this ministry. A preacher therefore is officially commissioned to proclaim the Good News, although outside liturgical functions no commission is required and even laypersons might preach, as was done often throughout the Middle Ages and Renaissance, although ecclesiastical authorities sometimes expressed strong misgivings about this and sometimes forbade it. Christian tradition, however, beginning with Paul, has always recognized charismatic speaking (1 Cor. 12:8–11, 28), as scripture made clear that the Holy Spirit chooses whom he will and causes him to speak as he will, as with the prophets of Israel.

Preaching Reforms. In the Middle Ages and Renaissance, preaching was commonly seen as fallen dismally below its ideal condition, and some church councils and synods sought to address this. The Fourth Lateran Council (1215) made clear that bishops were responsible for preaching and clerical education, and the subsequent approval of the Order of Preachers (Dominicans) and the Order of Friars Minor (Franciscans) gave a vigorous stimulus to a preaching revival in the Latin West. The Fifth Lateran Council's decree on preaching, *Supernae majestatis praesidio* (1516), warned of incompetent, self-styled preachers uttering apocalyptic messages and nonsense and made strong recommendations for dealing with such abuses, including excommunication. Fifth Lateran reminded clergy that "they preach and explain the evangelical truth and Sacred Scripture according to the declaration, interpretation and exposition of the doctors whom the Church or daily use has approved"; it also admonished bishops to keep watch over their preachers. The many complaints of synods and of other observers in this era about this impoverished condition of preaching suggest that in many areas of Europe, especially in the countryside, few competent individuals preached on a regular basis, and inhabitants of those areas were pitifully ignorant of the rudiments of Christian instruction. On the other hand, it is evident that much good preaching did occur.

The Council of Trent (1545–1563) went much further than any previous ecclesiastical assembly in addressing this state of preaching. Trent identified preaching as the "special duty of bishops" and enjoined them "to preach the holy Gospel of Jesus Christ, to feed the people entrusted to them . . . by teaching them those things necessary for all to know in order to be saved, and by impressing upon them with briefness and plainness of speech the vices they must avoid and the virtues they must cultivate, in order that they may escape eternal punishment and obtain the glory of heaven." Trent's directives were based on the conviction that an active preaching clergy has always been essential for a holy Christian community and that poor preaching was inevitably a clear sign of clerical ignorance and vice. Trent's directive came at a time when the understanding of preaching among Catholics and Protestants had in fact already begun to change dramatically, and a preaching revival was in full swing throughout Europe. Many of the new religious orders in the sixteenth century, such as the Jesuits, Theatines, and Capuchins, made preaching a priority, and many orders, above all the Jesuits, had discarded the medieval forms of preaching for the application of humanist rhetoric to sacred oratory. Many bishops, such as Cornelio Musso (1511–1575), Francisco Panigarola (1548–1594), and most notably Carlo Borromeo of Milan (1538–1584), preached regularly, thereby setting an example for the other bishops and clergy. In the mid-sixteenth century, numerous bishops, such as Gasparo Contarini (1483–1542) of Belluno, Gianmatteo Giberti (1495–1543) of Verona, and Gabriele Paleotti (1527–1597) of Bologna, as well as many superiors of religious orders, composed instructions for preachers on approved methods, content, and materials for preaching to the people. The idealized portrait of late sixteenth-century Rome in Gregory Martin's *Roma Sancta* (1581) illustrates this preaching revival and the effects of good preaching on a city that some years earlier had been sorely criticized for its crimes and vices.

Elements of Preaching. Since preaching itself has no prescribed format, each preacher is to seek ways to address his audience most effectively. As Desiderius Erasmus noted, quoting Paul, "the gift of proclaiming God's message should be under the speaker's control." Authors of treatises on preaching noted that in the early church inspired speakers arose spontaneously, but in the post-apostolic age preaching was regulated by ecclesiastical authorities, and unregulated preaching could be harmful. They emphasized that preaching required instruction, lengthy preparation in the liberal arts and scripture, and, most important, holiness in the preacher himself. Specifically, the theme, length and parts of the discourse, language, subject matter, style, and so on, though variable, should be appropriate for the occasion. In the Middle Ages and Renaissance these issues mattered, especially in more formal situations, and many homiletic resources were made available to assist preachers at all levels to advance in this ministry.

Preaching took many forms, but at Mass it was principally the sermon and the homily, both believed to have their origins in biblical and patristic tradition. The sermon was a more formal construction aimed at teaching moral and spiritual lessons with a moral exhortation based on the texts of scripture read at the Mass. By comparison, the homily was a more flexible form of discourse consisting of an opening address, a pious application of the liturgical text based on the allegorical sense of scripture, parenesis (moral exhortation), and doxology (praise to God). In the Renaissance the homily attracted many adherents among humanist-trained ecclesiastics both because of its flexibility and adaptability to classical rhetorical theory and practice and because the

Renaissance rediscovery of Christian antiquity had made clear how the eloquent fathers of the Greek and Latin churches (Gregory of Nazianzus, Gregory of Nyssa, Basil, John Chrysostom, Ambrose, Augustine, and others) had used this form so effectively.

The sermon (*sermo*) sometimes differed little from the homily, but in the Middle Ages it assumed a distinctively more formal structure. Scholastic theorists argued that the sermon should teach and convince the listener of the truths of the faith. Their treatises developed into the many medieval handbooks for preaching (*Artes praedicandi*) which systematized the sermon into a unified, organically developing whole and gave explicit rules for each of its formal elements, from invention and arrangement to delivery and rhetorical devices. Though scholastic in approach, the *Artes praedicandi* could occasion many lively sermons, depending on the preacher. The success of these manuals further suggests how popular the "scholastic" or "thematic" sermon became in the Middle Ages.

The thematic sermon regularly began with a theme (usually a short quotation from scripture read at Mass) resembling the statement of a proposition. After a protheme (prologue) to catch the audience's attention and a short prayer for God's assistance, the preacher repeated the theme, emphasized its significance, and proceeded to divide the sermon into parts. He then gave definitions, made distinctions, supported arguments with examples and proofs from scripture, the Fathers, and other authorities, and concluded. The scholastic method had a strong impact on medieval and Renaissance preaching, especially among members of the mendicant orders, the Dominicans and Franciscans, whose teachers and best preachers received their education disputing theological questions. But the thematic sermon held no exclusive monopoly and could be substantially altered when preachers addressed "the people" (*ad populum*).

Central to the homily and the sermon was the exposition of holy scripture. For the mendicants this could often mean a simple approach which abandoned the subtleties of scholastic disputations in order to shake sinners from their vices and instill a love of the virtues. Francis of Assisi's *regula bullata,* the definitive Second Rule of the Friars Minor (1223), set this direction, which not only characterized Franciscan preaching but was picked up by other religious orders and echoed loudly in Trent's decree on preaching: "I warn and remind friars that whenever they preach their words are to be well chosen and pure, so as to help and edify the people, and to define virtues and vices, punishment and glory. And let them be brief, for the Lord himself was brief while on earth." Franciscan preaching aimed at the spiritual needs of town dwellers in their own language and images, with concrete stories and clear lessons. This approach seemed more consistent with the preaching of St. Paul, for example, who shunned "lofty words or wisdom" (1 Cor. 2:1): it was brief, unostentatious, and simple, focused on the basics of Christian instruction (Ten Commandments, Apostles' Creed, Our Father) and on the Christian virtues and the vices to avoid, and used quotations from scripture and the Fathers to move the heart. These were the rudiments of Christian doctrine, the "things necessary for all to know in order to be saved," according to Trent.

The Papal Nuncio Preaching. The papal representative Cornelio Musso preaches before the emperor Ferdinand I in the Augustinerkirche, Vienna, in 1560. Painting by Jakob Seisenegger (1505–1567). Private Collection/The Bridgeman Art Library

Preaching Manuals. Though much criticism was heard throughout the Middle Ages and well into the Renaissance about poor preaching, there were nonetheless many good preachers who commanded wide followings and showed great diversity in their approach to preaching, from the thematic sermon to more mystical approaches. Among the more well-known preachers of this kind are the Dominicans Meister Eckhart (1260?–1327?) and Johannes Tauler (c. 1300–1361), Gerhart Groot (1340–1384), Jean de Gerson (1363–1429), the Franciscan Bernardino of Siena (1380–1444), Gabriel Biel (c. 1420–1495), the Dominican Girolamo Savonarola (1452–1498), and Johann Geiler von Kaisersberg (1445–1510).

To assist them, preachers often had abundant materials, such as sermon collections, summae of virtues and vices, books of exempla, the famous *Legenda aurea* (Golden legend) of Jacobus de Voragine, and treatises on preaching. Homiletic helps of this kind appeared frequently throughout the Middle Ages and Renaissance, especially among members of the mendicant orders.

By the sixteenth century the *Artes praedicandi* had begun to fall out of favor, especially in Italy. With the humanist revival of Roman rhetorical education, humanist-trained ecclesiastics came to understand preaching more broadly as "sacred eloquence" and to see it as falling in line with the three aims of classical rhetoric—to move, to teach, and to delight (*movere, docere, delectare*).

Arguably the single most important work to validate the application of classical rhetoric to Catholic preaching was Erasmus's massive treatise on homiletics, *Ecclesiastes sive de ratione concionandi* (Ecclesiastes, or the theory of preaching; 1535). Humanist-trained preachers in Rome and elsewhere in the mid-fifteenth century had long been preaching this way, but it was only in the next century that theoretical works, such as those of Johann Reuchlin, Erasmus, and Philipp Melanchthon, began to take up the subject systematically. Paradoxically, Erasmus's work found no enthusiastic response among Catholics, especially after some of his works were placed on the Index of Prohibited Books. Although few Catholic authors ever acknowledged his contribution, his work prompted the edition of numerous preaching manuals, the "ecclesiastical rhetorics," which appeared with the full endorsement of the Roman hierarchy from the end of the Council of Trent until well into the next century. Among the more popular manuals to follow Erasmus's work and come out in many editions are *Rhetorica christiana* (1574) by Diego Valades, *De rhetorica ecclesiastica* (1579) by Agostino Valier, bishop of Verona, *Rhetoricae ecclesiasticae* (1576) by Luis de Granada, *De ratione concionandi* (1576) by Diego de Estella, *Divinus orator* (1595) by Ludovico Carbone, *Orator Christianus* (1612) by Carlo Reggio, and *De eloquentia sacra et humana* (1617) by Nicholas Caussin. The popularity of these manuals became so great, especially in the late sixteenth and early seventeenth centuries, that the new manuals seem to have displaced completely the *Artes praedicandi,* though thematic sermons were still preached, mostly in settings for theological instruction.

The ecclesiastical rhetorics presented preaching as an activity intending "persuasion" (*persuadere*) in the broadest sense—to move the heart, will, and emotions. Depending on the occasion and context, they saw preaching as falling into one or more of the three *genera* of classical rhetoric: the *genus deliberativum* (the art of persuading and dissuading), as in persuading one to shun vice and grow in virtues; the *genus demonstrativum* (epideictic, the art of praise and blame), as with panegyrics of God, the saints and the angels, and deceased Christians; or, in rarer circumstances, the *genus iudiciale* (the art of accusing and defending). The new manuals also gave advice on the three *genera* of speaking styles (the humble, middle, and grand) and on their appropriateness in various homiletic contexts, in addition to dwelling on the parts of oratory, rhetorical devices, and so on. Above all, they reminded preachers that the end of preaching is not vain eloquence as it was with the pagan orators, but the "salvation of souls" and "the glory of God." One might apply the principles of pagan rhetoric, but proclaiming the Word was a completely different kind of speaking.

The popularity of the ecclesiastical rhetorics was not restricted to Catholic preachers. Across Europe, preachers of many Protestant denominations found them useful, and Catholic writers and teachers of rhetoric sometimes even commented that Protestant preachers were adopting the same rhetorical methods as Catholics. One had to learn well the elements of rhetoric to be an effective preacher.

Late Renaissance preachers also had a wealth of new homiletic resources for preaching. By the early sixteenth century, texts newly edited by Erasmus and others of the homilies and sermons of Jerome, Gregory the Great, Basil, Gregory Nazianzene, John Chrysostom, and others made clear the extraordinary power of the early church fathers. These provided timely models of excellent preaching. The printing press also made available collections of contemporary preaching, the Roman catechism, and numerous devotional materials that could be adapted for the pulpit.

The Protestant Reformation gave a renewed prominence to the preaching of the Word and a sense of urgency for a more systematic approach to improving preaching. The Reformers also called attention to the shortcomings in Catholic preaching. Martin Luther's concept of the true church where the Word is preached and the sacraments (baptism and the Eucharist) are dispensed made clear that effective preaching was central to the Protestant churches and a major challenge to Catholic clergy, who had often been remiss in their duty to preach at Mass and to their flocks. Interestingly, Protestants and Catholics seem to have been familiar with each others' manuals on preaching: both consciously sought to adapt classical rhetoric to preaching and both apparently borrowed from each other without acknowledgment.

The importance of Jewish preaching in the late sixteenth and seventeenth centuries has been given careful study by David Ruderman and other scholars who observe that "the Jewish preacher assumed a status unparalleled in any previous age, and the interest of a Jewish laity in hearing and reading sermons reached unprecedented heights." Despite wide differences in theology and communal practices, Jewish and Christian preaching had many affinities in style and intellectual content in mediating knowledge and culture to a community of believers. Studies now suggest they owed much more to one another than they ever acknowledged.

BIBLIOGRAPHY

Bayley, Peter. *French Pulpit Oratory, 1598–1650: A Study in Themes and Styles, with a Descriptive Catalogue of Printed Texts*. Cambridge, Mass., 1980.

Charland, Thomas Marie. *Artes praedicandi: Contribution à l'histoire de la rhétorique au moyen âge*. Paris, 1936.

Fumaroli, Marc. *L'âge de l'éloquence: Rhétorique et "res literaria" de la Renaissance au seuil de l'époque classique*. Paris, 1980.

McGinness, Frederick J. *Right Thinking and Sacred Oratory in Counter Reformation Rome*. Princeton, N.J., 1995.

Murphy, James J. *Rhetoric in the Middle Ages: A History of Rhetorical Theory from Saint Augustine to the Renaissance*. Berkeley, Calif., 1974.

O'Malley, John. *Praise and Blame in Renaissance Rome: Rhetoric, Doctrine, and Reform in the Sacred Orators of the Papal Court, c. 1450–1521*. Durham, N.C., 1979.

Ruderman, David B., ed. *Preachers of the Italian Ghetto*. Berkeley, Calif., 1992.

Schneyer, Johann Baptist. *Geschichte der katholischen Predigt*. Freiburg, Germany, 1968.

Shuger, Debora K. *Sacred Rhetoric: The Christian Grand Style in the English Renaissance*. Princeton, N.J., 1988.

Smith, Hilary D. *Preaching in the Spanish Golden Age: A Study of Some Preachers of the Reign of Philip III*. Oxford, 1978.

Taylor, Larissa. *Soldiers of Christ: Preaching in Late Medieval and Reformation France*. New York, 1992.

FREDERICK J. MCGINNESS

Jewish Preaching and Sermons

Detecting the influence of the Renaissance on Jewish preaching is not a simple matter. Most sermons from the late fifteenth and early sixteenth centuries reveal little evidence of a new cultural milieu. Spanish Jewish preachers from the generation of the 1492 expulsion, for example, preserve the continuities of the medieval homiletic tradition, including the influence of Christian scholasticism, with thematic sermons including syllogistic arguments and "disputed questions."

These sermons popularize philosophical material for a general audience. They do not reflect a rediscovery of the classics or the pulse of Italian humanism. While some scholarship has argued that the courtier-scholar Isaac Abravanel (1437–1508) reveals the impact of the Renaissance in his biblical commentaries, particularly in his historical method and his wide reading in classical and Christian sources, the few extant sermons attributed to him seem fully medieval. Not surprisingly, the best indications of a new spirit are Italian.

Rhetoric. An instructive contrast can be seen in two almost contemporary works dealing with rhetoric and the art of preaching. The first, "Ein ha-Kore" (The Proclaimer's Wellspring), written in the 1450s by the Castilian courtier and philosopher Joseph ibn Shem Tov, is rooted entirely in the medieval realm of Aristotle and his Muslim explicators (Avicenna, Averroes). In this work, rhetoric is identified as the art most appropriate for preaching, but it is clearly inferior to logical demonstration.

Nofet tsufim (The honeycomb's flow), written in the 1450s and 1460s by the Italian scholar Judah Messer Leon (and printed in Mantua in 1475/76), reveals a totally different cultural ambience. Suffused with the classical texts of Cicero and Quintilian, it exalts the ideals of eloquence, exemplified in the Hebrew Bible and therefore accessible to the contemporary preacher. This heightened emphasis on oratory is expressed in the fact that during the following century, perhaps for the first time in Jewish history, instruction and training in the preparation and delivery of sermons became an integral part of the curriculum for well-educated Jewish males in Italy and beyond. Child-prodigy preachers were celebrated in the Jewish community, and preaching manuals and aids proliferated.

Classical Sources. Preachers of late sixteenth-century Italy reveal aspects of Renaissance culture, although not as consistently as has sometimes been maintained. Occasionally, their syncretism got them into trouble, as can be seen in the example of one David Del Bene, who was censured by several Italian rabbis in 1598 for using mythological motifs in a sermon. The published sermons of the Mantuan rabbi Judah Moscato (c. 1530–c. 1593), however, show that a preacher could use such material effectively, as he illustrates a Talmudic passage by recourse to the stories of Sisyphus and the daughters of Danaus.

Moscato's sermons are filled with references to authorities from the classical and Christian worlds, all woven into a deeply Jewish texture, a practice justified by the medieval claim of a Hebraic source for the wisdom of the Gentiles. In his preaching, Plato and Aristotle, Pythagoras and Mercurio (Hermes) Trismegistus, Cicero and Quintilian, Giovanni Pico della Mirandola and Rudolph Agricola, are juxtaposed with the Talmud, Jewish mystical texts, and such philosophers as Moses Maimonides and Joseph Albo, in an all but seamless tapestry. While the true extent of the influence of Renaissance culture on his work remains a matter of scholarly debate, his eclectic reading is beyond doubt.

Most of Moscato's colleagues, including the Venetian polymath Leon Modena (1571–1648), whose personal library included many works by gentile authors, cite non-Jewish authorities far less in their pulpit discourse. Yet assuming that the written texts reflect what was said in the synagogue, these preachers, intellectuals of the first or second rank, would have made the congregation of listeners aware of an exciting intellectual world beyond the familiar classical Jewish texts. Unlike in fifteenth-century Christian Italy and eighteenth-century eastern Europe, there is little evidence of truly "popular" Jewish preaching in Italy at this time. Modena attracted many listeners, including Christian clergy, but we know of no renowned itinerant preachers whose appeal was directed toward the ordinary Jew.

Arts. Jewish preachers rarely cite contemporary Italian or Jewish belles lettres. Samuel Judah Katzenellenbogen (1521–1597), rabbi in Padua and Venice, does refer to the practice "of our contemporary poets" to illuminate a passage in Psalms, but the practice mentioned—ending a poem with an echo of its beginning—was characteristic of Hebrew poetry in Spain five centuries earlier. A dramatic use of the plastic arts occurs in the introduction to Modena's inaugural sermon, where he compares preaching to painting and sculpture. Moscato's first published sermon is devoted to the theme of music.

Funerary Preaching. Extant eulogy texts date from the early fifteenth century, but it was not until the sixteenth century that the eulogy became a major component of many sermons. One is tempted to link this development with the heightened emphasis on the individual associated with the Renaissance, except that these sermons generally explore standard exegetical and conceptual problems relating to the soul and its fate after death, often omitting from the printed version the discussion of the individual being eulogized, and rarely reflecting the humanistic transformation of funerary oratory that began considerably earlier. Modena includes some strikingly unusual material in his eulogies, overtly derived from Christian sources.

Language and Structure. While sermons were ordinarily delivered in the vernacular throughout the Middle Ages, preachers wrote their sermons for dissemination in Hebrew. The earliest known text written in a vernacular language (excluding Judeo-Arabic) is by the late-sixteenth-century Kabbalist Mordecai Dato. In the following generations, manuscripts in Italian become increasingly common.

In form, the late medieval structures and conventions of Jewish homiletics continue to prevail in Italy, but there are also innovations. Moscato may have been the first to give his sermons titles. Modena claims to have crafted an original form, reflecting a synthesis of the Christian sermon and the traditional Jewish homily, possibly influenced by a treatise on preaching by the bishop of Asti, Francesco Panigarola (Modena owned a copy). One novelty is a formal introduction, not just a conventional justification of the preacher's decision to deliver the sermon, as was common in the late Middle Ages, but an artistic presentation of a significant motif.

See also **Abravanel, Isaac**; **Modena, Leon**.

BIBLIOGRAPHY

Primary Works

Messer Leon, Judah. *The Book of the Honeycomb's Flow: Sēpher Nōpheth Sūphīm*. Edited by Isaac Rabinowitz. Ithaca, N.Y., 1983. Illustrates the tropes of classical rhetorical theory through the Bible.

Zahalon, Jacob. *A Guide for Preachers on Composing and Delivering Sermons: The Or ha-Darshanim of Jacob Zahalon*. Edited by Henry Adler Sosland. New York, 1987.

Secondary Works

Altmann, Alexander. "*Ars Rhetorica* as Reflected in Some Jewish Figures of the Italian Renaissance." In *Jewish Thought in the*

Sixteenth Century. Edited by Bernard Dov Cooperman. Cambridge, Mass., 1983. Pages 1–22.

Ruderman, David B., ed. *Preachers of the Italian Ghetto*. Berkeley, Calif., 1992. Collection of six articles on Italian Jewish preaching c. 1550–1650.

Saperstein, Marc. *Jewish Preaching, 1200–1800*. New Haven, Conn., 1989. Substantial survey of Jewish preaching, including sixteen translated and annotated sermons (one by Moscato) and other source material.

MARC SAPERSTEIN

PREGNANCY. There were certain nearly universal aspects of the reproductive life of women during the Renaissance, because biological imperatives were joined with the demands of a common culture. The subcultures of region and social rank produced some large differences, however.

Normal Patterns. There were significant differences in conception and pregnancy between upper-class and lower-class women. Wealthy and aristocratic women usually became pregnant for the first time in their late teens and early twenties, while peasants became pregnant in their late twenties. The difference was due to the age at which they married. Pregnancy at extremely young ages was rare, however, since the usual age of menarche seems to have been rather late. Poor nutrition and hard work may have helped to delay menarche in the lower ranks, but even noblewomen who married at age fourteen or younger apparently had to wait several years before conceiving.

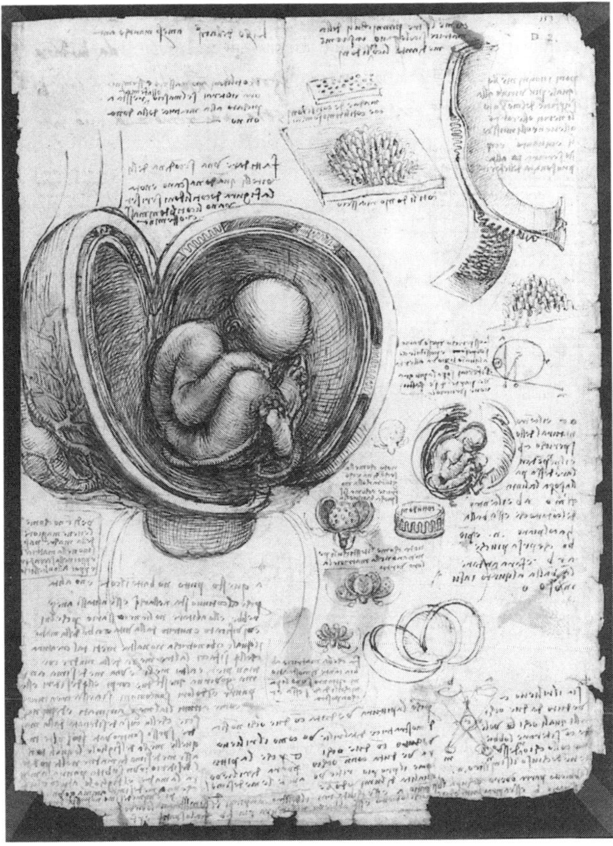

Embryo in the Womb. Drawing by Leonardo da Vinci, c. 1510. THE ROYAL COLLECTION © HER MAJESTY QUEEN ELIZABETH II

In most cases there was not a long wait between marriage and pregnancy. Most brides became pregnant within a year after the wedding—a pattern that transcended differences of geography and rank. A large number of brides had become pregnant, but rarely gave birth, before they got married. Many baptisms took place fewer than nine months after the wedding, but the number of illegitimate births was small.

A regular succession of pregnancies followed the first one. For well-to-do women the intervals were short, perhaps a few months. It was possible to have a baby every year, and some women did just that. Most women conceived much less frequently, however. The usual interval between births was two to three years. This was because the vast majority of women breast-fed their babies for at least a year or two—lactation has a contraceptive effect of varying duration, and there were taboos against sexual intercourse for nursing women.

Society often did not differentiate miscarriage and stillbirth, and both were confused with abortion. They made little difference in the rhythm of pregnancies for most elite women, who did not breastfeed but used wet nurses. For other women, the absence of a newborn to suckle would result in a shorter than usual interval before the next pregnancy. Some conditions affecting poor women in particular could also make conceptions less frequent. Poor harvests after frost, flood, or drought caused serious malnutrition, which could interfere with the menstrual cycle.

One nearly universal feature was the seasonal pattern of conception. The phenomenon was noticed by some contemporaries, among them the French author François Rabelais, who is said to have investigated local parish records. Couples might get married at various times of year, but after the first child most conceptions occurred in the spring.

Last pregnancies occurred either around menopause or just before the death of the husband. That is, women continued to conceive as long as they could. Nobody was amazed at the idea of a woman giving birth in her forties. On the other hand, widows might have their last babies in their early thirties. In families with dynastic concerns such a curtailment of potential fertility would be remedied by prompt remarriage, but there were many poor widows living with small children. Famine and an array of diseases killed off adult men an average of seven to ten years after marriage.

Scientific and Popular Beliefs. Although the sixteenth century saw the beginnings of biology as a modern science, knowledge about the process of conceiving and bearing a child was still extremely limited. What was known was a combination of the learned tradition handed down from antiquity and pragmatic guesswork. Scientific investigation was severely hampered by ignorance of what was invisible to the naked eye. Just as the presence of microscopic spermatozoa was unknown, so also was the function of the ovaries in manufacturing eggs. Aristotle's view of the woman's role in conception as a passive vessel was widely accepted in medicine during the Renaissance.

It was obvious that conception took place when a man's semen entered a woman's body. Semen meant "seed" and was thought to be sufficient, the womb being needed only as the place for the seed to grow. Except when equated with impotence, the notion of male infertility was nonexistent. Impotence was a matter of great concern, and doctors of medicine, church authorities, and ordinary people commonly attributed it to witchcraft. When a man seemed to have performed normally in his sexual relations with his wife, she was assumed to be responsible for the failure to conceive. If physical examination (usually by midwives) did not reveal any structural impediment, she too was assumed to be in the grip of forces beyond human understanding.

Another somewhat different view of conception, taken from the influential second-century physician Galen, held that a female seed joined with the male seed in the womb to form the fetus. Not until the sixteenth century was the anatomy of the female reproductive system described with much accuracy. Indeed, some of its parts were named for the first time. Gabriele Falloppio (1523–1562), Italian professor of anatomy and medicine, named the vagina, clitoris, and placenta, and he discovered the uterine tubes that connect the ovaries and the uterus, which are named for him. He was highly critical of Galen's notions of how the female body worked, but necessarily remained ignorant of the microscopic moment of conception.

The subject of female sexuality was dominated by the mysteries of menstrual blood. It was commonly thought that menstrual blood first nourished the seed developing in the womb, and that after birth it was diverted to the mother's breasts and became the milk that nourished the infant. The connection between lactation and menstruation helped to explain a number of common beliefs, and even a careful observer like Leonardo da Vinci drew the inner anatomy of the female body showing a duct (nonexistent in reality) leading from the uterus to the breasts.

There was a long Western tradition associating menstrual blood with filth and spiritual pollution. This made it likely that religious taboos against sexual intercourse during menstruation would be widely accepted. The fairly common ceremony of "churching" for women after childbirth probably derived from the ancient Jewish rite of "purification," based on the same attitude toward the unclean substances discharged by women.

Controlling Fertility. Late marriage, which was normal for most people, was the main form of family limitation. Any postponement of marriage, such as would be caused by a famine or other disaster, reduced the number of births. The decision not to marry at all was sometimes made in order to limit fertility, as some parents planned their children's futures with an eye to keeping family property intact. Hence a familiar upper-class strategy of sending some daughters to convents and some sons into the church or military service.

The control of fertility within marriage may have been primarily directed toward promoting conception, not preventing it. One approach was to follow the advice of physicians, as Henry II of France and his wife, Catherine de Médicis, did after twelve years of a childless marriage. Henry's physician, following the recommendation of a famous French surgeon of the time, Ambroise Paré (1510–1590), said that copulation should take place during a woman's fertile period, which he put right after menstruation. Henry and Catherine followed his advice, which produced results, in spite of the fact that scientists today say the fertile period is the two weeks before menstruation.

More commonly couples sought supernatural help. In addition to praying to the Virgin Mary and other female saints, women—and sometimes men—visited shrines associated with fertility, some since pagan times, many of which were on the sites of wonder-working springs. A few famous shrines attracted pilgrims from great distances, such as the one to the Virgin Mary at Walsingham in northern England, which Desiderius Erasmus (c. 1466–1536) described with some skepticism in his *Colloquies* but which both Henry VIII and his wife Catherine of Aragon visited.

Ordinary people and learned men alike also put their faith in remedies for barrenness that were based on theories of sympathetic magic. Eating crabs and lobsters, which were said to be extremely fecund creatures, was thought to promote conception, as was wearing amulets made of substances associated with fecundity. A powder made of the dried wombs of hares was said to be especially efficacious.

There were attempts to understand why, apart from sorcery, sexual intercourse did not always result in pregnancy. The female seed of Galen's theory was thought to be released only when the woman had an orgasm. In this way of thinking, women were not merely passive vessels, and a woman could not possibly conceive if she did not participate fully in coitus. It was recognized in law that rape could therefore not cause pregnancy.

Scholars agree that it does not seem likely that a considerable number of people tried to avoid pregnancy by conscious planning or artificial means. Married couples did not plan their families so that women stopped becoming pregnant at any point before menopause. The prevailing attitude was that respectable people would have nothing to do with contraceptive practices. The demimonde of prostitutes and courtesans, however, was supposed to be full of secret methods.

For a long time the most recognized way to have sexual intercourse and avoid pregnancy was coitus interruptus, or withdrawal before ejaculation. Moralists and theologians fulminated against it throughout the period, concerned that it was both sinful and widely used. It was surely widely known, but its association with illicit sex remained strong, and it barely began to gain respectability after the middle of the seventeenth century.

The only respectable way to avoid pregnancy was abstinence, which itself was of doubtful morality in the marital relationship, where the partners owed each other a "debt" of sexuality (*debitum conjugale*). On the other hand, the health of the mother was recognized as a legitimate concern, and some families were clearly overburdened by many children. The opinion of the time was ambivalent, made more so by the high mortality rate of young children, for which there was no obvious remedy except having more children.

As always, contraception was confused with abortion, since both were aimed at avoiding birth. Like coitus interruptus, abortion had shady associations, yet it may have been fairly common. Historians cannot be sure whether a miscarriage was spontaneous or induced. Certain substances were known as abortifacients (the herb rue, for example), and authorities warned that certain activities might destroy the fetus, among them strenuous work and overindulgence in sexual intercourse. There was little concern about the termination of a pregnancy in its very early stages before quickening (the point at which fetal motion could be felt), as this period might also be interpreted as amenorrhea (abnormal absence of menses). This was considered a serious condition, for which various medical remedies were prescribed.

Although the condom was first described in the middle of the sixteenth century in a work on syphilis by Falloppio (*De morbo gallico* [The French disease], 1564), for a long time it remained primarily a prophylactic associated with illicit sex, before being considered a contraceptive.

The effort to control fertility was sometimes directed to controlling the sex of the child. With the common preference for male children, couples may have heeded the warnings of learned men about the kinds of bad coitus that would result in malformed, ugly, defective, or female infants. Lustful desire, poor health, and, above all, copulation during menstruation were believed to have these undesirable results.

See also **Birth and Infancy**; **Motherhood**.

BIBLIOGRAPHY

Crawford, Patricia. "Attitudes to Menstruation in Seventeenth-Century England." *Past and Present* 91 (May 1981): 47–73. Ranges over more time and place than the title suggests.

Gélis, Jacques. *The History of Childbirth: Fertility, Pregnancy, and Birth in Early Modern Europe*. Cambridge, U.K., 1991. Translation of *L'arbre et le fruit*.

Hair, P. E. "Bridal Pregnancy in Rural England in Earlier Centuries." *Population Studies* 20 (1966): 233–243. There is a "further examination" of the subject by the author in the same journal, 24 (1970): 59–70.

Himes, Norman E. *Medical History of Contraception*. Baltimore, 1936. Reprint, New York, 1963, 1970. A pioneering work.

Laqueur, Thomas. *Making Sex: Body and Gender from the Greeks to Freud*. Cambridge, Mass., 1990. Especially interesting on the Renaissance period.

McLaren, Angus. *A History of Contraception from Antiquity to the Present Day*. Oxford and Cambridge, Mass., 1991.

McLaren, Angus. *Reproductive Rituals: The Perception of Fertility in England from the Sixteenth Century to the Nineteenth Century*. London and New York, 1984. A flawed work with nevertheless much interesting information.

Wrigley, Edward A. *Population and History*. New York, 1969. A good, clear introduction to historical demography.

BEATRICE GOTTLIEB

PRINCE. In discussing princes and princedoms in the Renaissance, it is important to clarify these terms. "Prince" (Latin: *princeps*) originally designated the Roman emperor. In the Middle Ages, with the twelfth-century revival of Roman law, the term was used to indicate the source of law, the universal monarch or Holy Roman Emperor. More particularly, it referred to the primacy of the emperor as the supreme power upon which all others depended, the implication being that kings and other potentates exercised their authority by right of concession from the divinely appointed world monarch. The emperor alone was invested with what is today called sovereignty.

In the twelfth century the concept of the prince, or *princeps,* insofar as it embodied the medieval notion of sovereignty, was initially reserved for the Holy Roman Emperor. The term itself was largely confined to Roman law: it was not at first an operative political concept. This changed dramatically, however, in the subsequent centuries known as the Renaissance. Papal claims to independent temporal authority over the Lands of St. Peter led canon lawyers to apply the term *princeps* to the popes. Meanwhile, the kings of France set their jurisconsults to work elaborating a theory of sovereignty in relation to the French kingdom, which resulted in the term *princeps* being allocated to the French king as well. By the mid-fourteenth century the Italian jurist Bartolo (Bartolus) di Sassoferrato (1313/4–1357) had coined the phrase "civitates sibi principes" (city-states as princes unto themselves) to encompass the increasingly independent position assumed by the Italian city-states vis-à-vis the empire as a political framework.

From this point on, the term *princeps* (Italian: *principe*) evolved, moving from the realm of jurisprudence to the emerging sphere of political discourse. The precise contours of this gradual development are difficult to chart. To some extent the process was foreshadowed in the medieval "mirror of princes" literature. No doubt it received new impetus from humanism. But the key moment came in fifteenth-century Italy with the emergence and consolidation of a system of independently governed territorial states. Within this context the term "prince" came to be used in diplomatic circles to designate the ruler of such a state, be it kingdom, duchy, or one of the more ill-defined lordships of northern and central Italy.

In reality, the term "prince" covered a host of variables, ranging from the legitimate monarchs of large kingdoms to petty rulers whose fleeting power was based on little more than sheer force; one might indeed argue that it came to apply more specifically to the latter. But the term retained something of its original connotation of sovereign power, albeit in its more modern form—that is, as appertaining to a plurality of polities of widely differing kinds. A prince could be, for example, legitimate or not, depending on his status with regard to the law. His right to rule might or might not be recognized by long tradition, by local authorities, or by a duly constituted superior such as the pope or the emperor. Yet in the end what mattered most was the possession of effective power, as demonstrated by the ability to legislate and enforce laws, impose and collect taxes, raise and command armies, make alliances, and declare and wage war. These and other features of the sovereign powers claimed and wielded by the Renaissance prince are familiar to modern readers through Niccolò Machiavelli's treatise *De principatibus* (*Il principe;* trans. *The Prince;* 1513).

Origins of the Renaissance Prince. Such abstract observations run the risk of concealing a wide variety of practical situations. In the Italian Peninsula, there were fundamental geographical distinctions. Not all of the peninsula was invested with the phenomenon of the prince in the higher sense outlined by Machiavelli. Venice and the southern kingdom of Naples may be set aside: the former because Venice did not follow the general pattern of evolution toward princely rule; the latter because the exercise of central power in the kingdom remained heavily dependent on feudal relationships.

The classic case of the prince occurred in the areas of the Italian Peninsula that were subject—in theory at least—to either the empire or the church. It is in the temporary weakness of these universal institutions that the seeds of the phenomenon must be sought.

The origins of the Renaissance princedom can best be seen as a process unfolding in three stages. The first stage was the rise of the communes, or self-governing towns, as de facto independent political entities in northern and central Italy. While often seen as due to increasing self-awareness allied to economic muscle, this development may have owed more to the virtual absence, in the later thirteenth century, of any effective form of political authority emanating from the theoretical sovereign. The resulting power vacuum left ample room for improvisation: the communes began to exercise powers usually reserved for a higher authority. Gradually, the right to exercise these powers came to be recognized as the prerogative of the communes through grants, or *privilegia,* conceded by the empire or the church, often under financial or political duress.

The second stage in the evolution toward the princedom came with the transfer of these powers from the communal organs to a specific individual, usually, though not always, a leading member of a prominent family in the ruling oligarchy. The reasons for such an act varied but in some cases were due to internal strife. In Verona, for example, the grant of lordship to Alberto della Scala in 1277 capped the efforts of the popular party to thwart the nobility's plans to establish control over the city. The Veronese example illustrates other features of this early stage in the transition from commune to *signoria* (lordship), including the limited nature of the initial grant of lordship. Strict parameters were set; there was no sense at this point that the grant would be extended to Alberto's heirs or even to other members of his family. In fact, Alberto was referred to in the documentation not as *signore,* or lord of Verona, but as *capitaneus generalis* (captain general) of the commune, albeit for life. While this title clearly carried with it extraordinary powers, the commune nevertheless retained its right to confer seigneurial authority. The continued priority of communal institutions restrained the early elaboration of seigneurial power.

The third stage in the evolution toward princely power requires more attention, for it leads to the transformation of the *signoria* into the principate. One aspect of this change involved a reversal of the relationship between commune and *signore.* The key to this reversal was the commune's recognition of the hereditary nature of authority within the seigneurial family. In the case of the Scala in Verona this occurred in 1359; elsewhere too it was a mid-fourteenth-century development. At one stroke, it would appear, the commune had relinquished its hold over the right of succession, thereby effectively relegating itself to a subsidiary status. But the commune was not merely an accessory to increasing princely power. The conferral of hereditary rights did not mean that the commune ceased to exist; its collegial bodies remained in operation, ready to resume their functions at times of crisis, such as the dying out of the princely line or the loss of confidence in a *signore*'s ability to guarantee peace and stability. In any case, the succession from one lord to the next often sparked a resurgence of the commune's latent claim to be the ultimate source of princely authority.

The increased competition for territory among *signori* as the fourteenth century wore on helps explain the grant of hereditary rights. Hereditary rights represented a strengthening of power and resources at the center, and thus conferred significant military and political advantages over rivals. The tendency was toward the expansion of the stronger *signore*'s control over a growing number of weaker territories. The prime example is the Visconti *signoria* of Milan, which reached its apogee under Giangaleazzo Visconti (1351–1402). At the height of his power, Giangaleazzo ruled nearly a third of the Italian Peninsula, holding sway over dominions stretching from Padua in the east, across the plains of Lombardy, north to the Alps, and south to the Apennines. By the time of his death he had begun to extend his influence into Tuscany.

The case of Giangaleazzo Visconti raises yet another general issue concerning Renaissance princes: their relations with the Holy Roman Empire. Giangaleazzo's efforts to establish a more permanent dynastic claim to his conquests were crowned in 1395, when he was made duke of Milan by the emperor Wenceslas. The emperor, however, was deposed soon afterward, partly as punishment for dealing too loosely with Italian potentates like Giangaleazzo Visconti. The ducal title was also revoked and its attribution to Giangaleazzo's successors suspended. It is easy to see why: formal, titular recognition provided a substantial increase in the prestige of Italian princes and thus considerably strengthened their dynastic pretensions. When it came to the Sforza—successors to the Visconti after 1450—all pleas for the ducal title were met with silence, until political pressures (in the form of the imminent French invasion) forced Maximilian I's hand in 1494 and he conferred the title duke of Milan on Lodovico Sforza to secure his assistance in the war.

With regard to the lands of the church, the situation was no different: the locally appointed *signori* received titles so long as they showed themselves useful to the papal cause. This was notably the case for the Este in Ferrara, strategically placed near the border with Venice, and for the Montefeltro, condottieri (mercenary captains) whose seat was in Urbino. A contrary case of a seigneurial family that never gained higher acceptance is that of the Malatesta, whose grip over Rimini was contested in the 1460s by Pope Pius II.

The Powers of the Prince. Although scholars have reached a consensus on the origins of the Renaissance princedom, they do not agree on how to interpret its significance. Early views took for granted the image of the prince as all-powerful, able to impose his will on a society that gradually had been deprived of its representative bodies. In his *Histoire des républiques italiennes du moyen âge* (History of the Italian republics in the Middle Ages; 1807–1818), the Swiss historian J.-C.-L. Simonde de Sismondi presented the rise of the prince as the end of a glorious tradition of republican government that had characterized the medieval Italian communes.

Jakob Burckhardt later took Sismondi as a useful guide in *The Civilization of the Renaissance in Italy* (1860). Burckhardt, however, saw the coming of the prince in a more positive light: it ushered in a new age in which powerful personalities came to the fore. To Burckhardt, princely culture was the defining feature of the Renaissance because it had fostered the cult of the individual. Politically speaking, Burckhardt both admired and feared the Renaissance prince. His portrait is filtered through the lens of concepts elaborated by early-nineteenth-century German historiography, especially the concept of enlightened monarchy as applied to the strong progressive rulers of the previous century (Frederick II of Prussia, Catherine II of Russia, Joseph II of Austria). As such, Burckhardt's portrait of the Renaissance prince as a political animal hinges on a few sweeping generalizations rather too swiftly erected into policies: among these are the centralization of power, the creation of an efficient bureaucracy responsible only to the prince, and the reform and standardization of outmoded fiscal and legal procedures.

Burckhardt baptized his model "the state as a work of art," which proved an influential paradigm well into the twentieth century. One finds it, for example, in the works of Cecilia M. Ady on the Bentivoglio of Bologna and the Sforza of Milan. In these studies Ady fell under the spell of Burckhardt's view of the Renaissance prince as despot. In *The Bentivoglio of Bologna: A Study in Despotism* (1937), she describes how "powers belonging to the commune were gradually accumulated in the hands of its first citizen" and how "republican institutions fell into decay, and those which survived became instruments of a single will." Such statements suggest how contemporary realities affected the way the consolidation of seigneurial power in medieval Italy was described. Indeed, the ideological conflicts of the twentieth century served to sharpen Burckhardt's notion of the Renaissance prince as a sort of all-powerful dictator. Over and against this portrait, scholars tended to pit the so-called republicanism of centers such as Florence and Venice, whose citizens were seen to have resisted the trend toward the centralization of power in the hands of a prince.

This picture has undergone a dramatic shift, and few modern scholars accept the validity of these early conceptions of princes and republics. It has been shown, for example, that the gap between the two ideal types was virtually nonexistent. Whether princedom or republic, Renaissance states tended to be governed by oligarchies of prominent citizens bound together not by ideology but by self-interest. Typical of this pattern was republican Florence in the fifteenth century. The early Medici—Cosimo de' Medici and Piero de' Medici, the leaders of Florence from 1434 to 1464 and from 1464 to 1469, respectively—perfected the system whereby a restricted group established control over electoral procedures, assuring that only loyal friends were selected for office.

From here it was but a short step to the more elaborate methods of Lorenzo de' Medici, Il Magnifico, whose tenure as leader lasted from 1469 to 1492. Lorenzo established an ever tighter grip over fiscal matters, foreign policy, and diplomacy. In fact, in the highly sophisticated studies of Riccardo Fubini, Lorenzo emerges as almost the archetypal Renaissance prince, even though he held no official status as such within Florence, where republican institutions continued to function alongside the newer, more authoritarian ones responsible to the Medici leader alone.

Students of Renaissance princedoms proper have revised the traditional paradigms. By shifting its focus to the feudal nobility, and to the persistence of local and regional forms of power, the new work has shown that the image of the Renaissance prince as an all-powerful despot is a myth perpetrated by humanist rhetoric and sustained largely out of convenience and convention. Archival research has revealed a much more complex web of power-sharing relationships, compromises, and mutual concessions as characteristic of princely politics. One example of this is found in the pacts made by Francesco Sforza with the governing bodies of the centers he gradually subdued in his drive to occupy the duchy of Milan in 1447–1450. The binding force of these agreements remained intact throughout Sforza's rule, and their terms came up for renegotiation and discussion with each crisis faced by the new regime.

Research has moved away from the prince and from the problems that interested earlier generations (such as the formation of bureaucratic cadres). Much of the new work begins with the assumption that the dynamics of power do not emanate from the center but are generated by encounters and agreements made on the periphery between new and traditional sources of authority. In the process of mediation that ensues, the prince and his supporters represent but one side of the equation. The older structures (commune, corporation, neighborhood) not only remain intact; they also continue to exercise control where it really counts, at the local and regional levels, where power intersects with people's lives.

The new model, however, does not explain everything; its focus is limited to the exercise of power within the boundaries of the princely state. It tends to neglect interstate relations, diplomacy, war, and foreign policy—all areas where the concentration of power in the hands of the prince was a significant development of the late fifteenth century. The newer scholarship focuses on post-1530s Italy, where the margins for individual action in the realm of foreign policy had been greatly reduced by the installment either of puppet regimes loyal to foreign masters (for example, Cosimo I in Florence) or of foreign masters (Milan was under direct Spanish rule from 1535). This later period is perhaps best viewed not as part of the age of Renaissance princes but as a time of reestablished monarchical legitimacy after more than two centuries during which Italy had been left free to forge its own political destinies. The end result of the earlier, independent evolution had been the territorial state ruled by a prince. No doubt debate will continue about the extent and character of the powers wielded by this enigmatic figure and his entourage.

See also **Despotism; Medici, House of; Political Thought; Renaissance, Interpretations of the,** *subentry on* **Jakob Burckhardt; Visconti, Giangaleazzo.**

BIBLIOGRAPHY

Ady, Cecilia M. *The Bentivoglio of Bologna: A Study in Despotism.* Oxford, 1937.

Albertini, Rudolf von. *Das florentinische Staatsbewusstsein im Übergang von der Republik zum Prinzipat.* Bern, Switzerland, 1955. Published in Italian as *Firenze dalla repubblica al principato: Storia e coscienza politica.* Translated by Cesare Cristofolini. Preface by Federico Chabod. Turin, Italy, 1970. Fundamental study of the transition to monarchy in Florence, 1492–1537.

Bueno de Mesquita, D. M. "Ludovico Sforza and His Vassals." In *Italian Renaissance Studies.* Edited by E. F. Jacob. London, 1960. Pages 184–216.

Chittolini, Giorgio. *La formazione dello stato regionale e le istituzioni del contado.* Turin, Italy, 1979. Pioneering study on the origins of the fifteenth-century northern Italian territorial states.

Dean, Trevor. *Land and Power in Late Medieval Ferrara.* Cambridge, U.K., 1988. Focuses on feudality as the basis of Este family power in Ferrara.

Ercole, Francesco. *Dal comune al principato: Saggi sulla storia del diritto pubblico del rinascimento italiano.* Florence, 1928. Still useful on many aspects of the passage from communes to prince.

Fubini, Riccardo. *Italia Quattrocentesca: Politica e diplomazia nell'età di Lorenzo il Magnifico.* Milan, 1994. A collection of the author's essays organized around the theme of fifteenth-century Italian statecraft.

Hay, Denys, and John E. Law. *Italy in the Age of the Renaissance, 1380–1530.* London and New York, 1989. A successful attempt in English to survey the period.

Lubkin, Gregory. *A Renaissance Court: Milan under Galeazzo Maria Sforza.* Berkeley, Calif., 1994. Explores the role of the court in the political strategy of the Sforza, 1466–1476.

The Origins of the State in Italy, 1300–1600. Supplement to *The Journal of Modern History* 67 (December 1995).

Partner, Peter. *The Lands of St. Peter: The Papal State in the Middle Ages and the Early Renaissance.* London, 1972. Covers papal policy with regard to *signori* within church lands.

Pennington, Kenneth. *The Prince and the Law, 1200–1600: Sovereignty and Rights in the Western Legal Tradition.* Berkeley, Calif., 1993. Examines theories of the prince in medieval legal thought.

Simeoni, Luigi. *Le signorie.* 2 vols. Milan, 1950. Classic, though somewhat dated, study of Italy, 1313–1559.

GARY IANZITI

PRINTING AND PUBLISHING. Printing concentrated and accelerated an operation that had involved a variety of materials, a series of independent processes, and an almost infinite number of individuals.

The Book before Printing. Until after 1100 the only available material for writing was calf-, goat-, or sheepskin first stretched and dried, then polished to offer a surface that was both attractive and durable. Described as parchment, vellum, or membrane, and available in widely different qualities, it was still used for prestigious copies after the invention of printing, but its cost—up to twenty-five *deniers* for a single skin in fourteenth-century Paris, when a loaf of bread, even in famine conditions, could be had for five—confined the possession of books for many centuries to institutions such as monasteries, or to very wealthy individuals. Paper formed from a pulp of shredded rags sieved through a metal screen, then pressed dry between sheets of felt and sealed with size, was introduced from the Islamic world early in the twelfth century. Mistrusted from the first because of its readiness to tear, and banned from use in public documents by Emperor Frederick II in 1231, it gained steadily in popularity because it helped to satisfy the demand for books in the expanding universities of the thirteenth century. The mills of Fabriano, near Ancona on the Adriatic coast, were well placed to supply Bologna, Padua, and Ferrara, and later facilitated the rise of Italian printing. Binding and illustration were separate processes that could range from plain wooden boards to jeweled velvet, from a few strokes of ink to the most expensive pigments. The individual buyer chose according to his (or her) means.

In the medieval universities the multiplication and circulation of manuscript books reached its fullest development. A licensed guild of *stationarii*—named from the stalls that they set up near the lecture halls—was entrusted with copies of the principal texts approved by the professors. Individual *stationarii* divided their copy into separate gatherings or *pecia,* each of which was let out to a different scrivener and recopied. Bologna provided work for 140 scribes between 1265 and 1267. When reassembled, the *pecia* could form books that were both cheap—four to six *deniers* each—and available in runs of up to four hundred copies, which the first printers made no attempt to surpass.

From the later fourteenth century a growing demand for books from secular magnates such as Jean, duc de Berri, or Humphrey, duke of Gloucester, encouraged a rise in the book trade outside universities. The fifteenth-century Florentine Vespasiano da Bisticci is the best known figure in the book trade. But he and others like him were entrepreneurs like the *stationarii,* coordinating the work of copyists and illuminators who often acquired an independent prestige. By the time printing was introduced, any interested scholar might act as his own copyist. More than two thousand copyists' names are known from the fifteenth century, many of them from single surviving copies, as several different copyists often worked on the same manuscript.

The Origins of Printing. The growth in demand for books is confirmed by evidence that experiments with "writing mechanically" were afoot in three separate areas by around 1440. In 1499, by a Cologne chronicler, Laurens Coster of Harlem was named as the inventor of printing. But the books attributed to him are undated, and no document confirms the claim. A document credits Procopius Waldvogel of Prague with owning "48 forms of tin for the art of writing" in Avignon in 1444, but no books have been traced to him. Court records show that Johann Gutenberg formed a company in Strasbourg between 1436 and 1439, and he is known to have formed another with Johann Fust in 1450 after returning home to Mainz. Printed indulgences show that the technique outlined in the documents was well developed by the end of 1454, and work on the forty-two-line Bible was probably in progress before then. Although some authorities have accepted the Coster tradition, most now give the credit to Gutenberg.

The invention combined known but separate technologies. The screw press had long been used in linen, paper, and wine making. Mints or goldsmiths used steel punches to impress images on a softer metal and so create a mold or "matrix": this was adapted to create molds for individual letters, whose "forms" were then cast in an alloy of lead, tin, and antimony. Early illustrations show three men operating a press. The compositor, who set letters for the next day's work in two frames, had a skilled and intellectually demanding task. The inker, who set the two frames one above the other in the press, smeared them, and inserted the sheets of paper between, needed a sense of touch and rhythm. The operator, who swung the lever to bring the two frames together and imprint two, four, or eight pages of the text on each side of the sheet, needed only a strong arm. The size of the book itself—the large folio for academic works, the smaller quarto for literary texts, and the still smaller octavo at first for Psalters or books of hours—depended on the number of times the full sheet was folded. Ideally, such a team could run off over one thousand sheets from a pair of frames in a day's work, thus completing one part of the edition while the compositors prepared the frames for the next. But that meant working in close coordination. It took time to train a press team, the equipment required—press, types, and paper—had to be bought and housed before the printer could count on getting any money back from sales of a completed book, and few of the first generation understood the problems of cash flow. Gutenberg was forced to sell out to Johann Fust in 1455, and many of his successors followed him into bankruptcy. Those who did not either had previous experience of commerce, like William Caxton, or could draw on the support of financiers.

The first years of printing were restricted to the Rhine river system by operators whose eagerness to reach buyers as distant as Avignon or Lübeck probably had to fight with their anxiety to keep the technique secret. Gutenberg's successors, Fust and Peter Schoeffer, along with contemporaries like Johann Mentelin in Strasbourg (c. 1459), Albrecht Pfister in Bamberg (1461), and Ulrich Zel in Cologne (c. 1464), used black letter, gothic types to present Vulgate Bibles, canon law, Latin patristic texts, and grammar books to the schools, monasteries, and universities of these cathedral cities. Early printing was anchored to established academic and religious traditions. The

Sack of Mainz in 1462 supplies a useful date to end this first phase, for the diaspora of craftsmen spread the technique to two new countries—Italy and France—and brought printing into the glare of publicity that humanists found necessary to their very existence.

Consolidation and Acceptance. In 1465 Conrad Sweynheim and Arnold Pannartz set up their press at the abbey of Subiaco, in the mountains some forty-seven miles (seventy-five kilometers) from Rome, before moving on to Rome itself. Their editor, Gianandrea de' Bussi, had studied with Vittorino da Feltre, their types were modeled on the humanist, "roman" script of the Italian chanceries rather than the angular gothic of the cathedral schools, and they were responsible for ten first editions of the Latin classics. By 1468 Bussi was boasting of an 80 percent reduction in the cost of books, which notarial records of the price paid for manuscripts a few years earlier have confirmed. His dedications to Popes Paul II and Sixtus IV, and the Greek cardinal Bessarion show that printers could could now appeal for patronage to persons of the highest status and were more anxious to advertise than conceal the potential of printing. Expansion became irresistible. There were printers in Venice by 1469, fourteen other Italian cities by the end of 1472, and fifty by the end of the decade. By this time Italy had outstripped Germany, which had about thirty centers. Paris had a press by 1470, but only eight other French towns followed its lead by 1480. Barcelona saw the first Spanish enterprise during 1473, and although he worked from Bruges until 1476, William Caxton was preparing to supply the English market by 1472.

During the 1470s and 1480s printing gained the acceptance of European literary society. Prices continued to spiral downward. The size of editions rose within ten years from the two to three hundred copies in the late 1460s to around a thousand, and rival publishers tempted buyers with smaller and cheaper versions of the same popular titles. In Venice, whose total output of more than four thousand editions before 1500 almost doubles that of any other center, the price of a reading primer dropped from four *soldi* to one between 1484 and 1488. Since a skilled craftsman earned the equivalent of sixty *soldi* per month, it is likely that introductory material was available to most of those who wanted it. The city's Ascension fairs quickly combined with others in Frankfurt am Main and Lyon to become foci of an international network where by the 1490s agents gathered with lists of "books in print" to exchange news of publications in France, Italy, and the empire. Progress was never steady. An outbreak of plague or a squeeze on credit could cut a city's output by more than half in a matter of months, as happened in Venice in 1473 and 1478.

Until well into the 1500s potential saboteurs—friars with puritanical objections to erotic Latin poetry, or disgruntled scribes with contacts on the city council—tried to kindle opposition to the growth of publishing. Just as a small number of cities—Venice, Cologne, Augsburg, Nürnberg, Basel, Paris, and Lyon—dominated production within individual countries, patterns of production reveal that a few publishers dominated the industry within those cities: 40 to 60 percent of the business was usually dominated by two or three large companies, while anywhere from five to twenty smaller publishers, often anonymous, scrambled for the remainder. But crises and hostility were short-lived. Merchants and investors—Barthelémy Buyer of Lyon, Giovanni Agostini of Venice, Anton Koberger of Nürnberg—moved into publishing by the mid-1470s. No level of society was unaffected. Established centers of education—schools, universities, and monasteries—continued to be the chief beneficiaries of grammars, textbooks, and service books available at prices which more and more students could afford. In the university city of Bologna, Platone de' Benedetti stocked around 10,000 books during the 1490s, including 278 Latin grammars and 1,000 reading primers. But aristocratic collectors seem to have welcomed the new books as exciting curiosities: many expensively bound, illuminated copies survive, and the number of miniaturists operating in Venice rose from one or two to around twenty in the ten years after 1469. At the other end of the social scale, the street singers of Florence were offering printed copies of their ballads by 1477.

Printing and the Renaissance. As the pioneers died out around 1490, their successors understood that the last two decades had brought problems as well as profit. Financiers, printers, and authors all sought to protect sales of particular titles through state monopolies, usually covering ten years and threatening confiscation and a fine to offenders. But enforcement was difficult, and price-cutting encouraged piracy. Ninety-seven appeals were submitted in Venice before 1500, and in 1496 one of them described the common abuses. Agents would bribe a printer's workmen to steal a copy of a promising text, then put several presses to work on a rival edition set to appear before the original, and so ruin its publisher. Teachers, once delighted at the flood of new material, now realized that setting one printed text from another compounded the errors of both, and began to worry that "many books made men less studious." Modern registers of legal volumes in German libraries suggest that cut-rate imports of key works were pushing locally produced editions out of one of their most profitable academic markets: hence, perhaps, the shift of printers in centers such as Mainz and Strasbourg toward vernacular texts, and the anxiety that the archbishop of Mainz expressed in 1485 about religious texts in German. New ideas and new markets were needed. As they were explored, the established commercial network became a web for the exchange of styles or techniques, and the sense of discovery already attached to printing merged into Europe's rediscovery of its own past and of an outside world unknown even to the ancient philosophers.

New types and new languages. There had been small ventures beyond the Latin alphabet since the earliest days. Sweynheim and Pannartz set extracts in a Greek type in 1467, and Tommaso Ferrando printed a complete text in a Greek type in Brescia in 1473. Hebrew printing, well financed and serving a limited but predictable market, became an established section of the industry from 1475. A glagolitic (Slavonic) type was used to print a missal at some unknown center in 1483, and an experiment with a similar font ten years later by the Venetian publisher Torresani, who was about to enter a partnership to print in Greek, shows the interest in a widening variety of languages. Cyrillic texts were being printed in Cracow by 1491. From 1494 these bridgeheads were expanded in Venice and Florence as Aldus Manutius and Lorenzo di Alopa sought to offer Greek texts to a widening circle of academic readers and, in Aldus's case, provide grammars and texts for the study of the Old Testament scriptures in the original language. Alopa's press languished when his main editor, Janus Lascaris, left for France in 1495, and Aldus never fulfilled the aim, which he announced in 1497, of printing parallel texts of the Bible in Greek, Latin, and Hebrew. There is no evidence that Democrito Terracina, who announced in 1498 that he was about to embark on a series of Arabic, Syriac, and Armenian editions, ever produced a book, but the recent discovery of a single copy of the Koran printed by Alessandro Paganino around 1537 shows that such material was not beyond the capacity of Venetian publishing.

From 1498 the primate of Spain, Cardinal Francisco Jiménez de Cisneros, was planning a university at Alcalá de Henares, near Madrid, where holy writ was to be studied in all its ancient languages, and it was here that the first Polyglot Bible was printed between 1514 and 1517. By 1500 a new generation of writers, mostly classical philologists, had become accustomed to using the press for self-advertisement and saw it as a means of realizing their wider hopes for reform of the church and of society at large. The arrival of the literary text in octavo form from 1501 smoothed their way by turning the book into a portable object.

Typescript and image. As the range of languages in print extended, the range of material in print extended beyond language. The woodcut image predated movable type by at least half a century but was an independent process using water-based rather than oil-based ink. The first publishers chose among several methods available to them, sometimes using woodcut capitals and illustrations, sometimes leaving space in the text that they or the customer could employ a miniaturist to fill, sometimes treating the woodcut as an outline to be colored in by hand. The risks and costs are shown in the career of Lienhart Holle, expelled from Ulm for debt in 1484 after only two years of production, including an edition of Ptolemy's *Cosmographia* (1482) illustrated with thirty-two woodcut maps, mostly hand colored.

By this time, however, illustration was becoming a matter of interest to individuals who were either skilled enough to solve the problems or rich enough to take the risks. Erhardt Ratdolt, son of an Augsburg woodcarver, printed in Venice in 1476, designing arabesques for marginal decoration, which could be printed in black or red to give the impression of illumination, and producing a first edition of Euclid's *Elements* (1482) with 420 woodcut figures to explain the theorems. Ratdolt enjoyed not only the patronage of the ducal Mocenigo family but also the friendship of the artists the family employed. At least one of the prospering crowd of miniaturists, Benedetto Bordon, was becoming interested in woodcut design as a supplementary field by the early 1490s. North of the Alps, Anton Koberger put up the money for the 645 blocks designed by Michael Wolgemut for Hartmann Schedel's *World Chronicle,* whose combination of illustration with both Latin and German versions showed a way to encourage new readers, as well as to tempt old ones.

Word and image were being drawn into closer alliance. In the 1490s only twenty-six illustrated books were printed in Strasbourg. Between 1500 and 1509 the number was up to ninety-one, the majority of them in German. Dividing a page equally between the picture of an incident in history or legend and

TYPOGRAPHIA HARLEMI PRIMVM INVENTA
Circa Annum 1440.
Zaenredam invent.
Currat penna licet, tantum vix scribitur anno,
Quantum uno reddunt prœla Batava die:
Addidit inventis aliquid Germania tantis:
Hollandus cœpit, Theuto peregit opus.
velde sculp.
P. Scriverius.

Printers at Work. The caption claims that printing was invented by Pieter Schrijver in Haarlem in 1440. Engraving from *P. Scriverii Laure-Crans voor L. Coster von Haelem, eerste Vinder vande Boeck-Druckerey.* BY PERMISSION OF THE BRITISH LIBRARY. 132A5 P

the lines of text needed to explain what was happening did much to expand the fluid boundaries of literacy.

At the same time the problems of musical printing were being solved. At first combining notes with staves and text proved so complex that it could be achieved only by incising both on blocks, or by leaving one element—either the staves or the notes—to be added by hand. Printed scores were in circulation at the latest by 1476, when Ulrich Han produced his Roman Missal, and possibly as early as 1473. But it was not until the 1490s that Ottaviano de' Petrucci, possibly benefiting from other experiments afoot in Venice at the time, designed movable types that fit together accurately enough to allow the three elements to be set on the page in three separate "pulls" of the press. Petrucci petitioned for a monopoly in 1498 and produced his first score in 1501. Although time-consuming and expensive, his system must have been successful, for he printed at least forty-three works before leaving Venice in 1511. His scores included not only the masses of Josquin des Prez (c. 1440–1521) but also popular songs that might otherwise have been lost.

Intellectuals, designers, and printers. The growing involvement of artists in the world of the book encouraged cross-fertilization between the various fields of human creativity. In earlier centuries the craftsman enjoyed access to books either through the generosity of a patron or through the collective ownership of his workshop. Leonardo da Vinci's notebooks list thirty-seven of his own, including printed works on botany, surgery, and military science. Michelangelo turned to an illustrated Italian Bible for some of the images on the Sistine Chapel ceiling. Albrecht Dürer was Koberger's godson and had worked with Wolgemut until 1489; from 1498 he issued his sequence of woodcuts of the *Apocalypse* above text in Koberger's types. He later incorporated a section on letter design in his *Manual for Painters* (1525). Dürer's many writings, their geometrical ideas derived partly from a Venetian edition of Euclid, show his belief in the correct design of letters as one part of a lost tradition of proportion known to the ancient artists but now within the grasp of his contemporaries through their reconstruction of classical culture. This notion of letterforms as symbols of precise design and mysterious significance was encouraged by the treatise of the Franciscan Luca Pacioli, *On the Divine Proportion,* which had circulated in manuscript from 1497 and was printed in Venice in 1509. Dürer could have come across the idea on either of his visits to Italy and was only one of many affected. Another was a French visitor named Geoffroy Tory. In 1527 he published his own treatise on the mystic quality of the letter entitled *Le champ fleury* (The field of flowers), but from 1507 he was editing texts for the Parisian printers Gilles de Gourmont, Henri Estienne the Elder, and Josse Bade. Not surprisingly, printers in northern Europe were encouraged to copy the roman fonts perfected in Italy, whose capitals bore the closest resemblance to the ideal designs of Pacioli.

By the early 1500s there was a triangular alliance between groups of intellectuals and designers eager to re-create the different aspects of ancient culture that interested them and the fashion-conscious printers who sought to keep abreast of their tastes. The full potential of print to carry out that task appeared during the second decade, particularly in the Basel workshop of Johann Froben, who printed the works of Erasmus and Thomas More alongside the woodcuts of Hans Holbein. Those committed to the principle of "revival" were never more than a minority in any part of Europe: there was always easier money to be made from books of hours, Bibles, or breviaries, and nearly half of the 1,656 editions printed in Paris during the first decade of the century were religious books. But the movements started by Bussi and Aldus had ensured that there were too many copies of the Latin and Greek classics in circulation for them to submerge as they had after 500 A.D., while the aesthetics of Pacioli, Dürer, and Tory turned what had been an Italian cult into a European movement. Printing did not create the cultural ferment of the High Renaissance: it added effervescence, and it guaranteed permanence. The full significance of text and image allied to a sense of revival appeared after 1517.

Printing and the Reformation. The availability of printing and the expansion of the reading public that it had fostered during the previous half century made the difference between Luther's Reformation and the earlier efforts made by John Wycliffe and Jan Hus.

The Protestants. At first it was the connection between the Reformers and the committed, scholarly printers of the previous two decades that was most evident. Elector Frederick (the Wise, 1463–1525) of Saxony had contacted Aldus Manutius to buy Greek texts for the University of Wittenberg. Andreas Carlstadt and Philipp Melanchthon were both Hellenists, and Luther used Erasmus's commentary on the Greek New Testament to develop his idea of penitence as a purely spiritual state. Some thought his attack on indulgences was a continuation of Johann Reuchlin's quarrel with the Dominicans over the study of Hebrew. Luther himself was astonished at the speed with which first his ninety-five theses and then his polemical tracts of 1520 were circulated in print, and the partial figures available for book production in Germany over the next few years have made the Protestant creeds appear creations of the printed word from the moment of their conception. Between 1518 and 1524 total output rose from about 150 publications per year to 990. In August 1520 alone the Wittenberg publisher Melchior Lotther distributed 4,000 copies of Luther's *Address to the Christian Nobility of the German Nation;* in 1522 the first printing of his German New Testament was exhausted within three months and another 252 editions were called for by 1546. Of 498 texts printed in 1523 in the German vernacular, 418 were either by Luther or concerned with the debates he had raised. The surge of publications receded after the Peasants' War of 1525: Strasbourg's output dwindled from 160 editions to less than 40 within a couple of years. But Luther had every reason to describe printing as "God's highest and extremest act of grace."

Scholarship in the late twentieth century, however, has tended to trace the impact of Luther's message more to the printed word in conjunction with a visual image than to the printed word in itself, and also to question if, in the longer term, printing brought the benefits Luther expected. A large number of the polemics in his favor consisted of woodcuts summarized by a few lines of text. The layout was similar to that of the small vernacular editions that had been gaining popularity since the turn of the century, and blocks that had depicted monsters a few years earlier could be put to use as "calf-monks" or demonic cardinals. Luther had the support of masters like Holbein and Lucas Cranach. The latter's *Passional Christi et Antichristi,* which showed Christ washing the disciples' feet opposite a pope extending his foot to be kissed, needed no text to deliver the powerful but short-lived sense of revulsion that both the statistics and the events of the 1520s reflect. When Luther was dead, and the principle of governments deciding the religion of their subjects was accepted at Augsburg in 1555, the ubiquity of printing left the Protestant churches divided by a plethora of different liturgies or catechisms in mutually incomprehensible vernacular languages and dialects. By this time the militant Rome of the Counter-Reformation had learned how to use the press as effectively as had its opponents.

Though less obvious, the relationship between the reformers and the press was as close in France and Italy as in Germany. Jacques Lefèvre d'Étaples, who translated the New Testament and the Psalms into French between 1523 and 1524, had worked with Paris publishers like Josse Bade, Simon de Colines, and Henri Estienne since before 1500. In the early 1530s either the example of Tory, or Francis I's interest in a royal college for the study of languages, prompted a number of printers (including Henri's son Robert Estienne), to redesign their types on the classical models of Italy. A printed denunciation of the Mass circulated by Protestant extremists during the "Affaires des Placards" of 1534–1535 turned the king decisively against the Reformers, and the printers were the first to feel his outrage. Under the influence of Guillaume Farel and John Calvin, some regrouped in Geneva and did much to make it the center not only of scholarly publication but also of a Protestant movement more cosmopolitan than Luther's. Between 1525 and 1550 six printers were operating in Geneva and only forty-two titles were published between 1533 and 1540. When Robert Estienne, by this time honored with the title of "Royal printer in Greek," brought his family to Geneva to escape harassment in 1550, Calvin noted the significance of the event by commenting in a letter that the Catholic theologians "would be raving." In the next few years thirty-seven refugees arrived from Lyon, by 1564 around forty presses were at work, and since 1550, 527 editions had been printed, 160 of them works of Calvin. The proximity of Lyon made it easy to supply books openly or secretly to the Protestant communities in France and to others farther afield in the Low Countries, England, and Italy. A tract entitled *Il beneficio di Cristo crocefisso* (the benefit of Christ crucified) had the backing of several influential ecclesiastics and is said to have sold 40,000 copies in Italy before it was realized in 1549 that most of the ideas came from Calvin's *Institutes*.

The Catholics. The Catholic hierarchy seems to have treated the printed book with suspicion almost from the beginning. From 1479 the University of Cologne was empowered by Sixtus IV to inspect the local printers, and seven years before Luther posted his theses John Colet was inspecting religious publications in London. In the 1520s and 1530s the theology faculty of the Sorbonne attacked publications as diverse as Lefèvre d'Étaples's Bible translations and François Rabelais's *Pantagruel*. When a papal inquisition was established in 1542 one of its main functions was to draw up indexes of prohibited books, those of 1559, 1564, and 1596 being the best known. The effect on Italian publishing was obvious, especially in subject matter. In Venice, for example, before 1560 the Giolito press had devoted more than half its capacity to secular literature: during the 1570s the proportion was down to 11.5 percent, and nearly 70 percent of output was religious. Prices steadied as production dwindled. A stock book of the internationally active Giunti company shows that in 1600 a moderately sized text in octavo cost 1.5 *lire,* as it had when Aldus Manutius popularized the format a century earlier. Inflation must have reduced the real price, but the downward spiral of prices that had marked the first fifty years of printing was clearly finished.

But the indexes could never have been enforced without a measure of collaboration from the printers, who made their own contribution to the Catholic revival of the later sixteenth century. Evidence for the expansion of literacy is no less impressive in Catholic than in Protestant countries. Between 1460 and 1510, of those asked by the Castilian Inquisition if they could read, only 9 percent replied that they could; the proportion was up to 54 percent between 1571 and 1590. Before the final session of the Council of Trent in 1562, the legate Girolamo Seripando wrote of the opportunity offered by the "amazing division" of the various Protestant sects and of the new Pope Pius IV's determination to "restore the printing of books to Rome."

The relations of the hierarchy with three great printers suggests that by the third quarter of the century such men saw themselves, and were seen, as an elite of super-communicators who could choose their own loyalties at will. In the early 1550s Henri Estienne II traveled throughout Italy collecting material and was entertained by a network of scholarly ecclesiastics who were well aware of his connections. When Paulus Manutius (1512–1574), the son of Aldus, was pressed to come to Rome as official printer to the papacy in 1560 he used an earlier offer from the Protestant Elector Palatine to improve his bargaining position. Then when Paulus found himself unable to satisfy the demand for new missals and breviaries, he sought the help of the Frenchman Christophe Plantin of Antwerp, it did not matter that Plantin had been suspected of heresy for at least six years or that all his partners were Calvinists. Between 1568 and 1576 Plantin collaborated with Philip II's chaplain Arias Montanus on a series of revised liturgical books and a new Polyglot Bible, sometimes sending proofs to the Escorial for the personal approval of the king. Between 1571 and 1575 Plantin's exports of books to the Spanish dominions were worth 110,136 *florins* and satisfied the need for uniformity which Seripando had seen lacking in the Protestant churches. When first the "Spanish fury" of 1576, then the advance of the duke of Parma's armies in the early 1580s, made Antwerp untenable, Plantin moved to Leiden; between 1583 and 1586 he served as printer to the new university founded by William of Orange to honor the city's resistance to Philip II. But he returned to end his life in Spanish-dominated Antwerp in 1589. His son-in-law Johannes Moretus kept the workshop in Antwerp going throughout the intervening years. The Moretus family continued to print until the nineteenth century, and Antwerp preserves their workshop as public museum.

Printing, Reading, and Society. Experiences like those of the Manutii, the Estienne, or the Plantin show that printing affected cultural or religious movements like the Renaissance and Reformation only insofar as its practitioners were affected by them. But it also shows the effect of concentrated book production; a small number of people could dominate taste and choice, laying the foundations of the modern cliché that "knowledge is power." Manuscripts could be copied anywhere. The rise of commerce and universities during the high Middle Ages made literacy a more urban skill, but markets, festivals, and wandering entertainers kept the boundaries between rural and urban, religious and civic, and court and street cultures essentially fluid through a common tradition of memorized themes and images.

Even the spread of printing did not change this at once. Nobles might commission manuscript books of hours worth hundreds of *ducats*. Artisans could and often did buy unbound printed versions for one *sou* (a skilled craftsman earned up to six *sous* per day, and even an agricultural worker could hope for two *sous*), and the Parisian dealer Loys Royer stocked 98,529 editions in 1528. But the illustrated polemics and placards of the Reformation circulated mainly in cities, where clergy and government disapproved of earlier practices because they were popish, or pagan, or fun. As the ballad singers departed and the churches were stripped, more learned books became available. Professional men expanded their libraries and reading became a solitary, silent occupation rather than a public lecture or a recitation. Printing widened the gulf between rural, "primitive" culture and literate, "urban" culture. It also encouraged a division between literary and "popular" cultures, as old romances reappeared with new saints' lives and almanacs in cheap editions during the early seventeenth century. These cheap editions could be recognized for what they were, and despised for it, by those higher up the social scale.

The adjustment produced one fortunate accident. In England, which had done little to develop its own printing industry, the government attempted in 1572 to deal with what it saw as a threat to public order and morality by compelling wandering entertainers either to place themselves under the protection of aristocratic patrons or be treated as vagabonds. Those affected tended to congregate around London during the winter months, close enough to seek the patronage they needed around the court, and far enough out to be beyond the reach of the Puritanical city authorities. Among the "bear-wards, minstrels, jugglers, peddlers and tinkers" came the "common players." They brought their repertoire in "prompt books" that had to be kept as a company's exclusive property to avoid piracy, and were also subject to whatever improvisation or "slapstick" the circumstances demanded. Theirs was still the fluid old world of memory and image. But such proximity to the capital, with its mixed audience of courtiers, lawyers, and rowdy apprentices, exposed plays and writers to the blandishment of such publishers as there were or the attention of sharks from a rival company. The combination of bigotry and confusion ensured the survival of English Renaissance drama in print.

See also **Bible**, *subentry on* **Printed Bibles; Catholic Reformation and Counter-Reformation; Caxton, William; Complutensian Polyglot Bible; Estienne Family; Gutenberg, Johann; Humanism; Index of Prohibited Books; Literacy; Protestant Reformation; Reuchlin Affair;** *and entries on specific presses mentioned in this article.*

BIBLIOGRAPHY

Overviews

Eisenstein, Elizabeth L. *The Printing Press as an Agent of Change.* 2 vols. Cambridge, U.K., and New York, 1979.

Febvre, Lucien P., and Henri Jean Martin. *The Coming of the Book: The Impact of Printing, 1450–1800.* Translated by David Gerard. London, 1976, 1984, 1990, and 1997.

On Origins and Early Years

De Bussi, Giovanni Andrea. *Prefazioni alle edizione di Sweynheym e Pannartz prototipografi romanii.* Edited by Massimo Miglio. Milan, 1978.

Hindman, Sandra, ed. *Printing the Written Word: The Social History of the Book, c. 1450–1520.* Ithaca, N.Y., and London, 1991.

Kapr, Albert. *Johann Gutenbuerg: The Man and His Invention.* Translated by Douglas Martin. Aldershot, U.K., 1996.

Lowry, Martin. *Nicholas Jenson and the Rise of Venetian Printing in Renaissance Europe.* Oxford, 1991.

Nuovo, Angela. *Il commercio librario nell'Italia del Rinascimento.* Milan, 1998.

On Linguistic Spread and Humanist Enthusiasm

Bentley, Jerry. *Humanists and Holy Writ: New Testament Scholarship in the Renaissance.* Princeton, N.J., 1983.

Chrisman, Miriam. *Lay Culture, Learned Culture: Books and Social Change in Strasbourg, 1480–1599.* New Haven, Conn., 1982.

Nuovo, Angela. *Alessandro Paganino (1509–1538).* Padua, Italy, 1990.

Zimmer, Szczepan K. *The Beginning of Cyrillic Printing in Crakow, 1491.* New York, 1983.

On the Reformation

Berthoud, Gabrielle, ed. *Aspects de la propagande religieuse.* Geneva, 1957.

Dickens, Arthur G. *The German Nation and Martin Luther.* New York and London, 1974.

Parker, G. "Success and Failure during the First Century of the Reformation." *Past and Present* 136 (1992): 43–82.

Scribner, R. *For the Sake of Simple Folk.* Oxford, 1994.

On the Counter-Reformation

Clair, Colin. *Christopher Plantin*. London, 1960.

Grendler, Paul F. *The Roman Inquisition and the Venetian Press, 1540–1605*. Princeton, N.J., 1977.

On Printing and Society

Chartier, Roger. *The Cultural Uses of Print in Early Modern France*. Translated by L. Cochrane. Princeton, N.J., 1987.

Davis, Natalie Zemon. *Society and Culture in Early Modern France*. Stanford, Calif., 1965.

Gurr, Andrew. *The Shakespearean Stage, 1574–1642*. Cambridge, U.K., 1980.

MARTIN J. C. LOWRY

PRINTMAKING. Printmaking in itself was not a creation of the Renaissance—the first printed images were late Gothic. During the Renaissance, however, printmaking expanded greatly, and prints either embodying Renaissance forms or depicting the visual material of antiquity became widely available. Views and maps and other printed material meeting a high standard of scientific accuracy are also an important component of Renaissance printmaking.

The Fifteenth Century. Around the middle of the fifteenth century, paper became available in quantities sufficient for the mass production of books and prints, thus providing the impetus for the labor-saving inventions of movable type and reusable matrices to print images.

Woodcuts. Wooden matrices could be created with a minimum of technological expertise. To make a woodcut, an image was drawn onto a flat plank of fairly hard wood, such as pearwood. The wood was cut away from the sides of the lines, leaving the linear image in relief; this was inked and printed in the same kind of press used to make wine. Woodcuts were probably being printed on paper by 1400, although few survive from before 1450. The great majority of fifteenth-century woodcuts are devotional images, late Gothic rather than Renaissance in spirit, from German-speaking areas.

Woodcuts were the natural medium to illustrate books, for they could be printed in the same kind of press, and by 1500 illustrated books were issued in great numbers north of the Alps. Only in Italy, however, did Renaissance forms appear in books: Francesco del Tuppo's edition of Aesop's *Vita et fabulae* (Naples, 1485) framed its subjects under classically inspired ornamental arches, and Venetian books of the 1490s were illustrated with elegant outline woodcuts in a style reminiscent of Gentile Bellini. The most influential Venetian illustrated book of the fifteenth century was Francesco Colonna's *Hypnerotomachia Poliphili* (Strife of love in a dream of Poliphilo), published by Aldo Manuzio in 1499 [see the illustrations in the "Aldine Press" and "Colonna" entries]. In this elaborate allegorical love story, written in a hybrid of Italian and classical languages, Polia (Poliphilo's lost love) symbolizes antiquity in both its civilized and its Arcadian aspects. Its grave yet graceful woodcuts are perhaps by Benedetto Bordon.

In the 1490s Albrecht Dürer singlehandedly elevated the woodcut to a level of high art, with numerous large prints and his galvanizing *Apocalypse* of 1498, although his imagery still had a Gothic component. Jacopo de' Barbari's astonishingly accurate aerial view of Venice, on six blocks measuring about five by eleven feet, was published in 1500, the precursor of even more ambitious projects in woodcut in the next decades.

Engravings. An engraving is made by incising lines into a metal plate, usually copper, with a burin, a tool that creates grooves of varying width and depth depending on the force behind it. Ink is applied to the plate, and the surface is then wiped clean. A dampened piece of paper is put on top of the plate, covered with a felt or blanket, and the two are run through a roller press. Because a much more complex technology was needed to manufacture a flat, smooth metal plate than a plank of wood, the production of engravings, as compared with woodcuts, was both more expensive and more concentrated in locale.

Engraving seems to have begun in the upper Rhine region, near Lake Constance. Hundreds of refined, even exquisite, engravings were produced in northern Europe in the fifteenth century, but like the woodcuts, these were still essentially Gothic. Again it was Dürer who brought the Renaissance to the North, expanding accepted boundaries in engraving with esoteric subjects like *The Dream of the Doctor* (c. 1498).

In Italy engraved images were produced in Florence and Ferrara in the 1460s. In Florence, Baccio Baldini engraved most of the so-called Fine Manner prints, characterized by strong outlines and very fine shading lines, from the mid-1460s into the 1480s. Among these are series of planets, prophets and sibyls, and the *Triumphs* of Petrarch. Francesco Rosselli engraved in the so-called Broad Manner, using a clean outline and extremely even parallel shading lines. In the 1490s he rendered Sandro Botticelli's *Assumption of the Virgin* on two plates. Only a fragment of Rosselli's map of Florence on six plates survives; his one signed and dated print is his map of the world, of 1506, reflecting knowledge of Columbus's discoveries. Along with his series of fifteen *Scenes from the Life of Christ and the Virgin* came a sheet of border pieces, in the form of classical foliate panels, to be cut and fit around the individual images; a few assembled sets, carefully hand-colored, are preserved.

From Ferrara the most famous prints, probably existing by 1467, were the fifty so-called *tarocchi,* a sort of cosmography in five groups of ten images, perhaps used as a game and surely used as models by other artists. The only fifteenth-century single-sheet Italian print for which a contract is known, dated 24 October 1481, is *Interior of a Ruined Church,* engraved by Bernardo Prevedari, inscribed BRAMANTV/S. FECIT/.IN M[I]L[AN]O. (fig. 1). The engraver was to finish this seventy-by-fifty-centimeter plate in two months, working on nothing else. Unusually, engravings, by Baldini, were used to illustrate Antonio Bettini's *Monte Sancto di Dio* in 1477 and the 1481 edition of Dante's *Divine Comedy* with commentary by Cristoforo Landino, both published by Nicolaus Laurentii in Florence; the Dante illustrations were designed by Botticelli. Cristofano Robetta made prints following designs by Antonio Pollaiuolo, Botticelli, and Filippino Lippi; a few prints after Leonardo were made by Giovanni Antonio da Brescia. More than twenty designs by Andrea Mantegna were engraved, his two extraordinary *Bacchanals* deriving from ancient sarcophagi he would have seen in Rome in the late 1480s. The traditional assumptions that some of these prints were engraved by Mantegna himself, and that the *Battle of the Nudes,* the largest engraving of a design by Pollaiuolo, inscribed .OPVS./.ANTONII.POLLA/IOLI FLORENT/TINI, was engraved by Pollaiuolo himself, have been questioned; no other major Italian artist of their generation, or even the subsequent one, made prints.

The Sixteenth Century. Very early in the century the first etchings were made. In etching a metal plate is covered with an acid-resistant substance, and the printmaker draws into this, exposing the plate. Acid is then used to etch (from the Dutch *etsen,* "to eat") the lines into the plate, and the plate is inked and printed as an engraving would be.

German-speaking areas. Dürer was the leading printmaker in northern Europe until his death in 1528. In his "books" the *Large Passion* and the *Life of the Virgin,* issued in 1511, the later woodcuts reflect the influence of the Italian Renaissance. Emperor Maximilian I, chronically short of money, hired Dürer, his chief court artist Hans Burgkmair, Albrecht Altdorfer, and others to perpetuate his fame by creating a triumphal arch, chariot, and procession printed on paper; these have outlasted many more expensive monuments in paint or stone. Whereas the prints by Dürer's contemporaries Lucas Cranach and Hans Baldung are more expressive than classical, the so-called Little Masters Sebald and Barthel Beham and Georg Pencz published engravings in classical idiom and on classical themes until about 1550.

Italy. Venice had a brief efflorescence of large-scale woodcuts, including Titian's majestic five-block *Triumph of Faith* of 1517, and the stupendous twelve-block *Submersion of Pharaoh's Army in the Red Sea* (fig. 2). One of the most important books of the century, Andreas Vesalius's *De humani corporis fabrica* (Basel, 1543) was illustrated with woodcuts designed in the circle of Titian, perhaps by Jan Stephan van Calcar, of skeletons and flayed figures startling in their naturalistic poses and settings.

If the work of Raphael represents a culminating point of Renaissance art, the engravings of Marcantonio Raimondi, purveyor of Raphael's designs to contemporaries and to posterity, may thus be the quintessential Renaissance prints. Arriving in Rome about 1509, Raimondi began reproducing Raphael's designs. Many had been made in preparation for frescoes, but some of the best known, *The Massacre of the Innocents* and *The Judgment of Paris,* apparently had been created expressly to be engraved. After Raphael's death in 1520, Raimondi reproduced designs by Baccio Bandinelli and Giulio Romano, including the licentious *I Modi* (1524), for which he spent several months in jail. Raimondi's assistants Agostino Veneziano and Marco Dente da Ravenna began the stream of renditions of antique statuary, architectural details, vases, and grotesques that diffused this imagery fundamental to the Renaissance all over Europe. Also in Rome, before the 1527 sack by mercenaries of Emperor Charles V, Jacopo Caraglio engraved designs of Giovanni Battista, Rosso, Perino del Vaga, and Francesco Parmigianino, and Ugo da Carpi and Antonio da Trento made brilliant chiaroscuro woodcuts—woodcuts printed in color from two, three, or even four blocks, creating the effect of a drawing in color with white highlights—after designs of Raphael and Parmigianino.

After the sack of 1527, Parmigianino fled from Rome to Bologna, where he took up etching, producing some sixteen prints of unmatched grace. Enea Vico of Parma, in the next generation, engraved nearly five hundred plates, including series

Figure 1. Bernardo Prevedari. *Interior of a Ruined Church.* Engraving; 1481; 70 × 50 cm (27.5 × 19.5 in.). © THE BRITISH MUSEUM, LONDON

Figure 2. Woodcut after Titian. *Pharaoh's Army Submerged in the Red Sea.* The woodcut illustrates the passage in Exodus 14:23–28. Anonymous woodcut on twelve sheets after a design by Titian; c. 1515; 122.5 × 221.5 cm (48 × 87 in.). Published by Domencho dalle Greche, 1549. THE METROPOLITAN MUSEUM OF ART, NEW YORK, HARRIS BRISBANE DICK FUND, 1927 (27.54.87–98)

of vases, trophies, friezes and grotesques, medals and gems, further disseminating the classical repertory. Giorgio Ghisi, the most influential engraver after Raimondi, brought the firm, clear style of Raimondi to Antwerp and later to France. The Netherlander Cornelis Cort brought Ghisi's style, with subtler handling, back to Italy about 1565, working in the style of both older and contemporary masters, especially Titian and the brothers Taddeo and Federico Zuccaro.

Antonio Salamanca, a book publisher in Rome, began issuing prints in 1538; among his first was an immense view of the Colosseum by the little-known Girolamo Fagiuoli, after a drawing by Domenico Giuntalodi. In 1543 Salamanca issued the first engraving of Michelangelo's *The Last Judgment,* in ten sections, by Niccolo della Casa. Antoine Lafréry from Lorraine eventually dominated print publishing, until his death in 1577. His *Speculum romanae magnificentiae* (Mirror of the magnificence of Rome), including antique architecture and sculpture as well as modern structures like the new St. Peter's, is a monument of the Renaissance.

France and the Netherlands. It was only in the 1530s, with the arrival of Rosso and Francesco Primaticcio at Fontainebleau, that Renaissance art reached France in full force. The four principal etchers of the school of Fontainebleau—the Master I♀V (possibly Jean Viset), Antonio Fantuzzi, Léon Davent, and Jean Mignon—disseminated designs of Giulio Romano, Rosso, Primaticcio, and Luca Penni. A French edition of the *Hypnerotomachia* was published in Paris by Jacques Kerver in 1546, with woodcuts copied from the original in the graceful French brand of mannerism. At midcentury in Paris, Pierre Milan and René Boyvin issued large engravings and Étienne Delaune, dozens of small sets. These, along with the etchings of Jacques Androuet Du Cerceau, assured that models of Renaissance art and ornament were accessible in France.

In 1549 Hieronymus Cock established his house Aux Quatre Vents in Antwerp, then the commercial center of northern Europe; he published large engravings by Giorgio Ghisi of Raphael's *School of Athens* and *The Dispute on the Holy Sacrament* in 1550 and 1552. Hendrik Goltzius in Haarlem, who engraved striking images based in classical mythology, epitomized the svelte products of northern mannerism. His abrupt cessation of engraving in 1600 may be seen as the end of Renaissance printmaking.

See also **Dürer, Albrecht; Parmigianino; Raphael.**

BIBLIOGRAPHY

Bartrum, Giulia. *German Renaissance Prints, 1490–1550.* Exhibition catalog, British Museum. London, 1995.

Bartsch, Adam. *Le peintre-graveur.* 21 vols. Leipzig, 1803–1821. *The Illustrated Bartsch.* Edited by Walter L. Strauss. University Park, Pa., and New York, 1971–.

Byrne, Janet S. *Renaissance Ornament Prints and Drawings.* Exhibition catalog, Metropolitan Museum of Art. New York, 1981.

The French Renaissance in Prints from the Bibliothèque Nationale de France. Exhibition catalog, Grunwald Center for Graphic Arts. Los Angeles, 1994.

Landau, David, and Peter Parshall. *The Renaissance Print, 1470–1550.* New Haven, Conn., 1994.

Levenson, Jay A., Konrad Oberhuber, and Jacquelyn L. Sheehan. *Early Italian Engravings from the National Gallery of Art.* Exhibition catalog. Washington, D.C., 1973.

SUZANNE BOORSCH

PRISONS. *See* **Crime and Punishment.**

PRIVACY. *See* **Daily Life.**

PROCESSIONS. *See* **Parades, Processions, and Pageantry.**

PROFESSIONS. Law, medicine, the civil service, the church, and teaching were the major professions of Renaissance Europe. Membership in them elevated a man above his contemporaries, except for rulers and aristocrats who enjoyed privileges based on birth. Becoming a professional required specialized training, often a university degree, and acceptance by a regulatory body.

Training and Career. Training to enter a profession began at an early age, because almost all of them required the ability to read, write, and sometimes speak Latin. Lawyers, physicians, university professors, clergymen, notaries, and governmental secretaries and administrators used Latin daily. A boy had to begin studying Latin as early as the age of six or seven in order to acquire such facility. Boys who attended Latin schools could aspire to enter the professions; those who did not were relegated to the world of work.

Most legists and some physicians had to have university degrees, preferably doctorates. In Italy and southern Europe a boy began university studies at the age of seventeen or eighteen and emerged five to eight years later with a doctorate in law or medicine. In northern Europe boys aged thirteen or fourteen began to attend a residence college in a university town, where masters and advanced students taught them. They obtained bachelor's degrees in arts after four or more years of study, then might continue to study for doctorates in law, medicine, or theology. In England residence at one of the London Inns of Court often completed the training of an aspiring lawyer or civil servant.

After receiving a degree, the new legist or physician had to be accepted by the professional association in the town in which he wished to practice. Called a guild (for example, the guild of physicians and apothecaries) or a college (for example, the college of lawyers and notaries), this body regulated the profession and determined who might practice. Local sons, especially of prominent families or those with male relatives in the guild, found easy acceptance. Anyone not locally born had more difficulty and was sometimes rejected. Once accepted, the young lawyer or jurist might establish a private practice or work for the town or state. Physicians practiced privately or were hired by the community to treat the impoverished ill.

Probably only a minority of medical practitioners were university trained. The rest included surgeons and empirics (practical doctors) who dealt with wounds, fractures, and rashes and barbers who did cupping and bleeding (that is, placing a cup on the skin in order to bring blood to the surface by creating a vacuum). These men learned as apprentices or were self-taught; they followed vernacular texts of practical medical advice. Medical guilds accepted surgeons and empirics if they passed a practical examination but rejected barbers. These members of the medical profession did not enjoy the prestige or income of university-trained physicians.

The expanding administrations of Renaissance states employed an increasing number of administrators, secretaries, judges, and prosecutors, all professionals with specialized training. Sometimes the state established special schools to train boys for careers in government. Notaries were also essential for both government and business, because they recorded partnerships, contracts, property sales, marriage agreements, and wills. Licensed by the state and members of a guild, notaries wrote a legalistic Latin in a handwriting so difficult to read and full of special formulas and abbreviations that it protected their professional status. Prospective notaries learned from established notaries and sometimes had university training.

The Clergy. Many men became religious professionals. The Roman Catholic church had a great variety of clergy—parish priests, priests who served bishops in many capacities, bishops, cardinals, diplomats, Vatican officials, and the pope. The church had its own courts, which required clergymen with legal training, and a large corps of secretaries, who served popes and bishops. Another group treated as clergymen were the nonordained monks, friars, and lay brothers who were members of religious orders.

While most clergymen were ordained priests, the training varied according to their professional aspirations in the church. Indeed, education helped determine how high a clergyman could rise. Parish priests often received just a few years' education in a local Latin school and informal guidance from an established priest. A priest who hoped to rise to the episcopacy or higher needed a university degree and often took a law degree, because law opened the door to the highest ranks of the ecclesiastical hierarchy, which involved administration and governance. The overwhelming majority of Italian popes, cardinals, and bishops in the fifteenth and sixteenth centuries held degrees in canon law or both civil and canon law. Clergymen expecting to become teachers and scholars of theology obtained theology degrees.

This situation changed somewhat by the late sixteenth century. In the Catholic world the development of seminaries and the schools of new religious orders, such as the Jesuits, gave future clergymen training in letters, philosophy, and theology, subjects more appropriate to the religious profession. Protestant churches also established schools for their clergy, which emphasized Bible study, theology, and preaching.

Social Position. The training and social position of teachers varied. University professors had degrees and shared the world of lawyers and physicians. Teachers at the secondary level, especially of Latin schools, came close to the training and social position of professors. But the humble elementary-school teachers, a few of them women, lacked social distinction and received low salaries. Anyone could become a teacher, because the profession lacked regulatory organizations.

The vast majority of lay professionals came from professional families. Hence, the Renaissance saw dynasties of lawyers and physicians, as father, son, grandson, and nephew all became lawyers or physicians. For example, numerous members of the Sozzini family of Siena became lawyers, jurists, and professors of law in fifteenth- and sixteenth-century Italy. Boys from nonprofessional or poor families had greater opportunities to rise in the church. For example, Pope Pius V (reigned 1566–1572) was the able and pious son of a peasant who joined the Dominican order, obtained a doctorate in theology, and rose through the hierarchy.

Professional men were privileged members of society. Most earned much higher incomes than nonprofessionals, except for very wealthy merchants, and nobles. However achieved, a professional position lifted a man (women were barred from the professions except for elementary teaching) above most of the rest of Renaissance society.

See also **Clergy**, *subentry on* **Catholic Clergy; Inns of Court; Law; Medicine; Notaries; Universities.**

BIBLIOGRAPHY

Grendler, Paul F. *Schooling in Renaissance Italy: Literacy and Learning, 1300–1600.* Baltimore, 1989. Discusses teachers and pre-university education.

Hoffman, Philip T. *Church and Community in the Diocese of Lyon, 1500–1789.* New Haven, Conn., 1984. Study of diocesan clergy, especially in the sixteenth century.

Martines, Lauro. *Lawyers and Statecraft in Renaissance Florence.* Princeton, N.J., 1968. A detailed study of the legal profession.

Park, Katharine. *Doctors and Medicine in Early Renaissance Florence.* Princeton, N.J., 1985. Good survey of all aspects of the medical profession.

Prest, Wilfrid, ed. *Lawyers in Early Modern Europe and America.* London, 1981. Legal profession in England, Scotland, and Spain.

Strauss, Gerald. *Law, Resistance, and the State: The Opposition to Roman Law in Reformation Germany.* Princeton, N.J., 1986. Chapters 1, 5, and 6 describe the legal profession and lawyers as civil administrators.

Turchini, Angelo. "La nascita del sacerdozio come professione." In *Disciplina dell'anima, disciplina del corpo e disciplina della società tra medioevo ed età moderna.* Edited by Paolo Prodi and Carla Penuti. Bologna, Italy, 1994. Pages 225–256.

PAUL F. GRENDLER

PROSE, ELIZABETHAN. The significant outpouring of prose works of considerable merit during the reign of Elizabeth I of England (1558–1603) was the consequence of humanist training and grammar schools founded in large numbers during and after the Reformation. Breaking from scholastic prose of an earlier period, humanism conveyed the radical idea that originality meant returning to origins rather than creating something wholly new, or rather that the best way to create something new was to modify antique texts by signaling deviation while imitating them. The Protestant prose of William Tyndale and

Miles Coverdale also demonstrated how classical languages might be translated. Vernacular prose came swiftly of age under this sense of personal relationship with classical works highly regarded, as Sir Philip Sidney's style was released by the power of Ciceronian figures and Sir Francis Bacon's by the model of Michel Montaigne (1533–1592) before him. Roger Ascham had advocated the use of the native tongue over Latin as early as 1545 in his *Toxophilus,* but it was ultimately Joachim Du Bellay's extended *Défense et illustration de la langue française* (The defense and illustration of the French language) in 1549 that prompted the admired teacher of Edmund Spenser and others, Richard Mulcaster, principal of the famed Merchant Taylors' School in London, to proclaim,

> I do write in my natural English tongue, because though I make the learned my judges, which understand Latin, yet I mean good to the unlearned, which understand but English. (*Positions,* 1581)

> For is it not indeed a marvelous bondage, to become servants to one tongue for learning sake, the most of our time, with loss of most time, whereas we may have the very same treasure in our own tongue, with the gain of most time? our own bearing the joyful title of our liberty and freedom, the Latin tongue remembering us, of our thraldom and bondage? I love *Rome,* but *London* better, I favor *Italy,* but *England* more, I honor the *Latin,* but I worship the *English.* (*The Elementarie,* 1582)

Under such a forceful plea for change, a philosopher like Bacon came to meditate not on scripture as his predecessors had, but on his own life.

Structure. Tudor prose poetics drew on the lessons of the grammar school in the arts of speaking: grammar, rhetoric, and logic (both for organization and for style). Inventing, or finding ideas (places, topoi), meant searching both classical texts and everyday experience, often recorded in commonplaces and proverbs, and combining these to form a new work. There were two fundamental principles of organization: that of the disputation or speech and that of the dialogue or debate (dialectic); and mythology and even unnatural natural history, drawn from Ovid or Pliny as well as from observation and close listening, helped to provide illustration. While many writers (especially those educated at Oxford and the Inns of Court, where logical debates were frequently staged) used a traditional rhetoric ultimately derived from Aristotle and involving the marriage of thought and style, many who studied at Cambridge (such as Robert Recorde, Thomas Digges, and John Dee) followed the newest trend, introduced by Petrus Ramus, that divorced style from substance.

Ornamentation thus became an end in itself, growing ever more elaborate through the use of schemes and tropes, patterned figures of speech and thought, of which alliteration and chiasmus became especially popular. George Puttenham's *Art of English Poesie* (1589) is an extant handbook of the most widely used stylistic devices presented with witty English names alongside the more traditional Latin ones, such as "Soraismus, or The Mingle Mangle"; "Apostrophe, or the Turn Tale." Such writing stressed simile and metaphor—that is, writing analogically and combining examples from different sources and fields of interest rather than analytically, as biblical exegesis had practiced in the earlier medieval period and would again in the later seventeenth century.

The Range of Styles. While it now seems possible to identify two lines of developing prose style that can be traced back to Cicero—the sparse, tight, sharply focused style he called Attic and the elaborate, florid, ornamental style he called Asiatic—the widespread acknowledgment of the possibilities of the vernacular and the sheer love of the native language this promoted in fact produced (in a writer like Thomas Nashe) heaps of neologisms, words newly coined in a spirit of excitement and adventure and boundless possibility: "high men and low men both prosper alike; langrets, fullams, and all the whole fellowshippe of them." Such exuberance perhaps reaches its limit, in fact, in a long list of "canting," or special rogue terms more invented than real, that Thomas Harman (fl. 1567) appended to his *Caveat for Common Cursitors Vulgarly Called Vagabonds* (1566). But in fact there was an extraordinary range of styles.

John Lyly created the most elaborate in an attempt to give the English court an elegance thought already to characterize its continental counterparts. It was soon called euphuism, after the title character of his first prose novel, *Euphues* (1578; 1580, complete), which opens this way: "There dwelt in Athens a young gentleman of great patrimony, and of so comely a personage, that it was doubted whether he were more bound to nature for the lineaments of his person, or to fortune for the increase of his possessions." This self-conscious way of writing (deliberately Asiatic) was based on an elaborate system of balancing (perhaps drawn from Aristotle's sense of the golden mean). The fundamental techniques were *isocolon* (clauses or phrases of equal length), *parison* (succeeding clauses or phrases of identical structure), and *paramoion* (succeeding clauses, phrases, or syllables alike in sound). While such patterns gave special premium to rhythm and sound, the sense was also delighted (and relieved) by frequent use of mythology and unnatural natural history. A somewhat less formal Ciceronianism, by which syntax was loosened though still complicated, and sound was not so predictable, was promoted as a superior courtly style by such writers as Sir Philip Sidney (1554–1586) in his novel *Arcadia* (1590) and Richard Hooker in his state-assigned *Lawes of Ecclesiastical Politie* (1597): "The laws which have been hitherto mentioned do bind men absolutely, even as they are men, although they have never any settled fellowship, never any solemn agreement amongst themselves what to do or not to do" is an example from book 1, chapter 10.

Contrarily, the Attic style derived from Tacitus signified writing that fostered force and precision. The best example of this style is in the essays of Bacon. Thus the famous one "Of Studies" begins, "Studies serve for delight, for ornament, and for ability. Their chief use for delight is in privateness and retiring; for ornament, is in discourse; and for ability, is in the judgment and disposition of business." Such directness and comparative simplicity were thought to produce clarity and objectivity—gone were the poetic tics that accompanied a more decorated style. While the syntactically normalized structure of Hooker's sentences transformed controversial and dialectical writing into something approaching philosophy (a new prose mode for which Hooker was the English pioneer), Bacon's deliberate sparseness was meant to give the illusion of unmediated accuracy. This was Bacon's aim, since he intended to write about science and its methodologies (as he did later in *Novum Organum;* 1620). But Bacon's style moves the vernacular back toward exegesis, the parsing of sentences that had been the basis of medieval sermonizing and was, under Puritan preachers, returning; it can even be found in the mature sermons of Lancelot Andrewes, whose prose style T. S. Eliot found especially praiseworthy. Both Lyly and Bacon, that is, move toward opposite extremes. Perhaps the best-known middle ground of Elizabethan prose is what has come down as the King James Bible (1611), in good measure an incorporation of earlier work by Tyndale and Coverdale, but somewhat expanded, utilized, and made even more poetic by Elizabethan preachers. Of these, putatively the best was "silver-tongued" Henry Smith, whose 1592 sermon on Jonah was reprinted for decades, eventually serving as a stylistic source for Shakespeare's *The Tempest*.

Conclusion. The court was not alone in enjoying fine prose, as literacy increased and people read to those who could not read, more popular works emerged: the reports of voyagers to the New World collected by Richard Hakluyt; chroniclers of England's glorious past summarized by Raphael Holinshed, Richard Grafton, and John Stow; and romances by Robert Greene and Thomas Lodge. More notoriously, cony-catching pamphlets (conies were the easily duped) exposed confidence games and the life of the underworld with all its special terms, and pamphlets about monsters and wonders and witchcraft anticipated our present tabloid newspapers. By the close of Elizabeth I's reign, it seemed the possibilities of vernacular prose had become limitless.

See also **Bible**, *subentry on* **The English Bible; Biography and Autobiography**, *subentry on* **England; Fiction, Elizabethan; Prayer Book, English;** *and biographies of figures mentioned in this article.*

BIBLIOGRAPHY

Bush, Douglas. *Classical Influences in Renaissance Literature.* Cambridge, Mass., 1952.

Colie, Rosalie L. *The Resources of Kind.* Edited by Barbara K. Lewalski. Los Angeles and Berkeley, 1973.

Croll, Morris W. *Style, Rhetoric, and Rhythm.* Edited by J. Max Patrick, Robert O. Evans, John M. Wallace, and R. J. Schoeck. Princeton, N.J., 1966.

Davis, Lloyd. *Guise and Disguise.* Toronto, 1993.

Elsky, Martin. *Authorizing Words.* Ithaca, N.Y., 1989.

Howell, Wilbur Samuel. *Logic and Rhetoric in England, 1500–1700.* Princeton, N.J., 1956.

Jones, Richard F. *The Triumph of the English Language.* Stanford, Calif., 1953.

Lewis, C. S. *English Literature in the Sixteenth Century, Excluding Drama.* Oxford, 1954.

Mueller, Janel. *The Native Tongue and the Word.* Chicago, 1984.

Ong, Walter J. *Ramus: Method and the Decay of Dialogue.* Cambridge, Mass., 1958.

Shuger, Debora Kuller. *Habits of Thought in the English Renaissance.* Los Angeles and Berkeley, 1990.

Trimpi, Wesley. *Muses of One Mind.* Princeton, N.J., 1983.

Tuve, Rosemond. *Elizabethan and Metaphysical Imagery.* Chicago, 1947.

ARTHUR F. KINNEY

PROSODY, ELIZABETHAN. Like a classical comedy, Elizabethan prosody begins in a state of unhappy instability and ends in one of satisfying and dynamic equilibrium. Successful versification involves the harmonization of fixed metrical law and variable speech rhythm, and in the middle of the sixteenth century, these two elements were at loggerheads in English poetry. Due to linguistic confusions that had arisen during the transition from Middle to Modern English, poets no longer understood the fluidly iambic prosody Geoffrey Chaucer had developed. Though they continued to write in iambic measure, they had lost the ability to manage it flexibly—particularly as far as the decasyllabic line was concerned—and their rhythms were either disorganized and awkward or correct but wooden. Nowhere is this unfortunate dichotomy clearer than in Thomas Wyatt's poems. The texts he left in manuscript at his death in 1542 are often metrically confused, yet they are hardly improved by the vigor-draining regularizations that they underwent when Richard Tottel edited and published them in his *Miscellany* of 1557. Complicating the metrical malaise was the concern that native prosody, which observed syllabic accent, was simply incapable of great poetry, and that if English verse were to advance, it would have to adopt, as ancient verse had, a prosody governed by syllabic quantity (that is, syllabic length or duration).

For several decades, poets grappled with these and related issues, and it is impossible to overestimate the genius of their collective effort. By 1600, not only had most of the practical and theoretical problems been resolved, writers were producing a poetry to rival, as Ben Jonson would later say in connection with William Shakespeare, "all that insolent Greece or haughty Rome / Sent forth, or since did from their ashes come."

Suppleness of Line. This triumph involved several factors. First, poets gradually rediscovered the suppleness of the iambic line and learned that using it effectively entailed not rigid replications of the prosodic grid, but rather continual modulations of its basic pattern. To be sure, the grid could be followed exactly, as in this iambic pentameter, which consists of five rear-stressed disyllabic units:

To *fawn,* to *crouch,* to *wait,* to *ride,* to *run*

(Edmund Spenser, "Mother Hubberd's Tale," line 905)

Or the grid could be followed closely, as in this pentameter, which features a fairly regular alternation of weak and strong syllables:

Al*though* the *course* be *turned* some *oth*er *way*

(Walter Ralegh, "The Ocean's Love to Cynthia," line 82)

Yet the sole requirement of an iamb is that its second syllable be weightier than its first, and, as poets discovered, it is possible to maintain the iambic fluctuation without making every metrically accented peak an Everest or every metrically unaccented dip a Grand Canyon. Some peaks can be lower than other peaks:

My nature and the terror of my name

(Christopher Marlowe, *Tamburlaine the Great,* Part 1, 5.1.176)

Some valleys may be higher than other valleys:

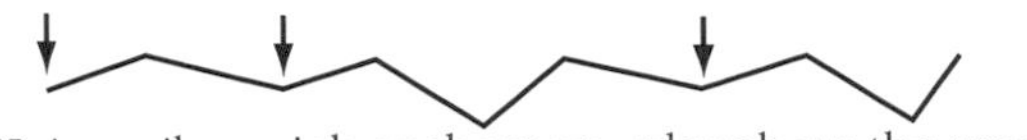

Hoise sails, weigh anchors up, plough up the seas

(George Peele, "A Farewell to Sir John Norris and Sir Francis Drake," line 51)

For that matter, a valley in one place may be higher than a peak in another:

Takes all for gold that glisters in the eye

(Barnaby Googe, "To Alexander Neville," line 12)

What is more, since the only requirement of an iamb is that its second syllable be weightier than its first, a light iamb can be followed with a heavy one to create a continuous rise of rhythm over two feet. In the example that follows, the rise is nicely expressive of the phenomenon the poet is describing:

With how sad steps, O moon, thou climb'st the skies

(Philip Sidney, *Astrophel and Stella,* Sonnet 31, line 1)

Equally important, in exploring these various modulatory capacities, poets learned that modern iambic meters were not restricted, to the extent that ancient meters had been, to particular tones and genres, but could accommodate a wide range of styles, from the grand to the melodic to the colloquial. And this did much to dispel anxieties that the native prosody might require overhauling or complexifying before it could deal with sophisticated subject matter.

Monosyllabic Words. Another factor crucial to the triumph of native meter involves the realization of the centrality of monosyllabic words in English. Many Elizabethan writers on prosody noted that English abounds in monosyllabic words. Even Roger Ascham and Thomas Campion, who advocated a quantitative metric for English, perceived that its monosyllables would forever prevent its being tuned to the well-knit polysyllabic intricacies of ancient quantitative measures such as the dactylic hexameter. By the same token, poets grew increasingly aware that, however unsuited English monosyllables are to classical meter, they are extraordinarily handy for the native prosodic system. More specifically, poets realized that any monosyllabic word can, given the right context, serve as either a metrical beat or a metrical offbeat. This awareness in turn produced a liberating distinction between ancient and modern meter: whereas ancient prosody can classify syllables as short or long according to their phonemic and phonetic nature, stress in English is not so abstractly determinable, but varies with sense and verbal environment. Admittedly, this distinction showed that modern prosody could never aspire to the exactitude of ancient metric. But the distinction also established that English poets could employ the metrical grid not only to organize rhythm but also to point meaning, and could thereby achieve a fluidity and rhetorical focus impossible under quantitative rules.

Illustration of this point is supplied by Shakespeare's comment (Sonnet 129, lines 13–14) about the destructive consequences of yielding to illicit sexual passion:

x / x / x / x / x /
All this | the world | well knows, | yet none | knows well

To shun the heaven that leads men to this hell.

In the scanned line, both the third and fifth feet consist of the adverb "well" plus the verb "knows," with the order of the words transposed from one foot to the other. And, paradoxically, both feet are iambs. Shakespeare points out that while everyone *knows* that lust is wrong, this knowledge is not always *sufficient* to prevent dishonorable conduct: "All this the world well *knows,* yet none knows *well.*"

To Rhyme or Not to Rhyme. Even the great prosodic question the Elizabethans could not settle—to rhyme or not to rhyme—proved fruitful in its irresolution. However hagglingly futile the debate about rhyme may at first blush appear—the pro-rhymers praising the device for bestowing surpassing beauties on modern poems, the anti-rhymers damning it as a corrupt embellishment that classical Greek and Latin writers sensibly avoided—the argument helped insure that Modern English poetry would enjoy lively traditions of both rhymed and rhymeless verse. And if on the one hand the Elizabethan period witnessed a flowering of rhymed verse in the modes of sonnet-lyric (for example, Sidney's *Astrophel and Stella*), romantic epic (Spenser's *Faerie Queene*), narrative (Marlowe's *Hero and Leander* and Shakespeare's *Venus and Adonis*), and elegy and epigram (the early poems of John Donne and Ben Jonson), on the other hand the period saw the development of a vital school of blank verse. From its modest beginnings in Henry Howard's translations (circa 1540) of Books 2 and 4 of the *Aeneid* and in Thomas Norton and Thomas Sackville's *Gorboduc* (1561), blank verse increased in significance until establishing itself, in the plays of Thomas Kyd, Robert Greene, Marlowe, and Shakespeare, as *the* medium for dramatic verse.

It is fascinating to compare the Elizabethan era with that other great epoch of prosodic restlessness, the twentieth century. Whereas the Elizabethans reconciled meter and rhythm, many twentieth-century poets subordinated the former to the latter or divorced the two altogether. Whereas the Elizabethans conducted a spirited dialectic with earlier prosodic tradition—assimilating useful elements and discarding those that proved unsuited to their language—twentieth-century poets all too often conducted their experiments on the negative principle of avoiding the past. Finally, whereas Elizabethan practice produced a vigorous consensus that allowed diverse voices a common basis of technique, twentieth-century verse grew decade by decade more fragmented. These comparisons not only underscore the Elizabethans' achievement but also suggest the lessons that that achievement may hold for poetry in the new millennium.

See also biographies of figures mentioned in this entry.

BIBLIOGRAPHY

Attridge, Derek. *Well-Weighed Syllables: English Verse in Classical Metres.* London, 1974. A thorough and admirably sympathetic discussion of attempts in the Elizabethan period to imitate or incorporate in English the methods of ancient quantitative versification.

Cunningham, J. V. "Lyric Style in the 1590s." In *The Collected Essays of J. V. Cunningham.* Chicago, 1976. Pages 311–324. An illuminating account, by a fine twentieth-century poet and metrist, of Donne's and Jonson's use in English of the classical genres of elegy, verse epistle, satire, and epigram.

Hardison, O. B., Jr. *Prosody and Purpose in the English Renaissance.* Baltimore, 1989. A treatment of miscellaneous topics in Renaissance verse, with special attention to the development of blank verse and to connections between English prosody and the more purely syllabic prosodies of French and Italian poetry.

Partridge, A. C. *Orthography in Shakespeare and Elizabethan Drama: A Study of Colloquial Contractions, Elision, Prosody, and Punctuation.* London, 1964. A helpful study of technical issues crucial to understanding Elizabethan verse. Also, a useful reminder of the ways in which current texts often obscure, by modernized spellings and word forms, the metrical intentions of Elizabethan poets.

Smith, G. Gregory, ed. *Elizabethan Critical Essays.* 2 vols. Oxford, 1904. A thoughtfully introduced and well-annotated anthology of seminal essays on prosody and poetics by such Elizabethan poets and scholars as Roger Ascham, George Gascoigne, Philip Sidney, George Puttenham, Thomas Campion, and Samuel Daniel.

Thompson, John. *The Founding of English Metre.* 1961. Reprint, with an introduction by John Hollander, New York, 1989. A classic study of the development of English prosody from Wyatt and Surrey to Spenser and Sidney.

Wright, George T. *Shakespeare's Metrical Art.* Berkeley, Calif., 1988.

TIMOTHY STEELE

PROSTITUTION. Although there were certainly women who traded sex for payment in both town and countryside throughout the Renaissance, most of these transactions have left no record; almost all sources about prostitution come from cities, where there were likely to be greater concentrations of prostitutes. During the fourteenth and fifteenth centuries, many cities and towns throughout Europe opened official municipal houses of prostitution or designated certain parts of the city, such as the area around the Mercato Vecchio in Florence, as places in which prostitution would be permitted. Generally this was done with little recorded discussion, but the city fathers sometimes justified their actions with reference to St. Augustine, who regarded prostitution as a necessary evil that protected honorable girls and women from the uncontrollable lusts of young men. In Italian cities prostitution was also viewed as a way of encouraging young men into acceptable heterosexual activity and away from homosexual liaisons. Prostitutes—or at least those who lived in municipal brothels—were integrated fairly well into urban society, appearing as a group at city festivals and publicly welcoming visiting dignitaries. Ordinances regulating municipal brothels attempted to guard the safety of the brothel's residents and customers by such measures as forbidding weapons, prohibiting brothel owners from selling women, and checking prostitutes for disease.

Prostitutes. Sixteenth-century depiction of women of the street and pimp. MUSÉE D'ART ET D'HISTOIRE, GENEVA

The integration of prostitutes into urban society was never complete, however, and during the later fifteenth century many cities, particularly in northern Europe, began to restrict the movements and appearance of prostitutes more sharply, requiring them to wear clothing that distinguished them from "honorable" women and to stay in the brothel at all times. Harsher penalties, including physical mutilation and banishment, were imposed on women who lived outside the official house or district. This process of marginalization culminated in the closing of official brothels, in Germany mainly during the period from 1520 to 1590 and in Spain in the early seventeenth century. Major Italian cities such as Florence and Venice did not outlaw prostitution entirely, but they regulated it more strictly. Until recently scholars linked this criminalization to the advent of syphilis in Europe, but it is now clear that although city and state authorities knew the new disease was generally transmitted sexually, moral rather than medical considerations were most important.

These moral concerns were in part a result of the Protestant and then Catholic Reformations. Martin Luther called prostitutes tools of the devil and accused them of bewitching students and other unmarried men; Catholic reformers joined him in preaching and writing against prostitution in vicious language. This moralism came to be shared by city authorities, who justified closing brothels with discussions of God's wrath toward unpurified communities, and even by journeymen's guilds, who rejected their earlier acceptance of brothel visits as normal for their unmarried members and now banned members who had simply stood next to a prostitute in a public place. The prohibition of prostitution was part of wider attempts at social control as authorities increasingly regarded everyone who did not live in stable, male-headed households as suspect. In some Catholic cities the criminalization of prostitution was accompanied by the opening of what were often termed Magdalene houses, convents for repentent prostitutes, though by the seventeenth century these had become primarily penal institutions and had largely lost their religious purpose.

During this period of first toleration and then repression—or, in some areas, alternating periods of toleration and repression—women continued to turn to prostitution as a source of income. Many women combined prostitution with other sorts of casual labor like laundering, seamstressing, or selling food and drink, moving from town to town with others of the laboring poor; the few sources we have from women indicate that they regarded prostitution primarily as work that paid relatively well, and that they were not shunned by their neighbors for their activities. During times of war and unrest, prostitutes accompanied bands of soldiers, providing both sexual and other sorts of services such as laundering or finding food. These "soldier's whores" were often banned by city authorities, although they fascinated artists such as Albrecht Dürer with their flamboyant clothing. Artists and writers were also attracted to women on the upper end of the prostitution spectrum, courtesans such as the Venetian poet Veronica Franco who offered their customers elegant literary refinement as well as sex; these Italian and French courtesans were often glamorized in portraits and poetry. For most women who traded sex for payment, however, life was not glamorous but filled with poverty, violence, and disease; because they did not belong to one man but were common to all, they were both exemplars and victims of male fears about uncontrolled female sexuality.

See also **Women,** *subentry on* **Women in the Renaissance.**

BIBLIOGRAPHY

Karras, Ruth. *Common Women: Prostitution and Sexuality in Medieval England*. New York. 1996. Sets changes in prostitution in England within the context of changing ideas about female and male sexuality.

Otis, Leah Lydia. *Prostitution in Medieval Society: The History of an Urban Institution in Languedoc*. Chicago, 1985. Traces the institutionalization and then restriction of municipal brothels in southern France; based on extensive archival sources.

Perry, Mary Elizabeth. "Deviant Insiders: Legalized Prostitutes and a Consciousness of Women in Early Modern Seville." *Comparative Studies in Society and History* 27 (1985):138–158.

Roper, Lyndal. "Discipline and Respectability: Prostitution and the Reformation in Augsburg." *History Workshop* 19 (1985): 3–28.

MERRY E. WIESNER

PROTESTANT REFORMATION. A religious upheaval originating in sixteenth-century Germany but affecting all of western and central Europe, the Protestant Reformation resulted in the permanent loss of religious unity and the establishment of several rival religious traditions. Historians regard the challenge by Martin Luther in 1517 to the theology underlying indulgences as its beginning. Although it began as a movement of religious reform, it had major effects on political, social, economic, and intellectual life; later in the century it generated civil wars in Germany, France, the Netherlands, and Scotland.

Backgrounds. The Protestant Reformation was rooted in medieval religious conditions and problems. Thus it closely parallels the Catholic Reformation. Traditional historiography depicted a pre-Reformation church on the verge of collapse, outwardly strong but spiritually moribund. This interpretation is supported by much evidence of corruption and pastoral incompetence among the leadership and by numerous expressions of discontent in art and literature. Especially in the 1980s and early 1990s, some historians, focusing more on the religious practices of ordinary people than on the failings of the leaders, contended that most people found traditional religion satisfying. Although this interpretation has merit, it exaggerates the role of compulsion in the Reformation and overlooks the fact that where the common people had a voice (for example, in independent German towns), pressure for reform often came from the bottom of society, not from the top. Rather than presenting the Reformation as an inevitable collapse or as the consequence of compulsion, it is more accurate to conclude that while the church was not on the verge of collapse, it was vulnerable to the kind of challenge that did occur. Many of the sources of this vulnerability lay in its own recent history, particularly in the failure of the Renaissance papacy to undertake comprehensive reform, leaving a residue of mistrust and cynicism that was increased by the popes' concentration on politics and neglect of spiritual problems.

Many who agitated for reform were traditional medieval figures—monks and preachers of repentance—but the most influential reformers just before 1517 were the humanists. Especially in northern Europe, reform came to be closely linked to Renaissance interest in antiquity. "Christian humanists" like Jacques Lefèvre d'Étaples and Desiderius Erasmus hoped to renew religion by a return to the sources of early Christianity.

The Career of Martin Luther. The Augustinian friar Martin Luther (1483–1546), professor of theology at Wittenberg, set off the religious revolution. Luther developed a new theology that challenged many current practices. His Ninety-five Theses (October 1517) questioned the theological foundations of indulgences (the remission of part or all of the temporal punishment due for sins after the eternal punishment has been remitted by the priest in confession). Accused of heresy, Luther articulated what he regarded as an "evangelical" (Bible-based) theology, emphasizing humanity's total dependence on God's grace and the uselessness of all supposedly meritorious human actions. He defended himself by developing a remarkable talent for writing popular tracts that attracted growing support.

Relation to Renaissance humanism. Luther's relationship to Renaissance humanism has been much debated. His education was scholastic, not humanistic. But his teaching impelled him toward a theology based on close exegesis of the Bible rather than traditional speculative theology. He knew and used the patristic and biblical scholarship of Lefèvre and Erasmus, especially Erasmus's Greek New Testament (1516).

While the role of humanism in Luther's new theological system was significant but limited, its role in the propagation of his ideas after 1517 was absolutely crucial. Some unidentified humanist was probably responsible for the first publication of the Ninety-five Theses, for humanists perceived in Luther (not quite correctly) an eloquent spokesman for their own reform program. Humanist editors diffused his books throughout Germany. By 1521, when he traveled to Worms for a hearing before the imperial Diet, Luther had become a national hero.

From Luther to Reformation. While Luther was in seclusion after being outlawed by the Diet, his associates in Wittenberg were bitterly divided over how fast and how far his ideas should be translated into religious changes. Eventually, the Lutheran Reformation produced a series of moderate but substantial changes. Many large German principalities and a majority of self-governing cities emulated his reforms. The close cultural and economic ties between Germany and the Scandinavian countries also facilitated the spread of Lutheran ideas in northern Europe, initially through the influence of students and preachers educated in Germany but, in the long run, mainly because ambitious kings in Denmark and Sweden exploited religious change to weaken the power of the bishops and to create Lutheran state churches that the kings could control.

The specter of religious disunity and the German Peasants' War of 1524–1525 confirmed the fears of conservative Germans that religious change would cause social upheaval. A number of humanists who had sympathized with Luther drew back. The most famous example was Erasmus, who in 1524 published an attack on Luther's denial of free will. Most older humanists turned against the Reformation because it endangered unity. Many younger humanists, however, became preachers of the new faith.

The Swiss Reformed Tradition. Former humanists took the lead in creating a distinct Reformation in the Swiss Confederation. Huldrych Zwingli (1484–1531) had admired Erasmus since meeting him in 1515, and he insisted that he had become a reformer before he heard of Luther. Between 1520 and 1525 his preaching persuaded the Zurich city council to adopt drastic reforms. In the years 1527–1529, other Swiss cities followed suit. In each of these places, the leader was a former humanist transformed into a reform preacher. No one planned to create a rival Reformation, but disagreement between Luther and Zwingli over Christ's presence in the Eucharist produced an irreconcilable split by the time of the Colloquy of Marburg (1529), and Protestantism remained divided.

The pace of change in Zurich was not rapid enough to satisfy Zwingli's most radical followers. Their rejection of infant baptism caused them to be called Anabaptists (rebaptizers). But their truly distinctive beliefs were their insistence on separation from a church that tolerated unbiblical practices and their organization of rival independent churches.

Protestant Map of Catholicism. Mountains of relics and images lie near a coffin of animal bones marked "Relics." From *Mappemonde novelle papistique* (1556) by Frangidelphe Escorche-Masses (pseudonym of Théodore de Bèze).

Fears that radicalism would lead to social upheaval were confirmed when extremists seized control of the city of Münster in 1534 and instituted an authoritarian dictatorship that adopted communism and polygamy, banned all books except the Bible, and expelled or massacred all "godless" persons. After the exiled Catholics and Lutherans stormed the city and killed all the defenders, Anabaptism survived only as a group of small, persecuted sects.

John Calvin and the Reformation in France. The French Reformation grew out of humanism. Lefèvre d'Étaples had turned humanistic scholarship toward concern with the Bible and the church fathers. By the 1520s idealistic young humanists, inspired by Lefèvre, Erasmus, and Luther, and often sheltered by the pious, highly intellectual sister of the king, Margaret of Navarre (also called Margaret of Angoulême), were known as evangelicals. Their reform aspirations had no clear theological foundation and no plan of action except the forlorn hope that the king would use his authority to initiate reform.

The person who provided French evangelicals with a coherent set of beliefs and a plan of action was John Calvin (1509–1564). Calvin began his career as a humanist but by 1533 was committed to the Reformation. In March 1536 he published *Institutio Christianae religionis* (Institutes of the Christian religion), a powerful restatement of theological ideas drawn from Luther, Zwingli, and other reformers. Settling at Geneva, he created a church organization that Protestants all over Europe regarded as a model. His Ecclesiastical Ordinances (1541) were notable for making religious discipline independent of control by the civic authorities. Education was central to Calvin's conception of reformed Christianity. At his urging, in 1559 the city founded the Genevan Academy, which provided humanistic education and theological training for future ministers and lay leaders from many lands. Its former students played leading roles in the later phases of the Reformation throughout Europe. For Calvin, Geneva was never an end in itself but a base for the spiritual conquest of the world, especially his native France, where Calvinism spread rapidly during the 1550s, assisted by the Genevan church's training and dispatching pastors to France.

Calvinism and Civil War. The proselytizing zeal of Calvinism and its powerful internal organization made its spread into Catholic societies a source of political as well as religious conflict, not only in France but also in the Netherlands and in Scotland. In each case, Calvinist churches, organized as autonomous and highly disciplined local congregations but tightly linked together by a hierarchy of representative assemblies, became associated with a political movement that opposed royal policy. The French Wars of Religion (1562–1598) ended with the

Edict of Nantes (1598), which legalized the French Reformed church, but only as a tolerated minority. In the Netherlands, the Dutch war for independence (1572–1609) from Spain began as a purely constitutional struggle against the authoritarian policies of King Philip II but divided on the religious issue. The north, controlled by Calvinists, became independent; the southern provinces accepted restoration of Spanish control. In Scotland Protestants led by the preacher John Knox opposed the pro-French and pro-Catholic policies of Queen Mary Stuart. By 1568 the queen had been driven into exile, the authority of the pope and the bishops had been abolished, and the Calvinist church had become a major force in Scottish life. Calvinism also gained a following in eastern Europe (Poland, Bohemia, and Hungary), where Lutheranism had attracted only the numerous colonies of ethnic Germans; but by the middle of the seventeenth century, it remained a significant movement only in Hungary.

Reformation and the Arts. Lutheran Protestantism substituted vernacular liturgies for Latin and reduced the power and independence of the clergy, but Luther was cautious about change except in cases where tradition seemed clearly contrary to scripture. The role of art and music in public worship was changed but not abolished. The Reformed (Zwinglian and Calvinist) tradition, however, insisted on more drastic change, not only in theology but also in forms of worship and the use of art. Zwingli and Calvin were fearful of the "idolatry" potentially linked to the use of art and music in the churches. Reformed worship restricted or abolished the use of music and insisted on simple liturgies that emphasized preaching rather than colorful ceremony. Reformed churches eliminated religious images, especially pictures of Christ and the saints, that might encourage "superstitious" and "idolatrous" acts. The arts could still flourish in a Reformed country (notably in the Netherlands) but must be secularized—relocated from the church to the home and changed in theme.

During the struggle for control in the Swiss and Netherlandish cities, violent acts of iconoclasm sometimes occurred. Yet traditional historiography exaggerates the frequency of such incidents. Rulers and preachers normally discouraged mob action, preferring orderly elimination of religiously offensive objects by official action.

The English Reformation. Although Lutheran and Erasmian criticism of the church was influential among educated English people during the 1520s, it is doubtful whether Protestantism could have triumphed if dynastic problems had not led Henry VIII (ruled 1509–1547) to attack papal authority in order to secure an annulment of his marrage to his queen. Henry employed Thomas Cromwell, who used parliamentary authority to abolish papal power. He then had the archbishop of Canterbury, Thomas Cranmer, dissolve the royal marriage. Although both Cranmer and Cromwell were influenced by Lutheran thought, the king was theologically conservative. The English church remained officially Catholic in doctrine during Henry's lifetime. Cromwell employed humanist writers to uphold royal religious policy, translating, for example, carefully chosen works of Erasmus. Cromwell's plan to publish and distribute the first legally authorized English Bible survived his fall from power in 1540.

Edward VI and Mary. The reign of Edward VI (ruled 1547–1553) was a decisive step toward making England a Protestant nation. In 1549 Archbishop Thomas Cranmer was authorized to publish an English-language liturgy, the Book of Common Prayer. This book retained much of the outer forms of the Catholic liturgy, but its doctrinal implications were Protestant, especially in the revised edition of 1552. Henry VIII's elder daughter Mary (ruled 1553–1558) came to the throne determined to undo these religious innovations. Although the nation as a whole accepted restored Catholicism readily, the brevity of her reign and her failure to give birth to an heir doomed the Catholic restoration.

The Elizabethan religious settlement. Mary's half-sister Elizabeth I (ruled 1558–1603) adopted a moderately Protestant policy. The Act of Supremacy (1559) again abolished the pope's authority and recognized the queen as "supreme governor" of the church. A slightly revised version of Cranmer's Prayer Book offended the returning Protestant exiles, but it facilitated acceptance of the settlement by ordinary people who were not strongly committed to either Protestant or Catholic theologies. The recusants, those who remained loyal to Roman Catholicism, were relatively few. Far more numerous were those English Protestants who objected to Elizabeth's control of the church, the authority of the bishops, and the Prayer Book. They were the nucleus of an outspoken Puritan minority, which persisted but never gained the upper hand in Elizabeth's time.

See also **Christianity**, *subentry on* **The Western Church**; **Prayer Book, English**; **Puritanism**; **Wars of Religion**; *and biographies of figures mentioned in this entry.*

BIBLIOGRAPHY

Bainton, Roland Herbert. *Here I Stand: A Life of Martin Luther*. New York, 1950. Best of the older biographies.

Bouwsma, William J. *John Calvin: A Sixteenth-Century Portrait*. New York, 1988.

Brady, Thomas A. *Ruling Class, Regime, and Reformation at Strasbourg, 1520–1555*. Leiden, Netherlands, 1978. A model prosopographical study of the social history of the Reformation in a major German city.

Cameron, Euan. *The European Reformation*. Oxford, 1991.

Dickens, A. G. *The English Reformation*. 2d ed. London, 1989.

Dickens, A. G., and John Tonkin, with Kenneth Powell. *The Reformation in Historical Thought*. Cambridge, Mass., 1985. A history of the writing of Reformation history.

Duffy, Eamon. *The Stripping of the Altars: Traditional Religion in England, 1400–1580*. New Haven, Conn., 1992.

Lindberg, Carter. *The European Reformations*. Oxford and Cambridge, Mass., 1996.

McConica, James. *English Humanists and Reformation Politics under Henry VIII and Edward VI*. Oxford, 1965.

McGrath, Alister. *The Intellectual Origins of the European Reformation*. Oxford, 1987.

McGrath, Alister. *A Life of John Calvin: A Study in the Shaping of Western Culture*. Cambridge, Mass., 1990.

Moeller, Bernd. *Imperial Cities and the Reformation: Three Essays*. Edited and translated by H. C. Erik Midelfort and Mark U. Edwards Jr. Philadelphia, 1972. The three German originals appeared in 1965, 1959, and 1962.

Oberman, Heiko A. *Luther: Man between God and the Devil*. Translated by Eileen Walliser-Schwarzbart. New Haven, Conn., 1989. The German original was published in 1982.

Ozment, Steven E. *The Reformation in the Cities*. New Haven, Conn., 1975.

Potter, G. R. *Zwingli*. Cambridge, U.K., and New York, 1976.

Spitz, Lewis W. *The Protestant Reformation, 1517–1559*. New York, 1985.

Strauss, Gerald. *Luther's House of Learning: Indoctrination of the Young in the German Reformation*. Baltimore, 1978.

CHARLES G. NAUERT

PSYCHOLOGY. During the Renaissance psychology was regularly taught as part of the natural philosophy course in the universities and relied principally upon Aristotle's *De anima* (On the soul) and his *Parva naturalia* (Short physical treatises). Renaissance analyses of the soul were influenced by medieval interpretations of Aristotle's views (Arabic and Latin), and by Aristotle's ancient Greek commentators (for example, Alexander of Aphrodisias, Simplicius, and Philoponus), as well as by such other ancient sources as Plato and Galen. Humanists concerned with literary elegance and with the recovery of classical sources provided new Latin translations of *De anima* and Latin translations and Greek editions of relevant works of Aristotle's Greek commentators. Some philosophers, such as Iacopo Zabarella (1533–1589), using these and the manuscripts of *De anima* and other related Greek texts not available in the medieval period, sought to provide clear and accurate analyses of Aristotle's text.

The study of human psychology had implications for both medicine and theology in light of the human soul's double role as the principle of vital and cognitive activities, and as the source of immortality. Renaissance developments in these two areas had a lasting impact on theories of psychology. Along with the foundation of Latin, Arabic, and Greek sources, they promoted a rich array of theories and lent to Renaissance psychology its unique character.

Rival Views of the Human Soul. It was commonly agreed that the subject of psychology is the soul, and that human understanding is an activity of the human soul that employs no bodily organ. But a key problem, the structure of the human soul and its relation to body, divided Renaissance theorists into two camps. The first maintained that each human being has one soul, with organic (vegetative, sensitive) and inorganic (intellective) faculties. A second camp maintained that the same soul cannot at the same time be organic and inorganic, dependent on organs and independent of organs. Further, some argued, an organic soul, like the souls of nonhuman living things, perishes with the body, but the human intellective soul or mind is immortal. So human beings must have two souls, an organic soul and mind. Those who claimed that human beings have more than one soul are called pluralists.

The second group was further divided into monopsychists (such as Paul of Venice, Tiberio Baccillieri, and Alessandro Achillini) and individualists (such as Philipp Melanchthon, Jacopo Zabarella, and Fortunius Licetus). The monopsychists, like the scholastic Jean of Jandun, maintained that Averroes (Ibn Rushd; 1126–1198) correctly claimed that the human *mind* is a single separated substance. That is, all human beings share one mind. This mind acts in conjunction with each human organic (cogitative) soul to produce, in each human being, intellective cognition. Individualists, like William of Ockham (1285–1349), maintained instead that each human being, like other animals, has a mortal organic soul as well as an individual and purely intellective mind. Further, some pluralists (such as Bernardino Telesio [1509–1588] and the Galenist physician Eustachius Rudius) claimed that the organic soul is corporeal. Others held that each human being has three souls, a vegetative soul, a sensitive soul, and a mind.

One-soul theorists were also further divided into monists (such as Chrisostomo Javelli, Franciscus Toletus, and Francisco Suarez) and dualists (such as

Gregor Reisch and Filippo Fabri). All maintained that each living thing is a substance, that each substance is composed of prime matter and substantial form, and that the soul is a substantial form. Dualists, like John Duns Scotus (1266–1308), claimed that the human body has its own substantial form or essence that is really distinct from the soul. Monists commonly adopted the Thomistic metaphysical argument that with two substantial forms (two "actualities") a thing will be two substances, not one. Hence, a soul must be the only substantial form of a living thing.

Professors of Thomistic and Scotistic metaphysics and theology and the New Scholasticism of such Jesuits as Toletus, the Coimbra Commentators, and Suarez contributed to the entrenchment of one-soul analyses. Averroist monopsychism, seen as denying personal immortality, and the Renaissance view, influenced by Alexander of Aphrodisias that, according to Aristotle and reason, the human soul is inseparable from the body and mortal, provoked the Fifth Lateran Council's condemnation of these views in 1513. This council proclaimed the human soul's immortality and required that philosophers demonstrate that the human soul is immortal. Nonetheless, in his *De immortalitate animae* (On the immortality of the soul; 1516), Pietro Pomponazzi supported Alexandrist mortalism and argued that Thomistic monism is inconsistent with the immortality of the human soul. In light of Lateran V's proclamation, Pomponazzi's work posed the problem of how the human soul's immortality can be demonstrated. One response was the pluralist view that a purely intellective human mind is really distinct from the mortal organic soul of the human body, and so it is separable and immortal. Pluralism also acquired a following among Protestants (such as Philipp Melanchthon and Petrus Bertius). It was seen by the influential late Renaissance adversaries Iacopo Zabarella and Francesco Piccolomini as the mainline interpretation of Aristotle's view, supported by his Greek commentators, by Averroes and Latin Averroists, and by Plato and Galen.

Thomists and Scotists. Renaissance philosophers generally provided similar classifications of organic powers, but differed on the body's role in their exercise. Hieronymus Wildenberg, a Thomistic monist, focusing principally upon the soul, its nature and powers, distinguished five faculties (vegetative, sensitive, motive, appetitive, and intellective), and three grades of souls (vegetative in plants, sensitive in animals, and rational in human beings), each higher grade having the powers of all lower grades. He then surveyed the different powers of each faculty (nutritive, visual, and others), their instruments, their objects, and their operations, and thereby delineated the natural activities of a bodily organism. The passive intellect, a power of the human soul, enables the soul to receive and experience intelligible species (universals), which were abstracted from sense images of the imagination by a companion power, the active intellect.

Some issues derived from Scotus commonly raised in opposition to Thomistic views by Renaissance dualists, from Gregor Reisch to Filippo Fabri, were the formation of human beings, the relation of the soul to its powers, and the intellectual cognition of singulars. Both Reisch and Fabri reject the Thomistic view that in human reproduction lower substantial forms are successively generated and destroyed to be replaced by a single rational soul that God creates *de novo,* because this view underestimates human heredity. Both maintained that parents, via seeds or semen, are sufficient to cause forms of the body, but not the human soul, which is superadded to the body and caused by God. Psychic powers are not qualitative forms employed by the soul, as Thomists claim, but principles identified with the soul's essence. Thus, since the whole soul is wholly in each part of the body, bodily organs play a significant role in determining the soul's operation. Finally, unlike Aquinas, who maintained that there is only indirect and reflexive intellectual cognition of singular things, Fabri and other Scotists claimed that the intellect apprehends singulars directly by intuitive cognition.

Pluralist Psychology. Melanchthon (1497–1560), an educator and Luther's principal associate, was eclectic, uniting Aristotle's general account of the human soul with views of Galen, Cicero, and Plato. Citing Ockham as his source, Melanchthon supported a real distinction between an organic soul and human mind. He stated that organic souls are entelechies (motions) or temperaments, whereas the mind is a spirit, and so a soul of a different sort. The organic soul is inseparable from the body and mortal. Its operations are distinguished by the organs that are empowered by the soul. Melanchthon, therefore, in explaining natural activities, provided a detailed study of each external and then each internal bodily part, such as organs, humors, and spirits, and then considered their functions. From this study, he explained, one can come to understand the powers attributed to the organic soul. The human mind, on the other hand, understands universals, has innate ideas, reflects upon itself, deliberates by lengthy ratiocination, and makes moral judgments. Such activities are impossible for an extended entity like the body. Thus the human mind must be unextended and incorporeal, and, as such, indestructible and so immortal.

Averroes retained a following in the Renaissance, especially at the universities of Padua and Bologna, a tradition inherited by Jacopo Zabarella and Francesco Piccolomini. Both, like the Averroists, distinguished organic soul and mind, but they disagreed on the structure of the organic soul, on the nature and cause of the human mind, active and passive intellect, and sensible and intelligible species. Zabarella, an eclectic Aristotelian, sided with the Thomistic view of the soul's relation to its powers and of sensible and intelligible species as real entities, and identified the opposing view, taken by Piccolomini, as that of the moderns (*recentiores*). Zabarella claimed, citing Jandun, that each animal has three souls, a vegetative soul, a sensitive soul, and a specific soul, which places it in its species and makes it what it is. The specific soul of each human being is a mind. He also maintained, following Pomponazzi, that the whole human soul is caused naturalistically by parents and celestial spirits in the seed, and that, as Alexander of Aphrodisias argued, the active intellect is God and the passive intellect is a personal human mind. Piccolomini claimed instead, like Ockham, that there are two human souls (organic soul and mind), that sensible and intelligible species are "acts" of cognition, and he recognized a distinction of reason, not a real distinction, between active and passive intellects. He said that Averroes's monopsychism correctly interprets Aristotle's view but Aristotle erred. In an extensive defense of the human mind's personal immortality, he held that the mind is created by God, and he supported the mind's purely intellective powers of abstraction, reflection upon itself, and moral judgment.

Renaissance theories of a purely intellective human mind and an increasing role for body in works on psychology were at least in part, a response to the immortality problem and developments in medicine. As a result, dualism and pluralism acquired a substantial following in the late Renaissance, and, in turn, provided the context for early modern dualisms of, for example, René Descartes, and double soul theories like that of Descartes's principal adversary, Pierre Gassendi.

See also **Humanity, Concept of**; **Immortality**; *and biographies of Melanchthon, Suarez, and Zabarella.*

BIBLIOGRAPHY

Primary Works

Casirer, Ernst, Paul Oskar Kristeller, and John Herman Randall, eds. *Renaissance Philosophy of Man.* Chicago, 1948. Selections in translation.

Kennedy, Leonard A., ed. *Renaissance Philosophy: New Translations.* The Hague, Netherlands, 1973. Includes selections in translation from Thomas de Vio (Cajetan) and Tiberius Baccillierius.

Reisch, Gregor. *Margarita Philosophica* (The pearl of philosophy). 1504. Reprint. Düsseldorf, 1973. Introduction by L. Geldsetzer.

Zabarella, Jacopo. *Commentaria in tres libros De anima* (Commentary on the three books of *De Anima*). 1606. Reprint. Frankfurt, 1966.

Secondary Works

Kristeller, Paul O. *Renaissance Thought II: Papers on Humanism and the Arts.* New York, 1965.

Kristeller, Paul O. *Renaissance Concepts of Man and Other Essays.* New York, 1972.

Mahoney, Edward P. "Nicoletto Vernia on the Soul and Immortality." In *Philosophy and Humanism: Renaissance Essays in Honor of Paul Oskar Kristeller.* Edited by E. P. Mahoney. New York, 1976. Pages 144–163.

Park, Katherine, and Eckhard Kessler. "The Organic Soul." In *The Cambridge History of Renaissance Philosophy.* Edited by Charles B. Schmitt, Quentin Skinner, Eckhard Kessler, and Jill Kraye. Cambridge, U.K., and New York, 1988. Pages 453–534. Appendix includes an extensive bibliography and biobibliographies.

EMILY MICHAEL

PTOLEMY (C. A.D. 100–C. A.D. 170), Alexandrian scholar important for his works on astronomy, geography, optics, and related sciences; of great influence in the early Renaissance.

We know very little about Claudius Ptolemy's life. Most of what is known comes from his own works and some from works of late antiquity and the Byzantine period. Since his name is a combination of a Roman (Claudius) and an Egyptian name (Ptolemy), he probably came from a mixed family. His observations in the *Mathematical Syntaxis,* or *Almagest,* come from the reigns of the Roman emperors Hadrian and Antoninus Pius, and the work was written around 150. Since he wrote several major works after the *Almagest,* he probably lived into the reign of Marcus Aurelius (d. 180). Ptolemy appears to have spent his whole life in Alexandria.

Ptolemy's works deal with many of the mathematical sciences of antiquity. His writings include the *Almagest* (his major work on astronomy), *Handy Tables* (a work listing all tables necessary for astronomical calculations and a description concerning their use), *Planetary Hypotheses* (another major work on astronomy), *Phases of the Fixed Stars* (on the risings

Ptolemaic Universe. The ptolemaic model of the universe towers over Ptolemy and Regiomontanus. Engraving from *Epytoma in Almagestum Ptolemaei* by Regiomontanus (1496). RARE BOOK DIVISION, NEW YORK PUBLIC LIBRARY, ASTOR, LENOX, AND TILDEN FOUNDATIONS

and settings of bright stars), *Analemma* (an application of mathematics to astronomy, including problems involving sundials), *Tetrabiblos* (a major work on astrology), *Geography, Planisphere, Optics, Harmonics* (a work on music theory), and *On the Faculties of Judgment and Command* (a short philosophical treatise; circulated under Ptolemy's name but possibly not by him). Several works have been lost and are known only through references in other ancient volumes. These include Ptolemy's work on mechanics, his *On Dimension* and *On the Elements.*

The *Almagest.* Ptolemy's views on the heavens are primarily developed in his masterpiece of mathematical astronomy, the *Almagest.* Originally called in Greek the *Mathematical Syntaxis* (Mathematical compilation), Ptolemy's work was given the Greek title of "great (or greatest) compilation" in late antiquity. Then in medieval Arabic the title became *al-majisti* and in medieval Latin *almagesti* or *almagestum,* producing the title *Almagest.*

The *Almagest* is written in thirteen books, covering all aspects of mathematical astronomy as it was understood in antiquity. In terms of Ptolemy's physical vision of the cosmos, one can say that it is largely Aristotelian in inspiration with some Stoic influence. To attain knowledge of the universe, Ptolemy argues, one must study astronomy. Physics deals with the world of corruption and change, but astronomy aids theology as it leads us to contemplation of the Prime Mover, the first cause of all heavenly motions—that is, God. Following earlier Greek thinkers, including Aristotle, Ptolemy argued for the spherical nature of the heavens and heavenly motions. Adopting arguments drawn largely from Aristotle, he also argued for the spherical nature of the earth, its centrality and its motionless nature. The earth, he proclaimed, is also insignificant in size in comparison to the heavens.

After this brief physical disquisition, Ptolemy proceeded to deal with the problems of mathematical astronomy in a masterful manner. He quite properly rejected the antiquated and inadequate homocentric system of Eudoxus (the fourth-century B.C. astronomer) and of Aristotle, in which all heavenly motions were truly centered on the earth. Instead he adopted the Hellenistic devices of eccentric circles and epicycles and deferent circles to handle many of the problems of planetary motion. To these traditional devices, Ptolemy added the equant point when calculating planetary motions.

Eccentric circles were devised to handle the classic problem of the sun's orbit around the earth and the inequality of the seasons. Realizing this fact, earlier Greek astronomers had moved the physical center of the sun's orbit (the earth) off center and had the sun moving on a circle that was not exactly centered on the earth. This accounted for the inequality of the seasons. Epicycles and deferents were primarily devised to handle the problem of the stations and retrogradations of the planets. Planets appeared to stop in their revolutions around the earth and then go backward before proceeding once again on proper circular orbits. Planets were placed on little circles (epicycles), which were placed on big circles (deferents) that moved and carried the epicycles with them. As the planet moved on the epicycle while it was carried by the deferent, it would appear from the vantage point of the earth that the planet would stop (station) and go backward for a time (retrogradation) before continuing in its proper circular orbit.

These devices of eccentric circles, epicycles, and deferents were combined by Ptolemy with the equant in his *Almagest.* In order to handle certain problems Ptolemy introduced the equant point, a point from which the planet's speed was always uniform while its distance was uniform from the center of an eccentric circle, which itself was a deferent. In this way Ptolemy hoped to abide by the principle of uniform circular motion for all heavenly bodies by having the distance be uniform in terms of one point and the speed uniform in terms of another (the equant point). Later critics charged that he had violated the ruling principle of Greek astronomy. However, by combining all these devices, Ptolemy managed to create mathematical models that fit very well with observations. His system was the basis for mathematical astronomy until the publication of Nicolaus Copernicus's *On the Revolutions of the Heavenly Spheres* (1543).

Other Works. Ptolemy offered only mathematical models in the *Almagest.* In his *Planetary Hypotheses,* however, he offered a physical depiction of the cosmos. In that work he argued that observations and the Aristotelian principle of a full universe supported his order of the planets (Moon, Mercury, Venus, Sun, Mars, Jupiter, Saturn) in which the furthest distance of one body from the earth equaled the least distance of the next. He also inveighed against Aristotle's mechanical system of interconnected, counteracting spheres and argued for a simpler machinery of spheres. In terms of the forces moving the planets, Ptolemy proposed two: the motion of necessity, which was the daily rotation of the entire heavens on its axis; and the free motion, which he likened to the flight of birds. Planets are impelled to move by an inner force that is transmitted to the epicycles and deferents. These arguments would become important in Renaissance cosmological debates.

Ptolemy's *Tetrabiblos,* or *Quadripartitum,* as it was known in the Latin West, was more influential. This work was a defense of astrology, predicated on the idea that the heavenly bodies affected all earthly matters, such as geography and climate, and human lives, by way of physical influences. It did not contain any of the mathematical information that was later needed for the making of horoscopes and the casting of houses that were such important parts of later medieval and Renaissance astrology.

Renaissance Criticisms. Two major types of criticism of Ptolemaic astronomy and cosmology appeared during the Renaissance. One was a revival of Aristotelian homocentric astronomy, in which attempts were again made to create physical systems that would center all heavenly spheres on a truly central earth. The most important figures associated with this school were both Italians. The famous doctor Girolamo Fracastoro (1478–1553) published a book entitled *Homocentrica sive de stellis* (Homocentric spheres; 1538) and Giovanni Battista Amico (1512–1538) issued a book *De motibus corporum coelestiu[m]* (On the motions of the heavenly bodies; 1536). Both created homocentric systems and both had been students at the University of Padua. Undoubtedly, they were influenced by the sharp criticisms of Ptolemaic astronomical devices to be found in works of Paduan Aristotelian philosophers, such as Agostino Nifo (1473–1538). This revived homocentrism was extremely cumbersome, greatly inferior to the astronomy of Ptolemy, and short lived. Far more fruitful was the heliocentrism of Copernicus (1473–1543). In his major work, *On the Revolutions of the Heavenly Spheres,* Copernicus offered a new sun-centered, geokinetic astronomy and cosmology that attempted to handle all the same problems as the system of Ptolemy, but in a simpler manner. It was this system that truly began the destruction of the Aristotelian and Ptolemaic visions of the universe.

See also **Astronomy; Geography and Cartography.**

BIBLIOGRAPHY

Primary Works

Ptolemy, Claudius. *Ptolemy's Almagest.* Translated and annotated by G. J. Toomer. Princeton, N.J., 1998. English translation of the Greek *Mathematical Syntaxis.*

Ptolemy, Claudius. *Tetrabiblos.* Edited and translated by F. E. Robbins. Cambridge, Mass., 1940. English translation and Greek edition of the *Tetrabiblos.*

Secondary Works

North, John. *The Fontana History of Astronomy and Cosmology.* London, 1994.

Rosen, Edward. *Copernicus and the Scientific Revolution.* Malabar, Fla., 1984.

Toomer, G. J. "Ptolemy." In *Dictionary of Scientific Biography.* Vol. 11, edited by Charles Coulston Gillispie. New York, 1975. Pages 186–206.

IRVING A. KELTER

PUBLIC WELFARE. *See* **Poverty and Charity.**

PUBLISHING. *See* **Printing and Publishing.**

PULCI, ANTONIA (1452–1501), Florentine playwright. Antonia, daughter of Francesco d'Antonio di Giannotto Tanini and Iacopa da Roma Tanini, was one of five siblings and two illegitimate half siblings. Because of confusions arising from her grandfather's patronymic "di Giannotto," Antonia has long been misidentified as a Giannotti.

At eighteen, possibly with the assistance of a dowry provided in response to Iacopa da Roma Tanini's plea to Lorenzo de' Medici's wife, Clarice Orsini, Antonia married Bernardo Pulci, twin of the renowned Luigi Pulci, author of the epic *Morgante*. Atypical but not unprecedented for a woman of her epoch, Antonia enjoyed educational advantages usually afforded the male children of merchants. Her studies included the usual curriculum of the *abacco* schools, the poems of Dante and Petrarch, the lives of saints, and something of vernacular humanism. Following Bernardo's death in 1487, Pulci resisted her brother Niccolò's insistence she remarry. She chose instead to found an order of Augustinian tertiaries, Le Monache della Misericordia (Nuns of Mercy). Using her dowry—restored to her when Bernardo died without issue—she purchased the sisters a house. She officially took vows in 1500.

Pressed by near penury early in their marriage, Antonia, who had mastered Italian prosody, and Bernardo collaborated in writing for the burgeoning Florentine printing industry to help eke out a living. Evidence of this collaboration appears in the 1490–1495 collection of *Sacre rappresentazioni* (devotional plays), published by Florentine printer Antonio Miscomini. Therein appear posthumously plays by Bernardo, and also drama, *Composta per Mona Antonia donna di Bernardo Pulci* (Authored by Antonia, wife of Bernardo Pulci).

Plays certainly hers include *Il figlio prodigale* (The prodigal son), *Santa Guglielma* (Saint Wilhelmena), *Santa Domitilla* (Saint Domitilla), *San Antonio abbate* (St. Anthony the abbot), and *San Francesco* (St. Francis of Assisi). The plays concerning male saints seem to have been performed at religious festivals staged by Florentine confraternities on the name days of their patrons. Those concerning female saints seem designed for production in convents, principally for female audiences, and with sisters playing the roles. Among other plays Pulci may have authored or coauthored are *Santa Teodora,* a two-part *Rosana, Susana,* and another St. Francis play.

Antonia Pulci's dramas, polished, one-act, verse plays, eschew the misogyny that often afflicts even the literary work of nuns. Grounded in hagiography, her drama regularly concerns issues of special interest to women: the dangers of childbearing, the disappointments of child rearing, the unwanted attentions of suitors, and the jealousy, unpredictability, and thoughtlessness of husbands. Her heroines are thoughtful, courageous, proactive problem-solvers. Pulci's charming plays remained in print in apparent acting editions for almost two hundred years. The convent drama that Pulci helped found developed into a healthy tradition among the nunneries of Italy and heralded the subsequent emergence of a secular vernacular theater with actresses and female playwrights like Isabella Andreini (1562–1604).

BIBLIOGRAPHY

Primary Works

Pulci, Antonia. *Florentine Drama for Convent and Festival: Seven Sacred Plays*. Translated by James Wyatt Cook. Edited by James Wyatt Cook and Barbara Collier Cook. Chicago, 1996.

Richa, Giuseppe. *Notizie istoriche delle chiese fiorentine,* vol. 5. Florence, 1757. See pages 249–251.

Secondary Works

Cardini, Franco. "La figura di Francesco D'Assisi nella 'Rappresentatione di sancto Francesco' di Antonia Pulci, *Il francescanesimo e il teatro medievale*." Proceedings from the Convegno Nazionale di Studi, San Miniato, 8–10 October 1982. Castelfiorentino, Italy, 1984. Pages 196–207.

Carrai, Stefano. "Lorenzo e l'umanismo volgare dei fratelli Pulci." In *Lorenzo De' Medici: New Perspectives*. Edited by Bernard Toscani. New York, 1993.

Weaver, Elissa. "The Convent Wall in Tuscan Drama." In *The Crannied Wall: Women, Religion, and the Arts in Early Modern Europe*. Edited by Craig A. Monson. Ann Arbor, Mich., 1995. Pages 73–86.

JAMES WYATT COOK

PULCI, LUIGI (1432–1484), Florentine poet. By the time of Luigi Pulci's birth, his family, believed to be of French descent, had lost almost all of its former wealth and influence. After the death of their father, Iacopo, Luigi and his brothers, Luca and Bernardo, who shared with him a love for poetry, were forced to sell their meager inheritance to cover Iacopo's debts. Luigi was unable to seek a public office because of his family's insolvency, but he had meanwhile earned a certain reputation as a poet of popular inspiration, and in 1460 he was admitted into the residence of Cosimo de' Medici. There he met Lucrezia Tornabuoni, wife of Cosimo's oldest son, Piero, and mother of Lorenzo the Magnificent. A devout person, Lucrezia took a great liking to Pulci and wanted him to write a poem that, by celebrating the figure of Charlemagne, would extol all the good deeds the emperor had done to defend and promote the faith. In response to her urging the poet started to work, possibly in the spring of 1461, on his *Morgante,* whose definitive edition in twenty-eight cantos was published in Florence in 1483 with the title of *Morgante maggiore.*

Morgante is a complex and multifaceted work, the product of the bizarre fantasy of a poet who defies any ready-made definition. Averse by nature to the lofty ideals of chivalry, Pulci's creativity was stimulated by an earthy, plebeian, picaresque view of reality. His main sources are *Chanson de Roland* and the *cantari popolari* (popular songs) of the fourteenth and fifteenth centuries, such as *Orlando* and *La Spagna,* of which he made an ingenious and often grotesque parody. *Morgante* retells the mock-epic adventures of Orlando and his giant friend Morgante and features a cast of other unforgettable characters, among them the demigiant Margutte and the devil-theologian Astarotte. The "motor" of the story is the forever scheming Gano, in whose hands the old emperor Charlemagne, deprived of the almost sacred aura that surrounds him in *Chanson de Roland,* becomes a virtual puppet—but he regains some of his former wisdom and leadership in the poem's last five cantos.

Although Pulci was sixteen years older than Lorenzo de' Medici, they became close friends, as attested to by the many letters the poet addressed to Lorenzo between 1465 and 1484. While Lorenzo was strongly influenced by the work of humanist scholars, Pulci had the knowledge typical of a man who lives more on the fringes than at the center of culture. An eccentric, sarcastic, and popularizing poet, Pulci showed no particular interest in philological studies. His *Vocabolista* (Lexicon; 1465), a work filled with classical names and affected diction, was probably inspired by his desire not to seem out of place in the learned humanistic circles of his city. Of the great men of letters of his time, Pulci admired and respected only Angelo Poliziano, whom he highly praises in his *Morgante.*

In about 1475 Pulci engaged in a damaging dispute with Marsilio Ficino, the revered philosopher then lecturing in Florence. Pulci attacked Ficino in five irreverent sonnets, mocking and even denying the immortality of the soul and the existence of a divine reward after death. These sonnets caused a scandal in Florence and provoked Ficino to accuse Pulci of waging war against God. Even though Pulci tried to make amends by writing a long poem, *Confessione,* as a public act of repentance, his polemic with Ficino cost him the friendship and the protection of Lorenzo the Magnificent. In 1475 Pulci entered the service of the Neapolitan count Roberto Sanseverino. Apparently his repentance and his repeated professions of orthodoxy did not succeed in convincing his contemporaries; when he suddenly died near Padua on his way to Venice, he was buried in unconsecrated ground.

In addition to *Morgante* and other already mentioned works, Pulci authored *La giostra di Lorenzo de' Medici* (Lorenzo's joust; 1482), a poem that describes a splendid tournament given in Florence by Lorenzo in 1469; *La Beca da Dicomano* (Beca from Dicomano), a parody of Lorenzo's *La Nencia da Barberino* (Nencia from Barberino); and at least one novella, several *rispetti* (rustic love songs), and two *frottole* (popular songs). *Morgante,* Pulci's masterpiece, was well known outside Italy long before the end of the seventeenth century. It is credited with having influenced Rabelais and Goethe, as well as several English writers, among them Lord Byron, who translated the first canto of Pulci's epic.

BIBLIOGRAPHY

Primary Works

Pulci, Luigi. *Morgante.* Edited by Franca Ageno. Milan and Naples, Italy, 1955.

Pulci, Luigi. *Morgante: The Epic Adventures of Orlando and His Giant Friend Morgante.* Translated by Joseph Tusiani. Introduction and Notes by Edoardo A. Lèbano. Bloomington, Ind., 1998.

Pulci, Luigi. *Opere minori.* Edited by Paolo Orvieto. Milan, 1986.

Secondary Works

De Robertis, Domenico. *Storia del "Morgante."* Florence, 1958.

Lèbano, Edoardo A. "Luigi Pulci and Late Fifteenth-Century Humanism in Florence." *Renaissance Quarterly* 27 (1974): 489–498.

Orvieto, Paolo. *Pulci medievale.* Rome, 1978.

Tetel, Marcel. "Pulci and Rabelais: A Revolution." *Studi francesi* 25 (1965): 89–93.

EDOARDO A. LÈBANO

PURITANISM. Few terms have been more controversial than "Puritanism," partly because "puritan" originated as a term of opprobrium in polemic debate. Its initial use apparently occurred in 1565, when the Catholic Thomas Stapleton employed it to describe his English Protestant opponents. Some scholars, including the church historian Thomas Fuller in 1655 and C. H. George in 1968, have called for the abolition of "puritan" and "Puritanism" because of wide variations in meaning. Most specialists use the terminology but are cognizant of the danger of defining "Puritanism" and then using the definition to determine which people were puritans. Historians normally examine the beliefs of individuals thought to be puritans (such as Edward Dering and Thomas Cartwright) before defining the term, but this methodology is also problematic because it begins by assuming the meaning of "puritan."

English religious groups are best understood in relationship to one another and as entities on a continuum. So conceived, Catholics are at one end of the continuum and Protestant separatists at the other, with conformists and puritans occupying the middle ground. The continuum enables us to distinguish differences within groups, such as the difference between moderate puritans, who embraced episcopalian polity, and presbyterians, who opposed it. Too often, puritans are depicted in negative terms, as opponents of perceived abuses in the Church of England, such as "popish" ceremonies and vestments. Such opposition was a manifestation of a positive religious experience rooted in a fervent quest for purity of heart, mind, and worship. Their experience typically took puritans from an early stage of anxiety about their religious state to a triumphant assurance of salvation. They concentrated on the first four of the Ten Commandments (for Roman Catholics, the first three), the commandments on obligations to God. Determined to ground their faith and practice in the Bible, they rejected anything lacking scriptural authority. Their quest to purify the church of nonessentials distinguished them from conformists.

The Sixteenth Century. The movement's roots were in Edward VI's reign (1547–1553), as reflected, for example, in John Hooper's opposition to the vestments prescribed in the Anglican Ordinal (the book of rites for the ordination of deacons, priests, and bishops) because they lacked biblical sanction. Exiles during the Catholic rule of Mary I continued the debate at Frankfurt, where John Knox and his supporters demanded further reform of the Prayer Book. The moderate Elizabethan settlement of the church did not satisfy reformist Protestants, and in 1563 Laurence Humphrey and Thomas Sampson attacked traditional ministerial dress, especially the surplice and outdoor clerical garb. When Matthew Parker, archbishop of Canterbury, failed to resolve the dispute, Elizabeth demanded conformity, thereby raising the question of how far the government could go in imposing religious views. Puritan hopes of obtaining reform through Parliament in 1566 were dashed; recent scholarship has shown that the House of Commons contained no puritan block.

The movement gained a new dimension in 1570 when Cartwright, lecturing at Cambridge, called for presbyterian polity; essentially democratic, his proposal would have abolished archbishops, bishops, and deacons. The challenge cost Cartwright his professorship. In 1571 Walter Strickland, a puritan M.P. (member of Parliament), introduced a bill to remove objectionable ceremonies from the Prayer Book, but his failure deepened the growing rift in the church. Against this background the ecclesiastical Court of High Commission ordered various young puritans, including Dering and John Field, to subscribe without qualification to the Prayer Book, the Thirty-Nine Articles, and the surplice. In 1572 Field and Thomas Wilcox submitted an *Admonition to Parliament* urging an end to episcopacy, the Prayer Book, church courts, and vestments. The radical *Admonition* split puritan ranks and incited a pamphlet war in which Cartwright and John Whitgift, bishop of Worcester, were the key protagonists.

As tensions heightened, a debate erupted over "prophesyings," which had originated in Zurich in the 1520s. Prophesyings, in which ministers and theology students met for Bible study, followed by a sermon to a partly lay audience, were popular among some conformists as well as puritans. In 1574 Elizabeth ordered their suppression at Norwich, apparently viewing them as platforms for puritans to demand reforms. After Edmund Grindal, the nearly puritan archbishop of Canterbury, refused her order to end all prophesyings in his province, she commanded the bishops to do so in 1576. (She permitted prophesyings to continue in the province of York, where educated clergy were needed to convert Catholics.) Puritan clergy responded to the attack on prophesyings by holding "exercises," in which one minister preached a sermon later discussed by other clerics. Soon referred to as "classes" (the plural of the Latin *classis,* class), these groups engaged in mutual instruction and the discussion of behavioral issues. Clergy from various classes convened as a synod at the shire level, somewhat emulating presbyterian polity.

By requiring clergy to subscribe to articles endorsing the Prayer Book in its entirety and by using the Court of High Commission to punish radical puritans, Whitgift, archbishop of Canterbury since 1583, crushed the classical movement. The puritan cause sustained further damage when a member, almost certainly the M.P. Job Throckmorton, published seven satirical attacks on conformist clergy under the pseudonym Martin Marprelate. Even Cartwright thought he had gone too far.

The Seventeenth Century. These setbacks notwithstanding, the puritans, still a potent force, outlined a reformist program in their Millenary Petition to James I shortly after he became king. He responded by convening a conference at Hampton Court (1604), in which he endorsed moderate reforms for a better-trained and better-paid clergy and a new translation of the Bible. But James never followed through, and his bishops ignored all meaningful reform except for publication of the Authorized Version of the Bible (1611).

The struggle for the established church's soul became a crisis in the 1630s when William Laud, successively bishop of London and archbishop of Canterbury, stressed liturgy rather than preaching, emphasized the English church's continuity with medieval Christendom rather than a sharp break at the Reformation, criticized the prevailing Calvinist theology, and repressed dissent. Puritan hostility to Laudianism was manifest in the Long Parliament in the early 1640s and contributed to the outbreak of civil war in 1642.

Puritan thought produced tensions because of the preeminence accorded scripture. Although separatists criticized traditional academic learning, puritans generally valued such pursuits, including the study of Hebrew, Greek, philology, and biblical exegesis. As heirs of the Calvinist tradition, puritans embraced its incorporation of one stream of humanism, and in their preoccupation with the Bible and primitive Christianity, puritans reflected their indebtedness to the Renaissance.

See also **Bible**, *subentry on* **The English Bible**; **Prayer Book, English**.

BIBLIOGRAPHY

Collinson, Patrick. *The Elizabethan Puritan Movement*. Berkeley, Calif., 1967. The standard study.

Collinson, Patrick. *The Religion of Protestants: The Church in English Society, 1559–1625*. Oxford, 1982.

Greaves, Richard L. *Society and Religion in Elizabethan England*. Minneapolis, Minn., 1981.

Lake, Peter. *Moderate Puritans and the Elizabethan Church*. Cambridge, U.K., and New York, 1982.

RICHARD L. GREAVES

QUEENS AND QUEENSHIP. Queenship is and was a less precise term than kingship, for royal women had a variety of functions. The question of whether they could or should be monarchs was a much debated issue, especially after Henry VIII divorced Catherine of Aragon in 1533 on the reasoning that their marriage was in violation of divine law or God would have blessed them with surviving male children. Only a few women actually held regal powers, but even where rules limited women's ability to inherit the throne, as in France and Aragon, the wives of monarchs still had considerable influence. Numerous regents, queen mothers, and surrogates also performed a variety of official and unofficial duties. The Renaissance is noteworthy for its exceptional number of royal women who contributed greatly to cultural and political changes in a narrow spectrum of time.

Queens Regnant. In at least three areas, women rulers had greater difficulties than their male counterparts. The first duty of every hereditary monarch was to marry and produce heirs to continue the dynasty. The queen regnant's selection of a spouse was especially controversial, for it was difficult for the members of a patriarchal society in which husbands were viewed as heads of households to distinguish between a woman's status as a private wife and as a public ruler. Some feared civil war if she married one of her subjects, and others feared an intrusion into the kingdom's diplomacy if she wed a foreigner. The political infrastructure posed other problems, for men dominated the royal bureaucracy as well as local offices. That a woman could rule through this phalanx of men was doubted, for, as the Scottish Calvinist John Knox asserted in 1558, a kingdom with a female governor was symbolically a monster with its feet where its head ought to be. Warfare created even more problems, for personal leadership on the battlefield was an essential part of the knightly culture that still extolled chivalric ideals.

Two queens regnant, Isabella of Castile (ruled 1474–1504) and Elizabeth I of England (ruled 1558–1603), responded to these difficulties in different ways. Isabella's marriage to Ferdinand II of Aragon in 1469 won acceptance because it led to the unification of their realms as the kingdom of Spain. Elizabeth lacked such a serendipitous choice. As she succeeded her half-sister Mary (ruled 1553–1558), who had wed Philip II of Spain in 1554, Elizabeth was personally aware of the discord that could result from a foreign marriage. Political divisions in her privy council over the selection of a husband prevented her from marrying; thus the succession issue remained unresolved during her reign. Her singleness did offer some advantages, for until late in life she could use her marriage as a diplomatic lever in negotiations with countries such as France. Unlike Mary, queen of Scots (ruled 1542–1568), whose husband was murdered in 1567, Elizabeth's domestic politics remained free of spousal entanglements.

As a married woman, Isabella's rule of a male-dominated system was less awkward than that of a single woman's. Her children, the crusade against the Moors in Granada, and her husband's authority in Aragon served to buttress her governance. In contrast, Elizabeth coped by presenting herself as both

Queen Elizabeth I in Coronation Robes. Anonymous portrait; c. 1559. NATIONAL PORTRAIT GALLERY, LONDON/ THE BRIDGEMAN ART LIBRARY

male and female in language and imagery. As she grew older, her subjects adopted the imagery of the Virgin Mary to honor her.

In warfare both queens assumed martial roles. Isabella accompanied the army in its campaigns to expel the Moors, and her husband's military leadership helped to soften her inability to wield the sword on the battlefield. Invoking the name of God in 1588, Elizabeth dressed in armor and gave a speech to her troops at Tilbury to inspire them to defeat the Spanish invaders.

Queens Consort. Like other wives, the prime responsibility of queens consort was to give birth to a male heir. If they failed in this duty, as did Anne Boleyn, mother of Elizabeth I, their husbands might divorce them or even have them executed. As consorts, they also had symbolic power, which was especially potent if they had been honored and blessed in a coronation ceremony. Without ruling authority, their influence depended on the survival of their male children, on the strength of their personalities, and on the status of their lineage, particularly if they hailed from foreign dynasties whose interests they could represent in their new lands.

Regents, Surrogates, Queen Mothers. Regents held somewhat limited legal authority to govern, since they acted on behalf of rulers, who were often relatives, as, for example, the regents Mary of Hungary (ruled 1531–1555), who controlled the Netherlands for her brother, Emperor Charles V, and Catherine de Médicis (1519–1589), who ruled France for her minor sons. Those with the least power were consorts, like England's Katherine Parr (1512–1548) in 1544, who served for short durations during their husbands' absences. Surrogates and queen mothers, such as Louise of Savoy (1476–1531), whose son Francis I was captured in battle in 1525, could provide much-needed stability during times of emergency. Mistresses, as, for example, Henry II of France's Diane de Poitiers (from 1547 to 1559), might also wield unofficial power by manipulating the actions of their royal lovers.

Patronage and Power. Regardless of her queenly status, a queen's position at court offered her the opportunity to patronize artists, musicians, humanists, and poets. One of the greatest patrons was Margaret of Austria, regent of the Netherlands (1507–1515; 1519–1530) for her nephew, the future emperor Charles V. She collected a fine library and supported outstanding artists and musicians. The many women who married rulers of foreign realms also could introduce political and economic connections and new cultural trends into their adopted lands.

The activities of these women established their importance as political and cultural leaders. In France, where they had helped to forge absolutism, surrogates, queen mothers, and consorts remained influential; ironically, in England, where queens regnant had made the greatest gains, the increase in parliamentary authority had led to a decrease in royal power when queens regnant once again succeeded to the throne near the end of the seventeenth century. At the close of the early modern period, the empresses Elizabeth (ruled 1741–1762) and Catherine the Great (ruled 1762–1796) wielded considerable authority in Russia, which emerged as a major European power in the eighteenth century.

See also biographies of queens mentioned in this entry.

BIBLIOGRAPHY

Levin, Carole. *"The Heart and Stomach of a King": Elizabeth I and the Politics of Sex and Power.* Philadelphia, 1994.

Liss, Peggy K. *Isabel the Queen: Life and Times.* New York, 1992.

McCartney, Elizabeth. "The King's Mother and Royal Prerogative in Early-Sixteenth-Century France." In *Medieval Queenship*. Edited by John Carmi Parsons. New York, 1993. Pages 117–141.

Parsons, John Carmi. "Family, Sex, and Power: The Rhythms of Medieval Queenship" and "Mothers, Daughters, Marriage, Power: Some Plantagenet Evidence, 1150–1500." In *Medieval Queenship*. Edited by John Carmi Parsons. New York, 1993. Pages 1–11, 63–78.

Warnicke, Retha. *The Rise and Fall of Anne Boleyn: Family Politics at the Court of Henry VIII*. Cambridge, U.K., 1989.

RETHA M. WARNICKE

QUERCIA, JACOPO DELLA. *See* **Siena,** *subentry on* **Art in Siena; Sculpture.**

QUERELLE DES FEMMES. The phrase "querelle des femmes" means the woman question and refers to the literary debate over the nature and status of women that began around 1500 and continued beyond the end of the Renaissance. The *querelle* is one topic within the broader framework of Renaissance feminism and should be understood in relation to it.

Heinrich Agrippa of Nettesheim's *Declamatio de nobilitate et praecellentia foeminei sexus* (Declamation on the nobility and preeminence of the female sex; Latin lecture 1509, publication 1529), dedicated to Margaret of Austria (daughter of the emperor Maximilian I and governor of the Netherlands), brought the woman question to center stage. Since the declamation was soon translated into English, French, German, and Italian, Agrippa's ideas were repeated endlessly by a broad spectrum of writers. Arguing that women were better off in the ancient world than since that time, he reinterpreted biblical, Greek, and Roman texts to "prove" women superior to men. Undermining a two-thousand-year-old male consensus regarding women, he reread the Bible to show, among many other things, that men and women were created equal in soul (appealing to Genesis 1 rather than Genesis 2, to which theologians had referred for centuries in arguing the inferiority and subordination of women to men) and that the New Testament makes it clear that women not only spoke (prophesied) in public but also served as church leaders.

Perhaps even more subversive was Agrippa's contention (anticipated by Mario Equicola's *De mulieribus* [On women] in 1500) that the oppression of women was based not on their (biological) nature but on social convention, thus establishing a distinction between the biologically given (sex) and the socially constructed (gender). Agrippa, however, did not advocate a social role for women. Book 3 of Baldassare Castiglione's *Il cortegiano* (1528; trans. *The Book of the Courtier*) summarized the issues in the *querelle* for a wide audience but was much less radical than Equicola or Agrippa. Castiglione neglected the public role of women (indeed, he robbed the women present of any role in the conversation itself). While acknowledging that male sovereignty places a limit on women's freedom, he never challenged the male right to this sovereignty. Much more pro-woman was Ludovico Ariosto, especially in his 1532 additions to *Orlando Furioso,* where he raised questions about whether women can be chaste (yes, cantos 4 and 5), whether women are morally inferior to men (no, cantos 27–29), and whether men have a greater potential for depravity than women (yes, cantos 42 and 43). Especially provocative was his urging women to write their own history instead of

THE
Parliament of VVomen.
With the merrie Lawes by them newly Enacted. To live in more Eaſe, Pompe, Pride, and wantonneſſe: but eſpecially that they might have ſuperiority and domineere over their husbands: with a new way found out by them to cure any old or new Cuckolds, and how both parties may recover their credit and honeſty againe

London, Printed for W.Wilſon and are to be ſold by him in Will-yard in Little Saint Bartholomewes. 1646.

Querelle des Femmes. Title page of *The Parliament of Women* (London, 1646). BY PERMISSION OF THE BRITISH LIBRARY. E1150(5)

depending on men to do it for them, an idea picked up in Italy by Luigi Dardano and in France by François de Billon and Guillaume Postel.

Discussion of the woman question in England turned initially on whether women should be rulers. Juan Luis Vives's *De institutione foeminae christianae* (1523; trans. *Instruction of a Christian Woman*), translated from Latin by Richard Hyrde in 1540 at the request of Queen Catherine for the guidance of her daughter Mary Tudor, concluded that Mary should not govern because women are weak, though Hyrde tried to put Vives's work in a more positive light. In *The Defence of Good Women* (1540) Thomas Elyot argued against Vives that women can rule as well as men, though they should do so only under special circumstances. John Knox's *First Blast of the Trumpet against the Monstrous Regiment of Women* (1558), which was written while three Catholic women governed France (Catherine de' Medici), Scotland (Mary of Guise), and England (Mary Tudor), but appeared only as the Protestant Elizabeth became queen of England, made the issue a critical one thereafter. John Aylmer's *Harborowe for Faithfull and Trewe Subjectes* (1559), written in response to Knox, contended that Elizabeth ruled by divine intervention—that is, she was an extraordinary woman, unlike other women, and so could not be used as a precedent for future practice. Edmund Spenser introduced a version of the same argument into books 3–5 of *The Faerie Queene* (1590; 1596), where Elizabeth is presented as beyond replication, her uniqueness deriving from her having been chosen by God.

Apart from the debate concerning Queen Elizabeth, a consensus was reached by the end of the sixteenth century that virtue was the same for both men and women. The question became how to make this equality real. During the seventeenth century emphasis shifted to education as the potential equalizer. Anna Maria van Schurman (1607–1678), regarded as the most learned woman of her age, wrote a tract in the form of a logical discourse *Dissertatio de ingenii muliebris ad doctrinam et meliores litteras aptitudine* (whether a Christian woman should be educated; 1638), affirming that women who have the leisure to study can be scholars, though she later abandoned the life of learning for one of religious piety. Marie de Gournay (1565–1645), who corresponded with Schurman, did not share her piety or her advocacy of limited access to education for women. In *Égalité des hommes et des femmes* (The equality of men and women; 1622) she argued for equality of mind between men and women and asserted that if women were educated as men are, they would excel to the same degree. In her later essay *Grief des dames* (The ladies' grievance; 1626) she satirized the failure of men to take women seriously and as equals in conversation. Gournay won this last argument, for in the second half of the seventeenth century social conversation between men and women was generally accepted as morally appropriate and pleasant. One of the best-known dialogues of the *querelle,* François Poulain de la Barre's *De l'égalité des deux sexes* (The equality of the two sexes; 1673), is a conversation in which women and men contribute much to the discussion.

During the same century, however, insistence on the subordination of women in marriage remained firm. Indeed, a major argument for Queen Elizabeth's single status was that as a ruler she governed all men but if she were to marry she would be subordinate (as wife) to her husband. Neither men nor women who participated in the *querelle* were able to bridge the gulf between arguments for the equality of the sexes in virtue and the subordination of women to men in the political and social (including marital) arena. The conclusions and problems of the *querelle* established the terms and arguments of the issue for the coming centuries.

See also **Feminism**; *and biographies of figures mentioned in this entry.*

BIBLIOGRAPHY

Agrippa, Heinrich. *Declamation on the Nobility and Preeminence of the Female Sex.* Translated by Albert Rabil. Chicago, 1996.

Beilin, Elaine V. *Redeeming Eve: Women Writers of the English Renaissance.* Princeton, N.J., 1987.

Benson, Pamela. *The Invention of the Renaissance Woman.* University Park, Pa., 1992.

Woodbridge, Linda. *Women and the English Renaissance: Literature and the Nature of Womankind, 1540 to 1620.* Urbana, Ill., 1984.

ALBERT RABIL

QUEVEDO, FRANCISCO DE (1580–1645), Spanish humanist and writer, active in politics during the reigns of Philip III (1598–1621) and Philip IV (1621–1665). Quevedo was born in Madrid to a family of minor gentry from the valley of Toranzo. He was raised at court, where his grandparents and parents had served the royal family. Quevedo was educated by the Jesuits, then studied at the University of Alcalá from 1596 to 1600, graduating with the degrees of bachelor and master of arts; he continued to study theology. He knew Latin, Greek and Hebrew, and he translated from French and Italian and read Portuguese.

From 1601 to 1606 Quevedo lived with the court in Valladolid, writing his first literary works and searching for social and economic advancement. Thus he dedicated his first works to the duke of Osuna, who called on Quevedo to accompany him to Italy when he became viceroy of Sicily in 1613. Quevedo remained in his service until Osuna's destitution and imprisonment in 1620, which interrupted his own ascending political career. Attempting to reposition himself within the new regime in 1621, Quevedo dedicated his *Carta de Fernando el católico* (Letter to Ferdinand the Catholic; 1621) to Baltazar de Zúñiga and the first part of *Política de Dios* (Duties of God; 1617, 1626) to the count of Olivares. In 1632 Quevedo was designated secretary to the king. However, his subsequent involvement with the duke of Medinaceli and a faction of high noblemen opposing Olivares led to his imprisonment in San Marcos de León (1639–1643). He spent his last years in La Torre and died in Villanueva de los Infantes.

Quevedo gained early recognition for his knowledge and humanistic interests and later for his neo-Stoic works. He became one of the best poets of the Spanish baroque, as well as a prolific satirist, who renovated the practice of Menippean and verse satire while casting his denunciation of vices in the context of neo-Stoic ideas. His works were written according to the aesthetics of wit, an ideal of language and style that he shaped while distancing himself from Luis de Góngora and his followers. Quevedo's influence was vast. Appreciated mostly as a satirist in the eighteenth and nineteenth centuries, his love poetry and moral poetry gained new recognition with the Generation of 1927 in Spain, especially with Jorge Luis Borges's (1899–1986) vindication of his style and erudition.

Francisco de Quevedo. Portrait by Velázquez (1599–1660). INSTITUTO DE VALENCIA DE DON JUAN, MADRID/ INDEX/THE BRIDGEMAN ART LIBRARY

Prose and Verse Satires. Quevedo became famous for his early short and comic prose satires, *Vida de la corte* (Court life) and *Cartas del Caballero de la tenaza* (The retentive knight and his epistles; 1664); *Pregmática del desengaño contra los poetas güeros, chirles y hebenes* (The lessons of experience of those dear insipid and insignificant poets) among others, was conceived as a parody of official documents. His literary satires focused on attacks against Góngora's style (*Aguja de navegar cultos* [Compass for navigating public worship; 1631]; *La culta latiniparla* [The learned latinaparla; 1629]), or against miscellanies (*Libro de todas las cosas,* [A treatise of all things whatsoever; 1626], *Perinola* [after 1633]), and against popular speech and proverbs (*Cuento de cuentos* [Teller of tales; 1626]). His *Sueños* (Visions; 1627), a cycle of Menippean prose satires written in imitation of Lucian, Erasmus, and Justus Lipsius, encompass dreams of the Last Judgment, Hell, and death, and two discourses in which the satirist condemns human folly and worldly ambition. *Discurso de todos los diablos* (Discourse of all the devils; 1627) presents, alongside moral and social types, historical characters who discuss political issues in Hell, the nature of monarchy, justice, and the perfect king. *La Fortuna con seso y la hora de todos* (Fortune in her wits, or the hour of all men; 1636) also combines social satire with a series of tableaux that enact scenes of national and international politics, within a parodic mythological framework.

Poetry and Drama. In 875 poems, 600 of which were published posthumously in 1648, Quevedo re-created meters and subgenres practiced in his time, among them two short epics, the religious

"Poema heroico a Cristo resucitado" (Heroic poem on Christ resurrected) and the parodic-satiric "Poema heroico de las necedades de Orlando el enamorado" (Heroic poem on the foolishness of Orlando the lovesick). His satirical poetry draws on Roman satire (Horace, Persius, and Juvenal) and epigram (the Greek Anthology and Martial) for his main motifs and devices. His love poetry encompasses a Petrarchan collection, *Canta sola a Lisi* (Songs for Lisi), and other poems, usually built on Neoplatonic motifs and themes. His moral poetry includes the religious collection "Heráclito cristiano" (Christian Heracleitus). Many circumstantial poems function as testimony of Quevedo's participation in court life, with descriptions of statues and houses in the tradition of Statius's poetry and epitaphs and sonnets in praise of heroes and kings. Quevedo's satirical interludes (*entremeses*) show his prodigious verbal inventiveness in his representation of comic types (*Diego Moreno, La vieja Muñatones* [The old Muñatones], and *La venta* [The sale]).

Picaresque Fiction. His narrative *Historia de la vida del Buscón* (The history of the life of a swindler), probably composed around 1605–1608, but edited and corrected for its 1626 publication, is one of three fundamental works of the genre in Spain. It presents the fictional autobiography of Pablo de Segovia—his birth, his life as a servant, and his gradual fall into delinquency, which motivates him to escape justice by traveling to America. Quevedo criticizes the idea of social ascent for his protagonist, at the same time making fun of his contemporaries and their vain hopes and superstitions.

Other Works. As a courtier, Quevedo wrote several books and pamphlets on contemporary domestic and international politics. He is best known for his treatises of political theory, *Política de Dios* (1617–1626, 1634, 1635) and *Marco Bruto* (1631, 1634), in which he developed his ideas on the ideal king and his ministers.

Quevedo translated and published Greek and Latin poetry and prose, and rendered from Hebrew the first chapter of the Lamentations attributed to Jeremiah, a work frequently set to music at that time. His philosophical works deal with stoicism and epicureanism, and he wrote several works on religious asceticism.

See also **Góngora, Luis de; Picaresque Novel; Spanish Literature and Language; Stoicism.**

BIBLIOGRAPHY

Primary Works

Quevedo, Francisco de. *The Choice Humorous and Satirical Works.* Translated into English by Sir Roger L'Estrange and John Stevens. Revised and edited by Charles Duff. Westport, Conn., 1978.

Quevedo, Francisco de. *Obra poética.* Edited by José Manuel Blecua. 4 vols. Madrid, 1969–1981.

Quevedo, Francisco de. *Obras.* Edited by A. Fernández-Guerra. 2 vols. Madrid, 1946 and 1953.

Quevedo, Francisco de. *Obras completas.* Edited and with a preliminary study and notes by Felicidad Buendía, 2 vols. in 3. Madrid, 1986.

Quevedo, Francisco de. *Política de Dios, Govierno de Cristo.* Edited by James O. Crosby. Madrid, 1966.

Quevedo, Francisco de. *Songs of Love and Death and in Between.* Edited and translated by David M. Gitlitz. Lawrence, Kans., 1980.

Quevedo, Francisco de. *Sueños y discursos.* Edited by James O. Crosby. 2 vols. Madrid, 1993.

Quevedo, Francisco de. *The Swindler.* In *Two Spanish Picaresque Novels.* Translated by Michael Alpert. Harmondsworth, N.Y., 1971.

Quevedo, Francisco de. *La vida del Buscón.* Edited by Fernando Cabo Aseguinolaza. Barcelona, Spain, 1993.

Secondary Works

Clamurro, William. *Language and Ideology in the Prose of Quevedo.* Newark, Del., 1991.

Dunn, Peter N. *Spanish Picaresque Fiction: A New Literary History.* Ithaca, N.Y., 1993.

Jauralde Pou, Pablo. *Francisco de Quevedo (1580–1645).* Madrid, 1998.

Olivares, Julián. *The Love Poetry of Francisco de Quevedo.* Cambridge, U.K., 1983.

Smith, Paul Julian. *Quevedo on Parnassus.* London, 1987.

LÍA SCHWARTZ

QUIROGA, VASCO DE (1470–1565), judge of the second Audiencia (high court) of Mexico and bishop of Michoacán (1537). Following the conquest of Mexico in 1521, the first Audiencia encouraged the cruel treatment and enslavement of the indigenous peoples. A system of government was imposed that undermined the native social system. Native men were taken to fight the wars of the colonists or to work in the mines. Quiroga and the second Audiencia arrived in Mexico in 1530 with the responsibility of ameliorating those oppressive conditions. Quiroga remarked that on his arrival he found hosts of Indians—orphaned children, women, and disabled men—looking for food left by the Spaniards' pigs and dogs.

Quiroga's reputation centers on two communities of Indians he established in Mexico City and Michoacán called pueblo-hospitals, which he hoped would become the model for civilizing and Christianizing Indian communities throughout the New World. In a letter he wrote to the Council of the Indies in August 1531, he argued that founding Indian communities in imitation of the Spanish municipal system was the most effective way to Christianize the

Indians. The ordinances he wrote for these communities show that he was inspired by the *Utopia* of the English humanist Thomas More. The Mexican scholar Silvio Zavala listed Quiroga among Spanish humanists and claimed that his pueblo-hospitals were inspired not only by More but also by Lucian's *Saturnalia,* suggesting that Quiroga's ideas anticipated the Renaissance notion of the noble savage.

The first pueblo-hospital of Santa Fe in Mexico City was founded on 14 September 1532. Built by Indian labor, the hospital of Santa Fe de Mexico provided a home for Indian children who were brought up in monasteries, functioning as a center of instruction in Christianity and a refuge for poor, sick, and orphaned Indians from other parts of Mexico. The care of the sick was its most important responsibility. In a document sent by Queen Isabella to Viceroy Antonio de Mendoza, Quiroga and his pueblo-hospitals came in for high praise and the Mexican authorities were urged to continue their support of the communities.

Quiroga established a second pueblo-hospital in Michoacán, where, because of the gold mines, the Indians suffered cruelly at the hands of the colonists and Spanish officials. In its project of bringing a more peaceful situation to Michoacán, Quiroga's Santa Fe de Michoacán complemented a Franciscan mission founded there in 1525. Quiroga was made bishop of Michoacán in 1537.

When the ordinances of the two communities were written between 1554 and 1565, it was clear that both communities were doing well. But Quiroga and his pueblo-hospitals were subjected to constant criticism from the colonists, who accused him of exploiting the Indians and reaping a huge profit from agriculture based on their labor. The divisive character of the Mexican political culture of his day accounts in large measure for these charges against Quiroga. The colonial system did not allow alternative systems such as his to thrive.

BIBLIOGRAPHY

Callens, Paul L. *Tata Vasco, un gran reformador del siglio dieciséis*. Mexico City, Mexico, 1959.

Warren, Fintan Benedict. *Vasco de Quiroga and His Pueblo-Hospitals of Santa Fe*. Washington, D.C., 1963.

Zavala, Silvio Arturo. "The American Utopia of the Sixteenth Century." *Huntington Library Quarterly* 10, no. 4 (1947): 337–347.

Zavala, Silvio Arturo. *Sir Thomas More in New Spain*. London, 1955.

DAVID M. TRABOULAY

RABBIS. Italian rabbis distinguished themselves by their great learning in all fields of classical and medieval biblical, rabbinic, and Hebrew literature, as well as in Italian and sometimes Latin, in addition to medical and scientific fields. The elite among the rabbis of Italy, aided by visiting instructors from Palestine, some of whom also spoke Hebrew and emphasized the study of early Hebrew rabbinic classics such as the Mishnah, wrote in beautiful, fluent Hebrew prose and poetry styles. By contrast, other Jewish males and virtually all Jewish females needed Judeo Italian translations of basic Jewish liturgical texts and, after whatever basic instruction they received in their youth, continued with only the limited education available as part of lectures at daily synagogue services and occasional series sponsored by various confraternities. A very few outstanding women entered this world of learning, not without rabbinic opposition, and earned the title of *rabbanit*.

Despite limitations placed by secular rulers on the dissemination of the Talmud text with the coming of the Counter-Reformation, especially at this time when the introduction of printing might have made it widely accessible (or perhaps because of that potential), rabbis nevertheless circulated tractates and made significant accomplishments in the study of the Talmud and even in Aramaic composition. In addition to writing in the usual genres of sermons, rabbinic decisions, religious polemics, letters, and commentaries on biblical and legal texts, rabbis in the Renaissance produced Hebrew works in the realms of music, dance, and theater, as well as in science, magic, and mysticism, and innovations in areas such as autobiography, New Testament studies, criticism of mystical texts, historiography, rhetoric manuals, and educational textbooks for children. Such a vast discrepancy in accomplishments between rabbis and others was due to the usual factors of cultural attitudes, economic means, individual abilities, and family aspirations, the best results often produced by private instruction at home rather than in large public classes which required truant officers armed with whips. In some families, rabbinic prominence recurred throughout the generations, often among the later-born children, as among Christians who entered the clergy; in other families, the rabbinic accomplishments of a father or mother did not necessarily inspire or financially enable all the children to pursue such a course.

The broadly based educational attainments of some rabbis, influenced in part by Italian and Latin culture, reflected the educational and cultural interactions between Jews and the society in which they lived. Indeed, the Italian institution of the Jewish ghetto may have made such intellectual as well as social closeness even easier for both Jews and Christians because the ghetto provided clear boundaries that diminished the sense of danger often inherent in situations of intimacy between members of the two groups. This intimacy occurred on a regular basis in Italy, especially between rabbis and priests.

Status and Authority of Italian Rabbis. To be a rabbi was not necessarily a profitable calling, but it was a respected and intellectually stimulating one. Rabbis as a class appear, based upon their own claims and demands, to have been entitled to privileges and prerogatives in the Jewish communities, perhaps accorded to them by some Jewish communal and Christian secular leaders out of religious respect, in part reflecting honors granted to doctors and to Catholic clergy. These roles included interpreting dreams; hearing the confession of the dying; censoring, authorizing, and condemning books; and ordaining other rabbis. The main exercise of their authority, according to the evidence of their diplomas, was to issue decisions in matters of Jewish law, supported by the theoretical traditional prerogatives to excommunicate, to fine, expel, and, in some cases, maim or kill those who did not abide by their authority in the Jewish community. This function created an impression that the Jewish community stood in a subordinate or dependent relation to its rabbis.

For the most part, however, the rabbis—lacking the necessary charismatic personalities, unrivaled authority in the Jewish community, and authorization from the Christian rulers because of the great theological difficulties connected with recognizing Jewish autonomy—held a subordinate position to lay leaders and did not function together as a cohesive body. In Italy the wealthy communal leaders, often of Iberian origin, limited the authority of the rabbis, often of Italian, French, or German origin, by imposing minimum age limits on ordinations, sometimes as high as fifty but regularly between thirty-five and forty, and controlling excommunications—a situation that reflected social, religious, economic, and ethnic tensions in the Jewish communities. Rabbis served as functionaries of the community, of societies such as confraternities, and of wealthy individuals, mainly preaching, teaching, and supervising the educational programs, while also, for lack of a full salary, keeping the record books and writing letters, usually in Hebrew. When circumstances allowed, they functioned more as lay arbitrators rather than as religious judges. To have done otherwise would have required the cooperation of all parties in the Jewish and Christian communities, a circumstance which did not occur on a regular basis, especially when those Jews whose interests were at stake chose to seek alternative venues, including Christian courts, for a more favorable decision.

Even the leading, influential rabbis of the period were often ignored, especially in their own communities, though they never stopped trying to spread their influence in other communities, often for a fee, usually in international controversies on symbolic matters, such as use of a particular ritual bath, the proper care of tephilin straps, consumption of non-Jewish wine, and a few celebrated marital controversies. But in actual practice the rabbis, squelched by outside forces and divided by internal squabbles and alliances, did not have the authority or the power to resolve many important matters satisfactorily. For example, in a limited number of rabbinic decisions they were reluctant or perhaps unable to force abusive men to divorce their wives, although a precedent for such a ruling existed in medieval Jewish sources. This precedent, however, came mainly from Islamic countries, which shows the lack of coercive powers, the inability to act in unison, and the influence of the Catholic position on the indissolubility of marriage among rabbis in Christian countries.

Rabbinic Decision Making. Italian rabbis often made their decisions in the spirit of the medieval view that later rabbinic authorities were more binding than earlier ones. This means that it cannot be taken for granted that the Bible and the Talmud were the ultimate arbiters of Jewish experience. Rather, these texts were mediated not only by (sometimes conflicting) later rabbinic views but also by each rabbi who saw his own views as potentially determinative. Such an approach to Jewish law essentially undermined any notion of an overriding precedent which must be followed. This practice reflects a principle of rabbinic Judaism that "custom takes precedence over law," a maxim that the Italian rabbis regularly drew upon to support their attempts to ratify what had become common practice among the Jews of their day. As Rabbi Azriel Diena (d. 1536) of Sabbioneta wrote in one decision, "it is necessary to know the custom of every single city, and one city cannot be judged according to the custom of surrounding countries . . . because in that state they do the opposite of what is custom in another place" (*Sheelot Uteshuvot,* no. 116). But such principles were only selectively invoked. Thus Rabbi Leon Modena of Venice (1571–1648) could both elaborate the criteria by which custom could be invoked—such as its being widespread and permanent—and elsewhere dismiss a widespread and permanent practice as "nothing but a custom."

One of the practical ramifications of rabbinic authority was that the rabbis could easily decide with partiality for various reasons, such as the connection between the rabbi and the petitioner. In one instance Modena carefully discussed the merits of a case with apparent objectivity but then concluded with the hope that since the orphans involved in the case were his relatives, everything possible would be done on their behalf. Thus ritual specifications could be adjusted in accordance with local economic and social imperatives. Rabbi Judah Minz of Padua (1408–1506) wrote,

> Thus it is that sometimes you will find a sage who forbids something contrary to his opinion for a reason or a purpose but his opinion inclines to permit it completely. Then if a question is sent to him and the person asking it is poor or if it is Friday close to the sabbath, even if he is rich, the honor of the sabbath causes him to consider him as he could consider the law for a poor person and permit him. At any rate, the custom is to say to them the reason for this is because of his poverty and for this, because of the honor of the sabbath so that they will not be surprised that sometimes he forbids and sometimes allows. (*Sheelot Uteshuvot,* no. 15)

Aware, often painfully, of this partiality, Jews—especially Jewish women, who had much reason to feel that they were not totally protected by the rabbis, who referred to their "Weakness and Imbecility" and who regularly ruled that it is the man who rules in his house—sought protection with Christian authorities, despite persistent rabbinic opposition. As amply documented in Venice, Jewish women left more testaments among Christian notaries than did Jewish men, who were probably more willing to rely upon the traditional lines of succession supported by the rabbis. Jewish testators, male and female, provide a compelling example of Jews who were willing and able to sidestep rabbinic authority in order to meet their personal needs, as the rabbis used their authority to meet their own. In this case, as also in other aspects of life, indicating the constant tensions between different groups in the community and between tradition and daily life strategies, the rabbis strove to uphold both the interests of their own class and tradition as they understood it.

BIBLIOGRAPHY

Adelman, Howard. "Rabbis and Reality: The Public Activities of Jewish Women in Italy during the Renaissance and Catholic Restoration." *Jewish History* 5, no. 1 (1991): 27–40.

Adelman, Howard. "Rabbi Leon Modena and the Christian Kabbalists." In *Renaissance Rereadings: Intertext and Context.* Edited by Maryanne C. Horowitz, Anne J. Cruz, and Wendy A. Furman. Urbana, Ill., and Chicago, 1988. Pages 271–286.

Adelman, Howard. "Wife-Beating among Early Modern Italian Jews, 1400–1700." In *Proceedings of the Eleventh World Congress of Jewish Studies.* Jerusalem, 1994. Vol. B, part 1, pp. 135–142.

Bonfil, Roberto. *Jewish Life in Renaissance Italy.* Translated by Anthony Oldcorn. Berkeley and Los Angeles, 1994.

Bonfil, Roberto. *Rabbis and Jewish Communities in Renaissance Italy.* Translated by Jonathan Chipman. London and Washington, D.C., 1993.

Rosenberg, Shalom. "Emunat Hakhamim." In *Jewish Thought in the Seventeenth Century.* Edited by Isadore Twersky and Bernard Septimus. Cambridge, Mass., 1987. Pages 285–341.

Ruderman, David B. *Kabbalah, Magic, and Science: The Cultural Universe of a Sixteenth-Century Jewish Physician.* Cambridge, Mass, 1988.

Ruderman, David B. *The World of a Renaissance Jew: The Life and Thought of Abraham ben Mordecai Farissol.* Cincinnati, Ohio, and New York, 1981.

HOWARD TZVI ADELMAN

RABELAIS, FRANÇOIS (1494?–1553), French humanist, physician, prose satirist. For a number of reasons, the life of François Rabelais does not lend itself to a simple narrative pattern. First, significant data are missing for several periods of his life. Second, from early on in his career, Rabelais moved about almost incessantly. And finally, although he is known primarily as the author of *Gargantua and Pantagruel,* he pursued a number of professional roles during his lifetime. These include Benedictine monk, humanist philologist, physician, and teacher.

Life and Career. Little is known of Rabelais's birth and early years. Some documentary evidence suggests 1483 as the year of birth, but most consider 1494 a more accurate approximation. Rabelais was the son of a well-established lawyer in the town of Chinon south of the Loire. He may have been a novice at the nearby Franciscan monastery of La Baumette as early as 1510 or 1511, where he would have received the traditional education in church Latin and scholastic disputation.

The first concrete documentary evidence of his life is a letter written by Rabelais in 1521 after he had joined the Franciscan order of the monastery at Fontenay-le-Comte. Here he belonged to a group of humanist scholars dedicated to the study of the classical languages and culture. Rabelais himself was one of a growing number of European scholars who could read Greek. In what would be the first in a lifelong series of conflicts between Rabelais and the conservative Faculty of Theology at the University of Paris, the Greek and Latin texts of Rabelais and his circle were confiscated in 1523. While the Faculty of Theology eventually returned the texts, Rabelais quickly moved on to the less restrictive Benedictine order and into the service of Abbot Geoffroy d'Estissac, later bishop of Maillezais, who would remain an important patron throughout much of his life.

In 1527 Rabelais left the Benedictine order and entered the world dressed in the habit of a secular priest. At some point in the next three years he must have spent considerable time studying medicine,

Pantagruel. Woodcut from *Pantagruel* by François Rabelais (Lyon, 1547).

perhaps at the University of Paris, since in 1530 he registered at Montpellier University and received a Bachelor of Medicine degree six weeks later. While he would practice medicine intermittently throughout the remainder of his life and even perform a public dissection of a body in 1537, Rabelais would distinguish himself in the profession through his linguistic skills. Medical school curricula relied heavily on the works of the early Greek medical writers Hippocrates and Galen. With his knowledge of Greek, Rabelais worked to produce editions of these ancient medical texts that were both accurate and free from an often overwhelming mass of scholastic commentary, following instead the humanist agenda of scholars like Budé and Erasmus, who worked with early secular and holy texts. In 1531 Rabelais lectured on Hippocrates at Montepellier citing the original Greek text, and in 1532 he published a new edition of Hippocrates's *Aphorisms*.

In that same year Rabelais published a much different and more enduring work. In *Pantagruel,* Rabelais chronicled the comic adventures of a race of giants. While it proved popular, the Paris theologians, Rabelais's lifelong nemeses, condemned the work for its indecency and anticlerical satire. In 1533 Rabelais published the first in a series of sham almanacs entitled *Pantagrueline Prognosticatio,* mockingly dedicated to "fools and idle dreamers."

Soon after this, Rabelais attached himself to one of his most important patrons, Cardinal Jean du Bellay, the bishop of Paris. But despite the support of du Bellay, Rabelais would spend the remainder of his life on the margins of political and financial stability. Having associated himself from early on with the religious and intellectual reformers, of whom Erasmus was perhaps the most notable, Rabelais would be subject both to the constant condemnations of the conservative Faculty of Theology of the University of Paris and to the political vacillations of the monarchy. It is at times difficult to distinguish between what must have been his natural proclivity for moving about with the very real need to flee the authorities. In 1534 Rabelais accompanied du Bellay to Rome as his personal physician and upon his return published *Gargantua,* the history and adventures of the father of the giant Pantagruel. Publication could not have come at a more inauspicious time. In 1534 a group of radical Protestant Reformers posted signs throughout Paris denouncing the Mass. In what became known as the Affair of the Placards, repression was swift and forceful. Booksellers and printers came under increased scrutiny and control, and those who had been openly critical of institutional practices of the church found themselves in a precarious situation.

For several years Rabelais had set aside his Benedictine habit without authorization from the church, and on a second trip to Rome he sought and received absolution for deserting his order. Freed from his monastic vows, Rabelais received upon his return an advanced medical degree from Montpellier in 1537. For the remainder of his life he would support himself in varying degrees through the practice of medicine, through patronage, and through the modest income from his popular writings. Although in 1543 *Gargantua and Pantagruel* was again condemned by the Faculty of Theology, Rabelais received in 1545 permission from the king to publish more tales of Pantagruel, and a third installment appeared the following year. After a third and final trip to Rome, Rabelais was made curate of two parishes from which he drew a modest income, finally achieving some degree of financial stability. In 1552 book 4 of *Gargantua and Pantagruel* was published, and in the following year, on a date unknown and in circumstances unclear, Rabelais died.

Gargantua and Pantagruel. Although Rabelais published a broad range of works during his career, his reputation rests on *Gargantua and Pantagruel*. The text comprises a collection of four books published separately over a twenty-year span and a fifth book published after the author's death. The order of the collection does not follow the chronology of its printing history. *Pantagruel,* which was published first in 1532, appears as the second book in the collection. *Gargantua,* or book 1, followed in 1534, book 3 in 1546, a partial edition of book 4 in 1548, and the complete book 4 in 1552. The first sixteen chapters of what is known as book 5 were published under the title *L'isle sonnante* (The ringing island) in 1562, nine years after the author's death, and the complete book 5 was published in 1564. Scholars remain divided over the authenticity of book 5. Books 1 and 2 were both published under the pseudonym Master Alcofibras, a partial anagram of the author's name. Rabelais published books 3 and 4, however, under his own name and dedicated book 3 to Margaret of Navarre, the sister of Francis I and a consistent supporter of religious reform.

Rabelais modeled *Pantagruel* on a popular collection of the fanciful tales of giants set against a background of Arthurian romance, which were called *Les grands et inestimables chroniques du géant Gargantua* (Chronicles of Gargantua). Rabelais's work was presented as a sequel to these tales, depicting the birth, education, and adventures of Pantagruel, the son of Gargantua. Two other characters play prominent roles. In *Gargantua,* Friar Jean represents a new type of monk, a worldly and dynamic one, who tills the earth and performs heroic feats against the army attacking his vineyards. In *Pantagruel,* Panurge is a comic prankster who becomes the giant's boon companion. Some scholars have argued that the birth and martial exploits of the giants in both *Pantagruel* and *Gargantua* provide an epic structure through which Rabelais asserts the values of Christian humanism and the reform movement. But Rabelais was also influenced by classical writers of what is often called Menippean satire, loosely collected parodies of intellectual, religious, and professional types. The influence of satirists like Petronius and Lucian is clearly present in what at times seems a hodgepodge of comic episodes, especially in *Pantagruel.* In book 3, published fourteen years later, Rabelais abandoned the giant motif and chronicle structure. Pantagruel and Panurge consult a series of religious seers and professional experts to determine if Panurge should run the risk of marriage. The role of Panurge shifts somewhat from that of clown to one who seeks certainty in the face of the world's mutability. Books 4 and 5 tell of the mock epic voyage of Pantagruel and Panurge to the oracle of the bottle, where they hope to discover the final answer to their question.

Rabelais wrote *Gargantua and Pantagruel* during a period of pronounced religious and intellectual turmoil. The Protestant Reformation, with its emphasis on individual faith rather than institutional worship, undermined traditional beliefs. Religious unrest and civil conflict produced royal attempts to suppress opposing views. Rabelais responded to the turmoil and the intolerance it regularly provoked with a text whose salient characteristic is to celebrate the violation of boundaries and the rejection of ideologically rigid and fixed points of view. This quality manifests itself in a number of ways. Rabelais conceals the authority of his own narrative voice behind an assortment of ironic masks. In the prologue to *Gargantua,* for instance, the narrator speaks with shifting irony, at one point presenting himself as a sage philosopher and at another as a carnival barker hustling his wares. Determining when or if the mask of the narrator comes off is one of the most difficult problems in reading *Gargantua and Pantagruel.* Moreover, on every page the richness and abundance of language spills over into excess. Rabelais draws his words from both the highest and lowest elements of his world, from the cloister to the street, and violates hierarchies of decorum by mixing them together. A call for an excess of eating and drinking complements Rabelais's excessive play of language. Rabelais celebrates the visceral energies of the body and their triumph over rational control. Laughter itself is one of these, and Rabelais incessantly mocks the seriousness of clerics, intellectuals, and ideologues of whatever variety. For instance, when an English scholar appears seeking a debate in which only hand signals may be used since words cannot penetrate the mysteries of truth, Panurge responds with a series of mostly obscene gestures to mock this learned fool.

And finally, Rabelais continually turns perspectives inside out by first offering the most serious commentary and then, sometimes in the same motion, just as quickly dismantling it. The well-known description of the Abbey of Thélème at the end of *Gargantua* provides a telling example. The abbey was built by Gargantua for Friar Jean, in recognition of his role in the wars against Picrochole. It has no walls and no regulations. In this most ideal environment, freedom and faith naturally lead to a spirit of community. But one is left wondering if the abbey represents the values of Christian humanism and a more biblically oriented Christianity or is simply a utopian fantasy of good taste and refined epicureanism. A prophetic riddle is discovered during the digging of the foundations of the abbey, which confirms this interpretive confusion. Gargantua reads the riddle as a revelation of Christian truth. Friar Jean, however, sees merely the thinly veiled rules for the game of tennis. Rabelais reverses this process in the episode of Judge Bridoye in book 3. At first Rabelais seemingly mocks this incompetent legal authority who makes decisions by rolling dice and then backs them up with legal jargon. But then Pantagruel praises Bridoye and acknowledges some influence of divine providence in the simplicity of his decisions. This play of interpretive perspectives and the concurrent exuberance and excess of the text itself reflect the fundamental comic spirit of *Gargantua and Pantagruel*. In Rabelais's world life cannot be contained by any single intellectual or religious perspective.

Although the Paris theologians routinely condemned *Gargantua and Pantagruel,* the work was an immediate popular success. Its influence is surely present in a range of subsequent works, perhaps most clearly in Cervantes's *Don Quixote,* Laurence Sterne's *Tristram Shandy,* and James Joyce's *Ulysses*. And while the text may currently be read more by academics than by the general reading public, the adjective Rabelaisian, used to describe a text marked by the characteristics of extravagant and coarse humor, has entered the English lexicon.

See also **Satire Ménippée**.

BIBLIOGRAPHY

Primary Works

Rabelais, François. *The Complete Works*. Translated by Donald M. Frame with an introduction by Raymond C. La Charite. Berkeley, Calif., 1991. Includes notes and a helpful glossary of people and places.

Rabelais, François. *The Histories of Gargantua and Pantagruel*. Translated by J. M. Cohen. Harmondsworth, U.K., 1955.

Secondary Works

Auerbach, Erich. *Mimesis: The Representation of Reality in Western Literature*. Translated by Willard Trask. Princeton, N. J., 1953. See chapter 11, "The World in Pantagruel's Mouth," pp. 262–284. Investigates Rabelais's playful manipulation of perceptions of reality.

Bakhtin, Mikhail. *Rabelais and His World*. Translated by Helene Iswolsky. Bloomington, Ind., 1984. Translation of *Tvorchestvo Fransua Rable* (1965). Important study of folk culture in the Middle Ages and Renaissance and its influence on Rabelais.

Bowen, Barbara C. *Enter Rabelais, Laughing*. Nashville and London, 1998.

Duval, Edwin M. *The Design of Rabelais's* Pantagruel. New Haven, Conn.,1991.

Febvre, Lucien. *The Problem of Unbelief in the Sixteenth Century: The Religion of Rabelais*. Translated by Beatrice Gottlieb. Cambridge, Mass., 1982. Translation of *Le problème de l'incroyance au seizième siècle: La religion de Rabelais* (1942). A seminal work refuting claims of Rabelais's atheism and placing his beliefs in the context of sixteenth-century religious thought.

Greene, Thomas M. *Rabelais: A Study in Comic Courage*. Englewood Cliffs, N.J., 1970. The best introduction to Rabelais and his work.

Plattard, Jean. *The Life of François Rabelais*. Translated by Louis P. Roche. London, 1930. Translation of *Vie de François Rabelais* (1928). The standard biography.

Screech, M. A. *Rabelais*. Ithaca, N.Y., 1979. A thorough and informative book-by-book study of *Gargantua and Pantagruel*.

DOUGLAS MCFARLAND

RAGUSA, REPUBLIC OF. *See* **Dubrovnik.**

RAIMONDI, MARCANTONIO. *See* **Raphael; Printmaking.**

RALEGH, WALTER (also Raleigh; 1554?–1618), English courtier, soldier, seaman, explorer, colonizer, poet, historian. Born in Devonshire, where both his father's and mother's families had seafaring connections, Walter Ralegh was educated at Oriel College, Oxford, and in London at the Middle Temple. He saw early military service in France and Ireland, where he participated in the Smerwick Mas-

Walter Ralegh and His Eldest Son, Walter. Anonymous portrait. NATIONAL PORTRAIT GALLERY, LONDON/SUPERSTOCK

sacre (1580), in which six hundred Spanish mercenaries on the side of the Irish were killed. His first seagoing venture was as captain of a ship in his half brother Sir Humphrey Gilbert's unsuccessful 1578 expedition intended for the coast of North America.

From 1581, when he caught the attention of Queen Elizabeth I, Ralegh's fortunes were determined by royal power. In the course of a very few years, he was knighted; granted large estates in Ireland and the west of England; made warden of the Cornish tin mines, lord lieutenant of Cornwall, and captain of the guard; and given two lucrative monopolies. But this sudden eminence was perilously subject to envy and to the fickleness of favor. Rivalry with the queen's new favorite, the young earl of Essex, sent Ralegh back to Ireland in 1589, a secret marriage, perhaps as early as 1588, to Elizabeth Throckmorton, a privy chamber attendant of the queen, landed him and his wife in the Tower when it came to light in 1592. He recovered from this fall, but shortly after James became king Ralegh was arrested and charged with treason. The king commuted the resulting death sentence to imprisonment, and Ralegh spent the next thirteen years in the Tower. He was released in 1616 to undertake an expedition to Guyana, but that expedition offended the Spanish and brought home no riches, so Ralegh was arrested and, on 29 October 1618, was executed in accordance with the original sentence for treason.

Hated in prosperity and loved in disgrace, Ralegh became a hero to anti-Spanish militants in England and on the Continent, as well as to English republicans of the mid-seventeenth century. As patron of and eventual participant in expeditions to Newfoundland, Virginia (where he sponsored the earliest attempts at settlement), and Guyana, Ralegh was also the Englishman most identified with the New World. Though none of his American enterprises succeeded, they prepared the way for successes that followed, and Ralegh is credited with bringing tobacco to England and the potato to Ireland and with fostering influential publications on overseas expansion by Richard Hakluyt, Theodore de Bry, and Thomas Hariot.

As a poet, Ralegh is known for the melancholy wit of such lyrics as "Farewell False Love," "The Nymph's Reply to the Shepherd," and "On the Life of Man," and for the plaintive extravagance of "The Ocean to Cynthia." His place in the history of English poetry has also been secured by his friendship with Edmund Spenser, memorialized in Spenser's *Colin Clout's Come Home Again*. In prose, Ralegh celebrated the suicidal bravery of his kinsman Sir Richard Grenville in his "Report of the Truth of the Fight about the Isles of Açores" (1591) and defended his own Guyana enterprise with the brilliantly unconvincing *Discoverie of . . . Guiana* (1596). During his many years in prison, he wrote treatises on ships, politics, war, and religion as well as his massive, though unfinished, *History of the World* (1614), a frequently reprinted work into which he poured his reflections on human power and divine providence.

BIBLIOGRAPHY

Greenblatt, Stephen J. *Sir Walter Ralegh: The Renaissance Man and His Roles*. New Haven, Conn., 1973.

May, Steven W. *Sir Walter Ralegh*. Boston, 1989

RICHARD HELGERSON

RAMUS, PETRUS (1515–1572), French philosopher, humanist educator, orator. Petrus Ramus was a controversial figure in sixteenth-century France. Attacking the educational establishment of his day, he used the lecture hall and the printing press to challenge the authority of Aristotle, disparage Cicero and Quintilian, the idols of earlier humanists, and advance his own reformulation of the arts and sciences. Ramus sought to reform the teaching of grammar, logic, and rhetoric, add physics to the liberal arts, increase appreciation for mathematics, and reconstruct the entire university curriculum. He argued with great passion that all knowledge was available to anyone willing to use the right method to discover it in his native language. He claimed that one method sufficed for all the arts and sciences, his new dialectics, which in reality carried further the simplification of Aristotle's dialectics begun by Rudolf Agricola (1443 or 1444–1485) fifty years earlier.

Career and Works. Ramus was born of a poor farming family at Cuts in the province of Picardy. Baptized Pierre de La Ramée, he later latinized his name to Petrus Ramus. He went to Paris in 1523, where he worked his way through school as a valet for richer students, entering the Collège de Navarre in 1527. His classmates included Charles de Bourbon, the future cardinal and archbishop of Rouen, and Charles de Guise, later the cardinal of Lorraine and Guise and his patron. Ramus completed his M.A. in 1536, arguing in his master's disputation that all that Aristotle wrote is inconsistent and contrived. Beginning his teaching career in Paris at the Collège du Mans the following year, he achieved notoriety by continuing to challenge the authority of Aristotle, whose logic had been predominant since the first curriculum created at the University of Paris in 1215.

Called by some contemporaries one of the greatest orators since Cicero, he filled lecture theaters, making his impact publicly decisive.

After teaching at the Collège du Mans, Ramus taught at the Collège de l'Ave Maria. He worked feverishly, seldom sleeping more than three hours a night. The result was the publication of his two defining, major works in 1543: *Dialecticae institutiones* (Training in dialectic) and *Aristotelicae animadversiones* (Remarks on Aristotle). These works infuriated many of his colleagues because of the virulent language he used in his criticism of ancient and modern Peripatetics and, even more importantly, because of his plan to change the courses and texts of the curriculum. In 1544, at the urging of his detractors, a royal commission composed of university faculty was established to hear a debate between the defender of tradition Antonio de Gouveia (c. 1505–1566?) and Ramus. After two days of disputation Ramus failed to win the field and was subsequently banned from teaching dialectics and philosophy on the command of King Francis I. A year later, however, Charles de Guise, the cardinal of Lorraine, succeeded in having him appointed principal of the Collège de Presles. His fortunes improved even more in 1547 with the accession of Henry II, who lifted the ban against him.

Ramus next confronted the other two ancient authorities revered by the establishment, Cicero and Quintilian. In 1547 he published *Brutinae quaestiones in Oratorem Ciceronis* (Questions of Brutus against Cicero's *Orator*), a critique of Cicero's *Orator,* wherein Cicero describes what he considers the best oratorical style in response to Brutus's queries. Ramus claims that Cicero does not understand true oratory at all. Taking on the person of Brutus, he proceeds to address Cicero in a supercilious manner, showing him to be confused and disorganized. This work was followed by an attack on Quintilian titled *Rhetoricae distinctiones in Quintilianum* (Arguments in rhetoric against Quintilian), which was published in 1549 along with a revised edition of *Brutinae quaestiones in* Oratorem *Ciceronis.*

Ramus embarked on an extraordinary career over the next twenty years. In 1551 he was appointed royal lecturer at the Collège de France, a platform he used for continuing attacks on Aristotelians. In 1561 he converted to the Protestant faith. His conversion caused him to break with his longtime patron, Charles de Guise, the cardinal of Lorraine. Armed with a new religion, he produced a plan for the reform of the University of Paris in 1562. This included firing professors, abolishing student fees, adding

Petrus Ramus. Portrait from *Testamentum Petri Rami* (Paris, 1576).

physics to the arts curriculum and clinical practice to the medical curriculum, adding the Old Testament in Hebrew and the New Testament in Greek to theology, and creating chairs of mathematics (which he later endowed from his own estate), anatomy, botany, and pharmacy. His plan, however, was short-lived. The Wars of Religion began that year, and he withdrew to Fontainebleau with the king's protection.

Ramus returned to Paris in 1563 and again in 1568, when he found his library ransacked. But during these war years he completed *Scholae in liberales artes* (Lectures on the liberal arts; 1569). The religious wars forced him to be on the move between France, Germany, and Switzerland. Returning to the Collège de Presles in 1570, he was condemned in 1572 by the Synod of Nîmes for advocating secular views of church government. He was murdered in his rooms on 26 August 1572 in the midst of the Saint Bartholomew's Day massacre, killed by assassins allegedly hired by his longtime academic adversary Jacques Charpentier, the new protégé of the cardinal of Lorraine.

Logic and Rhetoric. Aristotelian logic taught students at late medieval and Renaissance universities to find demonstrative truth or error in reasoning. Having learned the rules and forms of presentation and argument, the student used them when expressing the results of his research in other disciplines, especially philosophy. The study of rhetoric, by contrast, was less important in the university. But among humanist scholars, rhetoric attained the prominence it once had among the Romans. Cicero's and Quintilian's ideal orator, who felt it incumbent upon him to supply political leadership, was again embraced by civic leaders, such as the Florentine chancellors Coluccio Salutati and Leonardo Bruni, and Lorenzo Valla. A vogue of Ciceronianism, in which the language and style of Cicero were extolled and emulated, reached its height in the generation before Ramus. The cult was severely attacked by Desiderius Erasmus, and Ramus, as we have seen, soon took up the cudgel.

In the early Renaissance rhetoric was considered to consist of five parts: invention, arrangement, style, memory, and delivery. But style most often claimed the largest part of the exposition of the art, with invention a close second. Invention belonged, however, not only to rhetoric but also to dialectic, considered by late medieval scholars the essential art for investigating serious questions in the natural sciences, moral philosophy, and theology.

It is not surprising that Renaissance pedagogues, tired of the tedious exercises in dialectic and its abstruse applications, wished to reform the art. They recognized that dialectic as an art contained a fruitful technique for investigation, the system of the topics, but they saw no need to teach a derivative method in the art of rhetoric. The same method could be applied to both the abstract questions of philosophy and the practical ones of rhetoric, they reasoned. First, Valla sought to revise dialectics and its underpinnings in Aristotle's *Categories*. He was followed by Agricola. The new logic was derived, they said, from a knowledge of things obtained through personal observation. Developed by Agricola and embraced later by Juan Luis Vives (1492–1540), the first part of this "natural" logic was still invention or discovery, with a revised list of topics that would enable the inquiring mind to argue the question raised; the second part was judgment, which would aid in deploying these arguments correctly to resolve the question definitively. These concepts were well in place by the 1540s.

Ramus's Method. Ramus followed in the footsteps of these authors. His work on a method of dialectics was inspired and facilitated by Johann Sturm, who introduced Valla's and Agricola's works while teaching in Paris. Ramus owed his greatest debt to Agricola, who based his treatment of dialectics on Aristotle but did not disparage him, even as he modified his teachings. Ramus aimed to create a single method with easily memorized rules from which one could learn the common form and matter of any subject. Since traditional logic used several methods at different times for different subjects, his new logic would dispose of both the existing course structure and its textbooks for logic and rhetoric. Ramus stated also that his method served two purposes, teaching and prudence, which correspond broadly to Aristotle's doctrine (*docens*) and practice (*utens*).

Dialectics for Ramus is the method of discoursing well. Its two parts are invention and judgment. Following Aristotle, Cicero, and Agricola, Ramus conceived of invention as a means of resolving questions by searching for a middle term to join or dissociate subject and predicate. The means of finding the middle term is in the system of the topics. A student would be expected to run through his list of fourteen possible arguments to solve the problem proposed. Ramus's list includes five "first arguments"—causes, effects, subjects, adjuncts, and opposites—and nine "derived arguments": genus, form, name, notations, conjugates, testimonies, contraries, distributions, and definitions.

Judgment next assembles the arguments and orders them. The rhetorical term "arrangement" soon replaces judgment in Ramus's method. This consists of three steps. First, arguments are organized as to reasoning, being syllogisms (including induction), enthymemes, or examples. The second step is a lengthier sequence of arguments that employs definition and division. And the third step, oddly enough, is religion, which, in Ramus's 1543 *Dialecticae institutiones* (Training in dialectic), is assent to God. Thus for him the mind moves upward from grammar, to rhetoric, to dialectic, which comprises all subjects, and thence to their origin in the mind of God. In later revisions of the subject, the third step disappears. By 1569 Ramus had reduced his entire method to three laws: the law of universal application, or the law of truth; the law of essential application, or the law of justice; and the law of total application, or the law of wisdom.

Ramus's preoccupation with method, the second law of which prohibits redundancy, ordained his revision of the art of rhetoric. Having given to dialectics invention, arrangement, and memory, Ramus left only style and delivery to rhetoric. Although the trea-

P. RAMI DIALECTICA.

TABVLA GENERALIS.

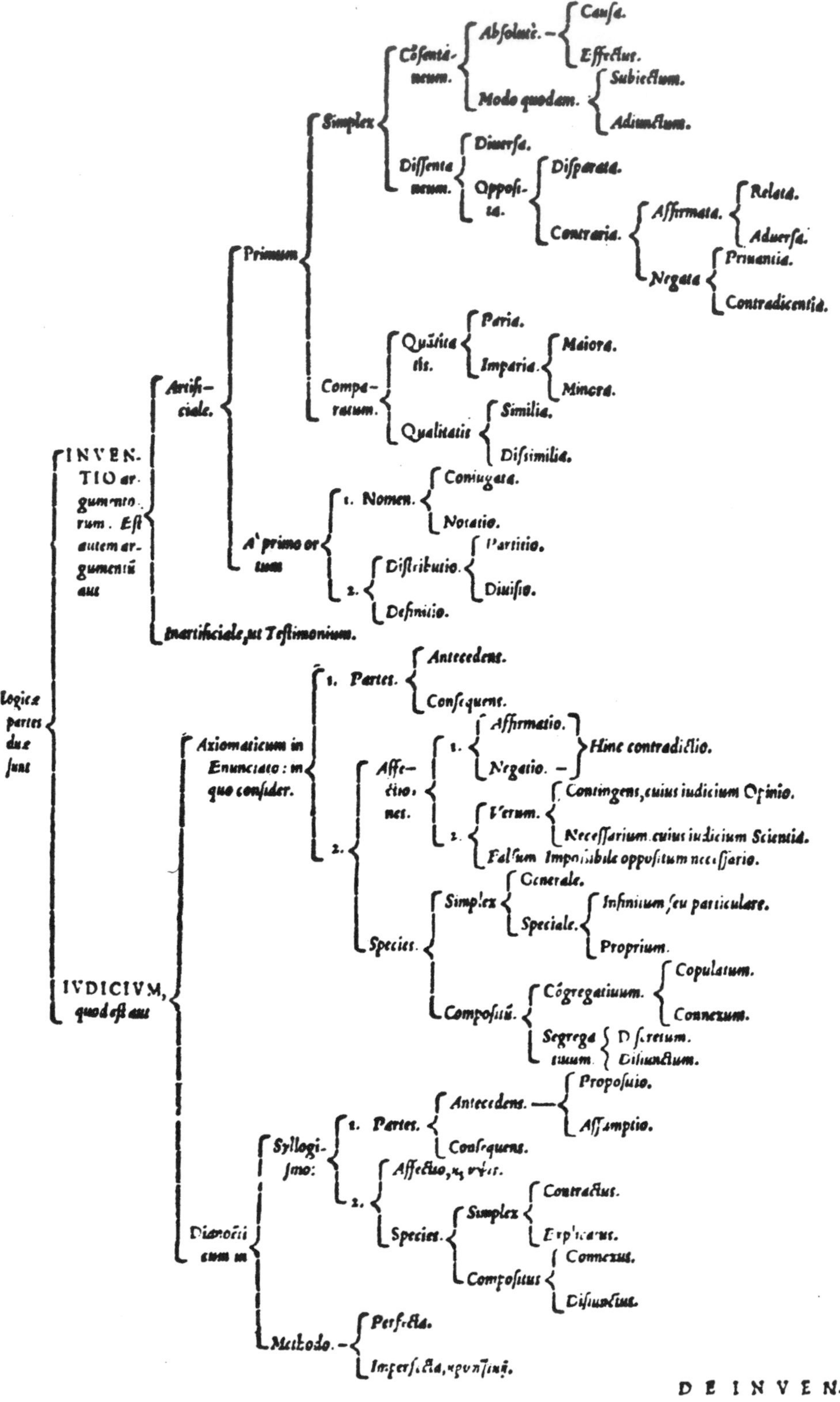

Ramus's Dialectic. General table showing Ramus's division and subdivision of dialectic from his *Scholae in liberales artes,* published under the title *Professio regia* (1576).

tise *Audomari talaei rhetorica* (Training in oratory; 1545) bears the name of Omer Talon (c. 1510–1562) as its author, it was undoubtedly written under Ramus's direction. Talon's name appears on other works written when Ramus was forbidden to write on or teach philosophy. The Talon-Ramus work defines rhetoric or eloquence as "the power of expressing oneself well" (Ong 1983, p. 271). Ironically, the content is based closely on Quintilian. The treatise has three parts: nature, art, and exercise, conceived as successive stages to eloquence. The first part of the work, devoted to *elocutio,* or style, treats of tropes and figures, while the second part addresses delivery, dividing it into voice and gesture. The last part drops out in the later *Rhetoric.*

Ramus's single method was viewed as a threat to the educational establishment. He further angered many of his contemporaries by stating that once one found the first principles of method and stripped away the ancient and medieval commentaries, one achieved "the truth." He established himself, with his group at Presles, as the representative of the new logic and rhetoric. Observing artisans first in Paris and then in Germany, where the wealth of independent cities cultivated the mechanical arts, he saw a connection between mechanical and philosophical theory and practical problem solving that gave focus to his ideas and contributed to the scientific revolution and empiricism.

Ramus's success was due largely to his being an educationalist who placed primary emphasis on the classroom. While much of his work can be seen as simplistic and derivative, his textbooks were a great printing and teaching success. He helped to transform humanism into the humanities. He advertised his classes not for philosophers but for young men who wanted success in the real world of commerce, government, and the professions. He trained them in orderly thought, showed them how his method fit the texts, how his method could resolve the problem, and how to cross-check the texts to prove that his method brought an unimpeachable conclusion. Once they abandoned the "stultifying errors" and "wretched confusions" of "the race of Aristotelians," children could learn to write and speak clearly, adults to interpret art, poetry, music, theology, government, law, and politics, and scholars to discover the boundaries of the liberal arts and sciences.

Publications and Influence. Ramus published more than fifty works in Latin and French in his lifetime, many of which were also abridged, anthologized, translated, and re-edited. A large number of unpublished works were looted from his study after his death. There were more than two hundred editions of his *Dialecticae institutiones* alone in the sixteenth century in six languages and numerous versions. Much of his work, however, proved inseparable from that of Talon, since it is often impossible to determine who wrote what. In addition, he was always rewriting his books, changing the phraseology and vocabulary. By 1650 there were more than eleven hundred printings of his works in Europe and hundreds of authors who wrote about him. The works of Ramus and Talon, along with their team members, adversaries, and supporters, spread to Germany, Switzerland, Denmark, Poland, the Low Countries, Scotland, and England by the early seventeenth century and from there to New England, where Ramus's logic may have been as influential as the theology of John Calvin.

The evidence from booksellers' catalogs demonstrates that the new logic and rhetoric were entrenched in Paris by the 1560s, with Philipp Melanchthon (1497–1560), Agricola, and Ramus the predominant writers. The formative years were the 1530s and 1540s, both before and during Ramus's apprenticeship as a young developing scholar. In this era the new logic and rhetoric were spreading throughout Europe, particularly northern Europe and the Protestant countries. Ramism was attractive chiefly to practicing orators, lawyers, and teachers. But the influence varied by academic level as well as by region. In central Europe the influence was strongest in primary and secondary schools (Freedman), where the work of Sturm was influential. In England it was strongest in the universities and among major writers such as Francis Bacon.

The English variety has been studied extensively. The pioneers Agricola and Melanchthon captured the attention of John Seton (1498?–1567), who incorporated their teachings in his lectures on dialectics at Cambridge in the 1540s. A Catholic, Seton was imprisoned in 1561, fled England, and died in Rome. But his lectures, which were published in 1572, became a major textbook into the 1600s. Seton was succeeded in 1568 as lecturer in dialectics at Cambridge by Laurence Chaderton (1546–1640) of Christ's College, who established Ramus in England. The works of Ramus were soon in rich supply. Gabriel Harvey (1545?–?1630) wrote the most influential Ramist works, *Rhetoric* (1575) and *Ciceronianus* (1577), which first were delivered as lectures at Cambridge. The lectures were later published as *Gabrielis Harveii rhetor* (Gabriel Harvey on rhetoric, 1577). Harvey's pupils Dudley Fenner (1558?–1587) and

Abraham Fraunce (fl. 1587–1633) went on to publicize the Ramist program. Walter Ong sees the influence of Ramus as predominant from the 1570s to the 1620s. The reaction against Ramus continued long after his initial outburst in Paris in the 1540s. Italian rhetorics often ignore him, while noting the innovations of Agricola and Melanchthon.

At the end of the twentieth century the influence of Ramus and his new logic and rhetoric was still a subject of debate (see the lists in Ong, *Inventory,* and the catalog of participants in Sharratt). This continuing debate was due to the difficulty of knowing who is responsible for much of the work: Ramus, his team, their predecessors, or their successors. In some subject areas, such as the sciences, the influence of Ramus and his team has been claimed for various classificatory schemes. Such claims are difficult to document. There can be no doubt that Ramus sought to retrieve arithmetic, geometry, physics, and astronomy from the neglect into which they had fallen in his day. As to his knowledge of science, he rejected Aristotle's *Physics,* the seedbed from which most of modern science sprang, without giving evidence of understanding its teachings. He was attracted to astronomy but undoubtedly was perplexed by the Ptolemaic and Copernican systems because of their use of hypotheses. His preference would have been a return to the astronomy of the Babylonians and the Egyptians and to build an astronomy simply on the observed regularities of the heavens. His successors, however, took his ideas in new directions. The first technical college in Europe, Gresham College, London, was founded by Ramists in 1597.

In other areas, such as law and theology, influences have been diffused by politics and religion. For example, Ramists tended to promote meritocracy rather than hereditary privilege, causing their method to be promoted by a Calvinist theologian such as William Perkins, and a Puritan poet like John Milton, while opposed by a royalist political theorist such as Thomas Hobbes. Ramus worked in an environment that was rich in changing philosophical traditions. His legacy is that he took the initiative to use them to make an impact on the intellectual, spiritual, and material worlds.

See also **Logic**; **Rhetoric**; **Scientific Method**.

BIBLIOGRAPHY

Primary Works

Ramus, Petrus. *Arguments in Rhetoric against Quintilian: Translation and Text of Peter Ramus's* Rhetoricae distinctiones in Quintilianum (1549). Translated by Carole Newlands. Edited by James J. Murphy. De Kalb, Ill., 1986.

Ramus, Petrus. *The Latin Grammar of P. Ramvs Translated into English*. Menston, U.K., 1971. Reprint of the 1585 translation of *Rudimenta grammaticae latinae* (1560).

Ramus, Petrus. *The Logike of the Moste Excellent Philosopher P. Ramus, Martyr.* Translated by Roland MacIlmaine (1574). Edited by Catherine M. Dunn. Northridge, Calif., 1969.

Secondary Works

Freedman, Joseph S. "The Diffusion of the Writings of Petrus Ramus in Central Europe, c. 1570–c. 1630." *Renaissance Quarterly* 46 (spring 1993): 98–152.

Grafton, Anthony, and Lisa Jardine. *From Humanism to the Humanities: Education and the Liberal Arts in Fifteenth- and Sixteenth-Century Europe.* London, 1986. The best modern work on dialectics and its context.

Howell, Wilbur S. *Logic and Rhetoric in England, 1500–1700.* Princeton, N.J., 1956. Reprint, New York, 1961. The most lucid description of his logic and rhetoric and their history in England.

Mack, Peter. *Renaissance Argument: Valla and Agricola in the Traditions of Rhetoric and Dialectic.* Leiden, Holland, 1993. Includes much material on Ramus.

Mahoney, Michael S. "Ramus, Peter." In *Dictionary of Scientific Biography.* Vol. 11. Edited by Charles Coulston Gillispie. New York, 1975. Pages 286–290. Good on Ramus's relation to modern science.

Miller, Perry. *The New England Mind: The Seventeenth Century.* New York, 1939. The classic study of Ramus's influence on northern American colonial society.

Nelson, Norman E. *Peter Ramus and the Confusion of Logic, Rhetoric, and Poetry.* Ann Arbor, Mich., 1947. Critical of Ramus and his purported influence.

Ong, Walter, J., S.J. *Ramus and Talon Inventory: A Short-Title Inventory of the Published Works of Peter Ramus (1515–1572) and of Omer Talon (ca. 1510–1562) in Their Original and in Their Variously Altered Forms with Related Material.* Cambridge, Mass., 1958. Reprint, Folcroft, Pa., 1969. The definitive list of the group's publications.

Ong, Walter J., S.J. *Ramus, Method, and the Decay of Dialogue: From the Art of Discourse to the Art of Reason.* Cambridge, Mass., 1958. Reprint, Cambridge, Mass., 1983. The most complete study of his work.

Sharratt, Peter. "Nicolaus Nancelius, *Petri Rami vita.* Edited with an English Translation." *Humanistica Lovaniensia: Journal of Neo-Latin Studies* 24 (1975): 161–277.

LOUIS A. KNAFLA with JEAN DIETZ MOSS

RAMUSIO, GIOVANNI BATTISTA (1485–1557), Italian geographer and humanist. Born in Treviso to an aristocratic family new to the Venetian mainland, Ramusio studied in Padua with Pietro Pomponazzi, a renowned philosopher. An expert in classical and modern languages, he was chosen as secretary to the Senate in 1515; in 1533 he was named to the Council of Ten and served the republic in various diplomatic missions to France, Rome, and Switzerland. Despite demanding political tasks, Ramusio lived the life of a literary gentleman and corresponded with the most learned individuals of his time, poets, physicians, and navigators.

Ramusio spent his final years in his villa near Padua, laboring on an enormous collection of travel reports, verifying the new routes opened by the Portuguese to the Indian Ocean, which were causing an irreversible decline in Venice's profitable spice trade. Two volumes of his *Delle navigationi et viaggi* (On navigations and travels), containing ancient travel accounts of Africa, the Portuguese discoveries, and voyages to the New World, were published, without the author's name, by Tommaso Giunti in Venice—volume 1 in 1550 and volume 3 in 1556. Volume 2, containing accounts of European and Middle Eastern journeys, appeared posthumously, under its author's name, in 1559. Numerous editions of the *Navigationi* were published in the sixteenth and seventeenth centuries.

Ramusio's work remains the first well-researched and critically accurate collection of travel accounts of the Renaissance. It is a vast compilation of previously published reports and newly found records, collected through a network of devoted informers. The goal of Ramusio's editorship, as he stated in his preface addressed to Girolamo Fracastoro, an eminent fellow scientist, was not only to improve upon Ptolemy's *Geographike hyphegesis* (Geography), but also to provide a wider readership. To these ends, he used Italian in the *Navigationi* and provided a much needed objective description of the world.

BIBLIOGRAPHY

Primary Work

Ramusio, Giovanni Battista. *Navigationi et viaggi*. 6 vols. Edited by Marica Milanesi. Turin, Italy, 1978–1983.

Secondary Work

Parks, George B. "The Contents and Sources of Ramusio's *Navigationi*." *Bulletin of the New York Public Library* 59 (1955): 279–313.

LUIGI MONGA

RAPE. Historians must confess uncertainty concerning the definition, incidence, circumstances, and motivation of rape in the Renaissance. Criminal documents are the best source for learning about rape (though other documents, such as women's diaries and treatises of various kinds on women's role in society, serve a corroborative function), but these only deliver information about reported incidents, which, as Elena Fasano Guarini has stated about Renaissance Florence, does not reflect the total occurrence of rape. Criminal documents filter truth through a glass darkly; it was the word of the man against that of the woman (or young boy, young males being the subjects of homosexual rape) unless there was a confession.

To jurists and lawmakers of the Renaissance the very definition of rape was something of a mystery. In Italy, for example, two Latin words could describe the crime: *raptus,* which implied the element of abduction; and *stupro,* which meant sexual violence. Thus a rape need not include a forced sexual act, according to the law. In practice, criminal prosecutions of rape always included at least the allegation of actual or attempted sexual violence. As was always the case with law in the medieval and Renaissance periods, punishments were calibrated to the seriousness of the crime, which was established by considering the social station of the victim and of the perpetrator, the time and place of the crime, and so on. Further considerations pertained to the use of force and/or weapons; likewise, the resistance shown or alleged by the female victim (claimed or demonstrated resistance does not seem to have been an issue in homosexual rape) was of crucial importance to the believability of the woman's story. Punishments varied from a medieval reliance on money payments, and perhaps a forced marriage to the rapist, to capital penalties that were very infrequently executed. In Florence in 1558, under the reign of Cosimo I Medici, a reformed statute was decreed stating the extreme gravity of the crime and equalizing the treatment of all those guilty of sexual violence, regardless of social status. It is not known whether punishments were actually executed in the evenhanded way announced by the new law.

Insofar as anything can be concluded concerning the incidence of rape, late twentieth-century research indicated that it formed only a minor fraction of all crimes. This conclusion may be the result of rape being underreported or of Renaissance society continuing the medieval practice of resolving these affairs privately between the families of the perpetrator and victim.

It is all but impossible to compose other than a sketchy profile of victim and perpetrator. Some preliminary indications point to victims being primarily young unmarried women and girls, though married women could also be victimized by rape (in rural areas in pursuit of a vendetta, for instance). Men, young and mature, were the perpetrators, singly or, in the cities, in groups. The places of attack varied from the open countryside to city streets or homes from which male protectors were absent. Victim and perpetrator were seldom completely unknown to each other, which raises the issue of motivation.

The question of motivation gives rape its historical interest. Some feminists in the second half of the twentieth century and some psychologists—for example, Susan Brownmiller and Sigmund Freud, respectively—argue that men are naturally disposed to actual or potential rape and, according to Freud, that women desire to be raped on some mental level. If these conclusions were true, then rape would be an ahistorical occurrence that could only be dealt with ultimately through the complete separation of men and women. Other researchers, including anthropologists and historians (Roy Porter, for example), have established that rape is historical, that it changes through time and in different societies in the same time.

According to some who wrote concerning the motivation for rape in the Renaissance and late medieval period, such as the thirteenth-century Italian judge Albertus of Brescia, a man might be led to attack the wife and daughter of his enemy due to a lack of self-control, to lust and cupidity. Similarly, in England rape was an expression of men's "lustfull Desires and pleasures," writes Garthine Walker, quoting a seventeenth-century jurist. This is the conclusion one would expect from men of the law writing in a strongly Christian context. But Walker cites a case which suggests that violence and control were more the issue for men: Francis Baker "forcibly and violently threw me [Jane Bingley] downe on the ground there and did hould both my hands in one of his hands, and lay upon my body, and had Carnal knowledge of my body against my will." This is a typical example of rape committed in a rural setting; rape in the urban arena was a group activity. In fact, most known cases of rape in Florence during the late Renaissance involved groups of men violating a woman who had no man about to protect her. These men were performing for the benefit of the group, demonstrating their manhood through violence and sex; rape was more a spectacle in the city than it was in the countryside. At the Renaissance court one might say with Edwin Mullins that rape was depicted as sport in painting. There were many examples drawn from myth, such as *The Rape of the Sabine Women,* painted by numerous artists, and *Rape of the Daughters of Leucippus,* one of Peter Paul Rubens's best-known paintings.

See also **Violence**.

BIBLIOGRAPHY

Brackett, John. *Criminal Justice and Crime in Late Renaissance Florence, 1537–1609.* New York, 1992.

Chaytor, Miranda. "Husband(ry): Narratives of Rape in the Seventeenth Century." *Gender and History* 7, no. 3 (November 1995): 378–407.

Dean, Trevor, and K. J. P. Lowe, eds. *Crime, Society, and the Law in Renaissance Italy.* Cambridge, U.K., 1994.

Johnson, Eric A., and Eric H. Monkkonen, eds. *The Civilization of Crime: Violence in Town and Country since the Middle Ages.* Urbana, Ill., 1996.

Mullins, Edwin. *The Painted Witch: How Western Artists Have Viewed the Sexuality of Women.* New York, 1985.

Porter, Roy, and Sylvana Tomaselli, eds. *Rape.* Oxford, 1986.

Walker, Garthine. "Rereading Rape and Sexual Violence in Early Modern England." *Gender and History* 10, no. 1 (April 1998): 1–25.

JOHN K. BRACKETT

RAPHAEL (1483–1520), painter and architect. Born in Urbino, Raphael Sanzio was the son of Giovanni Santi, a painter, in Giorgio Vasari's words, "of no great merit, but of good intelligence." Raphael was trained by his father, who died in 1494. Sometime thereafter he removed himself to Perugia to assist in the workshop of Perugino, the most renowned painter in central Italy at the time. Raphael, who would always be adept at learning from other artists, acquired Perugino's style so well that their paintings of this period are difficult to distinguish. Apparently because of Raphael's skill as a draftsman, Pinturicchio, another very successful painter of the time, had him draw some of the cartoons for the frescoes he was executing in the Piccolomini Library at the Siena Cathedral (commissioned in 1502). Raphael's first commissioned work was the altarpiece *St. Nicholas of Tolentino* (1500), which was later dismembered; parts are in Capodimonte, Naples; Pinacoteca Civica, Brescia; and the Louvre, Paris. He also painted *Crucifixion with Saints* (Mond Crucifixion; 1503; London, National Gallery) and *Coronation of the Virgin* (Vatican, Pinacoteca), both very close in style to Perugino. During this period he received commissions from the court of Urbino, notably the precious *St. George Fighting the Dragon* (Washington, D.C., National Gallery of Art; see the entry on England in volume 2; for another interpretation of this theme by Raphael, see the color plates in this volume), probably ordered when Guidobaldo da Montefeltro, duke of Urbino, was awarded the Order of the Garter in 1504.

In that year Raphael went to Florence with a letter of introduction from the duke's sister-in-law, Giovanna della Rovere, reportedly to see and study the works then being designed by Leonardo da Vinci and Michelangelo for the Sala di Consiglio at the Palazzo Vecchio. Although neither Leonardo's *Battle of Anghiari* nor Michelangelo's *Battle of Cascina* were

Raphael. *Coronation of the Virgin.* PINACOTECA VATICANA, VATICAN MUSEUMS AND GALLERIES, VATICAN CITY/ALINARI/ART RESOURCE

completed, the artists were then working on the cartoons. Raphael spent the next four years based in Florence, reworking his Peruginesque style under the influence of these two great masters. From Leonardo he learned the blurred contours and gentle shadow of his sfumato (a method of defining form by blending one tone into another rather than using abrupt outlines); from Michelangelo he learned to broaden his figures and attend to the underlying anatomy. He continued to study from antique sculpture when he went to Rome.

During his Florentine period (1504–1508), Raphael made a large number of holy-family paintings for private patrons. He systematically applied what he was deriving from his study of the Florentines, experimenting with the disposition of the figures. Some are two-figure groups, for example, *Madonna del Granduca* (Florence, Pitti Gallery), *Bridgewater Madonna* (Edinburgh, National Gallery of Scotland), *Small Cowper Madonna* and *Large Cowper Madonna* (1508; Washington, D.C., National Gallery of Art), *Colonna Madonna* (Berlin, Staatliche Museen), and *Madonna of the Carnations* (on loan to the National Gallery in London). In others, on the model of Leonardo's *Madonna of the Rocks* (Paris, Louvre), he added an infant St. John to broaden the base of his pyramidal composition and supply additional iconographic interest, for example in *Madonna of the Meadow* (1506; Vienna, Kunsthistorisches Museum), *La Belle Jardinière* (1507; Paris, Louvre), *Esterhazy Madonna* (Budapest, Szépmüvészeti Museum), and *Madonna of the Goldfinch* (Florence, Uffizi). Compositionally the most complex of this group is the five-figured *Canigiani Holy Family* (Munich, Alte Pinakothek). During his Florentine period, Raphael was commissioned to do a number of portraits. Especially in the pose of *Madalena Doni* (Florence, Pitti Gallery), one sees the influence of Leonardo's *Mona Lisa* (Paris, Louvre), then in the master's studio. In the altarpiece dated 1505, *Ansidei Madonna* (London, National Gallery), the lingering influence of Perugino is still evident, but it has nearly vanished by 1507, when Raphael executed *Entombment* (Rome, Borghese Gallery) on a commission from Atalanta Baglione for an altar in Perugia. By the time of his *Madonna del Baldacchino* (unfinished; Florence, Pitti Gallery) at the end of his Florentine sojourn, his first large commission for the Florentine church of Santo Spirito, his assimilation of the lessons of Leonardo, Fra Bartolommeo della Porta, and Michelangelo is apparent.

According to Vasari, Donato Bramante, a distant relative of Raphael's, sent him word that Pope Julius II had work for him decorating his apartment at the Vatican Palace. Raphael abandoned what he was working on and went to Rome. Frescoing the Stanza della Segnatura would occupy the painter until 1511, when Pope Julius was pleased enough with his accomplishment to assign him the adjacent room, the Stanza d' Eliodoro (the audience chamber). Julius died before its completion, but his successor, Leo X, ordered Raphael to continue and subsequently assigned him two more rooms, the Stanza dell' Incendio (the meeting room of the church's supreme court) and the Sala di Costantino. Very quickly, Raphael became popular with the Roman patrons, and he had more work of all genres than he could do: portraits, such as those of Pope Julius (London, National Gallery) and Cardinal Tommaso Inghirami (Florence, Pitti Gallery); altarpieces, such as *Madonna di Foligno,* originally for the high altar of Santa Maria in Aracoeli (1511–1512; Vatican, Pinacoteca), *Lo Spasimo di Sicilia,* for a church in Palermo (Madrid, Prado); and frescoes, such as *Isaiah,* in San Agostino, the decoration of the Chigi Chapel in Santa Maria della Pace, and *Galatea* and the loggia of Psyche for Agostini Chigi's Villa Farnesina.

The period between his arrival in Rome in 1508 and his premature death in 1520 was the most productive of his life and among the most productive of the Renaissance. While Raphael was at work in the Stanze, Michelangelo was painting the Sistine vault, Bramante was building the new St. Peter's and redesigning the Vatican Palace around the Cortile del Belvedere, and Peruzzi was designing Villa Farnesina, which was frescoed by Sebastiano del Piombo, Raphael, Sodoma, and Peruzzi himself. In his last half decade Raphael became the architect of St. Peter's, the Chigi Chapel (Santa Maria del Popolo), and Villa Madama, as well as several other palaces. Pope Leo commissioned him to design the cartoons for a set of tapestries to hang in the Sistine Chapel depicting the Acts of the Apostles (1515–1516), which were sent to Flanders to be woven (cartoons preserved in the Victoria and Albert Museum, London). In addition to local patrons, dukes and princes importuned him to create works for them, and Raphael was too polite ever to say no. In 1517 he promised Alfonso d'Este, duke of Ferrara, a *Triumph of Bacchus* for his *camerino* (dressing room); when its execution was repeatedly delayed, he sent cartoons of completed works in an attempt to placate the duke. *St. Michael* and *Holy Family of Francis I* (both 1518; Paris, Louvre) were commissioned as gifts for King Francis I of France. Raphael's last work, completed a few days before his death, was *Transfiguration*

Raphael. *Galatea.* Fresco in the Villa Farnesina, Rome ANDERSON/ALINARI/ART RESOURCE

(Vatican, Pinacoteca). It was installed above the bier at his funeral. He was buried in the Pantheon.

Contributions to Artistic Practice. Raphael invented new modes of composition and new modes of coloring, which were much imitated. Although he was often developing the methods of other painters, his formulations were the most influential and became definitive. Raphael was a master of linear perspective, the mode of composition that had defined the Renaissance treatment of space since Filippo Brunelleschi's and Leon Battista Alberti's work in the early fifteenth century. In his early *Marriage of the Virgin* (1504; Milan, Brera) he demonstrated his interest in and ability to invent an elaborate central-point perspective. In *School of Athens* and other frescoes in the Stanze [see the color plates in volume 5], linear perspective is an important element in unifying the compositions. In the last five years of his life, however, he explored two alternatives to linear perspective: the treatment of the wall as an ornamented surface and the relief-like style. According to Vasari, Raphael visited the underground grottoes today known to be Nero's palace, the Domus Aurea, in the company of his assistant, Giovanni da Udine. Giovanni was so fascinated by what he saw that he determined to reinvent the antique formula for making stucco. The experience was apparently a revelation for Raphael as well, for in 1516 he had Giovanni fresco the loggia of Cardinal Bernardo Dovizi Bibbiena in the Vatican Palace with *grotteschi* in imitation of the Domus Aurea and other surviving fragments of ancient Roman wall decoration. Raphael had his workshop apply this new mode of composition on the walls of the loggia known as "Raphael's Bible" the following year (1518–1519), in combination with scenes from the Bible, which were rendered in traditional perspective. For his next and last mural commission, the Sala di Costantino, Raphael employed yet another alternative to perspective. Scholars now attribute the invention of the scheme of this, the fourth, largest, and last of the Stanze, to Raphael, even though he died before his workshop executed it. The two narratives believed to have been designed by Raphael juxtapose traditional perspective *(Constantine Addressing His Troops)* with a new mode of composition based on imitation of antique relief *(Battle at the Milvian Bridge).* Michelangelo had earlier explored a relief-like organization of space in his *Battle of Cascina,* if surviving copies can be trusted. He switched to relief-like composition in the Genesis scenes on the Sistine vault after the perspectival recession of the first scene executed, *Deluge,* proved difficult to read from the floor. Raphael designed *Battle at the Milvian Bridge* to be treated like a procession, moving with the emperor Constantine and his army from left to right, with no middle ground and a background more like a backdrop and with dense overlapping of figures preventing views through. His decision may have been influenced by the long and narrow shape of the room, which would have so limited the viewing distance that a perspective construction would have appeared deformed. Equally important, however, would have been the fact that Constantine's battle was not a battle at all, for, as instructed in his vision, Constantine marched his troops onto the field under the sign of the cross, and his pagan enemy was swept away before them. These new modes of composition were much copied by Raphael's followers and became staples in the repertory of central Italian artists, alongside traditional perspective, for the rest of the century and beyond.

Raphael invented the concept of modes of coloring, in that he was the first to select a color style to match the conditions of the commission. In the traditional workshop of the fifteenth century, a master typically had only one color style, which he taught to his apprentices. Leonardo had explored more expressive coloring made possible by the elision of contours with his sfumato. During his Florentine years, Raphael developed a style of coloring that combined the qualities of Leonardo's sfumato with traditional Florentine *bellezza di colore,* that is, taste for beautiful effects of color. This *unione* mode he applied in the Stanza della Segnatura frescoes and in panel paintings of his earlier Roman years, such as *Madonna di Foligno, Sistine Madonna* (Dresden, Gemäldegalerie; see the color plates in this volume), and *Alba Madonna* (1509; Washington, D.C., National Gallery of Art). Whenever harmony rather than drama was called for, he would return to the *unione* mode, as in the *St. Cecilia* altarpiece (Bologna, Pinacoteca), his portraits of Donna Velata (Florence, Pitti Palace) and Baldassare Castiglione (Paris, Louvre), and the upper zone of *Transfiguration.* For the historical narratives in the Stanza d' Eliodoro and the Stanza dell'Incendio, he adopted the chiaroscuro mode, in which the heightened contrast of light and shade, blackish shadows, and more saturated colors help to dramatize the events. Michelangelo revived the color mode of *cangiantismo* (shifting to another hue in a modeling sequence) in the Sistine vault. Although *cangiantismo* had been in use since Giotto di Bondone for occasional variety, it had never before been used on such a large scale or so insistently. Like many of his contemporaries, Raphael had used *cangiantismo* for occasional variation throughout his career, but he experimented systematically with *cangianti* effects in his ceiling narratives of the Stanza d'Eliodoro at the time Michelangelo was painting the Sistine.

Sebastiano del Piombo was also using the chiaroscuro mode during these years. The competition set up by Cardinal Giulio de' Medici in late 1516 between the two painters to create a pair of panels for his titular church at Narbonne inspired Raphael to surpass Sebastiano's masterpiece in the chiaroscuro mode, *Raising of Lazarus* (London, National Gallery), by combining chiaroscuro with *unione* in his own *Transfiguration.* The upper zone depicting the vision of Christ transfigured is painted in the *unione* mode with transparent veils of liquid color and delicate touches of *cangiantismo.* The lower zone, which represents the apostles struggling unsuccessfully to heal a boy, is painted with the high contrasts, deep shadows, and intense, opaque colors of the chiaroscuro mode. Thus in his last painting Raphael demonstrated how to suit the color mode to the subject at the same time that he maximized the drama by contrasting the miracle above with the failed mir-

Raphael. ***The Transfiguration.*** The painting, in the Vatican Art Gallery, illustrates the passages in Matthew 17:1–8, Mark 9:2–8, and Luke 9:28–36. PINACOTECA VATICANA, VATICAN MUSEUMS AND GALLERIES, VATICAN CITY/ALINARI/ART RESOURCE

acle in the earthly zone below. As a result of Raphael's experimentations with color modes, the next generation of painters felt liberated to vary their choice of color mode with each commission and even to create hybrid modes, such as *unione-cangiantismo,* which became popular for large fresco cycles.

Working Practice and Workshop Organization. Raphael worked occasionally in egg tempera but primarily in oil, which he could have perfected with Perugino, who excelled in it. He prepared his compositions with studies of all kinds, including life studies. He did nude studies of figures composed in groups, all of which he later clothed in drapery. He studied drapery separately and with comparable attention. The habit of careful preparation with drawings made it possible for Raphael eventually to turn over the execution of a work to others. The tapestry cartoons presented a novel challenge because the paper had to support the weight and wetness of paint. For added strength, Raphael used relatively small sheets of paper glued together and a mixture of pigment, water, and animal glue with a high proportion of binder (something that promotes cohesion in loosely assembled substances).

A revolution in workshop organization was accomplished in the sixteenth century, and Raphael was its pioneer. Although Perugino, Andrea del Verrocchio, and Domenico Ghirlandaio all ran large *botteghe* (workshops), no one before Raphael delegated responsibility to the degree that he did. In his Florentine period and up to the later stages of the Stanza della Segnatura, he had no need for a large shop. The execution is mainly by his hand, as are the preparatory drawings. His large number of drawings reflects a new emphasis on invention. The new century would no longer tolerate Perugino's system of recycling cartoons that had been made for previous commissions. As his fame grew and the pressure on Raphael increased, he gathered about him more artists. Many were more collaborators than apprentices or assistants, some much older than he. By the middle of the second decade of the sixteenth century, he had what was probably the largest painting workshop that had ever been assembled: Vasari reported that fifty artists accompanied him daily to the Vatican.

He experimented with the division of responsibility and by trial and error discovered what did and did not work. He eventually developed a system in which he would participate in every stage of preparation and execution without being completely responsible for any stage after the initial conception. At times, he even required assistants to make studies from life and did not just assign them the secretarial tasks of transcription or of enlarging designs on cartoons. Although the usual picture given is of an artist too harried by the pressure of work to perform at top capacity, Raphael seems to have reconceived the workshop more as a cooperative and less as a master-apprentice relationship. He was remembered by Vasari, Giovanni Battista Armenini, and other sixteenth-century writers as the most generous of teachers.

Increasingly, the actual execution was delegated, and this began a trend that would be expanded by subsequent painters such as Giulio Romano, Perino del Vaga, Francesco Salviati (Cecchino), Vasari, and Taddeo Zuccaro, all of whom valued invention over execution. Raphael's pupil, Giulio Romano, reported to Vasari that the master would retouch the work of his assistants until they appeared entirely his. With frescoes, these retouchings were done in secco (dry plaster) and have therefore largely disappeared, leaving behind works that are much less well integrated than they were when Raphael ordered the scaffolding removed. Raphael experimented with oil murals as an alternative to fresco in the Sala di Costantino shortly before his death. Viewed today, the figures of Justice and Comity are darker and show deeper shadows than the surrounding images executed in true fresco. That Sebastiano del Piombo was painting *Flagellation* (Rome, San Pietro in Montorio) in oil on the wall at this time may have motivated this experiment, which would allow the kind of dramatic chiaroscuro in fresco that was the current taste in panel paintings in Rome.

Raphael and Classical Antiquity. The style Raphael forged, together with Leonardo and Michelangelo, is called by art historians the classical style of the High Renaissance. The term points to the style's relation to the style of classical antiquity and to certain qualities of heroic scale, grace, harmony, clarity, and unity. Whereas the modern concept of classical style posits a community between Raphael and Michelangelo in the first two decades of the sixteenth century, sixteenth-century writers often contrasted the two. Advocates of Raphael recognized in him an adherence to a Horatian mean and praised his moderation while they criticized Michelangelo for exercising too much artistic license and thereby straying too far from nature.

Two distinct approaches to antiquity existed among artists in the early years of the century. Antiquarians like Jacopo Ripanda (fl. 1490–1530) and Amico Aspertini (1474–1552) were mining the images of antiquity to reproduce the appearance of its material culture. Vasari and his contemporaries did not explore how Raphael's and Michelangelo's study of antiquity differed from that of the antiquarians. In *Dialogo della pittura* (1557; Dialogue of painting) Lodovico Dolce simply states that beauty should be derived from life and from the statues of the ancients. Modern scholars refer to their assimilation, more than imitation, of antique culture (Ernst Gombrich) and to their response to the aesthetic of the monuments of antiquity (S. J. Freedberg).

Pope Julius II surrounded himself with humanist men of letters who shared and fed his enthusiasm for reviving imperial Rome in a Christian form led by an enlightened papacy. He banished from the pulpit of his court traditional medieval preaching and favored priests like Egidio da Viterbo who styled their sermons on classical rhetoric (epideictic), couching their message in terms of praise and blame rather than admonition. Raphael must have been supplied with programs for his paintings such as those in the Stanza della Segnatura by learned men such as these. In other cases, the narratives he and his contemporaries were assigned to paint were based on ancient authors, as at Chigi's Villa Farnesina, where texts by Lucian, Ovid, and Apuleius were used. In this environment Raphael's classicism was nurtured. The style to which he aspired perfectly suited the ambitions of the patron and his court because it could express their lofty aspiration to re-create in idealized form the humanism of the ancient classical world. Such a coincidence of intellectual and artistic commitment to similar goals on the part of patrons and artist has been rare in the history of artistic endeavor and helps to account for the exalted and unprecedented achievements of the high Renaissance.

Under Pope Leo X, who was more of an antiquarian than Pope Julius, Raphael was pushed toward archaeological concerns. His interest in certain antique texts is reflected in his asking Marco Fabio Calvo, a physician and respected philologist, for assistance in translating Vitruvius's *De architectura*. This was in 1515, at about the same time that Leo put him in charge of all antiquities in Rome and asked him to create a topographical map of ancient Rome. The two loggias and the Sala di Costantino, executed in his last years for Leo, reflect the shift toward a more direct imitation of classical prototypes under this pope's patronage.

There exists a famous letter in which Raphael used a trope from classical texts to explain how he went about creating the image of a beautiful woman. The ancient painter Zeuxis asked that five beautiful women be assembled so that he might choose the most beautiful parts of each. Raphael says that lacking beautiful women he uses instead "a certain idea that comes into my head" to synthesize the image of the ideal woman. Although this letter is now understood to have been penned by Baldassare Castiglione in the name of Raphael, it nevertheless reflects a contemporary view of the nature of Raphael's ideality and points to its source in antique texts (Shearman, 1994).

Grace in Raphael's figures can serve as an example of how he baptized a pagan quality abounding in antique art and made it serve his Christian classicism. The theological concept of grace as the mark of God's favor becomes visualized by Raphael as a necessary aesthetic attribute of the hero. Thus, for example, his Galatea, St. Cecilia, St. Michael, Christ, and the apostles in the tapestry cartoons embody a superhuman component of beauty, grace, and loveliness. No distinction was made in this tolerant age between pagan and Christian heroes. By logical inversion, villains, such as Heliodorus, Ananias, and Lucifer, embody perfect ugliness and gracelessness. That this was an idea consonant with the humanism of the day is shown by Baldassare Castiglione's closely parallel statement in *Il cortegiano* (*The Book of the Courtier*): "A wicked soul rarely inhabits a beautiful body and for that reason outward beauty should be considered a true sign of inner goodness. And this grace is impressed upon the body in varying degrees as an index of the soul, by which it is outwardly known, as with trees the beauty of the blossoms is a token of the excellence of the fruit" (book 4, 57–58).

Esteem and Influence. Castiglione listed the five masters of painting, each of whom demonstrated his own perfection of style and might serve as a model for others. Raphael was included, along with Leonardo da Vinci, Michelangelo, Giorgione da Castelfranco, and Andrea Mantegna. Paolo Giovio, writing biographies in 1523–1527 of the three major artists shortly after the deaths of Leonardo and Raphael, ranked Leonardo first, Michelangelo second, and Raphael third. Sixteenth-century writers from Vasari on esteemed Raphael as equaled only by Michelangelo, if at all. Vasari considered Michelangelo to have perfected the means of art in *disegno* and Raphael to have provided a model for dealing with the goal of all art, narrative, in which he surpassed all others.

The comparison between Michelangelo and Raphael and the debate over which was the greater, and why, were the preoccupation of Lodovico Dolce (1557). He pits a proponent of Michelangelo against an advocate of Raphael, who praises him as the greater because of his versatility, his coloring, and the sweetness of his style (which he prefers to Michelangelo's awesomeness, or *terribilità*). Raphael's ability to paint every kind of figure and to make each look different is contrasted with Michelangelo's universally overmuscled figures. With respect to coloring, Raphael is said to have surpassed all those who practiced before him, whether in oil or in fresco, and on this point Michelangelo's advocate yields without contest. In the Counter-Reformation, critics blamed Michelangelo for showing off "the excellence of art" at the expense of devotional content and of providing a bad model for other painters, whereas Raphael's balance and moderation were praised. In *Dialogo nel quale si ragiona de gli errori e de gli abusi de' pittori circa l'historie* (Dialogue in which painters' errors and abuses are discussed; 1564), Giovanni Andrea Gilio, who cites Horace repeatedly, praises the appropriateness of the gestures and attitudes of Raphael's figures in his *Transfiguration*. In chapter 1 of book 1 in his *De' veri precetti della pittura* (On the true precepts of the art of painting; 1586), Giovanni Battista Armenini lists Raphael as one of the supreme masters of painting, along with Leonardo, Michelangelo, Titian, Correggio, Sebastiano del Piombo, Giulio Romano, and Andrea del Sarto. In *L'idea del tempio della pittura* (The idea of the temple of painting; 1590), Giovanni Paolo Lomazzo makes Raphael one of the seven governors, or canonical masters, of painting. To the five named by Castiglione (his source), Lomazzo adds Polidoro da Caravaggio and Gaudenzio Ferrari and substitutes Titian for Giorgione da Castelfranco. Each governor excels in one of the seven parts of art: proportion (Michelangelo), expression (Gaudenzio Ferrari), *forma,* meaning iconography (Polidoro), light (Leonardo), perspective (Mantegna), color (Titian), and composition (Raphael).

Raphael trained the next generation of artists in his large workshop, and after his death his style was disseminated throughout Italy by them. According to his testament, his pupils Giulio Romano and Gianfrancesco Penni (called Il Fattore) were the heirs of his workshop, which they attempted to keep intact while they continued and finished commissions that were under way, such as the Sala di Costantino. Members of the workshop went out on their own in the 1520s, practicing versions of Raphael's style. Giulio Romano, after completing the Sala di Costantino frescoes in autumn 1524, accepted the invitation of Federico II Gonzaga, the marquis of Mantua, to become court painter and moved to Mantua, where he stayed for the remainder of his life. Many of his designs, for the decoration of Palazzo del Te for example, were engraved and widely disseminated. Polidoro da Caravaggio (1490–1536 or 1499–1543) set up his own studio with Maturino da Firenze, and they became specialists in painted facades *all'antica,* a business that thrived until the sack of Rome in 1527 and that Polidoro transferred to Naples and even Messina. Perino del Vaga (1501–1547) received various commissions in Rome, but his career was similarly disrupted by the sack, after which he accepted the invitation of Andrea Doria to become court painter in Genoa. He stayed away for nearly a decade before returning to Rome to become the preferred artist of Pope Paul III until his death. Other artists who were not directly pupils of Raphael took up his style and imitated it. Parmigianino (1503–1540) did not go to Rome until 1524, but he was captivated by Raphael's style, which he copied, adding his own elongation of proportions to create figures of extreme sweetness and grace. The sack impelled him to Bologna and finally to his native Parma, from where his version of Raphael's style was widely influential. Francesco Salviati (Cecchino) (c. 1509–1563), a native of Florence and a pupil of Andrea del Sarto's, went to Rome in the early 1530s to study the antique remains and to draw after the modern masters, in particular Raphael. Taddeo Zuccaro (1529–1566) was a native of the area of Urbino, Raphael's birthplace. He made his career in Rome as the leading painter in the difficult years around mid-century, when Counter-Reformation demands for a retreat from the excesses of mannerism in religious images began to be heard. Taddeo, by emulating Raphael's constant rethinking of narrative and his moderation, forged a style that satisfied both the demands of the Counter-Reformation critics and the aesthetic requirements of his sophisticated patrons. His career, cut short by premature death, was continued by his less talented brother, Federico. Federico Barocci (c. 1535–1612) also came from Urbino. Like Taddeo Zuccaro, he imitated Raphael to shape a style that would answer the new needs of the Counter-Reformation church. Barocci returned to the kind of extensive drawing from life that Raphael had practiced but that had been largely abandoned in the intervening generations. The Carracci family—Lodovico (1555–1619), Annibale (1560–1609), and Agostino (1557–1602)—recognized the importance of drawing from life and instituted it in their Accademia degli Incamminati in Bologna and drew on Raphael in other respects as well as an important source for the reform of painting they undertook.

Raphael's collaboration with engravers was another way that his style was broadcast across Europe. Marcantonio Raimondi (c. 1480–c. 1534) went to Rome from Bologna in about 1510. He was already an accomplished engraver in the antiquarian mode when he and Raphael began their collaboration. The market for art prints was just then getting established, and Raphael was among the first to exploit it. In this groundbreaking enterprise, he allied himself with an entrepreneur, known as Il Bavieri, who was responsible for selling, and Marcantonio was associated with Agostino Veneziano and Marco Dente. Raphael appears to have set certain conditions with the engravers to control quality and his copyright. He retained ownership of the plates, which he left in his will to Il Bavieri. There were no reproductive engravings made until after his death: Raphael supplied unused drawings and designs for unexecuted projects. Usually they were in the form of *modelli,* which the engravers were required to follow closely with respect to direction, size, and image. The operation was carefully organized so that the profits accrued largely to the painter. Nevertheless, the antiquarian style of Marcantonio left its mark. He would shift the figures toward a more sculptural rendering, hardening the contours and flattening them to the plane with flat frontal light. Thus the style that was disseminated by means of the engravings was a classicistic version of Raphael's manner, which paved the way for the relief-like style that would become popular after his death.

Raphael's reputation has suffered in the twentieth century because of the use that was made of his style as the model for academic art, beginning in the French Academy in the seventeenth century. Principles were deduced from his style, which young painters were then taught as rules. This practice was at odds with the freedom Raphael allowed his students and collaborators and with his own experimental approach, in which he never repeated himself or set himself to the same problem twice. Nevertheless, he has always been recognized as one of the greatest European painters not just of the Renaissance but of all time.

See also **Classical Antiquity in Renaissance Art**; **Graphic Arts**; *and biographies of figures mentioned in this entry.*

BIBLIOGRAPHY

Ames-Lewis, Francis. *The Draftsman Raphael.* New Haven, Conn., 1986.

Bellori, Giovanni Pietro. *Descrizzione delle imagini dipinte da Rafaelle d'Urbino.* Rome, 1695.

Borsook, Eve. "Technical Innovation and the Development of Raphael's Style in Rome." *Canadian Art Review* 12, no. 2 (1985): 127–136.

Brown, David Alan. *Raphael and America.* Washington, D.C., 1983.

Fischel, Oskar. *Raphaels Zeichnungen.* 8 vols. Berlin, 1913–1941.

Freedberg, S. J. *Painting of the High Renaissance in Rome and Florence.* 2 vols. Cambridge, Mass., 1961. The definitive study of the classical style.

Golzio, Vincenzo. *Raffaello nei documenti nelle testimonianze dei contemporanei e nella letteratura del suo secolo.* Vatican City, 1936.

Gombrich, E. H. In *Norm and Form: Studies in the Art of the Renaissance.* London, 1966. See "The Style *all'antica:* Imitation and Assimilation," pp. 122–128.

Hall, Marcia B. *After Raphael: Painting in Central Italy in the Sixteenth Century.* New York, 1999.

Hall, Marcia B., ed. *Raphael's "School of Athens."* New York, 1997.

Joannides, Paul. *The Drawings of Raphael.* Oxford, 1983.

Jones, Roger, and Nicholas Penny. *Raphael.* New Haven, Conn., 1983.

Knab, Eckhart, Erwin Mitsch, and Konrad Oberhuber, with Sylvia Ferino Pagden. *Raphael: Die Zeichnungen.* Stuttgart, Germany, 1983.

Passavant, Johann David. *Raphael of Urbino and His Father Giovanni Santi.* 1872. New York, 1978. Translation of *Rafael von Urbino und sein Vater Giovanni Santi.* 3 vols. 1839. Rev. ed., Leipzig, 1858. The first monograph.

Pope-Hennessy, John. *Raphael: The Wrightsman Lectures.* London and New York, 1970.

Raffaello a Firenze: Dipinti e disegni delle collezioni fiorentine. Milan, 1984.

Raffaello a Roma: Il convegno del 1983. Rome, 1986.

Raffaello in Vaticano. Milan, 1984.

Raphael Invenit: Stampe da Raffaello nelle collezioni dell'Istituto Nazionale per la Grafica. Rome, 1985. Includes essays by Grazia Bernini Pezzini, Stefania Massari, Simonetta Prosperi Valenti Rodinò. The most complete compilation of prints after Raphael.

Salmi, Mario, ed. *The Complete Work of Raphael.* New York, 1968. Multiauthored volume, translated from Italian, with essays on every aspect of the artist.

Shearman, John. "Castiglione's Portrait of Raphael." *Mitteilungen des Kunsthistorischen Institutes in Florenz* 38, no. 1 (1994): 69–97. Presents the evidence that Castiglione, not Raphael, was the author of the famous letter "by Raphael to Castiglione."

Shearman, John. *Raphael's Cartoons in the Collection of Her Majesty the Queen and the Tapestries for the Sistine Chapel.* London, 1972.

Shearman, John, and Marcia B. Hall, eds. *The Princeton Raphael Symposium: Science in the Service of Art History.* Princeton, N.J., 1990. Studies by conservation scientists at major museums of Raphaels in their collections.

Vasari, Giorgio. *Le vite de' più eccelenti pittori, scultori, e architettori, nelle redazioni del 1550 e 1568.* Edited by Rosanna Bettarini and Paola Barocchi. 6 vols. Florence, 1966–1987.

Marcia B. Hall

RATIO STUDIORUM. The *Ratio studiorum,* or plan of studies, was the key document in Jesuit education. It established the curriculum and teaching methods in the hundreds of Jesuit colleges in Europe and mission countries until the suppression of the Jesuits in 1773. A modified version was adopted by the Jesuit colleges in 1832 after the restoration of the Jesuits.

The first Jesuit college for lay students was established at Messina, Sicily, in 1548. Ignatius Loyola set down general goals and rules for the Jesuit colleges in the fourth part of the Jesuit *Constitutions,* but as their network of colleges expanded (there were 372 by 1615) the Jesuits needed more detailed directives based on their practical experience in teaching. In 1584 Claudio Aquaviva, superior general from 1581 to 1615, formed a committee of six Jesuits to write a preliminary plan, or *ratio,* dealing with teaching methods, teacher formation, and curriculum. Aquaviva and his advisors went over the committee's directives and produced the *ratio* of 1591, which largely dropped the theoretical discussions in the committee's draft. The 1591 version was put into practice until the definitive version of the *Ratio studiorum* was drawn up and promulgated in 1599. It was more polished and drew on the added experience. Most of the text dictates concrete rules for the teachers of various subjects.

The Jesuit *Ratio* was not particularly innovative in curriculum content. It looked back to the experience of the first Jesuits who had studied at the University of Paris in the 1530s and previous humanist curricula, many built on Quintilian. The core curriculum was rhetoric and the study of classical Latin (above all Cicero's works) and to a lesser degree Greek writers. Advanced students studied some philosophy, basically Aristotle as interpreted by Thomas Aquinas. Theology played little direct role in the curriculum, but the Jesuit schools were steeped with religious practice and extracurricular religious activities such as plays and the Marian sodalities. The choice of readings from classical authors depended as much on moral content as literary excellence.

The Jesuit schools enjoyed enormous popularity among the elite of Catholic Europe because their teachers were well trained, the schools charged no tuition, firm discipline was established despite little use of the rod, and students progressed through a series of clearly defined steps. Because Jesuits frequently transferred from one school to another, they could compare teaching experiences. The *Ratio* encouraged contests to motivate students by pitting them as individuals or teams against one another. Large classes were divided into groups of ten with a student leader who drilled his fellows in fundamentals, thereby lessening this burden of Jesuit teachers so they could concentrate on lectures and correcting papers.

The main rival of the Jesuit schools in Italy were the *Scuole pie* of the Piarists, who developed their own plan of studies between 1604 and 1610. The Piarists concentrated on poorer students and hence on a more job-oriented curriculum that stressed accounting skills (*abbaco*) and the vernacular as well as Latin.

BIBLIOGRAPHY

Farrell, Allan P. *The Jesuit Code of Liberal Education: Development and Scope of the Ratio Studiorum.* Milwaukee, Wis., 1938.

Lukács, Ladislaus, ed. *Monumenta paedigogica Societatis Jesu.* Vols. 6 and 7. Rome, 1992.

Scaglione, Aldo. *The Liberal Arts and the Jesuit College System.* Amsterdam and Philadelphia, 1986.

JOHN PATRICK DONNELLY, S.J.

REASON OF STATE. "Reason of state" (in Italian, *ragion di stato*) refers to the rules of statecraft or the means by which rulers acquire or keep power, especially in emergencies.

Origins. Cicero had described methods of ruling in terms of *ratio reipublicae,* and some medieval writers had used the phrase *ratio communis utilitatis* (reason of the common good). The Italian term appears to have come into use in the first half of the sixteenth century. Francesco Guicciardini used the phrase "reasons of state" (*ragioni di stato*) around 1521, and in 1547 Giovanni Della Casa referred to the emperor Charles V's annexation of the city of Piacenza in similar terms. Arguing that the action cast a shadow on Charles's reputation, Della Casa contrasted honorable behavior with "the self-interest which they call today Reason of State" (*quell'utile che oggi si chiama Ragion di Stato*). The phrase was probably adopted as a euphemism, a way of avoiding Niccolò Machiavelli's over-frank discussion of "necessity" after his works were banned in the Roman Catholic world in 1559 and were attacked by Protestants.

However, "reason of state" became a fashionable term in the late Renaissance, especially in the decades following the publication of Giovanni Botero's book on the subject in 1589. This Piedmontese scholar's definition of reason of state stressed "such actions as cannot be considered in the light of *ragione ordinaria*"—a phrase that may be translated either as "ordinary reason" or "the normal process of law." By the late 1580s, according to Botero, ruling was a "constant subject of discussion" in the courts of some princes, the opinions of Machiavelli and Cornelius Tacitus being "frequently quoted." Botero's own book went through at least six Italian editions between 1589 and 1606, as well as being translated into German (1596), French (1599), Spanish (1599), and Latin (1602). The Spanish translation was made by the historiographer royal, Antonio de Herrera, at the command of Philip II himself.

Use of the Term. The novelty of the phrase "reason of state" in the 1590s may be judged from the fact that the German and Latin translations of Botero did not use it. By 1621, on the other hand, an Italian writer was claiming that "even the barbers and other base craftsmen discuss reason of state in their shops." We do not have to take this claim literally to infer that the phrase was spreading. By 1648 it had become so familiar that in the famous treatise on international relations by Henri, duc de Rohan, *De l'interest des princes et des estats de la Chrestienté* (The interest of princes and states in Christendom; 1638), the key term "interest" was translated into Latin as *ratio status*.

Botero was followed by a series of imitators. A few of them, almost all Italians, employed similar titles. There was Girolamo Frachetta's *Discorso della ragione di stato* (1592); Apollinare de'Calderini's *Discorsi sopra la ragion di stato* (1597); Giovanni Antonio Palazzo's *Discorso del governo e della ragion vera di stato* (1604); Pietro Andrea Canoniero's *Introduzione alla politica, alla ragione di stato* (1614); Fernando Alvia de Castro's *Verdadera razon de estado* (1616); Lodovico Zuccolo's *Della ragione di stato* (1621); Federico Buonaventura's *Della ragione di stato* (published in 1623 but written some twenty years earlier); Gabriele Zinano's *Della ragione degli stati* (1626); Ludovico Settala's *Della ragione di stato* (1627); Wilhelm Ferdinand von Efferhen's *Manuale politicum de ratione status* (1630); Antonio Mirandola's *Ragione di stato nella passione di Cristo* (1630); and Scipione Chiaramonti's *Della ragione di stato* (1635).

However, some authors preferred to speak of "secrets of state" (*mystères d'État* or *arcana imperii,* a phrase borrowed from the Roman historian Cornelius Tacitus); for example, the German professor Arnold Clapmar in his *De arcanis rerum publicarum* (1605). Others wrote about "prudence," "the prudence of governments" (*prudentia regnativa, prudencia de estado*), "civil prudence" (*prudentia civilis*), or "political prudence," like Jakob Bornitz in *De prudentia politica* (1602). Botero devoted the second part of his treatise to the subject, while the Flemish humanist Justus Lipsius stressed the importance of different kinds of prudence in his textbook, or anthology, of ancient writers, *Politicorum libri sex* (1589), described by a fellow academic as a work of philosophy the likes of which "has not been written or seen in a thousand years." (The book went through fifteen editions in ten years and was translated into seven languages.) Without using the term "reason of state," Lipsius discussed topics similar to those explored by Botero, notably deception, distinguishing minor lies (*deceptiunculae*) from major deceits (*magnae fraudes*), such as perfidy or injustice.

Yet other writers disguised their own ideas—or, more often, Machiavelli's—in the form of a commentary on the many political maxims to be found in Tacitus, as in the case of Scipione Ammirato's *Discorsi sopra Cornelio Tacito* (1594) and scores of later works. Ammirato devoted the twelfth book of his treatise to reason of state, noting that people were speaking of it "every day" and defining it in contrast to natural or civil law (*ragion di natura, ragion civile*) as "the contravention of ordinary law for the sake of the public good." The Spanish *arbitristas,* self-appointed advisers to the monarchy, also discussed reason of state in their texts but preferred titles such as Sancho de Moncada's *Restauración política de España* (The political restoration of Spain; 1619) or *The Conservation of Monarchies* (by Domingo Fernández Navarrete, 1626). Another important discussion of reason of state that avoided the term is Gabriel Naudé's *Considérations politiques sur les coups d'État* (1639). Naudé coined the term "coup," which was to have such success later, precisely to refer to extraordinary actions to be taken in emergencies (among which he specifically included the Saint Bartholomew's Day massacre).

Analysis of the Concept. It might be said that the late sixteenth century saw the rise or constitution of a "discourse" on reason of state, in the sense of a more or less closed intellectual universe structured around a small number of concepts, authorities, assumptions, and examples. Whether it was neutral or pejorative, the term "reason of state" was used especially widely in the period 1590–1630, particularly in Italian, Latin (*ratio status*), Spanish (*razó de estado*), and French (*raison d'État*).

The vogue for the phrase may be explained as a response to the civil wars of the previous generation, or to the rise of "absolute" monarchy (unconstrained by law). It also reveals an increasing interest in what rulers actually did rather than in what they ought to do, the rise of what was sometimes referred to in this period as "political science" (*scientia politica*). In this context it is worth remembering that Botero was the author not only of a treatise on reason of state but also of a comparative study of the political systems of the world, part of a still more ambitious global survey that he called *Relationi universali* (1591–1595).

To expound political science, the authors of the books mentioned above needed to reveal state secrets, a procedure often described at the time as "unmasking," "unveiling," or "anatomizing" the body politic. They frequently asserted that the *arcana imperii* were not to be revealed to "the vulgar," such as the barbers "and other base craftsmen." All the same, they contributed to a process of vulgarization by publishing their reflections.

Many writers preferred to carry out the task of unmasking by discussing the major events of the reigns of Roman emperors, especially Tiberius, as described by Tacitus, whether in homage to the prestige of ancient Rome or to be prudent. However, some of them were also prepared to draw parallels between the actions of Roman emperors and those of rulers in their own time. During his brief Protestant phase, Lipsius, for instance, compared the duke of Alba, who was governing the Netherlands for Philip II and persecuting heretics, to the cruel emperor Tiberius. Ammirato noted that just as Tiberius had his favorite, Sejanus, put to death without trial for reasons of state, so Henry III of France had Henri, duc de Guise, assassinated for the same motives.

Typical of the developing discourse of political science is the ambivalence many authors express about the political figures they cite as examples, condemning them as immoral while at the same time admiring their political skills. Botero, for example, began his treatise by describing Tiberius as a cruel and wicked tyrant but went on to cite him a number of times as an example of a successful ruler. Filippo Cavriana, author of one of the most important commentaries on Tacitus, described Tiberius as "a man of evil nature" but also as a prince of "great prudence." The French physician Rodolphe Le Maître devoted a whole treatise to the emperor, entitled *Tibère français* (1616), describing him as "a singular example of vigilance."

The main topics discussed in this genre of political treatises were violence and deceit, force and fraud—the opposite but complementary qualities of the lion and the fox that Machiavelli had recommended to his prince. On one side, for example, there was the necessity of using severe measures against rebels, a practice not infrequently compared to that of a physician who amputates a limb in order to preserve life. On the other side there were the advantages of simulation and dissimulation, exemplified (once again) by Tiberius, by Cesare Borgia (as Machiavelli noted), and by Louis XI of France, who is supposed to have coined the maxim "those who can't feign can't reign" (*qui nescit dissimulare, nescit regnare*). The authors of the political treatises walked an intellectual tightrope, praising severity but condemning cruelty, arguing against lying but in favor of dissimulation. Some of them, notably the Spanish Jesuit Pedro de Ribadeneira, distinguished two kinds of reason of state, the true and the false. The latter, also known as "devilish" or "hellish" reason (*ragion del diavolo, ragion d'inferno*), was associated with the doctrines of Machiavelli and sometimes those of Jean Bodin.

If it began as a euphemism, "reason of state" ultimately became a dirty word, associated with hypocrisy and murder and mocked on the seventeenth-century stage. At the end of the Renaissance it was gradually replaced by the new concept of "interest." Looking back on the Renaissance from the late twentieth century, it is tempting to view the many treatises on reason of state as so many examples of "Machiavellism," as a series of second-rate authors plagiarizing a single first-rate thinker. Even Giovanni Botero, the most famous of those authors, is not outstanding for his originality, and in the texts published after 1600 it is difficult to find an argument, a metaphor, or even an example that had not been used before, sometimes many times. However, it may be more illuminating to regard the authors as witnesses rather than thieves, and their treatises as examples of a collective attempt on the part of Renaissance academics and moralists to come to terms with the political realities of their time, a time of civil and ideological war. The important point, insofar as these writers were concerned, was to domesticate the insights of Machiavelli and Tacitus: to find a way of combining a measure of political realism with the precepts of Christian morality.

See also **Machiavelli, Niccolò,** *subentry on* **The Political Theorist; Political Thought;** *and biographies of Giovanni Botero, Justus Lipsius, Pedro de Ribadeneira, and Tacitus.*

BIBLIOGRAPHY

Primary Work

Botero, Giovanni. *The Reason of State.* Translated by P. J. Waley and D. P. Waley. London, 1956. Translation of *Ragion di stato* (1589).

Secondary Works

Baldini, A. Enzo, ed. *Botero e la "Ragion di stato."* Florence, 1992. A useful collective survey of recent research.

Birely, Robert. *The Counter-Reformation Prince: Anti-Machiavellianism; or, Catholic Statecraft in Early Modern Europe.* Chapel Hill, N.C., 1990.

De Mattei, Rodolfo. *Il problema della "ragion di stato" nell'età della Controriforma.* Milan and Naples, Italy, 1979.

Meinecke, Friedrich. *Machiavellism.* Translated by Douglas Scott. London, 1957. Translation of *Die Idee der Staatsräson* (1924). A classic study, now criticized but still indispensable.

Schnur, Roman, ed. *Staatsräson.* Berlin, 1975.

Stolleis, Michael. *Staat und Staatsräson in der frühen Neuzeit.* Frankfurt, 1990. Especially concerned with the German-speaking world.

Tuck, Richard. *Philosophy and Government, 1572–1651.* Cambridge, U.K., and New York, 1993. Places the problem of reason of state in the wider context of trends in the politics and philosophy of the period.

PETER BURKE

RECREATION. *See* **Daily Life.**

REFORMATION. *See* **Catholic Reformation and Counter-Reformation; Protestant Reformation.**

REGIOMONTANUS (Johannes Müller; 1436–1476), astronomer, mathematician. Regiomontanus's life is largely undocumented until he enrolled in the University of Vienna in 1450. The records there listed him as coming from "Künigsperg" (Königsberg, which means "King's Mountain") and the latinized form of that city became the standard designation of his name. He received his bachelor's degree in 1452 and in 1457 joined the faculty of the university. Georg Peurbach was also on the faculty, and the two became close friends and collaborators in the study of mathematical astronomy.

In 1460 Cardinal Johannes Bessarion, the papal legate to the Holy Roman Empire, came to Vienna. Bessarion was Greek and was interested in bringing Greek authors to the attention of Western intellectuals. He persuaded Peurbach to provide a Latin guide to Ptolemy's *Mathematical Syntaxis,* commonly known as the *Almagest,* the classical work of mathematical astronomy. Peurbach began the task, which Regiomontanus later titled the *Epitome,* but had only finished through book six when he died in 1461. On his deathbed he received Regiomontanus's promise that he would complete the work, which he did. The final version of the *Epitome* did more than summarize the *Almagest;* it also provided commentary. Its critique of Ptolemy's lunar theory, which required that the apparent diameter of the moon would vary much more than it did, was important to Nicolaus Copernicus in his rejection of Ptolemy.

During his association with Bessarion, Regiomontanus mastered Greek. Thus, unlike Peurbach, he could consult the *Almagest* in the original. He finished the *Epitome* in 1463, two years after Peurbach's death, and presented it to Bessarion, but the cardinal did not publish it. The *Epitome* was finally published in 1496, twenty years after Regiomontanus's death.

Regiomontanus began his work on trigonometry because he and Peurbach had perceived a need for systematic rules governing the ratios of the sides and angles in both plane and spherical triangles. In his book *De triangulis omnimodis* (On all classes of triangles), which was written in 1463–1464 but not published until 1533, he formulated the cosine law for spherical triangles. His *Tabulae directionum* (Tables of directions), written in 1467–1468, substituted base ten for the traditional sexagesimal division of the standard radius. The tables of sines and tangents included in this work helped to establish the decimal system.

By 1467 Regiomontanus was established in Hungary where he lectured at the new University of Pressburg, for the founding of which he had selected the most astrologically propitious moment. In 1471 he left for Nürnberg where he established a printing press for scientific writings, which existing houses were loath to publish, in part because it was expensive to print the diagrams in such publications. His first publication was Peurbach's *Theoricae novae planetarum* (New theory of the planets; 1454). In 1474 he produced his *Ephemerides,* the first book of its type to be published. It listed the positions of the heavenly bodies for each day from 1475 to 1506. Christopher Columbus took a copy on his fourth voyage and used the prediction of a lunar eclipse on 29 February 1504 to frighten the indigenous population in Jamaica. Regiomontanus died in 1476, probably from plague, on a trip to Rome.

See also **Astronomy** *and the biography of Peurbach, Georg.*

BIBLIOGRAPHY

Primary Work

Regiomontanus. *Opera collectanea.* Edited by F. Schmeidler. Osnabrück, Germany, 1972.

Secondary Work

Zinner, Ernst. *Leben und Wirken des Joh. Müller von Königsberg genannt Regiomontanus.* 2d ed. Osnabrück, Germany, 1968.

SHEILA J. RABIN

RÉGNIER, MATHURIN (1573–1613), French writer and poet. Born in Chartres to a bourgeois family, Mathurin Régnier was sent to learn Latin at college, where he began to write poetry at an early age. In 1587, he accompanied Cardinal François Joyeuse to Rome, where he spent ten years reading the works of the Pléiade poets. Régnier's life and career, like those of his illustrious poet uncle Philippe Desportes, interwove intimately with life at court, with courtly concerns and artistic preferences.

Régnier consciously imitated Francesco Berni and the *bernesque* poets: quirky, inexplicable developments, picturesque imagery, and quotidian references and turns of phrase typify his poetic voice. Another important influence, the Spanish picaresque novel, compounded the element of the macabre and the baroque excesses of his work.

Régnier's oeuvre includes *Les satires* (1596–1598); the *Premières oeuvres* (First works; 1608), composed of ten satires; *Les satyres* (1609); and some Petrarchan verse such as his "Cloris et Phylis" (1652). *Les satires,* the work most responsible for his acclaim at court, begins to grind the essential grist of Régnier's writer's mill: execrable poetasters and the hypocrisy and pretentiousness of life at court. These themes recur throughout his poetry; his *épîtres* (epistles), elegies, odes, and epigrams deflate bombast and dissembling through outrageous, often cynical, burlesque caricature. The witty ease of his poetry results from a meticulous craftsmanship: Régnier's highly cultivated poetry recalls and reworks erudite sources such as Horace, Ovid, and Juvenal, as well as contemporary influences such as Ariosto.

Because so much of Régnier's poetry draws sustenance and substance from scenes of daily existence, he avoids having to subjugate his poetic voice and meter to the prim constraints that François de Malherbe—who arrived at court shortly after the publication of the first of Régnier's *Satires*—promulgated in his new "modernist" doctrine of poetic sparseness and purity. Régnier instead remains faithful to the erotic subject matter and exalted voice that he had discovered in Pierre de Ronsard's poetry. He succeeds in wedding an audacious whimsy to a classical flavor. In addition, he should be credited with the first sustained attempt (since Joachim Du Bellay's attack on satire in the *Défense et illustration de la langue française*) to rehabilitate that genre as an effective, compelling vehicle for characterizing, criticizing, and perhaps even reforming, morals and lifestyle.

See also **Pléiade**.

BIBLIOGRAPHY

Mourgues, Odette de. *Metaphysical, Baroque, and Précieux Poetry*. Oxford, 1953.

Rubin, David Lee. *La poésie française du premier dix-septième siècle: Textes et contextes*. Tübingen, Germany, 1986.

Tiefenbrun, Susan. "Mathurin Régnier's 'Macette': A Semiotic Study in Satire." *Semiotica* 13 (1975): 131–153.

Vianey, Joseph. *Mathurin Régnier*. Paris, 1896.

CATHERINE RANDALL

RELIGIOUS LITERATURE. Because Christianity was socially and intellectually normative in the Renaissance as it is not today, almost every text used in Europe between 1350 and 1700 could be treated as essentially or potentially religious literature. Modern scholars narrow the field by distinguishing works of declared Christian content. A comparable if opposed distinction can be seen in the manuscript lists of books made in the late Middle Ages as library inventories: classical, that is pagan, authors were gathered under the single category of literature (*literae*). Declaredly Christian writings, in contrast, fell under many headings, such as spiritual writings (*spiritualia*), texts of Christian perfection (*ascetica*), Bibles and related doctrinal works (*Biblica, hagiographica, theologica*), sermons and preachers' aids (*sermones, predicabiles*), church histories, chronicles of religious orders, saintly biographies (*historiae, res gestae*), and liturgical documents (*liturgica, ecclesiastica*). These monastic categories were inherited by the Renaissance and were sometimes simplified: lay libraries might group all of them, for example, as ecclesiastical (*monastica, ecclesiastica*).

Renaissance literature of devotion, the focus here, draws on all the medieval religious genres. Indeed, Christians found spiritual nourishment in a striking variety of Latin and vernacular manuscript and printed texts: narrative, expository, and exhortative prose of all styles; lyric and epic poetry; dialogues; even lists. It seems useful, therefore, to define devotional literature by its intended or actual use in directing piety rather than by criteria of style, format, or content. The three letters of the Holy Name (I.H.U.) promoted by Bernardino of Siena, O.F.M. (1380–1444), for example, may be interpreted as the briefest of Christian devotional literatures, a script accessible to the illiterate. The multivolume critical editions of the Greek and Latin Fathers, edited by the northern humanist Erasmus (c. 1446–1536), provided devotional occasions for the learned. Between these extremes lies the abundant religious literature produced largely by and for the urban layperson, cleric, or professed religious to read and, importantly, to hear.

Contexts and Trends. Already by 1350 the success of vernaculars as artistic languages, the growing lay audiences for books, the influence of the mendicant orders, and the intellectual prominence of universities and Scholasticism had helped create new kinds of devotional texts. During the Renaissance, humanism, print, and confessional polemic wrought further change.

For two reasons, however, Renaissance devotional texts are a more conservative part of European literary history than we often think. First, patristic and medieval texts continued to be read and reproduced, and anonymous works continued to be attributed to earlier authors. Works by and attributed to Augustine, bishop of Hippo (354–430), and to Bernard of Clairvaux, O. Cist. (1090–1153), for example, were often copied, circulating in Latin and vernaculars.

Second, newly composed works took up traditional concerns. The most prominent of these for our period is the perennial interest in reform. Other continuities are also clear. As Lester Little has argued, the ideals of poverty, charity, and selfless service, so characteristic of early Franciscan spiritual writings, were further encouraged by Europeans' growing facility with a monetary economy. Apocalyptic meditations responded to famine, disease, social unrest, and war, although a new genre, instruction in Christian dying (*ars moriendi*), emerged in the early fifteenth century to address death by plague. Controversies in late scholastic philosophy and humanist rhetoric echoed in literature that treated the active and contemplative lives, the nature of body and soul, God's judgment and mercy, and the Neoplatonic hierarchy, none of which were new themes. The Pauline concerns of grace, free will, and predestination, all basic to an understanding of Renaissance spirituality, were also medieval ones, renewed by the recovery and retranslation of Plato and Aristotle. In hybrid ethical writings, servants of Renaissance courts and of the early nation-states composed works that mixed Christian devotion, civic virtue, and instruction in self-presentation or manners; these shared characteristics of medieval mirror literature (*specula*). Attention to the capacities of individuals as emotional and desiring beings, and to orderliness in spiritual training, evident in twelfth- and thirteenth-century monastic literature, was directed toward a broader audience in the late Middle Ages and Renaissance.

Five thematic continuities suggest that definitive features of late medieval piety coexisted with new developments in Renaissance devotional literature.

Devotion to the Second Person of the Trinity. The most popular devotional literature in Renaissance Europe advised the pious how to follow the example of Jesus. This theme, the imitation of Christ (*imitatio Christi*), reflected the ongoing force of twelfth-century eucharistic piety and its emphasis on the Passion. The discursive *Vita Christi* (Life of Christ), by Ludolph of Saxony (d. 1377), extant in innumerable Latin and vernacular manuscripts and more than eighty early printed editions, and the even more popular *De imitatione Christi* (Imitation of Christ) attributed to Thomas à Kempis (c. 1379/80–1471), represent this continuity most strongly. The possibility that believers might re-create Christ's suffering in their own minds and bodies also directed the spiritual exercises used by Catholics and some Protestants in the later Renaissance. For all confessions, devout reading continued to be centered on the Passion; for Roman Catholics, it focused especially on physical details of Christ's suffering, such as the Five Wounds and the Sacred Heart.

Marian devotion. From the late eleventh century, devotion to the Virgin increased in the West. Throughout the Renaissance, Catholics continued to invoke the Virgin, writing about her in epic and lyric, in sermons, and in meditative prose. Mary was represented as wife and mother, as miracle worker, and as intercessor. The Immaculate Conception, the Visitation, and the Assumption were favorite topics. The Carmelite Baptista Spagnuoli (Mantuanus; 1448–1516) composed a Virgilian epic, the *Parthenice mariana,* on the miraculous transport of her house to Loreto, and many authors, including some in the New World, wrote descriptions of miracles associated with her shrines and images. At the same time, devotion to other members of the Holy Family increased as well. Florentine confraternity members, for example, composed vernacular hymns, sermons, and meditations to honor Jesus's cousin, John the Baptist, who had been a city patron for centuries. The cult of Joseph was a newer development in the West, promoted not only because Jesus's earthly father was a model for Christian fathers, as the chancellor of the University of Paris, Jean de Gerson (1363–1429), pointed out, but also because Joseph was useful for dynastic propaganda. Especially in northern Europe, lives of and meditations on Ann and her mother, Emerentia, whose cults were not scriptural, praised holy and, increasingly, literate motherhood.

The desert hermitage. In part because Renaissance culture was an urban and courtly phenomenon, the solitary in the desert was an attractive devotional model. Both the transcription of older works and the composition of new ones demonstrate its popularity. A staggering number of Renaissance manuscript and printed editions recall the experiences of the Desert Fathers, the first Christian anchorites or hermits, who fled Roman persecution in the third and fourth centuries and settled in the deserts of Egypt, where they lived as holy hermits. Before print, and even after, as an act of piety, laypeople might copy out vernacular translations of these accounts for themselves, and will these manuscripts to their children. Extreme isolation was another form of piety; the anchorite Julian of Norwich (1342–after 1416) recorded its benefits in her *Revelations of Divine Love* (*Showings*). But anchoritic practice became less frequent over the course of the sixteenth century. While the observant Reforming movements of the fifteenth century encouraged meditative solitude, and while the need for structured isolation was further acknowledged in the seventeenth century by the Catholic literature of spiritual retreat, Catholics as well as Protestants increasingly directed their devotional activities to public spiritual benefit as well as personal renewal, and the literature reflected this double valuation.

Penitence and confession. The penitentials of the early Middle Ages were handbooks for priests who needed guidance in the care of souls, and Renaissance confessionals, such as that by Archbishop Antonino Pierozzi of Florence (1389–1459), took up this practical function. With print, such specialized texts became more available to laypeople, although their influence in shaping Reformation anxieties about spiritual self-examination is difficult to measure precisely. Life writings, lyric lament, and catalogs of virtues such as the Croatian Marko Marulić's *Bene vivendi instituta* (Instruction in good living; 1506 and many sixteenth-century printings) also reflected thoughtfulness about the health of the soul. The dialogue had not disappeared during the Middle Ages, but beginning with the *Secretum* (Secret book; 1342–1343), in which Petrarch recorded an imaginary conversation with Augustine, it found freedom to explore the self. The widely distributed vernacular dialogues between body and soul, Jesus and the sinner, and man and the devil continued more familiar patterns of discussion inherited from the Middle Ages. Sermon literature, with its exhortations and examples (*exempla,* brief didactic narratives), was often directed to acknowledgement and confession of sin. The *exemplum* was revived in the humanist use of classical, above all Stoic, models for virtue that might be seen as Christian. Suspicion of Stoicizing models is also evident, especially in confessors' attention to affectivity, or the state of the will.

Affectivity. A spirituality that emphasizes experience and emotion rather than speculation and intellect is customarily said to be affective. The word itself (*affectus,* love or emotion) was freely used in devotional works beginning at least as early as the twelfth century. It was relatively infrequent in early humanist religious writings, although evident in prayers and in vernacular sermons of the period; in the Catholic Reformation it reappeared with vigor. The literature of affectivity sought to engage the imagination and the senses, to induce sighs, groans, and tears. Its subjective language was understood to be feminine, although men often wrote and used these texts. The relationships of women and their male confessors also contributed to the popular literary expression of affectivity, as in the case of Raymond of Capua (1330–1399) and Catherine of Siena (1347–1380). Teresa of Avila (1515–1582) developed an especially complex rhetoric of affectivity in her mystical work *Castillo interior* (The interior castle; 1588).

While subjectivity or interiority was basic to late medieval and Renaissance devotional literature, there was disagreement on the degree to which it also ought to be enacted or performed. The influential movement known as the Devotio moderna (Modern devotion), for example, which produced a considerable body of devotional texts, generally disapproved pious theatricality, and Italian humanist authors did not often write about the charismatic and visionary living saints (*sante vive*) around them. Nevertheless, contemporary accounts of intense spiritual experiences circulated as devotional literature, as in the autobiography by the East Anglian laywoman Margery Kempe, completed in 1436, and mystical writings of the Florentine Carmelite nun Maria Maddelena Pazzi (1566–1607). When combined with increased attention to method in spiritual training, the warmth of affective language was powerful. Ignatius of Loyola's *Spiritual Exercises* (1548) registers its success.

These thematic continuities do not indicate stagnation or changelessness. Although the authority of tradition was, generally speaking, valued over innovation throughout this period, Renaissance authors sometimes violently or comically disparaged their predecessors' writings. And while it may seem that Renaissance devotional literature only modulated medieval spirituality, the authors' emphatic claims to novelty—including the novelty of returning to biblical or early Christian positions—were part of the reality of the period. The interplay of change and continuity, of novelty and accepted practice, is evident in the rich field of Renaissance writings on prayer.

The Literature of Prayer. For those who could use them, books were central to the Renaissance practice of prayer. From early Christian times, reading (*lectio*) referred at once to silent, solitary, meditative reading and to vocal, ritual, group reading or recitation as in the liturgy. Benedict's *Rule* (c. 530) required the liturgical "work of God" (*opus Dei*) but it did not explicitly value solitary reading. Benedict did, however, require of readers that ruminatory attention associated with devotional literature. From the later eleventh century, this slow, savoring reading was formalized as the first step of spiritual ascent. Between 1300 and 1700 the systematic movement from reading, to meditation, then prayer, and finally contemplation was elaborated, often on the basis of the *Scala claustralium* (Stairway of the enclosed), attributed to the twelfth-century Carthusian abbot Guido II and the *Epistola ad fratres de Monte Dei* (Golden letter), by the Cistercian William of St.-Thierry (c. 1085–1148).

Just as there were two kinds of reading, so there were two kinds of prayer: vocal and mental. The distinction between the two—one spoken, the other silent, but both of the heart—had been traced by the Fathers to the Bible, and remained significant throughout the Middle Ages and the Renaissance. Vital evidence of the place of vocal prayer can be seen in Catholic texts directing the Forty Hour and Forty Day devotions; these encouraged dramatic vocalizing and the intentionally startling use of gestures quite unlike the ritualized positions of medieval prayer. But in devotional literature emphasis increasingly fell on mental, that is, silent prayer. The two kinds of prayer were related, not opposed, as is evident from the many Renaissance editions of the *Paternoster* (Our Father) with instructional commentary; from advice on the performance and benefit of spontaneous, brief, even monosyllabic prayer (*jaculatoria*); and from encouragement on all sides to make life itself an act of prayer. Silent prayer, moreover, took different forms. The Spanish Carmelite, St. John of the Cross (1542–1591), described it, for example, as beginning in systematic conversation with God and proceeding to mystical abnegation. In the late Renaissance, Quietist devotional readings urged passive prayerfulness before the mystery of God's presence. The violence of the Reformation meant that the possibility of secrecy was also an important aspect of silent prayer. While there were basic disagreements both between Protestants and Catholics, and within each group, concerning some issues of prayer—notably intercession and display—Renaissance literature of prayer, like Renaissance devotional literature in general, took up that theme basic to modernity: the self.

See also **Bible; Book of Common Prayer; Catholic Reformation and Counter-Reformation; Chivalry,** *subentry on* **Romance of Chivalry; Hagiography; Liturgy; Patristics; Reformation;** *and biographies of* **John Colet** *and* **Philipp Melanchthon.**

BIBLIOGRAPHY

Bossy, John. *Christianity in the West, 1400–1700*. Oxford, 1985. Social history that includes attention to changes in the veneration of Mary and the Holy Family.

Constable, Giles. "The Ideal of the Imitation of Christ." In *Three Studies in Medieval Religious and Social Thought*. New York, 1995. Pages 143–248. Traces the conceptual framework of the imitation of Christ in the Middle Ages (there is no complementary work for the Renaissance).

Kieckhefer, Richard, "Major Currents in Late Medieval Devotion." In *Christian Spirituality: The High Middle Ages and Reformation*. Edited by Jill Raitt et al. New York, 1987. Pages 75–108. An alternative conceptual model to the one outlined above; locates devotional religion between public liturgical religion and private contemplative religion.

Kristeller, Paul Oskar. "The Contribution of the Religious Orders to Renaissance Thought and Learning." In *Medieval Aspects of Renaissance Learning: Three Essays*. Edited and translated by Edward P. Mahoney. Durham, N.C., 1974. Pages 93–158. A brief essay followed by an annotated list of religious participants in humanist culture.

Reinburg, Virginia. "Praying to Saints in the Late Middle Ages." In *Saints: Studies in Hagiography*. Edited by Sandro Sticca. Binghamton, N.Y., 1996. Pages 269–282. An excellent introductory study, through the issue of prayer, of the continuities of the imitation of Christ, Marian devotion, meditative solitude, and affectivity.

Schutte, Anne J. *Printed Italian Vernacular Religious Books, 1465–1550: A Finding List*. Geneva, 1983. The introduction defends a provocative expansion of the category of religious literature.

Vitz, Evelyn B. "From the Oral to the Written in Medieval and Renaissance Saints' Lives." In *Images of Sainthood in Medieval Europe*. Edited by Renate Blumenfeld-Kosinski and Timea Szell. Ithaca, N.Y., 1991. Pages 97–114. Based on an analysis of the *Legenda aurea* (*Golden Legend*), discusses how later readers responded to its perceived weaknesses.

ALISON KNOWLES FRAZIER

RELIGIOUS ORDERS. [This entry includes five subentries:

Orders of Men
Orders and Congregations of Women

New Religious Orders and Congregations in Italy
The Jesuits
New Religious Congregations in France]

Orders of Men

By the fifteenth century, all the religious orders with the exception of the order of Carthusians—the saying went that it was *nunquam deformatus* (never in need of reform)—had greatly fallen from their primitive ideals, though not entirely due to human frailty. The disasters of the fourteenth century, including the Black Death (1348), the residence of the popes at Avignon (1309–1378), and the Western Schism (1378–1417), had adversely affected all Christendom as well as the religious orders. Local events, such as the Hundred Years' War (1337–1453) between France and England had also affected the orders negatively.

For traditional monasticism (represented by the Benedictines), the thirteenth and fourteenth centuries were times of continued decline. The rise of the popular mendicant orders (the Franciscans, the Dominicans, the Carmelites, the Augustinians) in the thirteenth century attracted many desirable vocations and the patronage of the growing urban population. The universities that arose at this time, patronized largely by the mendicants, became the new centers of learning. Thus, the monasteries became increasingly isolated from contemporary society and without a proper function there. However, the most deleterious effect on the monasteries was the system of the *commenda* (the provision of a religious benefice to a layperson or such members of the secular clergy as cardinals, bishops, and curialists with dispensation from the regular life), which often placed persons whose only interest was personal gain to be placed at the head of abbeys, and of the great abbeys in particular.

In the course of the fourteenth century, the mendicants, too, fell away from their original ideals, particularly in the matter of poverty. Since the basic elements of the mendicant's vocation are a vow of poverty and the need to support oneself by begging, this deviation signaled a serious problem within the orders.

By this time, however, there was a growing sense within the church of the need of reform "in head and members," a need also felt by the religious orders. The age of the Renaissance, accordingly, was also a time of religious reform. How far this age, with its emphasis on the human spirit, contributed to this new religious spirit is a moot question. It certainly concerned itself with the textual criticism of the Bible and the Fathers and introduced a new method of theology inspired by its humanist values.

Benedictines. In the early Middle Ages, monasticism consisted of an amorphous mass of autonomous monasteries seemingly impervious to any organized effort at control or reform. This autonomy, though dictated by the Benedictine Rule, began to seem detrimental to the order. In 910 William the Pious, duke of Aquitaine, founded the abbey of Cluny, a reform abbey where a system developed that brought together in a loose union a number of monasteries committed to the same customs and usages, meeting regularly in general chapters and subject to canonical visitation. The Clunaic tradition became an accepted vehicle of reform but by the fifteenth century, Cluny had declined.

In Italy, the reform movement in 1424 at the congregation of Santa Giustina of Padua, later called the Cassinese congregation, was noteworthy. This reform tightened the union of abbeys, requiring, among other things, that monks take vows to the congregation, not to the individual abbeys. The Cassinese congregation eventually encompassed all of Italy and Sicily.

The reform movement spread throughout most areas of Europe. The great abbey of Melk (founded 1089) in northeastern Austria, though it did not head a congregation, had wide influence in Austria and Bavaria. The Union of Bursfeld, located in the south of Lower Saxony, became a flourishing congregation comprising more than one hundred abbeys—in part due to the polymath John Trithemius (1462–1516) who, as abbott of Sponheim, zealously promoted the union. In Hungary, Pannonhalma headed a reformed congregation. In Spain, the Congregation of St. Benedict of Valladolid numbered forty-five monasteries. The Benedictine movement of reform was one of the most significant in the period before the Catholic Reformation.

Cistercians. An independent order that sprang from a reform of the Benedictine order, the Cistercians were founded in 1098 by Robert of Molesme at Cîteaux near Dijon, France. The reform sought to observe the rule of St. Benedict in all its original austerity, a purpose reflected architecturally in its unadorned churches and artistically in the monocolored miniatures of its manuscripts. The order spread throughout Europe, especially through the influence of Bernard of Clairvaux (1090–1153), possibly the most influential personage of the times. It declined during the thirteenth and fourteenth centuries and, in spite of papal fulminations against the *commenda* during the fifteenth century, did not experience a movement of reform until the following century.

Canons Regular of St. Augustine. The clerical order of the Canons Regular of St. Augustine experienced—much like the monastic orders and for many of the same reasons, including the *commenda*—a decline during the thirteenth and fourteenth centuries. The fifteenth century witnessed the rise of reformed congregations such as St. Savior (Bologna), Lateran (Rome), St. John the Evangelist (Lisbon), and St. George in Alga (Venice).

Of particular importance among the reforms within the order was the establishment of the highly influential Windesheim Congregation, founded in 1387 by Florentius Radewyns (c. 1350–1400). Radewyns had been a follower of Gerhard Groote (1340–1384), who had established the lay order of the Brethren of the Common Life, based on the concept of *devotio moderna* (modern devotion). According to contemporary reports, Groote suggested on his deathbed that some of the members form an established order of Augustinian canons regular.

The ideals of the Windesheim congregation had a lasting influence on educational practices throughout Europe. Among prominent members of the congregation were Thomas à Kempis (1379/80–1471) and Johann Busch (1399–1480). Busch, whose zeal for reform along the lines of *devotio moderna* won over as many as forty-three monasteries belonging to several different orders—among them the Benedictine Congregation of the Union of Bursfeld—had a great influence on Canons Regular of St. Augustine, and the most prominent independent order of canons regular, the Premonstratensians.

The Premonstratensian order was founded by St. Norbert of Xanten in 1120 at Prémontré, France. As an offshoot of the Augustinian canons their rule was similar, but additions made by St. Norbert caused the order to be particularly austere. As with other orders, this austerity relaxed during the two centuries following its inception, and by 1460, when Johann Busch offered suggestions for reform, at least three Premonstratensian congregations adopted his ideas.

Even more eager to adopt the spirituality of the *devotio moderna* were the Canons Regular of the Holy Cross (or Crosiers), founded around 1210 at Clairlieu near Huy in Belgium by Theodore of Celles. In 1410, inspired by the success of Windesheim, the general chapter abrogated all former decrees in order to start a new reform based on Groote's teachings.

Augustinians. The Augustinians originated in the amalgamation of a group of eremitical orders in Italy. After the decline of religious observance, reform began in the convent of Lecceto near Siena. The general chapter of 1385 officially recognized Lecceto as the first house of the Observance. Two years later, it was withdrawn from the jurisdiction of the provincial superior and placed directly under the prior general.

In the course of the fifteenth century, there were eleven Observant congregations in the order: In Italy at Lecceto (Tuscany), Naples, Perugia, Monte Ortone (Venice), Lombardy, Dulceti (Puglia), Genoa; in Spain in Castile and at Toledo; in Germany in Saxony; and in Ireland at Callan in County Kilkenny. The Observance shared the order's interest in studies and the classical learning of the Renaissance. Giles of Viterbo (1469–1532), prior general from 1507 to 1517, was a leading scholar of Platonic and Hellenistic thought. Martin Luther was a member of the order. A famous Renaissance Augustinian church is that of the Holy Spirit in Florence, the work of Filippo Brunelleschi (1377–1446). Noteworthy paintings are the life cycles of St. Augustine by Ottaviano Nelli (c. 1370–1440) in Gubbio, Italy, and by Benozzo Gozzoli (1420–1497) in San Gimignano, Italy.

Carmelites. The Carmelites, as their name suggests, originated on Mount Carmel in Palestine at the end of the twelfth or the beginning of the thirteenth century. In the years 1206 to 1214, they received from Albert of Vercelli, patriarch of Jerusalem, a rule, which was modified in 1247 to permit foundations in populated areas. With time, they adopted the lifestyle of the mendicant orders, and during the fourteenth century experienced the negative effects of that period as well as its stirrings of reform. Two congregations were formed, one at Mantua, Italy, and the other at Albi, France. These were theoretically subject to the prior general, but the former in particular was practically independent. More effective was the reform carried out within the order by the prior general, John Soreth (c. 1395–1471).

Noteworthy among Carmelite artists are the painter Filippo Lippi (1406–1469) and the poet Baptist of Mantua (1447–1516). In Denmark, under the provincial Paul Helie (1480/85–1534?), the Carmelites led a movement away from Scholasticism toward a theology rooted in scripture and the Fathers.

Dominicans. At the end of the fourteenth century, the master general, Raymond of Capua, confessor of Catherine of Siena (Caterina Benincasa), undertook the reform of the Dominicans

(Ordo Predicatorum, Order of Preachers) with the aid of Conrad of Prussia (d. 1426) in Germany and John Dominici (1356–1420) in Italy. In each province, model convents were instituted after 1387 under a vicar general. When their number grew, congregations were formed, either within a province or independently. In the case of the Dominicans, these congregations, though outside the normal legislative structure of the order, remained united to it.

Beginning with Colmar in 1389, the reform spread through the province of Teutonia, the German province of the Dominicans. From Venice (1390), it spread though Lombardy, Dalmatia, Tuscany, Rome, and Naples, creating the congregations of Lombardy in 1459 and of San Marco, founded by Girolamo Savonarola, in 1493. From the convent of Scala Dei (1423) reform spread throughout Spain to Portugal. The congregation of Holland, beginning in Rotterdam (1444), included France, northern and eastern Germany, Denmark, and Poland. In the second half of the fifteenth century, reform began to prevail and eventually won out completely with the change of congregations into provinces and unreformed convents into vicariates. England remained outside the reform, but the province of Scotland was reformed between 1515 and 1518. After 1480, almost all the masters general were elected from the ranks of reformed friars.

The most famous of the Dominican artists of this period is the Fra Angelico (1378–1455). Tommaso di Vio, known as Cajetan (1469–1534), master general from 1508 to 1518, was a leading commentator on Thomas Aquinas and opponent of Martin Luther.

Franciscans. Reform among the Franciscans (Ordo Fratrum Minorum, Order of Friars Minor) began in 1368, when Paoluccio di Vagnozzo Trinci (d. 1390) founded a hermitage at Brugliano, Italy. His purpose was to restore Franciscan life as St. Francis of Assisi had conceived it in the twelfth century without the modifications subsequently granted by the popes. The reform prospered, and hermitages were founded in Umbria, Tuscany, Bologna, and Venice. In 1388, Paoluccio obtained from the minister general the title and powers of commissary general of the Observance. In 1418, the Observance numbered two hundred friars in thirty-four houses.

Around 1388, a reform arose in Mirabeau in Poitou, France. It spread and eventually achieved practical autonomy through a decree of the Council of Constance in 1415. The French Observance, unlike the Italian, accepted the papal mitigations, opted for communities rather than hermitages, and recommended studies and preaching.

The three Spanish provinces had separate movements of reform: Santiago around 1392, Castile in 1394, and Aragon in 1402. The most important, the reform of Villacreces, had many houses but remained subject to the provincials.

In the course of the fifteenth century, Observant houses appeared throughout Europe, in France, the Netherlands, Germany, Hungary, Austria, Bohemia, Poland, Lithuania, and England. In 1446, Pope Eugenius IV separated the Observance into cismontane (Italy) and ultramontane (north of the Alps), each with its own vicar general elected in their general chapters, over whom the minister general had only the right of visitation.

During this time, the separist tendency of the Observance aroused the opposition of the non-Observants, called Conventuals, who sought to maintain uniformity and unity in the order. The lengthy controversy was fuelled by the support or opposition of various popes. Several attempts at solution by compromise failed of their purpose, and in 1517, Pope Leo X divided the Franciscans into two orders, the Friars Minor and the Conventual Franciscans. The Friars Minor undertook the strict observance of the rule with the papal modifications.

The Minims (the "least" friars), founded by the miracle-working St. Francesco de Paola (1416–1507), were a separate order, approved in 1474 by Sixtus IV, that was dedicated to total abstinence and a simple lifestyle. The Capuchins (so called because of the pointed hood or *capuche* they wore) were founded by Matteo da Bascio (d. 1552) to be more strict than the Observant Franciscans and were formally approved by Clement VII in 1528 as a congregation of the Conventuals. The Capuchins survived the apostasy (1542) of their vicar general, Bernardino Ochino, became famous for their austerities and preaching, and in 1619 were established as a completely separate order.

Servites. The Servite order had greatly declined in religious observance, but, as in the other orders, the fifteenth century was marked by a definite effort at reform. The general chapter of 1404 decreed the restoration of Mount Senario, near Florence, the hermitage in which the order had originated and which had since been abandoned. An Observant congregation arose, consisting of new foundations in Brescia in 1430, Monte Berico in 1435, and Cremona in 1439. After the Council of Trent and subsequent reforms, the Observance lost its usefulness, and in 1570 Pope Pius V united it to the order.

See also **Clergy**, *subentry on* **Catholic Clergy**.

BIBLIOGRAPHY

Elm, Kaspar, ed. *Reformbemühungen und Observanzbestrebungen im spätmittelalterlichen Ordenswesen*. Berlin, 1989. "Reformatory Attempts within the Ordo Canonicus" by Ludo Milis (pages 61–69), on the Canons Regular of St. Augustine; "The Franciscan Regular Observance: The Culmination of Medieval Franciscan Reform" by Duncan B. Nimmo (pages 189–205); "Pretridentine Reform in the Carmelite Order" by Joachim Smet, O. Carm. (pages 293–323) "The Augustinian Observant Movement" by Francis Xavier Martin, O.S.A. (pages 325–345);

Gutiérrez, David, O.S.A. *History of the Order of St. Augustine*. Vol. 1, pt. 2: *The Augustinians in the Middle Ages, 1357–1517*. Translated by Arthur J. Ellis. Villanova, Pa., 1979.

Hinnebusch, William A. *The Dominicans: A Short History*. New York, 1975.

Holzapfel, H. *The History of the Franciscan Order*. Teutopolis, Ill., 1948.

Huber, Raphael M. *A Documented History of the Franciscan Order from the Birth of St. Francis to the Division of the Order, 1182–1517*. Milwaukee, Wis., 1944.

Lekai, Louis Julius. *The White Monks: A History of the Cistercian Order*. Okauchee, Wis., 1953.

Moorman, John. *A History of the Franciscan Order from Its Origins to the Year 1517*. Oxford, 1968.

New Catholic Encyclopedia. 19 vols. New York, 1967; supp. 1, 1974; supp. 2, 1979. "Augustinians" by A. C. Shannon (vol. 1, pages 1071–1076); "Benedictines" by A. G. Biggs (vol. 2, pages 288–295); "Canons Regular of St. Augustine" by J. C. Dickinson (vol. 3, pages 62–64); "Carmelites" by J. Smet (vol. 3, pages 118–121); "Cistercians" by L. J. Lekai (vol. 3, pages 885–889); "Crosier Fathers" by J. W. Rausch (vol. 4, pages 472–473); "Dominicans" by W. A. Hinnebusch (vol. 4, pages 974–982); "Franciscans" by C. J. Lynch (vol. 6, pages 38–46); "Premonstratensians" by R. J. Cornell (vol. 11, pages 737–739); "Servites" by J. M. Ryksa (vol. 13, pages 131–135).

Petit, François. *The Order of Canons Regular of Prémontré*. De Pere, Wis., 1961.

Schmitz, Philibert, O.S.B. *Histoire de l'ordre de Saint-Benoît*. 7 vols. Maredsous, Belgium, 1942–1956.

Smet, Joachim, O. Carm. *The Carmelites*. 4 vols. Darien, Ill., 1985–1988.

JOACHIM SMET

Orders and Congregations of Women

Between the mid-fifteenth and mid-seventeenth centuries the condition of women and the church's involvement in it changed profoundly. The humanistic culture and the religious currents of the fifteenth century influenced a model of active life, in opposition to cloistered life, and favored participation in charitable activities aimed at helping the poor, the sick, and orphans. The Catholic Reformation emphasized the active life, and women were directly engaged in the new apostolic activities (such as catechisms and missions) as well as in welfare services. Female institutions, both cloistered and those for the protection and reform of prostitutes, provided women with an alternative lifestyle or a substitute for the family. The new forms of secular religious life socially legitimized the unmarried condition, which had previously been considered dishonorable.

Devotio Moderna. The most significant example of the renewal of the religious vocation in the fifteenth century was the movement of the "devotio moderna" (modern devotion) and the foundation of religious institutions that observed the practices of the Sisters and the Brethren of the Common Life, inspired by Geert Groote (1340–1384) in Deventer in the Netherlands, and founded in 1379 and 1383 respectively. Groote's main goal was to promote renewal of the religious life based on meditation on scripture and mental prayer. Groote promoted a more emotional and christocentric spirituality aimed essentially at religious practice.

The Sisters of the Common Life were particularly widespread in Holland and northwest Germany, where ninety communities existed at the beginning of the fifteenth century. These women came mainly from aristocratic or bourgeois backgrounds, but there were no entry restrictions based on social condition or age. In addition, the women did not take vows and could maintain property rights. They divided their days between prayer and work. These religious communities, due to their secular features, were well accepted by the general public, which at times feared the multiplication of exempt ecclesiastical institutions or those holding unalienable property. But with time, the sisters' work with textiles was restricted as it became competitive with business activities of the community at large. Even the nature of women's secular congregations, groups in which women lived together without taking vows and without rules, eventually became contested. Both religious and civic authorities exhorted the sisters to adopt the rule of a religious order. Thus some adopted the rule of the Franciscan third order, others that of the Augustinian order. Some women adapted themselves to the monastic model of canonesses regular of the Windesheim congregation, an order founded by Groote for the Brethren disciple, Florenz Radewyns, and others who wished to become priests and lead a cloistered common life.

Mendicant orders also put pressure on the sisters to enter convents. And very few of their religious houses survived the crisis of the sixteenth century, when most of the lands in which they lived adopted

Protestantism. The way of life promoted by the sisters and the needs that inspired the foundation of their order reflected the social and religious aspirations of many women of the Renaissance. The order became part of the Beguine tradition of northwest Europe, which had an equivalent in third orders of some Mediterranean countries. The third orders had adapted themselves to one of the religious rules that the mendicant orders sanctioned for females; the women were thus subjected to ecclesiastical jurisdiction. The Beguines lived off their work, in their own homes or in small groups, and dedicated themselves to prayer and to assisting the needy; they professed simple or private vows. In fifteenth-century Italy the tertiary movement evolved toward a cloistered life, which made the women assume a way of life analogous to the monastic life. However, their way of life remained devoid of the obligation of *clausura* (cloister) canonically tied to the profession of solemn vows. In general, the religious needs of devotion in the female world manifested themselves in an inclination toward a mixed life that united prayer and contemplation with work and charitable service. Small groups living in common, often supported by widows, were also a result of women's social needs to be partially liberated from familial and paternal guardianship.

Reform and the Apostolic Life. In the Catholic world, there was a twofold need to reform old institutions and to increase the apostolic and missionary life. Women contributed to both ends. In the beginning of the sixteenth century, the most direct expression of new spiritual orientations was the foundation of the Company of Saint Ursula promoted by Angela Merici (1470/74–1540). It was a feminine confraternity composed of young women of a middle or low social condition and was protected and governed by noble widows. It was for girls who desired to dedicate themselves to God but who were unable to enter convents for lack of convent dowries. The rules dictated by the foundress included the intent to conserve girls' virginity, but the order did not demand the profession of vows.

The absence of monastic vows arose from an attraction to the early Christian church—when neither monasteries nor convents existed. The intention of conserving virginity while continuing to live with one's family, assisted materially and spiritually by other women, is the Renaissance expression of the attraction formerly felt by lay people toward the way of perfection.

The Company of St. Ursula was founded in 1535, and approved by the local bishop in 1536 and by the pope in 1544. In the period from 1545 to 1565, it spread in the diocese of Brescia but suffered much opposition, which eventually forced it to adopt more direct forms of institutionalization. For example, it became necessary to wear a special belt over one's clothes in order to signify dedication to God. A stronger dependence on one's spiritual father and local bishop was also adopted. In the period after the Council of Trent, as a result of conciliar decrees and successive legislation, many open female monasteries (that is, tertiaries) were forced into cloistered life, but the Brescian company succeeded in conserving its original structure. The bishop of Milan, Carlo Borromeo (1538–1584), promoted the Ursulines in his diocese. The Ursulines, who lived throughout the city, taught catechism to young girls. This apostolic aim was later paired with the need for female literacy and education, which marked the goal of other religious orders, especially those of the seventeenth century. The Ursulines became a cloistered order in France. In this form, it spread to Canada, where at the start of the seventeenth century the Ursuline nuns founded the first female mission.

Apostolic life and charitable activities also inspired the foundation of the Angelicals of St. Paul, under the patronage of the countess of Guastalla, Ludovica Torelli (1499–1569). Twice widowed as a young woman, Torelli sold her fief and gave part of her patrimony to the construction of the church of San Paolo in Milan, which became the home of the Angelic Sisters. The close relationship between the Barnabite Order of Clerks Regular and the Angelic Sisters was unique. It recalled the medieval European double cloister, where a strong female influence in the direction and discipline of the community existed. The Angelic sister Paola Antonia Negri was venerated as charismatic, and was called the "Divine Mother Mistress." The Angelic Sisters' apostolic activity was directed in various cities toward female participation in convent reform, and toward helping the sick, orphans, and former prostitutes. From 1552, following accusations made in Venice and particular opposition to Negri's administration, the congregation was forced to undergo papal investigation. Negri was then sent to live in a convent in Milan and the Angelic Sisters were subjugated to cloistered life. Torelli refused to accept the provision that denied the character of an apostolic life to the order. She founded a school for orphans in Milan and eventually retired to it. The idea of the monastery as an alternative home (in place of family life) for widows who did not intend to remarry was suggested by the presence of so many widows in the convent of San Paolo, some of whom were even members of the same family.

Cloister. The obligation of *clausura* was the most noteworthy decision regarding nuns made by the Council of Trent. In Spanish territory, and before the Tridentine decree was promulgated, Teresa de Cepada y Ahumada (1515–1582) of the Carmelite monastery of the Incarnation of Ávila, undertook a program of reform centered on poverty and cloister, which influenced the male branch of the Carmelites (Discalced) as well. With the support of King Philip II, the reform spread from Spain to France and Flanders. The Discalced Carmelite order of St. Teresa thus assumed a political role as it represented Spanish penetration into traditionally hostile or contested territories. It also engaged in missionary and Counter-Reformation activity in Europe and the New World. At the end of the sixteenth century, the Teresian reform even reached Italy. Thus it represented an exemplary model of life for Counter-Reformation nuns.

Missionary aspiration made female religious orders consider modeling their structure and goals on those of regular clerics. The Institute of the Blessed Virgin Mary, or the English Ladies of Mary Ward (1585–1645), came about in this manner: Its earliest constitutions were based on that of the Society of Jesus. Ward was an English noblewoman born in Yorkshire, who chose to dedicate herself to God first by joining a Poor Clare house in Saint-Omer, France. During her novitiate, however, she realized the cloistered life was in opposition to her own aspiration toward apostolic life. She committed herself to teaching girls, and between 1611 and 1628 she founded numerous colleges in various countries across the continent, including Italy. Although Ward appealed to the pope for recognition of her institute as a religious order, he refused on the grounds that her houses were not cloistered and her sisters attempted to accomplish tasks believed to be unfit for women. Despite twenty years of fruitful work and numerous foundations, the congregations of the Jesuitesses, as they were called, were suppressed by Urban VIII in 1631. But they survived in various places in modified form and were formally approved by Clement XI in 1703. From 1631 however, female aspiration toward an apostolic life and toward teaching had to find expression in secular institutions approved locally by bishops and not officially recognized as religious orders whose members could profess simple vows.

Even within the sphere of monastic life traditionally reserved for women, innovations directed toward the cultural and social needs of the times were not permitted. An example is the institute of the Visitation of Our Lady, founded in France in 1610 by Francis de Sales (1567–1622) and Jeanne-Françoise de Chantal (1572–1641). The institute intended to address itself to those women (such as widows with children or those with health problems) who could not profess vows in an ordinary monastery. The Visitation therefore defined itself as a monastic institute in which women professed simple and temporary vows, observed a mitigated cloister, and agreed to leave the cloister to perform charitable works. Under these terms, the congregation could not obtain papal recognition as a religious order. The institute was not accepted because a simple and temporary vow did not render a nun *tamque vere mortua* (as though really dead) from a legal point of view. That is, the women were permitted to inherit and eventually to marry. After the initial foundation of the Visitation at Annecy in Savoy, a second house at Lyon was to be opened, but the local bishop insisted on cloister. In 1618, the founders had to accept the transformation of the congregation into a cloistered order under the rule of Saint Augustine and with constitutions dictated by Francis de Sales. Through the founders' spirituality, the double aspiration to the contemplative and to the apostolic life was conserved in the Visitation.

The vitality of female religious movements and the prime role played by some founders, reformers, or religious masters of the Renaissance period are examples of women's adherence to the most innovative cultural and spiritual movements of their time. But the aspiration toward apostolic life could only be achieved by several congregations when they agreed to renounce formal recognition as religious orders. Although the church officially insisted on cloistered seclusion as the essential condition of the state of female perfection, it also acknowledged (through episcopal approval by entrusting to women such apostolic activities catechetics) that women hold a role and a social identity previously unrecognized.

See also **Devotio Moderna**; **Spirituality, Female**.

BIBLIOGRAPHY

General Works

Information about each order, institute, and founder mentioned above can be found in Giancarlo Rocca, ed., *Dizionario degli Istituti di Perfezione,* 9 vols. (Rome, 1974–1997); a description and bibliography of select female institutes (Ursulines, Barnabites, Angelic Sisters, Barefooted Carmelites, Visitandines) can be found in Richard L. DeMolen, ed., *Religious Orders of the Catholic Reformation: In Honor of John C. Olin on His Seventy-Fifth Birthday* (New York, 1994).

On new religious institutions and women's culture in France and Italy during the Renaissance, see Elizabeth Rapley, *The Dévotes: Women and Church in Seventeenth-Century France* (Montreal, Kingston, London, Buffalo, 1990); and Gabriella Zarri, ed., *Donna, disciplina, creanza cristiana dal XV al XVII secolo: Studi e testi a stampa* (Rome, 1996).

Specific Works

Bilinkoff, Jodi. *The Avila of Saint Teresa: Religious Reform in a Sixteenth-Century City*. Ithaca, N.Y., 1989.

Devos, Roger. *Vie religieuse feminine et société: L'origine sociale des Visitandines d'Annecy aux XVIIe et XVIIIe siècles*. Annecy, France, 1973.

Konrad, Anne. *Zwischen Kloster und Welt: Ursulinen und Jesuitinnen in der Katholischen Reformbewegung des 16./17. Jahrhunderts*. Mainz, Germany, 1991.

Koorn, Florence W. J. "Women without Vows: The Case of the Beguines and the Sisters of Common Life in Northern Netherlands." In *Women and Men in Spiritual Culture in the Fourteenth–Seventeenth Centuries: A Meeting of South and North*. Edited by Elisja Schulte van Kessel. The Hague, Netherlands, 1986. Pages 135–147.

Mariani, Luciana, Elisa Tarolli, and Maria Saynaeve. *Angela Merici: Contribution towards a Biography*. Milan, 1989.

Perry, Mary Elizabeth. *Gender and Disorder in Early Modern Seville*. Princeton, N.J., 1990.

Zagni, Aldo. *La contessa di Guastalla*. Reggiolo, Italy, 1987.

GABRIELLA ZARRI

Translated from Italian by Elizabeth Bernhardt

New Religious Orders and Congregations in Italy

The rise of new religious orders and congregations usually indicates religious revival among Catholics since new orders are a response of laypeople to felt religious needs. Official approval by bishops and popes comes only later. The Renaissance produced great artists and writers but few new religious orders until the sixteenth century, when some twenty new orders for men and women were founded, mostly in Italy. Many of them were a new kind of order—clerics regular. They were called regular because they lived under a rule (*regula* in Latin); they were priests living in community under a rule with the traditional vows of poverty, chastity, and obedience, and devoting themselves to active ministries, mostly in parishes and schools. The largest new order of clerics regular was the Jesuits; although the Jesuits were founded in Italy, most of their founding fathers were Spaniards, and most Jesuits worked outside Italy. The orders discussed here were small and overwhelmingly Italian.

The Theatines. Four members of a Roman confraternity, the Oratory of Divine Love, began a new religious community in 1524. Their leaders were St. Cajetan of Thiene (1480–1547); Gian Pietro Carafa (1476–1559), who later became Paul IV (1555–1559); Bonafacio de' Colli (d. 1558); and Paolo Consiglieri (d. 1557). Young Thiene worked as a priest in the papal curia and founded confraternities and hospitals in several north Italian cities. Carafa sprang from a noble Neapolitan family; as a young humanist he corresponded with Erasmus, who praised his friendliness and learning, but Carafa was alarmed by the rising tide of Protestantism and became Italy's most ardent supporter of repression. Carafa resigned his bishopric of Chieti ("Teate" in Latin, whence Theatines) when he and Thiene established their new order.

The founders saw a need for communities of austere, pious priests dedicated to preaching, hearing confessions, encouraging frequent communion, giving spiritual directions, and working with the sick in hospitals. Like the earlier orders of monks and friars, the Theatines took permanent vows of poverty, chastity, and obedience, but two practices set them apart. They refused to beg; they would live on stipends from their ministries and from free-will gifts. Also distinctive was their recitation of the divine office in common, but without singing. They did not wear a distinctive religious habit, but only the usual cassock and biretta of diocesan priests. For their first eighty years the Theatines had no official constitutions but depended on a long letter written by Carafa in 1526 that described their lifestyle. Annually elected superiors looked to his letter for guidance. In 1603 a general congregation of the order finally proposed official constitutions that were approved by Clement VIII in 1604.

The Theatines set up their first community at Rome, but when Charles V's army sacked Rome in 1527 they fled to Venice. They set up a second community at Naples in 1533 and returned to Rome in 1557. By 1550 they counted only twenty-seven members, but between 1565 and 1600 new residences were begun in Padua, Cremona, Piacenza, Milan, Genoa, Lecce, Verona, Florence, Bologna, and two additional ones in Naples. A total of 744 men had joined them by 1600; most were already priests when they entered, although the order had some lay brothers. During the next century the Theatines spread slowly to Austria, Germany, Spain, Portugal, and Poland. The Theatines were always an elite group. Probably their greatest contribution to Catholic re-

Plate 1. The Peasantry. *The Harvesters* by Pieter Brueghel the Elder (d. 1569). Oil on wood; 118 x 160.7 cm (46.5 x 63.25 in.). [See the entry on Peasantry in this volume.] METROPOLITAN MUSEUM OF ART, ROGERS FUND, 1919, 19.164

Plate 2. Philip II. King Philip II of Spain kneels in the right foreground of *Adoration of the Name of Jesus* (also called *The Dream of Philip II*), 1580, by Doménikos Theotokópoulos, called El Greco (1541–1614). The painting celebrates the victory of Spain, Venice, and the papacy at the Battle of Lepanto in 1571. [See the entry on Philip II in this volume and the entry on El Greco in volume 2.] ESCORIAL, MADRID/ ERICH LESSING/ART RESOURCE

Plate 3. Philosophy. In *The School of Athens,* Raphael depicts the philosophers of ancient Greece; Plato and Aristotle are in the center. Painted 1513. [See the entries on Philosophy and Raphael in this volume.] VATICAN MUSEUMS AND GALLERIES, VATICAN CITY/SUPERSTOCK

Plate 4. Piero della Francesca. *The Resurrection.* Painted c. 1460–1470. [See the entry on Piero della Francesca in this volume.] PINOCATECA COMMUNALE, SANSEPOLCRO, ITALY/SCALA/ART RESOURCE

Plate 5. **Piero della Francesca**. ***The Baptism of Christ.*** Egg tempera on poplar; 1450s; 167 x 116 cm (65.7 x 45.7 in.). [See the entry on Piero della Francesca in this volume.] NATIONAL GALLERY, LONDON/ERICH LESSING/ART RESOURCE

Plate 6. Pinturicchio. ***Disputa di Santa Caterina.*** St. Catherine of Alexandria argues against defenders of idolatry appointed by Maximinus (caesar, 305–308, emperor 308–313). She was martyred in 305. Mural in the Borgia Apartments in the Vatican Palace. [See the entry on Pinturicchio in this volume.] VATICAN MUSEUMS AND GALLERIES, VATICAN CITY/SCALA/ART RESOURCE

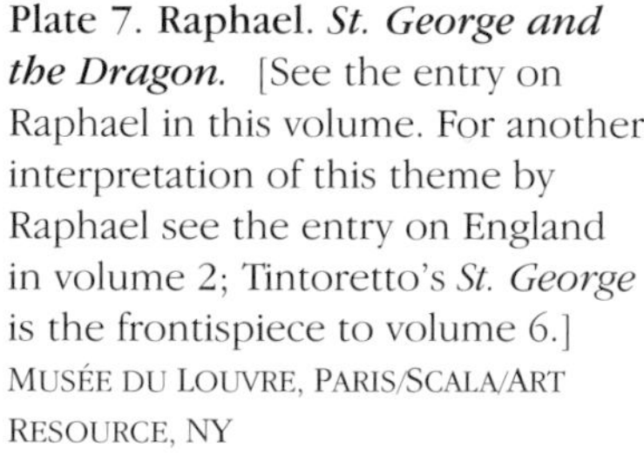

Plate 7. Raphael. ***St. George and the Dragon.*** [See the entry on Raphael in this volume. For another interpretation of this theme by Raphael see the entry on England in volume 2; Tintoretto's *St. George* is the frontispiece to volume 6.] MUSÉE DU LOUVRE, PARIS/SCALA/ART RESOURCE, NY

Plate 8. Raphael. ***The Sistine Madonna.*** Painted for Pope Julius II. The Madonna is flanked by Saint Sixtus I and Saint Barbara. Oil on canvas; 1513–1514; 269.5 x 201 cm (106 x 79 in.). [See the entry on Raphael in this volume.] STAADLICHE KUNSTSAMMLUNGEN, DRESDEN, GERMANY/ERICH LESSING/ART RESOURCE

Plate 9. The Protestant Reformation. *Four Holy Men*, painted by Albrecht Dürer (1471-1528) for the city council of Nürnberg. The panels may be interpreted as expressing the Reformation themes of the supremacy of God's word, the equality of all believers, and need of orderly reformation of the church. In the left panel, John the Evangelist shows the beginning of his gospel (in Martin Luther's German translation) to Peter (the symbol of the papacy in Roman Catholic iconography), who bows to the text of scripture. In the right panel are Paul (holding the book and sword), the inspiration of the Reformers, and Mark. Below the paintings, Dürer placed biblical texts that warn the Nürnberg city councilors against the errors of the Roman church and more radical Reformers. Oil on panel; 1526; each panel 215 x 76 cm (85 x 30 in.). [See the entry on the Protestant Reformation in this volume; for discussion of Dürer's art, see the article on him in volume 2.]

Plates 10 and 11. A Renaissance Theme Reinterpreted. Édouard Manet (1832–1883) shocked the nineteenth-century Paris art world with his portrayal of a nude woman in the company of men in *Le dejeuner sur l'herbe* (Luncheon on the grass; oil on canvas; *above*) in 1863. But the painting revived a classical theme, represented in *Concert champêtre* (Pastorale; open-air concert; oil on canvas; 105 x 36.5 cm. (41 x 54 in.); *below*) by Titian (also attributed to Giorgione). [See the entry Renaissance, subentries on The Influence of the Renaissance and The Renaissance in Popular Imagination in this volume, and the entry on Titian in volume 6.] MANET: MUSÉE D'ORSAY, PARIS/SUPERSTOCK; TITIAN: MUSÉE DU LOUVRE, PARIS/ERICH LESSING/ART RESOURCE

Plate 12. Art in Rome. *Christ Giving the Keys to Peter* by Perugino. The painting, in the Sistine Chapel, illustrates the passage in the gospel of Matthew (16:13–20); the golden key represents Peter's (and the popes') spiritual authority; the iron key hanging from it represents secular authority, which depends on the spiritual. Two other scenes from the gospel are depicted in the background: the tribute money *(left;* Matthew 17:24–27; for Masaccio's interpretation of this passage, see the color plates in volume 4) and opposition to Jesus *(right;* Luke 4:28–30 and the saying in Matthew 23:37–39 and Luke 13:34–35). VATICAN MUSEUMS AND GALLERIES, VATICAN CITY

Plate 13. Peter Paul Rubens. *Venus and Adonis* Venus attempts to restrain Adonis from setting out for the hunt, where she fears, correctly, that he will be killed. The painting depicts a scene from Ovid's *Metamorphoses.* Oil on canvas; c. 1635 or later; 197.5 x 242.9 cm (77.75 x 95.5 in.). [See the entry on Rubens in this volume; for a treatment of the death of Adonis, see the painting by Sebastiano del Piombo in the color plates in volume 6.] METROPOLITAN MUSEUM OF ART, GIFT OF HARRY PAYNE BINGHAM, 1937, 37.162

form was the forty-five bishops who came from their ranks between 1524 and 1624.

The Somascans. The Clerics Regular of Somasca held their first general meeting in 1534 and set up a motherhouse at the Somasca. Their founder, St. Jerome Emiliani (1481–1537), was a former soldier who recognized the need for a group of men to dedicate themselves to caring for orphaned boys and girls. This was the first and major purpose of the new order of priests and lay brothers, which Paul III approved in 1540 and Pius V reconfirmed in 1568. Constitutions were adopted in 1591 and approved with revisions by the papacy in 1626. Clement VIII (1592–1605) invited them to open schools, and soon they were also doing parish work. They had twenty-four residences by 1568 and forty-one by 1595 with some four hundred members. In 1599 they drew up a *Ratio studiorum* (Plan of studies) to guide their schools—the same year that the Jesuits approved their famous *Ratio studiorum*. At various points the Somascans discussed mergers with the Jesuits, Theatines, or Barnabites, but nothing came of these plans. The order was confined almost exclusively to Italy.

The Barnabites. The Clerics Regular of Saint Paul took their name from their motherhouse in Milan. Their founder, St. Antonio Maria Zaccaria (1502–1539), studied at the University of Padua; returning home to Cremona in 1524, he briefly practiced medicine but gradually became engaged in helping people in hospitals and the poor. In 1528 he was ordained and worked briefly in a local parish. About 1530 he came into contact with Battista Carioni da Cremona (c. 1460–1534), an aging Dominican. Carioni had been preaching religious reform through Milanese and Venetian territory, drawing his inspiration from the Bible and church fathers while condemning humanism for excessive concern with literary excellence. Carioni helped to draw up the Barnabite constitutions, but his role was a mixed blessing since he fell under the Inquisition's suspicion.

In 1531 Zaccaria wrote to two friends and proposed a community of clerics combining priestly ministry with a monastic lifestyle. Two years later the three friends set up such a community; six men joined them the next year, all living in a community but without formal vows. Zaccaria served as its superior until 1536.

He was confessor to Countess Ludovica Torelli (1500–1569), a wealthy widow, who began to gather devout women into a parallel order of women, the Angelic Sisters of Saint Paul the Converted (popularly known as the Angelics). Married people among Zaccaria's friends joined a new confraternity, the Devoted Married Laity of Saint Paul, founded about 1531. The three organizations, one for priests, one for nuns, and one for married couples, were closely linked in early Barnabite history and spirituality—too closely for many conservative churchmen.

The early years of the Barnabites were turbulent. In 1534 their public penances at Milan resulted in accusations of heresy and public disorder. Carioni's books were put on the Venetian Index of Prohibited Books in 1554 and on the Roman Indexes starting in 1557, and remained there for more than three centuries. What provoked this hostility? At Milan the priests and nuns mixed together to perform public acts of penance—painting their faces, whipping themselves, carrying heavy crosses, and openly confessing their sins. They also went into the marketplaces to beg donations for pregnant unwed mothers. Such behavior was even more shocking because so many Barnabites and Angelics came from the nobility at a time when Italy was growing increasingly aristocratic in government and mores. Zaccaria passionately defended his followers before the Milanese Inquisition in 1534: such attacks could be expected because his followers were trying to live a life of devotion to Christ; they were proud of being "fools" for Christ's sake. The Inquisition found no real evidence against the Barnabites but did not formally exonerate them.

Zaccaria turned to Rome for approval. In 1533 Clement VII approved their community under episcopal jurisdiction, and in 1543 Paul III put them under papal jurisdiction and praised their purpose and status as clerics who lived a common life and wore a distinctive habit. They received permission to take the three traditional vows and elect superiors to three-year terms. Still, new accusations of heresy kept cropping up so that they grew to only forty members during their first twenty years. In 1551 the new order set aside the constitutions drawn up by Carioni and Zaccaria and drafted new ones, which Julius III approved in 1553. The constitutions, revised by a committee starting in 1570, were approved by Gregory XIII in 1579. The Angelics received papal approval in 1535 but were forced to adopt cloister in 1552. Their new constitutions, drawn up by Carlo Bascapè (1550–1615), were approved by Urban VIII in 1625.

All the orders discussed in this article remained small, and partly for that reason possible mergers with other orders were discussed and sometimes undertaken, but such mergers were usually unhappy and short-lived. The Barnabites discussed or attempted unsuccessful mergers with the Jesuits, the Humiliati (mainly lay brothers), the Oratorians, and the Doctrinaires in France. In 1623 they absorbed the tiny order of the Fathers of Our Lady of the Annunciation founded by Antonio Pagni.

The spread of the Barnabites was slow, but between 1537 and 1544 they established communities at Vicenza, Verona, and Venice at the request of local bishops—in each case with a parallel convent of Angelics. The support of St. Charles Borromeo, archbishop of Milan, who put the Barnabites in charge of his minor seminary, largely stopped criticism and encouraged vocations. Seven permanent communities were set up in northern Italy between 1557 and 1599, plus one in Rome. In 1554 the Barnabites began admitting lay brothers. By 1608 there were 322 Barnabites, and they more than doubled in the next century when the order spread to southern Italy, France, and Austria. They also began to operate free day schools for boys, many of whom joined their ranks.

The Camillans, or Clerics Regular Ministering to the Sick. In 1582 St. Camillus of Lellis (1550–1614) convinced a group of men at Rome to minister to the sick in hospitals. Sixtus V approved the group in 1586 and Gregory XIV raised their twenty-six members to the status of an order in 1591. Members took a special fourth vow to assist physically and spiritually sick people, including plague victims. The Camillans took Christ and the Good Samaritan as their models. The order was highly centralized under a general and four consultors, who were elected every six years by a general congregation. Camillan lay brothers could both vote and be elected to office—two of the four consultors had to be brothers. The Camillans spread quickly from Rome to Milan, Genoa, Naples, Ferrara, and Mantua. In 1591 they accompanied papal troops campaigning in Hungary against the Turks. This and their distinctive habits with red crosses on front and back led to their being seen as precursors of the Red Cross.

The Piarists, or Poor Clerics Regular of the Mother of God of the Pious Schools. St. José Calasanz (1557–1648) was an Aragonese priest who came to Rome in 1592 seeking advancement at the papal curia. There his work with a confraternity that taught catechism to poor children made him aware of how poor children lacked effective schooling. He tried to get both city officials and the religious orders to provide better education for poor boys, but both claimed they lacked resources. In 1597 Calasanz and three friends opened a school where instruction was free of charge. Students flocked to its doors. Money came from the donations of wealthy prelates. The Jesuit colleges were also free of charge, but they accepted only students who already knew the rudiments of Latin, something poor boys rarely possessed. The Piarist schools taught catechism together with subjects that would enable the boys to get better jobs; prayer and the sacraments were integrated into the school day. The band of teachers, some priests, and other laymen grew to twenty. In 1604 Clement VIII authorized them to live as a religious community; in 1614 Paul V agreed to Calasanz's request that they be merged with the Matritani, a small order founded by St. Giovanni Leonardi (1541–1609). The marriage ended three years later, largely because the Matritani were not narrowly focused on education and cultivated a less austere religious poverty. The Piarists, popularly know as the Scolopi in Italian, were formally approved by Gregory XV in 1621. Calasanz was elected the first superior and wrote their constitutions, which received papal approval in 1622. To the traditional three vows the constitutions added a fourth—to teach. Calasanz did not allow his priests to preach; he discouraged their hearing confessions or any work that might distract them from teaching.

The Piarists resorted to begging funds from door to door, at least in time of need. Their schools filled a need, and the order grew rapidly. New schools were opened in thirteen Italian cities between 1617 and 1634. The first school outside Italy opened in Moravia in 1631. By 1646 the Piarists had five hundred members and thirty-seven houses, almost all with schools. In a few instances the Piarists took over existing municipal schools along with an annual subsidy from the town.

This growth caused severe problems for the Piarists; Calasanz seems to have lowered standards to rush candidates into the classroom after only a year's training. The Piarists had a large proportion of lay brothers. The priests taught the more advanced classes, especially those in Latin, and the brothers were restricted to the lower classes. To ease mounting tensions between the two groups, Calasanz authorized all the brothers to be ordained in 1627, but this caused its own problems and was rescinded ten years later. Calasanz's authoritarianism as general superior alienated other superiors. The Jesuits resented the Piarists as a rival teaching order, and many nobles saw free education as undermining traditional class structures. Some Piarists were denounced to the Inquisition, and in 1642 Calasanz was arrested briefly. Finally the order was forbidden to take in novices, and those with vows were allowed to join other orders. Two hundred members left, but three hundred persevered. The papacy relented and restored the Piarists as a congregation in 1656 and as a full order in 1669. Once more their ranks swelled, and new schools were opened, notably in eastern Europe and Spain. The Piarists, who fostered devotion to Mary and to the Eucharist, borrowed much of their spirituality from the Jesuits.

The Oratorians. Technically the Oratorians were not a religious order since they did not take the three traditional vows. They started as a community of priests and laymen that gathered under the charismatic leadership of St. Philip Neri (1515–1595) without vows or an elected superior. Individuals contributed to community expenses from their patrimony or income. Members served the church of San Giovanni dei Fiorentini at Rome, preaching, hearing confessions, encouraging frequent communion, and running discussion groups that sang hymns. From their practice the oratorio musical genre gradually evolved.

Neri wanted his followers to be a model for diocesan priests rather than to become a religious order. But a new Oratorian community at Naples wanted and needed more structure. At Rome most new members were already priests, but at Naples candidates were younger and rarely ordained. Candidates had to undergo training as novices similar to that in religious orders, but they did not take vows. Still other practices edged the Oratorians closer to religious orders. The Naples model prevailed in the sixty-one independent Oratorian communities that sprang up in Italy between 1591 and 1700.

Even closer to religious orders were the French Oratorians, who had a superior general and triennial general congregations. In Italy the Oratorians ran parishes, but in France they were largely schoolmasters who by 1700 operated at least nineteen seminaries and twenty-two colleges. Their schools had a more modern curriculum than those of their Jesuit rivals and were staffed by a remarkable number of outstanding scholars.

Conclusion. Renaissance Italy was never as pagan as Jakob Burckhardt painted it. The new religious orders helped to make the Italy of the late Renaissance more Christian than it had ever been. The clergy was better educated and preached more often. Going to confession and receiving the Eucharist became much more common. The new orders gave young men a better chance at an education and the opportunity to devote themselves to caring for orphans and the sick.

See also **Catholic Reformation and Counter-Reformation; Ratio Studiorum.**

BIBLIOGRAPHY

Primary Works

Hudon, William V., ed. and trans. *Theatine Spirituality*. New York and Mahwah, N.J., 1996.

Olin, John. *The Catholic Reformation: From Savonarola to Ignatius Loyola*. Bronx, N.Y., 1993. Includes texts of the rules of the Oratory of Divine Love and the Theatines.

Sántha, Georgius, and Claudius Vilá Palá, ed. *Epistolarium Coaetaneorum S. Iosephi Calasanctii, 1600–1648*. 6 vols. Rome, 1977–1981. Correspondence of the early Piarists.

Secondary Works

Cistellini, A. *San Filippo Neri: L'oratorio e la congregazione oratoriana, storia e spiritualità*. 3 vols. Brescia, Italy, 1989. Massive study of the Oratorians.

DeMolen, Richard L., ed. *The Religious Orders of the Catholic Reformation*. New York, 1994. The best overview in English, with chapters on the Theatines, Barnabites, Piarists, and Oratorians.

Donnelly, John Patrick. "The New Religious Orders, 1517–1648." In *Handbook of European History, 1400–1600*. Vol. 2. Edited by Thomas Brady et al. Leiden, Netherlands, 1995. Pages 283–315.

Evennett, H. Outram. *The Spirit of the Counter-Reformation*. Cambridge, U.K., 1968. A classic study.

Gentili, Pablo. *The Barnabites: A Historical Profile*. Translated by S. Zanchetta and A. Bianco. Youngstown, N.Y., 1980.

Le Bras, Gabriel. *Les ordres religieux*. 2 vols. Paris, 1979–1980.

Ponnelle, Louis, and Louis Bordet. *St. Philip Neri and the Roman Society of His Times, 1515–1595*. Translated by R. F. Kerr. London, 1937. Reprint, London, 1979. A detailed biography.

JOHN PATRICK DONNELLY, S.J.

The Jesuits

The Jesuits, formally known as the Society of Jesus, are a religious order of the Catholic church founded by Ignatius Loyola (1491–1556) and his companions. They were officially constituted by the bull of Pope Paul III *Regimini militantis ecclesiae* on 27 September 1540. While studying at the University of Paris (1528–1535), Ignatius attracted to himself six other students, including Francis Xavier (1506–1552), who would later become the great missionary to India and Japan, and Diego Laínez (1512–1565), who would be an important theologian at the future Council of Trent and succeed Ignatius as superior general of the order. In 1534 these seven men pronounced vows of poverty and chastity and determined to travel to Palestine to convert the Muslims or, if they could not secure passage, to offer themselves to the pope for ministry wherever he saw fit.

The reason they later gave for this fallback alternative was that they came from several nations and dioceses, so that they as a group had no local commitments. The whole project presaged the strongly missionary character the order would have from the beginning. At this point, however, the companions were uncertain how long they would stay together.

While awaiting passage in Venice and environs the now ten companions were ordained priests and began to call their band *Compagnía di Gesù* (Latin: Societas Jesu; Society of Jesus) because they had no superior but Jesus. They were thus one of the innumerable *compagnie,* or voluntary confraternities, found almost everywhere in Europe at the time. Prevented by war from traveling to Jerusalem, in 1539 they decided to found a new order dedicated "to the progress of souls in Christian life and doctrine and to the propagation of the faith," as the papal bull stated. They would accomplish these goals through ministries like preaching, guiding persons in Ignatius's *Spiritual Exercises,* teaching catechism, hearing confessions, and performing the spiritual and corporal works of mercy.

They envisaged an order dedicated largely to itinerant ministry after the model of Jesus's disciples and the evangelizing Paul. This scope induced them to preclude for their membership the recitation or chanting of the canonical hours in common, a practice their contemporaries considered the very essence of a religious order, and to stipulate for their members a special vow to obey the pope "concerning missions," equivalently a vow to be available as missionaries anywhere in the world. At this time they were not particularly concerned with confuting Protestants or with ecclesiastical reforms within the Catholic church, but countering the Reformation would later be a characteristic of their activities in many parts of Europe.

In 1548 the Jesuits entered a dramatically new phase when they opened their first school, in Messina, Sicily. Until that time they had avoided permanent teaching assignments, but, with the success of Messina and other schools like it designed in accordance with principles of Renaissance humanism, by 1560 they recognized such institutions as their primary ministry. They thus became the first teaching order in the Catholic church. Their most famous and prestigious school was the Roman College, also known as the Gregorian University, opened in 1551. The direct and indirect influence the Jesuits exercised in education was thus immense.

By the time of Ignatius's death in 1556 the Jesuits numbered about 1,000, about 3,500 ten years later, and 13,000 by 1615. They were originally recruited most strongly from Portugal and Spain, but then from other areas in Europe where they were active, especially Italy and Germany. Francis Xavier arrived in India in 1542, where the Jesuits soon established a strong missionary presence. In 1549 he entered Japan, where the same occurred. Later, under the leadership of the farsighted Alessandro Valignano (1539–1606), the Jesuits accepted Japanese into the Society, a departure from a more general policy of denying entrance to non-Europeans. Valignano was also responsible for the policy of accommodation to local rites and customs made famous in China by his disciple, Matteo Ricci (1552–1610), who entered Beijing in 1601. In 1549 the Jesuits landed in Brazil, and later in the century in Mexico and other parts of Spanish America. In the early seventeenth century they arrived in New France.

Character and Culture. The Jesuits strongly resembled the earlier mendicant orders like the Franciscans and Dominicans in their dedication to active ministry, their administrative division into provinces, their independence from the jurisdiction of bishops, and in the mobility on a global scale of their membership. Besides seemingly superficial differences from them in such matters as not celebrating the liturgical hours in common and having no distinctive habit or garb, they differed in more subtle ways.

In this regard the *Spiritual Exercises* was of fundamental importance. No other order had a book quite like it. It acted as a guide through a set of inner experiences every Jesuit underwent, thereby generating motivation and corporate coherence that help explain the order's survival through many vicissitudes. Ignatius, in the *Constitutions* he composed for the order, exhorted Jesuits to "find God in all things" (n. 288).

Ignatius's insistence on frequent correspondence between superiors and subjects established a tradition that also helped the Jesuits achieve a common outlook, and it provided an immense and invaluable resource for future historians of the era. The order experienced, nonetheless, some severe internal crises. The most protracted was the challenge to the fifth superior general Claudio Aquaviva (1543–1615) by a faction of Spanish Jesuits, finally resolved in the general's favor in 1593 by the fifth general congregation, the highest authority in the order.

The *Constitutions* is a sophisticated document showing the influence of humanism in the literary and theological coherence underlying its many prescriptions. It enjoined for members of the order a

Notable Jesuits. Ignatius Loyola holding the Constitutions of the Society of Jesus, flanked by noted Jesuit theologians of the late sixteenth and seventeenth centuries: Leonard Lessius (1554–1623), Luis de Molina (1535–1600), Gabriel Vázquez (1549–1604), and Antonio Escobar y Mendoza (1589–1669). HULTON GETTY/LIAISON AGENCY

careful and long training in pastoral practice and also a rigorous academic program in classical literature and in medieval philosophy and theology. Robert Bellarmine (1542–1621) and Francisco Suárez (1548–1617) were among the order's most outstanding theologians. The *Constitutions* prescribed Thomas Aquinas (1225–1274) as the principal theological authority in the Society, which confirmed and promoted the Jesuits' tendency to see grace as perfecting nature and moved them away from more Augustinian viewpoints. In the seventeenth century they therefore opposed the Jansenists, for which they earned Blaise Pascal's (1623–1662) enmity, articulated in his deliciously wicked satire *Les provinciales* (1656–1657; trans. *Provincial Letters*).

Through their schools the Jesuits were drawn into an ever-deepening relationship with drama, music, and the other arts. Lope de Vega, Pedro Calderón de la Barca, Andreas Greif (Gryphius); Jakob Biedermann, Pierre Corneille, and Molière received their first training in theater in Jesuit schools. Peter Paul Rubens in Antwerp and Giovanni Lorenzo Bernini in Rome, to mention only the most outstanding artists, were closely associated with the order's projects.

Humanism and the Renaissance. The impact of humanism on the Jesuits was pervasive and profound, and perhaps no other single institution was more important than the Society of Jesus as a vehicle for transmitting the humanistic legacy into the modern world. The Jesuits accomplished this transmission principally through their immense network of schools and through the schools they inspired others to undertake. Their own schools put the Jesuits into a relationship to humanism that was systemic, for they cultivated it as a program incumbent upon all their members. Moreover, their obligation to teach the humanistic disciplines turned them into professionals in pursuing them. The single most important document describing their methods is the *Ratio studiorum* (Plan of studies; 1599).

The Jesuits seem to have been more welcoming of the rhetorical component in Renaissance humanism than they were of the historico-critical, especially when the latter touched on the text of the Bible or similar matters. Nonetheless, they constructed their own biographical and historical works much under the influence of the humanists' respect for sources and literary principles, as is manifest in the Bollandists' great edition of the *Acta sanctorum* (*Lives of the Saints*) undertaken in the seventeenth century. Jesuit preaching, although it often retained scholastic underpinnings, was an obvious and vibrant medium for the propagation of elegant style that reached beyond the cultural elite.

See also **Confraternities; Humanism; Ignatius Loyola; Ratio Studiorum.**

BIBLIOGRAPHY

Primary Works

The Constitutions of the Society of Jesus. Translated and annotated by George E. Ganss. St. Louis, Mo., 1970. Ganss's notes and commentary make this among the most informative and useful edition in any language.

Monumenta historica Societatis Jesu. Madrid and Rome, 1894–. For the most part these documents are from the sixteenth century. Especially pertinent within the series are the volumes entitled *Monumenta paedagogica.*

Secondary Works

Alden, Dauril. *The Making of an Enterprise: The Society of Jesus in Portugal, Its Empire, and Beyond (1540–1750).* Stanford, Calif., 1996. A remarkable synthesis, with special attention to finances.

Bangert, William V. *A History of the Society of Jesus.* 2d ed. St. Louis, Mo., 1985. Comprehensive and factually reliable.

Giard, Luce, ed. *Les Jésuites à la Renaissance: Système éducatif et production du savoir.* Paris, 1995. Deals with Jesuit contributions to specific disciplines and cultural traditions.

Martin, A. Lynn. *The Jesuit Mind: The Mentality of an Elite in Early Modern France.* Ithaca, N.Y., 1988. A study of Jesuit attitudes on a variety of issues as derived from their correspondence.

O'Malley, John W. *The First Jesuits.* Cambridge, Mass., 1993. Covers practically every aspect of Jesuit activity from 1540 to 1565, with extensive bibliographical citations.

O'Malley, John W., et al., eds. *The Jesuits: Cultures, Sciences, and the Arts (1540–1773).* Toronto, 1999. Some thirty contributions, especially strong on historiographical issues.

Polgár, László. *Bibliographie sur l'histoire de la Compagnie de Jésus, 1901–1980.* 3 vols. in 6. Rome, 1981–1990. Indispensable guide, whose continuation since 1980 can regularly be found in the *Archivum historicum Societatis Jesu.*

Scaglione, Aldo. *The Liberal Arts and the Jesuit College System.* Amsterdam and Philadelphia, 1986. Brief but broad presentation of aspects of Jesuit schools in Italy and France.

JOHN W. O'MALLEY

New Religious Congregations in France

New religious orders arose in France in response to the problems of the Catholic Church, which was spiritually and physically exhausted by the Wars of Religion (ended 1598). Damage to church property made collection of revenues from benefices difficult. The diocesan priests' lack of education, inability to preach and hear confessions well, inability to give spiritual guidance to the laity, ignorance of canon law, concubinage, and pursuit of benefices (income-producing appointments) gave rise to a sense that they were not living up to the standards set by the Italian congregations of priests, the reform of the old monastic and mendicant orders, and the Council of Trent.

Influences. An initial impetus for reform came from the *dévots* (devout Catholics dedicated to personal and institutional reform), notably the circle that gathered in the Paris house of Barbe-Jeanne (Avrillot) Acarie (1566–1618). Acarie supported the introduction into France of the reformed Carmelites (the Spanish branch of the order to which Teresa of Ávila and John of the Cross belonged) and the Ursulines (the Italian congregation of women founded by Angela Merici), and she encouraged Pierre de Bérulle (1575–1629) to establish the Oratory (a priestly congregation) in France. On the death of her husband in 1613, she became a Carmelite, taking the name Marie de l'Incarnation (Mary of the Incarnation).

The spirituality of Bérulle was one of three major influences on French congregations; the other two were the organization of the Society of Jesus (Jesuits) and the work of Vincent de Paul.

Bérulle's thought emphasized the priesthood of Jesus Christ and the priesthood of ordained priests. The priesthood, not the vows of religious orders, was for him the source of all holiness in the church, through the celebration of mass, the administration of the sacraments, and the giving of spiritual direction to other priests and to laypeople. Bérulle recognized the need for practical reform of the clergy but was more dedicated to encouraging the holiness of priests. Bérulle was influenced by the Jesuits' emphasis on realizing the fruits of prayer and contemplation in practical action in the world. The organization of the Society of Jesus—its centralized government with a superior general elected for life—also appealed to him. However, he adapted the structure of the Society to the French situation, rejecting subordination to Rome. Vincent de Paul (1581–1660) followed Bérulle in emphasizing the central importance of the secular priesthood in the life of the church and sought ways to encourage priests to undertake active ministry.

Congregations of Men. The earliest French congregation of priests was the Congregation of Christian Doctrine, founded by César de Bus and Jean-Baptiste Romaillon in 1592. As their name implied, the Doctrinarians were a community of teachers dedicated to forming in piety boys of all social conditions, and educating them in the humanities. To do this, the teachers had themselves to be pious. The congregation was riven by debate over the suitability of solemn vows until 1647, when it ceased to require vows and became a community of secular priests.

The most influential congregation was the Oratory of Jesus and Mary, founded by Bérulle in 1611. Influenced more by the Society of Jesus than by the Italian Oratory of Philip Neri, Bérulle gave the Oratory a central administration headed by a general elected for life, a structured spirituality inspired by his theology of the priesthood, and a dedication to formation of the clergy. The debate over vows among the Doctrinarians moved many of them to join the Oratory in 1619. At Bérulle's death in 1629, there were about four hundred Oratorians, all secular priests without vows, living in sixty houses throughout France.

Other congregations arose either from Bérulle's inspiration or directly from the Oratory. Adrien Bourdoise founded the Congregation of Saint Nicholas-du-Chardonnet, which was devoted to seminary education, in 1620, and Jean Eudes left the Oratory to found the Congregation of Jesus and Mary (1643), which was devoted to the training of priests, the preaching of parish missions, and the direction of secondary schools.

Vincent de Paul founded the Congregation of the Mission in 1625. The Vincentians, also called Lazarists after the congregation's headquarters at the priory of Saint-Lazare, conducted missions in country parishes: they preached, taught catechism, heard confessions, and aided the sick. Led by a superior general and an assembly general, they had conducted 840 missions by 1660 and directed thirty seminaries by 1700. A disciple of Vincent, Jean-Jacques Olier, founded the Congregation of Saint-Sulpice in 1642; the seminary of Saint-Sulpice became the most important institution for the training of priests in France.

Congregations of Women. Although the Council of Trent had ordered that women's communities be enclosed and although the Ursulines in France were cloistered, many French communities engaged in limited apostolates, usually the education of girls. The earliest was the Congregation of Notre-Dame, founded by Alix Le Clerc and Pierre Fourier in 1598. Jeanne de Lestonnac (1556–1640) established the Company of Notre-Dame of Bordeaux in 1605; modeled on the Society of Jesus, the company was dedicated to the religious education of girls who were expected to influence society as grown women.

Vincent de Paul encouraged the establishment of the Sisters of Charity by Louise de Marillac in 1633. The mother superior was elected for a three-year term; the superior general of the Lazarists served as spiritual director. The sisters established their first school in 1638.

Institutions. Like the Italian congregations of secular clerics in the early sixteenth century and the Jesuits, French congregations of men intended to serve the church by improving the clergy. But by the early seventeenth century the number and types of their ministries—among them seminaries, secondary schools on the humanist model, institutions for the care of the sick and indigent, and missions for parishes—had expanded and their institutions had become more formal. Bérulle, for example, originally intended that the Oratory offer spiritual counseling and ways of improvement to priests, but Pope Paul V in 1613 required the congregation to operate schools. After Bérulle's death the Oratory developed the institutions of a formal religious organization: a permanent administration to assist the general, superiors of local houses appointed by the central administrators, a triennial general assembly to set policies and make rules, and institutions of training and formation for its own members.

BIBLIOGRAPHY

Primary Works

Bérulle, Pierre de, et al. *Bérulle and the French School: Selected Writings*. Edited by William M. Thompson. Translated by Lowell M. Glendon. New York and Mahwah, N.J., 1989.

Vincent de Paul and Louise de Marillac. *Rules, Conferences, and Writings*. Edited by Frances Ryan and John E. Rybolt. New York and Mahwah, N.J., 1995.

Secondary Works

Boureau, René. *L'Oratoire en France*. Paris, 1991.

Broutin, Paul. *La réforme pastorale en France au dix-septième siècle*. 2 vols. Tournai, Belgium, 1956.

Pisani, Paul. *The Congregations of Priests from the Sixteenth to the Eighteenth Century*. Translated by Mother Mary Reginald, O.P. London and St. Louis, Mo., 1930.

Viguerie, Jean de. *Une oeuvre d'éducation sous l'ancien régime: Les pères de la doctrine chrétienne en France et en Italie, 1592–1792*. Paris, 1976.

Walsh, Eugene Aloysius. *The Priesthood in the Writings of the French School: Bérulle, de Condren, Olier*. Washington, D.C., 1949.

Williams, Charles E. *The French Oratorians and Absolutism, 1611–1641*. New York, 1989.

STEPHEN WAGLEY

RELIGIOUS PIETY. Piety means the observance of religion in public and in private, communally and individually. The observance of religion includes any human activity involving the myths, rituals, and symbols of religion which aims to commune with the divine. Lay piety means the observance of the Christian religion by nonclerics and encompasses a wide array of practices, from liturgies, processions, and pilgrimages to private prayer and home devotional reading. But the line between laity and clergy should not be exaggerated. The religious life of the laity was never distinct from, or totally independent of, the clergy, and vice versa. They shared the same myths, rituals, and symbols. Though lay Christians could take the lead in the observance of religion, the clergy were always involved, directly or indirectly.

On the eve of the Renaissance, Europeans shared a religion that sought to establish links between earth and heaven, body and soul, the human and the divine. Lay piety was more practical than theoretical. Though informed by the theology of the church, it focused more on rituals, symbols, and ethics than beliefs.

Sacred Rites: The Seven Sacraments. The rites of the church known as sacraments, which were conferred by priests, were the basic structure of piety and the framework for devotion. In 1439 the Catholic Church proclaimed seven sacraments as official dogma: baptism (initiation), penance (purification and sanctification), the Eucharist (communion with the divine), confirmation, marriage, ordination as a cleric, and extreme unction (preparation for death). Five of the sacraments were rites of initiation and transition received once in a lifetime or more than once only in unusual circumstances (for example, marriage and extreme unction). But the Eucharist and penance were constantly celebrated. The Eucharist took place within the ritual, or liturgy, called the Mass, during which, according to the teaching of the Catholic Church, bread and wine were miraculously transformed into the body and blood of Christ and offered for consumption by the faithful. The sacrament of penance offered forgiveness of sins obtained by confessing one's misdeeds to a priest, expressing contrition, and obtaining absolution from the priest.

The Mass played a pivotal role in piety. As the most frequently celebrated rite, it brought communities together for prayer, instruction, and celebration. It allowed the laity to experience repeatedly a synthesis of the ultimate Christian values. The Mass also acquired a therapeutic value. Masses known as votive could be offered to ward off or correct as many ills as can befall the human race: to protect crops from hail or drought, to be spared by plagues, even to help find lost objects. Even though priests celebrated masses, these specific requests usually came from the laity.

The Mass also assumed a practical spiritual and social function connecting the living and the dead. Masses for the dead lessened the time spent in purgatory by the souls of the deceased; they also cemented relations among kin and neighbors. Masses for the dead were a key element of lay piety throughout Europe by the fifteenth century.

Within and beyond the ritual of the Mass, the consecrated bread became a focus of devotion. Consecrated hosts were displayed for adoration in special vessels known as monstrances, which could be taken out for processions. Hosts were believed to work wonders, especially when denigrated by skeptics or infidels. Reports of eucharistic miracles sharply increased in the fifteenth century, as did the number of shrines built to revere hosts that reportedly bled, levitated, or impaired their would-be assailants. The yearly feast devoted to the Eucharist, Corpus Christi or Corpus Domini (Body of Christ or God), assumed a privileged place in the Christian calendar in the fifteenth century. On Corpus Christi day (usually in June) priests and people in procession carried the consecrated host through the streets, making sacred the world outside the church.

The fact that sacramental ritual was conducted in Latin throughout western Europe bound together a vast array of disparate cultures in lay piety. Although the vast majority of the laity did not understand Latin, its use surrounded the ritual with an aura of mystery and holiness. In lay piety Latin assumed a sacred and mystical quality, an attribute that emphasized the different identities of the clergy and the laity.

Sacred Space. Lay piety fixed on specific earthly points which were believed to be closer to heaven. Divine power was believed to reside more strongly in churches where certain saints and martyrs were buried, or where divine apparitions and visions had been seen, or in churches that housed certain sacred objects. Called shrines, these special churches drew worshipers from far and near. Shrines were often places where miracles were expected. The promise of healings, especially physical, filled the map of Europe with urban and rural shrines.

Saints' graves and saints' relics were singularly sacred and powerful. Relics were the physical traces of human beings who had died and gone to heaven.

Devotion to relics had been part of Christianity since its earliest days, when the remains of martyrs began to be venerated. By the fifteenth century the cult of relics was deeply woven into the fabric of lay piety and thriving. But for every genuine relic there were many of doubtful origin. At least seven different shrines claimed to have the head of John the Baptist. Some clergy and laity resolved these conflicting claims by believing that God miraculously multiplied relics for the benefit of humankind. But others did not accept such reasoning by the fifteenth century.

Churches also contained visual representations of the holy, such as paintings and statues of saints which were the focus of veneration. Although the theology of the church distinguished between the worship offered to God alone and the reverence shown to images which reminded the viewer of God, lay piety did not always understand and observe the distinction. People knelt and prayed before images; they burned candles and incense or offered flowers to them. They wore stamped wax or metal images of Jesus, Mary, or the saints on their bodies, in remembrance and for personal protection. These created private points of contact with the divine. The Renaissance stands out as an extraordinary period of lay investment in sacred art. In Zurich, for example, the donation of sacred images increased a hundred fold between 1500 and 1518.

The cult of the saints expanded considerably in the fifteenth century through the creation of chapels and shrines, the donation of images, and the publication of lives of the saints, stories of miracles, and books of prayers. The most popular saint was the Virgin Mary, Mother of God and Queen of Heaven, who was considered the most effective advocate because she was closest to her son, Jesus. Mary was also considered the most tender and caring intercessor. Approached as a mother, her veneration balanced that of God the Father, endowing the divine with a feminine dimension. Mary was simultaneously the most universal and most local saint. She was often assigned a regional persona, especially at shrines where miraculous images were venerated. There she became "Our Lady of [place]," such as at Montserrat in Catalonia, Walsingham in England, or Altöting in Bavaria.

Being a member of the Catholic Church meant belonging to a community of both the living and the dead. Hence the saints in heaven were sought as patrons and intercessors, while the living sought through their prayers to shorten the stay of the deceased sinners in purgatory.

The pilgrimage and the procession were two prominent features of lay religion. Pilgrimages were journeys to sacred sites, where the divine was believed to be intensely present, in order to ask for divine assistance or forgiveness of sins. Processions were parades, group journeys going forth from churches and shrines, making a circuit with a definite path. Processions celebrated fixed feasts or dealt with crises such as plagues or drought. Processions usually carried and prominently displayed sacred objects.

Sacred Time. Much of lay piety was scheduled and predetermined according to the calendar. Sunday was a sacred day, a holy time when attendance at Mass was required and all work should cease. Friday was a day of penance, when all were required to abstain from eating meat. But clergy and laity celebrated many other days as events in salvation history: Epiphany, Good Friday, Easter, Pentecost, Christmas, and others. Saints were honored on specific days of the year set down by the church calendar. Special masses, processions, public celebrations, and the suspension of work marked saints' feast days. But the laity also sometimes celebrated saints' days with riotous behavior.

Fasting and feasting were a perpetual dialectic in piety, often balanced but sometimes prone to extreme swings. For example, carnival, not an official part of the church calendar, involved several days, sometimes weeks, in which people indulged in food, drink, partying, and sexual license. It preceded the penitential season of Lent, which consisted of forty days of fasting and prayer in preparation for the joyous celebration of Easter.

Piety was private as well as public. Personal devotion involved the repetition of short set prayers (Our Father—the Lord's Prayer—the Hail Mary, the Gloria, and the Creed). These might be said in a pattern of repetitions, especially that of the rosary, in which the devout person prayed a specific number of Hail Marys, Our Fathers, and Glorias according to the number and arrangement of the beads on the rosary.

Piety and Superstition. The line between piety and what the clergy termed the superstition of the laity was often crossed and led to tension. A constant irritant was the adaptation of ritual to "magical" or "superstitious" purposes, such as scattering consecrated hosts on the ground to ensure a good harvest. Clergy and laity clashed over attitudes toward symbols and rituals, such as the belief that an image of St. Christopher could protect one from accidents or that anyone who recovered his or her health after receiving extreme unction should remain barefoot and celibate thereafter. But some priests shared the beliefs of lay piety and acted on them, as when they performed rites of exorcism on swarms of locusts, seeking to drive away the demons that supposedly possessed the insects.

Exorcisms and other rites aimed against the devil were an integral part of lay piety because both the clergy and the laity believed that evil was personified in spiritual entities who had some degree of control over the material world and who could wreak havoc on the human race. Demons lurked everywhere, causing harm and constantly tempting humans to sin. Even worse, demons attracted veneration in exchange for magical or miraculous favors. Such beliefs were as old as Christianity itself and solidly grounded in the New Testament, but the line between Christian teachings and pre-Christian beliefs in evil forces had blurred in the Middle Ages, especially with ancestral folk customs. The clergy might label the latter as demonic. When that happened, the laity could turn toward the rites of the church which warded off demons or toward occult rites that tapped demonic powers.

Good spirits who sometimes communicated with the human race also populated the spiritual world. Monks, nuns, and lay people frequently reported apparitions of Christ, Mary, angels, and saints. These extraordinary religious experiences of the clergy and laity helped shape piety. Visionaries who claimed to see Christ, Mary, or an angel or saint could give rise to cults and shrines, which the clergy might approve or disapprove.

The Renaissance. The cultural renewal of the Renaissance contributed substantially to the unfolding of new attitudes toward religion. The Renaissance drive to return to the sources and origins of the Christian religion brought many aspects of piety under closer scrutiny, often finding them lacking in correctness. The restoration of Christianity to its primitive purity became the chief goal of many reform-minded scholars of the Renaissance. These so-called Christian humanists, found throughout Europe, criticized religious corruption and sought to reform piety. Of them, Desiderius Erasmus (c. 1466–1536) had the greatest impact on religion.

Erasmus summarized much of the Renaissance critique of medieval piety and publicized it in numerous books, often repeatedly published and translated. His *Enchiridion militis Christiani* (Handbook of the Christian knight; 1503), *Moriae encomium* (Praise of folly; 1511), and *Colloquia* (1518–1533) took aim against many of the chief expressions of lay piety, notably vows, pilgrimages, rote prayers, devotion to images and relics, and the invocation of the saints. The *Colloquia* contains some of the most biting satirical pieces written to that date against lay piety.

Although Erasmus never condemned outright any aspect of medieval piety, he lampooned lay devotion and called into question some of lay piety's most significant elements. He argued that they were a gross deviation from the spiritual, Christ-centered worship of the early church. Disparaging the cult of the saints, as well as all attempts to localize the divine, Erasmus urged the laity to turn away from the external elements of religion and to draw inward, to the realm of the soul.

The Protestant Reformation. The Protestant Reformation brought about a wholesale revolution in lay piety. The most pronounced change in lay piety, shared by all Protestants, was the acceptance of the Bible as the supreme guide for thought and behavior. Hence Protestants sought to do away with all aspects of piety that they deemed unbiblical, which included some of the distinguishing features of medieval religion.

Protestants no longer sought to tap the power of the divine by localizing it. They eliminated holy sites, together with apparitions, visions, and miracles. Sunday remained a holy day, but gone were the saints' feasts. Protestants eliminated the attempt to negotiate with the divine on legalistic terms, which meant that they denied the existence of purgatory and the cult of saints who might intercede for humankind. They replaced Latin with vernacular languages for prayer and ritual, and reduced the sacraments from seven to two (baptism and the Eucharist). Beyond these common traits, however, Protestant piety was as varied as the number of churches it produced.

Lutherans. The church established under the leadership of Martin Luther (1483–1546) strongly rejected any aspect of piety that focused on activities that should produce specific responses from God, including fasting, pilgrimages, vows, the celebration of saints' feasts, and masses for the dead. Lutherans rejected the intercession of the saints and the veneration of their relics and images but retained works of art in their churches and books. Because Luther firmly believed in the presence of demons and their power over the human race, Lutherans continued to practice exorcisms and to persecute witches.

The Reformed churches. The family of churches known as Reformed, whose major leaders were Huldrych Zwingli (1484–1531) and John Calvin (1509–1564), took further steps to spiritualize piety, stripping it further of material points of contact with the divine and purging it of any rituals that could lead to what they considered idolatry. Guided by a strict interpretation of the Old Testament passages forbidding the use of religious imagery, they destroyed sacred art and banned it from churches. Iconoclasm (the destruction of images) became an earmark of Reformed Protestantism. Although the Reformed were less inclined than Lutherans to stress the presence of the demonic in the world, they nevertheless believed in witches and sought to wipe them out.

The radicals. The two most distinctive features of those churches classified as radical or Anabaptist were their rejection of compulsory infant baptism and the high incidence of lay leaders, most of whom were artisans. The radicals sought the most thorough reform of lay piety by insisting that only the seriously committed could be considered true Christians. Because they were persecuted throughout western Europe, the ethic of martyrdom assumed a central place in their piety.

The Anglican Church. The Church of England eventually adopted a middle way between Reformed Protestantism and Catholicism. English lay piety centered on the reformed rituals found in the Book of Common Prayer (1549–1559). Reformed Protestants in England, known as Puritans, considered some of the external traces of medieval piety retained by the Anglican Church as "idolatrous" and waged a persistent campaign against the church.

The Catholic Reformation. Changes in lay piety were less pronounced among those who remained with the Roman Catholic Church, but they were still significant. The reformist impulses of Christian humanism, coupled with the need to combat defections to Protestantism, led to an intense reinvigoration of medieval religion. Most of what vanished in piety among Protestants continued to thrive among Catholics, especially after the Council of Trent (1545–1563) reaffirmed the value of traditional rituals. It defended the merits of shrines, images, relics, pilgrimages, rosaries, and acts of charity. The transition from Renaissance style to baroque art in Catholic cultures saw an intensification of external expressions of religion at all levels. Nevertheless, after Trent guidelines were clarified, and clerical control over the establishment of cults and objects of veneration increased. Stricter methods were applied to the authentication of visions, apparitions, and relics, and for the depiction of sacred images. Promotion to sainthood became a more rigorous process.

The Catholic Reformation also sparked a renewal of private devotion and especially the reading of catechisms, saints' lives, miracle accounts, prayer books, and devotional treatises. Many clerical authors promoted ascetic ideals to lay audiences by writing books which sought to teach the laity how best to approximate the monastic life while living in the world. *Il combattimento spirituale* (The spiritual combat; 1589) by Lorenzo Scupoli and *Introduction à la vie dévote* (Introduction to the devout life; 1609) by St. Francis de Sales were very widely read.

Conclusion. The Renaissance saw profound change in religion for all Christians, lay and clerical. Although the transformation of religion varied widely in time and place, it eventually led to a greater standardization of piety and to increased clerical control. All the various Reformations produced clergy who were more intent on supervising the piety of their lay flocks and on rooting out their vices, errors, and superstitions than in the past. The lines between "true" and "false" piety, as determined by the clergy, became clearer after 1600.

See also **Carnival, Catholic Reformation and Counter-Reformation; Christianity,** *subentry on* **The Western Church; Clergy; Liturgy; Parades, Processions, and Pageantry; Pilgrimage; Protestant Reformation;** *and biography of Erasmus.*

BIBLIOGRAPHY

Primary Works

Ciruelo, Pedro. *A Treatise Reproving All Superstitions and Forms of Witchcraft.* Translated by Eugene A. Maio and D'Orsay W. Pearson. Rutherford, N.J., 1977. Translation of *Reprobación de las supersticiones y hechicerias* (1530).

Erasmus, Desiderius. *Colloquies.* Vols. 39–40, *Collected Works of Erasmus.* Translated by Craig R. Thompson. Toronto; Buffalo, N.Y.; and London, 1997.

Sales, Francis de, St. *Introduction to the Devout Life.* Translated by Michael Day. Westminster, Md., 1956.

Scupoli, Lorenzo. *The Spiritual Combat.* Translated by William Lester and Robert Mohan. Revised ed. New York, 1978.

Spener, Philipp Jakob. *Pia Desideria.* Translated by Theodore G. Tappert. Philadelphia, 1964.

Thomas à Kempis. *The Imitation of Christ.* Translated by William Creasy. Macon, Ga., 1989.

Secondary Works

Bossy, John. *Christianity in the West, 1400–1700.* Oxford, 1985.

Christian, William A., Jr. *Apparitions in Late Medieval and Renaissance Spain.* Princeton, N.J., 1981.

Christian, William A., Jr. *Local Religion in Sixteenth-Century Spain.* Princeton, N.J., 1981.

Duffy, Eamon. *The Stripping of the Altars: Traditional Religion in England, c. 1400–c. 1580.* New Haven, Conn., 1992.

Eire, Carlos M. N. *From Madrid to Purgatory: The Art and Craft of Dying in Sixteenth-Century Spain.* New York, 1995.

Eire, Carlos M. N. *War against the Idols: The Reformation of Worship from Erasmus to Calvin.* New York, 1986.

Galpern, A. N. *The Religions of the People in Sixteenth-Century Champagne.* Cambridge, Mass., 1976.

Marsh, Christopher. *Popular Religion in England: Holding Their Peace.* New York, 1998.

Muir, Edward. *Ritual in Early Modern Europe.* New York, 1997.

Nalle, Sara T. *God in La Mancha: Religious Reform and the People of Cuenca, 1500–1650.* Baltimore, 1992.

Rubin, Miri. *Corpus Christi: The Eucharist in Late Medieval Culture.* Cambridge, U.K., 1991.

Scribner, R. W. *Popular Culture and Popular Movements in Reformation Germany.* London, 1987.

Strocchia, Sharon T. *Death and Ritual in Renaissance Florence.* Baltimore, 1992.

Trinkaus, Charles, and Heiko A. Oberman, eds. *The Pursuit of Holiness in Late Medieval and Renaissance Religion.* Leiden, Netherlands, 1974.

Whiting, Robert. *The Blind Devotion of the People: Popular Religion and the English Reformation.* Cambridge, U.K., 1989.

Carlos M. N. Eire

RELIGIOUS THEMES IN RENAISSANCE ART.

Religious art functions to reinforce faith and articles of doctrine; in this respect the expression of religious themes in Renaissance art was an extension of medieval practice. At the same time, the continued urbanization and developing economic strength of western Europe, the restoration of the Papal States and increasing centralization of the papacy in Rome, and a proliferation of new religious orders were among the significant factors that led to a growing demand for religious art in both public and private spheres.

Overview. Works of art as diverse as Jacopo della Quercia's Fonte Gaia (c. 1419), Siena's celebrated public fountain which featured the Madonna and Child flanked by Virtues, or the bronze St. Peter placed atop the Column of Trajan in Rome in 1588 remind us that Christian imagery was ubiquitous and deemed appropriate, if not necessary, for the ornamentation of public buildings and civic monuments in Renaissance culture until the Protestant Reformation. The renovation and ornamentation of the great cathedrals and the significant monastic establishments rising throughout Europe during the Renaissance were also regarded as a source of community pride and furnished numerous occasions for the public display of sacred art. The acquisition of family chapels, with the concomitant responsibility for their decoration, as well as the continuing practice of privately commissioning religious art and liturgical objects for donation to the church, allowed private patrons to use religious art as a public means of declaring their faith while also conveying an impression of their wealth and status to the community at large.

Similarly, religious images became a constant in the domestic realm, as preachers and authors advocated the usefulness of sacred imagery in the home. The wealthy constructed private chapels for personal devotions in or adjacent to their palatial residences. Merchants and other travelers carried portable altars. The fastidious might commission a private *pax,* a small plaque kissed during mass. Netherlandish Paternoster beads, worn on belts or attached to rosaries, could be opened to present elaborately carved scenes of Christ's Passion for private contemplation. Italian *deschi da parto,* traditional gift platters laden with delicacies to tempt new mothers after the rigors of childbirth, might be decorated with inspirational or celebratory religious scenes. Personal portraits, a growing genre of Renaissance art in all media, could allude to the piety of the sitter by means of attributes or allegory, at the same time that donor portraits appeared with increasing frequency in altarpieces. Art fairs in Bruges offered middle-class patrons their choice of subject. The less well-heeled hung wooden crucifixes above beds or purchased inexpensive woodcuts, and, by the end of the fifteenth century, engravings provided religious art for the most humble dwelling.

The ancillary contexts in which religious imagery was placed fostered a greater sense of God's presence in every area of human life. Through increased attention to narrative presentation, religious themes became less ethereal and more closely aligned to everyday experience, structured in time and physical place. This new emphasis on the concreteness of sacred history was enhanced by the development of artistic techniques such as linear and atmospheric perspective and experimentation with new media such as oil painting, which allowed greater visual realism and resulted in religious art of broad empathetic appeal. Religious themes underscoring the humanity of the biblical past became popular: scenes detailing the childhood of Christ, the heroism of David and Judith, and the model acts of saints appeared as frequently in the secular domain as in ecclesiastical settings. In addition, as Renaissance humanism intensified interest in all aspects of the ancient world, the classical past was increasingly viewed as a visual framework for religious themes. Architects from Filippo Brunelleschi through Andrea Palladio invoked the historical roots of Christianity by means of

Religious Themes. *The Tower of Babel* by Pieter Brueghel the Elder. The story of the Tower of Babel is in Genesis 11:1–9. Oil on oakwood; 1563; 114 × 155 cm (45 × 61 in.). KUNSTHISTORISCHES MUSEUM, VIENNA/ERICH LESSING/ART RESOURCE

ground plan or masonry ornament, saints became classical orators in the hands of Donatello, and Raphael's Vatican *stanze,* decorated for two successive early sixteenth-century popes, provided a manifesto of the close integration of Christian belief and humanist study.

The Renaissance witnessed an expansion of religious subjects as a means of elaborating Christian themes, as can be observed in microcosm by examining altarpieces. Although the purpose of the Renaissance altarpiece, like that of its medieval predecessors, was to stimulate devotion and focus the worship of the faithful on the miracle of God's continued presence, artists and patrons enlarged the repertoire of subjects and themes through which the miraculous significance of God's corporeality could be expressed. While subjects like the Madonna and Child accompanied by saints and occasional biblical narratives do appear before 1400, the majority of fourteenth-century altarpieces featured traditional iconic treatments of the Madonna and Child enthroned as celestial rulers, in addition to hieratically composed Crucifixions or the presentation of Christ as the Man of Sorrows. During the course of the fifteenth century, altarpiece imagery of the Madonna and Child expanded to include saints in the new format of the so-called *sacra conversazione* (holy conversation), initially developed in Italy but rapidly reported throughout western Europe, or offered stories from sacred history realistically presented for devotional purposes. Narrative episodes from the beginning and end of Christ's life on earth, his human birth and painful human death, were increasingly isolated for pictorial treatment on altars. Scenes of the Annunciation, the Nativity, and the Adoration of the Magi or of the Shepherds, as well as narratives related to Christ's Crucifixion, such as his Entombment, removal from the Cross (or Deposition), Resurrection, and Pietà (the lamentation of Mary over the body of her Son), proliferated as subjects during the fifteenth century and were given new emotional resonance through more dynamically active compositional treatments during the sixteenth century. The elegant pageanty of early fifteenth-century Coronation of the Virgin scenes gave way to those of Mary's Assumption, expressed as a moment of exquisite excitement and wonder.

The advent of the Protestant Reformation discouraged the visualization of religious themes through art and curtailed its production in northern Europe. The official response of the Roman church, reflected in the deliberations at the Council of Trent (1545–1563), continued to sanction the use of images to impart the mysteries of redemption. Although Tridentine reforms affected the nature of Renaissance piety as well as its image making by curbing some of the most exuberant of artistic excesses in expressing religious themes, they only strengthened the demand for even more concrete images of the miraculous.

Christian and Jewish Themes. The authority of scripture provided the principal themes for religious art. Christians valued the Judaic Testament particularly for what it revealed about the Christian Testament, understanding its messianic message as fulfilled in Christ. Comprehensive decorative cycles like that of the cathedral facade in Orvieto (c. 1310–1330) by Lorenzo Maitani depicted episodes from Genesis through the Last Judgment. Maitani's curling vines, which link narratives carved across four relief panels, underscored a continuous Judeo-Christian genealogy, identifying Christ as the fulfillment of Isaiah's prophecy (Isaiah 11:1–3) and the culmination of Judaic kingship in the family of Jesse, according to Matthew's Gospel. Another *Tree of Jesse,* painted by the Master of Calvary (1470; Darmstadt), included scenes of Gideon, Ezekiel, Moses, and Aaron foreshadowing Christianity within the Judaic past.

The Sistine Chapel offered a more encyclopedic scheme of God's plan for humanity. Decorated over a seventy-year period, each successive campaign expanded its sacred symbolism. Pope Sixtus IV commissioned Sandro Botticelli, Perugino, Cosimo Rosselli, Domenico del Ghirlandaio, and Luca Signorelli, to paint pairs of Judaic and Christian narratives which parallel Moses as the prototype of Christ (c. 1481–1483); accompanying inscriptions elucidate the prefiguration of Christianity in Hebrew history. This campaign also included a series of papal portraits, extending the genealogy of Moses and Christ into the contemporary church. Michelangelo's vault frescoes (1509–1512) recount Genesis from the beginning of time through Noah; their decreasing figural scale suggests a temporal and physical descent into the earthly present. Seven Hebrew prophets and five ancient Sibyls ring the vault, harnessing the testimony of both classical antiquity and Judaic prophecy for the truth of Christianity. Fictive medallions portraying Judaic Bible histories, each supported by pairs of classical nudes, further elaborate this theme as do four spandrel compositions which frequently serve Christian typologies: *Judith and Holophernes, David and Goliath,* the *Bronze Serpent,* and the *Punishment of Aman*. Michelangelo's lunette frescoes, painted at the same time as his *Last Judgment* (1536–1541), visually transcribe Christ's Judeo-Christian genealogy according to Matthew's Gospel. Tapestries designed by Raphael, hung below c. 1519, chronicle the evangelical lives of Saints Peter and Paul, respectively symbolizing the Church Universal and the Church Triumphant, and accentuate the church's historic role in promulgating Christian teachings. Michelangelo's prominent *Last Judgment* behind the altar marks the culmination of human time and Christian aspiration.

Christ and the Virgin were viewed as the perfected Adam and Eve. The legend of the True Cross, represented in fresco by Piero della Francesca in San Francesco, Arezzo (c. 1454–1458), linked Adam and Christ through the wood of the cross. By tracing the origins of Christ's crucifix to a cutting from the Tree of Knowledge and reminding viewers of Christ's crucifixion at the same site as Adam's burial, often indicated by a skull at the base of the cross in crucifixion narratives, the identity of Christ as redeemer of Adam's sin was symbolically secured. Original sin, imaged by Adam and Eve's expulsion from Eden, was the literal and figurative background of a number of Annunciation paintings like that by Fra Angelico (c. 1432; Cortona, Museo Diocesano), contrasting the fall from grace with the beginning of the redemptive process through Christ's incarnation. The primal parents similarly appear in fictive relief on the Virgin's prie-dieu in the Annunciation panel of the *Columba Altarpiece* by Rogier van der Weyden (c. 1450–1455; Munich, Alte Pinakothek), and on the architectural framework of Petrus Christus's *Nativity* (c. 1445; Washington, D.C., National Gallery). Masolino's *Temptation* and Masaccio's *Expulsion* introduced a series of frescoes thematically devoted to redemption portrayed in the acts of St. Peter as vicar of Christ (c. 1425–1428; Florence, Brancacci Chapel, Santa Maria del Carmine).

Popular typological texts like the *Biblia Pauperum* and *Speculum humanae salvationis* encouraged comprehension of scriptural parallels and prefigurations. Abraham's sacrifice of Isaac was understood to foreshadow that of Christ in reliefs by Lorenzo Ghiberti and Filippo Brunelleschi (1401–1402; Florence, Bargello Museum). Claus Sluter's *Well of Moses* (1395–1403; Dijon, Chatreuse de Champmol) represented Moses, David, Jeremiah, Zachariah, Isaiah, and Ezekiel, under a now-lost Crucifixion as the foundation of Christian salvation. The *Holy Sacrament Triptych,* by Dirck Bouts (1464–1468; Louvain, Sint-Pieterskerk), is a lexicon of sacred-meal typologies with subsidiary scenes of the *Gathering of Manna, Elijah Fed by an Angel, and Abraham and Melchizedek* surrounding a central *Last Supper.* Depictions of the Virgin alluded to the sagacity of Solomon by including the Throne of Wisdom, identified by its lions, as in the *Mérode Altarpiece,* by the Master of Flémalle (1425; New York, Cloisters).

Biblical Stories. Ambitious decorative cycles articulated the function of Renaissance religious architecture, edifying the faithful with representations drawn from scripture. Because Scripture was sacrosanct and not to be interpreted without instruction, established traditions of exegesis shaped the development of visual conventions. A fourfold system of exegetical interpretation, termed the *divina quaternitas,* read scripture for its literal truth as sacred history, explained its tropological and allegorical value and the underlying moral typologies and correspondences among diverse stories, and examined its anagogical significance, the sacred message hidden in its truth. Sacred representations required clear narrative and comprehensible symbols to convey its literal meaning as well as its didactic and doctrinal importance for all members of society.

The figurated reliefs on three sets of bronze doors created for the Florentine Baptistery translate these theological constructs to the viewer through detailed narration. The first set crafted by Andrea Pisano (c. 1330) illustrates the life of John the Baptist in twenty scenes, drawn largely from the Gospels; eight panels depicting the Virtues amplify the moral value of the narratives. The second set of doors, commissioned from Lorenzo Ghiberti in 1403, recounts the life of Christ; individual panels on the two lowest registers depict the fathers of the church and Evangelists, whose words illuminated the great mysteries of faith. The third set of doors, Ghiberti's so-called Gates of Paradise (1425–1452), presents Hebrew Testament stories from Genesis through Solomon and Sheba in ten large panels whose classically inspired figures and compelling spatial settings appear as an extension of the viewer's world. The frame, populated by saints and messianic visionaries, encourages viewers to perceive the theological unity of symbolic correspondences; the presence of the artist's self-portrait reflects his own status as exegete.

Renaissance believers framed their identity within biblical precedents, continuously translating its lessons into the present. Andrea Pisano's hexagonal Genesis reliefs for the Florentine Cathedral's bell tower (c. 1334–1337; Museo dell'Opera del Duomo), focused on themes of productive work, showing Adam plowing, Eve spinning, and their descendants inventing various labors. These were juxtaposed against scenes of modern labors like agriculture, woolens weaving, and sculpture, so that Genesis provided a direct paradigm of contemporary Florentine life, which depended on these trades. Biblical heroes also embodied contemporary civic ideals, as attested by the numerous Florentine statues of David as a youthful warrior, among them two by Donatello (c. 1412 and 1430; Florence, Bargello Museum), and one by Michelangelo (1501–1504; Florence, Accademia).

Lives of Christ and Mary. The lives of Christ and the Virgin became models for the ideal family, reflecting contemporary mendicant pedagogy, which sought to return Christianity to its populist origins by stressing Christ's humanity. Giotto's frescoes in the Scrovegni Chapel, Padua (1305–1306), treat their lives as a continuous whole, stimulating devotional empathy as they chronicle events from the Virgin's birth and Christ's childhood. Condensed cycles of their lives dominated the altarpieces of the early Renaissance, both public and private, as the numerous paintings by Taddeo Gaddi and Bernardo Daddi in the 1320s and 1330s attest. The era created new visions of the Virgin, as the Madonna nursing her child and the Madonna of Humility, seated upon the ground by the manger, to emphasize her maternal sensibilities. Fifteenth-century patrons sometimes preferred more regal imagery, as exemplified by Gentile da Fabriano's 1423 Strozzi Altarpiece (Florence, Ufizzi). Depicting the *Adoration of the Magi* in its main panel, with the *Nativity,* the *Flight into Egypt,* and the *Circumcision* below, the altarpiece presents its protagonists in opulent splendor. More typically, the Virgin and Christ appear aristocratic, as in the *Melun Diptych* by Jean Fouquet (c. 1450–1452), and the Santa Maria Novella frescoes in Florence, by Domenico del Ghirlandaio (1485), mirroring changes in Renaissance society, as newly prominent families commissioned works that spoke directly to their own class. Mannerist conceptions of the Virgin and Christ incorporated explorations of aesthetic grace, as the *Marriage of the Virgin* by Rosso Fiorentino (1523; Florence, San Lorenzo) shows in its hyperbolic gestures, anatomical stylization, and rarefied colors.

The *Nativity* and *Adoration of the Magi* panels by Dosso Dossi (c. 1519), in the Pinacoteca Nazionale of Ferrara, narrate their tales against vivid landscapes to heighten their drama. The development of aesthetic theory in the sixteenth century led artists to explore new models of biblical narration, aimed at a growing intellectual class. The *Life of St. John the Baptist,* by Andrea del Sarto (c. 1510–1526; Florence, Chiostro dello Scalzo) looks to the mystical account of the gospel of John for its source instead of the more temporal accounts of Luke and Mark. Breaking chronology, it emphasizes symbolic understandings. The Passion cycle in the monastery of Galluzzo by Pontormo (1522–1527) invited contemplation through eloquent coloration, graceful gestures, expressive figures, and compressed compositions. A Passion of Christ cycle in the oratory of Santa Lucia del Gonfalone in Rome, frescoed by painters working under Federico Zuccaro (1568–1576), similarly presumed educated viewers who would appreciate how its aesthetic qualities intensified its contemplative purpose.

The liturgical significance of Christ's last meal with his disciples assured its representation in numerous pictorial contexts. Duccio di Buoninsegna included the *Last Supper* within a comprehensive narrative of Christ's life on the reverse of his Maesta Altarpiece (c. 1308–1311; Siena, Museo dell'Opera del Duomo); works like Pietro Lorenzetti's fresco (c. 1320s–1330s) in the lower church of San Francesco, Assisi, and Hans Memlinc's Passion Panel (after 1468; Turin, Pinacoteca) presented the theme within cycles illustrating Christ's Passion. Famed for its narrative drama of betrayal, Leonardo da Vinci's *Last Supper* (c. 1495–1498; Milan, Santa Maria delle Grazie) was nevertheless typical in its placement within a monastic refectory, encouraging monks to contemplate spiritual sustenance during their meals. Tintoretto's monumental *Last Supper* (c. 1592–1594; Venice, San Giorgio Maggiore) portrayed Christ offering bread and wine to the apostles, thus inaugurating the central rite of the church; Tintoretto's canvas reflects the reemphasis of the theme's sacramental significance sanctioned by the Counter-Reformation and seen earlier in works such as the *Communion of the Apostles* (c. 1472–1475; Urbino, Palazzo Ducale) by Joos van Ghent.

Crucifixes and Crucifixions. Images of the Crucifixion, which marked the central mystery of faith, received particular attention. Large painted and carved crucifixes hung in ecclesiastical interiors to underscore the significance of Christ's sacrifice and the importance of the Mass. Mirroring a shift in devotional practice, images of an alert and living Christ, serenely transcended over death, the "Christus triumphans" type exemplified by Berlinghiero Berlinghieri's early-thirteenth-century *Crucifix* (Lucca, Pinacoteca), were increasingly supplanted by the "Christus patiens" type, a Christ whose anguish emphasized his humanity. The addition of Passion narratives in the side panels of Coppo di Marcovaldo's late-thirteenth-century *Crucifix* (San Gimignano, Museo Civico) was intended to accentuate Christ's suffering and evoke empathy. Crucifixes also appeared in Tree of Life imagery based on the writings of St. Bonaventure (c. 1217–1274), as in Taddeo Gaddi's refectory fresco (c. 1328–1330) for Santa Croce, Florence, and the anonymous image (c. 1450) in St. Lorenz, Nürnberg.

By the early fourteenth century, painted crucifixes were increasingly replaced in favor of more expansive compositions brimming with realistic detail. Narrative content varied, sometimes presenting the two thieves crucified with Christ as in Jan van Eyck's *Crucifixion* (c. 1430; New York, Metropolitan Museum), or contrasting the devastated mourners with the brutality of the Roman soldiers, as in the panel attributed to the Master of St. Veronica (c. 1430; Cologne, Wallraf-Richartz Museum). The anatomical realism of devotional works like Masaccio's *Trinity* (c. 1426; Florence, Santa Maria Novella) and Donatello's *Crucified Christ* (c. 1446; Padua, San Antonio) emphasized Christ's humanity; his face conveyed profound resignation. Later-fifteenth-century images such as Antonello da Messina's *Crucifixion* (1475; London, National Gallery) stressed spiritual contemplation over emotional tension by placing the narrative in a pastoral setting, witnessed by introspective saints.

Two consecutive scenes from the Passion commonly focused on dramatic expression: Christ's Deposition and the Lamentation, exemplified by Rogier van der Weyden's *Descent from the Cross* (c. 1440; Madrid, Prado) and Niccolò dell'Arca's painted terracotta *Lamentation over the Body of Christ* (c. 1463; Bologna, Santa Maria Della Vita). The Pietà, initially

Saints in *Sacra Conversazione*. A *sacra conversazione* depicts the Virgin and Child in the company of several saints. Giovanni Bellini (c. 1430–1516) painted the *sacra conversazione* above for the church of S. Zaccaria, Venice, in 1505.
MUSEO CIVICO, PESARO, ITALY/ALINARI/ART RESOURCE

a devotional variant of the Lamentation theme, originated in northern Europe, as evidenced in mid-fifteenth-century works such as the Avignon panel attributed to Enguerrand Quarton (Paris, Louvre). Matthias Grünewald placed a Pietà below the Crucifixion on the exterior of the *Isenheim Altarpiece* (1515; Colmar, Unterlinden Museum) to reinforce its emotional impact. In Italy, the theme first gained favor in painting, as demonstrated by Cosimo Tura's *Pietà* (1474?; Paris, Louvre); Michelangelo sculpted his acclaimed *Pietà* (c. 1498–1500; Vatican, St. Peter's) and returned twice to the theme in the mid-1550s (Florence, Museo dell'Opera del Duomo, Florence, and Milan, Castello Sforzesco). Albrecht Dürer's *Man of Sorrows* (c. 1494–1498; Karlesruhe, Kunsthalle) reflects yet another iconic distillation, as does the meditation on the Passion type seen in Vittore Carpaccio's panel from the late 1490s (New York, Metropolitan Museum).

Angels. The fifteenth century initiated a golden age of angels, increasingly present in all forms of religious imagery. Angels manifest themselves hundreds of times throughout the Bible, occurring as well in the Apocrypha and prophetic literature. Because of their roles as celestial attendants of God and agents of divine will and its execution on earth, as well as protectors and guardians of humanity, angels were frequently portrayed in Renaissance art. The immensely influential "Celestial Hierarchy," written in the sixth century by an unknown author now called Pseudo-Dionysius the Areopagite, ranked angels into three hierarchies, each further subdivided into three for a total of nine categories, or "choirs," which were occasionally presented surrounding the Madonna in early Renaissance art. The Christian Neoplatonism of Pseudo-Dionysius's works gave them an avid readership among Renaissance humanists, and they were translated by no less a figure than Marsilio Ficino (1433–1499), thus broadening the already enormous appeal of angel imagery for the entire spectrum of the Renaissance audience.

According to Pseudo-Dionysius, the highest orders of angels had the greatest affinity with God; the others became more corporeal as they descended the hierarchy. As a result, seraphim and cherubim were usually placed near the top of pictorial compositions, depicted closest to God. Identified by their disembodied heads and one to three sets of wings, the former are sometimes red while the latter could be blue or golden in color. Andrea Orcagna painted these types of seraphim and cherubim, along with their more embodied brethren, surrounding Christ in the *Enthroned Christ with Madonna and Saints* (1354–1357), for the Strozzi Chapel altar of Santa Maria Novella, Florence. The remaining angelic hierarchies were not consistently distinguished by appearance or attribute, with the notable exceptions of the manlike seraph who appeared in scenes like Giotto's *Stigmatization of St. Francis* (c. 1320s; Florence, Santa Croce), and the archangels. Jan van Eyck's *Adoration of the Lamb* (1432; Ghent, St. Bavo), depicting various types of angels in three of its panels, demonstrates how Renaissance artists embellished conventional imagery: angels had human bodies clothed according to the demands of theme or patronage, were generally youthful, adolescent or younger, frequently but not always winged, and often endowed with halos as a sign of their spiritual essence.

The three archangels named in scripture had distinct and recurrent attributes. Gabriel, the divine messenger who announced the Incarnation to Mary, appeared frequently with lily or flowering staff in scenes of the Annunciation. He was also identified with the angel who appeared to Samson's mother in the Judaic Testament, prefiguring the birth of Christ. Gabriel figured among the angels announcing Christ's Nativity and Resurrection and was occasionally presented as a trumpeter in Last Judgment scenes. Michael, the guardian warrior dressed in armor, appeared more frequently in Last Judgment scenes, either barring the damned from entry into Heaven with his sword or holding the scales that reflect his eschatological duty as the "weigher of souls," as seen on the interior of Rogier van der Weyden's *Last Judgment Altarpiece* (c. 1445–1448; Beaune, Musée de L'Hotel Dieu). Depicted alone as a narrative subject, Michael battles dragons and demons. He could also appear as part of a devotional ensemble, as presented in Perugino's altarpiece (c. 1499; London, National Gallery), commissioned by Lodovico Sforza of Milan for the Certosa di Pavia. The third archangel, Raphael, is also featured on the laterals of Perugino's altarpiece, accompanying Tobias on his filial journey. Raphael was the prototypical guardian angel whose name means "God heals," symbolized here by the fish hanging from Tobias's wrist, which will cure both the demons plaguing his future bride and his father's blindness. Raphael was often dressed as a pilgrim, depicted with a walking stick, a fish, or a medicine flask.

Following pictorial traditions inaugurated by Giotto, artists invested angels with a full range of human emotions, with which the spectator could empathize. Angels accompanied Jesus and Mary in Christological narratives, witnessing the Nativity, lending their support in Agony in the Garden scenes, proclaiming the Resurrection, or accompanying the Virgin's Assumption and Coronation, as they do in Andrea Mantegna's 1454 fresco in the Eremitani Church in Padua or Jobst Harrich's 1614 copy of Albrecht Dürer's no longer extant 1508 Heller Altarpiece (Frankfurt, Historisches Museum). Prominent in Last Judgment compositions, angels blow trumpets, carry implements of Christ's Passion, guide and welcome the righteous to Heaven, or drive the damned toward Hell. Beyond these scripturally determined roles, angels appeared as musicians and messengers, sometimes mediating between donor portraits and holy figures. They hover in images of martyrdom, prepared to bestow the martyr's palm and crown, as in Titian's *Martyrdom of St. Lawrence* (c. 1564–1567; Cambiaso, Escorial). Although the adolescent physiognomy of angels was initially derived from antique Roman genius figures or winged Etruscan death gods, angels as winged infants predominate in the sixteenth century, becoming virtually indistinguishable from the little cupids, or putti, pervasive in ancient Roman art.

Saints. The practice of venerating saints was consequential to Renaissance image making. Sharing in God's holiness, saints were intermediaries between the mortal and the divine; because their exceptional behavior earned them the privilege of God's direct protection, saints acted as advocates, protectors, and intercessors for the faithful, creating a bridge between worshiper and worshiped. Models for human conduct, saints' actions exemplified Christian virtue and their lives and deaths reinforced God's promise of salvation. The Virgin Mary is chief among the saints, and angels are also considered saintly in that they participate in holiness. In addition to scripture and apocryphal texts, testimony concerning saints was provided by medieval martyrologies and lexicons like Jacobus da Voragine's *Legenda sanctorum,* or *Golden Legend,* still popular in the Renaissance. The importance of imaging saints was sanctioned by a long liturgical and pictorial tradition dating from earliest Christianity, and underscored by the official adoption of the *Martyrologium Romanum* by the Roman church in 1584.

Beliefs concerning the efficacy and protective power of saints expanded in Renaissance culture. Saintly protectors of cities were objects of special veneration, often featured in cathedral decoration. Canonization of new saints in the thirteenth and fourteenth centuries, notably Anthony of Padua (c. 1195–1231), Nicholas of Tolentino (c. 1246–1305), Peter Martyr (c. 1205–1252), Thomas Aquinas (c. 1225–1274), and Catherine of Siena (c. 1347–1380), among others, prompted a fresh need for representation, while portrayals of founding saints like Benedict, Francis, and Dominic figured in monastic decoration. Guilds and confraternities commissioned works to honor patron saints, as witnessed by guild-funded statues outside Orsanmichele, Florence. Representation of personal saints was also popular, whether adopted onomastically, like the various images of Cosmas and Damian commissioned by Cosimo de' Medici, or resulting from personal experience, as reflected in Rogier van der Weyden's charming *St. Luke Drawing the Virgin* (c. 1435–1440; Boston, Museum of Fine Arts), believed to be a self-portrait of the artist as the patron saint of painters. Images were commissioned in gratitude or in hope of intervention, as evidenced by the numerous portrayals of Sebastian and Roch invoked against the plague.

Saints appeared in countless pictorial situations: by themselves, in groups surrounding the Virgin and Child, or in narratives illustrating their miracles. Many had well-defined attributes that served for identification as well as mnemonic purposes, encouraging remembrance of their professions or activities: Paul armed with his sword or the four fathers of the church dressed to connote ecclesiastical rank, as in the *Madonna and Child with Jerome, Gregory, Ambrose, and Augustine Altarpiece,* painted by Antonio Vivarini and Giovanni d'Alemagna (1446; Venice, Gallerie dell'Accademia). The fifteenth-century vogue for small-scale images of the learned Jerome is seen in Niccolò Colantonio's *St. Jerome in His Study Removing a Thorn from the Lion's Paw* (c. 1445; Naples, Museo e Gallerie Nazionale di Capodimonte), painted for Alfonso of Aragon following Flemish models; these were later supplanted in popularity by portrayals of Jerome as penitent hermit, like Lorenzo Lotto's *St. Jerome in the Wilderness* (1506; Paris, Louvre). Attributes like Peter's keys referred to an important event both in the saint's life and in the future of the worshiper, or recalled the means of martyrdom like Lucy's eyes or Dorothy's basket of fruit. The setting itself might serve as an attribute, as was the case with St. Joseph in scenes of the Nativity or Rest on the Flight to Egypt, popular after 1500. Germane to baptisteries or baptismal fonts, representations of John the Baptist marked liturgical function.

Images of saints also figured significantly in *sacra conversazione,* a new religious theme developed largely in Italy during the early fifteenth century. *Sacra conversazione* works featured the Madonna and Child in the company of saints and sometimes donors. Departing from earlier paintings of similar subjects, the Virgin and saints were unified by spatial setting, figural scale, and consistent representation of light, usually from a single source, as can be seen in the central panel of Domenico Veneziano's *St. Lucy* altarpiece (c. 1445–1447; Florence, Ufizzi), often considered the first of this type, and Giovanni Bellini's exquisite San Zaccaria Altarpiece of 1505, in its namesake church in Venice. Attempts to animate and dramatize this essentially static, devotional form are seen after 1500 in Andrea del Sarto's *Madonna of the Harpies* (1517; Florence, Ufizzi), for the high altar of San Francesco dei Macci in Florence and Correggio's two altarpieces for Modenese confraternities, the *Madonna with St. Sebastian* and the *Madonna with St. George* (c. 1524 and before 1530; both Dresden, Gemäldegalerie). Works such as Raphael's *Sistine Madonna* (1513; Dresden, Gemäldegalerie), and Parmigianino's *Vision of Saint Jerome* (1527; London, National Gallery) were elaborations of the theme, delineating the saints' roles as intermediaries whose visions allowed greater access to and understanding of Divinity.

Fifteenth-century imagery distinguished Mary Magdalen from other holy women by means of her unguent jar, copious hair, and placement near Christ's feet in scenes of Lamentation and Crucifixion, a reference to the woman who anointed Christ's feet (Luke 7:36). After 1500, Magdalen imagery broadened in scope as interest in depicting Resurrection themes like the so-called "Noli me tangere" (John 20:14–18) increased. Counter-Reformation piety stressed devotion to the sacraments, inspiring canvases like Titian's famous *Penitent Magdalen* (c. 1531–1533; Florence, Pitti Palace).

Andrea Mantegna's frescoed martyrdoms of James and Christopher (c. 1457; Padua, Ovetari Chapel, Eremitani Church) presaged the intensely dramatic presentations of saints popular with sixteenth-century audiences. Themes of martyrdom were presented above altars, like Giulio Romano's *Stoning of St. Stephen* (1520; Genoa, Santo Stefano), as lateral canvases in private chapels, like Caravaggio's *St. Matthew* series (1599–1600; Rome, Contarelli Chapel, San Luigi dei Francesi), and in monumental ensembles like Michelangelo's Pauline Chapel frescoes (1542–1550; Vatican).

Jerusalem. Although Jerusalem was lost to Christendom in 1187, the fall of Constantinople in 1453 intensified Europe's desire to retake Jerusalem for Christianity and magnified Jerusalem's hold on Renaissance imagination. Jerusalem signified more than David's royal city and the locus of Christ's earthly ministry: its recurrent identification in the Hebrew Bible as the dwelling place of God was transformed into a Christian eschatology that not only envisioned a heavenly Jerusalem as the eternal dwelling of those redeemed by Christ but also anticipated the establishment of a New Jerusalem, an ideal city that would come "down out of heaven from God" (Revelation 3:12; 21:2; 21:10). Renaissance artists envisioned their own burgeoning cities as Jerusalem: Bartolo di Fredi di Cini depicted the distinct, striped walls of Siena's Duomo in the distant Jerusalem of his *Adoration of the Magi* (1385–1389; Siena, Pinacoteca), the Dome of the Rock transformed the otherwise Flemish setting of an anonymous *Christ Bearing the Cross* (c. 1470), and Bruges appeared behind the Gate of Heaven in Gerard David's *Virgin and Child with Four Angels* (c. 1510–1515; both New York, Metropolitan Museum).

With the restoration of the papacy to Rome in 1420, Italian images of Jerusalem looked increasingly like Rome, which provided handy models for ancient city structures. The Flavian Colosseum and Column of Trajan appear within Jerusalem's walls in Andrea Mantegna's *Agony in the Garden* (c. 1460; London, National Gallery), and triumphal arches idealized from that of Constantine occur in Perugino's *Christ Giving the Keys to St. Peter* (1481; Vatican, Sistine Chapel). The idea of Jerusalem reborn in sixteenth-century Rome figured in papal imagery and was expounded by theologians like Giles of Viterbo and Thomas de Vio at the Fifth Lateran Council (1512–1517). Raphael's *Expulsion of Heliodorus* (c. 1512; Vatican, Stanza d'Eliodoro) equated the structure of the temple of Jerusalem with the rising vaults of Bramante's new St. Peter's. Further accentuating the link between the two cities, Raphael's later Sistine tapestry cartoon of *Christ Healing the Lame Man* (c. 1515–1516; London, Victoria and Albert Museum), presented this miracle before the famed spiraled columns of St. Peter's, believed to be spoils from Solomon's temple.

See also **Supernatural World in Renaissance Art**.

BIBLIOGRAPHY

Ainsworth, Maryan W., and Keith Christiansen, eds. *From Van Eyck to Bruegel: Early Netherlandish Painting in the Metropolitan Museum of Art.* Exhibition catalog, Metropolitan Museum of Art. New York, 1998.

Borsook, Eve. *The Mural Painters of Tuscany: From Cimabue to Andrea del Sarto.* Oxford, 1980.
Hall, James. *Dictionary of Subjects and Symbols in Art.* Rev. ed. New York, 1979.
Hall, Marcia B. *After Raphael: Painting in Central Italy in the Sixteenth Century.* Cambridge, U.K., 1999.
Hartt, Frederick. *History of Italian Renaissance Art: Painting, Sculpture, Architecture.* Edited by David G. Wilkins. 4th ed. New York, 1994.
Künstle, Karl. *Ikonographie der christlichen Kunst.* Freiburg im Breisgau, Germany, 1928.
Schiller, Gertrud. *Iconography of Christian Art.* Translated by Janet Seligman. New York, 1971.
Snyder, James. *Northern Renaissance Art: Painting, Sculpture, the Graphic Arts from 1350 to 1575.* Englewood Cliffs, N.J., and New York, 1985.

MAUREEN PELTA and MICHAEL GRILLO

RENAISSANCE. [This entry includes five subentries:

The Renaissance in Historical Thought
The English Renaissance in Literary Interpretation
The Renaissance in Popular Imagination
Influence of the Renaissance
Renaissance Studies

For discussion of the historical period that preceded the Renaissance, see Middle Ages. For discussion of the period that followed the Renaissance, see Baroque, Concept of the, and Early Modern Period.]

The Renaissance in Historical Thought

Scholars have been viewing the Renaissance as a unique period of history since the middle of the fourteenth century, making it a continuing chapter in the history of historiography.

The Renaissance View of the Renaissance. The notion of a new age of rebirth began with Petrarch in the fourteenth century. Fifteenth- and sixteenth-century scholars, especially Italians, amplified and developed Petrarch's periodization and belief in a Renaissance.

Petrarch (1304–1374) altered medieval historical periodization and initiated the view that the Middle Ages were a dark age. Earlier historians commonly made the birth of Christ a major turning point in history, the end of the dark pagan times and the beginning of the Christian age of salvation. But Petrarch rejected what he felt was the barbarous Latin and irrelevant university learning of the high Middle Ages. He preferred the ancients Cicero and Augustine. Hence he drew a line between the Roman era and the Christian and barbarian period that began when the Roman Empire adopted Christianity in the fourth century. He made the distinction on the basis of culture. In the Roman era, men wrote "good" Latin, that is, classical Latin, and, hence, were highly cultured. In the Christian era they wrote "bad" Latin, that is, the Latin of Scholasticism rather than the classical Latin of St. Augustine, as learning declined. Petrarch began to use the terms "ancient" and "modern" to separate the two eras.

The humanist historian Flavio Biondo (1392–1463) made the new periodization sharp and definite in his *Historiarum ab inclinatione Romanorum imperii decades* (History from the Decline of the Roman Empire; written 1439–1453). He took a dramatic event, the Sack of Rome by the Goths in 410, which Biondo mistakenly dated as 412, as the beginning of Rome's decline. He then narrated the history of Italy and the Eastern Empire to 1412. (The fact that he had already written a history of Italy for the period 1412–1442 may have influenced him.) Biondo did not see the centuries between 412 and 1412 as unrelievedly bleak. But his clear periodization, with a middle period lasting one thousand years and a new age beginning in the fifteenth century, had considerable impact on historians and humanists of the era.

The notion of medieval darkness followed by a rebirth of learning, literature, and the arts took hold among fifteenth- and sixteenth-century Italians, especially the humanists. They saw their own age as one of rebirth ("*rinascità*" in Italian) after a long and dark Middle Ages, although the latter term was not yet in use. For example, the Florentine Matteo Palmieri (1406–1474), writing in the 1430s, made the contrast very sharp. Describing arts and letters after ancient Rome, he wrote:

> Of letters and liberal studies at large it were best to be silent altogether. For these . . . have been lost to mankind for 800 years and more. It is but in our own day that men dare to boast that they see the dawn of better things. For example, we owe it to our Leonardo Bruni [c. 1370–1444, the leading Florentine humanist of his own time] that Latin, so long a by-word for its uncouthness, has begun to shine forth in its ancient purity, its beauty, its majestic rhythm.

In similar fashion Palmieri saw Giotto (d. 1337) as the artist who restored painting to life. And he praised his own age in fulsome tones:

> Now, indeed, may every thoughtful spirit thank God that it has been permitted to him to be born in this new age, so full of hope and promise, which already rejoices in a greater array of nobly-gifted souls than the world has seen in the thousand years that have preceded it. (Palmieri, *Della vita civile,* as quoted in translation in Hay, *The Renaissance Debate,* p. 9)

Palmieri considered the learning, literature, and art of the centuries after Rome and before the fourteenth century as unworthy of mention. But with Giotto in art, Petrarch in literature, and Bruni in Latin, a rebirth had occurred. This view became commonly accepted among Italians of the fifteenth and sixteenth centuries.

Northern European View of the Renaissance. Northern Europeans were also convinced that a new age had dawned after a dark medieval night. French humanist historians writing in the sixteenth and early seventeenth centuries repeated the Italian view that a rebirth of culture had occurred. They mostly agreed that the Italians had begun a Renaissance but also credited French heroes. For example, the French historian Jacques Amyot (1513–1593), writing in 1559, credited Francis I (ruled 1515–1547) with enabling good letters to be reborn and flourish.

Desiderius Erasmus (c. 1466–1536) and his followers accepted the periodization of the Italian humanists. They firmly believed that a Renaissance had occurred and added a religious reason. For inspiration Erasmus looked back to the secular learning of ancient Greece and Rome, and to Christianity of the first through fourth centuries. The former served as models of literature, culture, and good morality, while the church fathers through Jerome (d. 419/20) combined the purity of early Christianity with ancient learning. But then ancient literature and early Christianity fell prey to the barbarous Latin and theological confusion of medieval Scholastics. Erasmus and his followers were now engaged in a struggle to restore good literature (classical Greek and Latin literature) and good religion (early Christianity purified of Scholastic irrelevance and clerical abuses). Although the Erasmian humanist view of the ancient world, Middle Ages, and Renaissance was fundamentally the same as the Italian view, differences in tone separated them. The Italian humanists paid little attention to religious matters when describing the rebirth, and they did not feel the need to battle so strongly against Scholasticism as did Erasmus and the northern humanists.

After the Protestant Reformation began, sixteenth- and seventeenth-century Protestant historians adopted the concept of ancient and medieval periods giving way to a rebirth. But they further darkened the Middle Ages and blamed the papacy for its cultural obscurity and wrong religion. They also conceived of their own age as the period in which true religion (Protestantism) had been restored. Thus, Protestant historians often combined the restoration of good letters (humanism in northern Europe) with religious "reform" (the Latin *reformare* means to go back to the original shape, to restore), viewing them as one.

None of the figures mentioned above developed full historical accounts of the ancient, medieval, and Renaissance periods. Rather, they made comments, sometimes in passing, that expressed such views. Scholars in later centuries would develop their insights.

Enlightenment View of the Renaissance. Enlightenment intellectuals, especially Frenchmen, inherited from the humanists the division of history into three eras and a view of the Renaissance as an era of rebirth. They also believed in human progress through history, which predisposed them to accept the notion of a Renaissance following the Middle Ages. Consequently, they reinforced the contrast between medieval and modern.

The most important Enlightenment historical work to express these views was Voltaire's (1694–1778) *Essai sur les moeurs et l'esprit des nations* (Essay on the manners and spirit of nations; 1756), which narrated the history of civilization from the age of Charlemagne (c. 800) to the age of Louis XIV (ruled 1643–1715). Voltaire was the first to write about all aspects of civilization, including politics, ideas, arts, literature, and social history; he even made passing reference to the importance of economics. Although his book fell far short of being a comprehensive history in the modern sense, it offered ample scope for expression of Voltaire's views about the Renaissance.

Possibly Voltaire's most arresting innovation was his view that humanity's reason awakened during the Renaissance. Enlightenment intellectuals identified the Middle Ages as an era in which organized religion made common cause with tyrannical governments in order to oppress the reason and freedom of individuals. Then came a "renaissance and the progress of the human mind," according to Voltaire. Although Voltaire did not specifically identify a chronological period for a Renaissance, he saw Italians of the fourteenth, fifteenth, and sixteenth centuries beginning to shake off the chains of religion and taking rational steps forward. Italy, especially Florence, was the most enlightened land in Europe at that time. Voltaire saw Cosimo de' Medici and Lorenzo "il Magnifico" de' Medici of the fifteenth century as precursors of eighteenth-century enlightened despots, because they encouraged arts and letters and governed well. Voltaire also praised sixteenth-century France as a great age.

Following Voltaire's lead, the art historian Jean-Baptiste Seroux d'Agincourt (1730–1814), in a broad history of art (published 1810–1823), called "Renaissance" the art of the period between the Middle Ages and the eighteenth century. Thus, long before the mid-nineteenth century, all the elements for the Renaissance as a historical conception existed. But they had not been combined into a comprehensive historical picture.

The Nineteenth Century. Several scholars in the middle of the nineteenth century articulated a view of the Renaissance as a unique period in history. This is usually called the Burckhardtian interpretation of the Renaissance after its most famous and brilliant proponent, Jakob Burckhardt. But it really was the joint effort of several scholars working independently.

Michelet. In 1855 the French historian Jules Michelet (1798–1874) published *La renaissance,* the seventh volume in his seventeen-volume *Histoire de France* (History of France). Michelet was the first historian to conceive of the Renaissance as a distinct period embracing all of Europe and with a characteristic spirit that expressed itself in all areas of life. Michelet also wrote that the essence of the Renaissance was "the discovery of the world and the discovery of man," phrases that Burckhardt would make famous.

The revival of classical antiquity, scientific discoveries, and geographical exploration were the chief glories of the Renaissance for Michelet. He saw little rebirth in fifteenth-century Italy. But Columbus, Copernicus, and Luther were major Renaissance figures, the last because the Renaissance led directly to the Reformation in the progressive freedom of the individual breaking loose from the medieval past and the church. Michelet also emphasized the importance of the French invasion of Italy in 1494 for bringing Italian influences into France, a theme taken up by future historians. Long on rhetoric and anticlericalism, but short on facts, Michelet nevertheless exerted considerable influence.

Voigt. The German historian Georg Voigt (1827–1891) redirected attention to Italy in his *Die Wiederbelebung des classischen Alterthums, oder das erste Jahrhundert des Humanismus* (The revival of classical antiquity, or the first century of humanism; 1859). The book provided a comprehensive view of Italian Renaissance humanism and mentioned some characteristics of the period as a whole. Voigt credited a single person for beginning the Italian Renaissance: Petrarch, "the discoverer of the new world of humanism." According to Voigt, Petrarch broke completely with medieval Scholasticism, preferring to take his inspiration from antiquity. In contrast to medieval Scholastic philosophers who only represented an academic system, Petrarch became an individual expressing his own personal, human interests. He was "the prophet of the new age, the ancestor of the modern world." Following Petrarch's lead, other Italian humanists also rejected Scholasticism and turned to the classics of antiquity. Voigt discussed at length humanists—their writings, where they gathered (especially Florence)—through the middle of the fifteenth century. He then sketched northern European humanism. Voigt praised Renaissance humanists for their philological and historical studies, which unlocked antiquity's riches, and for creating classical education. He emphasized the individualism of the humanists, but was not impressed with much of their output. After Petrarch, in Voigt's judgment, much humanist literature was artificial, egoistic, and imitative.

Even though he focused on humanism rather than the period as a whole, Voigt saw the Italian Renaissance much like Burckhardt and later nineteenth-century historians. He saw a sharp break between medieval culture and Italian Renaissance culture, and viewed the latter as the beginning of modern culture. He emphasized individualism as a key characteristic of the Renaissance, even though it degenerated into egocentricity in later humanists. But he expressed his views in measured fashion. Voigt's book was the most scholarly and the best grounded in primary sources of the nineteenth-century treatments of the Renaissance. It can still be consulted today, especially in the revised and expanded edition of 1893, for information on the writings and movements of the Italian humanists.

Burckhardt. Jakob Burckhardt (1818–1897), who taught history and the history of art at the University of Basel, published *Die Kultur der Renaissance in Italien* (trans. *The Civilization of the Renaissance in Italy*) in 1860. Burckhardt saw his book as an exploratory essay to be followed by a comprehensive history of Renaissance art, which was never realized. It was simultaneously the culmination of the growth of the concept of the Renaissance as a distinct period of history and a work of stunning originality, "the masterpiece of a great historical artist," in the words of Wallace K. Ferguson.

Burckhardt had a unique approach. He made the assumption that a whole nation in a particular age possessed a distinctive spirit, character, or mentality. The task of the historian was to identify the spirit and to describe how the age manifested it. Burckhardt divided his book into six parts, each of which described one aspect of Italian civilization (*Kultur* in German) from about 1300 to about 1530. Part 1, "The State as a Work of Art," deals with the politics of the Italian city-states. According to Burckhardt, the state was the conscious creation of a man, rather than an institution embedded in laws and tradition. The Renaissance prince created his own state dependent on him alone. This was the origin of the modern European "state-spirit," that is, the state existing free and independent of moral considerations.

Part 2 addresses the development of the individual, "the evolution of the Italian into the modern man." Individualism was the key to the entire Italian Renaissance. In the Middle Ages, "man was conscious of himself only as a member of a race, people, party, family, or corporation." But Renaissance man was a self-conscious individual, "the first-born among the sons of modern Europe," a famous phrase (*The Civilization of the Renaissance in Italy,* p. 121). Renaissance individuals relied on their own resources for success in a difficult world; they gave full expression to every talent and facet of their personality. Burckhardt offered many examples of "the Renaissance man." Part 3 covers the revival of antiquity. Burckhardt did not see antiquity as essential to the Italian Renaissance, which would have developed anyway. But antiquity guided Renaissance man in realizing his potential.

Part 4 was "The Discovery of the World and of Man." After discovering himself, Renaissance man discovered natural beauty, the physical world through scientific discovery, and the non-European world through geographical exploration. Part 5, "Society and Festivals," describes the individual in his social setting, as Renaissance man created his own society. According to Burckhardt, the nobility and the middle class joined together in an urban society in which culture and wealth, rather than birth, determined place. Part 6 discusses religion. The excessive individualism of Renaissance Italians produced a breakdown in morals and lack of respect for religion. The loss of moral fiber was a major cause for Italy's decline in the sixteenth century. But the work of the Italian Renaissance was done. Italians had brought Western man into the modern world, and others would continue the task.

For Burckhardt the Italian Renaissance was a distinct period in history, different from the Middle Ages, but also the beginning of the modern world. The spirit of the age of the Renaissance was individualism manifested through all aspects of life. Even though all the elements for his synthesis existed previously, Burckhardt brought them together brilliantly. He knew the period well, and the work is steeped in primary historical and literary sources and a deep knowledge of Italy's art. Burckhardt probably had a better knowledge of the Italian Renaissance than any other scholar of the nineteenth century.

Today, it is easy to find fault with Burckhardt's book. Its contrast between the Renaissance and the Middle Ages is far too sharp. Burckhardt posited a unique spirit of the age, based on Hegelian philosophy and historical intuition, which few other historians have found. Burckhardt's picture was static and allowed for little historical development. He overemphasized the individualism, secularism, and immorality of the Renaissance.

Burckhardt's book immediately achieved both critical and popular success. It was enlarged, illustrated, reprinted, and translated; others echoed his views for the next hundred years. His book persuaded so well partly because it masterfully synthesized beliefs to which nineteenth-century intellectuals eagerly assented. Indeed, while it is common to speak of the Burckhardtian conception of the Renaissance, it would be more accurate to call it the nineteenth-century consensus view of the Italian Renaissance. This is a major reason why Burckhardt's interpretation won immediate acceptance.

The most important post-Burckhardtian synthesis was *Renaissance in Italy* (7 vols., 1875–1886) by John Addington Symonds (1840–1893). Symonds formulated his interpretation and had written a good deal before he became aware of Burckhardt's work. Nevertheless, his views mirrored those of Burckhardt. Through this work, his articles in the *Encyclopaedia Britannica,* and his many translations and monographs on Italian and English Renaissance figures, Symonds brought the nineteenth-century Renaissance synthesis to the English-speaking world.

The Northern Renaissance after Burckhardt. Burckhardt's conception of the Italian Renaissance found wide acceptance. But there was less agreement on the definition of a northern Renaissance among nineteenth- and twentieth-century historians. They usually agreed that the northern Renaissance was a break with, and reaction against, the intellectual system of the Middle Ages. They further agreed that the return to classical antiquity through humanism was a key element. But this was as far as agreement went.

For some historians, perhaps the majority, from northern Europe, the Italian Renaissance was the precursor of northern developments. But how to explain the differences between the Renaissance in Italy and the Renaissance in France, Germany, and England? There was the obvious difference that northern humanists, following the lead of Erasmus, were more religiously oriented than Italian humanists, whom Voigt and Burckhardt saw as worldly, even pagan. One solution was to postulate the Italian Renaissance and its humanism as the model, then demonstrate how humanism in France, Germany, England, Spain, or the Netherlands differed by taking on local coloring.

The Protestant Reformation especially complicated the issue. Nineteenth- and twentieth-century historians of northern Europe have found it difficult to agree on the relationship between the Renaissance and the Reformation. The majority of historians of Germany have viewed the northern Renaissance, including Erasmian humanism, as the beginning of the Reformation, which then absorbed it. Historians of England have often viewed Renaissance developments as a lesser part of the history of Tudor England in which the deeds and misdeeds of Henry VIII, Mary Tudor, and Elizabeth I determined the course of history. The inevitable consequence of a lack of consensus was, and is, that the conception and definition of a northern Renaissance was never so well established as the Italian Renaissance. Historians of northern Europe also tend to see sixteenth-century northern Europe, not fifteenth-century Italy, as the beginning of the modern world.

Revolt of the Medievalists. The one constant in the historical conception of the Renaissance from Petrarch through the nineteenth century was that it was viewed as a rebirth after the darkness of the Middle Ages. The excesses of the nineteenth-century Renaissance consensus produced a strong reaction from twentieth-century medieval scholars. Some accepted the existence of a Renaissance but pushed back its origins to earlier, medieval centuries. Others argued that there was nothing new in the Renaissance; medieval men had anticipated everything thought to be new in the Renaissance and had done it better. The Renaissance was nothing more than a continuation, even the decline, of the Middle Ages.

The strongest and most influential medievalist attack against the Renaissance was *The Renaissance of the Twelfth Century* (1927) by Charles Homer Haskins (1870–1937), longtime professor of history at Harvard University. Haskins's purpose was twofold: to equate the Renaissance of the twelfth century with the beginning of the modern world and to reduce the Italian Renaissance to a minor and derivative historical episode. He wrote a learned and attractive synthesis of intellectual developments of the twelfth century, which he liberally sprinkled with polemical asides attacking the fifteenth-century Italian Renaissance. Haskins trivialized and denied the originality of the later Renaissance but never pursued a serious comparison. Despite many brief comments comparing twelfth-century developments with Petrarch and Lorenzo Valla (1407–1457), to the disparagement of the latter pair, his book does not have a single reference to their works, nor to secondary scholarship on the two. Despite its scholarly shortcomings, Haskins's book spawned several general treatments of the intellectual history of the Middle Ages that also denied the significance or existence of the Italian Renaissance.

The Interpretation of Humanism after 1945. The period after World War II witnessed an unprecedented explosion of scholarship on the Renaissance, but scholars seldom attempted grand syntheses of the Renaissance as a whole. The majority accepted the existence of a period called the Renaissance without necessarily accepting or even making reference to the nineteenth-century synthesis. But this does not mean that their vision has been narrow, or their ambition limited. The most important contribution that historians of the Renaissance have made since the 1940s has been to identify humanism as the unifying force of the Renaissance across Europe, and to see it as the major intellectual and cultural movement that stimulated Renaissance men and women to express new ideas.

The emphasis on Italian humanism, begun in the nineteenth century with Georg Voigt, was renewed by the Italian historian Remigio Sabbadini (1850–1934) in some fifteen volumes and over three hundred articles. For Sabbadini the humanists were the discoverers, collectors, editors, disseminators, and teachers of classical learning. He insisted that the Italian humanists saved much of ancient learning from possible total loss. But he did not ask how the recovery of ancient learning changed culture and learning.

Baron. Historians since 1945 have concentrated on the influence of the classics on the thought of humanists and the links between humanism and other aspects of life in the Renaissance. Beginning with a series of studies in the late 1920s and culminating with *The Crisis of the Early Italian Renaissance* (1955), Hans Baron (1900–1988) argued that shortly after 1400 Florentine humanists combined their classical studies with a commitment to Florentine republican political values. According to Baron, humanism developed in two stages. First came the literary humanism of Petrarch and his fourteenth-century followers who counseled withdrawal from the active life in favor of study and contemplation. But this viewpoint changed in early fifteenth-century Florence. Led by Leonardo Bruni, several Florentine humanists believed that a scholar should also be a citizen involved in the affairs of his city. Hence they looked to their classical studies for examples of ancient authors who devoted themselves to the practical life of involvement in political and civic affairs. Humanism became civic.

Civic humanism articulated a new historical consciousness; a favorable moral attitude toward wealth, because a citizen needed a certain amount of wealth in order to fulfill his duties to family and state; and a new appreciation of Cicero as an active statesman. Why did this decisive change take place in early fifteenth-century Florence? Baron argued that the successful Florentine resistance against the political and military threat posed by Milan around 1400 convinced Florentine humanists that their classical studies and civic commitment had to be in harmony. That this happened when Florence was the most important center for humanistic scholarship influenced the entire Renaissance. "From that time on there would exist a kind of Humanism which endeavored to educate a man as a member of his society and state" (*The Crisis of the Early Italian Renaissance,* p. 460).

Garin. In similar fashion the Italian historian Eugenio Garin (b. 1909) in many books and articles beginning in the late 1930s saw humanism as a philosophy of humanity. Garin decisively rejected the view that the Italian Renaissance was a continuation of the Middle Ages and that Renaissance humanism was simply the study of ancient texts. Humanism was a questing and critical philosophical exploration of every aspect of humanity's life on earth. Humanism was a philosophy of humankind.

Garin sought to explain most of the original intellectual achievements of the Renaissance, however much they differed from each other, as manifestations of humanism. The major features of humanism were rejection of medieval Scholasticism, an acutely historical philology, a well-marked historical consciousness enabling humanists to avoid the anachronisms of medieval writers, a positive moral evaluation of human life on earth, Renaissance Platonism, and important scientific innovations. Although originating in Italy, humanism manifested itself in the unique intellectual achievements of major Italian and non-Italian Renaissance figures.

Kristeller. By contrast, Paul Oskar Kristeller (1905–1999) defined humanism through the studies, occupations, and writing of humanists.

> By the first half of the fifteenth century, the *studia humanitatis* [humanistic studies] came to stand for a clearly defined cycle of scholarly disciplines, namely grammar, rhetoric, history, poetry, and moral philosophy, and the study of each of these subjects was understood to include the reading and interpretation of its standard ancient writers in Latin and, to a lesser extent, in Greek. . . . Thus Renaissance humanism was not . . . a philosophical tendency or system, but rather a cultural and educational program which emphasized and developed an important but limited area of studies. (*Renaissance Thought,* pp. 9–10)

Humanists were the professors, teachers, scholars, and students of the *studia humanitatis*. They also found employment as secretaries to princes, prelates, and cities. From their studies and professional activities came their writing: public and personal letters, orations, treatises and dialogues on moral questions, the writing of history, commentaries on the Latin classics, and Latin poetry in classical form. Kristeller saw a professional continuity between the Middle Ages and the Renaissance. Both the medieval Italian *dictatores* (professional rhetoricians who taught and practiced the art of Latin letter writing) and Renaissance humanists composed documents, letters, and public speeches in Latin. But the Renaissance humanists followed classical models, while the medieval *dictatores* did not.

Because it followed classical models and was written in a new age, humanistic writing was different than medieval rhetoric. It placed "the emphasis on man, on his dignity and privileged place in the universe." Humanists also had "the tendency to express, and to consider worth expressing, the concrete uniqueness of one's feelings, opinions, experiences, and surroundings." And they possessed "a fundamental classicism," seen in "the taste for elegance, neatness, and clarity of style and literary form" (*Renaissance Thought,* pp. 20–21). Further, individuals' humanistic training in the classics usually influenced their philosophy, politics, theology, and medical scholarship. For example, a humanistic philosopher, that is, one who brought humanistic historical method and familiarity with classical texts to his philosophical writing, was not the same as a

Scholastic philosopher. Individual humanists might be monarchists or republicans, Aristotelians or Platonists, Catholics or Protestants, but all shared a commitment to humanistic studies.

Other studies of humanism. Baron, Garin, and Kristeller positioned humanism at the center of the Renaissance. Numerous additional studies have documented the key role of humanism and its adaptability to different political and institutional circumstances. There have been studies of Roman humanism (John F. D'Amico), Neapolitan humanism (Jerry H. Bentley), Venetian humanism (Margaret L. King), Milanese humanism, Spanish humanism (Luis Gil Fernández), humanism at the Tudor court in England (James K. McConica), numerous studies on French and German humanism, and a set of volumes covering Europe as a whole (edited by Albert Rabil Jr.), all influenced in greater or lesser degree by Baron, Garin, and Kristeller.

The Religious Renaissance. Although the nineteenth-century consensus interpretation of the Renaissance emphasized its secular, even pagan, nature, Charles Trinkaus's (1911–1999) *In Our Image and Likeness* (1970) demonstrated that major Italian humanists were profoundly religious. But they approached God and religious issues very differently from their medieval predecessors. They took seriously the message of Genesis 1:26, that God created man in his image and likeness, and constructed a humanistic theology that explained this likeness.

In similar fashion, scholars beginning with Roland Bainton's (1894–1984) aptly named *Erasmus of Christendom* (1969) have affirmed the centrality of Erasmus to the Renaissance. Christian ecumenism of the 1960s and later may have inspired scholars to look at Erasmus with fresh insight and greater sympathy than in the past. Instead of viewing him as a lukewarm Catholic, a cowardly Protestant, or first son of the Enlightenment (Johan Huizinga), they have emphasized his combination of humanism and religious insight. Two massive editorial projects, the *Opera omnia Desiderii Erasmi Roterodami* (the modern Latin critical edition of Erasmus's works) and the *Collected Works of Erasmus* (English translations of almost all of his works), have facilitated what might be called the Erasmus Renaissance. The flourishing of Erasmus studies has given renewed emphasis to scholarship that sees a strong northern Renaissance independent of the Protestant Reformation.

The Renaissance State. Was there a Renaissance state different from its medieval predecessors? Was it the beginning of the modern state? A number of historians have studied the functioning of Renaissance states in order to answer these questions. Federico Chabod (1901–1960), in a series of historiographical articles and studies of the Milanese state within the Spanish empire in the sixteenth century, documented the growth of an administrative organization of trained officials that increasingly regulated the lives of the inhabitants of the state. He saw this as distinctly modern. G. R. Elton (1921–1994) argued that the Tudor monarchs created an English national monarchy with an administrative structure recognizably modern. Marvin Becker (b. 1922) argued that the pluralistic late medieval Florentine state of the fourteenth century, with its many informal associations and personal ties, changed under the duress of fiscal crisis into a centralized state with modern fiscal structures by the early fifteenth century.

According to these historians and others, whether a particular Renaissance state was a monarchy, part of an empire, or an independent city-state, all types of states shared some common characteristics and were more modern than their medieval predecessors, although still far from the highly developed European states of later centuries. They see the state very differently from Burckhardt, who viewed the Renaissance state as the creation of a single prince manifesting Renaissance individualism. The renewed study of Machiavelli as one who analyzed the components of a successful state may also be seen as part of the interest in the Renaissance state.

The Rise of Social History. From the 1960s onward, more historians have practiced social history than any other kind of history. The starting point was probably the *Annales* school of French historians, named for a journal founded by Marc Bloch and Lucien Febvre in 1929 and called *Annales: Économies, sociétés, civilisations* since 1946. Dissatisfied with what they saw as too much emphasis on surface diplomatic and political events and persons in the writing of history, the *Annales* school called for "total history," meaning the study of all human activities. In addition, it rejected narrative history in favor of analyzing structures of the economy and society that changed little over decades and centuries. The best known work of the Annaliste school is *La Méditerranée et le monde méditerranéen à l'époque de Philippe II* (1949; trans. *The Mediterranean and the Mediterranean World in the Age of Philip II,* 1972) of Fernand Braudel (1902–1985), which emphasizes historical geography, climate, communications, sea and land transport, prices, and population movements in the Mediterranean basin over a century and more.

Two of the three most famous Annaliste historians, Lucien Febvre (1878–1956) and Braudel, focused their research on sixteenth-century Europe. Hence, the *Annales* school has had a considerable impact on Renaissance scholarship. It has been felt most strongly in the study of France and Spain, somewhat less, but still noticeable, in the study of Italy and Germany.

Over time, Annaliste history has become social history in general. Even though ideas, religion, and politics were part of the total history of the *Annales* school, and Febvre was a brilliant intellectual and religious historian, *Annales*-inspired social history normally excludes these. Instead, social historians have investigated a variety of issues and groups in order to determine how men and women fared during the fifteenth, sixteenth, and seventeenth centuries. How did they marry, reproduce, and die? What was the size and shape of different social classes and economic levels? What bonds drew men and women together or drove them apart? How did society treat poverty and crime? To find the answers to these questions, social historians have sifted mountains of historical data and often applied techniques from demography, economics, sociology, and cultural anthropology.

The great contribution of social history has been to provide detailed information on large areas of life previously little known. Social historians have looked into every nook and cranny of Renaissance life in town and country, have examined rich and poor, and have paid special attention to those on the margins of society. They have painted a more diverse picture of Renaissance society than previous historians imagined.

Social history as it has been practiced since the early 1960s has had very little to say about historiographical issues of the Renaissance. Social historians' preference for focusing on the long term (what the Annalistes call "la longue durée") de-emphasizes precise periodization, such as medieval, Renaissance, and modern. Instead, they tend to see the foundations of social and economic life changing little over the centuries.

Women in the Renaissance. In 1977 the historian Joan Kelly-Gadol (1928–1982) posed the question "Did women have a Renaissance?" She answered with a resounding "No." Kelly-Gadol dissented from an optimistic, if unexamined, view that the lot of women improved during the Renaissance. Although her article limited itself to the examination of noblewomen as seen through courtly literature, it was the opening statement of a large investigation into the history of Renaissance women.

Scholars initially echoed Kelly-Gadol's answer, describing the Renaissance period as a retrograde era for women—socially, politically, and intellectually. But after the initial reaction, the study of women in the Renaissance became a broad search into all areas of their lives. What kinds of lives did married women, widows, unmarried women, and religious women have? What were their roles? How much power did they have? Were they educated, and in what way? What was the legal position of women? Scholars have brought to light the work that women did, the literature that they wrote, the art they created, and the music that they composed and performed.

A comprehensive account of European women in the Renaissance (Margaret L. King, *Women of the Renaissance,* 1991) responds to Kelly-Gadol's question with the answer that Renaissance women did not escape the often harsh social conditions and restrictions imposed by a masculine society any more than did their medieval sisters. But they did develop a greater sense of themselves and exhibited a considerable amount of intellectual and spiritual achievement.

Anti-Renaissance Literary Theory. Beginning in the 1970s many scholars articulated an approach to English literature of the sixteenth and seventeenth centuries that rejects the notion of a Renaissance. The umbrella terms "new historicism" and "literary theorists" describe a diverse group of scholars and their approaches. Probably the single most-cited work of this movement is Stephen Greenblatt's *Renaissance Self-Fashioning: From More to Shakespeare* (1980), which coined the term "new historicism."

The new historicist or theoretical approach to literature begins with the proposition that it is impossible to understand fully and exactly what a sixteenth-century author meant to say. Hence the scholar must "decode" the text of the distant past. To do this, scholars assume that all texts are "embedded" in the culture of the period, which is seen as one of power and repression. The way to decode the sixteenth-century text is to apply one or several theoretical approaches, such as postmodernism, Marxism, psychoanalytic theory, notions of power and victimization borrowed from Michel Foucault

(1926–1984) or cultural anthropology, feminist theory, semiotics, or cultural materialism. Deconstructionism might be the best umbrella term to describe this approach. Much of this kind of scholarship is based on a theoretical analysis of the language used by Renaissance authors. It is also shaped by the view that the scholar can only find culturally determined perspectives, not universal truth or even historical reality. Finally, such scholarship often resonates with contemporary concerns. Although many North American scholars of English literature accept the perspectives of literary theory, others sharply challenge this approach.

Some literary theorists reject the term "Renaissance" for sixteenth- and seventeenth-century English literature. They repudiate the Renaissance, which they define narrowly in a neo-Burckhardtian way as meaning a small group of elite males who created works of literature as expressions of their individuality. This is a more limited view of the Renaissance than that of Burckhardt or, possibly, any historian of the twentieth century. Some literary theorists prefer the term "early modern," which means the formal and informal literature of the period as a whole, especially the writing of women and members of nonelite groups, whether or not it can be judged "great," that is, culturally transcendent.

Conclusion. Scholars have had a great deal to say about the Renaissance as a period of human history since Petrarch in the fourteenth century. The nineteenth century created a consensus view, usually labeled Burckhardtian for its most famous exponent. Scholars since 1945 have not written grand interpretations of the Renaissance but have emphasized defining aspects of the period. They still often view the Renaissance as different from the Middle Ages and as manifesting modernity, although in a more measured fashion than their nineteenth-century predecessors. And while much of the anti-Renaissance polemic of medievalists has disappeared, a new tendency to deny the existence of the Renaissance as a unique period, or to dismiss it as an era of elites and elite culture, has emerged. It remains to be seen how scholars of the twenty-first century will view the Renaissance.

See also **Early Modern Period; Historiography, Renaissance; Humanism; Middle Ages; Protestant Reformation; Renaissance, Interpretations of the.**

BIBLIOGRAPHY

Surveys of Renaissance Historiography

Bullen, J. B. *The Myth of the Renaissance in Nineteenth-Century Writing*. Oxford, 1994. Discusses French and English writing about the Renaissance, circa 1750–1860.

Ferguson, Wallace K. *The Renaissance in Historical Thought: Five Centuries of Interpretation*. Boston, 1948. A comprehensive study of Renaissance historiography since Petrarch and a classic in its own right.

The Renaissance Debate. Edited by Denys Hay. New York, 1965. Contains translated excerpts on the Renaissance from Palmieri, Voltaire, Michelet, Voigt, Burckhardt, Symonds, Haskins, Baron, Kristeller, Chabod, and others.

From Petrarch to 1945

Burckhardt, Jakob. *The Civilization of the Renaissance in Italy*. Translated by S. G. C. Middlemore. Edited and introduced by Irene Gordon. New York, 1960. Translation of *Die Kultur der Renaissance in Italien* (1860). Based on the German edition of 1868, the last one supervised by the author. This edition eliminates the many illustrations and footnotes often added to Burckhardt's spare original essay.

Haskins, Charles Homer. *The Renaissance of the Twelfth Century*. New York, 1957. First published 1927.

Symonds, John Addington. *Renaissance in Italy*. 7 vols. London, 1875–1886.

Voigt, Georg. *Die Wiederbelebung des classischen Alterthums, oder das erste Jahrhundert des Humanismus*. 2 vols. 3d ed. Berlin, 1893. First published 1859. Expanded two-volume edition: Berlin, 1880–1881. Third edition: Berlin, 1893.

Humanism since 1945

Baron, Hans. *The Crisis of the Early Italian Renaissance: Civic Humanism and Republican Liberty in an Age of Classicism and Tyranny*. Rev. ed. Princeton, N.J., 1966. First published 1955 in two volumes.

Bentley, Jerry H. *Politics and Culture in Renaissance Naples*. Princeton, N.J., 1987.

D'Amico, John F. *Renaissance Humanism in Papal Rome: Humanists and Churchmen on the Eve of the Reformation*. Baltimore, and London, 1983.

Garin, Eugenio. *Italian Humanism: Philosophy and Civic Life in the Renaissance*. Translated by Peter Munz. Oxford, 1965. First appeared in German in 1947 and in Italian in 1952.

Gil Fernández, Luis. *Panorama social del humanismo español (1500–1800)*. Madrid, 1981.

King, Margaret L. *Venetian Humanism in an Age of Patrician Dominance*. Princeton, N.J., 1986.

Kristeller, Paul Oskar. *Renaissance Thought: The Classic, Scholastic, and Humanist Strains*. New York and London, 1961.

McConica, James K. *English Humanists and Reformation Politics under Henry VIII and Edward VI*. Oxford, 1965

Renaissance Humanism: Foundations, Forms, and Legacy. Edited by Albert Rabil Jr. 3 vols. Philadelphia, 1988. A survey of humanism across Europe accompanied by studies of specific topics within humanism.

Sabbadini, Remigio. *Le scoperte dei codici latini e greci ne' secoli XIV e XV*. Edited by Eugenio Garin. 2 vols. Reprint, Florence, 1967. First published 1905–1914.

Erasmus

Bainton, Roland H. *Erasmus of Christendom*. New York, 1969.

Erasmus, Desiderius. *Collected Works of Erasmus*. Toronto, 1974–.

Erasmus, Desiderius. *Opera omnia Desiderii Erasmi Roterodami*. Amsterdam, 1969–.

Huizinga, Johan. *Erasmus and the Age of Reformation*. Translated by F. Hopman. New York and Evanston, Ill., 1957.

The Renaissance State

Becker, Marvin B. *Florence in Transition*. 2 vols. Baltimore, 1967–1968.

Chabod, Federico. *Storia di Milano nell'epoca di Carlo V*. Turin, Italy, 1971. First published in 1961 as *L'epoca di Carlo V*.

Chabod, Federico. "Was There a Renaissance State?" In *The Development of the Modern State*. Edited by Heinz Lubasz. New York, 1964. Pages 26–42. First published in French in 1958.

Elton, Geoffrey Rudolf. *The Tudor Revolution in Government*. Cambridge, U.K., 1953.

Social History

Braudel, Fernand. *The Mediterranean and the Mediterranean World in the Age of Philip II*. Translated by Siân Reynolds. 2 vols. New York, 1972.

Burke, Peter. *The French Historical Revolution: The Annales School, 1929–89*. Cambridge, U.K., 1990.

Women in the Renaissance

Kelly-Gadol, Joan. "Did Women Have a Renaissance?" In *Becoming Visible: Woman in European History*. Edited by Renate Bridenthal and Claudia Koonz. Boston, 1977. Pages 137–164.

King, Margaret L. *Women of the Renaissance*. Chicago and London, 1991.

Literary Theory

Greenblatt, Stephen. *Renaissance Self-Fashioning: From More to Shakespeare*. Chicago, 1980.

"The State of Renaissance Studies: A Special Twenty-fifth Anniversary Symposium in Honor of Dan S. Collins." In *English Literary Renaissance* 25, no. 3 (autumn 1995). Articles by twelve scholars assessing English Renaissance scholarship since the early 1970s. The majority endorse "new historicism" and other theory-driven approaches; a minority express strong dissent.

PAUL F. GRENDLER

The Renaissance in Literary Interpretation

Literary historians and critics have for more than a century applied the rubric "Renaissance" to their own material, but they have also criticized that application, sometimes fiercely. Two arenas of debate have been especially notable.

The English Renaissance. The pattern for speaking of an English Renaissance was set by Hippolyte Taine in his *History of English Literature* (1863–1864; translated 1871). Taine's was a specifically literary Renaissance, beginning in the early sixteenth century and running later than any of its continental siblings, primarily in order to include the key figure of Milton; it was also a conflicted Renaissance, a collision between the pagan spirit of the larger European Renaissance and the new influence of the German Reformation. This periodization was canonized by English and especially American usage in the course of the first half of the twentieth century, and it is still the periodization used in most American English departments (though there is often a curricular distinction between sixteenth- and seventeenth-century literature as well). The reference of the term "Renaissance" in connection with England remains largely confined to literature, with the fine arts—which figure so importantly in Jakob Burckhardt's picture—keeping a comparatively low profile.

Through the 1950s terminological controversies about the English Renaissance were often formulated as debates as to whether the event denoted by the period term did or did not occur. C. S. Lewis characterized his sixteenth-century volume in the *Oxford History of English Literature* (1954) as a polemical demonstration "that the Renaissance never happened in England," or at least "that if it did, *it had no importance*." Most of such dissent was rooted in a conviction that Burckhardt's originary contrast between the Middle Ages and the Renaissance was a dangerous oversimplification, and that the latter period needs to be understood primarily as a continuation of the former; the penultimate chapter of Wallace Ferguson's *The Renaissance in Historical Thought* (1948) is entitled "The Revolt of the Medievalists." In particular, critics such as Lewis distrusted the pagan innuendo that they felt attached to the term "Renaissance" and wanted to affirm the fundamentally Christian character of sixteenth- and seventeenth-century English culture. Perhaps the closest thing to a consensus to result is that offered by Douglas Bush in *The Renaissance and English Humanism* (1939), which kept the term "Renaissance" but allied it with a specifically "Christian humanism" in which piety toward antiquity was thoroughly integrated with commitment to the Christian religion; as in Taine, Milton figures as an important culmination. So conceptualized, the period term could be used to contest unguardedly modern interpretations of literary texts.

Renaissance or Early Modern. A different appeal to history has informed later controversies concerning the period category. The 1980s and 1990s saw calls by some literary scholars for the replacement of "Renaissance" by "early modern," the term that starting in the late nineteenth century gradually established itself as the preferred label among some historians. This usage itself is congruent with Burckhardt, who wrote of his Italians in *The Civilization of the Renaissance in Italy* as "the first-born among the sons of modern Europe" and who was never wholly comfortable with the term "Renaissance" (which he occasionally puts within quotation marks, an inflection lost in the Middlemore translation); placing the period on the far side of a bracket that opens toward the present rather than toward the Middle Ages effectively takes Burckhardt's part in what had been a major point of controversy over his work. The polemics of the 1980s and 1990s, however, tend to cast themselves in inclusive opposition to the Burckhardtian tradition, and are generally less concerned with the exact placement of the medieval/modern boundary than with the methodology and interests of contemporary literary critics.

At its most modest, the proposed shift in terminology enforced a useful distinction between a historical period (early modern) whose dates are fairly uniform across western Europe and an occasionally self-conscious cultural movement (the Renaissance) occurring within that period, on different schedules in different locales. Those interested in Italy and its formative influence on the culture of Europe from the fifteenth to the seventeenth century are naturally attracted to the humanists' own notion of rebirth, while proponents of the term "early modern period" are effectively opposing an Italocentric perspective on the age. In more expansive mode, advocates of the change seek to purge what they see as an ideological heritage carried by the word "Renaissance," a bias in favor of high culture, imperial politics, and combative individualism. A manifesto by Leah S. Marcus ("Renaissance/Early Modern Studies"; 1992) posits "early modern" as the more "egalitarian" rubric, under which numerous trends in contemporary work can find a sense of common cause: attention to previously uncanonical writers (especially women) and to nonliterary texts, alertness to matters of gender and especially to manifestations of homosexual desire, concern with issues related to European colonization (with particular sensitivity to the perspective of the colonized), respect for "the instability of literary texts" in editorial practice, and even such shifts of interest within the established roster of texts as that from the "elitist" lyric to the popular drama (though the special importance of Milton is specifically reaffirmed).

The alliance of causes here is a loose one, and not all participants assent to the terminological shift. Walter Cohen, for instance, writing on "The Discourse of Empire in the Renaissance" (1995), argues for retaining the older period term precisely because of its value in accounting for the crimes perpetrated by the European nations upon the inhabitants of the New World. Marcus herself in a later forum ("Cyberspace Renaissance"; 1995) reports a modest change of heart concerning the overtones of the word "Renaissance" and welcomes it back into general usage. William Kerrigan and Gordon Braden, in *The Idea of the Renaissance* (1989), do not address the matter directly, but find ideological distress at the Burckhardtian rubric overwrought and see few real hazards in the alert continuation of its established role. Individual practice at present varies widely.

See also **Early Modern Period; Renaissance,** *subentry on* **The Renaissance in Historical Thought.**

BIBLIOGRAPHY

Burckhardt, Jakob. *The Civilization of the Renaissance in Italy.* Translated by S. G. C. Middlemore. 2 vols. Reprint, New York, 1958. Translation of *Die Kultur der Renaissance in Italien* (1860).

Bush, Douglas. *The Renaissance and English Humanism.* Toronto, 1939.

Cohen, Walter. "The Discourse of Empire in the Renaissance." In *Cultural Authority in Golden Age Spain.* Edited by Marina S. Brownlee and Hans Ulrich Gumbrecht. Baltimore, 1995. Pages 260–283.

Ferguson, Wallace Klippert. *The Renaissance in Historical Thought: Five Centuries of Interpretation.* Boston, 1948.

Gibb, Jocelyn, ed. *Light on C. S. Lewis.* London, 1965.

Kerrigan, William, and Gordon Braden. *The Idea of the Renaissance.* Baltimore, 1989.

Lewis, C. S. *English Literature in the Sixteenth Century, Excluding Drama.* The Oxford History of English Literature, vol. 3. Oxford, 1954.

Marcus, Leah S. "Cyberspace Renaissance." *English Literary Renaissance* 25 (1995): 388–401.

Marcus, Leah S. "Renaissance/Early Modern Studies." In *Redrawing the Boundaries: The Transformation of English and American Literary Studies.* Edited by Stephen Greenblatt and Giles Gunn. New York, 1992. Pages 41–63.

Taine, Hippolyte. *History of English Literature.* Translated by Henri van Laun. 2 vols. Edinburgh, 1871. Translation of *Histoire de la littérature anglaise* (1863–1864).

Gordon Braden

The Renaissance in Popular Imagination

As an object of scholarly study, the Renaissance spurs historians, art historians, scholars of literature and the performing arts, and others to consult documents, texts, and objects from the period in order to reach considered judgments about what happened and why. These professionals normally communicate with each other by means of scholarly books, articles published in learned journals, and papers delivered at seminars and meetings of learned societies, such as the Renaissance Society of America. The majority, but not all, of such scholars are employed in universities and colleges, or work in museums and galleries. The entries in this encyclopedia present the results of their research.

But people not involved in academic and scholarly study also have an awareness of the Renaissance. Their perceptions may be informed by scholarly study, or independently of such formal study, or by a mixture of these two approaches. Members of the general public, museum goers, high school and university students, television viewers, artists, composers, novelists, filmmakers, and many others have a conception of the Renaissance. Indeed, a large number of people beyond the scholarly community have presented an image or a view of the Renaissance to a variety of audiences. An even greater number of people have read, viewed, heard, or participated in such presentations.

What follows is a brief survey with a few examples illustrating how the Renaissance appears outside of the academic community. The examples from literature, music, film, and commerce document what the Renaissance means to many in the general public. Some individuals and themes from the Renaissance appear repeatedly and have exerted great fascination.

The Word "Renaissance." The *Oxford English Dictionary* indicates that the French word "renaissance" (meaning "rebirth") entered the English language as an adjective with a pejorative connotation. In *A Summer in Brittany* (1840), Thomas A. Trollope (brother of the novelist Anthony Trollope) looked with horror at "that heaviest and least graceful of all possible styles, the 'renaissance,' as the French choose to term it." However, the style did not offend all eyes. Two years after Trollope, Queen Victoria reported in her journal that "we . . . saw the fine greenhouse the Duke has built, all in stone, in the Renaissance style." Nevertheless, the pejorative meaning of Renaissance persisted. In 1886 *The Church Times,* commenting on architectural styles, sniffed that "the Renaissant" is most appropriate "for gin-shops, theatres and restaurants."

The English noun "Renaissance" quickly acquired the positive meaning of rebirth of artistic achievement and novelty. Richard Ford's *Hand-book for Travellers in Spain* in 1845 wrote of basking in "the bright period of the *Renaissance* when fine art was a necessity and pervaded every relation of life." The term "Renaissance" has since been applied to numerous kinds of novelty and achievement far distant from the fifteenth and sixteenth centuries. Alain Locke wrote of a "Negro Renaissance" in *The New Negro* (1925), and the term "Harlem Renaissance" describes an outpouring of literary and artistic works by African-Americans in the 1920s.

The alternate spelling "renascence" (pronounced "ren NAYS ens") referred in the early eighteenth century to the rebirth of the soul. The English poet and essayist Matthew Arnold first used it as an alternate spelling for "Renaissance" in *Culture and Anarchy* in 1869. Whatever the spelling, it continues to be used to mean rebirth of some kind.

Renaissance suggests urban rebirth and renewal after a period of decline. For example, in the 1950s and 1960s the city of Pittsburgh called itself "the Renaissance city," because a refurbished central core of gleaming new buildings replaced a decaying urban center. In similar fashion, Detroit in the late 1970s created the Renaissance Center, a rebuilt downtown area featuring corporate headquarters, a circular hotel, and a building for the arts. In both cases, the label meant a rebirth of the spirit of the city as well as new buildings. Pittsburgh's civic leaders wished to tell the world that it was no longer a decaying industrial city full of smog and abandoned steel plants, but growing and vibrant. Detroit's Renaissance Center promised an urban area full of activity, rather than one marked by crime and abandoned buildings.

Renaissance Man. "Renaissance man" or "Renaissance woman," meaning someone very accomplished and successful in several, unconnected activities, is common usage. For example, a tribute to a successful and wealthy banker and philanthropist, who also wrote a scholarly book on the American civil war, called him a "Renaissance man, because his interests ranged far and wide, and everything he touched found success" (*The News & Observer* of Raleigh, N.C., 14 March 1998, p. B1). The same newspaper, relating news about Hollywood personalities, described the film actress Jodie Foster as a Renaissance woman because she "tackled acting, directing, and producing," and was about to become a mother (6 March 1998, p. A2).

A man searching for romantic love can take advantage of this favorable image by advertising himself as a "Renaissance man." In one such personal advertisement, the unidentified man describes himself as a former art student turned professional engineer, turned artist. He further calls himself "very handsome," honest, sensitive, sincere, sensual, self-aware, humorous, and financially secure. His additional interests range from the arts to gourmet cooking and skiing. (*The Washingtonian,* February 1998, p. 166). This ad produced four times as many responses as the normal personal ad. The editor of the personal ads section of *The Washingtonian* noted that a man advertised himself as a Renaissance man approximately once a month. But the editor could not remember a woman advertising herself as a "Renaissance woman," or a man searching for a "Renaissance woman" (telephone interview, 10 August 1998).

Shakespeare. The Renaissance figure with the greatest influence in the popular imagination of the English-speaking world has been William Shakespeare. From the early nineteenth century onward, schools and universities everywhere in the English-speaking world have taught one or several of his plays and sometimes his sonnets. Some phrases from his works, such as "To be or not to be" from *Hamlet,* are a permanent part of the English language. His plays are performed more often than any others in the language.

Shakespeare has always been popular outside the schoolroom. In nineteenth-century America, numerous touring companies brought his plays to large cities, small towns, frontier villages, even mining camps. Actors acquired reputations and earned large sums of money for their characterizations of Hamlet, Macbeth, and other well-known Shakespearean characters. Shakespeare was popular entertainment. This meant that his works had universal appeal, whatever the educational level of the members of the audience.

Shakespeare became popular with nineteenth-century Americans for several reasons. Just as they listened avidly for hours to political orators, so they loved the rhetorical flourishes in Shakespeare. This aspect of Shakespeare struck a deep chord, because oratory was an essential part of nineteenth-century education and culture. Indeed, Shakespeare was taught more as declamation and rhetoric than as literature in nineteenth-century schools. The emphasis on rhetoric is ultimately traceable to the humanistic education of the Renaissance period, of which Shakespeare was a product.

Shakespeare was also seen as a moralist. Much of the central action in his plays depends on moral issues. His characters reap the just consequences of their good, and especially their evil, actions. Again, this emphasis is found in the humanistic education of the Renaissance, which endured in schooling for centuries. Finally, Shakespeare's plays emphasize the individual, just as the American ideology of individualism does. The plays often revolve around the actions of towering individuals who strike out on their own against the advice of family and friends. The ambitious Richard III and the star-crossed lovers Romeo and Juliet take personal responsibility for their actions. The theme of individualism is so deeply ingrained in the American character that Shakespeare's plays could not fail to resonate.

While Shakespeare's plays continued to be performed on the stage in the twentieth century, popular Shakespeare intended for the broadest audiences moved from the stage to the motion picture theater, the new center of popular entertainment.

Filmmakers have produced numerous versions of Shakespeare's plays. (For lists of some of the better-known films of Shakespeare's plays and films based on Shakespeare's plays, see tables 1 and 2.) Possibly the best-known and most popular have been three British productions starring Laurence Olivier: *Henry V* (1944), which was partly intended to boost English morale during World War II, *Hamlet* (1948), and *Richard III* (1955). Every generation of filmmakers has produced new versions of *Romeo and Juliet.* The films faithfully reproduce Shakespeare's words, but often shorten the text. For example, Kenneth Branagh's *Hamlet* (1997) has a complete and an abridged version. Because the action is no longer limited to a theater stage, the filmmaker can create memorable physical scenes, such as full-scale battles, in which to convey Shakespeare's words and meaning.

Shakespeare's influence extends far beyond performances of his works. Numerous authors have borrowed the plots of his dramas, then adapted them to their own purposes and different settings. *Romeo and Juliet* may be the love story most evoked and retold in different contexts all over the world. A famous example in popular culture is the Broadway musical *West Side Story* (1957), which was followed by the 1961 film version. It retells the story of the doomed lovers in a New York City world of urban youth gangs that fight until tragedy strikes. While "Romeo" dies, "Juliet" lives to reconcile the gang members.

Nineteenth-century French, German, and Italian audiences loved Shakespeare in translation for the same reasons as did American and English audiences. They also transformed Shakespeare to fit other popular formats, above all, opera. Giacchino Rossini composed his *Otello* (1816), and Giuseppe Verdi (1813–1901) wrote a famous trio of operas based on Shakespeare's plays: *Macbeth* (1847), *Otello* (1887), and *Falstaff* (1893). Shakespeare continues to be the most important direct product of the Renaissance in the English-speaking world, and a significant one in non-English cultures.

Opera. The chief musical interpretation of the Renaissance has been through opera. Even though

TABLE 1. Movies of Shakespeare Plays

Antony and Cleopatra (Great Britain, Spain, Switzerland, 1972), Maurice Pelling; Charlton Heston, Hildegarde Neil
As You Like It (Great Britain, 1936), Paul Czinner; Elisabeth Bergner, Laurence Olivier.
Hamlet (Great Britain, 1948), Laurence Olivier; Laurence Olivier, Eileen Herlie, Basil Sydney.
Hamlet (USSR, 1964), Grigori Kozintsev.
Hamlet (Great Britain, 1969), Tony Richardson; Nicol Williamson.
Hamlet (Warner Brothers, 1991), Franco Zeffirelli; Mel Gibson, Glenn Close, Alan Bates, Ian Holm, Paul Scofield.
Hamlet (Great Britain, 1997), Kenneth Branagh; Kenneth Branagh, Derek Jacobi.
Henry V (Great Britain, 1944), Laurence Olivier; Laurence Olivier, Robert Newton.
Henry V (Great Britain, 1989), Kenneth Branagh; Kenneth Branagh, Derek Jacobi, Alec McCowan, Emma Thompson.
Julius Caesar (MGM, 1953), Joseph L. Mankiewicz; John Gielgud, James Mason, Marlon Brando, Greer Garson, Deborah Kerr; score by Miklos Rozsa.
King Lear (Great Britain, Denmark, 1970), Peter Brook; Paul Scofield, Irene Worth.
Macbeth (Republic, 1948), Orson Welles; Orson Welles, Jeanette Nolan, Dan O'Herlihy, Roddy McDowall. In Scots dialect.
Macbeth (Great Britain, 1971), Roman Polanski; Jon Finch, Francesca Annis.
A Midsummer Night's Dream (Warner, 1935), Max Reinhardt; James Cagney, Dick Powell, Olivia de Havilland, Victor Jory, Mickey Rooney.
Much Ado about Nothing (Great Britain, United States, 1993), Kenneth Branagh; Kenneth Branagh, Michael Keaton, Keanu Reeves, Emma Thompson, Denzel Washington.
Othello (United States, France, 1951), Orson Welles; Orson Welles, Michael MacLiammoir, Fay Compton.
Othello (United States, Great Britain, 1995), Oliver Parker; Laurence Fishburne, Kenneth Branagh, Irène Jacob.
Richard III (Great Britain, 1955), Laurence Olivier; Laurence Olivier, Claire Bloom, Ralph Richardson, Cedric Hardwicke, John Gielgud.
Richard III (United States, Great Britain, 1995), Richard Loncrain; Ian McKellen, Annette Bening.
Romeo and Juliet (MGM, 1936), George Cukor; Leslie Howard, Norma Shearer, John Barrymore, Basil Rathbone, Edna May Oliver.
Romeo and Juliet (Rank, 1954), Renato Castellani; Laurence Harvey, Susan Shentall.
Romeo and Juliet (Great Britain, 1968), Franco Zeffirelli; Leonard Whiting, Olivia Hussey.
The Taming of the Shrew (United Artists, 1929), Sam Taylor; Douglas Fairbanks, Mary Pickford.
The Taming of the Shrew (Columbia, 1967), Franco Zeffirelli; Richard Burton, Elizabeth Taylor.

Entries indicate title, studio or country of origin, director, and major actors.

opera began in late Renaissance Italy, opera plots did not depict Renaissance society or deal with Renaissance themes and stories before the nineteenth century. Beginning with Gioacchino Rossini (1792–1868) the Renaissance served as a source for plots that offered pretexts for elaborate singing and spectacular stage effects. Composers had little interest in interpreting the Renaissance, nor did their music have much relationship to Renaissance styles. For example, Rossini used the overture to an opera of his that dealt with a Roman emperor for *Elisabetta, Regina d'Inghilterra* (1815), an opera about Elizabeth I of England, and used it again for his *Il barbiere di Siviglia* (*The Barber of Seville;* 1816), a comic opera set in the eighteenth century. Gaetano Donizetti (1797–1848) also looked to English Renaissance history, for the plots of *Anna Bolena* (Anne Boleyn, 1830), *Maria Stuarda* (Mary Queen of Scots, 1834), and *Roberto Devereux* (1837), the latter concerning Elizabeth's reputed lover. *Beatrice di Tenda* (1834) by Vincenzo Bellini (1801–1835) dealt with the Visconti ruling family of early fifteenth-century Milan. Giacomo Meyerbeer (1791–1864) used sixteenth-century history for *Robert le diable* (1831), and French Reformation history for *Les Huguenots* (1836) and *Le prophète* (1849). None of these operas offered a penetrating look at Renaissance society.

Beginning in the 1840s, composers and librettists offered interpretations of the Renaissance period focusing on two aspects: the Renaissance as a society and the Renaissance as a period of artistic creativity.

Several operas saw Renaissance society and politics as decadent and immoral. Donizetti's *Lucrezia Borgia* (1833) titillated the audience with hints of

TABLE 2. Movies Based on Shakespeare's Plays

Hamlet Goes Business (Finland, 1987). Modern-day version of *Hamlet.*
Chimes at Midnight (Spain, Switzerland, 1966), Orson Welles; Orson Welles, John Gielgud, Margaret Rutherford, Jeanne Moreau. Based on the Falstaff episodes in *Henry IV* and *Henry V.*
King Lear (France, 1987), Jean-Luc Godard; Burgess Meredith, Peter Sellers, Molly Ringwald, Norman and Kate Mailer, Woody Allen.
Ran (Japan, 1985), Akira Kurosawa. Based on *King Lear.*
Throne of Blood (Japan, 1957), Akira Kurosawa; Toshiro Mifune. Based on *Macbeth.*
Les amants de Vérone (France, 1948), André Cayatte; Pierre Brasseur, Anouk Aimée. Same story as *Romeo and Juliet.*
West Side Story (United Artists, 1961), Robert Wise and Jerome Robbins; lyrics by Stephen Sondheim; music by Leonard Bernstein; Natalie Wood (sung by Marni Nixon), Richard Beymer (sung by Jimmy Bryant). Musical version of *Romeo and Juliet.*
Kiss Me Kate (MGM, 1953), George Sidney; songs by Cole Porter; Howard Keel, Kathryn Grayson, Ann Miller, Keenan Wynn, James Whitmore, Bob Fosse. Musical about a production of *The Taming of the Shrew.*
Forbidden Planet (MGM, 1956), Fred M. Wilcox; Walter Pidgeon, Anne Francis, Leslie Nielsen. Based on *The Tempest.*
The Tempest (Great Britain, 1980), Derek Jarman. A punk version.
Prospero's Books (Great Britain, Netherlands, 1991), Peter Greenaway; John Gielgud. Based on *The Tempest.*
Looking for Richard (Fox Searchlight, 1996), Al Pacino; Al Pacino, Alec Baldwin, Kevin Spacey, Estelle Parsons, Winona Ryder, Aidan Quinn. Documentary about actors working on *Richard III.*

Entries indicate title, studio or country of origin, director, and major actors.

incest and sexual immorality, and depicted a mass poisoning; although the work dazzled audiences with vocal fireworks, it did not offer a serious interpretation of the Renaissance. Giuseppe Verdi's *Rigoletto* (1851), based on Victor Hugo's play *Le roi s'amuse* (1832; trans. *The King Amuses Himself*), did present such an interpretation. It depicts a Renaissance prince who preys on the wives and daughters of his courtiers and subjects. Rigoletto, the hunchbacked court jester, aids the duke of Mantua in his seductions until his own daughter falls victim to the prince. By means of its memorable music, the opera describes serious social disorder in an Italian Renaissance court.

The librettists of Verdi's *Don Carlos* (1867; revised 1882–1883) ignored the facts of history in order to create an exciting story set in the court of Philip II of Spain (ruled 1556–1598). The opera depicts Carlos, Philip II's son, and Elisabeth de Valois, Philip's wife, as being in love, even though there was no historical attraction between the pair, who were quite mismatched in age. The librettists also inserted the character of the Grand Inquisitor. The alleged support of the Netherlands' battle for independence from Spain by Carlos and Rodrigue, another Spanish noble in the opera, appealed to the liberal political sentiments of the nineteenth-century opera-going bourgeoisie.

Other operas viewed the Renaissance positively as a period of artistic creativity: they depicted a historical Renaissance artist creating great works despite philistine contemporaries and uncomprehending patrons. Hector Berlioz (1803–1869) composed his *Benvenuto Cellini* (premiere 1838) for the Paris Opéra, a government-subsidized theater swirling with hostility against him. In the opera, Cellini struggles against the crass taste of the officials of the papal court, just as Berlioz struggled against the crass taste of the officials of the Opéra. Pope Clement VII orders Cellini to cast an immense statue of Perseus or be hanged. When Cellini succeeds, the pope pardons him and approves his marriage to the daughter of the papal treasurer. Thus, the artist succeeds at art and life. Unfortunately, Berlioz's opera did not. The opening-night audience booed the opera off the stage. *Benvenuto Cellini* lasted only three performances in its premiere run.

Richard Wagner's *Die Meistersinger von Nürnberg* (*The Mastersingers of Nürnberg;* composed 1862–1867; premiere 1868) is based on histories of the guild of singers in sixteenth-century Nürnberg and on a real poet, the cobbler Hans Sachs (1494–1576), who was the subject of many poems, dramas, and operas in the nineteenth century. In Wagner's opera, Sachs genially and with great heart struggles against his obscurantist fellow guild members, who require that the composition of music follow strict rules. In the opera Sachs broadens the circle of creative artists and stretches the rules of music making by championing an outsider, a knight uprooted by the changing fortunes of his class in mid-sixteenth-century Germany. Like Cellini, the knight creates a work of art (a *Meistergesang* or master's song) and wins the hand of a rich man's daughter. Wagner integrated traditional musical forms—songs, Lutheran chorale tunes, marches, and dances—into the score and evoked sixteenth-century music with a style employing Renaissance counterpoint and archaic harmonies.

Berlioz's and Wagner's works are joyous and exuberant celebrations of Renaissance artistic endeavor. Two twentieth-century operas paint a dark picture of Renaissance artists struggling against society. The libretto of *Palestrina* (1917) by Hans Pfitzner (1869–1949) departs from historical fact by using the character of Giovanni Palestrina (1525/26–1594), the composer of Catholic Church music, as an example of the artist who resists the new musical expression of his times, and who struggles unhappily against the demands of overweening institutional patrons. *Mathis der Maler* (Matthias the painter; 1938) by Paul Hindemith (1895–1963) sets the painter Matthias Grünewald (c. 1475–1528) in the court of Cardinal Albrecht of Mainz, who sees his patronage of artists as a way of building on the Rhine River a rival to Renaissance Rome. Matthias, moved more by the sufferings of the downtrodden during the Peasants' War (1525) than by Albrecht's pretensions, or by the avarice and philistinism of the rich, is unable to paint in a time of violence. But St. Paul tells him in a vision to paint for the glory of God. Matthias then creates his masterpiece, the *Isenheim Altarpiece,* which he actually painted between 1512 and 1515. Alberto Ginastera (1916–1983) harked back to Donizetti's plots with portrayal of monstrous Renaissance deeds—poisoning, incestuous rape, and torture—in *Bomarzo* (1967) and *Beatrix Cenci* (1971).

Historical Fiction and Films. The popular imagination sees the Renaissance period as one of great achievement and great excess. According to this view, larger-than-life individuals strode across the fifteenth and sixteenth centuries, creating great works of art, sometimes perpetrating cruel deeds, but always leaving a memorable legacy. This understanding of the Renaissance has strongly influenced historical fiction and films. (For a selective list of films dealing with the Renaissance, see table 3.)

The Italian-born Rafael Sabatini (1875–1950) wrote several historical novels with this approach: *The Life of Cesare Borgia* (1912), *Torquemada and the Spanish Inquisition: A History* (1913), *The Fortunes of Captain Blood* (1936), and *Columbus* (1942). But possibly the most widely read American author of Renaissance historical novels of the first half of the twentieth century was Samuel Shellabarger (1888–1954). His *Captain from Castile* (1945) is a fictional account of Hernán Cortés's invasion of Mexico (1519–1521) as seen through the eyes of a young Spanish soldier who joins Cortés's expedition in flight from unjust persecution by the Spanish Inquisition. Shellabarger's *Prince of Foxes* (1947) narrates the adventures of a young man of low birth who assumes the noble name of Andrea Orsini in 1500 in Italy. He begins by serving the unscrupulous Cesare Borgia, but then works to thwart Borgia's nefarious schemes, which imperil him and his beloved. *The King's Cavalier* (1950) is set in the France of Francis I (ruled 1515–1547). Shellabarger, who earned a Ph.D. and was a professor of English for some years, inserted a considerable amount of historical information about the Renaissance into his novels.

Two of Shellabarger's novels became films. *Captain from Castile* (1947) starred Tyrone Power as the young captain from Castile, Jean Peters as the servant girl whom he loves, and César Romero as Cortés. It is full of action and brave speeches, as the Spaniards conquer Mexico. The music composed by Alfred Newman includes the rousing march for orchestra "Captain from Castile," which continues to be performed. The black-and-white film *Prince of Foxes* (1949) is a very free adaptation of Shellabarger's novel. The film focuses on a rivalry between Cesare Borgia (acted by Orson Welles) and Orsini (Tyrone Power) for the love, or the body in the case of Borgia, of Camilla Verano (Wanda Hendrix), who is betrothed against her will to Borgia.

In the same year, Welles appeared in a quite different film, *The Third Man* (1949; directed by Carol Reed, screenplay by Graham Greene), a black-and-white thriller set in immediate post–World War II Vienna. In it Welles expressed the popular view that the Renaissance was an era of great extremes of human accomplishment and evil. The character he plays, a trafficker in adulterated penicillin whose actions lead to the deaths of children, justifies his actions by saying, "In Italy for thirty years, under the Borgias, they had warfare, terror, murder, and bloodshed, but they produced Michelangelo, Leonardo da Vinci, and the Renaissance. In Switzerland they had brotherly love. They had five hundred years

TABLE 3. Selected Movies Dealing with the Renaissance

Affairs of Cellini (Twentieth Century-Fox, 1934), Gregory La Cava; Fredric March.
The Agony and the Ecstasy (Twentieth Century-Fox, 1965), Carol Reed; Charlton Heston, Rex Harrison.
Anne of the Thousand Days (Universal, 1969), Charles Jarrott; Richard Burton, Geneviève Bujold.
Assassination of the duc de Guise (France, 1908), Charles Le Bergy. The duc de Guise was murdered in 1589.
The Beloved Rogue (United States, 1927), Alan Crosland; John Barrymore. About the French poet François Villon (1431-after 1463); same story as *The Vagabond King.*
Bride of Vengeance (Paramount, 1948), Mitchell Leisen; Paulette Goddard. About the Borgias.
Caravaggio (Great Britain, 1986), Derek Jarman.
Cervantes (Spain, Italy, France, 1968), Vincent Sherman; Horst Buchholz, Gina Lollobrigida, Louis Jourdan, José Ferrer, Fernando Rey.
Diane (MGM, 1956), David Miller; Lana Turner. About Diane de Poitiers, mistress of Henry II of France.
Don Juan (Warner, 1926), Alan Crosland; John Barrymore. Don Juan at the court of Lucrezia Borgia.
Don Quixote. There are eleven versions.
El Greco (Italy and France, 1964), Luciano Salce; Mel Ferrer.
Ever After (Twentieth Century-Fox, 1998), Andy Tennant; Anjelica Huston, Drew Barrymore, Dongray Scott. A Cinderella is aided by Leonardo da Vinci.
Fire over England (Great Britain, 1936), William K. Howard; Flora Robson, Laurence Olivier, Raymond Massey. Deals with the English defeat of the Spanish Armada.
If I Were King (Paramount, 1938), Frank Lloyd; script by Preston Sturges; Ronald Colman, Basil Rathbone. On François Villon.
Intolerance (United States, 1916), D. W. Griffith. Includes a depiction of the Saint Bartholomew's Day massacre.
Lady Jane (Great Britain, 1986), Trevor Nunn; Helena Bonham-Carter. About Lady Jane Grey.
A Man for All Seasons (Columbia, 1966), Fred Zinnemann; Paul Scofield, Wendy Hiller, Susannah York, Robert Shaw, Orson Welles. Life of Thomas More.
Mary of Scotland (RKO, 1936), John Ford; Katharine Hepburn. Based on a Maxwell Anderson play.
Mary Queen of Scots (Universal, 1971), Charles Jarrott; Vanessa Redgrave, Glenda Jackson.
Les perles de la couronne (France, 1937), Sacha Guitry. Includes episodes dealing with Clement VII, Catherine de Médicis, Henry VIII of England, and Henry IV of France.
Prince of Foxes (Twentieth Century-Fox, 1949), Henry King; Tyrone Power, Orson Welles, Everett Sloane. Concerns Cesare Borgia.
The Private Life of Henry VIII (Great Britain, 1933), Alexander Korda; Charles Laughton, Elsa Lanchester.
Private Lives of Elizabeth and Essex (Warner, 1939), Michael Curtiz; Bette Davis, Errol Flynn. Based on Maxwell Anderson's *Elizabeth the Queen.*
Queen Elizabeth (France, 1912), Henri Desfontaines; Sarah Bernhardt.
The Return of Martin Guerre (France, 1982), Daniel Vigne; Gérard Depardieu, Nathalie Baye.
Shakespeare in Love (Miramax, 1998), John Madden; Joseph Fiennes, Gwyneth Paltrow, Judi Dench, Geoffrey Rush.
Tower of London (Universal, 1939), Rowland V. Lee; Basil Rathbone, Boris Karloff, Vincent Price.
Tower of London (American International, 1962), Roger Corman; Vincent Price.
Tudor Rose (Great Britain, 1936), Robert Stevenson; Cedric Hardwicke, Nova Pilbeam, John Mills. The life and reign of Lady Jane Grey.
The Vagabond King (Paramount, 1956), Michael Curtiz; Oreste, Kathryn Grayson. A musical about François Villon; same story as *The Beloved Rogue.*
The Virgin Queen (Twentieth Century-Fox, 1955), Henry Koster; Bette Davis, Richard Todd. Elizabeth I of England.
Young Bess (MGM, 1953), George Sidney; Jean Simmons, Stewart Granger, Charles Laughton. Early years of Elizabeth I.

Entries indicate title, studio or country of origin, director, and major actors.

of democracy and peace, and what did they produce? The cuckoo clock!"

Irving Stone's (1903–1989) *The Agony and the Ecstasy: A Novel of Michelangelo* (1961) is a fictional life with invented dialogue and scenes. The author based his "biographical novel," as he called it, on extensive research into Michelangelo's artistic and literary works, the locations in which he lived and worked, and scholarly sources. It enjoyed considerable popular success and large sales.

The color film *The Agony and the Ecstasy* (1965) concentrates on the years in which Michelangelo created the Sistine Chapel ceiling (1508–1512). The film portrays the creation of Michelangelo's masterpiece as a personal duel between Pope Julius II (played by Rex Harrison) and Michelangelo (Charlton Heston). The pope demands: "When will you make an end of it?" Michelangelo responds through clenched teeth: "When it is finished." The film also emphasizes the greatness of the creative artist, and adds the notion dear to the nineteenth and twentieth centuries that the artist must struggle to realize his or her vision against an uncomprehending society. The film introduces historical events and individuals, including the painter Raphael and the architect Donato Bramante.

A more artistically successful film based on the Renaissance was the French film *Retour de Martin Guerre* (The Return of Martin Guerre; 1982). The film is based on true events first described by the sixteenth-century judge who presided over the trial that ended the story. Set in a French village between about 1539 and 1560, it is the story of a man who claimed to be returning to his wife, son, and village after an absence of many years. All accept him as Martin Guerre, until his suspicious uncle denounces him as an imposter. A trial reveals that he is a fraud, as the true Martin Guerre appears. The film concentrates on village life and the ambiguity of relationships: does the wife know that the pretender, who shares her bed, is not her husband?

As the examples indicate, novels and films about the Renaissance are of two kinds: some portray real individuals and events of the Renaissance more or less faithfully, while others use a Renaissance setting or historical characters as the setting for a wholly imaginative story. An example of the latter is the romantic comedy *Shakespeare in Love* (1998). Suffering writer's block, Shakespeare falls in love with a young woman who inspires him to write *Romeo and Juliet*. And *Ever After* (1998) is a Cinderella tale set in Renaissance France about 1515. It features Leonardo da Vinci as a friend to the Cinderella character, who reads Thomas More's *Utopia*.

Whether artistically successful or not, Renaissance films share several characteristics. They create visually stunning scenes, especially in color, because they are often filmed on location or in sets that evoke the historical period. The films present authentic-looking interiors and clothing by relying on the visual record found in Renaissance artifacts and paintings. Second, the films invariably take greater or lesser liberties with the historical record. They simplify, streamline, and personalize the story. They add fictional characters and situations, typically a love interest. Historical facts that get in the way of a clear narrative are omitted or changed. Third, the films commonly endow the historical characters with attitudes and views designed to make them more appealing to twentieth-century film audiences, even if such attitudes and views might not be found in the Renaissance period.

Artistic Interpretations. As in music, the nineteenth century marked the beginning of interpretations of the Renaissance in the visual arts, especially painting. A few artists painted Renaissance historical scenes. Frederick Leighton's *Cimabue's Madonna Carried in Procession through the Streets of Florence* (1853–1855; National Gallery, London) depicts a story in Giorgio Vasari's *Lives of the Artists* (1550), although the Madonna is not by Cimabue. Jane Beham Hay's *A Florentine Procession* (1867; Homerton College, Cambridge, England) shows followers of Girolamo Savonarola preparing for a bonfire of the vanities, which occurred in Florence in the late 1490s.

Nineteenth- and twentieth-century painters tend to reinterpret, allude to, or quote Renaissance works of art, rather than depict scenes from Renaissance history. Thus, Dante Gabriel Rossetti's *Annunciation* (1850; Tate Gallery, London) alludes to Lorenzo Lotto's *Annunciation* (c. 1527–1529; S. Maria sopra Mercanti, Recanati, Italy). Édouard Manet's *Déjeuner sur l'herbe* (1862–1863; Musée d'Orsay, Paris) shocked mid-nineteenth-century sensibilities by portraying a nude woman in the company of clothed men. But the scene, including the postures of the figures, resembles Giorgione's *La tempesta* (The Storm; c. 1503; Accademia, Venice) and Titian's *Pastorale* (c. 1510–1511; Louvre, Paris). The setting and composition of Manet's *Olympia* (1863; Musée d'Orsay, Paris) recalls Titian's *Venus of Urbino* (c. 1518; Florence, Uffizi).

Giorgione. *The Tempest.* Painted c. 1505. The posture of the woman—a female nude in a landscape—at the right inspired that of the seated woman in Édouard Manet's *Déjeuner sur l'herbe* (1863; see the color plates in this volume). GALLERIA DELL'ACCADEMIA DI BELLE ARTI, VENICE/ALINARI/ART RESOURCE

Thanks to the public's acquaintance with the most familiar Renaissance works of art, twentieth-century artists can reinterpret them with some assurance that their references will be recognized. In 1919 Marcel Duchamp penciled a beard and mustache on a postcard of the *Mona Lisa* and the letters L.H.O.O.Q. (a lewd remark when read aloud in French) below her (private collection, Paris). Pablo Picasso reinterpreted Grünewald's *Isenheim Altarpiece* in a series of drawings in 1932 and Lucas Cranach the Elder's *David and Bathsheba* in a series of lithographs in 1947–1948. The following year he painted *Portrait of a Painter after El Greco* (Collection Angela Rosengart, Lucerne, Switzerland). In 1957 he made a drawing of *Venus and Cupid after Cranach the Elder*. Sometimes the quotation is tongue in cheek. In 1996 the National Gallery, London, exhibited work in progress by the British artist Peter Blake (b. 1932), *The Venuses' Outing to Weymouth*. This pastiche shows nine Venuses—three by Titian, two by Correggio, and one each by Sandro Botticelli, Agnolo Bronzino, Lucas Cranach the Elder, and the Baroque painter Diego Velazquez—lolling on the beach, while Cupids borrowed from two of the paintings play cricket in the background.

Leonardo da Vinci's painting *La Gioconda* or *Mona Lisa* even entered the ephemeral world of popular music. The portrait of the slightly smiling woman inspired the lyrics to an American popular song called *Mona Lisa* (1949; music and words by Jay Livingston and Ray Evans). The refrain voices a longing to understand the enigmatic woman with the smile, by comparing a mysterious and distant real woman with the portrait: "Mona Lisa, Mona Lisa, men have named you. You're so like the lady with the mystic smile. . . . Do you smile to tempt a lover, Mona Lisa? . . . Are you warm, are you real Mona Lisa? Or just a cold and lonely, lovely work of art?" The 1950 recording by Nat "King" Cole (1919–1965), one of the best-known male vocalists in popular music at the time, made the song a hit heard by a very large audience.

Popular Imagination and Commerce. Modern advertising and commerce have noted the fascination with the Renaissance in the popular imagination. Advertisers use Renaissance art, or sometimes just names from the era, in order to give their products the aura of high quality and the glamour of an admired era.

Merchandisers sometimes attach names and labels from the Renaissance to merchandise that has little or nothing to do with the period in order to convey the impression that it conveys the quality and spirit of the Renaissance. In 1998 Bertolli olive oil was advertised as "another Italian masterpiece" against a photograph of Leonardo's *Virgin, Child, and St. Anne.* In the late 1980s four Teenage Mutant Ninja Turtles (children's toys and cartoon characters) boasted the names Leonardo, Raphael, Michelangelo, and Donatello. The marketing use of these names without identification or explanation means that the advertisers believe that certain individuals and artworks of the Renaissance are instantly recognizable and are admired.

They can do this, and be sure that the viewer understands the allusion, because almost everyone in the Western world is familiar with at least five or six key Renaissance works of art. They may have seen the original works in museums in Italy or Paris, or have seen or purchased photographic reproductions.

Telephone directories, newspaper advertisements, and television and radio commercials in major and minor North American cities offer a variety of products and services with the name "Renaissance" attached: Renaissance Auto Care, Renaissance Business Interiors, Renaissance Garden Cafe, Renaissance Hotels, Renaissance Interior Design, Renaissance Physiotherapy Clinic, Renaissance Roofing, Renaissance Securities, Renaissance Translations, and so on.

Experiencing the Renaissance. Seeing works of art and experiencing vicariously some aspects of Renaissance life is part of the era's appeal. Art lovers visit the great art centers of Italy, the rest of Europe, and the Mediterranean, sometimes in trips sponsored by American museums. Those unable to travel abroad can see Renaissance art in museums in most large and medium-sized cities in North America. For those who want their own copies, North American garden supply stores frequently offer smaller reproductions of Renaissance sculptures, especially of Michelangelo's *David,* to be purchased and displayed as garden statuary.

People wishing a vicarious "Renaissance experience" can visit one of twenty-two annual Renaissance Faires held around the United States, run by Renaissance Entertainment Corporation, a publicly traded company. Renaissance Faires consist of fun, games, and outdoor eating. In 1998 the twenty-first New York Faire (held at Tuxedo, N.Y.) focused on Queen Elizabeth I and featured an entertainment called Instant Shakespeare. At this Faire patrons could use privies with full plumbing called "da Vinci's latest invention."

Conclusion. The historical era of the Renaissance and especially its major artistic figures have resonated in the popular imagination since the beginning of the nineteenth century. The term has become a metaphor for rebirth and achievement. There is no sign that the hold of the Renaissance on the popular imagination is weakening.

But Renaissance has both a positive and a negative meaning in the popular imagination. Renaissance art is admirable; Renaissance politics are seen as deceptive and murderous. There are unanswered questions in the public response to the Renaissance. Why is it that a democratic society finds the literary and artistic products of an aristocratic society so attractive? Are the larger-than-life figures, such as Leonardo da Vinci and Michelangelo, admired because modern man and woman feel stripped of significance in mass society? Why does Renaissance art, with its classical themes, nudity, and portrayal of idealized human figures, attract such high prices in a world of commerce and computers? The ambiguities and dissonances in attitudes toward the Renaissance remain to be explored in learned articles, dissertations, and student term papers.

BIBLIOGRAPHY

Carnes, Mark C., Ted Mico, and John Miller-Monzon, eds. *Past Imperfect: History According to the Movies.* New York, 1995. Includes Carla Rahn Phillips, "Christopher Columbus: Two Films"; Antonio Fraser, "Anne of the Thousand Days"; and Richard Marius, "A Man for All Seasons."

Cox-Rearick, Janet. "Imagining the Renaissance: The Nineteenth-Century Cult of François I as Patron of Art." *Renaissance Quarterly* 50 (1997): 207–250.

Fraser, George Macdonald. *The Hollywood History of the World.* Rev. ed. London, 1996.
Jellinek, George. *History through the Opera Glass: From the Rise of Caesar to the Fall of Napoleon.* New York and London, 1994.
Levine, Lawrence W. *Highbrow/Lowbrow: The Emergence of Cultural Hierarchy in America.* Cambridge, Mass., 1988. See pp. 13–81, "William Shakespeare in America."

PAUL F. GRENDLER and STEPHEN WAGLEY

Influence of the Renaissance

The two most significant movements associated with the Renaissance, humanism and art, are closely related. The Renaissance, through its return to classical antiquity, brought about revolutions in both areas that spread through virtually every cultural expression and far into the future.

Education. During the Renaissance a classical school curriculum was created that dominated education in Europe, North America, and some parts of the rest of the world until well into the twentieth century. This development began with Italian humanists who recovered numerous texts of classical antiquity. Between Petrarch's discovery of Cicero's *Pro Archia* in 1333 and Giovanni Aurispa's discovery of Pliny's panegyric on Trajan in 1433, virtually all of Latin antiquity now known to us was recovered, including texts by Cicero—*Ad Atticum* (Letters to Atticus), *Epistularum ad familiares* (Familiar letters), *De oratore* (On oratory), and *Orator*—and Quintilian.

These discoveries coincided with the development of a self-consciously humanist curriculum, the *studia humanitatis* (grammar, poetry, rhetoric, history, moral philosophy). Classical grammar and usage, based on Quintilian and Cicero, formed the foundation of this curriculum, transforming the emphasis of Latin education from logic to rhetoric (oratory). Humanist schools were established to teach the new curriculum using the newly discovered texts; by 1450 humanist schools and the *studia humanitatis* took over Latin schools in northern Italy and by the end of the century the entire peninsula.

From Italy humanist education spread north, so that between 1500 and 1600 the educational landscape changed throughout western Europe. Greek and Latin proficiency remained the basis of university admission and education throughout the region into the twentieth century. When the American colonies were settled by the English and French, the humanist curriculum was established in North America as well. Harvard, Yale, and Columbia, among the elite institutions of North America, required proficiency in classical Latin as a basis for admission until shortly after the beginning of the twentieth century.

Philology. Out of the humanist practice of copying, emending, and publishing classical manuscripts grew modern philology. Lorenzo Valla (1405–1457) revealed its possibilities in his treatise *De falso credita et ementita Constantini donatione declamatio* (Declamation on the falsely believed and forged Donation of Constantine; 1440) in which he proved that what purported to be the fourth-century will of the emperor Constantine bequeathing the western half of his empire to Pope Sylvester could not have been composed in the fourth century.

The principles of a philological science were first set forth by Angelo Poliziano (1454–1494) in *Miscellanea* (1480), where he elaborated a set of rules for judging his own and others' attempts to correct and explicate texts. These rules included naming the sources from which he drew, even if they were at secondhand; developing criteria for discriminating among manuscripts and proving that one was the parent of others, then using these "best" manuscripts to emend texts; using ancient inscriptions to establish correct orthography; and looking for Greek models behind Latin works, especially poetry, and in the process mastering the secondary tradition related to Greek texts that had developed in the Hellenistic period. Through these methods, Poliziano developed ways of viewing texts in their own context rather than in terms of their possible relevance to contemporary life; thus he eliminated moral interpretations and contemporary applications from classical studies, a practice followed by the seventeenth-century antiquarians who were the direct descendants of this humanist tradition, as well as by more modern scholars.

History. Humanists wrote many histories—of cities, wars, families, dynasties, individuals—which differed from those of their medieval predecessors in several important ways. Petrarch was the first to regard the collapse of the Roman Empire, rather than the birth of Christ, as a significant dividing point in Western history. He and his successors initiated the dividing of history into ancient, medieval, and modern (Petrarch identified what we call medieval with the dark age and is probably the source of the continued use of that label in some quarters). Further, humanists treated history as a fully human activity, sharply reducing the importance of divine causes in explanations of events. Like classical historians (Livy was their chief model), they wrote history as rhetorical narrative, using literary devices like orations and dialogues to lend verisimilitude and to extract moral and political lessons from the reconstructed past.

They also developed the practice of studying archival documents. With the development of libraries and then of printing, these new methods and research tools led to the proliferation of various kinds of historical study.

During the sixteenth century the relation between historical narrative and historical truth became acute, leading to discussions of whether history was an art or a science. In Germany and France emphasis shifted to the latter, and the idea emerged of universal history, of total inclusiveness. The late sixteenth through the seventeenth century was the heroic age of textual emendation. Antiquarians extended the notion that first appeared in Poliziano of separating the study of the past from its contemporary lessons. Renaissance historians thus began the process by which the writing of history became a learned and sometimes technical discipline in which the historian strives for as much objectivity as possible.

Moral Philosophy. Humanist moral philosophy embraced ethical issues (questions of behavior, both private and public or political) and philosophical issues related to cosmic and social order (is the soul immortal? in what does human dignity consist? what is nobility and who is noble? are men superior to women or vice versa?). The humanists regarded history as moral philosophy taught by example and often viewed it as a branch of moral philosophy. But discussions of the human condition and the nature of politics had the most long-lasting influence on moral philosophy.

The human condition. In didactic discussions of human dignity, the humanists viewed human nature in a positive light; when those discussions became profound the humanists used irony, paradox, and humor to convey their views. Erasmus's *Moriae encomium* (trans. *Praise of Folly;* 1511), an imitation of the irony of Lucian's satires, with the additional ingredient of paradox derived from the Pauline epistles in the New Testament, brought the wise fool onto the historical stage. During the following century others, including Rabelais, Shakespeare, and Cervantes, followed Erasmus's lead in equally brilliant productions. Martin Luther and the Protestant Reformers interpreted the wise fool in tragic rather than in comic terms as one who recognizes human sinfulness and submits to the grace of God. During the same century the notion of the wise fool, together with Pyrrhonian skepticism (skepticism that does not claim that we can know nothing, but that we must suspend judgment), made known by humanists through the rediscovered text of Sextus Empiricus (published 1562), assisted in the birth of Montaigne's three books of *Essays* written between 1572 and his death in 1592, in which he explored what he could know about himself. The psychological novel, which emerged first in France (for example, Madame de La Fayette's *La Princesse de Clèves,* 1678), in turn owes much to the introspection generated by Montaigne.

The nature of politics. Two strands of moral philosophical discussion are discernible. The first is Machiavelli's discussion of politics as power in *The Prince* (1513, published 1532), a book of advice for a prince in which Machiavelli explains how to attain power and rule successfully with a series of principles based on history and his own experience and observation. But Machiavelli did not frame those principles in the traditional terms of the "mirror of princes" literature written in preceding ages and by humanists of his own time; his conclusions were those of a man involved in government. He analyzed the successful and unsuccessful actions of rulers and states. Above all, he raised the question of whether a ruler could survive politically by following a traditional moral code and answered no. Hence he distinguished personal and political morality, the latter concerned only with what must be done for a ruler and state to survive and prosper. Machiavelli's was a new, pragmatic approach to politics. Many other writers in the sixteenth century followed his lead (if not always or even usually his conclusions) in discussing the nature of politics and how a ruler should act. All modern writers on politics owe a great deal to him.

Machiavelli's counterpoint and foil was Thomas More. Like Machiavelli, More knew that change had to be factored into politics, but he did so in his *Utopia* (1516) by stopping time altogether, as it were, by eliminating power and substituting administration for it, assuming that if money (and so greed) were abolished the desire for power could also be eliminated and stasis established. More's treatise, an imitation of a classical model, Plato's *Republic,* gave rise to an entire stream of literature. Utopias have been common in every century since More's own (and in twentieth-century dystopias as well), and they have inspired many attempts to bridge the gap between the way things are and the way they might be or served as platforms for the expression of more pessimistic, even apocalyptic, views.

Literary Theory. Humanists, through their innumerable treatises on the art of poetry in the sixteenth and seventeenth centuries, laid the groundwork for modern theories of aesthetics. Many discussions were devoted to Horace's *Ars poetica* and his view that the purpose of art is to instruct and to entertain. Even more were devoted to Aristotle's *Poetics,* which, unlike Horace's poem, passed almost unnoticed in antiquity; sixteenth-century critics literally invented the *Poetics* of Aristotle (published 1498 in Latin, 1508 in Greek). Critics of the *Poetics* focused on poetry as the art of imitating nature and elaborated the meaning of the unities of time and place. A few treatises focused on the artistic imagination and were based on the Platonic notion that poets were inspired by the gods. The Horatian, Aristotelian, and Platonic theories were developed by Italian humanist critics in relation to works of Italian literature by Dante, Sperone Speroni, Ludovico Ariosto, and Torquato Tasso, so that theorists were able to reach more precise ideas about tragedy, comedy, the epic poem, tragicomedy, and pastoral drama. Subsequent aesthetic discussions in other European nations were dependent on Renaissance Italian critics.

Music. The most significant Renaissance innovation in music was the wedding of words and notes; that is, musical proportion (number) gave place to rhetoric and meaning. The first to effect this change was Josquin des Prez (1440–1521), whose music was generated by texts rather than by numerical form. He accomplished this end through several devices: through retaining polyphony but having each part sing the same words or having the sopranos sing the words first in a higher key followed by others imitating them in a lower key (as in a round); and through changing the musical style to reflect a change in the context of the words (for example, in music created for the mass, having the soprano sing higher than anyone else at the point when the host is elevated, so that the text is the key to the music). The madrigal—the hallmark of secular Renaissance music—presupposes a close interaction between text and music. Word painting, or writing music to fit the meaning of notes, has been a part of music since the Renaissance.

Art. Renaissance art developed in tandem with humanism. The humanist recovery and imitation of classical antiquity were paralleled by the artistic revolution that occurred in Florence between 1400 and 1440, associated with the names of Donatello, Masaccio, and Filippo Brunelleschi. Brunelleschi invented a technique for creating the illusion of three-dimensional space in two dimensions, first used by Masaccio (*The Holy Trinity with the Virgin and St. John,* 1425; see the entry on Christian theology, in volume 1) and codified by Leon Battista Alberti in *Della pittura* (On painting; 1435, Latin; 1436, Italian), that became the stock-in-trade of virtually all painters and is still taught today. In his book Alberti also commends *istoria,* or narrative painting (later commended by Leonardo da Vinci in his *Notebooks*), in which the movements of the body express emotions and thought. Seventeenth- and eighteenth-century academies in France and England regarded history painting as the highest form of that art; reality was literally defined as scenes from history, especially from the Bible or classical antiquity.

The marble portrait bust, a revival of a classical type, first reappeared in Florence in the work of Donatello (*St. Mark,* 1413) and has had a continuous history since. Both sculptors and painters—inspired by portraits on coins from ancient Rome—paid attention to the representation of individuals. Portrait painters sought to reveal an individual in appearance and demeanor—an important meaning of Renaissance individualism. Donatello also created the first full-scale equestrian statue, a monument to the mercenary captain Gattamelata (Padua, 1445–1450), which has inspired many in every century since the fifteenth. The reclining female nude, invented by Giorgione da Castelfranco and Titian in Venice in the early sixteenth century, became an extremely popular and long-lived type. It was imitated by artists as diverse as Cranach the Elder, Velázquez, Goya, Ingres, Wesselman, and Manet. Manet's *Olympia* and *Déjeuner sur l'herbe* (1860s), for example, both portray nude figures; the first is an interpretation of Titian's *Venus of Urbino* (1538), which the artist had copied in the Uffizi, the second a landscape that draws on Giorgione's *Pastoral Symphony* (*Concert champêtre,* 1508). [Manet's *Olympia* and Giorgione's *Pastoral Symphony* appear in the color plates in this volume; Titian's *Venus of Urbino* appears in the color plates in volume 6.] But the most influential Renaissance artists during the following two centuries were undoubtedly Raphael and Michelangelo Buonarroti. Both were esteemed as examples of what art should be: rooted in nature, but a nature idealized and ennobled. The Pre-Raphaelites in nineteenth-century England, seeking to escape the conventions taught at the Royal Academy, rejected this ideal and developed a realism owing much to earlier Renaissance artists, northern European as well as fifteenth-century Florentine (Sandro Botticelli, for example).

Renaissance adaptations of classical architecture have been extremely influential. Alberti was the first to study seriously Vitruvius's *De architectura* (On architecture), the only extant classical architectural text, and published his own *De re aedificatoria* (Treatise on architecture; 1452). But among Renaissance architects none was more influential, especially in England and colonial America, than Andrea Palladio (1508–1580), who has been called the most influential architect ever. He wrote *I quattro libri dell' architettura* (Four books on architecture; 1570). He designed many villas in the Veneto, the mainland north of Venice (nineteen of which are still standing), which were studied and copied by later architects. [A photograph of one of Palladio's villas appears in the color plates in volume 4.] His influence is pervasive in the design of English country houses from the seventeenth century up to the Gothic Revival in the nineteenth century. In the United States, the White House is a Palladian palace; Monticello and the University of Virginia, designed by Thomas Jefferson, are Palladian in inspiration; southern plantation homes were often Palladian. The architectural firm of McKim, Mead, and White led a Renaissance revival in New York City; the Villard Houses (1882) are good examples. A late example is the Italianate palazzo designed for Henry Clay Frick, which now houses the Frick Collection.

Modern Science and Medicine. Both humanists and artists influenced the development of modern science. Humanists questioned the authority of Aristotle, the great ancient authority in matters scientific. They recovered and disseminated ancient scientific works (by Galen, Ptolemy, Pliny, Theophrastus, Dioscorides), leading to controversy over whether information provided by these writers was scientifically accurate. They discovered other texts that had been virtually unknown (by Lucretius, Celsus), especially those of mathematicians (Archimedes, Hero, Pappus, Apollonius, Diophantus), which they translated into Latin, greatly increasing attention devoted to mathematics. They composed numerous works on technology between the fourteenth and the sixteenth centuries—on military matters (Conrad Kyeser, Mariano Taccola, and Roberto Valturio, all influenced by Vegetius), on the body (Andreas Vesalius), on metals (Rudolf Agricola), on plants (Leonhard Fuchs), on animals (Conrad Gesner). Translations of the Platonic corpus, including a corpus of occult texts dating from the Greco-Roman period and attributed to Hermes Trismegistus (who proposed the idea of a heliocentric universe), offered a cosmology opposing that of Aristotle.

The union of the experimental and the theoretical in the collaboration between artists and humanists in fifteenth-century Italy was significant for science in the use of perspective to generate maps for navigation, in the scientific study of the human body by Leonardo and Vesalius, and in Vitruvius's treatise on architecture. All of these works are concerned with the unity of theory and practice, the notion that the universe is a uniform and mathematically harmonious entity, the necessity of precise measurement and the significance of practical mathematics, and the idea that technical progress is possible and that it is achieved through cooperation and sharing knowledge. These Renaissance innovations were instrumental in the development of modern scientific practice.

During the sixteenth century medical teaching and practice were revolutionized through a greater emphasis on the study of anatomy and the beginning of clinical medicine, that is, bringing students to the hospital, where the professor explained diseases with the use of patients, practices that are still important to medical training today. University lectureships were established in the medicinal use of plants in Italian universities, and the first university botanical gardens were established almost simultaneously at the universities of Pisa and Padua in 1545. Other universities in Italy and beyond quickly followed their lead.

See also **Aristotle and Aristotelianism; Classical Antiquity, Discovery of; Historiography; Humanism; Humanity, Concept of; Individualism; Middle Ages; Poetics; Political Thought; Renaissance,** *subentry on* **The Renaissance in Popular Imagination; Resistance, Theory of; Skepticism.**

BIBLIOGRAPHY

General Works

Hale, John. *The Civilization of Europe in the Renaissance.* London, 1993.

Rabil, Albert, Jr., ed. *Renaissance Humanism: Foundations, Forms, and Legacy.* 3 vols. Philadelphia, 1988. See the articles on history, poetics, and science.

Schmitt, Charles B., et al., eds. *The Cambridge History of Renaissance Philosophy.* Cambridge, U.K., 1988. See, especially, the articles on science.

Works on Education

Grafton, Anthony, and Lisa Jardine. *From Humanism to the Humanities: Education and the Liberal Arts in Fifteenth- and Sixteenth-Century Europe.* Cambridge, Mass., 1986.

Grendler, Paul F. *Schooling in Renaissance Italy: Literacy and Learning, 1300–1600.* Baltimore, 1989.

Works on Philology

Sandys, John Edwin. *A History of Classical Scholarship.* 3 vols. New York, 1958.

Wilson, Nigel Guy. *From Byzantium to Italy: Greek Studies in the Italian Renaissance.* Baltimore, 1992.

Work on History

Cochrane, Eric. *Historians and Historiography in the Italian Renaissance.* Chicago, 1981.

Works on Moral Philosophy

Manuel, Frank, and Fritzie Manuel. *Utopian Thought in the Western World.* Cambridge, Mass., 1979.

Skinner, Quentin. *The Foundations of Modern Political Thought.* 2 vols. Cambridge, U.K., 1978.

Trinkaus, Charles. *In Our Image and Likeness: Humanity and Divinity in Italian Humanist Thought.* 2 vols. Chicago, 1970.

Work on Literary Theory

Greene, Thomas. *The Light in Troy: Imitation and Discovery in Renaissance Poetry.* New Haven, Conn., 1982.

Works on Music

Lowinsky, Edward. "Music in the Culture of the Renaissance." In *Renaissance Essays from the* Journal of the History of Ideas. Edited by Paul Oskar Kristeller and Philip P. Wiener. New York, 1968. Pages 337–381.

Owens, Jessie Ann. "Music Historiography and the Definition of 'Renaissance.' " *Notes: Quarterly Journal of the Music Library Association* 47 (December 1990): 305–330.

Works on Art

Baxandall, Michael. *Giotto and the Orators: Humanist Observers of Painting in Italy and the Discovery of Pictorial Composition, 1350–1450.* Oxford, 1971.

Panofsky, Erwin. *Renaissance and Renascences in Western Art.* New York, 1969.

Vasari, Giorgio. *The Lives of the Painters, Sculptors, and Architects.* 4 vols. Translated by A. B. Hinds. New York, 1927.

Work on Medicine

Siraisi, Nancy G. *Medieval and Early Renaissance Medicine: An Introduction to Knowledge and Practice.* Chicago, 1990.

ALBERT RABIL

Renaissance Studies

Renaissance studies is the study and teaching of the period running approximately from 1350 to 1650, usually called the Renaissance. Scholars sometimes focus on one aspect, such as the era's art, politics, thought, or social life; on one group, such as women; or on a single author, such as Shakespeare. Alternatively, the focus may be chronological, involving the relationship of a Renaissance topic, such as the family, to the preceding medieval or succeeding modern centuries. All these possibilities make for many approaches. National traditions contribute to various ideological perspectives as well.

The Renaissance Society of America. North American scholars teaching and studying the Renaissance as a common enterprise coalesced with the recognition during the 1930s of the need for a "synthesis of departmentalized researches" (*Renaissance News* 7 [1954]: 1). The American Council of Learned Societies (ACLS) sponsored a conference of interested scholars in eight fields (history, English, French, German, classics, philosophy, Italian, and bibliography) in 1937, which debated Jakob Burckhardt's thesis and issued a report on the state of scholarship. The conference rejected the idea of founding a new society, but in 1938 the ACLS established the Committee on Renaissance Studies. This committee in turn established the New England Renaissance Conference in 1939; five other regional groups soon followed. (In 1999 there were eight.) In 1944 the ACLS reorganized the Committee on Renaissance Studies. *Renaissance News (RN)* was published in 1946 and 1947 within the *Journal of Renaissance and Baroque Music,* and beginning in 1948 as a separate journal. *RN* listed new books, conferences, and works in progress in history, literature, music, and the visual arts.

With 1,200 *RN* subscribers by 1952, the question of establishing a national society became critical, and out of the deliberations that followed, the Renaissance Society of America (RSA) was incorporated in 1954. Publication of *RN* became quarterly, though still largely confined to information. Longer articles were published separately in *Studies in the Renaissance* (1954–1974). But in 1967 *RN* changed its name to *Renaissance Quarterly (RQ)* and the journal began to publish longer articles as well as reviews. By the late 1990s *RN* published about twenty major articles and about three hundred book reviews annually, as well as annual review essays on books in French, Spanish, Italian, and German; it is the premier journal in Renaissance studies.

North America. The situation of Renaissance studies in North America reflects the enormous changes that have occurred in the academy since the inception of the RSA. At the end of the twentieth century there were nineteen officially recognized disciplines, each with its own discipline representative, and thirty-three constituent societies, including university centers, which are often umbrellas for undergraduate majors; seminars in various regions for the presentation of scholarly papers; centers for Renaissance studies independent of university affiliation; and regional conferences, each of which holds its own annual meeting. In addition the RSA holds a national meeting annually. The proliferation resulted in part from the growth of the entire academic enterprise in North America since World War II. But it was spearheaded by a talented group of German émigré Renaissance scholars who arrived from Europe during the 1930s and 1940s and who were primarily concerned with matters of intellectual culture.

Hans Baron, Ernst Cassirer, Felix Gilbert, Paul Oskar Kristeller, and Erwin Panofsky were notable among them. They helped shape the agenda for future studies with their investigations, respectively, into the relation between Renaissance Platonism and the rise of modern science, the emergence of "civic humanism" in early fifteenth-century Florence, the interpretation of politics and history in Renaissance Italy, the identification of humanism as a literary movement distinguishable from both scholastic and Renaissance Platonic philosophies, and the characteristics that distinguish medieval from Renaissance art. This focus on intellectual culture fitted closely with the interests of scholars in comparative literature, the visual arts, and music. Scholars in these fields identified the Renaissance as a distinguishable period within their disciplines before it became a general period designation in virtually all academic disciplines.

Italian archives were invaded by North American scholars beginning in the early 1950s, aided by the Fulbright Act, which first made it possible for graduate students to spend extended time in Europe. The pioneers in this endeavor were Marvin Becker, Gene Brucker, Frederic Lane, and Donald Weinstein. American scholars rivaled Italians in archival research in Florentine, Venetian, and other collections, and produced a host of original books and monographs focusing particularly on the political and social structures of Renaissance cities and institutions. Most of these scholars had no Italian ancestry but were drawn by their intellectual interests.

Since the 1960s the desire to stress less-studied groups has led to an increasing emphasis on race, gender, and sexual orientation as well as "material culture"; this interest has generated translations of texts, as well as numerous scholarly articles and monographs. The result of trends in both the 1950s and 1960s has been a proliferation of subfields in historical studies and an expanding canvas on which to test questions about the nature and definition of the Renaissance. The term "Renaissance" itself has come under increasing scrutiny. Some have abandoned it in favor of "Early Modern Europe" as a period designation. For example, the *Journal of Medieval and Renaissance Studies* changed its name in 1996 to *Journal of Medieval and Early Modern Studies,* and the New York Society for the Study of Women in the Renaissance, organized by women in 1993, became within a year the Society for the Study of Early Modern Women. But there have also been countertendencies. In the early 1990s Theodore Rabb, a Renaissance historian, produced for public television a six-hour series entitled *Renaissance.* The series sought to present innovations that give the period its clarity, but employed more inclusive frames of reference, indicated by the six segments on "The Scientist," "The Dissenter," "The Artist," "The Prince," "The Warrior," and "The Merchant." This method of framing allowed the retention of the designation "Renaissance" while making it inclusive as a period marker. The debate over terminology is in part a reflection of more extensive and intensive coverage of the period.

Several universities offer special programs in art history on site in Florence, notably Syracuse University and New York University, where college students study abroad for a summer or semester. Harvard University's Villa I Tatti, located just outside of Florence, has for some time been a center for Renaissance studies, awarding fellowships usually to younger scholars in a variety of fields. There are also combined programs, such as the Medieval and Renaissance Studies Program of the University of California at Los Angeles and the Centre for Reformation and Renaissance Studies of Victoria University in the University of Toronto.

Institutes for Renaissance studies also exist outside universities in museums and libraries. The Folger Shakespeare Library in Washington, D.C., offers seminars, workshops, and lectures by and for college and university teachers on Renaissance themes, as well as summer institutes for high school teachers focusing on Shakespeare in performance. The Newberry Library in Chicago has several major programs, one of which is its Center for Renaissance Studies. Particular strengths of the library are in early printed literature from the fifteenth through the seventeenth centuries. Graduate programs are offered in various disciplines—religion, literature, history, and art—through a consortium of thirty midwestern universities. The designations Early Modern Europe and Renaissance are both used, but the center's name has not been changed because the library's strength is printed literature rather than archival sources (usually available only on location in any case).

The term "Renaissance" is retained in secondary school teaching, because there the notion of a clearly demarcated period distinguished from what precedes and what follows is pedagogically more effective, and also because many teachers are interested in Renaissance art and in Shakespeare, who is identified as the preeminent Renaissance playwright and poet. But the rearrangement of the secondary school curriculum to deemphasize European culture has shortened the time formerly allotted to European history in general and the Renaissance in particular

(Shakespeare excepted). To compensate, the RSA has sponsored several national summer institutes (funded by the National Endowment for the Humanities) on the Renaissance for high school teachers and has begun the development of web sites to reach a wider audience.

Britain and Australia. Renaissance studies in England, as in North America, received a great boost from the transference of the Aby Warburg Institute from Germany to London in 1945. The Institute was joined with the Courtauld art collection to form the Warburg and Courtauld Institutes. E. H. Gombrich, Erwin Panofsky, and Edgar Wind, all German émigré scholars, together with English scholars D. P. Walker and Frances Yates, all of whom published significant original work on the art, music, and philosophy of the Renaissance, made the Institutes a world center of Renaissance studies. Connected to University College, London, it pioneered the Ph.D. in Renaissance studies in England. Its two principal aims have remained the development of a library and archive in which scholars can pursue research, and a fellowship program for young scholars from all over the world. But the Institute also teaches, publishes, and runs a program of open lectures, seminars, and colloquiums. A second pole of Renaissance studies in England is the Shakespeare Institute at Stratford-on-Avon, where Shakespeare in production remains a lively topic, even more lively now that the Globe Theater has been reconstructed.

In Australia, only the Australian National University has formally instituted postgraduate teaching faculties, and European history is not among them. All other universities in Australia are undergraduate institutions, though in these there are a number of prominent Renaissance scholars who have a postgraduate following. There is still, however, no journal of Renaissance studies, and the major historical journal in the country does not publish articles or reviews of books on Renaissance studies, because the field is not represented in the graduate faculties.

Europe. Italian universities do not have institutes for Renaissance studies. Rather, the study of the Renaissance has always been a major part of the study of Italian national history, literature, and thought. In the nomenclature of Italian history departments, the major divisions of Italian history are ancient, medieval, modern (which means Renaissance to the risorgimento), risorgimento (nineteenth century), and contemporary. In the teaching of Italian literature, the Renaissance is a very important area. The great authors of the fourteenth century (Dante, Petrarch, and Boccaccio especially) and of the sixteenth century (Machiavelli, Ariosto, and Tasso especially) receive a great deal of attention. In addition, Italian universities often have several professors teaching the history of philosophy, which sometimes means an intensive study of Italian Renaissance humanism.

In France, Rabelais and Montaigne have received more attention than any other Renaissance figures. The Centre d'Études Supérieures de la Renaissance at Tours has spearheaded a number of publishing projects at Livre de Poche (a French publisher) for sixteenth-century editions. The division of "Textes et documents" at the University of Paris (Jussieu) is developing a section on Renaissance studies. The Société Française des Seiziémistes publishes bibliographies in addition to a journal. The Librairie Droz in Geneva, Switzerland, has published several hundred books in Renaissance studies, as well as the *Bibliothèque d'Humanisme et Renaissance,* a major journal in the field.

Because the majority of scholars in Germany have viewed the Protestant Reformation initiated by Martin Luther as the major event of the fifteenth and sixteenth centuries, the study of the Renaissance has been less cultivated. Nevertheless, several major Reformation figures were simultaneously important humanists. Publication of the works of Phillip Melanchthon, Willibald Pirckheimer, and Johann Reuchlin is under way. Albrecht Dürer remains a topic of perennial interest. The Herzog August Bibliothek in Wolfenbüttel, Germany, helped establish in 1976 the Wolfenbütteler Arbeitskreis für Renaissanceforschung, and has supported the publication of a series of studies. These books frequently result from conferences on the Renaissance held at the library with participants from many countries. In the Netherlands, publication of the critical edition of the works of Erasmus is in progress.

Renaissance studies in Spain have been vigorously pursued only since the end of the Franco regime in the 1970s. No institutes for Renaissance studies exist, only a literary association on the Siglo de Oro (Golden Age). In addition to studying the Renaissance in Spain, many North American scholars studying the Spanish Renaissance concentrate on the New World.

See also **Early Modern Period; Renaissance, Interpretations of the; Villa I Tatti.**

BIBLIOGRAPHY

Cochrane, Eric. *Historians and Historiography in the Italian Renaissance.* Chicago, 1981.

Ferguson, Wallace K. *The Renaissance in Historical Thought: Five Centuries of Interpretation*. Boston, 1948.

Grafton, Anthony, and Lisa Jardine. *From Humanism to the Humanities: Education and the Liberal Arts in Fifteenth- and Sixteenth-Century Europe*. Cambridge, Mass., 1986.

Kerrigan, William, and Gordon Braden. *The Idea of the Renaissance*. Baltimore, 1989.

Proctor, Robert. *Education's Great Amnesia: Reconsidering the Humanities from Petrarch to Freud, with a Curriculum for Today's Students*. Bloomington, Ind., 1988.

Rabil, Albert, Jr., ed. *Renaissance Humanism: Foundations, Forms, and Legacy*. 3 vols. Philadelphia, 1988.

ALBERT RABIL

RENAISSANCE, INTERPRETATIONS OF THE.

[This entry includes fifteen subentries on major interpreters of the Renaissance (in roughly chronological order they are Giorgio Vasari, Jules Michelet, Jakob Burckhardt, John Ruskin, John Addington Symonds, Walter Pater, Bernard Berenson, Aby Warburg, Johan Huizinga, Erwin Panofsky, Hans Baron, Eugenio Garin, Remigio Sabbadini, Georg Voigt, and Paul Oskar Kristeller) and one subentry on economic interpretations.]

Giorgio Vasari

Born into the artisan class of Arezzo, a subject city of Florence, the painter, architect, and art historian Giorgio Vasari (1511–1574) was the son of a dealer in small goods. His educational background was unusually good for someone of his origins; he began his schooling under the humanist Giovanni Lappoli, known as Pollastra, a skilled Latinist and ardent Medicean. Although not "literate" in the Renaissance sense—that is, able to write Latin—Vasari could read and write fluently in the vernacular and appreciate the value of literary forms.

Possibly through the intervention of Pollastra, Vasari came to the attention of Cardinal Silvio Passerini, the tutor of the Medici heirs and the governor of Florence. When he moved to Florence in 1524, Vasari was affiliated with the household of Alessandro and Ippolito de' Medici. Throughout his career Vasari maintained close associations with the literary men he met in the court circles where he was employed: such figures as Pietro Aretino, Claudio Tolomei, Paolo Giovio, Annibale Caro, and Vincenzo Borghini, all of whom influenced his ambitions and his desire to give them literary form.

Vasari the Artist. Vasari's primary profession was that of a painter. He was trained first in Arezzo by Guillaume de Marcillat, a French glass painter. Vasari's training as an artist was itinerant and involved associations with Andrea del Sarto, Baccio Bandinelli, and Rosso Fiorentino, and the inspiration of Michelangelo. He was phenomenally productive throughout his life, in part because of his ability to manage groups of assistants and because of his prodigious energy and dedication to work.

Vasari's *Lives of the Artists*. Title page of part 1 of the second, enlarged edition of *Le vite de piú eccelenti pittori, scultori, et architecttori* published by the Giunti Press (Florence, 1568). YALE CENTER FOR BRITISH ART, PAUL MELLON COLLECTION

Personally, politically, and professionally, Vasari had an abiding loyalty to his early protectors, the Medici, working successively for Cardinal Ippolito, Duke Alessandro, and Duke Cosimo I. He was also employed by Cardinal Alessandro Farnese and Popes Julius III, Pius IV, Pius V, and Gregory XIII, and received numerous commissions from religious orders and other patrons throughout Italy. A fair copy of his business records, his *ricordanze,* has 368 entries between 1527 and 1572. But the book is a selective summary and only a partial record of his total commissions. He did all types of painting, from small devotional works and portraits to large-scale altarpieces and massive schemes, such as the *Deeds of Pope Paul III* in the great hall of the Cancelleria (the Sala de' Cento Giorni), done for Pope Paul's grandson, Cardinal Alessandro Farnese, in 1546, and the decorative ensemble of the Palazzo Vecchio, done for Duke Cosimo de' Medici between 1555 and 1572. Vasari was also active as an architect and designed the magistrate's offices, the Uffizi, for Cosimo I, which was but one of his many projects in Rome, Florence, and Arezzo. In the early 1560s he helped to promote the foundation of the Accademia del Disegno, officially approved by Duke Cosimo I in 1563, an important moment for the prestige of the visual arts, giving them a recognized association that paralleled earlier literary and philosophical academies.

Vasari the Art Historian. In addition to his career as a painter Vasari had begun to write polished letters in the late 1520s. He fully realized the potential of writing to advance the "arts of design" (painting, architecture, and sculpture) in his book of artists' biographies published in 1550, *Le vite de' più eccellenti architetti, pittori, et scultori italiani* (trans. *The Lives of the Most Excellent Architects, Painters, and Sculptors*). Written with the guidance of the biographer and historian Paolo Giovio, this work presents the history of art schematically and observes the conventions of humanist eulogistic biography. In it, Vasari expressed his admiration for ancient art but noted its decline in the fourth century. Medieval art, which followed, was poor in quality because, under Byzantine influences, its human figures were flat and distorted rather than natural. Vasari then described the beginning of the rebirth (*rinascita*), when the Florentine painter Cimabue (c. 1240–c. 1302) kindled "the first lights of painting." The key figure in the rebirth was the painter and architect Giotto (c. 1267–1337), who "restored the art of design, of which his contemporaries knew little or nothing." Again the criterion was that art should resemble nature.

Vasari divided Renaissance art from Giotto through Michelangelo into three successive eras. In the first (middle of the thirteenth century to the end of the fourteenth) artists replaced the Byzantine style with that of Giotto, although their art still had many imperfections. In the second era (the fifteenth century) artists matured in technique and made tremendous progress. Masaccio (1401–c. 1428) improved the art of painting, while Donatello (1386–1466) sculpted lifelike human figures of great perfection. The culmination of Renaissance art came in the third period (the sixteenth century), which began with Leonardo da Vinci and reached divine perfection in Michelangelo. Overall, Vasari used the imitation of nature as a means of judging art and emphasized following the models of the best works of antiquity.

The Lives offered a breathtaking panorama of more than 250 years of activity by more than 142 artists in the second edition. Vasari had no precedent for the scale of his work or for the systematic application of the metaphor of rebirth, even though he was not the first to use it. His book was original in giving biographical form, and therefore status, to artists' careers. Vasari established a canon that defined and dominated the study of the visual arts of the Renaissance in his day and that continues to be influential. At the same time, modern art historians do not dismiss medieval art as Vasari did, and many episodes in his biographies cannot be verified.

In 1568 Vasari published a considerably expanded second edition of *The Lives,* which became the standard version. Vasari added more information to extant biographies, inserted new biographies, and included a section on living artists as well as a description of his own works. The second edition, at 1,500 pages, is three times longer than the first and includes portraits of the artists.

Both versions are formed of Vasari's experiences, convictions, and prejudices. Vasari created a paradigm of achievement based on the style of central Italian artists, notably Raphael and Michelangelo. He expounded on the aims of his biographies, including their value as examples of good behavior and good style, in the preambles to each of the three eras. For the wealth of information and critical insight into the arts of the Renaissance, Vasari's *Lives* has remained a standard source.

BIBLIOGRAPHY

Primary Works

Brown, Gerard Baldwin, ed. *Vasari on Technique; Being the Introduction to the Three Arts of Design, Architecture, Sculpture, and Painting.* Translated by Louisa S. Maclehose. London, 1907. Reprint, New York, 1960. Provides a translation of the technical introduction.

Vasari, Giorgio. *Le vite de' più eccellenti architetti, pittori, et scultori italiani: Da Cimabue insino a' tempi nostri: Nell'edizione per i tipi di Lorenzo Torrentino, Firenze 1550.* Edited by Luciano Bellosi and Aldo Rossi. Turin, Italy, 1986. First reprint of the 1550 edition.

Vasari, Giorgio. *Le vite de' più eccellenti pittori, scultori ed architettori scritte da Giorgio Vasari pittore aretino con nuove annotazioni e commenti.* 9 vols. Edited by Gaetano Milanesi. Florence, 1878–1885. Repr., Florence, 1973. Remains important for its notes and commentaries to the text based on extensive archival research.

Vasari, Giorgio. *Le vite de' più eccellenti pittori scultori e architettori: Nelle redazioni del 1550 e 1568.* Edited by Rosanna Bettarini and Paola Barocchi. Florence, 1966–. Parallel-text edition of the *Lives,* with commentary and comprehensive indexes; the text volumes are complete, the indexes are still appearing.

Vasari, Giorgio. *Lives of the Most Eminent Painters, Sculptors, and Architects.* Translated by Gaston du C. de Vere. 10 vols. London, 1912–1915. Reprinted as *Lives of the Painters, Sculptors, and Architects,* with an introduction by David Ekserdjian. 2 vols. London, 1996. The most faithful translation, but it includes only the biographies, not the technical introduction.

Secondary Works

Barolsky, Paul. *Giotto's Father and the Family of Vasari's* Lives. University Park, Pa., 1992.

Barolsky, Paul. *Michelangelo's Nose: A Myth and Its Maker.* University Park, Pa., 1990.

Barolsky, Paul. *Why Mona Lisa Smiles and Other Tales by Vasari.* University Park, Pa., 1991.

Boase, T. S. R. *Giorgio Vasari: The Man and the Book.* Princeton, N.J., 1979.

Giorgio Vasari: Principi, letterati e artisti nelle carte di Giorgio Vasari, Casa Vasari, pittura vasariana dal 1532 al 1554, Sottochiesa di S. Francesco. Florence, 1981. Exhibition catalog containing much new and unfamiliar material on Vasari.

Rubin, Patricia Lee. *Giorgio Vasari: Art and History.* New Haven, Conn., 1995.

Satkowski, Leon George. *Giorgio Vasari: Architect and Courtier.* Princeton, N.J., 1993.

Jules Michelet

Jules Michelet (1798–1874) is the most celebrated historian among the French romantics. Born into an artisan family, he idolized the people of France. He had a brilliant academic career, becoming professor of history at the Collège de France in 1838. In 1852 his hostility to Napoleon III resulted in his dismissal from his professorship as well as from his post at the Archives Nationales. He published many historical and other works, of which the best known is his *Histoire de France* (History of France; Paris, 1833–1867). He interrupted this multivolume work in the years 1847–1853 to compose his *Histoire de la Révolution française* (History of the French Revolution).

By the time Michelet resumed his national history with the publication of his volume on the Renaissance in 1855, his earlier praise of the role of the church in the Middle Ages had been replaced with a strong anticlericalism. He now regarded feudal and Catholic institutions as alienating humankind from its roots in nature, and the Renaissance, which he called "the discovery of the world and of man," as liberating the human spirit from the trammels of the medieval past. Like the nymph Daphne, who was transformed into a tree in Greek myth, humanity could become one with nature.

Science, geographic discovery, and the revival of classical antiquity were the hallmarks of the new age. Italy was its birthplace and Leonardo da Vinci, Michelangelo, and Raphael its principal artistic exemplars. The Protestant Reformation seconded the Renaissance in breaking the medieval mold and establishing a self-reliant individualism, while pagan classicism vied with a new biblical erudition through the medium of the printing press. Columbus, Copernicus, and Luther were the heroes of Michelet's vision of the Renaissance.

BIBLIOGRAPHY

Primary Work

Michelet, Jules. *Renaissance et réforme: Histoire de France au seizième siècle.* Edited by Claude Mettra. Paris, 1982.

Secondary Works

Kippur, Stephen A. *Jules Michelet: A Study of Mind and Sensibility.* Albany, N.Y., 1981.

Mitzman, Arthur. *Michelet, Historian: Rebirth and Romanticism in Nineteenth-Century France.* New Haven, Conn., 1990.

J. H. M. SALMON

Jakob Burckhardt

Burckhardt (1818–1897) was born in Basel, the son of a Protestant minister. The family belonged to the local patriciate, but Burckhardt was not concerned with worldly possessions and was never wealthy. Educated at the civic gymnasium (classical high school), he acquired a thorough knowledge of classical and romance languages and literatures. In 1837 he began to study theology at the University of Basel, but two years later, after a crisis, he abandoned theology. While he never lost sight of the fact that Christianity was an unavoidable part of his cultural heritage, he could no longer accept religious doctrines supported solely by divine revelation. From 1839 to 1843 he studied at the University of Berlin with such teachers as Leopold von Ranke, Johann Gustav Droysen, and Franz Kugler, immersing himself in the history and the art of all ages from ancient Greece to modern times. During a summer spent at Bonn, Burckhardt embraced the romantic patriotism of his German friends, who were fiercely opposed to the bourgeois and clerical establishments. Subsequently, after his return to Basel, he veered in a considerably more conservative direction, at least in his political views.

In 1843 the University of Basel conferred a doctorate degree on Burckhardt and authorized him to teach in a junior (and mostly unsalaried) position. In

1855 he moved to Zurich and taught history at the recently founded Federal Institute of Technology. In 1858 he was offered the chair of history (later including art history) in his home university and returned to Basel, henceforward devoting his best energies to his academic teaching and a long series of public lectures for a general audience. Serving his fellow citizens in this office was to him "a steady source of happiness." He declined offers to fill prestigious chairs at the Universities of Tübingen, Heidelberg, and Berlin. The intimate atmosphere of Basel allowed him to engage in research and independent thinking reminiscent of the surge in creativity that he attributed to Florence and other city-states of the Italian Renaissance. Burckhardt retired in 1893 and died four years later. He had never married; his leisure hours were spent with a small circle of devoted friends. He also liked to travel, exploring the great museums and monuments of western and central Europe, especially Italy.

Burckhardt as Historian. Among the wide range of Burckhardt's publications, the most original and influential is *Die Kultur der Renaissance in Italien* (1860; trans. *The Civilization of the Renaissance in Italy*). Burckhardt first conceived the plan for this book in Rome during the winter of 1847–1848, amid the swell of popular agitation that led to the republican insurrection of 1848. As late as 1868, when he prepared the text for the second, slightly revised edition, Burckhardt added a dedication to his old friend Luigi Picchioni, who had fought in the 1848 revolution and was later saddened by the diplomatic bartering that led to an incomplete Kingdom of Italy instead of the all-inclusive republic he had longed for. Although Burckhardt's own sympathy with radical politics had vanished by the time he actually wrote the book (1858–1859), his revolutionary leanings had not; they found expression in the bold concept of the work and in its many uncompromising phrases.

In 1848 Burckhardt set himself the goal of producing an entire library of cultural history consisting of monographs devoted to climactic periods from Periclean Athens to the "Age of Raphael," and possibly beyond. A typical feature of such outstanding periods was, he suggested, their ability to "achieve renaissances." He never pursued this grand project in a systematic fashion, but some of his books, for example, *The Age of Constantine the Great* (1853), can be seen to correspond with it. It is significant that this plan anticipated on a grand scale the method Burckhardt applied throughout his *Civilization*. He wished to make the past comprehensible by creating a sequence of synchronous tableaux that would capture the essential character of each age. This approach, which Burckhardt modestly described as unmethodical, was chosen in sharp and often explicit contrast to the prevailing rules among contemporary historians in Germany and elsewhere. To give an account of events in linear chronology, analyzing them in terms of cause and effect, seemed to Burckhardt unprofitable. Tracing a specific development tended to prevent the reader from understanding the society and its culture as a whole. What interested him was not the outstanding event but the continually repeated typical feature. The prevailing method of *Quellenforschung* (the study of sources) claimed to be scientific in that it interpreted preferably archival sources with rules that ensured factuality and objectivity. Burckhardt realized that these goals were unreachable. He made a point of finding his evidence predominantly in chronicles and other literary sources. Factuality mattered little; what had actually happened might well elude the historian, but how contemporaries saw and experienced it was illuminating.

Most of the evidence presented by Burckhardt ranges chronologically from the reign of Emperor Frederick II in the middle of the thirteenth century to the Sack of Rome in 1527. His purpose did not call for a chronological order; rather, the scheme of consecutive synchronous cross sections is unobtrusively applied to the Renaissance itself. The reader is gradually made aware of the changes in outlook that occurred between the generation of Dante and that of Machiavelli.

The Civilization of the Renaissance. The book divides into six sections, among which the aspect most commonly associated with the Renaissance, "The Revival of Antiquity," is relegated to third place. Important as the recovery of classical style and literature was, Burckhardt believed that to do it justice one had first to understand that it was undertaken by minds of a new type with results that had no precedent in the Middle Ages. To analyze that new mentality, as Burckhardt did in his second section, "The Development of the Individual," it was advisable to turn initially to the civic framework that fostered the new ways of thinking. This Burckhardt did in his first section, "The State as a Work of Art."

He argued that Italy's Renaissance culture developed under two radically new forms of government, the despotic and the republican state, both normally centered upon a specific city. The despots particularly fascinated him; their refined mechanism of state control reminded him of artfully crafted clockwork. Lapsing into the terminology of romanticism, Burckhardt contrasted the organically grown state of the Middle Ages with its Renaissance successor, which launched "the great modern delusion that a constitution can be made." Here began what he sarcastically termed "the typically modern fiction of the omnipotence of the state. The prince is to take care of everything." Where before there had been a "people," there was now a "mass of subjects" liable to manipulation. Unable to function as a people, the Italians became, to a degree hitherto unknown, conscious of their individuality. Rightly feared by the tyrants, individualism, with its concomitant wealth of imagination and thirst for fame, brought forth the artistic creativity that to Burckhardt was both the crowning achievement and the saving grace of Renaissance Italy. Individuality is not only the theme of Burckhardt's second section; it is emphasized continually throughout the book.

Borrowing the term from Jules Michelet, Burckhardt entitled his fourth section "The Discovery of the World and of Man." Here is Burckhardt at his best. Using such examples as Petrarch and Pope Pius II, he analyzed a new awareness of nature that, with the aid of his descriptive dexterity, uncovered intricate connections between the scientific universe, the beauty of landscape, and humanity's inner nature. In the fifth section, "Society and Festivals," Burckhardt's treatment is more fragmentary than elsewhere, but later, when social history and sociology came into their own, the somewhat disjointed findings of this section proved seminal.

Burckhardt's last section, "Morality and Religion," is the most provocative and controversial. Burckhardt was of course aware of this and frequently cautioned the reader not to expect a conclusive judgment. Such caveats notwithstanding, Burckhardt's verdict is clear: immorality was prevalent in Italian society, while the church was ripe with corruption and unable to stem the flood of popular superstitions.

From a mass of evidence Burckhardt selected stunning examples that may be troubling to some readers. Pleas for reform by a few honest and pious souls had little impact; most intellectuals turned to "Epicurean" skepticism. A healthy secular spirit might eventually have done away with the despicable friars and perhaps even the papacy, but that was prevented by the arrival of Spanish armies and a Catholicism revitalized by the German Reformation. Why did Renaissance Italy, with all its intellectual vitality, not precede Germany in bringing about a true spiritual reform? Burckhardt asked the question only to submit that it eluded the powers of historical analysis. What he did find "attested by abundant historical proof" was that what he considered to be the modern world's departure from faith in immortality had begun in Renaissance Italy, not as a systematic, ideologically founded atheism, but as "a wavering between freethinking and the remnants of Catholic upbringing."

Assessment. Burckhardt's tableau of Italian Renaissance culture is incomplete. Economic conditions are neglected, as he regretfully noted. To fill that gap much patient research in the archives was needed, which Burckhardt was in no position to undertake. Renaissance art, while frequently instanced in the *Civilization,* also did not receive the extensive treatment that might have been expected in view of Burckhardt's expertise in that field. For many years he planned a comprehensive monograph on art as a companion volume to the *Civilization,* but only his treatment of architecture, arranged by types and forms of buildings and their parts, was published in his lifetime (*Die Geschichte der Renaissance in Italien* [1868; trans. *The Architecture of the Italian Renaissance,* 1985]). Burckhardt's views on painting and sculpture must be gleaned from texts not always available in English translation. According to Burckhardt, Raphael (and in some measure, Rubens) achieved the perfect Renaissance balance between aesthetic beauty, compositional order, and emotional energy, but in Michelangelo such a balance was lacking.

It may be added that Burckhardt had no use for philosophies of history and that subsequent attempts to interpret his work in theoretical terms did not prove helpful. Inevitably, diverse aspects of his work on the Renaissance were later criticized, but his most cogent critics praised the imposing ensemble of insight and myth he had created. For the educated public of the early twentieth century, fascination with the Renaissance turned into a fashion. This intense interest was due largely to Burckhardt's *Civilization,* although it was not an outcome he had intended.

See also **Renaissance,** *subentry on* **The Renaissance in Historical Thought.**

BIBLIOGRAPHY

Critical Editions

Briefe. 10 vols. Edited by M. Burckhardt. Basel, Switzerland, 1949–1986.

Jacob Burckhardt: Gesamtausgabe. 14 vols. Edited by E. Dürr et al. Stuttgart, Leipzig, and Berlin, 1929–1934.

Über das Studium der Geschichte. Der Text der Weltgeschichtlichen Betrachtungen. Edited by P. Ganz. Munich, 1982.

English Translations of Burckhardt's Works Relevant to the Renaissance

The Architecture of the Italian Renaissance. Translated by J. Palmes. Chicago, 1985. Translation of *Die Geschichte der Renaissance in Italien* (1868, 1878).

The Cicerone, or, Art Guide to Painting in Italy. Translated by A. H. Clough. London, 1873. Translation of *Der Cicerone* (1855).

The Civilization of the Period of the Renaissance in Italy. Translated by S. G. C. Middlemore. London, 1878. Translation of *Die Kultur der Renaissance in Italien* (1860). Middlemore's correct but uninspiring translation has been republished many times, with and without Burckhardt's notes and sometimes with additional notes by an editor.

The Altarpiece in Renaissance Italy. Translated by P. Humfrey. New York, 1988.

Secondary Works

Brown, Alison. "Jacob Burckhardt's Renaissance." *History Today* 38 (October 1988): 20–26.

Ferguson, Wallace K. *The Renaissance in Historical Thought*. Boston, 1948.

Gilbert, Felix. *History: Politics or Culture? Reflections on Ranke and Burckhardt*. Princeton, N.J., 1990.

Gossman, Lionel. "Jacob Burckhardt." In *The Dictionary of Art*. Edited by Jane Turner. Vol. 5: 189–190. New York, 1996.

Guggisberg, Hans R., ed. *Umgang mit Jacob Burckhardt: Zwölf Studien*. Basel, Switzerland, and Munich, 1994.

Kaegi, Werner. *Jacob Burckhardt: Eine Biographie*. 7 vols. Basel, Switzerland, 1947–1982.

Noll, Thomas. *Vom Glück des Gelehrten: Versuch über Jacob Burckhardt*. Göttingen, Germany, 1997.

PETER G. BIETENHOLZ

John Ruskin

John Ruskin (1819–1900), English writer, art critic and theorist, and painter, was born in London to an affluent Scottish family. A breakdown in 1840 was followed by a seminal trip to Italy, where he found himself as enamored of Venetian painting and architecture as he was appalled by Saint Peter's Basilica in Rome. He graduated from Christ Church, Oxford, in 1842. In 1848 he married Euphemia Chalmers Gray; the union, never consummated, was annulled in 1854. In 1869 he was elected Oxford's first Slade Professor of Fine Art, a position in which he was active intermittently, in the face of increasingly severe mental breakdowns, until 1885. In 1871 he founded at Oxford the Ruskin Drawing School, where instruction was based on the study of items from his personal collection, which was particularly rich in works by early Italian Renaissance artists, the Pre-Raphaelites, and the nineteenth-century English artist J. M. W. Turner. Ruskin asserted that students, by copying these works, would acquire a sense of humility, one of the spiritual values that, though prerequisite to the creation of truly great art, had almost completely disappeared since the advent of the Renaissance and its aesthetic of egoism.

Ruskin's opinions on Renaissance art and architecture, among the most influential of the nineteenth century, are scattered throughout his works, particularly *Modern Painters* (5 vols., 1843–1860), *The Seven Lamps of Architecture* (1849), and *The Stones of Venice* (3 vols., 1851–1853). Among the works that influenced Ruskin's views on the merits of medieval versus Renaissance art was Alexis-François Rio's *De la poésie chrétienne dans son principe, dans sa matière et dans ses formes* (1836; trans. *The Poetry of Christian Art*). Like Ruskin after him, Rio establishes an aesthetic hierarchy in which Italian Renaissance painters, whose paganism he decries, are placed below "pre-Renaissance" (today we would use the term "early Renaissance") painters such as Sandro Botticelli and Fra Angelico (Guido di Pietro), whose works he finds imbued with the religious feeling essential to the loftiest forms of art.

Ruskin claims that High Renaissance painters (like Raphael in all but his earliest works) are guilty of the sin of pride, in that they view artistic endeavor as an opportunity for the display of virtuoso technique rather than as a quest for the truth. For Ruskin, the truth is to be found in the firsthand experience of nature rather than in the rational application of the laws of perspective. He declares that the discovery of mathematical tenets for the depiction of reality has had the unhealthy consequence of tempting artists to eschew direct contemplation of the natural world, whose beauties are a divine gift. In Renaissance art, this leads to a gradual fading of faith and subsequently of feeling. According to Ruskin, Michelangelo's *Last Judgment* (1536–1541) is mere stage decoration, a display of originality for its own sake.

In sculpture, the decline into the "mathematical" style occurs as early as Lorenzo Ghiberti, whose manner in the celebrated *Gates of Paradise* (1403–1424) Ruskin finds emphatic, even operatic, but devoid of spiritual feeling, for too often the observer marvels at the exquisite rendering of the flesh and forgets the religious raison d'être of the work. In architecture, Ruskin extols the Venetian Gothic style (for example, that of Saint Mark's Basilica, begun 1063) as the quintessential expression of communal humility and devotion. In contrast, he portrays Andrea Palladio's design for the church of San Giorgio Maggiore (begun 1566) in Venice as the willful, gross, and contemptible result of an overintellectualized architectural aesthetic based on too many rules and too little feeling.

The crisis of faith that Ruskin suffered in the 1850s and 1860s inspired him to revisit some of his opinions: he appears more willing, for example, to concede a moral dimension to the work of an artist such as Titian, whose output comprises both religious and profane subjects. Always drawn to the sensual appeal of this artist's use of color, Ruskin relates the breadth of Titian's oeuvre to the artist's understanding that the happiness of human beings depends on acceptance of their animal passions as well as the cultivation of their spiritual tendencies.

BIBLIOGRAPHY

Primary Work

Ruskin, John. *The Works of John Ruskin*. 39 vols. Edited by E. T. Cook and Alexander Wedderburn. London and New York, 1903–1912.

Secondary Works

Abse, Joan. *John Ruskin: The Passionate Moralist*. London and New York, 1980.

Landow, George P. *The Aesthetic and Critical Theories of John Ruskin*. Princeton, N.J., 1971.

PAUL ALBERT FERRARA

John Addington Symonds

Author of the largest and most influential history of the Italian Renaissance in English, John Addington Symonds was born in Bristol, England, on 5 October 1840. After schooling at Harrow and Oxford, he married in 1864 and fathered four daughters. When a blood vessel in his lungs burst, Symonds moved to the high mountain town of Davos Platz in eastern Switzerland in 1877. He died of pneumonia on 19 April 1893.

In the early 1870s, Symonds conceived a multivolume history of the Italian Renaissance. *The Age of the Despots* appeared in 1875, followed by *The Revival of Learning* (1877), *The Fine Arts* (1877), *Italian Literature from the Beginnings to Ariosto* in two volumes (1881), and *The Catholic Reaction* in two volumes (1886). Symonds also wrote articles on "Renaissance" and "History of Italy" for the ninth edition of the *Encyclopaedia Britannica* (issued 1875–1889).

Symonds's interpretation reflected a general nineteenth-century conception of the Renaissance based on Jules Michelet and like-minded authors. Symonds had formulated his views and had written a good deal before he became aware of Jakob Burckhardt's book, probably in the English translation (*The Civilization of the Renaissance in Italy*) of 1878. Later, Symonds exuberantly echoed Burckhardt's conception of the Italian Renaissance. For Symonds the Italian Renaissance

> was the emancipation of the reason for the modern world. During the Middle Ages man had lived enveloped in a cowl. . . . He had not seen the beauty of the world, or had seen it only to cross himself, and turn aside and tell his beads and pray. . . . At a time when the rest of Europe was inert, Italy had already begun to organise the various elements of the modern spirit. . . . Thus, what the word Renaissance really means is new birth to liberty—the spirit of mankind recovering consciousness and the power of self-determination, recognizing the beauty of the outer world, and of the body through art, liberating the reason in science and conscience in religion, restoring culture to the intelligence, and establishing the principle of political freedom. . . . The great achievements of the Renaissance were the discovery of the world and the discovery of man.

Symonds then described the politics, art, humanism, and literature of the Italian Renaissance, often by focusing on individuals.

After leading humanity into the modern world, the Italian Renaissance fell victim to the reactionary forces, as Symonds saw them, of the Catholic Reformation, spearheaded by the Spanish Inquisition. The Renaissance spirit then passed to the Elizabethans and into modern times. In Symonds's conception, the spirit of the Renaissance and modernity progressed from the Italian Renaissance to the Protestant Reformation, the Elizabethan era, and into the nineteenth century. It was a classic formulation of history as the story of liberty and progress.

Symonds's work was based on the best available printed primary and secondary sources in several languages. It presents an immense amount of information in vivid language. The two volumes on Italian literature are the best of the set. The obvious faults are Symonds's exaggerations, his preference for colorful descriptions ahead of analysis of causes, and hostility toward the Middle Ages and the Catholic Church.

Symonds published numerous other works on Italian and English Renaissance figures, including Giovanni Boccaccio, Benvenuto Cellini, Ben Jonson, and Sir Philip Sidney. He translated the poetry of Tommaso Campanella and Michelangelo. Symonds's scholarship was the most important channel through which a Burckhardtian view of the Italian Renaissance reached scholars and the general public of the English-reading world.

BIBLIOGRAPHY

Primary Work

Symonds, John Addington. *Renaissance in Italy*. 7 vols. London, 1875–1886. After the first edition, it is difficult to disentangle new editions, reprints of previous editions, and reprints of individual volumes. The work was continuously in print between the 1890s and the late 1930s, with one or more volumes reissued every three or four years. The last reprint (in paperback) of all seven volumes appeared in the 1960s. A one-volume condensed version appeared in 1893 and was also reprinted several times. A one-volume Italian translation was published in Turin in 1900.

Secondary Works

Grosskurth, Phyllis. *John Addington Symonds: A Biography.* London, 1964. Standard biography that focuses on his life as a man of letters and his struggle as a homosexual in Victorian society.

Hale, John R. *England and the Italian Renaissance: The Growth of Interest in Its History and Art.* London, 1954. Pages 169–196. Perceptive evaluation of Symonds's *Renaissance in Italy.*

PAUL F. GRENDLER

Walter Pater

One of the greatest prose stylists in the history of English literature, the English critic, novelist, and scholar Walter Pater (1839–1894) is most widely appreciated today as a father of literary modernism, his influence felt by Oscar Wilde, W. B. Yeats, James Joyce, Virginia Woolf, and D. H. Lawrence, among others. Living a remarkably uneventful, austere, and private life, primarily at Oxford, as a scholar and teacher, Pater published his first book, *Studies in the History of the Renaissance,* in 1873 (revised editions 1877, 1888, and 1893), probably his greatest and most influential work. Pater's book was based on a series of essays that he began publishing in the late 1860s, just several years after the appearance of Jakob Burckhardt's *The Civilization of the Renaissance in Italy.* Although Pater's concept of "universal culture" in the Renaissance seems to echo Burckhardt's concept of the Renaissance "universal man," there has been almost no discussion of Pater's possible indebtedness to Burckhardt.

Like Burckhardt, Pater dwells on the revival of antiquity and the development of the individual in the Renaissance. He is profoundly concerned with the inwardness of his subjects, with what came to be called Renaissance "subjectivity" or "psychology." Pater's influence on our understanding of the Renaissance and cultural history generally is poorly understood because his poetic prose, aestheticism, and impressionistic criticism make scholars uneasy. Yet he has had a considerable influence.

His first essay, "Two Early French Stories," is more broadly about the classical spirit of the twelfth century, which foretells that of the Italian Renaissance. Rooted in Jules Michelet's *History of France,* Pater's view of the continuity between the twelfth-century "renaissance" and that of the fifteenth century stands behind Charles Homer Haskins's classic *The Renaissance of the Twelfth Century* as it informs Erwin Panofsky's *Renaissance and Renascences in Western Art.*

Pater's essay on Giovanni Pico della Mirandola is one of the foundations for the modern study of Neoplatonism in the artistic culture of the Renaissance, influencing Nesca Robb's *Neoplatonism of the Italian Renaissance* and a large body of writings by Panofsky, Ernst Gombrich, André Chastel, and others. Pater played the principal role in the nineteenth-century rediscovery of Sandro Botticelli. His treatment of Botticelli and Dante—particularly of Botticelli's Neoplatonism, elegiac spirit, and "poetry"—has dominated the literature on Botticelli from John Addington Symonds to Panofsky. Pater's interpretation of Luca Della Robbia and the Tuscan sculptors of the fifteenth century also deeply informs the writings of John Pope-Hennessy.

Pater's poetic insights into Leonardo da Vinci's childhood found their way into Sigmund Freud's psychoanalytic investigation of the artist. In a similar way, Pater's chapter on the poetry of Michelangelo, "the greatest phenomenological writing on the artist ever undertaken," is reflected in David Summers's *Michelangelo and the Language of Art,* and his essay on Leonardo is fundamental to Kenneth Clark's *Leonardo da Vinci,* one of the few truly great art historical monographs. Pater's "The School of Giorgione" haunts the modern scholarship on Venetian painting and is especially alive in S. J. Freedberg's celebration of "Giorgionismo" (*Painting in Italy, 1500–1600*). Finally, the essay on Joachim du Bellay and the decline of the Renaissance presages Johan Huizinga's riposte to Burckhardt, *The Waning of the Middle Ages,* which emphasizes the theme of decline: Pater's emphasis on the courtly grace of art here is an important, still largely unacknowledged, antecedent to twentieth-century discussions of mannerism, *maniera,* and their courtly milieu.

BIBLIOGRAPHY

Primary Work

Pater, Walter. *The Renaissance: Studies in Art and Poetry.* Edited with notes by Donald L. Hill. Berkeley, Los Angeles, and New York, 1980. A modern edition of the 1893 version of *Studies in the History of the Renaissance.*

Secondary Works

Barolsky, Paul. *Walter Pater's Renaissance.* University Park, Pa., and London, 1987.

Monsman, Gerald. *Walter Pater.* Boston, 1977.

PAUL BAROLSKY

Bernard Berenson

The foremost authority on Italian Renaissance painting for more than half a century, Bernard Berenson (1865–1959) was born into a poor Lithuanian family that emigrated to Boston in 1875. There young Berenson received his formal education at Harvard University. During a postgraduate study trip to Europe sponsored by Isabella Stewart Gardner, among others, and meant to prepare him as a literary critic, Berenson found his true vocation as a connoisseur. Adopting the new "scientific" method of his mentor Giovanni Morelli, which relied on the comparison of ears, hands, and other morphological details to determine the authorship of works of art, Berenson quickly established himself as an expert. He did so partly through his publications, particularly the four essays and lists of works he accepted as authentic (1894–1907), which later became *Italian Painters of the Renaissance* (1952) and *Italian Pictures of the Renaissance* (1957–1968), as well as his *Drawings of the Florentine Painters* (1903, 1938). No less important was Berenson's role in guiding wealthy Americans to form collections of Italian paintings. In addition to his first patron, Mrs. Gardner, he advised such collectors as John G. Johnson and P. A. B. and Joseph Widener in Philadelphia; Henry Walters in Baltimore; and Benjamin Altman, Robert Lehman, and Samuel H. Kress in New York. The fact that there are now more Italian Renaissance paintings in the United States than anywhere else outside Italy is largely due to Berenson's influence.

Having inherited from Walter Pater and others the concept of the Renaissance as a golden age, Berenson never wavered in his conviction of the superiority of the early Italian masters over those of other schools. Though initially drawn to the Venetians, he soon came to prefer the Florentine artists for what he called their "tactile values." The central Italian masters, headed by Perugino, were distinguished by their ability at "space composition." Working as an independent scholar (he never held a museum or teaching post) at his Villa I Tatti outside Florence, Berenson combined the pursuit of scholarship with a strenuous social life among a distinguished circle of friends, including Edith Wharton, all supported by the remuneration he obtained for his services from collectors and dealers, especially Sir Joseph Duveen.

In his incessant labors as a connoisseur, forming, expanding, and revising the famous "lists" (the indices of artists and locations that originally supplemented the turn-of-the-century essays), Berenson was aided by his wife, Mary Logan, who also edited her husband's earlier writings. At first these writings centered on scholarly problems, as Berenson sought not only to establish painters' oeuvres, but also to define their "artistic personalities." His appraisals of artists, while always pertinent, are often quite subjective: Berenson praised Leonardo's draftsmanship, for example, at the same time that he clearly disliked his paintings, now more than ever a heretical view. Over the years his writings became broader in scope, as he expounded on such issues as the "decline of art" after the Renaissance. His various publications also became more and more autobiographical, to the extent that his persona as a sage who had survived two world wars eventually overshadowed, among the public at least, his initial and still highly significant contribution to the study and interpretation of Renaissance art. A legend in his own lifetime, Berenson bequeathed his house, with its vast library, to his alma mater. Villa I Tatti now flourishes as the Harvard University Center for Italian Renaissance Studies.

Apart from I Tatti and the collections he helped to form (all now on public view), Berenson's legacy is mixed. That he made a major contribution to expanding knowledge in the field of Italian painting no one would deny. His willingness to reconsider his opinions, furthermore, formed the basis for the concept of attribution as a working hypothesis commonly accepted today. Nor was his approach to connoisseurship limited to mere questions of authorship; he always maintained the importance of quality in evaluating works of art. But Berenson undoubtedly neglected artists' techniques and the social and intellectual milieux in which they worked, factors that loom large for present-day students of the Renaissance. Immensely erudite, Berenson was well equipped to deal with such contextual matters, but he preferred—and this is characteristic of early twentieth-century scholarship in general—to focus on the formal values of the objects he chose to study. Not surprisingly, therefore, he believed that the iconographic researches of Erwin Panofsky and his disciples were unrelated or even inimical to the appreciation of art. With his gaze fixed unswervingly on the actual artwork, the example Berenson set, together with his earlier publications, epitomizes what has come to be called an object-oriented approach to the study of Renaissance art.

See also **Villa I Tatti**.

BIBLIOGRAPHY

Primary Works

Berenson, Bernard. *The Drawings of the Florentine Painters.* Rev. ed. 3 vols. Chicago, 1938.

Berenson, Bernard. *The Italian Painters of the Renaissance.* London, 1952. Combined edition of the author's original essays of 1894, 1896, 1897, and 1907.
Berenson, Bernard. *Italian Pictures of the Renaissance: Central Italian and North Italian Schools.* 3 vols., London, 1968.
Berenson, Bernard. *Italian Pictures of the Renaissance: Florentine School.* 2 vols., London and New York, 1963.
Berenson, Bernard. *Italian Pictures of the Renaissance: Venetian School.* 2 vols., London, 1957.
Berenson, Bernard. *Sketch for a Self-Portrait.* London, 1949.
Berenson, Bernard. *The Study and Criticism of Italian Art.* 3 vols. London, 1901–1916.

Secondary Works
Brown, David Alan. *Berenson and the Connoisseurship of Italian Painting.* Washington, D.C., 1979. Exhibition catalog, National Gallery of Art.
Calo, Mary Ann. *Bernard Berenson and the Twentieth Century.* Philadelphia, 1994.
Samuels, Ernest. *Bernard Berenson: The Making of a Connoisseur.* Cambridge, Mass., 1979.
Samuels, Ernest. *Bernard Berenson: The Making of a Legend.* Cambridge, Mass., 1987.

DAVID ALAN BROWN

Aby Warburg

Aby Warburg (1866–1929) was a German cultural historian who left a legacy for Renaissance art history that far exceeds his few but highly influential published essays. The library that he founded with his family banking fortunes in Hamburg at the end of the nineteenth century, Kulturwissenschaftliche Bibliothek Warburg, remains in London (where it was moved on the eve of World War II), where it is still a fabled institute for ancient and Renaissance studies. Warburg's lifelong intellectual project was devoted to the study of the "afterlife" (*Nachleben*) of antiquity and its role in determining the underlying psychology of Renaissance artifacts and attitudes. A disciple of Jakob Burckhardt, Warburg directed his early investigations into the Florentine archives, which alerted him to the mythological and astrological symbolism that ran through Medici art and politics; in Ferrara he came to know elaborate and enigmatic fresco cycles, such as those in the Schifanoia Palace. Warburg was dismissive of the aesthetes and formalists who then dominated the history of Renaissance art and disparagingly dubbed these scholars "border police." He sought, rather, to "trespass" disciplinary boundaries as he explored the meanings of Renaissance imagery. He crossed national borders as well, journeying in 1895 to the southwestern United States to study the Hopi snake dance, believing that its arcane symbolism might provide clues to the meaning of certain ritualistic appearances in Renaissance art.

An iconographer by disposition, Warburg always sought out the cultural and sociological context to explain the image, the written text to decipher the visual meaning. By 1912, the year in which "iconology was born," however, he had effectively challenged the new discipline of art history to range even wider in its inquires into the Renaissance visual imagination. He did not actually have a method, but, as his biographer Ernst Gombrich put it, "he had a message." Warburg advocated the reading of objects of art as testimonies of underlying cultural and psychological predispositions and was interested neither in the spiritual world of the Middle Ages nor the excesses of the baroque worldview. Rather, he was fascinated with enduring ancient gestures (such as the frenzied waving of the "Nympha" in Ghirlandaio's *Birth of the Virgin,* 1485–1490) that periodically resurfaced in fifteenth-century painting. Warburg's own imagination was haunted, in particular, by the survival of pagan astrological gods and demons long after the enlightened thinkers of the Renaissance had believed them vanquished.

Warburg's intellectual preoccupations interacted with his mental state. Subject all his life to his own spells of psychic torment, he was obsessed with articulating the struggle between the forces of reason and unreason that fixed the Renaissance character (and, by extension, the modern character) in its psychological polarities. On the verge of mental collapse, Warburg was confined in 1921 to a closed ward in Ludwig Binswanger's sanatorium in Kreuzlingen, Switzerland.

In his three-year professional absence, his private library was transformed into a public research institute by his able assistants, Fritz Saxl and Gertrud Bing. They initiated a publication series, and many famed scholars of the Renaissance, such as Ernst Cassirer (1874–1945), Ernst Curtius (1814–1896), Francis Yates (1899–1981), and Erwin Panofsky (1892–1968) were openly indebted to its idiosyncratic resources. The last five years of Warburg's own life were devoted to assembling his vast Mnemosyne project. This project consisted of a series of large, canvas exhibition screens on which he compulsively arranged and rearranged a collection of images from the past and the present, all in the attempt to chart the routes through which the sublime serenity that Renaissance artists achieved was derived from the taming of pagan passions.

BIBLIOGRAPHY

Primary Works
Warburg, Aby. *Ausgewählte Schriften und Würdigungen* (Collected writings). Edited by Dieter Wuttke. Baden-Baden,

Germany, 1980. Also see D. Wuttke's *Aby Warburg-Bibliographie 1866 bis 1995: Werk und Wirkung*. Baden-Baden, Germany, 1998.

Warburg, Aby. *The Renewal of Pagan Antiquity Contributions to the Cultural History of the European Renaissance (Texts and Documents)*. Introduction by Kurt W. Forster. Translated by David Britts. Los Angeles, 1999.

Warburg, Aby. *Images for the Region of the Pueblo Indians of North America*. Edited and translated by Michael Steinberg. Ithaca, N.Y., 1995.

Secondary Works

Bredekamp, H., M. Diers, and C. Schoell-Glass, eds. *Aby Warburg: Akten des internationalen Symposions*. Hamburg, 1990. A series of conference reports by well-known scholars.

Diers, Michael. "Warburg and the Warburgian Tradition of Cultural History." Translated by Thomas Girst and Dorothea von Moltke. *New German Critique* (spring/summer 1995): 59–73.

Ferretti, Silvia. *Cassirer, Panofsky, and Warburg: Symbol, Art, and History*. Translated by Richard Pierce. New Haven, Conn., and London, 1989.

Forster, Kurt. "Aby Warburg: His Study of Ritual and Art on Two Continents." Translated by David Britt. *October* 77 (summer 1996): 5–24.

Ginzburg, Carlo. "From Aby Warburg to E. H. Gombrich." In *Clues, Myths, and the Historical Method*. Translated by John Tedeschi and Anne C. Tedeschi. Baltimore, 1989.

Galitz, Robert, and Brita Reimers, eds. *Aby M. Warburg: "Ekstatische Nymphe . . . trauernder Flussgott": Porträt eines Gelehrten*. Hamburg, 1995.

Gombrich, Ernst. *Aby Warburg: An Intellectual Biography*. 2d ed. Chicago, 1986.

Heckscher, William. "The Genesis of Iconology." *Stil und Überlieferung in der Kunst des Abendlandes: Akten des 21. International Kongresses für Kunstegeschichte in Bonn, 1964*. Vol. 3, *Theorien und Probleme*. Berlin, 1967.

Rampley, Matthew. "From Symbol to Allegory: Aby Warburg's Theory of Art." *Art Bulletin* 79 (1997): 41–55.

Weigel, Sigrid. "Aby Warburg's *Schlangenritual:* Reading Culture and Reading Written Texts." *New German Critique* (spring/summer 1995): 135–153.

MICHAEL ANN HOLLY

Johan Huizinga

Johan Huizinga (1872–1945) studied linguistics and Sanskrit at the University of Groningen and took his doctorate in 1897. He then became a high school teacher in Haarlem and worked as a docent for Indic studies at the University of Amsterdam. He became a professor of history in 1905 at the University of Groningen and in 1915 at the University of Leiden, where he stayed until the Nazis closed the university in 1942. He was one of a number of prominent citizens imprisoned by the Nazis to guarantee the good behavior of his countrymen. He and his fellow hostages were to be shot at any sign of Dutch resistance. He was released from the camp by the intervention of the Swedish Red Cross but was banished to the small town of De Steeg, where he died on 1 February 1945 during a harsh winter.

Huizinga's interest in history was aroused when, as a child, he witnessed a re-creation of a medieval procession in Groningen. His interest in the Renaissance was theoretical, as is shown by his thoughtful consideration of Jakob Burckhardt's *Die Kultur der Renaissance in Italien* (*The Civilization of the Renaissance in Italy*; 1860), which he felt identified the Renaissance too strongly with the discovery of the individual.

In his early training in Indic studies, Huizinga was influenced by the work of the seminal anthropologist Sir Edward Burnett Tylor, who thought that all human cultures were basically the same and that apparent differences were but variations on this basic form. In part based on his study of Tylor's work, Huizinga developed the idea that the most defined moments in the history of culture come when a civilization becomes focused on a central teleology, when the "tone" of an age becomes clear, as in the Enlightenment, when the focus was on "the improvement of the world." In Huizinga's view, Burckhardt's thesis, that the central point of the Italian Renaissance was the discovery of the individual, would have depicted such a moment, if the thesis were true.

Huizinga argued that defining the Renaissance in terms of such a single characteristic not only is inaccurate (there are many individuals, knowing themselves to be such, in the Middle Ages) but has the effect of robbing the term "Middle Ages" of any significance for history, since it requires that any striking individual—Dante, Saint Francis of Assisi, Saint Bernard of Clairvaux—be seen as a precursor to the Renaissance rather than exemplary of his own time. What is true of "individualism" is also true of other attempts to define the Renaissance around a single term or strictly delimited group of terms, such as "realism," "antireligiosity," "objectivity," or "reliance on the model of antiquity," since all of those things were strongly present in the Middle Ages. Even so, Huizinga agreed that there was an important difference between medieval and Renaissance culture, that the tone of each was at a different pitch.

Huizinga felt that the way to distinguish the Middle Ages from the Renaissance was by clearly differentiating the Middle Ages from modern times and situating the Renaissance as a period of transition between them. His method requires that the historian show how the "forms of life" vary from era to era. Huizinga's theoretical contribution to this project was *Homo Ludens* (1938), which posits that the forms of life are rooted in play. But he most successfully applied his theory in *Herfsttij der middeleeuwen* (*The Autumn of the Middle Ages*; 1919), where he demonstrates that the art of the brothers van Eyck is thoroughly medieval in tone although it has frequently been mistaken for Renaissance realism (notably by Burckhardt).

Huizinga, who was a great literary stylist, suggests that the metaphor for the movement from the Middle Ages to the Renaissance needs to be reconceived: instead of thinking, as Burckhardt did, of the ripping aside of the veil of illusion, Huizinga proposes thinking of the change as the turning of a tide, which does not happen everywhere at once. Each place that the tide touches the shore is affected in a slightly different way, but eventually all the waters run in the same direction: the tone of life changes, and the teleology of the age becomes apparent. *The Autumn of the Middle Ages* concludes:

> The Renaissance only arrives when the "tone of life" is changing, when the ebb tide of the deadly denial of life has given way to a new flood and a stiff fresh breeze is blowing; it arrives only when the joyful insight (or was it an illusion?) has ripened that all the glories of the ancient world, of which for so long men had seen themselves the reflection, could be reclaimed.

Huizinga's other book on the Renaissance, *Erasmus,* was completed in 1924, five years after *The Autumn of the Middle Ages.* The book was commissioned by the philanthropist Edward Bok, a commission Huizinga accepted in spite of his lack of sympathy for Erasmus. Huizinga's goal in this book was, he said, "to see of that great Erasmus as much as the petty one permits."

This highly critical stance led Huizinga to present Erasmus as a man far too susceptible to aesthetic considerations (in questions of reform, for instance), too reluctant to enter into contention, and too lacking in passion about his deepest convictions: Erasmus's weaknesses, therefore, negatively mirror Luther's strengths. However, if Erasmus was too weak for his times, he does foreshadow the future in his "enunciation of the creed of education and perfectability, of warm social feeling and of faith in human nature, of peaceful kindliness and toleration." In these he is a precursor of "Rousseau, Herder, Pestalozzi and of the English and American thinkers." In short, Erasmus early exemplifies the form of life of the Enlightenment, explained in *The Autumn of the Middle Ages,* when the mind turned definitively to the improvement of the world. Huizinga thus is faithful to the analysis of the forms of life and at the same time emphasizes his view of the Renaissance, and one of the major figures in it, as a transition between the Middle Ages and modern times.

See also **Erasmus, Desiderius; Renaissance, Interpretations of the,** *subentry on* **Jakob Burckhardt.**

BIBLIOGRAPHY

Primary Works

Huizinga, Johan. *The Autumn of the Middle Ages.* Translated by Rodney Payton and Ulrich Mammitzsch. Chicago, 1996.

Huizinga, Johan. *Dutch Civilisation in the Seventeenth Century, and Other Essays.* Selected by Pieter Geyl and F. W. N. Hugenholtz. Translated by Arnold J. Pomerans. New York, 1968. Contains the biographical sketch "My Path to History."

Huizinga, Johan. *Erasmus and the Age of Reformation.* Translated by F. Hopman. Princeton, N.J., 1984.

Huizinga, Johan. *Homo Ludens: A Study of the Play-Element in Culture.* Boston, 1962.

Huizinga, Johan. *Men and Ideas.* Translated by James S. Holmes and Hans van Marle. New York, 1959. Contains the two Renaissance essays "The Problem of the Renaissance" and "Renaissance and Realism."

Huizinga, Johan. *Verzamelde Werken.* 9 vols. Edited by L. Brummel, W. R. Juynboll, Th. J. G. Locher. Haarlem, Netherlands, 1948–1953. Volume 9 contains a bibliography, including translations of Huizinga's works.

Secondary Works

Kaegi, Werner. *Das historische Werk Johan Huizingas.* Leiden, Netherlands, 1947.

Krul, W. E. *Historicus tegen de tijd: Opstellen over leven en werk van J. Huizinga.* Groningen, Netherlands, 1990.

Lem, Anton. *Het eeuwige verbeeld in een afgebaald bed: Huizinga en de Nederlandse beschaving.* Amsterdam, 1997.

Weintraub, Karl J. *Visions of Culture.* Chicago, 1966.

RODNEY J. PAYTON

Erwin Panofsky

Born in Germany, Erwin Panofsky (1892–1968) was an art historian who had an enormous impact on the Anglo-American study of Renaissance art history after he was compelled to emigrate to the United States on the eve of World War II. Educated in law at the University of Freiburg, he taught at the newly founded University of Hamburg during the Weimar Republic. His intellectual home in Hamburg was Aby Warburg's private library of cultural studies (Kulturwissenschaftliche Bibliothek Warburg), and his closest colleagues there were a number of influential scholars of Renaissance studies: Aby Warburg, Edgar Wind, Gertrud Bing, Fritz Saxl, Rudolf Wittkower, and Ernst Cassirer (Cassirer, in particular, exerted a lasting influence on the way he interpreted the philosophical underpinnings of his work).

Panofsky was dismissed from his university post by the National Socialists in 1933 for being Jewish. By that time, he was well known for both theoretical and historical studies of medieval and Renaissance imagery. Panofsky had already surveyed a prodigious list of topics, including Albrecht Dürer's engravings as an index of the connections between the northern and southern Renaissance, representations of the humor of melancholy, a survey of medieval German sculpture, the Platonic conception of ideal forms and their connection to Renaissance art, the function of devotional images, Galileo's impact on the visual arts, a study of proportions and their implications for visual representations, and perhaps most characteristic, a study of the Renaissance system of perspective as a culturally conditioned (that is, conventional) symbol. All these early works attest to Panofsky's lifelong commitment to deciphering "meaning" and historical content in both northern and Italian Renaissance art. This was an approach that countered the aesthetic and formalist inquiries pursued by many art historians who were his contemporaries.

Panofsky started his career in the United States as a visiting professor of fine arts at New York University in 1934. In 1935 he began serving as a member of the Institute for Advanced Study in Princeton, New Jersey. He taught and wrote principally in English. His influence on the young discipline of art history was both strong and swift, as was his impact on both literary and historical studies. Although his American essays are less theoretical in tone and content than his early German texts (in which he appears to be as much a philosopher of art as an art historian), they singlehandedly initiated a passion for the iconographic and iconological inquiry that dominated studies of Renaissance art throughout most of the rest of the twentieth century. The preface to his 1939 *Studies in Iconology* codifies his famed three-tiered approach to Renaissance images by reference to Leonardo da Vinci's *Last Supper* (1495–1497/98). The "pre-iconographic" first level depends on commonsensical recognition, apart from historical or symbolic associations (for example, the identification of thirteen animated men seated at a banquet table). The "iconographic" second stage deciphers the image according to its textual meanings as it identifies the subject of Leonardo's painting, for example, by reference to the biblical story, at the same time as it seeks out other artistic precedents. An "iconological" analysis, the third level, is classified as "iconography turned interpretive." For this reading, the art historian must comprehend the work as a cultural document, one that is expressive of "the essential tendencies of the human mind" as they have become embodied in this particular historical, personal, and social monument. At this level, the *Last Supper,* for example, is read not only as a testimony to Leonardo's rather idiosyncratic vision but also as a supreme product of Renaissance religious, philosophical, and intellectual ideals.

Over the course of a fifty-year scholarly career, Panofsky's other sustained studies included such topics as Michelangelo's Neoplatonism, the "hidden symbolism" in early Netherlandish art, the late works of Titian, the history of late medieval manuscript illumination, the Scholasticism of Gothic architects and their patrons, and Dürer's Italianate humanism. This formidable body of scholarship can be reduced to two pervasive interpretive commitments: Panofsky drew attention to the cultural and historical links between Renaissance words and images, and he unceasingly placed works of visual art back into their historical and ideological contexts.

Panofsky's influence is still strong in Renaissance studies, even if his confidence in humanistic inquiry and historical transparency has come under scrutiny from a variety of poststructuralist directions. Adamant about distinguishing the subjects of the humanities from the objects of science, he possessed an abiding faith in the rationality and protocols of historical scholarship: "The humanist, dealing as he does with human actions and creations, has to engage in a mental process of a synthetic and subjective character; he has mentally to re-enact the actions and to re-create the creations. It is in fact by this process that the real objects of the humanities come into being" (Panofsky, "The History of Art as a Humanistic Discipline," *Meaning in the Visual Arts,* p. 14). It is virtually impossible to conceive of the present state of Renaissance art history apart from Panofsky's formative influence.

BIBLIOGRAPHY

Primary Works

Panofsky, Erwin. "Die Perspektive als 'symbolische Form.'" *Vorträge Bibliothek Warburg* (1924–1925): 258–230. Translated by Christopher Wood as *Perspective as Symbolic Form.* New York, 1991.

Panofsky, Erwin. *Early Netherlandish Painting: Its Origins and Character.* 2 vols., 1953; New York, 1971.

Panofsky, Erwin. *Gothic Architecture and Scholasticism: An Inquiry into the Analogy of the Arts, Philosophy, and Religion in the Middle Ages.* Latrobe, Pa., 1951; New York, 1957.

Panofsky, Erwin. *The Life and Art of Albrecht Dürer.* 1943; Princeton, N.J., 1955.

Panofsky, Erwin. *Meaning in the Visual Arts.* 1955; Chicago and Garden City, N.Y., 1982.

Panofsky, Erwin. *Renaissance and Renascences in Western Art.* 1960; New York, 1969.

Panofsky, Erwin. *Studies in Iconology: Humanistic Themes in the Art of the Renaissance.* 1939; New York, 1962.

Secondary Works

Bonnet, Jacques, ed. *Erwin Panofsky.* Cahiers pour un temps. Paris, 1983.

Holly, Michael Ann. *Panofsky and the Foundations of Art History*. Ithaca, N.Y., 1984.
Lavin, Irving, ed. *Meaning in the Visual Arts: Views from the Outside: A Centennial Commemoration of Erwin Panofsky, 1892–1968*. Princeton, N.J., 1995.
Podro, Michael. *The Critical Historians of Art*. New Haven, Conn. 1982.

MICHAEL ANN HOLLY

Hans Baron

Hans Baron (1900–1988) was an important scholar of Renaissance history. Born in Berlin in 1900 of Jewish parents, he studied at Leipzig and Berlin and received his doctorate from the latter university in 1922. Following several years of postdoctoral study at Berlin and in Italy, he served as research assistant on the Historical Commission of the Munich Academy of Sciences from 1928 to 1933. Barred from academic advancement because of his Jewish heritage, he suffered the indignities and dangers common to Jews living in Nazi Germany. In 1937 Baron, his wife Edith, and their two children went to England, and in 1938 to the United States. He taught at Queens College in New York City (1939–1942) and then became a member of the Princeton Institute for Advanced Study (1944–1948). In 1949, he was appointed research fellow and bibliographer at the Newberry Library, where he remained until retirement in 1970. He continued his research and writing until just a few weeks before his death on 26 November 1988.

Baron's earliest book, *Calvins Staatsanschauung und das konfessionelle Zeitalter*, was published in 1924, and four years later his *Leonardo Bruni Aretino: Humanistisch-philosophische Schriften mit einer Chronologie seiner Werke und Briefe* appeared. In this same period he edited and published two volumes of his teacher Ernst Troeltsch's essays (1924 and 1925). In 1955 he published his master work, *The Crisis of the Early Italian Renaissance* and a supporting volume, *Humanistic and Political Literature in Florence and Venice*. *The Crisis* appeared in a revised edition in 1966 and a second revised version in Italian in 1970. He followed these volumes with *From Petrarch to Leonardo Bruni: Studies in Humanistic and Political Literature* (1968), *Petrarch's "Secretum": Its Making and Its Meaning* (1985), and, just before his death, a collection of new and revised essays *In Search of Florentine Civic Humanism: Essays on the Transition from Medieval to Modern Thought* (1988).

Baron's *Crisis of the Early Italian Renaissance* revolutionized the study of early Italian Renaissance humanism across a wide range of fields and was doubtless the most controversial book on the Renaissance written in the twentieth century. The product of decades of research and numerous specialized articles, the book imposed a broad interpretive framework on Italian humanism, endeavoring to relate intellectual change to political and sociological development. In place of the relatively vague evolutionary approach to humanism characteristic of pre–World War II scholarship, Baron sharply contrasted fourteenth-century with fifteenth-century humanism, explaining the passage from the first to the second as the result of a political crisis. He buttressed his thesis with substantial documentation from literary sources, many of them hitherto neglected.

Baron characterized Petrarch and his immediate fourteenth-century disciples as envisaging humanistic studies within a Christian context that valued the contemplative life and political quietism over the active life of the citizen. In the early years of the fifteenth century, however, Baron identified a new humanism stressing the importance of civic life and political participation. This new movement Baron called "civic humanism" and saw it as beginning in Florence. In Baron's view the titanic struggle between Florence and Milan from 1389 to 1402, which nearly ended in the destruction of the Florentine republic, made Florentine humanists realize the value of their civic culture and led to a sudden change in attitude. The earliest manifestation of this new position, Leonardo Bruni's *Laudatio urbis florentinae* (Praise of the city of Florence; 1404), marked the beginning of a republican interpretation of history and politics that, diffused over the Alps in the sixteenth century, became a source of the republican tradition in Western European culture down to the nineteenth century. Furthermore, the humanists' new positive assessment of lay life, together with their justification of wealth, laid a theoretical foundation for the modern secular view of society. Despite the controversial nature of some of his arguments, Baron's basic distinctions between fourteenth- and fifteenth-century Italian humanism continue to dominate the interpretation of the movement in these centuries.

Closely tied to the central theses of *The Crisis*, Baron's subsequent writings on Machiavelli significantly altered contemporary concepts of Machiavelli's intellectual development and the character of his thought. His now widely accepted dating of the *Prince* as prior to the *Discourses* suggests an evolution of Machiavelli's ideas from the largely amoral position of the first work to the republican convictions of the second. Baron's later contributions to

Petrarch studies, however, have been less important. Committed to the assumption that a close reading of Petrarch's texts against a background of the biography would allow scholars to demonstrate the precise evolution of Petrarch's thought, his work largely overlooked the rhetorical element so prominent in the humanist's writings.

BIBLIOGRAPHY

Primary Works

Baron, Hans. *Leonardo Bruni Aretino: Humanistisch-Philosophische Schriften met einer Chronologie seiner Werke und Briefe.* Leipzig, Germany, 1928. Collection of Bruni's works with an extended introduction by Baron.

Baron, Hans. *The Crisis of the Early Italian Renaissance: Civic Humanism and Republican Liberty in an Age of Classicism and Tyranny.* 2 vols. Princeton, N.J., 1955. Revised, one-volume edition, Princeton, N.J., 1966.

Baron, Hans. *Humanistic and Political Literature in Florence and Venice.* Cambridge, Mass., 1955. Reprint, New York, 1968.

Baron, Hans. *From Petrarch to Leonardo Bruni: Studies in Humanistic and Political Literature.* Chicago and London, 1968.

Baron, Hans. *In Search of Florentine Civic Humanism: Essays on the Transition from Medieval to Modern Thought.* 2 vols. Princeton, N.J., 1988. Collects and revises his major articles.

Secondary Works

Fubini, Riccardo. "Renaissance Historian: The Career of Hans Baron." *Journal of Modern History* 64 (1992): 541–574.

Rabil, Albert. "The Significance of 'Civic Humanism' in the Interpretation of the Italian Renaissance." *Renaissance Humanism: Foundations, Forms and Legacy.* 3 vols. Edited by Albert Rabil. Philadelphia, 1988. Pages 141–172.

Witt, Ronald, John N. Najemy, Craig Kallendorf, and Werner Gundersheimer. "AHR Forum: Hans Baron's Renaissance Humanism." *American Historical Review* 101 (1996): 107–144.

RONALD G. WITT

Eugenio Garin

Professor of the history of philosophy emeritus at the University of Florence, and later at the Scuola normale superiore di Pisa, Garin (b. Rieti, Italy, 1909) developed a comprehensive picture of Italian cultural unity, c. 1400–1600. Sometimes he labels this entire culture "humanism," as in *Italian Humanism* (1947); at other times, he calls the 1400s—beginning slightly before 1400 with Petrarch (1304–1374) and extending to Marsilio Ficino (1433–1499)—the "age of humanism;" and the 1500s—Pietro Pomponazzi (1462–1525) to Galileo Galilei (1564–1642)—"the Renaissance," as in *Storia della filosofia italiana* (History of Italian philosophy; 1966). By either designation Garin describes a transition from an essentialist culture, one that searches for eternal truths, to a historicist culture, one that focuses on the problems encountered in building a human or "civic" world. The same culture that produced Petrarch (humanist) also produced Ficino (philosopher) and Galileo (scientist), which is to say that Garin emphasizes the unity of Italy's cultural achievement (and leadership); he assumes that the same cultural impulse gave rise to them all. He regards the humanists as philosophers and believes that "philosophers" emerged for the first time in Renaissance Italy. Thinkers who took the entire historical world, human and natural, as their domain, "philosophers" differ fundamentally from the "intellectuals" of the Middle Ages who wanted above all else to understand heaven, and who elevated the contemplative life over the active life.

Petrarch initiated the new impulse, most vividly in *On His Own Ignorance and That of Many Others* (1368), in which he rejected the veneration of Aristotle as an "authority" and put forward the alternative of multiple responses to the world, each with its own contribution to the whole. Petrarch's humanist followers discussed many "worldly" problems—primacy of the will (and its ability to triumph over Fortune), the importance of individual virtue, the (positive) value of business and the wealth it generates, reasons for preferring Epicureanism and criticizing Stoicism, human dignity, and a host of others—and in doing so not only introduced new topics but a new method, rhetorical rather than logical, built on the foundation of the *studia humanitatis* (grammar, rhetoric, poetry, history, moral philosophy, politics). Although the "civic humanists" of the fifteenth century differ from the Platonists, the latter also contributed to the same worldly (if not civic) impulse in their valuation of the mathematical understanding of nature, affirmed by Ficino and developed by Galileo and others; and in the energy for religious reform evident especially in Giovanni Pico della Mirandola (1463–1494) and Ficino, put into practice first in Italy by Girolamo Savonarola (1452–1498) and subsequently in the northern European Reformation. Although Garin's vision involves a kind of "cultural nationalism," it is based on an attentive reading of sources in many areas of Italian culture during these centuries. Moreover, he modified and developed the idea of "civic life" first introduced by Hans Baron. His way of seeing humanism and the Italian Renaissance has deeply informed discussions of both in the twentieth century.

BIBLIOGRAPHY

Garin's vision of Italian Renaissance culture was first developed in *Italian Humanism: Philosophy and Civic Life in the Renais-*

sance (New York, 1965). This is a translation of *Umanesimo italiano: Filosofia e vita civile nel Rinascimento* (Bari, Italy, 1952, 1958), which was first published in German as *Die italienische Humanismus: Philosophie und bürgerliches Leben in Renaissance,* translated by G. Zamboni (Bern, Switzerland, 1947). His many other books reflect broad and deep interests in the period, for example: *L'educazione in Europa (1400–1600)* (Bari, Italy, 1957), *Scienza e vita civile nel Rinascimento italiano* (Bari, Italy, 1965), *Storia della filosofia italiana,* 3 vols. (Turin, Italy, 1967). Garin has also edited numerous texts, including *Prosatori Latini del quattrocento* (Milan, 1952). Also available in English are *Portraits from the Quattrocento* (New York, 1972), and *Renaissance Characters* (Chicago, 1991)—chapter 5, "The Philosopher and the Magus" is a clear statement of his point of view. For an extensive bibliography of his writings (edited works excluded), see *The Cambridge History of Renaissance Philosophy* (Cambridge, U.K., 1988), pp. 888–889, and *Bibliografia degli Scritti di Eugenio Garin* (Bari, Italy, 1969).

ALBERT RABIL JR.

Remigio Sabbadini

One of the greatest and most prolific modern students of Italian humanism, with a bibliography of 492 items, Remigio Sabbadini (1850–1934) was born the son of peasants in the village of Sarego between Vicenza and Verona. (Late in his career he dedicated the two volumes of his *Scoperte* to his younger brother, "who plows the sod of the little family farm.") After graduating as a scholarship student from the University of Florence in 1874, Sabbadini spent twelve years as a high school classics teacher in various towns in Sicily and mainland Italy. Finally, in 1886 he gained the chair of Latin at the provincial University of Catania. In 1900, he transferred to the Accademia Scientifico-Letteraria of Milan, which became a university faculty in 1924, only two years before Sabbadini's retirement. Thus, despite his scholarship, Sabbadini was effectively never in a position to train the next generation of university professors in Renaissance studies. In the eight years between retirement and death he lived in Pisa. Born in a part of Italy that was then part of the Austrian Empire, he learned German at a young age. He also reviewed English books and talked of going to London, which held important sources for him. Able to obtain manuscripts on interlibrary loan (virtually unthinkable today, but not uncommon then), he never left Italy during his very long life.

Sabbadini approached the Renaissance as a professor of classical philology and, particularly, of classical Latin literature (throughout his life he published works on Virgil). His focus explains his strengths and weaknesses. His three-volume edition of the letters of the humanist educator Guarino da Verona is itself a classic, as are his two books on Guarino's life, teaching practice, and scholarship. His *Metodo degli umanisti* (Methods of the humanists) is filled with insights on the style and scholarship of the humanists and has not yet been superseded; his *Scoperte* remains a fundamental study of the discovery of classical texts; and his *Storia del ciceronianismo* (History of Ciceronianism) still is required reading for anyone interested in Neo-Latin literature and Renaissance literary theory. To these one can add a great quantity of first-rate work on the manuscripts of classical texts and on individual humanists such as Lorenzo Valla and Giovanni Aurispa, which has put future scholars permanently in his debt, even when they correct him in detail. In all these works, Sabbadini's great common sense, rigorous standard of scholarship, and immense erudition shine through.

On the other hand, one searches in vain throughout Sabbadini's writings for an overarching interpretation of the Renaissance apart from the opinion that it was a revival of classical languages and literature. He had no scholarly interest in other aspects of humanism or in the broader social and intellectual trends of the Renaissance. As he said in the preface to his biography of Guarino da Verona in 1895 and repeated in the preface to first volume of his *Scoperte* in 1905, "the natural cultivators of [Renaissance] humanism would have to be the students of classicism." In short, for Sabbadini, to study the Renaissance was to study the classical tradition in the Renaissance.

BIBLIOGRAPHY

Selected Works of Remigio Sabbadini

Carteggio di Giovanni Aurispa. Rome, 1931.

"Cronologia della Vita del Panormita e del Valla." In *Studi sul Panormita e sul Valla* (with Luciano Barozzi). Florence, 1891. Reprinted in Lorenzo Valla. *Opera Omnia*. Vol. 2. Edited by Eugenio Garin. Turin, Italy, 1962. Pages 355–464.

Epistolario di Guarino Veronese. 3 vols. In *Reale Deputazione veneta di storia patria. Miscellanea di storia veneta*. 3d series. Vols. 8, 11, and 14. Venice, 1914, 1915, 1919. Reprint, Turin, 1959.

Guariniana. Edited by Mario Sancipriano. Turin, Italy, 1964. Reprints "Vita di Guarino Veronese" (1891) and *La scuola e gli studi di Guarino Veronese* (1896).

Il metodo degli umanisti. Florence, 1922.

Le scoperte dei codici latini e greci ne' secoli quattordici e quindici. 2 vols. Florence, 1905–1914. Reprint, with author's corrections and additions and a summary of Sabbadini's contributions by Eugenio Garin, editor. Florence, 1967.

Storia del ciceronianismo e di altre questioni letterarie nell' età della rinascenza. Turin, Italy, 1885.

Secondary Work

Billanovich, Eugenio and Myriam. "Bibliografia di Remigio Sabbadini." *Opere minori* by Remigio Sabbadini. Vol. 1. Edited by Tino Foffano. Padua, Italy, 1995. Pages liii–lxxxiii. Also includes Billanovich, Giuseppe. "Presentazione." Pages ix–xlv.

JOHN MONFASANI

Georg Voigt

Georg Voigt was the first historian to see humanism as the determining intellectual principle of the Italian Renaissance and very important for the European Renaissance. Because he published his pioneering work in 1859, one year before Jakob Burckhardt's *The Civilization of the Renaissance in Italy* (1860), it is often overlooked.

Voigt, the son of a historian, was born in Königsberg, Prussia, on 5 April 1827. He began his career as a university librarian in Königsberg, served on a historical commission at the University of Munich in 1854, and became a professor of history at the University of Rostock by 1862. He published a three-volume study of Enea Silvio Piccolomini (1856–1863) and other works. He died in 1891.

His major work is *Die Wiederbelebung des classischen Alterthums, oder das erste Jahrhundert des Humanismus* (The revival of classical antiquity, or The first century of humanism; 1859). The book provides a comprehensive view of Italian Renaissance humanism beginning with Petrarch. Voigt identified Petrarch as the first humanist, "the discoverer of the new world of humanism." Voigt contrasted Petrarch's "genial learning" with the "aridity" and "pedantry" of medieval Scholasticism. Future humanists took their cue from Petrarch, acting as individual personalities pursuing their own human interests, in contrast with Scholastic philosophers who were only representatives of the medieval academic system. Voigt also emphasized the importance of Florence in the development of humanism, the first scholar to do so.

Voigt praised humanists for their philological and historical studies, which unlocked antiquity's riches and created a new kind of education based on the classics. But after Petrarch, Voigt judged much humanist literature to be artificial, egoistic, and an imitative reiteration of classical commonplaces. After studying Italian humanists and humanism through the middle of the fifteenth century, Voigt sketched northern European humanism. He concluded by listing the general tendencies and literary genres of humanism.

Voigt emphasized the individualism of humanists and insisted that humanism marked a sharp break with medieval culture and the beginning of modern culture. Voigt and Burckhardt independently reached similar conclusions about humanism and the Renaissance as the beginning of the modern world. But there were differences, especially in historical approach. Voigt wrote a compelling analytical narrative with clear chronological and geographical signposts. Burckhardt rejected narrative history in favor of interpretive essays on different areas of Renaissance life, each intended to illustrate "the spirit of the age."

Voigt mapped the development of Renaissance humanism in a way that is still recognizable. No scholar today disputes the importance of Petrarch and Florence in the origins and history of humanism. On the other hand, Voigt's view of humanists as free individuals lacking institutional or civic ties, and his negative judgment on their literary efforts, are not widely accepted today.

BIBLIOGRAPHY

The Renaissance Debate. Edited by Denys Hay. New York, 1965. Pages 29–34. The sole English translation of Voigt's major work (a few pages only), taken from the Berlin, 1893, edition.

Voigt, Georg. *Enea Silvio de' Piccolomini als Papst Pius der Zweite und sein Zeitalter*. 3 vols. Berlin, 1856, 1862, 1863. Photographic reprint, Berlin, 1967.

Voigt, Georg. *Die Wiederbelebung des classischen Alterthums, oder das erste Jahrhundert des Humanismus*. Berlin, 1859. Expanded edition, 2 vols., Berlin, 1880–1881. 3d edition, Berlin, 1893. Italian translation with additional material, 3 vols., Florence, 1888–1897; reprint, Florence, 1968. French translation, Paris, 1894.

PAUL F. GRENDLER

Paul Oskar Kristeller

The most important student of Renaissance humanism of the twentieth century, Paul Oskar Kristeller (1905–1999) was raised in a middle-class Jewish family in Berlin. He received his doctorate in 1929 from the University of Heidelberg for his dissertation on Plotinus, and after seminar work with the classicists Werner Jaeger and Eduard Norden in Berlin, he proceeded to Freiburg, where, with the approval of Martin Heidegger, he chose the Renaissance philosopher Marsilio Ficino as the subject of his *Habilitationsschrift* (a dissertation that qualifies one to teach at a German university). The Nazis' ascension to power in 1933 ended his German career, and in 1934 he moved to Italy.

After a period as instructor in a school for German Jews near Florence, Kristeller was appointed in 1935 as a lecturer in German at the elite Scuola Normale Superiore of Pisa with the support of its director, the former minister of education Giovanni Gentile. At the Scuola Normale, Kristeller inspired some of the most talented students to take up Renaissance studies, but the anti-Semitic laws of 1938 cost Kristeller his post and his Italian career. In February 1939, Gentile and American friends helped him to emigrate to the United States. That autumn he joined the philosophy department of Columbia University; he remained at Columbia for the rest of his professional life.

Kristeller's massive scholarship (his bibliography fills seventy-three printed pages) encompasses three areas of Renaissance studies: the history of philosophy, manuscript research, and the culture of humanism. His initial interest was the Platonist Ficino. After coming to America, he published *The Philosophy of Marsilio Ficino*. He then also became interested in Renaissance Aristotelianism and published a string of fundamental works on the subject, in particular on Pietro Pomponazzi. While still in Italy he realized that there remained an enormous amount of work to be done on the manuscripts of Ficino and other Renaissance figures. The first fruits of this bibliographical research were the two volumes of the *Supplementum Ficinianum* in 1937, which were a revelation for the amount of new information they contained. In 1945, after meeting in New York with Fritz Saxl, the director of London's Warburg Institute, he embarked on the *Iter Italicum,* a finding list of manuscripts of Renaissance authors that, when completed, consisted of more than 200,000 manuscript descriptions. The *Iter Italicum,* in conjunction with *Latin Manuscript Books* (see below), has probably enabled more original research than any other modern work on the Renaissance by a single scholar. At this time Kristeller also launched the *Catalogus translationum et commentariorum,* a cooperative venture tracing the commentary and translation history of every classical author, Christian as well as pagan, in the Middle Ages and Renaissance. The catalog of manuscript catalogs and inventories he first prepared for this project (*Latin Manuscript Books*) is the essential reference tool of every serious manuscript scholar today.

Kristeller's most provocative theme is his conception of Renaissance humanism as "a characteristic phase in what may be called the rhetorical tradition in Western culture" (*Renaissance Thought and Its Sources,* pp. 23–24). For him, Renaissance humanism was not a philosophy or an ideology or even simply the beginning of modern classical scholarship. The power of Kristeller's thesis lies in its capacity to locate Renaissance humanism in the sociopolitical setting of medieval Italy, which produced several forms of secular oratory and a form of medieval rhetoric (*dictamen,* the art of letter writing), as well as a professional interest in rhetoric on the part of Italian notaries, jurists, chancery officials, and *dictatores* (the teachers of *dictamen*). This interest in rhetoric led to growing interest in classical literary texts, and those who avidly pursued this second interest became increasingly expert in classical languages, literature, and history; they became, in short, what the Renaissance itself called "humanists." Kristeller's theory explains why humanism was an educational movement focused on rhetoric and classical literature and based on the curriculum of the *studia humanitatis* ("the humanities")—rhetoric, grammar, poetry, history, and moral philosophy. Kristeller's view of Renaissance humanism as a cultural rather than an ideological movement explains why some excellent humanists could be secular-minded and others Christian reformers; some Platonists and others Aristotelians or not interested in philosophy at all; some Protestants and others Catholic; some supporters of republics ("civic humanists") and others of tyrants and monarchs, and so forth. Finally, Kristeller's theory gives renewed meaning to the conception of the Renaissance as the Renaissance of Italy, since, according to his theory, humanism did not displace Scholasticism, but rather competed with it as each movement grew simultaneously in Italy, humanism having been indigenous to Italy, and Scholasticism having been imported from northern Europe. The Renaissance was the golden age not only of Italian humanism but also of Italian Scholasticism. The result was that in the Renaissance, Italy gained "a kind of intellectual empire that extended in its time from Lisbon to Uppsala and from Edinburgh to Cracow" (*Studies in Renaissance Thought and Letters,* vol. 2, p. 8).

BIBLIOGRAPHY

Works by Kristeller

Iter Italicum: A Finding List of Uncatalogued or Incompletely Catalogued Humanistic Manuscripts of the Renaissance in Italian and Other Libraries. 6 vols. Leiden, Netherlands, and London, 1963–1997.

The Philosophy of Marsilio Ficino. Translated by Virginia Conant. New York, 1943. Now to be read in the second (revised) Italian edition, *Il pensiero filosofico di Marsilio Ficino* (Florence, 1986).

Renaissance Thought and Its Sources. Edited by Michael Mooney. New York, 1979. Another useful collection of articles.

Studies in Renaissance Thought and Letters. 4 vols. Rome, 1956–1996. The most extensive, though only partial, collection of his articles.

Secondary Work

Mahoney, Edward P. "Paul Oskar Kristeller and His Contribution to Scholarship." In *Philosophy and Humanism: Renaissance*

Essays in Honor of Paul Oskar Kristeller. Edited by Edward P. Mahoney. New York, 1976. Pages 1–16.

JOHN MONFASANI

Economic Interpretations

The discourse among economic historians has been one of the most contentious in Renaissance historiography. The debate has focused not only on the nature of the economy, but on whether the term "Renaissance," coined by intellectual, cultural, and art historians, is at all applicable to the study of economic history. Many have rejected the term and the assumptions inherent in it in favor of a division of time that stresses larger, cyclical economic patterns.

Economic history itself is a relatively recent discipline. The work touching on the Renaissance goes back to the initial decades of the twentieth century. Studies followed two basic lines, one focusing on specific structures such as trade and industry, the other on theoretical issues such as the rise of capitalism. Both owed much to German scholars, who took the lead in economic history as they had in other aspects of Renaissance historiography. The discourse on capitalism took its inspiration from Karl Marx, Georg Wilhelm Friedrich Hegel, and Wilhelm Dilthey. The most influential works were those of Werner Sombart (1863–1941) and Max Weber (1864–1920). Sombart dated the emergence of capitalism to the fifteenth century, distinguishing it from petty trade in wares by artisans and craftsmen of the Middle Ages. Weber, in his famous formulation, placed capitalism at the beginning of the sixteenth century, linking it with the appearance of Calvinism and the so-called Protestant ethic.

Subsequent years saw a de-emphasis on theoretical approaches in favor of more empirical studies. The much greater use of archival materials by scholars after World War II encouraged such researches, which produced a wealth of detailed information. Scholars gave emphasis to specific industries such as wool cloth and banking—subjects that now fall under the heading of "business history"—and to specific regions and urban centers. Many of the studies have dealt with Italy, the commercial leader of the era. Of these, the work of Frederic C. Lane (1900–1984) on Venice and Raymond de Roover (1904–1972) on Florence stand out as among the most influential.

Italy has likewise been the focus of Marxist interest. Studies have centered on the relationship between city and countryside, that is, whether cities, to sustain themselves, oppressed their rural lands, and on the meaning of popular uprisings. Viktor Rutenberg has interpreted the social disturbances in urban centers in the fourteenth and fifteenth centuries as proto-proletarian movements.

The impetus toward accumulation of quantifiable data was greatly stimulated by a group of social historians, most of them French, known collectively by the name of the journal in which they often published, *Annales: Économies, sociétés, civilisations.* Gathering masses of statistical information, their adherents, such as Fernand Braudel (1902–1985), pointed out larger trends. At the same time, however, the Annalists tended to minimize the Renaissance as an operative concept and stressed more the *longue durée,* or long duration, usually meaning more than a century, linking data to cyclical patterns such as prices and population.

Statistical information coupled with economic theory has yielded important results in determining monetary trends. Bringing together his calculations (now disputed) of the influx of gold and silver to Spain from the Americas together with the quantity theory of money, Earl J. Hamilton called attention to the "price revolution" in Europe in the sixteenth century, which saw increases on goods of as much as 300 and 400 percent. Meanwhile, monetary theorists using mint records and other data have assessed the availability of specie for the fourteenth and fifteenth centuries. Several historians, such as Harry Miskimin, have spoken of a bullion famine in Europe in these years, a finding that continues to be debated.

The biggest controversy regarding the Renaissance economy occurred as a result of Robert Lopez's assertion (1953) that the period was one of economic depression. Lopez (1910–1987), who defined the Renaissance as dating from the middle of the fourteenth century to the end of the fifteenth, "give or take a decade or two on either side," drew on the work of the Belgian economic historian of the Middle Ages, Henri Pirenne (1862–1935), and several like-minded contemporaries. His thesis focused on the demographic disaster brought on by the Black Death of 1348 and its aftershocks, as well as the concomitant contraction of trade and overseas markets. He backed his assertions with what he apologetically called "disreputable" statistics, including evidence of steep declines in yields at the port of Genoa and the contraction of two of the largest industries of the era: wool cloth and banking.

Lopez's thesis had wide appeal because he tied the economic downturn directly to the production of Renaissance art and culture. With business flagging and opportunity lacking, people stopped pouring their money into their unprofitable financial ventures and invested in art. Lopez was opposed by Carlo M. Cipolla (b. 1922), who asserted that the demographic crisis did not depress the economy, but brought about a new equilibrium in which per capita earnings were the same or perhaps higher than before.

The debate proceeded from there, with Lopez and Cipolla providing the two poles. It dominated study of economic history, particularly of Italy, where the implications were most apparent, for nearly a quarter of a century. The debate had positive results, because it proved the broad applicability of economic history and made cultural and art historians more sensitive to the economy and economic historians more aware of culture and art. The discussion also added to the sophistication of the discipline. Malthusian analysis (economic decline is the inevitable result of increasing population) had its play, as did quantitative methods and, eventually, computer analysis. A high point in the application of computers was the appearance in 1978 of *Les Toscans et leur familles* (Tuscans and their families) by David Herlihy (a student of Robert Lopez) and Christiane Klapisch-Zuber. The work involved analysis of the great Florentine tax assessment (*catasto*) of 1427. It exhibits much Annalist influence and demonstrates the strong connections between economic history and social history.

The last ten years have seen a progressive shift away from economic history toward social history. Interesting work nevertheless continues to be done, particularly on cities and industries. Reinhold Mueller has produced a magisterial study of the money market in Venice, a sequel to his influential collaborative study (with Frederic Lane) on Venetian money and banking. Important studies have been devoted to the Italian silk industry and the countryside. Richard Goldthwaite has presented an generally positive view of the economy of Florence, the first city of the Renaissance, finding there a flourishing market for art as well as consumerism that foreshadowed that of the present day. His views serve as a point of reference for continued debate.

See also **Banking and Money**.

BIBLIOGRAPHY

Braudel, Fernand. *The Mediterranean and the Mediterranean World in the Age of Philip II.* 2 vols. Translated by Sian Reynolds. London and New York, 1973.

Braudel, Fernand. "Histoire et sciences sociales: La longue durée." *Annales: Économies, sociétés, civilisations* 13 (1958): 725–753.

Brown, Judith. "Prosperity and Hard Times in Renaissance Italy." *Renaissance Quarterly* 53 (1989): 760–780.

Cipolla, Carlo M. "Economic Depression of the Renaissance?" *Economic History Review* 4 (1964): 519–524.

De Roover, Raymond. *The Rise and Fall of the Medici Bank.* New York, 1966.

Ferguson, Wallace K. "Recent Trends in the Economic Historiography of the Renaissance." *Studies in the Renaissance.* Vol. 7. New York, 1960. Pages 10–26.

Goldthwaite, Richard A. *The Building of Renaissance Florence.* Baltimore, 1980.

Hamilton, Earl J. *American Treasure and the Price Revolution in Spain, 1501–1650.* Cambridge, Mass., 1934.

Herlihy, David, and Christiane Klapisch-Zuber. *Les Toscans et leurs familles: Une étude du catasto florentin de 1427.* Paris, 1978.

Lopez, Robert S. "Hard Times and the Investment in Culture." In *The Renaissance: A Symposium.* New York, 1953. Pages 19–34.

Lopez, Robert S., and Harry Miskimin. "The Economic Depression of the Renaissance." *Economic History Review* 3 (1962): 408–426.

Miskimin, Harry. *The Economy of Early Renaissance Europe, 1300–1460.* Englewood Cliffs, N.J., 1969.

Miskimin, Harry. *The Economy of Later Renaissance Europe 1460–1600.* Cambridge, U.K., and New York, 1977.

Mueller, Reinhold C. *The Venetian Money Market: Banks, Panics, and the Public Debt, 1200–1500.* Baltimore, 1997.

Rutenberg, Viktor I. *Popolo e movimenti popolari nell'Italia del '300 e '400.* Bologna, 1971.

WILLIAM CAFERRO

RENÉE OF FERRARA (1510–1575), French princess and duchess of Ferrara. Renée was the second daughter of Louis XII and Anne of Brittany and sister-in-law to Francis I. She was educated at the French court at a time when the influence of Margaret of Angoulême and her circle of humanist reformers was strong. In 1528 Renée married Ercole II d'Este as part of Francis I's search for allies against Holy Roman Emperor Charles V. Ercole became duke of Ferrara six years later. Long a center of Renaissance culture, now the court of Ferrara also became a refuge for many reform-minded humanists and Protestants who had fled from France. Among them were Clément Marot and Lyon Jamet, who stayed at Ferrara for over a year, and John Calvin, who arrived at Ferrara in 1536 but remained only a short time before making his way to Geneva. Renée carried on an extensive correspondence with Calvin until his death, although a major theme of it was Calvin's annoyance with her for not espousing the Reform openly enough. She was too committed to it for her husband, who forced her to abjure her beliefs in 1554. She remained faithful to them, nonetheless, and when her husband died in 1559, she returned to her French château of Montargis, where she maintained a Calvinist household. She avoided taking sides during the early Wars of Religion but suffered the indignity of having her château sacked by her daughter

Anne's husband, Francis of Guise. She died at Montargis in 1575.

BIBLIOGRAPHY

Blaisdell, Charmarie Jenkins. "Politics and Heresy in Ferrara, 1534–1559." *The Sixteenth Century Journal* 6 (1975): 67–93. The only readily accessible source in English.

FREDERIC J. BAUMGARTNER

REPRESENTATIVE INSTITUTIONS. Representative institutions in Europe were the product of the later Middle Ages; their widespread development, from Scandinavia to Sicily and from Portugal to Poland, owed little to the Renaissance or to a humanistic admiration for the institutions of ancient Rome or Greece (where direct democracy was more common than representation). But representative institutions did not disappear during the Renaissance: French kings avoided convening the Estates General between 1484 and 1560, but in neither France nor Spain did the king become an absolute ruler until the seventeenth century.

During the earlier Middle Ages, kings throughout Europe relied on the advice and support of the clergy (the first estate) and the nobility (the second estate), which were institutionalized in a Council of State. Events in the thirteenth century prompted kings to include representatives of towns (the third estate), which marked the beginning of the institution called Estates in France and the Netherlands, Parliament in England, Cortes in the Iberian Peninsula, and other names in central and eastern Europe.

Before turning to the history of the bodies representing estates at the national or provincial level, it is appropriate first to examine institutions of representation in the towns. Towns were everywhere subject in theory to the higher authority of a territorial prince, king, or emperor but in practice exercised varying degrees of autonomy. Those that attained the greatest independence were the cities of northern and central Italy, for example Florence and Venice.

Florence. From the seventh to the eleventh century, the bishop ruled Italian towns in both the secular and spiritual realms, but he was displaced from the secular during the eleventh century, in Florence and elsewhere in Italy, by the commune (*Comune*). While this institution purported to represent the entire community, its councils were in fact dominated by the urban nobility.

The communal form of government was threatened during the twelfth and thirteenth centuries from both within and without. In Florence and many other cities a new form of government, based on the guilds, was introduced. It was called a government "of the people" (and later dubbed "republican" by those who saw it as the heir of the ancient Roman republic), but it excluded from participation all who were not members of a guild. At one end of the social scale nobles were disqualified; at the opposite end employees of the textile industry, numbering perhaps a third of the population, were forbidden to form guilds and were therefore not considered citizens. The Florentine republic survived until the sixteenth century, interrupted only once (1342–1343) by the eleven-month rule of a despot (the duke of Athens). Within the guild community, however, the governing bodies of the city were generally dominated by men from the greater guilds. After 1382 the minor guilds were allowed only three, and later two, representatives on the Signoria, the executive council of eight priors. After 1434 the Medici were the actual rulers, but during the fifteenth century they worked through the representative institutions of the republic.

In many other towns, however, when the communal government was unable to cope with internal dissension, it gave way to the rule of a despot, who often succeeded in founding a dynasty: that of the della Scala in Verona, of the Carrara in Padua, and above all of the Visconti in Milan. Giangaleazzo Visconti (1351–1402) conquered the principal states of the Po Valley up to the borders of Venice. In Tuscany the cities of Pisa, Lucca, and Siena accepted his dominion. He did not govern his subject cities under a common code of law but contracted with each of them to observe his authority in foreign and military affairs, while preserving their self-government in local matters through their traditional representative institutions. Nevertheless, he came close to making himself king of northern and central Italy and was hailed as a Caesar by the humanists in his service. However, the *style* of the Renaissance was not born under the despots of northern Italy but in the Republic of Florence.

Venice. Republican government was more enduring in Venice, where it survived until 1797, but this was not a government of the people. Under a doge, who was elected for life, was the Great Council, which elected him and the other magistrates who administered the affairs of the city. These included an overseas empire and, from the fifteenth century on, an empire on terra firma, extending up the Po Valley to Brescia and Bergamo. The Great Council numbered more than two thousand in the fifteenth century, and since 1297 its ranks had been closed to newcomers. All political power thus belonged to a hereditary aristocracy, whose sources of revenue were, however, not landed estates but trade and municipal bonds.

A senate was formed toward the end of the fourteenth century; its approximately two hundred members were elected annually by the Great Council. Questions of foreign and military policy were discussed by this body in the presence of the doge.

Netherlandish Towns. Netherlandish towns most nearly attained the autonomy of the Italian city-state. Most of these provinces (for example, Brabant and Holland) were legally within the Holy Roman Empire until 1648, while others (notably Flanders) were originally attached to the crown of France.

Patricians dominated the towns of the Netherlands from the middle of the twelfth century until the end of the thirteenth. During the fourteenth century weavers and fullers attempted to take power, especially in the Flemish centers of the textile industry, but ending the political monopoly hitherto enjoyed by their masters did not render them less dependent on the merchant-clothiers for employment. The revolutionary dictatorships gave way to regimes that included representatives of the merchants and of the lesser crafts.

In Ghent, alongside the *poorters* (burghers) fifty-nine (later fifty-three) guilds were represented. In Brussels, the capital of Brabant, the magistracy was composed of a first burgomaster and the *échevins* (magistrates) representing the seven *lignages* (aristocratic clans) plus an underburgomaster and six councilors chosen from a list drawn up by the nine *nations* (groups of the forty-nine guilds). But such urban constitutions, typical of Flanders and Brabant, were quite different from those found in the northern provinces. In Holland and Zealand, the magistracy was composed of a *vroedschap* or *raad* (council) and burgomasters were always chosen from among the city's wealthiest citizens by the *stadhouder* (governor) of the province from a list drawn up by the incumbents.

In Flanders, the towns of Ghent, Bruges, and Ypres presumed to represent the whole county and, calling themselves the three members (*leden*) of Flanders, arrogated to themselves, from the mid-fourteenth century onward, the authority elsewhere accorded to the three estates. The three towns pursued protectionist policies that subjected the inhabitants of surrounding small towns and the peasants of the countryside to the domination of the metropolis. After 1385 a fourth member was added from the territorial conscription called the Franc de Bruges. When Flanders came into the possession of Philip le Hardi (1342–1404), duke of Burgundy, representatives of the clergy and the nobility were added, and such assemblies were called *Staten* (*États* or Estates). Flanders was the extreme case, but in the rest of the Netherlands, too, the third estate, though the least in social rank, came to eclipse the upper two estates by virtue of economic power. The ruler of the land, such as the count of Holland or the duke of Brabant, had to permit the chief towns to be represented in the Estates and to respond to their grievances in return for the revenues they could supply.

The Netherlands under the Dukes of Burgundy and the Habsburgs. The duchy of Burgundy was part of the French realm, but its dukes added most of the Low Countries to their possessions during the second half of the fifteenth century, creating a state between Germany and France that was often in contention with France. To obtain the revenues required by their foreign policy, the dukes would convene the three estates of the provinces separately and often together as the Estates General of the Netherlands. At such assemblies the deputies of the provincial Estates would hear the propositions of their sovereign but then return to their constituents to obtain authorization to consent. A new tax required the consent of all provinces, which therefore voted in the Estates General by province rather than by head. Within each province, the veto of one of the three estates, or even of a single member of a single commune, could prevent the central government from raising new taxes.

This was the system that confronted the Habsburgs when they came to rule the Netherlands in the sixteenth century. Charles I (later the emperor Charles V) was born in Ghent and during his reign as king of Spain (1516–1556) was generally able to gain the support of the Estates. When challenged by the revolt of 1540 in Ghent, however, he abolished its liberties and privileges. Under his son Philip, who was brought up in Spain, a fundamental contention developed between the crown and the Estates General. The cost of war with France led Philip to ask extra taxes of his Netherlandish subjects. To cope with religious dissent and the political opposition in the Estates, Philip in 1567 sent the duke of Alva at the head of a Spanish army into the Netherlands to restore order and reestablish royal authority. For a time the duke was successful, but the period of absolutism was short-lived. In 1572 William of Orange and his followers seized the provinces of Holland and Zealand and summoned their Estates to serve as the basis of a government that defied Spanish control. In 1576 revolutions in the southern provinces of Brabant and Flanders led to a convocation of the Estates General of all the Low Countries, and for a time the government of the whole country was in their hands. This failed when the southern provinces were reconciled with the king of Spain on the promise that the privileges of their Estates would be respected.

The seven provinces north of the Rhine and Meuse Rivers, each governed by its own provincial estates, sent delegates to the Estates General, which served as the governing body of an independent republic that lasted until the French Revolution. During that period, except for a "republican" interlude (1650–1672), the executive power was actually exercised by successive rulers of the House of Orange.

The Iberian Peninsula. By the close of the fifteenth century the Iberian Peninsula consisted of three principal kingdoms: Castile, with 65 percent of the area and 73 percent of the population, Portugal, and Aragon. Cortes were present in each but with very unequal powers. The Cortes of Castile suffered from several weaknesses. Though originally composed of the usual three orders, after 1480 it was rare for the clergy or the nobility to attend, as they were exempt from taxation and lacked the motive of the third estate, which was left to confront the crown alone. The Cortes therefore consisted of thirty-six *procuradores,* two from each of the eighteen towns entitled to representation. They were originally elected by a general assembly (*concejo*) of the heads of families, but already in the fourteenth century most of the powers of the *concejo* had been transferred to *regidores* appointed by the crown. The crown's power over the towns was strengthened under Isabella (ruled 1474–1504) by the appointment of *corregidores.*

Royal electoral mandates required the *regidores* to make sure suitable *procuradores* were elected with "sufficient and complete" powers. The mandate made residents of the city as good as present themselves in the Cortes. *Procuradores* who arrived with defective powers could not sit as representatives because they lacked the legal powers to vote taxes and otherwise act on behalf of their constituents. But despite all attempts of the crown to guarantee their complaisance, there were disputes over the powers of the *procuradores* throughout the sixteenth century. Cortes after Cortes proclaimed the principle that no aid should be voted until after the crown had responded to their grievances, only in the end to back down. Nevertheless, Castilian codes of law embodied many provisions that had originally been demanded by the Cortes.

Yet their power of the purse was limited, as the crown had sources of revenue immune to their control. No one was exempt from the *alcabala* (a sales tax), for example, but it incurred less protest because it was paid by the vendor. A large share of American silver was reserved for the crown as well. According to some historians, the Cortes temporarily gained an effective power of the purse under Philip III (1598–1621). This power lay in the *millones,* a subsidy—not a tax—granted for limited periods of time and for specific amounts of money (expressed in millions of ducats). From 1601 onward, this subsidy was resorted to regularly. Revisionist historians claim that political power was thus shifted from the crown to the Cortes and the cities, but this radical reinterpretation of Castilian constitutional history has been challenged by those who argue that the alleged gains were either only partial and provisional or nonexistent. In any case, Philip IV and Gaspar de Guzmán y Pimental, the count of Olivares, broke the power of the Cortes in 1632.

The king of Aragon ruled over three realms—Aragon proper, Valencia, and the principality of Catalonia—with a separate Cortes in each. In the Cortes the nobles of Aragon were divided into two members, one for the higher nobility and one for the *infanzones* (lower nobility). Unanimity was required in each of the four members. In Catalonia the Cortes had rigid control over legislation. A standing committee, called the Diputacio, controlled all taxation and also guarded the principality's liberties against the crown. This control was not quite as rigid in Aragon proper or in Valencia, but the sharp contrast was with Castile and Portugal. It is noteworthy that the Aragonese established parliamentary institutions in their Mediterranean possessions (Sicily, Sardinia, and Naples), whereas the Castilians chose not to export such institutions to the Americas. In the crisis of 1626 the Cortes of Aragon and Valencia voted subsidies but refused to supply troops, while Catalonia refused both. Resistance there led to the revolution that broke out in 1640 under the leadership of the Diputacio. But while the Portuguese revolution of 1640 was successful, the Catalans' was crushed.

France. French kings began to summon representatives of towns to join with members of the clergy and nobility early in the fourteenth century.

The three estates might represent a province or a region. Estates General met frequently in the fifteenth century. Deputies to the Estates General had no power to vote taxes but could recommend them to the provincial Estates that had elected them.

Between 1484 and 1560 there were no assemblies of the Estates General (though the king did consult other bodies), and their absence has led some historians to say that this was the beginning of French absolutism and somehow connected with the Renaissance. But without consulting Estates, Francis I (1515–1547) was unable to levy taxes except in the central generalities of Langue d'Oïl and Outre-Seine; elsewhere, and especially in the peripheral provinces of Normandy, Brittany, Languedoc, Dauphiné, Burgundy, and Provence, he had to ask the consent of the provincial Estates, who could therefore bargain for the satisfaction of their grievances. Their assent was also required to ratify treaties.

The Estates, however, represented not the general population but only its privileged members. In most of the Provincial Estates, the third estate was outvoted by the two higher estates. The exception was Normandy, where the three orders sat together and voted by local district (*baillage*) instead of by order, thus giving the third estate a majority. In Normandy representatives of the countryside were also included in the third estate, but elsewhere in France, as in Europe generally, the countryside went unrepresented except by the nobility. Within the third estate only designated towns had the privilege of representation. Here the deputies were generally elected by a town council, which represented established interests, not the whole resident population.

Francis I was succeeded by Henry II (ruled 1547–1559), who died leaving three minor sons. The monarchy was thus weak for the ensuing thirty years. The followers of Calvin attained considerable influence in the Estates General of 1560 but never again. However, their hopes of making profitable use of the Estates were nurtured at the provincial level by their success in Languedoc, where their forces predominated in the eastern half of the province. Their Estates professed to be the legitimate representatives of the province, though they were countered by Catholic Estates in Toulouse.

In 1574 the Estates representing Calvinist areas met at Millau and asked the king to convene an assembly of the Estates, both general and provincial, where both Catholics and Calvinists could present their respective grievances, but nothing came of this. Instead the Estates came increasingly under the domination of their adversaries organized in the Catholic League. At the Estates General of 1588 the king embraced the League and issued an Edict of Union calling for permanent war on the Calvinists. This persuaded not only the victims but also the Politiques (a party of moderate Catholics), who put the State above religious affiliation, to despair of the Estates. Politique support went to Henry of Navarre, the Calvinist leader, when he became heir to the throne, and he made it easier for the Politiques by accepting conversion to Catholicism. Henry's original Calvinist supporters, represented through their own assemblies, negotiated with him to protect their cause and finally in 1598 reached a successful conclusion embodied in the Edict of Nantes. This edict of relative religious toleration rested, however, on the will of the monarch rather than on any Estates General. There was no assembly of the Estates General after 1615 until 1789. Cardinal Richelieu was only partly successful in his efforts to destroy the provincial Estates, and Louis XIV completed the structure of absolutism.

England. The English Parliament is bicameral, with the Lords Spiritual and Temporal sitting together in the House of Lords. The House of Commons was made up of two knights elected in each county and two burghers chosen by the council of each borough enjoying the privilege of representation. By the sixteenth century at least, it became customary for the boroughs to choose as their representative a knight rather than a burgher, which resulted in the House of Commons being transformed into a gentlemen's club.

Between the accession of Henry VII in 1485 and the convening of the Parliament in 1529 by Henry VIII, there were only twenty sessions, but the Parliament summoned in 1529 sat for five years and was the major instrument in Henry's Reformation. To sever relations with Rome and to carry out the reformation of the Church of England, including the dissolution of the monasteries, the government required the support of Parliament. Likewise Elizabeth I made use of Parliament to lay the permanent foundations of the Church of England, though in her later years the demands of the Puritans for further reform caused her displeasure.

Under the Stuarts, however, contentions between king and Parliament—over religion, taxation, and the administration of justice—led, after the failure of Charles I to rule as an absolute monarch without summoning Parliament (1629–1640), to civil war, the execution of the king (1649), and the short-lived experiment with republican government. The Levelers and their supporters in Oliver Cromwell's army advocated universal male suffrage, but they were suppressed by Cromwell, and reform of the Parliament to achieve democratic representation was postponed to the nineteenth century.

Denmark. In fourteenth- and fifteenth-century Denmark an annual assembly of nobles and clergy (Danehof) forced the king into concessions, including the provision that he would rule in concert with them. The monarchy grew further isolated, so that in 1468 the king attempted to counteract the nobility by sanctioning representation for commoners. Thus a new diet, the Rigsdag, took the place of the Danehof. The new body was made up of delegates from four estates: the clergy, nobles, burghers, and free peasants. The diet's wide-ranging powers prevented the king from waging war or generating new taxes without its approval. The peasants' representatives kept their place in the Rigsdag until the end of the sixteenth century, when they were subjected to serfdom.

Sweden. In Sweden, too, delegates of commoners came to have a place in the deliberations of councils. In the first half of the fifteenth century, great assemblies were called by leaders of a Swedish rebellion, who wanted widespread support for independence from the monarchical Scandinavian union. Representatives of town burghers, miners, and free peasants joined the land's nobles and high clergy in a parliamentary setting. After a 1471 victory against the union, the Swedish regent frequently summoned this diet, which continued to seat burghers and peasants. The sixteenth-century Swedish king Gustavus Vasa, himself elected by the Diet, extended this legacy. In 1527 Gustavus called on the parliament to accept the tenets of the Reformation in Sweden. The assembly is usually referred to as the Riksdag, although this term was not used for meetings until the 1560s.

Switzerland. By 1513 the Swiss Confederation (Bund) consisted of seven city-states and six rural cantons that existed autonomously from any overlord other than the Holy Roman Emperor. As the confederation expanded, its more rural cantons featured general assemblies of peasant citizens. Town cantons had their own assemblies of burghers with an elected executive. A statewide diet (Bundestag) seated delegates from the cantons, and its decisions over war and finance had to be unanimous. Though some town assemblies symbolically included all male citizens, the more powerful councils were elected from members of each city's elite. Even the guilds, which gained the privilege of selecting a number of council members during the fourteenth century, sent their wealthiest and most powerful members as representatives, so that the magistracy remained in the hands of a wealthy few. Council members had authority over citizens and territorial subjects, but their power did not always go unchallenged. The perception of lost freedoms and privileges did impel revolts by peasants or guilds, such as the peasant revolt in 1653 in the cities of Lucerne and Bern. This oligarchical representation survived internal religious disputes and threats to its autonomy from the dukes of Burgundy and the Habsburgs and continued until the eighteenth century.

The German Principalities. Among the diverse entities of the German-speaking world there was a variety in the character of representative institutions and in who attended them. The clergy usually formed the first estate. However, they did not attend the diet (Landtag) in some places, such as the duchies on the lower Rhine, and in many cases only the two other estates, the nobility and the towns, met in the diets. In areas such as Baden, Württemberg, the Palatinate, Bamberg, and Trier, however, the nobility in the early sixteenth century gained the status of free imperial knights (*Reichsritter*); they disdained to answer the local prince's summons to attend the Landtag and left this assembly to the clergy and towns. To display their independence vis-à-vis the prince, the knights chose to appear only at the imperial Reichstag. The German peasants did not have direct representation in a Landtag, except in a few areas where the peasantry had won some economic independence. This was the case for certain frontier areas near Switzerland, the margravate of Baden, and the counties of Frisia and Mörs on the North Sea.

Many Germanic towns attained a high degree of self-government. Like their Italian counterparts, they profited from the weakness of imperial or other authority. Towns originally dominated by patricians experienced revolutions that resulted in regimes that have been called popular or democratic; however, these regimes represented the guilds rather than individuals. The representation of a particular guild depended on its economic power, but this varied from town to town, and no two towns exhibited the same balance of economic interests. Moreover, the relative importance of a particular guild varied over time, and such a shift in the balance of economic power produced perennial demands, often accompanied by violence, for modifications of the constitution to reflect the new economic reality.

Most German towns were subject to a territorial prince, but some towns were powerful enough to gain the status of "imperial cities," independent of any superior but the emperor. The all-important matter of finance controlled the balance of power between the estates and the local ruler. In Bavaria, for instance, the prince sometimes raised enough revenues on his own, undercutting the main function of a gathering of the Estates so that he could rule without them. In some cases a prince was able to establish a permanent tax. Because the Estates then were not needed to vote for a new tax, their privileges declined. However, in places such as Württemberg taxes were levied only for a limited period and were administered by the Estates, so that their privileges remained.

The Estates not only raised new funds; often they provided the control and administration of these moneys. They gathered the money and maintained records, fulfilling the functions of a state bureaucracy that did not yet exist. This situation helped strengthen the Estates during the fourteenth and fifteenth centuries.

The religious factor increased the power of the Estates in Protestant areas during the sixteenth century. In fact, the Estates became dominant in the secularized duchy of Prussia. Princes took over monasteries and other church holdings only in consultation with the diets and usually had to sell them quickly. The Estates gained new privileges and influence in religious matters and became the champions of orthodox Lutheranism. On the other hand, the enduring Catholic status of Bavaria served to keep the prince strong and erode the power of the Estates there as the sixteenth century progressed.

Eastern Europe. The predominance of the nobility and weakness of the towns in the parliaments of eastern Europe have in broad terms been explained as reflections of the division of labor that set Europe east and west of the Elbe on opposite but complementary courses from the beginning of the sixteenth century. In exchange for the manufactured products of the west, landlords in the east turned to the production of grain for export from their extensive estates. To secure the necessary labor, they resorted to serfdom with the support of the state. The towns built by German-speaking immigrants were islands in this Slavic sea and unable to compete with the imported products from the west.

Bohemia. Diets in the Bohemian Crown Lands (Bohemia proper, Moravia, Silesia, Upper and Lower Lusatia) consisted of the high clergy, higher and lesser nobility (knights), and royal townsmen. The General Diet (*Sněm*) was composed either of delegations from each Land or of the entire Bohemian Diet together with elected representatives from the other Lands. The General Diet had the power to approve taxes and raise armies. It guarded the prerogatives of the nobility, for example, by preventing the codification of the law proposed by the emperor Charles IV (ruled 1346–1378).

The composition of the diets was transformed by the turmoil of the Hussite wars (1420–1436). In the Bohemian Diet the clergy lost their representation. They retained it in Moravia and the other Lands but were lumped together for voting purposes with the representatives of the towns.

The Bohemian Diet's ratification was required for important treaties and for the reception of a new king. The kingdom of Bohemia was governed by an executive council of the Diet from 1419 to 1436, when the Hussites prevented a Roman Catholic from taking the throne.

The upper nobility had to attend the Diet in person but knights sent representatives. The knights gathered in district congresses (*sjezdy*) to elect six of their number as delegates to the Diet. Meeting regularly in the fifteenth century, these congresses also drafted proposals for the Diet and executed its decrees. In the sixteenth century, however, the Habsburg emperor restricted the *sjezdy* and thus the power of the lesser nobility. Representatives of the royal free towns were elected in town councils dominated by patrician families. Assemblies of all the burghers could be held only with royal permission under the Habsburgs.

Hungary. From 1445 on, the Diet in Hungary met at least once a year. It was eventually composed of two houses; the upper was made up of the great landowners (magnates) and high clergy, the lower of representatives of the very numerous lesser nobility. The latter were elected in county assemblies, where votes were weighted by property. Delegates of the free royal towns also sat in the lower house, but with only one vote among them. Their influence was further limited by the fact that business was conducted in Magyar, whereas most townsmen were German-speaking.

The consent of the Diet was required for legislation or the imposition of new taxes, but the Diet was not involved in administration. Treaties altering the country's borders required ratification by the Diet. At the death of the king, the Diet had the power to confirm his successor.

Croatia. The Croatians, linked with Hungary and subjects of the Hungarian king until 1526, retained their *Sabor,* traditionally dominated by upper nobles and church officials. The *Sabor* certified tenure of a new king and established laws for Croatian territory. Most of Croatia was taken by the Turks in 1526; the remaining part accepted Habsburg rule in 1527.

Poland. The Diet (*Sejm*) in Poland was composed of magnates and lesser nobility (*szlachta*), bishops and lesser clergy, and officials of noble birth, such as governors (*voivodes*). By the end of the fifteenth century, the *Sejm* met in two houses: the upper, or Senate, for bishops, magnates, and governors; and the lower, or Chamber of Deputies, for representatives of the lesser nobility, who were elected in provincial diets, and for representatives of some towns, but these members had been deprived of the power to vote. The *Sejm* also acted as a supreme court, empowered to examine allegations of wrongdoing on the part of the king or his officials and to demand redress. In 1505 the statute *Nihil Novi* was enacted, requiring the Diet's consent for the enforcement of new legislation.

The Jewish community, large in many Polish towns in the sixteenth century, obtained a charter from the king in 1551. This granted representation at the local level in the *kahal,* whose members were elected annually and which collected taxes, operated schools, and exercised local self-government in general.

After the 1569 formal union of Poland and Lithuania, the kingdom developed into a parliamentary monarchy. The nobility governed the state almost entirely on its own, and laws could be made only by the *Sejm*.

Walachia and Moldavia. The diets in the Romanian principalities of Walachia and Moldavia closely resembled institutions in other parts of Europe. During the Renaissance period the Walachian state at times fell under Ottoman rule or allied itself with Hungary to resist the Turks. A considerable Hungarian influence was manifested in a rather powerful diet (*Sobor*) that demanded privileges for the nobility and the clergy. A council of bovars (barons) also existed. The diet in Moldavia sometimes adopted the Polish designation *Sejm,* as Moldavia looked to Poland (as well as to Hungary) for support against the Ottomans. As this assembly sanctioned the rule of some princes and undermined others, it secured benefits for nobles and clergy, the estates that it represented.

Russia. The tsar of Russia from time to time summoned church and lay officials during the sixteenth century to give him military and economic advice and support. These assemblies (*Zemski Sobor*) sometimes included merchants involved in matters of state finance. Upon the death of the last member of the dynasty, it fell to the patriarch of the Russian Orthodox Church to summon a *sobor* to elect a new tsar. Representatives of merchants and peasants were invited to take part, as they did for the years immediately following the election.

Inherited from the Middle Ages, subjected to increasing pressure from monarchs, and in many cases losing authority, representative institutions nevertheless endured through the Renaissance period to bequeath their legacy of representative principles to following centuries.

See also **City-State.**

BIBLIOGRAPHY

Primary Works

Kossmann, E. H., and Albert Fredrik Mellink. *Texts Concerning the Revolt of the Netherlands.* Cambridge, U.K., 1974.

Rowen, Herbert Harvey, comp. *The Low Countries in Early Modern Times: A Documentary History.* New York, 1972.

General Secondary Works

Griffeth, Robert, and Carol G. Thomas. *The City-State in Five Cultures.* Santa Barbara, Calif., 1981. See chapter 3, "The Italian City-State," by Gordon G. Griffiths, and chapter 4, "The Swiss and German City-States," by Christopher R. Friedrichs.

Griffiths, Gordon. "Humanists and Representative Government in the Sixteenth Century: Bodin, Marnix, and the Invitation to the Duke of Anjou to Become Ruler of the Low Countries." In *Representative Institutions in Theory and Practice.* Brussels, Belgium, 1970. Pages 59–83.

Griffiths, Gordon. *Representative Government in Western Europe in the Sixteenth Century.* Oxford, 1968.

Koenigsberger, H. G. *Estates and Revolutions: Essays in Early Modern European History.* Ithaca, N.Y., 1971.

Myers, A. R. *Parliaments and Estates in Europe to 1789.* London, 1975.

Parliaments, Estates, and Representation. London, 1981–. Journal of the International Commission for the History of Representative and Parliamentary Institutions.

England

Elton, G. R. *The Tudor Constitution.* Cambridge, U.K., 1960.

Neale, Sir J. E. *The Elizabethan House of Commons.* London, 1949.

France

Doucet, Roger. *Les institutions de la France au XVIe siècle.* 2 vols. Paris, 1948.

Griffiths, Gordon. "Estates and Revolution among the Huguenots." In *Studies Presented to the International Commission*

for the History of Representative and Parliamentary Institutions. Warsaw and Moscow, 1975.
Major, J. Russell. *The Deputies to the Estates General in Renaissance France.* Madison, Wis., 1960. Included in *Studies Presented,* vol. 21.
Major, J. Russell. *Representative Institutions in Renaissance France, 1421–1559.* Madison, Wis., 1960. Included in *Studies Presented,* vol. 22.
Prentout, Henri. *Les états provinciaux de Normandie.* Vol. 2, *Organisation et compétence.* Caen, France, 1925. See appendix: "Essai d'histoire comparée: Les États Provinciaux de la région française."

Germany and the Holy Roman Empire
Barraclough, Geoffrey. *The Origins of Modern Germany.* New York, 1984.
Carsten, F. L. *Princes and Parliaments in Germany, from the Fifteenth to the Eighteenth Century.* Oxford, 1959.
Dillon, Kenneth J. *King and Estates in the Bohemian Lands, 1526–1564.* Brussels, Belgium, 1976. Included in *Studies Presented,* vol. 57.

The Netherlands
Geyl, Pieter. *The Revolt of the Netherlands, 1555–1609.* London, 1932.
Gilissen, John. *Le régime représentatif avant 1790 en Belgique.* Brussels, Belgium, 1952.
Juste, Theodore. *Histoire des États Généraux des Pays-Bas, 1465–1790.* Brussels, Belgium, 1864.

Poland
Miller, James. "The Polish Nobility and the Renaissance Monarchy: The 'Execution of the Laws' Movement: Part Two." *Parliaments, Estates, and Representation* 4 (June 1984): 1–24.

Spain
Elliott, John Huxtable. *Imperial Spain, 1469–1716.* London, 1963.
Ladero Quesada, Miguel-Angel. "Les Cortes de Castille et la politique financière de la monarchie, 1252–1369." *Parliaments, Estates, and Representation* 4 (December 1984): 107–124.
Lynch, John. *Spain under the Habsburgs.* 2 vols. Oxford, 1964.

Sweden
Metcalf, Michael F., and Herman Schuck, eds. *The Riksdag: A History of the Swedish Parliament.* New York, 1987.

GORDON GRIFFITHS

REPUBLICANISM. In politics and political thought, Italy in the late Middle Ages and the Renaissance shared with other areas of Europe the growing concern with the constitutional nature of government and notions of consent, representation, and the common good. But two distinctive features of Italian politics and culture—the number and strength of the independent city-states and the prominence of the classical tradition and the memory of Rome—resulted in a vigorous republicanism that is the essential link between the republics of antiquity and those of the modern age.

The origins of Renaissance republicanism lie in the medieval communes—self-governing associations of citizens that were increasingly disinclined to recognize any superior authority. The efforts to conceptualize and defend the philosophical and legal foundations of these governments led political theorists back to Roman law and ancient political thought. Only with the growth of humanism and the cult of antiquity in the fourteenth and fifteenth centuries did it become fashionable to refer to the city-states and their Renaissance successors as republics, but the fundamental institutions and attitudes that underlay Renaissance republicanism first emerged in the medieval communes.

The Communes. Between the eleventh and thirteenth centuries the economic growth of Italy and the long conflict between the papacy and the Holy Roman Empire created the conditions in which scores of north and central Italian cities freed themselves from imperial, episcopal, and other forms of overlordship and declared the institution of a commune—a sworn association of citizens (usually from the wealthy and military classes) that gradually absorbed the administrative and jurisdictional functions formerly belonging either to the bishops or to the counts who had represented imperial authority.

Two basic institutions defined the early communes: an executive committee of consuls elected for limited terms of office and the larger deliberative councils or assemblies that the consuls were expected to consult. These acquired the power to approve laws, which were soon gathered into compilations of statutes to which all citizens, including the consuls, were bound. Short terms of office allowed for the participation, over several years, of hundreds—and, in larger communes like Venice, Padua, Milan, Genoa, Siena, and Florence, perhaps thousands—of citizens in one office or another.

In legal terms communes defined themselves as a species of *universitas,* the term used by medieval lawyers for associations, or corporations, created by the mutual oaths of their members and endowed with jurisdiction over the members and the legal authority to represent them. The notion of representation permitted a minority of members organized in the council or assembly to make decisions on behalf of the full body. The principle by which a council could "represent the mind of the people," as the jurist Bartolus of Sassoferrato (1314–1357) put it in the fourteenth century, made it possible for the communes to claim the consent of the people as the foundation of their legitimacy without the necessity of having to consult all citizens on every decision.

The emergence of republican thought in the second half of the thirteenth century involved two distinct although sometimes overlapping currents: the growth of interest in the history of the Roman republic, especially through Cicero and Sallust, and the development of constitutionalist theory stimulated by the Latin translation of Aristotle's *Politics* in the 1260s. The authors of thirteenth-century treatises on rhetoric and instructional manuals for city magistrates defined the ideals and objectives of the communes in Ciceronian and Roman republican terms: justice, the common good, civic peace, the equality of citizens before the law, and the willingness of magistrates to "render to each person his due," which was the definition of justice in Roman law. Brunetto Latini (c. 1220–1295), chancellor of Florence during the city's first popular government from 1250 to 1260, argued in his *Tresor* (Book of the treasure) that of the three kinds of government, "that of kings, of the best men, and of the communes," the last is by far the best because it is elected and advised by the citizens themselves, adheres strictly to the communal statutes, and must never fail to embrace justice and the common good.

The impact of Aristotle's *Politics* led to a more analytical approach to the different kinds of government and modes of rule. Particularly influential was his distinction between the "regal" or unlimited rule of one man over a free people (and its "despotic" variant of one-man rule over an unfree people) and the "political" rule exercised among a free people by citizens who assume and relinquish office by turns. It was through Thomas Aquinas (1225?–1274) and the other commentators on Aristotle that the term *politicus* entered Italian and European thought as a way of talking about governments limited by law, dedicated to the common good, and characterized by alternation of office among citizens.

The most original of those who applied this language to the Italian communes was Ptolemy of Lucca (c. 1236–1327), who completed Thomas's *De regimine principum* (On the government of rulers) possibly around 1300, and redirected its argument to a fully elaborated republicanism that rejected regal rule as in essence always despotic. Governance "according to the statutes" was the essence of political rule for Ptolemy: "Political rectors are bound by laws, nor can they proceed beyond them in the pursuit of justice." Ptolemy's analysis of political rule as the expression of the collective virtue of a people, his praise of the ancient Roman republic as the ideal model for such rule, and his condemnation of Caesar as the one who "converted a polity into a despotic or tyrannical rule" mark the real beginning of Renaissance republican thought.

Guild Republicanism. At different times in different places, most communes underwent the revolution of the *popolo*—the rise to power of coalitions of nonelite merchants, notaries, artisans, and shopkeepers organized in guilds and federations of guilds. Guilds too were formal corporations, or *universitates,* which exercised jurisdiction over their members and held them accountable to standards of professional conduct and to the fulfillment of their contractual obligations. Like the communes, guilds also developed a constitutional structure of elected executive consuls and legislative councils, whose powers were defined and limited by written statutes. With the thirteenth century rise in population, expansion of the urban economies, and increasing specialization of mercantile and artisanal activities, guilds grew enormously in both number and size. In dozens of cities this grassroots republicanism gave expression to the collective identities and interests of thousands of persons who had had no part to play in the original communes dominated by the social elites. The phenomenon of the *popolo* significantly recast communal politics in dozens of cities, including Padua, Piacenza, Bergamo, Genoa, Bologna, Pistoia, Lucca, Florence, Siena, and Perugia.

Guilds organized in alliances and petitioned the communes for the representation of their interests and some role in government. In at least three of the largest communes—Bologna, Padua, and Florence—they periodically assumed control of the government. In Florence coalitions of guilds succeeded in creating popular governments on three occasions: 1292–1295, when a federation of twenty-one guilds promulgated the *Ordinamenta iustitie* (Ordinances of justice) and excluded seventy-two upper-class families, designated as magnates, from communal and guild offices; 1343–1348, when it was openly asserted that the "Florentine *respublica* is ruled and governed by the guilds and guildsmen" of the city; and 1378–1382, when a resurgence of guild republicanism inspired the unincorporated working classes to demand guilds of their own and a share of communal offices as members of the guild federation. The brief government of the summer of 1378, created by the demands of the Ciompi for three new guilds of workers, was no doubt the most democratic moment in the history of Renaissance republicanism.

Guild republicanism found theoretical underpinnings in Roman law, particularly in the dictum "that which touches all must be approved by all" (*quod omnes tangit debet ab omnibus approbari*), which was echoed in the Florentine *Ordinances* of 1293. The *Ordinances* justified the new political role assigned to the guilds by declaring that "that is judged most perfect which consists of all its parts"—the guilds being the parts of the whole—"and which is approved by the judgment of them all." Implicitly, this asserted a theory of the consent and representation of a multiplicity of autonomous interests and voices within the commune.

The greatest theorist of popular republicanism, and indeed the most important political thinker of the Renaissance before Machiavelli, was Marsilius of Padua (c. 1275–1342), whose *Defensor pacis* (Defender of peace; completed in 1324) argues for a popular sovereignty built on the distinction between the people as the sovereign legislator and the government, or "ruling part," which (whether one person or many) must be subordinate to the laws approved by the legislator. Marsilius's idea of the state recalls the guild republics of his time in the notion that the most "perfect" and advanced political communities are those that exhibit the highest degree of differentiation among the "artes" (skills, but also guilds) and the "parts" of the state (1.3–4), which he identifies as the agricultural, artisan, military, financial, priestly, and judicial, deliberative, or ruling part (1.5). The necessary distinction and ordering of the parts is the work of the legislator, which makes the laws and regulates all the parts.

For Marsilius "well-tempered" governments rule by the consent of voluntary subjects and for their common benefit. Thus "the elected kind of government is superior to the non-elected" (1.9). Consent and representation are at the heart of Marsilius's notion of the sovereign lawmaking power of the legislator, which he defines (1.12) as the "people or *universitas* of the citizens, or the weightier part thereof." The people is thus a corporation that can delegate its powers to representatives, and the "weightier part"—whether large or small—"represents [*repraesentat*] the whole *universitas*." Marsilius echoes the *popolo*'s recognition of the right of each guild to an autonomous representation of its interests by suggesting that each of the "primary parts of the state" may elect some of the men delegated to draft the laws (1.13). Paraphrasing *quod omnes tangit,* he insists that "those matters which can affect the benefit and harm of all must be known and heard by all" (1.12). Not to leave the final approval of the laws to the people, he says, would be to open the door to "oligarchy" or "tyranny" (1.13).

If this early republicanism succeeded in creating and theorizing a set of practices that brought the notions of consent and representation firmly into the political discourse of the city-states, it must nonetheless be recognized that one of its notable failures was the unwillingness of the city-republics to extend the concept of representation beyond the cities themselves to the surrounding territories. Hence the irony that Renaissance republics proclaimed and defended their own liberty while they treated the populations under their control as subjects to be ruled, an attitude that helps to explain why these territorial dominions so frequently broke apart during military crises.

Republicanism and Humanism. The Renaissance alliance of republicanism and humanism was adumbrated by the Paduan classical scholar and poet Albertino Mussato (1261–1329), who dramatized Padua's defense of its endangered liberty in the first secular tragedy since antiquity, *Ecerinis* (1315); and, two decades later, by Cola di Rienzo (1314–1354), the enthusiastic investigator of Roman antiquities who led a revolt against the city's baronial families and eventually declared the restoration of the republic against papal rule. Petrarch (Francesco Petrarca), who had praised the republic of Scipio's time in his *Africa,* celebrated the news of Cola's action by comparing his liberation of Rome to the heroic deeds of the two Brutuses, the one who freed Rome from its tyrant kings and established the republic, and the one who tried to save Roman liberty by assassinating Julius Caesar. Petrarch hailed Cola as Rome's third Brutus and urged the Roman people to emulate the many defenders of the ancient republic's liberty.

From 1375 to 1378 the Florentine republic found itself at war with the papacy and asked its newly appointed chancellor Coluccio Salutati (1331–1406), the most important of the scholars influenced by Petrarch, to defend the war in the court of Italian public opinion. In his public letters Salutati extolled republican liberty as the "mother of laws" and "teacher of virtues" and made it clear that the liberty he spoke of was found only in republics: "in a republic that flourishes with liberty, no one hesitates to show how much a virtuous man can do." He praised those "happy republics" ruled by "merchants and guildsmen who naturally love liberty, desire civic peace in which they can exercise their skills [*artes*], and love and promote equality among citizens," and "who in every popular republic strive after justice . . . and do not glory in dominating others. Taking turns, they command when they are called upon to fill public offices and willingly obey as private persons when others are in power."

Salutati's language mixes the Aristotelian concept of the alternation of citizens in office with the *popolo*'s conviction that liberty was guaranteed by the civic virtues of peace-loving guildsmen. By contrast, he argued, kings, no matter how just they may be, do not rule but only punish their subjects. Indeed, "anyone who thinks himself worthy of lordship is actually confessing himself guilty of great crimes." To all this Salutati added examples from ancient history and the claim that the Florentine defense of liberty was an inheritance from their Roman progenitors. His denunciation of monarchy, his idealization of the social and psychological foundations of republican liberty, and the link to antiquity became central features of the civic humanism of the next generation.

By the end of the fourteenth century, popular and guild republicanism was everywhere on the decline as elites and aristocracies regained control. North of the Appenines the aristocratic reaction against the *popolo* took the form of the so-called despotisms, and in the remaining republics a new oligarchical republicanism took hold. In both Venice and Florence power was broadly shared within the upper class, but entrance into this ruling class became far more difficult. In Florence the consolidation of oligarchy concentrated power in the hands of several score elite families while at the same time the size of the office-holding class actually expanded. The number of Florentines approved for the highest executive offices increased from between six and seven hundred in the 1380s and 1390s to over one thousand in 1411 and then to over two thousand in 1433.

Dependent on elite patronage and relegated to occasional participation in offices without the opportunity for any organized representation of their interests, the middle-class officeholders developed attitudes of deference and subservience to the "patrician" families and the government. Family metaphors began to dominate the political discourse of this patriarchal republicanism, in which the city was thought of as a family writ large and the ruling elite as benevolent fathers to the civic family. The assumption of consensus delegitimated opposition, dissent, or even any notion of divergent interests among the parts of the civic community. In this ideological construct, the unity of the republic and the loyalty of its citizens were ensured by bonds of duty and affection. Civic humanism was heavily conditioned by these attitudes.

The study of Florentine civic humanism has been dominated by the famous thesis of Hans Baron, who argued that a new ethic of republicanism, the active life, and patriotism emerged among both citizens and humanists as a consequence of the threat to Florentine liberty posed by the expansion of Milan's power into Tuscany by its duke, Giangaleazzo Visconti. According to Baron, Florence's escape from the threat of imminent invasion in 1402 had the effect of turning the attention of the humanists, in particular Leonardo Bruni (1369–1444), away from scholarly classicism to civic themes and a spirited defense of Florence's republican tradition.

Bruni extolled the Roman republican origins of the city, denounced the emperors as "plagues and destroyers of the Roman Republic," and lauded the Brutus who killed Caesar as a republican hero. The Florentines, Bruni claimed, were the sons and heirs of the Roman Republic, entrusted with a historical mission to defend the republican liberty once enjoyed by the Roman people. To their love of liberty Bruni attributed the Florentines' cultural and literary preeminence, arguing that the talents of citizens are stimulated by the chance to serve in public offices and that only in the active life of a free republic does the individual citizen gain identity and realize his human excellence. Bruni thus turned republican liberty into a cultural and moral ideal: the political participation that republics offered to citizens was a theater for the actualization of "virtue"; and the task of education and learning was to produce the good citizen who loved his republic and was ready to serve it in whatever role he was needed.

These ideas were widely shared within the Florentine political class, as is evident from the writings of the merchant Gregorio Dati (1362–1436), whose *Istoria di Firenze* (History of Florence from 1380 to 1406) presented the war against Visconti Milan as having been waged "for the liberty of Italy" against the "tyrant of Lombardy"; and from those of the merchant and humanist Matteo Palmieri (1406–1475), whose dialogues in *Vita civile* (On civic life; written in the 1430s) are a compendium of ancient sources and authorities adduced in support of the civic humanist ethic of good republican citizenship.

Most historians now concur that the idealized picture of Florentine politics and society found in the civic humanist texts does not accurately represent what we know of the political realities of the period and obscures the fact that Florence was an oligarchic republic in which all citizens did not enjoy equal access to office. But Bruni's purpose was not so much the accurate representation of Florentine politics as the promotion of attitudes of unity and consensus. His best-known short political writings—*Laudatio Florentinae urbis* (Panegyric of the city of Florence; 1403–1404), *Vita di Dante* (Life of Dante; 1436), and *Oratio in funere Nannis Strozae equitis Florentini* (Funeral oration for Nanni Strozzi; 1427–1428)—were widely read works of exhortation in which he sought to inculcate the values and assumptions central to the new configuration of Florentine domestic politics: the republic as a homogeneous family; the paternalistic benevolence of elite leadership; and the decorous conformity of the good citizen, eager to serve but completely loyal to the policies of his political betters. And in the monumental *Historiarum florentini populi libri XII* (Florentine histories; 1415–1444) Bruni recast the history of Florence to persuade his readers that Florentine unity and consensus had deep roots, that political opposition was always disloyal, and that protests from the lower classes were nothing more than the violence of the mob.

By the middle of the fifteenth century the realities of Medici control, and especially the decision by Cosimo de' Medici to abandon the anti-Milanese alliance between the sister republics of Florence and Venice and to align Florence with the new duke of Milan, Francesco Sforza, who had crushed the attempt of the Milanese people in 1447–1450 to restore republican government, seriously weakened the enthusiasm for republicanism. The Medici continued their formal respect for the republican framework of their unofficial rule, even as they were treated as quasi-princes by citizens and foreigners. It was in the occasional protests and opposition to the Medici from upper-class families who lamented their own political marginalization that republican ideas continued to find expression. In his 1479 dialogue *De libertate* (On liberty), Alamanno Rinuccini (1426–1499), once a member of the Medici circle, openly denounced the Medici as tyrants who had subverted republican institutions.

Revival and Demise of the Florentine Republic. Florentine civic and republican ideas reemerged suddenly and with great strength in 1494 when the French invasion of Italy resulted in the banishment of the Medici. For some time admiration of the Venetian constitution had been growing in Florence among the elite families, or *ottimati,* many of whom now urged the creation of an aristocratic regime modeled on Venice. But the charismatic Dominican preacher Girolamo Savonarola (1452–1498) persuaded the Florentines to emulate the Venetians in the most popular feature of their constitution, the Great Council. With his backing, the law of 23 December 1494 abolished the old legislative councils and created the Great Council as the republic's central legislative assembly with broad powers over elections and taxes. An astonishing total of over 3,200 citizens, including many from the middle classes, were eligible for membership. Although attendance eventually fell to manageable levels, the council was still a huge body that became and remained the heart of the restored republic.

In his many and impassioned sermons and in his 1498 *Trattato circa il reggimento e governo della città di Firenze* (Treatise on the constitution and government of the city of Florence), Savonarola exhorted the Florentines to protect their new constitution against the dangers of tyranny from both the exiled Medici and the hostile upper-class families. He argued that the particular character of the Florentines (their boldness, vitality, and intelligence) and their history of civic freedom made it impossible for them to live under any other but a "civil form of government." He preached the necessity of a constitution in which the "whole people," represented by the council, would control the distribution of offices. Perhaps his most significant contribution to Florentine republicanism was the prophetic and millenarian message of regeneration and reform of both society and church that he mixed with political liberty. He promised the Florentines that if they carried out these political reforms, their city would become a new Jerusalem and a "paradise on earth" of just power and wealth, political liberty, and "spiritual beatitude." Savonarola infused Florentine popular republicanism with an eschatological fervor that made the republic a vessel of Christian salvation—an ideology that reemerged with particular force in the last republic of 1527–1530.

The government inaugurated by Savonarola's reforms lasted until the return of the Medici in 1512, and it was in the next two decades that Florentines and Venetians brought republicanism to new levels of theoretical sophistication. In Florence republican thought now grappled with the question of why the republic of 1494 had failed, and whether, or when, the triumphant Medici would officially end the republic and institute a principate—which did in fact happen in 1530–1532. In these years there was an explosion of debate and writing on republics: their strengths and weaknesses, historical development, and social foundations. Republic and principate were now more than ever real and theoretical alternatives: *repubblica* came closer to its modern meaning of constitutional government in which the people is sovereign (whereas *respublica* had often meant "commonwealth" or the "common weal"), and *principato* moved away from the Latin *principatus* (which means preeminence, rule, or dominion) and came more often to designate a state in which sovereignty is vested in a single head. This linguistic clarification is immediately evident in the first sentence of Machiavelli's *Il principe* (1513; trans. *The Prince*), which proclaims that "all states and all dominions . . . have been or are either republics or principalities."

Machiavelli's chief contribution to republican thought is the *Discorsi sopra la prima deca di Tito Livio* (Discourses on Livy; 1515–1517). The originality of his analysis of republics lies above all in his emphasis on their social foundations. He argued that republics are incompatible with the presence in their midst of "lords and gentlemen" who "without working live in luxury on the returns from their landed possessions" and who "command castles and have subjects who obey them." Republics, he said, must rest on equality of legal status among citizens (1.55). Social conditions and class relationships largely determine what kind of political regime is feasible in a given territory.

Machiavelli took polemical aim at the prevailing admiration of Venice and stated his preference for ancient Rome as the model for modern republics, essentially because Rome granted the people, or plebs, both arms and a share of political power and thus laid the foundation for its victories and conquests. Venice, by contrast, was an unarmed republic that ensured its military weakness by excluding the people from both politics and the army and by concentrating political authority in a closed and hereditary upper class. His preference for Rome led Machiavelli to the claim that well-ordered republics allowed for competition and constitutionally channeled conflicts among social classes: in Rome the tumults between the nobility and the plebs, far from being a source of weakness, were actually the chief reason why Rome was both free and powerful. "All the laws made in favor of liberty resulted from . . . the discord" between the *grandi* and the *popolo* (1.4). This was an astonishing argument in its time. The weight of all conventional political wisdom was that republics needed above all peace and concord, and no one had ever asserted that social conflicts could actually be beneficial. For Machiavelli, dissent and disunion—expressed of course in public councils and forums, and not through factions and private armies—were necessary to a healthy and free republic.

Machiavelli's criticism of aristocracies and his preference for republics in which the people had a major political and military role was unacceptable to political thinkers from the upper class. His younger contemporary Francesco Guicciardini (1483–1540), diplomat, lawyer, historian, administrator of papal territories under the Medici, and member of an elite Florentine family, rejected the thesis concerning the beneficial effects of social conflict with the memorable quip in his *Considerazioni intorno ai Discorsi del Machiavelli* (Considerations on the *Discourses* of Machiavelli; 1529–1530) that "to praise these conflicts is akin to praising the illness of a sick man because of the effectiveness of the treatment given him." For Guicciardini, the prudence and skills necessary for governing a republic belonged to the aristocracy of great families who had long experience in such matters. But he also recognized that events had gone beyond the point where a purely aristocratic government on the Venetian model was possible in Florence. In the *Dialogo del reggimento di Firenze* (Dialogue on the government of Florence), written in the early 1520s, he acknowledged that the *ottimati* no longer had the political strength to rule on their own. They could only share power, either with the popular republicans or with the Medici, and the great question that he and his class faced—for as long as the choice was open to them—was that of deciding between these alternatives. While in his early works Guicciardini elaborated the possibilities for an alliance with the *popolo* that would have kept the republic alive and Medici dominance at bay, by the 1530s he and most of the *ottimati* realized that they could only survive in alliance with Medici supremacy.

The third party to this conflict of ideas and constitutional realities were the Mediceans—not the Medici themselves, who seem to have been uninterested in the theorizing that swirled around the facts of their power in Rome and Florence, but their advisers and supporters who wondered by what means the Florentines could be "weaned" from their stubborn republican sympathies. In 1516 Lodovico Alamanni, a Medici partisan, penned a memorandum recommending that the Medici forget about the older generation, whose attachment to republican customs was too deeply ingrained, and concentrate on the younger members of the great families. The prince should invite them one by one and promise to each the rank and privileges he merits. "As soon as they come into his service, he should make them remove their civic dress and accept courtly garments" and then enroll them into one or another form of courtly service. Thus "he will wean them from civic customs in such a way that those who for His Excellency's sake will put on capes and set aside their hoods, almost as if they were becoming monks, will be renouncing the republic and making a profession [of loyalty] to his order of things. . . . All their ambition will turn to winning the favor of His Excellency." The strategy of wooing the *ottimati* away from the republican *popolo* eventually succeeded in the 1530s as the elite families, frightened by the radicalism of the last republic, finally gave up their republicanism and became courtiers under a Medici duke.

The last major theorist of Florentine republicanism was Donato Giannotti (1492–1573), whose early work evinces admiration for the hierarchical structure of Venetian government. But with the reestablishment of the republic in Florence in 1527, Giannotti returned there and was soon appointed secretary to the Ten of War. Under the impact of the increasing radicalism of the last republic, he turned to a popular republicanism in which the militia emerged as the central element of good citizenship by making men equal and more disposed to accept and obey public authority. Such citizens would have to be accepted into the Great Council, and an armed people thus led inexorably to an expanding popular republic. In his most important work, *Della repubblica fiorentina* (The Florentine republic), written in the 1530s after the fall of the last republic, Giannotti hypothesized an Aristotelian mixed constitution apparently like that of Venice—Great Council, Senate, and executive committees culminating in a lifetime chief executive—except that he located ultimate sovereignty in the council. Like Venice, Giannotti's republic sought stability and tranquillity; but like Machiavelli's Rome, it did so through the participation of the people and the political role of the militia.

However, Giannotti was planning his new republic when the cold facts had moved beyond any possibility of its realization. The symbolic end of Florentine republicanism as a political movement is the story of Filippo Strozzi (1489–1538), a disaffected Medici in-law and former political adviser, who led a band of republicans into the hills to prepare an attack against Duke Cosimo in 1537. Captured and imprisoned, he took his own life in imitation of Cato the Younger and, in his own epitaph, asked the living to "shed copious tears if the Florentine Republic means anything at all to you."

The Myth of Venice. Venice's republican tradition was admired and praised from at least the early fourteenth century. In an early vision of the myth of Venice, Henry of Rimini (c. 1300) described the "polity of the Venetian people" as a mixed constitution and stressed the elective nature of the government, the alternation in office of citizens, and the Venetians' adherence to "their own statutes": they "are most faithful to the republic, which everyone strives to maintain in opulence and honor; but the republic also itself conserves and carefully preserves its citizens, even the plebeians, in great liberties and singular immunities." Benzo of Alessandria (c. 1320) praised Venice for its popular aspects when he wrote that "not the nobility, but the assent of all citizens, prevails."

In fact, Venetian republicanism around 1300 could be seen from either perspective. The power of the doges and the old popular general assembly had been displaced by the Great Council and its powerful inner body, the Senate. In the late thirteenth century, pressure from new families seeking membership in the Council resulted, in 1297, first in its expansion from about 400 to over 1,100 members (from 150 to 200 families), and then in the "Closing" (*Serrata*), which made the admission of new members very difficult and rare. Thus the membership of the enlarged council became permanent and hereditary. The jurist Bartolus in his *Tractatus de regimine civitatis* commented that Venice "is said to be ruled by a few, but I say that they are few with respect to the whole population of the city, but many when compared with other cities; and because they are many, the multitude does not resent being governed by them."

Despite the admission of thirty new families in 1381 (the last additions until the seventeenth century) and the growth of the Council to 2,600 members by the early sixteenth century, the much smaller Senate became the real center of power. By 1400 the aristocratic nature of Venetian republicanism was generally recognized by, among others, the Capodistrian humanist Pier Paolo Vergerio (1370–1444) who commented (in his *De republica veneta;* c. 1400) that "the power of both the Council and the whole city resides in the Senate."

In the fifteenth century, Venetian republican thought came more fully under the influence of humanists, who, like their Florentine counterparts, were interested less in constitutional analysis and more in the republic as a locus of virtue. In *De praestantia Venetae politiae* (On the excellence of the Venetian polity; 1463) the nonnoble Giovanni Caldiera (c. 1400–1474) defined virtue as devotion to the republic: mutual faith among citizens "renders the republic immortal." He juxtaposed republic and family and saw patriarchal authority in both spheres as justified by the same principles of natural hierarchy. George of Trebizond (1395–1484) and Marcantonio Sabellico (1436–1506) praised Venice for having achieved the perfect republic as defined by Plato and for having ensured the "eternal concord of the social orders." Sabellico and Francesco Negri (1452–1523) in his *De aristocratia* (On aristocracy; 1493–1495) particularly lauded the aristocratic character of Venetian government.

Within the nobility as well there was much self-congratulation for the republic's social harmony and benevolent leadership, especially once Venice began to be feared and resented in the rest of Italy because of its expansion onto the mainland. Paolo Morosini (1406–1482) defended the nobility's innate virtues—devotion to liberty, peace, and law—and the republican constitution that in his view blunted personal ambition. Lauro Quirini (c. 1420–c. 1475) affirmed the legitimacy of aristocratic government in *De republica* (On the republic; c. 1449–1450) by arguing that since both monarchy and the "mutable vulgar souls" of the people are prone to corruption, only those whose aim is honor and glory are fit to rule. Like the Florentine civic humanists, Quirini advocated the "studies of humanity"—chiefly history and moral philosophy—in the education of the nobility and measured Venetian excellence against the Roman model. At the end of the century Domenico Morosini (1417–1509), in *De bene instituta re publica* (On the well-managed republic; begun in 1497), outlined an ideal polity run by a sober and wise gerontocracy devoted to public, not private, utility.

The invasions of Italy by the European powers beginning in 1494 made Venice vulnerable to new dangers and intensified the myth of the city's ideal government. In 1509 Venice suffered a catastrophic military defeat at the hands of a league of European states and the sudden (though temporary) loss of most of its territorial dominion. In the responses to this disaster some historians are inclined to see the full elaboration of the "myth of Venice"—the idealization of the republic's free origins, perfect and mixed government, selfless and civic nobility, its devotion to liberty, stability, and social concord, and its longevity. But the key elements of the myth were present and even prominent before the early sixteenth century, and much of Venetian republican thought after 1509 recycled old ideas to shore up the republic's image in a time of doubt and worry.

Gasparo Contarini (1483–1542) brought together all the aspects of the myth in a famous book that caught the attention of northern Europeans and was even translated into English at the end of the century. Contarini was a Venetian nobleman with a long record of political and diplomatic service to the republic. His *De magistratibus et republica Venetorum* (On the magistrates and the republic of the Venetians), begun in the mid-1520s and first published in 1543, lauded Venice's perfect constitution and peaceful social order, but rejected the exemplarity of the Roman Republic promoted by Machiavelli and by some Venetian humanists as well. Certain republics have indeed exceeded Venice in power, authority, military discipline, and glory in war, wrote Contarini, but "none can be compared with ours in the institutions and laws suitable for living well and happily." He criticized Rome's militarism and factionalism as the causes of its loss of liberty. By contrast, the founders of Venice, "from whom we have received this illustrious republic, united themselves as one in their zeal to establish and expand the fatherland, without any regard for private gain or honor."

In challenging the model of Rome and offering Venice as an alternative, Contarini was implicitly taking part in the great debate of the early sixteenth century on the nature of republics. As the "guardian, vicar, and minister of the laws, who governs the republic according to the rule of law," he preferred "the government of the multitude" over monarchy, because the latter often degenerates into tyranny, whereas "republics are known to flourish for centuries through peace and war." But because the "multitude" is unable to govern on its own, a republic must be "tempered" by a mixture of aristocratic rule of the few and popular rule of the "many."

Contarini's notion of the "many" excluded workers and artisans, who "should be considered public servants." The responsibilities of government must be restricted to "free men" who do not perform "servile work" and who are distinguished by the nobility of their blood, exceptional virtue, and service to the state: "This assembly of citizens, or, as they say, this Great Council, which has supreme authority within the republic, and on which the authority of the Senate and the magistracies depends, represents the element of popular rule." Its main role is to elect the members of other councils and magistracies. The doge represents the monarchical principle and is the symbol of the republic's unity, but his role is strictly subordinated to the laws. And the Senate represents the "rule of the few" that is the fulcrum of Contarini's republic.

The people's "great love for and obedience to the nobility" was the result of the decision to reserve to their higher and more deserving ranks certain offices with administrative responsibilities but without any share in rule. This satisfied the popular desire for some role in public affairs without disturbing the "state of the nobles." For these reasons, Contarini concluded, Venice achieved what none of the illustrious republics of antiquity was ever able to do: it endured for twelve hundred years, without succumbing to either foreign tyrants or civil discord. Contarini's vision of Venetian society and government is both deeply conservative and fundamentally ahistorical. Saying little about the actual development of institutions, he gives a mostly static picture of the republic's timeless solutions to the problems of social disorder and dissent.

The historical dimension missing in Contarini is the central feature of the thought of the last of Venice's great republican political thinkers, Paolo Paruta (1540–1598) and Paolo Sarpi (1552–1623). Paruta's *Discorsi politici* (Political discourses; first published 1599) are a sustained argument with Machiavelli about the criteria for evaluating republics. Machiavelli was wrong, he wrote, to praise the Romans for their social conflicts and for their constant attention to war. Much more explicitly than Contarini, Paruta rejected the Roman model—especially the prominence of the people—and offered Venice as the ideal republic, precisely for its devotion to peace and social concord. In fact, for Paruta, Rome became a negative model—the complete demonstration of what republics ought not to be. But he makes this argument with much attention to the history of both Rome and Venice: to the phases of their evolution, growth, and, in the case of Rome, corruption and decline, the inevitable implication being that Venice, too, lived in history.

Paolo Sarpi is a bridge to the republicanism of the Enlightenment, given the popularity of his writings in northern Europe. In Venice's dramatic conflict with the papacy over the question of who had jurisdiction over the Venetian clergy, a conflict that culminated with the papal interdict of 1606–1607, Sarpi was entrusted with defending the republic's rights and liberties in a series of polemical writings. When the crisis was over, he wrote his *Istoria del concilio tridentino* (History of the Council of Trent; 1619), which denounces the church for falling into papal tyranny and provides an extended historical critique of its failure to preserve the republican principles on which it was founded and—in Sarpi's view—should still function. In defending Venice's defiance of the papal interdict, Sarpi vindicated the rights of secular and sovereign republics to rule unchallenged in their own territories against the pretensions of allegedly universal powers claiming superior jurisdiction. In so doing, he brought Renaissance republicanism full circle to the assertion by the medieval communes of their independence from emperors and popes alike.

See also **Florence; Humanism,** *subentry on* **Italy; Political Thought; Renaissance, Interpretations of the,** *subentry on* **Hans Baron; Venice;** *and biographies of figures mentioned in this essay.*

BIBLIOGRAPHY

Primary Works

Bruni, Leonardo. *The Humanism of Leonardo Bruni.* Translations and introductions by Gordon Griffiths, James Hankins, and David Thompson. Binghamton, N.Y., 1987. Translations of many of Bruni's works.

Contarini, Gasparo. *Commonwealth and Government of Venice.* Translated by Lewes Lewkenor. London, 1599. Translation of *De magistratibus et republica venetorum.*

Giannotti, Donato. *Opere politiche.* Edited by Furio Diaz. Milan, Italy, 1974. Includes *Della repubblica fiorentina.*

Guicciardini, Francesco. *Dialogue on the Government of Florence.* Edited and translated by Alison Brown. Cambridge, U.K., and New York, 1994. Translation of the *Dialogo del reggimento di Firenze.*

Kohl, B. G., and R. G. Witt. *The Earthly Republic.* Philadelphia, 1978. Translations of texts by Salutati, Bruni, Poggio, and others.

Latini, Brunetto. *The Book of the Treasure.* Translated by Paul Barrette and Spurgeon Baldwin. New York, 1993. Translation of *Li livres dou tresor.*

Machiavelli, Niccolò. *Machiavelli: The Chief Works and Others.* 3 vols. Translated by Allan Gilbert. Durham, N.C., 1989. See vol. 1, *Discourses on the First Decade of Titus Livius.*

Marsilius of Padua. *The Defender of Peace.* Translated by Alan Gewirth. New York, 1979. Translation of *Defensor pacis.* Original publication (New York, 1951–1956) also contains a separate volume of solid and learned analysis by Gewirth.

Palmieri, Matteo. *Vita civile.* Edited by Gino Belloni. Florence, 1982.

Paruta, Paolo. *Discorsi politici.* Edited by Giorgio Candeloro. Bologna, Italy, 1943.

Ptolemy of Lucca and Thomas Aquinas. *On the Government of Rulers.* Edited and translated by James M. Blythe. Philadelphia, 1997. Translation of the *De regimine principum.*

Sarpi, Paolo. *History of the Council of Trent.* London, 1676. Translation of the *Istoria del concilio tridentino.*

Watkins, Renée Neu. *Humanism and Liberty: Writings on Freedom from Fifteenth-Century Florence.* Columbia, S.C., 1978. Translations of texts by Bruni, Poggio, Rinuccini, Savonarola, and others.

Secondary Works

Albertini, Rudolf von. *Firenze dalla repubblica al principato.* Translated by Cesare Cristofolini. Turin, Italy, 1970. Translation of *Das florentinische Staatsbewusstsein im Übergang von der Republik zum Prinzipat.* A classic overview of the great debates on the fate of the republic from 1494 to the creation of the principate.

Baron, Hans. *The Crisis of the Early Italian Renaissance.* 2d ed. Princeton, N.J., 1966. The influential book whose two-volume first edition of 1955 defined the historical problem of Florentine civic humanism.

Blythe, James M. *Ideal Government and the Mixed Constitution in the Middle Ages.* Princeton, N.J., 1992. An invaluable study of medieval constitutionalism that traces the roots of much of Italian republican thought to Aristotle and his thirteenth-century commentators.

Bock, Gisela, Quentin Skinner, and Maurizio Viroli. *Machiavelli and Republicanism.* Cambridge, U.K., 1990. Essays on the origins and context of Machiavelli's republicanism.

Bouwsma, William J. *Venice and the Defense of Republican Liberty: Renaissance Values in the Age of the Counter Reformation.* Berkeley, Calif., 1968. A magisterial synthesis of Venetian political ideas in their historical context, with special attention to Sarpi.

Brucker, Gene. *The Civic World of Early Renaissance Florence.* Princeton, N.J., 1977. The best treatment of Florentine politics in the period of oligarchic consolidation and civic humanism, with an indispensable analysis of the ruling group.

Canning, J. P. *The Political Thought of Baldus de Ubaldis.* Cambridge, U.K., and New York, 1987. Excellent analysis of the role of corporation law in the emergence of the theory of city-state sovereignty.

Davis, Charles T. *Dante's Italy, and Other Essays.* Philadelphia, 1984. Illuminating essays on Brunetto Latini, Ptolemy of Lucca, Dante, and others.

Finlay, Robert. *Politics in Renaissance Venice.* New Brunswick, N.J., 1980. Looks behind the myth to the sometimes less attractive realities of Venetian politics.

Gilbert, Felix. *Machiavelli and Guicciardini: Politics and History in Sixteenth-Century Florence.* Princeton, N.J., 1965. Important treatment of the establishment of the Great Council in 1494 and the debates over the form of the republic.

King, Margaret L. *Venetian Humanism in an Age of Patrician Dominance.* Princeton, N.J., 1986. Invaluable guide to fifteenth-century humanism in Venice, with much attention to political thought.

Muir, Edward. *Civic Ritual in Renaissance Venice.* Princeton, N.J., 1981. Elegant study of the myth of Venice in ritual and ceremony.

Najemy, John M. *Corporatism and Consensus in Florentine Electoral Politics, 1280–1400.* Chapel Hill, N.C., 1982. A case study of the republicanism of the guild-based *popolo.*

Nederman, Cary J. *Community and Consent: The Secular Political Theory of Marsiglio of Padua's* Defensor Pacis. Lanham, Md., 1995. The most recent treatment of Marsilius in English.

Peterson, David S. "Conciliarism, Republicanism, and Corporatism: The 1415–1420 Constitution of the Florentine Clergy." *Renaissance Quarterly* 42 (1989): 183–226. Penetrating demonstration of the important links between secular republicanism and conciliarism in the short-lived corporation of Florence's clergy.

Pocock, J. G. A. *The Machiavellian Moment: Florentine Political Thought and the Atlantic Republican Tradition.* Princeton, N.J., 1975. A magisterial inquiry into the philosophical and theoretical issues surrounding Renaissance republicanism in Florence and Venice and their legacy in England and America.

Quaglioni, Diego. *Politica e diritto nel trecento italiano.* Florence, 1983. Contains the text of Bartolus's *De regimine civitatis.*

Robey, D., and J. Law. "The Venetian Myth and the 'De Republica Veneta' of Pier Paolo Vergerio." *Rinascimento* 15 (1975): 3–59. Traces the myth of Venice back to the fourteenth century and contains the relevant passages from Henry of Rimini, Benzo of Alessandria, and Pier Paolo Vergerio.

Rubinstein, Nicolai. *The Government of Florence under the Medici (1434–1494).* Oxford and New York, 1997. Second and revised edition of the classic work on Medici government first published in 1966.

Rubinstein, Nicolai. "Marsilius of Padua and Italian Political Thought of His Time." In *Europe in the Late Middle Ages.* Edited by J. R. Hale, J. R. L. Highfield, and B. Smalley. London, 1965. Pages 44–75. Connects Marsilius to his historical context.

Skinner, Quentin. *The Foundations of Modern Political Thought.* 2 vols. Cambridge, U.K., and New York, 1978. Volume 1 provides a comprehensive survey of Italian political thought from the thirteenth to the sixteenth century, including an excellent chapter on republicanism.

Tierney, Brian. *Religion, Law, and the Growth of Constitutional Thought, 1150–1650.* Cambridge, U.K., and New York, 1982. Wide-ranging essays on the medieval roots of much of modern political thought, with particular attention to the origins in canon law of constitutionalist ideas.

Weinstein, Donald. *Savonarola and Florence: Prophecy and Patriotism in the Renaissance.* Princeton, N.J., 1970. Still the best book on Savonarola, with much attention to his political thought.

Witt, Ronald G. *Coluccio Salutati and His Public Letters.* Geneva, 1976. Includes a valuable analysis of the political ideas in the chancery letters.

JOHN M. NAJEMY

RESISTANCE, THEORY OF. The modern idea of resistance had important precedents in classical and biblical antiquity as well as in the Middle Ages, but it came into clear maturity during the sixteenth century. The possibility of resistance was implied by notions of feudal, ecclesiastical, and communal liberties whenever a question of tyranny on the part of a superior arose. The Old Testament was filled with examples of protest and of just wars against tyranny, and the authority of Roman law was based on the semilegendary *lex regia,* according to which sovereignty had originally been invested in the Roman people and under certain conditions might be reclaimed by them. Germanic custom, too, recognized the legitimacy of resistance to kings and judges if they do wrong. In the sixteenth century resistance might be called for if a ruler violated the rights of the church, nobility, or even chartered towns, and likewise if a lord failed in his compact with his feudal vassals. Down to the seventeenth century, moreover, peasant revolts were often grounded on claims that ancient customs had been violated, and so armed resistance was justified.

Theoretician of Resistance. George Buchanan wrote *De jure regni apud Scotos* in 1568 to oppose the rule of Mary, queen of Scots. Scottish National Portrait Gallery

Medieval and Renaissance Development. Medieval ecclesiology was also a rich source of resistance ideas. It was churchmen like John of Salisbury and Jean de Gerson who proposed regicide as an effective, if extreme, remedy for secular tyranny. "No sacrifice is more pleasing to God," Jean de Gerson declared in 1405, "than the death of a tyrant." Within the church, too, the principle of resistance received expression, especially in the form of conciliar theory. The Great Schism of the late fourteenth century produced two lines of popes and provoked a radical questioning of papal authority, signaled especially by the deposition of two popes and subsequent election of Martin V by the Council of Constance (1417). The conciliarist challenge to papal rule brought not only a new, in a sense constitutional, notion of church government but also resistance to papal supremacy in the form of resurgent national churches. In the long view the Anglican and Lutheran churches of the next century were only radical examples of national secession from papal authority.

The great age of resistance in Europe occurred in the wake of the Protestant Reformation, when religious enthusiasm inflamed secular issues of social discontent and constitutional complaint. The original Protestants were the German princes who opposed Charles V's violation of their ecclesiastical rights by outlawing Luther, and in the Schmalkaldic wars beginning in 1530 their position was reinforced by the claims to liberty of conscience asserted by Luther and other reformers. Luther himself believed in the divine right of rulers, never pretended to authority in secular matters, and opposed the radicalism that fueled the peasant wars of 1524–1525. Yet "if one may resist the pope," he declared, "one may also resist all the emperors and dukes who contrive to defend the pope." Further support for Lutheran resistance theories was given by the civil law maxim that force might legitimately be opposed by force (*vi vim repellere licet*) and by the arguments presented on behalf of Strasbourg, Magdeburg, and other cities on the grounds that their ancient civic liberties had been violated.

Another rich field for the cultivation of resistance thought was the experience of English Protestants fleeing persecutions initiated by Mary I. "Wo be unto you . . . that make unryghteous laws"—so John Ponet, one of these Marian exiles, in 1556 invoked the words of the prophet Isaiah; Ponet added that the threat "of everlasting damnation was spoken not only to Jerusalem but also to Germanie, Italie, Fraunce, Spayne, Englande, Scotlande, and all other countreyes and nacions." Before Mary, English Protestants had also demanded liberty of conscience, and with the resurgence of popery (and Protestant martyrdoms) in the 1550s they began to articulate some of the most radical ideas about political resistance of early modern times; these ideas were based especially on conceptions of popular sovereignty in which the voice of the people was identified with the English Parliament.

The principal source of modern resistance theory after Luther was John Calvin (1509–1564), whose *Institutio christianae religionis* (Institutes of the Christian religion; 1536), provided the foundational text for English as well as continental Protestants. Like Luther, Calvin accepted divine right and denied the right of private persons to rise up against sovereign authority; Calvin recommended only passive resistance (in practice, martyrdom or exile) to his persecuted followers. Yet he, too, left the door open to more subversive action by adding that obedience to secular authority should never take precedence over obedience to the will of God. He also invoked some of the biblical examples of active resistance and veiled threats of God's vengeance descending on the enemies of the true religion. Both the exception to secular obedience and the inflammatory biblical rhetoric were extended by the next generation of Protestants caught up in the turmoil of religious war: both concepts promoted more active forms of resistance.

French Theories of Resistance. Active resistance occurred most conspicuously during the French Wars of Religion and the Dutch war of liberation. In France the issue was provoked by the death of Henry II in 1559, when the government fell into the hands of Catherine de Médicis and the Guise family and when the Huguenots—followers of the so-called reformed religion, Protestantism—became the target of renewed persecution. "We are often asked," wrote Théodore de Bèze (Beza) in 1559 referring also to Calvin, "whether it is permitted to rise up against those who are enemies not only of religion but also of the realm." The standard Calvinist answer had been that such rebellion was justified only as a response to the leadership of inferior magistrates (meaning blood peers in the case of France), but this essential ingredient unfortunately was lacking in the first episode of resistance before the Wars of Religion, the conspiracy of Amboise (1560). This crisis provoked the first upsurge in the production of literature devoted to resistance and constitutionalism, which defined the Huguenot agenda for the next generation.

The problem of legitimate leadership was finally resolved in April 1562, when Louis I de Bourbon, prince of Condé, a member of the royal family, gathered with other Huguenot leaders and feudal retainers and with his legal consultants (including Beza and François Hotman), drew up a treaty of association and a justification for the resort to violence—in effect a declaration of a just war. The arguments were that Condé was not a rebel or a traitor but rather a patriot who wanted to liberate the underage king from his evil advisers, to relieve the poor from unjust taxation, and to defend the principle of liberty of conscience. This defense remained, in general, the Huguenots' party line for a generation, throughout seven agonizing civil wars.

After 1572 circumstances acted to radicalize ideas of resistance, when the massacre on Saint Bartholomew's Day led some critics to conclude that the French king, Charles IX—who had acknowledged responsibility for the assassination of the Huguenot leader Gaspard II de Coligny and so for the subsequent killings—had indeed shown himself to be a tyrant. "How can one accept as king a man who has spilled the blood of 30,000 persons in eight days?" asked Hotman in a 1573 letter. His old friend Beza, now Calvin's successor, concluded that "we must honor as martyrs not only those who have conquered without resistance, and by patience only, against tyrants who have persecuted the truth, but those also who, authorized by law and by competent authorities, [have] devoted their strength to the defense of true religion" (1574). So Beza took the step from passive to active resistance that his great predecessor had always avoided.

In the wake of the Saint Bartholomew's Day massacre three classic statements of French resistance theory were made by Hotman, Beza, and Philippe Duplessis-Mornay. Hotman's *Francogallia* (1573) was a learned survey of French history that, although the product of years of research, confronted the issues of the day—asserting the original elective character of kingship, defending the central place maintained by the Estates General in the French monarchy, setting the ancient constitution above the bloody tyranny of the Valois kings, and in general praising the Germano-Celtic heritage of France (as opposed to the foreign influences of Romanism and papism). Beza's *Du droit des magistrats* (Right of magistrates; 1574), recalling and extending Calvin's classic statement of resistance theory, brought together a wide range of sacred and secular learning in support of his arguments concerning the popular basis for sovereignty and the right, indeed the duty, of subjects to resist ungodly tyranny. Still more radically, Duplessis-Mornay's *Vindiciae contra tyrannos* (Defense of liberty against tyrants; 1579) extended Beza's theory of the contractual nature of government, according to which subjects are unconditionally justified in taking up arms against "a prince who violates God's law and desolates His church" and even in applying for help from neighboring princes. A variant of Huguenot resistance theory was expressed by the Scottish humanist George Buchanan, whose *De jure regni apud Scotos* (The law of the kingdom among Scots) was composed in 1568 (and published in 1579) to justify the deposition of Mary Stuart.

The Netherlands and the French Catholic League. Resistance ideas took a parallel course in the Netherlands, where the Estates opposed first the evil advisers of their king, Phillip II, and then the sovereign himself. Once again there was a mixture of constitutional, economic, and religious grounds for protest—the Dutch Calvinists making common cause with their coreligionists in France. When the Spanish king placed a price on his head, the Dutch Calvinist leader, William of Orange, issued a personal apology (1581), justifying his actions in much the same terms as Condé did at the outset of the French Wars of Religion. William's statement was followed by a more principled protest by the Estates General, which published its abjuration of Spanish sovereignty on the grounds that, in oppressing his subjects and violating their ancient liberties, the king had become a tyrant and so forfeited all claims to obedience. The abjuration was in effect a declaration of independence, and it was accepted in international law in 1648 in the Treaties of Westphalia.

An extraordinary ideological turnabout occurred in the 1580s, as Catholics were put on the defensive—for example, the Catholic martyrs under Elizabeth I and the Catholic defenders of resistance to Henry III and to the succession of Henry of Navarre. Louis d'Orléans, an advocate for the Catholic League, drew on Huguenot resistance theory for such purposes; Louis, however, celebrated the Parlement of Paris rather than the Estates General as a check on tyranny, asserted that Catholicism was a fundamental law of the kingdom, and warned that Protestant heresy was akin to tyranny. Jean Boucher, who was a preacher for the Catholic revolutionary group in Paris known as the Sixteen, shared the radical views of that group and defended not only the political role of the Estates General but also the legitimacy of deposing a king in principle as well as in the particular case of Henry III. Some League theorists went so far as to resurrect the theory of elective kingship that had been proposed by Hotman (though Hotman himself dropped it in a later edition of *Francogallia* published after Henry of Navarre became the legitimate successor of the Valois line).

In general, resistance theory was a mirror image of sovereignty, just as "treason" (lèse majesté) was the opposite of sovereignty (majesté)—*majestas* being the Latin term for sovereignty, as Jean Bodin famously pointed out. Like resistance, constitutionalism—the role of the Estates—tended to question the comfortable idea of absolute sovereignty, which to many observers of the troubles of the sixteenth-century wars seemed perilously close to unbridled tyranny. Compounding the confusion was the question of where sovereignty resided—in the monarch, as Bodin argued, or in the people, as the Dutch theorist Johannes Althusius concluded, adding that even private persons had the right to resist force with force. But in any case there was always the danger of an abuse of power: constitutional arrangements were inadequate to remedy such abuse, so resistance—with its modern offspring, civil disobedience—continued to be a theory of last resort at least.

See also **Conciliarism; Constitutionalism; Protestant Reformation; Tyrannicide; Wars of Religion;** *and biographies of figures mentioned in this entry.*

BIBLIOGRAPHY

Primary Works

Bèze, Théodore de. *Du droit des magistrats.* Edited by Robert M. Kingdon. Geneva, 1971. Critical edition of Beza's *Right of Magistrates* (1574).

Duplessis-Mornay, Philippe. *Vindiciae contra tyrannos; or, Concerning the Legitimate Power of a Prince over the People, and of the People over a Prince.* Edited and translated by George Garnett. Cambridge, U.K., and New York, 1994. Written perhaps in collaboration with Hubert Languet and translated in 1648 as *A Defense of Liberty against Tyrants.*

Franklin, Julian H., ed. and trans. *Constitutionalism and Resistance in the Sixteenth Century: Three Treatises by Hotman, Beza, and Mornay.* New York, 1969. Translated selections from the books listed in this section.

Hotman, François. *Francogallia.* Edited by Ralph E. Giesey. Translated by J. H. M. Salmon. Cambridge, U.K., 1972. Variorum edition and modern translation of Hotman's most influential work.

Secondary Works

Caprariis, Vittorio de. *Propaganda e pensiero politico in Francia durante le guerre di religione.* Naples, Italy, 1959. Detailed study of French pamphlet literature before the Saint Bartholomew's Day massacre.

Gelderen, Martin van. *The Political Thought of the Dutch Revolt, 1555–1590.* Cambridge, U.K., 1992. Ideas and arguments developed by Dutch Calvinists in their war of liberation.

Kelley, Donald R. *The Beginning of Ideology: Consciousness and Society in the French Reformation.* Cambridge, U.K., 1981. Study of psychological, social, cultural, and political dimensions of Protestantism in France.

Kelley, Donald R. "Kingship and Resistance." In *The Origins of Modern Freedom in the West.* Edited by Richard W. Davis. Stanford, Calif., 1995. Pages 235–268, 359–364. The dialectic between royal and individual will and the conflict between authoritarian and resistance thought and behavior from late medieval to early modern times.

Kingdon, Robert M. "Calvinism and Resistance Theory, 1550–1580." In *The Cambridge History of Political Thought 1450–1700.* Edited by J. H. Burns. Cambridge, U.K., 1991. Pages 193–218. Up-to-date, scholarly survey of the subject.

Parrow, Kathleen A. *From Defense to Resistance: Justification of Violence during the French Wars of Religion.* Philadelphia, 1993. Arguments from civil law, including trespass, for active resistance.

Salmon, J. H. M. "Catholic Resistance Theory, Ultramontanism, and the Royalist Response, 1580–1620." In *The Cambridge History of Political Thought.* Cambridge, U.K., 1991. Pages 219–253. Up-to-date, scholarly survey of the subject.

DONALD R. KELLEY

REUCHLIN, JOHANN (1455–1522), German humanist. Although best known for his involvement in the Reuchlin affair, Johann Reuchlin also gained fame as a pioneer in the study of Hebrew language and literature.

Born at Pforzheim in Baden, he matriculated at the University of Freiburg in 1470, moved to the University of Paris as tutor to a young prince, then to Basel (1474), taking B.A. and M.A. degrees (1475, 1477). He next studied law in France, at Orléans and Poitiers, receiving his licentiate at Poitiers in 1481. At an undetermined date he acquired a doctorate in law, probably at Heidelberg. He began a successful legal career as a counselor to Count Eberhard of Württemberg (ruled 1457–1495) and later served as judge in the imperial court at Stuttgart (from 1484) and in the court of the Swabian League (from 1502). He visited Italy in 1482 and again in 1490 and 1498, meeting such influential scholars as Marsilio Ficino (1433–1499), Giovanni Pico della Mirandola (1463–1494), Ermolao Barbaro (1453/54–1493), and Aldus Manutius (1449–1515). The Neoplatonic and kabbalist interests of Ficino and Pico strongly influenced his intellectual development.

Other humanists revered Reuchlin as the first German to master all three ancient languages, Latin, Greek, and Hebrew. At the age of twenty he compiled a Latin dictionary, which went through many editions. He published Latin translations of Greek works by St. Athanasius, Demosthenes, Hippocrates, and Homer. But his study of Hebrew language and literature was his unique contribution. He began this study in 1486 with an unidentified teacher, but in 1492 he met his real master, Jakob ben Jehiel Loans, a Jewish physician to the emperor. Reuchlin's two major contributions to Hebrew studies were his grammar book, *De rudimentis Hebraicis* (The rudiments of Hebrew; 1506), and an advanced treatise on accents and orthography, *De accentibus et orthographia linguae Hebraicae* (On the accents and orthography of the Hebrew language; 1518).

Reuchlin was convinced that mastery of Hebrew language and religious literature would unlock the treasures of the Old Testament for Christian scholars. Like his Florentine friends, he believed in an ancient tradition of religious wisdom, revealed by God to the sages of every ancient nation but kept secret from the ignorant masses. For the Greeks, this wisdom culminated in the mystical arithmetic of Pythagoras and the philosophy of Plato. Even more holy was the secret wisdom revealed to Moses, transmitted only orally until the Babylonian captivity, but then written down in the kabbalistic books. Study of these books would reveal that Jewish religion, if properly understood, was compatible with Christian faith, and even that Jesus must be the Messiah. He first developed these ideas in *De verbo mirifico* (On the wondrous word; 1494) and in 1517 brought out a far more learned Kabbalistic book, *De arte cabalistica* (On the kabbalistic art). Although his kabbalistic ideas were criticized by his enemies, Reuchlin was an exceedingly pious Christian. His goal in kabbalistic study was to reinforce Catholic truth and to advance the cause of converting the Jews, through persuasion rather than force. During the Reuchlin affair he came into conflict with certain scholastic theologians and Dominican friars, but he was never an outspoken critic of Scholasticism and had served as legal adviser to the Dominican order.

In 1511, when his conflict with the Cologne Dominicans began, he was a central figure in German humanism, in touch with nearly all of the leading humanists. For the Palatine court at Heidelberg, he composed two Latin comedies. *Scaenica progymnasmata* (A play for schools), also known as *Henno,* was adapted from an anonymous French farce known as *Pathelin,* staged at Heidelberg in 1497, and printed the following year. *Sergius* was published in 1504 but was never staged because it sharply criticized devotion to religious relics and the role of the monastic orders in promoting that devotion. Yet Reuchlin never challenged orthodox doctrine or hierarchical authority.

When the Luther affair arose in 1517, Reuchlin refrained from any endorsement of a man who might turn out to be a heretic. He did recommend his precocious great-nephew, Philipp Melanchthon (1497–1560), whose education he had directed, for the new professorship of Greek at Wittenberg in 1518. Reuchlin, however, became distressed by Melanchthon's support of Luther's doctrines and urged him to leave Wittenberg for Ingolstadt, where Reuchlin himself served as professor of Hebrew and Greek (1520–1522), residing as a guest in the home of Luther's archenemy, Johann Eck (1486–1543). Since Melanchthon refused to leave, in 1521 Reuchlin commanded him never to write again; and although he had promised to will his valuable library to Melanchthon, he instead left it to a monastery in his native town of Pforzheim.

See also **Kabbalah**; **Reuchlin Affair**.

BIBLIOGRAPHY

Primary Work

Reuchlin, Johannes. *De verbo mirifico, 1494. De arte cabalistica, 1517.* Stuttgart, Germany, 1964. Facsimile reprint of Reuchlin's two principal kabbalistic books (in Latin).

Secondary Works

Geiger, Ludwig. *Johann Reuchlin: Sein Leben und seine Werke.* Leipzig, 1871. Reprint, Nieuwkoop, Netherlands, 1961. Despite its age, still the best book-length biography; never translated into English.

Overfield, James H. *Humanism and Scholasticism in Late Medieval Germany*. Princeton, N.J., 1984. Biographical sketch, pp. 159–163; account of Reuchlin affair, pp. 247–297.

Spitz, Lewis W. *The Religious Renaissance of the German Humanists*. Cambridge, Mass., 1963. See chapter 4, "Reuchlin: Pythagoras Reborn," pp. 61–80.

CHARLES G. NAUERT

REUCHLIN AFFAIR. This controversy, pitting the German humanist Johann Reuchlin against theologians from the University of Cologne, culminated in a famous anticlerical satire, *Epistolae obscurorum virorum* (Letters of obscure men; 2 vols., 1515–1517).

The affair began with the efforts of a converted Jew, Johannes Pfefferkorn (1469–c. 1522), to convert his former coreligionists. Backed by the Dominicans at Cologne, he claimed that Jews' religious literature encouraged their resistance. In 1509 the emperor Maximilian I (ruled 1493–1519) authorized him to examine Jewish books and to destroy any books that impeded conversion. In 1510, however, the archbishop of Mainz, who had friendly relations with the local Jewish community, persuaded the emperor to authorize a study by a group of experts. He sought written opinions from four German theology faculties and three individuals. Reuchlin, the leading Christian expert on Hebrew, was one of those consulted. All the others endorsed confiscation, but Reuchlin opposed it. Maximilian followed Reuchlin's advice, which argued that destruction of Hebrew books would harm biblical scholarship, and also that confiscation would violate property rights established under imperial law. Pfefferkorn reacted with a polemic, *Handt spiegel* (Hand mirror; 1511), alleging that Reuchlin had been bribed by rich Jews. Reuchlin retorted with his equally abusive *Augenspiegel* (Eye mirror; 1511).

Some Cologne theologians then charged that *Augenspiegel* had damaged Christianity by upholding the Jews. Arnold von Tongern published a list of its alleged theological errors, and the inquisitor Jacob Hoogstraeten (c. 1460–1527) initiated an investigation. Reuchlin then appealed to the papal curia. Pope Leo X (1513–1521) remanded the case to the bishop of Speyer, who ruled in March 1514 that *Augenspiegel* was not heretical. He ordered Hoogstraeten to abandon his attacks. Although the theologians appealed the decision to Rome, the pope had no desire to condemn either Reuchlin or the Cologne theologians, and in 1516 he issued a mandate imposing silence on both sides. Hoogstraeten, however, continued his attacks and launched a renewed appeal.

The Reuchlin Controversy. Reuchlin is depicted with a duplicitous double tongue. Engraving by Johannes Kapnion, 1516.

Although most German humanists respected Reuchlin as a good and learned man and resented the attacks, few of them shared his zeal for Hebrew. Even some who sympathized with him and despised his critics thought that *Augenspiegel* was unduly provocative, although they expressed these reservations only in private. None of them wanted to be perceived as a defender of the Jews.

One small group of humanists, however, felt differently. They secretly wrote and published a savage satire, *Epistolae obscurorum virorum* (1515). This was not a conventional rebuttal. Instead, it contained fictitious letters supposedly exchanged between a Cologne humanist, Ortwin Gratius (c. 1480–1542), and various members of the Cologne faculty and the mendicant orders. The supposed authors reveal themselves as ignorant, morally depraved, and hypocritical scoundrels. The book did something even more dangerous to the theologians than denounce them: it transformed them into objects of ridicule. The Latin style is itself a major part of the satire—not only unclassical but blatantly ungrammatical. The letters present the correspondents as motivated by hostility to the new humanist learning, blind devotion to obsolete medieval textbooks, and unscrupulous pursuit of pleasure, wealth, and prestige.

Modern scholarship has identified the authors. The basic plan came from the Erfurt humanist Crotus Rubeanus (c. 1480–c. 1539), who wrote all or nearly all of the letters in the first edition. The anticlerical humanistic knight Ulrich von Hutten (1488–1523) added seven letters in an edition of 1516 and wrote all or nearly all of the letters in the second volume (1517). Whereas Crotus maintained a light, bantering, humorous tone and avoided references to real persons (except for Gratius), Hutten's letters are much harsher in tone and frequently name real persons. A third humanist, Hermann von dem Busche (1468–1534), may have written a few of the letters, and he probably arranged the clandestine publication. The title, with its reference to "obscure" men, is both a commentary on the Scholastics and a reference to the title of Reuchlin's collection of character references, *Clarorum virorum epistolae* (Letters of famous men; 1514).

Reactions to the satire varied. Reuchlin himself never commented but probably did not welcome its pugnacious tone, which was contrary to his desire to bring the conflict to an end. The influential Erasmus (1466–1536) admitted that some sections were witty but deplored its abusive tone, fearing that it would only increase hostility to humanistic scholarship. There was no vernacular translation of the *Letters* into German, so most of the polemics were accessible only to the Latin-reading elite. The early Protestant Reformation deflected attention from the case, and the book dropped out of print. Nevertheless, while only a few humanists endorsed *Letters of Obscure Men,* virtually all must have read it.

So the broader significance of the Reuchlin case may lie not in demonstration of an inevitable humanist-scholastic conflict but in the negative impression that it created about the competence, sincerity, and moral integrity of the same theologians who soon undertook to defend orthodoxy against Martin Luther (1483–1546). Traditional historical scholarship was more right than wrong in viewing the Reuchlin affair as a prelude to the Reformation. As for the equally traditional view that it represents an irrepressible conflict between humanists and Scholastics, the verdict of scholarship is mixed, but James Overfield has demonstrated that the original quarrel over Hebrew books had nothing at all to do with humanism and that most humanists did not view the affair as an attack on humanism and did not want to get personally involved.

In the end, Reuchlin lost his legal case. The theologians renewed their appeal, and in 1520, reacting to religious revolution in Germany, the pope condemned *Augenspiegel* as a scandalous book. The sentence required Reuchlin to make public apology and to pay the heavy costs of the appellate procedure. Reuchlin, always an obedient son of the church, submitted quietly and paid the expenses.

See also **Humanism,** *subentry on* **Germany and the Low Countries; Reuchlin, Johann; Satire.**

BIBLIOGRAPHY

Primary Work

Epistolae obscurorum virorum. Edited and translated by Francis Griffin Stokes. London, 1909. Original Latin text with English translation on facing pages. English text alone, with new introduction by Hajo Holborn, was reprinted under the title *On the Eve of the Reformation.* New York, 1964.

Secondary Works

Mehl, James V. "Language, Class, and Mimic Satire in the Characterization of Correspondents in the *Epistolae obscurorum virorum.*" *Sixteenth Century Journal* 25 (1994): 289–305.

Oberman, Heiko A. *The Roots of Anti-Semitism in the Age of Renaissance and Reformation.* Translated by James I. Porter. Philadelphia, 1984. See pp. 24–37.

Overfield, James. *Humanism and Scholasticism in Late Medieval Germany.* Princeton, N.J., 1984. See pp. 159–163, 247–297.

Overfield, James. "A New Look at the Reuchlin Affair." *Studies in Medieval and Renaissance History* 8 (1971): 165–207.

Peterse, Hans. *Jacobus Hoogstraeten gegen Johannes Reuchlin: Ein Beitrag zur Geschichte des Antijudaismus im 16. Jahrhundert.* Mainz, Germany, 1995.

Spitz, Lewis W. *The Religious Renaissance of the German Humanists.* Cambridge, Mass., 1963. See chapter 4, "Reuchlin: Pythagoras Reborn," pp. 61–80.

Zika, Charles. "Reuchlin and Erasmus: Humanism and Occult Philosophy." *Journal of Religious History* 9 (1977): 223–246.

CHARLES G. NAUERT

RHENANUS, BEATUS. *See* **Beatus Rhenanus.**

RHETORIC. In the proper sense, "rhetoric" either means the art of persuasive discourse as taught and described in manuals or refers to the presence of rhetoric in spoken and written discourse.

Classical Rhetoric in the Renaissance. In the Renaissance, rhetoric recovered the preeminence it had once had in the classical period. Cicero (106–43 B.C.E.) furnished the principles of the art through his writings and served as a revered model of civic responsibility and rhetorical elegance. He claimed that when rhetoric combined wisdom with eloquence it produced and preserved civil government and justice, a sentiment echoed throughout the Renaissance.

The best-known sources of the classical art in the Middle Ages and the Renaissance were two Roman texts, Cicero's *De inventione* (On invention) and the anonymous *Rhetorica ad Herennium* (The art of rhetoric for Herennius), which had often been attributed to Cicero. Both books describe rhetoric as the art of persuasion and note that it is concerned with controversial issues. It includes five canons or subdivisions: invention, arrangement, style, memory, and delivery. Although rhetoric is said to be applicable to any subject, it is traditionally divided into three kinds: judicial, political, and epideictic or demonstrative. In judicial oratory, orators use arguments to accuse or defend clients before a jury. Political rhetoric employs arguments to exhort or dissuade the audience on issues in which action needs to be taken. Epideictic rhetoric applies praise or blame to persons or things on birthdays, funerals, and other ceremonial events. In this way it serves to deepen community values. During the Renaissance epideictic oratory was the kind most frequently used both for classroom exercises and in public life.

The parts of rhetoric that engaged the most enthusiastic attention of Renaissance scholars were invention and style. Invention comprises methods for the discovery of arguments; these techniques are referred to as topics or commonplaces (*koinoi topoi* in Greek, *loci communes* in Latin). The topics have both a philosophical as well as a rhetorical origin, a fact that created great controversy in the Renaissance. Techniques of invention were treated in detail by Aristotle in both the *Rhetoric* and in his work on dialectics, the *Topics,* the art of logical inquiry and debate. The disparate threads were absorbed by Cicero, who attempted to explain Aristotle's philosophical approach in his own treatise, *Topics,* and the rhetorical applications in his writings on rhetoric.

In writing on rhetorical invention, Cicero first takes up the method of determining the point at issue in a judicial case (Latin, *constitutiones;* Greek, *stasis*). The four questions employed in the method ask whether the fact, the definition, or the quality of the act is in question or whether the jurisdiction of the court is being challenged. He next considers the commonplaces or topics (Greek, *topoi*), which he says are based upon either persons or actions. Under persons fall topics of ancestry, education, appearance, and character; under topics of actions, manner of life, deeds, and words. Cicero mentions also extrinsic topics, those not invented by the orator but used by him, such as witnesses, circumstances, and testimony. In addition, Cicero's *Topics* provides logical topics: definition, division, similarities, opposites, relationship, antecedent, and consequent. This panoply of topics, along with others noted by Themistius (c. 317–388 C.E.), were passed on by Boethius (c. 480–524 C.E.), but he complicated matters in his texts on dialectics by adding maxims based on common assumptions suggested in Aristotle. Under these maxims he listed individual topics (*differentiae*). These versions of the topics were passed on to the Renaissance. The complexity and redundancy of teaching the topics in rhetoric and dialectics eventually so exasperated such influential teachers as Lorenzo Valla (1407–1457), Rudolph Agricola (1443/44–1485), and Peter Ramus (1515–1572) that they attempted a complete renovation of both arts, as noted below.

The second canon of the traditional art considered the arrangement of the parts of an oration. Ancient practice conceived of an oration as consisting of six parts: an introduction; a narration presenting the facts of the matter; a partition announcing the thesis and order of the ensuing arguments; a confirmation offering arguments in support of the thesis; a refutation of the other side; and a peroration or conclusion. This conception of the oration furnished the structure not only of the elaborate orations of the humanist era but also of written discourse from formal letters to essays.

Treatments of style by Renaissance authors owed much to the *Ad Herennium*'s elaborate discussion. It includes descriptions of sixty-four figures of speech, which it divides into figures of words and tropes and figures of thought. Under style, diction and the three levels of style—plain, middle, and grand—are also explicated. The figures and tropes fascinated Renaissance authors, who delighted in producing even longer lists of these. Brian Vickers explains that in the Renaissance these stylistic devices were viewed as a repertoire essential to the expression of emotion and were not intended merely to exhibit versatility.

In its chapters on memory and delivery, the *Ad Herennium* preserved ancient techniques of mnemonics and advice on using voice and gesture. Renaissance authors were not much concerned with memory, but delivery was accorded some attention in Ciceronian rhetorics.

Rhetoric in Transition from the Middle Ages. Always the product of need, the rhetorical art had lost its position as the capstone of education in the Middle Ages. By the twelfth and thirteenth centuries, the more elementary arts of the trivium (grammar, rhetoric, and logic) gave pride of place to logic. Principles of rhetoric were taught as ancillary to the basic subject of grammar and preliminary to the more utilitarian discipline of logic. Rhetorical concepts of organization and style were useful for understanding literary works studied with the grammarian.

The part of logic called dialectics, based on Aristotle's description of inventive logic in the *Topics,* was employed to do the work of exploring and solving problems in natural and moral philosophy and theology by scholars who generally taught in the universities. Although both dialectics and rhetoric in scholastic teaching were used to investigate issues where certain truth was not forthcoming and probabilities had to furnish the premises of arguments, the content and aims of the two arts differed. The content of dialectics was concerned with universal questions and its aim was the discovery of probable truth, while rhetoric's content was concerned with particular cases and its aim was the creation of persuasive arguments to convince an audience. Dialectics posed questions and conjectured answers, while rhetoric offered cohesive units of oratory and prose. Audiences were different as well; dialectic engaged a single opponent before an audience of experts in the field, while rhetoric addressed the common man. Dialectical disputation, thus, was the medium of choice for scholars engaged in speculative inquiry in the sciences, not rhetoric.

These distinctions began to erode in the Renaissance, not only because scholars questioned the need for two forms of inquiry and argument, but because audiences interested in scholarly questions grew beyond the academic forums. The printing press made what were stimulated by the recovery of Cicero's letters. This revived form, the epistle, was conceived as conversation between absent friends. Humanist authors often adopted the form but with the design of publishing such letters to reach wider audiences.

The third medieval art, which had undertaken in the *nova poetria* to teach the principles of narrative poetic structure and style, flowered in the Renaissance into a separate art of poetic composition that continued to make use of rhetorical elements but applied them to various poetic forms. Rhetoric and poetics were closely knit in the period, each affecting the expression of the other. The interaction of commonplaces and figures, described in detail by Sister Miriam Joseph, served poet, dramatist, orator, and essayist in amplifying thought.

Humanism and Rhetoric. In the Renaissance, teachers and practitioners of letter writing and its specialized legal form, the notarial art, were in great demand. Students of *ars dictaminis* were sought after and attained positions of prominence in secular and ecclesiastical courts and city governments. In centers of commercial and spiritual power, which had been expanding since the tenth century, primary or spoken rhetoric also became a valuable political skill. Among the first humanists were Colluccio Salutati (1331–1406), Leonardo Bruni (c. 1370–1444), and Poggio Bracciolini (1380–1459), men who were skilled in *dictamen* and familiar with Cicero's orations and letters. Serving as chancellors of the papal court and also of Florence, they witnessed the practical value of instruction in the classical art of rhetoric and sought to revive the central part it played in ancient Greece and Rome.

The rise of humanism was to affect the place of rhetoric in education. Petrarch (1304–1374) was a critical influence in the revival of classical culture and the development of humanism. He revered the high culture of ancient Greece and Rome and saw issues formerly for specialists accessible to a wider public. Scholars began to apply rhetoric to disputations for orations and letters, in which philosophical and theological issues were treated in a more open and continuous style.

Although the older conception of rhetoric as central to education had faded in the Middle Ages, three subsidiary disciplines came into being then and were expanded and changed significantly in the Renaissance: *ars praedicandi,* the art of preaching; *ars dictaminis,* the art of letter writing; and *ars poetria,* the new art of poetry.

The university-style sermon of the late Middle Ages with its thematic structure was loosened in Renaissance usage and a Christian classical oratory developed that favored the grand style, which played upon emotions to move its hearers to virtue. The Reformation brought with it increased attention to preaching the Word. Elaborate new texts were issued devoted to ecclesiastical oratory. These departed from the medieval manuals of preaching in analyzing the role of particular emotions and dwelling on style. Erasmus's *Ecclesiastes, sive concionator evangelicus* (Ecclesiastes, or the evangelical preacher; 1535) treats the emotions suited to the Christian life—love, joy, hope, and sorrow—and recommends the use of figures of speech and vivid description to elicit these. Other popular treatments were Philipp Melanchthon's writings on preaching; Luis de Granada's *Ecclesiastica rhetorica* (Ecclesiastical rhetoric; 1576), issued after the Council of Trent and calling for more intense attention to preaching; and William Perkins's *Art of Prophesying* (1607), conveying the English Puritan emphasis on inspired plain style. Another popular text, Nicholas Caussin's *De eloquentia sacra et humana* (On sacred and human eloquence; 1617), knit together all oratory, covering sacred eloquence as expressed in

Scripture; heroic oratory, as in the oratory of the fathers of the church; and human or secular oratory.

The medieval art of writing formal letters, which had emerged under the ecclesiastical and judicial needs of the late Middle Ages, in the Renaissance spawned another, quite different variety, an informal approach that took Cicero as the epitome of eloquence.

Recovery of Latin Rhetorical Manuscripts. Central to the revival of interest in classical rhetoric was Petrarch's recovery of lost manuscripts of Cicero's letters to Atticus, Brutus, and Quintus in 1345 and his discovery in 1333 of Cicero's oration *Pro Archia poeta* (In defense of the poet Archias), extolling the value of poetry and literature. These along with the recovery of other works of Cicero—the *Epistola ad familiares* (Letters to friends), a collection of letters to friends; *De oratore* (On oratory), a mature discussion in dialogue form of the art of rhetoric; *Brutus,* a history of rhetoric; *Orator,* the modeling of the *orator perfectus;* and *De officiis* (On duties), on the duties of the statesman—brought new vitality to the rhetorical genres of letter writing and oratory and fueled the desire to emulate the virtues of the statesman-orator as well as his elegant style.

The search for more manuscripts in monasteries and obscure libraries yielded other finds significant for the revival of rhetoric. Bracciolini found more of Cicero's orations and, most importantly, discovered in 1416 a complete manuscript of Quintilian's *De institutione oratoria* (On the education of the orator), for which only fragments had previously been known. This lengthy work of twelve books described the education of the model orator, "the good man speaking well," as Quintilian put it. Its description of the formation of the orator influenced the design of rhetorical education and its relation to other liberal arts as advocated by humanist educators as diverse as Agricola, Juan Luis Vives (1492–1540), and Philipp Melanchthon (1497–1560).

Quintilian's text also provided a detailed outline of the grammatical and rhetorical exercises of the *progymnasmata,* inherited from Greek practice, in which the student learned through imitation of models to progress by easy stages to writing more and more complicated pieces. A version of the *progymnasmata* by Apthonius was translated by Agricola from Greek into Latin. His popular translation was used by schoolmasters for two centuries. Imitation of models, part of the Sophistic heritage, was favored by pedagogues from antiquity onward. It yielded the familiar "commonplace book" of the Renaissance in which students recorded passages of note, often classifying them by themes and organizing them alphabetically. The aim was not simply to use the originals but to emulate them by building a supply or storehouse of ideas and stylistic devices. Erasmus was to show the way in his *De copia* (On copiousness) described below.

Rhetorician. Guillaume Fichet presents a manuscript of his *Rhetorica* to Cardinal Bessarion. Miniature from a printed copy of *Rhetorica* (1471). BIBLIOTECA NAZIONALE MARCIANA, VENICE. MEMBR. 53, FOL. 1R

Recovery of the Greek rhetorical heritage. Another important influence for the direction of rhetorical studies in the Renaissance was that provided by Greek scholars. As early as 1396 Manuel Chrysolores (c. 1353–1415), ambassador from the Byzantine emperor, had begun to teach Greek in Florence.

The Greek rhetorical heritage was enlarged by Bruni, who besides acting as chancellor of Florence, translated into Latin Plato's dialogues, *Gorgias* and *Phaedrus,* in which the value of rhetoric was debated. He also translated orations of Demosthenes and Aeschines.

The invention of printing made it possible to publish the recovered works of Greek rhetoricians. No press was more active than that of Aldus Manutius in Venice, which published in 1508 the *Rhetores graeci.* In all he printed ninety manuscripts, making them available to scholars throughout Europe. Thus, to the newly published Latin classics of rhetoric were added works of Plato, Aristotle, Hermogenes, Apthonius, Demosthenes, Isocrates, Aeschines, and other Attic orators. These two rhetorical traditions served to reorient the textual focus of educators in the new course of studies developing as the *studia humanitatis.*

New interest in Aristotle's teachings on rhetoric was awakened in the period. Although Aristotle's *Rhetoric* was recovered and translated into Latin in the high Middle Ages, it was taught as a part of the logical arts of Aristotle's *Organon* and as ancillary to his *Politics.* Aristotle's contribution to the discipline of rhetoric had been imperfectly assimilated by the Roman rhetoricians.

In the Renaissance, new translations and commentaries on Aristotle's *Rhetoric* were published, which helped to fill out ambiguous parts. In 1445 George of Trebizond (1395–1486) became the first to translate the *Rhetoric* in the period. The differences in the logical arts of dialectic and rhetoric so important to medieval scholars were reemphasized by Antonio Riccobono (1541–1599), who in his *Aristotelis ars rhetorica* (Aristotle's art of rhetoric; 1579) distinguished between the probable argument of dialectics and the "persuasible" proofs of rhetoric. Aristotle's definition of rhetoric as the art of finding or seeing all the means of persuasion, which may or may not persuade, differed from the Sophistic and Ciceronian view in which rhetoric was defined as the art of persuasion. The sources of persuasion, which Aristotle characterized as artistic and inartistic, had not been noted in the two Roman texts described earlier. The artistic proofs, those invented by the orator, rest on three appeals: *ethos,* the character of the speaker as projected in the speech; *logos,* the rational argument of the speech; and *pathos,* the emotion of the audience. The inartistic proofs referred to are the "extrinsics" mentioned by Cicero. In the *Rhetoric,* Aristotle describes the rhetorical topics or commonplaces, which he says are means of generating ideas that are then expressed in inductive or deductive arguments. He separates the rhetorical forms of induction and deduction, the example and the enthymeme, from the more formal arguments of logic suited to the speculative sciences.

Aristotle's teachings were most appreciated in Italy, where they were conveyed by pedagogues from George to Riccobono, Jacopo Brocardo, and Ludovico Carbone (d. 1597). Carbone studied in the Collegio Romano of the Jesuits shortly after it opened in 1551. The college curriculum, which called for a blending of Aristotelian and humanistic education, was adopted throughout the widespread Jesuit system.

Latin and vernacular oratory. Oratory was also affected by the recovery of these ancient texts. While opportunities for deliberative rhetoric increased to some degree in this period and judicial rhetoric always had had a place in civic life, epideictic rhetoric, the rhetoric of occasion, was exercised most vigorously. Orations in Ciceronian Latin for visiting dignitaries, for anniversaries, and for inaugurating new terms of office or academic terms were delivered by most of the humanists. Bruni, as the official orator of Florence, and Bartolomeo Ricci, as public orator of Ferrara, were prone to speak in imitation of Cicero. In his lectures and in his oratory on religious feasts, Marc-Antoine Muret (1526–1585) preferred the more briskly complex style of Tacitus. Prelates and religious and secular priests were expected to provide appropriate funeral oratory. Orations in praise of famous men were so popular that the collection *Orationes clarorum virorum,* published in Cologne, was widely imitated and even parodied in the *Epistolae obscurum virorum* (Letters of obscure men; 1515–1517) by Johann Reuchlin in his controversy with Scholastics over the importance of the study of Hebrew literature.

Orations in Italian were numerous as well. Francesco Sansovino published a collection in Venice in 1561. Four-fifths of the work consists of epideictic oratory, including funeral orations, imaginary addresses (*prosopopoeia*), and several orations of praise and one of blame.

***Rhetoric within the* studia humanitatis.** The growth of interest in rhetoric and its application not only to classical literature but to civic life wedded the discipline even more closely to moral philosophy and to the study of history, especially Roman history, where occasions of its use were brought to life through Cicero's letters and speeches. During the first half of the fifteenth century, with rhetoric as the central core, the studies of the trivium metamorphosed into the *studia humanitatis,* which included grammar, poetics, rhetoric, history, and moral philosophy. Logic is conspicuously absent as a formal subject in the panoply. The humanists had tired of its domination of education, and although it eventually was taught as preliminary to rhetoric in some grammar schools and had a place in university education, it was unimportant to the majority of schools in late-fifteenth-century Italy.

Within the *studia humanitatis,* classical works were studied in the ancient languages, chiefly in Latin, but supplemented with a few Greek texts, some illuminated by humanist Latin commentaries. The most popular Latin rhetorical works were the epistles and orations of Cicero, especially his *Pro Milone* and *Pro M. Marcello,* his treatises on rhetoric, *De officiis,* and the *Rhetorica ad Herennium.* Required reading in the Greek classics of rhetoric included Aristotle's *Rhetoric* and Isocrates's orations.

Three pedagogues influential in the shift to the new humanist studies were Gasparino Barzizza (1360–1430), teaching in Venice, Padua, and Bologna; Guarino Guarini (1374–1460), instructing in Venice, Verona, Florence, and Ferrara; and Vittorino da Feltre (c. 1373–1446), teaching in Padua, Venice, and Mantua. All three had illustrious students, some of whom became rulers of city-states, others reputable scholars and teachers themselves. These teachers, who taught mainly in communal and private schools and at times in universities, made rhetoric as imparted by Cicero and Quintilian central to their reforms of the curriculum.

One of the greatest of the later humanist reformers of educations was Desiderius Erasmus. For him the aim of education was eloquence, with all that implied for wisdom, style, and moral character. His *De ratione studii* (On a course of studies; 1512) laid out a curriculum that combined mastery of Latin, imitation of the ancients, and original work. Both oral and written discourse was stressed, which included various genres of rhetoric from orations to epistles. The book was influential in reforming education on the Continent and in England, where John Colet (1466 or 1467–1519) adopted his approach for St. Paul's School, the English grammar school he started. Erasmus wrote his famous rhetorical text *De copia* (On copiousness; 1512) for use in Colet's new school. The aim of the book was to awaken in students the knowledge that eloquence lies in the richness of ideas (*res*) expressed in a variety of appropriate, imaginative words (*verba*). Acquaintance with the possibilities open to the author would lead to facility of expression, to copiousness that could yield eloquence.

Although Erasmus's interest in style was Ciceronian in its basic theme, he deplored the cult of Ciceronianism that advocated slavish imitation of Cicero's style and even the sole use of his vocabulary. His dialogue *Ciceronianus* (The Ciceronian; 1528) satirized such pedantic imitation while recommending emulation of Cicero's ideals and his concern for elegant expression.

Realizing that classical epistles, orations, dialogues, poetry, and historical works could not be fully appreciated without a thorough understanding of the rhetorical discipline, other pedagogues had also turned to writing textbooks. The Renaissance added to the technical legacy new sources drawing on both Greek and Roman works. Some of these books covered the entire art, while some treated only invention or style.

George of Trebizond, mentioned above, was a Greek emigrant who wrote the first and most comprehensive rhetoric of the Renaissance, *Rhetoricorum libri V,* published about 1433. In it he conveyed the Greek and Byzantine tradition and preserved the Roman, using illustrations from Hermogenes, Dionysius of Halicarnassus, Cicero, Quintilian, and Virgil. His work was instrumental in illustrating the prevalence of stylistic devices throughout all eloquent expression regardless of genre. Hermogenes's seven "ideas" of style, which George explained, extended the register beyond the three levels. Other comprehensive manuals in Latin spread the expanded humanistic teachings on rhetoric throughout Europe. Prominent among these were a *Rhetorica* (1471) written by the rector of the University of Paris, Guillaume Fichet; Lorenzo Guglielmo Traversagni's *Nova rhetorica* (1478), published while the author visited England; Melanchthon's *Institutiones rhetoricae* (Training in rhetoric; 1521) and its revised version, *Elementa rhetorica* (Elements of rhetoric; 1531), which extended the humanistic rhetorical art to Germany and other northern countries; Joannes Cesarius's *Rhetorica* (1542); and Cypriano Soarez's *De arte rhetorica libri tres ex Aristotele, Cicerone, et Quintiliano deprompti* (Three books on the art of rhetoric drawn from Aristotle, Cicero, and Quintilian; 1562). This last text, written by a Spanish Jesuit, was adopted by the Collegio Romano, reprinted continuously into the eighteenth century, and circulated throughout the Jesuit *studia* around the world.

In the sixteenth century, comprehensive rhetorics in the vernacular also began to appear. The most notable are Bartolomeo Cavalcanti's *La retorica* in seven books, published in Italian in 1559, and in English, Thomas Wilson's *The Arte of Rhetorique* (1553), the first original rhetoric in English. Both of these present the art as primary rhetoric, which is conceived as oratory, secular and ecclesiastical.

Many authors published texts treating style alone. Vives, a Spaniard educated at the University of Paris and an influential humanist educator, believed that the most significant part of rhetoric was style. He claimed in *De ratione dicendi* (On the art of oratory; 1532) that the complete art of rhetoric was really not a subject suitable for boys. In this work he devoted himself to stylistic elements such as the composition of sentences, amplification and concision, tone, and the levels of style.

Reforms of Rhetoric. The study of rhetoric, now central to the new humanities curriculum, began to undergo reform also. Pedagogues in the century before Vives were concerned with simplifying their subjects. The most prominent early reformer was Valla, who taught rhetoric at the University of Pavia and at Rome, and as many humanists did, served as secretary to secular and ecclesiastical authorities. His interest in language led to a new critical method of analyzing texts. In his *Disputationes dialecticae* (1439) he claims that there is no need for a separate art of invention, that rhetorical invention suffices for all kinds of argumentation.

The Dutch scholar Agricola carried back to northern Europe his enthusiasm for humanist learning when he returned there in 1479 after his studies in Italy. Like Valla he saw no need for two arts of invention. In his *De inventione dialecticae* (On dialectical invention; 1479) he combines rhetoric with dialectic, giving to logic all the commonplaces used for inquiry in all subjects. Agricola saw dialectic as the sole component of logic, thus discarding the demonstrative reasoning of scientific argument, an important part of Aristotle's *Organon*. Nevertheless, his teachings depend on Aristotelian dialectic in conceiving the task of invention as supplying middle terms to make convincing arguments. His list of twenty-four topics drew from Aristotle's *Topics* and *Rhetoric,* from Cicero and Themistius. The second part of the scholastic study of dialectic, judgment, he treats only briefly. He returns to currency the Aristotelian notion of probabilities as the foundation of all arguments and removes the weighty Boethian version with its application of maxims. For Agricola rhetoric furnished only methods of organization, emotional appeals, and stylistic embellishment. Taking his cue from the three duties of the orator, noted by Cicero (to teach, to charm, and to move), Agricola taught that the purpose of discourse was first to teach, but that to charm might also be useful in fulfilling its main duty. Rhetoric's task in discourse was to provide ornamentation, charm. In his scheme, then, both dialectic and rhetoric are at work in discourse and are applicable to any subject matter. Agricola's work was especially popular in Paris and inspired other prominent scholars such as Johann Sturm (1507–1589), who introduced students at the University of Paris to the work.

Ramus, who became a pupil of Sturm, was to carry the ideas of Agricola to greater extremes. Bent upon simplifying rhetoric, Ramus found fault with the icons of humanism, Cicero and Quintilian, and with the scholastics' worship of Aristotle, writing polemical works against all three: *Brutinae questiones* (Brutus's problems; 1547), *Rhetoricae distinctiones in Quintilianum* (Evaluations of Quintilian's rhetoric; 1549), and *Aristotelicae animadversiones* (Remarks on Aristotle; 1543), respectively. He announced a new method of teaching dialectic in his *Dialectical partitiones* (The structure of dialectic; 1543), which overturned Aristotelian logic.

Ramus sought to avoid any overlap in his vision of the liberal arts. The parts taught in dialectic, he believed, should be separate and different from those of rhetoric. Building on Agricola's innovation in his *Dialecticae institutiones* (Training in dialectics; 1543) he reserved invention for dialectics alone and detached arrangement from rhetoric, transmuting it into judgment. The topics of invention are based largely on Agricola's topical logic, reduced to fourteen and arranged dichotomously as Ramus preferred. Under judgment, which he views as managing arguments found in invention, he treats enthymeme and example, definition and division. Memory, he argues, is absorbed in the practice of judgment, which aids recall of arguments. Thus, to rhetoric is left only delivery and style.

An innovation in Ramus's amalgamated rhetoric and dialectic was his introduction of use, or exercise, which interpreted writing or speaking. Interpretation meant the analysis of readings, whether oratory, poetry, or philosophy, for the nature of the questions taken up in the work, the topics employed, and the soundness of the arguments. The actual practice of writing and speaking was barely touched upon. Ramism most affected Protestant Europe, his influence perhaps spurred on by his assassination following the St. Bartholomew's Day massacre of Protestants in France in 1572.

Ramist rhetoric, as conveyed by Ramus's colleague Omer Talon (c. 1510–1562) in *Institutiones oratoriae* (Training in oratory; 1545), is mainly concerned with ornamentation through *elocutio,* that is, language or style. It includes detailed distinctions of figures and tropes. The tropes are classified dichotomously into four master tropes: metonymy, synecdoche, metaphor, and irony. Figures are also divided and subdivided into twelve figures of diction and fourteen figures of thought. Poetry in the Ramist system is treated under style. Talon and his disciples, however, recommended the plain style and words decorously chosen in keeping with the subject matter. Delivery is accorded a brief treatment of voice and gesture.

Sympathetic to the reforms of Ramus was the northern European scholar Bartholomeus Keckermann (1571–1608/9). He taught in the German cities of Wittenberg, Heidelberg, and Danzig (now Gdansk in Poland). Moderately Ramist, Keckerman used the dichotomous approach to order principles of the art. His *De rhetorica ecclesiastica* (On ecclesiastical rhetoric) was widely used on the Continent and in England.

Another eminent northern European, Gerhard Johann Vossius (1577–1649), who taught in Leiden and Amsterdam, was anti-Ramist in his views. He addressed the full Ciceronian art of rhetoric in his *Commentaria rhetorica* (1605) and wrote three other very popular works on rhetoric. Both authors emphasized the importance of the emotions in the moving of the will.

Rhetoric in England. The Renaissance spread last to England. Texts in Latin at first provided the chief instruction in rhetoric, including the ubiquitous *De inventione* and the *Rhetorica ad Herennium.* Vernacular rhetorics appeared early in the sixteenth century. Contemporary Continental influences were strong, as the first English rhetoric, Leonard Cox's *Arte or Crafte of Rhetoryke* (1532), demonstrates. His treatise, which focuses on invention, is based primarily on Melanchthon's *Institutiones rhetoricae.*

As W. S. Howell has shown, Renaissance English rhetorics generally fall into three types: Ciceronian, stylistic, and formulary. Wilson's Ciceronian rhetoric, *The Arte of Rhetorique,* contains all five canons of rhetoric. He attacks the material in a fresh manner, however, including biblical, classical, and contemporary dilemmas as illustrations of the application of commonplaces to issues. In his lengthy treatment of style, Wilson stresses plainness and aptness of expression.

Stylistic rhetorics were numerous and varied in their approaches. Richard Sherry's *A Treatise on Schemes and Tropes* (1550) was the first stylistic text in English and owes much to Cicero and Quintilian. Henry Peacham's popular *Garden of Eloquence* (1577) recasts the categories in the *Ad Herennium*'s discussion of style, classifying figures into tropes of words and thoughts, and dividing schemes into those of grammar (orthography and syntax) and of rhetoric (words, thoughts, amplification).

Formulary rhetorics provided an overview of the five parts of rhetoric and furnished models. Richard Rainolde, in *A Booke Called the Foundacion of Rhetorike* (1563), used Apthonius's *Progymnasmata* as the basis of his model speeches. Other popular formularies were *The Enemie of Idleness* (1568), by William Fulwood, and *The English Secretorie* (1586), by Angel Day.

The height of Ramist influence was felt from 1575 to 1600. Gabriel Harvey was the best known Ramist, lecturing on this approach to rhetoric at Cambridge and publishing the lectures in 1575. A Latin edition and an English translation of Ramus's work were published by Roland MacIlmaine in 1574. Dudley Fenner's *The Artes of Logicke and Rhetorike* (1584) summarized both Ramus's logic and Talon's rhetoric. Others followed, but neo-Ciceronian rhetorics soon appeared, among the most famous being George Puttenham's *Arte of English Poesie* (1589).

Among those reacting negatively to the rhetoric of Ramus was Francis Bacon. In a number of his works he reasserts the importance of the complete art of rhetoric to civic life, noting its relation to philosophy. He defines "the duty and office of rhetoric" in the *Advancement of Learning* (1605) as "to apply reason to imagination for the better moving of the will." In this he emphasizes its faculty of "setting things before the eyes," as recommended by Aristotle and Quintilian. Its civic purpose was central to his reappraisal of the art, leading him to stress its role as the handmaid of wisdom, and requiring of it clarity rather than excessive display and honesty rather than sophistry. In his reappraisal, however, Bacon departs from tradition in seeing invention as simply recalling from memory what has been stored there. True invention, he says, belongs to science. Rhetoric becomes for him the instrument or means of transmission of wisdom, an active participant not in its development but in its presentation. Later in the seventeenth century, members of the Royal Society who adopted Bacon as their guide in the scientific enterprise went much further than he and denied a place for rhetoric even in the presentation of science.

Throughout the Renaissance interest in rhetoric remained high. Whatever the intent of reformers to reconfigure the art, the effects were to reassert its importance. Educators taught students to invent ideas and expressions, whether with dialectical or with rhetorical techniques, and to analyze the inventions of others. Principles of organization, classical or Ramean, the tropes and schemes were so familiar to the erudite of the high Renaissance that they could deploy them at will. Eloquence became the key to renown in all the professions as well as in the courts of kings and prelates. But by the end of the Renaissance reaction against artifice of pen, tongue, and dress had begun to alter the notions of style in favor of plain, unadorned discourse. And that too, as both Talon and Wilson recognized, is a style of its own.

See also **Commonplace Books**; **Education**; *and biographies of figures mentioned in this entry.*

BIBLIOGRAPHY

Baldwin, Charles S. *Renaissance Literary Theory and Practice.* New York, 1939.

Baron, Hans. *The Crisis of the Early Italian Renaissance: Civic Humanism and Republican Liberty in an Age of Classicism and Tyranny.* 2 vols. Princeton, N.J., 1955; rev. ed. of vol. 1, Princeton, 1966.

Bolgar, R. R., ed. *Classical Influences on European Culture, A.D. 1500–1700.* Cambridge, U.K., 1976.

Camporeale, Salvatore. *Lorenzo Valla: Umanesimo e teologia.* Florence, 1972.

Clark, Donald L. *John Milton at St. Paul's School: A Study of Ancient Rhetoric in English Renaissance Education.* New York, 1948.

Fumaroli, Marc. *L'age de l'éloquence: rhétorique et "res literaria" de la Renaissance au seuil de l'époque classique.* Geneva, 1980.

Gray, Hannah H. "Renaissance Humanism: The Pursuit of Eloquence." *Renaissance Essays from the* Journal of the History of Ideas. Edited by Paul O. Kristeller and Philip P. Wiener. New York, 1968. Pages 192–216.

Grendler, Paul. *Schooling in Renaissance Italy: Literacy and Learning, 1300–1600.* Baltimore, 1989. Discusses humanistic education in the schools of Italy.

Howell, Wilbur S. *Logic and Rhetoric in England, 1500–1700.* New York, 1961.

Jardine, Lisa. *Francis Bacon: Discovery and the Art of Discourse.* London, 1974.

Kristeller, Paul Oskar. *Renaissance Thought: The Classic, Scholastic, and Humanist Strains.* New York, 1961. Revised and enlarged edition of *The Classics and Renaissance Thought,* Cambridge, Mass., 1955.

Kristeller, Paul Oskar. *Renaissance Thought II: Papers on Humanism and the Arts.* New York, 1965.

Miriam Joseph, Sister. *Rhetoric in Shakespeare's Time: Literary Theory of Renaissance Europe.* 1947. Reprint, New York, 1962.

Monfasani, John. *George of Trebizond: A Biography and a Study of His Rhetoric and Logic.* Leiden, Netherlands, 1976.

Moss, Jean Dietz. *Novelties in the Heavens: Rhetoric and Science in the Copernican Controversy.* Chicago, 1993.

Murphy, James J., ed. *Renaissance Eloquence: Studies in the Theory and Practice of Renaissance Rhetoric.* Berkeley, Calif., 1983.

O'Malley, John W. *Praise and Blame in Renaissance Rome: Rhetoric, Docrine, and Reform in the Sacred Oratory of the Papal Court, c. 1450–1521.* Durham, N.C., 1979.

Ong, Walter J. *Ramus: Method and the Decay of Dialogue, from the Art of Discourse to the Art of Reason.* Cambridge, Mass., 1958. A thorough examination of Ramus and Ramism.

Patterson, Annabel M. *Hermogenes and the Renaissance: Seven Ideas of Style.* Princeton, N.J., 1970.

Seigel, Jerrold E. *Rhetoric and Philosophy in Renaissance Humanism.* Princeton, N.J., 1968.

Shuger, Debora K. *Sacred Rhetoric: The Christian Grand Style in the English Renaissance.* Princeton, N.J., 1988.

Struever, Nancy. *The Language of History in the Renaissance: Rhetoric and Historical Consciousness in Florentine Humanism.* Princeton, N.J., 1970.

Vasoli, Cesare. *La dialettica e la retorica dell'Umanesimo: "Invenzione" e "Metodo" nella cultura del XV e XVI secolo.* Milan, 1968.

Vickers, Brian. *In Defence of Rhetoric.* Oxford, 1988.

JEAN DIETZ MOSS

RHÉTORIQUEURS. The term *rhétoriqueurs* (or *grand rhétoriqueurs*) was first applied in the nineteenth century to a group of poets active during the reign of Louis XII (1498–1515). The name (improperly borrowed from the fifteenth-century satiric poet Guillaume Coquillart) soon referred to an entire school of late-fifteenth- and early-sixteenth-century courtly writers, spanning several francophone countries (the duchies of Burgundy and Brittany, and the kingdom of France) and three generations, from the historiographer of the Burgundian house, Georges Chastellain (c. 1405/15–1474), to his successor, Jean Molinet (1435–1507), to Molinet's successor, Jean Lemaire de Belges (1473–1525), who switched from Burgundian to French allegiance.

Defining the *Rhétoriqueurs*. Despite its inappropriateness, the name stuck. For one thing, its derogatory overtones suited the contempt that turn-of-the-century French scholars felt for writers who, more often than not, were not French in the national sense, and whose entire output seemed dedicated to praising their masters in an absurdly ornate language. At the same time, it made sense to think of them as a group, because they did so themselves, at least after the first generation; and it made sense to call them *rhétoriqueurs,* because rhetoric was their craft and their claim to glory. Upon his death Chastellain was hailed, notably by Jean Robertet (d.c.

1503), as a humanist's hero, whose *rhétorique,* in prose and verse, had single-handedly put French language and northern culture on a par with ancient and Italian models: here was a new Cicero, a new Livy, a new Petrarch. Lavish mutual compliments and growing lists of worthy fellow writers confirm that the *rhétoriqueurs,* in addition to being politically Xfaithful to their rulers, were aesthetically loyal to one another (at times across national divisions) and had a keen sense of their cultural distinction. They behaved in the self-conscious and self-promoting manner that would characterize later groups of Renaissance poets.

But they were not poets in the specialized sense that would apply first to Clément Marot (1496–1544; son of a *rhétoriqueur* who steered clear of his father's kind of rhetoric and, by so doing, reinvented French poetry), and then, even more emphatically, to the stars of the Pléiade. What defined the *rhétoriqueurs* was (1) an official courtly role, not only as encomiastic writers, but also as historiographers and propagandists at the service of a royal or princely house, and (2) a commitment to carry out this duty both in verse (*séconde rhétorique*) and in prose, twin registers for an extremely elaborate, flamboyant conception of eloquence, in which the pleasant and the persuasive, the beautiful and the efficient, were often envisioned as one and the same effect. The *rhétoriqueurs* used prose in their daily chronicles and in more synthetic historical works such as Jean Lemaire's *Illustrations de Gaule et singularitez de Troyes* (Illustrations of Gaul and singularities of Troy, c. 1510). They used verse in their work for the theater—an important aspect of their production—from Jean Molinet's *Mystère de saint Quentin* (Mystery of St. Quentin) to Pierre Gringore's (c. 1475–1528) *Sottie du jeu du prince des sots* (Play of the prince of fools; 1512), and in traditional, highly technical forms such as the ballad or the *chant royal,* with subjects of praise and blame ranging from the holy to the bawdy. Yet verse was also employed in pieces that were historical in nature: Chastellain and Molinet used it not only to celebrate, satirize, or deplore a significant political moment, but also to narrate—in an allusive, symbolic, enigmatic manner—entire sequences of events that they also reported in the prose of their chronicles; see, for example, the *Recollection des merveilleuses advenues en nostre temps* (Collection of wonderful events of our time), begun by Chastellain and continued by Molinet. The French *rhétoriqueurs* tried to outdo their Flemish rivals by writing extensive chronicles in which verse was dominant. Jean Marot's (c. 1463–1526) *Voyage de Gênes* and *Voyage de Venise,* for example, are annals of Louis XII's Italian successes with bits of prose inserted in a system of *variatio metrica* (metric variation) and mythological fictions. In some cases, such as Guillaume Cretin's (c. 1465–1525) *Chronique française,* verse even became the sole medium of historical narration.

Rhétoriqueur. Jean Marot presents his *Voyage de Gênes* to Queen Anne de Bretagne. BIBLIOTHÈQUE NATIONALE, PARIS

Allegories of Praise. In the hybrid *prosimetrum,* prose and verse together produced complex allegories built upon an analogical model, whereby the prince was shown as being to this world what God is to the spiritual one. Thus, Maximilian I of Austria, savior of the Burgundian heritage, is another Christ for Molinet, while Louis XII, in the eyes of Jean Marot, is the "messiah of France." The analogical hierarchy was often reversed; claiming to use the prince as an image of God, the *rhétoriqueur* ended up drawing on divine images to extoll the achievements of the prince and touting his own ingenuity at discovering correspondences, often based on puns and homonymy (between Mary of Burgundy and the Virgin Mary, for example). The increasingly precise classical culture of the last *rhétoriqueurs* would allow them to combine the abstraction of moral personifications with the more plastic presence of mythological figures; Jean Lemaire, the most Italianized of them, was the main agent of change in this domain.

The practice of eloquence of the *rhétoriqueurs* was based on the assumption that the prince, incarnating God's will and the aristocratic ideal of *chevalerie* (chivalry), had the power to make the world less impure, more prosperous, peaceful, and beautiful—what Molinet called a *paradis terrestre* (earthly paradise), a new garden of Eden. The ultimate figure of this dream was the universal monarchy that would follow a reconciliation of the Christian houses and a crusade against the Turks. When the prince failed (as Charles the Bold did so spectacularly in 1477, with his defeat and death at Nancy), the *rhétoriqueur* would castigate his blinding pride and vividly depict the roaring wheel of fortune. These partisan writers fundamentally perceived themselves as agents of concord and magnificence, announcing the victory of order over chaos, of *facture* (composition) over *fracture* (fracture), creating in words the kind of radiant harmony that the prince's deeds were expected to bring into the world.

The *prosimetrum* usually hails or deplores a particular event, such as the birth of Philip of Austria in Jean Molinet's *Chapelet des dames* (The garland of the ladies) or the death of Philibert, duke of Savoy, in Jean Lemaire's *Couronne margaritique* (The crown of Margaret). But there was no *éloge* without *conseil,* no high-ringing praise without high-minded sermonizing: the *prosimètre* was above all an *opus magnum,* a triumphant piece of *pleine rhétorique* ("full" rhetoric, in both verse and prose) designed to describe, explain, celebrate, and promote the cardinal virtues of good government (the paradigmatic example of this is Jean Meschinot's *Lunettes des princes* [The princes' spectacles; c. 1461]). The point was to "do it all," in a fashion that would soon become unintelligible to narrower practitioners of speech—poets, orators, and historians, each taking pride in the purity of their specific ethical and formal rules. Not that the *rhétoriqueurs* had no sense of a difference between verse and prose, or history and poetry, but such contrasts were superseded by an assumption of complementarity.

Their practice, however, was not stable; in fact, within the corpus of the *rhétoriqueurs,* the utilizations of prose and verse, of history and poetry, of political persuasion and aesthetic pleasure, manifest contradictory tendencies, and there are alternating urges to merge and diverge. These shifts can be seen in Molinet's brilliant introduction of metric rhythms and rhyme effects in the prose of his *Chroniques* (whereas nothing of the sort is found in Chastellain's meandering sentences); or the rarefaction of stylistic colors in the last books of Lemaire's *Illustrations,* as though the austere historian, guided by Pallas, had to split from the frivolous ear-charmer, the Venus-bound poet; or the attempts by André de La Vigne (c. 1470–c. 1515), Guillaume Cretin, and Jean Marot to keep together the task of the chronicler and the art of rhyme.

The *rhétoriqueurs,* with Molinet at their epicenter, embody a first moment of humanist vernacular writing among French-speaking nations, a period in which *rhetoric* as such reigns, in all the glory of florid elocution—every verbal ornament jubilantly applied to every possible argument. In a second phase, a more refined cultural perception, a more exact practice of imitation would proceed to divide rhetoric's kingdom into many principalities, making the encomiastic utopia of the *rhétoriqueurs*' appear naive and "still medieval" by comparison (one has to keep in mind, however, that the long-lived Jean Bouchet [1476–c. 1558] was able to carry their composite aesthetics well into the reign of Henry II). For centuries, until their rehabilitation at the hands of twentieth-century poets and scholars, they were lambasted for having produced bad history and bad poetry. In truth, their sin was to have had the highest sense of both.

See also **French Literature and Language**; **Historiography, Renaissance**, *subentry on* **French Historiography**; **Marot, Clément**.

BIBLIOGRAPHY

Primary Works

Auton, Jean d'. *Chroniques de Louis XII.* Edited by R. de Maulde La Clavière. 4 vols. Paris, 1889–1895.

Bouchet, Jean. *Le temple de bonne renommée.* Edited by Giovanna Bellati. Milan, 1992.

Chastellain, Georges. *Œuvres.* Edited by J. Kervyn de Lettenhove. 8 vols. Brussels, 1963–1966.

Cretin, Guillaume. *Œuvres poétiques.* Edited by Kathleen Chesney. Paris, 1932. Reprint, Geneva, 1977.

Fabri, Pierre. *Le grand et vray art de pleine rhetorique.* Edited by A. Héron. Rouen, France, 1889. Reprint, Geneva, 1972.

Gringore, Pierre. *Œuvres complètes.* Edited by Ch. d'Héricault and A. de Montaiglon. Paris, 1858–1877.

La Vigne, André de. *La ressource de la Chrestienté.* Edited by Cynthia J. Brown. Montreal, 1989.

Lemaire de Belges, Jean. *Œuvres*. Edited by Joseph Stecher. 4 vols. Louvain, Belgium; 1882. Reprint, Geneva, 1969.
Marot, Jean. *Œuvres complètes*. Edited by Gérard Defaux and Thierry Mantovani. Geneva, 1999.
Meschinot, Jean. *Les lunettes des princes*. Edited by Christine Martineau-Génieys. Geneva, 1972.
Molinet, Jean. *Chroniques*. Edited by Georges Doutrepont and Omer Jodogne. 3 vols. Brussels, 1935.
Molinet, Jean. *Faictz et dictz*. Edited by N. Dupire. 3 vols. Paris, 1937.
Parmentier, Jean. *Œuvres poétiques*. Edited by Françoise Ferrand. Geneva, 1971.
Recueil d'Arts de Seconde Rhétorique. Edited by Ernest Langlois. Paris, 1902. Reprint, Geneva, 1974.
Robertet, Jean. *Œuvres*. Edited by Margaret Zsuppán. Geneva, 1970.
Saint-Gelais, Octavien de. *Le séjour d'Honneur*. Edited by Joseph A. James. Chapel Hill, N.C., 1977.

Secondary Works

Brown, Cynthia J. *The Shaping of History and Poetry in Late Medieval France: Propaganda and Artistic Expression in the Works of the Rhétoriqueurs*. Birmingham, Ala., 1985.
Cigada, Sergio, and Anna Slerca, eds. *Les grands rhétoriqueurs*. Milan, 1985.
Cornilliat, François. *"Or ne mens": Couleurs de l'éloge et du blâme chez les "grands rhétoriqueurs."* Paris, 1994.
Devaux, Jean. *Jean Molinet, indiciaire bourguignon*. Paris, 1996.
DiStefano, Giuseppe, and Rose M. Bidler, eds. *La grande rhétorique* (*Le moyen français* 34). Montreal, 1994.
Grands rhétoriqueurs. Paris, 1997.
Guy, Henry. *Histoire de la poésie française au XVIe siècle*. Reprint, Paris, 1968.
Jodogne, Pierre. *Jean Lemaire de Belges, écrivain franco-bourguignon*. Brussels, 1972.
Koopmans, Jelle, et al., eds. *Rhetoric, Rhétoriqueurs, Rederijkers*. Amsterdam, 1995.
Randall, Michael. *Building Resemblance: Analogical Imagery in the Early French Renaissance*. Baltimore, 1996.
Thiry, Claude. "La poétique des grands rhétoriqueurs." *Le Moyen Âge* 86 (1980): 117–133.
Zumthor, Paul. *Le masque et la lumière: La poétique des grands rhétoriqueurs*. Paris, 1978.

FRANÇOIS CORNILLIAT

RIBADENEIRA, PEDRO DE (Ortiz de Cisneros; 1526–1611), Jesuit humanist, ascetical writer, biographer, historian, translator. Born in Toledo, Pedro de Ribadeneira arrived in Rome as the page of Cardinal Alexander Farnese in 1539. He entered the Society of Jesus in 1540 at age thirteen. He was educated from 1542 to 1549 in the humanities, philosophy, and theology in Paris and Padua. Ribadeneira's career had three major phases. First, he was a professor of rhetoric in Palermo and later at the Roman College and the Germanicum in Rome (1549–1555). He then served in various administrative posts for the Jesuit order (1555–1574). In the final phase of his career, he returned to Spain where he wrote his most important works (1574–1611).

Ribadeneira was an accomplished biographer. His work notably includes the biographies of men and women, a collection of hagiographical lives, and an autobiography. *Vita Ignatii Loiolae* (*Vida del padre Ignacio de Loyola;* The life of Ignatius Loyola; Latin, 1572; Spanish, 1583), his most important biography, was the first of Loyola sanctioned by the Society of Jesus. It also includes a thorough history of the foundation of the Jesuits. Ribadeneira wrote biographies of other leading sixteenth-century Jesuits, including Saint Francisco de Borja (1592) and Diego Laínez (1594), as well as of the generous patronesses of Jesuit works in Spain, Estafanía Manrique Castilla and María de Mendoza. These biographies of holy men and women are most notable for their humanist style, which can be found in the historical objectivity and the sense of human agency and autonomy that mark the narrative as well as in the rhetorical devices and structures that Ribadeneira borrowed from the norms of classicized rhetoric so popular among Renaissance humanists. Ribadeneira's biographical efforts contributed significantly to the development of a type of hagiography that met the standards of humanist biography.

He published an autobiography, modeled on Augustine's *Confessions,* in 1595. His collection of the lives of the saints, *Flos sanctorum,* was written in Latin, published in two volumes (1599–1604), and quickly translated into several vernacular languages. Other writings include histories, for example, *Historia ecclesiástica del cisma del reyno de Inglaterra* (Ecclesiastical history of the schism in England; 1588); Christian political thought, such as *Tratado de la Religion y Virtudes que deue tener el Principe Christiano, para gouernar y conseruar sus estados. Contra lo que Nicolás Machiauelo y los politicos deste tiempo enseñan* (Treatise on the religion and virtues of a Christian prince for the sake of his states; 1595); and his own ascetical reflections in *Tratado de la tribulación* (Treatise on tribulation; 1589) and *Manuale de oraciones y exercicios, para e uso y approveechamiento de la gente devoto* (Manual of prayer 1604). Ribadeneira was also an accomplished translator of Christian texts into Castilian Spanish. These include the ascetical writings of Saint Albert the Great in *Tratado de las virtudes* (1594) and a broad selection of Saint Augustine in two volumes: *Las meditaciones, soliloquios, y manual del bienaventurado sant Augustín* (The meditations, soliloquies, and manual of the Blessed Saint Augustine; 1553) and *Las confessiones* (1598). The style of Ribadeneira's Castilian Spanish in all his writings, but especially in the translations, is considered a preeminent example of Spain's literary golden age.

BIBLIOGRAPHY

Primary Works

Ribadeneira, Pedro de. *Fontes narrativi de S. Ignatio de Loyola et de Societatis Iesu Initiis*. Vol. 4, *Monumenta historica Societatis Iesu*. Rome, 1965.

Ribadeneira, Pedro de. *Historias de la Contrarreforma*. Edited with notes and introduction by Eusebio Rey. Madrid, 1945.

Ribadeneira, Pedro de. *Monumenta Ribadeneira*. 2 vols. Rome, 1920–1923, reprinted 1969.

Secondary Works

Bilinkoff, Jodi. "The Many 'Lives' of Pedro de Ribadeneira." *Renaissance Quarterly* 52 (1999): 180–196.

Bireley, Robert. "Pedro de Ribadeneira: Origins of the Tradition in Spain (1595)." In his *The Counter-Reformation Prince: Anti-Machiavellianism or Catholic Statecraft in Early Modern Europe*. Chapel Hill, N.C., 1990. Pages 111–135.

Gómez-Menor, José. "La Progenie Hebrea del Padre Pedro de Ribadeneira S.I." *Sefarad* 36 (1976): 307–332.

DAVID J. COLLINS

RIBEIRO, BERNARDIM (1482?–1552?), Portuguese novelist and poet, creator of the Portuguese version of the sentimental romance. Documentary claims about Ribeiro's life have proven fraudulent, so much remains a mystery. The Ferrara editor of Ribeiro's works was an exiled Portuguese Jew, and this has led to speculations that Ribeiro may himself have been a converted Jew. He is thought to have been born in the village of Torrão, Alentejo, and may have been a companion of Francisco de Sá de Miranda. Someone with his name is known to have attended the University of Lisbon between 1507 and 1511 and to have been named Royal Scribe to João III in 1524. Ribeiro may have been in Italy and is thought to have died in Lisbon two years before the publication of his works in Ferrara, Italy (1554).

His *Menina e moça* (Young girl), also known as *Livro das saudades* (Book of sorrowful longing), combines elements of sentimental, chivalric, and pastoral romance, using them all as vehicles of sentiment. The last sentimental romance of the Renaissance, *Menina e moça* was probably written between 1530 and 1540 and was proscribed by the Portuguese Inquisition in 1581. The work established the sensibility of *saudade* as a distinctive feature of Portuguese artistic expression. The central characters are tragic sufferers who refuse to renounce the frustrated claims of almost morbidly intense strivings to attain their ideals in love, preferring instead the anguish of self-imposed exile in a bucolic setting that also constitutes a brutally impersonal natural order. Ribeiro was influenced by Ovid, Virgil, the *roman courtois,* Castilian sentimental romance, the Italian poets of the *dolce stil nuovo* (sweet new style), Dante, Petrarch, Boccaccio, Jacopo Sannazaro, courtly and folk amatory lyric, Fernando de Rojas, and the romance of chivalry.

Menina e moça's most striking features are its tragic and even fatalistic atmosphere, its deep feeling and unaffected sincerity, its emphasis on the feminine point of view, its avoidance of sensationalism and of artificially literary qualities, its subtle analysis of love sentiment, its poetic and allegorical use of imagery, its delicacy and originality of language, and the rhythmic musicality of its prose. *Menina e moça's* mannerist style may be seen in its exotic fusion of genres, its counterpoint between fantasy and realism and between archaism and a realistic emphasis on familiar detail, its association of love and death, the tension between the beauty of its natural settings and the extreme inward strife of its characters, and its unexpected ellipses and truncated ending.

By conceiving a tragic sense of life that arises from love's being regarded as the only truly important value, the spirit of Ribeiro's work militates against a repressive atmosphere of distrust and enmity such as was fomented by domineering and fantastical elements in the Reformation–Counter-Reformation struggle. In its portrayal of the afflictions of tragic love, *Menina e moça* both captures and places in a critical perspective the climate of violence and repression that by the middle of the sixteenth century came more and more to be directed against the opponents of authoritarian dogma, particularly those who favored cultured humanism or a civic-minded and evangelical emphasis on compassion and tender humanity. In Ribeiro's work, unrelieved suffering in love is a sign of distinction and becomes almost a romantic and secular ideal of morality. Ribeiro's interest in purity of heart and in the figure of the passionate, somber, homeless wanderer make him a precursor of the eighteenth-century cult of sensibility, romanticism, and modernism.

An accomplished lyric poet, Ribeiro also introduced the eclogue into Portuguese literature and is thought by many to be the true author of the *Écloga de Crisfal* (instead of Cristovão Falcão). He wrote a dense, cryptic lyric as sophisticated in its unconventional use of symbolic imagery as it is psychologically penetrating and complexly metaphysical. Anticipating the lyric of Luíz Vaz de Camoës and others, nothing in the Iberian lyric of Ribeiro's day is more original.

BIBLIOGRAPHY

Primary Works

Ribeiro, Bernardim. *História de menina e moça*. Edited by D. E. Grockenberger. Lisbon, Portugal, 1947. The most carefully prepared and scholarly edition of Ribeiro's masterpiece.

Ribeiro, Bernardim. *Obras completas*. Edited by Aquilino Ribeiro and M. Marques Braga. 2 vols. Lisbon, Portugal, 1972. Ribeiro's poetry is collected in volume 2.

Secondary Works

Asensio, Eugenio. *Estudios portugueses*. Paris, 1974. Contains three essays on Ribeiro. Lucid perceptions place all previous critical opinion and its shortcomings in perspective.

Creel, Bryant. "Bernardim Ribeiro and the Tradition of Renaissance Pastoral." In *Renaissance and Golden Age Essays in Honor of D. W. McPheeters*. Edited by Bruno Damiani. Potomac, Md., 1986. Pages 27–48. An interpretation of *Menina e moça* in relation to its cultural-historical and political context.

Salgado Júnior, António. *A* Menina e moça *e o romance sentimental no renascimento*. Aveiro, Portugal, 1940. The essential critical study of Bernardim Ribeiro.

BRYANT CREEL

RICCI, MATTEO (Li Ma-tou, Li Madou; 1552–1610), founder of the Roman Catholic missions in China during the modern era. Born in Macerata, Italy, Ricci attended the new Jesuit college in his hometown and went to Rome in 1568 to study law. He entered the Jesuit novitiate at S. Andrea al Quirinale in Rome on 15 August 1571. As part of his training he did chores in the Professed House located not far from the Farnesian Church of the Gesù. He studied philosophy at the Collegio Romano from 1573 to 1577. As a student of Christopher Clavius (1538–1612), the Jesuit from Bamberg who was instrumental in developing the Gregorian calendar, Ricci pursued courses on mathematics and astronomy, including the making of sundials, clocks, and astrolabes. In his last year at the college Ricci was enrolled in the Course of Controversies that Robert Bellarmine (1542–1621) inaugurated.

As a volunteer missionary to the Indies, Ricci, with Michele Ruggieri (1543–1607) and two other Jesuits, arrived in Goa, India, in September 1578. Ordained a priest at Cochin in 1580, Ricci returned to Goa for additional theological studies. Alessandro Valignano (1539–1606), the superior of the Jesuit missions in Asia, ordered Ruggieri to come to Macao (Aomen) to learn Chinese. After several months in Macao Ruggieri suggested to Valignano, then in Japan, that Ricci join him in the language program. When Ricci reached Macao in 1582, Ruggieri was in Canton (Guangzhou), where he showed the Portuguese merchants how to adapt themselves to Chinese etiquette. One year later Chinese officials invited Ruggieri and Ricci to settle at Chao-ch'ing (Zhaoqing), west of Canton. The interest of visitors in the world map displayed in the Jesuit residence led Ricci to translate into Chinese its place names, many of them still in use today. Although a new governor-general ordered him expelled in 1589—Ruggieri left for Rome the previous year to arrange for a papal embassy to be sent to Peking (Beijing)—Ricci persuaded officials to allow him to move to Shao-chou (Shaozhou) in the same province.

Matteo Ricci. The Jesuit missionary to China with Li Paul, a Chinese convert. CORBIS/BETTMANN

Ricci is the founder of sinology because of his translation of the Four Books, into Latin, which included the works of Confucius and Mencius, and his development of the first standard system of romanizing Chinese. He introduced Western clocks and astronomical instruments that attracted the intellectual curiosity of the Chinese literati. Ricci's first Chinese book *Chiao-yu lun* (*Jiaoyou lun;* On friendship) appeared in 1595 and established his reputation as a virtuous and talented scholar. A dialogue in imitation of Cicero, this essay was based on Andreas d'Evera's *Sententiae et exempla* and other Latin and Greek works. In that same year Ricci published *Hsi-kuo chi-*

fa (*Xiguo jifa;* Art of memory in the West), drawn from such authors as Cypriano Soarez and his *De arte rhetorica,* Pliny's work on natural history, the *Ad Herrenium* then attributed to Cicero, and the works of Quintilian. The next year the first edition of his catechism, *T'ien-chu shih-i (Tianzhu shiyi;* True meaning of the Lord of Heaven), appeared. In this dialogue with a Chinese scholar, Ricci presented concepts of natural theology from the works of Aristotle and St. Thomas Aquinas.

With letters of introduction from several Chinese friends, Ricci arrived in Peking in 1598. Court officials considered all foreigners as possible spies because Japan had invaded Korea, which the Chinese government supported with military aid. Forced to return to central China, Ricci continued to meet more scholars and to write essays. With the restoration of Sino-Japanese relations, Ricci entered Peking in 1601, and in a few years his Chinese friends included several officials, such as Hsü Kuang-ch'i (Xu Guangqi; 1562–1633), the prime minister who became a convert to Christianity in Nanking (Nanjing) in 1603. Hsü supported the views of Ricci concerning the compatibility of Christian and Confucian teachings. Assisted by Hsü, Ricci translated books on astronomy, geography, and mathematics, including the first six chapters of Euclid's *Elementa.* Such works attracted the literati who came to Peking for the metropolitan civil service examinations and wanted to meet the Western scholar. With official permission to live in the capital, Ricci established a residence that became the center of the growing Christian community. He presented clocks and other gifts to the emperor. When the clocks needed rewinding, the imperial court summoned him to train eunuchs to do so. Through his ministers the emperor learned about Ricci's world map, so Ricci forwarded a special copy to the palace. Not long before his death in Peking, Ricci completed an Italian history of the introduction of Christianity into China that first appeared in Europe in a Latin translation in 1615. The emperor, whom Ricci never met, granted a burial place at Zhalan (Chala), just outside the old western city gate. This recently restored site, known today as the Li Madou mu (Matteo Ricci cemetery), includes the tombstones of Ricci and more than sixty Jesuits and other missionaries. By his profound knowledge and appreciation of Chinese culture, Ricci became the bridge connecting China to late Renaissance Europe.

BIBLIOGRAPHY

Primary Works

Chou K'ang-hsieh (Zhou Kangxie), ed. *Li-ma-tou yen chiu lun chi.* Hong Kong, 1971.

Fonti Ricciane. Edited by Pasquale M. d'Elia. 3 vols. Rome, 1942–1949.

Lettere dei Manoscritto Maceratese. Edited by C. Zeuli. Macerata, Italy, 1985.

Ricci, Matteo. *China in the Sixteenth Century: The Journals of Matthew Ricci, 1583–1610.* New York, 1953.

Ricci, Matteo. *Opere storiche del P. Matteo Ricci, S. I.* Edited by Pietro Tacchi-Venturi. 2 vols. Macerata, Italy, 1911–1913.

Ricci, Matteo. *The True Meaning of the Lord of Heaven (T'ien-chu shih-i).* Edited by Edward J. Malatesta. St. Louis, Mo., and Taipei, Taiwan, 1985.

Secondary Works

Bernard, Henri. *Matteo Ricci's Scientific Contribution to China.* Beijing, 1935.

Cronin, Vincent. *The Wise Man from the West.* New York, 1955.

Dunne, George H. *Generation of Giants: The Story of the Jesuits in China in the Last Decades of the Ming Dynasty.* Notre Dame, Ind., 1962.

Lo, Kuang, ed. *International Symposium of Chinese-Western Cultural Interchange in Commemoration of the Four Hundredth Anniversary of the Arrival of Matteo Ricci, S. J., in China.* Taipei, Taiwan, 1983.

Malatesta, Edward J., and Gao Zhiyu, eds. *Departed, Yet Present: Zhalan, The Oldest Christian Cemetery in Beijing.* Macao, China, 1995.

Ronan, Charles E., and Bonnie B. C. Oh, eds. *East Meets West: The Jesuits in China, 1582–1773.* Chicago, 1988.

Spence, Jonathan D. *The Memory Palace of Matteo Ricci.* New York, 1984.

Witek, John W. "Principles of Scholasticism in China: A Comparison of Giulio Aleni's *Wanwu zhenyuan* with Matteo Ricci's *Tianzhu shiyi.*" In *"Scholar from the West." Giulio Aleni S.J. (1582–1649) and the Dialogue between Christianity and China.* Edited by Tiziana Lippiello and Roman Malek. Nettetal, Germany, 1997. Pages 273–289.

JOHN W. WITEK, S.J.

RICCIO, ANDREA BRIOSCO, IL (1470–1532), north Italian sculptor. Riccio (the nickname means curly-haired) trained as a goldsmith under his father, who had moved to Padua by 1492. In this year, due to health problems, it is related that Riccio abandoned the art of the goldsmith to work in bronze and terra-cotta sculpture under Bartolomeo Bellano, Donatello's former assistant. On Bellano's death in around 1497, Riccio is believed to have completed his master's monument to *Pietro Roccabonella* (Padua, San Francesco) with three figures of the theological virtues (*Faith, Hope,* and *Charity*), which, if compared to Bellano's work, are characterized by a refined classicism. In 1506 Riccio worked on another of Bellano's unfinished projects: a cycle of reliefs on Old Testament subjects for the choir screen of the basilica of Sant' Antonio in Padua. Riccio executed two bronze reliefs of the *Story of Judith* and *David and the Ark of the Covenant,* which display a keen awareness of classical sculpture and Roman relief style, well depicted human emotion and expression, and, in line with the art of Andrea Mantegna, an interest in the archaeological reconstruction of antique items.

After completing these reliefs in 1507, Riccio was commissioned to work on a monumental bronze Paschal candlestick, also for the basilica of Sant' Antonio. This item, generally regarded as the sculptor's masterpiece, was not finished until 1516. The complex iconography comprises subjects from classical mythology, including satyrs, sphinxes, and centaurs, and should be viewed in the context of Paduan humanist culture. In fact, the philosopher Giambattista Leone, who was involved in awarding the commission to Riccio, is thought to have had some part to play in the choice of subject matter, an amalgam of the Christian and the pagan. The varied surfaces of the candlestick, incorporating both friezes and statuettes, bear witness to Riccio's superb technical gifts: he was precise in the casting and meticulous in the chasing, and he enlivened the texture of the bronze by filing and hammering.

Pagan references, so abundant in the candlestick, reappear in a freestanding funerary monument executed by Riccio in the Veronese church of San Fermo Maggiore (undated; c. 1510–1520?). The latter work, devoid of Christian iconography, was designed as a joint tomb for Girolamo and Marcantonio della Torre, both distinguished professors of medicine at the University of Padua. Riccio catered to the tastes of Paduan humanists and scholars, such as the della Torre, with statuettes of figures from pagan mythology. The sculptor frequently returned to the satyr as a subject, and he took delight in depicting the wild emotions associated with the mythological figure. Riccio conveyed human emotion in his terra-cotta sculptures also: contrast the sorrowful expressions of the surviving figures of the *Entombment* (Padua, San Canziano; 1530) with the wistful Madrid *Virgin and Child* (1520s; Thyssen-Bornemisza Museum).

Riccio's statuettes, plaquettes and domestic pieces in bronze, which embody humanist ideals, were widely copied in the Veneto well after his death. Bridging the gap between Donatello (1386?–1466) in Padua and Jacopo Sansovino (1486–1570) in Venice, Riccio played an important role in the development of bronze sculpture in northeast Italy.

BIBLIOGRAPHY

Planiscig, Leo. *Andrea Riccio*. Vienna, 1927.

Pope-Hennessy, John. *Italian Renaissance Sculpture*. 4th ed. London, 1996.

Radcliffe, Anthony. "Riccio." In *The Genius of Venice, 1500–1600*. Edited by Charles Hope and Jane Martineau. Exhibition catalog, Royal Academy of Arts. London, 1983. Pages 371–380.

FLAVIO BOGGI

RIEMENSCHNEIDER, TILMAN (c. 1460–1531), German sculptor. Riemenschneider was among the most prolific of Germany's pre-Reformation sculptors. He was born in Heiligenstadt in Thuringia, the son of Tilman the Elder (d. 1483), later the mint master in Osterode. Nothing secure is known about his training. Before 1479 Riemenschneider moved to Würzburg, where his uncle Niklaus worked for the bishop. He registered in the Guild of St. Luke in 1483 and two years later became a master and citizen. In the same year he wed Anna Schmidt, a wealthy widow of a goldsmith, the first of his four wives. Riemenschneider enjoyed great success, especially within the Würzburg bishopric. Between 1501 and 1517 twelve apprentices are recorded under his direction. His large workshop included joiners, sculptors, and painters, as the artist controlled all aspects of altarpiece production. Riemenschneider was an officeholder in Würzburg's local government beginning in 1505; in 1509 he was named a member of the Upper Council and in 1520–1521 he served as burgomaster. In 1525 he and other council members unsuccessfully supported the peasants' revolt against Prince-Bishop Konrad von Thungen. The artist was subsequently imprisoned for two months, fined, and expelled briefly from Würzburg. His activities as a sculptor waned considerably in the years prior to his death in Würzburg.

Working in both wood and stone, Riemenschneider carved large altarpieces, tombs and epitaphs, and single figures, but many of these creations were destroyed, damaged, or dismembered in the peasants' revolt and subsequent upheavals. Such was the fate of the *Mary Magdalen Altar* that he prepared between 1490 and 1492 for the parish church in Münnerstadt, his first documented project. Fragments include the exquisite life-size corpus statue of the saint with angels who accompany her heavenward. Riemenschneider chose to stain rather than polychrome his figures. One of the extant wing reliefs showing the *Noli me tangere* (Berlin, Skulpturengalerie) reveals Riemenschneider's frequent reliance on contemporary prints, especially those of Martin Schongauer, as models.

The artist's best known altarpieces are *Holy Blood* in Rothenburg (Sankt Jakobskirche; 1501–1505) and *Assumption of the Virgin* in Creglingen (Herrgottskirche; c. 1505–1510). Both are unpolychromed winged altars, which, including their intricate super-

Tilman Riemenschneider. ***Jesus Announces His Betrayal.*** Detail from *The Altar of the Holy Blood* in Sankt Jakobskirche, Rothenburg, Tauber, Germany. Limewood; 1501–1505. ST. JACOB'S CHURCH, ROTHENBURG, TAUBER, GERMANY/ERICH LESSING/ART RESOURCE

structures, are about nine meters (thirty feet) high. Riemenschneider made dramatic use of light by piercing the back wall of the corpus. In the *Holy Blood Altarpiece* light streaming through the windows behind the Last Supper heightens the moment as Christ stares at Judas. The brighter illumination permitted Riemenschneider to draw attention to the apostles' varied expressions and poses. Justus Bier credits Riemenschneider with producing ten documented altarpieces plus another eleven that are attributed on the basis of style. Most of these are collaborative products of his large workshop.

Among Riemenschneider's other notable projects are the sandstone *Adam* and *Eve* of 1491–1493, commissioned by the Würzburg town council for the portal of their Marienkapelle, and the lime- and sandstone *Tomb of Emperor Henry II and Empress Kunigunde* (1499–1513), which originally adorned the eastern nave of Bamberg Cathedral. Prince-Bishop Lorenz von Bibra commissioned the artist to carve two imposing tombs for himself (1519–1522) and for his predecessor Rudolf von Scherenberg (1496–1499) in Würzburg Cathedral. Although Riemenschneider's style was quite influential within the diocese until 1525, his subsequent legacy was severely limited by the advent of the Reformation and its attendant political uncertainties.

See also **Decorative Arts,** *subentry on* **Religious Arts; Germany, Art in; Sculpture.**

BIBLIOGRAPHY

Bier, Justus. *Tilman Riemenschneider.* 4 vols. Würzburg and Augsburg, Germany; and Vienna, 1925–1978.

Bier, Justus. *Tilman Riemenschneider: His Life and Work.* Lexington, Ky., 1981.

Chapuis, Julien, ed. *Tilman Riemenschneider.* New Haven, Conn., 1999.

Muth, Hanswernfried. *Tilman Riemenschneider: Die Werke des Bildschnitzers und Bildhauers, seiner Werkstatt und seines Umkreises im Mainfränkischen Museum Würzburg.* Würzburg, Germany, 1982.

Smith, Jeffrey Chipps. *German Sculpture of the Later Renaissance, c. 1520–1580: Art in an Age of Uncertainty.* Princeton, N.J., 1994.

JEFFREY CHIPPS SMITH

RIOTS. *See* **Violence.**

RITUAL, CIVIC. The word "ritual" when applied to the localized cults of the saints, urban processions, and princely or episcopal entries into Renaissance cities is anachronistic. Before the sixteenth century there were similar words in circulation, such as *ritus* (rite) and *caerimonia* (ceremony), that identified the liturgical practices of the church as a distinct kind of activity, but the generic conception of ritual or ceremonial derives from the upheaval in the theology of rites associated with the Protestant Reformation of the sixteenth century. The word "ritual" began as a pejorative term in English, first appearing about 1570 to refer to religious practices that supposedly duped people by creating insubstantial appearances and employing meaningless words. Even in the Romance languages of the Catholic world, the term developed similar connotations of inflated pomp.

Modern Definitions and Approaches. Late-twentieth-century scholars of the Renaissance have been kinder, treating rituals as especially revealing of social structures, political conflicts, and collective understandings that were otherwise obscure in civic life. They have understood civic rituals as repetitive and standardized actions that combined movements, gestures, and sometimes words to create civic and corporate identities or to resist them. Such rituals have been interpreted in two basic ways: as models and as mirrors. As models, they demonstrated an idealized scheme for the construction of society: when civic officials calmly walked in an ordered procession, they modeled the behavior expected of them in the conduct of public affairs. As mirrors, rituals reflected society as it actually was, revealing the distribution of power and challenges to the political and social hierarchy. The creative tension between the modeling and mirroring aspects of civic rituals accounts for their allure.

Different academic disciplines emphasize different aspects of civic rituals. Some scholars emphasize ritual as a form of behavior, as an enactment that either created social solidarity, such as propitiatory processions during a time of plague, or formed social identities, such as the collective self-flagellation sessions of confraternity members. Others emphasize ritual as a form of communication that allowed citizens to tell stories about themselves, such as when they commemorated a military victory against a neighbor. Still others emphasize ritual as a special kind of performance, akin to drama, that constructed, maintained, and modified society through the very act of performing, especially the improvisations of popular festivals, such as Carnival, or of the rites of violence, such as the bread riots organized by women or vendetta murders perpetrated by men.

Types of Civic Rituals. Among the vast array of practices labeled "rituals," three were distinctively civic: the local celebrations of saints' cults; the regular processions of civic groups, such as public officials, nuns, clergymen, parishioners, confraternity members, guildsmen, and militia companies; and the formal entries into cities of princes or bishops.

Each city had its own patron saint or sometimes several patron saints who were thought to favor the city and to act as intercessors with God. For their part, citizens were obliged to ensure the favor of the patron saint through regular prayer before the saint's relics, celebration of the saint's feast day, and public supplicatory processions. Although towns all across Europe adopted patron saints, the independent city-states of Italy most notably deployed the cults of patron saints to combat internal divisions and to bolster civic identities. The practices associated with these patron saints varied widely, from the tumultuous liquefactions of the blood of St. Januarius in Naples to the special church liturgies devoted to St. Ambrose in Milan and St. Mark in Venice.

On the patron saint's feast day, priests and town officials would characteristically join an elaborate public procession through the streets of the town. The object of the procession was either to visit the relics in the titular church of the saint or to display them publicly by carrying them along. In Siena all citizens of the city and subject towns were required by law to participate in the processions in honor of the Virgin. The very notion of citizenship, then, was linked to public participation in the cult rituals of the patron saint.

The orderly, measured progress of the civic procession, which derived from processions in honor of the patron saints, became a model for good government, and the ranked order of the participants mirrored the distribution of authority among officials.

The association between civic processions and civic authority became so inextricable that any alteration in the ranking of participants had serious political implications and was often the source of public disputes. Dissatisfied citizens or subjects resisted authority by breaking up or lampooning processions or staging counter-processions. Especially during the fifteenth and sixteenth centuries, civic processions provided the rigging for more elaborate public displays called "pageants." Pageants came in three types: allegorical *tableaux vivants,* in which actors maintained static poses; pantomimes, in which they moved but did not speak; and set pieces, in which they delivered lines to an audience. Pageants either were carried along on floats in the procession or appeared on fixed stages that the procession passed by. During the Renaissance, pageants became the principal means by which civic officials propagandized the population and made political or diplomatic pronouncements to outsiders.

Cities were most vulnerable to external threat and most sensitive to symbolic representations of their autonomy at their gates. Officials protected their cities through the rigid protocol and ritual of formal entries when powerful persons, such as foreign princes, diplomats, and important ecclesiastics, visited the city. Entries fell into three types: receptions, at which a visitor was treated with honor but as a formal equal; advents, in which Christ's Palm Sunday entry into Jerusalem provided a model for expressing authority over the city; and triumphs, in which the imitation of the victorious entry of an ancient Roman general implied that the visitor had conquered the city.

In order to clarify the meaning of various ritual actions, many towns began, as early as the fourteenth century, to keep books of ceremonies that codified precedents in rituals. Much of the rigidity of ceremonial entries derives from the fear that unanticipated or unregulated gestures and words might compromise the political privileges or autonomy of the city. No matter how interpreted, civic rituals in their frequency, cost, and magnificence stood at the very center of civic life during the Renaissance.

See also **Parades, Processions, and Pageants.**

BIBLIOGRAPHY

Bryant, Lawrence M. *The King and the City in the Parisian Royal Entry Ceremony: Politics, Ritual, and Art in the Renaissance.* Geneva, 1986.

Hanawalt, Barbara A., and Kathryn L. Reyerson, eds. *City and Spectacle in Medieval Europe.* Minneapolis, Minn., 1994.

Muir, Edward. *Ritual in Early Modern Europe.* Cambridge, U.K., 1997.

Trexler, Richard C. *Public Life in Renaissance Florence.* New York, 1980.

EDWARD MUIR

ROBBIA, LUCA DELLA. *See* **Della Robbia, Luca.**

ROBERTI, ERCOLE DE'. *See* **Ferrara,** *subentry on* **Art in Ferrara.**

ROJAS, FERNANDO DE (c. 1475–1541), Spanish dramatist. Born in La Puebla de Montalbán, province of Toledo, and a third-generation converso (his grandfather was a convert, perhaps involuntarily, from Judaism to Christianity), Fernando de Rojas studied law in the humanist environment of the University of Salamanca in the 1490s and finished there the sixteen-act *Comedia de Calisto y Melibea* (Burgos, 1499; Toledo, 1500; Seville, 1501). The origins of the work may or may not lie in an unfinished manuscript that Rojas, in his "Letter from the Author to a Friend," claims fell unexplainedly into his hands. He slyly attributes it to either Juan de Mena or to Rodrigo Cota, deceased poets of a slightly earlier generation of writers. A series of acrostic verses, however, states that Rojas is its author. Whether the anonymous first author is a literary fiction, and Rojas the true and only author of the work, is an unresolved scholarly issue.

Considered independently, this allegedly anonymous manuscript, representing act 1 of the work, compares favorably with works of Renaissance humanistic comedy and, as such, is the first written in the Spanish vernacular. In his "Letter," Rojas claims that several readings of this manuscript—which, typically, deals with a male lover who must resort to the stratagems of servants, including a go-between, in order to overcome the obstacles to a desired union with an inaccessible love object—impressed and inspired him to "finish" the work. In so doing, he transcends his literary model and delivers an anguished moral reading of a rudderless society whose proclaimed values are shown to be undermined by hypocrisy, concupiscence, and self-interest at all levels. Rojas does not provide the happy ending associated with humanist comedies. Rather, we witness the deaths of the go-between, Celestina (by assassination), of Calisto's two servants (by execution), and, finally, of the two lovers themselves: Calisto in a fall from the ladder that gains him access to his lover's walled garden, and Melibea in a suicide leap from a tower, just moments after their first physical union. Thus, Rojas does not spare, in his bleak denoue-

Tragicomedia de Calisto y Melibea. En la qual se contienen (de mas de su agradable y dulce estilo) muchas sentencias filosofales: y auisos muy necessarios para mancebos: mostrandoles los engaños q̃ estan encerrados en seruientes y alcahuetas.
¶ Y nueuamẽte añadido el tratado de Centurio y el auto de Traso y sus cõpañeros. Nueuamẽte hystoriado.

Fernando de Rojas. Title page of *Calisto y Melibea* (1526).

ment, the old nobility (Calisto), nor the newly rich and successful bourgeoisie, products of the Renaissance in Spain (Melibea and her family), nor the resentful servant class, imbued with radical new humanist views of their own worth. Rojas's work rejects the recent failures of a hierarchical patterning of society inherited from the Middle Ages, while still reflecting it. By paying close attention to the portrayal of the social damage and moral chaos produced by characters whose highest value is self-interest, we glimpse the reform-minded, albeit bitterly disillusioned, author at work.

Rojas's *Comedia* enjoyed immediate editorial and popular success. In about 1502, Rojas expanded the work by adding five new acts, and it was retitled the *Tragicomedia de Calisto y Melibea,* a designation that takes into account his ominous mix of comedy and tragedy. In the prologue to this expanded version, Rojas claims that it was lack of reader satisfaction with the brevity of Calisto and Melibea's love affair that occasioned this revision. By increasing the time the lovers enjoy their illicit tryst to a month and adding a subplot of revenge for Celestina's murder, organized by the prostitutes left "motherless," Rojas succeeded in darkening his negative portrait of society. On another front, he devised a dramatic scene in which Melibea, now deeply committed to her affair, and overhearing her parents planning her marriage, speaks out for freedom of choice and against marriage. Her own choice of loving freely, against societal norms, is preferable to any form of acquiescence to them. It illuminates Melibea's inner struggles and dramatizes Calisto's importance to her and her willingness to take her own life, in a mimetic fall. Her father's lament before her broken body, the concluding act of both versions, is traditionally seen as embodying Rojas's condemnation of the false values of this world, a view supported by the didactic tone of the materials that both precede and follow the work proper.

But because Rojas's masterpiece revolves chiefly around the compelling character of Celestina, the aging go-between, the *Tragicomedia* in time came to be printed with her name usurping both of its previous titles. Its success with the public was responsible for the more than eighty editions printed in Spanish up to 1640 (in Spain, Italy, and the Low Countries), with only minor censorship applied by the Inquisition, principally directed at courtly hyperboles comparing the love of a woman to the love of God. Its appeal to Renaissance tastes occasioned translations into Italian (1505), German (1520, 1534), French (1527, 1578), English (c. 1530, 1631), Dutch (1550), Hebrew (mid-sixteenth century), and Latin (1624).

Once the twenty-one-act *Tragicomedia* was in circulation, Rojas, the trained jurist, assumed duties in Talavera de la Reina as mayor. He died there, never again turning his hand to literary endeavors. *La Celestina* is today considered to be Spain's second masterpiece, ceding pride of place only to Cervantes's *Don Quixote*. The work has exerted its fascination on creative artists and their public for five hundred years, inspiring continuations, imitations, translations, verse and stage adaptations, operas, ballets, woodcut illustrations, paintings and lithographs, and more—a phenomenon known as "*la celestinesca*." Additional homage is paid to Rojas's work in that "celestina" has passed into the language as a common noun for a go-between.

BIBLIOGRAPHY

Primary Works

Rojas, Fernando de. *The Celestina: A Novel in Dialogue*. Translated by Lesley Byrd Simpson. Berkeley and Los Angeles, 1955. Translation of *Comedia de Calisto y Melibea*.

Rojas, Fernando de. *Celestina: A Play in Twenty-One Acts*. Introduced and translated by Mack Hendricks Singleton. Madison, Wis., 1958. Translation of *Tragicomedia de Calisto y Melibea*.

Rojas, Fernando de. *Celestina. With the Translation of James Mabbe (1631)*. Edited with introduction and notes by Dorothy S. Severin. Warminster, U.K., 1987. Translation of *Tragicomedia de Calisto y Melibea*. The oldest complete version, in Elizabethan English.

Secondary Sources

Corfis, Ivy A., and Joseph T. Snow, eds. *Fernando de Rojas and "Celestina."* Madison, Wis., 1993.

Deyermond, Alan. *The Petrarchan Sources of "La Celestina."* Westport, Conn., 1975.

Fothergill-Payne, Louise. *Seneca and "Celestina."* Cambridge, U.K., 1988.

Gilman, Stephen. *The Spain of Fernando de Rojas*. Princeton, N.J., 1972.

Joseph T. Snow

ROMAN POETS. *See* **Classical Scholarship; Ovid; Horace; Virgil.**

ROME. [This entry includes two subentries, the first on the city of Rome and the second on artists active in Rome and the surrounding territory. For discussion of the government of Rome and the Papal States, see the entry on the Papacy.]

The City of Rome

In 1350 Rome was an agricultural town of about thirty thousand with a turbulent feudal nobility and, due to the papacy's removal to Avignon in 1309, no resident prince. In 1347, hoping to bring the barons under control and inspired by the city's classical past, the notary Cola di Rienzo (1313–1354) declared himself tribune, an official who represented the Roman people in antiquity. Cola's short-lived attempt to revive the political institutions of ancient Rome briefly excited the humanist Petrarch (1304–1374) but did not leave an enduring local legacy. However, by 1410 a viable set of municipal institutions similar to those found in contemporary Italian towns had been established in Rome and were recognized by the papacy.

Government and Population. The most important civic officials were the senator and three conservators. The senator, who had to be a foreigner, was appointed by the pope to head the Capitoline tribunal, the highest lay court in the city. The three conservators, who were chosen by lot from lists drawn up in the city's fourteen urban districts (*rioni*), held office for three months; their duties were to oversee the markets and guilds, govern Rome's four vassal towns, preside at meetings of the civic councils, and represent the Senate and Roman People (*senatus populusque Romanus,* or simply SPQR), as Rome's civic government was called, on ceremonial occasions. The senator and conservators had their seats in two urban palaces on the Capitoline hill, redesigned by Michelangelo as a unified urban ensemble centered on an ancient bronze equestrian statue of the emperor Marcus Aurelius given to the city by the pope in 1538.

The relationship of the SPQR to the popes was subordinate but not spineless; it represented the local landowning class, which hoped to prosper under papal rule, especially after 1420, when the popes once again resided in Rome. In the course of the fifteenth century two civic councils, called the "public council" and the "private council," were formalized. They were recognized in the definitive set of municipal statutes published in 1580 and occasionally served as a forum for local grievances. The larger "public council" was open to any Roman citizen over twenty years old who was considered eligible by five gentlemen from his urban district. In contrast to practices in other Italian towns this flexible standard opened civic offices and institutions to immigrants, as long as they acquired Roman citizenship and were not artisans or servants. To an unusual degree Renaissance Rome welcomed and absorbed newcomers of all classes.

The city tripled its population between 1350 and 1600. In 1420 the population of Rome had sunk to around twenty thousand, but it more than doubled in the next century to around fifty-five thousand. The sack of Rome in 1527 caused a sharp temporary drop, but after 1550 Rome participated in the pan-European demographic upswing, doubling its population to one hundred thousand by 1600. This included a small (three to four thousand) Jewish community with roots in antiquity; after 1555 the Jews were forced to live in the ghetto, a gated enclosure that was locked at night. Rome grew through immigration, but unlike most cities it attracted more male than female migrants; men exceeded women in the city's population not only because of the presence of numerous male clerics but also because households composed of unmarried laymen (from cardinals' servants to artists' assistants) were not uncommon. The curia, the papacy's bureaucracy, was gradually Italianized during the Renaissance, and af-

ter 1500 successful curial officials often allied with local families, while the reinvigoration of the university of Rome after 1431 provided an educated native elite who also sought papal employ. Roman patrician families grew to depend on both their landed estates and curial offices. Commerce and manufactures were relatively weak in Rome.

The Renaissance in Rome. To the extent that the Renaissance was a revival of interest in Roman antiquity the city became a place for humanists to visit, to study, and to scavenge for antiquities. From 1400 the curia provided jobs for humanists, whose characteristic script, chancery cursive, became the ancestor of the italic hand, one of the most enduring legacies of the Renaissance. The humanists hunted through ruins for ancient inscriptions, a source for the Roman capital letters whose use they revived. When a curial humanist became Pope Nicholas V in 1447, the resources of the papacy were enlisted in collecting ancient texts; his successors, like Cardinal Giuliano della Rovere (1443–1513), the future Pope Julius II, collected ancient objects and statues, often unearthed in Rome. In 1474, della Rovere's predecessor and uncle, Pope Sixtus IV, gave a group of ancient sculptures to the SPQR in a gesture meant to underline the vivid new connection between civic institutions and the city's ancient past. Roman cardinals and patrician families followed in the footsteps of the popes as collectors of classical authors and antiquities. Humanists, and architects whom they inspired with their enthusiasm, also contributed to the archaeological understanding of the ancient city that lay below Renaissance Rome.

While humanist intellectuals influenced the tastes of the urban elite, it was classicizing architecture and urbanism that displayed Renaissance principles to the broadest number of Romans and visitors. Urban palaces built for cardinals and papal relatives in the latest style introduced symmetry, the classical orders, and the notion of the facade to the streetscape. Beginning in the 1490s straight streets, in imitation of the ancients, were cut through the city's serpentine fabric. Domes, revived by Florentines in the 1420s, crowned new churches in Rome after 1500. Ancient statues and obelisks were dug up and put to new public uses as fountains, places to post anonymous lampoons, or foci for axial urban vistas. In its deployment of monuments and adornment of public spaces Rome set an example for all later European capital cities. On the domestic side, Renaissance artists found work decorating patrician family chapels and palace interiors in the new style, and helped patrons construct suburban villas with gardens designed on ancient Roman principles. By 1585, however, Christian polemics began to reclaim a city landscape that had been given unparalleled magnificence under the influence of classical models and ideals. Under Pope Sixtus V between 1585 and 1590 ancient columns that had never fallen were topped with statues of Rome's patron saints and relocated obelisks were labeled with inscriptions in revived ancient capitals proclaiming the Christian victory over paganism.

See also **Papacy**; **Urbanism**.

BIBLIOGRAPHY

D'Amico, John. *Renaissance Humanism in Papal Rome: Humanists and Churchmen on the Eve of the Reformation*. Baltimore, 1983.

Delumeau, Jean. *Vie économique et sociale de Rome dans la seconde moitié du seizième siècle*. 2 vols. Paris, 1957–1959.

Jacks, Philip. *The Antiquarian and the Myth of Antiquity: The Origins of Rome in Renaissance Thought*. Cambridge, U.K., 1993.

Nussdorfer, Laurie. *Civic Politics in the Rome of Urban VIII*. Princeton, N.J., 1992.

Partner, Peter. *Renaissance Rome, 1500–1559*. Berkeley, Calif., 1976.

LAURIE NUSSDORFER

Art in Rome and Latium

Renaissance art in Rome, as well as throughout the province of Latium (Lazio), was remarkable for the provincial and progressive tendencies that coexisted at its formative period, and the conscious juxtaposition of tradition and experimentation at its peak. Provincial artists clung to medieval formulas for iconography and composition, but others were open to progressive approaches, represented by the emergence of humanist-scholars and collectors of antiquities. During the fifteenth century, both strands flourished in Rome and its outlying area, as the city recovered its stability after its abandonment by the papacy in the fourteenth and early fifteenth centuries. Even in the early sixteenth century, when the dynamism of the high Renaissance ushered in new artistic forms and values, the juxtaposition of the old with the new was evident throughout Latium, propelling Rome to the forefront as the recovery of antiquity took hold. The humanist revival of classical learning and the rediscovery of ancient monuments fed directly into the development of the visual arts. Wealthy patrons connected with the newly aggrandized papal court to pour funds into the embellishment of the city's monuments, and the construction and decoration of their own residences. These combined factors, sustained by Rome's growing political power, infused new life into the culture of the city, and to a lesser extent the province of Latium, so that by the early sixteenth century Rome had become a mecca for the most prominent artists of the era.

The Early Renaissance. After a long hiatus, Roman artists regained a sense of identity by the mid-fifteenth century, excelling in the technical aspects of fresco decoration, large-scale construction, and marble carving. Painting flourished under the leadership of Antoniazzo Romano (Antoniazzo Aquili; active c. 1460–1508), whose long career spawned a unique blend of medieval themes and forward-looking formal qualities. Impressive works of architecture and sculpture, like the monumental Palazzo Venezia (1455–1503) built by Francesco del Borgo and the marble Ciborium (c. 1475) for the Church of St. Peter's, were created by unidentified artists, obscure or still unknown. Local artists were clearly familiar with progressive trends; they were influenced by the brief visits and, increasingly, by the extended stays of masters from the north. The steady influx of outsiders began in the third decade under Pope Martin V (1417–1431), gained momentum under Nicholas V (1447– 1455), and culminated on a grand scale under Pope Sixtus IV (1471–1484). The Florentine architect Baccio Pontelli (c. 1450–1492), credited with numerous building projects for Sixtus, devised fortifications, if not innovative church

Art in Rome. *The Raising of Lazarus* by Sebastiano Luciani, known as Sebastiano del Piombo (c. 1485–1547). The painting illustrates the passage in John 11:1–44. Oil on panel transferred to canvas; c. 1517–1519; 381 × 289 cm (12.5 × 9.5 ft.). NATIONAL GALLERY, LONDON/ANDERSON/ALINARI/ART RESOURCE

designs, like Santa Maria del Popolo (1472–1480), and public buildings like the Hospital of Santo Spirito in Sassia (1472–1478); and the most famous fresco artists of Tuscany and Umbria arrived to decorate the walls of the Sistine Chapel. Thus the finest painters, sculptors, and architects from the leading artistic centers of northern Italy worked in Rome, albeit temporarily, during the fifteenth century. The cultural life of Rome further was enriched by the activities of individual artists, like Andrea Bregno and Melozzo da Forlì who set up practice in their adopted city.

Andrea (di Cristoforo) Bregno (1418–1503), from Lombardy, arrived in Rome in the 1460s to perfect a consciously classicizing manner. A skilled marble-carver, he was acknowledged as the designer of cardinals' tombs, which included the Tomb of Cardinal Pietro Riario (1474–1477; Church of SS. Apostoli) and the Tomb of Cardinal Diego de Coca (c. 1477;

Church of Santa Maria sopra Minerva). Bregno ran a large workshop, but his fame was due less to technical competence than to his activities as an antiquarian. He kept ancient sculpture and epigraphy in his home on the slopes of the Quirinal Hill—a renowned collection that he made available to artists and scholars, but that was dispersed after his death.

Melozzo da Forlì's (1438–1494) earliest residence in Rome may have been in the 1460s, but he certainly was established in the city by the mid-1470s, drawn to the Sistine court through association with the Riario and Della Rovere branches of the papal family. The painter's distinctive style showed a command of spatial illusionism and color harmonies, suggesting connections with the older Piero della Francesco (c. 1420–1492), whom Melozzo probably encountered in either Rome or Urbino. Melozzo's first documented commission in Rome was for the new Vatican library, where he painted the imposing fresco of *Sixtus IV and Platina* (1476–1477; Vatican, Pinacoteca), an incisive group portrait that includes the papal nephews within a classically inspired setting. Soon thereafter Melozzo signed the statutes of the Company of St. Luke—the guild of painters—as the painter of the pope.

Melozzo's other major work in Rome was for the choir of the Church of SS. Apostoli, where he executed a monumental scene of the *Ascension* (1479–1480). Commissioned by the papal nephew and future Julius II, Cardinal Giuliano della Rovere, the fresco cycle featured the triumphant figure of Christ surrounded by a host of airborne angels. The cycle was destroyed as the result of later renovations to the church, yet the surviving fragments rank among the most impressive examples of Roman painting of the fifteenth century: the *Musical Angels* (Vatican, Pinacoteca) and the figure of *Christ Blessing* (Rome, Quirinal Gallery). The sixteenth-century theorist Sebastiano Serlio justly praised Melozzo for his mastery of perspective and foreshortening, features consistent with the fresco design for the Sacristy of St. Mark, in the basilica of the Holy House (Casa Santa) at Loreto. Commissioned from Melozzo in 1477–1478 by another papal nephew, Cardinal Girolamo Basso della Rovere, these *Prophets and Angels* were likely executed by an assistant. No other certain traces of Melozzo's Roman career remain. He departed abruptly after 1481, abandoning Latium altogether and moving north to his native Forlì until his death.

The High Renaissance. Experimentation in the visual arts intensified at the turn of the century, surging ahead under the papacy of the ambitious, visionary Julius II (1503–1513). It is likely that the architect Donato Bramante (1444–1514) moved to Rome from Milan even before his formidable patron summoned other great artists of the era, including Raphael and Michelangelo. They initially came to work at the Vatican—painting the Stanze in the papal apartments and the Sistine ceiling, designing the new Church of St. Peter's and the pope's own tomb. But their impact was felt throughout all aspects of Roman culture, as their own work took on monumental dimensions, classicizing form, and expressive content. Both local and émigré artists followed in their wake, including Leonardo da Vinci, who stayed from 1513 to 1517, with the result that a dynamic generation came to maturity in the city.

The Tuscan sculptor Andrea Sansovino (Andrea dal Monte Sansovino; c. 1467–1529) settled in Rome from 1505 to 1513, assisted by Jacopo Sansovino (Jacopo d'Antonio; Rome, c. 1506–1510, 1518–1527), who adopted his master's surname. Like the architect Bramante, Sansovino surely was encouraged by Pope Julius II to revive classical motifs and triumphal forms for the pair of marble tombs in the choir of the Church of Santa Maria del Popolo. In the Church of Sant'Agostino, the sculptor produced a *Virgin and Child with St. Anne*—a work intended as a metaphor for the arts of sculpture, painting, and poetry—whose design reflects close study of Leonardo's cartoon of the same theme (London, National Gallery) as well as the dynamic grouping of the recently excavated *Laocoön*. From 1513 to 1527, Sansovino worked on marble revetment for the Holy House (Casa Santa) at Loreto, which comprised exquisitely carved reliefs of considerable narrative power, such as the *Annunciation*.

The painter Polidoro da Caravaggio (Polidoro Caldara; c. 1500–1543) built an artistic reputation as a decorator on a grand scale. Like other artists who adopted Rome as their native city, he came from northern Italy and received specialized training in the workshop of Raphael. He participated in the fresco decoration of the papal apartments and the Vatican loggias, where he worked with his contemporaries Giulio Romano and Perino del Vaga. Polidoro subsequently developed his career in response to the growing demand for classically inspired designs. Time has stripped palace facades of his famed monochromatic frescoes simulating sculptural friezes of ancient history. Only vestiges remain, such as on the Facade of the Palazzo Ricci (c. 1524–1525), but his designs survive in drawings and engravings. His subtle landscape scenes for the Chapel of Fra Mariano (c. 1525) in the Church of San Silvestro al Quirinale derive from a profound knowledge of ancient wall paintings. As a result of the Sack, he left Rome in 1527 for Naples, and eventually relocated in Messina.

Due to their entrenched position in professional and patronage circles, members of the Sangallo family came to dominate the Roman architectural scene, filling the void created by the death of Raphael in 1520, and profiting from the resurgence in ecclesiastical commissions beginning in the late 1530s. Initially, however, the older members of the family came to Rome from their native Florence, only to find their authority usurped by more illustrious architects. Giuliano da Sangallo (c. 1445–1516), a favorite architect of Cardinal Giuliano della Rovere, arrived in Rome in 1505, but soon was displaced by the brilliant Bramante. Giuliano worked on plans for the new Church of St. Peter's and in the Vatican Borgo, and later produced a project for a Palace on Piazza Navona for the Medici pope, Leo X (1513–1521). Antonio da Sangallo the Younger (1483–1546), a nephew of Giuliano and his brother Antonio the Elder, fared better, ascending the professional ladder with steady success. Like other family members, he trained as a carpenter, but he also acquired knowledge of engineering and draftsmanship in the *fabbrica* (works) of the new Church of St. Peter's where he was in contact with the elderly Bramante and Raphael, not to mention Vitruvian scholars like Fra Giocondo of Verona.

After approximately fifteen years on the site, Antonio the Younger was appointed architect of St. Peter's at Raphael's death in 1520. He had already produced numerous independent projects such as the Palazzo Farnese (1516), the Palazzo Baldassini (1521–1522), and the Church of Santa Maria in Monserrato (1518–1520). He later assumed responsibility for fortifications, festival designs, and public-works projects in Rome. After the Sack, he continued as papal architect to Paul III (1534–1549), garnering an ever higher public profile, only to be ridiculed by the incomparable Michelangelo on account of his ungainly wooden model for the Church of St. Peter's (1539–1545). Nonetheless, the Sangallo family members (called the "sect" by Giorgio Vasari) secured sufficient prestige as draftsmen, woodworkers and theorists, not to mention architects. Bastiano (Aristotile, 1481–1551) and Battista (Giovanni Battista, also called "Il Gobbo" 1496–1548) da Sangallo continued to practice, after the death of Antonio the Younger, transmitting the classical idiom into the mid-sixteenth century.

One of the rare Roman artists with a career that continued after the Sack, Sebastiano del Piombo (Sebastiano Luciani; 1485–1547) thrived as a painter who adapted to stiff competition and demanding circumstances. He left his native Venice in 1511 to execute mythological frescoes in Agostino Chigi's villa in Rome (Villa Farnesina), working in proximity with Baldassare Peruzzi and Raphael. Sebastiano's famous altarpiece of the *Raising of Lazarus* of 1517–1519 (London, National Gallery) was commissioned by Cardinal Giulio de' Medici for the Cathedral of Narbonne, France. It was a sophisticated, dramatic composition, which Sebastiano produced in rivalry with Raphael, and with the assistance of Michelangelo. His muscular scene of the *Flagellation* of 1516–1524 (Rome, Church of San Pietro in Montorio) was executed in oil, again with the help of the great artist. (Michelangelo nonetheless later disparaged his former friend when he referred to oil painting as a technique suitable only "for women and rich do-nothings like Fra Bastiano.") Sebastiano's star ascended further under Pope Clement VII (1523–1534), and he formed contacts with other gifted painters like Rosso Fiorentino (Giovanni Battista di Jacopo; 1494–1540), Il Parmigianino (Francesco Maria Mazzola; 1503–1540), Perino del Vaga (Pietro Bonaccorsi; 1500/01–1547) and Polidoro da Caravaggio. Sebastiano acquired deserved prominence as a portrait painter with bold, insightful studies typified by his portraits of Clement VII (Naples, Capodimonte Museum; Parma, Pinacoteca; Los Angeles, Getty Museum). His production fell off sharply after 1531, when he took religious vows in order to receive a papal appointment as keeper of the seal, and when he turned almost exclusively to haunting biblical themes like *Christ Bearing the Cross* (Madrid, Prado).

The Sack of Rome by the imperial troops brought this immense artistic flowering to an abrupt halt in 1527. The energy of the high Renaissance dissipated, as artists and patrons fled the devastated city, and the papacy confronted its loss of temporal authority. When the artistic life of the city revived under the Counter-Reformation popes, Roman art and architecture took on a different set of cultural values, practical priorities, and aesthetic forms.

Ecclesiastical design and decoration tended toward simplicity. The longitudinal basilica became a desirable plan, with sacred cycles and altarpieces planned for side chapels. The formula employed by the Sangallo circle for churches constructed after the Sack of Rome found logical expression in the most influential basilican plan of the century, *Il Gesù*, designed by Giacomo da Vignola (1507–1573) and

Giacomo della Porta (c. 1537–1602) for the Jesuit order. As a result of the Council of Trent (1545–1563), Catholic theologians, like Gabriele Paleotti and St. Charles Borromeo, emphasized the need for clarity and legibility. The Maniera, the strain of mannerism calculated for a sophisticated audience, was also practiced in Rome by artists like Perino del Vaga and the brothers Taddeo (1529–1566) and Federico Zuccari (c. 1540–1609). Equally strong was the influence of Michelangelo, whose *Last Judgment* (1536–1541) for the altar wall of the Sistine Chapel provoked criticism for its nude figures and general lack of decorum from conservative elements, but also inspired fresco artists like Cecchino Salviati (1510–1563) and Jacopino del Conte (c. 1510–1598). Civic design, exemplified by Michelangelo's complex for the Capitoline Hill (1538–1564), became increasingly ambitious, culminating in the urban plan commissioned by Sixtus V (1585–1590) from his architect, Domenico Fontana (1543–1607). The building of St. Peter's continued throughout the sixteenth century, with each new pope shifting the direction of the project. When Michelangelo took over as architect of the basilica in 1547, he instituted a return to a dynamic, simplified version of the centralized plan. Although his design for a hemispherical cupola was altered by his successors, Giacomo della Porta and Domenico Fontana, Michelangelo's imprint survives in the area of the crossing, the dome, the lantern, and the apse.

BIBLIOGRAPHY

Ackerman, James S. "Architectural practice in the Italian Renaissance." In his *Distance Points: Essays in Theory and Renaissance Art and Architecture*. Cambridge, Mass., 1991. Pages 361–384.

Bober, Phyllis P., and Ruth O. Rubenstein. *Renaissance Artist and Antique Sculpture: A Handbook of Sources*. London and New York, 1986.

Chastel, André. *The Sack of Rome, 1527*. Translated by Beth Archer. Princeton, N.J., 1983.

Hall, Marcia B. *After Raphael: Painting in Central Italy in the Sixteenth Century*. Cambridge, U.K., 1999.

Hollingsworth, Mary. *Patronage in Renaissance Italy from 1400 to the Early Sixteenth Century*. London and Baltimore, 1994.

Müntz, Eugène. *Les arts à la cour des papes pendant le quinzième et le seizième siècles: Recueil de documents inédits*. Paris, 1878–1882.

Partridge, Loren. *The Art of Renaissance Rome, 1400–1600*. New York, 1996.

EUNICE D. HOWE

ROME, SACK OF. Contemporaries viewed the Sack of Rome as a unique cataclysm. While its profound and lasting cultural repercussions justify viewing the event in the long term as a watershed in Renaissance history, the brutality and excesses of the victorious imperial soldiers at once fixated the attention of a stunned Christendom.

The Attack. Around dawn on 6 May 1527, troops of the emperor Charles V (ruled 1519–1556) laid siege to Rome. Despite the death early on of their commander, Charles, the constable of Bourbon, within a day they had conquered virtually the entire city. His successor, Philibert de Chalon, the prince of Orange, proved unable to control the victorious army, which included contingents of French and Italian soldiers as well as German Landsknechts and Spanish regulars. Pope Clement VII (Giulio de' Medici; reigned 1523–1534) fled to the Castel Sant' Angelo, where he was joined by around a thousand other refugees. From that fortress, they could but watch as the imperial troops sacked Rome and terrorized its remaining citizens, torturing, ransoming, raping, and plundering at will over a period of months. If Lutherans among the German troops desecrated relics and profaned sacred objects, the Spaniards demonstrated equal disregard for the holy and gained particular infamy for wanton cruelty.

Once Clement ascertained that his allies would not risk attempting his rescue, he capitulated on 5 June, agreeing to the exorbitant ransom of 400,000 *ducats*. Using gold that the sculptor and goldsmith Benvenuto Cellini had recovered by melting down papal crowns and ornaments, the pope paid out 70,000 *ducats*, guaranteeing the rest by giving over seven hostages, including Jacopo Salviati and Gian Matteo Giberti. Clement himself, along with thirteen cardinals, remained in the papal fortress under direct imperial guard until 7 December, when further payments and assurances made possible his escape to Orvieto. In mid-February 1528 the occupying army at last quit the ruined city, to which the pontiff returned only that autumn, on 6 October.

The sack marked the collapse of the papacy's efforts to maintain political autonomy even as France and Spain competed for hegemony over the Italian Peninsula. Whether haphazardly or by design, in the early years of his pontificate Clement repeatedly switched allegiance between the two sides. In retrospect, his greatest error appears to have been joining with France, Florence, Venice, and Milan in the League of Cognac (22 May 1526) against Charles V, thus prompting the emperor to dispatch into Italy the army led by Bourbon. In March 1527, as that army menaced Tuscany, Clement concluded an armistice with the imperial viceroy of Naples, Charles de Lannoy, but Bourbon and his men refused to honor it and instead marched on Rome. Once the city had been taken, Clement awaited assistance from a League army under the command of Francesco Maria della Rovere, the duke of Urbino. But della Rovere, safeguarding the interests of his Venetian employers rather than those of the papacy, came no closer than Isola Farnese, several miles from Rome, and on 2 June ordered his army to retreat even from there. Three days later Clement came to terms with the occupying troops. The following months brought no relief from either Francis I of France or Charles V, but only a visitation of the plague, a heat wave, food shortages, and continued efforts to extort concessions from the captives. Once safely in Orvieto, Clement VII briefly inclined again toward the French, but by May 1529 he had concluded a lasting peace with Charles V, whom he crowned as Holy Roman Emperor in Bologna in February 1530. Thereafter, Clement remained allied with the emperor, who provided an army to besiege Florence and restore the Medici, who had been ousted from power there soon after the Sack of Rome. Thus, family gains compensated Clement, a Medici, somewhat for his losses as pontiff.

Whether or not Charles V authorized the attack on Rome—a point on which historians disagree—he was appalled by the destruction that ensued and sought to dissociate himself from it. Alfonso de Valdés, Charles's Latin secretary, wrote a dialogue blaming the sack on those among the pope's advisers who had counseled him to join in the League of Cognac. Valdés claimed that the troops had proceeded to Rome against the emperor's will, but that the sumptuary excesses and corruption of the Roman clergy then incited them to commit atrocities. Clement's supporters, too, conveniently came to pin the blame on Bourbon and his men, treating them as renegades who had acted against the emperor's wishes. Yet they shared the sense that the moral failings of the clergy had helped to bring on the catastrophe, a position that Pope Clement himself voiced in a sermon delivered on Palm Sunday in 1528. The sense of historic destiny in the event was underscored by pamphlets trumpeting prophecies and prodigies, such as a blade-shaped comet, that were said to have anticipated the disaster. The sack also gave seeming confirmation and therefore renewed life to earlier apocalyptic preaching that had heralded Rome's imminent punishment for corruption. Even the poet and pornographer Pietro Aretino, hardly a moral exemplar, exploited such rhetoric so as to rub salt in Clement's wounds.

The Consequences. The sack dealt a severe blow to Rome's artistic and literary community. Some humanists, such as Paolo Bombace and Cristoforo Marcello, died at the hands of the invaders. Others, such as Johann Küritz, fled Rome at their earliest opportunity, never to return. Among the artists and architects, Jacopo Sansovino and Sebastiano Serlio found refuge in Venice, Giovanni da Udine fled to the Friuli, Baldassare Peruzzi to Siena, Perino del Vaga to Genoa, and Parmigianino to Bologna. Rosso Fiorentino went initially to Borgo San Sepolcro, then to Venice and to France. Sebastiano del Piombo, who soon returned from Venice to Rome and to papal service, wrote to Michelangelo in February 1531 about his own disengagement and dispiritedness, saying that he was no longer the same Sebastiano he had been before the sack. Many humanists, including the papal secretary and future cardinal, Jacopo Sadoleto, similarly perceived the event as marking a personal turning point.

Beyond its effects on specific individuals, the sack prompted a general shift in conceptions of Renaissance Rome and its historic significance. In the decades before 1527, humanists and artists celebrated Rome's role as *caput mundi,* the head of the world, and predicted the imminent onset of a golden age that the papacy would initiate. The sack muted these claims, forcing more sober appraisals of what Renaissance Rome could accomplish. Giles of Viterbo, the head of the Augustinian order and a confidant of popes from Julius II to Clement VII, now looked to Charles V as the leader destined to initiate the new age. Curial humanists such as Pietro Corsi attenuated their claims on behalf of Clement, defending his integrity and the dignity of his office rather than predicting triumphs. Elsewhere in the republic of letters, a range of meanings was attached to the sack. While Protestants viewed the event as the sort of divinely mandated retribution that Luther had predicted, Thomas More interpreted the atrocities of the German Lutheran troops in Rome as evidence of the debilitating effects of heresy upon human character. Yet humanists both in Catholic and in Protestant camps, and from within Italy as well as beyond it, joined in lamenting the destruction of libraries and the damage done to Rome as a center of learning.

Under Clement's successor, Paul III (reigned 1534–1549), Rome regained political and economic strength and again became a magnet for artistic and literary talent. But the sack cast a pall over subsequent efforts at renewal, tempering any optimism with an awareness of the contingency of the city's political welfare and with nostalgia for a golden age of Renaissance Roman culture that many perceived as having ended decisively in May 1527.

See also **Charles V**; **Clement VII**; **Wars of Italy**.

BIBLIOGRAPHY

Primary Works

Guicciardini, Francesco. *The History of Italy.* Edited and translated by Sidney Alexander. New York, 1969. Translation of *La storia d'Italia.* Book 18, first printed in 1564, includes an account of the sack.

Guicciardini, Luigi. *The Sack of Rome.* Edited and translated by James H. McGregor. New York, 1993. Translation of *Il Sacco di Roma.* Paris, 1664. Adequate English rendition marred by a misleading critical apparatus.

Valdés, Alfonso de. *Alfonso de Valdés and the Sack of Rome: Dialogue of Lactancio and an Archdeacon.* Edited by John E. Longhurst. Albuquerque, N. Mex., 1952. Translation of *Dialogo en que particularmente se tratan de las cosas ocurridas en Roma el año de MDXXVII.* Printed c. 1529.

Secondary Works

Chastel, André. *The Sack of Rome, 1527.* Translated from the French by Beth Archer. Princeton, N.J., 1983.

De Caprio, Vincenzo. *La tradizione e il trauma: Idee del Rinascimento romano.* Manziana, Italy, 1991.

Firpo, Massimo. *Il Sacco di Roma del 1527: Tra profezia, propaganda politica e riforma religiosa.* Cagliari, Italy, 1990.

Gouwens, Kenneth. *Remembering the Renaissance: Humanist Narratives of the Sack of Rome.* Leiden, Netherlands; Boston; and Cologne, 1998.

Hook, Judith. *The Sack of Rome, 1527.* London, 1972.

KENNETH GOUWENS

RONSARD, PIERRE DE (1524–1585), French poet. Pierre de Ronsard became the most celebrated and most influential poet of sixteenth-century France. His family claimed nobility dating at least from the fourteenth century; in any event its noble lifestyle was assured by his father Loys de Ronsart's military career and intermittent success at the court. Pierre de Ronsard was born in the ancestral manor La Possonnière in the Vendôme. He became a page in the service first of Charles de Valois (third son of Francis I), then of Madeleine de France, and accompanied her to Scotland in 1537 when she married James I, returning to France in 1538. He then reentered the service of Charles, who became duke of Orléans.

Having been tutored in Latin, Ronsard began composing poetry in that language in the early 1540s and set about learning Greek. His French compositions began in this period as well. When his patron, Charles d'Orléans, died of the plague in 1545, the young Pierre was welcomed by the humanist Lazare de Baïf, in whose home he studied Greek and Latin poetry with Baïf's son Jean-Antoine, under the guidance of the humanist scholar and poet Jean Dorat. Between 1547 and 1549 Ronsard was a student at the Collège de Coqueret in Paris, where Dorat seems to have begun teaching.

In this period and during the 1550s, a group of young poets whose members varied but included Ronsard, Jean-Antoine de Baïf, Joachim du Bellay, Étienne Jodelle, and Pontus de Tyard, identified themselves as the "Brigade" (later known as the "Pléiade") and set out to fashion a new poetic "high" tradition in the vernacular, based on imitation of classical and Italian models and valorizing the role of the poet as an inspired seer. In 1549 du Bellay published his Italianate sonnet collection *L'olive* and his stirring manifesto for French poetry, *Deffense et illustration de la langue françoise* (Defense and illustration of the French language). Ronsard followed by publishing his first collection, *Les quatre premiers livres des odes de Pierre de Ronsard, vandomois. Ensemble son Bocage* (The first four books of the odes of Pierre de Ronsard, of the Vendôme. Together with the Bocage; 1550).

The ode was a favorite form for the young poet, who kept augmenting and rearranging his editions. In the ode addressed to Michel de l'Hospital, published in 1552, Ronsard demonstrates, in ways that recall Italian Neoplatonism, both the divine origin of poetry and the divine foundation of the political order that poetry praises. This poem incarnates most clearly the poetic aspirations of the mid-century Pléiade poets.

Les amours. Turning from imitation of classical models and elevated forms to the more intimate, Italian-inspired form of the sonnet, Ronsard published his most celebrated work, *Les amours,* in 1552. It was modeled on Petrarch's *Canzoniere,* a collection of sonnets and longer poems that sing the praises of the poet's beloved, Laura, and explore the evolution and intricacies of his love and his mourning after her death. Ronsard chose the name "Cassandre" to designate his beloved, referring apparently to the daughter of a wealthy Italian merchant, Cassandre Salviati, whom he had met at a dance in April 1543. However, the decasyllabic sonnets play on the mythological connotations of the name. The entire collection is suffused with mythological allusions, so much so that the humanist Marc Antoine Muret published a commentary in 1553 explaining the allusions and the "argument" of the poems. Ronsard's erudition is combined with conventional topics of Petrarchan love poetry: the intensity of the gaze, the fatal moment of the first encounter, metaphors of heat and cold incarnating the antitheses of suffering and joy, the tortuous paths of unrequited love, and the exalted inwardness of poetry. Yet throughout the collection Ronsard retains an eroticism and a sense of the rhythm and musicality of language that distinguish his poetry from the more artificial imitations of Petrarch.

Les amours was followed in 1555 by the *Continuation des amours,* a collection much augmented during the next few years, which found its definitive form under the title *Second livre des amours* only in 1560, when Ronsard first published his collected works. The 1555 continuation of his love sonnets adopted the alexandrine verse and a more accessible, familiar style, as well as a new mistress, Marie (an anagram of *aimer,* to love); apparently Marie was a peasant from Bourgueil. Rémy Belleau, a fellow poet, provided commentary on Ronsard's second book of love sonnets. In the 1578 edition of his collected works Ronsard published two other cycles of love poems: *Sonnets et madrigals pour Astrée,* dedicated to Françoise d'Estrées, mother of Gabrielle d'Estrées, and the substantial two books of the *Sonnets pour Hélène,* inspired by Hélène de Surgères, a lady at the court of Catherine de Médicis. The Hélène cycle, while playing on the mythological connections with Helen of Troy, represents a change from the self-obsessed early poems. Ronsard incorporates dialogue, places his poems in historical contexts and precise settings, and is concerned with his own aging.

Pierre de Ronsard. THE STATE HERMITAGE MUSEUM, ST. PETERSBURG, RUSSIA

While his love poetry constitutes Ronsard's most celebrated achievement, his ambitions lay in epic poetry. The emergence of French as a viable literary language, rivaling Latin and Italian, demanded a national epic, and at mid-century no one was acknowledged to be more talented and better placed than Ronsard. He announced his project in 1550, in the "Ode de la paix, au roi" (Ode to peace, to the king), and began composition in 1552. Serious work on the epic depended, however, on generous royal patronage, which was only assured by Charles IX after 1564. In 1572, in the weeks following the Saint Bartholomew's Day massacre, the first four books of his epic, *La Franciade,* appeared. Written in decasyllabic verse, seemingly at the request of Catherine de Médicis, the epic celebrates Francus, alias Astyanax (who survives the sack of Troy by divine intervention), as the progenitor of French royalty. Although inspired by Virgil, Ronsard's poem recalls Hellenistic epic, even Ludovico Ariosto's *Orlando furioso,* in its sense of decoration, details, and marvelous adventures. But Ronsard never finished the work. *La Franciade* does not seem to have enjoyed the critical success the poet had hoped for, and after Charles IX's death in 1574 royal patronage of the epic was no longer available, so Ronsard abandoned his project. Indeed, at the court of Henry III Ronsard was eclipsed by the younger Philippe Desportes; although he still received a royal pension and had some success as an organizer of court festivities, he spent increasing time at his priories of Croixval and Saint-Cosme, outside Tours.

Ronsard was associated with the French court in other ways, as panegyrist and composer of sonnets and other poems "on command" and as a defender of Catherine de Médicis's policy toward French Protestants. In 1562–1563 Ronsard wrote a series of polemical poems against the Huguenots and their leader, Théodore de Bèze, ending with the celebrated "Responce aux injures et calomnies." This long "reply" to Protestant accusations of paganism, flattery, debauchery, and various other vices stands as an intricate account of the relationship between poetry, rhetoric, politics, and religion, and was widely read in the early years of the religious wars.

Influence. The prolific Ronsard is well known for many other poems: the early ambitious cosmological hymns celebrating gold, the sky, the stars, and death (1555–1556); the hymns of the seasons (1563); pastoral poetry; circumstantial court pieces; and the melancholic sonnets he composed on his deathbed in 1585, *Les derniers vers* (Last verses). In an age in which poetry was becoming increasingly self-conscious Ronsard contributed to poetic theory, especially in his prefaces (such as the *Abbregé de l'art poëtique françois* [Summary of French poetics]; 1565), which gave practical advice concerning composition in French and insisted above all on the pleasure of variety. Finally, Ronsard was a tireless editor of his own works, which he gathered, corrected, and republished frequently, often in magnificent editions.

Although Ronsard became partially deaf at an early age, in 1542, the musicality of his short poems has inspired many composers, from Pierre Certon to Clément Jannequin. Poets of the late sixteenth century, such as the Protestants Théodore-Agrippa d'Aubigné and Guillaume de Salluste du Bartas, admired and emulated Ronsard. By the early seventeenth century, however, Ronsard's abundant and archaic language was widely criticized in literary and court circles. His influence beyond French borders was considerable: the neo-Latin poet Melissus (Paul Schede), Jan van der Noot in the Netherlands, Georg Rudolf Weckherlin and Martin Opitz in Germany, Gabriello Chiabrera in Italy, and Thomas Lodge in England are examples of the European resonance of Ronsard's *Amours* and *Odes,* particularly.

See also **Pléiade**.

BIBLIOGRAPHY

Primary Work

Ronsard, Pierre de. *Oeuvres complètes.* 2 vols. Edited by Jean Céard, Daniel Ménager, and Michael Simonin. Paris, 1993.

Secondary Works

Bellenger, Yvonne et al., eds. *Ronsard en son quatrième centenaire.* Vol. 1: *Ronsard hier et aujourd'hui.* Geneva, 1988. Vol. 2: *L'art de poésie.* Geneva, 1989.

Cave, Terence, ed. *Ronsard the Poet.* London, 1973.

Ménager, Daniel. *Ronsard: Le roi, le poète et les hommes.* Geneva, 1979.

Nilges, Annemarie. *Imitation als Dialog: Die europäische Rezeption Ronsards in Renaissance und Frühbarock.* Heidelberg, Germany, 1988.

Raymond, Marcel. *L'influence de Ronsard sur la poésie française (1550–1585).* Rev. ed. 2 vols. Geneva, 1965.

Silver, Isidore. *Ronsard and the Hellenic Renaissance in France.* Vol. 1, *Ronsard and the Greek Epic.* St. Louis, Mo., 1961. Vol. 2, *Ronsard and the Grecian Lyre.* Geneva, 1981.

Simonin, Michel. *Pierre de Ronsard.* Paris, 1990.

ULLRICH LANGER

ROPER, MARGARET MORE (1505–1544), British scholar and translator. Margaret More Roper was the daughter of Sir Thomas More and his first wife, Jane Colt. Educated by humanist tutors including William Gonell and Richard Hyrde in Greek, Latin, theology, astronomy, philosophy, mathematics, poetry, logic, grammar, and rhetoric, Roper was the star pupil in her father's school for his children and wards. In 1521 she married William Roper, a lawyer and later the author of *The Life of Sir Thomas More;* the names of two sons and three daughters are recorded.

A Devout Treatise upon the "Pater Noster" (written c. 1524; first published 1526), her skillful translation of Erasmus's *Precatio dominica,* is significant as an early popularization of the Erasmian devotional meditation on the "seven petitions" in the Lord's Prayer. Richard Hyrde's preface commends Roper's "judgment in expressing lively the Latin" and praises her as an exemplary woman whose learning increases her virtue as a daughter and wife, terms reiterated in More's letters and by his biographers. In his *Life* of More (1588), Thomas Stapleton also refers to other works by Roper now apparently lost: Latin and Greek prose and verse, Latin speeches, a response to an oration by Quintilian, and a treatise on *The Four Last Things,* a topic she shared with her father. The correspondence between father and daughter during More's imprisonment in the Tower of London (1534–1535) reveals their mutual devotion and the great extent to which More depended on Roper to preserve and disseminate his reasons for opposing Henry VIII's divorce and the Act of Succession. A letter to Alice Alington, apparently written by Roper in August 1534, is a dialogue between father and daughter that details More's conscientious objections.

BIBLIOGRAPHY

Primary Work

Roper, Margaret More, trans. *A Devout Treatise upon the "Pater Noster."* In *Erasmus of Rotterdam: A Quincentennial Symposium.* Edited by Richard L. DeMolen. New York, 1971. Pages 93–124.

Secondary Works

Beilin, Elaine. *Redeeming Eve: Women Writers of the English Renaissance.* Princeton, N.J., 1987.

McCutcheon, Elizabeth. "Margaret More Roper: The Learned Woman in Tudor England." In *Women Writers of the Renaissance and Reformation*. Edited by Katharina M. Wilson. Athens, Ga. 1987. Pages 449–480.

Verbrugge, Rita. "Margaret More Roper's Personal Expression in the *Devout Treatise upon the Pater Noster*." In *Silent but for the Word: Tudor Women as Patrons, Translators, and Writers of Religious Works*. Edited by Margaret Patterson Hannay. Kent, Ohio, 1985. Pages 30–40.

ELAINE V. BEILIN

ROSSELLINO, BERNARDO (1409–1464), Italian sculptor and architect. Born into a family of stonecutters from Settignano (near Florence), he was principally involved in a series of projects in the Tuscan towns of Florence, Siena, Arezzo, Pistoia, and Pienza. His fame, however, extended beyond his native borders, and he received important commissions in Rome from Popes Nicholas V and Pius II.

Sculpture. Bernardo Rossellino and his brothers Giovanni and Tommaso operated an important sculpture workshop in fifteenth-century Florence. Probably the best-known work produced under Bernardo's supervision was the tomb of Florentine chancellor Leonardo Bruni in Santa Croce (after 1444). The classically conceived sarcophagus, upon which the figure of the deceased is displayed in effigy, and the attendant putti (angels) and medallions are set inside an elegantly carved shallow niche cut into the wall of the church. The semicircular arch with the sculpted *tondo* (medallion) representing the Madonna and Child at its apex and framed by delicately carved pilasters sets up a vertical axis that balances the horizontal thrust of the tomb and lends a contemplative and serene mood to the ensemble.

The space implied by the niche as well as the ornamental detail is in keeping with Filippo Brunelleschi's and Leon Batista Alberti's classicizing architecture and constitutes a break from the late medieval forms of the church itself. With this work Bernardo modified a surviving medieval tradition and established the Renaissance wall tomb type. The chapel of the cardinal of Portugal at San Miniato al Monte on the periphery of Florence by Bernardo's younger brother Antonio (with Antonio Manetti) represents its most immediate and highly acclaimed successor.

Architecture. Despite the significance of his sculptural projects, Bernardo's fame rests chiefly on his architectural work. Entrusted with major commissions for the Vatican and Roman churches (for example, the rehabilitation of San Stefano Rotondo) by two popes, he was also the architect in charge of the Duomo in Florence (1461). Undoubtedly, his most important architectural achievement was the rebuilding of the city of Pienza for Pope Pius II (1460–1462). As one of the very few Renaissance urban renewal schemes to be completed, Pienza offers a unique example of contemporary conceptions of the ideal city.

Bernardo Rossellino. ***Virgin of the Annunciation.*** Statue in the Chapel della Misericordia, Empoli, Italy. ALINARI/ART RESOURCE

Arranged around a trapezoidal square, the cathedral, the pope's palace, the *palazzo communale* (city hall), and bishop's palace constitute the real and symbolic heart of the city. Through siting and facade treatment, each building contributes to a harmonious and coherent ensemble; the visual unfolding of the square from one privileged vantage point additionally enhances its unity and suggests that the design was perspectivally conceived. Bernardo's fine classical detailing and flat, incised rustication recall the delicate ornamental style of Michelozzo and Lucca della Robbia, although other projects ascribed to him (Palazzo delle Papesse and Palazzo Piccolomini, Siena) show him able to create powerful, monumental effects.

According to Renaissance chroniclers, Bernardo collaborated with Alberti on several projects, notably on Pienza and the Palazzo Rucellai in Florence. Indeed, authorship for both projects continues to be debated. The most recent proposals attribute Pienza to Rossellino as well as the execution and interior design changes to the Palazzo Rucellai; the facade of the palace is ascribed to Alberti.

See also **Urbanism**.

BIBLIOGRAPHY

Mack, Charles. *Pienza. The Creation of a Renaissance City*. Ithaca, N.Y., and London, 1987.

Preyer, Brenda. "The Rucellai Palace." In *Giovanni Rucellai ed il suo zibaldone* (A Florentine patrician and his palace). Edited by Alessandro Perosa. London, 1981. Volume 2, pages 156–225.

Saalman, Howard. "The Palazzo Rucellai." *Journal of the Society of Architectural Historians* 47, no. 1 (1988): 82–90.

Schulz, Anne Markham. *The Sculpture of Bernardo Rossellino and His Workshop*. Princeton, N.J., 1977.

Tavernor, Robert. *On Alberti and the Art of Building*. New Haven, Conn., and London, 1998.

ALINA A. PAYNE

ROSSO FIORENTINO, GIOVANNI BATTISTA DI JACOPO, IL. *See* **Florence,** *subentry on* **Art of the Sixteenth Century.**

ROUEN. A wide range of commercial, manufacturing, and administrative activities made Rouen the second-largest city of Renaissance France, behind only Paris. Its population was around 40,000 in 1500, 75,000 in 1550, and 68,000 in 1600.

Economy. Rouen was France's busiest port in the sixteenth century. Ocean-going vessels were able to navigate the Seine as far as Rouen, where they unloaded their cargoes for distribution to the vast Paris basin. Rouen's merchants were active on the great Antwerp market, in trade with England, in the salt and wine trade with France's west coast ports, in commerce with the Iberian peninsula, and in the alum trade with Italy. With the expansion of Europe's horizons, they also moved into cod fishing off the Newfoundland Banks and began regular trade with the west coast of Africa by 1511 and with Brazil by 1518. In 1528 a vessel outfitted by Rouen merchants was captured in the Indian Ocean. Trade brought an important colony of Spanish merchants to the city, many of whose members obtained letters of naturalization and married into the city's elite. A few Italian banking families also had representatives in the city. Indigenous merchants nonetheless controlled the lion's share of commerce.

Metalwares, leather goods, woolens, and stockings were particularly important products manufactured in Rouen, with the cloth and hosiery trades occupying the largest number of workers. Restrictive guild regulations, however, caused a growing number of woolen manufacturers to abandon the city for nearby localities beyond the reach of these regulations during the first half of the sixteenth century. A comparable trend diminished the ranks of stocking makers from the 1540s on, reversing several decades of vigorous expansion for that industry. Nearby regions of Normandy were also major centers for production of linen and paper, which were marketed in Rouen and contributed significantly to its international commerce.

Rouen was no less important as an administrative center for the province of Normandy. Rouen's archbishop oversaw France's largest diocese, with 1,338 parishes. A parlement, or high court of appeals, was established in Rouen in 1499. It headed a panoply of royal courts in the city that expanded steadily in size and competency over the course of the century.

Municipal Government. With so many royal courts and officials in the city, the governing authority over Rouen was contested. Rouen had a city government known as the Council of Twenty-four that was elected by the more prominent inhabitants of the town. The city's law courts also claimed considerable responsibility for urban governance. Rouen's Parlement in particular played a growing role in regulating markets, public health, sanitation, and poor relief as the sixteenth century advanced. A governor or lieutenant general represented the king and was also an influential figure in local politics and peacekeeping.

Intellectual and Artistic Life. Despite Rouen's size, wealth, and wide commercial contacts, it was not a noteworthy center of Renaissance intellectual or artistic activity. The central event in local literary life was the annual poetic competition in honor of the Virgin Mary known as the Puy des Palinods. Established in 1484, the competition gained new luster after Pope Leo X confirmed its statutes and conferred new privileges on it in 1520. It attracted entries from nonresident participants of the caliber of Clément Marot.

While judges in the Parlement and canons of the cathedral chapter are known to have pursued scholarly or literary interests, and while small neo-Latin poetic circles grouped jurists, doctors, clerics, and merchants, virtually the only author of any note to reside in Rouen for an extended period of time was the minor poet Claude Chappuys, canon from 1536 to 1575. Chappuys played an important role in designing the royal entry of 1550 that was one of the most elaborate of these splendid period festivities.

Most public construction undertaken amid the commercial prosperity of this era was in the late Gothic style, although a few townhouses and funerary monuments display Renaissance stylistic influences. Rouen was France's third most active printing center in the sixteenth century, but its production paled in comparison with that of Paris and Lyon.

Reformation and Wars of Religion. Normandy was one of the hotbeds of Protestantism in France. After a long period when Protestant ideas circulated underground, a Reformed church was formed in Rouen in 1557 and quickly grew in size. The Protestants seized control of the city on 15 April 1562. After a wave of iconoclasm several weeks later, Catholic services ceased. Royal and Catholic troops retook the city on 26 October 1562, sacked it for three days, and executed several leaders of the Calvinist regime, including the noted minister Augustin Marlorat (on 30 October), one of the Huguenot movement's most prominent theologians. The Reformed church reestablished itself after the 1563 Peace of Amboise and soon counted 16,500 members. Relations between Catholics and Protestants remained troubled for the next decade. On 17–20 September 1572, Rouen witnessed a local reenactment of the Saint Bartholomew's Day massacre. Hundreds of Protestants were killed, and many more fled or returned to the Catholic church.

Although intermittent civil war continued elsewhere in France, Rouen escaped most of the turmoil for the next fifteen years and even saw a revival of its pre-1562 prosperity. But the crisis of the Bourbon succession saw the city taken over by supporters of the Catholic League on 5 February 1589. Warfare returned. Between 11 November 1591 and 21 April 1592, Rouen was besieged by Henry IV, assisted by English troops under the Earl of Essex. The city held out despite great suffering until delivered by Spanish troops under the duke of Parma. On 30 March 1594 Rouen recognized Henry IV's authority, effectively ending the era of the civil wars in the region.

See also **Wars of Religion**.

BIBLIOGRAPHY

Benedict, Philip. *Rouen during the Wars of Religion*. Cambridge, U.K., 1981.

Mollat, Michel. *Le commerce maritime normand à la fin du Moyen Age*. Paris, 1952.

Mollat, Michel, et al. *Histoire de Rouen*. Toulouse, France, 1979.

PHILIP BENEDICT

ROYAL ICONOGRAPHY, ENGLISH. In order to praise the Tudor and Stuart monarchs, artists fashioned an elaborate royalist iconography (that is, the symbolic representation of meaning by use of artistic and literary images) out of a dense network of elements derived from biblical, classical, and European heraldic traditions.

Henry VII and Henry VIII. Henry Tudor faced the iconographical problem of proclaiming the legitimacy of the dynasty that he founded only by victory at Bosworth Field in 1485. As Henry VII (reigned 1485–1509), he projected a composite image of regal magnificence and pious orthodoxy. In return for his fealty, the pope proclaimed him Defender of the Faith, a title claimed by British monarchs to the present day. Thomas More's *History of Richard III* contributed to Henry's image-building project by transmitting a defamatory portrayal of the slain Yorkist king as a murderous hunchback. Passing that legend on to posterity, William Shakespeare's *Richard III* enshrines a Tudor myth. In line with a supposed prophecy of the Tudor succession uttered by Henry VI, who received veneration as both saint and martyr, Henry VII claimed inheritance from the Lancastrian kings. By marrying the Yorkist heiress, Princess Elizabeth, King Henry seemed to reunite the warring Houses of York and Lancaster, symbolized respectively by white and red roses. A fusion of those emblems produced the Tudor rose, a powerful symbol of dynastic unity that often accompanied the portcullis device of the king's mother, Margaret Beaufort.

During the early decades of his reign, Henry VIII (reigned 1509–1547) emulated his father's image. Exploiting their Welsh origins, both father and son used the red dragon of Wales as a Tudor emblem and claimed descent from King Arthur. Playwrights such as John Heywood and John Skelton cultivated Henry VIII's image of regal magnificence. Like his father and preceding English monarchs, he adopted the closed royal crown as a sign of "imperial" majesty. Triggered by the pope's refusal to annul the king's marriage to Catherine of Aragon, England's schism from Rome entailed a searching reconfiguration of royal iconography. The imperial crown

The English "Pope," Henry VIII. Receiving homage from kneeling bishops and nobles for his unification of church and state, Henry VIII transmits the Bible, symbolic of Protestant kingship. Henry's sword of justice is a traditional regal figure, but it undergoes modification by association with "the sword of the spirit, which is the Word of God" (Ephesians 6:17) in the hand of the flanking figure of Paul, the "Protestant saint" who here symbolizes the New Testament. The text in the right-hand banderole, "I am not ashamed of the Gospel of Christ, for it is the power of God" (Romans 1:16), appears in other portraits of the Protestant Tudors. Symbolic of the Old Testament, King David's playing on the harp represents both "godly" kingship and his supposed authorship of Psalms. The definitive image of Reformation kingship at the center recurs in works such as John Bale's *King John,* an allegorical drama that urged continuing ecclesiastical reform. From the Coverdale Bible (1535). BY PERMISSION OF THE BRITISH LIBRARY. C132H46

now symbolized England's independence from papal overlordship. Royal clients such as Hans Holbein the Younger, the German artist, and Miles Coverdale, the evangelical Bible translator, fashioned a new image of Henry VIII as an English "pope" who headed both church and state without clerical intercession.

Edward and Mary. The accession of Edward VI (reigned 1547–1553) precipitated an iconographical problem because the Protestant lords who dominated his government reconstructed the Church of England along Protestant lines despite the boy's legal incapacity to rule as a minor. Claiming that Edward possessed biblical warrant to initiate ecclesiastical reforms despite his youth, preachers and propagandists fashioned his image as a new Josiah. The suppression of pagan idolatry by that boy king of Judah afforded a precedent for iconoclastic attack on Roman Catholic altars, shrines, and religious images. Thomas Cranmer, archbishop of Canterbury, constructed the Josiah myth in his coronation sermon, and Protestant writers such as Coverdale and John Bale disseminated it in Bible prefaces, commentaries, ballads, allegorical plays, and popular pamphlets. On the model of late medieval royal iconography, King Edward also received praise as a new Solomon, wise in his youth. Solomon's erection of the Temple in Jerusalem, a figure for Edward's reputed role as the architect of a newly reformed church, received considerable emphasis.

The accession of Mary I (reigned 1553–1558) entailed reversal of Protestant royal iconography. For example, her assumption of the motto of *Veritas filia temporis* (Truth, the daughter of Time) conferred new meaning on an adage previously associated with Reformation theology. As the Roman Catholic daughter of Catherine of Aragon, she complemented the Tudor rose with her mother's emblems of the pomegranate or castle. The first Virgin Queen of England, she adopted the pose of a second Virgin Mary

A "New Josiah," Edward VI. Protestant iconoclasm dominates this woodcut allegory of the reign of Edward VI. The king bears the Sword and the Book at the lower left in emulation of his father's pose in Holbein's woodcut for the Coverdale Bible. The top panel portrays the "Burning of Images" and "The Papists packing away their paultry," which consists of elements used in the celebration of the Mass. A Protestant iconoclast pulls a saint's image down from a church wall as "papists" load their "trinkets" aboard "The ship of the Romish Church." Portraying "The Temple well purged," the scene at the lower right displays the essential elements of Protestant worship: preaching, Bible reading, and the reduction of the seven Roman Catholic sacraments to the rites of the Lord's Supper (Holy Communion) and baptism. From John Foxe's *Actes and Monuments* (1570). BY PERMISSION OF JOHN N. KING

(a stance assumed by late-medieval queens consort) and mother of the reconstructed Catholic church in England. After she married her Habsburg cousin, Philip of Spain, royal portraits conferred emblems of kingship (such as the sword of justice) upon her rather than her consort, thus proclaiming the ability of a woman to govern, a vexed issue in the Renaissance. Her image as a second Mary enabled publicists to proclaim her capacity to bear a royal heir through divine intervention despite the likelihood that she had passed the age of childbearing. Poets such as John Heywood and Miles Hogarde and the court playwright, Nicholas Udall, praised her as a pious handmaiden or England's marigold (attributes of the Virgin Mary).

Elizabeth. Contrary to popular opinion, Elizabeth I (reigned 1558–1603) never took a youthful vow to remain unmarried as the spouse and mother of her country, but she did embrace her late sister's style as a Virgin Queen. Early in her reign she cultivated an image of maidenly eligibility for marriage and childbearing. In addition to standard Tudor devices, she assumed the emblem of her mother, Anne Boleyn, the white falcon on a stake. In precoronation pageantry in celebration of her entry into London,

Elizabeth appropriated her late sister's motto by performing the role of Truth, the daughter of Time, and accepting a gift copy of a large Bible, an important symbol of Protestant monarchy. Texts such as John Foxe's *Book of Martyrs* exploited biblical models, notably Deborah, the female judge, to craft her image as a defender of Protestant reform at the same time that Mary Tudor underwent vilification as a new Jezebel, whose persecution of Protestants earned her enduring reputation as "Bloody Mary." By assuming the motto *Semper eadem* (Always the same), Elizabeth proclaimed the unchangeability of her decrees in matters of church and state. After the breakdown of her final marriage negotiations, midway through her reign, she received adulation as Diana, virgin goddess of the hunt, in esoteric allegorical portraits. As Venus Virgo she combined unapproachable virginity with erotic allure. Poets such as Shakespeare, Sir Walter Ralegh, and Edmund Spenser contributed to the image of the aging queen as a perpetual virgin.

Elizabeth I and Her Symbols. Ascribed to Isaac Oliver, this picture's arcane symbolism epitomizes the final phase of Elizabethan iconography. Wearing the "mask of youth" that denied the aged queen's vulnerability to death, Elizabeth grasps the rainbow symbolic of both peace and her claim to govern as the chosen of God. The motto, *Non sine sole iris* (No rainbow without the sun), associates her with the Sun, a symbol for Christ and Christlike kings. Nonetheless, she receives adulation as Diana, the virgin goddess of the Moon who is symbolized by the bejeweled crescent atop the elaborate headpiece. Onetime attributes of the Virgin Mary, pearls sewn onto the elaborate costume glorify the Virgin Queen of England. The queen holds a heart-shaped ruby that represents her as an object of unfulfillable desire, and the jeweled serpent on her sleeve symbolizes wisdom or prudence. The floral bodice signifies fertility, and the eyes, ears, and mouths on her cloak celebrate the widespread dissemination of the queen's fame through hearing, sight, and speech. Portrait of Queen Elizabeth by Taddeo Zucarri (1529–1566), called the Rainbow Portrait. BY COURTESY OF THE MARQUESS OF SALISBURY

The Stuarts. The extinction of the Tudor dynasty at the death of Elizabeth I brought to the throne a descendant of Henry VIII's eldest sister. When James VI of Scotland became James I of England (reigned 1603–1625), the Scottish thistle joined the Tudor rose as a monarchic emblem. Jacobean iconography heightened emphasis upon Roman imperial models such as Caesar Augustus, who was renowned for finding Rome made of brick and leaving it marble. Unlike Elizabethan poets such as Ralegh and Spenser, whose works fell out of favor in courtly circles, Shakespeare's dramatic company cultivated royal patronage by performing plays such as *Macbeth,* which celebrated the Stuart monarch's Scottish descent. Ben Jonson collaborated with Inigo Jones, a designer of elaborate scenic effects, in staging courtly masques whose arcane symbolism complemented the king's pose as Schoolmaster of the Realm, many of whose writings went into print. James's reputation for wisdom led him to pose as a new Solomon, but he also emulated David to the point of versifying Psalms ascribed to the Hebrew king. Although Jacobean iconography emphasized continuity with the Tudors, the royal motto of *Beati pacifici* (Blessed are the peacemakers) stressed his goal of achieving a peace settlement with foreign Catholic powers.

Charles I (reigned 1625–1649) inherited elements of his father's iconography. In concert with pacifistic policies toward Spain, the king's swerve toward Catholicism alarmed Puritan members within the religio-political establishment. They also took issue with increasingly esoteric courtly masques, which violated convention by including female dancers, and with the vogue for mildly pornographic Cavalier verse. Equally unpopular was the Neoplatonic cult inspired by Henrietta Maria, the king's foreign Catholic consort. After the birth of an heir, the fleur-de-lis of the French royal house supplemented the English rose in courtly paintings, which also included olive branches symbolic of Stuart pacifism. The Bible symbolic of Tudor Protestant militancy, which enjoyed a vestigial place in Jacobean iconography, disappeared during the Caroline era. John Milton's *A Mask at Ludlow* and *Lycidas* typified opposition to the king's religious policies. After the unprecedented execution of Charles I during the revolutionary era, Milton found occasion to attack the late king's poses as a suffering martyr, a Christlike king, and a new David who composed Psalmlike meditations. Milton's polemical pamphlets compared him instead to idolatrous monarchs of the Old Testament such as Pharaoh and Ahab, whom Protestant militants vilified as prototypes for Catholic tyranny. By contrast, the Restoration instituted celebration of Charles I as a saintly royal martyr.

See also **Monarchy**; **Queens and Queenship**.

BIBLIOGRAPHY

King, John N. "Queen Elizabeth I: Representations of the Virgin Queen." *Renaissance Quarterly* 43 (1990): 30–74. Analyzes successive phases in Elizabethan iconography of marriageable, perpetual, and goddesslike virginity.

King, John N. *Tudor Royal Iconography: Literature and Art in an Age of Religious Crisis*. Princeton, N.J., 1989. Considers iconography of "godly" monarchy across the Tudor dynasty.

Kipling, Gordon. *Enter the King: Theatre, Liturgy, and Ritual in the Medieval Civic Triumph*. Oxford, 1998.

Smuts, R. Malcolm. *Court Culture and the Origins of a Royalist Tradition in Early Stuart England*. Philadelphia, 1987. Considers courtly culture under James I and Charles I.

Yates, Francis A. *Astraea: The Imperial Theme in the Sixteenth Century*. London, 1975. See "Queen Elizabeth I as Astraea," pp. 29–87. Classic study of late-Elizabethan iconography.

JOHN N. KING

RUBENS, PETER PAUL (1577–1640), Flemish painter. Rubens represents the culmination of the Renaissance tradition in art. The most successful and influential of seventeenth-century northern artists, he synthesized in his glowing, painterly treatments of mythology, religious subjects, portraits, and landscapes the classical contours and heroic vision of the Italian Renaissance masters. His robust, sensual representation of the human body epitomizes the baroque style—shimmering in color, pulsating with energy, in every sense larger than life.

Yet art was but one facet of his fame. His contemporary and friend the Italian general Ambrogio Spinola said of him, "Of all his talents, painting is the least." Rubens was renowned throughout Europe as a diplomat. A true Renaissance man, he was a scholar and Christian humanist, a classicist and antiquarian, a prodigious correspondent (in Latin, Italian, and French, as well as his native Flemish), and an amateur architect. As a shrewd businessman and impresario of vast decorative programs, he organized the most famous and productive painter's studio in Europe. His inventive powers were paralleled by his extraordinary energy and versatility. The Danish court physician Otto Sperling recalled seeing the master at work on a painting, "in the course of which he was read to from Tacitus while, at the same time, he dictated a letter. As we did not disturb him by talking, he began to speak with us, carrying on his painting without stopping, still being read to and going on with the dictation."

A devout Catholic, devoted husband, and father of eight children, Rubens was unwavering in loyalty to his Spanish sovereigns and the Church. This prosperous, energetic, life-embracing, thoroughly balanced man in tune with his time represents the antithesis of the struggling artist who pays dearly—economically, spiritually, and socially—for exerting his genius. These very qualities have confounded critics who prefer to find genius in a tormented Michelangelo, a rebellious Caravaggio, a withdrawn and introspective Rembrandt. The collaborative nature of Rubens's studio productions likewise runs counter to the modern notion of solitary genius. Like the Renaissance poets Petrarch and Shakespeare, Rubens drew deeply from a once-common wellspring of imagery and allusions—biblical, theological, and mythological—much of which is unfamiliar to present-day viewers. The eighteenth-century archaeologist Johann Winckelmann compared him to the ancient Homer in his "great fertility of imagination." Rubens's art, like his life, reveals the epic quality of a giant who towers over his age.

Early Career. Rubens was born on 28 June 1577 in the small German town of Siegen, in Westphalia, to parents living in exile following the religious persecutions in the Netherlands in the late sixteenth century. After his father's death, the family returned to Antwerp, where young Peter Paul received a solid, classical education. His formal artistic training began in 1591 with his apprenticeship first to Tobias Verhaecht, then Adam van Noort, and finally Antwerp's leading master of the day, Otto van Veen, who contributed much to Rubens's early style and, more important, his development as an artist grounded in an ambitious, humanistic ideal of painting.

Rubens's *Portrait of a Young Man* (New York, Metropolitan Museum) is his earliest dated work, inscribed 1597, a year before his admission into the painters' guild of St. Luke. Following a long-established tradition among Netherlandish artists, he set off on an Italian sojourn in 1600. In Venice he studied the luminosity and dramatic expressiveness of masterpieces by Titian, Tintoretto, and Paolo Veronese. Hired by Vincenzo I Gonzaga, duke of Mantua, he proceeded to the Mantuan court, where the current music master was Claudio Monteverdi, the father of Italian opera, and where the duke's gallery of masterpieces by Titian, Andrea Mantegna, Correggio, Raphael, and Giulio Romano furthered his artistic education.

Rubens's arrival in Rome in 1601 coincided with the dawn of the baroque style heralded there by Annibale Carracci's sensual and erudite Renaissance revival in his frescoes for the ceiling of the gallery in the Palazzo Farnese and by Caravaggio's bold new naturalism and metaphysical chiaroscuro. Both left lasting imprints on Rubens. In the Vatican he sketched copies of Michelangelo's and Raphael's frescoes and of ancient sculpture, which appear drawn from live models rather than marble, as he infused them—Pygmalion-like—with immediacy and life. In his Latin treatise *De imitatione statuarum* (On the imitation of [ancient] statues), Rubens wrote that one must "above all else, avoid the effect of stone." His full-blooded transformations of classical antiquity exemplified his underlying credo of such artistic metamorphosis.

Rubens's first major Roman commission in 1601, three large murals for the chapel of Saint Helena in Santa Croce in Gerusalemme, was followed two years later by his first diplomatic assignment as Gonzaga's emissary bearing princely gifts to King Philip III of Spain. For Philip's prime minister, the duke of Lerma, Rubens painted his first major equestrian portrait (1603; Madrid, Prado), an early baroque variation on the Renaissance models of Titian and Tintoretto. In 1605 Rubens made his second trip to Rome and together with his brother Philip undertook an intensive study of classical art and philology. Rubens soon became an avid antiquarian and collector of Roman sculpture, reliefs, portrait busts, and ancient coins.

Work in Antwerp for Court and Church. A year later Rubens won the most sought-after commission in Rome: the high altar of the Oratorian church, Santa Maria in Vallicella. But before its unveiling he dashed home to Antwerp in October 1608 upon receiving word—too late—that his mother was gravely ill. Despite his personal loss, Rubens's arrival home was most timely. The Twelve Years' Truce between the United Provinces (the Dutch separatists) and Spain promised economic recovery for war-weary Flanders. The commission to paint for the signing of the truce in the Town Hall a celebratory *Adoration of the Magi* (Madrid, Prado; 1609) served as an epiphany of the young baroque master fresh from Rome. Before he could return to Rome, the coregents Albert and Isabella appointed Rubens their new court painter, exempted him from all taxes and court duties, and allowed him to organize his own studio in Antwerp. Two weeks later Rubens married the nineteen-year-old Isabella Brant. Among the many religious commissions that fell to Rubens during this period of Antwerp's economic optimism and church restoration were two great triptychs, the *Raising of the Cross* (Antwerp, Cathedral), commissioned in 1610 for the high altar of Saint Walburga, and the *Descent from the Cross* (1611–1614) for Antwerp's cathedral.

For his own home Rubens designed a magnificent studio, portico, and classical garden pavilion—an Italian Renaissance villa transplanted to the heart of Antwerp. The decade from 1610 to 1620 witnessed an enormous production of altarpieces—Assumptions of the Virgin, Adorations of Shepherds and Magi, lives of the saints, Nativities, Crucifixions, Last Judgments—establishing Rubens as the paramount painter of Counter-Reformation themes in northern Europe. Yet his output of secular pieces—mythologies, hunting scenes, portraits, history, and allegory—was equally prodigious.

Rubens's thriving studio of assistants, collaborators, and engravers disseminated his compositions throughout Europe. The Danish physician Sperling recalled "a large hall which had no windows but was lighted through an opening in the ceiling. In this hall were a number of young painters, all at work on different pictures, for which Rubens had made the drawings in chalks indicating the tones here and there which Rubens would afterwards finish himself. The work would then pass for a Rubens." Several of his outside collaborators were themselves distinguished painters, such as Jan Wildens, Paul de Vos, Frans Snyders, and Jan Brueghel.

Among his assistants was the precocious Anthony van Dyck, twenty-two years younger than Rubens. Van Dyck quickly absorbed Rubens's style and faithfully imitated it when executing full-scale works under the master's supervision, such as the huge cartoons in oil on canvas (Vaduz, Liechtenstein Collection) for the Decius Mus tapestries, designed in 1616. Based on Livy's account of the heroic consul who sacrificed his life in battle to save Rome, this

Peter Paul Rubens. ***Descent from the Cross.*** Oil on panel; c. 1611. COURTAULD GALLERY, LONDON/THE BRIDGEMAN ART LIBRARY

first multicomposition commission reflected on a grandiose scale Rubens's adherence to the neo-Stoicism of the late Christian humanist and philosopher Justus Lipsius (1547–1606), his reconciliation of ancient Roman *virtus* with Christianity. Rubens's treatments of ancient themes—historical or mythological—served as prefigurations of Christianity in general and Roman Catholic doctrine in particular. In Rubens's eyes, Rome remained Rome: history was a continuum of tradition and revelation.

The seventeenth-century biographer Filippo Baldinucci credited the Italian baroque master Gian Lorenzo Bernini as being "the first to unite painting, sculpture, and architecture in such a way that together they form a pleasing whole." That claim may be made for Rubens, a generation earlier, in view of his multiple contributions in all three media to Antwerp's new Jesuit church. In 1620 Rubens contracted to furnish a series of thirty-nine ceiling paintings, for which he undertook to paint the preparatory oil sketches himself. The full-scale canvases were to be executed by Van Dyck and other assistants. The ceiling paintings were finished in a year—the first northern revival of the Venetian Renaissance tradition of Titian, Tintoretto, and Veronese—but perished by fire in the eighteenth century. Yet Rubens's autograph *modelli* (detailed oil sketches that served as models) offer glimpses into his creative genius and extraordinary verve—what the seventeenth-century Italian critic Giovanni Bellori called "the great speed and frenzy of his brush."

The day after the church dedication Rubens wrote that he was "by natural instinct, better fitted to execute very large works than small curiosities. Everyone according to his gifts; my talent is such that no undertaking, however vast in size or diversified in subject, has ever surpassed my courage." Vast new decorative cycles would soon prove the validity of this boast.

Diplomacy and International Commissions. After the expiration of the Twelve Years' Truce and the death of Archduke Albert in 1621, the widowed infanta Isabella engaged Rubens as her confidential agent in the clandestine diplomatic maneuvers for peace between the two Netherlands. His widespread fame, like Titian's, as "the painter of princes and prince of painters" permitted Rubens to travel freely among royal courts while disguising ulterior motives for his meetings with sovereigns and their ministers, who often discussed matters of state while sitting for portraits.

In January 1622 Rubens was called to Paris by the dowager queen of France, Maria de' Medici (Marie de Médicis), widow of Henry IV, to decorate the two main galleries in her new Luxembourg Palace, wherein she sought to promote, through Rubens's persuasive brush, her life and former regency of France in epic fashion. Maria's lackluster career required an unprecedented dose of poetic license and allegory—a display of Rubens's fertile powers of invention. Comprising twenty-four scenes, the Medici cycle (Paris, Louvre; see the frontispiece to this volume) was prepared by autograph oil sketches and figure drawings before being enlarged by assistants, and retouched by Rubens, in the final canvases. Maria's adviser, the abbé de Saint-Ambroise, commented that "two Italian painters would not carry out in ten years what Rubens will do in four." In fact, he took only three.

Rubens exploited his encyclopedic knowledge of classical mythology, emblems, and allegory to raise Maria's melodramatic life to the stage of grand opera, to a mythic plane on which mortals meet Olympian gods. While in Paris, Rubens met George Villiers, duke of Buckingham, who had been sent to escort Maria's daughter, Henrietta Maria, to London as the new English queen and bride of Charles I. Buckingham was a first-rate connoisseur, and he wasted no time in persuading Rubens to paint his equestrian portrait (destroyed; oil sketch, 1625; Fort Worth, Kimbell Museum), the high baroque fulfillment of the early portrait of Lerma.

Back in Antwerp, Rubens continued to accept important commissions from churches and private patrons. His great *Adoration of the Magi* (Antwerp, Royal Museum) was installed in 1624 at the high altar of the Abbey of Saint Michael in Antwerp, crowned by freestanding sculptures designed by Rubens. For the high altar of the Antwerp Cathedral he designed a marble portico to frame his definitive *Assumption of the Virgin,* painted from 1624 to 1627. Nor did Rubens neglect smaller-scale works of portraiture and landscape. The 1620s gave rise to his masterly portraits of his physician and friend *Ludovicus Nonnius* (c. 1627; London, National Gallery), his future sister-in-law *Susanna Fourment* (c. 1622–1625; London, National Gallery), and the double portrait of his sons *Albert and Nicolaas Rubens* (c. 1625; Vaduz, Liechtenstein Collection). His development as portraitist was paralleled by an expansive, narrative approach to landscape: the *Landscape with Philemon and Baucis* (c. 1625; Vienna, Kunsthistorisches Museum) presents a cataclysmic view of nature with only the faint beginnings of a rainbow at the far left to suggest abatement and the restoration of benign order.

Following the Dutch defeat at Breda in June 1625, a Pyrrhic victory for Spain in the Netherlands, the infanta Isabella commissioned from Rubens a vast tapestry cycle of more than twenty panels, the *Triumph of the Eucharist* (1626–1628; Madrid, Descalzas Reales), which Rubens unified by an architectural framework within which he depicted illusionistic tapestries within tapestries, an unprecedented display of baroque illusionism. In view of the several preparatory stages of design—*bozzetti* (preliminary oil sketches), *modelli,* cartoons—as well as the enormous expense of the weavings parceled out to several Brussels workshops, the cycle of allegory

Peter Paul Rubens. ***Adoration of the Magi.*** Oil on canvas; 1624; 447 × 184 cm (14.5 × 6 ft.). KONINKLIJK MUSEUM VOOR SCHONE KUNSTEN, ANTWERP/SCALA/ART RESOURCE

and propaganda may be seen as the sacred equivalent of the Medici cycle and as Rubens's thoroughly baroque expression of his Catholic faith.

Following the death of his wife in 1626, Rubens embarked on a diplomatic odyssey. Negotiations with Buckingham over the sale of Rubens's collection of antiquities served as a convenient cover for diplomatic meetings in search of peace among England, Spain, and the Dutch Republic. In August 1628 Rubens left for Madrid, ostensibly to paint a portrait of King Philip—but deceiving few about the real purpose of the visit. There he took full advantage of the royal gallery of paintings, especially the extensive collection of Titian's paintings, which he had not seen in twenty-five years. He proceeded to paint copies after Titian, to whose style, with its vibrant brushwork and luminous modeling, he was now completely attuned. Proceeding to England, Rubens prevailed against court intrigues and achieved an exchange of ambassadors between England and Spain as a prelude to a formal peace treaty. He was awarded an honorary master of arts degree from Cambridge. Before departing for home he received from the king both a knighthood and the long-coveted commission to decorate the ceiling of the Banqueting House in Whitehall Palace with nine vast canvases of royal propaganda.

Later Career. Back in Antwerp, Rubens devoted himself to his "beloved profession" of painting. The peace treaty signed in November between England and Spain was followed by the fifty-three-year-old Rubens's marriage to the sixteen-year-old Helena Fourment. As Rubens later confided, "I have taken a young wife of honest but middle-class family, although everyone tried to persuade me to make a court marriage. But I feared Pride, that inherent vice of the nobility, particularly in that sex, and that is why I chose one who would not blush to see me take my brushes in hand." Far from blushing, Helena was to inspire a late series of personal and poignant portraits as well as some of the most exuberant works of the rejuvenated master.

The marriage was as fruitful as it was blissful, producing five children. In Rubens's poetic *Garden of Love* (c. 1630–1632; Madrid, Prado), marital allegory is imbued with personal significance. If Venus is the reigning goddess of the late mythologies, she is often identified with Helena Fourment, as in the glowing *Venus and Adonis* (c. 1635; New York, Metropolitan Museum; see the color plates in this volume), Rubens's reinterpretation of Ovid's ancient poetry in the light of Titian.

Rubens soon lost all taste for political diplomacy: "I made the decision to force myself to cut this golden knot of ambition, in order to recover my liberty. . . . I seized the occasion of a short, secret journey to throw myself at Her Highness' feet and beg, as the sole reward for so many efforts, exemption for such assignments and permission to serve her in my own home. This favor I obtained with more difficulty than any other she ever granted me . . . and I have never regretted this decision."

In 1631 Philip IV knighted Rubens—the only painter so honored by kings of both England and Spain. Rubens now turned his attention to glorifying the English king James I, Charles I's father. During this decade of his renewed interest in Titian, the Whitehall commission offered a parallel revival of the Venetian Renaissance ceilings of Tintoretto and Veronese, a field of carved and gilded wood frames enclosing three primary scenes devoted to King James, flanked by six subsidiary allegories—a high baroque fanfare for the ill-fated Stuart dynasty. It represents the first successful translation of monumental Italianate decorative painting into England. Upon his arrival in there in 1629, Rubens had written that "in this island I find none of the crudeness which one might expect from a place so remote from Italian elegance." The ceiling paintings were completed in 1634 and shipped to London for installation two years later. Italy was less "remote" after Rubens brought Renaissance Venice to the Thames.

In December 1633 the infanta Isabella died. Her nephew and successor, the cardinal-infante Ferdinand, was to be welcomed with unsurpassed grandeur in a series of nine triumphal arches and stages erected along the processional route through the streets of Antwerp. These temporary architectural monuments of wood, sculpture, cutout figures, and paintings required an army of carpenters, sculptors, and painters, all working under the direction of Rubens. He was now spending the summer months at his Flemish country estate, Het Steen, where he painted the most expansive and glowing landscapes of his career—poetic odes in oil to the natural order of creation.

For Philip IV's new hunting lodge, the Torre de la Parada outside Madrid, Rubens was commissioned in 1636 to paint a vast series of mythologies. It was an enormous undertaking requiring the employment of virtually every able painter in Antwerp. Rubens painted some sixty-odd oil sketches inspired by Ovid's *Metamorphoses* as he approached afresh these stories of the loves, conflicts, and passions of ancient gods and mortals. The masterly oil sketches

Peter Paul Rubens. ***Assumption of the Virgin.*** THE ROYAL COLLECTION © HER MAJESTY QUEEN ELIZABETH II

for the Torre de la Parada rank among his liveliest and most spontaneous, charged as they are with all the powers of his literary imagination and fecundity of invention.

Despite frequently incapacitating attacks of gout, Rubens continued to accept a wide range of commissions. His allegorical *Horrors of War* (Florence, Pitti Palace), painted in 1638 for the duke of Tuscany, expresses the passionate, if pessimistic, yearnings of the former diplomat and seeker of peace. At the same time, Rubens painted, either for his own pleasure or for private patrons, glowing mythologies and portraits. Two late masterpieces offer a dramatic contrast of the public man and private life: in the official stately image of his *Self-Portrait* of c. 1638–1640 (Vienna, Kunsthistorisches Museum), Rubens presents himself not as an artist but as a knight—self-confident and proud, if now aging and visibly weary—wearing his jeweled sword from Charles I. In *Het Pelsken* (c. 1636–1638; Vienna, Kunsthistorisches Museum) he admits the viewer to an unguarded moment as Helena modestly wraps herself—like the ancient "Venus Pudica" statue—in fur, his revival of Titian's *Young Woman in a Fur Cloak* (Vienna, Kunsthistorisches Museum), which he had copied earlier.

Following a severe attack of gout, Rubens died on May 30, 1640. Over his tomb was placed his last and most resonant *sacra conversazione*, the *Virgin and Child with Saints* (c. 1638–1640; Antwerp, Jacobskerk). Rubens's artistic legacy extended far beyond the Netherlands. In Italy his influence was decisive among such high and late baroque masters as Pietro da Cortona, Luca Giordano, and Giovanni Battista Gaulli ("Il Baciccio"); it may even be detected in the most painterly of sculptors, Gian Lorenzo Bernini. In Spain, Rubens's early impression on the young Diego Velázquez was superseded by his impact on the art of Bartolomé Murillo, the most Rubensian of Spanish painters. In France, the champions of color over line, the baroque over the classical, found in Rubens their model. The leader of the Rubénistes at the French Royal Academy of Painting, Roger de Piles, ranked the Fleming first (in a tie with Raphael) in the entire history of painting. Rubens's recurrent impact on artists places him beside his Renaissance forebears Raphael, Michelangelo, and Titian. At the same time, as the preeminent *uomo universale* of his age—painter, diplomat, impresario, scholar, antiquarian, architect, humanist—Peter Paul Rubens represents the baroque fulfillment of the Renaissance man.

See also **Baroque, Concept of the.**

BIBLIOGRAPHY

General (life and work):
Christopher White, *Peter Paul Rubens: Man and Artist* (New Haven, Conn., 1987); Charles Scribner III, *Peter Paul Rubens* (New York, 1989); Kerry Downes, *Rubens* (London, 1980); Martin Warnke, *Peter Paul Rubens, Life and Work* (New York, 1980). *Special studies:* Svetlana Alpers, *The Making of Rubens* (New Haven, Conn., 1995); Julius S. Held, *The Oil Sketches of Peter Paul Rubens* (Princeton, N.J., 1980); Julius S. Held, *Rubens: Selected Drawings* (London and New York, 1986); Julius S. Held, *Rubens and His Circle* (Princeton, N.J., 1982); Michael Jaffe, *Rubens and Italy* (Oxford, 1977); Ruth S. Magurn, trans. and ed., *The Letters of Peter Paul Rubens* (Cambridge, Mass., 1955); John Rupert Martin, *Rubens: The Antwerp Altarpieces* (New York, 1969); John Rupert Martin, *The Ceiling Paintings for the Jesuit Church in Antwerp* (London and New York, 1968); John Rupert Martin, *The Decorations for the Pompa Introitus Ferdinandi* (London and New York, 1972); John Rupert Martin, ed., *Rubens Before 1620* (Princeton, N.J., 1972); Ronald F. Millen and Robert E. Wolf, *Heroic Deeds and Mystic Figures: A New Reading of Rubens' Life of Maria de' Medici* (Princeton, N.J., 1990); Jeffrey M. Muller, *Rubens: The Artist as Collector* (Princeton, N.J., 1989); Charles Scribner III, *The Triumph of the Eucharist: Tapestries Designed by Rubens* (Ann Arbor, Mich., 1982); Wolfgang Stechow, *Rubens and the Classical Tradition* (Cambridge, Mass., 1968); Roy Strong, *Brittania Triumphans: Inigo Jones, Rubens, and Whitehall Palace* (London, 1980); Lisa Vergara, *Rubens and the Poetics of Landscape* (New Haven, Conn., 1982); C. V. Wedgwood, *The Political Career of Peter Paul Rubens* (London, 1975); Ludwig Burchard, *Corpus Rubenianum Ludwig Burchard* (London and New York, 1968–) is a monumental *catalogue raisonné* in progress.

CHARLES SCRIBNER III

RUDOLF II (1552–1612), king of Hungary (as Rudolf, 1572–1608), king of Bohemia (as Rudolf II, 1575–1608/1611), archduke of Austria (as Rudolf V, 1576–1608), and Holy Roman Emperor (as Rudolf II, 1576–1612).

Rudolf was the eldest surviving son of Holy Roman Emperor Maximillian II and Maria, a daughter of Charles V. Although he spent eight formative years (1563–1571) at the court of his uncle, Philip II of Spain, Rudolf failed to become a Counter-Reformation crusader in the Spanish Habsburg mold. He emerged as a figure far more mysterious and complex, traditionally viewed in three quite different ways: as a final great patron of the late mannerist phase of Renaissance art; as an obsessive devotee of occult learning; and as a misguided, ineffectual, and impoverished ruler whose ineptitude led directly to the disasters of the Thirty Years' War.

Patronage of Arts and Learning. When Rudolf moved the Habsburg capital from Vienna to Prague in 1583, he brought with him several leading artists inherited from his father's service, including Bartholomäus Spranger, Hans Mont, and Giuseppe Arcimboldo, whose famous painting of Rudolf II as the Etruscan god of orchards and gardens, *Vertumnus*—a portrait composed entirely of fruits, vegetables, and flowers—is a characteristically exotic icon of Rudolf's court. Other artists were lured to Prague from the Netherlands, notably Hans von Aachen and Adriaen de Vries, whose portraits on canvas and in bronze offer more traditional repre-

Emperor Rudolf II. Portrait of the emperor as the Etruscan god Vertumnus by Giuseppe Arcimboldo (c. 1530–1593). Oil on wood; 1590; 70.5 × 57.5 cm (28 × 22.5 in.). SLOTT, SKOKLOSTERS, SWEDEN/ERICH LESSING/ART RESOURCE

sentations of the emperor. Those leading mannerists such as Giovanni da Bologna and Federigo Zuccaro whom Rudolf failed to lure to Prague he patronized at a distance, and he collected earlier masters with equal relish, especially Albrecht Dürer and Pieter Brueghel the Elder. Cosmopolitan, pan-European, and marvelously comprehensive, Rudolf's galleries were the wonder of his age and the last and greatest collection of European mannerism.

Rudolf's insatiable appetite for collecting, moreover, ranged well beyond painting and sculpture. He commissioned the most lavish and extraordinary decorative objects imaginable as well as mechanical contrivances of great variety, from ceremonial weapons and musical instruments to clocks, waterworks, and scientific devices. His menagerie, botanical gardens, and unrivalled "cabinet of curiosities" likewise collected natural objects—living, dead, and in artistic representations—especially the precious, the curious, and the exotic. Alongside painters and sculptors he patronized leading natural philosophers; from his father's court he retained the leading botanist of the day, the Belgian Charles de l'Ecluse. As imperial mathematicians he employed the two greatest astronomers of the age: the Dane Tycho Brahe and the Swabian Johannes Kepler, whose jointly compiled astronomical data, the *Rudolphine Tables* (1627), remained a standard work for a century.

Occult Learning. In Rudolphine Prague, fascination with arcane symbolism and unchecked curiosity about nature shaded off imperceptibly into metaphysical speculation and occult learning. Astronomical investigation blended with astrological prognostication. Fascination with clockwork, *automata,* and the heavenly spheres merged into the search for the secret of perpetual motion. Mineralogy and botany passed via pharmacology into the alchemical pursuit of the universal medicine and the philosopher's stone. The learned emblems of mannerist art reflected and encouraged an approach to the whole of nature as an intricate set of symbols awaiting decipherment. A generation of leading occult philosophers were drawn to Prague by this aspect of Rudolphine culture: the Englishman John Dee, the Italian Giordano Bruno, the Pole Michael Sendivogious, the Saxon Oswald Croll, and many others. Underlying much of their activity was a passionate search in the microcosm of the emperor's collections for the harmonies of nature that could restore order to an increasingly factionalized church and empire. It was a search increasingly tinged with melancholy, desperation, and doubt: Rudolf's Prague was at once the capital of the final phase of Renaissance art and learning and its last redoubt in a period when that culture was already under attack from all sides.

Politics. Traditionally historians have identified Rudolf's preoccupation with artistic and intellectual pursuits at the cost of practical affairs, together with the bouts of depression verging on madness that plagued the Habsburg ruler, as a major cause of the inconsistency and eventual paralysis that infected his politics. A more subtle and sympathetic recent approach links Rudolf's triumphs as patron and disasters as politician to an underlying striving after harmony and universality in an age of religious, intellectual, and political disintegration.

Rudolf inherited the Habsburg resolve to rule a united Christendom in an era increasingly ill suited to it. Revolted by the revived temporal claims of the papacy and the uncompromising reassertion of its spiritual authority, Rudolf neglected the patronage of religious art, withdrew eventually from normal Catholic observance, and died without receiving the last rites. No less alienated by Spain's intransigent and repressive religious policy, he hesitated to take the advantageous step of marrying the Spanish infanta; yet despite periods of serious illness, he made no concerted effort to provide the dynasty with a legitimate heir. Unwilling on the other hand to use Protestantism as anything except a counterweight to Rome and Madrid, he promoted instead the last generation of conciliarists, irenicists, and humanists. When papal and Spanish agents nevertheless insinuated the Counter-Reformation program into his court he reacted by cultivating those figures who appeared independent of the warring camps, even at the cost of political chaos. He last attended the German diet in 1594, and as his mental instability and political procrastination increased in subsequent years, he exercised little effective restraint on the series of religious confrontations that threatened to provoke civil and European war within the Empire.

It was affairs on the Turkish front, however, that eventually proved Rudolf's undoing. His unwillingness to compromise, together with a quixotic desire to unify Christendom in a great crusade against its archenemy, led him into a protracted and indecisive war with the Turks (1593–1606), which in 1604 prompted his exhausted Hungarian subjects to revolt. Alarmed by his growing detachment and incompetence, the other members of the Habsburg family forced Rudolf to cede control of Hungarian affairs in 1605 to his ambitious younger brother Matthias, who laboriously concluded a peace first with the Hungarian rebels, then with the Turks in 1606. Appalled by his brother's extensive concessions, Rudolf prepared to renew war with the Turks; but Matthias rallied support among the disaffected in Hungary and in 1608 compelled Rudolf to cede to him the crowns of Hungary, Austria, and Moravia. The predominantly Protestant Bohemian estates seized the moment of royal weakness to demand greater religious liberty, which Rudolf reluctantly granted in the fateful *Letter of Majesty* in 1609. But when Rudolf sought to repress further disorder militarily, the Bohemians appealed to Matthias, whose army held Rudolf a virtual prisoner in Prague until he yielded the crown of Bohemia to his brother in 1611. Nine months later Rudolf died, stripped of all but a now-empty imperial title, which likewise passed to Matthias five months after his death.

Politically as well as culturally, Rudolf II thus represents the end of an era. In May 1618 the Bohemian estates, acting in defence of the *Letter of Majesty,* flung Matthias's ambassadors from the window of their Chancery in Prague—the famous "defenestration" of Prague that began the Thirty Years' War (1618–1648). In the chaos that followed, the collections that Rudolf had intended to become one of the permanent glories of his dynasty were looted and dispersed as far afield as Stockholm and Rome.

See also **Prague**.

BIBLIOGRAPHY

Evans, R. J. W. *Rudolf II and His World: A Study in Intellectual History.* 2d ed. Oxford, 1984. The fundamental synthetic work on the subject, with a new bibliography.

Fučíková, Eliška, James M. Bradburne, et al., eds. *Rudolf II and Prague: The Court and the City.* London, New York, and Prague, 1997. A huge and lavishly illustrated exhibition catalog with thirty introductory essays on various aspects of Rudolphine Prague.

Kaufmann, Thomas DaCosta. *The School of Prague: Painting at the Court of Rudolf II.* Chicago and London, 1988. An important scholarly treatment of a key aspect of Rudolf's patronage.

Prag um 1600: Beiträge zur Kunst und Kultur am Hofe Rudolfs II. 2 vols. Freren, 1988. A lavish and learned exhibition catalog.

Trevor-Roper, Hugh. *Princes and Artists: Patronage and Ideology at Four Habsburg Courts, 1517–1633.* London, 1976. A lively introduction. See in particular chapter 3, "Rudolph in Prague."

Volcelka, Karl. *Rudolf II und seine Zeit.* Vienna, 1985. The most recent survey, beautifully illustrated.

HOWARD HOTSON

RUIZ DE ALARCÓN Y MENDOZA, JUAN

(c. 1581–1639), Spanish dramatist and lawyer. Alarcón studied law in his youth, earning his licentiate degree in 1608 in Mexico and practicing law until 1613, when he went to live in Madrid. There he wrote plays, which were well received by the public, and moved in literary circles until 1626, when he was appointed court reporter on the Council of the Indies. In 1628 he published eight of his plays and in 1634, twelve more. During these years as a dramatist he endured ridicule by other writers because of his hunchback and because he was a Creole, an "intruder" from the colonial empire.

Although Alarcón employed the three-act new comedy form created by Lope de Vega, he adapted it in new ways, with a critical view of Spanish society honed by his Creole background.

Among his seven historical dramas, *Ganar amigos* (Winning friends; 1634) stands out for its manipulation of plot and characters and illustrates some of Alarcón's major themes: the supreme value of friendship; virtue as the necessary component even of nobility acquired by birth; and the role of law as the stabilizing force in society, a law proclaimed by the king, but which he himself must obey.

Some of Alarcón's eleven comedies of manners and customs deepen into genuine comedies of character. The best known of these is *La verdad sospechosa* (Suspect truth; 1634), whose protagonist, García, fails to win the women he loves because of the flaw in his character, his compulsive, gratuitous lying. Pierre Corneille, who adapted this play for his *Menteur* (The liar; 1644), wrote that he had never read anything in the Spanish language that pleased him more.

Among the dramatists of his period Alarcón was the only representative of Spain's small professional bourgeoisie, and his plays speak to and for them in the importance given to marriage and the family, father-and-son relationships, the sturdy moral sense and strength of women, not idealized but never punished violently for their failings. Alarcón was the creator in his time of urban comedy at its best.

BIBLIOGRAPHY

Primary Work

Ruiz de Alarcón, Juan. *Obras completas*. Edited by Agustín Millares Carlo. 3 vols. Mexico, 1957–1968.

Secondary Works

Alatorre, Antonio. "Para la historia de un problema: La mexicanidad de Ruiz de Alarcón." *Anuario de Letras* 4 (1964): 161–202.

King, Willard F. *Juan Ruiz de Alarcón, letrado y dramaturgo: Su mundo mexicano y español*. Mexico City, Mexico, 1989.

WILLARD F. KING

RUSKIN, JOHN. *See* **Renaissance, Interpretations of the,** *subentry on* **John Ruskin.**

RUSSIA. Most historians agree that Russia missed the Renaissance and, later, much of the Enlightenment. They interpret these successive failures as a partial explanation of Russia's traditional backwardness. However, some scholars argue that isolation was not detrimental to Russia's development, and others (especially those in the Slavophile tradition) enthusiastically embrace the notion that Russia sought its own path toward cultural development. This debate eventually spills into that morass dividing those who believe in the decisive importance of ideas from those who attribute progress and change to economic forces.

Art and Ideas. There were numerous obstacles to Russia's accepting Renaissance concepts. First and foremost, the Orthodox church was hostile to everything Western, including the realistic religious art of the fifteenth and sixteenth centuries; its anti-book tradition hindered the print revolution that had spread Renaissance ideas across the West; and the church's emphasis on salvation caused potential readers to conclude that it was a waste of time to study secular Renaissance writers. Second, the Poles—the great carriers of Renaissance thought, art, and architecture in east central Europe—were the chief political rivals of Moscow in the struggle for domination of the southern woodlands and steppe. Lastly, these crucial centuries were filled with external wars and internal crises; and, as Enea Silvio Piccolomini—the Renaissance humanist (later Pope Pius II) best acquainted with the eastern borderlands of the West—noted in his book *De Prutheorum origine,* "when war appears, the muses become mute."

Russian art. Moscow's isolationism became deeper after the Council of Florence (1439), when the Greek Orthodox church sought a compromise with Rome that would bring military aid to beleaguered Constantinople. Already regional art had begun to develop a distinctive Russian style under the influence of the monk Andrei Rublev (c. 1370–c. 1430). As Moscow became the center of political and religious life, contacts with the Byzantine and Western worlds through Kiev, Novgorod, and Smolensk became less important.

Italian architects. The occasional Italian who appeared in Moscow was expected to conform to architectural conventions that combined antiquarianism with colossalism. Aristotele Fioravanti used his technical skill in constructing the Dormition cathedral in the Kremlin (1475), but other than a general spaciousness and logical geometric order, he contributed relatively little stylistically that one would recognize as Renaissance. Other Italians worked on the Faceted Palace (1487) and the bell tower (1505). Alevisio Novi managed to combine some Italian themes, especially in the exterior decoration, with Russian traditionalism in the Cathedral of the Archangel Michael (1505) in a way that later generations admired greatly and occasionally copied.

Literary criticism. Maximus the Greek (c. 1475–1556), a monk from Mount Athos who had studied in Florence, arrived in Moscow in 1518 and was given the task of correcting adulterated religious texts. His application of literary criticism was violently denounced, and in 1525 he was subjected to trial, torture, and lifelong imprisonment. He was nevertheless the most important theologian of the era and was later canonized. Moreover, Russians

Ivan the Terrible. Ivan IV, ruler of Russia (ruled 1533–1584; tsar after 1547), is depicted as a ruthless tyrant, holding the severed head of one of his subjects.The image dates from 1582, the year after Ivan killed his son and heir, Ivan. COLLECTION, VISUAL CONNECTION

thereafter studied Greek, if only to improve their ability to work with religious texts, not to study the Greco-Roman classics.

Foreign Visitors. Influenced by Renaissance-era interest in foreign cultures, sixteenth-century diplomats from central Europe and England wrote remarkable memoirs of their visits to Muscovy. Sigismund von Herbertstein and Heinrich von Staden were struck by the exotic character of the Russians, who shared so little of the culture that was the pride of Western nobles and clerics.

Foreign residents. The number of foreigners living in Russian cities increased dramatically during the reign of Ivan III (1462–1505), who may have been influenced by his wife, Zoë Palaeologus, to employ their talents. Several thousand Westerners were in the grand duke's service, some as artisans, a few as diplomats, and twenty-five hundred in an elite military unit. Thousands more were independent merchants and artisans. However, Russians were slow to learn from their example. Russians were jealous and suspicious of Catholics, Protestants, and Jews, and traditionally disliked foreign ways. Since few Russians traveled abroad, they could not see what emulation of Western ways might do for Russia; or, if they did understand it, they feared it.

Moscow's fear of foreigners. The great rival of Moscow for supremacy in Russia was Lithuania. The Polish-Lithuanian state represented Catholicism and the Uniate church, a powerful gentry and growing merchant class, Western art and architecture, and the hegemony of the Latin language. The grand dukes of Moscow deliberately contrasted their Russian values with those foreign ones. They forced the choice between traditional, stable Russia and the innovative, dynamic state of Poland—and they could point to the Polish inability to deal with Tartars and Turks as proof that Moscow offered what Russia needed. The grand dukes could not afford to be seen as halfhearted or willing to compromise in this choice: the Renaissance did not have a chance in the heartland.

Belarus and Ukraine. The states of Kievan Rus' that were long under Polish-Lithuanian influence had a separate cultural and political development from Moscow that could never be eradicated by later efforts at Russification. Renaissance humanism had taken root there, however weakly, so that today those people are organized as independent states with closer ties to Western traditions (Christian, Jewish, and secular) and to Greco-Roman literature and culture than are found in the Russian heartland.

Russia
Principality of Muscovy, c. 1300
Grand Principality of Muscovy, 1462
Acquired by Ivan III, 1462–1505
Acquired by Basil III, 1505–1533
Acquired by Ivan IV the Terrible and Fyodor, 1533–1598
Semi-independent lands
Acquired 1689
Losses, 1618–1624, regained 1667–1686
Boundary 1689
150 300 Miles
150 300 450 Kilometers
WHITE SEA
Arkhangelsk
FINLAND
SWEDEN
CARELIA 1617 to Sweden
Lake Onega
Lake Ladoga
Helsingfors
INGRIA 1617 to Sweden
Stockholm
Reval
Narva
ESTONIA
Novgorod
BALTIC SEA
Dorpat
Pskov
GRAND PRINCIPALITY OF MUSCOVY
Riga
LIVONIA
Moscow
Nizhniy Novgorod
Kazan 1552
Vyazma
LITHUANIA
Danzig
Smolensk
Dnieper River
Orel
Don River
Volga River
Warsaw
POLAND
Cracow
VOLHYNIA
GALICIA
PODOLIA
JEDISAN
KHANATE OF CRIMEA
Astrakhan 1556
HUNGARY
OTTOMAN EMPIRE
CASPIAN SEA
BLACK SEA

Russian Icon. *Vladimir Mother of God* (also called *Our Lady of Kazan*), the most venerated icon in Russia, expresses the divinity and humanity of Christ in the arms of the Virgin Mary. It may have been brought to Kiev from Constantinople around 1135. In 1355 it was taken to Vladimir and from there to Moscow in 1395. Housed in the Cathedral of the Dormition (Assumption) in the Moscow Kremlin, it was the symbol of Russian unity and resistance to foreign invasion. Tretyakov Gallery, Moscow/Scala/Art Resource

Summary. The reign of Ivan IV (the Terrible, 1533–1584) illustrates the complex and contradictory attitude of the Muscovite state. On the one hand, there was more contact with foreigners and an expansion outward into non-Russian lands; on the other hand, the tsar created the *oprichnina* (an early form of secret police) and allowed it to destroy the most Westernized segments of Russian society—slaughtering the merchant community of Novgorod and annihilating several great noble families that had defected from Poland-Lithuania. This eliminated the best opportunity for that combination of learning, manners, and taste we call the Renaissance to take root in Russian soil.

See also **Baltic States; Poland.**

BIBLIOGRAPHY

Primary Work

Fennell, J. L. I., ed. *The Correspondence between Prince A. M. Kurbsky and Tsar Ivan IV of Russia, 1564–1579.* Cambridge, U.K., 1955.

Secondary Works

Auty, Robert, and Dimitri Obolensky. *An Introduction to Russian Art and Architecture.* Cambridge, U.K., 1980.

Hamilton, George Heard. *The Art and Architecture of Russia.* Baltimore, 1954.

Medlin, William K., and Christos G. Patrinelis. *Renaissance Influences and Religious Reforms in Russia: Western and Post-Byzantine Impacts on Culture and Education (Sixteenth–Seventeenth Centuries).* Geneva, 1971.

Okenfuss, Max J. *The Rise and Fall of Latin Humanism in Early-Modern Russia: Pagan Authors, Ukrainians, and the Resiliency of Muscovy.* New York, 1995.

WILLIAM L. URBAN

RUZZANTE (Angelo Beolco; 1496?–1542), Italian playwright, actor, musician. Known to contemporaries by his stage name of Ruzzante ("Ruzante" in *pavano,* his stage dialect), Angelo Beolco was acclaimed the Plautus and Roscius of his age. He performed in his native Padua and in Venice from 1520 to 1526 until political enmities between Venice and Padua made him unwelcome. In Padua, the wealthy landowner Alvise Cornaro sponsored his performances and commissioned a theater meant to imitate the open-air theaters of antiquity. Ruzzante also performed at the ducal court in Ferrara, where he collaborated with Ludovico Ariosto. At the time of his premature death, probably due to malaria contracted while working in the swamplands between Padua and Venice, he was preparing to perform and direct Sperone Speroni's academic tragedy, *Canace.*

Information about Ruzzante's life is derived from a few legal documents, some contemporary references, and whatever information his writings reveal. Central to every interpretation of his life and work is the fact that Angelo Beolco was an illegitimate child raised in his father's Paduan home in the care of his paternal grandmother; a maid-servant in the upper-class household may have been his mother. Although Angelo managed Beolco family properties and inherited a small sum from his father, he depended financially upon Cornaro and the fruits of his own labor. He married a woman of modest circumstances named Giustina Palatino, but she remained in her parents' home while Ruzzante resided with Cornaro.

Modern scholarship has searched Ruzzante's biography to help interpret his theatrical representation of the *contadino,* a farmer native to the countryside near Padua (the *pavano*). Ruzzante portrayed the *contadino* in a series of plays that reflect events during and after the Cambraic wars (1509–1517), when farmers from the region were recruited to fight for Venice. Separated from their families, their land overrun by mercenary soldiers, beset by drought and famine, many farmers were finally forced to give up their land. Their passage from contentment to despair unfolds in a series of fourteen works that offer a changing image of the rustic.

The series begins with *Pastoral,* written in verse and performed about 1518, in which Ruzzante and his companion rustics appear alongside classical shepherds, the rustics speaking in *pavano,* the shepherds in Tuscan. A farcical doctor from Bergamo adds a third language to the mixture of languages and styles that continues throughout the playwright's work. Both *Pastoral* and a rustic *mariazo* (marriage play) called *Betìa* (1524–1525) show the influence of the university environment at Padua. A subsequent group of plays from 1529 to 1531 dramatize the agony of the rustic world with stunning realism. In *Dialogo facetissimo* (Witty dialogue; 1529) a starving rustic is saved by the intervention of a holy man; in *Parlamento,* or *Reduce* (The veteran; 1529), a vainglorious rustic is defeated in battle and then at home; in *Bilora* (Weasel; 1530) the cowardly protagonist stabs to death an elderly Venetian rival for his wife. A five-act comedy, *La Moscheta* (The well-spoken lady; 1530–1531), presents a foolish rustic who unwittingly devises his own cuckoldry. More positively, the memory of better times, the expression of future hopes, and the vivid personality of rustic speech claim lasting attention. The lost rustic homeland and a devastated present are the subjects of two *Orations* (1521 and 1528), the first describing an earthly paradise inhabited by the rustic community, the second a barren wasteland.

After a final all-rustic comedy, *La Fiorina* (Flora; 1531–1532), Ruzzante wrote plays in imitation of ancient Roman comedy. Both *La Piovana* (The girl from Piove; 1532), written entirely in *pavano,* and *La vaccaria* (Cow-play; 1533), combining *pavano* and standard Italian, are in the humanist tradition of erudite comedy. *L'Anconitana* (The woman from Ancona; 1534–1535); although similar to the classicizing plays, has an original plot involving Tuscan-speaking aristocrats, a Venetian merchant, and Ruzzante, who plays a scheming servant prototypical of the comic mask soon to appear in the commedia dell'arte. The play has been claimed both as an early work and as the playwright's last comedy. *L'Anconitana* celebrates the author-actor's singing voice, having numerous songs for Ruzzante (the character) to sing throughout the comedy. He sang to improvised musical settings or to popular tunes in a high range now called countertenor. The author of twelve lyrics and an early *Lettera giocosa* (Playful letter), Ruzzante closed his writing career with a performable letter to his acting-companion Marco Alvarotto, in which he recounts a dream vision of an allegorical realm of Gaiety, a place resembling the theater. Guided to that realm by a former dialect comedian, Ruzzante speaks for the first time in Italian, signing his letter "Ruzante" and dating it the day of Epiphany 1536.

BIBLIOGRAPHY

Primary Works

Ruzzante. *I dialoghi, La seconda oratione, I prologhi alla Moschetta*. Edited by Giorgio Padoan. Padua, Italy, 1981.

Ruzzante. *La pastoral, La prima oratione, Una lettera giocosa*. Edited by Giorgio Padoan. Padua, Italy, 1978.

Ruzzante. *Teatro*. Edited and translated by Ludovico Zorzi. Turin, Italy, 1967.

Secondary Works

Carroll, Linda L. *Angelo Beolco (Il Ruzante)*. Boston, 1990.

Dersofi, Nancy. *Arcadia and the Stage: An Introduction to the Dramatic Art of Angelo Beolco, called Ruzante*. Washington, D.C., 1978.

Fido, Franco. "An Introduction to the Theater of Angelo Beolco." *Renaissance Drama* 6 (1973): 203–218.

Padoan, Giorgio. "Angelo Beolco da Ruzante a Perduoçimo." *Medioevo e umanesimo* 31 (1978): 94–283.

NANCY DERSOFI

SABBADINI, REMIGIO. *See* **Renaissance, Interpretations of the,** *subentry on* **Remigio Sabbadini.**

SACHS, HANS (1494–1576), German shoemaker, poet, playwright, leading champion of the Lutheran Reformation. An author of unparalleled literary productivity—he wrote more than six thousand works—Hans Sachs was also a leading propagandist of the Lutheran cause and a critical chronicler of his time.

Sachs's life was relatively uneventful. Born in the old imperial city of Nürnberg—at that time an important center of commerce, trade, and the arts—as the son of a tailor, Sachs attended Latin school for eight years. Apprenticed at age fifteen to a shoemaker, he traveled through Germany as a journeyman from 1511 to 1516. Upon his return he settled in his hometown and married Kunigunde Kreuzer, who bore him seven children (none survived him). He became a master shoemaker in 1520. In the early 1520s, he became a fervent follower of Martin Luther. With the exception of short trips to trade fairs in Frankfurt am main, he spent the rest of his life in Nürnberg. He never wavered in his loyalty to his native city and his devotion to the Lutheran cause.

After immersing himself in Luther's writings, Sachs wrote a seven-hundred-verse allegorical poem, *Die Wittenbergisch Nachtigall* (The Wittenberg nightingale; 1523). In it he forcefully denounced the church, its fiscal exploitation, and its cult of relics, and he used rhymed couplets to expound Luther's teaching. The work went through numerous editions, securing its author instant fame in Germany.

Sachs continued his support for the Reformation with four prose dialogues (1524). Through lively discussions, vivid depiction of characters, and dramatic structure, they attempted to influence public opinion in Nürnberg, which at that time had not officially embraced Lutheranism. The best known of these works is the *Disputation zwischen einem Chorherren und Schuchmacher* (Disputation between a canon and a shoemaker; 1524), in which a Bible-quoting shoemaker represents the "common man." Though consistently on the side of the Lutheran cause, Sachs in later dialogues also articulated his uneasiness with some of the radical changes taking place.

Today Sachs is primarily remembered as the jovial cobbler-poet and leader of the Meistersinger in Richard Wagner's opera *Die Meistersinger von Nürnberg* (The master singers of Nürnberg; 1862–1867). Although Wagner presents a fictional view of these singing craftsmen, it is true that the Meistergesang was at the center of Sachs's creative work and that Sachs was its undisputed leader from 1524 to 1560. The Meistersinger were literary and musical artisans in Nürnberg and other southern German cities who organized themselves into guilds or associations. Their songs, which they performed solo and unaccompanied, were judged not according to originality but according to conformity with the strict rules and conventions of their schools. In his more than four thousand songs (the majority of which have not yet been edited), Sachs dealt with a broad spectrum of topics, ranging from the religious to the farcical, drawing his material from the Bible and from ancient, medieval, and contemporary literature.

Although Sachs is celebrated today as the quintessential Meistersinger, it is not his Meisterlieder that are performed today but rather some of his eighty-five *Fastnachtspiele,* or carnival plays. In these short plays (rarely longer than half an hour), Sachs created a colorful cast of characters: greedy merchants, simple-minded peasants, merciless inquisitors, and cruel tyrants. Marriage, with its daily problems, jealousies, and large and small deceptions, became a rich topic for these playlets. Sachs's humor is always good-natured, mild, and conciliatory. These plays have traveled well through the centuries, retaining much of their humor and freshness.

Nearly forgotten, on the other hand, are his almost 130 tragedies and comedies, genres that he pioneered in German literature. The function of these plays was, in addition to entertainment, to provide guidelines for correct moral behavior. To this end, Sachs transformed all his characters, whether drawn from the Bible, ancient, medieval, or contemporary literature, into contemporary Nürnberg citizens. The message in these plays, as in his two thousand poems (*Spruchgedichte*), was always the same: he denounced self-interest, envy, greed, and egotism, and praised moderation, work, devotion to the commonweal, and faith in God.

Nearly forgotten for two hundred years, Sachs was rehabilitated by young Johann Wolfgang von Goethe (1749–1832). In the nineteenth century, Sachs became the subject of poems, dramas, and operas, of which Wagner's is the one that has shaped the modern image of Sachs. Only in recent decades has a less idealized and more historical view of the Nürnberg poet emerged.

BIBLIOGRAPHY

Primary Works

Hans Sachs Werke. Edited by Adelbert von Keller and Edmund Goetze. 26 vols. Stuttgart, Germany, 1870–1908. Reprint, Hildesheim, Germany, 1964.

Translations of the Carnival Comedies of Hans Sachs (1494–1576). Translated and edited by Robert Aylett. Lewiston, N.Y./Queenston/Lampeter, Canada, 1994. Contains translations of nine carnival plays.

Secondary Works

Bernstein, Eckhard. "Hans Sachs." In *Dictionary of Literary Biography.* Vol. 179, *German Writers of the Renaissance and Reformation, 1280–1580.* Detroit, Mich., Washington, D.C., and London, 1959. Pages 241–252.

Bernstein, Eckhard. *Hans Sachs.* Rheinbek, Germany, 1993. Illustrated biography with extensive bibliography.

Hahn, Reinhard. "Hans Sachs." In *Deutsche Dichter der frühen Neuzeit (1450–1600).* Edited by Stephan Füssel. Berlin, 1993. Pages 406–427.

ECKHARD BERNSTEIN

SACRA RAPPRESENTAZIONE. *See* **Religious Drama.**

SÁ DE MIRANDA, FRANCISCO DE (1480 or 1490–1558), Portuguese poet and dramatist. Francisco de Sá de Miranda was the illegitimate son of a canon of Coimbra Cathedral. He was brought up in the court at Lisbon, where he studied law and received his doctorate. Some of his early poems were published in the *Cancioneiro geral* (General songbook) of 1516. Around 1520 he began a prolonged tour of Italy, not returning to Portugal until 1526. His two comedies, *Os estrangeiros* (The foreigners; 1527) and *Os Vilhalpandos* (1538), both probably written while he was abroad, give a vivid portrait of life in Sicily and in Rome. References in his eclogue *Nemoroso* suggest that he met the poet and writer Giovanni Rucellai and the Sienese humanist Lattanzio Tolomei (1487–1543); he was also a distant relative of the poet Vittoria Colonna. Although detailed information about his time in Italy is lacking, it was nevertheless clearly a turning point in the poet's life and marks the beginning of the literary Renaissance in Portugal.

By 1530 Sá de Miranda had married and exchanged court life for that of a country gentleman in the northern province of Minho. It was there that he produced the bulk of his literary work. Many theories have been advanced to explain his decision to leave the court, but he did not lose touch with it altogether, for around 1552 he sent three collections of his poems to Prince John, heir to the throne of Portugal, at the latter's request. He was in contact, too, with the younger generation of poets, especially Diogo Bernardes, António Ferreira, and Pero de Andrade Caminha.

Sá de Miranda was the first Portuguese to write sonnets, eclogues, elegies, and other poems in the Italian Renaissance style, using the Italian decasyllabic line. Many of these poems are in Spanish, the language of the court, but he also composed in the new style in Portuguese, albeit with some difficulty. His position in Portuguese literature is similar to that of Garcilaso de la Vega and Juan Boscán in Spain. He alludes to their work, and the eclogue *Nemoroso* contains an elegy on the death of Garcilaso, which occurred in 1536.

Sá de Miranda is a transitional figure. Throughout his career he continued to compose poetry in the traditional Iberian forms, as well as in the new Italian ones. Although he tried to write erotic and pastoral verse in the manner of Petrarch and Virgil, he had the moralist's distrust of the beauties of nature and of the passion of love. His best work, his satires, combines the old and the new. These poems, five verse letters and the eclogue *Basto,* employ the traditional Iberian meter but are full of references to classical and Italian literature. In them, sometimes in passages of great epigrammatic force, Sá de Miranda presents himself as a Stoic individualist, bitterly but wittily opposed to the materialism that had gripped Portuguese life in the epoch of the discoveries.

Sá de Miranda changed the course of Portuguese literature. Although later poets only rarely imitated his poems, they could not fail to be influenced by his example. He remains to this day exemplary in another, moral sense, as the archetype of the upright man of unbending principle.

BIBLIOGRAPHY

Primary Works

Sá de Miranda, Francisco de. *Obras Completas.* Edited by Rodrigues Lapa. Lisbon, 1937. The only accessible edition, several times reprinted, of the first edition (1595).

Sá de Miranda, Francisco de. *Poesias.* Edited by Carolina Michaëlis de Vasconcelos. Lisbon, 1989. A classic edition of a manuscript containing many important variants, first published in 1885.

Secondary Work

Earle, T. F. *Theme and Image in the Poetry of Sá de Miranda.* Oxford and New York, 1980.

T. F. Earle

SADOLETO, JACOPO (1477–1547), Italian churchman and humanist. For two generations, young men of the Sadoleto family were expected to study civil and canon law at Modena-Ferrara to qualify for positions in the court of the d'Este dukes. Jacopo was an exception, leaving Ferrara in 1497 in order to continue his studies of the classics in Rome. There he won recognition as a classical scholar and poet, and there he died a cardinal, still celebrated for his elegant Latin, and equally well known for his exertions in the reform movement in the hierarchy.

One of the first acts of Leo X (pontificate 1513–1521) was the appointment of Sadoleto and his Venetian friend Pietro Bembo (1470–1547) to the papal secretariat. The two Latin secretaries were drawn into matters of diplomacy and governance and also into the rich and lavish patronage of the Medici pope. But Leo had summoned Jacopo to the Vatican not as a priest but as an ornamental Latinist in the service of a prodigal patron.

The pope rewarded Sadoleto with the diocese of Carpentras in 1517. Remote and rural "without obligation of residence," Carpentras, in Provence, became the turning point of Sadoleto's life and work; he moved there in 1527 to escape from the confusion of the papal court where reports abounded of distant wonders and oddities about Turks, Lutherans, and Waldensians. Carpentras marked the beginning of Sadoleto's mature development—with all its contradictions—as a humanist scholar.

His long-standing literary plans were divided between the explication of scripture and the defense of the liberal arts, demonstrating the connections between theology and philosophy, wisdom and knowledge, nature and grace. During his most productive years at Carpentras (1527–1535), he addressed himself to two distinctive publics—his university friends at Padua and his humanist friends of Erasmian persuasion—Reginald Pole (1500–1558), Federigo Fregoso (d. 1541), and Gasparo Contarini (1483–1542). Each in turn was uneasy about Sadoleto's treatise on the *Hortensius* (a lost dialogue [45 B.C.] of Cicero on philosophy), which marks his failure as a humanist theologian. While the *Hortensius* is a major work in the literature of sixteenth-century humanism, it is trifling as a work of philosophy, his rejection of Augustine too great and his qualifications of Pelagius too small. What often remains is a series of Neoplatonic declarations. In concluding the *Hortensius,* Sadoleto abruptly asserts that the effect of philosophy is to make a man "*similem Deo*" (like God), while nothing is offered to show the affinity between philosophy and theology. In his *In Pauli epistolam ad Romanos commentarium* (Commentaries on Romans; 1535) he promises a theological *altera via,* a new path with which to navigate safely between Augustine and Pelagius, promising Contarini that the *Commentaries* would "illuminate and open up the whole mystery of the cross."

Assertions like this brought forth "corrections" from humanist friends, censure from the theological faculty at the University of Paris and from the Master of the Sacred Palace in the Vatican. And Sadoleto's letter to the *Senate and People of Geneva* (1539) provoked John Calvin (1509–1564) to respond with one of his best treatises. Martin Luther (1483–1546) recognized an accomplished classicist in Sadoleto, but found no understanding of theology in him. Sadoleto's knowledge of patristic and scholastic theology was almost entirely autodidactic, acquired only in retirement and thus after fifty. While Erasmus saw in Sadoleto "the glory of the age" he added that "brilliance of style dulled the edge of piety."

BIBLIOGRAPHY

Primary Works

Calvin, John, and Jacopo Sadoleto. *A Reformation Debate: Sadoleto's Letter to the Genevans and Calvin's Reply.* Edited by John C. Olin. New York, 1966.

Sadoleto, Jacopo. *Epistolae quotquot extant proprio nomine scriptae nunc primum duplo auctiores in lucem editae.* Edited by V. A. Costanzi. 3 vols. Rome, 1760–1764.

Sadoleto, Jacopo. *Opera quae extant omnia*. 4 vols. Verona, Italy, 1737–1738.

Secondary Works

Douglas, Richard M. *Jacopo Sadoleto, 1477–1547: Humanist and Reformer*. Cambridge, Mass., 1959.

Reinhard, Wolfgang. *Die Reform in der Diözese Carpentras unter den Bischofen Jacopo Sadoleto, Paolo Sadoleto, Jacopo Sacrati und Francesco Sadoleto, 1517–1596*. Münster, Germany, 1966.

RICHARD M. DOUGLAS

SAHAGÚN, BERNARDINO DE O.F.M. (1499?–1590), linguist and missionary to the Nahuas (Aztecs). Sahagún was born in Spain and educated at Salamanca and was one of the early Franciscans in Mexico. He is best known for his twelve-volume encyclopedic compendium on Aztec culture, *Historia general de las cosas de Nueva España* (published in English as the *Florentine Codex*), written in parallel columns of Spanish and Nahuatl, with accompanying pictorials. It was designed to aid Spanish missionaries evangelizing the Nahuas; the Franciscan order saw having precise knowledge of indigenous religion and customs as key to their efforts' effectiveness. The *Historia general* also includes information on social structure and natural history; the final volume has a full-length account of the Conquest from the defeated Indians' viewpoint. Sahagún chose as his informants Indian noblemen born before the Spanish conquest of central Mexico (1519–1521). His scribes were graduates of the Colegio de Santa Cruz in Tlatelolco, founded by Franciscans to train elite Indian men for the Christian priesthood and where Sahagún taught. Sahagún wrote numerous other texts for friars' use in evangelization, such as sermons, works on Christian doctrine, a psalmody, and a manual for new converts. Only the *Psalmodia Christiana* was published in his lifetime and remained in use until the eighteenth century. Sahagún was highly skeptical of the success that some early Franciscans claimed in converting Indians to Christianity. His lasting contribution is the preservation of information about pre-Hispanic Aztec culture from the indigenous viewpoint, an invaluable source for scholars.

BIBLIOGRAPHY

Primary Works

Sahagún. Bernardino de. *Florentine Codex: General History of the Things of New Spain*. Translated and edited by Arthur J. O. Anderson and Charles Dibble. 12 vols. Santa Fe, N.Mex., and Salt Lake City, Utah, 1950–1982.

Sahagún, Bernardino de. *Historia general de las cosas de Nueva España*. Edited by Angel Maria Garibay K. 4 vols. Mexico City, 1981.

Secondary Works

Cline, Howard F. "Sahagún Materials and Studies." In *Handbook of Middle American Indians*. Vol. 13. Austin, Tex., 1973. Pages 218–232.

Klor de Alva, J. Jorge, H. B. Nicholson, and Eloise Quinones Keber. *The Work of Bernardino de Sahagún*. Albany, N.Y., and Austin, Tex., 1988.

Olwer, Luis Nicolau d', and Howard F. Cline. "Sahagún and His Works." In *Handbook of Middle American Indians*. Vol. 13. Austin, Tex., 1973. Pages 186–207.

SARAH CLINE

SAINT ANDREWS UNIVERSITY. In 1410 the city of Saint Andrews in Scotland became the home of a Studium Generale Universitatis, founded by King James I and the city's bishop (Henry Wardlaw), prior, and archdeacon. Although Saint Andrews had been a center of education since the twelfth century, it was European politics and Scotland's strained relationship with England in the early fifteenth century that forced Scotland to found its first university. Before the fifteenth century Scottish students had often traveled to universities in Italy and France, but when the antipope Benedict XIII was deposed by the Council of Pisa in 1409—a decision supported in Europe but ignored in Scotland—it became impossible for students to study on the Continent.

Growth and Consolidation, 1450–1560. The earliest teachers at Saint Andrews were associated with the city's church, but they were joined by other masters from France. Students were taught theology, canon and civil law, arts, and medicine. As at continental universities, bachelor's degrees in arts at Saint Andrews generally involved two years of study, and students became masters after four years. Theological students attained bachelor status in their fourth year; master's degrees and doctorates took four more years of study.

The university became more institutionalized as the fifteenth century progressed. The Faculty of Arts began to keep formal records in 1413, and the Faculty of Theology had detached itself from the city's priory by 1429. Canon law was taught from the foundation of the university, but a reference to a school for the subject appeared in 1457.

The chancellor of the university was responsible for the supervision of the rector, who maintained order and discipline within the community. Rectors were elected at annual congregations in which all members of the university voted. Early teaching took place in the rooms and lodgings of students and teachers, although beginning in 1415 the Faculty of

Arts met in the Chapel of Saint John on South Street. Patronage and support were crucial for the university's continued growth. As chancellor, Bishop Wardlaw granted land for the teaching of arts in 1430. Twenty years later Bishop James Kennedy founded Saint Andrews's first college, Saint Salvator's, for the teaching of arts and theology. It was established as an independent community in which members of the college became canons and choristers in the collegiate church built as part of the southern perimeter of Saint Salvator's.

At the end of the fifteenth and the beginning of the sixteenth century, academic subjects were coordinated by the university faculties, but most of the teaching was done in an increasingly collegiate environment. Saint Leonard's College was founded in 1512. The third foundation, Saint Mary's, was founded in 1537 as a college of "theology, canon and civil law, physic, medicine, and other liberal disciplines." Saint Mary's became, in effect, a training college for men entering the priesthood, but the curriculum was in no sense limited: one of its earliest provosts, Archibald Hay, wanted students to study Latin, Greek, and Hebrew and expected them to have a thorough grounding in grammar and rhetoric as foundations for the study of philosophy and theology.

Reformation, 1560–1600. During the late fifteenth and the early sixteenth century, Saint Andrews was associated with some of the leading figures in the intellectual life of Europe and the religious history of Scotland. John Mair (Major) was provost of Saint Salvator's College between 1531 and 1539. Possibly John Knox and certainly George Buchanan—poet, political theorist, and the tutor of James VI (James I of Great Britain)—experienced college and university life at Saint Andrews. There were upheavals in academic and religious life in the early sixteenth century. The Lutheran student Patrick Hamilton was burned at the stake outside the gates of Saint Salvator's College in 1528. Saint Andrews—and a number of its graduates—was very much part of the Reformation in Scotland after 1560. A plan for Protestant reform in 1561 wanted to reinforce Saint Andrews as the "first and principal" of Scotland's universities.

The university's financial difficulties became opportunities for Protestant reform and experiment. In the 1560s Buchanan wrote out a humanist and classical curriculum for students in a "College of Humanity." In 1574 proposals were made for lectures in theology, Greek, rhetoric, Hebrew, mathematics, and civil law. In an attempt to sustain Scottish Protestantism and replace the surviving elements of the medieval curriculum, Andrew Melville turned Saint Mary's College into a theological seminary and pressed for the study of rhetoric, Latin, Greek, logic, ethics and politics, and natural philosophy. Melville's career at Saint Andrews between 1580 and 1606 underlines the university's European links: Melville had been a pupil of Petrus Ramus and (like other teachers) had taught in France.

The Seventeenth Century and After. In the early seventeenth century, the university settled into comfortable middle age. Acknowledged as the ecclesiastical capital of Scotland, it attracted money—enough to finance the repair of college buildings in the 1620s—and the sons of the realm's nobility. In 1608 royal commissioners suggested a plan to remodel Saint Andrews on the examples of Cambridge and Oxford. The university, rather than its colleges, received more interest. A common library was founded in 1611, and the university was very much part of the royal visit to Saint Andrews by James VI and I in 1617. But there were also political dimensions to the university's life. In 1633 Archbishop William Laud tried to reintroduce common university services, less than a decade later, after an initial refusal by Saint Andrews to sign the National Covenant against Charles I (1638), members of the university became involved in the Scottish covenanting movement.

The southern walls and the Church of Saint Salvator's College survive, but the original fifteenth-century cloister and hall fell into disrepair and were replaced in the eighteenth and nineteenth centuries. Although the college steeple and gate of Saint Leonard's were demolished, the church, hall, and college buildings still exist. The same is true of Saint Mary's College on South Street: the old hall was destroyed, but the western side of the original college and the library of 1643 survive.

See also **Universities**.

BIBLIOGRAPHY

Primary Works

Anderson, James Maitland, ed. *Early Records of the University of St. Andrews*. Edinburgh, 1926. The graduation roll (1413–1579) and the matriculation roll (1473–1579) of the university.

Hannay, Robert Kerr, ed. *The Statutes of the Faculty of Arts and the Faculty of Theology at the Period of the Reformation*. Saint Andrews, Scotland, 1910.

Secondary Work

Cant, Ronald Gordon. *The University of St. Andrews: A Short History*. Edinburgh and London, 1946. 3d ed., 1992. The standard history of the university, with a detailed bibliography.

STEPHEN ALFORD

SAINT-GELAIS, MELLIN DE (1491–1558), French court poet. Mellin de Saint-Gelais was an important transitional figure between the poetic school of Clément Marot and the reforms of Pierre de Ronsard. Raised by his grandfather, Pierre de Saint-Gelais, and further instructed by his uncle, the poet Octavien de Saint-Gelais, Mellin received a humanistic education. His lengthy stay in Italy, where he learned to recite verse set to the accompaniment of the lute, placed him in contact with contemporary Italian poets whom he later introduced to France. At age twenty-four, Saint-Gelais began composing poems for and with Francis I and became his official court poet and chaplain. So popular were his brief poems for gentlemen to give to their ladies at court parties that they were inscribed on books of hours, portraits, even precious boxes. In addition, he gave music and mathematics lessons to the royal children. He then became court poet for Henry II and in 1544 was put in charge of the royal libraries at Blois and Fontainebleau. His public quarrel with Ronsard, of whose rising popularity he was jealous, ended in the latter seeking reconciliation.

Saint-Gelais was among the first to translate and adapt works by Ludovico Ariosto, Pietro Aretino, and Petrarch as well as epigrams by Horace and Martial. His translation of Gian Giorgio Trissino's *Sophonisba* (1554) was performed posthumously in 1559 and influenced the development in France of the genre of the humanist tragedy. Saint-Gelais collaborated with Clément Marot in composing the *Blason anatomique de l'oeil* (Anatomical blazon of the eye; 1536) and the *Blason du bracelet de cheveux* (Blazon of the hair ornament; 1536). His only published work, the philosophical prose poem *Advertissement sur les jugemens d'astrologie* (Warning on the judgments concerning astrology) appeared anonymously in Lyon in 1546.

BIBLIOGRAPHY

Primary Works

Saint-Gelais, Mellin de. *Oeuvres complètes*. Edited by Prosper Blanchemain. 3 vols. Paris, 1873.

Saint-Gelais, Mellin de. *Oeuvres poétiques françaises*. Edited by Donald Stone, Jr. Paris, 1993.

Secondary Works

Molinier, Henri Joseph. *Mellin de Saint-Gelays (1490?–1558): Étude sur sa vie et ses oeuvres*. 1910. Reprint, Geneva, 1968. Classic study of Saint-Gelais.

Stone, Donald. *Mellin de Saint-Gelais and Literary History*. Lexington, Ky., 1983.

ANNE R. LARSEN

SAINTS. *See* **Hagiography; Religious Themes in Renaissance Art.**

SALAMANCA, UNIVERSITY OF. Salamanca was the leading university in medieval and Renaissance Spain and a center of Spanish intellectual life, especially during its heyday in the sixteenth century. Founded c. 1218 by Alfonso IX of León, it was chartered in 1254 by Alfonso X of Castile. The medieval university relied mainly on the church for protection and patronage and was governed by papal-sanctioned constitutions; those of Martin V (1422) remained in force through the sixteenth century. The governing structure combined elements of the Bolognese student-controlled and the Parisian master-controlled systems. A rector (an aristocratic student) and chancellor presided over governing councils composed of masters and students. Few records survive from the fifteenth century, when university life was plagued by chronic violence at the hands of partisan bands, reflecting the civil unrest in Castile at large. After Ferdinand and Isabella restored peace in the 1470s, royal influence on the university steadily increased. The papal constitutions were supplemented by crown-sanctioned statutes, which were periodically revised (1538, 1561, 1594) under the supervision of royal visitors. In 1641, crown reformers abolished Salamanca's traditional system of *oposiciones,* elections that selected permanent lecturers by vote of the student body.

Salamanca's traditional curriculum combined arts and sciences with Aristotelian philosophy and the "higher faculties" of law, theology, and medicine. The late fifteenth century brought some curricular innovations, as new teaching chairs were established (for example, astronomy in 1467; Greek in 1495; Arabic in 1542) and the first foreign-born teachers appeared. Spain's leading humanist, Antonio de Nebrija, taught grammar there from about 1476 to 1487 and intermittently from 1505 to 1512. But many of these innovations were short-lived, and Salamanca never became a mecca for humanist studies like the newer University of Alcalá. The liberal arts continued to serve mainly as preparation for studies in the three higher faculties. A trilingual college (teaching Latin,

Greek, and Hebrew), opened in 1554, proved an embarrassing failure.

The faculty of canon and civil law dominated university life and politics, partly because legal studies allowed entry into Spain's large political and ecclesiastical bureaucracies. This trend grew more pronounced after 1600, as Salamanca's other faculties fell into decay. Theology, the second most important faculty, was dominated by the Dominican order, which housed its masters and students in the monastery of San Esteban (whose present structure was built 1524–1630). Dominican influence made Thomism the leading school of theology after 1500. The Dominican neo-Thomist Francisco de Vitoria, perhaps Salamanca's most famous teacher, held the principal chair of theology from 1526 to 1546. The Jesuits, incorporated into the university in 1570, contributed to grammar, arts, and theology instruction. Rivalry between the Dominicans and other orders was a constant feature of university life, figuring, for example, in the persecution of Augustinian Luis de León by the Inquisition in the 1570s. Medicine was the smallest of the three superior faculties. A chair of anatomy was created in 1551; a chair of surgery in 1566. An anatomical theater was built in the 1550s.

The late fourteenth century saw the foundation of the first residential colleges for secular students. These numbered twenty-eight by 1600. Limited at first to poor students, these houses soon became the preserve of an aristocratic elite. Most prestigious and exclusive were the four *colegios mayores*, which admitted bachelors (that is, graduates) only: San Bartolomé (also known as Anaya), established 1401; Cuenca, established 1510; San Salvador de Oviedo, established 1517; Colegio del Arzobispo, established about 1521. Graduates of these colleges (and their counterparts in Alcalá and Valladolid) held a near monopoly on the highest bureaucratic posts in Habsburg Spain.

Before 1400 most instruction at the university took place either in monastic houses or in Salamanca's cathedral, but the fifteenth and sixteenth centuries brought a spate of new construction. The *escuelas mayores* ("major schools," where arts, theology, and law were taught) were begun in 1415 and completed in the 1520s. Their famous plateresque facade depicting Ferdinand and Isabella was completed in 1529. The *escuelas menores* ("minor schools," for grammar instruction) were begun in 1428 and completed by 1533. This era of architectural expansion also saw the total number of students grow, from perhaps six hundred in 1400 to perhaps three thousand in 1500, to a peak of nearly seven thousand in the 1580s, at the apogee of Salamanca's intellectual prestige. Thereafter the university's fortunes declined with those of the monarchy, reaching a state of irreversible decay by 1650.

See also **Universities.**

BIBLIOGRAPHY

Primary Work

Beltrán de Heredia, Vicente, O.P., ed. *Cartulario de la Universidad de Salamanca (1218–1600).* 6 vols. Salamanca, Spain, 1970–1972.

Secondary Works

De Ridder-Symoens, Hilde, ed. *A History of the University in Europe.* Vol 2, *Universities in Early Modern Europe (1500–1800).* Cambridge, U.K., 1996.

Fernández Álvarez, Manuel, et al., eds., *La Universidad de Salamanca.* 3 vols. Salamanca, Spain, 1989–1990.

Kagan, Richard L. *Students and Society in Early Modern Spain.* Baltimore, 1974.

Rodríguez Cruz, Agueda María, O.P. *Historia de la Universidad de Salamanca.* Madrid and Salamanca, Spain, 1990.

KATHERINE ELLIOT VAN LIERE

SALERNITANO, MASUCCIO (Tommaso Guardati; c. 1410–1475), Italian writer. The son of a secretary to the prince of Salerno and a woman of nobility, Masuccio Salernitano became familiar with the classics, Latin, and the works of Dante and Boccaccio at a young age and without a formal course of studies. Like his father, he became secretary to a prince (Roberto Sanseverino, whose death in 1474 Masuccio mourned at the end of his *Novellino*).

Novellino is a highly structured collection of fifty tales, with a *cornice* (frame) that consists of a prologue and a conclusion. The tales were probably written separately and then gathered and grouped (in imitation of Boccaccio) into five days of ten tales each, according to preestablished topics. Each tale is preceded by a *dedicatoria* (dedication), identifying the person to whom the tale is addressed and the reason for having written it, and followed by a commentary.

The topics for each of the five days are, first, criticism of the clergy; second, amusing pranks or jests; third, criticism of women's lust; fourth, alternating tragic and comic tales; and fifth, examples of magnanimous virtue (in imitation of the *Decameron*'s final day).

Novellino was already circulating in manuscript form around 1460, but it was not published until 1476, a year after the author's death. Between 1484 and 1539, seven Venetian editions were printed, which shows the rapid popularity the tales achieved, not only in northern Italy, but also in the kingdom of Naples.

BIBLIOGRAPHY

Primary Works

Salernitano, Masuccio. *Il novellino*. Edited by Luigi Settembrini. Milan, 1990.

Smarr Levarie, Janet, trans. and ed. *Italian Renaissance Tales*. Rochester, Mich., 1983.

Secondary Work

Pirovano, Donato. *Modi narrativi e stile del* Novellino *di Masuccio Salernitano*. Florence, 1996.

MAUDA BREGOLI-RUSSO

SALONS. The salon was a site of sociability whose roots stretched back to medieval and Renaissance courts and that assumed its definitive form in the seventeenth century. Forerunners of the salon can be found in fifteenth-century Italy, in the court over which Isabella d'Este presided, for example, and in the literary gatherings where the Brescian humanist Laura Cereta engaged in conversation and delivered her orations. Pioneers of the salon were the gatherings of Mesdames Catherine and Madeleine des Roches in Poitiers before 1600 and Madame de Rambouillet's *chambre bleue* in the 1630s in Paris. The salon made a particularly strong impression on Parisian cultural development, but salons were also found, at various times, in other European capitals, such as Berlin, Vienna, and London. The terms "salon" and "*salonnière*" were coined only in the nineteenth century to denote gatherings that contemporaries had referred to as "companies" or "*ruelles*."

The feature that defined a salon and distinguished it from other social forms such as learned academies or leisure entertainments was its structured mixing of diverse elements that were held together through the discursive practices it established: women with men, writers with members of the power elite, oral culture with written texts, sociability with intellectual substance, private with public.

The salon was the only one of the convivial loci for discussion (including coffeehouses, academies, clubs, and masonic lodges) that actively embraced the participation of women. A woman led each salon, inviting guests of both sexes to the gathering in her home, presiding over the conversation, and invoking the etiquette that tamed rivalries (social, ideological, or professional) that in less regulated settings impeded communication. For the *salonnière,* the salon might serve as a means of education as well as a source of influence. Among the salon's most important connections with the Renaissance were the conceptions of civilization and femininity it borrowed from such works as Baldassare Castiglione's *Il cortegiano* (1528; trans. *The Book of the Courtier*). The portrayal of women as delicate, sensitive, beauteous, and selfless was used to justify *salonnières*' exercise of cultural authority and brokering of esteem and favor. Nonetheless, the prominence of women was one of the most severely criticized aspects of salons; Michel de Montaigne, Molière, Nicolas Boileau, and Jean-Jacques Rousseau were but the best-known critics to lament that the influence salons placed in the hands of women threatened manly virtues, the seriousness of intellectual work, and the stability of social hierarchies.

The salon was a place where writers might gain patronage for advancing in their careers, either from the social elite with whom they mixed there or from the *salonnière* herself. It was at the same time a venue for both the creation and the dissemination of new knowledge through oral interactions: authors reading their writings aloud and commenting on each other's works, focused debates, dramatic performances, and practice in the art of conversation. Such interchanges had a far-reaching effect on letters and the dissemination of ideas. As the philosophe Denis Diderot would remark in the eighteenth century, the combination of etiquette and ideas "accustoms us to discuss with charm and clarity the driest and thorniest of subjects." Before the nonlearned salon audience, then, intellectual innovations and technical advances were recast in clear terms accessible to expanding circles of the population of both sexes, thus facilitating the gradual maturation of new ideas into accepted ways of thinking.

What varied over time and from place to place was the subject matter of the salon's discussions and the nature of its collaborative activity. In seventeenth-century Paris, for example, salon gatherings were devoted to refining the language, to promoting a clarity of style and precision of expression. Discussions probed (often in quite radical terms) the nature of love, marriage, and patriarchal authority. Several literary genres originated or matured in those social settings (portrait, novel, maxim, occasional verse, newsletter). A number of women in seventeenth-century salons—notably Madeleine de Scudéry, Marie-Madeleine de La Fayette, Antoinette du Ligier de la Garde Deshoulières, Madame d'Aulnoy—published their own writings, many of which incorporated the interactive dynamics of salon conversations and the themes common to them. In the eighteenth century, by contrast, the topics in which women were thought to have special insight receded in importance, somewhat lessening their participation in intellectual discourse.

Paris salons promoted a series of cultural transformations. In the seventeenth century the prominence in salons of individuals from outside the traditional nobility gave rise to an ideology—again, in part traceable to the Renaissance through Castiglione—of open access and of talent's superiority to birth. As arenas of demanding personal discipline and yet far more socially inclusive than courts, these urban centers of sociability were the key agencies through which a broad segment of the population would be socialized in new expectations of self-control and the narrowed range of acceptable behavior that came to characterize Western cultures from the Renaissance onward.

In the eighteenth century, the salon's extension of new ideas to larger circles of men and women had far-reaching social and political consequences. Meeting in a home, a private space separate from the state (by contrast, for example, with the royal court or even the academies chartered by the king), the salon could air new ideas fettered only by its own rules. This privacy of the salon was instrumental in the birth of the public and of public opinion: of an enlarged set of notables who developed a body of thought independent of official political control, which could be appealed to over and against authorities on the basis of the common good. Down to the end of the Old Regime, the salon was controversial, subject to ridicule as well as to hostile criticism from those who contested women's participation in the republic of letters and the remaking of the social order that salons advanced.

See also **Feminism**; **Women**.

BIBLIOGRAPHY

Goldsmith, Elizabeth C. *Exclusive Conversations: The Art of Interaction in Seventeenth-Century France*. Philadelphia, 1988.

Goodman, Dena. "Enlightenment Salons: The Convergence of Female and Philosophic Ambitions." *Eighteenth-Century Studies* 22, no. 3 (1989): 329–350.

Harth, Erica. *Cartesian Women: Versions and Subversions of Rational Discourse in the Old Regime*. Ithaca, N.Y., 1992.

Hertz, Deborah. *Jewish High Society in Old Regime Berlin*. New Haven, Conn., 1988.

Lougee, Carolyn C. Le paradis des femmes: *Women, Salons, and Social Stratification in Seventeenth-Century France*. Princeton, N.J., 1976.

CAROLYN LOUGEE CHAPPELL

SALUTATI, COLUCCIO (1331–1406), Italian humanist and chancellor of Florence. Salutati was the most important humanist between Petrarch (1304–1374) in the mid-fourteenth century and the humanist movement of the early fifteenth century. He also played a dominant role in the intellectual life of Florence.

Origins and Political Career. Born into a Guelf family of Stignano, a small village in Florentine territory on the border with Lucca, Salutati was carried into exile as a newborn when Stignano was taken over by local Ghibellines a few days after his birth. He received his formal education in Bologna where his father served the local tyrant, Taddeo dei Pepoli. After grammar school and a course in rhetoric with Pietro da Moglio, later a follower of Petrarch, he took classes in the notarial art between 1348 and 1350. His father having died in the meantime, Salutati together with his mother and siblings returned to their ancestral home in Stignano, which after 1339 was firmly in Florentine hands.

For the next sixteen years Salutati worked as a private notary in the area around Stignano and had a number of short-term appointments as secretary of communal governments in the region. At least by 1358 he was the leading political figure in his local commune, which included Stignano and three neighboring villages. After marrying in 1366 he decided to seek a wider world and in 1367–1368 served as chancellor of Todi before moving on to Rome, where he worked in the office of Francesco Bruni, one of four papal secretaries. Rather than return to Avignon with the papacy in 1370, he obtained through Bruni's good offices a year's appointment as chancellor of Lucca, newly liberated from Pisan control. He almost certainly became involved in party politics, and, because his political faction suffered defeat during his term, he was not given a renewal in 1371. After lingering in Lucca for months without work, Salutati, whose wife died in giving birth to their second child in 1371, returned disconsolate to Stignano with his little son. His second marriage, probably in 1373, signals a revival of self-confidence. His wife, Piera Riccomi, bore him at least eight more children.

Early in 1374 Salutati was summoned to Florence to take up the newly created position of secretary of the Tratte, charged with overseeing the republic's elaborate procedures for electing government officials by lot. Very probably an instrument of the political faction bent on firing the controversial chancellor, Niccolò Monachi, Salutati combined the Tratte with the chancellorship the following year when Monachi was ousted. Taking up office in the very months when Florence went to war with the papacy, the new chancellor made himself internationally famous almost immediately by the brilliance of his *missive,* or public letters, written in justification of Florence's cause. Over the next thirty-one years Salutati may have produced tens of thousands of letters of which about five thousand remain. Despite the turbulent political life of the republic, Salutati, who had learned his lesson at Lucca, successfully maintained a position of neutrality, which, coupled with his fame as a writer, insured his long tenure of the office. His last *missive* were written only a few days before his death in early May 1406.

A Leading Humanist. Although Salutati showed an interest in ancient literature and history as early as 1352 when he heard Zanobi da Strada lecture in Florence, serious contact with Florence's Petrarchan circle did not begin much before 1359–1361. Even then, the character of Salutati's approach to the ancients during the next ten years linked him not to Petrarchan humanism but to the earlier secular humanism of the region around Venice in northern Italy. Only in 1369, when in Rome with access to the library of Francesco Bruni, a correspondent of Petrarch, did Salutati betray an interest in religious issues reflecting the influence of Petrarch. The contradictions of Salutati's mature writings mainly result from the tension between his Florentine patriotism and commitment to the lay life and the Petrarchan preference for political quietism and scholarly seclusion.

Salutati's stature as a leader of Italian humanism in his generation owes much to the early fame he acquired as author of Florence's public *missive.* Most of his public letters are brief, written in an unexceptional humble style of *ars dictaminis* (a medieval style of writing formal letters in Latin), and deal with routine matters, but perhaps a hundred scattered throughout the collection are brilliant defenses of Florentine foreign policy, rich in citations of historical precedents taken from ancient and medieval sources. For his purpose he revived and brought to perfection the *stilus rhetoricus* or oratorical style developed by the papal and imperial chanceries in the first half of the thirteenth century. If his style remained medieval, his grasp of appropriate precedents was humanistic and his lesson that knowledge of history was essential for a political leader made a strong argument for a politician's need of a humanist education. Because as chancellor he had a corps of government messengers to carry his personal writings along with public correspondence to the corners of western Europe, the lines of communication for Italian humanism soon ran through Florence.

Petrarch had been an itinerant, but Salutati remained fixed in Florence. Over the decades he nurtured a group of disciples, Leonardo Bruni and Poggio Bracciolini from Tuscany, and from northern Italy, Pier Paolo Vergerio and Antonio Loschi, who became the leaders of the next generation of Italian humanists. Florence became the capital of the movement in the first half of the fifteenth century largely owing to Salutati's efforts. Particularly important was his role in reintroducing Greek learning to western Europe in 1397 after the abortive experiment of the Florentines with Leonzio Pilato in 1360–1362. Due to Salutati's relentless pressure on the Florentine government, Manuel Chrysoloras (1350–1415) was lured to Florence on generous financial terms and when, after less than three years, he departed, the brilliant teacher left behind students who could work in the Greek language on their own.

Unlike Petrarch, who felt nostalgia for the ancient world and abhorred the thousand years which separated him from antiquity, Salutati, better adjusted and more gregarious, felt relatively comfortable as a denizen of the fourteenth century. Nor did he embrace Petrarch's notion of the "dark ages." For him the intervening centuries between antiquity and the present had witnessed only a gradual decay in learning, the thirteenth century being akin to an Arctic summer night before a new sunrise in the fourteenth with Albertino Mussato (1261–1329) and Geri d'Arezzo (c. 1270–1327). His only quarrel with Scholasticism concerned logicians who often took verbal constructions for reality, thereby obscuring the truth. Whereas Petrarch showed no interest in history after the early second century A.D., Salutati began to describe the intervening period by tracing several developments through successive centuries. Beginning with the first century A.D. he sketched a history of Latin literature down to his own time and attempted to determine in which period *vos* had replaced *tu* for the second person singular.

Scholarly Interests. Among his other achievements, he anticipated Lorenzo Valla (1407–1457) by articulating a theory of linguistic development as dependent on change in popular speech and therefore accessible to historical analysis. He was the first to state unequivocally that Caesar, not Celsus, was the author of the *Commentarii,* and he identified Germanicus as the author of the *Aratrea.* Although he could not designate the author, he doubted the attribution of the *Epistola Valerii ad*

Ruffinum (Letter of Valerius to Ruffinus) either to St. Jerome or Valerius and rejected the attribution of the medieval *Manuale sive speculum Augustini* (Handbook or mirror of St. Augustine) to St. Augustine. If he shared with Antonio Loschi and Pasquino Capelli the honor of bringing Cicero's *Ad familiares* from hiding, he alone was responsible for putting the pseudo-Ciceronian *Synonyma* and *Differentiae* into circulation, as well as discovering Cato's *De re rustica* (On rural life), Servius's *De centum metris,* Pompeius's *Commentum artis Donati* (Comment on the art of Donatus), and Maximianus's *Elegiae.* He put all his philological talent to use in the *Invectiva contra Antonium Luschum* (Harangue against Antonio Loschi; 1403) where he presented his argument that Florence had not been founded by Caesar, as tradition had it, but in the time of Sulla decades earlier.

Salutati had a dialectical turn of mind. Well trained in dialectic in his youth, he invited his correspondents to raise issues for him to resolve. Once having chosen his side in a debate, he mustered all the favorable arguments and threw himself into the fray, often assuming exaggerated stances. The unqualified defense of the superiority of monastic seclusion to life in the world made in his *De saeculo et religione* (On matters secular and religious; 1381–1382), composed in response to a monk's request to strengthen his resolve to remain loyal to the monastic life, could not have been entirely sincere.

His interests in formal theology and philosophy, together with a growing tendency to emphasize the superiority of Christian over pagan wisdom led in Salutati's last years to tensions between the master and his disciples, who obviously felt his approach and views were old-fashioned. His *De fato et fortuna* (On fate and fortune; 1396) devoted to reconciling divine predestination with freedom of the human will was largely unoriginal, but in the *De nobilitate medicine et legum* (On the nobility of medicine and law; 1399), Salutati developed Petrarch's stress on the centrality of the will in the human personality into a respectable philosophical position. Relying heavily on the Scholastic, Duns Scotus, he maintained that medicine, representing the intellect and—unable to criticize the contemplative life directly—the speculative life, was vastly inferior to law, identified with the will and the active life of the legislator and citizen. Poggio and Bruni would have found the conclusions attractive, but the manner of proof uncongenial.

Salutati, moreover, was deeply attracted to allegorical interpretation and relied heavily on etymological analyses to unlock the truth encoded in words, especially proper names. In his *De laboribus Herculis* (On the labors of Hercules), extant in two editions, he explored poetic fictions relating to the labors of Hercules for truth about God and created beings. The first edition, limited to analyzing Seneca's *Hercules furens* and *Hercules oeteus,* was left unfinished about 1382, while the bulk of the second, concerned with all twelve labors of the hero, belongs to 1381–1391. Although he continued work on the second manuscript, it was left unfinished at his death.

Monarchy and Pagan Culture. Perhaps what most bothered the younger men, who were just beginning to exploit Cicero's Latin, was Salutati's eclectic style. At its best Salutati's epistolary style, like that of Petrarch, generally reflected at varying distances the Senecan model in form, content, and tone, but his sententious discourse lacked Seneca's pithy wisdom and Petrarch's occasional narrative quality. In discussing philosophical and theological issues, moreover, he abandoned any pretense of classicized style: *De nobilitate medicine et legum* was constructed as a scholastic discourse.

Politically, the two generations lived in different worlds. Whereas for the younger men Florence was a republic acting autonomously amid a group of other independent political powers, for the elder Salutati it had not yet emerged from the communal organization of central and northern Italy, living within the shadow of pope and emperor. If republican sentiments were only rarely expressed in his private and public writings, it is because he could not bring himself to make the assault on monarchy which a theoretical defense of republicanism required.

The increasing influence of Dante's *Commedia* from the early 1390s, moreover, augmented Salutati's tendency to see political and cultural issues in terms of a divinely willed progress generally from paganism to Christianity and more specifically from Roman republic to empire. This tendency obviously underlay Salutati's approach in the *De tyranno* (A treatise on tyrants; 1400), a work with the patriotic aim of vindicating the condemnation of Brutus and Cassius to the lowest circle of Hell by Dante, Florence's beloved poet. Reaching his goal by constructing a chain of dubious arguments to prove that in murdering Caesar these men had killed a legitimate monarch, Salutati added that God himself caused the death of the murderers with a view to establishing an era of peace under a monarchy so as to facilitate the diffusion of the Christian message and that in any case monarchy was the best form of government.

The consequences of his evolving negative appraisal of pagan culture and politics emerged in his exchange of letters in 1405–1406 with Poggio, now employed at the papal court in Rome. Reacting to Poggio's stance that modern writers, epitomized by Petrarch, were incomparably inferior to the ancients in eloquence, and sensing an element of religious scepticism in the critique, Salutati responded that an author could only be eloquent to the degree that he knew the truth. Consequently, he concluded, the ancients, ignorant of the Christian god, could never be truly eloquent.

Salutati was an immensely influential figure in the development of Italian humanism and in the establishment of Florence as the capital of Italian humanism. His classical studies, his civic position, his influence on younger humanists, and the scholarly projects that he supported enabled the humanist movement to continue unchallenged throughout the next generation.

BIBLIOGRAPHY

De Rosa, Daniela. *Coluccio Salutati: Il cancelliere e il pensatore politico.* Florence, 1980.

Langkabel, Hermann. *Die Staatsbriefe Coluccio Salutatis. Untersuchungen zum Frühhumanismus in der Florentiner Staatskanzlei und Auswahleditions,* Archiv für Diplomatik, Beiheft 3. Cologne, Germany, 1981.

Petrucci, Armando. *Coluccio Salutati.* Biblioteca biographica, 7. Rome, 1972.

Trinkaus, Charles. "Coluccio Salutati's Critique of Astrology in the Context of His Natural Philosophy." *Speculum* 64 (1989): 46–68.

Trinkaus, Charles. *In Our Image and Likeness: Humanity and Divinity in Italian Humanist Thought.* 2 vols. London, 1970. Reprint, 1995.

Ullman, Berthold L. *The Humanism of Coluccio Salutati.* Medioevo e umanesimo, 4. Padua, Italy, 1963.

Witt, Ronald. *Coluccio Salutati and His Public Letters.* Travaux d'humanisme et renaissance, 151. Geneva, 1976.

Witt, Ronald. *Hercules at the Crossroads: The Life, Works, and Thought of Coluccio Salutati.* Duke Monographs in Medieval and Renaissance Studies, 6. Durham, N.C., 1983.

RONALD G. WITT

SALVIATI, LEONARDO (1540–1589), Florentine philologist and literary critic. Born into a distinguished family long involved in the government of Florence, Salviati received a solid education and participated actively in literary circles beginning in his youth, gaining fame for his oratorical eloquence. He found favor with Benedetto Varchi and other learned individuals, assuming the post of consul of the Accademia Fiorentina (Florentine academy) by the age of thirty. Using the pseudonym *Infarinato* (Covered with flour), Salviati attained prominence in the Accademia della Crusca (Bran academy), to which he was admitted a year after its establishment in 1582. He was charged by the administration of Francesco I de' Medici, the grand duke of Tuscany, with the preparation of an artfully expurgated version of Boccaccio's *Decameron* designed to replace a previous infelicitous bowdlerization and to restore the work's former influence. In addition to critical and philosophical writings, he published poetry and two comedies, *Il granchio* (The crab; 1566) and *La spina* (The thorn; 1592).

Salviati's lifelong aspiration was the exaltation of his native tongue. His youthful *Orazione in lode della fiorentina lingua* (Oration in praise of the Florentine language; 1564) reflects the attempt to reconcile two contrasting positions then current: one stressing the inherent superiority of the spoken language (an outlook championed especially by Varchi), the other emphasizing the need for adherence to sanctioned literary tradition (a perspective underlying the pronouncements of Pietro Bembo). Salviati followed his *Orazione* with twenty years of reflection on linguistic affairs and on ideas held by other scholars. What is probably his most important work, the incomplete disquisition *Degli avvertimenti della lingua sopra il Decamerone* (Remarks on the language of the *Decameron;* first published 1584–1586) consists of two volumes comprising five books. The first volume treats philological issues surrounding Boccaccio's tales, the widespread controversies subsumed under the heading *Questione della lingua* (Question of the language), and orthography, while the other volume is devoted to grammatical problems. Particularly in the *Avvertimenti*'s second book, Salviati insists on the exemplary nature not only of the language employed in the *Decameron,* but also of that used in fourteenth-century texts of a nonliterary nature, all of which he saw as demonstrative of the natural beauty and purity of the Florentine speech of that earlier era. Although Salviati's observations on grammar are largely derivative, his comments on spelling—which precede a noteworthy illustration of Italian dialectal differences—show an original and reasoned approach.

Salviati involved the Accademia della Crusca in a protracted dispute over the merits of Torquato Tasso's epic poem *Gerusalemme liberata* (Jerusalem delivered; 1580). Penning two attacks on the work under his academic alias, Salviati harshly criticized Tasso's love of conceit and his excessive use of Latinisms and of elements foreign to common Tuscan speech. Salviati's most significant contribution to the achievements of this academy lies in lexicography. In the *Avvertimenti* he proposed the creation of a dictionary, and his highly influential views are reflected in the criteria fundamental to compilation of the first edition of the *Vocabolario degli accademici della Crusca* (Dictionary by the members of the Crusca academy; 1612).

BIBLIOGRAPHY

Primary Works

Salviati, Leonardo. *Degli avvertimenti della lingua sopra il Decamerone.* Edited by Lorenzo Ciccarelli. Naples, Italy, 1712.

Salviati, Leonardo. *Opere complete del cavaliere Lionardo Salviati.* 5 vols. Milan, 1809–1810.

Secondary Works

Brown, Peter Melville. *Lionardo Salviati: A Critical Biography.* London, 1974.

Sozzi, Bortolo Tommaso. "Leonardo Salviati nella questione linguistica cinquecentesca." In his *Aspetti e momenti della questione linguistica.* Padua, Italy, 1955. Pages 101–173.

MICHAEL T. WARD

SANCHES, FRANCISCO (1551–1623), Portuguese philosopher and doctor of medicine and the only sixteenth-century skeptic, apart from Michel de Montaigne, to win fame for his radical skepticism. Born of Jewish parents in the Spanish town of Túy but christened and educated in the Portuguese city of Braga, Sanches emigrated with his family in 1562 to Bordeaux, France. After studying at the famous Collège de Guyenne (1562–1571), Sanches left for a tour of universities in northern Italy before taking up his medical studies at the University of Rome, renowned for its progressive medical curriculum.

Rome was an important turning point in Sanches's intellectual and professional life. The Galenic tradition, which emphasized the union between medicine and philosophy, was honored in Italian universities. The question of scientific method was hotly debated. New research in the fields of anatomy and botany, and the pharmacological use of plants, furthered the belief that scientific knowledge might advance through the observation of natural phenomena. Medical empirical knowledge, as Sanches later demonstrated in his works, presented a possible way out of the skeptic's dilemma. Sanches's medical works, which constitute the bulk of his publications, were published posthumously in Toulouse (*Opera medica,* 1636).

In 1573 Sanches returned to France, completed a doctorate in medicine at the University of Montpellier in 1574, then moved to Toulouse, where he spent the rest of his life as a doctor at the Hôtel-Dieu (hospital) and held first a professorship in philosophy (1585) and then a professorship in medicine (1612) at the University of Toulouse.

During the period 1574–1581 Sanches reflected deeply on philosophical issues. His first publication in 1578, the *Carmen de cometa M.D. LXXVII* (Poem about the comet of 1577), mocked the absurd predictions of astrologers and the Aristotelian theory of comets that common sense and scientific facts had proved false. His major work, *Quod nihil scitur* (trans. *That Nothing Is Known;* 1581), written in Latin for an academic audience, gained him a reputation in Europe as a complete skeptic. Sanches's forceful exposition of the impossibility of attaining perfect scientific knowledge and his devastating critique of the universally accepted Aristotelian system of knowledge—based on what Sanches called scientific instruction in syllogisms—led him to propose writing a new book, *De modo sciendi* (On the method of knowing). Sanches insisted that it was necessary to reject authority, to look at the facts with an open, inquiring mind, using reason and sensory information as guides. He believed that with the aid of judgment and experience (experimentation), one may arrive at a kind of scientific knowledge.

Unlike Montaigne, Sanches did not develop his skepticism by means of the traditional skeptical arguments that belittle the certainty of human knowledge and invoke the variety, inconstancy, and relativity of human beliefs and customs. Rather, Sanches questioned the foundations of Aristotelianism that dominated university teaching. His advocacy of methodological doubt certainly influenced René Descartes's *Discours de la méthode* (trans. *Discourse on Method;* 1637). Pierre Bayle originated the myth of Sanches's Pyrrhonism in his *Dictionnaire historique et critique* (1697). But philosophically, Sanches's skepticism belongs to the school of the ancient Greek skeptic Carneades.

BIBLIOGRAPHY

Primary Works

Sanches, Francisco. *That Nothing Is Known.* Edited by Elaine Limbrick and Douglas F. S. Thomson. Cambridge, U.K., 1988. Translation of *Quod nihil scitur.*

Sanchez, Franciscus. *Opera philosophica.* Edited by Joaquim de Carvalho. Coimbra, Portugal, 1955.

Secondary Work

Popkin, Richard H. *The History of Scepticism from Erasmus to Spinoza.* Berkeley, Calif., 1979. Classic study of Renaissance and seventeenth-century skepticism.

E. LIMBRICK

SANDOVAL Y ROJAS, FRANCISCO GÓMEZ DE (c. 1553–1625), marques of Denia and grandee of Castile (1575), duke of Lerma (1599), cardinal of San Sisto (1617). Sandoval y Rojas is best known as the favorite and chief minister of Philip III of Spain, a role he occupied from 1598 to 1618. An obscure courtier until he rose to power, Lerma in time became the first of an influential group of seventeenth-century European favorites–cum–prime ministers who played powerful roles in the internal and international policies of their respective monarchies.

Lerma's rise to power in 1598, concurrent with Philip III's accession to the throne, led to important changes in the Spanish monarchy. Under his leadership the Spanish monarchy sought to redefine its role in European politics and conflicts by promoting—in clear contrast to the policies of the previous king, Philip II (ruled 1556–1598)—conservation over territorial expansion and diplomatic over military solutions to impending conflicts in the Low Countries and England. Internally, Lerma and his faction were proponents of absolutist principles and administrative and political reforms aimed at reinforcing royal authority throughout the Spanish monarchy.

The role of the duke of Lerma as the king's chief minister had its most lasting impact, however, in the realm of contemporary theories on royal favorites. Responding to the need to legitimate his actions as a de-facto prime minister, Lerma and his supporters developed a complex and all-encompassing positive theory on the nature and role of the royal favorite, who from then on was depicted as the king's friend and, thus, as the king's other self. This theory, in turn, allowed seventeenth-century political theorists to integrate the royal favorite into the formal structure of the monarchy without having to question the monarch's role as the sole sovereign.

Lerma, who became the most important patron and art collector of his times, fell from power in October 1618 after losing Philip III's confidence. He died in Valladolid on 17 May 1625, portrayed as a currupt favorite and accused, together with Philip III, of being responsible for the precipitous decline of Spanish power in Europe.

See also **Philip III**.

BIBLIOGRAPHY

Feros, Antonio. *Kingship and Favoritism in the Spain of Philip III, 1598–1621*. Cambridge, U.K., 2000.

ANTONIO FEROS

SANNAZARO, JACOPO (1458–1530), Neapolitan writer. Born to a noble family that had emigrated from Pavia, Sannazaro grew up in and around Naples. By 1478 he was associated with a small group of humanists that formed the Accademia napoletana and that included Giovanni Pontano, Benedetto Gareth (known as il Cariteo), and Tristano Caracciolo. Throughout the 1480s Sannazaro composed Petrarchan poetry, farces for the duke of Calabria's court, and the first ten chapters of his innovative romance *Arcadia.* In the next decade he turned his attention to Latin poetry, in which he is arguably more distinguished. A number of his epigrams and elegies are from the period before 1501, when Sannazaro joined Frederick of Aragon, king of Naples, in exile in France. He remained in France until Frederick's death in 1504, then returned to his villa of Mergellina, a gift from Frederick, where he lived in semiretirement until his death. His major Latin works from this period are *Piscatorial Eclogues,* five eclogues written in Virgilian style but set among fishermen along the coast of Naples, and the epic *De partu Virginis* (On giving birth by the Virgin; 1526), which tells of the annunciation and birth of Christ.

Sannazaro is best known for his work in pastoral, and his engagement in this genre is apparent in far more than *Arcadia.* Published first in a pirated edition in 1502 and with two additional chapters in 1504, *Arcadia* was one of the more popular works of the sixteenth century. It is first and foremost a pastiche of allusions to Virgil, Tibullus, Pliny, Ovid, Dante, and Petrarch, among others; it also pays homage to the circle of poets with whom Sannazaro was closely associated. A series of sketches of pastoral life, *Arcadia* features bucolic games and competitions, wizards who can cure lovesickness, rural feast days, and singing shepherds. Much like Giovanni Boccaccio's *Comedia delle ninfe fiorentine* (Comedy of the Florentine nymphs; 1341–1342), it is divided into chapters that conclude with canzones characterized by great metrical variety. Yet even though *Arcadia* has pretensions to an encyclopedism that suggests Sannazaro did not always wear his learning lightly, it also exhibits what was to become a highly influential narrative line for Renaissance pastoral. A thinly disguised autobiographical tale of a forlorn Neapolitan lover named Sincero (Sannazaro's academic name was Actius Sincerus), the romance stages Sincero's entrance into Arcadia and his gradual incorporation into the culture and customs of the poetic shepherds he finds there. Such an incorporation, however, is never complete; Sannazaro handles with particular subtlety the speaker's distance from the rustic world. Only in the final chapters, probably written while Sannazaro was in exile, does Sincero return to his homeland in a dreamlike vision and learn that the woman whom he loved has died, prompting him to say, "I cursed the hour that ever I left Arcadia."

Such a pattern of immersion in and return from a bucolic sphere that doubles as a training ground for poets would have a long history in European pastoral. It is evident not only in the English work most closely patterned after Sannazaro's, Philip Sidney's *Old Arcadia,* but in romances by Jorge de Montemayor, Miguel de Cervantes Saavedra, and Honoré d'Urfé. Although the epic elements in these latter texts threaten to displace the simplicity of the pastoral setting, Sannazaro's work also displays an impulse toward epic and a clear chafing at pastoral constraints even as he praises them in the epilogue. Much of this can be explained by Sannazaro's explicit Virgilian ambitions. A great deal of his work is characterized by a strong and self-conscious poetic voice that exhibits (like Virgil's) both a keen awareness of its place in literary tradition and a deeply felt commitment to the political conditions that support literary pursuits.

Sannazaro's epic, *De partu Virginis,* written in Virgilian hexameters, is a profound meditation on the affinity of the lowly and simple pastoral style for the mystery of the virgin birth. While Sannazaro's starting point for linking pastoral to Christ's nativity was Virgil's fourth eclogue, he vividly imagines the community of shepherds as they gather to listen to the angel and hold rustic festivities; he celebrates Christ as a kind of Pan, whose songs will be echoed by the woods; and toward a stunning and abrupt close, he has Proteus prophesize a Christ who will call simple fishermen—*colonos*—to join him. Sannazaro also makes the elegiac tonalities that are so central to his *Arcadia* a notable feature of *De partu Virginis;* one of the poem's more moving passages is a portrait of Mary at Christ's death, weeping bitterly at the foot of the cross. Sannazaro's masterful five *Piscatorial Eclogues* (and one fragment) are in turn remarkably fluid with respect to genre. The fourth eclogue is dedicated to Frederick's son, Ferdinand of Aragon, duke of Calabria, and sings of the glories of Naples; all of them dwell on exile, death, metamorphosis, and fluvial deities. At the same time, there are tales of lovers who seek rustic havens to assuage their grief.

In these evocative geographical details, one finds Sannazaro's most salient contribution to Italian poetry. Like Horace, Sannazaro is a poet of place for whom Naples and its surrounding seascape and islands become both powerfully suggestive metaphors for the rise and fall of cities and sources of natural beauty and poetic inspiration. As in epigram I.2, in which Sannazaro transforms Villa Mergellina into a domain of nymphs and numinous forces, or the memorable twelfth eclogue of *Arcadia* with its evocations of the warm springs of Baia and its grief that "Naples is no longer Naples" (l. 117), much of the poetry is dedicated to imbuing Sannazaro's beloved local haunts with historical and mythological meaning. Assuredly one reason for Sannazaro's influence is his success in detailing in the landscape a profound depth and otherness of its own, at once responsive to human inhabitants and resistant to appropriation by them.

Jacopo Sannazaro. Raphael included a portrait of Sannazaro looking at the viewer from above the heads of the Greek poets Homer and Anacreon in *Parnassus* (detail) in the Stanza della Segnatura in the Vatican Palace. Painted c. 1510. VATICAN MUSEUMS AND GALLERIES, VATICAN CITY/ ALINARI/ART RESOURCE

Rightly called the inventor of melancholy by the critic Erwin Panofsky, Sannazaro best elicits that melancholy when intimating the distance Greek or Roman past of a savage woodland, as in the elegy "Ad ruinas Cumarum" (To the ruins of Cumae). Such melancholy is indicative of his profound sense of the elusiveness of local cultures even when one is in their midst.

BIBLIOGRAPHY

Primary Works

Arcadia and Piscatorial Eclogues. Translated and with an introduction by Ralph Nash. Detroit, Mich., 1966.

De partu Virginis. Edited by Charles Fantazzi and Alessandro Perosa. Florence, 1988.

Opere di Iacopo Sannazaro. Edited by Enrico Carrara. Turin, Italy, 1963.

The Piscatory Eclogues of Jacopo Sannazaro. Edited by Wilfred Pirt Mustard. Baltimore, 1914.

Secondary Works

Kennedy, William. *Jacopo Sannazaro and the Uses of Pastoral.* Hanover, N.H., 1983.

Panofsky, Erwin. *Meaning in the Visual Arts.* Garden City, N.Y., 1955. See "*Et in Arcadia Ego:* Poussin and the Elegiac Tradition," pp. 295–320.

Percopo, E. *Vita di Jacopo Sannazaro.* Naples, Italy, 1931. Extract from *Archivio storico per le provincie napoletane* 17 (1931): 87–198.

Quint, David. *Origin and Originality in Renaissance Literature: Versions of the Source.* New Haven, Conn., 1983.

JANE TYLUS

SARDINIA. The Renaissance marked an important stage in Sardinia's history, for it was at this time that the island achieved, however briefly, a measure of political autonomy, which in later centuries proved a foundation of Sard nationalism. At the same time, however, there was no meaningful change in the lives of the Sards in terms of economic growth, cultural attainment, or religious development. Like most of the Mediterranean islands, Sardinia's ancient and medieval history was one of subjugation to a series of continental rulers. Roman control gave way in the fifth century to domination from North Africa—first by the Vandals, then, in the seventh century (after a brief Byzantine interlude) to the Arabs of Maghreb. A joint Pisan and Genoese invasion drove the Muslims from the island in 1016, and they themselves were eventually driven out by the Catalans in 1323.

Throughout these centuries, and indeed throughout the Renaissance, Sardinia was arguably the poorest region in Europe. The extraordinary ruggedness of the terrain was primarily responsible for this. With relatively little arable land available, the island's wheat production was modest; and since much of whatever was produced quickly found its way en route to the markets controlled by the island's current rulers, near-famine conditions kept the indigenous population very low. Animal herding and its products (meat, cheese, leather, wool) comprised the second major export. Neither the grain nor the animal products, however, were renowned for their quality. Some wine was produced, all for local consumption; a small amount of salt was mined, and an even smaller amount of coral was fished. In the region around Iglesias, in the southwest, some modestly productive silver mines existed. The reasons for the repeated struggles to control the island, therefore, had more to do with its strategic location: until western navigational skills developed to the point where sailing within the sight of land was not a fundamental necessity, Sardinia served as a reference point and staging area for Mediterranean fleets.

Since the bulk of the island's population lived along the coast, foreign control was relatively easy to maintain. The island was divided into four administrative regions called *giudicati* (judgeships), which Sards sometimes fancifully refer to as "kingdoms": Gallura, Logudoro, Arborea, and Cagliari. The "judges" who governed these were often local urban magnates who were allied with whichever continental power controlled the island at the time, and sometimes were representatives of the foreign rulers themselves.

In 1355 Peter IV "the Ceremonious" of Catalonia-Aragon granted legislative autonomy to the island and established its first parliament, but this, coupled with the continuing rapacious policies of the Catalans toward the island, only resulted in Sard rebellion. Leadership of this revolt centered in Arborea, and specifically with a single "judge" or "queen," Eleanora (ruled 1383–1404), who has since acquired near mythical stature with the Sardinian people. The rebellion was so successful that by 1408 the Catalans had to mount what was essentially a second conquest of the island. Martin "the Younger," son of Catalonia-Aragon's ruler Martin I, nearly succeeded, but after several months of campaigning he succumbed to one of the island's frequent malarial epidemics. Since the younger Martin was the only direct heir to the Catalan throne, his death opened the door to a new Catalan-Aragonese dynasty, the Trastamara. The island remained under their close control thereafter, and under that of their eventual successors the Spanish Habsburgs, until 1720.

BIBLIOGRAPHY

Casula, Francesco Cesare. *La Sardegna aragonese.* 2 vols. Sassari, Italy, 1988.

CLIFFORD R. BACKMAN

SARPI, PAOLO (1552–1623), Venetian intellectual, historian of the Council of Trent. Sarpi entered the religious order of the Servants of Mary (the Servites) at age fourteen. His doctorate, awarded by the University of Padua in 1578, was in theology, but he was intellectually omnivorous and continued to study science, philosophy, and history throughout his life. In the late 1560s and early 1570s Sarpi resided in Bologna, Mantua, and Milan, while in 1585–1588 he was a member of the Roman court of Sixtus V. Within the Servite order he rose to high office and engaged in factional politics, but after the turn of the century he abandoned this commitment and sought appointment to a bishopric, unsuccessfully.

While continuing to live as a religious and a priest, Sarpi silently defected from allegiance to the papacy during the last decades of the sixteenth century and then, to some greater or less degree (this is a matter of debate), from orthodox Catholicism. He engaged in speculation leading to libertine views on the history of religions and their role in societies, and he became deeply interested in the Council of Trent (1545–1563) as the focal point of the European history of the sixteenth century and began to collect information relating to it.

Sarpi's Philosophy. Sarpi's intellectual influences included Epicureanism, Stoicism (especially the *Essais* of Montaigne and *De la sagesse* of Pierre Charron), William of Ockham, Niccolò Machiavelli, Ibn Rushd (Averroes) and Paduan Averroism, and the most advanced scientific culture of the time, including the new discoveries in medicine and physiology and the mechanics and astronomy of Galileo Galilei. To put it another way, he was influenced by all the currents that ran counter to the Aristotelian-Thomist synthesis.

Sarpi's own philosophical papers, which he kept private, include a short treatise on cognition and three series of *Pensieri* (Aphorisms). Like all aphorisms, Sarpi's were experiments in thinking, and this qualifies their value as evidence. But their tendency was materialist and determinist, and in them he virtually abandons any belief in an afterlife of punishments and rewards, or a God of providence. He retained belief in the social utility of religion, which he viewed as the medicine that remedies the ignorance and superstition of the majority, and thus as an instrument of government. These libertine ideas were not shocking ones to many of the contemporaries with whom Sarpi conversed, nor beyond that circle to a broad stratum of the European elite; but they would have been shocking if uttered or printed in public. Sarpi was most unconventional when he posited that the fear of eternal punishment was not indispensable for social life, since it really had no deterrent effect on bestial men. This position contradicted a view universally held at that time and allows David Wootton to conclude in his book that Sarpi was one of the first modern moral atheists of whom we know.

Service to the Venetian State. In May 1606 Pope Paul V excommunicated the doge and other leaders of the Venetian state, and in an interdict prohibited the clergy from performing the sacraments in the Venetian dominion. This was a reprisal against Venetian laws that limited the acquisition of property by the church, and against the arrest of two delinquent clerics. The Venetians reacted by banning the publication of the papal interdict, which they regarded as null, and ordering all clergy to continue their regular functions. The major European powers engaged in diplomacy to prevent the outbreak of war, and in April 1607 France arranged to have Paul V and Venice back down simultaneously, in what amounted to a defeat for Rome.

Sarpi, as theological consultant to Venice, advised the Venetian leaders, abetted their intransigence, and published works that defended Venetian jurisdiction over the property and personnel of the church. He was excommunicated in January 1607. In the early seventeenth century every national and territorial state was driven by the inner dynamic of European history to evolve toward absolutism by monopolizing power and jurisdiction within its borders, but it was naturally more difficult for an Italian territorial state like Venice, a neighbor of the papacy, to dominate the Catholic church on its territory than it was for a northern national monarchy like France. Sarpi, inspired by Venetian patriotism and aversion to the papacy, wrote powerfully in defense of Venetian jurisdiction and became a significant ideologist of absolutism.

He turned to ecclesiastical history in his *Trattato delle materie beneficiarie* (Treatise on benefices; 1675), extolling the poverty, powerlessness, and submission to political authority of the Christians in the apostolic age, and recounting with polemical force the acquisition (portrayed as abusive) of wealth and power by the western papal church. These partisan works involved Sarpi in erudite research into history and law, while in the *Istoria dell'Interdetto* (History of the interdict; 1624)—his history of the diplomatic and military stratagems of Venice, Rome, France, and Spain during the crisis—he displayed mastery of a very different genre, that of "pragmatic" historiography, the dynamic narrative of complex sequences of events as they unfolded rapidly and often simultaneously.

Sarpi had enough support among the Venetian patricians to keep his post as consultant to the government for the rest of his life and to promote policies that he and his supporters favored: strong Venetian jurisdictionalism, political resistance to the papacy and the Habsburgs of Spain and Austria, military resistance to those powers in the Adriatic, and friendly relations with non-Catholic states like England and Holland. But Sarpi went further, cultivating semisecret contacts with Protestant ambassadors in Venice and influential Protestants in Germany, France, and England. His correspondence with these men reveals a vague general consensus on the desirability of converting Venice to Calvinism, but although Sarpi certainly encouraged hard-line Calvinism abroad, there was never a moment when he thought it was actually feasible or desirable to bring it to Venice. By joining the international Calvinist network and giving its members reason to hope for such a revolution, he attracted practical support for Venice against the papacy.

Sarpi's Religion. Sarpi's religious identity is a subject of endless debate because he was a man of many facets but austere reserve, and because like many intellectuals of the sixteenth and seventeenth centuries he lived by the precept of conforming outwardly to the beliefs and customs established in one's society, while thinking independently of them. Was Sarpi an Augustinian Catholic reformer? a fideist like Montaigne? one of the Italian religious radicals defined by Italian historian Delio Cantimori (d. 1966)? a Calvinist? or a libertine and virtual atheist? The last two possibilities are the ones most strongly represented in late twentieth-century scholarship. Sarpi lived ascetically and when he does refer to the divinity he expresses a sense of its remote majesty and the comparative impotence of human free will that resembles the code of Calvinism; but these references occur in letters and published works and so may be more conventional and less authentic than the aphorisms Sarpi wrote entirely for himself. If he could have guided the religious evolution of Europe along the lines that he preferred, the primacy of the Roman papacy would have been abolished and there would have existed a number of European churches completely subordinated to the national and territorial states. But that hypothetical outcome conforms more closely to the political libertinism of his aphorisms, and to the absolutist model, than it does to Calvinism.

Sarpi is best known for his *Istoria del Concilio Tridentino* (*History of the Council of Trent;* 1619). Its protagonist is the papacy of the sixteenth century, from Leo X to Pius IV (1513–1565). The aim of the work is to show that Rome at various times convoked, deferred, or suspended the council, and manipulated its agenda and decisions, for the purpose of defeating the challenge to its primacy from reformers within the Catholic world. Sarpi's model, in style and method, was Francesco Guicciardini's *Storia d'Italia* (*History of Italy;* written 1537–1540), which had analyzed the motives and calculations of the princes of Italy and the rest of Europe during the wars of 1494–1530. But Sarpi's subject matter was novel, for there was no previous example of a pragmatic narrative that focused on a crucial event in ecclesiastical and doctrinal history and applied the penetrating analysis of Guicciardini to the motives and calculations of the leaders of the church.

The contrast between the theological dogmas and anathemas that were debated and voted at Trent under the watchful eyes of the papal legates, and the constant negotiation between Rome and the European powers that conditioned that legislation, allowed Sarpi to exploit an ironic register far deeper and more varied than that available to any previous historian. For this and allied reasons the work was influential as Europe moved from the Renaissance to the Enlightenment and has been combated unremittingly in Catholic historiography. Among the masterpieces of European historical literature, perhaps only Edward Gibbon's *History of the Decline and Fall of the Roman Empire* (1776–1788) has had a similar capacity to polarize judgment and sentiment from its first publication down to the present.

BIBLIOGRAPHY

Primary Works

Sarpi, Paolo. *Istoria del Concilio Tridentino*. 2 vols. Edited by C. Vivanti. Turin, Italy, 1974.

Sarpi, Paolo. *Istoria dell'Interdetto e altri scritti editi e inediti*. 3 vols. Edited by M. D. Busnelli and G. Gambarin. Bari, Italy, 1940.

Sarpi, Paolo. *Lettere ai protestanti*. 2 vols. Edited by M. D. Busnelli. Bari, Italy, 1931.

Sarpi, Paolo. *Opere*. Edited by G. and L. Cozzi. Milan, 1969. Contains excerpts from Sarpi's works and correspondence; a selection from his aphorisms, including the first edition of many; the fullest modern interpretive biography; and bibliography.

Sarpi, Paolo. *Pensieri*. Edited by G. and L. Cozzi. Turin, Italy, 1976. Reproduces the aphorisms, biography, and bibliography from *Opere*.

Sarpi, Paolo. *Scritti filosofici e teologici editi e inediti*. Edited by R. Amerio. Bari, Italy, 1951.

Sarpi, Paolo. *Scritti giurisdizionalistici*. Edited by G. Gambarin. Bari, Italy, 1958.

Secondary Works

Frajese, Vittorio. *Sarpi scettico. Stato e chiesa a Venezia tra cinque e seicento*. Bologna, Italy, 1994. With full bibliography.

Wootton, David. *Paolo Sarpi: Between Renaissance and Enlightenment.* Cambridge, U.K., 1983.

WILLIAM MCCUAIG

SASSETTA, STEFANO DI GIOVANNI, IL. *See* **Siena,** *subentry on* **Art in Siena.**

SATIRE. [This entry includes five subentries, an overview of satire on the Continent followed by subentries on satire in England, France, Germany, and Italy.]

Satire on the Continent

Satirical writing in the European Renaissance took many forms, but in its initial revival along classical lines in Italy the brief epigram, the longer verse satire, and the Lucianic fable or dialogue are among satire's dominant modes. Many authors took their lead from the Roman verse satirists Horace, Juvenal, Persius, and the epigrammatist Martial. The humanist scholars of the Renaissance had already in the fifteenth century produced lengthy commentaries and editions of these poets (Cristoforo Landino on Horace, Niccolò Perotti on Martial, and Angelo Poliziano on Persius, for example). More creative humanist authors like Francesco Filelfo directly imitated classical satire in his Neo-Latin poetry, though his efforts tended more in the direction of invective directed against individuals than in the more generalizing praise of virtue and excoriation of vice traditionally characteric of classical satire. By the sixteenth century satirical writing had achieved somewhat greater decorum, and literary theorists like Francesco Robortello (*De satyra* [On satire]; 1548) and Julius Caesar Scaliger (*Poetices libri septem* [Poetics]; 1561) began defining satire as a literary genre in stricter terms, though they still misunderstood its origins as deriving from the ancient Greek satyr play. These authors especially criticized satire that tended toward the obscene and scurrilous, thereby anticipating neoclassical literary standards. Satire provided a foundation for some of the most inventive writing of the Renaissance, as is evident from its use and transformation by major writers such as Ludovico Ariosto and Pietro Aretino in Italy, François Rabelais in France, and Erasmus and Thomas More in England.

See also **Filelfo, Francesco.**

BIBLIOGRAPHY

Albanese, Gabriella. "Le raccolte poetiche Latine di Francesco Filelfo." In *Francesco Filelfo nel quinto centenario della morte.* Medioevo e Umanesimo 58. Padua, Italy, 1986. Pages 389–458.

Poliziano, Angelo. *Commento inedito alle satire di Persio.* Edited by Lucia Cesarini Martinelli and Roberto Ricciardi. Florence, 1985.

Weinberg, Bernard. *A History of Literary Criticism in the Italian Renaissance.* 2 vols. Chicago, 1961.

W. SCOTT BLANCHARD

Satire in England

Satirical writing in the English Renaissance assumed a variety of forms and was influenced by both medieval antecedents and classical literary models, but common themes in most Renaissance authors of satire make possible a few generalizations about the period. While medieval traditions remained strong in some authors, humanistic interest in classical models for satire derived from the Roman writers Horace, Juvenal, and Martial dominated the English Renaissance. Satire's tendency to focus on current issues especially suited an increasingly literate public eager for what the Roman satirist Juvenal had defined as the subject of satire: "whatever men do" (*Satire 1*). With the rise of court culture in the Tudor period, courtiers and their habits came under a great deal of attack from the satirists, much in the manner that the abuses of the clerical class had been the topic of much medieval satire or "complaint." From the Roman satirists Renaissance authors found important warrants for conducting social and political critique, and in their literary theories about satire they associated satire (wrongly, as it turned out) with the ancient figure of the satyr and with that figure's coarse appearance and uncivilized demeanor. Such an association strengthened satire's connection with the more colloquial or "low" style reserved for comic writing, but also with the satyr figure's special freedom to criticize. The satirist's function has always been to unmask the hypocrisies and follies of his or her age, and Renaissance authors often employed a medical analogy to define their therapeutic role in restoring humoral balance to the diseased body politic through satiric writing.

Verse Satire. In early Tudor writers like John Skelton (c. 1460–1529), medieval literary forms, such as the "estates satire" (satire directed against particular classes in society), a pervasive feature in medieval writers like Chaucer and William Langland, are still a noticeable influence. Skelton's satires show him demonstrating some dependence on medieval complaint, which often used allegory or dream vision as a technique (*The Bowge of Court*), and Skelton frequently adopts a religious attitude of contempt for the worldliness and corruption of his society. His satires can even take on a prophetic dimension in the manner of the religious "jeremiad," and the later satires of the 1520s are highly political. Skelton's poetry is somewhat idiosyncratic, and much of it is characterized by a unique type of versification that has come to be known as "Skeltonics," but in him we still see the survival of the medieval alliterative tradition.

In the three satires of Sir Thomas Wyatt (1503–1542), an author from the next generation, virtually all traces of the medieval inheritance have vanished, and the classical Horatian satire is directly imitated. Wyatt's analysis of the new values of the court of Henry VIII in "Mine owne John Poynz" is especially revealing, as is his contrast, also found in Roman satire, between the corrupt, urban court and the more honest countryside.

In the later sixteenth century, the pastoral eclogues in Edmund Spenser's *The Shepheardes Calendar* (1579) contain some satiric content, but in other poems from his volume of *Complaints* (1591) we find Spenser (1552/53–1599) at his most satiric, relying on the figure of the rustic Colin Clout (borrowed from Skelton) to voice opinions that praise Queen Elizabeth as the inaugurator of a golden age of pastoral innocence and bliss while blaming the grasping court establishment for its vices of envy, malice, and idleness. Spenser's reliance on the literary form of the beast fable in the political satire of *Mother Hubberd's Tale* (1591) and his archaizing language are neomedieval elements in an author who showed an interest in classical genres but largely remained faithful to native traditions.

Verse satire in the English Renaissance reached its greatest development in the satires of John Donne (1572–1631) and in the epigrams and epistles of Ben Jonson (1572–1637). Donne's lively and conversational style, closely resembling that of Juvenal, exposes the follies of the London cityscape, where encounters with various upstart courtier types, influenced by foreign customs in both language and fashion, are detailed. In Donne's *Satire 4,* the world of the court and the city of London become imagined as a hell on earth, while the alternative of "true religion" as a cultural remedy serves the same function as Juvenal's endorsement of a saner "path of virtue." Ben Jonson was one among many Elizabethan and Jacobean writers to use the brief epigram, adapted from the Roman poet Martial, for satiric purposes, while his longer satires, such as "To Robert Wroth," urge in a calmer and more measured manner than Donne's the adoption of the Horatian values of country simplicity, friendship, and honesty as alternatives to the commercial values ascendant in his society. The verse satires of Joseph Hall (1574–1656), Thomas Lodge (1557–1625), and others demonstrate the wide appeal of verse satire in the late Elizabethan and Jacobean periods. Hall's *Virgidemiarum,* published in two parts as *Tooth-lesse Satyrs* (1597) and *Byting Satyres* (1598), demonstrate a familiarity with the full range of his classical models, from the gently moralizing Horatian satires of the earlier volume to the latter volume's more critical, mordant tone in the manner of Juvenal. Hall's satires display a socially responsible concern for abuses such as enclosures and rural poverty alongside their analysis of the character defects of individuals.

Prose Satire. In the mid-Tudor period, the Protestant polemicist John Bale, working in exile, composed a number of prose works of a clearly satiric character that later earned him the epithet "bilious Bale," but prose satire awaited the latter part of the sixteenth century for its full development.

Satirical purposes infiltrated the prose writers of the Elizabethan age in works that are to a certain extent unprecedented and in which some scholars have detected the earliest roots of the picaresque novel. The satirical prose of Thomas Nashe (1567–1601), Robert Greene (c. 1558–1592), Thomas Lodge, and Philip Stubbes (c. 1555–c. 1610) is best described as being journalistic, and its function is twofold: to expose or anatomize criminal or depraved elements in society (with a somewhat voyeuristic appeal resembling the modern tabloid), and to lament such changes by advocating a return to the conservative values that existed prior to the onset of urban decadence. Additionally, the prose satires of the period often engage in personally directed invectives, as authors competed for recognition in a market hungry for the latest pamphlet. The ecclesiastical establishment, concerned with the challenges that satire presented to social decorum and with its use in religious controversies dating back to the Marprelate pamphlets of the late 1580s, issued a restraining order in 1599. The Archbishop of Canterbury and the Bishop of London ordered that the works of Thomas Nashe and his rival, Gabriel Harvey (1545?–1630?), were to be burned, and furthermore prohibited the publication of any satires or epigrams whatsoever. The prose writers as a group employ a racy, earthy style filled with colloquialisms, and for all of its satiric exaggeration, their work is in its own way an early form of novelistic realism.

Satire in Drama. In 1599 Ben Jonson inaugurated the genre of "comicall satyre" with his play

Every Man Out of His Humor, expanding his dramatic conceptions from their earlier dependence on the conventions and stock character types of the Roman comedies of Plautus. Also termed "city comedy," this dramatic form shares with verse and prose satire a resolutely urban setting and tends to focus on social types—exaggerated caricatures that represent specific cultural or moral tendencies. In these city comedies Jonson seems to draw more on the didactic methods of the medieval drama for his satiric purposes, sketching stereotyped characters who are dominated by a particular "humor," a secular reworking of the vice tradition of the Middle Ages. Usurers, courtier gallants, sanctimonious Puritans, and urban scoundrels inhabit these plays, whose purpose is to display the "enormities" or deformities of the world of London. Jonson's experiments in this form were followed by those of Thomas Middleton (1580–1627), John Marston (1576–1634), and other playwrights. Shakespeare's *Troilus and Cressida* (c. 1601–1602) is an especially trenchant example of satire given a dramatic form in a play depicting the moral dissolution that follows from the pursuit of individual passions.

BIBLIOGRAPHY

Blanchard, W. Scott. *Scholars' Bedlam.* Lewisburg, Pa., 1995.

Campbell, Oscar James. *Shakespeare's Satire.* London, 1943.

Gibbons, Brian. *Jacobean City Comedy: A Study of Satiric Plays by Jonson, Marston, and Middleton.* Cambridge, Mass., 1968.

Gransden, K. W. *Tudor Verse Satire.* London, 1970.

Hester, M. Thomas. *Kinde Pitty and Brave Scorn: John Donne's Satyres.* Durham, N.C., 1982.

Kernan, Alvin. *The Cankered Muse: Satire of the English Renaissance.* New Haven, Conn., 1959.

Rhodes, Neil. *Elizabethan Grotesque.* London, 1980.

W. SCOTT BLANCHARD

Satire in France

Though often not bearing the formal title of "satire," satirical writing in the French Renaissance was pervasive and can be found in virtually all of the major authors of the period. One of the sixteenth century's greatest imaginative works, François Rabelais's *Gargantua and Pantagruel* (1532), is thoroughly marked by satirical intentions, and satire also pervades Montaigne's innovative *Essais* (Essays, 1572–1580; 1588). Satire in verse shows a combination of medieval influences alongside an increasingly classicizing taste for greater decorum in the choice of subject matter.

The figure of François Villon (1431–c. 1463) is among the most fascinating of the satirists. Villon's work in many ways derives from the medieval traditions of goliardic poetry, the targets of which were often clerics, but in Villon the cynical patron of taverns and brothels also lashes out against the pretensions of the courtly love tradition. His *Testament* (1461), a mock legal bequest written from his prison cell after his arrest for theft, endorses a countercultural worldview that exposes the values of the dominant classes by juxtaposing them to the world of Parisian lowlife. In many ways a student of Villon and also his first editor, Clément Marot (c. 1497–1544) continued the tradition of legal satire in a poem also written from prison, *L'Enfer* (Hell; 1526). Marot relied on allegory in this poem, but in a series of poems that take the form of verse letters, the *Epîtres du coq à l'asne* (Letters written from the cock to the ass; c. 1530s), Marot, who was suspected of Lutheranism for much of his adult life, lashed out against a variety of subjects in a poetic form (the *coq à l'âne*) that allowed for the informal treatment of contemporary topics. Much of his satire has as its immediate context the religious conflicts that so dominated French civilization in the sixteenth century.

Although he generally eschewed a "low" genre like satire, Pierre Ronsard (1524–1585) drifted toward satire in donning the mantle of the poet-prophet in a series of poems lamenting the religious novelties of his age from a conservative viewpoint. His *Discours des misères de ce temps* (Discourse on the misery of our times; 1562) and several related poems lash out in the manner of the biblical jeremiad against the arrogance of religious reformers whose upending of tradition has turned "the world upside-down." His attacks especially single out the Calvinist Theodore Beza and frequently appeal to nationalist sentiment to overcome the divisive effects of Reformation teachings. Less focused on religion but nationalistic in other respects, the satirical sonnets included in Joachim du Bellay's (1522–1560) lyrical sequence *Les regrets* (Regrets; 1558) satirize the corrupt and worldly habits of the Roman Curia. Du Bellay, who spent four years in the service of his cousin, a cardinal at Rome, wrote much of this "sweet satire" ("doulce satyre") to compensate for his bitter feelings of alienation and exile from his beloved France, though even upon his return to France he found it difficult not to write satire about his own countrymen in the closing poems of the sequence. Du Bellay also endorsed, in his prose *Deffence et Illustration de la langue Françoise* (Defense and illustration of the French language; 1549), the imitation of the classical satirists, though in his own work the more personal and introspective form of the sonnet was brought into service to expose the vanities of human nature in a satirical manner. A late work, *Le poète courtisan*

(1559), mocks the affected and parasitical behavior of courtiers in a manner similar to many other writers of the Renaissance.

Les satyres (The satires; 1608 and later) of Mathurin Régnier (1573–1613) come closer to the classical models of Juvenal and Horace than those of any of the sixteenth-century poets. In Regnier, a satirical treatment of courtiers often is counterbalanced by a more positive admonition to practice Stoic resignation and Horatian detachment from the world. Additionally, in Regnier we see satire's ability to migrate into issues of a more strictly literary nature. In several of his satires he champions a more natural and informal style against the stricter, emerging neoclassicism of François de Malherbe. Regnier especially shows the influence of his countryman Michel Montaigne and of the Italian satirist Francesco Berni (c. 1497–1535).

See also biographies of figures mentioned in this entry.

BIBLIOGRAPHY

Primary Work

Marot, Clément. *Oeuvres Satiriques.* Edited by Claude-Albert Mayer. London, 1962.

Secondary Works

Aulotte, Robert. *Mathurin Regnier. Les Satires.* Paris, 1983.

Tomarken, Annette. *The Smile of Truth: The French Satirical Eulogy and Its Antecedents.* Princeton, N.J., 1990.

W. SCOTT BLANCHARD

Satire in Germany

Renaissance Germany saw an unprecedented flourishing of satires. Written both in Latin and the vernacular and drawing on classical and native traditions, satires appeared in various guises: as carnival plays, farces, dialogues, ironic encomia, and verse narratives. A number of satires of that period found their way into world literature, such as *Das Narrenschiff* (Ship of fools; 1494) by Sebastian Brant, the *Encomium moriae* (1511; trans. *In Praise of Folly*) by Erasmus of Rotterdam, the *Epistolae obscurorum virorum* (Letters of obscure men; 1515–1517) by Crotus Rubianus and Ulrich von Hutten, the *Grobianus* (1549) by Friedrich Dedekind, and the anonymous *Reynke de Vos*.

The reasons for the thriving of satire lie in the social, political, ideological, and religious tensions that tore Germany apart: the feudal order was challenged by the emerging middle class; humanism clashed with Scholasticism; and Luther challenged the authority of the Catholic Church. Satire became a powerful weapon in these conflicts.

Pre-Reformation Satire Written in the last decade of the fifteenth century, Sebastian Brant's (1457–1521) *Narrenschiff* introduced into European literature the figure of the fool as a powerful metaphor of the time. Sparing no one, Brant parades before the readers' eyes an almost endless variety of fools ranging from beggars to bishops and from peasants to princes. The figure of the fool was taken up by Brant's fellow Alsatian Thomas Murner (1475–1537) in his *Die Narrenbschwerung* (Exorcism of fools; 1512). In it, as in three other satires—*Der Schelmen zunfft* (The fools' guild; 1512), *Die Mülle von Schwyndelszheym* (The mill of Swindeleton; 1515), and *Die Geuchmatt* (The lovers' meadow; 1519)—Murner pillories human weakness, follies, and vices.

The Low German *Reynke de Vos* (Reinike the fox; 1498) represents the most comprehensive social satire of the time. Clothed in the form of an animal epic, it chronicles the triumphal rise of the fox who, with cunning and deception, outwits his stronger competitors and finally becomes the chancellor of the kingdom. It is a bitter satire on the clerical-feudal hierarchy and what the author saw as a warped system of justice.

While Murner, Brant, and the anonymous author of *Reynke de Vos* wrote in German for a broad audience, the humanists composed their Latin satires for a small educated elite. Drawing on ancient traditions, Erasmus's *Encomium moriae* is based on the simple literary device of ironic praise. While Erasmus's satire is a sophisticated and urbane satire on the folly of man in general, the *Epistolae obscurorum virorum* are directed against a specific group of men, scholastic theologians, who through their correspondence—allegedly written by themselves but in reality by the humanist authors—and through their barbarous Latin demask themselves in their folly, immorality, and complacency.

Reformation Satire Marking the transition from the humanist to the Reformation satire, *Eccius Dedolatus* (The planed-down Eck; 1520, published anonymously but probably written by the Nürnberg humanist Willibald Pirckheimer) foreshadows the more aggressive tone of the Reformation period when satire frequently assumed the function of a "ceremonial slaying" (Stopp, p. 56). In this Latin work, Johann Eck (1486–1543), Luther's principal opponent in the early phase of the Reformation, is forced to undergo a violent cure: he is planed down (hence the title), beaten, shaved, purged, and cut open for the removal of destructive character faults.

By 1521, however, public discourse was conducted primarily in the vernacular, with the Protestants being more skillful in using literature for their propagandistic purposes. Satirical elements can be found in Hans Sachs's poems, dialogues, and carnival plays, in Ulrich von Hutten's dialogues, and in the thousands of pamphlets that inundated the German market after 1520. A major propagandist for the (Swiss) Reformation was Niklaus Manuel (1484–1530). His play *Vom Papst und seiner Priesterschafft* (On the pope and his priests; 1523), for instance, was staged as a public event in Bern in 1523. Using the revue-technique of the carnival play—the succession of only loosely connected individual scenes—Manuel satirizes the splendor of the pope and his retinue, and the abuse of indulgences, especially the custom of requiem masses. One of the few Catholic satirists of note was the Franciscan Thomas Murner. In this satire *Von dem Grossen Lutherischen Narren* (Of the great Lutheran fool; 1522) he created a work that was just as drastic as *Eccius Dedolatus* in its grotesque exaggeration and its symbolic killing of its opponent, in this case Luther.

In spite of the prevalence of the vernacular in Reformation literature, Latin satires continued to be written. Dedekind described and ironically endorsed the coarse and boorish behavior of his protagonist in his *Grobianus: De morum simplicitate libri duo* (Grobianus: Two books on the simplicity of manners), and the Lutheran pastor Thomas Naogeorg (1508–1563) ridiculed all who follow the wrong doctrines, in his *Satyrarum libri quinque priores* (Five books of satires; 1555).

See also biographies of figures mentioned in the entry.

BIBLIOGRAPHY

Primary Work

Schade, Oskar, ed. *Satiren und Pasquille aus der Reformationszeit.* 3 vols. Hanover, Germany, 1863. Reprint, Hildesheim, Germany, 1966. Most comprehensive collection of Reformation satires.

Secondary Works

Best, Thomas W., ed. *Eccius Dedolatus: A Reformation Satire.* Lexington, Ky., 1971.

Hess, Günter. *Deutsch-lateinische Narrenzunft: Studien zum Verhältnis von Volkssprache und Latinität in der satirischen Literatur des 16. Jahrhunderts.* Munich, 1971.

Könneker, Barbara. *Satire im 16. Jahrhundert: Epoche, Werke, Wirkung.* Munich, 1991. Best study on German satire in the sixteenth century.

Stopp, F. J. "Reformation Satire in Germany. Nature, Conditions, and Form." *Oxford German Studies* 3 (1968): 53–68.

ECKHARD BERNSTEIN

Satire in Italy

The canon of classical satire was available by the close of the fifteenth century and attracted humanist scholarship and commentary. Despite this, with the exceptions of Lodovico Ariosto's Horatian satires (1517–1525), formal verse satire was not much imitated. Much of the neglect resulted from the pervasive acceptance of the false etymology deriving "satire" from "satyr." In consequence, satire was believed to be not only concerned with the condemnation of human vice, but—like the satyr himself—rough, uncouth, low in diction, and preoccupied with sexuality. The definition was loose enough to accommodate a variety of writings in verse and prose; and the Victorian judgment of John Addington Symonds, that the Renaissance was an age of burlesque and parody but lacked satire, ignores the contemporary standard.

Verse satire may be said to have been reborn in Rome with the custom of attaching anonymous, vituperative poems to the statue of Pasquino, at first on his feast day of 25 April and later whenever the spirit moved. These pasquinades, usually sonnets and *capitoli* (satiric verse in terza rima), were politicized during the papal elections of the 1520s. Pietro Aretino claimed public credit for his pasquinades, causing an unlikely number to be attributed to him. Francesco Berni (c. 1497?–1535), Aretino's enemy, wrote satiric *capitoli* and sonnets, but was most famous for his burlesque praises of insignificant objects, usually with bawdy double entendres. Teofilo Folengo (c. 1491–1544), Annibale Caro (1507–1566), and many others also produced burlesques and paradoxes that shade into satire.

A powerful contemporary example came from Erasmus, whose *Encomium moriae* (1511; trans. *Praise of Folly*) and colloquies, often bubbling with social and clerical criticism, taught vernacular writers how to use irony and dialogue between fictive speakers for self-protection. Until the Roman Inquisition began enforcing censorship rigorously, the Reformist sympathies common in the circles of vernacular writers and printers gave a focus to the satiric dialogues that they produced. The conditions of life following the Sack of Rome (1527)—foreign dominance, despotism, class inequities—fostered an outpouring of social criticism in prose dialogues. Aretino's *Ragionamenti,* dialogues on prostitution (1534, 1536), excoriate the luxury and vice of church and court, audaciously arguing that the whore's life is the only honest one. Ortensio Lando (c. 1512–1553), Nicolò Franco (1515–1570), who was hanged for his pasquinades against Paul IV, and Anton Francesco Doni (1513–1574) all used satire to delineate their targets for reform. The sixth world of Doni's *I Mondi* (1552), the "World of Fools," shows the influences of Erasmus's *Folly* and of Thomas More's *Utopia* (1516); Doni's utopian New World satirizes the follies of his own society without projecting an alternative.

If satiric expression found an effective instrument in the dialogue form, it has an obvious affinity with comedy as well, drama being all dialogue. The New Comedy formulas of Plautus and Terence, mother's milk in the humanist schools, lent themselves readily to social criticism. Niccolò Machiavelli's *Mandragola* (The mandrake; 1518) exploits the character types and situations to devastating effect in an unblinking analysis of amorality masked by hypocrisy. Although institutions such as law, church, and family receive some attention, Machiavelli's primary thrust is an exposure of human nature. The balance shifts in the other direction with the satiric comedies of Aretino and of Angelo Beolco (known as Ruzzante; 1502–1542). Aretino typically uses a New Comedy plot, which he embellishes with incidental satire on courts, church, and urban society. Beolco's many comedies present sympathetically the naturalness and hardships of peasant life, while directing their barbs against the oppression of the ruling class and its culture.

The theoretical accounts of satire in this period—for example, those by Lodovico Dolce (1559), Francesco Sansovino (1560), even Francesco Patrizi (1586)—may seem rudimentary or banal; but, indisputably, the practice of satire was vigorous and abundant, at its best producing works of enduring value.

See also Pasquino *and biographies of figures mentioned in this entry.*

BIBLIOGRAPHY

Primary Works

Ariosto, Lodovico. *The Satires of Ludovico Ariosto: A Renaissance Autobiography.* Translated by Peter DeSa Wiggins. Athens, Ohio, 1976. With a useful introduction.

Berni, Francesco. *Renaissance Humanism at the Court of Clement VII: Francesco Berni's* Dialogue against Poets *in Context.* Edited and translated by Anne Reynolds. New York, 1997.

Secondary Works

Grendler, Paul F. *Critics of the Italian World, 1530–1560: Anton Francesco Doni, Nicolò Franco, and Ortensio Lando.* Madison, Wis., 1969.

Radcliff-Umstead, Douglas. *The Birth of Modern Comedy in Renaissance Italy.* Chicago, 1969. Reprint, 1992. Commentary on individual plays with plot summaries.

Symonds, John Addington. *Renaissance in Italy.* Vols. 4–5, *Italian Literature.* London, 1881. Reprint, New York, 1935. Dated opinions, but rich in detail.

RAYMOND B. WADDINGTON

SATIRE MÉNIPPÉE. *La satire ménippée,* first published in 1594, is the most celebrated pamphlet of the French Wars of Religion. It was composed by a group of ecclesiastics, poets, scholars, and judicial officers meeting secretly at the house of the Parisian magistrate Jacques Gillot in 1593. The satire was directed against the ultra-Catholic Holy League, which at the time was holding in Paris a meeting of the Estates General, or representative assembly, to elect a Catholic candidate to replace the then-Protestant king, Henry IV. The first two parts of the satire circulated in manuscript as a parody of the Leaguer estates and an imaginary account of two charlatans, representing the Spanish and Lorrainer allies of the League, who set up a stall to sell to the deputies their panacea, the Catholicon, which would enable the buyer to rob and pillage at will, betray fortresses, assassinate enemy princes, or become cardinals. A third and later part was added containing facetious verses and epigrams.

The contributors were Politique supporters of Henry IV who put the need for peace before religious uniformity. Apart from Gillot, they were Pierre Le Roy, a canon of Rouen who conceived the project; Nicolas Rapin (1535–1608), a poet from Poitou who fought for Henry IV at the Battle of Ivry; Gilles Durant (1550–1615), a jurist who added to the third section of the satire a piece called "The Donkey of the League" in imitation of Apuleius's *Golden Ass,* a satirical romance of the second century A.D.; Florent Chrestien (1541–1596), a former tutor to Henry IV; Pierre Pithou (1539–1596), a humanist and antiquary best known for his defense against Rome of the independence of the French Catholic, or Gallican, church, which he was composing at the time; and Jean Passerat (1534–1602), a learned humanist professor at the Collège Royal.

Either Pithou or Passerat was responsible for the second of two introductory discourses that explained the Menippean mode of satire. Sixteenth-century humanists were agreed that the term referred to the third-century B.C. Cynic philosopher Menippus of Gadara, who influenced Varro, the Roman literary polymath and satirist two centuries later. Scholars differed, however, as to whether satire was primarily Greek or Roman, and this disagreement was reflected in an etymological debate on the derivation of the word from either the Greek "satyr" or the Latin *satura lanx,* a dish of mixed foods. An important criterion of Menippean satire was that it consisted of a mixture of verse and prose, and could incorporate dialogue. While it often depicted imaginary allegorical contexts, such as dreams and fantastic voyages, it also satirized real people, their politics and fallibilities. On the other hand, the standard classical Roman satirists, Lucilius, Horace, Juvenal, and Persius, wrote in hexameters and tended to compose satire about abstract vices and virtues. It was they who were the principal objects of literary criticism and emulation by French humanists until the time of the League, when the *Satire ménippée* was the most prominent among many polemical examples of the alternate mode. Moreover, the Menippean genre offered an opportunity to combine Renaissance interest in classical satire with medieval French *gauloiseries* that contained elements of broad popular farce. This, after all, was the practice of Rabelais, who was mentioned in the second introductory discourse. This discourse also referred to Justus Lipsius's *Satyrae menippeae* of 1581, which launched the conscious imitation of the Menippean form and alluded to a bevy of ancient satirists.

Among the highlights of the *Satire ménippée* was a mock account of the procession of the deputies to the estates, showing the radical clergy of the League armed to the teeth and its leader, the duke of Mayenne, as Phaëthon, who, according to Greek myth, was struck down by Zeus for driving his father's chariot through the heavens. Another imaginary scene in the satire was the assembly hall of the estates, hung with tapestries depicting the anarchic revolt of the lower classes inspired by the League. The best-known section provided the fictitious speeches of those present at the estates, when the orators confessed that they were using religion as a pretext for continuing the civil war for their own profit. The one serious speech, written by Pithou, was put into the mouth of Claude Daubray, a former mayor of Paris, who denounced the policies of the League as leading France into chaos. While the *Satire ménippée* contained a great deal of farce and bawdy, it was also replete with classical allusions reflecting the scholarly aspect of the French Renaissance.

See also **Wars of Religion**.

DISCREPAT A PRIMA FACIES HÆC ALTERA VATUM
Cornelius Severus.

Satire Ménipée. Engraving from an early edition of *Satire Ménippée.* The Latin tag from the epic poet Cornelius Severus reads: "This other version of the prophets is very different from the original." The print shows a fiery preacher of the Catholic League wearing a mask thrown back and brandishing a cross of Lorraine, symbol of one of the leaders of the League. He stands beneath the so-called infernal fig tree, symbolizing Spanish-inspired sedition. In the right foreground are two conspirators beside bags of gold and a crevasse spewing forth fire from hell. Behind them are the pope and a Leaguer bishop, possibly Guillaume Rose of Senlis. In the left foreground a monk picks up an assassin's dagger for Madame de Montpensier, sister to the duc de Mayenne, leader of the League. In the background Leaguer forces sack a city. PHOTO COURTESY OF J. H. M. SALMON

BIBLIOGRAPHY

Primary Work

Read, Charles, ed. *La satyre ménippée; ou, La vertu du Catholicon selon l'édition princeps de 1594.* 2d ed. Paris, 1880.

Secondary Works

Salmon, J. H. M. *Renaissance and Revolt: Essays in the Intellectual and Social History of Early Modern France.* Cambridge, Mass., 1987. Pages 73–97.

Smet, Ingrid A. R. de. *Menippean Satire and the Republic of Letters, 1581–1655.* Geneva, 1996.

J. H. M. SALMON

SAVONAROLA, GIROLAMO (1452–1498), Dominican preacher, reformer, apocalyptic prophet. One of the singular personalities of the Renaissance, Girolamo Savonarola was a mendicant friar whose claim to the divine gift of prophecy thrust him into the glare of Florentine and Italian—even European—affairs. Although as a foreigner and cleric he was excluded from Florence's political forum, he came to be hailed, and vilified, as the champion of the people and the guiding spirit of the post-Medicean republic.

Protesting his submissiveness to papal authority, Savonarola nonetheless turned aside repeated summons to Rome, hinted at the illegitimacy of Alexander VI's election, and, in letters to princes, dared advocate church reform by a council. He condemned the pursuit of reputation, wealth, and power, yet rallied Florentines to his vision of a New Jerusalem by promising that God would make them "more glorious, richer, more powerful than ever." Whether Savonarola achieved his ascendancy over the Florentines by divine mandate, opportunism, or a series of circumstances neither planned nor foreseen were questions passionately debated during his lifetime and long afterward.

Girolamo Savonarola. Profile protrait by Fra Bartolommeo (1472–1517). MUSEO DI SAN MARCO, FLORENCE/ALINARI/ART RESOURCE

Early Career. Girolamo Savonarola was born in Ferrara. His father, Niccolò, was a faltering banker; his grandfather, Michele Savonarola, a noted physician and medical writer. After a humanistic education Girolamo received an M.A. and studied medicine. In April 1475 he entered the Dominican convent of San Domenico in Bologna vowing to become "a knight of Christ" to battle "the great wretchedness of the world and the wickedness of men." Having had "to fight cruelly to keep the devil off [his] back," he was ready to sacrifice his body for his immortal soul.

After he took his vows Fra Girolamo was ordained and studied theology until 1482, when he was assigned to San Marco in Florence, where he began to preach. The dominant themes of his early sermons were penitential and Christocentric: human sin, divine punishment, Christ's redemptive love, and the contemplation of his passion ("the food of the soul"). He was not a success. His voice and Ferrarese speech grated on fastidious Florentine ears, and the dogmatic content of his sermons aroused little interest. Away from Florence, however, his preaching was more dramatic. In San Gimignano, where he was a Lenten preacher in 1485 and 1486, he announced that God was about to scourge the sinful world, particularly the church, and bring about a great reform. In 1487 he was called back to San Domenico in Bologna as master of studies. He also preached in various cities of Lombardy, where he repeated his prophecies of the coming scourge and reform.

In 1490 Savonarola was reassigned to San Marco in Florence at the request of Lorenzo de' Medici. Lorenzo seems to have sought the transfer on behalf of his friend, Giovanni Pico della Mirandola, a great admirer of the friar, but he also had a personal interest in the matter. San Marco was a showplace for Medici patronage and enlightened piety, and the return of the budding reformer-prophet would enhance the prestige both of the convent and its benefactors.

The Savonarola who returned to San Marco in 1490 preached "with a new message and a new style." A Dominican critic, Fra Giovanni Caroli, recalled that Savonarola's sensational preaching on the Book of Revelation appealed to the common people, and, "since it appeared that he spoke not with his own words but those of the spirit, the fame of his teaching and his goodness grew, and all the people followed him." Well-born ladies and gentlemen also attended his sermons, however, and pressed him with requests for private attention. Artists and literati of Lorenzo's circle, most notably Girolamo and Domenico Benivieni, Pico della Mirandola himself, Angelo Poliziano, Marsilio Ficino, Sandro Botticelli, and Michelangelo flocked to hear him, many describing themselves as spellbound by his eloquence.

Elected prior of San Marco, Savonarola's restoration of strict Observantist rule (insisting on a literal and austere observance of the order's founding Rule of 1215) and his resounding sermons gave the convent new visibility and standing in Florence and the region. San Marco swelled with new recruits, some from prominent families. In 1493, in league with the agents of Piero de' Medici, who had succeeded his father as first citizen, San Marco won papal permission to form its own Congregation of Tuscany, subsequently renamed the Congregation of San Marco.

Savonarola became more outspoken, excoriating tyrants who exploited the poor and attacking the unholy alliance of wealth, power, and religion. Although critics dismissed him as "the preacher of the desperate," there was no breakdown of relations with either Lorenzo or Piero. Savonarola attended Lorenzo on his deathbed in April 1492 and gave him his blessing. Long afterward he claimed that he had privately predicted Lorenzo's death as well as the death of Pope Innocent VIII in the same year. Between 1492 and 1494 he boldly proclaimed that God had directly inspired him with the knowledge that "someone like Cyrus" (2 Chron. 36:22) was coming across the Alps to conquer Italy, and he illustrated these prophecies with figures from dreams and apparitions—the sword of God poised over the earth and crosses in the sky over Rome and Jerusalem.

The French Invasion. In late summer 1494 King Charles VIII of France embarked on the conquest of the kingdom of Naples. Unopposed, he crossed the northern border of Tuscany in late October. The Florentines were in panic. Piero de' Medici had denied Charles's request for free passage through Florentine territory, and now the king was poised to retaliate by sacking the city.

Piero rushed to the king's camp, but paid a high price for peace: surrender of Florentine fortresses and strategic towns and a huge financial subvention. The news ignited rebellion in Florence. Returning with an armed escort, Piero was denied admission to the Palazzo della Signoria. The following day he and his brothers fled the city.

The Medici nemesis was Savonarola's triumph. Charles VIII, the friar asserted, was the Cyrus of his prophecies, the sword of God, come to scourge Italy and the church. With terrifying images of the Flood he exhorted the Florentines to build a spiritual ark for all true penitents. Chosen by the seat of the executive branch of government, the Signoria, to lead a special embassy to the king's camp, he insisted that Charles bypass Florence, but the French army entered the city on 17 November. When Charles demanded the restoration of his new ally, Piero de' Medici, the Florentines adamantly refused. After days of tense bargaining, an anti-French riot, and more talks with Savonarola, the king accepted a reduced subsidy and, on 28 November, left Florence.

Florence: The New Jerusalem. One crisis was over, a second was beginning. The populace angrily rejected the limited reforms proposed by a "false and fraudulent" *parlamento,* or mass assembly, and, aided by a few sympathetic patricians, forced the leadership to consider serious constitutional change.

At this point Savonarola entered the debate. Before proceeding to the matter of moral and spiritual renewal, he said, Florence must provide a new form for its government, "either as the Venetians do it, or in some better way as God will inspire you." The Venetian way, long admired in Florence, was represented by the proposal to replace the city's patchwork of councils with a single sovereign body on the order of Venice's Maggior Consiglio (great council) of 1,500 to 2,000 nobles. With increasingly enthusiastic support from Fra Girolamo, this was adopted in late December 1494. Aptly called the Consiglio Maggiore, the new deliberative body was the largest Florence had ever had, with about 3,000 members, all of them male. Savonarola hailed the measure as the foundation of the *governo popolare* (popular government) and claimed credit for it. So relieved were Florentines with the resolution of the constitutional crisis and so persuasive was Savonarola's holy eloquence, that the irony of labeling as "popular" a design modeled on Venetian oligarchy seems to have been lost.

From December 1494, preaching almost daily, Savonarola adumbrated a vision in which political form and spiritual matter were interdependent. The city was safe and free, a double blessing he proclaimed as evidence of his own godly ministry and the city's divine election. Now the Florentines must "reform their consciences," make good laws, and fulfill the city's destiny as the New Jerusalem. The fourth age of the world, the state of the tepid Christians, he said, was ending; the fifth age, of Antichrist, was about to begin. Florence, in partnership with the French crusader king, would lead the world into the sixth and final age of universal Christianity and peace. On 10 December he announced, for the first time, "the good news": the new, reformed Florence will be "glorious in the sight of God and men" and "have innumerable riches." "Spread your empire, and thus you will have power temporal and spiritual."

With this incantatory vow Savonarola came into his vocation as Florence's own prophet and theorist of its political theology. His millenarian vision (Florence as the New Jerusalem, center of a radiant Christian spirituality) resonated with early founding myths of the city's special destiny (Florence, the daughter of Rome) and themes of worldly hegemony. Florence would extend its empire, but it would be a sacred imperium; its people must first join him in building a holy republic, such a polity as would elect no other king but Christ.

For the next three years Savonarola struggled to keep the Florentines on course to the New Jerusalem. Together with the zealot Fra Domenico da Pescia and the somnambulist visionary Fra Silvestro Maruffi, and helped by a legion of devoted clerical and lay followers—dubbed Piagnoni (wailers) by their enemies—he and his lieutenants took the campaign directly to the people with frequent, intense, and often lurid sermons, marshaling Florence's riotous youth, staging religious processions, and organizing the notorious "bonfires of the vanities"—flaming pyres of suggestive books and pictures, immodest clothing and female ornament, and playing cards and dice—all considered dangerous to good morals.

Although Savonarola appears to have been satisfied that the constitutional reforms of December had brought the men of the artisan class into active political life, modern scholars have found little evidence that new men replaced the established political leadership, the *primati,* to any significant extent. Still, led by patricians such as Francesco Valori, the Frateschi (friar's party) pressed Savonarola's agenda in the Consiglio Maggiore and the Signoria with considerable success: an amnesty for former Mediceans to promote *la pace universale* (general peace), a law of appeal to discourage the use of the death sentence as a political weapon, the establishment of a public loan bank (Monte di Pietà) to extirpate Jewish pawnbroking, and other measures designed to remake Florence into a model of puritan Christianity. Abroad, they adhered to the French alliance and waged an unrelenting campaign to reconquer Pisa, which had broken free of Florentine rule.

None of this, the campaign for Pisa excepted, was unopposed. Conservative clerics challenged the friar's militant Observantism, criticized his involvement in politics, and were as skeptical of his claims to prophetic inspiration as any of the more secular-minded laity. Opponents in the Signoria and the Consiglio blocked favorite Savonarolan measures, including further electoral and fiscal reforms and the regulation of women's dress and ornamentation. A gang of young aristocrats, the Compagnacci (bad companions), resenting infringements on their pleasures, disrupted the friar's sermons and harassed Piagnoni processions. Opposition fortunes, like Savonarola's popularity, were contingent on numerous imponderables: the health of the economy, the price of bread, the recurrence of plague, the prospect of Charles VIII returning to resume his prophetic role, and pressure from Rome.

By summer 1497, after Pope Alexander VI had excommunicated Savonarola and all who supported him or listened to him preach, the tension between obedience to the pope and loyalty to the friar became increasingly difficult to bear, especially when Alexander retaliated against Italian merchants abroad and threatened an interdict on the city. In the same summer a plot to restore Piero de' Medici was discovered. The execution of the respected patrician Bernardo del Nero and four other conspirators without giving them their right to appeal was a severe blow to Savonarola's moral standing.

Trial by Fire. Early in 1498 Fra Domenico da Pescia accepted a rival preacher's challenge to test the validity of Savonarola's actions by an ordeal by fire. Public excitement forced Savonarola to give his consent. By the appointed day the affair had escalated into a broader test of the friar's apostolate. On 7 April, Florentines avid to see "the miracle" packed the Piazza della Signoria. Hours passed as the two parties bickered over details. A sudden downpour extinguished the waiting flames, an apparent sign of God's disapproval. Finally the government's men at arms dispersed the angry crowd. The fiasco was disastrous to Savonarola's credibility, and the next day a mob besieged San Marco. Again the Signoria's guard intervened, this time arresting Savonarola, Fra Domenico da Pescia, and Fra Silvestro Maruffi.

Questioned under torture, the three friars gave up damaging information. Savonarola confessed that he had falsified his prophecies, then recanted, then confessed again. On 23 May 1498, in the Piazza della Signoria, the three were hung and their bodies burned. Although their remains were collected and their ashes scattered over the Arno, devotees retrieved bits of bone and scraps of clothing as relics

Execution of Savonarola. Savonarola was hanged and his body burned in the Piazza della Signoria on 23 May 1498. Anonymous painting. MUSEO DI SAN MARCO, FLORENCE/ ALINARI/ART RESOURCE

of their three martyrs; after a brief period of persecution San Marco resumed its role as the center of Piagnonism. The forcible return of the Medici in 1512 was followed by a succession of populist prophets and ever more extreme millenarian schemes. In 1527 Piagnone radicals were active in the expulsion of the Medici and the establishment of the new republic. Once again Florentines proclaimed Christ their king and declared war on sin, but in 1530 troops of the Emperor Charles V restored the Medici. This time they gave up any pretense of republicanism, quashing dissent and transforming Florence into a hereditary dukedom. Piagnonism ceased to be an active political force for the next three centuries.

Outside Florence interest in Savonarola's prophecy had been widespread, with sixteenth-century Venice the major center for the publication of his sermons and writings. Through his meditations, devotional tracts, and doctrinal treatises, many translated into Italian and European vernaculars, Savonarola's reputation as a spiritual mentor as well as reformer grew steadily. His Christocentric, evangelical, and fideist ideas were an important influence on the Spirituali, sixteenth-century Catholic reformers. Luther and other Protestants regarded him as a forerunner, although the theory that he directly influenced Luther's doctrine of salvation by faith alone is surely overstated.

In post-Napoleonic Europe Savonarola again became an icon of liberation and spiritual rebirth and the protagonist of numerous historical dramas and biographies. In Italy, where he was hailed as a prophet and forerunner of the risorgimento, a group of San Marco scholars, dubbed the New Piagnoni, began the modern, archive-based study of his life and work that continues to enrich our knowledge and understanding of the friar and his times. Meanwhile, members of his order and other devotees are pressing for the reversal of his excommunication, the first step toward officially proclaiming him a saint.

Savonarola and Renaissance Art. Savonarola's relation to Renaissance art is very controversial. On one hand, his attacks on "pagan" influences in philosophy, morals, literature, and the arts and his consignment to flames of "immodest" paintings have earned him the reputation of a philistine as well as a puritan, the enemy of art—and of the

Renaissance *tout court*. On the other hand, some believe his religious teachings exerted a major influence on religious art at the turn of the sixteenth century. Both positions are exaggerated and imprecise. If Savonarola thought about art at all, he did so in instrumental and didactic terms. He was keenly aware of the power of visual images to convey meaning and insisted that painting and sculpture should lead viewers from the representation of nature to the contemplation of the Maker. Nudes and other images that aroused lascivious feelings and unworthy emotions were to be condemned. These views were neither original nor unique to Savonarola, although his vigorous assertion of them seems to have influenced some contemporary painters and sculptors. In the paintings of Fra Bartolommeo at San Marco, themes from Savonarola's sermons are evident. Sandro Botticelli's *Mystic Nativity* and *Mystic Crucifixion* contain apocalyptic themes apparently Piagnone in inspiration. Michelangelo's declared esteem for Savonarola has persuaded some scholars that his work is permeated with the friar's religious teachings, but the analysis is vague. Beyond these and a few lesser examples, evidence for Savonarola's influence stems mainly from his appearance in contemporary painting. In his Orvieto fresco of the Apocalypse, Luca Signorelli unflatteringly portrayed him as the Antichrist. Fra Bartolommeo's classic portrait depicts him as an inspired visionary, while some discern his baleful countenance among the prophets and sibyls in Michelangelo's *Last Judgment* in the Sistine Chapel. That Savonarola made a deep impression on some important artists is obvious, that his influence upon their art was uniformly important is less so.

In one Renaissance art, the making of books, Savonarola's historic place is assured. He was one of the first to understand the potential of printed books, not only for the dissemination of doctrine but also as a polemical tool. Working closely with printers and artists, he presided over the marriage of visual images with printed text, employing narrative scenes, meditational images, and schematic diagrams. Among the many editions of his sermons and works are some of the finest exemplars of Renaissance *incunabula* (books printed before 1500).

See also **Florence; Medici, House of.**

BIBLIOGRAPHY

Primary Works

The collected sermons and writings of Savonarola in Latin and Italian, *Opere di Girolamo Savonarola,* began publication in 1955 and is nearly complete in more than two dozen volumes. Very few texts are available in English, other than excerpts in anthologies.

Savonarola, Girolamo. *Prison Meditations on Psalms 51 and 31.* Edited and translated by John Patrick Donnelly. Milwaukee, Wis., 1994.

Secondary Works

Gaston, Vivian. "The Prophet Armed: Machiavelli, Savonarola, and Rosso Fiorentino's *Moses Defending the Daughters of Jethro.*" *Journal of the Warburg and Courtauld Institutes* 51 (1988): 220–225.

Gewirtz, Isaac. "Savonarola and Fifteenth-Century Printing." In *Girolamo Savonarola: Piety, Prophecy, and Politics in Renaissance Florence.* Edited by Donald Weinstein and Valorie R. Hotchkiss. Dallas, Tex., 1994.

Meltzoff, Stanley. *Botticelli, Signorelli, and Savonarola.* Florence, 1987.

Polizzotto, Lorenzo. *The Elect Nation: the Savonarolan Movement in Florence, 1494–1545.* Oxford, 1994.

Ridolfi, Roberto. *The Life of Girolamo Savonarola.* Translated by Cecil Grayson. New York, 1959.

Steinberg, Roland M. *Fra Girolamo Savonarola, Florentine Art, and Renaissance Historiography.* Athens, Ohio, 1977.

Trexler, Richard C. *Public Life in Renaissance Florence.* New York, 1980.

Villari, Pasquale. *The Life and Times of Girolamo Savonarola.* Translated by Linda Villari. London, 1889.

Weinstein, Donald. *Savonarola and Florence: Prophecy and Patriotism in the Renaissance.* Princeton, N.J., 1970.

DONALD WEINSTEIN

SAVOY. *See* **Piedmont-Savoy.**

SAXONY. A principality in northeastern Germany, Saxony's Renaissance history began in 1423 when Emperor Sigismund bestowed the vacant electoral duchy Saxony-Wittenberg upon Frederick, landgrave of Meissen and Thuringia. The "partition of Leipzig" in 1485 divided the Wettin territories between Frederick's grandsons, Ernest and Albert, resulting in the foundation of the two main lines of the Saxon house. The lands were never again united. Ernest, the elder brother, obtained Saxony-Wittenberg with the electoral title, central and southern Thuringia, the Franconian lands (Coburg), and parts of the Vogtland. Albert received Meissen and northern Thuringia. This arrangement created complex and deliberately confusing boundaries that became the root of future conflicts.

Of the two, Ernestine Saxony, centered in Wittenberg, initially overshadowed Albertine Saxony, governed from Dresden. Under the able leadership of Elector Frederick III, "the Wise" (ruled 1486–1525), Saxony-Wittenberg prospered and quickly became the most influential principality in the Holy Roman Empire. With the University of Leipzig under Albertine control, Frederick in 1502 founded a new university at Wittenberg, the Leucorea, for the training of future civil and ecclesiastical servants. The university offered a scholastic curriculum but welcomed champions of the new Renaissance learning. Among these was the Erfurt humanist Nicholas Marschalk, who set up a printing shop in Wittenberg and generated much enthusiasm for the Greek language and classical antiquity.

The arrival of the Augustinian Hermit Martin Luther (1483–1546) gave humanistic studies an even greater boost. Luther possessed qualities of intellect and leadership that soon made him the unchallenged leader of the Wittenberg academic community. Although not a humanist, he used humanist methods of biblical exegesis and in the process became a relentless critic of Scholasticism. His close friendship with Georg Spalatin, a student of Marschalk's, who was the elector's advisor responsible for the university, magnified Luther's influence. By the summer of 1518 when the indulgence controversy, kindled by the posting of his famous Ninety-Five Theses (31 October 1517), was beginning to attract attention to Luther as a religious reformer, he already had initiated a number of humanistic curricular reforms.

The appointment of Philipp Melanchthon (1497–1560) in 1518 to the newly created professorship in Greek lent further impetus to these changes. His inaugural lecture was a stirring manifesto of the humanists' pedagogical principles that now would dominate the Leucorea. As Luther found himself increasingly embroiled in religious controversies, Melanchthon not only became his chief theological supporter but also the leader of educational reform. These reforms changed Wittenberg from a scholastic and Roman Catholic school into a humanistic and Evangelical one by 1521, and made it one of the the most popular universities in Germany.

Frederick and his successors, John the Constant (ruled 1525–1532) and John Frederick the Magnanimous (ruled 1532–1554, elector until 1547), protected Luther's movement against the decrees of the church and emperor, making Ernestine Saxony the center of Reformation. By contrast, Duke George of Albertine Saxony (ruled 1500–1539) remained a staunch defender of the old church; deeply shaken by the Peasants' Revolt (1524–1525), he joined with the rulers of Brunswick and Brandenburg in the anti-Lutheran League of Dessau (1525).

Economic and political differences enhanced this confessional duality. While Ernestine Saxony was essentially agricultural, more densely populated Albertine Saxony profited greatly from textile production, mining, and trade. Duke Henry V (ruled 1539–1541) finally introduced the Lutheran Reformation in Albertine Saxony. His son and heir, Maurice (ruled 1541–1553), continued to push church reform but did not join the Schmalkaldic League, siding with the emperor Charles V instead. He was rewarded by the transferal of the electoral title and most of the Ernestine lands, including Wittenberg and its university, to the Albertine branch of the House of Wettin. In 1548 Maurice supported the Augsburg Interim of 1548, which would provoke a series of confessional controversies.

When Charles reneged on some of his earlier promises and as Maurice became increasingly alarmed about the emperor's ambitions in Germany, he entered into a secret alliance with King Henry II of France. In 1552 Maurice suddenly attacked Charles, leading a rebellion of German princes that forced the emperor, in the Treaty of Passau (1552), to give up his plans for imperial and religious restoration. The dominant position formerly enjoyed by the Wittenberg court had shifted to Dresden. Albertine Saxony, ably administered and benefiting from administrative reforms and a thriving economy, became the empire's leading Protestant state. Its universities flourished with Joachim Camerarius (1500–1574), a prolific classical scholar regarded by many as Erasmus's heir, generating new prominence for the University of Leipzig, and Philipp Melanchthon and his disciples, while increasingly controversial, assuring Wittenberg's continued popularity, notably among sympathizers of the Reformed creed.

Elector August I (ruled 1553–1586), brother and successor of Maurice, was one of the best rulers Saxony ever had. Leipzig especially benefited and became a center of arts during his reign. While increasingly critical of the Melanchthonian efforts to bridge the gap between the old and new faiths and the Wittenberg and Genevan reformations, August worked hard for greater inner-Lutheran confessional harmony. These efforts resulted in the Formula of Concord (1577) and the eventual banishment of all suspected Calvinists from Saxony, making the University of Wittenberg a bastion of Lutheran orthodoxy by the end of the century.

Saxony entered the seventeenth century with its Protestant leadership position eroded by the Calvinist Palatinate that had assumed an increasingly militant stance in the confessional controversies that were dividing Germany at this time. In the Thirty Years' War (1618–1648), elector John George (ruled 1611–1656) first sided with Emperor Ferdinand II, then attempted to lead a neutral third-party block, temporarily fought on the side of the Swedes, and signed a separate peace with the Habsburgs (1635), only to see his lands devastated during the last decade of the war. When the lengthy conflict finally ended with the Peace of Westphalia (1648), neighboring Brandenburg had replaced Saxony as the leading state in northern Germany.

See also **Holy Roman Empire** *and biographies of Martin Luther and Philipp Melanchthon.*

BIBLIOGRAPHY

Bachmann, Manfred, et al., eds. *Der silberne Boden: Kunst und Bergbau in Sachsen.* Stuttgart and Leipzig, Germany, 1990.

Blaschke, Karlheinz. *Sachsen im Zeitalter der Reformation.* Gütersloh, Germany, 1970.

Grossmann, Maria. *Humanism in Wittenberg, 1485–1517.* Nieuwkoop, Netherlands, 1975.

Junghans, Helmar, ed. *Das Jahrhundert der Reformation in Sachsen.* Berlin, 1989.

Kötzschke, Rudolf, and Hellmut Kretzschmar. *Sächsische Geschichte.* 1935. Reprint, Frankfurt am Main, Germany, 1965.

BODO NISCHAN

SCALIGER, JOSEPH JUSTUS (1540–1609), French philologist and historical chronologer. Scaliger believed the fable invented by his father, Julius Caesar Scaliger, that they were descendants of the lords of Verona. Moving from his home in Gascony to Paris at age eighteen, he learned Greek on his own in a prodigiously short time, and progressed to Hebrew and other oriental languages. His masters included Adrien Turnèbe, Denys Lambin, and Jacques Cujas. In 1562 Scaliger converted to Calvinism, and in 1593 he left France for the University of Leiden, where he remained until his death.

Scaliger made his reputation as a philologist with his editions of, and commentaries on, the extant fragments of the Latin dictionary of Festus (1575), the poets Catullus, Tibullus, and Propertius (1577), and the astronomical poem of Manilius (1579). His intellectual power startled his contemporaries and made him the leading scholar of his time. His conduct towards his fellow scholars on the printed page was ambitious and competitive, partly because of his exaggerated sense of personal honor but mostly because of the rules of the genre, for late Renaissance scholarship was still conducted as a rhetorical contest. His private character was humane and won him lasting friendships, especially among the learned magistrates of Paris.

Scaliger's work on historical chronology began with *De emendatione temporum* (On the emendation of chronology; 1583) and was crowned by *Thesaurus temporum* (Treasury of chronology; 1606). These works laid a new foundation for the history of civilization in the ancient Near East and Mediterranean, and embedded Judaism and Christianity in that context.

BIBLIOGRAPHY

Grafton, Anthony. *Joseph Scaliger: A Study in the History of Classical Scholarship.* 2 vols. Oxford, 1983–1993.

WILLIAM MCCUAIG

SCALIGER, JULIUS CAESAR (1484–1558), Italian scholar, polemicist, and theorist. His father, Benedetto Bordone of Padua, was a miniature painter who moved his family to Venice soon after the birth of his son Giulio in 1484. In his teens, Giulio Bordone joined the Franciscan order for a time and later frequented the printing house of Aldo Manuzio. In the years 1509–1515 Giulio served as a soldier in the wars of Italy, then studied at the University of Padua, graduating in 1519. Subsequently he must have studied medicine, the profession he was practicing by the mid-1520s. His translation of some of the *Lives* of Plutarch into Italian was published at Venice in 1525 under his native name—but thereafter Giulio Bordone reinvented himself as Julius Caesar Scaliger, a scion of the clan (the della Scala or Scaliger) that had once ruled Verona. The humiliating truth leaked out before the end of the sixteenth century, but Joseph Justus Scaliger, the famous son of Julius Caesar, defended the imaginary descent of his father and himself. The question remained open until the research of Myriam Billanovich established conclusively the singular identity of Giulio Bordone and Julius Caesar Scaliger in 1968.

At the end of 1524 Scaliger migrated from Italy to southwest France in the service of Antonio Della Rovere, who had received the bishopric of Agen. Scaliger married, settled, and raised his family there, earning a solid reputation and a comfortable living from the practice of medicine, and participating, despite his isolation, in literary and intellectual life. In 1538 he was investigated on suspicion of heresy, but the case was quashed. As an intellectual Scaliger belongs to the Aristotelian tradition. He wrote on a variety of topics (including botany and zoology) and was also a prolific but undistinguished poet; some of his writings were published posthumously.

Scaliger gained notoriety for the militancy of his polemics against Erasmus and Gerolamo Cardano. In 1531 and 1537 Scaliger published two *Orationes* (Diatribes) against Erasmus's dialogue *Ciceronianus* (1528), which had condemned the excessive devotion of European Christians, especially Italians, to classical Latin, and by extension, to pagan values. Scaliger himself was not an exponent of pure and classical Latin, however. Indeed, he practiced and justified the incorporation of scholastic terms from medieval Latin into the modern vocabulary. In 1550 Cardano, a noted physician and mathematician, published the first edition of his *De subtilitate rerum* (On subtlety), a miscellaneous and highly idiosyncratic work of natural philosophy. Scaliger attacked it from an Aristotelian stance in his *Exotericae exercitationes* (Exercises for nonspecialists; 1557). Another opponent of Scaliger was François Rabelais; their dislike of one another arose out of their mutual disdain for the other's medical competence. Scaliger's *De causis linguae Latinae* (On the causes of the Latin language; 1540) discussed the philosophy and principles of grammar and language. His *Poetics* (1561) was built on Aristotle's theory of literature and greatly influenced French classicism in the seventeenth century. It is today the most widely studied of his works.

BIBLIOGRAPHY

Primary Work

Scaliger, Julius Caesar. *Poetices libri septem* (Sieben Bücher über die Dichtkunst; Poetics in seven books). Edited by Luc Deitz, Gregor Vogt-Spira, and Manfred Fuhrmann. Stuttgart, Germany, 1994–. A multivolume critical edition of the Latin text with German translation.

Secondary Works

Jensen, Kristian. *Rhetorical Philosophy and Philosophical Grammar: Julius Caesar Scaliger's Theory of Language.* Munich, 1990. Includes a biographical chapter on Scaliger.

Maclean, Ian. "The Interpretation of Natural Signs: Cardano's *De subtilitate* Versus Scaliger's *Exercitationes*." In *Occult and Scientific Mentalities in the Renaissance.* Edited by Brian Vickers. Cambridge, U.K., 1984. Pages 231–252.

WILLIAM MCCUAIG

SCAMOZZI, VINCENZO (1548–1616), Italian architect, theorist, writer. In addition to numerous extant architectural drawings, Vincenzo Scamozzi's built works survive throughout the Veneto, and his architectural writings were widely diffused in many successive editions, compendia, and translations from the original Italian into English, French, German, and Dutch. His importance as a late Renaissance figure lies in his profound classical erudition, both textual and architectural, and his ability to incorporate that understanding into his architectural and literary practice.

Family, Education, and Early Career. Vincenzo's father, Giandomenico Scamozzi (1526–1582), moved from Lombardy to Vicenza in 1546 and enjoyed a modest career in the building trades and as a surveyor. His enduring contribution to the history of sixteenth-century culture lay in providing the initial impetus for the first collected and annotated edition of the architectural writings of Sebastiano Serlio, *Tutte l'opere d'architettura di Sebastiano Serlio Bolognese,* which Vincenzo completed and published in 1584. The precedent for this enterprise was the edition with extensive learned commentary by Daniele Barbaro of Vitruvius's *Ten Books on Architecture,* which was first published in Italian in 1556. This work, with woodcut illustrations by Andrea Palladio, was one of the principal formative influences on the young Vincenzo, whose copy of the second edition of 1567 (Vatican Library) is full of marginal comments made when he read this work in 1574. Vincenzo's privileged upbringing and education, which probably included attendance at the Bishop's Seminary and Olympic Academy in Vicenza, was completed by the most formative event of his early maturity: an extended study tour south, between 1578 and 1580, to Naples and then Rome, where he stayed for over a year, taking mathematics classes with Christopher Clavius at the Collegio Romano and immersing himself in the study of both ancient and modern buildings.

In 1580 Scamozzi published an engraving illustrating his proposed reconstruction of the baths of Diocletian; after establishing himself in Venice about that time, following the death of Palladio, Scamozzi published his *Discorsi sopra l'antichità di Roma* (Discourse on the antiquities of Rome) in 1582, comprising forty commentaries to accompany a series of engravings of ancient Roman buildings by Gianbattista Pittoni. With his extensive citation of ancient authors, including Horace, Livy, Pliny, and Vitruvius, Scamozzi established his literary credentials and displayed his classical erudition. The first collected edition of Serlio's works, which followed in 1584, secured Scamozzi's reputation.

Architectural Practice. After early training and practice in the art of building undertaken with his father in the late 1560s, Scamozzi emerged as an independent architect in the 1570s, when he obtained several commissions for palaces in Vicenza and villas in the Veneto. The villa Rocca Pisani of 1576–1579 is his best work, revealing Scamozzi's ability to successfully design a variety of spatial volumes for practical purposes within a square plan, thus improving upon the celebrated prototype of Palladio's Villa Rotonda (which Scamozzi himself

Vincenzo Scamozzi. Design of a Tuscan arch from *L'idea della architettura universale* (1615).

later completed, 1581–1589) by replacing its rigorous, ideal symmetry with a coherent, workable plan which was more functional and comfortable for its inhabitants. In the early 1580s Scamozzi also completed Palladio's Olympic Theater in Vicenza by sensitively adding perspective scenery, based on a woodcut by Palladio, to re-create the seven avenues of Thebes for the inaugural performance of 1585, when Sophocles's *Oedipus Rex* was performed in Italian translation. In 1588, on commission from Vespasiano Gonzaga, the duke of Sabbioneta (near Mantua), Scamozzi designed the first autonomous theater building of the Renaissance. It had an independent facade, together with an innovative horseshoe-shaped auditorium. Scamozzi also designed several temporary displays of architecture based on classical models, most notably for the coronation ceremony in Venice of the dogaressa Morosina Grimani in 1597.

However, Scamozzi's reverence for the fundamental tenets of classical design impeded his success in Venice. The inclusion of roundheaded Roman arches in his proposal for the rebuilding of the Rialto Bridge in the 1580s resulted in a design which was unsuited to the site and function the bridge was required to serve. Scamozzi justified his design in a written memorial through references to Vitruvius and Leon Battista Alberti, but the project was rightly rejected, although his second design with a single nonclassical arch is very close to that actually built in 1588 by Antonio da Ponte. Scamozzi's rigid beliefs about correct architectural design also exacerbated the problems surrounding his completion of Jacopo Sansovino's Public Library in Venice because the extra story he wished to add would have ruined the building and its harmonious relation to the other buildings in Piazza San Marco. Problems also arose with Scamozzi's overtly Romanist church of Santa Maria della Celestia in Venice of 1582, which was directly based on the ancient Pantheon. Construction at the Celestia was interrupted when it was only half-built, and it was then abandoned for over a decade until 1605, when it was demolished and replaced with a different design by another architect. One of the Celestia nuns described Scamozzi's building as a "monster of architecture—a body without its head."

Scamozzi's difficult personality and possible incompetence led to him being dismissed as architect for the church of San Nicolò da Tolentino, Venice, of 1590–1595. He was also antagonistic to his gifted sixteenth-century predecessors whose work he had to complete. In his treatise of 1615 Scamozzi openly disparaged Sansovino's Library, and he simply ignored the influential treatise and built works of Palladio. Scamozzi was equally unhelpful when he met Inigo Jones in Vicenza in 1613, and Jones described Scamozzi as "purblind." An impression of arrogance is also created in the index to his treatise, which includes entries such as "Tasteless patrons always build badly." And yet Scamozzi was also one of the first architects able to see beyond classical norms, demonstrating a remarkable appreciation of French Gothic architecture in the sketches and commentary of his travel diary, which record his voyage from Paris to Venice in 1599–1600.

Late Theoretical Career and Influence. Following in the footsteps of Serlio and Palladio, Scamozzi distinguished himself as an architectural theorist through publication. In the second edition of Serlio's collected works (1600), Scamozzi included an important "Discourse on Architecture." A thinly disguised self-penned description of his buildings was also included in a 1604 guide to the city of Venice. Scamozzi's most important publication is his treatise of 1615, *L'idea della architettura universale,* of which only six of the projected ten books were ever published. Scamozzi's treatise is justly considered the last project to represent exhaustively the science of architecture following the Vitruvian model. Rather than simply focusing on the hierarchy of the orders as Giacomo Barozzi da Vignola had, Scamozzi, like Palladio before him, aimed to cover the whole intellectual and practical spectrum of architectural thought and knowledge.

Scamozzi directly influenced two important seventeenth-century architects. Inigo Jones read and annotated the treatises of Palladio and Scamozzi in tandem (Worcester College, Oxford), and in the last few years of his life Scamozzi probably had a hand in teaching the young Baldassare Longhena (1597–1682). His name was taken up by Ottavio Bertotti-Scamozzi (1719–1790) of Vicenza, who became the most famous recipient of the endowment established by Scamozzi in his will. Ironically, Bertotti-Scamozzi is remembered for his measured drawings and commentary on Palladio's works. Although Scamozzi's treatise was not greatly influential in its original form, his hierarchy of the architectural orders was widely diffused in many publications, and they were as often cited and used as those of his more famous predecessors.

BIBLIOGRAPHY

Primary Works

Scamozzi, Vincenzo. *Discorsi sopra l'antichità di Roma di Vincenzo Scamozzi Architetto Vicentino, con quaranta tavole in rame* (Discourse on the antiquities of Rome by Vincenzo Scamozzi, Vicentine architect, with forty engraved plates). Venice, 1582. Facsimile, with an introduction by Loredana Olivato, Milan, 1991.

Scamozzi, Vincenzo. "Discorso intorno alle parti dell'architettura" (Discourse on the parts of architecture) In *Tutte l'opere d'architettura di Sebastiano Serlio Bolognese* (All the works of architecture of Sebastiano Serlio of Bologna) Venice, 1584. 2d ed. Venice, 1600. Facsimile, Bologna, Italy, 1987.

Scamozzi, Vincenzo. *L'idea della architettura universale di Vincenzo Scamozzi architetto veneto divisa in dieci libri* (Toward a universal architecture, by Vincenzo Scamozzi, architect of the Veneto, divided into ten books). 2 vols. Venice, 1615. Facsimile, Ridgewood, N.J., 1964.

Scamozzi, Vincenzo. *Taccuino di viaggio da Parigi a Venezia (14 marzo–11 maggio 1600).* (Travel diary from Paris to Venice, 14 March–11 May 1600). Edited by Franco Barbieri. Venice, 1959.

Secondary Works

Barbieri, Franco. *Vincenzo Scamozzi.* Vicenza, 1952.

Franz, Rainald. *Vincenzo Scamozzi, 1548–1616: Der Nachfolger und Vollender Palladios.* Petersberg, Germany, 1999.

Oechslin, Werner. "Premesse a una nuova lettura dell'*Idea della architettura universale* di Scamozzi." In *L'idea della architettura universale di Vincenzo Scamozzi architetto Veneto.* 2 vols. Venice, 1615. Facsimile, Vicenza, Italy, 1997. Vol. 1, pp. xi–xxxviii.

ANDREW JAMES HOPKINS

SCANDINAVIAN KINGDOMS. During the high Middle Ages the Scandinavian kingdoms had been united under Danish sovereignty. After the collapse of the Kalmar Union in 1448, the following centuries were characterized by constant rivalry between Sweden and Denmark, who managed to keep Finland and Norway-Iceland, respectively, under their control (see table).

Initially Denmark tended to be dominant, but Sweden emerged victorious from the 1657–1660 war, and Denmark lost significant parts of its territory. For Sweden the seventeenth century was a period of political and cultural flowering, with expansion into Russian, Polish, and German territories.

The population consisted mainly of farmers and fisherman. A modest surplus was achieved, and Scandinavia exported cattle, herring, and timber. In the cities, merchants were gradually developing new wealth

Reigns of Scandinavian Monarchs

Sweden (with Finland)	
Sten Sture the Younger	1512–1520
Christian II (king of Denmark)	1520–1523
Gustav Vasa	1523–1560
Erik XIV	1560–1568
Johan III	1568–1592
Sigismund	1592–1599
Charles IX	1599–1611
Gustav II Adolf	1611–1632
Christina	1632–1654
Denmark (with Norway and Iceland)	
Christian II	1513–1523
Frederick I	1523–1533
Christian III	1534–1559
Frederick II	1559–1588
Christian IV	1588–1648

Beginnings. The Renaissance reached Scandinavia during the first decades after 1500. German and Flemish artists were invited by kings and noblemen; the first individualizing portraits known in Scandinavia represent the Danish king Christian II.

Humanists were inspired by the desire to reestablish classical Latin and demonstrate to the rest of the world the virtues and venerable age of the local cultures. The Dane Christiern Pedersen had Saxo's national history *Gesta Danorum* (The deeds of the Danes; c. 1200) printed in Paris in 1514, and the Swedes Johannes and Olaus Magnus published monumental descriptions of Nordic geography and customs in Venice: *Carta marina* (A map of the sea; 1539) and *Historia de gentibus septentrionalibus* (A history of the Nordic peoples; 1555). Johannes Magnus's *Historia de omnibus Gothorum Sveonumque regibus* (History of all the kings of the Goths and Swedes) of 1554 asserts that the Swedish people stem from Noah's grandchild Magog, and this "Gothic theory" was firmly maintained.

The printing press had been introduced toward the end of the fifteenth century and played a significant role in the vernacular discussions leading to the adoption of Protestantism. In Denmark, Paul Helgesen defended Catholicism, Hans Tausen and Christiern Pedersen Lutheranism. The Swedish humanist Olaus Petri published Protestant sermons, hymns, and educational works for his compatriots, as well as *En swensk cröneka* (The Swedish chronicle; c. 1535).

But the main initiative for religious reform came from the kings: Gustav Vasa declared Sweden Lutheran in 1527, and Christian III did the same for

Denmark in 1536. Only the Icelanders offered energetic resistance. There the last Catholic bishop, Jón Arason, a powerful Renaissance figure who was both a great poet and a secular lord with his private merchant ships trading on the Continent, was beheaded by the Danish authorities in 1550.

Lutheran Renaissance. After the establishment of Lutheranism, Philipp Melanchthon became the great inspiration for generations of German and Scandinavian students with his ideas of harmonizing Christian faith with pagan classicism. To promote individual piety, the Bible was translated into the vernaculars. Olaus Petri and his brother Laurentius Petri published a Swedish translation in 1541. Christiern Pedersen's Danish translation was published in 1550 and imposed on Norwegian readers, too. Michael Agricola translated the New Testament into Finnish in 1548, and an Icelandic translation of the Bible by Gudbrandur Thorláksson was published in 1584.

Ecclesiastical and educational institutions were reformed in accordance with Wittenberg ideas, which organized them into a centralized system with the king at its head. The universities of Uppsala and Copenhagen had been closed, but that of Copenhagen was reopened, and Latin schools for the elementary education of boys were established all over Danish territory. Copenhagen had the only university in that territory, while the Swedes gradually opened new universities in their dependent areas: Dorpat in 1632, Åbo in 1640, and Lund in 1668. Little science was taught, as the main purpose was to educate teachers and clergymen; those who had higher career ambitions had to go abroad. In medicine, the ideas of Paracelsus (Theophrast Bombast von Hohenheim, 1493–1541), who emphasized the chemical basis of medicine, were breaking the monopoly held by Galen, whose medicine was based on the four humors. The Dane Peder Sørensen and the Swede Johannes Bureus led the way.

Under Melanchthon's auspices a great classicizing Latin literature developed with almost all typical Renaissance genres represented. Kings and other patrons paraded as Augustus reincarnated (the Swedish royal name Gustauus even offered itself as an anagram), and their court poets were new Virgils and Horaces. There were many occasions for prose, too, mostly in the form of orations. In addition, rhetorical, political, and moral philosophical theory was cultivated, and important themes were the vindication of local eminence and national history. The vernaculars were largely confined to religious literature; they also remained the women's medium for both speaking and writing.

The Danish Efflorescence, c. 1550–1600. The death of Christian III and coronation of Frederick II were occasions for orations and poems by Erasmus Laetus and others, and a majestic funeral monument in Roskilde cathedral was made by the Netherlander Cornelis Floris. In Sweden, Gustav Vasa was celebrated at his funeral as the ideal monarch by Peder Swart in a Swedish oration and by Laurentius Petri Gothus in a Latin poem, and the king rests in the cathedral of Uppsala with an elaborate funerary monument, also Netherlandic. His son's coronation was eulogized by the German poet Henricus Mollerus.

In Denmark, Frederick II was a great patron, attracting artists, architects, and musicians and supporting the education of promising students. His castles, especially Kronborg, were important Renaissance buildings magnificently decorated. The nobility took up the challenge both in building activities and in the luxurious celebration of family events, and gradually lavish funeral monuments invaded the churches. Leading poets were Erasmus Laetus with huge Latin epics, Hans Jørgensen Sadolin and Hans Frandsen with lyrics, and Hans Thomessøn and Hans Christensen Sthen with Danish hymns. Peder Hegelund and Hieronymus Justesen Ranch composed comedies on biblical themes; Ranch's *Kong Salomons hylding* (Coronation of King Solomon) was written for the coronation of Frederick II's son in 1584. Jakob Madsen did pioneering work in the study of the Danish language. Noblemen and noblewomen collected folk ballads, and the historiographer Anders Sørensen Vedel edited the world's first ballad collection in 1591. Arild Huitfeldt wrote his *Danmarckis rigis krønicke* (Chronicle of Denmark; 1604). Tycho Brahe (1546–1601) established a brilliant research center, Uraniborg, which attracted leading scientists from the whole of Europe. With his versatile talent in all branches of learning, he is the towering Renaissance genius of Scandinavia, and his Latin poems are unrivaled. His sister Sophie participated in his activities and became famous as the first erudite woman in Scandinavia.

While Danish culture thrived, Norway and Iceland were in a less favored position. But humanist circles survived: in Bergen, Mats Størssøn, Laurents Hanssøn, and Absalon Pederssøn Beyer studied Norse literature and history; and Jens Nielssøn, Jacob Jacobssøn Wolf, and Halvard Gunnarssøn were active at the Latin school in Oslo. When in 1589 a storm

Stockholm. View of the city in 1535 (detail). STOCKHOLMS STADSMUSEUM

compelled the Scottish king James VI to celebrate his marriage to the Danish princess Anne in Oslo, it was a great occasion for poetry and speeches. In Iceland, the cathedral schools of Hólar and Skálholt were centers of learning. Oddur Einarsson and Arngrímur Jónsson were eager to defend their country against foreign prejudice, and the latter's *Brevis commentarius de Islandia* (Brief comment on Iceland; 1593) and *Crymogaea* (1609) became famous.

Meanwhile in Sweden, Gustav Vasa had felt little obligation to support culture, although he did take care to have his own deeds described by Peder Swart, also the author of a drama, *Tobie comedia* (Tobias's comedy; 1550). But important building projects were undertaken, such as the castle of Gripsholm, the city of Kalmar, and the monastery of Vadstena.

Under Gustav Vasa's sons arts and scholarship developed. Erik XIV reopened the University of Uppsala in 1566, and regulations were laid down for Latin grammar schools. Laurentius Petri Gothus, Petrus Michaelis Ostrogothus, and Ericus Jacobi Skinnerus composed historical and panegyric poetry, and as late as 1620 Sylvester Johannis Phrygius remembered Johan III's death with *Threnologia dramatica* (Dramatic tearful description). Erik Sparre published a political treatise, *Pro lege, rege, et grege* (For the law, the king, and the commoners), in 1585 and Gothus published works on theology and philosophy.

In Finland, Paulus Juusten and Erik Herkepaeus established a modest scholarly milieu around the cathedral school of Turku. Juusten's edition of *Catalogus et ordinaria successio episcoporum Finlandensium* (Chronicle of medieval bishops; printed in 1728) was a significant humanistic work, similar in kind to Christiern Pedersen's edition of Saxo. He also wrote a vivid description of an embassy to Moscow. Theodoricus Petri Rutha edited *Piae cautiones* (Pious songs; 1582), a students' songbook, in which many of the most delightful medieval poems from Scandinavia have been preserved with their melodies.

The Swedish Efflorescence, c. 1600–1650. Both Scandinavian kings engaged themselves in the German Thirty Years' War, the Danish Christian IV with disastrous results, while for the Swedes Gustav II Adolf's campaigns marked the beginning of a steady political and cultural expansion.

During the reigns of Gustav Adolf and his daughter, Christina, artists and other intellectuals gathered in Stockholm, among them John Amos Comenius, René Descartes, Hugo Grotius, and Nicolaus Heinsius. Christina retained a French court painter and a German architect, and she had Drottningholm Castle built near Stockholm. Danish Christian IV also engaged in magnificent construction projects: the castle of Rosenborg and various other elegant buildings in Copenhagen, as well as in Frederiksborg in northern Zealand. When Oslo was destroyed by fire in 1624, Christian IV rebuilt the city and modernized its castle, Akershus, in Renaissance fashion. In the cities, rich burghers built impressive houses.

Foreign poets—Bohemian, Netherlandic, and French—celebrated Gustav Adolf's deeds in Latin epics. Learning thrived, and the rivalry between Sweden and Denmark influenced scholarship: for example, the Swede Johannes Bureus and the Dane Ole Worm competed in collecting runic inscriptions. Johannes Messenius wrote a massive general history of Scandinavia. Lars Wivallius was a charming poet, who was unusual in treating Latin and Swedish with equal ease and elegance, even now and then mixing the two into a hilarious macaronic idiom. By now, the revolt against Latin dominance was manifesting itself, as in the pseudonymous work *Thet swenska språketz klagemål* (Lament of the Swedish Language) of 1658.

In Denmark, the poet Claus Christoffersen Lyschander was active. He composed for the nobility and the king in Danish, producing, for example, *Den grønlandske Chronica* (The Greenlandic chronicle; 1608) and *Den Calmarnske Triumph* (The Triumph of Calmar; 1611); his *Her Christian den Feurtis Udvellelsis oc Hyldings Historia* (History of Christian V's coronation; 1623) saw this event in a framework derived from Herodotus and Xenophon. Anders Arrebo paraphrased the Bible's story of the creation *Hexaemeron rhytmico-danicum* (The six days), and Anders Bording wrote the first great lyrics in the Danish language.

In Norway almost all influential posts had gradually been taken over by Danes, whereas in Iceland the local population, though poor, was left in charge. There, the tradition of anonymous poetry, *rimur,* flourished, and poets such as Einar Sigurdsson composed hymns. In Finland, the opening of the Academy of Åbo in 1640 stimulated intellectual life, and Enevald Svenonius was reviving classical Latin in his dissertations.

The courts of Christian IV and Christina excelled in elegant entertainment. Christian IV inherited his father's musicians and attracted new ones; most famous were the Dane Mogens Pedersen and the German Heinrich Schütz, the latter being in charge of the music for an extravagant princely wedding in 1634. Court "ballets" were popular, such as Georg Stiernhielm's Swedish *Freds-afl* (Fruits of peace; 1649); he also celebrated Christina in a number of poems and is considered the first great vernacular poet in Sweden with his *Hercules* (1647) and *Musae suethizantes* (Swedish-speaking muses; 1668).

How much of this cultural activity affected the everyday life of the commoners? Very little, no doubt. In the medieval churches, wall paintings had appealed directly to them as part of the religious teaching, but Renaissance art moved out of the churches and into the palaces. Most literature and music was composed for courtly occasions. In a way, the Latin schools were the most democratic feature of Renaissance culture, since they were open to pupils of relatively humble backgrounds and gave intelligent boys a chance of climbing the social ladder.

At the death of Christian IV in 1648, the Danish state was bankrupt, and six years later Sweden was shocked by Queen Christina's conversion to Catholicism and ensuing abdication. But art, literature, and

The King of Sweden. Gustavus Vasa hears the petition of Stockholm after taking the city in 1523. THE ROYAL LIBRARY, NATIONAL LIBRARY OF SWEDEN, STOCKHOLM

learning had made their impact. The first steps had been taken from collectivism to individualism and from piety to secularism, and Scandinavian ambitions of playing a respected role in the civilized world remained.

Book Collections. Only in Sweden and Denmark were notable book collections built up. Most of the Danish ones have since been scattered, but in Sweden, Elias Palmskiöld's collection in Uppsala and Samuel Älf's in Linköping are preserved. Skokloster Castle near Uppsala has a rich and beautiful library. But the bulk of Finnish and Swedish Renaissance books are now in the Royal Library of Stockholm and the University Library of Uppsala, while Norwegian, Icelandic, and Danish books are mainly in the Royal Library of Copenhagen.

BIBLIOGRAPHY

Åkerman, Susanna. *Queen Christina of Sweden and Her Circle: The Transformation of a Seventeenth-Century Philosophical Libertine*. Leiden, Netherlands, 1991.

Boyer, Régis. *Histoire des littératures scandinaves*. Paris, 1996.

Derry, T. K. *A History of Scandinavia: Norway, Sweden, Denmark, Finland, and Iceland*. London, 1979.

Friese, Wilhelm. *". . . Am Ende der Welt": Zur skandinavischen Literatur der frühen Neuzeit*. Leverkusen, Germany, 1989.

Jensen, Minna Skafte, ed. *A History of Nordic Neo-Latin Literature*. Odense, Denmark, 1995.

Merisalo, Outi, and Raija Sarasti-Wilenius, eds. *Mare Balticum, Mare Nostrum: Latin in the Countries of the Baltic Sea (1500–1800)*. Helsinki, 1994.

Toyne, S. M. *The Scandinavians in History*. Port Washington, N.Y., 1970.

Wade, Mara R. *Triumphus nuptialis danicus: German Court Culture and Denmark: The "Great Wedding" of 1634*. Wiesbaden, Germany, 1996.

MINNA SKAFTE JENSEN

SCEPTICISM. *See* **Skepticism.**

SCÈVE, MAURICE (1500?–1560?), French poet. Maurice Scève headed the Renaissance movement in Lyon and introduced mathematical and precise Neoplatonic and emblematic imagery into the poetic canon.

Born into a well-known bourgeois family in Lyon, Scève received a scholar's education and became a humanist rather than following in his father's footsteps as a magistrate. In 1536 Scève won the prize for the best *blason,* a descriptive poem on a part of the human body—in this instance, the eyebrow—in Clément Marot's collection of that year. This Renaissance fascination with the body and with anatomizing it through writing was to continue throughout his career. It was believed that Scève had discovered the tomb of Petrarch's Laura in the city of Avignon by deciphering the characters 'M.L.M.I.' on a tomb as *Madonna Laura Morta Iace* ('Here lies Lady Laura'). The female cadaver returns in his sonnet sequence *Délie,* an emblem book of 449 ten-line poems with fifty emblems and 9 poems inserted between them, first published in 1544. In *Délie* the beloved, whose name is the title of the work, is alternately a strong, sadistic lover who cruelly withholds her favors from the poet and the lost object of the poet's mourning, enshrined perhaps in emblem 50, that of the tomb and the candles. There has been speculation that Délie was actually Scève's fellow poet of the Lyon school, Pernette du Guillet, but no direct link has been established.

Scève's other major works include *La saulsaye* (The willow grove; 1547) and *Microcosme* (Microcosm; 1562), both works continuing his interest in visual imagery and in parallels between the human and natural worlds, as well as in the enigmatic nature of the sonnet sequence. Active in cultural movements of the time, Scève supervised the 1548 entry of Henry II into Lyon, a weeklong spectacle of living emblemata and a visual montage of French Renaissance culture.

BIBLIOGRAPHY

Primary Works

Scève, Maurice. *Délie*. Edited by Ian McFarlane. Cambridge, U.K., 1966. Critical edition with notes and introductory essay in English. Includes the emblems from the 1544 edition. Most accessible edition available to speakers of English, since *Délie* has never been translated.

Scève, Maurice. *Oeuvres complètes*. Edited by Pascal Quignard. Paris, 1974. Does not contain emblems, but does contain *Saulsaye* (The willow grove) and *Microcosme* (Microcosm).

Secondary Works

Coleman, Dorothy G. *Maurice Scève, Poet of Love: Tradition and Originality*. Cambridge, U.K., 1975. Ties Scève into the Petrarchan tradition of love poetry, how he subtends and subverts this tradition.

Giudici, Enzo. *Maurice Scève: Poeta della "Délie"*. Vol. 1. Rome, 1965. Vol. 2. Naples, Italy, 1967. Introduces Scève to modern scholarship. Provides historical, cultural, and literary contextualization of *Délie*.

de Mourgues, Odette. *Metaphysical, Baroque, and Précieux Poetry*. Oxford, 1953. Reads Scève as announcing baroque and précieux movements in French poetry. Classic study of lesser-read writers of the early modern period.

Tetel, Marcel. *Lectures scéviennes: L'emblème et les mots*. Paris, 1983. One of the few readings that fully takes into account the dual—that is, visual and verbal—nature of *Délie*. A poststructuralist account of how meaning is figured through both language and image.

MARIE MICHELLE STRAH

SCHEGK, JAKOB (Jakob Degen; 1511–1587), German philosopher and physician. The son of Bernhard Degen (Schegk), Jakob was born in Schorndorf, Württemberg, and attended school there. He studied at the University of Tübingen in the faculty of arts (Magister Artium, 1530) and subsequently in the faculty of theology, being ordained priest before 1534. After the introduction of the Reformation into Württemberg in 1534, Schegk studied law and then medicine at Tübingen (Doctor of Medicine, 1539). From c. 1532 he was *Konventor* (tutor) at the realist hostel of Tübingen's Arts Faculty. He taught Greek (1535), physics (1536–1552), dialectics (1564–1577), and medicine (1533–1577) at Tübingen, then retired due to blindness. In 1539 Schegk married Corona Vogler of Cannstatt (near Stuttgart), with whom he had a daughter and two sons. In 1553 he was appointed physician to Duke Christoph (1515–1568). He died in Tübingen.

An Aristotelian in the humanist tradition, Schegk taught Aristotle without recourse to scholastic commentaries. He published commentaries on the analytic part of the *Organon* (*Commentaria in Organi Aristotelis libros;* Tübingen, 1570); the *Topics* (*Perfecta et absoluta definiendi ars;* Tübingen, 1556; and *Commentaria in VII libros Topicorum Aristotelis;* Strasbourg, 1585); the *Physics* and *On the Soul* (*Erotemata in physica Aristotelis;* Tübingen, 1538; and *In octo physicorum sive de auditione physica libros Aristotelis commentaria;* Basel, 1546); and other related works on natural philosophy (*In reliquos naturalium Aristotelis libros commentaria;* Basel, 1550). In defense of Aristotle, Schegk was drawn into controversy with Petrus Ramus, rejecting the latter's theories of rhetorical proof while complementing his own Aristotelian logic with references to Galen.

Schegk's major work, *De demonstratione libri XV* (a commentary on Aristotle's *Posterior Analytics;* Basel, 1564), sets out his theory of knowledge and demonstration. Schegk distinguishes between analysis, concerned with the pure theory of syllogism or proof, and the topics, "popular and common knowledge." Following Plato, Schegk distinguishes between four levels of knowledge, of which the upper two, *dianoia* (thought) and *nous* (mind) attain to the intelligible world. Three levels of proof lead to different levels of perfection in knowledge: imperfect or incomplete proofs, complete proofs, and the "most perfect" proofs of metaphysics, which are of the mind and free of hypothesis. Hypotheses are not necessarily true but empirically probable, and the distinction between hypothetical and nonhypothetical principles reflects the degree of truth that can be attained in subsequent demonstration. Against Ramus, Schegk argued that most proofs cannot be free of hypothesis, so that definition and proof must be seen as separate.

Schegk also brought his understanding of physics to bear in the eucharistic controversies of the second half of the sixteenth century and the associated theological conflicts about the nature of Christ (see, for example, his *De una persona et duabus naturis Christi,* published in 1565). Arguing that Christ's corporeal body, glorified through being united with divinity, is not confined by space or time, he offered a philosophical basis for the Lutheran conviction of the real presence of Christ in the Eucharist, and the ubiquity of Christ's presence. His reservations about the omnipresence of Christ's ascended physical body, however, rendered him vulnerable to accusations that he espoused a Zwinglian theology of the Eucharist. Besides his commentaries on the Aristotelian corpus and his contributions to the Eucharistic controversy and other theological discussions of his day, Schegk published a number of works on medicine and at least one on jurisprudence.

Apart from the dispute with Ramus, Schegk's influence can be traced primarily within the University of Tübingen. He taught almost all the professors who were later to teach Johannes Kepler, notably Andreas Planer (later professor of logic), George Liebler (physics), and Michael Maestlin (mathematics and astronomy). Schegk's theory of proof and his understanding of the relationship between empirical proof and hypothesis influenced the work of his students and thus, albeit indirectly, Kepler's thinking.

BIBLIOGRAPHY

Primary Works

Schegk, Jakob. *Explicatio in priorem librum Priorum Analyticorum Aristotelis* (1565). In *Ein Collegium logicum im 16. Jahrhundert. Mittheilungen aus einer Handschrift der k. Universitätsbibliothek Tübingen*. Edited by Christoph Sigwart. Tübingen, Germany, 1890. Lecture notes taken by Martin Crusius, transcribed by Christoph Sigwart.

Schegk, Jakob. *Hyperaspistes responsi ad quatuor epistolas Petri Rami*. Tübingen, Germany, 1570. Facsimile ed., Frankfurt am Main, Germany, 1976.

Secondary Works

Kusukawa, Sachiko. "Lutheran Uses of Aristotle: A Comparison between Jacob Schegk and Philip Melanchthon." In *Philosophy in the Sixteenth and Seventeenth Centuries: Conversations with Aristotle*. Edited by Constance Blackwell and Sachiko Kusukawa. Forthcoming.

Risse, Wilhelm. *Die Logik der Neuzeit*. Vol. 1, *1500–1640*. Stuttgart-Bad Cannstatt, Germany, 1964.

CHARLOTTE METHUEN

SCHOLASTICISM. A term first used in a derogatory sense by sixteenth-century humanists, "scholasticism" has come to mean a historical movement or a system of thought bequeathed by that movement. Renaissance scholasticism was a revival of medieval scholasticism, which had systematized the learning of the schools, mainly in philosophy and theology, to a lesser extent in law and medicine. It may be characterized in general by its method, language, and proponents, then by various schools into which it was divided in the early and later Renaissance.

General Characteristics. "Scholastic method" means literally a common way of teaching and learning in the schools. It was often caricatured as an arid verbalism, a closed and a priori system of thought perpetuated by rote memorization. To the contrary, it proposed itself as a rational method of investigating problems in any discipline, examined from opposing points of view, to reach an intelligent, scientific solution consistent with known facts, accepted authorities, human reason, and, ultimately, Christian faith. Its main instruments were definition, division (or distinction), and argumentation, and its ideal goal was *scientia* (science) in the Aristotelian sense, though frequently it could reach only probable or dialectical conclusions.

Factors that shaped Renaissance Scholasticism include the invention of printing (c. 1450), the fall of Constantinople (1453) and the resulting influx of Greek scholars to the West, the discovery of America (1492), and the Protestant Reformation (from c. 1517). The rise of humanism was also a factor, since humanist denunciations were directed against the late medieval penchant for barbarous Latinity, subtle distinctions, principally in the *summulae* (summary works on logic) treatment of sophisms, and disregard for sources, mainly in the use of the Bible.

By the Renaissance a stylized format for meeting these challenges had been generally adopted. It consisted of presenting, in order, difficulties and matters presupposed (*praenotamina*), contrary opinions and theses to be defended, proofs, and replies to objections, the latter to meet instructional or apologetic needs. Its language was a technical Latin, medieval in its grammatical forms, but with a specialized vocabulary suited to particular subject matters. With growing knowledge of the Greek Aristotle and awareness of the limitations of the Vulgate Bible's Latin, both philosophers and theologians became more concerned with accurate translations from Greek sources. Humanistic Latin ("Neo-Latin") was generally eschewed, though it was employed for decorative purposes in dedications and encomiums.

The main proponents of the movement were clergymen, both Catholic and Protestant. Among members of religious orders Dominicans, Franciscans, and Jesuits were the most influential, although members of other orders, such as Augustinians and Carmelites, along with the diocesan clergy, made substantial contributions. Order affiliations were very important, for they resulted in a variety of teachings that were distinctive and carefully guarded as part of the orders' respective traditions.

Geographically, Scholasticism flourished in Italy and on the Iberian peninsula, in France, Germany, and the Low Countries, and in the British Isles. The locus of its teachings was generally in universities and religious houses of studies. Scholasticism was also transplanted to the New World by members of religious orders and with the founding of institutions of higher learning in North and South America and the Philippines. American colleges, such as Harvard, Yale, and William and Mary, reflected the teachings current in Protestant universities in England, Scotland, Germany, and the Low Countries.

The Early Renaissance. There were three major schools of thought within early Renaissance Scholasticism: the Thomist, elaborating the thought of Thomas Aquinas (1225–1274); the Scotist, elaborating that of John Duns Scotus (c. 1266–1308); and the nominalist, drawing on that of Durand of Saint-Pourçain (c. 1275–1334) and William of Ockham (c. 1285–1347).

Thomism. Among the Dominicans, the major commentators on St. Thomas were the Italians Thomas de Vio Cajetan (1469–1534) and Francesco Silvestri (Ferrariensis; c. 1474–1528), and the Portuguese Jean Poinsot, better known as John of St. Thomas (1589–1644). Early followers of Aquinas were Giovanni Dominici (c. 1356–1419), who inveighed against paganizing humanists, the moral theologian Antoninus (Antonio Pierozzi; 1389–1459; archbishop of Florence), and the French John Capreolus (c. 1380–1444), who defended St. Thomas against Scotus and Ockham. Also in France, the secular master Johannes Versor (d. c. 1485) promoted Thomism largely through his many commentaries on Aristotle.

In Italy the foremost Thomists were Giovanni Crisostomo Javelli (1470–c. 1538), whose manuals were frequently reprinted, and Bartholomaeus Spina (c. 1479–1547) and Ambrogio Catarino (1487–1553), both opposing Cajetan's views. More numerous still were the Spanish Thomists: Domingo de Soto (1495–1560), Melchior Cano (1509–1560), Domingo Bañez (1528–1604), and Diego Mas (1553–1608). Soto is well known for his part in the Council of Trent, Cano for his work on theological sources, Bañez for his way of reconciling human freedom with divine causality, and Mas for his compendious accounts of scholastic teachings in the *Physics* and *Metaphysics* of Aristotle. In Germany, Conrad Köllin (c. 1476–1536) wrote Thomistic commentaries and defended Catholic doctrine against the Lutherans.

Scotism. The Franciscans were less enthusiastic in their embracing of Scotism, early because of their attachment to the traditional Augustinianism of St. Bonaventure (c. 1217–1274), later because of the new type of Aristotelianism presented by Ockham. The first Scotists, such as John of Bassolis (d. c. 1347) and Francis of Marchia (d. after 1344) adhered to Scotus's main teachings, and Peter of Aquila (1275–1361), who called himself Scotellus (little Scotus), composed a compendium of his thought.

Major contributors to a later Scotist revival were the Irish Maurice O'Fihely (c. 1460–1513), the French Pierre Tartaret (d. c. 1522), the Italians Francesco Liceto (d. 1520) and Antonio Trombeta (1436–1517), the second of whom was prominent at Padua as a foe of Averroism and a critic of Cajetan, and the Dutch Frans Titelmans (1502–1537), whose compendiums became important teaching tools. In 1539 the Franciscan Order officially adopted Scotus as their doctor, and shortly thereafter manuals were prepared for use in their schools. Another Irish Franciscan, Luke Wadding (1588–1657), played an important role in this task. By the end of the sixteenth century Scotism had become a vital force at major universities in Spain, Italy, France, and elsewhere.

Nominalism. As a movement this first appeared at Paris in the thought of Peter Abelard (1079–1142). Its revival in the later Middle Ages was prompted by Ockham's reaction to Scotus's teaching that "common natures" exist in things as universals, where they must be modified by the form of "thisness" (*haecceitas*) to become individual. For Ockham natures do not exist as universals; they can be known only through names (*nomina*) or terms (*termini*) by which they are referenced as singulars—whence "nominalism" or "terminism," alternate labels for his system. In the Renaissance, nominalism was advanced in logic, particularly in teaching the *Summulae* of Peter of Spain, and in Aristotelian philosophy and scholastic theology, where it was used to dispose of what were regarded by many as superfluous conceptual entities.

Nominalist thought radiated out from the University of Paris to the Iberian peninsula and the Low Countries, often as part of eclectic philosophies that were open to various types of realism. The principal figures were George of Brussels (d. 1502), Thomas Bricot (d. 1516), and the Scot John Major (1469–1550), all of whom taught in Paris, and Johann Eck (1486–1543), whose career was mainly in Germany. Among those taught or influenced by Major were Jacques Alamain (c. 1480–1515), Luis Nuñez Coronel (d. 1531), Pedro Ciruelo (1470–1554), and Gaspar Lax (1487–1560). Major's school made important contributions in mathematics and the study of motion, preparing the way for the scientific revolution of the seventeenth century.

Other schools. In the early fifteenth century small groups of thinkers at Paris and Cologne, identifying themselves as Albertists, set up a school opposed to Thomism. They took their lead from Johannes de Nova Domo, who taught at Paris before 1420 and made use of Albertus Magnus's commentaries on the *Liber de causis* and the works of Pseudo-Dionysius. Johannes saw existence as flowing from essence and thus denied Aquinas's real distinction between the two. His student, Heymericus de Campo (van de Velde; 1395–1460), taught at Cologne after 1424 and developed emanationist views of knowledge that include distinctive teachings on universals; the latter are contained in his *Tractatus problematicus,* published at Cologne in 1428 and again in 1496. Otherwise the school had few adherents and seems to have been short lived.

The Augustinians, or Hermits of St. Augustine, in 1560 adopted Giles of Rome (c. 1243–1316), who had been a student of Aquinas, as their special doctor. They retained their links with Thomism, but generally incorporated the positions of earlier Augustinians into their teachings, especially those of the nominalist Gregory of Rimini (1300–1358) and the logician and natural philosopher, Paul of Venice (c. 1370–1428/29). Their most important Renaissance scholar was Giles of Viterbo (1469–1532), a reformer of the order and later cardinal. Especially significant were the Spanish friars Diego de Zuñiga (c. 1536–1599), a systematic philosopher and theologian, and Alonso Gutierrez de la Vera Cruz (c. 1504–1584), a missionary who became known as "the father of Mexican philosophy." The secular master John Dullaert of Ghent (c. 1470–1513) also advanced their teachings at Paris.

More closely associated with Thomism were the Spanish Carmelites, whose John of the Cross (1542–1591) based his mystical teachings on the theology he had studied at Salamanca. Carmelite professors at Alcalá (Complutum) and Salamanca published their courses of studies in philosophy and theology in the early seventeenth century. Known respectively as the *Complutenses* and *Salmanticenses,* these have become, along with the *Conimbricenses* (see below), the best sources of scholastic Renaissance teachings in these disciplines. The *Summa philosophiae* of the French Cistercian Eustachius a Sancto Paulo (1573–1640) is also noteworthy for its systematic treatments of logic, ethics, physics, and metaphysics.

The Later Renaissance. The most significant development in the later Renaissance was the foundation of the Jesuit order (Society of Jesus) in 1540. This group blended humanism with scholasticism and introduced new systems of thought that had profound effects, first on Catholic thinkers, then on Protestants, the latter mainly in northern Europe.

The Jesuits. The order came into being five years before the Council of Trent, in time to take part in the flowering of Spanish Scholasticism. Its founder, Ignatius of Loyola (1491–1556), prescribed that the order take its intellectual roots from Aristotle and Thomas Aquinas, but its brand of Thomism was more liberal and eclectic than the Dominican. The first teachers at the school Loyola founded, the Collegio Romano, were Iberians, their preeminent leader being Franciscus Toletus (1532–1596), who had studied under Soto at Salamaca. Others who taught there include Gabriel Vazquez (1549–1604), Francisco Suarez (1548–1617), and Gregory of Valencia (c. 1549–1634). The Italian Jesuit Cosmo Alamanni (1559–1634), who had studied under Vazquez and Suarez, wrote *summae* of philosophy that were being reedited at Paris as late as 1894. Also important was the Portuguese Pedro da Fonseca (1528–1599), who taught at Coimbra and initiated the publication of the entire philosophical course taught there, the *Conimbricenses*. Fonseca's student, Luis de Molina (1535–1600), proposed his teaching on God's "middle science" (*scientia media*), which became the Jesuit alternative to Bañez's way of reconciling God's foreknowledge with free human action.

Suarez turned out to be the most influential of these teachers, and his system of thought in both philosophy and theology, Suarezianism, became standard Jesuit teaching in later centuries. It may be regarded as a relaxed but original species of Thomism that meets Scotist and nominalist critiques of Aquinas's teachings. Suarez's most important work, *Disputationes metaphysicae* (Metaphysical disputations), was published at Salamanca in 1597. His political views, joined to those of Molina and Robert Bellarmine (1542–1621), plus their Dominican predecessors Vitoria and Soto, constitute a body of legal theory still being studied.

Protestant Scholasticism. Although Martin Luther objected to Scholasticism in 1517, within a hundred years scholastic metaphysics had come to occupy a central place in Protestant universities, whether they leaned to Calvinism, as in Heidelberg and Marburg, or to Lutheranism, as in Wittenberg, Altdorf, and Helmstedt. In the background of this movement was the 1543 *Dialecticae institutiones* (Dialectical teachings) of Petrus Ramus (1515–1572), which substituted a humanist logic for that of Aristotle. Basic approaches were those of Philip Melanchthon (1497–1560), who composed textbooks on physics, psychology, and ethics at Wittenberg, and Jakob Schegk (1511–1587), who wrote commentaries on Aristotle's logic and natural philosophy at Tübingen.

For metaphysics, Jesuit textbooks, particularly Suarez's, were used initially and then replaced by Protestant manuals. Johannes Caselius (1535–1613) and Cornelius Martini (1568–1621), working at Helmstedt, wrote early texts in the Aristotelian tradition pioneered by Schegk. Works showing Suarez's influence include those of Jakob Martini (1570–1649) at Wittenberg and Christoph Scheibler (1589–1653) at Giessen, the latter called the Protestant Suarez.

For systematic thought, most notable are the works of Bartholomaeus Keckermann (1571–1608), who taught at Heidelberg and Danzig and elaborated manuals for all of philosophy and science. Johann Heinrich Alsted (1588–1638) published a complete edition of Keckermann's works in 1613 under the title of *Systema systematum* (System of systems), and followed this by his own *Encyclopediae* in 1620 and 1630. At Leyden, Franco Burgersdijk (1590–1635) wrote similar compendiums for scholastic philosophy, widely used throughout Protestant Europe.

In natural theology, Lutherans treated God under the science of being, whereas Calvinists or Reformed theologians tended to distinguish two sciences, one of God and the other of being. The Lutheran approach may be seen in the works of Daniel Cramer (1568–1637) and those of the two Martinis and Scheibler, the Calvinist in the works of Rodolphus Goclenius (1547–1628), Clemens Timpler (1567/68–1624), Keckermann, and Alsted.

Humanism. Scholasticism is frequently seen in opposition to humanism, the most distinctive movement of the Renaissance. Surely there was opposition in their types of discourse. For Scholastics, discourse was logically structured and systematic, aimed at abstract truths found in speculative disciplines such as philosophy and theology. For humanists, its locus was in epistles, dialogues, and epideictic treatises, aimed at practical knowledge to guide human living. Claims have been made for philosophical opposition also, seeing humanism as a new philosophy based on individual human nature and ordered only to natural, as opposed to supernatural, goals. Such claims have been difficult to justify on the historical record.

Humanism is perhaps better understood as a developed version of Cicero's *studia humanitatis,* the type of broad general education that prepared one for effective participation in public life. This was found in courses on grammar, rhetoric, poetry, history, and the reading of classics encouraging moral virtue. Ramus's simplified logic, along with mathematics, further provided stimulus to correct thinking. None of these was opposed to, nor was it a substitute for, the serious study of philosophy and theology; on the other hand, they could be an excellent propadeutic for such study. Much of their content was incorporated in the *ratio studiorum* (course of studies) of the Jesuits' Collegio Romano toward the end of the sixteenth century. That result may be attributed to the pedagogical efforts of humanists in the preceding two centuries.

Such an irenic statement is not intended to cover up the many invectives and diatribes between humanists and Scholastics over that period. These were serious, and involved much more than literary and pedagogical debate, reaching into such areas as inter-faculty relationships and prolonged disputes over methodology, academic qualifications, dogmatic teachings, and the interpretation of Scripture.

See also **Aristotle and Aristotelianism**; **Humanism**; **Philosophy**; *and biographies of figures mentioned in this entry.*

BIBLIOGRAPHY

Farge, James K. *Biographical Register of Paris Doctors of Theology, 1500–1536.* Toronto, 1980

Giacon, Carlo. *La seconda scolastica.* 3 vols. Milan, 1944–1950.

Lohr, Charles H. *Latin Aristotle Commentaries.* II. *Renaissance Authors.* Florence, 1988. Brief biographies, detailed listings of publications.

McDonald, William J., et al., eds. *New Catholic Encyclopedia.* 15 vols. Washington, D.C., 1967. For a comprehensive treatment of scholasticism, see vol. 12, pp. 1145–1170. Also a good source for coverage of individual schools and their members.

Nauert, Charles G. *Humanism and the Culture of Renaissance Europe.* Cambridge, U.K., 1995.

Rummel, Erika. *The Humanist-Scholastic Debate in the Renaissance and Reformation.* Cambridge, Mass., and London, 1995.

Schmitt, Charles B., et al., eds. *The Cambridge History of Renaissance Philosophy.* Cambridge, U.K., 1988.

White, Kevin, ed. *Hispanic Philosophy in the Age of Discovery.* Washington, D.C., 1997.

WILLIAM A. WALLACE

SCHONGAUER, MARTIN (c. 1450–1491), German engraver and painter. Martin Schongauer was praised during his lifetime as "*pictorum gloria,*" and his refined art earned him the epithet "Martin Hübsch" (Beautiful Martin). The quincentenary of his death in 1991 was commemorated with renewed scholarly interest and major exhibitions, particularly in Germany and France.

His father, the goldsmith Caspar Schongauer the Elder (d. 1482/83), originally came from Augsburg and settled in Colmar, Alsace, around 1440. Martin, during his years as an apprentice, possibly traveled to the Netherlands and Spain. After living in Colmar most of his life, he resided in Breisach in 1486/87 and returned there in 1489. During his last years he worked on monumental frescoes in the cathedral of Saint Stephen in Breisach (where he died), depicting scenes from the Last Judgment (rediscovered in 1932, incomplete and badly damaged).

A total of 116 copperplate engravings bear his monogram. Schongauer was, in fact, the first artist to sign his prints on a consistent basis, but none was originally dated by him. These technically brilliant works spread his fame across Europe, influencing, among others, Hans Burgkmair (his only documented pupil), Albrecht Dürer, Michelangelo, and Raphael. Schongauer perfected the relatively new graphic medium of engraving, treating it with the same meticulous care and imaginative complexity as painting. He also developed a sculptural and, at times, dramatic use of chiaroscuro. These qualities make him a pioneer of the northern Renaissance. Schongauer's images, both sacred and secular, are traditional rather than innovative, representing the visual tradition and pictorial convention of the late Middle Ages. His most familiar engraving, *St. Anthony Tormented by Demons* (also called *The Temptation of St. Anthony*), is probably an early work (c. 1470–1475) and is representative of the popular cult of the saint, especially in Alsace.

Schongauer's fame during his lifetime was based on his paintings. Six or seven panels appear to be authentic, among them two in large format, the Orlier Altar of c. 1470 (Colmar, Museum Unterlinden) and the *Virgin in the Rose Garden* of 1473 (Colmar, Dominican Church), one of the most famous paintings of the German School before Dürer. Exquisite small paintings of the *Holy Family* are in the museums of Munich, Vienna, and Berlin; they are regarded as early works, showing strong Netherlandish influence.

A number of pen and ink drawings (from fifteen to fifty-five) are considered to be authentic, but none of these was originally dated (the date 1469 on three drawings was added later, almost certainly by Dürer). These works constitute the first significant body of drawings created by a German artist.

See also **Germany, Art in.**

BIBLIOGRAPHY

Bernhard, Marianne, ed. *Martin Schongauer und sein Kreis: Druckgraphik, Handzeichnungen*. Munich, 1980.

Glaubrecht, Friedrich. *Martin Schongauer zum 500. Todestag*. Edited by Susan Tipton. Dresden, Germany, 1991.

Minott, Charles I. *Martin Schongauer*. New York, 1971.

Winzinger, Franz. *Die Zeichnungen Martin Schongauers*. Berlin, 1962.

ILSE E. FRIESEN

SCHURMAN, ANNA MARIA VAN (1607–1678), learned Dutch proponent of female education. The daughter of Frederick van Schurman, who had fled the Netherlands during the duke of Alba's persecution of Protestants, and Eva van Harff, who belonged to Germany's lesser nobility, Schurman spent her early years in and near Cologne. Her father recognized her exceptional gift for languages and tutored her as well as her brothers in Latin and Greek. Around 1615 the family set up permanent residence in Utrecht, moving only temporarily to Franeker in 1623 so that Schurman's brother, Johan Godschalck, could study medicine. Her father, who had intended to study there with the English puritan theologian William Ames, died soon after the move. Anna Maria, meanwhile, continued her education not only in letters but also in the arts, including painting, miniature carving, intricate paper cutting, and calligraphy.

Schurman's most significant humanistic contribution was her logic exercise on women's education, *Whether a Christian Woman Should Be Educated,* first published in 1638 together with her correspondence on this question with theologian André Rivet. The study of grammar, logic, rhetoric, physics, metaphysics, history and languages, she argued, is valuable for women because it contributes to moral virtue and knowledge of God, even if it serves no utilitarian purpose. Her defense of women's education occasioned correspondence with other women such as Marie le Jars de Gournay of France, Dorothy Moor of Ireland, and Bathsua Makin of England, to whom she wrote in French, Hebrew, and Greek, respectively. Her admirers included theologians and philosophers, most notably René Descartes, but in the 1640s, under the tutelage of Utrecht theologian and professor of Semitic languages Gisbertus Voetius, she allied herself firmly with Reformed Scholasticism and its opposition to Cartesian philosophy.

During most of the 1650s and 1660s Schurman was out of the public eye, caring for two elderly aunts and devoting herself to charitable works. Disillusioned with the state church, she looked to the work of the Reformer Jean de Labadie. (He had been invited from Geneva to the Netherlands largely through the influence of Johan Godschalck van Schurman.) Labadie's ideas proved incompatible with a territorial church, so in 1669 he gathered his followers into a house church in Amsterdam. Anna van Schurman's decision to leave her home in Utrecht to live with Labadie and his followers scandalized many of her previous supporters. Critics forced the community to migrate from Amsterdam to Herford to Altona and finally to Wieuwerd in Friesland, where Schurman died. In her autobiographical work defending the Labadist community against its detractors, she testified that she had found in this community the true Christian faith and love that were lacking in the state church. She also bemoaned her youthful pursuit of intellectual accomplishments, even those of theology, insofar as they diverted her from the lived experience of faith.

Having mastered a dozen languages, Schurman was widely acclaimed in her own time as a woman unequaled in learning. She advanced the cause of female education not only by advocating it but also by serving as a model of women's intellectual capabilities. She was the first woman to study at a Dutch university, although she attended lectures hidden in a cubicle from other students. Her vision of woman's role did not challenge male leadership, however, nor did it include any practical application for women's education outside the home.

BIBLIOGRAPHY

Primary Work

Schurman, Anna Maria van. *Whether a Christian Woman Should Be Educated and Other Writings from Her Intellectual Circle*. Edited and translated by Joyce L. Irwin. Chicago, 1998.

Secondary Works

Baar, Mirjam de, et al., eds. *Choosing the Better Part: Anna Maria van Schurman (1607–1678).* Dordrecht, Netherlands, 1996.

Birch, Una (Una Pope-Hennessy). *Anna van Schurman: Artist, Scholar, Saint.* London, 1909.

JOYCE L. IRWIN

SCIENCE. The English term "science" is a translation of the Greek *epistēmē,* the Latin *scientia,* and the Italian *scienza,* and in these forms it occurs frequently throughout the Renaissance. It is also used by historians to speak of "Renaissance science," just as they speak of "ancient science" or "medieval science," connoting periods of transition from the earlier phases to "modern science." In such usage the focus is mainly on investigations that may be seen as orthodox in that they anticipate the methods of modern science. Intertwined with these were disciplines—including alchemy, astrology, and magic—that do not meet this standard. Since the orthodox line grew out of the Aristotelian tradition, the meaning of science in that tradition, along with the associated notion of demonstration, is basic for understanding the Renaissance development.

The Concept of Science.

For Aristotle (384–322 B.C.), *scientia* designated a type of perfect knowing, the attainment of knowledge that is certain and unchanging. He asserted that one obtained such knowledge of any object when one knew its cause, that this cause made the object be what it is, and therefore that the object could not be otherwise. In this sense science was true and necessary, not open to radical revision. From Aristotle onward, however, the concept was extended to cover less perfect types of knowing, including those based on probable explanations and that merely save the appearances, such as predicting eclipses without explaining why they occur. These grew during the Middle Ages and more rapidly during the Renaissance, each time coming closer to the modern notion of science.

Speculative Sciences.

An early extension of the concept saw science divided into two types: speculative sciences, concerned with knowing alone, and practical sciences, concerned with knowing as ordered to practice (*praxis*). Speculative sciences were further differentiated according to the ways they attained knowledge of the subjects they treated. On this basis speculative sciences were divided into three broad genera: natural science, mathematics, and metaphysics.

Natural science. This discipline had nature for its subject, that is, material or sensible or changeable being. Its general principles were taught as part of philosophy in courses on Aristotle's *Physics,* whose teachings were explored with the aid of Greek and Latin commentators by nominalists and realists. Humanist reactions to Aristotle, plus novel speculations about the universe, also led to new concepts of nature itself.

The special branches of natural science saw the greatest growth. With regard to the cosmos as a whole, considerable data became available for theorizing about its size and structure. Advances were also made in studies of material substances, with speculation about their atomic components and how they enter into combination. Also, a great deal of knowledge was gained about the earth and the minerals and metals beneath its surface.

The general study of life and its processes remained largely in philosophy, where new light was shed on the soul through Greek commentaries on Aristotle's *De anima* (On the soul), and the nature of man and immortality were addressed anew. The special study of plant life benefited from voyages of exploration and the related interest in herbals and botanical gardens. Animal studies benefited similarly with bestiaries and zoos and from the use of dissection in medical practice.

Mathematics and metaphysics. Mathematics had quantity, or quantified being, for its subject, and its pure branches were seen as two: arithmetic, treating of discrete quantity or number, and geometry, treating of continuous quantity or magnitude. Both saw advances in the Renaissance, mainly through the recovery of ancient sources, the development of algebraic notation, new solutions of equations, advances in trigonometry, and the invention of logarithms. But whether mathematics is a strict science in the Aristotelian sense came to be disputed during the period.

Metaphysics, finally, had all of being for its consideration. It was taught in philosophy and also in theology, the latter because of disputes arising from the Reformation. Its subject was intensely debated in the Renaissance, the main problem being whether it was one science or many. The consensus gradually developed that it must be at least two, a science of being, now called ontology, and a science of God.

Mixed sciences. A further division of the speculative sciences arose from the fact that the principles discovered in one subject of investigation could fruitfully be applied to another subject, thus giving rise to a mixed or middle science (Latin *scientia mixta, scientia media*). The classical example of a mixed science was what is now called mathematical physics. This was a science intermediate between mathematics and physical science, which examined the same subject as natural science but considered it under the light of mathematical principles. Already known to Aristotle and well exemplified in Euclidean optics and Ptolemaic astronomy, this type of science expanded greatly during the Renaissance.

Major advances were made in astronomy through more accurate determination of star positions, revised tables, and the consideration of new systems of the world. The invention and use of the telescope, plus the beginnings of "celestial" physics and the determination of elliptical orbits, brought astronomy to the verge of the modern period. Allied to this development were more refined methods of measuring time and mapping the earth's surface. Optics likewise gained through the recovery of earlier sources, the study of mirrors and lenses, and improved theories of human vision.

Practical Sciences. Like speculative sciences, practical sciences sought knowledge through causes. What distinguished them was that speculative sciences sought universal knowledge of what humans can only know, that is, universals, whereas practical sciences sought causal knowledge of what humans can do or make, that is, singular operables. This required that they be supplemented by prudence (*phronēsis*) or skill (*technē*), both dealing with singulars, to do so. Because of this close association with art, practical sciences were difficult to distinguish from art, and during the Renaissance some disciplines, such as logic and medicine, were commonly regarded as both.

The most notable practical sciences were the moral, medical, and engineering sciences. Of the moral sciences, ethics and politics were of major interest in the Renaissance. Basically the same system of ethics was followed by humanists, Platonists, and Aristotelians, though with different emphases in their approaches. Politics came to be divorced from ethics and religion, with force and wealth replacing them as determining factors in political life.

Medicine made great strides in the cure and prevention of disease and in the improvement of medicines, medical instruments, and hospital care. Allied with these were advances in dissection, surgery, and the study of organisms, notably the motion of the heart and blood.

Finally, engineering came into its own as a discipline, combining the pseudo-Aristotelian *Mechanica* (Mechanics) with the principles of Vitruvian architecture. Machines of all types, both mechanical and hydraulic, were invented and put to use in civic and cathedral construction.

Demonstration in Science. The principal logical instrument for attaining science in the Aristotelian sense was demonstration (Greek *apodeixis,* Lat. *demonstratio*), a term designating a proof concerned with necessary subject matter that yields truth and certitude. In Aristotle's *Analytica posteriora* (Posterior Analytics) demonstration was equated with causal reasoning and defined as "a syllogism productive of scientific knowledge, a syllogism, that is, the grasp of which actually constitutes such knowledge" (71b17–19). Stringent requirements were placed on the premises of such a syllogism, which "must be true, primary, immediate, better known than and prior to the conclusion, which is further related to them as effect to cause" (71b20–22). These requirements differentiate Aristotelian science from much of modern science, which has given up the search for causes and replaced them by mathematical or functional correlations. It also rejects Aristotle's demand that the premises be better known than the conclusions arrived at, thus effectively reducing science to probable reasoning.

Types of demonstration. Demonstrations were divided into two broad types: ostensive demonstrations, which prove a true conclusion from true premises, and negative demonstrations, which show that a conclusion is impossible by reducing it to another impossibility that is more known. Ostensive demonstrations were then of two further types: one resulted in knowledge of the fact (Greek *to hoti,* Latin *quia*), the other, in knowledge of the reasoned fact (Greek *to dioti,* Latin *propter quid*).

Demonstration of the reasoned fact assigned the proper ontological cause of a property's inhering in, and being attributed to, the subject. This type of cause is always prior to its effect, so the demonstration was said to be *a priori*. In the most perfect type of *propter quid* demonstration, all of the terms of the syllogism were commensurately universal. In a less perfect type only the middle term and the predicate or attribute were convertible, but this sufficed to satisfy the requirements listed above.

Demonstration of the fact was had whenever the middle term was not the proper cause of the attribute but was either its remote cause or one of its effects. If the first, it was *a priori;* if the second, it was *a posteriori,* since effects are posterior to, or follow from, their causes. If the effect was not convertible with the cause, the demonstration yielded knowledge of the existence of the cause and some of its conditions. If cause and effect were convertible, the demonstration made known the proper cause, and the terms could without circularity be recast as a *propter quid* demonstration. The process wherein this is done was known as the demonstrative regress.

With suitable qualifications the Aristotelian requirements for demonstration could be seen to apply to *a posteriori* demonstrations and to demonstrations in the mixed sciences. For example, if the proof required a mathematical premise that was presupposed as demonstrated in, say, geometry, this was like an "immediate" premise in physics, for there was no middle term in that discipline through which it could be demonstrated. Again, in the order of nature, causes are "more known" than their effects, but in human knowing this is not the case, since in sense experience effects are more readily knowable than their causes. Thus, "causes of" need not mean causes of the being of the effect, but only causes of our knowing it, and this sufficed for an *a posteriori* demonstration.

Transition to probable reasoning. This shift was effected by several factors. The first was the growing awareness in the Renaissance of the close connection between Aristotle's *Topica* (Topics), his treatise on probable reasoning, and his *Analytica posteriora.* In that period commentaries on the *Topica* far outnumbered those in the Middle Ages. Significant is the fact that they drew on Latin topical traditions other than the Aristotelian, specifically those of Cicero (106–43 B.C.) and Boethius (c. 480–524). Both of the latter enumerated "cause-effect" along with such topics as "antecedent-consequent," thus drawing attention to the fact that causal arguments need not be apodictic. Another factor was the increased concern over recognizing *a posteriori* arguments as valid demonstrations, since they always seemed to involve an element of conjecture. This led to intense debates over the validity of the demonstrative regress, for this involved a combination of *a posteriori* and *a priori* reasoning. And finally, there was the growth of the mixed sciences, with their use of mathematics, whose scientific status was suspect for many.

Mathematicians made extensive use of postulation or supposition (Greek *hupothesis,* Latin *suppositio*), and this led to a similar use in the mixed sciences of what was usually called demonstration *ex suppositione* (from a supposition), less frequently demonstration *ex hypothesis* (from a hypothesis). Galileo Galilei (1564–1642) favored the former expression and offered observational or experimental proof of his suppositions, thus claiming scientific status for his conclusions. Nicolaus Copernicus (1473–1543) offered similar demonstrations of the earth's motion, but these were seen as based on unproved hypotheses, and thus as probable arguments. The latter are not unlike those yielded by modern scientific method, which in this sense was already anticipated in the Renaissance.

See also **Anatomy; Astronomy; Dignity of Man; Inventions; Logic; Mathematics; Mechanics; Medicine; Metaphysics; Moral Philosophy; Natural Philosophy; Nature, New Philosophies of; Optics; Physics; Political Thought; Science, Epistemology of; Technology; Scientific Instruments; Scientific Method; Virtù;** *and biographies of Copernicus and Galileo.*

BIBLIOGRAPHY

Primary Work

Apostle, Hippocrates G., trans. *Aristotle's Posterior Analytics. Translation with Commentaries and Glossary.* Grinnel, Iowa, 1981.

Secondary Works

Butts, Robert E., and Joseph C. Pitt, eds. *New Perspectives on Galileo.* The University of Western Ontario Series in Philosophy of Science, no. 14. Dordrecht, Netherlands, and Boston, 1978.

Glutz, Melvin A. "Demonstration." In *New Catholic Encyclopedia,* vol. 4. New York, 1967. Pages 757–760.

Green-Pedersen, Niels J. *The Tradition of the Topics in the Middle Ages: The Commentaries on Aristotle's and Boethius' "Topics."* Munich and Vienna, 1984.

Nagel, Ernest. *The Structure of Science: Problems in the Logic of Scientific Explanation.* New York and London, 1961. See pages 42–46.

Schmitt, Charles B., ed. *The Cambridge History of Renaissance Philosophy.* Cambridge, U.K., 1988. See especially chapters 8 and 19.

Wallace, William A. "Aristotle and Galileo: The Uses of *Hupothesis (Suppositio)* in Scientific Reasoning." In *Studies in Aristotle.* Edited by D. J. O'Meara. Washington, D.C., 1981. See pages 47–77.

Wallace, William A. *Galileo's Logic of Discovery and Proof: The Background, Content, and Use of His Appropriated Treatises on Aristotle's* Posterior Analytics. Dordrecht, Netherlands; Boston; and London, 1992.

WILLIAM A. WALLACE

SCIENCE, EPISTEMOLOGY OF. Several problems associated with the emerging science of the Renaissance bear on the validity of knowledge claims, the province of epistemology. Chief among them are the ontological status of hypotheses in astronomy, the characterization of mathematics as a science of the real world, and a possible circularity of reasoning in regressive demonstrations. What follows is a brief consideration and resolution of each.

Hypotheses in Astronomy. Prior to Nicolaus Copernicus (1473–1543), the accepted system of the world was earth-centered or geocentric, and it was presented in different, though compatible, ways by philosophers and mathematicians. The main philosophical source was Aristotle's *De caelo* (On the heavens) and Book XII (Lambda) of his *Metaphysica* (Metaphysics), which differentiated the terrestrial from the celestial regions and saw the latter as composed of fifty-odd heavens or spheres in uniform circular motions around the earth's center. This was referred to as a physical astronomy, mainly because Aristotle's *Physics* provided principles that could explain motions on earth and in the heavens. The mathematical sources were twofold and gave rise to two mathematical astronomies. The earlier derived from Eudoxus (c. 400–c. 350 B.C.), who provided a precise geometrical model of the movement of the sun, moon, and planets against the background of the fixed stars, employing a system of homocentric spheres rotating on different axes to do so. The later derived from Ptolemy (c. 100–165), who replaced Eudoxian spheres with off-center spheres (eccentrics) and added spheres rotating around spheres (epicycles), plus imaginary centers around which rotations took place (equants), to model more accurately the observed movements in the heavens. The Eudoxian system was easily reconciled with Aristotle's physical astronomy whereas the Ptolemaic system was not, despite its being geocentric.

More radical was the world system proposed by Copernicus, which used most of Ptolemy's constructions but was sun-centered or heliocentric, having all celestial movements around the sun and setting the earth in motion as a planet in the fourth heaven. This directly contradicted Aristotelian physics and was offensive to common sense, since the earth is perceived as at rest in the center of the universe. More importantly, for Protestants and Catholics alike it went contrary to the teachings of Scripture. To head off biblical objections to Copernicus's *De revolutionibus orbium coelestium* (On the revolutions of the heavenly orbs; 1543), an unsigned preface was added to it by Andreas Osiander (1498–1552), a Lutheran theologian, without Copernicus's knowledge. Osiander stressed that the work did not contain a true description of the heavens but rather fictive entities that simplified the calculations of astronomers. Later, Tycho Brahe (1546–1601) proposed a compromise geo-heliocentric system, which put the earth with its orbiting moon at the world's center and placed the sun, with all the other planets orbiting it, in revolution around the earth, while retaining Copernicus's constructions.

This situation provoked intense debate in the Renaissance between so-called fictionalists and realists. Fictionalists saw entities like eccentrics and epicycles as simply *fictitia,* or mental constructs. The more significant among them were Averroist philosophers at Padua, notably Agostino Nifo (c. 1473–1538); Peter Ramus (1515–1572); Osiander; Nicolaus Reimarus Ursus (1551–1600), who published a treatise on hypotheses in 1597; and the Jesuits Benito Pereira (1535–1610) and Robert Bellarmine (1542–1621). Realists saw these entities and the motions they explained as real (*realia*), in varying senses. Included in their number were Copernicus; Brahe; the Jesuit Christopher Clavius (1538–1612); Michael Maestlin (1550–1631); and Johannes Kepler (1571–1630), who in 1600 composed a treatise against Ursus. The debate was never resolved in the Renaissance, though Kepler's later discovery of the laws of planetary motion provided the bases for its ultimate resolution. Eccentrics and epicycles are imaginative constructs, but the motions they approximate are real and actually take place in the heavens. Empirical evidence for the earth's motion was harder to come by, not becoming available until the nineteenth century.

Mathematics as a Science. Obviously, what was then at stake was the scientific value of mathematics. In his *Analytica posteriora* (Posterior analytics) Aristotle had numbered mathematics among the sciences and used its proofs to illustrate various requirements for demonstration. The Renaissance debate on the subject originated with the publication in 1533 of a commentary on Euclid's *Elements* by Proclus (c. 410–485), which offered a Platonic reading of geometrical proofs. The topic was taken up by Alessandro Piccolomini (1508–1578) in *Commentarium de certitudine mathematicarum disciplinarum* (The certitude of mathematical disciplines; Rome, 1547), a treatise in which he rejected the Aristotelian view that certitude in mathematics derives from its demonstrations. His arguments were taken up by Pereira, who inaugurated a campaign against mathematics at the Collegio Romano. Counterarguments were developed by Francesco Barozzi (1537–1604), who held that mathematical demonstrations were not only certain but most powerful (*potissimae*). His side was taken up by Clavius, who successfully countered Pereira's attack at the Collegio, and by his students, principally Giuseppe Biancani (1566–1624). Additional contributions to the debate were made by Pietro Catena (fl. 1547–1576) and Niccolò Tartaglia (1499–1557), and also by Galileo's friend, Jacopo Mazzoni (1548–1598), who fused Aristotelian and Platonic ideas to see mathematics as an indispensable instrument for studying the world of nature.

In summary, the arguments against mathematics being a science were that geometers base their arguments on suppositions (*suppositiones*) and do not attain to the essence of quantity or to true causes (*verae causae*), and that mathematical entities do not exist in the physical world but only in the mind abstracting them, and so are fictitious. The counterarguments were that mathematicians furnish essential definitions of the objects they treat, even while supposing them, and so demonstrate through formal and material causes, and that they deal with entities that exist in an intelligible matter (*materia intelligibilis*)—entities that, though abstracted from sensible matter, are possible beings and even acquire a perfection not found in terrestrial objects.

However these arguments are evaluated, throughout the Renaissance pure mathematics was regarded as the most certain of the sciences and expanded continuously. Mathematical physics also flourished, as groundwork was being laid for the Scientific Revolution of the seventeenth century.

Circularity and the Demonstrative Regress. For Aristotle, the causes of physical objects are usually hidden and must be disclosed through study of their effects. Effects are more known to us, he argued, whereas causes are more knowable to nature or in themselves. This situation requires that demonstrations in physical science proceed first from effect to cause, and then, when the cause has been uncovered, to go back or regress to the effect, showing why and how the cause produces that particular effect, a procedure known as the demonstrative regress. This procedure is not needed in mathematics because the causes of mathematical objects are immediately known to us and need not be demonstrated through their effects. Aristotle also cautioned against circularity in reasoning, and this caused concern among his commentators over whether the transition from effect to cause and from cause to effect again was not itself circular, in violation of Aristotle's own teaching.

The problem has a long history, mainly at the University of Padua, where it began with Pietro d'Abano (1257–1315), in *Conciliator differentiarum philosophorum, et precipue medicorum* (Conciliator of the differences among philosophers and principally physicians), written in 1310 and published at Venice in 1476. This work recovered teachings on the *regressus* in Galen (129–c. 199) and Averroes (Ibn Rushd; 1126–1198) and attempted to reconcile the two. The subject was taken up by Paul of Venice (c. 1369–1429), who explicitly addressed the question of circularity in *Expositio super octo libros phisicorum Aristotelis* (Exposition of the eight books of Aristotle; *Physics*), his commentary on the *Physics*. The work was published at Venice in 1499 and answered the question in the negative. Knowledge of an effect through what causes it, for him, is not the same as knowledge of the effect by itself, and thus two different knowings are involved. A long string of commentators took up the problem, the more notable being Francesco Securo di Nardó (fl. 1480), a Dominican known as Neritonensis; Nifo; Girolamo Balduino (fl. 1550); and Jacopo Zabarella (1533–1589). All saw the *regressus* as made up of two main processes, one from effect to cause, the other from cause to effect. The debate centered on which of the two was truly demonstrative and on how the transition between them could be effected. Zabarella is usually credited with the best solution, namely, that both processes are demonstrative but in different ways, and that a third stage must intervene between the processes, one of mental examination (*examen mentale*) in which the investigator convinces himself that the cause is the unique and proper cause of the given effect.

In a gloss on his commentary on the *Analytica posteriora,* Zabarella cites, as an example of the *regressus,* Aristotle's proof that the moon is a sphere because it exhibits phases. It turns out that Galileo's discoveries with the telescope of mountains on the moon, satellites of Jupiter, and Venus's revolution around the sun parallel that proof exactly. In his 1615 letter to the Grand Duchess Christina, Galileo claimed for these discoveries the status of "necessary demonstrations based on sensible experience." Whether he consciously employed the *regressus* in elaborating them may be open to debate, but there is no doubt that Galileo knew of the technique. His discoveries, now universally acknowledged as such, show that it could be used to document genuine scientific progress.

See also **Astronomy; Mathematics; Science; Scientific Method;** *and biographies of Tycho Brahe, Nicolaus*

Copernicus, Galileo Galilei, Johannes Kepler, Jacopo Mazzoni, Alessandro Piccolomini, and Jacopo Zabarella.

BIBLIOGRAPHY

De Pace, Anna. *Le Matematiche e il mondo: Ricerche su un diattito in Italia nella seconda metà del Cinquecento.* Milan, 1993.

Duhem, Pierre. *To Save the Phenomena: An Essay on the Idea of Physical Theory from Plato to Galileo.* Translated by Edmund Doland and Chaninah Maschler. Chicago and London, 1969.

Jardine, Nicholas. *The Birth of History and Philosophy of Science: Kepler's* A Defence of Tycho against Ursus *with Essays on Its Provenance and Significance.* Cambridge, U.K., 1984.

Jardine, Nicholas. "Epistemology of the Sciences." In *The Cambridge History of Renaissance Philosophy.* Edited by Charles B. Schmitt. Cambridge, U.K., 1988. Pages 685–711.

Wallace, William A. "Circularity and the Demonstrative *Regressus:* From Pietro d'Abano to Galileo Galilei." *Vivarium* 33, no. 1 (1995): 76–97.

Wallace, William A. *Galileo and His Sources: The Heritage of the Collegio Romano in Galileo's Science.* Princeton, N.J., 1984. Pages 126–148, 202–216.

WILLIAM A. WALLACE

SCIENTIFIC INSTRUMENTS. Devices used in the study of nature mainly for observation and measurement, but also for teaching, scientific instruments were already available in antiquity and were perfected throughout the Middle Ages. The Renaissance contribution consisted in further improving them and then, as experimentation and quantification increased, devising new instruments. These may be classified in various ways, as observing, measuring, drawing, calculating, and teaching instruments, or as those used in various fields of study. The following is an historical-systematic account that touches on these different categories.

Astronomy. Basic instruments for astronomy in the early Renaissance were the astrolabe, the quadrant, and the armillary sphere, to which might be added the astronomical ring, the torquetum, and the equatorium. The astrolabe was very common and of various types. Usually in the form of a small brass disk, it could be held in a vertical position on the thumb by means of a ring and used to sight the altitude of a heavenly object. It was known as a planispheric astrolabe because the markings on the disk showed various projections of a sphere on a plane. Calibrated scales on the instrument then enabled one to read off the hour, when the date was known, or vice versa. Much rarer was the spherical astrolabe, which used the celestial globe itself as a measuring instrument. Quadrants were basically devices for measuring angles up to 90 degrees and likewise were used for determining altitudes. As with astrolabes, there were various types.

Scientific Instrument. Trigonic sextant of Tycho Brahe, 1602. MARY EVANS PICTURE LIBRARY

The armillary sphere was a sphere made of rings, to which supplementary concentric and movable rings were added to show the supposed orbits of the heavenly bodies. A similar but simpler device, the astronomical ring, consisted of two circles for the equator and meridian respectively, and a third ring pivoted on the earth's axis that could be used to sight a star and find the angle between it and the meridian. More complex was the torquetum, or "Turkish instrument," a three-dimensional teaching device that could be used to demonstrate angles in different systems of celestial coordinates. The equatorium was a planar instrument inscribed with various circles that could be used to find the positions of planets in the Ptolemaic system without having to make calculations.

An early instrument maker was Jean Fusoris (c. 1355–1436), a canon of Paris, who made astrolabes, quadrants, "solid" spheres, and an equatorium. Early fifteenth-century craftsmen at Oxford and Cambridge in England also made instruments of these types. In Vienna, the Dominican friar Hans Dorn (c. 1430–1509), who had studied under Georg Peurbach (1423–1461), was particularly productive and innovative as an instrument maker.

In the early sixteenth century Gemma Frisius (1508–1555) and Gerard Mercator (1512–1594) had workshops in the Low Countries from which these instruments flowed constantly. At Nürnberg, Georg Hartmann (1489–1564) produced numerous astrolabes and other devices, in some cases making them in batches from identical molds. And in London, English astronomers were similarly supplied by Humphrey Cole (c. 1520–1591) and Elias Allen (fl. 1602–1653).

In the later Renaissance the most important observational astronomers were Bernard Walther (1430–1504) and Tycho Brahe (1546–1601). Walther, who had worked with Regiomontanus (1436–1476) at Nürnberg, continued making precise measurements for thirty years. He used a cross staff that was nine feet long and graduated in 1,300 equal divisions, as well as an armillary sphere three feet in diameter and graduated to five minutes of arc.

The young Brahe, working at Wittenberg in 1589, constructed a quadrant of nineteen-foot radius, of wood but with a brass scale graduated to one minute of arc. Later he built an eight-foot equinoctial armillary sphere that read to fifteen seconds of arc, and a mural quadrant that read to ten seconds of arc. In his observatory at Uraniborg, Brahe consistently made angular measurements with an accuracy within one minute of arc, which should be contrasted with an accuracy within ten minutes by the Mongol astronomer Ulugh Beg (1394–1449) in Uzbekistan and an accuracy within twenty minutes by Hipparchus of Rhodes, attained between 141 and 127 B.C. With the data supplied by Brahe's instruments, by 1609 Johannes Kepler (1571–1630) was able to detect that the orbit of Mars is not circular, as had always been believed, but elliptical.

The greatest advance, however, came at the end of the Renaissance with the invention of the telescope. This device was first made sometime during 1608 by Zacharias Jansen (1580–c. 1638), a spectacle maker in the Netherlands. During 1609 the news spread to Thomas Harriot (c. 1560–1621) in England and Galileo Galilei (1564–1642) in Italy. Harriot made the first recorded use of the telescope in July 1609, and Galileo later that year. The latter's publication of the *Sidereus nuncius* (The sidereal messenger) in 1610 revolutionized astronomy with its account of mountains on the moon, the moons of Jupiter, and the many stars making up the Milky Way. Galileo's telescope had a small concave lens for its objective and a single convex lens for its eyepiece. By 1611 Kepler had worked out the optics of the telescope, which were unknown to Galileo, and proposed a superior astronomical instrument that employed concave lenses at both ends.

Navigation and Geodesy. Astronomical instruments were readily applied in other ways. The cross staff employed for navigation was equipped with sighting vanes and gave direct readings in degrees. Usually made of wood and about three feet long, it was used to measure the sun's midday altitude or that of a star above the horizon. Later models had more than one crosspiece to increase the accuracy of measurement. When the astrolabe was adapted for seaboard use its center portion was cut away to make it easier to hold in the wind. The mariner's astrolabe was also heavy, made of metal, so that it could define the perpendicular by its own weight. It was usually equipped with an alidade whose sighting vanes were set close together to facilitate reading under conditions at sea.

The magnetic compass was readily adapted for nautical use. Instead of the needle being pivoted over the compass card, the compass card itself was pivoted and highly ornamented. The course of the ship was then indicated by the card's position relative to the ship's axis. Speed was measured by a log, a weighted rectangular plate attached to a long cord, that when thrown overboard set itself crosswise and remained that way while the cord unwound. By the end of the sixteenth century, log cords were knotted at regular intervals so that the number of "knots" could be counted. Time was measured at half-minute intervals by a sandglass or log glass. The distance a ship traveled and its position could then be indicated on a peg compass or "traverse board." This consisted of a board pierced with holes in which pegs could be inserted every half hour, thus providing a track of the ship's course.

Land surveying increased during the Renaissance, stimulated by the demand for new charts and maps, by military needs, and by changes in landownership. Since both surveying and navigation involved the measurement of heights, bearings, and distances, there was some similarity of methods and some common instruments such as the cross staff. The tendency, however, was toward specific instruments for specific purposes. Measuring rods and chains were

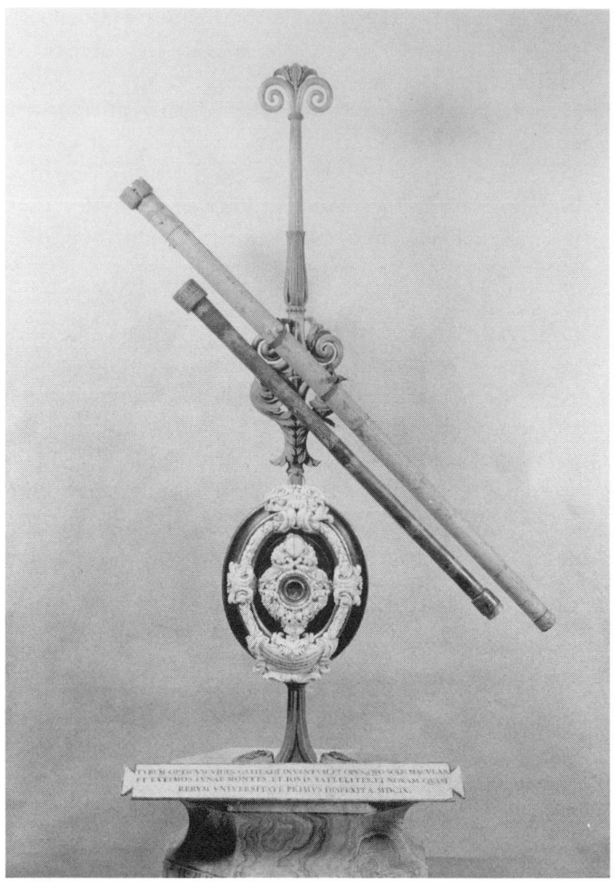

Galileo's Telescope. MUSEUM OF SCIENCE, FLORENCE/SCALA, ART RESOURCE

inherited from the Middle Ages, but triangulation became more common and led to the development of new instruments. Gemma Frisius invented one of the first devices for measuring horizontal angles. This was a horizontal circular disk graduated into four quadrants of 90 degrees, with an alidade pivoted at the center, to which a small compass was later added. This led to the theodolite, described by Thomas Digges (c. 1546–1595) in his *Geometrical Practise* of 1571. A further development was the geometrical square, a square-shaped board of wood or metal with a scale graduated along the two sides opposite the corner where the alidade was pivoted. A related instrument was the plane table, first described in the mid-sixteenth century, which quickly came into common use among surveyors. The latter also used hodometers or pedometers, also known as way wisers, to provide quick estimates of distances.

Drawing and calculating instruments were also improved during the Renaissance. The camera obscura, a dark chamber with a lens or opening through which an image is projected on an opposing wall, has a long history, but from the fifteenth century onward it was used as an aid by artists. As knowledge of optics increased, the pinhole was replaced by a lens to concentrate the image the camera produced. Dividers and compasses of various types were also produced, the more important being the reduction compass and the proportional compass. The reduction compass was invented around 1554 and consisted of two legs attached at one end by a pivot and fitted with both fixed and adjustable points. It was used to divide straight lines or circles into integral parts and to find the proportions of unequal lines. The proportional compass was a further development proposed in 1568 by Federico Commandino (1509–1575). It consisted of two slotted arms with points at each end, held together by a cursor that acted as a pivot. A further improvement was Galileo's geometrical and military compass, which he developed between 1595 and 1599. It may be described as the first mechanical mathematical calculator of all-around applicability, not restricted to one or even several specific tasks. A similar device was invented around the same time by the London mathematician Thomas Hood (fl. 1582–1598), who called it a sector and described it in a work published in 1598.

Although mathematicians and merchants did most of their mathematical calculations on paper with the aid of handbooks of mathematical problems, the frame counter or abacus also continued to be used. Logarithms were discovered by John Napier (1550–1617), who described them in a work published in 1614. Three years later he invented a calculating aid known as Napier's rods or Napier's bones, which provided in effect an arrangement of the multiplication table that shortened ordinary calculations. From these it was a short step to the slide rule. The idea of calibrating a length logarithmically and then multiplying simply by adding lengths was proposed in 1623 by Edmund Gunter (1581–1626). The circular slide rule was invented by William Oughtred (1575–1660) and described in a book published in 1631 by Richard Delamain (fl. 1610–1645). The straight slide rule as used in the twentieth century is attributed to Edmund Wingate (1596–1677), although others participated in its invention.

Precision in reading instruments was greatly improved by the invention of two devices, the nonius and the vernier, a short graduated scale that slides along a longer graduated scale and enables one to make fractional divisions in units of the longer scale. The vernier, the work of Pierre Vernier (1584–1638), came later and was the same as verniers used in the present day. The nonius was more complicated, for where the vernier usually had ten subdivisions to take into account, the nonius had well over thirty. It was the work of the Portuguese mathematician Pedro Nuñez (1502–1578) and was improved by the Jesuit mathematician Christopher Clavius (1537–1612). The latter's improvement anticipated the principle on which the vernier is based.

Physics and Medicine. Other instruments of the Renaissance pertain mainly to the physical or natural sciences and to medicine. The microscope did not gain the utility or popularity of the telescope in the Renaissance, but medical scholars began to use the microscope and to make new discoveries in the middle of the seventeenth century. Also, there is indirect evidence that before 1624 Galileo had adapted the telescope to make a compound microscope that would make a fly appear as large as a hen. Galileo also invented or experimented with other instruments, including the *pulsilogium,* a pendulum type of pulse watch; the *bilancetta,* a small hydrostatic balance; the *thermoscopium,* in effect a thermometer without a scale; the *giovilabio,* a paper instrument that could be used to determine the positions of Jupiter's satellites; and an escapement for the pendulum clock.

In the field of magnetism, the English physician William Gilbert (1544–1603) was the major pioneer. Among the instruments with which he experimented was the *terrella,* or "earthkin," a small spherical magnet that simulated the earth, the dipmeter, which measured magnetic dip and which he thought, incorrectly, could be used to determine latitude; and the *versorium,* a pivoted needle that could be used for identifying "electrics."

In medicine the foremost instrument maker was the Venetian physician Santorio Santorio (1561–1636). Santorio perfected two instruments that had already been anticipated by Galileo: the clinical thermometer, which Santorio equipped with a scale whose extreme points were determined by the temperatures of snow and a candle flame, and the pulsimeter, which measured pulse by the length of a pendulum whose swing matched the pulse's beat. He also invented a hygrometer for measuring humidity; the trocar, a special syringe for extracting bladder stones; a bathing bed; and a weighing chair. With the last named, Santorio systematically investigated the variation in weight experienced by the human body as a result of ingestion and excretion.

See also **Calendars; Clocks; Geography and Cartography; Weights and Measures.**

BIBLIOGRAPHY

Anderson, R. G. W., J. A. Bennett, and W. F. Ryan, eds. *Making Instruments Count: Essays on Historical Scientific Instruments Presented to Gerard L'Estrange Turner.* Aldershot, Hampshire, U.K., 1993.

Bedini, Silvio. "Galileo's Scientific Instrumentation." In *Reinterpreting Galileo.* Studies in Philosophy and the History of Philosophy, vol. 15. Edited by William A. Wallace. Washington, D.C., 1986. Pages 127–153.

Bud, Robert, and Deborah J. Warner, eds. *Instruments of Science: An Historical Encyclopedia.* New York and London, 1998. Mainly modern instruments, but contains concise and authoritative information for earlier periods.

Hawkes, Nigel. *Early Scientific Instruments.* New York, 1981. Contains about eighty color photographs, with commentary, many from the Renaissance.

Michel, Henri. *Scientific Instruments in Art and History.* Translated by R. E. W. Maddison and Francis R. Maddison. London and New York, 1967. Contains over one hundred color plates, with descriptions, and also line drawings, many from the Renaissance.

Mills, John FitzMaurice. *Encyclopedia of Antique Scientific Instruments.* New York, 1983. Contains a good introduction, with individual entries arranged alphabetically, some illustrated.

Turner, Anthony. *Early Scientific Instruments: Europe, 1400–1800.* London, 1987. The best overall introduction, with many illustrations, some colored.

Turner, Gerard L'Estrange. *Scientific Instruments and Experimental Philosophy, 1550–1850.* Aldershot, Hampshire, U.K., 1990. Collected studies by the author.

Turner, Gerard L'Estrange. *Scientific Instruments, 1500–1900: An Introduction.* London and Berkeley, Calif., 1998. Originally published in 1980 as *Antique Scientific Instruments.*

William A. Wallace

SCIENTIFIC METHOD. The term scientific "method" derives from the postclassical Latin *methodus,* a transliteration of the Greek *methodos,* taken from *meta,* meaning "after" or "following," and *hodos,* meaning "way," and thus signifying the way or order to be followed in rational inquiry. Interest in method revived during the Renaissance, when it joined with a changing interest in "science" to give rise to the notion of "scientific method." The modern concept differs from the Renaissance concept, the development of which occurred mainly within Aristotelianism and climaxed in the work of Galileo Galilei (1564–1642). Significant contributions were also made outside the Aristotelian tradition, most notably by Petrus Ramus (1515–1572) and Francis Bacon (1561–1626).

Aristotelian Development. The Greek teaching on method originated with the medical writer Hippocrates of Cos (c. 460–c. 377 B.C.). It is described in Plato's *Phaedrus* as a technique of dividing and collecting. Platonic "dialectical method" grew out of this and was itself a composite of four different methods: the analytical, the definitive, the divisive, and the probative, all of which were closely associated with art or *technē*. Aristotle extended Plato's idea to all rational inquiry, not merely that of the arts. For the sciences, which aimed at certain knowledge, Aristotle wrote the *Analytics,* which provides detailed methods of analysis and definition. For less stringent inquiries he wrote the *Topics,* which describes methods of probable reasoning. When method is taken broadly as coextensive with logic, as it sometimes is, all of Aristotle's books in his *Organon* ("instrument") may be seen as treatises on methodology.

A further influence came from Galen (129–c. 199), who was fundamentally Aristotelian but took inspiration also from Hippocrates and Plato. Galen focused first on analysis, then on synthesis, and associated both with definition and division. The Alexandrian mathematician Pappus (fl. 300–350), likewise wrote on methods, though he used the term *hodoi* rather than *methodoi* and confined his attention to geometry. His account influenced Renaissance mathematicians. Finally, Greek commentators on Aristotle were a major source of renewed interest in method among the Aristotelians. Many of them were also Platonists, and so they sought to correlate the four dialectical methods of Plato with Aristotle's various logical teachings.

The Latin tradition. In classical Latin many philosophical terms derived from Cicero, who did not use either *methodus* or *methodos,* with the result that the Latins never stressed "method" to the same extent as the Greeks. In classical writers one usually finds *via* or *ratio* in place of "method." Latin translations of the many commentaries on Aristotle by Averroës (1126–1198) avoided the term also. Medieval writers such as Boethius (c. 480–524), John of Salisbury (c. 1115–1180), and Albertus Magnus (c. 1200–1280) did use "method," but *via* and *ratio* became more common in the Middle Ages. To these were added the terms mode (*modus*), order (*ordo*), and process (*processus*). Albertus's student, Thomas Aquinas (1224–1274), spoke of resolution and composition (the Latin cognates of analysis and synthesis) as modes, differentiating the resolutive mode (*modus resolutivus*) from the compositive mode (*modus compositivus*). Resolution also became for him a *processus resolutivus,* or resolutive process. Order had similar connotations; thus one could speak of the order of resolution (*ordo resolutionis*) and the order of composition (*ordo compositionis*).

Jacopo Zabarella (1533–1589) gave order a more precise meaning by relating it directly to method and thereby stimulated discussion among Renaissance Aristotelians. For Zabarella order means simply that one thing should be learned before another, whereas method adds that what is known first will lead to or produce scientific knowledge of a second concept. One of Galileo's teachers at the University of Pisa, Girolamo Borro (1512–1592), published in 1584 "a defense of the peripatetic method of teaching and learning" in which he notes that method is a more precise term than order and signifies a short way whereby one ascends as quickly as possible to a particular knowledge or skill. Yet another of Galileo's teachers, Francesco Buonamici (d. 1603), placed great stress on *methodus* as the means whereby one can proceed progressively from things known to humans to those that are more knowable by nature. This process, for him, involves two stages, one resolutive and the other compositive; when both of these are completed, this closes a circle that is commonly referred to as the demonstrative regress. And Galileo's friend and colleague Jacopo Mazzoni (1548–1598) invoked the distinction found in Zabarella: order implies that one thing is learned after another, whereas method implies that one thing is learned from another and so connotes a demonstrative process.

Galileo's contribution. Galileo's clearest account of scientific method is given in his *Logical Treatises,* which he appropriated from a Jesuit logic course early in his career (c. 1589) and which became for him a logic of discovery and proof. Based on Zabarella's account of the demonstrative regress, it employed a twofold order or process, one of resolution and the other of composition. The first reasons from an effect to its cause. The second moves in the reverse order (hence a regress) from the cause to its effect. But between the two processes a third stage must intervene, and this requires the work of the intellect to be assured that the cause arrived at is the unique and proper cause of the effect.

As explained by Zabarella this third stage was based on an intellectual insight into the conditions of the conjectured cause and its accompanying effect that would be sufficient to ground a strict demonstration in Aristotle's sense and so would result in epistemic knowing, that is, in *epistēmē* or *scientia*. Galileo's development consisted in augmenting this third stage to include geometrical reasoning and experimentation. For this he also claimed epistemic results, as in his discoveries of mountains on the moon, the satellites of Jupiter, and the laws of falling bodies. He also went beyond Zabarella in extending the regress method to cover probable reasoning, as in his argument for the tides as a probable cause of motion of the earth. The latter usage is preserved in modern hypothetico-deductive reasoning, commonly referred to as "scientific method," which consists in formulating a hypothesis and deriving from it consequences that can be put to empirical test. This technique makes no claim for apodictic results, as does the regressive method, and its predominant use explains why most recent science is regarded as fallible and revisable.

Other Developments. Two other influences on scientific method in the Renaissance, as already mentioned, derive from Petrus Ramus and Francis Bacon. Both of these thinkers regarded themselves as anti-Aristotelians, as did Galileo in his physics, but their opposition, like his, was more to the Aristotelians of their day than it was to Aristotle himself.

Ramus was an educational reformer and a humanist who reacted against the Aristotelian logic he had been taught at the University of Paris and sought to replace it by the dialectical and rhetorical logic of Rudolf Agricola (1443/44–1485). He especially wished to revive the mathematical arts of the quadrivium (arithmetic, geometry, astronomy, and physics) and to show the practical uses to which they could be put. Aristotle's *Physics* was too abstruse and theoretical, in his mind, for educational purposes; better to start with his *Mechanical Problems* and his *Meteorology,* or even his biological works. Ramus also thought that classical authors on mathematics and natural history should be integrated into the curriculum. He placed great emphasis on method, but what he meant by this was more a method of teaching than of doing science. Even as the first it remained largely programmatic throughout his life.

Bacon took inspiration from Ramus, for he too was interested in the reform of human learning and had practical concerns. Despite being a contemporary of Galileo and other founders of modern science, he knew little of their achievements. Instead, he based his ideas on classical sources, with the result that his own contributions were mainly literary in character. His goal was to provide a new *Organon* that would make use of induction and experiment, but within which mathematics did not figure, as it had for Ramus. This was set out in his *Novum Organum* of 1620. The foundation for Bacon's science was to be natural history, which would serve as the base of a "ladder of axioms," above which would be physics, which in turn would lead to metaphysics, actually a kind of a universal physics. Both physics and metaphysics would then supply causal explanations of the world of nature. Bacon's concept of induction began with a simple enumeration of particulars, now known of as "Baconian induction," which was to be corrected by recourse to tables of presence, absence, and comparison, by consideration of numerous "prerogative instances" (including *instantiae crucis,* or "crucial instances"), and the performance of "fit and apposite experiments"—foreshadowing the notion of "crucial experiments." In practice, Bacon's method failed to achieve the results he claimed for it. Yet both it and his insistence on experimentation set an ideal for the Royal Society of England that bore much fruit throughout the seventeenth century.

See also **Mechanics; Science; Science, Epistemology of.**

BIBLIOGRAPHY

Blake, Ralph M., Curt J. Ducasse, and Edward H. Madden. *Theories of Scientific Method: The Renaissance through the Nineteenth Century*. Seattle, Wash., 1960.

Galilei, Galileo. *Galileo's Logical Treatises: A Translation, with Notes and Commentary, of his Appropriated Latin Questions on Aristotle's* Posterior Analytics. Translated and annotated by William A. Wallace. Dordrecht, Netherlands, and Boston, 1992.

Gilbert, Neal W. *Renaissance Concepts of Method*. New York and London, 1960.

Kargon, Robert H. *Atomism in England from Hariot to Newton*. Oxford, 1966.

Larsen, Robert E. "The Aristotelianism of Bacon's *Novum Organum*." *Journal of the History of Ideas* 23 (1962): 435–450.

Wallace, William A. *Galileo's Logic of Discovery and Proof: The Background, Content, and Use of His Appropriated Treatises on Aristotle's* Posterior Analytics. Dordrecht, Netherlands; Boston; and London; 1992.

Weisheipl, James A. "The Evolution of Scientific Method." In *Nature and Motion in the Middle Ages*. Edited by William E. Carroll. Washington, D.C., 1985. Pages 239–260.

WILLIAM A. WALLACE

SCOTLAND. Viewed from the Mediterranean centers of Renaissance civilization, Scotland appeared remote and semibarbarous, a kingdom notable less for its cultural achievements than for its ferocious internal feuding and longstanding animosity to England. It was a perception of which the Scots themselves were keenly aware and which they tried hard to combat. Precisely because Scotland was a small and relatively poor kingdom, situated "far from the sun" on the northwestern fringes of the known world, its political and cultural elite was deter-

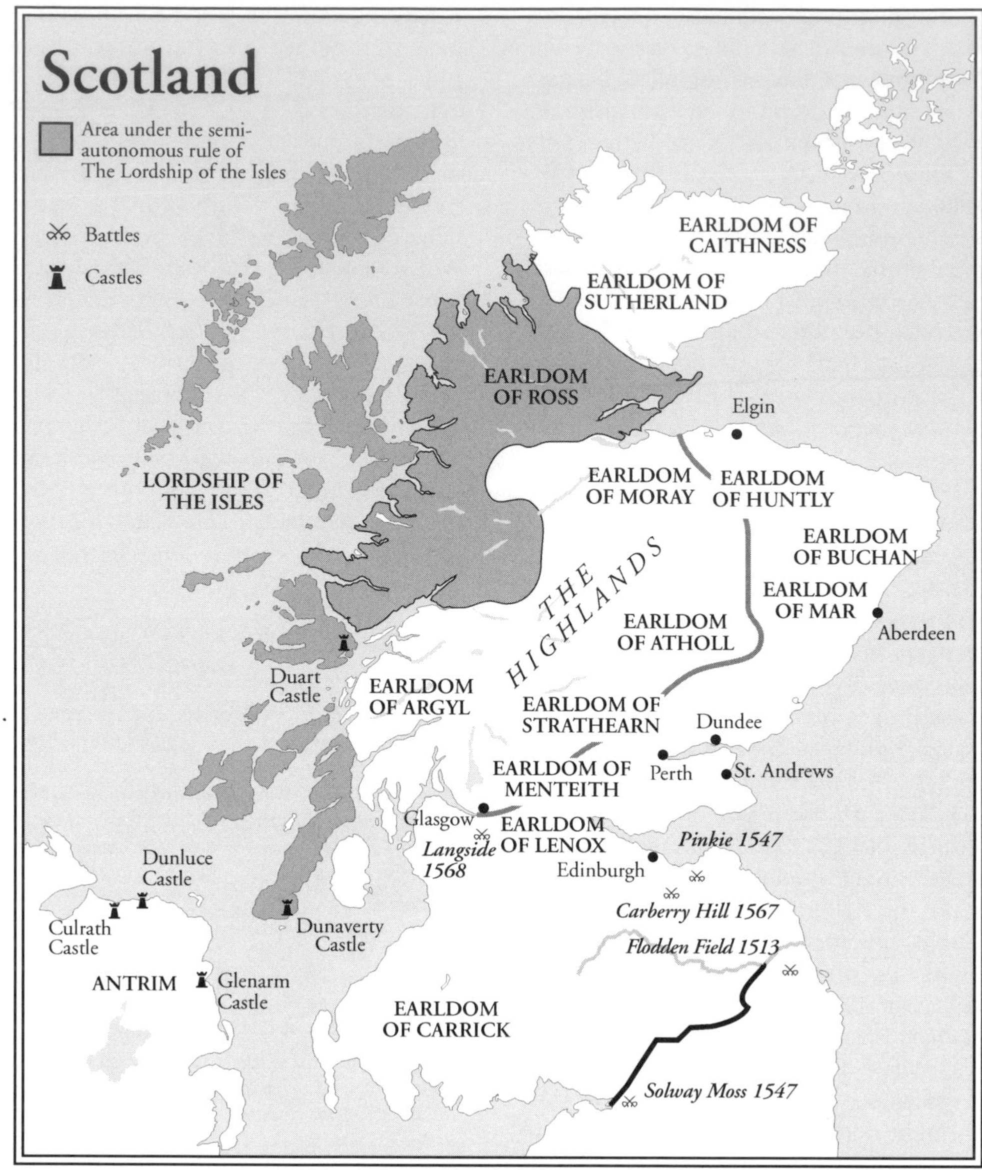

minedly European in outlook. Such cosmopolitanism was encouraged by extensive trade links across the North Sea with the Baltic states, the Low Countries, and France. Although not a rich country, Scotland sustained a growing population (rising from some 600,000 in 1450 to 900,000 in 1650), while also generating an agricultural surplus that enabled it to export primary products such as wool, hides, and salt fish in return for manufactured and luxury goods. Cultural commerce followed the trade routes but also went far beyond them. Despite the foundation of three universities in the fifteenth century (Saint Andrews in 1411, Glasgow in 1451, and Aberdeen in 1495), Scots continued to seek further education in the intellectual centers of Europe. Through their willingness to travel, the Scots' apparent remoteness did little to inhibit the impact of either the Renaissance or the Reformation on the cultural life of the kingdom.

Renaissance Monarchy. These influences are reflected in the aspirations of the Stuart dynasty, which dominated Scotland for three centuries following the family's accession to the throne in 1371. After a faltering start, a succession of energetic monarchs steadily imposed the crown's authority on what was not only a geographically fragmented kingdom but also a highly localized one in which military and jurisdictional power was vested in regional magnates. In the course of the fifteenth century, despite a succession of royal minorities, the balance of power gradually shifted in favor of the monarchy. By the reign of James IV (1488–1513), the power of the regional magnates was largely broken, and the territorial consolidation of the Stuart patrimony was all but complete.

Success at home was accompanied by a desire to make an impact abroad. While the early Stuart monarchs contented themselves with marriage alliances among the aristocracy, their successors forged ever more ambitious European unions. Thus in 1449 James II (1437–1460) married into the ducal house of Gueldres, while in 1469 James III (1460–1488) married into the Danish royal house. Such unions consolidated Scotland's close links with the Low Countries and the Baltic states, while also reflecting the Stuart dynasty's increasing significance on the European marriage market. The marriage in 1503 of James IV to Margaret Tudor, daughter of Henry VII of England, may be seen as a further step in this process of dynastic aggrandizement. Yet this marriage was significant for other reasons. The Scots' traditional hostility to England had ensured both that Scotland remained allied to France throughout the later Middle Ages and that the defense of the realm against English aggression was perceived as the key function of the Scottish crown. A policy of rapprochement with England was thus deeply unpopular in Scotland and 1503 did not mark the end of the "auld alliance" with France. In fact, it was in fulfillment of his obligations to the French king, Louis XII, that James IV embarked on the invasion of England which led to his defeat and death at the battle of Flodden in 1513.

The marriage of James IV to Margaret Tudor resulted a century later in the union of the Scottish and English crowns under James I (James VI of Scotland). Yet such a dynastic union was neither inevitable nor planned. By the early sixteenth century Scotland had emerged as a consolidated kingdom under a dynasty that was both well established and determined to play a part on the European stage. Significantly, it was during James IV's reign that the royal coat of arms was first embellished by an arched or closed "imperial" crown. The arched crown, the visual expression of the Roman law doctrine that "the king is emperor in his own kingdom," was a key symbol of the complete territorial and jurisdictional sovereignty claimed by the monarchies of Renaissance Europe. Well known in Italy and France, the idea was transmitted from French law schools to Scotland, where in 1469 Parliament first declared that the king possessed "full jurisdiction and free empire within his realm." By the end of the century, when Bishop William Elphinstone (1431–1514) embellished the chapel of his new university at Aberdeen with a steeple in the form of an imperial crown, the idea was being vigorously exploited as a means of encapsulating the integrity of the kingdom and the Stuart monarchy's jurisdictional supremacy within it. James IV, the most charismatic of the Stuart monarchs, presided over a flamboyant court, animated by the king's own passion for elaborate chivalric display as well as his interest in architecture, alchemy, and medicine. However, underpinning the vitality of his court was the Scottish community's strong sense of itself as an imperial monarchy claiming parity of status with those of Renaissance Europe as a whole.

The Impact of Humanism. Self-confidence such as this stemmed in part from the Scottish elite's exposure to European life and learning. Although more influential than most, William Elphinstone was not untypical among Scottish clerics in using a continental education as a stepping-stone to advancement in the royal bureaucracy as well as the church. Trained in law at Glasgow, Paris, and Orléans, he became both bishop of Aberdeen and a leading figure in James IV's government. Education abroad also ensured that the Scottish intelligentsia kept abreast of such intellectual developments as the renewed interest in classical literature associated with the humanist movement. Just as Elphinstone possessed a copy of Lorenzo Valla's celebrated *Elegantiae Latinae linguae* (Elegances of the Latin language; c. 1440), so the Cologne-educated Archibald Whitelaw, archdeacon of Saint Andrews and royal secretary from 1462 to 1493, amassed a classical library which included printed editions of Horace, Lucan, and Sallust as well as a manuscript copy of Cicero's philosophical works. It was Whitelaw's long tenure as royal secretary that ensured that humanist rhetorical skills became institutionalized in the Scottish chancery just as they were in the chanceries of Europe generally.

Yet the impact of humanism extended well beyond its practical application in government. Among Whitelaw's successors as royal secretary was the highly accomplished Patrick Paniter, who held the post from 1505 until 1519. Paniter was among a remarkable group of Scots who in the 1490s were fellow students of Desiderius Erasmus at the College of Montaigu in Paris. Among them was Hector Boece (c. 1465–1536), author of the first humanist history of Scotland, *Scotorum historia* (Paris, 1527), who served for thirty years as principal of Elphinstone's new university at Aberdeen, establishing it as the main Scottish center for the dissemination of the "new learning." Not all the Scottish universities were as open to humanist influences as Aberdeen. The dominant figure at Saint Andrews was John Mair or Major (c. 1467–1550), who, like Boece and Paniter, had studied with Erasmus at Montaigu but who remained deeply skeptical of the humanist movement's championing of rhetoric over dialectic. Major taught in Paris for twenty-five years, establishing a European reputation as a logician, philosopher, and theologian before returning to Scotland in 1518 to teach at Glasgow and Saint Andrews. For all his commitment to scholastic method, however, Major was not unsympathetic to the humanists' desire to create an educated lay elite. Gradually Saint Andrews and Glasgow were to follow Aberdeen's example and fashion an arts curriculum that, owing much to the *studia humanitatis,* was aimed at serving the laity as well as the clergy.

The emergence of a literate, often highly educated lay elite was among the most significant cultural developments of the period. The spread of literacy from the upper nobility and merchants to a wider population of lesser landowners and burgesses is reflected in the adoption in the fifteenth century of vernacular Scots as the language of government as well as in a remarkable explosion of vernacular poetry, written for or by the laity, and best exemplified in the work of Robert Henryson (c. 1430–c. 1500), William Dunbar (c. 1460–c. 1514), and Gavin Douglas (1474–1522). Douglas was also touched by humanism, translating Virgil's *Aeneid* into vernacular Scots for his lay patron, Henry, Lord Sinclair. Yet many laymen were becoming sufficiently accomplished in the language of learning to read such Latin texts for themselves. By the 1530s it was common enough for laymen not only to have graduated in arts but also to have gone on to study law, often in France or Italy. Thus Sir James Foulis of Colinton, the son of an Edinburgh burgess and an accomplished Latin poet, studied law in Paris and Orléans before serving as clerk-register from 1532 until 1549. Likewise, from 1526 to 1543, the post of royal secretary was held by Sir Thomas Erskine, a minor landowner who had studied law at Pavia.

Lay lawyers such as Erskine and Foulis played a prominent role in the government of James V, who, coming to the throne in 1513 when barely a year old, took personal control in 1528 and, in the aftermath of a turbulent minority, exploited the legal resources at his disposal to reimpose the crown's authority with ruthless efficiency. At the same time, following Henry VIII's break with Rome in 1533, he took advantage of Scotland's unwonted diplomatic significance to extort lucrative financial concessions from the papacy and to persuade the French king, Francis I, to permit his marriage in 1537 to his eldest surviving daughter, Madeleine. Although Madeleine died within months, the king's subsequent marriage to Mary of Guise reinforced Scotland's ties with Valois France while simultaneously lending weight to James V's self-image as an imperial monarch of European stature. Appropriately, the huge financial rewards of his successful diplomacy were invested in the royal palaces of Stirling, Falkland, and Holyrood, using French masons to create some of the first and finest Renaissance buildings in Britain.

Within these spectacular architectural settings, however, the glittering court of James V was fraught with tension. The clerical hierarchy felt threatened by the influence of educated laymen receptive both to evangelical humanism and to emergent Protestantism. The king may well have been tempted to follow the example of Henry VIII, and the logic of his own imperial pretensions, by overthrowing the authority of Rome and establishing the crown's supremacy over the church in Scotland. Certainly, he became an astute if fickle patron of anticlerical sentiment, commissioning from George Buchanan (1506–1582) the series of blistering attacks on the Franciscans which both established the young humanist's reputation as a Latin poet of prodigious talent and forced him into continental exile. More fortunate was the lay poet Sir David Lindsay (c. 1490–1555), a lifelong confidant of the king, whose vernacular verse was increasingly characterized by a scathing Erasmian anticlericalism which, spilling beyond the confines of the royal court, rapidly took hold in lay society more generally.

The Reformation. The unexpected death of James V in 1542, aged only thirty, left as his sole legitimate heir the week-old Mary, queen of Scots (1542–1587), and precipitated a prolonged crisis for the Stuart dynasty from which it did not recover until James VI (1566–1625) took personal control of the government in the mid-1580s. The intervening decades witnessed the Scots' final rejection of their ancient ties with France and Rome and their emergence as a Protestant kingdom closely allied with England. Yet the transformation was neither as inevitable nor as decisive as this suggests. In religious terms, while lay anticlericalism stoked up the pressure for reform, committed Protestants remained in a distinct minority in the two decades before 1560. The Protestant settlement of that year was more a product of international diplomacy than of overwhelming domestic support for the "godly" society envisaged by the leading Scottish Reformer and former Genevan exile, John Knox (1514–1572). While France's inability to respond to England's intervention in Scottish affairs in 1560 led to a precarious Protestant settlement, this was immediately jeopardized by the return of the adult and Catholic Mary Stuart to her native kingdom in 1561. Even the queen's deposition in 1567, on the grounds of adultery rather than idolatry, failed to place Scotland securely within the Protestant camp. Exiled and imprisoned in England, nursing her claim to the Tudor as well as to the Stuart inheritance, Mary continued to hold out the promise of a Counter-Reformation, which would see her established as the Catholic queen of Britain.

Dynastic stability was only restored by Mary's execution in 1587, an event that paved the way for her son, James VI, to succeed peacefully to the English throne on the death of the childless Elizabeth Tudor in 1603. Born in 1566, James was actually baptized a Catholic in a ceremony at Stirling, accompanied by a lavish Renaissance spectacle, which was the undoubted high point of Mary's brief personal rule. However, despite this baptism, James was brought up a Protestant. In 1570, in the midst of the civil war which racked the country following Mary's deposition, the king was placed in the care of George Buchanan, the most distinguished Scottish humanist of the age, who had returned to Scotland to grace the court of Mary Stuart but who emerged as the leading ideologue of the revolution against her. For twelve years, between 1570 and his death in 1582, Buchanan presided over the king's schooling, successfully instilling in his royal pupil a lifelong respect for classical learning and literature, while unsuccessfully impressing upon him the virtues of limited, elective monarchy.

James VI's subsequent development of a theory of divine right kingship was partly a reaction against Buchanan's subversive political ideas and partly a reaction to their adoption by his presbyterian critics who, determined to maintain the church's independence of state control, were opposed to the idea of the royal supremacy and the king's efforts to control ecclesiastical affairs through royally appointed bishops. Among the latter was the brilliant Calvinist-humanist academic Andrew Melville (1545–1622), who, in addition to reforming the Scottish universities along lines suggested by the work of French philosopher Petrus Ramus, became an outspoken defender of the church's independence from crown control. Such a stance inevitably brought Melville into conflict with a monarch committed to reasserting the crown's supremacy in both church and state. Yet James's opposition to presbyterianism owed less to an ideological commitment to imperial monarchy and episcopacy per se than to his desire to impose order and obedience on a kingdom destabilized by decades of civil and confessional strife. Insofar as presbyteries proved a vehicle for the pacification of the localities, James was prepared to support the work of his zealous Protestant clergy. At the same time, however, he remained tolerant of Catholics who, if they did not share the king's faith, shared his commitment to the rule of law. Though constantly strapped for cash and unable to re-create the stylish court life enjoyed by his predecessors, James was a significant patron of literature, as happy to extend royal favor to a Catholic poet like Alexander Montgomerie (c. 1548–1598) as to relish the Protestant epics of the French Huguenot Guillaume de Salluste Du Bartas. Likewise, Catholicism proved no bar to crown service: among James's most trusted and longest-serving counselors, appointed chancellor in 1605, was the cultivated Catholic lawyer, Alexander Seton, earl of Dunfermline (1555–1622).

In fact, it was neither Calvinism nor absolutism that lent coherence to James's policies but rather an overriding concern with the extension of law, order, and civility throughout his realm. Increasingly, such priorities resonated with a landed elite for whom a humanist education was now the norm and who, as local society was slowly demilitarized, began to extend and embellish their stark but defensible tower houses or to abandon them altogether in favor of the more luxurious country dwellings of a leisured aristocracy. Such developments predated 1603, though James's removal to England doubtless accelerated the process. Yet, despite the greater congruity of Scottish and English society, and despite the king's efforts to promote a common British polity and identity, what occurred in 1603 remained simply a union of the crowns, not a union of the kingdoms. Scotland retained its distinct political identity as well as a distinct cultural style and voice—the product of the interaction of native traditions with the transformative influence of the Renaissance and Reformation.

See also **James I; Major, John; Mary Stuart; Stuart Dynasty.**

BIBLIOGRAPHY

Donaldson, Gordon. *Scotland: James V to James VII.* Edinburgh, 1965. A dated but still useful survey.

Fawcett, Richard. *Scottish Architecture: From the Accession of the Stewarts to the Reformation, 1371–1560.* Edinburgh, 1994.

Howard, Deborah. *Scottish Architecture: Reformation to Restoration, 1560–1660.* Edinburgh, 1995.
Jack, R. D. S., ed. *The History of Scottish Literature.* Vol. 1, Origins to 1660. Aberdeen, U.K., 1988.
Lynch, Michael. *Scotland: A New History.* London, 1991. A comprehensive history of Scotland, particularly strong on the sixteenth century.
MacMillan, Duncan. *Scottish Art, 1460–1990.* Edinburgh, 1990.
Mason, Roger A. *Kingship and the Commonweal: Political Thought in Renaissance and Reformation Scotland.* East Linton, U.K., 1998.
Wormald, Jenny. *Court, Kirk, and Community: Scotland, 1470–1625.* London, 1981. The best short introduction to the period.

ROGER A. MASON

SCRIPTURE. *See* **Bible.**

SCULPTURE. Renaissance sculpture in Italy and in northern Europe have essential differences in their roots and development. They must be considered as separate units.

Italian Renaissance Sculpture. The development of Italian Renaissance sculpture can be divided into three periods. The first covers the transition from the later Middle Ages and lasted until around 1400. The second corresponds roughly to the fifteenth century and was dominated by Florentine art and artists. Sculptors carefully examined the appearance and behavior of man, including how the body functioned. They also studied the individual portrait (primarily the face), and powerful dramatic expression, greatly influenced by the Roman antique and humanistic man-centered ideas then prevalent. The first part of this phase is strongly connected to Florence's civic pride, linked to the democratic values attributed to the Roman Republic. The third phase covers the sixteenth century, beginning with the high Renaissance and Michelangelo (1475–1564). At this point, grandeur and power assumed a major role, and influenced sculptors' personal and artificial interpretations of human bodies and actions, often referred to as mannerist. Italian sculpture was used as a display of wealth that accompanied the expanding autocratic rule and its luxury, this leading to the sculptural embellishment of cities.

The early phase: c. 1250–1400. During this period Italian sculpture accommodated diverse trends. The first was the continuity of traditional massive form reverting to the Romanesque period. The second was the absorption of Gothic realism imported from northern Europe. The third, setting the stage for the Renaissance proper, was a direct awareness of ancient Roman art. These tendencies are already visible in the sculpture created for Emperor Frederick II (1220–1250) in southern Italy, and especially in the works of Nicola Pisano (c. 1220–1278/84), the leading Tuscan sculptor of his time. His pulpit reliefs in the Baptistery of Pisa (completed in 1260) use Roman sources that still exist: an ancient marble vase and a Phaedra sarcophagus. Nicola's Siena Cathedral pulpit (completed in 1268) reflects northern French sculpture in the softer, realistic treatment of figures. Nicola's son Giovanni Pisano (c. 1245/1250–1319), equally indebted to northern Gothic sculpture, preferred powerful, dramatic expression and violent movement, as can be seen in his pulpit reliefs in Sant' Andrea in Pistoia (1289–1301) and the Cathedral of Pisa (completed in 1312). In contrast, Arnolfo di Cambio (c. 1245–1302), who, like Giovanni, learned his art in Nicola's workshop, preferred simplified monumental form, as can be seen in his *Virgin and Child* from the facade of Florence Cathedral (after 1296; in the museum of the cathedral). The reliefs of *Genesis* and the *Last Judgment* on the facade piers of Orvieto Cathedral, usually attributed to Lorenzo Maitani (dated between 1310 and 1330), reveal a detailed understanding of the human form generally not seen this early, ranging from delicate relief treatment to active movement and intense emotion in the scene of the damned souls in hell. Andrea Pisano produced the first bronze door for the Baptistery of Florence, representing the Life of Saint John (completed in 1336).

The second period: the fifteenth century. Many outstanding sculptors were at work during the first half of the century, a time when Florence dominated. The start of this phase is usually generally considered to be the competition for the second bronze door of the Baptistry of Florence (1402), won by Lorenzo Ghiberti (c. 1378–1455). A superb craftsman, his competition relief of the *Sacrifice of Isaac* was cast in one piece, and the lithe body of his young Isaac demonstrates his full control over the depiction of human anatomy. Ghiberti's reliefs of *The Life of Christ* on the second Baptistery door (1403–1424) offer a transition from Gothic decorative conventions, clearly evident in the scoop folds of the Angel Gabriel's dress in the *Annunciation* scene, to the creation of agitated, packed crowd scenes, as in *Christ Driving the Moneylenders from the Temple.* Many elements on the door are derived from ancient Roman sarcophagi. Early in this period the influence of the Roman antique extends to the putti (cherubic children) carrying festoons on Jacopo della Quercia's (1374–1438) elegant sarcophagus of

Lorenzo Ghiberti. ***Sacrifice of Isaac.*** Ghiberti (c. 1378–1455) made the relief of the sacrifice of Isaac for a competition to complete the doors of the Baptistery of Florence Cathedral. The panels were to be the same size and shape as those made by Andrea Pisano (for a view of the doors, see the biography of Pisano in volume 5). Ghiberti received the commission to make new doors in 1403 (for a view of Ghiberti's doors, see the color plates in volume 3). The panel illustrates the text of Genesis 22:1–19. MUSEO NAZIONALE DEL BARGELLO, FLORENCE/ALINARI/ART RESOURCE

Ilaria del Carretto in Lucca Cathedral (1406), and Nanni di Banco's formal *Four Crowned Saints* (c. 1414) at Or San Michele, Florence. After completing the second bronze Baptistery door, Ghiberti was commissioned to make the third: the *Doors of Paradise* (1425–1452). The two wings show ten large squarish scenes from the Old Testament. These reliefs represent the culmination of his skill in control of bronze casting technique and perfect finish. The rhythmic grace of the three midwives in the *Jacob and Esau* panel [see the illustration to the entry on Space and Perspective] recalls the ancient group of the Three Graces, and in the architectural setting Ghiberti makes use of linear perspective.

Donatello's (1386?–1466) genius sets him above the other sculptors of his time. His early *Saint Mark* (1411–1413) at Or San Michele, Florence, firmly rests its weight on one leg, in the manner of ancient statuary. In the course of Donatello's career, the extreme range of his artistic curiosity reaches from the powerful drama of the bronze *Dance of Salome* relief in the Baptistery of Siena Cathedral (c. 1425) and the dynamic abandon of the dancing putti that appear on his choir balcony made for Florence Cathedral (mid-1430s), to the coarse realism of his *Zuccone* in the museum of Florence Cathedral (1423–1425), the idealizing *Cavalcanti Annunciation* in S. Croce, Florence (c. 1433), and the captivating perfect anatomy of the adolescent bronze *David* in the Bargello, Florence, made for the Medici (1440?). He also investigates the effects of perspective in low relief (*rilievo schacciato*) on his relief of *Saint George Fighting the Dragon* at Or San Michele (1415–1417). His interest in drama comprises vast panoramic architectural settings and scenes packed with agitated figures difficult to disentangle, as is evident in his bronze reliefs on the high altar of the Sanctuary of Saint Anthony at Padua of the *Miracle of the Believing Donkey* and the *Miracle of the Irascible Son* (1446–1453) and his two bronze pulpits, completed by his shop after his death, in San Lorenzo, Florence (1460s). He also made the monumental bronze commemorative equestrian statue of the Gattamelata in Padua (1445–1453), inspired by that of Marcus Aurelius in Rome. His bronze statue of Judith standing on the severed head of Holophernes (c. 1455) in the Piazza della Signoria, Florence, demonstrates his interest in statuary that is located in the open, where it can be seen effectively from various directions. And his *Mary Magdalen,* carved in wood and painted, in the museum of Florence Cathedral (1450s?), her worn body testifying to her penance, radiates spirituality. Donatello experimented widely with decorative effects

Donatello. ***Mary Magdalen.*** The statue, of wood, was originally in the Baptistery, Florence. MUSEO DELL'OPERA DEL DUOMO, FLORENCE/ALINARI/ART RESOURCE

and even abstraction, as can be seen in the reduced setting of the *Cavalcanti Annunciation,* and also the gold mosaic inlay in back of the wildly dancing white marble putti on his Choir Balcony.

Two other sculptors, both Florentine, active in the second half of the fourteenth century deserve notice. Antonio Pollaiuolo (c. 1431–1498) investigated bodies interlocked in movement in the small bronze of Hercules lifting Antaeus off the ground (1470s?) in the Bargello, Florence. And on his tomb of Sixtus IV in the Vatican he carefully renders the gerontic features of the old pope. The second, Andrea del Verrocchio (1435–1488), a master of precise detail, followed diverse interests, comprising the tender marble portrait of a young woman holding a nosegay to her chest, in the Bargello, Florence (c. 1475), the bronze statuary group of the *Doubting Thomas* at Or San Michele which extends out of its niche into the public space (1465–1483), and the delightful fountain sculpture of the putto with a fish in the Palazzo Vecchio, Florence (c. 1470). He also made the theatrical bronze equestrian monument of Bartolommeo Colleoni (1481–1496) in Venice, completed by Alessandro Leopardi, where the walking horse raises one foot off the ground.

Although female portraiture was usually idealized, in this period male portrait sculpture followed the everyday realism of the Roman Republic, with likenesses respecting unflattering detail of aging, as in Antonio Rossellino's bust of Matteo Palmieri, in the Bargello, Florence (1468). The tomb sculpture of this period puts the ancient triumphal arch motif to Christian use, as in Bernardo Rossellino's (1409–1464) elegant tomb of Leonardo Bruni, former chancellor of the Florentine republic, in Santa Croce, Florence (1446–1447). During the later fifteenth century, sculptors also expanded production of bronzes that copied the antique to satisfy the interests of humanist collectors. A battle relief by Bertoldo di Giovanni (c. 1430/40–1491), which pitted Roman against barbarian, in the Bargello, Florence (before 1491), is directly based on an ancient battle sarcophagus in Pisa, and in northern Italy Pier Jacopo Alari Bonacolsi (c. 1460–1528), called Antico, made bronze statuettes reflecting the antique style for the Gonzaga at Mantua.

The high Renaissance and the sixteenth century. This period is dominated by the overwhelming presence of Michelangelo di Lodovico Buonarroti Simoni (1475–1564), whose artistic career spans more than sixty years. Giorgio Vasari, in his two editions of the *Lives of the Artists* (published in 1550 and 1568) considers Michelangelo's work and concludes that it outperforms the great masters of antiquity and represents the climax of Renaissance art. His sculpture defies simple description. Michelangelo used the human body as the instrument of his artistic expression. Eager for recognition, the young sculptor strived for perfect finish and precise detail, visible in his early *Bacchus* (1497–1498) in the Bargello, Florence, and especially the Vatican *Pietà* (1498–1499; see the biography of Michelangelo in volume 4). Completed some years after, his colossal *David* in the Accademia, Florence (1501–1504; see the color plates in volume 3), more than fourteen feet high, is usually considered the ideal Renaissance male nude. In its stable pose and calculating sideward look, and especially its considerable scale, the statue expresses immanent power. A decade later Michelangelo followed with the two Louvre *Slaves* (1513–1516), intended for the tomb of Pope Julius II, whose tense muscular poses and emotionless faces suggest inner struggle. Completed shortly after, the overpowering *Moses* (1515), the centerpiece of the pope's tomb in San Pietro in Vincoli, Rome, introduces an element of theatrical exaggeration.

Michelangelo continued to investigate the allegorical use of the human form in the Medici tombs in the new sacristy of San Lorenzo, Florence (1519–1534). The two seated portraits of the deceased Lorenzo and Giuliano de' Medici, representing thought and action, are idealized and bear no resemblance to the actual persons. Michelangelo's four unfinished *Slaves* in the Accademia, Florence (1527–1528), intended for the tomb of Pope Julius II, present roughly defined, struggling bodies confined in their marble blocks. They invite comparison with the Platonic concept of the soul imprisoned in the earthly body, yearning to return to heaven. Altogether, Michelangelo's metaphorical use of the human body departs from the unquestioned realism of the previous century. As a consequence, sculptors are invited to follow personal inclinations, referred to as mannerist. Curvilinear movement often prevails, uplifting, defying gravity, visible in Michelangelo's *Medici Madonna* (1524–1534) in the new sacristy, San Lorenzo, Florence (the *figura serpentinata*), and his last, unfinished, sculpture: the *Rondanini Pietà* (1554–1564) in Milan.

Of the many outstanding Italian sculptors active around the middle of the sixteenth century, we know more of Benvenuto Cellini's (1500–1571) life than any other because he left an autobiography. Trained as a goldsmith, he also engaged in monumental sculpture, represented by his gigantic bronze *Per-*

Nicholas Gerhaerts of Leiden. ***Self-Portrait.*** Gerhaerts (d. 1473) was a stonemason and architect. Sculpted c. 1467. MUSÉE DE L'OEUVRE NÔTRE DAME, STRASBOURG, FRANCE/ ERICH LESSING/ART RESOURCE

seus in the Loggia dei Lanzi, Florence (1545–1554). In the latter part of the century Giovanni Bologna, born in Douai but active in Italy, investigated dynamic movement in monumental figure groups, such as his *Rape of the Sabines* (completed in 1583) and his *Hercules Fighting a Centaur* (1594–1599), both in the Loggia dei Lanzi, Florence.

As the sixteenth century progressed, autocratic rule, its propaganda, and its luxurious, ceremonial way of life made effective use of sculpture. Giovanni Bologna's dignified equestrian bronze portrait of Duke Cosimo I de' Medici (completed in 1595) was raised in the Piazza della Signoria, Florence. Classical allegory assumed a leading role in public commissions, including grand fountain sculpture. Giovanni Angelo Montorsoli's (c. 1507–1563) fountains of Orion and Neptune in Messina (completed respectively in 1551? and 1557) gave impetus to Bartolomeo Ammanati's (1511–1592) *Fountain of Neptune* in the Piazza della Signoria, Florence (completed in 1575), with its many bronze figures of sea divinities. Sculptural decoration of buildings also became prominent. Once established in Venice, Jacopo Sansovino (1486–1570) freely integrated sculpture with his architecture, thus contributing to its luxurious appearance. This can be seen in the relief of putti carrying festoons along the attic of the library of Saint Mark (begun in 1537) and the sculptures on the balustrade rising from the roof, motifs frequently repeated thereafter. And Sansovino richly adorned the facade of the *Loggetta* beneath the bell tower in the Piazza San Marco (1537–1540) with reliefs and niche statues of virtues and ancient gods. Altogether, much of sixteenth-century Italian sculpture offers conventions that were further developed in the baroque style of the seventeenth century and had a wide influence on the rest of Europe.

Northern European Sculpture. The rise of detailed realism visible in the leading sculpture in northern Europe of the later fourteenth and early fifteenth centuries lacks the decisive connection to the Roman antique found in Italy. Thus, it is questionable whether here the title of "Renaissance" really applies, or whether northern sculpture of this period should be considered late medieval.

In general, northern realism in sculpture reverts to the thirteenth-century rise of the great Gothic cathedrals and their vast sculptural decoration. This realism extends through the fourteenth century and includes a remarkable range in styles and media: large figures in wood and stone and exquisite ivory carvings. They offer a full range of emotional expression, from dramatic exaggeration in representations of the Passion of Christ, as in the Roettgen *Pietà* in Bonn (c. 1370), where Christ's blood gushes from his wounds, to the tender so-called beautiful *Madonnas* produced in central Europe around the turn of the century, including the Krumau *Madonna* in Vienna (c. 1390). In the latter part of the century, sculptors turned more toward a detailed realism, and works by known sculptors become more prevalent. The real portrait emerged, including Peter Parler's *Self-Portrait* in Prague Cathedral (1375–1379), and Jean de Liège's statues of Charles V in the Louvre (before 1381). This upsurge in realism reaches a climax in Claus Sluter's *Old Testament Prophets* from the Moses Fountain at the Carthusian Monastery at Champmol, near Dijon (1395–1406). Surely based on real models, the figures' realism is accentuated by animated expressions of thought, speech, and movement, the detailed treatment of the aging face, and also by their color, contributed by the painter Jean Malouel. Another example of painted northern sculpture is found in the firm *Annunciation* group of Jean Delemer (fl. c. 1428–1459) at the Ste. Marie-Madeleine, Tournai (1428), the painter being Robert Campin (1378–1444). These masters were of Netherlandish origin. In the first half of the fifteenth century, the development of Netherlandish painting and sculpture were intimately connected.

It is generally believed that Nicolaus Gerhaert (d. c. 1473), who came from Leiden, transferred Claus Sluter's (c. 1340/50–1406) realism to Germany and Austria, where he worked during the third quarter of the fifteenth century (he died in Vienna). His animated realism is evident in the elaborate twisted pose of his so-called *Self-Portrait* in Strasbourg (c. 1467). Hans Multscher of Swabia was another significant sculptor active for many years in southern Germany around mid-century.

German-speaking lands of the later fifteenth and early sixteenth centuries witnessed the production of exceptional monumental altarpieces carved in wood, often rising close to the choir vault, created by many outstanding wood-carvers. Michael Pacher's (1435–1498) altarpiece of the *Coronation of the Virgin* in the parish church of Saint Wolfgang, where he also served as the painter (1471–1481), is an outstanding example. Both the work's figures and the intricately carved canopy with its delicate Gothic tracery inspire admiration. Consider also Tilman Riemenschneider's *Altar of the Holy Blood* in Saint James's Church, Rothenburg (1499–1505; see the biography of Riemenschneider in this volume); Veit Stoss's *Death of the Virgin* Altar in Saint Mary's, Cracow (c. 1477–1489); the Altar of the *Coronation of the Virgin* by the Master H. L. in the Minster at Breisach (1523–1536), where the Virgin's smooth face and hands emerge from an extreme fill of swirling detail; and Bernt Notke's monumental statue of *Saint George Killing the Dragon* in the Storkyrka, Stockholm (completed in 1489). In a notable example that combines painting with sculpture, the Isenheim Altarpiece, painted by Matthias Grünewald (d. 1528; see the color plates in volume 3) reveals in its open state Nicholas of Hagenau's sculpture of Saint Anthony in the center (before c. 1509). The piece is in the museum of Colmar.

Sixteenth-century sculpture in northern Europe. In sculpture as in the other arts, the sixteenth century brought the influence of the Italian Renaissance into northern Europe in various ways. In the lowlands and German-speaking countries, Renaissance concepts and practices arrived after local artists traveled to Italy for practicum and inspiration, following the example of Albrecht Dürer. In contrast, in France and Spain, the respective rulers Francis I and Charles I adopted the idealism and rhetoric of Italian high Renaissance art for propagandistic ends. They commissioned leading works from Italian masters and employed them in their own countries. As a result, leading French masters quickly adopted Italianate conventions, an assimilation process that eventually evolved into seventeenth-century French classicism. Its formative stage can be followed, from Francesco Primaticcio's elegant stucco nudes in the room of the Duchesse d'Estampes at the royal Château at Fontainebleau (c. 1541–1545) to Jean Goujon's sinuous reliefs of nymphs from the Fountain of the Innocents in the Louvre (1548–1549). Germain Pilon's Italianate idealized *Gisants* (the deceased reclining just after death) from the Tomb of Henry II and Catherine de Médicis in the Abbey Church of St.-Denis, Paris (1563–1570), reverse the late Gothic tradition of showing the dead in a state of natural decay. And the rich sculptural decor of the upper story of Pierre Lescot's Louvre Court (after 1546) follows Italian examples such as Jacopo Sansovino's Library of Saint Mark in Venice. Leone Leoni (1509–1590), favored by Charles V, represented the emperor standing on a defeated and chained Fury (Prado, Madrid, 1549–1564).

In German-speaking lands, the rise of the Protestant Reformation terminated the vital production of religious sculpture. From 1520 to 1555, virtually none of consequence was produced. During the early Reformation the most virulent Protestant reformers turned iconoclasts. They included Huldrych Zwingli and his followers (who established the Reformation in Switzerland), who systematically cleansed Zurich's churches of their art in 1525. Luther's position was moderate, and gradually a Lutheran iconography developed, an early example being Peter Dell the Elder's *Allegory of Faith* relief in the Germanisches Nationalmuseum, Nürnberg (1534). It contributed to the re-emergence of German religious sculpture in the second half of the sixteenth century.

BIBLIOGRAPHY

Primary Works

Alberti, Leon Battista. *On Painting and Sculpture.* Edited and translated by Cecyl Grayson. London, 1972.

The Autobiography of Benvenuto Cellini. Translated by John Addington Symonds. Edited by Charles Hope and Alessandro Nova. Oxford, 1983.

I trattati dell'oreficeria e della scultura di Benvenuto Cellini. Edited by Carlo Milanesi. Florence, 1857.

Vasari, Giorgio. *Le vite de' piu eccellenti pittori scultori e architettori: nelle redazioni del 1550 e 1568.* Edited with commentary by Rosanna Bettarini and Paola Barocchi. 11 vols. Florence, 1966–.

Secondary Works

Babelon, Jean. *Germain Pilon*. Paris, 1927.

Baxandall, Michael. *The Limewood Sculptors of Renaissance Germany*. New Haven, Conn., and London, 1980.

Bier, Justus. *Tilman Riemenschneider*. 4 vols. Augsburg, Vienna, and Würzburg, 1925–1978.

Blunt, Anthony. *Art and Architecture in France, 1500–1700*. 3d ed. Harmondsworth, U.K., 1970.

De Tolnay, Charles. *Michelangelo*. 5 vols. Princeton, N.J., 1969–1975.

Du Colombier, Pierre. *Jean Goujon*. Paris, 1949.

Henderson, George H. *Nicola Pisano and the Revival of Sculpture in Italy,* Cambridge, U.K., 1938.

Janson, Horst W. *The Sculpture of Donatello*. Princeton, N.J., 1963.

Krautheimer, Richard, and Trude Krautheimer-Hess. *Lorenzo Ghiberti*. Princeton, N.J., 1956.

Lutze, Eberhart. *Veit Stoss*. 4th ed. Berlin, 1968; reprint of 1938 edition.

Morand, Kathleen. *Claus Sluter*. Austin, Tex., 1991.

Müller, Theodor. *Sculpture in the Netherlands, Germany, France, and Spain 1400–1500*. Harmondsworth, U.K., 1966.

Osten, Gert von der, and Horst Vey. *Painting and Sculpture in Germany and the Netherlands 1500–1600*. Translated by Mary Hotlinger. Harmondsworth, U.K., 1969.

Pinder, Wilhelm. *Die deutsche Plastik vom ausgehenden Mittelalter bis zum Ende der Renaissance* and *Die deutsche Plastik der Hochrenaissance*. Berlin, 1929.

Pope-Hennessy, John W. *An Introduction to Italian Sculpture*. 3 vols. I: *Italian Gothic Sculpture,* II: *Italian Renaissance Sculpture,* III: *Italian Renaissance and Baroque Sculpture*. 4th ed. London, 1996.

JOSEPH POLZER

SECUNDUS, JOHANNES (Jan Everaerts; 1511–1536), Neo-Latin poet born in The Hague. His father, Nicholas Everaerts, was a famous jurist and president of the States of Holland and Zealand at The Hague and of the Grand Council at Mechlin. Johannes Secundus paid tribute to him at his death in 1532 in a Neo-Latin dirge. Secundus himself took a law degree, and both father and son served the emperor Charles V. Secundus studied with the lawyer and poet Andrea Alciati and was acquainted with Erasmus. In 1533 Secundus went to Spain as secretary to Joannes Tavera, bishop of Toledo. Thereafter, he returned to Holland to serve as secretary to George Egmond, bishop of Utrecht. Called upon to take the post of private Latin secretary to Emperor Charles V, he departed for Italy, dying en route. He was buried at St. Amand under a Latin epitaph.

Although circulated during his lifetime, his poems (except for a few in a friend's collection) were not published until after his death, first in 1539, then in an expanded volume in 1541 edited by his poet-brothers. His poetry was reprinted in anthologies, in collections in 1561 and 1582 with the poet Michael Marullus, and in Leiden by Scriverius in 1619 (second edition, 1631). The authoritative version of his poetry was edited by Peter Burmann and Peter Bosscha in 1821. Secundus was first admired for the three books of love elegies composed in imitation of Propertius, Ovid, and Tibullus, the first book of which was addressed to Julia, a mistress briefly loved and lost. His more famous amatory sequence, the *Basia,* is a series of nineteen "kiss poems" addressed to Neaera, which imitates Catullus 5, 7, and 9 and contemporary Neo-Latin kiss poems by Marullus, Jacopo Sannazaro, and Giovanni Pontano. Secundus also wrote funeral odes, eclogues, epistles, epigrams, and an epithalamium. His Latin prose works include travel diaries of his three journeys to Bourges and Spain, letters to his brothers, his sister Isabella, and friends. His Orpheus eclogue is both a lament for Orpheus's death and an amatory piece on the cruel Neaera. His monody on the death of Thomas More indicates his sympathy for the Catholic cause, as does his ode to God Omnipotent against the Anabaptists. The elegies and the *Basia* had considerable influence on the Latin and vernacular poets who followed him. In France the Pléiade poets—particularly Pierre de Ronsard, Antoine de Baïf, Joachim Du Bellay, and Rémy Belleau—and later Marc Antoine Moret, Philippe Desportes, and Jean Bonnefons (*Pancharis*) were the first to imitate Secundus's love poems. In Germany Caspar Barth (*Eropaegnion*) was an admirer and in the Netherlands Joannes Dousa the elder and Albert Eufren; in Italy Gasparo Murtola and Giambattista Marino. Not until the seventeenth century was there much imitation of Secundus in England, with Ben Jonson, William Drummond of Hawthornden ("Kisses Desired"), Giles Fletcher, and Robert Herrick. The first, partial translation into English of Secundus's *Basia* is a chaste, but elegant version by Thomas Stanley in 1651. Goethe was the last major poet to take an interest in Secundus. Georg Ellinger's edition of the *Basia* (Berlin, 1899) includes a generous sample of these imitations and translations.

BIBLIOGRAPHY

Primary Works

An Anthology of Neo-Latin Poetry. Edited and translated by Fred J. Nichols. New Haven, Conn., 1979.

Secundus, Johannes. *The Love Poems of Joannes Secundus*. Translated by F. A. Wright. New York, 1930.

Secondary Works

Crane, Dougall. *Johannes Secundus: His Life, Work, and Influence on English Literature*. London, 1931.

Endres, Clifford. *Joannes Secundus: The Latin Love Elegy in the Renaissance*. Hamden, Conn., 1981.
Schoolfield, George. *Janus Secundus*. Boston, 1970.

STELLA P. REVARD

SEMINARIES. Seminaries are colleges or schools dedicated to the spiritual and intellectual formation of the clergy. Although the term "seminary" is usually associated with the Roman Catholic tradition, parallel institutions are found in the academies, colleges, and theological faculties maintained by Protestant churches, as both Protestants and Catholics are intent on training priests and ministers dedicated to the performance of pastoral duties. In varying degrees, Catholics and Protestants also share the humanist conviction that learning—rooted in the classical languages and the scriptures—and good character go hand in hand.

Medieval Antecedents. Clerical training took a variety of forms in the Middle Ages. From the seventh to the thirteenth century, cathedral and monastic schools provided candidates for the priesthood, living in community, with spiritual and moral discipline and lessons in church doctrine and liturgy. The rise of universities in the twelfth and thirteenth centuries was accompanied by the decline of cathedral and monastic schools and falling educational standards for the parish clergy. Only a small percentage of parish priests studied at the universities, and even these lacked spiritual formation and practical training for the cure of souls. Many prospective priests studied at the remaining cathedral and monastic schools, with parish priests, and at civic schools; but the failures of this system led to a general consensus, shared by both Roman Catholic and Protestant reformers, that the training of young men for the cure of souls was grossly inadequate.

Educational Reform in the Lutheran Territories. In the late 1520s Lutheran churches began to grapple with the low educational standards and performance of the clergy, exposed by a series of visitations of the rural parishes. Lutheran princes and towns diverted the funds of former monastic houses to the foundation of German and Latin schools in their towns and villages, and of secondary institutions called "gymnasiums." The intent was to provide civil servants, teachers, and capable pastors. After studies at gymnasiums, Lutheran ministers completed their training in the theological faculties of universities such as Wittenberg, Erfurt, Leipzig, and Marburg, and at institutions such as the "Preachers' Colleges" attached to the academy of Johann Sturm at Strasbourg and the "theological seminaries" that operated out of former monastery schools at Württemberg. Under the direction of Martin Luther and Philipp Melanchthon, the religious reformation was accompanied by a change in the curriculum, away from logic, scholastic theology, and canon law toward a more humanistic program consisting of grammar, rhetoric, Latin, Greek, Hebrew, and a scriptural-based theology. The lessons of the grammar schools and theological faculties did not, at this early date, include much practical training for the pastorate. The quality of the clergy gradually improved, however, because the churches insisted that pastors study throughout their careers, and they used frequent visitations to enforce this goal.

Reformed Academies. In Zurich, Huldrych Zwingli responded to the need for a preaching ministry by establishing the Prophezei (prophecy), which began to function in 1525. Clergy, students, and even laity gathered in the choir stalls of the Grossmünster to hear the scriptures explained in their Latin, Greek, and Hebrew texts. After Zwingli's death in 1531, the Prophezei evolved into the Lectorium or Pfarrerschule, which followed a more structured curriculum, still based, however, on the classical languages and the scriptures. Zurich's Lectorium did not develop faculties of law or medicine and remained an institution of local or regional significance.

By the middle of the sixteenth century, leadership in the Reformed tradition passed to Geneva. In 1559 the Geneva Academy was founded under the rectorship of Théodore de Bèze, who was joined by a group of exiles from the Academy of Lausanne. The Geneva Academy included the *schola privata* (private school), which offered classes in Latin grammar and elementary Greek, and the *schola publica* (public school), which provided lectures in Greek, Hebrew, the arts, and theology. The Genevan magistracy attempted to enhance the academy's reputation and attract students by establishing chairs of law and medicine, but the influence of the Company of Pastors was such that the primary role of the academy remained the training of ministers for the mission fields of France, and to a lesser extent of the Netherlands and Germany. Although the academy enjoyed immense prestige in the Calvinist churches, in the long run its development was inhibited by the fact that it did not grant degrees.

The Geneva Academy maintained close ties with Zurich's *Lectorium* and with the universities of Heidelberg in the Palatinate and Leiden in the northern

Netherlands. The two universities differed from the Geneva Academy in that they were under the control of the lay magistrates and princes, and the church played a negligible role. With a broader range of programs than Geneva and a wider appeal, the universities provided instruction in languages and theology but did not offer practical training for the ministry. The latter need was filled by colleges created to serve as seminaries. At Leiden, the States College and the Walloon College offered financial assistance, guidance, and practical training to a limited number of theology students destined for the ministry, while a similar role was played by the Collegium Sapientiae of Heidelberg.

Catholic Seminaries. Efforts to reform morals and educational standards of Catholic priests coalesced in the Council of Trent. After an early, unsatisfactory effort to revive cathedral lectureships in sacred scripture (Session 5, 17 June 1546), Session 23 of the council (15 July 1563) required the establishment of seminaries in each diocese. Seminaries were to include boys and young men twelve years of age and older, with a preference given to the sons of poor parents. They were to receive a proper moral and spiritual formation. The council prescribed the study of Latin, ecclesiastical song, rites and ceremonies, sacred scriptures, and the administration of the sacraments, especially penance.

In the years following the closure of the council in 1563, Rome, Milan, Bologna, Venice, Naples, and many smaller Italian dioceses established seminaries. Finances were often inadequate, however, and attendance at a seminary was not an obligation for ordination to the priesthood. Carlo Borromeo, archbishop of Milan, set a brilliant example by founding a network of major and minor seminaries that catered to students of varying ages and backgrounds. At Pavia, Cremona, Brescia, and other dioceses in the ecclesiastical province of Milan, however, seminaries remained small, housing only between twenty and forty students, and it was only after 1680 that the number of seminary spaces was significantly increased. The majority of students lived outside the seminaries and obtained their training with the religious orders or at the side of parish priests. In many of Italy's smaller dioceses, especially in the south and center of the peninsula, size and poverty mitigated against the foundation of seminaries.

In the early days, the seminaries of northern Italy focused on the practical matters most necessary for the administration of the cure of souls. Religious orders, especially new ones, played prominent roles in the early Italian seminaries. The humanities-based *Ratio studiorum* (Plan of studies) of the Jesuits was influential as seminarians often received their instructions at Jesuit colleges.

In Spain, the sixteenth century witnessed a proliferation of Jesuit colleges and universities founded with the financial support of the church. However, these remained the preserve of an elite of civil servants, bishops, and cathedral canons. Lack of funds, the impoverished conditions of the parish clergy, and the hostility of the cathedral chapters to new taxation prevented the establishment of seminaries in the majority of Spanish dioceses. The seminaries that were founded were small and often failed to weather the financial crises of the seventeenth century. Bishops were forced to adopt stopgap measures such as encouraging potential priests to study at the schools of the mendicant orders, with cathedral chapters, and at civic schools.

In Germany and Poland diocesan seminaries on the Tridentine model were slow to develop. The establishment of the German College at Rome in 1552 provided an alternative, as did the creation of "pontifical" seminaries at Vienna, Dillingen, Gratz, Olomouc, Braniewo, Fulda, and Ingolstadt between 1574 and 1600. The Jesuits played prominent roles in founding and staffing these institutions. Due to poverty and frequent wars, many bishoprics lacked proper diocesan seminaries until the eighteenth century. Colleges and seminaries were also established for English exiles, at Rome in 1578 and at various times at Douai, Paris, Louvain, and other centers.

In France religious wars and shortages of teachers and money impeded the establishment of seminaries in the sixteenth century. Although efforts were made to found seminaries and to revive cathedral schools, the majority of clerics studied with parish priests or with clerical relatives. Despite the pioneering efforts of Vincent de Paul, Jean Eudes, and Jean Jacques Olier (the founder of the Sulpician society of priests), in the first half of the seventeenth century, it was only after 1650 that French diocesan seminaries came to play a prominent role in the education of the parish clergy.

English Universities. In England, the greatest changes came between approximately 1540, when few of the parish clergy studied at universities, and the 1620s and 1630s, when the great majority of those appointed to parishes were graduates of Oxford and Cambridge. Through endowments and scholarships, both the crown and the ecclesiastical hierarchy promoted universities as seminaries for the

Anglican clergy. Students and their families came to view educational qualifications as the avenue to promotion in the church.

See also **Clergy; Ratio Studiorum.**

BIBLIOGRAPHY

Forster, Marc R. *The Counter-Reformation in the Villages: Religion and Reform in the Bishopric of Speyer, 1560–1720.* Ithaca, N.Y., 1992. Describes the development of the Catholic Reformation among the rural clergy.

Hoffman, Philip T. *Church and Community in the Diocese of Lyon, 1500–1789.* New Haven, Conn., and London, 1984. Places the urban and rural clergy of one of France's largest dioceses within the context of Tridentine reform.

Karant-Nunn, Susan C. *Luther's Pastors: The Reformation in the Ernestine Countryside.* Philadelphia, 1979. Gives a detailed account of the Lutheran clergy based largely on church visitations.

Maag, Karin. *Seminary or University? The Genevan Academy and Reformed Higher Education, 1560–1620.* Aldershot, U.K., and Brookfield, Vt., 1995. Provides essential information on the Geneva Academy and its sister institutions at Zurich, Heidelberg, and Leiden.

Martin Hernandez, Francisco. *Los seminarios españoles: Historia y pedagogia.* Vol. 1, *1563–1700.* Salamanca, Spain, 1964. Gives a detailed account of the foundation and statutes of Spanish seminaries.

O'Day, Rosemary. *The English Clergy: The Emergence and Consolidation of a Profession, 1558–1642.* Leicester, U.K., and Atlantic Highlands, N.J., 1979. Views the development of the pastoral role of the English clergy in the context of university training and the development of a sense of professionalism.

O'Donohue, James A. *Tridentine Seminary Legislation: Its Sources and Its Formation.* Louvain, Belgium, 1957. Dated but seminal for understanding the gestation of Tridentine seminary decrees.

Toscani, Xenio. "I seminari e il clero secolare in Lombardia nei secoli sedici–diciannove." In *Chiesa e società: Appunti per una storia delle diocesi lombarde.* Edited by A. Caprioli, A. Rimoldi, and L. Vaccaro. Vol. 1, *Storia religiosa della Lombardia.* Brescia, Italy, 1986. Basic institutional background on the development of seminaries in Lombardy, pp. 215–262.

THOMAS B. DEUTSCHER

SEPHARDIC JEWS. *See* **Conversos; Jews,** *subentry on the* **Jewish Community.**

SERLIO, SEBASTIANO (1475–1554), Bolognese author, architect, woodcutter, and painter. Sebastiano Serlio trained as a woodcutter and painter, first in Pesaro (1511–1514) and then in Rome under Baldassare Peruzzi, assisting Peruzzi in Bologna (Serlio's hometown) on the (unexecuted) project for the facade of the church of San Petronio (1522–1523). Following the Sack of Rome in 1527 Serlio moved to Venice, where he became part of a circle centered on Pietro Aretino that included Titian and Jacopo Sansovino. He executed a ceiling design in the Palazzo Ducale library (1527–1531) and provided Federico Priuli with designs for his villa at Treville and Pietro Zen with a design for his palace in Venice.

Between 1534 and 1535 Serlio collaborated with Titian and Fortunio Spira in the revisions made by the Neoplatonist Francesco di Giorgio to the proportioning of Jacopo Sansovino's church of San Francesco della Vigna, and some time before March 1535 he was commissioned to set the level of payment for the completed wooden ceiling that he had designed for the Scuola Grande di San Rocco. In 1539 Serlio submitted a design (as would Michele Sanmicheli and Giulio Romano) in the famous competition to renovate the basilica at Vicenza, won by Andrea Palladio.

During this period in Venice, Serlio published the first installment of his treatise, "book 4" on the architectural orders, supported by Ercole II d'Este. For the subsequent work, entitled "book 3," Serlio gained the patronage of the king of France, Francis I, and moved to France in 1541, where he was installed as *premier peintre et architecte* (royal painter and architect) at Fontainebleau. This period in the French king's employment coincided with the majority of Serlio's actual built work, although most of it was for members of the court rather than for the king himself. Serlio is thought to have designed the Grotte des Pins at Fontainebleau, although the grotto was not built following his scheme as drawn in book 6 on domestic architecture, and he is also traditionally credited with the chateau's Salle de Bal. This was begun by Giles Le Breton in 1541 and completed by Philibert de l'Orme in 1548; concerning the design of its loggia Serlio notes that he was not asked for the "smallest piece of advice" (Serlio, *Il settimo libro d'architettura* [The seventh book of architecture], p. 96). His project for the Louvre, rejected in favor of Pierre Lescot's, was illustrated in book 6 as a model "palace for a king."

In Fontainebleau Serlio executed a design (1544–1546) for the residence of Ercole II d'Este's brother, Ippolito II, which was called the Grand Ferrara (now destroyed, but illustrated in book 6), and it was here that Serlio was destined to spend the last few years of his life. In Burgundy from 1541 he designed the chateau of Ancy-le-Franc for Count Antoine de Clermont-Tonnerre, while his unexecuted project to amend the chateau at Lourmarin in Provence was represented as the ideal chateau of "Rosmarino" in book 7 on problems confronting architects. On the accession of Henry II in 1547 a wave of French nationalistic feeling largely hostile to Italian artists led to Serlio being replaced in his post by de l'Orme in April 1548.

Sometime before 1550 Serlio moved to Lyons, a center for printing, possibly following Ippolito II d'Este, who had been archbishop of the town since 1540. Here Serlio designed a merchants' courtyard (apparently unbuilt) and a merchants' exchange, or "loggia" (possibly built). Of Serlio's built work in France only Ancy-le-Franc has survived, but with its three wings enclosing an approximately square court fronted by a low wall, the Grand Ferrara helped establish a characteristic type in French domestic architecture.

Serlio's architecture, although limited in scope and quantity, was destined to enjoy wide influence through its illustration in his popular treatise, *Tutte l'opere d'architettura et prospetiva* (Complete works on architecture and perspective; 1537–1575). For in presenting his own work as models, Serlio graphically underlined the interrelationship between architectural theory and practice. His principles were intended to be universally applicable, irrespective of local styles and building traditions, as his domestic architecture in France clearly demonstrated in including medieval forms and ornament. The popularity of Serlio's treatise was greatly assisted by this emphasis on continuity rather than revolutionary change. Indeed the illustration of the Grand Ferrara and Ancy-le-Franc among examples of French domestic "types" in book 6 emphasizes the fact that both houses were built to reflect Serlio's faith in the existing feudal fabric of French society, with its clearly defined classes ranging from peasant to prince. Serlio equally sought to recommend a middle path in the choice of ornamentation, choosing to avoid the temptation of licentious excess while exploiting the expressive potential of the architectural orders as the context demanded. Hence the Serlian architect should, in all matters, "proceed very modestly and be very cautious, especially in public and solemn works, where it is praiseworthy to preserve decorum" (Serlio, *Regole generali,* fol. 3v/126v).

See also **Architecture**, *subentry on* **Architectural Treatises**.

BIBLIOGRAPHY

Primary Works

Serlio, Sebastiano. *Architettura civile. Libri sesto, settimo e ottavo nei manoscritti di Monaco e Vienna.* Transcription and notes of books 6–7, and (unnumbered) 8, by Francesco Paolo Fiore and Tancredi Carunchio. Milan, 1994.

Serlio, Sebastiano. *Il trattato di architettura di Sebastiano Serlio.* Edited by Marco Rosci and Anna Maria Brizio. 2 vols. Milan, 1966. Volume 2 is a facsimile of the "Munich" manuscript of Serlio's book 6.

Serlio, Sebastiano. *Sebastiano Serlio on Architecture.* Vols. 1 and 2. Translated by Vaughan Hart and Peter Hicks. New Haven, Conn., 1996–. Translation of books 1–5 and 6–8 of *Tutte l'opere d'architettura et prospetiva* (1537–1575).

Serlio, Sebastiano. *Sebastiano Serlio on Domestic Architecture.* Edited by Myra Nan Rosenfeld. New York, 1978. Facsimile of the "Avery" manuscript of Serlio's book 6. Republished without Serlio's Italian text, New York, 1996.

Secondary Works

Carpo, Mario. *La maschera e il modello. Teoria architettonica ed evangelismo nell'Extraordinario Libro di Sebastiano Serlio (1551).* Milan, 1993.

Carpo, Mario. *Metodo ed ordini nella teoria architettonica dei primi moderni: Alberti, Raffaello, Serlio e Camillo.* Geneva, 1993.

Dinsmoor, William Bell. "The Literary Remains of Sebastiano Serlio." *Art Bulletin* 24 (1942): 55–91, 115–154.

Frommel, Sabine. *Sebastiano Serlio.* Milan, 1998.

Hart, Vaughan, and Peter Hicks, eds. *Paper Palaces: The Rise of the Renaissance Architectural Treatise.* New Haven, Conn., and London, 1998.

Howard, Deborah. "Sebastiano Serlio's Venetian Copyrights." *Burlington Magazine* 115, no. 2 (1973): 512–516.

Johnson, June Gwendolyn. *Sebastiano Serlio's Treatise on Military Architecture (Bayerische Staatsbibliothek, Munich, Codex Icon. 190).* Ann Arbor, Mich., 1985. Facsimile reprint of her Ph.D. diss., University of California, Los Angeles, 1984.

Onians, John. *Bearers of Meaning: The Classical Orders in Antiquity, the Middle Ages, and the Renaissance.* Princeton, N.J., 1988.

Payne, Alina. *The Architectural Treatise in the Italian Renaissance.* New York, 1999.

Thoenes, Christof, ed. *Sebastiano Serlio.* Milan, 1989.

VAUGHAN HART

SERMONS. *See* **Preaching and Sermons.**

SERVANTS. Throughout the Renaissance servants were an important occupational group. By the early sixteenth century one-third of all households had live-in servants. Most great aristocratic and wealthy households employed as many as one hundred servants of both sexes, but these were not representative; the majority of households employing servants could afford only one or two. Even wealthy merchants in seventeenth-century Amsterdam rarely employed more than two servants. Usually servants were women—maids of all work. Servants of both sexes were employed by English farmers from the fifteenth century onward. One or two servants usually worked on each farm; they lived in and were provided with board and lodging and a small wage when they left, in exchange for general tasks on the farm and in the house.

Although girls as young as seven or eight and unmarried women formed the majority of servants, it

Servants. Detail from *Life of the Virgin* by Domenico Ghirlandaio (1449–1494). Alinari/Art Resource, NY

was male servants who gave status to a household. Women servants were employed in less public tasks behind the scenes, helping in the kitchen and cleaning the bedchambers. The lowlier the household employing servants the more likely it was the servant was a woman. In many European cities female servants constituted as much as 12 percent of the population. In mid-seventeenth-century Florence, servants may have comprised 17 percent of the population.

Many of the female servants found in cities were migrants from the countryside. The majority came from poor households and often, as in France, from poverty-stricken villages in backward agricultural areas. These young women saw domestic service as a way of saving enough money for a dowry to attract a husband. This could involve many years in service, and some never achieved the goal, but marriage almost always meant leaving service. In many areas servants were forbidden to marry either by custom or law, and pregnancy was usually grounds for instant dismissal.

Servants could be recruited at local hiring fairs, where they were usually hired for a year, but it was more common for servants to be hired by recommendation of neighbors, local tradesmen, or especially relatives. Some areas of Europe had employment agencies. Conditions of service varied greatly. Although in theory employers provided board and lodging, the latter rarely consisted of separate quarters—it could even be a cupboard under the stairs or a space on the kitchen floor. Employers and servants lived in very close proximity, which made female servants very vulnerable to the attentions of the men in the household, whether it was the master, his son, or fellow servants. Wages varied but were consistently low. Female servants received about half a male servant's wage. Servants generally received little to no time off and were expected to work long hours. They were totally dependent on their employers and could be punished or dismissed at will.

BIBLIOGRAPHY

Fairchilds, Cissie. *Domestic Enemies: Servants and Their Masters in Old Regime France*. Baltimore; 1983.

Hanawalt, Barbara, ed. *Women and Work in Preindustrial Europe*. Bloomington, Ind., 1986.

Bridget Hill

SERVETUS, MICHAEL (c. 1510–1553), Spanish scientist, humanist, theologian. Servetus was born to a minor Aragonese noble family. His education in Spain is undocumented. He left Spain in 1528 or 1529 and studied anatomy and medicine in Paris, where he also taught astrology. In 1530 he attended the coronation of Charles V in Bologna. This experience transformed Servetus into an antipapal theologian. In France he edited geographical and biblical works, including the *Ptolemaei geographicae* (1535) and the *Biblia sacra* of Sante Pagnini (1542), and practiced medicine.

Science and reason informed Servetus's vision of God and the cosmos. With his knowledge of classical and Semitic languages, he was able to ground his theology in history. The result of his approach was a radical new concept of God, Christology, and cosmology. In *De trinitatis erroribus* (1531) and *Dialogi de Trinitate* (1532) he attacked the dogmas of the Trinity, Christology, cosmology, and anthropology. In his last theological work, *Christianismi restitutio* (1553), he stated his radical ideas of reform, centering his thesis on restitution.

Servetus's antitrinitarian ideas provided the foundation of unitarianism as well as radical anabaptism. His Neoplatonism was modified by a historical, nonallegorical exegesis. This paradoxical methodology initiated the foundations for modern biblical studies. For Servetus, science and theology were one; and therefore in this last work, for the first time in the Western world he explained the pulmonary circulation of the blood.

Servetus's escape from the French Inquisition only to be burned by John Calvin in Geneva made his life and work even more controversial and forced the debate on religious freedom.

BIBLIOGRAPHY

Primary Works

Servetus, Michael. *Descripciones geográficas del estado moderno de las regiones, en la geografía de Claudio Ptolemeo Alejandrino.* Edited by José Goyanes. Madrid, 1932. Spanish translation of *Ptolemaei geographicae enarrationis libri octo* (1535).

Servetus, Michael. *The Discourse in Favor of Astrology* and *The Syrups.* In *Michael Servetus: A Translation of His Geographical, Medical, and Astrological Writings.* Edited and translated by Charles Donald O'Malley. Philadelphia, 1953. Translation of *Disceptatio pro astrologia* (1538) and *Syruporum universa ratio* (1537).

Servetus, Michael. *The Two Treatises of Servetus on the Trinity.* Translated and edited by Earl Morse Wilbur. Cambridge, Mass., 1932. Translation of *De Trinitatis erroribus* (1531), *Dialogi de Trinitate* (1532), and *Christianismi restitutio* (1553).

Secondary Works

Friedman, Jerome. *Michael Servetus: A Case Study in Total Heresy.* Geneva, 1978.

Nieto, José C. *El Renacimiento y la otra España: Visión cultural socioespiritual.* Geneva, 1997.

JOSÉ C. NIETO

SEVILLE. Even before the opening up of trade with the Western Hemisphere, Seville had served as an economic, administrative, and ecclesiastical center of the fertile agricultural and highly urbanized region of Andalusia. Its location on the Guadalquivir River, approximately seventy miles upriver from the Atlantic coast, also made it an attractive port for regulating the vigorous Atlantic trade that followed in the wake of the Columbian voyages. This link to Spain's transoceanic empire profoundly shaped Seville's Renaissance identity, indelibly marking the city's economic, cultural, and social development. Thanks to a royal monopoly, from 1503 to 1717 all people and merchandise bound for Spain's American territories were to be registered at Seville. The Casa de Contratación (House of Trade) oversaw the commerce, navigation, and population movement between Spain and its overseas empire, while the prominent Casa Lonja de Mercaderes (Merchant Hall), opened in 1598, accommodated the traders and transactions that supplied the empire. As an international entrepôt, Seville attracted population from throughout Spain and Europe, including numerous foreign merchant communities. It also supplied many of Spain's emigrants and colonial personnel, ranging from common seamen to senior administrators; Bartolomé de Las Casas (1474–1566) was among the most outspoken *Sevillanos* who witnessed and participated in early contacts between the "Old" and "New" Worlds. With a population exceeding 80,000 (some have estimated as many as 130,000), Seville was one of Europe's largest cities in the late sixteenth century. Plague epidemics in 1599–1601 and in 1649, combined with the ascendancy of Madrid as the seat of royal government and the displacement of transatlantic shipping to Cádiz, eclipsed Seville's prominence in the seventeenth century.

Seville's role as the hub of the Indies traffic shaped its cultural and intellectual development. The Casa de Contratación collected and studied geographic and cartographic reports from returning ship pilots; it also employed a chief cosmographer, chief pilot (the first was Amerigo Vespucci), and professor of navigation and cosmography to improve Spanish mariners' navigational tools and training. The Crombergers and other printers made Seville the most active publishing center in early-sixteenth-century Spain, while Christopher Columbus's son Hernando Colon collected humanist texts and other works from throughout Europe, which now form the core of the Biblioteca Colombina at the Cathedral of Seville. Educational initiatives included the University of Seville, established during the reign of Ferdinand and Isabella, and institutions founded by the Society of Jesus, including some specifically intended for the religious instruction of English and Irish Catholics.

It was also in Seville where Ferdinand and Isabella first revived the Inquisition during the 1480s, initially targeting conversos (Jewish converts to Christianity). In the sixteenth century the Seville Tribunal also increasingly targeted Protestants and mystics. This trend was fueled by the discovery of a group of Protestants in Seville during the 1550s and the apparent ease with which ideas and printed material entered this international city.

Seville's literary elite included the humanist Juan de Mal Lara (1524–1571), founder of Seville's Escuela de Humanidades y Gramática (School of Humanities and Grammar), and the poet Fernando de Herrera (1534?–1597), but readers of Spanish Golden Age literature will also be familiar with less refined dimensions of Seville. Both Miguel de Cervantes (1547–1616) and Mateo Alemán (1547–1614) spent time in the city, including stays in the royal prison there for debts incurred, and Seville was a common stop in the travels of mischievous *pícaros* (rascals). The popular plays of Lope de Rueda (1510?–1565) and Juan de la Cueva (1543–c. 1612) also helped make Seville an important center of sixteenth-century drama.

Ubiquitous period architecture perhaps best manifests Renaissance Seville. The Casa Lonjade Mercaderes was designed by Juan de Herrera (c. 1530–1597); since the late eighteenth century it has housed the Archivo General de Indias, the archives of Spain's Atlantic empire. Pedro Enríquez, his wife Catalina de Ribera, and their son Fadrique Enríquez de Ribera sponsored some of Seville's best known Renaissance architecture, including the immense Hospital de las Cinco Llagas (Hospital of the five wounds), also known as the Hospital de la Sangre (Hospital of blood). The hospital was begun by Martín de Gaínza and finished by Benvenutto Tortello, Francisco Sánchez, and Juan de Minjares. Located just outside Seville's walls, it now houses the Andalusian Parliament. The same family also commissioned the Casa de Pilatos (House of Pilate), an example of Spanish Renaissance domestic architecture exhibiting both classical and local, especially Mudejar (Muslim-inspired) elements. Seville's *ayuntamiento* (city hall) remains in the Plateresque building designed as such by Diego de Riaño (d. 1534), begun in 1527.

To Seville's medieval cathedral were added such Renaissance features as the *sacristía mayor* (main sacristy) of Diego de Riaño, the Royal Chapel of Martín de Gaínza, the Sala Capitular (Chapter Room) of Hernán Ruiz, and the weather vane added to the minaret-turned-belltower, which gives this city landmark its popular name: La Giralda. The Jesuit Casa Noviciado de San Luis (1609) provides an early example of Spanish baroque, while the wooden sculptures and *retablos* (altar retables) of the renowned sculptor Juan Martínez Montañés (1568–1649) adorn many of Seville's churches and religious houses. Some of the most highly regarded painters of Spain's Golden Age also worked in seventeenth-century Seville. These included Rodríguez de Silva Velázquez (1599–1660), Bartolomé Esteban Murillo (1617–1682), Francisco de Zurbarán (1598–1664), and Juan de Valdés Leal (1622–1690).

See also **Cromberger Press**; **Libraries**; **Spain and Portugal, Art in**.

BIBLIOGRAPHY

Chaunu, Pierre, and Huguette, Chaunu. *Seville et l'Atlantique, 1504–1650*. 8 vols. Paris, 1955–1959.

Griffin, Clive. *The Crombergers of Seville: The History of a Printing and Merchant Dynasty*. Oxford and New York, 1988.

Kubler, George, and Martin Soria. *Art and Architecture in Spain and Portugal and Their American Dominions, 1500–1800*. Baltimore, 1959.

Morales Padrón, Francisco. *La ciudad del quinientos*. Vol. 3 of *Historia de Sevilla*. Seville, Spain, 1977.

Perry, Mary Elizabeth. *Crime and Society in Early Modern Seville*. Hanover, N.H., and London, 1980.

Perry, Mary Elizabeth. *Gender and Disorder in Early Modern Seville*. Princeton, N.J., 1990.

Pike, Ruth. *Aristocrats and Traders: Sevillian Society in the Sixteenth Century*. Ithaca, N.Y., 1972.

VALENTINA K. TIKOFF

SEXUALITY. Sexuality comprises a range of human characteristics and behaviors, from sexual morphology, reproduction and sexual difference, and gender, to sexual desire and object choice. As such, it is both a familiar concept and one that is difficult to define: some argue that sexuality has a specific and distinctive historical genesis in the nineteenth century and thus that before the emergence of modernity, sexuality as such did not exist; instead, the object of investigation would be the history of sex, a set of experiences of the flesh related to reproduction, anatomical difference, and pleasure.

Reproduction and Sexual Dimorphism. For much of the Renaissance, ancient Greek sources (such as Galen, Hippocrates, and Aristotle) served as the authorities on sexual dimorphism and reproduction. According to the Galenic-Hippocratic model, men and women each contributed "seed" to the formation of the infant (female orgasm, which was thought to be responsible for the emission of seed, was perceived as crucial to successful conception). The Aristotelian model, on the other hand, viewed women as incubators, contributing nourishing matter and a warm place for the fetus to develop, while the male seed provided the formal principle or soul.

Both models of sexual dimorphism and human reproduction seem to support the contention that gender, the social meaning accorded to sexual difference, was already embedded within the notion of sex, for Renaissance theories of sexual difference incorporated ideologies of gender into their notions of the female as inferior to, or an imperfect version of, the male. Indeed, Thomas Laqueur (1990) has argued that early modernity subscribed to a "one sex model" of sexual difference, whereby a single morphology—male—constituted the reproductive system of both sexes; in this model, women's genitalia and reproductive system were considered internalized inversions of men's.

In the sixteenth century in particular, a fascination with anatomical anomalies called hermaphrodites, appearing in medical and popular literature, indicated an interest in sexual ambiguity and boundary-crossing. Civil courts were often called upon to adjudicate the sex of a particular individual, after which he or she was bound by law to adhere to the designated gender role. It was also during the sixteenth century (in 1559) that a professor of anatomy, Realdo Colombo, believed he was the first to discover the clitoris.

Sexual Desire, Marriage, and the Family. Throughout the Middle Ages and the Renaissance, the dominant approach to human sexual desire was theological. From Saint Augustine in the fifth century onward, human desire was thought to be a motivating force both for the attainment of the divine and for perversion, a turning away or detour from the path of salvation toward the sins of the flesh. Christian theology ranked celibacy and virginity ahead of active sexual practice, which was to be confined to marriage for the sake of procreation, and to be limited to one "natural" position for intercourse (face to face, with the man on top). Citing Paul, Christian theorists (notably Saint Thomas Aquinas, in his *Summa theologica,* 1267–1273) condemned homosexuality as a subcategory of nonprocreative sex acts, deemed as crimes "against nature." Medieval penitentials outlined a hierarchy of sexual offenses, from worst to least serious: incest, sodomy, bestiality, adultery, fornication (sex between unmarried persons), and masturbation.

A shift in the church's attitude toward marriage and family occurred during the Renaissance, resulting in part from struggles with the landed aristocracy and the emergent nation-states for control over property and inheritance, and also from competition with the rival doctrine of Protestantism, which endorsed marriage for priests and laypeople alike. Love and companionship came to be promoted as components within marriage, and moderate sexual pleasure not directly associated with conception was permitted. While contraception was not officially condoned, it seems to have been widely practiced.

Fornication, clandestine marriage, and adultery were sexual offenses related to marriage. The punishment for fornication was not severe, as fornication was often regarded as a prelude to marriage. Clandestine or secret marriage existed primarily because marriage itself was a complex procedure lacking clearly defined boundaries. The penalties for adultery varied according to the status and gender of the persons committing the act. Men were often punished less severely than women, and differences in social station determined the visibility of the crime in the first place. A married aristocrat having sexual relations with his servants, for instance, was not normally charged with adultery.

Gender. Most Renaissance families and societies were patriarchal: the male head of the household controlled the economic resources of the family and made all principal decisions. Male preeminence was due in part to the fact that men were often considerably older than women at marriage and in part to the frequent rate of female death in childbirth. It was also supported by canon and Roman law, which presented the family as a microcosm of the state, in which the sovereign served as father to his people. Nevertheless, women exercised limited independence by a variety of means. The convent, often an option for girls whose parents could not afford the higher cost of a marital dowry, could provide a measure of autonomy. In addition, widowhood, although usually accompanied by extreme hardship, might provide a degree of economic independence and a certain social standing. Perhaps on this account, widows tended not to remarry, while their male counterparts usually did.

The courtesan, a notable sixteenth-century Italian social figure, also carved out for herself a degree of financial and social independence, although this went along with a certain measure of moral disapproval, since she made her living from offering sexual services to wealthy clients. Some women engaged in the practice of cross-dressing, an answer to women's physical vulnerability and the restrictions placed on their mobility, in order to gain access to places and spaces from which they were normally barred.

Women's social station determined the way in which they experienced themselves and were treated as gendered. In Renaissance Venice, for instance, adult noblewomen shared certain social attributes with boys, servants, and slaves, if only as one of the possible objects of a nobleman's sexual desire.

Sex Crimes, Illicit Sexual Practices, Pornography. Civil and canon law criminalized certain sexual practices, from fornication to sodomy (understood primarily as same-sex sexual practice). In Italy and France, both men and women could be accused of sodomy. In England, there is no evidence for this period that women were prosecuted under sodomy statutes. The penalties for sodomy were severe, although a distinction was drawn between the lesser criminality of the younger, construed as passive, partner and the more culpable older, or active, partner. In Italy, particularly, male homosexual subcultures may have flourished in many urban centers. In fifteenth-century Florence cross-generational male same-sex relations were not uncommon, spurring magistrates to form a special organization to prosecute sodomy, while moralists and theologians lamented its incidence.

Prosecution of the crime of rape depended on the relative social stations and ages of the perpetrator and the victim. A rich literary tradition, from courtly love to the *pastourelle* (a poem in dialogue typically involving a young knight attempting to rape a peasant girl), describes male sexual violence toward women. A certain amount of violence was generally associated with male heterosexual desire, and thus penalties for rape—unless they involved breaches of social station or violence against very young girls—tended not to be as severe as penalties for sodomy.

Prostitution was widely practiced and, until the Protestant and Catholic Reformations, many towns throughout Europe funded municipal brothels. Prostitution was often regarded as a means of safely containing young men's sexual desires, considered uncontrollable. Unlike courtesans, prostitutes tended to be poor women who earned low wages.

Sodomites and whores figure prominently in the emergence of Renaissance literary pornography. Their status as social and sexual marginals made them ideal vehicles through which to satirize the family, the state and the clergy. The works of Pietro Aretino (1492–1556) are an important landmark in the development of pornography. His *Sonnetti lussuriosi* (Lewd sonnets; 1524), describing sexual positions and accompanying a series of obscene engravings, and his *Ragionamenti* (Dialogues; 1536, 1556), featuring satirical conversations among prostitutes about their profession, provide a wealth of information regarding sexual attitudes and practices. The *Ragionamenti* feature whores and sodomites as emblems of populist and aristocratic sexual practices, respectively. Thus pornography exposed and demystified the culture's official pronouncements regarding itself, while at the same time commenting on and contributing to the commodification of sex in an increasingly capitalist society.

See also **Homosexuality; Pornography.**

BIBLIOGRAPHY

Daston, Lorraine, and Katharine Park. "The Hermaphrodite and the Orders of Nature: Sexual Ambiguity in Early Modern France." In *Premodern Sexualities.* Edited by Louise Fradenburg and Carla Freccero. New York, 1996. Pages 117–136.

Findlen, Paula. "Humanism, Politics, and Pornography in Renaissance Italy." In *The Invention of Pornography: Obscenity and the Origins of Modernity, 1500–1800.* Edited by Lynn Hunt. New York, 1993. Pages 49–108.

Foucault, Michel. *The History of Sexuality.* Vol. 1. *An Introduction.* New York, 1978. Translation of *La volonté de savoir* (1976).

Laqueur, Thomas. *Making Sex: Body and Gender from the Greeks to Freud.* Cambridge, Mass., and London, 1990.

Park, Katharine. "The Rediscovery of the Clitoris: French Medicine and the Tribade, 1570–1620." In *The Body in Parts: Fantasies of Corporeality in Early Modern Europe.* Edited by David Hillman and Carla Mazzio. New York and London, 1997. Pages 171–193.

Richards, Jeffrey. *Sex, Dissidence, and Damnation: Minority Groups in the Middle Ages.* London and New York, 1991.

Ruggiero, Guido. *The Boundaries of Eros: Sex Crime and Sexuality in Renaissance Venice.* New York and Oxford, 1985.

Turner, James Grantham, ed. *Sexuality and Gender in Early Modern Europe: Institutions, Texts, Images.* Cambridge, U.K., 1993.

CARLA FRECCERO

SFORZA, HOUSE OF. *See* **Milan,** *subentry on* **Milan in the Renaissance.**